The Official
SCRABBLE
Players

DICTIONARY

FOURTH EDITION

Merriam-Webster

Merriam-Webster, Incorporated

Springfield, Massachusetts

Copyright © 2005 by Hasbro, Inc.

Library of Congress Cataloging-in-Publication Data

The official Scrabble players dictionary.—4th ed.
     p.   cm.
ISBN-13: 978-0-87779-420-2 (hardcover)
ISBN-10: 0-87779-420-0 (hardcover)
1. Scrabble (Game)—Glossaries, vocabularies, etc. I. Merriam-Webster, Inc.
GV1507 .S3.O36 2005
793.734—dc22

                          2005005110

Made in the United States of America

6 7 8 9 NK:RRD 11 10 09

P₃ **REFACE** • This is the fourth edition of the enormously popular Official SCRABBLE® Players Dictionary, and it includes some 4,000 words not included in the previous edition. This dictionary has been prepared especially for lovers of SCRABBLE® crossword games and is endorsed by the National SCRABBLE® Association for recreational and school use.

It is important to remember that The Official SCRABBLE® Players Dictionary was edited solely with this limited purpose in mind. It is not intended to serve as a general dictionary of English; thus, such important features of general dictionaries as definitions of multiple senses, pronunciation respellings, etymologies, and usage labels are omitted.

It is the intention of the makers of SCRABBLE® crossword games that they be enjoyed by children and adults alike. With this consideration in mind, words likely to offend players of the game have been omitted from this edition. The words omitted are those that would qualify for a warning usage note on the basis of standards applied in other Merriam-Webster™ dictionaries.

The detailed organization and special features of the dictionary are explained in the Introduction which follows. It should be read with care by all who use the dictionary. Now that this new updated work is available, we are confident that it will afford satisfaction and enjoyment to SCRABBLE® crossword game players everywhere.

OUR TRADEMARK • **SCRABBLE®** • Milton Bradley Company takes pride in offering this dictionary to owners of its SCRABBLE® Brand line of word games. The SCRABBLE® trademark, registered in the United States Patent and Trademark Office, is one of our most valued assets as it represents our seal and reputation for excellence and quality.

As a trademark, it must be capitalized, and when describing products, be followed by a generic name of the game, such as SCRABBLE® crossword game. The SCRABBLE® trademark means "made by" or "sponsored by" the Milton Bradley Company, a division of Hasbro, Inc.

Your cooperation in the continued proper use of our trademark is appreciated and we hope that this dictionary will enhance enjoyment of our products.

Hasbro, Inc.
443 Shaker Road
East Longmeadow, MA 01028

The Official SCRABBLE® Players Dictionary
has been endorsed by the
National SCRABBLE® Association.

For information on SCRABBLE® clubs, tournaments, publications, school programs, and other activities, contact:

National SCRABBLE® Association
Box 700
Greenport, NY 11944
Phone: (631) 477-0033
Fax: (631) 477-0294
info@scrabble-assoc.com

NTRODUCTION ● **MAIN ENTRIES** ● Main entries are listed in boldface type and are set flush with the left-hand margin of each column. Except for an occasional cross-reference (such as **UNDERLYING** present participle of underlie), main entries contain from two to eight letters, since words within this range are considered to be most useful to SCRABBLE® crossword game players. Words that are not permissible in SCRABBLE® crossword games have not been included in this dictionary. Thus, proper names, words requiring hyphens or apostrophes, words considered foreign, and abbreviations have been omitted. Because dictionaries have different criteria for selecting entries, several standard dictionaries were consulted in preparing the list of main entries for this book. Obsolete, archaic, slang, and nonstandard words are included because they are permitted by the rules of the game. All variant forms of a main entry are shown at their own alphabetical places and defined in terms of the principal form. Words that exceed eight letters in length and are not inflected forms of words entered in this dictionary should be looked up in a standard dictionary. The National SCRABBLE® Association recommends Merriam-Webster's Collegiate Dictionary, Eleventh Edition, as a reference for additional words.

PARTS OF SPEECH ● An italic label indicating a part of speech follows each main entry except cross-references, for which the label is given at the root word. The eight traditional parts of speech are indicated as follows:

n	noun
v	verb
adj	adjective
adv	adverb
pron	pronoun
prep	preposition
conj	conjunction
interj	interjection

When a word can be used as more than one part of speech, each part of speech is entered separately if the inflected forms are not spelled alike. For example, both the adjective *mean* and the verb *mean* are entered because the inflected forms vary.

MEAN	*adj* **MEANER, MEANEST** inferior in grade, quality, or character
MEAN	*v* **MEANT, MEANING, MEANS** to intend

On the other hand, the verb *garlic* is entered while the noun *garlic* is not because the inflected form *garlics* at the verb is spelled the same as the plural form of the noun. In a dictionary for SCRABBLE® crossword game players, entry of the noun is therefore redundant. Homographs (words spelled alike) which may be used as the same part of speech are treated in the same way. For example, *lie* is entered as a verb twice because the inflected forms are spelled differently.

LIE	*v* **LIED, LYING, LIES** to speak falsely
LIE	*v* **LAY, LAIN, LYING, LIES** to be or get into a horizontal position

If both sets of inflected forms were spelled alike, only one *lie* would be entered in this dictionary. In this way the dictionary includes as many different spellings as possible yet avoids wasting space with repeated entry of words spelled in the same way. The SCRABBLE® crossword game player, after all, needs only one entry to justify a play.

INFLECTED FORMS ● Inflected forms include the past tense, past participle, present participle, and present tense third person singular of verbs, the plural of nouns, and the comparative and superlative of adjectives and adverbs. They are shown in boldface capital letters immediately following the part-of-speech label. Irregular inflected forms are listed as main entries when they fall four or more alphabetical places away from the root word (see **Cross-References** below). All inflected forms are allowable for play in SCRABBLE® crossword games.

The principal parts of the majority of verbs are shown as **-ED, -ING, -S** (or **-ES** when applicable). This indicates that the past tense and past participle are formed simply by adding *-ed* to the entry word, that the present participle is formed simply by adding *-ing* to the entry word, and that the present third person singular is formed simply by adding *-s* (or *-es*) to the entry word.

MURMUR	*v* **-ED, -ING, -S** to speak unclearly

When inflection of an entry word involves any spelling change in addition to the suffixal ending (such as the dropping of a final *-e*, the doubling of a final consonant, or the changing of a final *-y* to *-i-*) or when the inflection is irregular, the inflected forms given indicate such changes.

POSE	*v* **POSED, POSING, POSES** to assume a fixed position
ROT	*v* **ROTTED, ROTTING, ROTS** to decompose
SHY	*v* **SHIED, SHYING, SHIES** to move suddenly back or aside, as in fear
RIDE	*v* **RODE, RIDDEN, RIDING, RIDES** to sit on, control, or be conveyed by an animal or machine

For verbs of more than one syllable, either the last syllable or the last two syllables are shown to indicate spelling changes.

LABEL   *v* **-BELED, -BELING, -BELS** or **-BELLED, -BELLING, -BELS** to describe or designate

EDUCATE   *v* **-CATED, -CATING, -CATES** to teach

The plurals of nouns are preceded by the abbreviation "pl." Most plurals are shown as **-S** (or **-ES** when applicable) to indicate that the plural is formed simply by adding the given suffix to the entry word.

LION   *n* pl. **-S** a large, carnivorous feline mammal

When pluralizing a noun involves any spelling change in addition to the suffixal ending (such as the changing of a final -*y* to -*i*- or a final -*f* to -*v*-) or when the plural is irregular, the plural form shown indicates such change.

PIXY   *n* pl. **PIXIES** a playfully mischievous fairy or elf

DWARF   *n* pl. **DWARFS** or **DWARVES** an extremely small person

OTITIS   *n* pl. **OTITISES** or **OTITIDES** inflammation of the ear

In such cases involving polysyllabic nouns at least the last syllable is shown.

THERAPY   *n* pl. **-PIES** the treatment of illness or disability

For the sake of clarity, two groups of nouns that are confusing to many, those ending in -*o* and those ending in -*y*, are always indicated in this dictionary by showing at least the last syllable, even though no spelling change is involved.

HIPPO   *n* pl. **-POS** a hippopotamus
CAY   *n* pl. **CAYS** a small low island

Variant plurals are shown wherever they add another word permissible in SCRABBLE® crossword games.

JUNCO   *n* pl. **-COS** or **-COES** a small finch

Plurals which have the same form as the singular are shown only when they are the only plural for that entry. This is done to show that for the entry in question it is not permissible to add **-S** (or **-ES**) to the singular to create a plural.

MOOSE   *n* pl. **MOOSE** a ruminant mammal
TAXUS   *n* pl. **TAXUS** an evergreen tree or shrub

Otherwise, they are omitted and only the plural with the inflection is shown.

DEER   *n* pl. **-S** a ruminant mammal

The italic label *n/pl* is given to two kinds of nouns. One is the plural noun that has no singular form.

TINSNIPS   *n/pl* a tool for cutting sheet metal

The other is the plural noun of which the singular form contains more than eight letters and is not entered in this dictionary.

TENTORIA   *n/pl* the internal skeletons of the heads of insects

Tentorium, the singular form, has nine letters and therefore is not entered.

The comparative and superlative forms of adjectives and adverbs are shown, when applicable, immediately following the part-of-speech label. Any spelling changes are indicated in the forms shown.

CLEAR   *adj* **CLEARER, CLEAREST** clean and pure

FAR   *adv* **FARTHER, FARTHEST** or **FURTHER, FURTHEST** at or to a great distance

CAGEY   *adj* **CAGIER, CAGIEST** shrewd

Not all adjectives or adverbs can be inflected, and only those inflected forms shown are acceptable. None of the adjectives and adverbs listed as run-on entries in this dictionary have inflected forms.

RUN-ON ENTRIES ●

A main entry may be followed by one or more derivatives in boldface type with a different part-of-speech label. These are run-on entries. Run-on entries are not defined since their meanings are readily derivable from the meaning of the root word.

AKINESIA   *n* pl. -S loss of muscle function
     AKINETIC *adj*

PLEON   *n* pl. -S the abdomen of a crustacean
     PLEONAL, PLEONIC *adj*

No entry has been run on at another if it would fall alphabetically four or more places from the entry. **When you do not find a word at its own place, it is always wise to check several entries above and below to see if it is run on.**

CROSS-REFERENCES ●

A cross-reference is a main entry that is an inflected form of another word (such as the plural form of a noun, the past tense form of a verb, or the comparative form of an adjective). An inflected form is entered as a main entry if it undergoes a spelling change in addition to or instead of suffixation *and* if it falls alphabetically four or more places away from the root word.

For example, in the entries reproduced below, **DICING** is a main entry because it involves a spelling change (the final *-e* of *dice* is dropped) besides the addition of the **-ING** ending and because it falls four or more places from the entry **DICE**. On the other hand, *dices* is not a main entry because it involves no spelling change beyond the addition of the ending **-S**. The word *diced*, although involving a spelling change (the final *-e* of *dice* is dropped), is not a main entry because it does not fall four or more places from **DICE**. **DICIER** and **DICIEST** are main entries because they involve a spelling change (the *-e-* is dropped and the final *-y* is changed to *-i-*) besides the addition of the **-ER**, **-EST** endings and they fall four or more places from the entry **DICEY**.

DICE	*v* **DICED, DICING, DICES** to cut into small cubes
DICENTRA	*n* pl. **-S** a perennial herb
DICER	*n* pl. **-S** a device that dices food
DICEY	*adj* **DICIER, DICIEST** dangerous
DICHASIA	*n/pl* flower clusters
DICHOTIC	*adj* affecting the two ears differently
DICHROIC	*adj* having two colors
DICIER	comparative of dicey
DICIEST	superlative of dicey
DICING	present participle of dice

This policy is intended to make the word desired as easy to find as possible without wasting space. Nevertheless, many inflected forms will appear only at the main entry. **You should always look several entries above and below the expected place if you do not find the desired word as a main entry.**

Cross-reference entries for present tense third person singular forms of verbs use the abbreviation "sing."

DEFINITIONS ● In most cases, only one very brief definition is given for each main entry since definitions do not play a significant role in the SCRABBLE® crossword game. This definition serves only to orient the player in a general way to a single meaning of the word. It is not intended to have all the precision and detail of a definition in a good general dictionary.

When a word consisting of eight letters or less appears in a definition but is not an entry in this dictionary, it is glossed in parentheses. For example, at the entry for the adjective *drifty*, the noun "drifts" is used in the definition and is glossed because the noun *drift* is not a separate entry.

DRIFTY	*v* **DRIFTIER, DRIFTIEST** full of drifts (masses of wind-driven snow)

A main entry that is a variant form of another entry is defined in terms of the most common form, which is entered and defined at its own alphabetical place.

SCHMALTZ	*n* pl. **-ES** excessive sentimentality
SCHMALZ	*n* pl. **-ES** schmaltz
SHMALTZ	*n* pl. **-ES** schmaltz

SCRABBLE® crossword game players in Canada will be pleased to learn that variant forms such as *honour*, *centre*, and *cheque*, which are often omitted from general dictionaries, have also been included in this book.

LISTS OF UNDEFINED WORDS ● Two separate lists of undefined words appear below the entries that begin with RE- and with UN-. These words are not defined because they are self-explanatory: their meanings are simply the sum of a meaning of the prefix *re-* or *un-* and a meaning of the root word. All of their inflected forms are given, however.

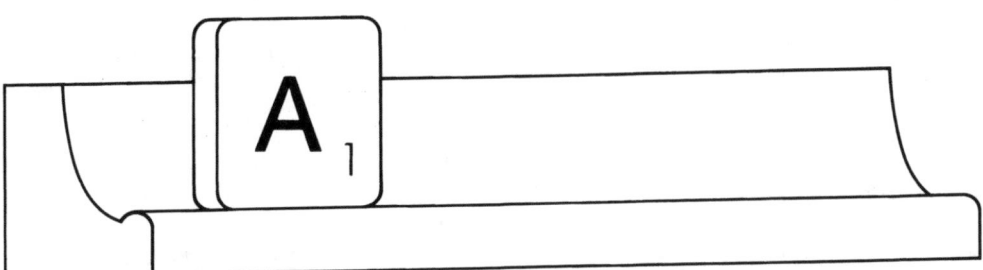

AA *n* pl. **-S** rough, cindery lava

AAH *v* **-ED, -ING, -S** to exclaim in amazement, joy, or surprise

AAL *n* pl. **-S** an East Indian shrub

AALII *n* pl. **-S** a tropical tree

AARDVARK *n* pl. **-S** an African mammal

AARDWOLF *n* pl. **-WOLVES** an African mammal

AARGH *interj* — used to express disgust

AARRGH *interj* aargh

AARRGHH *interj* aargh

AASVOGEL *n* pl. **-S** a vulture

AB *n* pl. **-S** an abdominal muscle

ABA *n* pl. **-S** a sleeveless garment worn by Arabs

ABACA *n* pl. **-S** a Philippine plant

ABACK *adv* toward the back

ABACUS *n* pl. **-CUSES** or **-CI** a calculating device

ABAFT *adv* toward the stern

ABAKA *n* pl. **-S** abaca

ABALONE *n* pl. **-S** an edible shellfish

ABAMP *n* pl. **-S** abampere

ABAMPERE *n* pl. **-S** a unit of electric current

ABANDON *v* **-ED, -ING, -S** to leave or give up completely

ABAPICAL *adj* directed away from the apex

ABASE *v* **ABASED, ABASING, ABASES** to lower in rank, prestige, or esteem **ABASEDLY** *adv*

ABASER *n* pl. **-S** one that abases

ABASH *v* **-ED, -ING, -ES** to make ashamed or embarrassed

ABASIA *n* pl. **-S** a defect in muscular coordination in walking

ABASING present participle of abase

ABATE *v* **ABATED, ABATING, ABATES** to reduce in degree or intensity **ABATABLE** *adj*

ABATER *n* pl. **-S** one that abates

ABATIS *n* pl. **-TISES** a barrier made of felled trees

ABATOR *n* pl. **-S** one that unlawfully seizes an inheritance

ABATTIS *n* pl. **-TISES** abatis

ABATTOIR *n* pl. **-S** a slaughterhouse

ABAXIAL *adj* situated away from the axis

ABAXILE *adj* abaxial

ABAYA *n* pl. **-S** a long loose robe worn by Arab women

ABBA *n* pl. **-S** father — used as a title of honor

ABBACY *n* pl. **-CIES** the office of an abbot

ABBATIAL *adj* pertaining to an abbot

ABBE *n* pl. **-S** an abbot

ABBESS *n* pl. **-ES** the female superior of a convent of nuns

ABBEY *n* pl. **-BEYS** a monastery or convent

ABBOT *n* pl. **-S** the superior of a monastery

ABBOTCY *n* pl. **-CIES** abbacy

ABDICATE *v* **-CATED, -CATING, -CATES** to give up formally

ABDOMEN *n* pl. **-MENS** or **-MINA** the body cavity containing the viscera

ABDUCE *v* **-DUCED, -DUCING, -DUCES** to abduct

ABDUCENS *n* pl. **-CENTES** a cranial nerve

ABDUCENT *adj* serving to abduct

ABDUCING present participle of abduce

ABDUCT *v* **-ED, -ING, -S** to draw away from the original position

ABDUCTEE *n* pl. **-S** one that has been abducted

ABDUCTOR *n* pl. **-S** or **-ES** an abducent muscle

ABEAM *adv* at right angles to the keel of a ship

ABED *adv* in bed

ABEGGING *adj* begging

ABELE *n* pl. **-S** a Eurasian tree

ABELIA *n* pl. **-S** an Asian or Mexican shrub

ABELIAN *adj* being a commutative group in mathematics

ABELMOSK *n* pl. **-S** a tropical herb

ABERRANT *n* pl. **-S** a deviant

ABET *v* **ABETTED, ABETTING, ABETS** to encourage and support

ABETMENT *n* pl. **-S** the act of abetting

ABETTAL *n* pl. **-S** abetment

ABETTED past tense of abet

ABETTER *n* pl. **-S** abettor

ABETTING present participle of abet

ABETTOR *n* pl. **-S** one that abets

ABEYANCE *n* pl. **-S** temporary inactivity

ABEYANCY *n* pl. **-CIES** abeyance

ABEYANT *adj* marked by abeyance

ABFARAD *n* pl. **-S** a unit of capacitance

ABHENRY *n* pl. **-RYS** or **-RIES** a unit of inductance

ABHOR *v* **-HORRED, -HORRING, -HORS** to loathe

ABHORRER *n* pl. **-S** one that abhors

ABIDANCE *n* pl. **-S** the act of abiding

ABIDE *v* **ABIDED** or **ABODE, ABIDING, ABIDES** to accept without objection

ABIDER *n* pl. **-S** one that abides

ABIGAIL *n* pl. **-S** a lady's maid

ABILITY *n* pl. **-TIES** the quality of being able to do something

ABIOSIS *n* pl. **-OSES** absence of life **ABIOTIC** *adj*

ABJECT *adj* sunk to a low condition **ABJECTLY** *adv*

ABJURE *v* **-JURED, -JURING, -JURES** to renounce under oath

ABJURER *n* pl. **-S** one that abjures

ABLATE *v* **-LATED, -LATING, -LATES** to remove by cutting

ABLATION *n* pl. **-S** surgical removal of a bodily part

ABLATIVE *n* pl. **-S** a grammatical case

ABLATOR *n* pl. **-S** one that ablates

ABLAUT *n* pl. **-S** a patterned change in root vowels of verb forms

ABLAZE *adj* being on fire

ABLE *adj* **ABLER, ABLEST** having sufficient power, skill, or resources

ABLE *n* pl. **-S** a communications code word for the letter A

ABLED *adj* capable of unimpaired function

ABLEGATE *n* pl. **-S** a papal envoy

ABLEISM *n* pl. **-S** prejudice or discrimination against disabled people

ABLEIST *n* pl. **-S** one that practices ableism

ABLER comparative of able

ABLEST superlative of able

ABLINGS *adv* ablins

ABLINS *adv* perhaps

ABLOOM *adj* blooming

ABLUENT *n* pl. **-S** a cleansing agent

ABLUSH *adj* blushing

ABLUTED *adj* washed clean

ABLUTION *n* pl. **-S** a washing

ABLY *adv* in an able manner

ABMHO *n* pl. **-MHOS** a unit of electrical conductance

ABNEGATE *v* **-GATED, -GATING, -GATES** to deny to oneself

ABNORMAL *n* pl. **-S** a mentally deficient person

ABOARD *adv* into, in, or on a ship, train, or airplane

ABODE *v* **ABODED, ABODING, ABODES** to forebode

ABOHM *n* pl. **-S** a unit of electrical resistance

ABOIDEAU *n* pl. **-DEAUS** or **-DEAUX** a type of dike

ABOIL *adj* boiling

ABOITEAU *n* pl. **-TEAUS** or **-TEAUX** aboideau

ABOLISH *v* **-ED, -ING, -ES** to do away with

ABOLLA *n* pl. **-LAE** a cloak worn in ancient Rome

ABOMA *n* pl. **-S** a South American snake

ABOMASAL *adj* pertaining to the abomasum

ABOMASUM *n* pl. **-SA** the fourth stomach of a ruminant

ABOMASUS *n* pl. **-MASI** abomasum

ABOON *adv* above

ABORAL *adj* situated away from the mouth **ABORALLY** *adv*

ABORNING *adv* while being born

ABORT   v **-ED, -ING, -S** to bring forth a fetus prematurely

ABORTER   n pl. **-S** one that aborts

ABORTION   n pl. **-S** induced expulsion of a nonviable fetus

ABORTIVE   adj failing to succeed

ABORTUS   n pl. **-ES** an aborted fetus

ABOUGHT   past tense of aby and abye

ABOULIA   n pl. **-S** abulia **ABOULIC** adj

ABOUND   v **-ED, -ING, -S** to have a large number or amount

ABOUT   adv approximately

ABOVE   n pl. **-S** something that is above (in a higher place)

ABRACHIA   n pl. **-S** a lack of arms

ABRADANT   n pl. **-S** an abrasive

ABRADE   v **ABRADED, ABRADING, ABRADES** to wear away by friction

ABRADER   n pl. **-S** a tool for abrading

ABRASION   n pl. **-S** the act of abrading

ABRASIVE   n pl. **-S** an abrading substance

ABREACT   v **-ED, -ING, -S** to release repressed emotions by reliving the original traumatic experience

ABREAST   adv side by side

ABRI   n pl. **-S** a bomb shelter

ABRIDGE   v **ABRIDGED, ABRIDGING, ABRIDGES** to reduce the length of

ABRIDGER   n pl. **-S** one that abridges

ABROACH   adj astir

ABROAD   adv out of one's own country

ABROGATE   v **-GATED, -GATING, -GATES** to abolish by authoritative action

ABROSIA   n pl. **-S** a fasting from food

ABRUPT   adj **-RUPTER, -RUPTEST** rudely brief **ABRUPTLY** adv

ABSCESS   v **-ED, -ING, -ES** to form an abscess (a localized collection of pus surrounded by inflamed tissue)

ABSCISE   v **-SCISED, -SCISING, -SCISES** to cut off

ABSCISIN   n pl. **-S** a regulatory substance found in plants

ABSCISSA   n pl. **-SAS** or **-SAE** a particular geometric coordinate

ABSCOND   v **-ED, -ING, -S** to depart suddenly and secretly

ABSEIL   v **-ED, -ING, -S** to rappel

ABSENCE   n pl. **-S** the state of being away

ABSENT   v **-ED, -ING, -S** to take or keep away

ABSENTEE   n pl. **-S** one that is not present

ABSENTER   n pl. **-S** one that absents himself

ABSENTLY   adv in an inattentive manner

ABSINTH   n pl. **-S** absinthe

ABSINTHE   n pl. **-S** a bitter liqueur

ABSOLUTE   adj **-LUTER, -LUTEST** free from restriction

ABSOLUTE   n pl. **-S** something that is absolute

ABSOLVE   v **-SOLVED, -SOLVING, -SOLVES** to free from the consequences of an action

ABSOLVER   n pl. **-S** one that absolves

ABSONANT   adj unreasonable

ABSORB   v **-ED, -ING, -S** to take up or in

ABSORBER   n pl. **-S** one that absorbs

ABSTAIN   v **-ED, -ING, -S** to refrain voluntarily

ABSTERGE   v **-STERGED, -STERGING, -STERGES** to cleanse by wiping

ABSTRACT   adj **-STRACTER, -STRACTEST** difficult to understand

ABSTRACT   v **-ED, -ING, -S** to take away

ABSTRICT   v **-ED, -ING, -S** to form by cutting off

ABSTRUSE   adj **-STRUSER, -STRUSEST** difficult to understand

ABSURD   adj **-SURDER, -SURDEST** ridiculously incongruous or unreasonable **ABSURDLY** adv

ABSURD   n pl. **-S** the condition in which man exists in an irrational and meaningless universe

ABUBBLE   adj bubbling

ABULIA   n pl. **-S** loss of will power **ABULIC** adj

ABUNDANT   adj present in great quantity

ABUSE   v **ABUSED, ABUSING, ABUSES** to use wrongly or improperly **ABUSABLE** adj

ABUSER   n pl. **-S** one that abuses

ABUSIVE   adj characterized by wrong or improper use

ABUT   v **ABUTTED, ABUTTING, ABUTS** to touch along a border

ABUTILON   n pl. **-S** a flowering plant

ABUTMENT   n pl. **-S** something that abuts

ABUTTAL   n pl. **-S** an abutment

ABUTTED   past tense of abut

ABUTTER *n* pl. **-S** one that abuts

ABUTTING present participle of abut

ABUZZ *adj* buzzing

ABVOLT *n* pl. **-S** a unit of electromotive force

ABWATT *n* pl. **-S** a unit of power

ABY *v* **ABOUGHT, ABYING, ABYS** to pay the penalty for

ABYE *v* **ABOUGHT, ABYING, ABYES** to aby

ABYSM *n* pl. **-S** an abyss

ABYSMAL *adj* immeasurably deep

ABYSS *n* pl. **-ES** a bottomless chasm **ABYSSAL** *adj*

ACACIA *n* pl. **-S** a flowering tree or shrub

ACADEME *n* pl. **-S** a place of instruction

ACADEMIA *n* pl. **-S** scholastic life or environment

ACADEMIC *n* pl. **-S** a college student or teacher

ACADEMY *n* pl. **-MIES** a secondary school

ACAJOU *n* pl. **-S** a tropical tree

ACALEPH *n* pl. **-LEPHS** or **-LEPHAE** a jellyfish

ACALEPHE *n* pl. **-S** acaleph

ACANTHA *n* pl. **-THAE** a sharp spiny part

ACANTHUS *n* pl. **-THUSES** or **-THI** a prickly herb

ACAPNIA *n* pl. **-S** a lack of carbon dioxide in blood and tissues

ACARBOSE *n* pl. **-S** a drug for treating diabetes

ACARI pl. of acarus

ACARID *n* pl. **-S** a type of arachnid

ACARIDAN *n* pl. **-S** acarid

ACARINE *n* pl. **-S** acarid

ACAROID *adj* resembling an acarid

ACARPOUS *adj* not producing fruit

ACARUS *n* pl. **-RI** a mite

ACAUDAL *adj* having no tail

ACAUDATE *adj* acaudal

ACAULINE *adj* having no stem

ACAULOSE *adj* acauline

ACAULOUS *adj* acauline

ACCEDE *v* **-CEDED, -CEDING, -CEDES** to consent

ACCEDER *n* pl. **-S** one that accedes

ACCENT *v* **-ED, -ING, -S** to pronounce with prominence

ACCENTOR *n* pl. **-S** a songbird

ACCEPT *v* **-ED, -ING, -S** to receive willingly

ACCEPTEE *n* pl. **-S** one that is accepted

ACCEPTER *n* pl. **-S** one that accepts

ACCEPTOR *n* pl. **-S** accepter

ACCESS *v* **-ED, -ING, -ES** to get at

ACCIDENT *n* pl. **-S** an unexpected or unintentional occurrence

ACCIDIA *n* pl. **-S** acedia

ACCIDIE *n* pl. **-S** acedia

ACCLAIM *v* **-ED, -ING, -S** to shout approval of

ACCOLADE *v* **-LADED, -LADING, -LADES** to praise

ACCORD *v* **-ED, -ING, -S** to bring into agreement

ACCORDER *n* pl. **-S** one that accords

ACCOST *v* **-ED, -ING, -S** to approach and speak to first

ACCOUNT *v* **-ED, -ING, -S** to give an explanation

ACCOUTER *v* **-ED, -ING, -S** to equip

ACCOUTRE *v* **-TRED, -TRING, -TRES** to accouter

ACCREDIT *v* **-ED, -ING, -S** to give official authorization to

ACCRETE *v* **-CRETED, -CRETING, -CRETES** to grow together

ACCRUAL *n* pl. **-S** the act of accruing

ACCRUE *v* **-CRUED, -CRUING, -CRUES** to come as an increase or addition

ACCURACY *n* pl. **-CIES** the quality of being accurate

ACCURATE *adj* free from error

ACCURSED *adj* damnable

ACCURST *adj* accursed

ACCUSAL *n* pl. **-S** the act of accusing

ACCUSANT *n* pl. **-S** an accuser

ACCUSE *v* **-CUSED, -CUSING, -CUSES** to make an assertion against

ACCUSER *n* pl. **-S** one that accuses

ACCUSTOM *v* **-ED, -ING, -S** to make familiar

ACE *v* **ACED, ACING, ACES** to score a point against in a single stroke

ACEDIA *n* pl. **-S** apathy

ACELDAMA *n* pl. **-S** a place of bloodshed

ACENTRIC *adj* having no center

ACEQUIA *n* pl. **-S** an irrigation ditch or canal

ACERATE	*adj* acerose
ACERATED	*adj* acerose
ACERB	*adj* **ACERBER, ACERBEST** sour
ACERBATE	*v* **-BATED, -BATING, -BATES** to make sour
ACERBIC	*adj* acerb
ACERBITY	*n* pl. **-TIES** sourness
ACEROLA	*n* pl. **-S** a West Indian shrub
ACEROSE	*adj* needle-shaped
ACEROUS	*adj* acerose
ACERVATE	*adj* growing in compact clusters
ACERVULI	*n/pl* spore-producing organs of certain fungi
ACESCENT	*n* pl. **-S** something that is slightly sour
ACETA	pl. of acetum
ACETAL	*n* pl. **-S** a flammable liquid
ACETAMID	*n* pl. **-S** an amide of acetic acid
ACETATE	*n* pl. **-S** a salt of acetic acid **ACETATED** *adj*
ACETIC	*adj* pertaining to vinegar
ACETIFY	*v* **-FIED, -FYING, -FIES** to convert into vinegar
ACETIN	*n* pl. **-S** a chemical compound
ACETONE	*n* pl. **-S** a flammable liquid **ACETONIC** *adj*
ACETOSE	*adj* acetous
ACETOUS	*adj* tasting like vinegar
ACETOXYL	*n* pl. **-S** a univalent radical
ACETUM	*n* pl. **-TA** vinegar
ACETYL	*n* pl. **-S** a univalent radical **ACETYLIC** *adj*
ACHE	*v* **ACHED, ACHING, ACHES** to suffer a dull, continuous pain
ACHENE	*n* pl. **-S** a type of fruit **ACHENIAL** *adj*
ACHIER	comparative of achy
ACHIEST	superlative of achy
ACHIEVE	*v* **ACHIEVED, ACHIEVING, ACHIEVES** to carry out successfully
ACHIEVER	*n* pl. **-S** one that achieves
ACHILLEA	*n* pl. **-S** yarrow
ACHINESS	*n* pl. **-ES** the state of being achy
ACHING	present participle of ache
ACHINGLY	*adv* in an aching manner
ACHIOTE	*n* pl. **-S** a yellowish red dye

ACHIRAL	*adj* pertaining to a symmetrical molecule
ACHOLIA	*n* pl. **-S** a lack of bile
ACHOO	*interj* ahchoo
ACHROMAT	*n* pl. **-S** a type of lens
ACHROMIC	*adj* having no color
ACHY	*adj* **ACHIER, ACHIEST** aching
ACICULA	*n* pl. **-LAS** or **-LAE** a needlelike part or process **ACICULAR** *adj*
ACICULUM	*n* pl. **-LUMS** or **-LA** a bristlelike part
ACID	*n* pl. **-S** a type of chemical compound
ACIDEMIA	*n* pl. **-S** a condition of increased acidity of the blood
ACIDHEAD	*n* pl. **-S** one who uses LSD
ACIDIC	*adj* sour
ACIDIFY	*v* **-FIED, -FYING, -FIES** to convert into an acid
ACIDITY	*n* pl. **-TIES** sourness
ACIDLY	*adv* sourly
ACIDNESS	*n* pl. **-ES** acidity
ACIDOSIS	*n* pl. **-DOSES** an abnormal condition of the blood **ACIDOTIC** *adj*
ACIDURIA	*n* pl. **-S** a condition of having excessive amounts of acid in the urine
ACIDY	*adj* sour
ACIERATE	*v* **-ATED, -ATING, -ATES** to turn into steel
ACIFORM	*adj* needle-shaped
ACING	present participle of ace
ACINUS	*n* pl. **-NI** a small, saclike division of a gland **ACINAR, ACINIC, ACINOSE, ACINOUS** *adj*
ACKEE	*n* pl. **-S** akee
ACLINIC	*adj* having no inclination
ACME	*n* pl. **-S** the highest point **ACMATIC, ACMIC** *adj*
ACNE	*n* pl. **-S** a skin disease **ACNED** *adj*
ACNODE	*n* pl. **-S** an element of a mathematical set that is isolated from the other elements
ACOCK	*adj* cocked
ACOELOUS	*adj* lacking a true body cavity
ACOLD	*adj* cold
ACOLYTE	*n* pl. **-S** an assistant
ACONITE	*n* pl. **-S** a poisonous herb **ACONITIC** *adj*

ACONITUM *n pl.* **-S** aconite

ACORN *n pl.* **-S** the fruit of the oak tree **ACORNED** *adj*

ACOUSTIC *n pl.* **-S** a hearing aid

ACQUAINT *v* **-ED, -ING, -S** to cause to know

ACQUEST *n pl.* **-S** something acquired

ACQUIRE *v* **-QUIRED, -QUIRING, -QUIRES** to come into possession of

ACQUIREE *n pl.* **-S** one that is acquired

ACQUIRER *n pl.* **-S** one that acquires

ACQUIT *v* **-QUITTED, -QUITTING, -QUITS** to free or clear from a charge of fault or crime

ACRASIA *n pl.* **-S** a lack of self-control

ACRASIN *n pl.* **-S** a substance secreted by the cells of a slime mold

ACRE *n pl.* **-S** a unit of area

ACREAGE *n pl.* **-S** area in acres

ACRED *adj* owning many acres

ACRID *adj* **-RIDER, -RIDEST** sharp and harsh to the taste or smell

ACRIDINE *n pl.* **-S** a chemical compound

ACRIDITY *n pl.* **-TIES** the state of being acrid

ACRIDLY *adv* in an acrid manner

ACRIMONY *n pl.* **-NIES** sharpness or bitterness of speech or temper

ACROBAT *n pl.* **-S** one skilled in feats of agility and balance

ACRODONT *n pl.* **-S** an animal having rootless teeth

ACROGEN *n pl.* **-S** a plant growing at the apex only

ACROLECT *n pl.* **-S** a high form of a language

ACROLEIN *n pl.* **-S** a flammable liquid

ACROLITH *n pl.* **-S** a type of statue

ACROMION *n pl.* **-MIA** the outward end of the shoulder blade **ACROMIAL** *adj*

ACRONIC *adj* occurring at sunset

ACRONYM *n pl.* **-S** a word formed from the initials of a compound term or series of words

ACROSOME *n pl.* **-S** a thin sac at the head of a sperm

ACROSS *prep* from one side of to the other

ACROSTIC *n pl.* **-S** a poem in which certain letters taken in order form a word or phrase

ACROTISM *n pl.* **-S** weakness of the pulse **ACROTIC** *adj*

ACRYLATE *n pl.* **-S** an acrylic

ACRYLIC *n pl.* **-S** a type of resin

ACT *v* **-ED, -ING, -S** to do something

ACTA *n/pl* recorded proceedings

ACTABLE *adj* suitable for performance on the stage

ACTIN *n pl.* **-S** a protein in muscle tissue

ACTINAL *adj* having tentacles

ACTING *n pl.* **-S** the occupation of an actor

ACTINIA *n pl.* **-IAS** or **-IAE** a marine animal

ACTINIAN *n pl.* **-S** actinia

ACTINIC *adj* pertaining to actinism

ACTINIDE *n pl.* **-S** any of a series of radioactive elements

ACTINISM *n pl.* **-S** the property of radiant energy that effects chemical changes

ACTINIUM *n pl.* **-S** a radioactive element

ACTINOID *n pl.* **-S** an actinide

ACTINON *n pl.* **-S** an isotope of radon

ACTION *n pl.* **-S** the process of acting

ACTIONER *n pl.* **-S** a film with exciting action

ACTIVATE *v* **-VATED, -VATING, -VATES** to set in motion

ACTIVE *n pl.* **-S** a participating member of an organization

ACTIVELY *adv* with activity

ACTIVISM *n pl.* **-S** a doctrine that emphasizes direct and decisive action

ACTIVIST *n pl.* **-S** an advocate of activism

ACTIVITY *n pl.* **-TIES** brisk action or movement

ACTIVIZE *v* **-IZED, -IZING, -IZES** to activate

ACTOR *n pl.* **-S** a theatrical performer **ACTORISH, ACTORLY** *adj*

ACTRESS *n pl.* **-ES** a female actor **ACTRESSY** *adj*

ACTUAL *adj* existing in fact **ACTUALLY** *adv*

ACTUARY *n pl.* **-ARIES** a statistician who computes insurance risks and premiums

ACTUATE *v* **-ATED, -ATING, -ATES** to set into action or motion

ACTUATOR *n pl.* **-S** one that actuates

ACUATE *adj* sharp

ACUITY *n pl.* **-ITIES** sharpness

ACULEATE *adj* having a sting

ACULEUS *n pl.* **-LEI** a sharp-pointed part

ACUMEN *n pl.* **-S** mental keenness

ACUTANCE *n* pl. **-S** a measure of photographic clarity

ACUTE *adj* **ACUTER, ACUTEST** marked by sharpness or severity **ACUTELY** *adv*

ACUTE *n* pl. **-S** a type of accent mark

ACYCLIC *adj* not cyclic

ACYL *n* pl. **-S** a univalent radical

ACYLATE *v* **-ATED, -ATING, -ATES** to introduce acyl into

ACYLOIN *n* pl. **-S** a type of chemical compound

AD *n* pl. **-S** an advertisement

ADAGE *n* pl. **-S** a traditional saying expressing a common observation **ADAGIAL** *adj*

ADAGIO *n* pl. **-GIOS** a musical composition or movement played in a slow tempo

ADAMANCE *n* pl. **-S** adamancy

ADAMANCY *n* pl. **-CIES** unyielding hardness

ADAMANT *n* pl. **-S** an extremely hard substance

ADAMSITE *n* pl. **-S** a lung-irritating gas

ADAPT *v* **-ED, -ING, -S** to make suitable

ADAPTER *n* pl. **-S** one that adapts

ADAPTION *n* pl. **-S** the act of adapting **ADAPTIVE** *adj*

ADAPTOR *n* pl. **-S** adapter

ADAXIAL *adj* situated on the same side as

ADD *v* **-ED, -ING, -S** to combine or join so as to bring about an increase **ADDABLE** *adj*

ADDAX *n* pl. **-ES** a large antelope

ADDEDLY *adv* additionally

ADDEND *n* pl. **-S** a number to be added to another

ADDENDUM *n* pl. **-DUMS** or **-DA** something added or to be added

ADDER *n* pl. **-S** a venomous snake

ADDIBLE *adj* capable of being added

ADDICT *v* **-ED, -ING, -S** to devote or surrender to something habitually or compulsively

ADDITION *n* pl. **-S** something added

ADDITIVE *n* pl. **-S** a substance added to another to impart desirable qualities

ADDITORY *adj* making an addition

ADDLE *v* **-DLED, -DLING, -DLES** to confuse

ADDRESS *v* **-DRESSED** or **-DREST, -DRESSING, -DRESSES** to speak to

ADDUCE *v* **-DUCED, -DUCING, -DUCES** to bring forward as evidence

ADDUCENT *adj* serving to adduct

ADDUCER *n* pl. **-S** one that adduces

ADDUCING present participle of adduce

ADDUCT *v* **-ED, -ING, -S** to draw toward the main axis

ADDUCTOR *n* pl. **-S** an adducent muscle

ADEEM *v* **-ED, -ING, -S** to take away

ADENINE *n* pl. **-S** an alkaloid

ADENITIS *n* pl. **-TISES** inflammation of a lymph node

ADENOID *n* pl. **-S** an enlarged lymphoid growth behind the pharynx

ADENOMA *n* pl. **-MAS** or **-MATA** a tumor of glandular origin

ADENOSIS *n* pl. **-NOSES** abnormal growth of glandular tissue

ADENYL *n* pl. **-S** a univalent radical

ADEPT *adj* **ADEPTER, ADEPTEST** highly skilled **ADEPTLY** *adv*

ADEPT *n* pl. **-S** an adept person

ADEQUACY *n* pl. **-CIES** the state of being adequate

ADEQUATE *adj* sufficient for a specific requirement

ADHERE *v* **-HERED, -HERING, -HERES** to become or remain attached or close to something

ADHEREND *n* pl. **-S** the surface to which an adhesive adheres

ADHERENT *n* pl. **-S** a supporter

ADHERER *n* pl. **-S** one that adheres

ADHERING present participle of adhere

ADHESION *n* pl. **-S** the act of adhering

ADHESIVE *n* pl. **-S** a substance that causes adhesion

ADHIBIT *v* **-ED, -ING, -S** to take or let in

ADIEU *n* pl. **ADIEUS** or **ADIEUX** a farewell

ADIOS *interj* — used to express farewell

ADIPOSE *n* pl. **-S** animal fat **ADIPIC** *adj*

ADIPOSIS *n* pl. **-POSES** obesity

ADIPOUS *adj* pertaining to adipose

ADIT *n* pl. **-S** an entrance

ADJACENT *adj* next to

ADJOIN   *v* **-ED, -ING, -S** to lie next to

ADJOINT   *n* pl. **-S** a type of mathematical matrix

ADJOURN   *v* **-ED, -ING, -S** to suspend until a later time

ADJUDGE   *v* **-JUDGED, -JUDGING, -JUDGES** to determine judicially

ADJUNCT   *n* pl. **-S** something attached in a subordinate position

ADJURE   *v* **-JURED, -JURING, -JURES** to command solemnly

ADJURER   *n* pl. **-S** one that adjures

ADJUROR   *n* pl. **-S** adjurer

ADJUST   *v* **-ED, -ING, -S** to bring to a more satisfactory state

ADJUSTER   *n* pl. **-S** one that adjusts

ADJUSTOR   *n* pl. **-S** adjuster

ADJUTANT   *n* pl. **-S** an assistant

ADJUVANT   *n* pl. **-S** an assistant

ADMAN   *n* pl. **-MEN** a man employed in the advertising business

ADMASS   *n* pl. **-ES** mass-media advertising

ADMIRAL   *n* pl. **-S** a high-ranking naval officer

ADMIRE   *v* **-MIRED, -MIRING, -MIRES** to regard with wonder, pleasure, and approval

ADMIRER   *n* pl. **-S** one that admires

ADMIT   *v* **-MITTED, -MITTING, -MITS** to allow to enter

ADMITTEE   *n* pl. **-S** one that is admitted

ADMITTER   *n* pl. **-S** one that admits

ADMIX   *v* **-MIXED** or **-MIXT, -MIXING, -MIXES** to mix

ADMONISH   *v* **-ED, -ING, -ES** to reprove mildly or kindly

ADNATE   *adj* joined to another part or organ

ADNATION   *n* pl. **-S** the state of being adnate

ADNEXA   *n/pl* conjoined anatomical parts **ADNEXAL** *adj*

ADNOUN   *n* pl. **-S** an adjective when used as a noun

ADO   *n* pl. **ADOS** bustling excitement

ADOBE   *n* pl. **-S** an unburnt, sun-dried brick

ADOBO   *n* pl. **-BOS** a Philippine dish of fish or meat

ADONIS   *n* pl. **-ISES** a handsome young man

ADOPT   *v* **-ED, -ING, -S** to take into one's family by legal means

ADOPTEE   *n* pl. **-S** one that is adopted

ADOPTER   *n* pl. **-S** one that adopts

ADOPTION   *n* pl. **-S** the act of adopting **ADOPTIVE** *adj*

ADORABLE   *adj* worthy of being adored **ADORABLY** *adv*

ADORE   *v* **ADORED, ADORING, ADORES** to love deeply

ADORER   *n* pl. **-S** one that adores

ADORN   *v* **-ED, -ING, -S** to add something to for the purpose of making more attractive

ADORNER   *n* pl. **-S** one that adorns

ADOWN   *adv* downward

ADOZE   *adj* dozing

ADRENAL   *n* pl. **-S** an endocrine gland

ADRIFT   *adj* drifting

ADROIT   *adj* **ADROITER, ADROITEST** skillful **ADROITLY** *adv*

ADSCRIPT   *n* pl. **-S** a distinguishing symbol written after another character

ADSORB   *v* **-ED, -ING, -S** to gather on a surface in a condensed layer

ADSORBER   *n* pl. **-S** one that adsorbs

ADULARIA   *n* pl. **-S** a mineral

ADULATE   *v* **-LATED, -LATING, -LATES** to praise excessively

ADULATOR   *n* pl. **-S** one that adulates

ADULT   *n* pl. **-S** a fully developed individual

ADULTERY   *n* pl. **-TERIES** voluntary sexual intercourse between a married person and someone other than his or her spouse

ADULTLY   *adv* in a manner typical of an adult

ADUMBRAL   *adj* shadowy

ADUNC   *adj* bent inward

ADUNCATE   *adj* adunc

ADUNCOUS   *adj* adunc

ADUST   *adj* scorched

ADVANCE   *v* **-VANCED, -VANCING, -VANCES** to move or cause to move ahead

ADVANCER   *n* pl. **-S** one that advances

ADVECT   *v* **-ED, -ING, -S** to convey or transport by the flow of a fluid

ADVENT   *n* pl. **-S** arrival

ADVERB   *n* pl. **-S** a word used to modify a verb, adjective, or other adverb

ADVERSE   *adj* acting in opposition

ADVERT   *v* **-ED, -ING, -S** to call attention

ADVICE *n* pl. **-S** recommendation regarding a decision or action

ADVISE *v* **-VISED, -VISING, -VISES** to give advice to

ADVISEE *n* pl. **-S** one that is advised

ADVISER *n* pl. **-S** one that advises

ADVISING present participle of advise

ADVISOR *n* pl. **-S** adviser

ADVISORY *n* pl. **-RIES** a report giving information

ADVOCACY *n* pl. **-CIES** the act of advocating

ADVOCATE *v* **-CATED, -CATING, -CATES** to speak in favor of

ADVOWSON *n* pl. **-S** the right of presenting a nominee to a vacant church office

ADWOMAN *n* pl. **-MEN** a woman employed in the advertising business

ADYNAMIA *n* pl. **-S** lack of physical strength **ADYNAMIC** *adj*

ADYTUM *n* pl. **-TA** an inner sanctuary in an ancient temple

ADZ *v* **-ED, -ING, -ES** to shape (wood) with an adz (a cutting tool)

ADZE *v* **ADZED, ADZING, ADZES** to adz

ADZUKI *n* pl. **-S** the edible seed of an Asian plant

AE *adj* one

AECIA pl. of aecium

AECIAL *adj* pertaining to an aecium

AECIDIAL *adj* pertaining to an aecium

AECIDIUM *n* pl. **-IA** an aecium

AECIUM *n* pl. **-IA** a spore-producing organ of certain fungi

AEDES *n* pl. **AEDES** any of a genus of mosquitoes

AEDILE *n* pl. **-S** a magistrate of ancient Rome

AEDINE *adj* pertaining to an aedes

AEGIS *n* pl. **-GISES** protection

AENEOUS *adj* having a greenish gold color

AENEUS *adj* aeneous

AEOLIAN *adj* eolian

AEON *n* pl. **-S** eon

AEONIAN *adj* eonian

AEONIC *adj* eonian

AEQUORIN *n* pl. **-S** a protein secreted by jellyfish

AERATE *v* **-ATED, -ATING, -ATES** to supply with air

AERATION *n* pl. **-S** the act of aerating

AERATOR *n* pl. **-S** one that aerates

AERIAL *n* pl. **-S** an antenna

AERIALLY *adv* in a manner pertaining to the air

AERIE *n* pl. **-S** a bird's nest built high on a mountain or cliff **AERIED** *adj*

AERIER comparative of aery

AERIES pl. of aery

AERIEST superlative of aery

AERIFORM *adj* having the form of air

AERIFY *v* **-FIED, -FYING, -FIES** to aerate

AERILY *adv* in an aery manner

AERO *adj* pertaining to aircraft

AEROBAT *n* pl. **-S** one that performs feats in an aircraft

AEROBE *n* pl. **-S** an organism that requires oxygen to live **AEROBIC** *adj*

AEROBICS *n/pl* exercises for conditioning the heart and lungs by increasing oxygen consumption

AEROBIUM *n* pl. **-BIA** aerobe

AERODUCT *n* pl. **-S** a type of jet engine

AERODYNE *n* pl. **-S** an aircraft that is heavier than air

AEROFOIL *n* pl. **-S** airfoil

AEROGEL *n* pl. **-S** a highly porous solid

AEROGRAM *n* pl. **-S** an airmail letter

AEROLITE *n* pl. **-S** a meteorite containing more stone than iron

AEROLITH *n* pl. **-S** aerolite

AEROLOGY *n* pl. **-GIES** the study of the atmosphere

AERONAUT *n* pl. **-S** one who operates an airship

AERONOMY *n* pl. **-MIES** the study of the upper atmosphere

AEROSAT *n* pl. **-S** a satellite for use in air-traffic control

AEROSOL *n* pl. **-S** a gaseous suspension of fine solid or liquid particles

AEROSTAT *n* pl. **-S** an aircraft that is lighter than air

AERUGO *n* pl. **-GOS** a green film that forms on copper

AERY *adj* **AERIER, AERIEST** airy

AERY *n* pl. **AERIES** aerie

AESTHETE *n* pl. **-S** esthete

AESTIVAL *adj* estival

AETHER *n* pl. **-S** the upper region of the atmosphere **AETHERIC** *adj*

AFAR *n* pl. **-S** a great distance

AFEARD *adj* afraid

AFEARED *adj* afeard

AFEBRILE *adj* having no fever

AFF *adv* off

AFFABLE *adj* easy to talk to **AFFABLY** *adv*

AFFAIR *n* pl. **-S** anything done or to be done

AFFAIRE *n* pl. **-S** a brief amorous relationship

AFFECT *v* **-ED, -ING, -S** to give a false appearance of

AFFECTER *n* pl. **-S** one that affects

AFFERENT *n* pl. **-S** a nerve that conveys impulses toward a nerve center

AFFIANCE *v* **-ANCED, -ANCING, -ANCES** to betroth

AFFIANT *n* pl. **-S** one who makes a written declaration under oath

AFFICHE *n* pl. **-S** a poster

AFFINAL *adj* related by marriage

AFFINE *n* pl. **-S** a relative by marriage

AFFINED *adj* closely related

AFFINELY *adv* in the manner of a type of mathematical mapping

AFFINITY *n* pl. **-TIES** a natural attraction or inclination

AFFIRM *v* **-ED, -ING, -S** to state positively

AFFIRMER *n* pl. **-S** one that affirms

AFFIX *v* **-ED, -ING, -ES** to attach

AFFIXAL *adj* pertaining to a prefix or suffix

AFFIXER *n* pl. **-S** one that affixes

AFFIXIAL *adj* affixal

AFFLATUS *n* pl. **-ES** a creative inspiration

AFFLICT *v* **-ED, -ING, -S** to distress with mental or physical pain

AFFLUENT *n* pl. **-S** a stream that flows into another

AFFLUX *n* pl. **-ES** a flowing toward a point

AFFORD *v* **-ED, -ING, -S** to have sufficient means for

AFFOREST *v* **-ED, -ING, -S** to convert into forest

AFFRAY *v* **-ED, -ING, -S** to frighten

AFFRAYER *n* pl. **-S** one that affrays

AFFRIGHT *v* **-ED, -ING, -S** to frighten

AFFRONT *v* **-ED, -ING, -S** to insult openly

AFFUSION *n* pl. **-S** an act of pouring a liquid on

AFGHAN *n* pl. **-S** a woolen blanket or shawl

AFGHANI *n* pl. **-S** a monetary unit of Afghanistan

AFIELD *adv* in the field

AFIRE *adj* being on fire

AFLAME *adj* flaming

AFLOAT *adj* floating

AFLUTTER *adj* nervously excited

AFOOT *adv* on foot

AFORE *adv* before

AFOUL *adj* entangled

AFRAID *adj* filled with apprehension

AFREET *n* pl. **-S** an evil spirit in Arabic mythology

AFRESH *adv* anew

AFRIT *n* pl. **-S** afreet

AFT *adv* toward the stern

AFTER *prep* behind in place or order

AFTERS *n/pl* dessert

AFTERTAX *adj* remaining after payment of taxes

AFTMOST *adj* nearest the stern

AFTOSA *n* pl. **-S** a disease of hoofed mammals

AG *n* pl. **-S** agriculture

AGA *n* pl. **-S** a high-ranking Turkish military officer

AGAIN *adv* once more

AGAINST *prep* in opposition to

AGALLOCH *n* pl. **-S** the fragrant wood of a tropical tree

AGALWOOD *n* pl. **-S** agalloch

AGAMA *n* pl. **-S** a tropical lizard

AGAMETE *n* pl. **-S** an asexual reproductive cell

AGAMIC *adj* asexual

AGAMID *n* pl. **-S** an Old World lizard

AGAMOUS *adj* agamic

AGAPE *n* pl. **-PES** or **-PAE** or **-PAI** a communal meal of fellowship **AGAPEIC** *adj*

AGAR *n* pl. **-S** a viscous substance obtained from certain seaweeds

AGARIC *n* pl. **-S** any of a family of fungi

AGAROSE *n* pl. **-S** a sugar obtained from agar

AGATE	*n* pl. **-S** a variety of quartz **AGATOID** *adj*
AGATIZE	*v* **-IZED, -IZING, -IZES** to cause to resemble agate
AGAVE	*n* pl. **-S** a tropical plant
AGAZE	*adj* gazing
AGE	*v* **AGED, AGING** or **AGEING, AGES** to grow old
AGEDLY	*adv* in the manner of an old person
AGEDNESS	*n* pl. **-ES** oldness
AGEE	*adv* to one side
AGEING	*n* pl. **-S** aging
AGEISM	*n* pl. **-S** discrimination based on age
AGEIST	*n* pl. **-S** an advocate of ageism
AGELESS	*adj* never growing old
AGELONG	*adj* lasting for a long time
AGEMATE	*n* pl. **-S** a person of the same age as another
AGENCY	*n* pl. **-CIES** an organization that does business for others
AGENDA	*n* pl. **-S** a list of things to be done
AGENDUM	*n* pl. **-S** an item on an agenda
AGENE	*n* pl. **-S** a chemical compound used in bleaching flour
AGENESIA	*n* pl. **-S** agenesis
AGENESIS	*n* pl. **AGENESES** absence or imperfect development of a bodily part **AGENETIC** *adj*
AGENIZE	*v* **-NIZED, -NIZING, -NIZES** to treat with agene
AGENT	*v* **-ED, -ING, -S** to act as a representative for **AGENTIAL** *adj*
AGENTING	*n* pl. **-S** the business or activities of an agent
AGENTIVE	*n* pl. **-S** a word part that denotes the doer of an action
AGENTRY	*n* pl. **-RIES** the office or duties of an agent
AGER	*n* pl. **-S** one that ages
AGERATUM	*n* pl. **-S** a flowering plant
AGGADA	*n* pl. **-DAS** or **-DOT** or **-DOTH** haggadah
AGGADAH	*n* pl. **-DAHS** or **-DOT** or **-DOTH** haggadah
AGGADIC	*adj* haggadic
AGGER	*n* pl. **-S** a mound of earth used as a fortification
AGGIE	*n* pl. **-S** a type of playing marble
AGGRADE	*v* **-GRADED, -GRADING, -GRADES** to fill with detrital material
AGGRESS	*v* **-ED, -ING, -ES** to commit the first act of hostility
AGGRIEVE	*v* **-GRIEVED, -GRIEVING, -GRIEVES** to distress
AGGRO	*n* pl. **-GROS** a rivalry or grievance
AGHA	*n* pl. **-S** aga
AGHAST	*adj* shocked by something horrible
AGILE	*adj* able to move quickly and easily **AGILELY** *adv*
AGILITY	*n* pl. **-TIES** the quality of being agile
AGIN	*prep* against
AGING	*n* pl. **-S** the process of growing old
AGINNER	*n* pl. **-S** one that is against change
AGIO	*n* pl. **AGIOS** a premium paid for the exchange of one currency for another
AGIOTAGE	*n* pl. **-S** the business of a broker
AGISM	*n* pl. **-S** ageism
AGIST	*v* **-ED, -ING, -S** to feed and take care of for a fee, as livestock
AGITA	*n* pl. **-S** a feeling of agitation
AGITATE	*v* **-TATED, -TATING, -TATES** to move with a violent, irregular action **AGITABLE** *adj*
AGITATO	*adj* fast and stirring — used as a musical direction
AGITATOR	*n* pl. **-S** one that agitates
AGITPROP	*n* pl. **-S** pro-Communist propaganda
AGLARE	*adj* glaring
AGLEAM	*adj* gleaming
AGLEE	*adv* agley
AGLET	*n* pl. **-S** a metal sheath at the end of a lace
AGLEY	*adv* awry
AGLIMMER	*adj* glimmering
AGLITTER	*adj* glittering
AGLOW	*adj* glowing
AGLY	*adv* agley
AGLYCON	*n* pl. **-S** a type of chemical compound
AGLYCONE	*n* pl. **-S** aglycon
AGMA	*n* pl. **-S** eng
AGMINATE	*adj* clustered together

AGNAIL   *n* pl. **-S** a piece of loose skin at the base of a fingernail

AGNATE   *n* pl. **-S** a relative on the father's side **AGNATIC** *adj*

AGNATION   *n* pl. **-S** the relationship of agnates

AGNIZE   *v* **-NIZED, -NIZING, -NIZES** to acknowledge

AGNOMEN   *n* pl. **-MENS** or **-MINA** an additional name given to an ancient Roman

AGNOSIA   *n* pl. **-S** loss of ability to recognize familiar objects

AGNOSTIC   *n* pl. **-S** one who disclaims any knowledge of God

AGO   *adv* in the past

AGOG   *adv* in a state of eager curiosity

AGON   *n* pl. **-S** or **-ES** the dramatic conflict between the main characters in a Greek play

AGONAL   *adj* pertaining to agony

AGONE   *adv* ago

AGONIC   *adj* not forming an angle

AGONIES   pl. of agony

AGONISE   *v* **-NISED, -NISING, -NISES** to agonize

AGONIST   *n* pl. **-S** one that is engaged in a struggle

AGONIZE   *v* **-NIZED, -NIZING, -NIZES** to suffer extreme pain

AGONY   *n* pl. **-NIES** extreme pain

AGORA   *n* pl. **-RAS** or **-RAE** a marketplace in ancient Greece

AGORA   *n* pl. **AGOROT** or **AGOROTH** a monetary unit of Israel

AGOUTI   *n* pl. **-S** or **-ES** a burrowing rodent

AGOUTY   *n* pl. **-TIES** agouti

AGRAFE   *n* pl. **-S** agraffe

AGRAFFE   *n* pl. **-S** an ornamental clasp

AGRAPHA   *n/pl* the sayings of Jesus not found in the Bible

AGRAPHIA   *n* pl. **-S** a mental disorder marked by inability to write **AGRAPHIC** *adj*

AGRARIAN   *n* pl. **-S** one who favors equal distribution of land

AGRAVIC   *adj* pertaining to a condition of no gravitation

AGREE   *v* **AGREED, AGREEING, AGREES** to have the same opinion

AGRESTAL   *adj* growing wild

AGRESTIC   *adj* rural

AGRIA   *n* pl. **-S** severe pustular eruption

AGRIMONY   *n* pl. **-NIES** a perennial herb

AGROLOGY   *n* pl. **-GIES** the science of soils in relation to crops

AGRONOMY   *n* pl. **-MIES** the application of scientific principles to the cultivation of land

AGROUND   *adv* on the ground

AGRYPNIA   *n* pl. **-S** insomnia

AGUACATE   *n* pl. **-S** an avocado

AGUE   *n* pl. **-S** a malarial fever **AGUELIKE, AGUISH** *adj* **AGUISHLY** *adv*

AGUEWEED   *n* pl. **-S** a flowering plant

AH   *v* **-ED, -ING, -S** aah

AHA   *interj* — used to express surprise, triumph, or derision

AHCHOO   *interj* — used to represent the sound of a sneeze

AHEAD   *adv* at or to the front

AHEM   *interj* — used to attract attention

AHI   *n* pl. **-S** a marine food fish

AHIMSA   *n* pl. **-S** the Hindu principle of nonviolence

AHOLD   *n* pl. **-S** a hold or grasp of something

AHORSE   *adv* on a horse

AHOY   *interj* — used in hailing a ship or person

AHULL   *adj* abandoned and flooded, as a ship

AI   *n* pl. **-S** a three-toed sloth

AIBLINS   *adv* ablins

AID   *v* **-ED, -ING, -S** to help

AIDE   *n* pl. **-S** an assistant

AIDER   *n* pl. **-S** one that aids

AIDFUL   *adj* helpful

AIDLESS   *adj* helpless

AIDMAN   *n* pl. **-MEN** a corpsman

AIGLET   *n* pl. **-S** aglet

AIGRET   *n* pl. **-S** aigrette

AIGRETTE   *n* pl. **-S** a tuft of feathers worn as a head ornament

AIGUILLE   *n* pl. **-S** a sharp, pointed mountain peak

AIKIDO   *n* pl. **-DOS** a Japanese art of self-defense

AIL   *v* **-ED, -ING, -S** to cause pain or discomfort to

AILERON *n* pl. **-S** a movable control surface on an airplane wing

AILMENT *n* pl. **-S** a physical or mental disorder

AIM *v* **-ED, -ING, -S** to direct toward a specified object or goal

AIMER *n* pl. **-S** one that aims

AIMFUL *adj* full of purpose **AIMFULLY** *adv*

AIMLESS *adj* lacking direction or purpose

AIN *n* pl. **-S** ayin

AINSELL *n* pl. **-S** own self

AIOLI *n* pl. **-S** garlic mayonnaise

AIR *adv* **AIRER, AIREST** early

AIR *v* **-ED, -ING, -S** to expose to the air (the mixture of gases that surrounds the earth)

AIRBAG *n* pl. **-S** an inflatable safety device in an automobile

AIRBOAT *n* pl. **-S** a boat used in swampy areas

AIRBORNE *adj* flying

AIRBOUND *adj* stopped up by air

AIRBRUSH *v* **-ED, -ING, -ES** to apply in a fine spray by compressed air, as paint

AIRBURST *n* pl. **-S** an explosion in the air

AIRBUS *n* pl. **-BUSES** or **-BUSSES** a passenger airplane

AIRCHECK *n* pl. **-S** a recording made from a radio broadcast

AIRCOACH *n* pl. **-ES** the cheaper class of accommodations in commercial aircraft

AIRCRAFT *n* pl. **AIRCRAFT** any machine or device capable of flying

AIRCREW *n* pl. **-S** the crew of an aircraft

AIRDATE *n* pl. **-S** the scheduled date of a broadcast

AIRDROME *n* pl. **-S** an airport

AIRDROP *v* **-DROPPED, -DROPPING, -DROPS** to drop from an aircraft

AIRER *n* pl. **-S** a frame on which to dry clothes

AIRFARE *n* pl. **-S** payment for travel by airplane

AIRFIELD *n* pl. **-S** an airport

AIRFLOW *n* pl. **-S** a flow of air

AIRFOIL *n* pl. **-S** a part of an aircraft designed to provide lift or control

AIRFRAME *n* pl. **-S** the framework and external covering of an airplane

AIRGLOW *n* pl. **-S** a glow in the upper atmosphere

AIRHEAD *n* pl. **-S** a stupid person

AIRHOLE *n* pl. **-S** a hole to let air in or out

AIRIER comparative of airy

AIRIEST superlative of airy

AIRILY *adv* in an airy manner

AIRINESS *n* pl. **-ES** the state of being airy

AIRING *n* pl. **-S** an exposure to the air

AIRLESS *adj* having no air

AIRLIFT *v* **-ED, -ING, -S** to transport by airplane

AIRLIKE *adj* resembling air

AIRLINE *n* pl. **-S** an air transportation system

AIRLINER *n* pl. **-S** a large passenger aircraft

AIRMAIL *v* **-ED, -ING, -S** to send mail by airplane

AIRMAN *n* pl. **-MEN** an aviator

AIRN *n* pl. **-S** iron (a mineral element)

AIRPARK *n* pl. **-S** a small airport

AIRPLANE *n* pl. **-S** a winged aircraft propelled by jet engines or propellers

AIRPLAY *n* pl. **-PLAYS** the playing of a record on a radio program

AIRPORT *n* pl. **-S** a tract of land maintained for the landing and takeoff of aircraft

AIRPOST *n* pl. **-S** a system of conveying mail by airplane

AIRPOWER *n* pl. **-S** the military strength of a nation's air force

AIRPROOF *v* **-ED, -ING, -S** to make impermeable to air

AIRSCAPE *n* pl. **-S** a view of the earth from an aircraft or a high position

AIRSCREW *n* pl. **-S** an airplane propeller

AIRSHED *n* pl. **-S** the air supply of a given region

AIRSHIP *n* pl. **-S** a lighter-than-air aircraft having propulsion and steering systems

AIRSHOT *n* pl. **-S** an aircheck

AIRSHOW *n* pl. **-S** an exhibition of aircraft stunts

AIRSICK *adj* nauseated from flying in an airplane

AIRSPACE *n* pl. **-S** the portion of the atmosphere above a particular land area

AIRSPEED	*n* pl. **-S** the speed of an aircraft with relation to the air	**ALAMO**	*n* pl. **-MOS** a softwood tree
AIRSTRIP	*n* pl. **-S** a runway	**ALAMODE**	*n* pl. **-S** a silk fabric
AIRT	*v* **-ED, -ING, -S** to guide	**ALAN**	*n* pl. **-S** a large hunting dog
AIRTH	*v* **-ED, -ING, -S** to airt	**ALAND**	*n* pl. **-S** alan
AIRTIGHT	*adj* not allowing air to escape or enter	**ALANE**	*adj* alone
AIRTIME	*n* pl. **-S** the time when a broadcast begins	**ALANG**	*adv* along
		ALANIN	*n* pl. **-S** alanine
AIRWARD	*adv* toward the sky	**ALANINE**	*n* pl. **-S** an amino acid
AIRWAVE	*n* pl. **-S** the medium of radio and television transmission	**ALANT**	*n* pl. **-S** alan
		ALANYL	*n* pl. **-S** a univalent radical
AIRWAY	*n* pl. **-WAYS** a passageway in which air circulates	**ALAR**	*adj* pertaining to wings
		ALARM	*v* **-ED, -ING, -S** to frighten by a sudden revelation of danger
AIRWISE	*adj* skillful in aviation	**ALARMISM**	*n* pl. **-S** the practice of alarming others needlessly
AIRWOMAN	*n* pl. **-WOMEN** a female aviator		
AIRY	*adj* **AIRIER, AIRIEST** having the nature of air	**ALARMIST**	*n* pl. **-S** one who alarms others needlessly
AISLE	*n* pl. **-S** a passageway between sections of seats **AISLED** *adj*	**ALARUM**	*v* **-ED, -ING, -S** to alarm
		ALARY	*adj* alar
AISLEWAY	*n* pl. **-WAYS** an aisle	**ALAS**	*interj* — used to express sorrow or regret
AIT	*n* pl. **-S** a small island		
AITCH	*n* pl. **-ES** the letter H	**ALASKA**	*n* pl. **-S** a heavy fabric
AIVER	*n* pl. **-S** a draft horse	**ALASTOR**	*n* pl. **-S** an avenging deity in Greek tragedy
AJAR	*adj* partly open		
AJEE	*adv* agee	**ALATE**	*n* pl. **-S** a winged insect
AJIVA	*n* pl. **-S** inanimate matter	**ALATED**	*adj* having wings
AJOWAN	*n* pl. **-S** the fruit of an Egyptian plant	**ALATION**	*n* pl. **-S** the state of having wings
		ALB	*n* pl. **-S** a long-sleeved vestment
AJUGA	*n* pl. **-S** a flowering plant	**ALBA**	*n* pl. **-S** the white substance of the brain
AKEE	*n* pl. **-S** a tropical tree		
AKELA	*n* pl. **-S** a leader of a cub scout pack	**ALBACORE**	*n* pl. **-S** a marine food fish
		ALBATA	*n* pl. **-S** an alloy of copper, nickel, and zinc
AKENE	*n* pl. **-S** achene		
AKIMBO	*adj* having hands on hips and elbows bent outward	**ALBEDO**	*n* pl. **-DOS** or **-DOES** the ratio of the light reflected by a planet to that received by it
AKIN	*adj* related by blood		
AKINESIA	*n* pl. **-S** loss of muscle function **AKINETIC** *adj*	**ALBEIT**	*conj* although
		ALBICORE	*n* pl. **-S** albacore
AKVAVIT	*n* pl. **-S** aquavit	**ALBINAL**	*adj* albinic
AL	*n* pl. **-S** an East Indian tree	**ALBINIC**	*adj* pertaining to albinism
ALA	*n* pl. **ALAE** a wing or winglike part	**ALBINISM**	*n* pl. **-S** the condition of being an albino
ALACHLOR	*n* pl. **-S** an herbicide		
ALACK	*interj* — used to express sorrow or regret	**ALBINO**	*n* pl. **-NOS** an organism lacking normal pigmentation
ALACRITY	*n* pl. **-TIES** cheerful promptness	**ALBITE**	*n* pl. **-S** a mineral **ALBITIC** *adj*
ALAE	pl. of ala	**ALBIZIA**	*n* pl. **-S** a tropical tree
ALAMEDA	*n* pl. **-S** a shaded walkway	**ALBIZZIA**	*n* pl. **-S** albizia

ALBUM	n pl. **-S** a book for preserving photographs or stamps
ALBUMEN	n pl. **-S** the white of an egg
ALBUMIN	n pl. **-S** a simple protein
ALBUMOSE	n pl. **-S** a proteose
ALBURNUM	n pl. **-S** sapwood
ALCADE	n pl. **-S** alcalde
ALCAHEST	n pl. **-S** alkahest
ALCAIC	n pl. **-S** a type of verse form
ALCAIDE	n pl. **-S** the commander of a Spanish fortress
ALCALDE	n pl. **-S** the mayor of a Spanish town
ALCAYDE	n pl. **-S** alcaide
ALCAZAR	n pl. **-S** a Spanish fortress or palace
ALCHEMY	n pl. **-MIES** a medieval form of chemistry **ALCHEMIC** adj
ALCHYMY	n pl. **-MIES** alchemy
ALCID	n pl. **-S** a diving seabird
ALCIDINE	adj pertaining to a family of seabirds
ALCOHOL	n pl. **-S** a flammable liquid
ALCOVE	n pl. **-S** a recessed section of a room **ALCOVED** adj
ALDEHYDE	n pl. **-S** a type of chemical compound
ALDER	n pl. **-S** a shrub or small tree
ALDERFLY	n pl. **-FLIES** a winged insect
ALDERMAN	n pl. **-MEN** a member of a municipal legislative body
ALDICARB	n pl. **-S** a pesticide
ALDOL	n pl. **-S** a chemical compound
ALDOLASE	n pl. **-S** an enzyme
ALDOSE	n pl. **-S** a type of sugar
ALDRIN	n pl. **-S** an insecticide
ALE	n pl. **-S** an alcoholic beverage
ALEATORY	adj pertaining to luck
ALEC	n pl. **-S** a herring
ALEE	adv toward the side of a vessel sheltered from the wind
ALEF	n pl. **-S** aleph
ALEGAR	n pl. **-S** sour ale
ALEHOUSE	n pl. **-S** a tavern where ale is sold
ALEMBIC	n pl. **-S** an apparatus formerly used in distilling
ALENCON	n pl. **-S** a needlepoint lace
ALEPH	n pl. **-S** a Hebrew letter

ALERT	adj **ALERTER, ALERTEST** ready for sudden action **ALERTLY** adv
ALERT	v **-ED, -ING, -S** to warn
ALEURON	n pl. **-S** aleurone
ALEURONE	n pl. **-S** protein matter found in the seeds of certain plants
ALEVIN	n pl. **-S** a young fish
ALEWIFE	n pl. **-WIVES** a marine fish
ALEXIA	n pl. **-S** a cerebral disorder marked by the loss of the ability to read
ALEXIN	n pl. **-S** a substance in the blood that aids in the destruction of bacteria
ALEXINE	n pl. **-S** alexin
ALFA	n pl. **-S** a communications code word for the letter A
ALFAKI	n pl. **-S** alfaqui
ALFALFA	n pl. **-S** a plant cultivated for use as hay and forage
ALFAQUI	n pl. **-S** a teacher of Muslim law
ALFAQUIN	n pl. **-S** alfaqui
ALFORJA	n pl. **-S** a leather bag
ALFREDO	adj served with a white cheese sauce
ALFRESCO	adv outdoors
ALGA	n pl. **-GAS** or **-GAE** any of a group of primitive aquatic plants **ALGAL** adj
ALGAROBA	n pl. **-S** the mesquite
ALGEBRA	n pl. **-S** a branch of mathematics
ALGERINE	n pl. **-S** a woolen fabric
ALGICIDE	n pl. **-S** a substance used to kill algae
ALGID	adj cold
ALGIDITY	n pl. **-TIES** coldness
ALGIN	n pl. **-S** a viscous substance obtained from certain algae
ALGINATE	n pl. **-S** a chemical salt
ALGOID	adj resembling algae
ALGOLOGY	n pl. **-GIES** the study of algae
ALGOR	n pl. **-S** coldness
ALGORISM	n pl. **-S** the Arabic system of arithmetic notation
ALGUM	n pl. **-S** almug
ALIAS	n pl. **-ES** an assumed name
ALIASING	n pl. **-S** the appearance of distortions in computer graphics
ALIBI	v **-BIED, -BIING, -BIS** or **-BIES** to make excuses for oneself

ALIBLE	*adj* nourishing
ALIDAD	*n* pl. **-S** alidade
ALIDADE	*n* pl. **-S** a device used in angular measurement
ALIEN	*v* **-ED, -ING, -S** to transfer to another, as property
ALIENAGE	*n* pl. **-S** the state of being foreign
ALIENATE	*v* **-ATED, -ATING, -ATES** to make indifferent or unfriendly
ALIENEE	*n* pl. **-S** one to whom property is transferred
ALIENER	*n* pl. **-S** alienor
ALIENISM	*n* pl. **-S** alienage
ALIENIST	*n* pl. **-S** a physician who treats mental disorders
ALIENLY	*adv* in a foreign manner
ALIENOR	*n* pl. **-S** one that transfers property
ALIF	*n* pl. **-S** an Arabic letter
ALIFORM	*adj* shaped like a wing
ALIGHT	*v* **ALIGHTED** or **ALIT, ALIGHTING, ALIGHTS** to come down from something
ALIGN	*v* **-ED, -ING, -S** to arrange in a straight line
ALIGNER	*n* pl. **-S** one that aligns
ALIKE	*adj* having close resemblance
ALIMENT	*v* **-ED, -ING, -S** to nourish
ALIMONY	*n* pl. **-NIES** an allowance paid to a woman by her divorced husband
ALINE	*v* **ALINED, ALINING, ALINES** to align
ALINER	*n* pl. **-S** aligner
ALIPED	*n* pl. **-S** an animal having a membrane connecting the toes
ALIQUANT	*adj* not dividing evenly into another number
ALIQUOT	*n* pl. **-S** a number that divides evenly into another
ALIST	*adj* leaning to one side
ALIT	a past tense of alight
ALIUNDE	*adv* from a source extrinsic to the matter at hand
ALIVE	*adj* having life
ALIYA	*n* pl. **-S** aliyah
ALIYAH	*n* pl. **-YAHS** or **-YOS** or **-YOT** the immigration of Jews to Israel
ALIZARIN	*n* pl. **-S** a red dye
ALKAHEST	*n* pl. **-S** the hypothetical universal solvent sought by alchemists
ALKALI	*n* pl. **-LIS** or **-LIES** a type of chemical compound **ALKALIC** *adj*
ALKALIFY	*v* **-FIED, -FYING, -FIES** to alkalize
ALKALIN	*adj* alkaline
ALKALINE	*adj* containing an alkali
ALKALISE	*v* **-LISED, -LISING, -LISES** to alkalize
ALKALIZE	*v* **-LIZED, -LIZING, -LIZES** to convert into an alkali
ALKALOID	*n* pl. **-S** a type of chemical compound
ALKANE	*n* pl. **-S** a type of chemical compound
ALKANET	*n* pl. **-S** a European plant
ALKENE	*n* pl. **-S** a type of chemical compound
ALKIE	*n* pl. **-S** alky
ALKIES	pl. of alky
ALKINE	*n* pl. **-S** alkyne
ALKOXIDE	*n* pl. **-S** a type of chemical salt
ALKOXY	*adj* containing a univalent radical composed of alkyl united with oxygen
ALKY	*n* pl. **-KIES** one who is habitually drunk
ALKYD	*n* pl. **-S** a synthetic resin
ALKYL	*n* pl. **-S** a univalent radical **ALKYLIC** *adj*
ALKYLATE	*v* **-ATED, -ATING, -ATES** to combine with alkyl
ALKYNE	*n* pl. **-S** a type of chemical compound
ALL	*n* pl. **-S** everything that one has
ALLANITE	*n* pl. **-S** a mineral
ALLAY	*v* **-ED, -ING, -S** to reduce in intensity or severity
ALLAYER	*n* pl. **-S** one that allays
ALLEE	*n* pl. **-S** a tree-lined walkway
ALLEGE	*v* **-LEGED, -LEGING, -LEGES** to assert without proof or before proving
ALLEGER	*n* pl. **-S** one that alleges
ALLEGORY	*n* pl. **-RIES** a story presenting a moral principle
ALLEGRO	*n* pl. **-GROS** a musical passage played in rapid tempo
ALLELE	*n* pl. **-S** any of several forms of a gene **ALLELIC** *adj*
ALLELISM	*n* pl. **-S** the state of possessing alleles

ALLELUIA	*n* pl. **-S** a song of praise to God
ALLERGEN	*n* pl. **-S** a substance capable of inducing an allergy
ALLERGIC	*adj* pertaining to allergy
ALLERGIN	*n* pl. **-S** allergen
ALLERGY	*n* pl. **-GIES** a state of hypersensitive reaction to certain things
ALLEY	*n* pl. **-LEYS** a narrow passageway
ALLEYWAY	*n* pl. **-WAYS** an alley
ALLHEAL	*n* pl. **-S** a medicinal herb
ALLIABLE	*adj* capable of being allied
ALLIANCE	*n* pl. **-S** an association formed to further the common interests of its members
ALLICIN	*n* pl. **-S** a liquid compound
ALLIED	past tense of ally
ALLIES	present 3d person sing. of ally
ALLIUM	*n* pl. **-S** a bulbous herb
ALLOBAR	*n* pl. **-S** a change in barometric pressure
ALLOCATE	*v* **-CATED, -CATING, -CATES** to set apart for a particular purpose
ALLOD	*n* pl. **-S** allodium
ALLODIUM	*n* pl. **-DIA** land held in absolute ownership **ALLODIAL** *adj*
ALLOGAMY	*n* pl. **-MIES** fertilization of a flower by pollen from another
ALLONGE	*n* pl. **-S** an addition to a document
ALLONYM	*n* pl. **-S** the name of one person assumed by another
ALLOPATH	*n* pl. **-S** one who treats diseases by producing effects incompatible with those of the disease
ALLOSAUR	*n* pl. **-S** a large dinosaur
ALLOT	*v* **-LOTTED, -LOTTING, -LOTS** to give as a share or portion
ALLOTTEE	*n* pl. **-S** one to whom something is allotted
ALLOTTER	*n* pl. **-S** one that allots
ALLOTYPE	*n* pl. **-S** a type of antibody
ALLOTYPY	*n* pl. **-TYPIES** the condition of being an allotype
ALLOVER	*n* pl. **-S** a fabric having a pattern extending over the entire surface
ALLOW	*v* **-ED, -ING, -S** to put no obstacle in the way of
ALLOXAN	*n* pl. **-S** a chemical compound

ALLOY	*v* **-ED, -ING, -S** to combine to form an alloy (a homogenous mixture of metals)
ALLSEED	*n* pl. **-S** a plant having many seeds
ALLSORTS	*n/pl* assorted small candies
ALLSPICE	*n* pl. **-S** a tropical tree
ALLUDE	*v* **-LUDED, -LUDING, -LUDES** to make an indirect reference
ALLURE	*v* **-LURED, -LURING, -LURES** to attract with something desirable
ALLURER	*n* pl. **-S** one that allures
ALLUSION	*n* pl. **-S** the act of alluding **ALLUSIVE** *adj*
ALLUVIA	a pl. of alluvium
ALLUVIAL	*n* pl. **-S** soil composed of alluvium
ALLUVION	*n* pl. **-S** alluvium
ALLUVIUM	*n* pl. **-VIUMS** or **-VIA** detrital material deposited by running water
ALLY	*v* **-LIED, -LYING, -LIES** to unite in a formal relationship
ALLYL	*n* pl. **-S** a univalent radical **ALLYLIC** *adj*
ALMA	*n* pl. **-S** almah
ALMAGEST	*n* pl. **-S** a medieval treatise on astrology or alchemy
ALMAH	*n* pl. **-S** an Egyptian girl who sings and dances professionally
ALMANAC	*n* pl. **-S** an annual publication containing general information
ALMANACK	*n* pl. **-S** almanac
ALME	*n* pl. **-S** almah
ALMEH	*n* pl. **-S** almah
ALMEMAR	*n* pl. **-S** a bema
ALMIGHTY	*adj* having absolute power over all
ALMNER	*n* pl. **-S** almoner
ALMOND	*n* pl. **-S** the edible nut of a small tree **ALMONDY** *adj*
ALMONER	*n* pl. **-S** one that distributes alms
ALMONRY	*n* pl. **-RIES** a place where alms are distributed
ALMOST	*adv* very nearly
ALMS	*n* pl. **ALMS** money or goods given to the poor
ALMSMAN	*n* pl. **-MEN** one who receives alms
ALMUCE	*n* pl. **-S** a hooded cape
ALMUD	*n* pl. **-S** a Spanish unit of capacity
ALMUDE	*n* pl. **-S** almud

ALMUG *n* pl. **-S** a precious wood mentioned in the Bible

ALNICO *n* pl. **-COS** an alloy containing aluminum, nickel, and cobalt

ALODIUM *n* pl. **-DIA** allodium **ALODIAL** *adj*

ALOE *n* pl. **-S** an African plant **ALOETIC** *adj*

ALOFT *adv* in or into the air

ALOGICAL *adj* being outside the bounds of that to which logic can apply

ALOHA *n* pl. **-S** love — used as a greeting or farewell

ALOIN *n* pl. **-S** a laxative

ALONE *adj* apart from others

ALONG *adv* onward

ALOOF *adj* distant in interest or feeling **ALOOFLY** *adv*

ALOPECIA *n* pl. **-S** baldness **ALOPECIC** *adj*

ALOUD *adv* audibly

ALOW *adv* in or to a lower position

ALP *n* pl. **-S** a high mountain

ALPACA *n* pl. **-S** a ruminant mammal

ALPHA *n* pl. **-S** a Greek letter

ALPHABET *v* **-ED, -ING, -S** to arrange in the customary order of the letters of a language

ALPHORN *n* pl. **-S** a wooden horn used by Swiss herdsmen

ALPHOSIS *n* pl. **-SISES** lack of skin pigmentation

ALPHYL *n* pl. **-S** a univalent radical

ALPINE *n* pl. **-S** a plant native to high mountain regions

ALPINELY *adv* in a lofty manner

ALPINISM *n* pl. **-S** mountain climbing

ALPINIST *n* pl. **-S** a mountain climber

ALREADY *adv* by this time

ALRIGHT *adj* satisfactory

ALSIKE *n* pl. **-S** a European clover

ALSO *adv* in addition

ALT *n* pl. **-S** a high-pitched musical note

ALTAR *n* pl. **-S** a raised structure used in worship

ALTER *v* **-ED, -ING, -S** to make different

ALTERANT *n* pl. **-S** something that alters

ALTERER *n* pl. **-S** one that alters

ALTERITY *n* pl. **-TIES** the state of being other or different

ALTHAEA *n* pl. **-S** althea

ALTHEA *n* pl. **-S** a flowering plant

ALTHO *conj* although

ALTHORN *n* pl. **-S** a brass wind instrument

ALTHOUGH *conj* despite the fact that

ALTITUDE *n* pl. **-S** the vertical elevation of an object above a given level

ALTO *n* pl. **-TOS** a low female singing voice

ALTOIST *n* pl. **-S** one who plays the alto saxophone

ALTRUISM *n* pl. **-S** selfless devotion to the welfare of others

ALTRUIST *n* pl. **-S** one that practices altruism

ALUDEL *n* pl. **-S** a pear-shaped vessel

ALULA *n* pl. **-LAE** a tuft of feathers on the first digit of a bird's wing **ALULAR** *adj*

ALUM *n* pl. **-S** a chemical compound

ALUMIN *n* pl. **-S** alumina

ALUMINA *n* pl. **-S** an oxide of aluminum

ALUMINE *n* pl. **-S** alumina

ALUMINUM *n* pl. **-S** a metallic element **ALUMINIC** *adj*

ALUMNA *n* pl. **-NAE** a female graduate

ALUMNUS *n* pl. **-NI** a male graduate

ALUMROOT *n* pl. **-S** a flowering plant

ALUNITE *n* pl. **-S** a mineral

ALVEOLAR *n* pl. **-S** a sound produced with the tongue touching a place just behind the front teeth

ALVEOLUS *n* pl. **-LI** a small anatomical cavity

ALVINE *adj* pertaining to the abdomen and lower intestines

ALWAY *adv* always

ALWAYS *adv* at all times

ALYSSUM *n* pl. **-S** a flowering plant

AM present 1st person sing. of be

AMA *n* pl. **-S** amah

AMADAVAT *n* pl. **-S** an Asian songbird

AMADOU *n* pl. **-S** a substance prepared from fungi for use as tinder

AMAH *n* pl. **-S** an Oriental nurse

AMAIN *adv* with full strength

AMALGAM *n* pl. **-S** an alloy of mercury with another metal

AMANDINE *adj* prepared with almonds

AMANITA *n* pl. **-S** any of a genus of poisonous fungi

AMANITIN *n* pl. **-S** a chemical compound

AMARANTH *n* pl. **-S** a flowering plant

AMARELLE *n* pl. **-S** a variety of sour cherry

AMARETTI *n/pl* macaroons made with bitter almonds

AMARETTO *n* pl. **-TOS** a kind of liqueur

AMARNA *adj* pertaining to a certain historical period of ancient Egypt

AMARONE *n* pl. **-S** a dry red wine

AMASS *v* **-ED, -ING, -ES** to gather

AMASSER *n* pl. **-S** one that amasses

AMATEUR *n* pl. **-S** one that engages in an activity for pleasure

AMATIVE *adj* amorous

AMATOL *n* pl. **-S** a powerful explosive

AMATORY *adj* pertaining to sexual love

AMAZE *v* **AMAZED, AMAZING, AMAZES** to overwhelm with surprise or wonder **AMAZEDLY** *adv*

AMAZON *n* pl. **-S** a tall, powerful woman

AMBAGE *n* pl. **-S** a winding path

AMBARI *n* pl. **-S** ambary

AMBARY *n* pl. **-RIES** an East Indian plant

AMBEER *n* pl. **-S** tobacco juice

AMBER *n* pl. **-S** a fossil resin

AMBERINA *n* pl. **-S** a type of glassware

AMBEROID *n* pl. **-S** ambroid

AMBERY *n* pl. **-BERIES** ambry

AMBIANCE *n* pl. **-S** ambience

AMBIENCE *n* pl. **-S** the character, mood, or atmosphere of a place or situation

AMBIENT *n* pl. **-S** ambience

AMBIT *n* pl. **-S** the external boundary of something

AMBITION *v* **-ED, -ING, -S** to seek with eagerness

AMBIVERT *n* pl. **-S** a person whose personality type is intermediate between introvert and extravert

AMBLE *v* **-BLED, -BLING, -BLES** to saunter

AMBLER *n* pl. **-S** one that ambles

AMBO *n* pl. **AMBOS** or **AMBONES** a pulpit in an early Christian church

AMBOINA *n* pl. **-S** amboyna

AMBOYNA *n* pl. **-S** the mottled wood of an Indonesian tree

AMBRIES pl. of ambry

AMBROID *n* pl. **-S** a synthetic amber

AMBROSIA *n* pl. **-S** the food of the Greek and Roman gods

AMBRY *n* pl. **-BRIES** a recess in a church wall for sacred vessels

AMBSACE *n* pl. **-S** bad luck

AMBULANT *adj* ambulating

AMBULATE *v* **-LATED, -LATING, -LATES** to move or walk about

AMBUSH *v* **-ED, -ING, -ES** to attack from a concealed place

AMBUSHER *n* pl. **-S** one that ambushes

AMEBA *n* pl. **-BAS** or **-BAE** amoeba **AMEBAN, AMEBIC, AMEBOID** *adj*

AMEBEAN *adj* alternately responding

AMEER *n* pl. **-S** amir

AMEERATE *n* pl. **-S** amirate

AMELCORN *n* pl. **-S** a variety of wheat

AMEN *n* pl. **-S** a word used at the end of a prayer to express agreement

AMENABLE *adj* capable of being persuaded **AMENABLY** *adv*

AMEND *v* **-ED, -ING, -S** to improve

AMENDER *n* pl. **-S** one that amends

AMENITY *n* pl. **-TIES** the quality of being pleasant or agreeable

AMENT *n* pl. **-S** a mentally deficient person

AMENTIA *n* pl. **-S** mental deficiency

AMERCE *v* **AMERCED, AMERCING, AMERCES** to punish by imposing an arbitrary fine

AMERCER *n* pl. **-S** one that amerces

AMESACE *n* pl. **-S** ambsace

AMETHYST *n* pl. **-S** a variety of quartz

AMI *n* pl. **-S** a friend

AMIA *n* pl. **-S** a freshwater fish

AMIABLE *adj* having a pleasant disposition **AMIABLY** *adv*

AMIANTUS *n* pl. **-ES** a variety of asbestos

AMICABLE *adj* friendly **AMICABLY** *adv*

AMICE *n* pl. **-S** a vestment worn about the neck and shoulders

AMICUS *n* pl. **AMICI** one not party to a lawsuit but permitted by the court to advise it

AMID	*n* pl. **-S** amide
AMIDASE	*n* pl. **-S** an enzyme
AMIDE	*n* pl. **-S** a type of chemical compound **AMIDIC** *adj*
AMIDIN	*n* pl. **-S** the soluble matter of starch
AMIDINE	*n* pl. **-S** a type of chemical compound
AMIDO	*adj* containing an amide united with an acid radical
AMIDOGEN	*n* pl. **-S** a univalent chemical radical
AMIDOL	*n* pl. **-S** a chemical compound
AMIDONE	*n* pl. **-S** a chemical compound
AMIDSHIP	*adv* toward the middle of a ship
AMIDST	*prep* in the midst of
AMIE	*n* pl. **-S** a female friend
AMIGA	*n* pl. **-S** a female friend
AMIGO	*n* pl. **-GOS** a friend
AMIN	*n* pl. **-S** amine
AMINE	*n* pl. **-S** a type of chemical compound **AMINIC** *adj*
AMINITY	*n* pl. **-TIES** the state of being an amine
AMINO	*adj* containing an amine united with a nonacid radical
AMIR	*n* pl. **-S** a Muslim prince or governor
AMIRATE	*n* pl. **-S** the rank of an amir
AMISS	*adj* being out of proper order
AMITIES	pl. of amity
AMITOSIS	*n* pl. **-TOSES** a type of cell division **AMITOTIC** *adj*
AMITROLE	*n* pl. **-S** an herbicide
AMITY	*n* pl. **-TIES** friendship
AMMETER	*n* pl. **-S** an instrument for measuring amperage
AMMINE	*n* pl. **-S** a type of chemical compound
AMMINO	*adj* pertaining to an ammine
AMMO	*n* pl. **-MOS** ammunition
AMMOCETE	*n* pl. **-S** the larva of a lamprey
AMMONAL	*n* pl. **-S** a powerful explosive
AMMONIA	*n* pl. **-S** a pungent gas
AMMONIAC	*n* pl. **-S** a gum resin
AMMONIC	*adj* pertaining to ammonia
AMMONIFY	*v* **-FIED, -FYING, -FIES** to treat with ammonia

AMMONITE	*n* pl. **-S** the coiled shell of an extinct mollusk
AMMONIUM	*n* pl. **-S** a univalent chemical radical
AMMONO	*adj* containing ammonia
AMMONOID	*n* pl. **-S** ammonite
AMNESIA	*n* pl. **-S** loss of memory
AMNESIAC	*n* pl. **-S** one suffering from amnesia
AMNESIC	*n* pl. **-S** amnesiac
AMNESTIC	*adj* pertaining to amnesia
AMNESTY	*v* **-TIED, -TYING, -TIES** to pardon
AMNIO	*n* pl. **-NIOS** a surgical insertion of a needle into the uterus
AMNION	*n* pl. **-NIONS** or **-NIA** a membranous sac enclosing an embryo **AMNIC, AMNIONIC, AMNIOTIC** *adj*
AMNIOTE	*n* pl. **-S** a vertebrate that develops an amnion during the embryonic stage
AMOEBA	*n* pl. **-BAS** or **-BAE** a unicellular microscopic organism **AMOEBAN, AMOEBIC, AMOEBOID** *adj*
AMOEBEAN	*adj* amebean
AMOK	*n* pl. **-S** a murderous frenzy
AMOLE	*n* pl. **-S** a plant root used as a substitute for soap
AMONG	*prep* in the midst of
AMONGST	*prep* among
AMORAL	*adj* lacking a sense of right and wrong **AMORALLY** *adv*
AMORETTO	*n* pl. **-TOS** or **-TI** a cupid
AMORINO	*n* pl. **-NI** an amoretto
AMORIST	*n* pl. **-S** a lover
AMOROSO	*adv* tenderly — used as a musical direction
AMOROUS	*adj* pertaining to love
AMORT	*adj* being without life
AMORTISE	*v* **-TISED, -TISING, -TISES** to amortize
AMORTIZE	*v* **-TIZED, -TIZING, -TIZES** to liquidate gradually, as a debt
AMOSITE	*n* pl. **-S** a type of asbestos
AMOTION	*n* pl. **-S** the removal of a corporate officer from his office
AMOUNT	*v* **-ED, -ING, -S** to combine to yield a sum
AMOUR	*n* pl. **-S** a love affair
AMP	*v* **-ED, -ING, -S** to amplify

AMPERAGE *n* pl. **-S** the strength of an electric current expressed in amperes

AMPERE *n* pl. **-S** a unit of electric current strength

AMPHIBIA *n/pl* organisms adapted for life both on land and in water

AMPHIOXI *n/pl* lancelets

AMPHIPOD *n* pl. **-S** a small crustacean

AMPHORA *n* pl. **-RAS** or **-RAE** a narrow-necked jar used in ancient Greece **AMPHORAL** *adj*

AMPLE *adj* **-PLER, -PLEST** abundant **AMPLY** *adv*

AMPLEXUS *n* pl. **-ES** the mating embrace of frogs

AMPLIFY *v* **-FIED, -FYING, -FIES** to make larger or more powerful

AMPOULE *n* pl. **-S** ampule

AMPUL *n* pl. **-S** ampule

AMPULE *n* pl. **-S** a small glass vial

AMPULLA *n* pl. **-LAE** a globular bottle used in ancient Rome **AMPULLAR** *adj*

AMPUTATE *v* **-TATED, -TATING, -TATES** to cut off by surgical means

AMPUTEE *n* pl. **-S** one that has had a limb amputated

AMREETA *n* pl. **-S** amrita

AMRITA *n* pl. **-S** a beverage that bestows immortality in Hindu mythology

AMTRAC *n* pl. **-S** a military vehicle equipped to move on land and water

AMTRACK *n* pl. **-S** amtrac

AMU *n* pl. **-S** a unit of mass

AMUCK *n* pl. **-S** amok

AMULET *n* pl. **-S** an object worn to protect against evil or injury

AMUSE *v* **AMUSED, AMUSING, AMUSES** to occupy pleasingly **AMUSABLE** *adj* **AMUSEDLY** *adv*

AMUSER *n* pl. **-S** one that amuses

AMUSIA *n* pl. **-S** the inability to recognize musical sounds

AMUSIVE *adj* amusing

AMYGDALA *n* pl. **-LAE** an almond-shaped anatomical part

AMYGDALE *n* pl. **-S** amygdule

AMYGDULE *n* pl. **-S** a small gas bubble in lava

AMYL *n* pl. **-S** a univalent radical

AMYLASE *n* pl. **-S** an enzyme

AMYLENE *n* pl. **-S** a flammable liquid

AMYLIC *adj* pertaining to amyl

AMYLOGEN *n* pl. **-S** amylose

AMYLOID *n* pl. **-S** a hard protein deposit resulting from degeneration of tissue

AMYLOSE *n* pl. **-S** the relatively soluble component of starch

AMYLUM *n* pl. **-S** starch (a solid carbohydrate)

AN *indefinite article* — used before words beginning with a vowel sound

ANA *n* pl. **-S** a collection of miscellaneous information about a particular subject

ANABAENA *n* pl. **-S** a freshwater alga

ANABAS *n* pl. **-ES** a freshwater fish

ANABASIS *n* pl. **-ASES** a military advance

ANABATIC *adj* pertaining to rising wind currents

ANABLEPS *n* pl. **-ES** a freshwater fish

ANABOLIC *adj* pertaining to a process by which food is built up into protoplasm

ANACONDA *n* pl. **-S** a large snake

ANADEM *n* pl. **-S** a wreath for the head

ANAEMIA *n* pl. **-S** anemia **ANAEMIC** *adj*

ANAEROBE *n* pl. **-S** an organism that does not require oxygen to live

ANAGLYPH *n* pl. **-S** a type of carved ornament

ANAGOGE *n* pl. **-S** a spiritual interpretation of words **ANAGOGIC** *adj*

ANAGOGY *n* pl. **-GIES** anagoge

ANAGRAM *v* **-GRAMMED, -GRAMMING, -GRAMS** to transpose the letters of a word or phrase to form a new one

ANAL *adj* pertaining to the anus

ANALCIME *n* pl. **-S** analcite

ANALCITE *n* pl. **-S** a mineral

ANALECTA *n/pl* analects

ANALECTS *n/pl* selections from a literary work or group of works

ANALEMMA *n* pl. **-MAS** or **-MATA** a type of graduated scale

ANALGIA *n* pl. **-S** inability to feel pain

ANALITY *n* pl. **-TIES** a type of psychological state

ANALLY *adv* at or through the anus

ANALOG *n* pl. **-S** analogue

ANALOGIC *adj* pertaining to an analogy

ANALOGUE *n* pl. **-S** something that bears an analogy to something else

ANALOGY *n* pl. **-GIES** resemblance in some respects between things otherwise unlike

ANALYSE *v* **-LYSED, -LYSING, -LYSES** to analyze

ANALYSER *n* pl. **-S** analyzer

ANALYSIS *n* pl. **-YSES** the separation of a whole into its parts

ANALYST *n* pl. **-S** one that analyzes

ANALYTE *n* pl. **-S** a substance being analyzed

ANALYTIC *adj* pertaining to analysis

ANALYZE *v* **-LYZED, -LYZING, -LYZES** to subject to analysis

ANALYZER *n* pl. **-S** one that analyzes

ANANKE *n* pl. **-S** a compelling necessity in ancient Greek religion

ANAPAEST *n* pl. **-S** anapest

ANAPEST *n* pl. **-S** a type of metrical foot

ANAPHASE *n* pl. **-S** a stage of mitosis

ANAPHOR *n* pl. **-S** a word or phrase that takes reference from a preceding word or phrase

ANAPHORA *n* pl. **-S** the repetition of a word or phrase at the beginning of several successive verses or sentences

ANARCH *n* pl. **-S** an advocate of anarchy

ANARCHY *n* pl. **-CHIES** absence of government **ANARCHIC** *adj*

ANASARCA *n* pl. **-S** a form of dropsy

ANATASE *n* pl. **-S** a mineral

ANATHEMA *n* pl. **-MAS** or **-MATA** a formal ecclesiastical ban or curse

ANATOMY *n* pl. **-MIES** the structure of an organism **ANATOMIC** *adj*

ANATOXIN *n* pl. **-S** a toxoid

ANATTO *n* pl. **-TOS** annatto

ANCESTOR *v* **-ED, -ING, -S** to be an ancestor (a person from whom one is descended) of

ANCESTRY *n* pl. **-TRIES** a line or body of ancestors

ANCHO *n* pl. **-CHOS** a chili pepper

ANCHOR *v* **-ED, -ING, -S** to secure by means of an anchor (a device for holding a floating vessel in place)

ANCHORET *n* pl. **-S** a recluse

ANCHOVY *n* pl. **-VIES** a small food fish

ANCHUSA *n* pl. **-S** a hairy-stemmed plant

ANCHUSIN *n* pl. **-S** a red dye

ANCIENT *adj* **-CIENTER, -CIENTEST** of or pertaining to time long past

ANCIENT *n* pl. **-S** one who lived in ancient times

ANCILLA *n* pl. **-LAS** or **-LAE** a helper

ANCON *n* pl. **-ES** the elbow **ANCONAL, ANCONEAL, ANCONOID** *adj*

ANCONE *n* pl. **-S** ancon

ANCRESS *n* pl. **-ES** a female recluse

AND *n* pl. **-S** an added condition or stipulation

ANDANTE *n* pl. **-S** a moderately slow musical passage

ANDESITE *n* pl. **-S** a volcanic rock

ANDESYTE *n* pl. **-S** andesite

ANDIRON *n* pl. **-S** a metal support for holding wood in a fireplace

ANDRO *n* pl. **-DROS** a steroid sex hormone

ANDROGEN *n* pl. **-S** a male sex hormone

ANDROID *n* pl. **-S** a synthetic man

ANE *n* pl. **-S** one

ANEAR *v* **-ED, -ING, -S** to approach

ANECDOTE *n* pl. **-DOTES** or **-DOTA** a brief story

ANECHOIC *adj* neither having nor producing echoes

ANELE *v* **ANELED, ANELING, ANELES** to anoint

ANEMIA *n* pl. **-S** a disorder of the blood **ANEMIC** *adj*

ANEMONE *n* pl. **-S** a flowering plant

ANEMOSIS *n* pl. **-MOSES** separation of rings of growth in timber due to wind

ANENST *prep* anent

ANENT *prep* in regard to

ANERGIA *n* pl. **-S** anergy

ANERGY *n* pl. **-GIES** lack of energy **ANERGIC** *adj*

ANEROID *n* pl. **-S** a type of barometer

ANESTRUS *n* pl. **-TRI** a period of sexual dormancy

ANETHOL *n* pl. **-S** anethole

ANETHOLE *n* pl. **-S** a chemical compound

ANEURIN *n* pl. **-S** thiamine

ANEURISM *n* pl. **-S** aneurysm

ANEURYSM *n* pl. **-S** an abnormal blood-filled dilation of a blood vessel

ANEW *adv* once more

ANGA	*n* pl. **-S** any of the eight practices of yoga
ANGAKOK	*n* pl. **-S** an Eskimo medicine man
ANGARIA	*n* pl. **-S** angary
ANGARY	*n* pl. **-RIES** the right of a warring state to seize neutral property
ANGEL	*v* **-ED, -ING, -S** to support financially
ANGELIC	*adj* pertaining to an angel (a winged celestial being)
ANGELICA	*n* pl. **-S** an aromatic herb
ANGELUS	*n* pl. **-ES** a Roman Catholic prayer
ANGER	*v* **-ED, -ING, -S** to make angry
ANGERLY	*adv* in an angry manner
ANGINA	*n* pl. **-S** a disease marked by spasmodic attacks of intense pain **ANGINAL, ANGINOSE, ANGINOUS** *adj*
ANGIOMA	*n* pl. **-MAS** or **-MATA** a tumor composed of blood or lymph vessels
ANGLE	*v* **-GLED, -GLING, -GLES** to fish with a hook and line
ANGLEPOD	*n* pl. **-S** a flowering plant
ANGLER	*n* pl. **-S** one that angles
ANGLICE	*adv* in readily understood English
ANGLING	*n* pl. **-S** the sport of fishing
ANGLO	*n* pl. **-GLOS** a white North American of non-Hispanic or non-French descent
ANGORA	*n* pl. **-S** the long, silky hair of a domestic goat
ANGRY	*adj* **-GRIER, -GRIEST** feeling strong displeasure or hostility **ANGRILY** *adv*
ANGST	*n* pl. **-S** a feeling of anxiety or dread
ANGSTROM	*n* pl. **-S** a unit of length
ANGUINE	*adj* resembling a snake
ANGUISH	*v* **-ED, -ING, -ES** to suffer extreme pain
ANGULAR	*adj* having sharp corners
ANGULATE	*v* **-LATED, -LATING, -LATES** to make angular
ANGULOSE	*adj* angular
ANGULOUS	*adj* angular
ANHINGA	*n* pl. **-S** an aquatic bird
ANI	*n* pl. **-S** a tropical American bird
ANIL	*n* pl. **-S** a West Indian shrub
ANILE	*adj* resembling an old woman
ANILIN	*n* pl. **-S** aniline
ANILINE	*n* pl. **-S** a chemical compound
ANILITY	*n* pl. **-TIES** the state of being anile
ANIMA	*n* pl. **-S** the soul
ANIMACY	*n* pl. **-CIES** the state of being alive
ANIMAL	*n* pl. **-S** a living organism typically capable of voluntary motion and sensation **ANIMALIC** *adj*
ANIMALLY	*adv* physically
ANIMATE	*v* **-MATED, -MATING, -MATES** to give life to
ANIMATER	*n* pl. **-S** animator
ANIMATO	*adv* in a lively manner — used as a musical direction
ANIMATOR	*n* pl. **-S** one that animates
ANIME	*n* pl. **-S** a resin obtained from a tropical tree
ANIMI	*n* pl. **-S** anime
ANIMISM	*n* pl. **-S** the belief that souls may exist apart from bodies
ANIMIST	*n* pl. **-S** an adherent of animism
ANIMUS	*n* pl. **-ES** a feeling of hostility
ANION	*n* pl. **-S** a negatively charged ion **ANIONIC** *adj*
ANISE	*n* pl. **-S** a North African plant
ANISEED	*n* pl. **-S** the seed of the anise used as a flavoring
ANISETTE	*n* pl. **-S** a liqueur flavored with aniseed
ANISIC	*adj* pertaining to an anise
ANISOLE	*n* pl. **-S** a chemical compound
ANKERITE	*n* pl. **-S** a mineral
ANKH	*n* pl. **-S** an Egyptian symbol of enduring life
ANKLE	*v* **-KLED, -KLING, -KLES** to walk
ANKLET	*n* pl. **-S** an ornament for the ankle
ANKUS	*n* pl. **-ES** an elephant goad
ANKUSH	*n* pl. **-ES** ankus
ANKYLOSE	*v* **-LOSED, -LOSING, -LOSES** to unite or grow together, as the bones of a joint
ANLACE	*n* pl. **-S** a medieval dagger
ANLAGE	*n* pl. **-GES** or **-GEN** the initial cell structure from which an embryonic organ develops
ANLAS	*n* pl. **-ES** anlace
ANNA	*n* pl. **-S** a former coin of India and Pakistan
ANNAL	*n* pl. **-S** a record of a single year

ANNALIST	*n* pl. **-S** a historian
ANNATES	*n/pl* the first year's revenue of a bishop paid to the pope
ANNATTO	*n* pl. **-TOS** a yellowish-red dye
ANNEAL	*v* **-ED, -ING, -S** to toughen
ANNEALER	*n* pl. **-S** one that anneals
ANNELID	*n* pl. **-S** any of a phylum of segmented worms
ANNEX	*v* **-ED, -ING, -ES** to add or attach
ANNEXE	*n* pl. **-S** something added or attached
ANNONA	*n* pl. **-S** a tropical tree
ANNOTATE	*v* **-TATED, -TATING, -TATES** to furnish with critical or explanatory notes
ANNOUNCE	*v* **-NOUNCED, -NOUNCING, -NOUNCES** to make known publicly
ANNOY	*v* **-ED, -ING, -S** to be troublesome to
ANNOYER	*n* pl. **-S** one that annoys
ANNUAL	*n* pl. **-S** a publication issued once a year
ANNUALLY	*adv* once a year
ANNUITY	*n* pl. **-TIES** an allowance or income paid at regular intervals
ANNUL	*v* **-NULLED, -NULLING, -NULS** to make or declare void or invalid
ANNULAR	*adj* shaped like a ring
ANNULATE	*adj* composed of or furnished with rings
ANNULET	*n* pl. **-S** a small ring
ANNULI	a pl. of annulus
ANNULLED	past tense of annul
ANNULLING	present participle of annul
ANNULUS	*n* pl. **-LUSES** or **-LI** a ring or ringlike part **ANNULOSE** *adj*
ANOA	*n* pl. **-S** a wild ox
ANODE	*n* pl. **-S** a positively charged electrode **ANODAL, ANODIC** *adj* **ANODALLY** *adv*
ANODIZE	*v* **-IZED, -IZING, -IZES** to coat with a protective film by chemical means
ANODYNE	*n* pl. **-S** a medicine that relieves pain **ANODYNIC** *adj*
ANOINT	*v* **-ED, -ING, -S** to apply oil to as a sacred rite
ANOINTER	*n* pl. **-S** one that anoints
ANOLE	*n* pl. **-S** a tropical lizard
ANOLYTE	*n* pl. **-S** the part of an electricity-conducting solution nearest the anode
ANOMALY	*n* pl. **-LIES** a deviation from the common rule, type, or form
ANOMIE	*n* pl. **-S** a collapse of the social structures governing a given society **ANOMIC** *adj*
ANOMY	*n* pl. **-MIES** anomie
ANON	*adv* at another time
ANONYM	*n* pl. **-S** a false or assumed name
ANOOPSIA	*n* pl. **-S** a visual defect
ANOPIA	*n* pl. **-S** anoopsia
ANOPSIA	*n* pl. **-S** anoopsia
ANORAK	*n* pl. **-S** a parka
ANORETIC	*n* pl. **-S** anorexic
ANOREXIA	*n* pl. **-S** loss of appetite
ANOREXIC	*n* pl. **-S** one affected with anorexia
ANOREXY	*n* pl. **-OREXIES** anorexia
ANORTHIC	*adj* denoting a certain type of crystal system
ANOSMIA	*n* pl. **-S** loss of the sense of smell **ANOSMIC** *adj*
ANOTHER	*adj* one more
ANOVULAR	*adj* not involving ovulation
ANOXEMIA	*n* pl. **-S** a disorder of the blood **ANOXEMIC** *adj*
ANOXIA	*n* pl. **-S** absence of oxygen **ANOXIC** *adj*
ANSA	*n* pl. **-SAE** the projecting part of Saturn's rings
ANSATE	*adj* having a handle
ANSATED	*adj* ansate
ANSERINE	*n* pl. **-S** a chemical compound
ANSEROUS	*adj* silly
ANSWER	*v* **-ED, -ING, -S** to say, write, or act in return
ANSWERER	*n* pl. **-S** one that answers
ANT	*n* pl. **-S** a small insect
ANTA	*n* pl. **-TAS** or **-TAE** a pilaster formed at the termination of a wall
ANTACID	*n* pl. **-S** a substance that neutralizes acid
ANTALGIC	*n* pl. **-S** an anodyne
ANTBEAR	*n* pl. **-S** an aardvark
ANTE	*v* **ANTED** or **ANTEED, ANTEING, ANTES** to put a fixed stake into the pot before the cards are dealt in poker

ANTEATER *n* pl. **-S** any of several mammals that feed on ants

ANTECEDE *v* **-CEDED, -CEDING, -CEDES** to precede

ANTEDATE *v* **-DATED, -DATING, -DATES** to be of an earlier date than

ANTEFIX *n* pl. **-FIXES** or **-FIXAE** or **-FIXA** an upright ornament at the eaves of a tiled roof

ANTELOPE *n* pl. **-S** a ruminant mammal

ANTENNA *n* pl. **-NAS** or **-NAE** a metallic device for sending or receiving radio waves **ANTENNAL** *adj*

ANTEPAST *n* pl. **-S** an appetizer

ANTERIOR *adj* situated in or toward the front

ANTEROOM *n* pl. **-S** a waiting room

ANTES present 3d person sing. of ante

ANTETYPE *n* pl. **-S** an earlier form

ANTEVERT *v* **-ED, -ING, -S** to displace by tipping forward

ANTHELIA *n/pl* halolike areas seen in the sky opposite the sun

ANTHELIX *n* pl. **-LIXES** or **-LICES** the inner curved ridge on the cartilage of the external ear

ANTHEM *v* **-ED, -ING, -S** to praise in a song

ANTHEMIA *n/pl* decorative floral patterns used in Greek art

ANTHEMIC *adj* pertaining to an anthem (a song of praise)

ANTHER *n* pl. **-S** the pollen-bearing part of a stamen **ANTHERAL** *adj*

ANTHERID *n* pl. **-S** a male reproductive organ of certain plants

ANTHESIS *n* pl. **-THESES** the full bloom of a flower

ANTHILL *n* pl. **-S** a mound formed by ants in building their nest

ANTHODIA *n/pl* flower heads of certain plants

ANTHOID *adj* resembling a flower

ANTHRAX *n* pl. **-THRACES** an infectious disease

ANTI *n* pl. **-S** one that is opposed

ANTIACNE *adj* effective against acne

ANTIAIR *adj* directed against attacking aircraft

ANTIAR *n* pl. **-S** an arrow poison

ANTIARIN *n* pl. **-S** antiar

ANTIATOM *n* pl. **-S** an atom comprised of antiparticles

ANTIBIAS *adj* opposed to bias

ANTIBODY *n* pl. **-BODIES** a body protein that produces immunity against certain microorganisms or toxins

ANTIBOSS *adj* opposed to bosses

ANTIBUG *adj* effective against bugs

ANTIC *v* **-TICKED, -TICKING, -TICS** to act in a clownish manner

ANTICAR *adj* opposed to cars

ANTICITY *adj* opposed to cities

ANTICK *v* **-ED, -ING, -S** to antic

ANTICLY *adv* in a clownish manner

ANTICOLD *adj* effective against the common cold

ANTICULT *n* pl. **-S** a group opposed to a cult

ANTIDORA *n/pl* holy breads

ANTIDOTE *v* **-DOTED, -DOTING, -DOTES** to counteract the effects of a poison with a remedy

ANTIDRUG *adj* opposed to illicit drugs

ANTIFAT *adj* preventing the formation of fat

ANTIFLU *adj* combating the flu

ANTIFOAM *adj* reducing or preventing foam

ANTIFOG *adj* preventing the buildup of moisture on a surface

ANTIFUR *adj* opposed to the wearing of animal furs

ANTIGANG *adj* opposed to gangs

ANTIGAY *adj* opposed to homosexuals

ANTIGEN *n* pl. **-S** a substance that stimulates the production of antibodies

ANTIGENE *n* pl. **-S** antigen

ANTIGUN *adj* opposed to guns

ANTIHERO *n* pl. **-ROES** a protagonist who is notably lacking in heroic qualities

ANTIJAM *adj* blocking interfering signals

ANTIKING *n* pl. **-S** a usurping king

ANTILEAK *adj* preventing leaks

ANTILEFT *adj* opposed to leftism

ANTILIFE *adj* opposed to life

ANTILOCK *adj* designed to prevent the wheels of a vehicle from locking

ANTILOG *n* pl. **-S** the number corresponding to a given logarithm

ANTILOGY *n* pl. **-GIES** a contradiction in terms or ideas

ANTIMALE *adj* opposed to men

ANTIMAN *adj* antimale

ANTIMASK *n* pl. **-S** a comic performance between the acts of a masque

ANTIMERE *n* pl. **-S** a part of an organism symmetrical with a part on the opposite side of the main axis

ANTIMINE *adj* effective against mines

ANTIMONY *n* pl. **-NIES** a metallic element

ANTING *n* pl. **-S** the deliberate placing, by certain birds, of living ants among the feathers

ANTINODE *n* pl. **-S** a region between adjacent nodes

ANTINOME *n* pl. **-S** one that is opposite to another

ANTINOMY *n* pl. **-MIES** a contradiction between two seemingly valid principles

ANTINUKE *n* pl. **-S** a person who opposes the use of nuclear power plants or nuclear weapons

ANTIPHON *n* pl. **-S** a psalm or hymn sung responsively

ANTIPILL *adj* opposing the use of contraceptive pills

ANTIPODE *n* pl. **-S** an exact opposite

ANTIPOLE *n* pl. **-S** the opposite pole

ANTIPOPE *n* pl. **-S** one claiming to be pope in opposition to the one chosen by church law

ANTIPORN *adj* opposed to pornography

ANTIPOT *adj* opposing the use of pot (marijuana)

ANTIPYIC *n* pl. **-S** a medicine that prevents the formation of pus

ANTIQUE *v* **-TIQUED, -TIQUING, -TIQUES** to give an appearance of age to

ANTIQUER *n* pl. **-S** one that antiques

ANTIRAPE *adj* concerned with preventing rape

ANTIRED *adj* opposed to communism

ANTIRIOT *adj* designed to prevent or end riots

ANTIROCK *adj* opposed to rock music

ANTIROLL *adj* designed to reduce roll

ANTIRUST *n* pl. **-S** something that prevents rust

ANTISAG *adj* designed to prevent sagging

ANTISERA *n/pl* serums that contain antibodies

ANTISEX *adj* opposed to sexual activity

ANTISHIP *adj* designed for use against ships

ANTISKID *adj* designed to prevent skidding

ANTISLIP *adj* designed to prevent slipping

ANTISMOG *adj* designed to reduce pollutants that cause smog

ANTISMUT *adj* opposed to pornography

ANTISNOB *n* pl. **-S** one that is opposed to snobbery

ANTISPAM *adj* designed to block spam (unsolicited email)

ANTISTAT *n* pl. **-S** an agent for preventing the buildup of static electricity

ANTITANK *adj* designed to combat tanks

ANTITAX *adj* opposing taxes

ANTITYPE *n* pl. **-S** an opposite type

ANTIWAR *adj* opposing war

ANTIWEAR *adj* designed to reduce the effects of long or hard use

ANTIWEED *adj* concerned with the destruction of weeds

ANTLER *n* pl. **-S** the horn of an animal of the deer family **ANTLERED** *adj*

ANTLIKE *adj* resembling an ant

ANTLION *n* pl. **-S** a predatory insect

ANTONYM *n* pl. **-S** a word opposite in meaning to another

ANTONYMY *n* pl. **-MIES** the state of being an antonym

ANTRA a pl. of antrum

ANTRAL *adj* pertaining to an antrum

ANTRE *n* pl. **-S** a cave (a hollow place in the earth)

ANTRORSE *adj* directed forward or upward

ANTRUM *n* pl. **-TRUMS** or **-TRA** a cavity in a bone

ANTSY *adj* **-SIER, -SIEST** fidgety

ANURAL *adj* anurous

ANURAN *n* pl. **-S** a frog or toad

ANURESIS *n* pl. **-RESES** inability to urinate **ANURETIC** *adj*

ANURIA *n* pl. **-S** absence of urine **ANURIC** *adj*

ANUROUS *adj* having no tail

ANUS *n* pl. **-ES** the excretory opening at the end of the alimentary canal

ANVIL *v* **-VILED, -VILING, -VILS** or **-VILLED, -VILLING, -VILS** to shape on an anvil (a heavy iron block)

ANVILTOP *n* pl. **-S** an anvil-shaped cloud mass

ANXIETY *n* pl. **-ETIES** painful or apprehensive uneasiness of mind

ANXIOUS *adj* full of anxiety

ANY	*adj* one, no matter which
ANYBODY	*n* pl. **-BODIES** a person of some importance
ANYHOW	*adv* in any way
ANYMORE	*adv* at the present time
ANYON	*n* pl. **-S** a subatomic particle
ANYONE	*pron* any person
ANYPLACE	*adv* in any place
ANYTHING	*n* pl. **-S** a thing of any kind
ANYTIME	*adv* at any time
ANYWAY	*adv* in any way
ANYWAYS	*adv* anyway
ANYWHERE	*n* pl. **-S** any place
ANYWISE	*adv* in any way
AORIST	*n* pl. **-S** a verb tense **AORISTIC** *adj*
AORTA	*n* pl. **-TAS** or **-TAE** a main artery **AORTAL, AORTIC** *adj*
AOUDAD	*n* pl. **-S** a wild sheep
APACE	*adv* swiftly
APACHE	*n* pl. **-S** a Parisian gangster
APAGOGE	*n* pl. **-S** establishment of a thesis by showing its contrary to be absurd **APAGOGIC** *adj*
APANAGE	*n* pl. **-S** appanage
APAREJO	*n* pl. **-JOS** a type of saddle
APART	*adv* not together
APATETIC	*adj* having coloration serving as natural camouflage
APATHY	*n* pl. **-THIES** lack of emotion
APATITE	*n* pl. **-S** a mineral
APE	*v* **APED, APING, APES** to mimic
APEAK	*adv* in a vertical position
APEEK	*adv* apeak
APELIKE	*adj* resembling an ape (a large, tailless primate)
APER	*n* pl. **-S** one that apes
APERCU	*n* pl. **-S** a brief summary
APERIENT	*n* pl. **-S** a mild laxative
APERITIF	*n* pl. **-S** an alcoholic drink taken before a meal
APERTURE	*n* pl. **-S** an opening
APERY	*n* pl. **-ERIES** the act of aping
APETALY	*n* pl. **-ALIES** the state of having no petals
APEX	*n* pl. **APEXES** or **APICES** the highest point
APHAGIA	*n* pl. **-S** inability to swallow
APHANITE	*n* pl. **-S** an igneous rock
APHASIA	*n* pl. **-S** loss of the ability to use words
APHASIAC	*n* pl. **-S** one suffering from aphasia
APHASIC	*n* pl. **-S** aphasiac
APHELION	*n* pl. **-ELIONS** or **-ELIA** the point in a planetary orbit farthest from the sun **APHELIAN** *adj*
APHESIS	*n* pl. **-ESES** the loss of an unstressed vowel from the beginning of a word **APHETIC** *adj*
APHID	*n* pl. **-S** any of a family of small, soft-bodied insects
APHIDIAN	*n* pl. **-S** an aphid
APHIS	*n* pl. **APHIDES** an aphid
APHOLATE	*n* pl. **-S** a chemical used to control houseflies
APHONIA	*n* pl. **-S** loss of voice
APHONIC	*n* pl. **-S** one affected with aphonia
APHORISE	*v* **-RISED, -RISING, -RISES** to aphorize
APHORISM	*n* pl. **-S** a brief statement of a truth or principle
APHORIST	*n* pl. **-S** one that aphorizes
APHORIZE	*v* **-RIZED, -RIZING, -RIZES** to write or speak in aphorisms
APHOTIC	*adj* lacking light
APHTHA	*n* pl. **-THAE** a small blister in the mouth or stomach **APHTHOUS** *adj*
APHYLLY	*n* pl. **-LIES** the state of being leafless
APIAN	*adj* pertaining to bees
APIARIAN	*n* pl. **-S** an apiarist
APIARIST	*n* pl. **-S** a person who raises bees
APIARY	*n* pl. **-ARIES** a place where bees are kept
APICAL	*n* pl. **-S** a sound articulated with the apex (tip) of the tongue
APICALLY	*adv* at or toward the apex
APICES	a pl. of apex
APICULUS	*n* pl. **-LI** a sharp point at the end of a leaf
APIECE	*adv* for each one
APIMANIA	*n* pl. **-S** an excessive interest in bees
APING	present participle of ape
APIOLOGY	*n* pl. **-GIES** the study of bees
APISH	*adj* slavishly or foolishly imitative **APISHLY** *adv*

APLASIA   *n* pl. **-S** defective development of an organ or part

APLASTIC   *adj* not plastic

APLENTY   *adj* being in sufficient quantity

APLITE   *n* pl. **-S** a fine-grained rock **APLITIC** *adj*

APLOMB   *n* pl. **-S** self-confidence

APNEA   *n* pl. **-S** temporary cessation of respiration **APNEAL, APNEIC** *adj*

APNOEA   *n* pl. **-S** apnea **APNOEAL, APNOEIC** *adj*

APO   *n* pl. **APOS** a type of protein

APOAPSIS   *n* pl. **-APSIDES** or **-APSES** the high point in an orbit

APOCARP   *n* pl. **-S** a fruit having separated carpels

APOCARPY   *n* pl. **-PIES** the state of being an apocarp

APOCOPE   *n* pl. **-S** an omission of the last sound of a word **APOCOPIC** *adj*

APOCRINE   *adj* pertaining to a type of gland

APOD   *n* pl. **-S** an apodal animal

APODAL   *adj* having no feet or footlike appendages

APODOSIS   *n* pl. **-OSES** the main clause of a conditional sentence

APODOUS   *adj* apodal

APOGAMY   *n* pl. **-MIES** a form of plant reproduction **APOGAMIC** *adj*

APOGEE   *n* pl. **-S** the point in the orbit of a body which is farthest from the earth **APOGEAL, APOGEAN, APOGEIC** *adj*

APOLLO   *n* pl. **-LOS** a handsome young man

APOLOG   *n* pl. **-S** apologue

APOLOGAL   *adj* pertaining to an apologue

APOLOGIA   *n* pl. **-GIAS** or **-GIAE** a formal justification or defense

APOLOGUE   *n* pl. **-S** an allegory

APOLOGY   *n* pl. **-GIES** an expression of regret for some error or offense

APOLUNE   *n* pl. **-S** the point in the orbit of a body which is farthest from the moon

APOMICT   *n* pl. **-S** an organism produced by apomixis

APOMIXIS   *n* pl. **-MIXES** a type of reproductive process

APOPHONY   *n* pl. **-NIES** ablaut

APOPHYGE   *n* pl. **-S** a concave curve in a column

APOPLEXY   *n* pl. **-PLEXIES** a sudden loss of sensation and muscular control

APORIA   *n* pl. **-S** an expression of doubt for rhetorical effect

APORT   *adv* on or toward the left side of a ship

APOSPORY   *n* pl. **-RIES** a type of reproduction without spore formation

APOSTACY   *n* pl. **-CIES** apostasy

APOSTASY   *n* pl. **-SIES** an abandonment of one's faith or principles

APOSTATE   *n* pl. **-S** one who commits apostasy

APOSTIL   *n* pl. **-S** a marginal note

APOSTLE   *n* pl. **-S** a disciple sent forth by Christ to preach the gospel

APOTHECE   *n* pl. **-S** a spore-producing organ of certain fungi

APOTHEGM   *n* pl. **-S** a maxim

APOTHEM   *n* pl. **-S** the perpendicular from the center to any side of a regular polygon

APP   *n* pl. **-S** a computer program for a major task

APPAL   *v* **-PALLED, -PALLING, -PALS** to appall

APPALL   *v* **-ED, -ING, -S** to fill with horror or dismay

APPANAGE   *n* pl. **-S** land or revenue granted to a member of a royal family

APPARAT   *n* pl. **-S** a political organization

APPAREL   *v* **-ELED, -ELING, -ELS** or **-ELLED, -ELLING, -ELS** to provide with outer garments

APPARENT   *adj* easily seen

APPEAL   *v* **-ED, -ING, -S** to make an earnest request

APPEALER   *n* pl. **-S** one that appeals

APPEAR   *v* **-ED, -ING, -S** to come into view

APPEASE   *v* **-PEASED, -PEASING, -PEASES** to bring to a state of peace or contentment

APPEASER   *n* pl. **-S** one that appeases

APPEL   *n* pl. **-S** a feint in fencing

APPELLEE   *n* pl. **-S** the defendant in a type of judicial proceeding

APPELLOR   *n* pl. **-S** a confessed criminal who accuses an accomplice

APPEND   *v* **-ED, -ING, -S** to add as a supplement

APPENDIX   *n* pl. **-DIXES** or **-DICES** a collection of supplementary material at the end of a book

APPESTAT   *n pl.* **-S** the mechanism in the central nervous system that regulates appetite

APPETENT   *adj* marked by strong desire

APPETITE   *n pl.* **-S** a desire for food or drink

APPLAUD   *v* **-ED, -ING, -S** to express approval by clapping the hands

APPLAUSE   *n pl.* **-S** the sound made by persons applauding

APPLE   *n pl.* **-S** an edible fruit

APPLET   *n pl.* **-S** a computer program for a simple task

APPLIED   past tense of apply

APPLIER   *n pl.* **-S** one that applies

APPLIQUE   *v* **-QUED, -QUEING, -QUES** to apply as a decoration to a larger surface

APPLY   *v* **-PLIED, -PLYING, -PLIES** to bring into contact with something

APPOINT   *v* **-ED, -ING, -S** to name or assign to a position or office

APPOSE   *v* **-POSED, -POSING, -POSES** to place side by side

APPOSER   *n pl.* **-S** one that apposes

APPOSITE   *adj* relevant

APPRAISE   *v* **-PRAISED, -PRAISING, -PRAISES** to set a value on

APPRISE   *v* **-PRISED, -PRISING, -PRISES** to notify

APPRISER   *n pl.* **-S** one that apprises

APPRIZE   *v* **-PRIZED, -PRIZING, -PRIZES** to appraise

APPRIZER   *n pl.* **-S** one that apprizes

APPROACH   *v* **-ED, -ING, -ES** to come near or nearer to

APPROVAL   *n pl.* **-S** the act of approving

APPROVE   *v* **-PROVED, -PROVING, -PROVES** to regard favorably

APPROVER   *n pl.* **-S** one that approves

APPULSE   *n pl.* **-S** the approach of one moving body toward another

APRAXIA   *n pl.* **-S** loss of the ability to perform coordinated movements **APRACTIC, APRAXIC** *adj*

APRES   *prep* after

APRICOT   *n pl.* **-S** an edible fruit

APRON   *v* **-ED, -ING, -S** to provide with an apron (a garment worn to protect one's clothing)

APROPOS   *adj* relevant

APROTIC   *adj* being a type of solvent

APSE   *n pl.* **-S** a domed, semicircular projection of a building **APSIDAL** *adj*

APSIS   *n pl.* **-SIDES** an apse

APT   *adj* **APTER, APTEST** suitable

APTERAL   *adj* apterous

APTERIUM   *n pl.* **-RIA** a bare area of skin between feathers

APTEROUS   *adj* having no wings

APTERYX   *n pl.* **-ES** the kiwi

APTITUDE   *n pl.* **-S** an ability

APTLY   *adv* in an apt manner

APTNESS   *n pl.* **-ES** the quality of being apt

APYRASE   *n pl.* **-S** an enzyme

APYRETIC   *adj* having no fever

AQUA   *n pl.* **AQUAS** or **AQUAE** water (a transparent, tasteless, odorless liquid)

AQUACADE   *n pl.* **-S** a swimming and diving exhibition

AQUAFARM   *v* **-ED, -ING, -S** to cultivate food fish

AQUANAUT   *n pl.* **-S** a scuba diver trained to live in underwater installations

AQUARIA   a *pl.* of aquarium

AQUARIAL   *adj* pertaining to an aquarium

AQUARIAN   *n pl.* **-S** a member of the old sects that used water rather than wine in religious ceremonies

AQUARIST   *n pl.* **-S** one who keeps an aquarium

AQUARIUM   *n pl.* **-IUMS** or **-IA** a water-filled enclosure in which aquatic animals are kept

AQUATIC   *n pl.* **-S** an organism living or growing in or near water

AQUATINT   *v* **-ED, -ING, -S** to etch, using a certain process

AQUATONE   *n pl.* **-S** a type of printing process

AQUAVIT   *n pl.* **-S** a Scandinavian liquor

AQUEDUCT   *n pl.* **-S** a water conduit

AQUEOUS   *adj* pertaining to water

AQUIFER   *n pl.* **-S** a water-bearing rock formation

AQUILINE   *adj* curving like an eagle's beak

AQUIVER   *adj* quivering

AR   *n pl.* **-S** the letter R

ARABESK   *n pl.* **-S** a design of intertwined floral figures

ARABIC   *adj* derived from gum arabic

ARABICA   *n* pl. **-S** an evergreen shrub that produces coffee beans

ARABIZE   *v* **-IZED, -IZING, -IZES** to cause to acquire Arabic customs

ARABLE   *n* pl. **-S** land suitable for cultivation

ARACEOUS   *adj* belonging to the arum family of plants

ARACHNID   *n* pl. **-S** any of a class of segmented invertebrate animals

ARAK   *n* pl. **-S** arrack

ARAME   *n* pl. **-S** an edible seaweed

ARAMID   *n* pl. **-S** a type of chemical compound

ARANEID   *n* pl. **-S** a spider

ARAPAIMA   *n* pl. **-S** a large food fish

ARAROBA   *n* pl. **-S** a Brazilian tree

ARB   *n* pl. **-S** a type of stock trader

ARBALEST   *n* pl. **-S** a type of crossbow

ARBALIST   *n* pl. **-S** arbalest

ARBELEST   *n* pl. **-S** arbalest

ARBITER   *n* pl. **-S** one chosen or appointed to judge a disputed issue **ARBITRAL** *adj*

ARBOR   *n* pl. **-ES** a tree when contrasted with a shrub

ARBOR   *n* pl. **-S** a shady garden shelter

ARBOREAL   *adj* living in trees

ARBORED   *adj* having trees

ARBORETA   *n/pl* places for the study and exhibition of trees

ARBORIST   *n* pl. **-S** a tree specialist

ARBORIZE   *v* **-IZED, -IZING, -IZES** to form many branches

ARBOROUS   *adj* pertaining to trees

ARBOUR   *n* pl. **-S** a shady garden shelter **ARBOURED** *adj*

ARBUSCLE   *n* pl. **-S** a dwarf tree

ARBUTE   *n* pl. **-S** an evergreen tree **ARBUTEAN** *adj*

ARBUTUS   *n* pl. **-ES** an evergreen tree

ARC   *v* **ARCED, ARCING, ARCS** or **ARCKED, ARCKING, ARCS** to move in a curved course

ARCADE   *v* **-CADED, -CADING, -CADES** to provide with an arcade (a series of arches)

ARCADIA   *n* pl. **-S** a region of simple pleasure and quiet

ARCADIAN   *n* pl. **-S** one who lives in an arcadia

ARCADING   *n* pl. **-S** an arcade

ARCANE   *adj* mysterious

ARCANUM   *n* pl. **-NUMS** or **-NA** a mystery

ARCATURE   *n* pl. **-S** a small arcade

ARCH   *v* **-ED, -ING, -ES** to bend like an arch (a curved structure spanning an opening)

ARCHAEA   *n/pl* a large group of microorganisms **ARCHAEAL** *adj*

ARCHAEAN   *n* pl. **-S** a microorganism of the archaea

ARCHAEON   *n* pl. **-CHAEA** archaean

ARCHAIC   *adj* pertaining to an earlier time

ARCHAISE   *v* **-ISED, -ISING, -ISES** to archaize

ARCHAISM   *n* pl. **-S** an archaic word, idiom, or expression

ARCHAIST   *n* pl. **-S** one that archaizes

ARCHAIZE   *v* **-IZED, -IZING, -IZES** to use archaisms

ARCHDUKE   *n* pl. **-S** an Austrian prince

ARCHER   *n* pl. **-S** one that shoots with a bow and arrow

ARCHERY   *n* pl. **-CHERIES** the sport of shooting with a bow and arrow

ARCHFOE   *n* pl. **-S** a principal foe

ARCHIL   *n* pl. **-S** orchil

ARCHINE   *n* pl. **-S** a Russian unit of linear measure

ARCHING   *n* pl. **-S** a series of arches

ARCHIVE   *v* **-CHIVED, -CHIVING, -CHIVES** to file in an archive (a place where records are kept) **ARCHIVAL** *adj*

ARCHLY   *adv* slyly

ARCHNESS   *n* pl. **-ES** slyness

ARCHON   *n* pl. **-S** a magistrate of ancient Athens

ARCHWAY   *n* pl. **-WAYS** a passageway under an arch

ARCIFORM   *adj* having the form of an arch

ARCKED   a past tense of arc

ARCKING   a present participle of arc

ARCO   *adv* with the bow — used as a direction to players of stringed instruments

ARCSINE   *n* pl. **-S** the inverse function to the sine

ARCTIC   *n* pl. **-S** a warm, waterproof overshoe

ARCUATE   *adj* curved like a bow

ARCUATED   *adj* arcuate

ARCUS   *n* pl. **-ES** an arch-shaped cloud

ARDEB *n* pl. **-S** an Egyptian unit of capacity

ARDENCY *n* pl. **-CIES** ardor

ARDENT *adj* characterized by intense emotion **ARDENTLY** *adv*

ARDOR *n* pl. **-S** intensity of emotion

ARDOUR *n* pl. **-S** ardor

ARDUOUS *adj* involving great labor or hardship

ARE *n* pl. **-S** a unit of surface measure

AREA *n* pl. **-S** a particular extent of space or surface **AREAL** *adj* **AREALLY** *adv*

AREA *n* pl. **AREAE** a section of the cerebral cortex having a specific function

AREAWAY *n* pl. **-WAYS** a sunken area leading to a basement entrance

ARECA *n* pl. **-S** a tropical tree

AREIC *adj* pertaining to a region of the earth contributing little surface drainage

ARENA *n* pl. **-S** an enclosed area for contests

ARENE *n* pl. **-S** an aromatic compound

ARENITE *n* pl. **-S** rock made up chiefly of sand grains

ARENOSE *adj* sandy

ARENOUS *adj* arenose

AREOLA *n* pl. **-LAS** or **-LAE** a small space in a network of leaf veins **AREOLAR, AREOLATE** *adj*

AREOLE *n* pl. **-S** areola

AREOLOGY *n* pl. **-GIES** the study of the planet Mars

AREPA *n* pl. **-S** a cornmeal cake

ARETE *n* pl. **-S** a sharp mountain ridge

ARETHUSA *n* pl. **-S** a flowering plant

ARF *n* pl. **-S** a barking sound

ARGAL *n* pl. **-S** argol

ARGALA *n* pl. **-S** a type of stork

ARGALI *n* pl. **-S** a wild sheep

ARGENT *n* pl. **-S** silver **ARGENTAL, ARGENTIC** *adj*

ARGENTUM *n* pl. **-S** silver

ARGIL *n* pl. **-S** a white clay

ARGINASE *n* pl. **-S** an enzyme

ARGININE *n* pl. **-S** an amino acid

ARGLE *v* **-GLED, -GLING, -GLES** to argue

ARGOL *n* pl. **-S** a crust deposited in wine casks during aging

ARGON *n* pl. **-S** a gaseous element

ARGONAUT *n* pl. **-S** a marine mollusk

ARGOSY *n* pl. **-SIES** a large merchant ship

ARGOT *n* pl. **-S** a specialized vocabulary **ARGOTIC** *adj*

ARGUABLE *adj* capable of being argued about **ARGUABLY** *adv*

ARGUE *v* **-GUED, -GUING, -GUES** to present reasons for or against

ARGUER *n* pl. **-S** one that argues

ARGUFIER *n* pl. **-S** one that argufies

ARGUFY *v* **-FIED, -FYING, -FIES** to argue stubbornly

ARGUING present participle of argue

ARGUMENT *n* pl. **-S** a discussion involving differing points of view

ARGUS *n* pl. **-ES** an East Indian pheasant

ARGYLE *n* pl. **-S** a knitting pattern

ARGYLL *n* pl. **-S** argyle

ARHAT *n* pl. **-S** a Buddhist who has attained nirvana

ARIA *n* pl. **-S** an elaborate melody for a single voice

ARIARY *n* pl. **ARIARY** a monetary unit of Madagascar

ARID *adj* **-IDER, -IDEST** extremely dry **ARIDLY** *adv*

ARIDITY *n* pl. **-TIES** the state of being arid

ARIDNESS *n* pl. **-ES** aridity

ARIEL *n* pl. **-S** an African gazelle

ARIETTA *n* pl. **-S** a short aria

ARIETTE *n* pl. **-S** arietta

ARIGHT *adv* rightly; correctly

ARIL *n* pl. **-S** an outer covering of certain seeds **ARILED, ARILLATE, ARILLOID** *adj*

ARILLODE *n* pl. **-S** a type of aril

ARIOSE *adj* characterized by melody

ARIOSO *n* pl. **-SOS** or **-SI** a musical passage resembling an aria

ARISE *v* **AROSE, ARISEN, ARISING, ARISES** to get up

ARISTA *n* pl. **-TAS** or **-TAE** a bristlelike structure or appendage **ARISTATE** *adj*

ARISTO *n* pl. **-TOS** an aristocrat

ARK *n* pl. **-S** a large boat

ARKOSE   *n* pl. **-S** a type of sandstone **ARKOSIC** *adj*

ARLES   *n/pl* money paid to bind a bargain

ARM   *v* **-ED, -ING, -S** to supply with weapons

ARMADA   *n* pl. **-S** a fleet of warships

ARMAGNAC   *n* pl. **-S** a French brandy

ARMAMENT   *n* pl. **-S** a military force equipped for war

ARMATURE   *v* **-TURED, -TURING, -TURES** to furnish with armor

ARMBAND   *n* pl. **-S** a band worn around an arm (an upper appendage of the human body)

ARMCHAIR   *n* pl. **-S** a chair with armrests

ARMER   *n* pl. **-S** one that arms

ARMET   *n* pl. **-S** a medieval helmet

ARMFUL   *n* pl. **ARMFULS** or **ARMSFUL** as much as the arm can hold

ARMHOLE   *n* pl. **-S** an opening for the arm in a garment

ARMIES   pl. of army

ARMIGER   *n* pl. **-S** one who carries the armor of a knight

ARMIGERO   *n* pl. **-GEROS** armiger

ARMILLA   *n* pl. **-LAS** or **-LAE** a thin membrane around the stem of certain fungi

ARMING   *n* pl. **-S** the act of one that arms

ARMLESS   *adj* having no arms

ARMLET   *n* pl. **-S** an armband

ARMLIKE   *adj* resembling an arm

ARMLOAD   *n* pl. **-S** an armful

ARMLOCK   *n* pl. **-S** a hold in wrestling

ARMOIRE   *n* pl. **-S** a large, ornate cabinet

ARMONICA   *n* pl. **-S** a type of musical instrument

ARMOR   *v* **-ED, -ING, -S** to furnish with armor (a defensive covering)

ARMORER   *n* pl. **-S** one that makes or repairs armor

ARMORIAL   *n* pl. **-S** a treatise on heraldry

ARMORY   *n* pl. **-MORIES** a place where weapons are stored

ARMOUR   *v* **-ED, -ING, -S** to armor

ARMOURER   *n* pl. **-S** armorer

ARMOURY   *n* pl. **-MOURIES** armory

ARMPIT   *n* pl. **-S** the hollow under the arm at the shoulder

ARMREST   *n* pl. **-S** a support for the arm

ARMSFUL   a pl. of armful

ARMURE   *n* pl. **-S** a woven fabric

ARMY   *n* pl. **-MIES** a large body of men trained and armed for war

ARMYWORM   *n* pl. **-S** a destructive moth larva

ARNATTO   *n* pl. **-TOS** annatto

ARNICA   *n* pl. **-S** a perennial herb

ARNOTTO   *n* pl. **-TOS** a tropical tree

AROID   *n* pl. **-S** a flowering plant

AROINT   *v* **-ED, -ING, -S** to drive away

AROMA   *n* pl. **-S** a pleasant odor

AROMATIC   *n* pl. **-S** a fragrant plant or substance

AROSE   past tense of arise

AROUND   *prep* on all sides of

AROUSAL   *n* pl. **-S** the act of arousing

AROUSE   *v* **AROUSED, AROUSING, AROUSES** to stimulate

AROUSER   *n* pl. **-S** one that arouses

AROYNT   *v* **-ED, -ING, -S** to aroint

ARPEGGIO   *n* pl. **-GIOS** a technique of playing a musical chord

ARPEN   *n* pl. **-S** arpent

ARPENT   *n* pl. **-S** an old French unit of area

ARQUEBUS   *n* pl. **-ES** an early portable firearm

ARRACK   *n* pl. **-S** an Oriental liquor

ARRAIGN   *v* **-ED, -ING, -S** to call before a court of law to answer an indictment

ARRANGE   *v* **-RANGED, -RANGING, -RANGES** to put in definite or proper order

ARRANGER   *n* pl. **-S** one that arranges

ARRANT   *adj* outright **ARRANTLY** *adv*

ARRAS   *n* pl. **-ES** a tapestry **ARRASED** *adj*

ARRAY   *v* **-ED, -ING, -S** to place in proper or desired order

ARRAYAL   *n* pl. **-S** the act of arraying

ARRAYER   *n* pl. **-S** one that arrays

ARREAR   *n* pl. **-S** an unpaid and overdue debt

ARREST   *v* **-ED, -ING, -S** to seize and hold by legal authority

ARRESTEE   *n* pl. **-S** one that is arrested

ARRESTER   *n* pl. **-S** one that arrests

ARRESTOR   *n* pl. **-S** arrester

ARRHIZAL   *adj* rootless

ARRIBA — *interj* — used to express pleasure

ARRIS — *n* pl. **-RISES** a ridge formed by the meeting of two surfaces

ARRIVAL — *n* pl. **-S** the act of arriving

ARRIVE — *v* **-RIVED, -RIVING, -RIVES** to reach a destination

ARRIVER — *n* pl. **-S** one that arrives

ARROBA — *n* pl. **-S** a Spanish unit of weight

ARROGANT — *adj* overly convinced of one's own worth or importance

ARROGATE — *v* **-GATED, -GATING, -GATES** to claim or take without right

ARROW — *v* **-ED, -ING, -S** to indicate the proper position of with an arrow (a linear figure with a wedge-shaped end)

ARROWY — *adj* moving swiftly

ARROYO — *n* pl. **-ROYOS** a brook or creek

ARSENAL — *n* pl. **-S** a collection or supply of weapons

ARSENATE — *n* pl. **-S** a chemical salt

ARSENIC — *n* pl. **-S** a metallic element

ARSENIDE — *n* pl. **-S** an arsenic compound

ARSENITE — *n* pl. **-S** a chemical salt

ARSENO — *adj* containing a certain bivalent chemical radical

ARSENOUS — *adj* pertaining to arsenic

ARSES — pl. of arsis

ARSHIN — *n* pl. **-S** archine

ARSINE — *n* pl. **-S** a poisonous gas

ARSINO — *adj* containing a certain univalent chemical radical

ARSIS — *n* pl. **ARSES** the unaccented part of a musical measure

ARSON — *n* pl. **-S** the malicious or fraudulent burning of property **ARSONOUS** *adj*

ARSONIST — *n* pl. **-S** one that commits arson

ART — *n* pl. **-S** an esthetically pleasing and meaningful arrangement of elements

ARTAL — a pl. of rotl

ARTEFACT — *n* pl. **-S** artifact

ARTEL — *n* pl. **-S** a collective farm in Russia

ARTERIAL — *n* pl. **-S** a type of highway

ARTERY — *n* pl. **-TERIES** a vessel that carries blood away from the heart

ARTFUL — *adj* crafty **ARTFULLY** *adv*

ARTICLE — *v* **-CLED, -CLING, -CLES** to charge with specific offenses

ARTIER — comparative of arty

ARTIEST — superlative of arty

ARTIFACT — *n* pl. **-S** an object made by man

ARTIFICE — *n* pl. **-S** a clever stratagem

ARTILY — *adv* in an arty manner

ARTINESS — *n* pl. **-ES** the quality of being arty

ARTISAN — *n* pl. **-S** a trained or skilled workman

ARTIST — *n* pl. **-S** one who practices one of the fine arts

ARTISTE — *n* pl. **-S** a skilled public performer

ARTISTIC — *adj* characteristic of art

ARTISTRY — *n* pl. **-RIES** artistic quality or workmanship

ARTLESS — *adj* lacking cunning or guile

ARTSY — *adj* **-SIER, -SIEST** arty

ARTWORK — *n* pl. **-S** illustrative or decorative work in printed matter

ARTY — *adj* **ARTIER, ARTIEST** showily or pretentiously artistic

ARUGOLA — *n* pl. **-S** arugula

ARUGULA — *n* pl. **-S** a European annual herb

ARUM — *n* pl. **-S** a flowering plant

ARUSPEX — *n* pl. **-PICES** haruspex

ARVAL — *adj* pertaining to plowed land

ARVO — *n* pl. **-VOS** afternoon

ARYL — *n* pl. **-S** a univalent radical

ARYTHMIA — *n* pl. **-S** an irregularity in the rhythm of the heartbeat **ARYTHMIC** *adj*

AS — *adv* to the same degree

ASANA — *n* pl. **-S** a posture in yoga

ASARUM — *n* pl. **-S** a perennial herb

ASBESTOS — *n* pl. **-ES** a mineral **ASBESTIC** *adj*

ASBESTUS — *n* pl. **-ES** asbestos

ASCARED — *adj* afraid

ASCARID — *n* pl. **-S** a parasitic worm

ASCARIS — *n* pl. **-RIDES** ascarid

ASCEND — *v* **-ED, -ING, -S** to go or move upward

ASCENDER — *n* pl. **-S** one that ascends

ASCENT — *n* pl. **-S** the act of ascending

ASCESIS — *n* pl. **-CESES** the conduct of an ascetic

ASCETIC — *n* pl. **-S** one who practices extreme self-denial for religious reasons

ASCI — pl. of ascus

ASCIDIAN — *n* pl. **-S** a small marine animal

ASCIDIUM   *n* pl. **-DIA** a flask-shaped plant appendage

ASCITES   *n* pl. **ASCITES** accumulation of serous fluid in the abdomen **ASCITIC** *adj*

ASCOCARP   *n* pl. **-S** a spore-producing organ of certain fungi

ASCORBIC   *adj* relieving scurvy

ASCOT   *n* pl. **-S** a broad neck scarf

ASCRIBE   *v* **-CRIBED, -CRIBING, -CRIBES** to attribute to a specified cause, source, or origin

ASCUS   *n* pl. **ASCI** a spore sac in certain fungi

ASDIC   *n* pl. **-S** sonar

ASEA   *adv* at sea

ASEPSIS   *n* pl. **-SEPSES** the condition of being aseptic

ASEPTIC   *adj* free from germs

ASEXUAL   *adj* occurring or performed without sexual action

ASH   *v* **-ED, -ING, -ES** to convert into ash (the residue of a substance that has been burned)

ASHAMED   *adj* feeling shame, guilt, or disgrace

ASHCAKE   *n* pl. **-S** a cornmeal cake

ASHCAN   *n* pl. **-S** a metal receptacle for garbage

ASHEN   *adj* consisting of ashes

ASHFALL   *n* pl. **-S** a deposit of volcanic ash

ASHIER   comparative of ashy

ASHIEST   superlative of ashy

ASHINESS   *n* pl. **-ES** the condition of being ashy

ASHLAR   *v* **-ED, -ING, -S** to build with squared stones

ASHLER   *v* **-ED, -ING, -S** to ashlar

ASHLESS   *adj* having no ashes

ASHMAN   *n* pl. **-MEN** one who collects and removes ashes

ASHORE   *adv* toward or on the shore

ASHPLANT   *n* pl. **-S** a walking stick

ASHRAM   *n* pl. **-S** a secluded dwelling of a Hindu sage

ASHTRAY   *n* pl. **-TRAYS** a receptacle for tobacco ashes

ASHY   *adj* **ASHIER, ASHIEST** covered with ashes

ASIDE   *n* pl. **-S** a comment by an actor intended to be heard by the audience but not the other actors

ASININE   *adj* obstinately stupid or silly

ASK   *v* **-ED, -ING, -S** to put a question to

ASKANCE   *adv* with a side glance

ASKANT   *adv* askance

ASKER   *n* pl. **-S** one that asks

ASKESIS   *n* pl. **ASKESES** ascesis

ASKEW   *adv* to one side

ASKING   *n* pl. **-S** the act of one who asks

ASKOS   *n* pl. **ASKOI** an oil jar used in ancient Greece

ASLANT   *adj* slanting

ASLEEP   *adj* sleeping

ASLOPE   *adj* sloping

ASLOSH   *adj* covered with water

ASOCIAL   *n* pl. **-S** one that avoids the company of others

ASP   *n* pl. **-S** a venomous snake

ASPARKLE   *adj* sparkling

ASPECT   *n* pl. **-S** appearance of something to the eye or mind

ASPEN   *n* pl. **-S** any of several poplars

ASPER   *n* pl. **-S** a Turkish money of account

ASPERATE   *v* **-ATED, -ATING, -ATES** to make uneven

ASPERGES   *n* pl. **ASPERGES** a Roman Catholic rite

ASPERITY   *n* pl. **-TIES** acrimony

ASPERSE   *v* **-PERSED, -PERSING, -PERSES** to spread false charges against

ASPERSER   *n* pl. **-S** one that asperses

ASPERSOR   *n* pl. **-S** asperser

ASPHALT   *v* **-ED, -ING, -S** to coat with asphalt (a substance used for paving and roofing)

ASPHERIC   *adj* varying slightly from an exactly spherical shape

ASPHODEL   *n* pl. **-S** a flowering plant

ASPHYXIA   *n* pl. **-S** unconsciousness caused by lack of oxygen

ASPHYXY   *n* pl. **-PHYXIES** asphyxia

ASPIC   *n* pl. **-S** the asp

ASPIRANT   *n* pl. **-S** one that aspires

ASPIRATA   *n* pl. **-TAE** a type of plosive

ASPIRATE   *v* **-RATED, -RATING, -RATES** to pronounce with an initial release of breath

ASPIRE   *v* **-PIRED, -PIRING, -PIRES** to have an earnest desire or ambition

ASPIRER   *n* pl. **-S** an aspirant

ASPIRIN   *n* pl. **-S** a pain reliever

ASPIRING   present participle of aspire

ASPIS   *n* pl. **-PISES** aspic

ASPISH   *adj* resembling an asp

ASQUINT   *adv* with a sidelong glance

ASRAMA   *n* pl. **-S** ashram

ASS   *n* pl. **-ES** a hoofed mammal

ASSAGAI   *v* **-GAIED, -GAIING, -GAIS** to pierce with a light spear

ASSAI   *n* pl. **-S** a tropical tree

ASSAIL   *v* **-ED, -ING, -S** to attack

ASSAILER   *n* pl. **-S** one that assails

ASSASSIN   *n* pl. **-S** a murderer

ASSAULT   *v* **-ED, -ING, -S** to attack

ASSAY   *v* **-ED, -ING, -S** to attempt

ASSAYER   *n* pl. **-S** one that assays

ASSEGAI   *v* **-GAIED, -GAIING, -GAIS** to assagai

ASSEMBLE   *v* **-BLED, -BLING, -BLES** to come or bring together

ASSEMBLY   *n* pl. **-BLIES** the act of assembling

ASSENT   *v* **-ED, -ING, -S** to express agreement

ASSENTER   *n* pl. **-S** one that assents

ASSENTOR   *n* pl. **-S** assenter

ASSERT   *v* **-ED, -ING, -S** to state positively

ASSERTER   *n* pl. **-S** one that asserts

ASSERTOR   *n* pl. **-S** asserter

ASSESS   *v* **-ED, -ING, -ES** to estimate the value of for taxation

ASSESSOR   *n* pl. **-S** one that assesses

ASSET   *n* pl. **-S** a useful quality or thing

ASSIGN   *v* **-ED, -ING, -S** to set apart for a particular purpose

ASSIGNAT   *n* pl. **-S** one of the notes issued as currency by the French revolutionary government

ASSIGNEE   *n* pl. **-S** one to whom property or right is legally transferred

ASSIGNER   *n* pl. **-S** one that assigns

ASSIGNOR   *n* pl. **-S** one who legally transfers property or right

ASSIST   *v* **-ED, -ING, -S** to give aid or support to

ASSISTER   *n* pl. **-S** one that assists

ASSISTOR   *n* pl. **-S** assister

ASSIZE   *n* pl. **-S** a session of a legislative or judicial body

ASSLIKE   *adj* resembling an ass

ASSOIL   *v* **-ED, -ING, -S** to pardon

ASSONANT   *n* pl. **-S** a word or syllable that resembles another in sound

ASSORT   *v* **-ED, -ING, -S** to distribute into groups according to kind or class

ASSORTER   *n* pl. **-S** one that assorts

ASSUAGE   *v* **-SUAGED, -SUAGING, -SUAGES** to make less severe

ASSUAGER   *n* pl. **-S** one that assuages

ASSUME   *v* **-SUMED, -SUMING, -SUMES** to take on

ASSUMER   *n* pl. **-S** one that assumes

ASSURE   *v* **-SURED, -SURING, -SURES** to insure

ASSURED   *n* pl. **-S** an insured person

ASSURER   *n* pl. **-S** one that assures

ASSURING   present participle of assure

ASSUROR   *n* pl. **-S** assurer

ASSWAGE   *v* **-SWAGED, -SWAGING, -SWAGES** to assuage

ASTASIA   *n* pl. **-S** inability to stand resulting from muscular incoordination

ASTATIC   *adj* unstable

ASTATINE   *n* pl. **-S** a radioactive element

ASTER   *n* pl. **-S** a flowering plant

ASTERIA   *n* pl. **-S** a gemstone cut to exhibit asterism

ASTERISK   *v* **-ED, -ING, -S** to mark with an asterisk (a star-shaped printing mark)

ASTERISM   *n* pl. **-S** a property of certain minerals of showing a starlike luminous figure

ASTERN   *adv* at or toward the rear of a ship

ASTERNAL   *adj* not connected to the sternum

ASTEROID   *n* pl. **-S** a type of celestial body

ASTHENIA   *n* pl. **-S** lack of strength

ASTHENIC   *n* pl. **-S** a slender, lightly muscled person

ASTHENY   *n* pl. **-NIES** asthenia

ASTHMA   *n* pl. **-S** a respiratory disease

ASTIGMIA   *n* pl. **-S** a visual defect

ASTILBE   *n* pl. **-S** an Asian perennial

ASTIR   *adj* moving about

ASTOMOUS   *adj* having no stomata

ASTONISH *v* **-ED, -ING, -ES** to fill with sudden wonder or surprise

ASTONY *v* **-TONIED, -TONYING, -TONIES** to astonish

ASTOUND *v* **-ED, -ING, -S** to amaze

ASTRAGAL *n* pl. **-S** a convex molding

ASTRAL *n* pl. **-S** a type of oil lamp

ASTRALLY *adv* in a stellar manner

ASTRAY *adv* off the right course

ASTRICT *v* **-ED, -ING, -S** to restrict

ASTRIDE *adv* with one leg on each side

ASTRINGE *v* **-TRINGED, -TRINGING, -TRINGES** to bind or draw together

ASTUTE *adj* shrewd **ASTUTELY** *adv*

ASTYLAR *adj* having no columns

ASUNDER *adv* into pieces

ASWARM *adj* swarming

ASWIRL *adj* swirling

ASWOON *adj* swooning

ASYLUM *n* pl. **-LUMS** or **-LA** an institution for the care of the mentally ill

ASYNDETA *n/pl* omissions of certain conjunctions

AT *prep* in the position of

ATABAL *n* pl. **-S** a type of drum

ATABRINE *n* pl. **-S** a drug to treat malaria

ATACTIC *adj* showing no regularity of structure

ATAGHAN *n* pl. **-S** yataghan

ATALAYA *n* pl. **-S** a watchtower

ATAMAN *n* pl. **-S** a hetman

ATAMASCO *n* pl. **-COS** a flowering plant

ATAP *n* pl. **-S** the nipa palm tree

ATARAXIA *n* pl. **-S** peace of mind

ATARAXIC *n* pl. **-S** a tranquilizing drug

ATARAXY *n* pl. **-RAXIES** ataraxia

ATAVIC *adj* pertaining to a remote ancestor

ATAVISM *n* pl. **-S** the reappearance of a genetic characteristic after several generations of absence

ATAVIST *n* pl. **-S** an individual displaying atavism

ATAXIA *n* pl. **-S** loss of muscular coordination

ATAXIC *n* pl. **-S** one suffering from ataxia

ATAXY *n* pl. **ATAXIES** ataxia

ATE *n* pl. **-S** blind impulse or reckless ambition that drives one to ruin

ATECHNIC *adj* lacking technical knowledge

ATELIC *adj* pertaining to a type of verb form

ATELIER *n* pl. **-S** a workshop or studio

ATEMOYA *n* pl. **-S** a fruit of a hybrid tropical tree

ATENOLOL *n* pl. **-S** a drug to treat hypertension

ATHANASY *n* pl. **-SIES** immortality

ATHEISM *n* pl. **-S** the belief that there is no God

ATHEIST *n* pl. **-S** a believer in atheism

ATHELING *n* pl. **-S** an Anglo-Saxon prince or nobleman

ATHENEUM *n* pl. **-S** a literary institution

ATHEROMA *n* pl. **-MAS** or **-MATA** a disease of the arteries

ATHETOID *adj* affected with a type of nervous disorder

ATHIRST *adj* having a strong desire

ATHLETE *n* pl. **-S** one skilled in feats of physical strength and agility **ATHLETIC** *adj*

ATHODYD *n* pl. **-S** a type of jet engine

ATHWART *adv* from side to side

ATILT *adj* being in a tilted position

ATINGLE *adj* tingling

ATLAS *n* pl. **ATLASES** or **ATLANTES** a male figure used as a supporting column

ATLATL *n* pl. **-S** a device for throwing a spear or dart

ATMA *n* pl. **-S** atman

ATMAN *n* pl. **-S** the individual soul in Hinduism

ATOLL *n* pl. **-S** a coral island

ATOM *n* pl. **-S** the smallest unit of an element **ATOMIC, ATOMICAL** *adj*

ATOMICS *n/pl* the science dealing with atoms

ATOMIES pl. of atomy

ATOMISE *v* **-ISED, -ISING, -ISES** to atomize

ATOMISER *n* pl. **-S** atomizer

ATOMISM *n* pl. **-S** the theory that the universe is composed of simple, indivisible, minute particles

ATOMIST *n* pl. **-S** an adherent of atomism

ATOMIZE   *v* **-IZED, -IZING, -IZES** to reduce to a fine spray

ATOMIZER   *n* pl. **-S** a device for atomizing liquids

ATOMY   *n* pl. **-MIES** a tiny particle

ATONAL   *adj* lacking tonality **ATONALLY** *adv*

ATONE   *v* **ATONED, ATONING, ATONES** to make amends or reparation **ATONABLE** *adj*

ATONER   *n* pl. **-S** one that atones

ATONIA   *n* pl. **-S** atony

ATONIC   *n* pl. **-S** an unaccented syllable or word

ATONING   present participle of atone

ATONY   *n* pl. **-NIES** muscular weakness

ATOP   *adj* being on or at the top

ATOPY   *n* pl. **-PIES** a type of allergy **ATOPIC** *adj*

ATRAZINE   *n* pl. **-S** an herbicide

ATREMBLE   *adj* trembling

ATRESIA   *n* pl. **-S** absence or closure of a natural bodily passage **ATRESIC, ATRETIC** *adj*

ATRIA   a pl. of atrium

ATRIAL   *adj* pertaining to an atrium

ATRIP   *adj* aweigh

ATRIUM   *n* pl. **ATRIUMS** or **ATRIA** the main room of an ancient Roman house

ATROCITY   *n* pl. **-TIES** a heinous act

ATROPHIA   *n* pl. **-S** a wasting away of the body or any of its parts **ATROPHIC** *adj*

ATROPHY   *v* **-PHIED, -PHYING, -PHIES** to waste away

ATROPIN   *n* pl. **-S** atropine

ATROPINE   *n* pl. **-S** a poisonous alkaloid

ATROPISM   *n* pl. **-S** atropine poisoning

ATT   *n* pl. **ATT** a monetary unit of Laos

ATTABOY   *interj* —used to express encouragement or approval

ATTACH   *v* **-ED, -ING, -ES** to connect as an associated part

ATTACHE   *n* pl. **-S** a diplomatic official

ATTACHER   *n* pl. **-S** one that attaches

ATTACK   *v* **-ED, -ING, -S** to set upon violently

ATTACKER   *n* pl. **-S** one that attacks

ATTAGIRL   *interj* —used to express encouragement or approval

ATTAIN   *v* **-ED, -ING, -S** to gain or achieve by mental or physical effort

ATTAINER   *n* pl. **-S** one that attains

ATTAINT   *v* **-ED, -ING, -S** to disgrace

ATTAR   *n* pl. **-S** a fragrant oil

ATTEMPER   *v* **-ED, -ING, -S** to modify the temperature of

ATTEMPT   *v* **-ED, -ING, -S** to make an effort to do or accomplish

ATTEND   *v* **-ED, -ING, -S** to be present at

ATTENDEE   *n* pl. **-S** an attender

ATTENDER   *n* pl. **-S** one that attends

ATTENT   *adj* heedful

ATTEST   *v* **-ED, -ING, -S** to affirm to be true or genuine

ATTESTER   *n* pl. **-S** one that attests

ATTESTOR   *n* pl. **-S** attester

ATTIC   *n* pl. **-S** a story or room directly below the roof of a house

ATTICISM   *n* pl. **-S** a concise and elegant expression

ATTICIST   *n* pl. **-S** one who uses atticisms

ATTICIZE   *v* **-CIZED, -CIZING, -CIZES** to use atticisms

ATTIRE   *v* **-TIRED, -TIRING, -TIRES** to clothe

ATTITUDE   *n* pl. **-S** a state of mind with regard to some matter

ATTORN   *v* **-ED, -ING, -S** to acknowledge a new owner as one's landlord

ATTORNEY   *n* pl. **-NEYS** a lawyer (a member of the legal profession)

ATTRACT   *v* **-ED, -ING, -S** to cause to approach or adhere

ATTRIT   *v* **-TRITTED, -TRITTING, -TRITS** to lose by attrition

ATTRITE   *v* **-TRITED, -TRITING, -TRITES** to attrit

ATTUNE   *v* **-TUNED, -TUNING, -TUNES** to bring into harmony

ATWAIN   *adv* in two

ATWEEN   *prep* between

ATWITTER   *adj* twittering

ATYPIC   *adj* atypical

ATYPICAL   *adj* not typical

AUBADE   *n* pl. **-S** a morning song

AUBERGE   *n* pl. **-S** an inn

AUBRETIA   *n* pl. **-S** aubrieta

AUBRIETA   *n* pl. **-S** a flowering plant

AUBURN   *n* pl. **-S** a reddish brown color

AUCTION   *v* **-ED, -ING, -S** to sell publicly to the highest bidder

AUCUBA   *n* pl. **-S** a shrub of the dogwood family

AUDACITY   *n* pl. **-TIES** boldness

AUDAD   *n* pl. **-S** aoudad

AUDIAL   *adj* aural

AUDIBLE   *v* **-BLED, -BLING, -BLES** to call a substitute play in football

AUDIBLY   *adv* in a way so as to be heard

AUDIENCE   *n* pl. **-S** a group of listeners or spectators

AUDIENT   *n* pl. **-S** one that hears

AUDILE   *n* pl. **-S** one whose mental imagery is chiefly auditory

AUDING   *n* pl. **-S** the process of hearing, recognizing, and interpreting a spoken language

AUDIO   *n* pl. **-DIOS** sound reception or transmission

AUDIT   *v* **-ED, -ING, -S** to examine with intent to verify

AUDITEE   *n* pl. **-S** one that is audited

AUDITION   *v* **-ED, -ING, -S** to give a trial performance

AUDITIVE   *n* pl. **-S** an auditory

AUDITOR   *n* pl. **-S** one that audits

AUDITORY   *n* pl. **-RIES** a group of listeners

AUGEND   *n* pl. **-S** a number to which another is to be added

AUGER   *n* pl. **-S** a tool for boring

AUGHT   *n* pl. **-S** a zero

AUGITE   *n* pl. **-S** a mineral **AUGITIC** *adj*

AUGMENT   *v* **-ED, -ING, -S** to increase

AUGUR   *v* **-ED, -ING, -S** to foretell from omens

AUGURAL   *adj* pertaining to augury

AUGURER   *n* pl. **-S** one that augurs

AUGURY   *n* pl. **-RIES** the practice of auguring

AUGUST   *adj* **-GUSTER, -GUSTEST** inspiring reverence or admiration **AUGUSTLY** *adv*

AUK   *n* pl. **-S** a diving seabird

AUKLET   *n* pl. **-S** a small auk

AULD   *adj* **AULDER, AULDEST** old

AULIC   *adj* pertaining to a royal court

AUNT   *n* pl. **-S** the sister of one's father or mother

AUNTHOOD   *n* pl. **-S** the state of being an aunt

AUNTIE   *n* pl. **-S** aunt

AUNTIES   pl. of aunty

AUNTLIKE   *adj* resembling an aunt

AUNTLY   *adj* **-LIER, -LIEST** of or suggesting an aunt

AUNTY   *n* pl. **AUNTIES** aunt

AURA   *n* pl. **-RAS** or **-RAE** an invisible emanation

AURAL   *adj* pertaining to the sense of hearing **AURALLY** *adv*

AURALITY   *n* pl. **-TIES** the quality of being aural

AURAR   pl. of eyrir

AURATE   *adj* having ears

AURATED   *adj* aurate

AUREATE   *adj* golden

AUREI   pl. of aureus

AUREOLA   *n* pl. **-LAS** or **-LAE** a halo

AUREOLE   *v* **-OLED, -OLING, -OLES** to surround with a halo

AURES   pl. of auris

AUREUS   *n* pl. **-REI** a gold coin of ancient Rome

AURIC   *adj* pertaining to gold

AURICLE   *n* pl. **-S** an ear or ear-shaped part **AURICLED** *adj*

AURICULA   *n* pl. **-LAS** or **-LAE** an auricle

AURIFORM   *adj* ear-shaped

AURIS   *n* pl. **AURES** the ear

AURIST   *n* pl. **-S** a specialist in diseases of the ear

AUROCHS   *n* pl. **-ES** an extinct European ox

AURORA   *n* pl. **-RAS** or **-RAE** the rising light of the morning **AURORAL, AUROREAN** *adj*

AUROUS   *adj* pertaining to gold

AURUM   *n* pl. **-S** gold

AUSFORM   *v* **-ED, -ING, -S** to subject steel to a strengthening process

AUSPEX   *n* pl. **-PICES** a soothsayer of ancient Rome

AUSPICE   *n* pl. **-S** a favorable omen

AUSTERE   *adj* **-TERER, -TEREST** grave in disposition or appearance

AUSTRAL   *n* pl. **-ES** or **-S** a former monetary unit of Argentina

AUSUBO   *n* pl. **-BOS** a tropical tree

AUTACOID   *n* pl. **-S** a hormone

AUTARCH *n* pl. **-S** an absolute ruler

AUTARCHY *n* pl. **-CHIES** absolute rule

AUTARKY *n* pl. **-KIES** national economic self-sufficiency **AUTARKIC** *adj*

AUTECISM *n* pl. **-S** the development of the entire life cycle of a parasitic fungus on a single host

AUTEUR *n* pl. **-S** the creator of a film

AUTHOR *v* **-ED, -ING, -S** to write

AUTISM *n* pl. **-S** extreme withdrawal into fantasy

AUTIST *n* pl. **-S** an autistic

AUTISTIC *n* pl. **-S** one who is affected with autism

AUTO *v* **-ED, -ING, -S** to ride in an automobile

AUTOBAHN *n* pl. **-BAHNS** or **-BAHNEN** a German superhighway

AUTOBUS *n* pl. **-BUSES** or **-BUSSES** a bus

AUTOCADE *n* pl. **-S** a parade of automobiles

AUTOCOID *n* pl. **-S** autacoid

AUTOCRAT *n* pl. **-S** an absolute ruler

AUTODYNE *n* pl. **-S** a type of electrical circuit

AUTOGAMY *n* pl. **-MIES** fertilization of a flower by its own pollen

AUTOGENY *n* pl. **-NIES** the production of living organisms from inanimate matter

AUTOGIRO *n* pl. **-ROS** a type of airplane

AUTOGYRO *n* pl. **-ROS** autogiro

AUTOHARP *n* pl. **-S** a type of zither

AUTOLYSE *v* **-LYSED, -LYSING, -LYSES** to autolyze

AUTOLYZE *v* **-LYZED, -LYZING, -LYZES** to break down tissue by the action of self-contained enzymes

AUTOMAN *n* pl. **-MEN** an automobile maker

AUTOMAT *n* pl. **-S** a type of cafeteria

AUTOMATA *n/pl* robots

AUTOMATE *v* **-MATED, -MATING, -MATES** to convert to a system of automatic control

AUTOMEN *n* pl. of automan

AUTONOMY *n* pl. **-MIES** the state of being self-governing

AUTONYM *n* pl. **-S** a name by which a people refers to itself

AUTOPEN *n* pl. **-S** a device for imitating signatures

AUTOPSIC *adj* pertaining to an autopsy

AUTOPSY *v* **-SIED, -SYING, -SIES** to examine a dead body to determine the cause of death

AUTOSOME *n* pl. **-S** a type of chromosome

AUTOTOMY *n* pl. **-MIES** the shedding of a damaged body part

AUTOTYPE *n* pl. **-S** a type of photographic process

AUTOTYPY *n* pl. **-TYPIES** autotype

AUTUMN *n* pl. **-S** a season of the year **AUTUMNAL** *adj*

AUTUNITE *n* pl. **-S** a mineral

AUXESIS *n* pl. **AUXESES** an increase in cell size without cell division

AUXETIC *n* pl. **-S** a substance that promotes auxesis

AUXIN *n* pl. **-S** a substance used to regulate plant growth **AUXINIC** *adj*

AVA *adv* at all

AVADAVAT *n* pl. **-S** a small songbird

AVAIL *v* **-ED, -ING, -S** to be of use or advantage to

AVANT *adj* culturally or stylistically new

AVARICE *n* pl. **-S** greed

AVAST *interj* — used as a command to stop

AVATAR *n* pl. **-S** the incarnation of a Hindu deity

AVAUNT *interj* — used as an order of dismissal

AVE *n* pl. **-S** an expression of greeting or farewell

AVELLAN *adj* having the four arms shaped like filberts — used of a heraldic cross

AVELLANE *adj* avellan

AVENGE *v* **AVENGED, AVENGING, AVENGES** to exact retribution for

AVENGER *n* pl. **-S** one that avenges

AVENS *n* pl. **-ES** a perennial herb

AVENTAIL *n* pl. **-S** ventail

AVENUE *n* pl. **-S** a wide street

AVER *v* **AVERRED, AVERRING, AVERS** to declare positively

AVERAGE *v* **-AGED, -AGING, -AGES** to calculate the arithmetic mean of

AVERMENT *n* pl. **-S** the act of averring

AVERRED past tense of aver

AVERRING present participle of aver

AVERSE   *adj* opposed; reluctant **AVERSELY** *adv*

AVERSION   *n* pl. **-S** a feeling of repugnance

AVERSIVE   *n* pl. **-S** a punishment

AVERT   *v* **-ED, -ING, -S** to turn away

AVERTER   *n* pl. **-S** one that averts

AVGAS   *n* pl. **-GASES** or **-GASSES** gasoline for airplanes

AVIAN   *n* pl. **-S** a bird

AVIANIZE   *v* **-IZED, -IZING, -IZES** to make less severe by repeated culture in a chick embryo, as a virus

AVIARIST   *n* pl. **-S** the keeper of an aviary

AVIARY   *n* pl. **-ARIES** a large enclosure for live birds

AVIATE   *v* **-ATED, -ATING, -ATES** to fly an aircraft

AVIATION   *n* pl. **-S** the act of aviating **AVIATIC** *adj*

AVIATOR   *n* pl. **-S** one that aviates

AVIATRIX   *n* pl. **-TRICES** or **-TRIXES** a female aviator

AVICULAR   *adj* pertaining to birds

AVID   *adj* eager

AVIDIN   *n* pl. **-S** a protein found in egg white

AVIDITY   *n* pl. **-TIES** the state of being avid

AVIDLY   *adv* in an avid manner

AVIDNESS   *n* pl. **-ES** avidity

AVIFAUNA   *n* pl. **-NAS** or **-NAE** the bird life of a particular region

AVIGATOR   *n* pl. **-S** one that navigates aircraft

AVION   *n* pl. **-S** an airplane

AVIONICS   *n/pl* the science of electronics applied to aviation **AVIONIC** *adj*

AVISO   *n* pl. **-SOS** advice

AVO   *n* pl. **AVOS** a monetary unit of Macao

AVOCADO   *n* pl. **-DOS** or **-DOES** the edible fruit of a tropical tree

AVOCET   *n* pl. **-S** a shore bird

AVODIRE   *n* pl. **-S** an African tree

AVOID   *v* **-ED, -ING, -S** to keep away from

AVOIDER   *n* pl. **-S** one that avoids

AVOSET   *n* pl. **-S** avocet

AVOUCH   *v* **-ED, -ING, -ES** to affirm

AVOUCHER   *n* pl. **-S** one that avouches

AVOW   *v* **-ED, -ING, -S** to declare openly **AVOWABLE** *adj* **AVOWABLY, AVOWEDLY** *adv*

AVOWAL   *n* pl. **-S** an open declaration

AVOWER   *n* pl. **-S** one that avows

AVULSE   *v* **AVULSED, AVULSING, AVULSES** to tear off forcibly

AVULSION   *n* pl. **-S** the act of avulsing

AW   *interj* — used to express protest, disgust, or disbelief

AWA   *adv* away

AWAIT   *v* **-ED, -ING, -S** to wait for

AWAITER   *n* pl. **-S** one that awaits

AWAKE   *v* **AWAKED** or **AWOKE, AWOKEN, AWAKING, AWAKES** to wake up

AWAKEN   *v* **-ED, -ING, -S** to awake

AWAKENER   *n* pl. **-S** one that awakens

AWAKING   present participle of awake

AWARD   *v* **-ED, -ING, -S** to grant as due or merited

AWARDEE   *n* pl. **-S** one that is awarded something

AWARDER   *n* pl. **-S** one that awards

AWARE   *adj* having perception or knowledge

AWASH   *adj* covered with water

AWAY   *adv* from a certain place

AWAYNESS   *n* pl. **-ES** the state of being distant

AWE   *v* **AWED, AWING** or **AWEING, AWES** to inspire with awe (reverential fear)

AWEARY   *adj* weary

AWEATHER   *adv* toward the windward side of a vessel

AWED   past tense of awe

AWEE   *adv* awhile

AWEIGH   *adj* hanging just clear of the bottom — used of an anchor

AWELESS   *adj* lacking awe

AWESOME   *adj* inspiring awe

AWFUL   *adj* **-FULLER, -FULLEST** extremely bad or unpleasant **AWFULLY** *adv*

AWHILE   *adv* for a short time

AWHIRL   *adj* whirling

AWING   a present participle of awe

AWKWARD   *adj* **-WARDER, -WARDEST** lacking skill, dexterity, or grace

AWL *n* pl. **-S** a pointed tool for making small holes

AWLESS *adj* aweless

AWLWORT *n* pl. **-S** an aquatic plant

AWMOUS *n* pl. **AWMOUS** alms

AWN *n* pl. **-S** a bristlelike appendage of certain grasses **AWNED, AWNLESS, AWNY** *adj*

AWNING *n* pl. **-S** a rooflike canvas cover **AWNINGED** *adj*

AWOKE a past tense of awake

AWOKEN a past participle of awake

AWOL *n* pl. **-S** one who is absent without leave

AWRY *adv* with a turn or twist to one side

AX *v* **-ED, -ING, -ES** to work on with an ax (a type of cutting tool)

AXAL *adj* axial

AXE *v* **AXED, AXING, AXES** to ax

AXEL *n* pl. **-S** a jump in figure skating

AXEMAN *n* pl. **-MEN** axman

AXENIC *adj* free from germs

AXES pl. of axis

AXIAL *adj* pertaining to or forming an axis **AXIALLY** *adv*

AXIALITY *n* pl. **-TIES** the state of being axial

AXIL *n* pl. **-S** the angle between the upper side of a leaf and its supporting stem

AXILE *adj* axial

AXILLA *n* pl. **-LAE** or **-LAS** the armpit

AXILLAR *n* pl. **-S** a feather on the undersurface of a bird's wing

AXILLARY *n* pl. **-LARIES** an axillar

AXING present participle of axe

AXIOLOGY *n* pl. **-GIES** the study of values and value judgments

AXIOM *n* pl. **-S** a self-evident truth

AXION *n* pl. **-S** a hypothetical subatomic particle

AXIS *n* pl. **AXES** a straight line about which a body rotates **AXISED** *adj*

AXIS *n* pl. **AXISES** an Asian deer

AXITE *n* pl. **-S** a fiber of an axon

AXLE *n* pl. **-S** a shaft upon which a wheel revolves **AXLED** *adj*

AXLETREE *n* pl. **-S** a type of axle

AXLIKE *adj* resembling an ax

AXMAN *n* pl. **-MEN** one who wields an ax

AXOLOTL *n* pl. **-S** a salamander of Mexico and western United States

AXON *n* pl. **-S** the central process of a neuron **AXONAL** *adj*

AXONE *n* pl. **-S** axon

AXONEMAL *adj* pertaining to an axoneme

AXONEME *n* pl. **-S** a part of a cilium

AXONIC *adj* pertaining to an axon

AXOPLASM *n* pl. **-S** the protoplasm of an axon

AXSEED *n* pl. **-S** a European herb

AY *n* pl. **AYS** aye

AYAH *n* pl. **-S** a native maid or nurse in India

AYE *n* pl. **-S** an affirmative vote

AYIN *n* pl. **-S** a Hebrew letter

AYURVEDA *n* pl. **-S** a Hindu system of medicine

AZALEA *n* pl. **-S** a flowering shrub

AZAN *n* pl. **-S** a Muslim call to prayer

AZIDE *n* pl. **-S** a type of chemical compound **AZIDO** *adj*

AZIMUTH *n* pl. **-S** an angle of horizontal deviation

AZINE *n* pl. **-S** a type of chemical compound

AZLON *n* pl. **-S** a textile fiber

AZO *adj* containing nitrogen

AZOIC *adj* pertaining to geologic time before the appearance of life

AZOLE *n* pl. **-S** a type of chemical compound

AZON *n* pl. **-S** a radio-controlled aerial bomb

AZONAL *adj* pertaining to a type of a soil group

AZONIC *adj* not restricted to any particular zone

AZOTE *n* pl. **-S** nitrogen **AZOTED** *adj*

AZOTEMIA *n* pl. **-S** an excess of nitrogenous substances in the blood **AZOTEMIC** *adj*

AZOTH *n* pl. **-S** mercury

AZOTIC *adj* pertaining to azote

AZOTISE	*v* **-TISED, -TISING, -TISES** to azotize
AZOTIZE	*v* **-TIZED, -TIZING, -TIZES** to treat with nitrogen
AZOTURIA	*n* pl. **-S** an excess of nitrogenous substances in the urine
AZUKI	*n* pl. **-S** adzuki
AZULEJO	*n* pl. **-JOS** a type of ceramic tile
AZURE	*n* pl. **-S** a blue color
AZURITE	*n* pl. **-S** a mineral
AZYGOS	*n* pl. **-ES** an azygous anatomical part
AZYGOUS	*adj* not being one of a pair

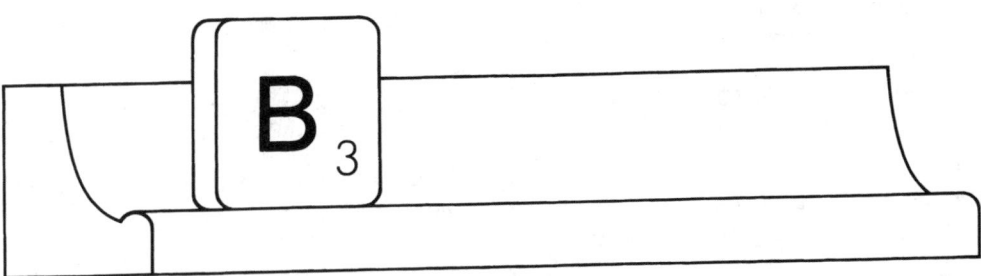

BA	*n* pl. **-S** the eternal soul, in Egyptian mythology
BAA	*v* **-ED, -ING, -S** to bleat
BAAL	*n* pl. **BAALS** or **BAALIM** a false god
BAALISM	*n* pl. **-S** the worship of a baal
BAAS	*n* pl. **-ES** master; boss
BAASKAAP	*n* pl. **-S** baaskap
BAASKAP	*n* pl. **-S** the policy of domination by white people in South Africa
BAASSKAP	*n* pl. **-S** baaskap
BABA	*n* pl. **-S** a rum cake
BABASSU	*n* pl. **-S** a palm tree
BABBITRY	*n* pl. **-RIES** conventional middle-class attitudes and behavior stressing respectability and material success
BABBITT	*v* **-ED, -ING, -S** to line with babbitt (an alloy of tin, copper, and antimony)
BABBLE	*v* **-BLED, -BLING, -BLES** to talk idly or excessively
BABBLER	*n* pl. **-S** one that babbles
BABBLING	*n* pl. **-S** idle talk
BABE	*n* pl. **-S** a baby
BABEL	*n* pl. **-S** confusion
BABESIA	*n* pl. **-S** a parasitic protozoan
BABICHE	*n* pl. **-S** rawhide thongs
BABIED	past tense of baby
BABIER	comparative of baby
BABIES	present 3d person sing. of baby
BABIEST	superlative of baby
BABIRUSA	*n* pl. **-S** a wild pig
BABKA	*n* pl. **-S** a coffee cake
BABOO	*n* pl. **-BOOS** a Hindu gentleman
BABOOL	*n* pl. **-S** babul
BABOON	*n* pl. **-S** a large ape
BABU	*n* pl. **-S** baboo
BABUL	*n* pl. **-S** a North African tree
BABUSHKA	*n* pl. **-S** a woman's scarf
BABY	*adj* **BABIER, BABIEST** resembling a baby (an infant)
BABY	*v* **-BIED, -BYING, -BIES** to coddle
BABYDOLL	*n* pl. **-S** short, sheer pajamas for women
BABYHOOD	*n* pl. **-S** the state of being a baby
BABYISH	*adj* resembling a baby
BABYSIT	*v* **-SAT, -SITTING, -SITS** to care for a child temporarily
BACALAO	*n* pl. **-LAOS** codfish
BACCA	*n* pl. **-CAE** a berry
BACCARA	*n* pl. **-S** baccarat
BACCARAT	*n* pl. **-S** a card game
BACCATE	*adj* pulpy like a berry
BACCATED	*adj* baccate
BACCHANT	*n* pl. **-S** or **-ES** a carouser
BACCHIC	*adj* riotous
BACCHIUS	*n* pl. **-CHII** a type of metrical foot
BACH	*v* **-ED, -ING, -ES** to live as a bachelor
BACHELOR	*n* pl. **-S** an unmarried man
BACILLAR	*adj* rod-shaped
BACILLUS	*n* pl. **-LI** any of a class of rod-shaped bacteria
BACK	*v* **-ED, -ING, -S** to support
BACKACHE	*n* pl. **-S** a pain in the back
BACKBEAT	*n* pl. **-S** a type of rhythm in music
BACKBEND	*n* pl. **-S** an acrobatic feat
BACKBITE	*v* **-BIT, -BITTEN, -BITING, -BITES** to slander
BACKBONE	*n* pl. **-S** the spine
BACKCAST	*n* pl. **-S** a backward movement in casting a fishing line
BACKCHAT	*n* pl. **-S** repartee

BACKDATE *v* **-DATED, -DATING, -DATES** to predate

BACKDOOR *adj* secretive

BACKDROP *v* **-DROPPED** or **-DROPT, -DROPPING, -DROPS** to provide with a scenic background

BACKER *n* pl. **-S** a supporter

BACKFILL *v* **-ED, -ING, -S** to refill

BACKFIRE *v* **-FIRED, -FIRING, -FIRES** to produce undesirable effects

BACKFIT *v* **-FITTED, -FITTING, -FITS** to retrofit

BACKFLIP *v* **-FLIPPED, -FLIPPING, -FLIPS** to perform a backward somersault

BACKFLOW *n* pl. **-S** a flowing back toward a source

BACKHAND *v* **-ED, -ING, -S** to strike with the back of the hand

BACKHAUL *v* **-ED, -ING, -S** to return after delivering a load

BACKHOE *v* **-HOED, -HOEING, -HOES** to use a backhoe (a type of excavating machine)

BACKING *n* pl. **-S** support

BACKLAND *n* pl. **-S** a region remote from cities

BACKLASH *v* **-ED, -ING, -ES** to cause a reaction

BACKLESS *adj* having no back

BACKLIST *v* **-ED, -ING, -S** to include in a publisher's list of older book titles

BACKLIT *adj* illuminated from behind

BACKLOAD *v* **-ED, -ING, -S** to defer a financial obligation

BACKLOG *v* **-LOGGED, -LOGGING, -LOGS** to accumulate

BACKMOST *adj* hindmost

BACKOUT *n* pl. **-S** a reversal of launching procedures

BACKPACK *v* **-ED, -ING, -S** to hike with a pack on one's back

BACKREST *n* pl. **-S** a back support

BACKROOM *n* pl. **-S** a place for meeting inconspicuously

BACKRUSH *n* pl. **-ES** the seaward return of water from a wave

BACKSAW *n* pl. **-S** a type of saw

BACKSEAT *n* pl. **-S** a rear seat

BACKSET *n* pl. **-S** a setback

BACKSIDE *n* pl. **-S** the hind part

BACKSLAP *v* **-SLAPPED, -SLAPPING, -SLAPS** to show much approval

BACKSLID past tense of backslide (to revert to sin)

BACKSPIN *n* pl. **-S** a backward rotation

BACKSTAB *v* **-STABBED, -STABBING, -STABS** to attack or betray behind one's back

BACKSTAY *n* pl. **-STAYS** a support for a mast

BACKSTOP *v* **-STOPPED, -STOPPING, -STOPS** to bolster

BACKUP *n* pl. **-S** a substitute

BACKWARD *adv* toward the back

BACKWASH *v* **-ED, -ING, -ES** to spray water backward

BACKWOOD *adj* uncouth

BACKWRAP *n* pl. **-S** a wraparound garment that fastens in the back

BACKYARD *n* pl. **-S** an area at the rear of a house

BACLOFEN *n* pl. **-S** a muscle relaxant

BACON *n* pl. **-S** a side of a pig cured and smoked

BACTERIA *n* pl. **-S** a group of microscopic organisms

BACTERIN *n* pl. **-S** a vaccine prepared from dead bacteria

BACULINE *adj* pertaining to a rod

BACULUM *n* pl. **-LUMS** or **-LA** a bone in the penis of many mammals

BAD *adj* **BADDER, BADDEST** very good

BAD *adj* **WORSE, WORST** not good

BAD *n* pl. **-S** something that is bad

BADDIE *n* pl. **-S** a bad person

BADDY *n* pl. **-DIES** baddie

BADE past tense of bid

BADGE *v* **BADGED, BADGING, BADGES** to supply with an insignia

BADGER *v* **-ED, -ING, -S** to harass

BADGERLY *adj* bothersome

BADINAGE *v* **-NAGED, -NAGING, -NAGES** to banter

BADLAND *n* pl. **-S** a barren, hilly area

BADLY *adv* in a bad manner

BADMAN *n* pl. **-MEN** an outlaw

BADMOUTH *v* **-ED, -ING, -S** to criticize

BADNESS *n* pl. **-ES** the state of being bad

BAFF *v* **-ED, -ING, -S** to strike under a golf ball

BAFFIES pl. of baffy

BAFFLE   *v* **-FLED, -FLING, -FLES** to confuse

BAFFLER   *n* pl. **-S** one that baffles

BAFFY   *n* pl. **-FIES** a wooden golf club

BAG   *v* **BAGGED, BAGGING, BAGS** to put into a bag (a flexible container)

BAGASS   *n* pl. **-ES** bagasse

BAGASSE   *n* pl. **-S** crushed sugarcane

BAGEL   *n* pl. **-S** a ring-shaped roll

BAGFUL   *n* pl. **BAGFULS** or **BAGSFUL** as much as a bag can hold

BAGGAGE   *n* pl. **-S** luggage

BAGGED   past tense of bag

BAGGER   *n* pl. **-S** one that bags

BAGGIE   *n* pl. **-S** the stomach

BAGGING   *n* pl. **-S** material for making bags

BAGGY   *adj* **-GIER, -GIEST** loose-fitting **BAGGILY** *adv*

BAGHOUSE   *n* pl. **-S** a facility for removing particulates from exhaust gases

BAGLIKE   *adj* resembling a bag

BAGMAN   *n* pl. **-MEN** a traveling salesman

BAGNIO   *n* pl. **-NIOS** a brothel

BAGPIPE   *v* **-PIPED, -PIPING, -PIPES** to play a bagpipe (a wind instrument)

BAGPIPER   *n* pl. **-S** one that plays bagpipes

BAGSFUL   a pl. of bagful

BAGUET   *n* pl. **-S** baguette

BAGUETTE   *n* pl. **-S** a rectangular gem

BAGWIG   *n* pl. **-S** a type of wig

BAGWORM   *n* pl. **-S** the larva of certain moths

BAH   *interj* — used to express disgust

BAHADUR   *n* pl. **-S** a Hindu title of respect

BAHT   *n* pl. **-S** a monetary unit of Thailand

BAIDARKA   *n* pl. **-S** bidarka

BAIL   *v* **-ED, -ING, -S** to transfer property temporarily **BAILABLE** *adj*

BAILEE   *n* pl. **-S** a person to whom property is bailed

BAILER   *n* pl. **-S** bailor

BAILEY   *n* pl. **-LEYS** an outer castle wall

BAILIE   *n* pl. **-S** a Scottish magistrate

BAILIFF   *n* pl. **-S** a court officer

BAILMENT   *n* pl. **-S** the act of bailing

BAILOR   *n* pl. **-S** a person who bails property to another

BAILOUT   *n* pl. **-S** the act of parachuting from an aircraft

BAILSMAN   *n* pl. **-MEN** one who provides security for another

BAIRN   *n* pl. **-S** a child **BAIRNISH** *adj*

BAIRNLY   *adj* **-LIER, -LIEST** childish

BAIT   *v* **-ED, -ING, -S** to lure

BAITER   *n* pl. **-S** one that baits

BAITFISH   *n* pl. **-ES** a fish used as bait

BAITH   *adj* both

BAIZA   *n* pl. **-S** a monetary unit of Oman

BAIZE   *n* pl. **-S** a green, woolen fabric

BAKE   *v* **BAKED, BAKING, BAKES** to prepare food in an oven

BAKEMEAT   *n* pl. **-S** a pastry

BAKER   *n* pl. **-S** one that bakes

BAKERY   *n* pl. **-ERIES** a place where baked goods are sold

BAKESHOP   *n* pl. **-S** a bakery

BAKEWARE   *n* pl. **-S** dishes used for baking

BAKING   *n* pl. **-S** a quantity baked

BAKLAVA   *n* pl. **-S** a Turkish pastry

BAKLAWA   *n* pl. **-S** baklava

BAKSHISH   *v* **-ED, -ING, -ES** to give a tip

BAL   *n* pl. **-S** a balmoral

BALANCE   *v* **-ANCED, -ANCING, -ANCES** to weigh

BALANCER   *n* pl. **-S** one that balances

BALAS   *n* pl. **-ES** a red variety of spinel

BALATA   *n* pl. **-S** a tropical tree

BALBOA   *n* pl. **-S** a monetary unit of Panama

BALCONY   *n* pl. **-NIES** an elevated platform

BALD   *adj* **BALDER, BALDEST** lacking hair

BALD   *v* **-ED, -ING, -S** to become bald

BALDHEAD   *n* pl. **-S** a bald person

BALDIES   pl. of baldy

BALDISH   *adj* somewhat bald

BALDLY   *adv* in a plain and blunt manner

BALDNESS   *n* pl. **-ES** the state of being bald

BALDPATE   *n* pl. **-S** a baldhead

BALDRIC   *n* pl. **-S** a shoulder belt

BALDRICK   *n* pl. **-S** baldric

BALDY   *n* pl. **BALDIES** a bald person

BALE   *v* **BALED, BALING, BALES** to form into tightly compressed bundles

BALEEN *n* pl. **-S** whalebone

BALEFIRE *n* pl. **-S** a bonfire

BALEFUL *adj* menacing

BALER *n* pl. **-S** one that bales

BALING present participle of bale

BALISAUR *n* pl. **-S** a long-tailed badger

BALK *v* **-ED, -ING, -S** to stop short and refuse to proceed

BALKER *n* pl. **-S** one that balks

BALKLINE *n* pl. **-S** the starting line in track events

BALKY *adj* **BALKIER, BALKIEST** stubborn **BALKILY** *adv*

BALL *v* **-ED, -ING, -S** to form into a ball (a spherical object)

BALLAD *n* pl. **-S** a narrative poem or song **BALLADIC** *adj*

BALLADE *n* pl. **-S** a type of poem

BALLADRY *n* pl. **-RIES** ballad poetry

BALLAST *v* **-ED, -ING, -S** to stabilize

BALLER *n* pl. **-S** one that balls

BALLET *n* pl. **-S** a classical dance form **BALLETIC** *adj*

BALLGAME *n* pl. **-S** a game played with a ball

BALLHAWK *n* pl. **-S** a very good defensive ballplayer

BALLIES pl. of bally

BALLISTA *n* pl. **-TAE** an ancient weapon

BALLON *n* pl. **-S** lightness of movement

BALLONET *n* pl. **-S** a small balloon

BALLONNE *n* pl. **-S** a ballet jump

BALLOON *v* **-ED, -ING, -S** to swell out

BALLOT *v* **-ED, -ING, -S** to vote

BALLOTER *n* pl. **-S** one that ballots

BALLPARK *n* pl. **-S** a facility in which ballgames are played

BALLROOM *n* pl. **-S** a large room for dancing

BALLUTE *n* pl. **-S** a small inflatable parachute

BALLY *n* pl. **-LIES** a noisy uproar

BALLYARD *n* pl. **-S** a ballpark

BALLYHOO *v* **-ED, -ING, -S** to promote by uproar

BALLYRAG *v* **-RAGGED, -RAGGING, -RAGS** to bullyrag

BALM *n* pl. **-S** a fragrant resin **BALMLIKE** *adj*

BALMORAL *n* pl. **-S** a type of shoe

BALMY *adj* **BALMIER, BALMIEST** mild **BALMILY** *adv*

BALNEAL *adj* pertaining to baths

BALONEY *n* pl. **-NEYS** bologna

BALSA *n* pl. **-S** a tropical tree

BALSAM *v* **-ED, -ING, -S** to anoint with balsam (an aromatic, resinous substance)

BALSAMIC *adj* containing balsam

BALUSTER *n* pl. **-S** a railing support

BAM *v* **BAMMED, BAMMING, BAMS** to strike with a dull resounding noise

BAMBINO *n* pl. **-NOS** or **-NI** a baby

BAMBOO *n* pl. **-BOOS** a tropical grass

BAN *n* pl. **BANI** a monetary unit of Romania

BAN *v* **BANNED, BANNING, BANS** to prohibit

BANAL *adj* ordinary **BANALLY** *adv*

BANALITY *n* pl. **-TIES** something banal

BANALIZE *v* **-IZED, -IZING, -IZES** to make banal

BANANA *n* pl. **-S** an edible fruit

BANAUSIC *adj* practical

BANCO *n* pl. **-COS** a bet in certain gambling games

BAND *v* **-ED, -ING, -S** to decorate with flexible strips of material

BANDA *n* pl. **-S** a style of Mexican dance music

BANDAGE *v* **-DAGED, -DAGING, -DAGES** to cover a wound with a strip of cloth

BANDAGER *n* pl. **-S** one that bandages

BANDAID *adj* providing superficial relief

BANDANA *n* pl. **-S** bandanna

BANDANNA *n* pl. **-S** a large, colored handkerchief

BANDBOX *n* pl. **-ES** a lightweight box

BANDEAU *n* pl. **-DEAUS** or **-DEAUX** a headband

BANDER *n* pl. **-S** one that bands

BANDEROL *n* pl. **-S** a streamer

BANDIED past tense of bandy

BANDIES present 3d person sing. of bandy

BANDIT *n* pl. **-DITS** or **-DITTI** a robber

BANDITO *n* pl. **-TOS** a bandit

BANDITRY *n* pl. **-TRIES** robbery by bandits

BANDMATE *n* pl. **-S** a fellow member of a band

BANDOG	*n* pl. **-S** a watchdog
BANDORA	*n* pl. **-S** bandore
BANDORE	*n* pl. **-S** an ancient lute
BANDSAW	*n* pl. **-S** a type of power saw
BANDSMAN	*n* pl. **-MEN** a member of a musical band
BANDY	*v* **-DIED, -DYING, -DIES** to throw to and fro
BANE	*v* **BANED, BANING, BANES** to kill with poison
BANEFUL	*adj* poisonous
BANG	*v* **-ED, -ING, -S** to hit sharply
BANGER	*n* pl. **-S** a sausage
BANGKOK	*n* pl. **-S** a straw hat
BANGLE	*n* pl. **-S** a bracelet
BANGTAIL	*n* pl. **-S** a racehorse
BANI	pl. of ban
BANIAN	*n* pl. **-S** a Hindu merchant
BANING	present participle of bane
BANISH	*v* **-ED, -ING, -ES** to expel
BANISHER	*n* pl. **-S** one that banishes
BANISTER	*n* pl. **-S** a handrail
BANJAX	*v* **-ED, -ING, -ES** to damage or ruin
BANJO	*n* pl. **-JOS** or **-JOES** a musical instrument
BANJOIST	*n* pl. **-S** one who plays the banjo
BANK	*v* **-ED, -ING, -S** to keep money in a bank (an institution dealing in money matters) **BANKABLE** *adj*
BANKBOOK	*n* pl. **-S** a depositor's book
BANKCARD	*n* pl. **-S** a credit card issued by a bank
BANKER	*n* pl. **-S** one who works in a bank **BANKERLY** *adj*
BANKING	*n* pl. **-S** the business of a bank
BANKIT	*n* pl. **-S** a raised sidewalk
BANKNOTE	*n* pl. **-S** a promissory note
BANKROLL	*v* **-ED, -ING, -S** to fund
BANKRUPT	*v* **-ED, -ING, -S** to impoverish
BANKSIA	*n* pl. **-S** an Australian plant
BANKSIDE	*n* pl. **-S** the slope of a river bank
BANNABLE	*adj* liable to be banned
BANNED	past tense of ban
BANNER	*v* **-ED, -ING, -S** to furnish with a flag
BANNERET	*n* pl. **-S** a small flag
BANNEROL	*n* pl. **-S** a banderol
BANNET	*n* pl. **-S** a bonnet
BANNING	present participle of ban
BANNOCK	*n* pl. **-S** a type of cake
BANNS	*n/pl* a marriage notice
BANQUET	*v* **-ED, -ING, -S** to feast
BANSHEE	*n* pl. **-S** a female spirit
BANSHIE	*n* pl. **-S** banshee
BANTAM	*n* pl. **-S** a small fowl
BANTENG	*n* pl. **-S** a wild ox
BANTER	*v* **-ED, -ING, -S** to exchange mildly teasing remarks
BANTERER	*n* pl. **-S** one that banters
BANTLING	*n* pl. **-S** a very young child
BANTY	*n* pl. **-TIES** a bantam
BANYAN	*n* pl. **-S** an East Indian tree
BANZAI	*n* pl. **-S** a Japanese battle cry
BAOBAB	*n* pl. **-S** a tropical tree
BAP	*n* pl. **-S** a small bun or roll
BAPTISE	*v* **-TISED, -TISING, -TISES** to baptize
BAPTISIA	*n* pl. **-S** a flowering plant
BAPTISM	*n* pl. **-S** a Christian ceremony
BAPTIST	*n* pl. **-S** one who baptizes
BAPTIZE	*v* **-TIZED, -TIZING, -TIZES** to administer baptism to
BAPTIZER	*n* pl. **-S** a baptist
BAR	*v* **BARRED, BARRING, BARS** to exclude
BARATHEA	*n* pl. **-S** a silk fabric
BARB	*v* **-ED, -ING, -S** to furnish with a barb (a sharp projection)
BARBAL	*adj* pertaining to the beard
BARBARIC	*adj* uncivilized
BARBASCO	*n* pl. **-COS** or **-COES** a tropical tree
BARBATE	*adj* bearded
BARBE	*n* pl. **-S** a medieval cloth headdress
BARBECUE	*v* **-CUED, -CUING, -CUES** to cook over live coals or an open fire
BARBEL	*n* pl. **-S** an organ of a fish
BARBELL	*n* pl. **-S** an exercise apparatus
BARBEQUE	*v* **-QUED, -QUING, -QUES** to barbecue
BARBER	*v* **-ED, -ING, -S** to cut hair
BARBERRY	*n* pl. **-RIES** a shrub
BARBET	*n* pl. **-S** a tropical bird
BARBETTE	*n* pl. **-S** a platform

BARBICAN n pl. **-S** an outer fortification

BARBICEL n pl. **-S** a part of a feather

BARBIE n pl. **-S** a portable fireplace for cooking

BARBITAL n pl. **-S** a sedative

BARBLESS adj having no barbs

BARBULE n pl. **-S** a small barb

BARBUT n pl. **-S** a type of helmet

BARBWIRE n pl. **-S** barbed wire

BARCA n pl. **-S** a double-ended boat

BARCHAN n pl. **-S** a type of sand dune

BARD v **-ED, -ING, -S** to armor a horse

BARDE v **BARDED, BARDING, BARDES** to bard

BARDIC adj poetic

BARE adj **BARER, BAREST** naked

BARE v **BARED, BARING, BARES** to expose

BAREBACK adv without a saddle

BAREBOAT n pl. **-S** a pleasure boat rented without personnel

BAREFIT adj barefoot

BAREFOOT adj being without shoes

BAREGE n pl. **-S** a sheer fabric

BAREHAND v **-ED, -ING, -S** to catch with a bare hand

BAREHEAD adv without a hat

BARELY adv scarcely

BARENESS n pl. **-ES** the state of being bare

BARER comparative of bare

BARESARK n pl. **-S** an ancient warrior

BAREST superlative of bare

BARF v **-ED, -ING, -S** to vomit

BARFLY n pl. **-FLIES** a drinker who frequents bars

BARGAIN v **-ED, -ING, -S** to discuss terms for selling or buying

BARGE v **BARGED, BARGING, BARGES** to move by barge (a long, large boat)

BARGEE n pl. **-S** a bargeman

BARGELLO n pl. **-LOS** a needlepoint stitch that makes a zigzag pattern

BARGEMAN n pl. **-MEN** the master or a crew member of a barge

BARGHEST n pl. **-S** a goblin

BARGING present participle of barge

BARGUEST n pl. **-S** barghest

BARHOP v **-HOPPED, -HOPPING, -HOPS** to visit a number of bars during an evening

BARIC adj pertaining to barium

BARILLA n pl. **-S** a chemical compound

BARING present participle of bare

BARISTA n pl. **-S** one who makes and serves coffee to the public

BARITE n pl. **-S** a mineral

BARITONE n pl. **-S** a male singing voice

BARIUM n pl. **-S** a metallic element

BARK v **-ED, -ING, -S** to cry like a dog

BARKEEP n pl. **-S** a bartender

BARKER n pl. **-S** one that barks

BARKLESS adj having no bark; unable to bark

BARKY adj **BARKIER, BARKIEST** covered with bark (tough outer covering of a root or stem)

BARLEDUC n pl. **-S** a fruit jam

BARLESS adj having no restraints

BARLEY n pl. **-LEYS** a cereal grass

BARLOW n pl. **-S** a jackknife

BARM n pl. **-S** the foam on malt liquors

BARMAID n pl. **-S** a female bartender

BARMAN n pl. **-MEN** a male bartender

BARMIE adj barmy

BARMY adj **BARMIER, BARMIEST** full of barm; frothy

BARN v **-ED, -ING, -S** to store in a barn (a large storage building)

BARNACLE n pl. **-S** a shellfish

BARNEY n pl. **-NEYS** a noisy argument

BARNLIKE adj resembling a barn

BARNY adj **BARNIER, BARNIEST** resembling a barn in size, shape, or smell

BARNYARD n pl. **-S** a yard near a barn

BAROGRAM n pl. **-S** a barometric reading

BARON n pl. **-S** a lower member of nobility

BARONAGE n pl. **-S** the rank of a baron

BARONESS n pl. **-ES** the wife of a baron

BARONET n pl. **-S** the holder of a rank below that of a baron

BARONG n pl. **-S** a broad knife

BARONIAL adj pertaining to a baron

BARONNE n pl. **-S** a baroness

BARONY n pl. **-ONIES** the domain of a baron

BAROQUE	*n* pl. **-S** an ornate object
BAROSAUR	*n* pl. **-S** a large dinosaur
BAROUCHE	*n* pl. **-S** a type of carriage
BARQUE	*n* pl. **-S** a sailing vessel
BARRABLE	*adj* capable of being barred
BARRACK	*v* **-ED, -ING, -S** to shout boisterously
BARRAGE	*v* **-RAGED, -RAGING, -RAGES** to subject to a massive attack
BARRANCA	*n* pl. **-S** a steep ravine
BARRANCO	*n* pl. **-COS** barranca
BARRATER	*n* pl. **-S** barrator
BARRATOR	*n* pl. **-S** one who commits barratry
BARRATRY	*n* pl. **-TRIES** fraud committed by a master or crew of a ship
BARRE	*v* **BARRED, BARRING, BARRES** to play a type of guitar chord
BARRED	past tense of bar
BARREL	*v* **-RELED, -RELING, -RELS** or **-RELLED, -RELLING, -RELS** to move fast
BARREN	*adj* **-RENER, -RENEST** unproductive **BARRENLY** *adv*
BARREN	*n* pl. **-S** a tract of barren land
BARRET	*n* pl. **-S** a flat cap
BARRETOR	*n* pl. **-S** barrator
BARRETRY	*n* pl. **-TRIES** barratry
BARRETTE	*n* pl. **-S** a hair clip
BARRIER	*n* pl. **-S** an obstacle
BARRING	present participle of bar and barre
BARRIO	*n* pl. **-RIOS** a district
BARROOM	*n* pl. **-S** a room where liquor is sold
BARROW	*n* pl. **-S** a type of cart
BARSTOOL	*n* pl. **-S** a stool in a barroom
BARTEND	*v* **-ED, -ING, -S** to tend a barroom
BARTER	*v* **-ED, -ING, -S** to trade
BARTERER	*n* pl. **-S** one that barters
BARTISAN	*n* pl. **-S** bartizan
BARTIZAN	*n* pl. **-S** a small turret
BARWARE	*n* pl. **-S** barroom equipment
BARYE	*n* pl. **-S** a unit of pressure
BARYON	*n* pl. **-S** a type of subatomic particle **BARYONIC** *adj*
BARYTA	*n* pl. **-S** a compound of barium **BARYTIC** *adj*
BARYTE	*n* pl. **-S** barite
BARYTON	*n* pl. **-S** a stringed instrument
BARYTONE	*n* pl. **-S** baritone
BASAL	*adj* pertaining to the foundation **BASALLY** *adv*
BASALT	*n* pl. **-S** a volcanic rock **BASALTIC** *adj*
BASALTES	*n* pl. **BASALTES** unglazed stoneware
BASCULE	*n* pl. **-S** a type of seesaw
BASE	*adj* **BASER, BASEST** morally low
BASE	*v* **BASED, BASING, BASES** to found
BASEBALL	*n* pl. **-S** a type of ball
BASEBORN	*adj* of low birth
BASED	past tense of base
BASELESS	*adj* having no foundation
BASELINE	*n* pl. **-S** a line at either end of a court in certain sports
BASELY	*adv* in a base manner
BASEMAN	*n* pl. **-MEN** a certain player in baseball
BASEMENT	*n* pl. **-S** the part of a building below ground level
BASENESS	*n* pl. **-ES** the state of being base
BASENJI	*n* pl. **-S** a barkless dog
BASER	comparative of base
BASES	pl. of basis
BASEST	superlative of base
BASH	*v* **-ED, -ING, -ES** to smash
BASHAW	*n* pl. **-S** a pasha
BASHER	*n* pl. **-S** one that bashes
BASHFUL	*adj* shy; timid
BASHING	*n* pl. **-S** an act of beating
BASHLYK	*n* pl. **-S** a cloth hood
BASIC	*n* pl. **-S** a fundamental
BASICITY	*n* pl. **-TIES** the state of being alkaline
BASIDIUM	*n* pl. **-IA** a structure on a fungus **BASIDIAL** *adj*
BASIFIER	*n* pl. **-S** one that basifies
BASIFY	*v* **-FIED, -FYING, -FIES** to alkalize
BASIL	*n* pl. **-S** an aromatic herb
BASILAR	*adj* basal
BASILARY	*adj* basilar
BASILECT	*n* pl. **-S** the least prestigious language of an area
BASILIC	*adj* pertaining to a basilica
BASILICA	*n* pl. **-CAS** or **-CAE** an ancient Roman building

BASILISK	*n* pl. **-S** a fabled serpent	**BATCH**	*v* **-ED, -ING, -ES** to bring together
BASIN	*n* pl. **-S** a large bowl **BASINAL, BASINED** *adj*	**BATCHER**	*n* pl. **-S** one that batches
BASINET	*n* pl. **-S** a medieval helmet	**BATE**	*v* **BATED, BATING, BATES** to reduce the force of
BASINFUL	*n* pl. **-S** as much as a basin can hold	**BATEAU**	*n* pl. **-TEAUX** a flat-bottomed boat
BASING	present participle of base	**BATFISH**	*n* pl. **-ES** a batlike fish
BASION	*n* pl. **-S** a part of the skull	**BATFOWL**	*v* **-ED, -ING, -S** to catch birds at night
BASIS	*n* pl. **BASES** the foundation of something	**BATGIRL**	*n* pl. **-S** a girl who minds baseball equipment
BASK	*v* **-ED, -ING, -S** to lie in a pleasant warmth	**BATH**	*n* pl. **-S** a washing
BASKET	*n* pl. **-S** a wooden container	**BATHE**	*v* **BATHED, BATHING, BATHES** to wash
BASKETRY	*n* pl. **-RIES** basket weaving	**BATHER**	*n* pl. **-S** one that bathes
BASMATI	*n* pl. **-S** a long-grain rice	**BATHETIC**	*adj* trite
BASOPHIL	*n* pl. **-S** a type of cell	**BATHLESS**	*adj* not having had a bath
BASQUE	*n* pl. **-S** a bodice	**BATHMAT**	*n* pl. **-S** a mat used in a bathroom
BASS	*n* pl. **-ES** an edible fish	**BATHOS**	*n* pl. **-ES** triteness
BASSET	*v* **-SETED, -SETING, -SETS** or **-SETTED, -SETTING, -SETS** to outcrop	**BATHROBE**	*n* pl. **-S** a housecoat
		BATHROOM	*n* pl. **-S** a room in which to bathe
BASSI	a pl. of basso	**BATHTUB**	*n* pl. **-S** a tub in which to bathe
BASSINET	*n* pl. **-S** a basket used as a baby's crib	**BATHYAL**	*adj* pertaining to deep water
BASSIST	*n* pl. **-S** a person who plays a double bass	**BATIK**	*v* **-ED, -ING, -S** to dye fabric by a particular process
BASSLY	*adv* in a low-pitched manner	**BATING**	present participle of bate
BASSNESS	*n* pl. **-ES** lowness in pitch	**BATISTE**	*n* pl. **-S** a sheer fabric
BASSO	*n* pl. **-SOS** or **-SI** a low-pitched singer	**BATLIKE**	*adj* resembling a bat (a flying mammal)
BASSOON	*n* pl. **-S** a low-pitched instrument	**BATMAN**	*n* pl. **-MEN** an orderly
BASSWOOD	*n* pl. **-S** a linden tree	**BATON**	*n* pl. **-S** a short rod
BASSY	*adj* low in pitch	**BATSMAN**	*n* pl. **-MEN** one who bats
BAST	*n* pl. **-S** a woody fiber	**BATT**	*n* pl. **-S** a sheet of cotton
BASTARD	*n* pl. **-S** an illegitimate child	**BATTALIA**	*n* pl. **-S** a military unit
BASTARDY	*n* pl. **-TARDIES** the state of being a bastard	**BATTEAU**	*n* pl. **-TEAUX** bateau
		BATTED	past tense of bat
BASTE	*v* **BASTED, BASTING, BASTES** to sew loosely together	**BATTEN**	*v* **-ED, -ING, -S** to fasten with strips of wood
BASTER	*n* pl. **-S** one that bastes	**BATTENER**	*n* pl. **-S** one that battens
BASTILE	*n* pl. **-S** bastille	**BATTER**	*v* **-ED, -ING, -S** to beat repeatedly
BASTILLE	*n* pl. **-S** a prison	**BATTERER**	*n* pl. **-S** one that batters
BASTING	*n* pl. **-S** the thread used by a baster	**BATTERIE**	*n* pl. **-S** a ballet movement
		BATTERY	*n* pl. **-TERIES** a device for generating an electric current
BASTION	*n* pl. **-S** a fortified place	**BATTIER**	comparative of batty
BAT	*v* **BATTED, BATTING, BATS** to hit a baseball	**BATTIEST**	superlative of batty
BATBOY	*n* pl. **-BOYS** a boy who minds baseball equipment	**BATTIK**	*n* pl. **-S** a fabric dyed by batiking
		BATTING	*n* pl. **-S** a batt

BATTLE	*v* **-TLED, -TLING, -TLES** to fight
BATTLER	*n* pl. **-S** one that battles
BATTU	*adj* pertaining to a ballet movement
BATTUE	*n* pl. **-S** a type of hunt
BATTY	*adj* **-TIER, -TIEST** crazy
BATWING	*adj* shaped like a bat's wing
BAUBEE	*n* pl. **-S** bawbee
BAUBLE	*n* pl. **-S** a cheap trinket
BAUD	*n* pl. **-S** a unit of data transmission speed
BAUDEKIN	*n* pl. **-S** a brocaded fabric
BAUDRONS	*n* pl. **-ES** a cat
BAUHINIA	*n* pl. **-S** a small tropical tree
BAULK	*v* **-ED, -ING, -S** to balk
BAULKY	*adj* **BAULKIER, BAULKIEST** balky
BAUSOND	*adj* having white marks
BAUXITE	*n* pl. **-S** an ore of aluminum **BAUXITIC** *adj*
BAWBEE	*n* pl. **-S** a Scottish coin
BAWCOCK	*n* pl. **-S** a fine fellow
BAWD	*n* pl. **-S** a madam
BAWDIER	comparative of bawdy
BAWDIES	pl. of bawdy
BAWDIEST	superlative of bawdy
BAWDILY	*adv* in a bawdy manner
BAWDRIC	*n* pl. **-S** baldric
BAWDRY	*n* pl. **-RIES** obscenity
BAWDY	*adj* **BAWDIER, BAWDIEST** obscene
BAWDY	*n* pl. **BAWDIES** obscene language
BAWL	*v* **-ED, -ING, -S** to cry loudly
BAWLER	*n* pl. **-S** one that bawls
BAWSUNT	*adj* bausond
BAWTIE	*n* pl. **-S** a dog
BAWTY	*n* pl. **-TIES** bawtie
BAY	*v* **-ED, -ING, -S** to howl
BAYADEER	*n* pl. **-S** bayadere
BAYADERE	*n* pl. **-S** a dancing girl
BAYAMO	*n* pl. **-MOS** a strong wind
BAYARD	*n* pl. **-S** a horse
BAYBERRY	*n* pl. **-RIES** a berry tree
BAYMAN	*n* pl. **-MEN** a person who fishes on a bay

BAYONET	*v* **-NETED, -NETING, -NETS** or **-NETTED, -NETTING, -NETS** to stab with a dagger-like weapon
BAYOU	*n* pl. **-S** a marshy body of water
BAYWOOD	*n* pl. **-S** a coarse mahogany
BAZAAR	*n* pl. **-S** a marketplace
BAZAR	*n* pl. **-S** bazaar
BAZOO	*n* pl. **-ZOOS** the mouth
BAZOOKA	*n* pl. **-S** a small rocket launcher
BDELLIUM	*n* pl. **-S** a gum resin
BE	*v* present sing. 1st person **AM,** 2d **ARE** or **ART,** 3d **IS,** past sing. 1st and 3d persons **WAS,** 2d **WERE** or **WAST** or **WERT,** past participle **BEEN,** present participle **BEING** to have actuality
BEACH	*v* **-ED, -ING, -ES** to drive ashore
BEACHBOY	*n* pl. **-BOYS** a male beach attendant
BEACHY	*adj* **BEACHIER, BEACHIEST** sandy or pebbly
BEACON	*v* **-ED, -ING, -S** to warn or guide
BEAD	*v* **-ED, -ING, -S** to adorn with beads (round pieces of glass)
BEADER	*n* pl. **-S** one that beads
BEADIER	comparative of beady
BEADIEST	superlative of beady
BEADILY	*adv* in a beady manner
BEADING	*n* pl. **-S** beaded material
BEADLE	*n* pl. **-S** a parish official
BEADLIKE	*adj* beady
BEADMAN	*n* pl. **-MEN** beadsman
BEADROLL	*n* pl. **-S** a list of names
BEADSMAN	*n* pl. **-MEN** one who prays for another
BEADWORK	*n* pl. **-S** beading
BEADY	*adj* **BEADIER, BEADIEST** resembling beads
BEAGLE	*n* pl. **-S** a small hound
BEAK	*n* pl. **-S** a bird's bill **BEAKED, BEAKLESS, BEAKLIKE** *adj*
BEAKER	*n* pl. **-S** a large cup
BEAKY	*adj* **BEAKIER, BEAKIEST** resembling a beak
BEAM	*v* **-ED, -ING, -S** to emit in beams (rays of light)
BEAMIER	comparative of beamy
BEAMIEST	superlative of beamy
BEAMILY	*adv* in a beamy manner

BEAMISH *adj* cheerful

BEAMLESS *adj* having no beam

BEAMLIKE *adj* resembling a beam

BEAMY *adj* **BEAMIER, BEAMIEST** beaming

BEAN *v* **-ED, -ING, -S** to hit on the head

BEANBAG *n* pl. **-S** a small cloth bag

BEANBALL *n* pl. **-S** a baseball thrown at the head

BEANERY *n* pl. **-ERIES** a cheap restaurant

BEANIE *n* pl. **-S** a small cap

BEANLIKE *adj* resembling a bean

BEANO *n* pl. **BEANOS** a form of bingo

BEANPOLE *n* pl. **-S** a thin pole

BEAR *v* **BORE, BORNE** or **BORN, BEARING, BEARS** to endure **BEARABLE** *adj* **BEARABLY** *adv*

BEARCAT *n* pl. **-S** a small mammal

BEARD *v* **-ED, -ING, -S** to oppose boldly

BEARER *n* pl. **-S** one that bears

BEARHUG *n* pl. **-S** a rough tight embrace

BEARING *n* pl. **-S** demeanor

BEARISH *adj* resembling a bear (a large mammal)

BEARLIKE *adj* bearish

BEARSKIN *n* pl. **-S** the skin of a bear

BEARWOOD *n* pl. **-S** a small tree of the buckthorn family

BEAST *n* pl. **-S** an animal

BEASTIE *n* pl. **-S** a tiny animal

BEASTLY *adj* **-LIER, -LIEST** resembling a beast

BEAT *v* **BEAT, BEATEN, BEATING, BEATS** to strike repeatedly **BEATABLE** *adj*

BEATER *n* pl. **-S** one that beats

BEATIFIC *adj* blissful

BEATIFY *v* **-FIED, -FYING, -FIES** to make happy

BEATING *n* pl. **-S** a defeat

BEATLESS *adj* having no rhythm

BEATNIK *n* pl. **-S** a nonconformist

BEAU *n* pl. **BEAUS** or **BEAUX** a boyfriend **BEAUISH** *adj*

BEAUCOUP *n* pl. **-S** an abundance

BEAUT *n* pl. **-S** something beautiful

BEAUTIFY *v* **-FIED, -FYING, -FIES** to make beautiful

BEAUTY *n* pl. **-TIES** one that is lovely

BEAUX a pl. of beau

BEAVER *v* **-ED, -ING, -S** to work hard

BEBEERU *n* pl. **-S** a tropical tree

BEBLOOD *v* **-ED, -ING, -S** to cover with blood

BEBOP *n* pl. **-S** a type of jazz

BEBOPPER *n* pl. **-S** one that likes bebop

BECALM *v* **-ED, -ING, -S** to make calm

BECAME past tense of become

BECAP *v* **-CAPPED, -CAPPING, -CAPS** to put a cap on

BECARPET *v* **-ED, -ING, -S** to cover with a carpet

BECAUSE *conj* for the reason that

BECHALK *v* **-ED, -ING, -S** to cover with chalk

BECHAMEL *n* pl. **-S** a white sauce

BECHANCE *v* **-CHANCED, -CHANCING, -CHANCES** to befall

BECHARM *v* **-ED, -ING, -S** to hold under a spell

BECK *v* **-ED, -ING, -S** to beckon

BECKET *n* pl. **-S** a securing rope

BECKON *v* **-ED, -ING, -S** to signal by sign or gesture

BECKONER *n* pl. **-S** one that beckons

BECLAMOR *v* **-ED, -ING, -S** to clamor loudly

BECLASP *v* **-ED, -ING, -S** to embrace

BECLOAK *v* **-ED, -ING, -S** to place a cloak on

BECLOG *v* **-CLOGGED, -CLOGGING, -CLOGS** to clog thoroughly

BECLOTHE *v* **-CLOTHED, -CLOTHING, -CLOTHES** to clothe

BECLOUD *v* **-ED, -ING, -S** to make cloudy

BECLOWN *v* **-ED, -ING, -S** to cause to appear ridiculous

BECOME *v* **-CAME, -COMING, -COMES** to come to be

BECOMING *n* pl. **-S** a process of change

BECOWARD *v* **-ED, -ING, -S** to accuse of cowardice

BECRAWL *v* **-ED, -ING, -S** to crawl over

BECRIME *v* **-CRIMED, -CRIMING, -CRIMES** to make guilty of a crime

BECROWD *v* **-ED, -ING, -S** to crowd closely

BECRUST *v* **-ED, -ING, -S** to cover with a crust

BECUDGEL *v* **-GELLED, -GELLING, -GELS** or **-GELED, -GELING, -GELS** to cudgel thoroughly

BECURSE   *v* **-CURSED** or **-CURST, -CURSING, -CURSES** to curse severely

BED   *v* **BEDDED, BEDDING, BEDS** to provide with a bed (a piece of furniture used for sleeping)

BEDABBLE   *v* **-BLED, -BLING, -BLES** to soil

BEDAMN   *v* **-ED, -ING, -S** to swear at

BEDARKEN   *v* **-ED, -ING, -S** to darken

BEDAUB   *v* **-ED, -ING, -S** to besmear

BEDAZZLE   *v* **-ZLED, -ZLING, -ZLES** to confuse

BEDBOARD   *n* pl. **-S** a board placed between a mattress and bedspring

BEDBUG   *n* pl. **-S** a bloodsucking insect

BEDCHAIR   *n* pl. **-S** a chair near a bed

BEDCOVER   *n* pl. **-S** a cover for a bed

BEDDABLE   *adj* suitable for taking to bed

BEDDED   past tense of bed

BEDDER   *n* pl. **-S** one that makes up beds

BEDDING   *n* pl. **-S** material for making up a bed

BEDEAFEN   *v* **-ED, -ING, -S** to deafen

BEDECK   *v* **-ED, -ING, -S** to clothe with finery

BEDEL   *n* pl. **-S** an English university officer

BEDELL   *n* pl. **-S** bedel

BEDEMAN   *n* pl. **-MEN** beadsman

BEDESMAN   *n* pl. **-MEN** beadsman

BEDEVIL   *v* **-ILED, -ILING, -ILS** or **-ILLED, -ILLING, -ILS** to harass

BEDEW   *v* **-ED, -ING, -S** to wet with dew

BEDFAST   *adj* confined to bed

BEDFRAME   *n* pl. **-S** the frame of a bed

BEDGOWN   *n* pl. **-S** a dressing gown

BEDIAPER   *v* **-ED, -ING, -S** to ornament with a kind of design

BEDIGHT   *v* **-ED, -ING, -S** to bedeck

BEDIM   *v* **-DIMMED, -DIMMING, -DIMS** to make dim

BEDIMPLE   *v* **-PLED, -PLING, -PLES** to dimple

BEDIRTY   *v* **-DIRTIED, -DIRTYING, -DIRTIES** to make dirty

BEDIZEN   *v* **-ED, -ING, -S** to dress gaudily

BEDLAM   *n* pl. **-S** confusion

BEDLAMP   *n* pl. **-S** a lamp near a bed

BEDLESS   *adj* having no bed

BEDLIKE   *adj* resembling a bed

BEDMAKER   *n* pl. **-S** one that makes beds

BEDMATE   *n* pl. **-S** a bed companion

BEDOTTED   *adj* covered with dots

BEDOUIN   *n* pl. **-S** a nomadic Arab

BEDPAN   *n* pl. **-S** a toilet pan

BEDPLATE   *n* pl. **-S** a frame support

BEDPOST   *n* pl. **-S** a post of a bed

BEDQUILT   *n* pl. **-S** a quilt for a bed

BEDRAIL   *n* pl. **-S** a board at bedside

BEDRAPE   *v* **-DRAPED, -DRAPING, -DRAPES** to drape

BEDRENCH   *v* **-ED, -ING, -ES** to drench thoroughly

BEDRID   *adj* bedfast

BEDRIVEL   *v* **-ELLED, -ELLING, -ELS** or **-ELED, -ELING, -ELS** to cover with saliva

BEDROCK   *n* pl. **-S** the rock under soil

BEDROLL   *n* pl. **-S** a portable roll of bedding

BEDROOM   *n* pl. **-S** a room for sleeping

BEDRUG   *v* **-DRUGGED, -DRUGGING, -DRUGS** to make sleepy

BEDSHEET   *n* pl. **-S** a sheet for a bed

BEDSIDE   *n* pl. **-S** the side of a bed

BEDSIT   *n* pl. **-S** a one-room apartment

BEDSONIA   *n* pl. **-S** a virus

BEDSORE   *n* pl. **-S** a type of sore

BEDSTAND   *n* pl. **-S** a table next to a bed

BEDSTEAD   *n* pl. **-S** a support for a bed

BEDSTRAW   *n* pl. **-S** a woody herb

BEDTICK   *n* pl. **-S** the cloth case of a mattress

BEDTIME   *n* pl. **-S** a time for going to bed

BEDU   *n* pl. **BEDU** a bedouin

BEDUIN   *n* pl. **-S** bedouin

BEDUMB   *v* **-ED, -ING, -S** to render speechless

BEDUNCE   *v* **-DUNCED, -DUNCING, -DUNCES** to make a dunce of

BEDWARD   *adv* toward bed

BEDWARDS   *adv* bedward

BEDWARF   *v* **-ED, -ING, -S** to cause to appear small by comparison

BEE   *n* pl. **-S** a winged insect

BEEBEE   *n* pl. **-S** a pellet

BEEBREAD   *n* pl. **-S** a pollen mixture

BEECH   *n* pl. **-ES** a type of tree **BEECHEN** *adj*

BEECHNUT *n* pl. **-S** the nut of a beech

BEECHY *adj* **BEECHIER, BEECHIEST** abounding in beeches

BEEDI *n* pl. **-DIES** bidi

BEEF *n* pl. **BEEFS** or **BEEVES** a steer or cow fattened for food

BEEF *v* **-ED, -ING, -S** to add bulk to

BEEFALO *n* pl. **-LOS** or **-LOES** the offspring of an American buffalo and domestic cattle

BEEFCAKE *n* pl. **-S** pictures of male physiques

BEEFIER comparative of beefy

BEEFIEST superlative of beefy

BEEFILY *adv* in a beefy manner

BEEFLESS *adj* being without beef

BEEFWOOD *n* pl. **-S** a hardwood tree

BEEFY *adj* **BEEFIER, BEEFIEST** brawny

BEEHIVE *n* pl. **-S** a hive for bees

BEELIKE *adj* resembling a bee

BEELINE *v* **-LINED, -LINING, -LINES** to go in a straight direct course

BEEN past participle of be

BEEP *v* **-ED, -ING, -S** to honk a horn

BEEPER *n* pl. **-S** a signaling device

BEER *n* pl. **-S** an alcoholic beverage

BEERY *adj* **BEERIER, BEERIEST** affected by beer

BEESWAX *n* pl. **-ES** a type of wax

BEESWING *n* pl. **-S** a crust that forms on wines

BEET *n* pl. **-S** a garden plant

BEETLE *v* **-TLED, -TLING, -TLES** to jut out

BEETLER *n* pl. **-S** one that operates a cloth-finishing machine

BEETROOT *n* pl. **-S** the root of the beet

BEEVES a pl. of beef

BEEYARD *n* pl. **-S** an apiary

BEEZER *n* pl. **-S** the nose

BEFALL *v* **-FELL, -FALLEN, -FALLING, -FALLS** to happen to

BEFINGER *v* **-ED, -ING, -S** to touch all over

BEFIT *v* **-FITTED, -FITTING, -FITS** to be suitable to

BEFLAG *v* **-FLAGGED, -FLAGGING, -FLAGS** to deck with flags

BEFLEA *v* **-ED, -ING, -S** to infest with fleas

BEFLECK *v* **-ED, -ING, -S** to fleck

BEFLOWER *v* **-ED, -ING, -S** to cover with flowers

BEFOG *v* **-FOGGED, -FOGGING, -FOGS** to envelop in fog

BEFOOL *v* **-ED, -ING, -S** to deceive

BEFORE *adv* previously

BEFOUL *v* **-ED, -ING, -S** to foul

BEFOULER *n* pl. **-S** one that befouls

BEFRET *v* **-FRETTED, -FRETTING, -FRETS** to gnaw

BEFRIEND *v* **-ED, -ING, -S** to act as a friend to

BEFRINGE *v* **-FRINGED, -FRINGING, -FRINGES** to border with a fringe

BEFUDDLE *v* **-DLED, -DLING, -DLES** to confuse

BEG *v* **BEGGED, BEGGING, BEGS** to plead

BEGALL *v* **-ED, -ING, -S** to make sore by rubbing

BEGAN past tense of begin

BEGAZE *v* **-GAZED, -GAZING, -GAZES** to gaze at

BEGET *v* **-GOT** or **-GAT, -GOTTEN, -GETTING, -GETS** to cause to exist

BEGETTER *n* pl. **-S** one that begets

BEGGAR *v* **-ED, -ING, -S** to impoverish

BEGGARLY *adj* very poor

BEGGARY *n* pl. **-GARIES** extreme poverty

BEGGED past tense of beg

BEGGING present participle of beg

BEGIN *v* **-GAN, -GUN, -GINNING, -GINS** to start

BEGINNER *n* pl. **-S** one that begins

BEGIRD *v* **-GIRDED** or **-GIRT, -GIRDING, -GIRDS** to surround

BEGIRDLE *v* **-DLED, -DLING, -DLES** to surround

BEGLAD *v* **-GLADDED, -GLADDING, -GLADS** to gladden

BEGLAMOR *v* **-ED, -ING, -S** to dazzle with glamor

BEGLOOM *v* **-ED, -ING, -S** to make gloomy

BEGONE *v* to go away —this is the only form in use

BEGONIA *n* pl. **-S** a tropical herb

BEGORAH *interj* begorra

BEGORRA *interj* — used as a mild oath

BEGORRAH *interj* begorra

BEGOT a past tense of beget

BEGOTTEN past participle of beget

BEGRIM *v* **-GRIMMED, -GRIMMING, -GRIMS** to begrime

BEGRIME *v* **-GRIMED, -GRIMING, -GRIMES** to dirty

BEGROAN *v* **-ED, -ING, -S** to groan at

BEGRUDGE *v* **-GRUDGED, -GRUDGING, -GRUDGES** to concede reluctantly

BEGUILE *v* **-GUILED, -GUILING, -GUILES** to deceive

BEGUILER *n* pl. **-S** one that beguiles

BEGUINE *n* pl. **-S** a lively dance

BEGULF *v* **-ED, -ING, -S** to engulf

BEGUM *n* pl. **-S** a Muslim lady of high rank

BEGUN past participle of begin

BEHALF *n* pl. **-HALVES** interest, support, or benefit

BEHAVE *v* **-HAVED, -HAVING, -HAVES** to act properly

BEHAVER *n* pl. **-S** one that behaves

BEHAVIOR *n* pl. **-S** demeanor

BEHEAD *v* **-ED, -ING, -S** to cut off the head of

BEHEADAL *n* pl. **-S** the act of beheading

BEHEADER *n* pl. **-S** one that beheads

BEHELD past tense of behold

BEHEMOTH *n* pl. **-S** a large beast

BEHEST *n* pl. **-S** a command

BEHIND *n* pl. **-S** the buttocks

BEHOLD *v* **-HELD, -HOLDING, -HOLDS** to view

BEHOLDEN *adj* indebted

BEHOLDER *n* pl. **-S** one that beholds

BEHOOF *n* pl. **-HOOVES** use, advantage, or benefit

BEHOOVE *v* **-HOOVED, -HOOVING, -HOOVES** to be proper for

BEHOVE *v* **-HOVED, -HOVING, -HOVES** to behoove

BEHOWL *v* **-ED, -ING, -S** to howl at

BEIGE *n* pl. **-S** a tan color

BEIGNE *n* pl. **-S** beignet

BEIGNET *n* pl. **-S** a type of fritter or doughnut

BEIGY *adj* of the color beige

BEING *n* pl. **-S** something that exists

BEJABERS *interj* bejesus

BEJEEZUS *interj* bejesus

BEJESUS *interj* — used as a mild oath

BEJEWEL *v* **-ELED, -ELING, -ELS** or **-ELLED, -ELLING, -ELS** to adorn with jewels

BEJUMBLE *v* **-BLED, -BLING, -BLES** to jumble

BEKISS *v* **-ED, -ING, -ES** to cover with kisses

BEKNIGHT *v* **-ED, -ING, -S** to raise to knighthood

BEKNOT *v* **-KNOTTED, -KNOTTING, -KNOTS** to tie in knots

BEL *n* pl. **-S** a unit of power

BELABOR *v* **-ED, -ING, -S** to discuss for an absurd amount of time

BELABOUR *v* **-ED, -ING, -S** to belabor

BELACED *adj* adorned with lace

BELADY *v* **-DIED, -DYING, -DIES** to apply the title of lady to

BELATED *adj* late or too late

BELAUD *v* **-ED, -ING, -S** to praise

BELAY *v* **-ED, -ING, -S** to fasten a rope

BELAYER *n* pl. **-S** one that belays

BELCH *v* **-ED, -ING, -ES** to expel gas through the mouth

BELCHER *n* pl. **-S** one that belches

BELDAM *n* pl. **-S** an old woman

BELDAME *n* pl. **-S** beldam

BELEAP *v* **-LEAPED** or **-LEAPT, -LEAPING, -LEAPS** to leap upon

BELFRY *n* pl. **-FRIES** a bell tower **BELFRIED** *adj*

BELGA *n* pl. **-S** a former Belgian monetary unit

BELIE *v* **-LIED, -LYING, -LIES** to misrepresent

BELIEF *n* pl. **-S** acceptance of the truth or actuality of something

BELIER *n* pl. **-S** one that belies

BELIEVE *v* **-LIEVED, -LIEVING, -LIEVES** to accept as true or real

BELIEVER *n* pl. **-S** one that believes

BELIKE *adv* perhaps

BELIQUOR *v* **-ED, -ING, -S** to soak with liquor

BELITTLE *v* **-TLED, -TLING, -TLES** to disparage

BELIVE *adv* in due time

BELL *v* **-ED, -ING, -S** to provide with a bell (a ringing device)

BELLBIRD *n* pl. **-S** a tropical bird

BELLBOY *n* pl. **-BOYS** a hotel's errand boy

BELLE   *n* pl. **-S** an attractive woman

BELLEEK   *n* pl. **-S** a very thin translucent porcelain

BELLHOP   *n* pl. **-S** a bellboy

BELLIED   past tense of belly

BELLIES   present 3d person sing. of belly

BELLING   *n* pl. **-S** a mock serenade for newlyweds

BELLMAN   *n* pl. **-MEN** a town crier

BELLOW   *v* **-ED, -ING, -S** to shout in a deep voice

BELLOWER   *n* pl. **-S** one that bellows

BELLPULL   *n* pl. **-S** a cord pulled to ring a bell

BELLWORT   *n* pl. **-S** a flowering plant

BELLY   *v* **-LIED, -LYING, -LIES** to swell out

BELLYFUL   *n* pl. **-S** an excessive amount

BELON   *n* pl. **-S** a flat oyster

BELONG   *v* **-ED, -ING, -S** to be a member of

BELOVED   *n* pl. **-S** one who is loved

BELOW   *n* pl. **-S** something that is beneath

BELT   *v* **-ED, -ING, -S** to fasten with a belt (a strap or band worn around the waist)

BELTER   *n* pl. **-S** one that belts

BELTING   *n* pl. **-S** material for belts

BELTLESS   *adj* having no belt

BELTLINE   *n* pl. **-S** the waistline

BELTWAY   *n* pl. **-WAYS** a highway around an urban area

BELUGA   *n* pl. **-S** a white sturgeon

BELYING   present participle of belie

BEMA   *n* pl. **-MAS** or **-MATA** a platform in a synagogue

BEMADAM   *v* **-ED, -ING, -S** to call by the title of madam

BEMADDEN   *v* **-ED, -ING, -S** to madden

BEMEAN   *v* **-ED, -ING, -S** to debase

BEMINGLE   *v* **-GLED, -GLING, -GLES** to mix together

BEMIRE   *v* **-MIRED, -MIRING, -MIRES** to soil with mud

BEMIST   *v* **-ED, -ING, -S** to envelop in a mist

BEMIX   *v* **-MIXED** or **-MIXT, -MIXING, -MIXES** to mix thoroughly

BEMOAN   *v* **-ED, -ING, -S** to lament

BEMOCK   *v* **-ED, -ING, -S** to mock

BEMUDDLE   *v* **-DLED, -DLING, -DLES** to confuse completely

BEMURMUR   *v* **-ED, -ING, -S** to murmur at

BEMUSE   *v* **-MUSED, -MUSING, -MUSES** to confuse

BEMUZZLE   *v* **-ZLED, -ZLING, -ZLES** to muzzle

BEN   *n* pl. **-S** an inner room

BENAME   *v* **-NAMED, -NEMPT** or **-NEMPTED, -NAMING, -NAMES** to name

BENCH   *v* **-ED, -ING, -ES** to take a player out of a game

BENCHER   *n* pl. **-S** a magistrate

BENCHTOP   *adj* suitable for use on a workbench

BEND   *v* **BENDED** or **BENT, BENDING, BENDS** to curve **BENDABLE** *adj*

BENDAY   *v* **-ED, -ING, -S** to reproduce using a certain process

BENDEE   *n* pl. **-S** bendy

BENDER   *n* pl. **-S** one that bends

BENDWAYS   *adv* bendwise

BENDWISE   *adv* diagonally

BENDY   *n* pl. **-DYS** okra

BENDY   *adj* **BENDIER, BENDIEST** flexible

BENE   *n* pl. **-S** benne

BENEATH   *prep* under

BENEDICK   *n* pl. **-S** benedict

BENEDICT   *n* pl. **-S** a newly married man

BENEFIC   *adj* kindly

BENEFICE   *v* **-FICED, -FICING, -FICES** to endow with land

BENEFIT   *v* **-FITED, -FITING, -FITS** or **-FITTED, -FITTING, -FITS** to be helpful or useful to

BENEMPT   a past participle of bename

BENEMPTED   a past participle of bename

BENIGN   *adj* kind **BENIGNLY** *adv*

BENISON   *n* pl. **-S** a blessing

BENJAMIN   *n* pl. **-S** benzoin

BENNE   *n* pl. **-S** the sesame plant

BENNET   *n* pl. **-S** a perennial herb

BENNI   *n* pl. **-S** benne

BENNY   *n* pl. **-NIES** an amphetamine tablet

BENOMYL   *n* pl. **-S** a chemical compound

BENT   *n* pl. **-S** an inclination

BENTHAL   *adj* benthic

BENTHIC   *adj* pertaining to oceanic depths

BENTHON   *n* pl. **-S** the organisms living in the benthos

BENTHOS *n* pl. **-ES** the bottom of the sea

BENTO *n* pl. **-TOS** obento

BENTWOOD *n* pl. **-S** wood bent for use in furniture

BENUMB *v* **-ED, -ING, -S** to make numb

BENZAL *adj* pertaining to a certain chemical group

BENZENE *n* pl. **-S** a volatile liquid

BENZIDIN *n* pl. **-S** a hydrocarbon

BENZIN *n* pl. **-S** benzine

BENZINE *n* pl. **-S** a volatile liquid

BENZOATE *n* pl. **-S** a chemical salt

BENZOIN *n* pl. **-S** a gum resin **BENZOIC** *adj*

BENZOL *n* pl. **-S** a benzene

BENZOLE *n* pl. **-S** benzol

BENZOYL *n* pl. **-S** a univalent chemical radical

BENZYL *n* pl. **-S** a univalent chemical radical **BENZYLIC** *adj*

BEPAINT *v* **-ED, -ING, -S** to tinge

BEPIMPLE *v* **-PLED, -PLING, -PLES** to cover with pimples

BEQUEATH *v* **-ED, -ING, -S** to grant by testament

BEQUEST *n* pl. **-S** a legacy

BERAKE *v* **-RAKED, -RAKING, -RAKES** to rake all over

BERASCAL *v* **-ED, -ING, -S** to accuse of being a rascal

BERATE *v* **-RATED, -RATING, -RATES** to scold severely

BERBERIN *n* pl. **-S** a medicinal alkaloid

BERBERIS *n* pl. **-ES** a barberry

BERCEUSE *n* pl. **-S** a lullaby

BERDACHE *n* pl. **-S** an American Indian male transvestite

BEREAVE *v* **-REAVED** or **-REFT, -REAVING, -REAVES** to deprive

BEREAVER *n* pl. **-S** one that bereaves

BERET *n* pl. **-S** a soft, flat cap

BERETTA *n* pl. **-S** biretta

BERG *n* pl. **-S** an iceberg

BERGAMOT *n* pl. **-S** a citrus tree

BERGERE *n* pl. **-S** an upholstered armchair

BERHYME *v* **-RHYMED, -RHYMING, -RHYMES** to compose in rhyme

BERIBERI *n* pl. **-S** a thiamine deficiency disease

BERIMBAU *n* pl. **-S** a Brazilian musical instrument

BERIME *v* **-RIMED, -RIMING, -RIMES** to berhyme

BERINGED *adj* adorned with rings

BERK *n* pl. **-S** a foolish person

BERLIN *n* pl. **-S** a type of carriage

BERLINE *n* pl. **-S** a limousine

BERM *v* **-ED, -ING, -S** to provide with a berm (a ledge)

BERME *n* pl. **-S** berm

BERMUDAS *n/pl* knee-length walking shorts

BERNICLE *n* pl. **-S** a wild goose

BEROBED *adj* wearing a robe

BEROUGED *adj* obviously or thickly rouged

BERRETTA *n* pl. **-S** biretta

BERRY *v* **-RIED, -RYING, -RIES** to produce berries (fleshy fruits)

BERSEEM *n* pl. **-S** a clover

BERSERK *n* pl. **-S** a fierce warrior

BERTH *v* **-ED, -ING, -S** to provide with a mooring

BERTHA *n* pl. **-S** a wide collar

BERYL *n* pl. **-S** a green mineral **BERYLINE** *adj*

BES *n* pl. **BESES** beth

BESCORCH *v* **-ED, -ING, -ES** to scorch

BESCOUR *v* **-ED, -ING, -S** to scour thoroughly

BESCREEN *v* **-ED, -ING, -S** to screen

BESEECH *v* **-SEECHED** or **-SOUGHT, -SEECHING, -SEECHES** to implore

BESEEM *v* **-ED, -ING, -S** to be suitable

BESET *v* **-SET, -SETTING, -SETS** to assail

BESETTER *n* pl. **-S** one that besets

BESHADOW *v* **-ED, -ING, -S** to cast a shadow on

BESHAME *v* **-SHAMED, -SHAMING, -SHAMES** to put to shame

BESHIVER *v* **-ED, -ING, -S** to break into small pieces

BESHOUT *v* **-ED, -ING, -S** to shout at

BESHREW *v* **-ED, -ING, -S** to curse

BESHROUD *v* **-ED, -ING, -S** to cover

BESIDE *prep* next to

BESIDES *adv* in addition

BESIEGE *v* **-SIEGED, -SIEGING, -SIEGES** to surround

BESIEGER *n* pl. **-S** one that besieges

BESLAVED *adj* filled with slaves

BESLIME *v* **-SLIMED, -SLIMING, -SLIMES** to cover with slime

BESMEAR *v* **-ED, -ING, -S** to smear over

BESMILE *v* **-SMILED, -SMILING, -SMILES** to smile on

BESMIRCH *v* **-ED, -ING, -ES** to dirty

BESMOKE *v* **-SMOKED, -SMOKING, -SMOKES** to soil with smoke

BESMOOTH *v* **-ED, -ING, -S** to smooth

BESMUDGE *v* **-SMUDGED, -SMUDGING, -SMUDGES** to smudge

BESMUT *v* **-SMUTTED, -SMUTTING, -SMUTS** to blacken with smut

BESNOW *v* **-ED, -ING, -S** to cover with snow

BESOM *n* pl. **-S** a broom

BESOOTHE *v* **-SOOTHED, -SOOTHING, -SOOTHES** to soothe

BESOT *v* **-SOTTED, -SOTTING, -SOTS** to stupefy

BESOUGHT a past tense of beseech

BESPEAK *v* **-SPOKE** or **-SPAKE, -SPOKEN, -SPEAKING, -SPEAKS** to claim in advance

BESPOUSE *v* **-SPOUSED, -SPOUSING, -SPOUSES** to marry

BESPREAD *v* **-SPREAD, -SPREADING, -SPREADS** to spread over

BESPRENT *adj* sprinkled over

BEST *v* **-ED, -ING, -S** to outdo

BESTEAD *v* **-ED, -ING, -S** to help

BESTIAL *adj* pertaining to beasts

BESTIARY *n* pl. **-ARIES** a collection of animal fables

BESTIR *v* **-STIRRED, -STIRRING, -STIRS** to rouse

BESTOW *v* **-ED, -ING, -S** to present as a gift

BESTOWAL *n* pl. **-S** a gift

BESTOWER *n* pl. **-S** one that bestows

BESTREW *v* **-STREWED, -STREWN, -STREWING, -STREWS** to scatter

BESTRIDE *v* **-STRODE** or **-STRID, -STRIDDEN, -STRIDING, -STRIDES** to straddle

BESTROW *v* **-STROWED, -STROWN, -STROWING, -STROWS** to bestrew

BESTUD *v* **-STUDDED, -STUDDING, -STUDS** to dot

BESWARM *v* **-ED, -ING, -S** to swarm all over

BET *v* **BET** or **BETTED, BETTING, BETS** to wager

BETA *n* pl. **-S** a Greek letter

BETAINE *n* pl. **-S** an alkaloid

BETAKE *v* **-TOOK, -TAKEN, -TAKING, -TAKES** to cause to go

BETATRON *n* pl. **-S** an electron accelerator

BETATTER *v* **-ED, -ING, -S** to tatter

BETAXED *adj* burdened with taxes

BETEL *n* pl. **-S** a climbing plant

BETELNUT *n* pl. **-S** a seed chewed as a stimulant

BETH *n* pl. **-S** a Hebrew letter

BETHANK *v* **-ED, -ING, -S** to thank

BETHEL *n* pl. **-S** a holy place

BETHESDA *n* pl. **-S** a chapel

BETHINK *v* **-THOUGHT, -THINKING, -THINKS** to consider

BETHORN *v* **-ED, -ING, -S** to fill with thorns

BETHUMP *v* **-ED, -ING, -S** to thump soundly

BETIDE *v* **-TIDED, -TIDING, -TIDES** to befall

BETIME *adv* betimes

BETIMES *adv* soon

BETISE *n* pl. **-S** stupidity

BETOKEN *v* **-ED, -ING, -S** to indicate

BETON *n* pl. **-S** a type of concrete

BETONY *n* pl. **-NIES** a European herb

BETOOK past tense of betake

BETRAY *v* **-ED, -ING, -S** to aid an enemy of

BETRAYAL *n* pl. **-S** the act of betraying

BETRAYER *n* pl. **-S** one that betrays

BETROTH *v* **-ED, -ING, -S** to engage to marry

BETTA *n* pl. **-S** a freshwater fish

BETTED a past tense of bet

BETTER *v* **-ED, -ING, -S** to improve

BETTING present participle of bet

BETTOR *n* pl. **-S** one that bets

BETWEEN *prep* in the space that separates

BETWIXT *prep* between

BEUNCLED *adj* having many uncles

BEVATRON *n* pl. **-S** a proton accelerator

BEVEL *v* **-ELED, -ELING, -ELS** or **-ELLED, -ELLING, -ELS** to cut at an angle

BEVELER *n* pl. **-S** one that bevels

BEVELLER	*n* pl. **-S** beveler
BEVERAGE	*n* pl. **-S** a liquid for drinking
BEVIES	pl. of bevy
BEVOMIT	*v* **-ED, -ING, -S** to vomit all over
BEVOR	*n* pl. **-S** a piece of armor for the lower face
BEVY	*n* pl. **BEVIES** a group
BEWAIL	*v* **-ED, -ING, -S** to lament
BEWAILER	*n* pl. **-S** one that bewails
BEWARE	*v* **-WARED, -WARING, -WARES** to be careful
BEWEARY	*v* **-WEARIED, -WEARYING, -WEARIES** to make weary
BEWEEP	*v* **-WEPT, -WEEPING, -WEEPS** to lament
BEWIG	*v* **-WIGGED, -WIGGING, -WIGS** to adorn with a wig
BEWILDER	*v* **-ED, -ING, -S** to confuse
BEWINGED	*adj* having wings
BEWITCH	*v* **-ED, -ING, -ES** to affect by witchcraft or magic
BEWORM	*v* **-ED, -ING, -S** to infest with worms
BEWORRY	*v* **-RIED, -RYING, -RIES** to worry
BEWRAP	*v* **-WRAPPED** or **-WRAPT, -WRAPPING, -WRAPS** to wrap completely
BEWRAY	*v* **-ED, -ING, -S** to divulge
BEWRAYER	*n* pl. **-S** one that bewrays
BEY	*n* pl. **BEYS** a Turkish ruler
BEYLIC	*n* pl. **-S** the domain of a bey
BEYLIK	*n* pl. **-S** beylic
BEYOND	*n* pl. **-S** something that lies farther ahead
BEZANT	*n* pl. **-S** a coin of ancient Rome
BEZAZZ	*n* pl. **-ES** pizazz
BEZEL	*n* pl. **-S** a slanted surface
BEZIL	*n* pl. **-S** bezel
BEZIQUE	*n* pl. **-S** a card game
BEZOAR	*n* pl. **-S** a gastric mass
BEZZANT	*n* pl. **-S** bezant
BHAKTA	*n* pl. **-S** one who practices bhakti
BHAKTI	*n* pl. **-S** a selfless devotion to a deity in Hinduism
BHANG	*n* pl. **-S** the hemp plant
BHANGRA	*n* pl. **-S** a form of popular Punjabi dance music
BHARAL	*n* pl. **-S** a goatlike Asian mammal
BHEESTIE	*n* pl. **-S** bheesty
BHEESTY	*n* pl. **-TIES** a water carrier
BHISTIE	*n* pl. **-S** bheesty
BHOOT	*n* pl. **-S** bhut
BHUT	*n* pl. **-S** a small whirlwind
BI	*n* pl. **-S** a bisexual
BIACETYL	*n* pl. **-S** a chemical flavor enhancer
BIALI	*n* pl. **-S** bialy
BIALY	*n* pl. **-ALYS** or **-ALIES** an onion roll
BIANNUAL	*adj* occurring twice a year
BIAS	*v* **-ASED, -ASING, -ASES** or **-ASSED, -ASSING, -ASSES** to prejudice **BIASEDLY** *adv*
BIASNESS	*n* pl. **-ES** the state of being slanted
BIATHLON	*n* pl. **-S** an athletic contest
BIAXAL	*adj* biaxial
BIAXIAL	*adj* having two axes
BIB	*v* **BIBBED, BIBBING, BIBS** to tipple
BIBASIC	*adj* dibasic
BIBB	*n* pl. **-S** a mast support
BIBBED	past tense of bib
BIBBER	*n* pl. **-S** a tippler
BIBBERY	*n* pl. **-BERIES** the act of bibbing
BIBBING	present participle of bib
BIBCOCK	*n* pl. **-S** a type of faucet
BIBELOT	*n* pl. **-S** a trinket
BIBLE	*n* pl. **-S** an authoritative publication **BIBLICAL** *adj*
BIBLESS	*adj* having no bib (a cloth covering)
BIBLIKE	*adj* resembling a bib
BIBLIST	*n* pl. **-S** one who takes the words of the Bible literally
BIBULOUS	*adj* given to drinking
BICARB	*n* pl. **-S** sodium bicarbonate
BICAUDAL	*adj* having two tails
BICE	*n* pl. **-S** a blue or green pigment
BICEP	*n* pl. **-S** biceps
BICEPS	*n* pl. **-ES** an arm muscle
BICHROME	*adj* two-colored
BICKER	*v* **-ED, -ING, -S** to argue
BICKERER	*n* pl. **-S** one that bickers
BICOLOR	*n* pl. **-S** something having two colors
BICOLOUR	*n* pl. **-S** bicolor
BICONVEX	*adj* convex on both sides

BICORN	*n* pl. **-S** bicorne
BICORNE	*n* pl. **-S** a type of hat
BICRON	*n* pl. **-S** one billionth of a meter
BICUSPID	*n* pl. **-S** a tooth
BICYCLE	*v* **-CLED, -CLING, -CLES** to ride a bicycle (a two-wheeled vehicle)
BICYCLER	*n* pl. **-S** one that bicycles
BICYCLIC	*adj* having two cycles
BID	*v* **BADE, BIDDEN, BIDDING, BIDS** to make a bid (an offer of a price)
BIDARKA	*n* pl. **-S** an Eskimo canoe
BIDARKEE	*n* pl. **-S** bidarka
BIDDABLE	*adj* obedient **BIDDABLY** *adv*
BIDDEN	past participle of bid
BIDDER	*n* pl. **-S** one that bids
BIDDING	*n* pl. **-S** a command
BIDDY	*n* pl. **-DIES** a hen
BIDE	*v* **BIDED** or **BODE, BIDING, BIDES** to wait
BIDENTAL	*adj* having two teeth
BIDER	*n* pl. **-S** one that bides
BIDET	*n* pl. **-S** a low basin used for washing
BIDI	*n* pl. **-S** a cigarette of India
BIDING	present participle of bide
BIELD	*v* **-ED, -ING, -S** to shelter
BIENNALE	*n* pl. **-S** a biennial show
BIENNIAL	*n* pl. **-S** an event that occurs every two years
BIENNIUM	*n* pl. **-NIUMS** or **-NIA** a period of two years
BIER	*n* pl. **-S** a coffin stand
BIFACE	*n* pl. **-S** a stone tool having a cutting edge
BIFACIAL	*adj* having two faces
BIFF	*v* **-ED, -ING, -S** to hit
BIFFIN	*n* pl. **-S** a cooking apple
BIFFY	*n* pl. **-FIES** a toilet
BIFID	*adj* divided into two parts **BIFIDLY** *adv*
BIFIDITY	*n* pl. **-TIES** the state of being bifid
BIFILAR	*adj* having two threads
BIFLEX	*adj* bent in two places
BIFOCAL	*n* pl. **-S** a type of lens
BIFOLD	*adj* twofold
BIFORATE	*adj* having two perforations
BIFORKED	*adj* divided into two branches
BIFORM	*adj* having two forms
BIFORMED	*adj* biform
BIG	*adj* **BIGGER, BIGGEST** of considerable size
BIG	*n* pl. **-S** one of great importance
BIGAMIES	pl. of bigamy
BIGAMIST	*n* pl. **-S** one who commits bigamy
BIGAMOUS	*adj* guilty of bigamy
BIGAMY	*n* pl. **-MIES** the crime of being married to two people at once
BIGARADE	*n* pl. **-S** a citrus tree
BIGAROON	*n* pl. **-S** a type of cherry
BIGEMINY	*n* pl. **-NIES** the state of having a double pulse
BIGEYE	*n* pl. **-S** a marine fish
BIGFOOT	*n* pl. **-FOOTS** or **-FEET** an influential person
BIGFOOT	*v* **-ED, -ING, -S** to apply one's influence as a bigfoot
BIGGER	comparative of big
BIGGEST	superlative of big
BIGGETY	*adj* biggity
BIGGIE	*n* pl. **-S** one that is big
BIGGIES	pl. of biggy
BIGGIN	*n* pl. **-S** a house
BIGGING	*n* pl. **-S** biggin
BIGGISH	*adj* somewhat big
BIGGITY	*adj* conceited
BIGGY	*n* pl. **-GIES** biggie
BIGHEAD	*n* pl. **-S** a disease of animals
BIGHORN	*n* pl. **-S** a wild sheep
BIGHT	*v* **-ED, -ING, -S** to fasten with a loop of rope
BIGLY	*adv* in a big manner
BIGMOUTH	*n* pl. **-S** a talkative person
BIGNESS	*n* pl. **-ES** the state of being big
BIGNONIA	*n* pl. **-S** a climbing plant
BIGOS	*n* pl. **-ES** a Polish stew
BIGOT	*n* pl. **-S** a prejudiced person
BIGOTED	*adj* intolerant
BIGOTRY	*n* pl. **-RIES** prejudice
BIGSTICK	*adj* threatening military force
BIGTIME	*adj* pertaining to the highest level
BIGWIG	*n* pl. **-S** an important person
BIHOURLY	*adj* occurring every two hours
BIJOU	*n* pl. **-JOUS** or **-JOUX** a jewel

BIJUGATE *adj* two-paired

BIJUGOUS *adj* bijugate

BIKE *v* **BIKED, BIKING, BIKES** to bicycle

BIKER *n* pl. **-S** one that bikes

BIKEWAY *n* pl. **-WAYS** a route for bikes

BIKIE *n* pl. **-S** biker

BIKING present participle of bike

BIKINI *n* pl. **-S** a type of bathing suit **BIKINIED** *adj*

BILABIAL *n* pl. **-S** a sound articulated with both lips

BILANDER *n* pl. **-S** a small ship

BILAYER *n* pl. **-S** a film with two molecular layers

BILBERRY *n* pl. **-RIES** an edible berry

BILBO *n* pl. **-BOS** or **-BOES** a finely tempered sword

BILBOA *n* pl. **-S** bilbo

BILBY *n* pl. **-BIES** a small nocturnal mammal

BILE *n* pl. **-S** a fluid secreted by the liver

BILEVEL *n* pl. **-S** a house having two levels

BILGE *v* **BILGED, BILGING, BILGES** to spring a leak

BILGY *adj* **BILGIER, BILGIEST** smelling like seepage

BILIARY *adj* pertaining to bile

BILINEAR *adj* pertaining to two lines

BILIOUS *adj* pertaining to bile

BILK *v* **-ED, -ING, -S** to cheat

BILKER *n* pl. **-S** one that bilks

BILL *v* **-ED, -ING, -S** to present a statement of costs to **BILLABLE** *adj*

BILLBUG *n* pl. **-S** a weevil

BILLER *n* pl. **-S** one that bills

BILLET *v* **-ED, -ING, -S** to lodge soldiers

BILLETER *n* pl. **-S** one that billets

BILLFISH *n* pl. **-ES** a fish with long, slender jaws

BILLFOLD *n* pl. **-S** a wallet

BILLHEAD *n* pl. **-S** a letterhead

BILLHOOK *n* pl. **-S** a cutting tool

BILLIARD *n* pl. **-S** a carom shot in billiards (a table game)

BILLIE *n* pl. **-S** a comrade

BILLIES pl. of billy

BILLING *n* pl. **-S** the relative position in which a performer is listed

BILLION *n* pl. **-S** a number

BILLON *n* pl. **-S** an alloy of silver and copper

BILLOW *v* **-ED, -ING, -S** to swell

BILLOWY *adj* **-LOWIER, -LOWIEST** swelling; surging

BILLY *n* pl. **-LIES** a short club

BILLYCAN *n* pl. **-S** a pot for heating water

BILOBATE *adj* having two lobes

BILOBED *adj* bilobate

BILSTED *n* pl. **-S** a hardwood tree

BILTONG *n* pl. **-S** dried and cured meat

BIMA *n* pl. **-S** bema

BIMAH *n* pl. **-S** bema

BIMANOUS *adj* two-handed

BIMANUAL *adj* done with two hands

BIMBETTE *n* pl. **-S** an attractive but empty-headed young woman

BIMBO *n* pl. **-BOS** or **-BOES** a disreputable person

BIMENSAL *adj* occurring every two months

BIMESTER *n* pl. **-S** a two-month period

BIMETAL *n* pl. **-S** something composed of two metals

BIMETHYL *n* pl. **-S** ethane

BIMODAL *adj* having two statistical modes

BIMORPH *n* pl. **-S** a device consisting of two crystals cemented together

BIN *v* **BINNED, BINNING, BINS** to store in a large receptacle

BINAL *adj* twofold

BINARISM *n* pl. **-S** a mode of thought based on oppositions

BINARY *n* pl. **-RIES** a combination of two things

BINATE *adj* growing in pairs **BINATELY** *adv*

BINAURAL *adj* hearing with both ears

BIND *v* **BOUND, BINDING, BINDS** to tie or secure **BINDABLE** *adj*

BINDER *n* pl. **-S** one that binds

BINDERY *n* pl. **-ERIES** a place where books are bound

BINDI *n* pl. **-S** a dot worn on the forehead by women in India

BINDING *n* pl. **-S** the cover and fastenings of a book

BINDLE *n* pl. **-S** a bundle

BINDWEED *n* pl. **-S** a twining plant

BINE *n* pl. **-S** a twining plant stem

BINER *n* pl. **-S** a soldier armed with a carbine

BINGE *v* **BINGED, BINGEING** or **BINGING, BINGES** to indulge in something without restraint

BINGER *n* pl. **-S** one that binges

BINGO *n* pl. **-GOS** or **-GOES** a game of chance

BINIT *n* pl. **-S** a unit of computer information

BINNACLE *n* pl. **-S** a compass stand

BINNED past tense of bin

BINNING present participle of bin

BINOCLE *n* pl. **-S** a binocular

BINOCS *n/pl* binoculars

BINOMIAL *n* pl. **-S** an algebraic expression

BINT *n* pl. **-S** a woman

BIO *n* pl. **BIOS** a biography

BIOASSAY *v* **-ED, -ING, -S** to test a substance (as a drug) in order to determine its strength

BIOCHIP *n* pl. **-S** a hypothetical computer component that uses proteins to store or process data

BIOCIDE *n* pl. **-S** a substance destructive to living organisms **BIOCIDAL** *adj*

BIOCLEAN *adj* free of harmful organisms

BIOCYCLE *n* pl. **-S** a life-supporting region

BIOETHIC *adj* pertaining to ethical questions arising from advances in biology

BIOFILM *n* pl. **-S** a thin layer of microorganisms

BIOFUEL *n* pl. **-S** fuel composed of biological raw materials

BIOG *n* pl. **-S** a biography

BIOGAS *n* pl. **-GASES** or **-GASSES** fuel gas produced by organic waste

BIOGEN *n* pl. **-S** a hypothetical protein molecule

BIOGENIC *adj* produced by living organisms

BIOGENY *n* pl. **-NIES** the development of life from preexisting life

BIOHERM *n* pl. **-S** a mass of marine fossils

BIOLOGIC *n* pl. **-S** a drug obtained from an organic source

BIOLOGY *n* pl. **-GIES** the science of life

BIOLYSIS *n* pl. **-YSES** death **BIOLYTIC** *adj*

BIOMASS *n* pl. **-ES** an amount of living matter

BIOME *n* pl. **-S** an ecological community

BIOMETER *n* pl. **-S** a device for measuring carbon dioxide given off by living matter

BIOMETRY *n* pl. **-TRIES** the statistical study of biological data

BIOMORPH *n* pl. **-S** an art form resembling a living organism in shape

BIONICS *n/pl* a science joining biology and electronics **BIONIC** *adj*

BIONOMY *n* pl. **-MIES** ecology **BIONOMIC** *adj*

BIONT *n* pl. **-S** a living organism **BIONTIC** *adj*

BIOPIC *n* pl. **-S** a biographical movie

BIOPLASM *n* pl. **-S** living matter

BIOPSIC *adj* pertaining to the examination of living tissue

BIOPSY *v* **-SIED, -SYING, -SIES** to examine living tissue

BIOPTIC *adj* biopsic

BIOSCOPE *n* pl. **-S** an early movie projector

BIOSCOPY *n* pl. **-PIES** a type of medical examination

BIOSOLID *n* pl. **-S** solid organic matter obtained from treated sewage

BIOTA *n* pl. **-S** flora and fauna

BIOTECH *n* pl. **-S** applied biology

BIOTIC *adj* pertaining to life

BIOTICAL *adj* biotic

BIOTICS *n/pl* a life science

BIOTIN *n* pl. **-S** a B vitamin

BIOTITE *n* pl. **-S** a form of mica **BIOTITIC** *adj*

BIOTOPE *n* pl. **-S** a stable habitat

BIOTOXIN *n* pl. **-S** poison made by a plant or animal

BIOTRON *n* pl. **-S** a climate control chamber

BIOTYPE *n* pl. **-S** a group of genetically similar organisms **BIOTYPIC** *adj*

BIOVULAR *adj* derived from two ova

BIPACK *n* pl. **-S** a pair of films

BIPAROUS *adj* producing offspring in pairs

BIPARTED *adj* having two parts

BIPARTY *adj* of two parties

BIPED *n* pl. **-S** a two-footed animal **BIPEDAL** *adj*

BIPHASIC *adj* having two phases

BIPHENYL *n* pl. **-S** a hydrocarbon

BIPLANE *n* pl. **-S** a type of airplane

BIPOD *n* pl. **-S** a two-legged support

BIPOLAR *adj* having two poles

BIRACIAL *adj* having members of two races

BIRADIAL *adj* having dual symmetry

BIRAMOSE *adj* biramous

BIRAMOUS *adj* divided into two branches

BIRCH *v* **-ED, -ING, -ES** to whip

BIRCHEN *adj* made of birch wood

BIRD *v* **-ED, -ING, -S** to hunt birds (winged, warm-blooded vertebrates)

BIRDBATH *n* pl. **-S** a bath for birds

BIRDCAGE *n* pl. **-S** a cage for birds

BIRDCALL *n* pl. **-S** the call of a bird

BIRDDOG *v* **-DOGGED, -DOGGING, -DOGS** to follow closely

BIRDER *n* pl. **-S** a bird hunter

BIRDFARM *n* pl. **-S** an aircraft carrier

BIRDFEED *n* pl. **-S** birdseed

BIRDIE *v* **BIRDIED, BIRDIEING, BIRDIES** to shoot in one stroke under par in golf

BIRDING *n* pl. **-S** bird-watching

BIRDLIFE *n* pl. **BIRDLIFE** avifauna

BIRDLIKE *adj* resembling a bird

BIRDLIME *v* **-LIMED, -LIMING, -LIMES** to trap small birds

BIRDMAN *n* pl. **-MEN** one who keeps birds

BIRDSEED *n* pl. **-S** a mixture of seeds used for feeding birds

BIRDSEYE *n* pl. **-S** a flowering plant

BIRDSHOT *n* pl. **BIRDSHOT** small shot for shooting birds

BIRDSONG *n* pl. **-S** the song of a bird

BIREME *n* pl. **-S** an ancient galley

BIRETTA *n* pl. **-S** a cap worn by clergymen

BIRIANI *n* pl. **-S** biryani

BIRK *n* pl. **-S** a birch tree

BIRKIE *n* pl. **-S** a lively person

BIRL *v* **-ED, -ING, -S** to rotate a floating log

BIRLE *v* **BIRLED, BIRLING, BIRLES** to carouse

BIRLER *n* pl. **-S** one that birls

BIRLING *n* pl. **-S** a lumberjack's game

BIRR *n* pl. **BIRROTCH** a monetary unit of Ethiopia

BIRR *v* **-ED, -ING, -S** to make a whirring noise

BIRRETTA *n* pl. **-S** biretta

BIRSE *n* pl. **-S** a bristle

BIRTH *v* **-ED, -ING, -S** to originate

BIRTHDAY *n* pl. **-DAYS** an anniversary of a birth

BIRTHING *n* pl. **-S** the act of giving birth

BIRYANI *n* pl. **-S** an Indian dish of meat, fish, or vegetables and rice

BIS *adv* twice

BISCOTTO *n* pl. **-COTTI** a crisp, anise-flavored cookie

BISCUIT *n* pl. **-S** a small cake of shortened bread **BISCUITY** *adj*

BISE *n* pl. **-S** a cold wind

BISECT *v* **-ED, -ING, -S** to cut into two parts

BISECTOR *n* pl. **-S** something that bisects

BISEXUAL *n* pl. **-S** one who is attracted to both sexes

BISHOP *v* **-ED, -ING, -S** to appoint as a bishop (the head of a diocese)

BISK *n* pl. **-S** bisque

BISMUTH *n* pl. **-S** a metallic element

BISNAGA *n* pl. **-S** a type of cactus

BISON *n* pl. **-S** an ox-like animal

BISQUE *n* pl. **-S** a thick soup

BISTATE *adj* pertaining to two states

BISTER *n* pl. **-S** a brown pigment **BISTERED** *adj*

BISTORT *n* pl. **-S** a perennial herb with roots used as astringents

BISTOURY *n* pl. **-RIES** a surgical knife

BISTRE *n* pl. **-S** bister **BISTRED** *adj*

BISTRO *n* pl. **-TROS** a small tavern **BISTROIC** *adj*

BIT *v* **BITTED, BITTING, BITS** to restrain

BITABLE *adj* capable of being bitten

BITCH *v* **-ED, -ING, -ES** to complain

BITCHEN *adj* excellent

BITCHERY *n* pl. **-ERIES** bitchy behavior

BITCHY *adj* **BITCHIER, BITCHIEST** malicious **BITCHILY** *adv*

BITE *v* **BIT, BITTEN, BITING, BITES** to seize with the teeth **BITEABLE** *adj*

BITER *n* pl. **-S** one that bites

BITEWING	*n* pl. **-S** a dental X-ray film
BITING	present participle of bite
BITINGLY	*adv* sarcastically
BITMAP	*n* pl. **-S** an array of binary data
BITSTOCK	*n* pl. **-S** a brace on a drill
BITSY	*adj* **-SIER, -SIEST** tiny
BITT	*v* **-ED, -ING, -S** to secure a cable around a post
BITTED	past tense of bit
BITTEN	a past participle of bite
BITTER	*adj* **-TERER, -TEREST** having a disagreeable taste **BITTERLY** *adv*
BITTER	*v* **-ED, -ING, -S** to make bitter
BITTERN	*n* pl. **-S** a wading bird
BITTIER	comparative of bitty
BITTIEST	superlative of bitty
BITTING	*n* pl. **-S** an indentation in a key
BITTOCK	*n* pl. **-S** a small amount
BITTY	*adj* **-TIER, -TIEST** tiny
BITUMEN	*n* pl. **-S** an asphalt
BIUNIQUE	*adj* being a type of correspondence between two sets
BIVALENT	*n* pl. **-S** a pair of chromosomes
BIVALVE	*n* pl. **-S** a bivalved mollusk
BIVALVED	*adj* having a two-valved shell
BIVINYL	*n* pl. **-S** a flammable gas used in making synthetic rubber
BIVOUAC	*v* **-OUACKED, -OUACKING, -OUACKS** or **-OUACS** to make a camp
BIWEEKLY	*n* pl. **-LIES** a publication issued every two weeks
BIYEARLY	*adj* occurring every two years
BIZ	*n* pl. **BIZZES** business
BIZARRE	*n* pl. **-S** a strangely striped flower
BIZARRO	*n* pl. **-ROS** one that is strikingly unusual
BIZE	*n* pl. **-S** bise
BIZNAGA	*n* pl. **-S** bisnaga
BIZONE	*n* pl. **-S** two combined zones **BIZONAL** *adj*
BLAB	*v* **BLABBED, BLABBING, BLABS** to talk idly
BLABBER	*v* **-ED, -ING, -S** to blab
BLABBY	*adj* talkative
BLACK	*adj* **BLACKER, BLACKEST** being of the darkest color
BLACK	*v* **-ED, -ING, -S** to make black
BLACKBOY	*n* pl. **-BOYS** an Australian plant
BLACKCAP	*n* pl. **-S** a small European bird
BLACKEN	*v* **-ED, -ING, -S** to make black
BLACKFIN	*n* pl. **-S** a food fish
BLACKFLY	*n* pl. **-FLIES** a biting fly
BLACKGUM	*n* pl. **-S** a tupelo
BLACKING	*n* pl. **-S** black shoe polish
BLACKISH	*adj* somewhat black
BLACKLEG	*n* pl. **-S** a cattle disease
BLACKLY	*adv* in a black manner
BLACKOUT	*n* pl. **-S** a power failure
BLACKTOP	*v* **-TOPPED, -TOPPING, -TOPS** to pave with asphalt
BLADDER	*n* pl. **-S** a saclike receptacle **BLADDERY** *adj*
BLADE	*v* **BLADED, BLADING, BLADES** to skate on in-line skates
BLADER	*n* pl. **-S** one that blades
BLADING	*n* pl. **-S** the act of skating on in-line skates
BLAE	*adj* bluish-black
BLAFF	*n* pl. **-S** a West Indian stew
BLAGGING	*n* pl. **-S** informal talk in public
BLAH	*n* pl. **-S** nonsense
BLAIN	*n* pl. **-S** a blister
BLAM	*n* pl. **-S** the sound of a gunshot
BLAMABLE	*adj* being at fault **BLAMABLY** *adv*
BLAME	*v* **BLAMED, BLAMING, BLAMES** to find fault with
BLAMEFUL	*adj* blamable
BLAMER	*n* pl. **-S** one that blames
BLAMING	present participle of blame
BLANCH	*v* **-ED, -ING, -ES** to whiten
BLANCHER	*n* pl. **-S** a whitener
BLAND	*adj* **BLANDER, BLANDEST** soothing **BLANDLY** *adv*
BLANDISH	*v* **-ED, -ING, -ES** to coax by flattery
BLANK	*adj* **BLANKER, BLANKEST** empty
BLANK	*v* **-ED, -ING, -S** to delete
BLANKET	*v* **-ED, -ING, -S** to cover uniformly
BLANKLY	*adv* in a blank manner
BLARE	*v* **BLARED, BLARING, BLARES** to sound loudly
BLARNEY	*v* **-NEYED, -NEYING, -NEYS** to beguile with flattery
BLASE	*adj* indifferent

BLAST	*v* **-ED, -ING, -S** to use an explosive	**BLEED**	*v* **BLED, BLEEDING, BLEEDS** to lose blood
BLASTEMA	*n* pl. **-MAS** or **-MATA** a region of embryonic cells	**BLEEDER**	*n* pl. **-S** one that bleeds
BLASTER	*n* pl. **-S** one that blasts	**BLEEDING**	*n* pl. **-S** the act of losing blood
BLASTIE	*n* pl. **-S** a dwarf	**BLEEP**	*v* **-ED, -ING, -S** to blip
BLASTIER	comparative of blasty	**BLEEPER**	*n* pl. **-S** one that bleeps
BLASTIEST	superlative of blasty	**BLELLUM**	*n* pl. **-S** a babbler
BLASTING	*n* pl. **-S** the act of one that blasts	**BLEMISH**	*v* **-ED, -ING, -ES** to mar
BLASTOFF	*n* pl. **-S** the launching of a rocket	**BLENCH**	*v* **-ED, -ING, -ES** to flinch
BLASTOMA	*n* pl. **-MAS** or **-MATA** a type of tumor	**BLENCHER**	*n* pl. **-S** one that blenches
BLASTULA	*n* pl. **-LAS** or **-LAE** an early embryo	**BLEND**	*v* **BLENDED** or **BLENT, BLENDING, BLENDS** to mix smoothly and inseparably together
BLASTY	*adj* **BLASTIER, BLASTIEST** gusty	**BLENDE**	*n* pl. **-S** a shiny mineral
BLAT	*v* **BLATTED, BLATTING, BLATS** to bleat	**BLENDER**	*n* pl. **-S** one that blends
		BLENNY	*n* pl. **-NIES** a marine fish
BLATANCY	*n* pl. **-CIES** something blatant	**BLENT**	a past tense of blend
BLATANT	*adj* obvious	**BLESBOK**	*n* pl. **-S** a large antelope
BLATE	*adj* timid	**BLESBUCK**	*n* pl. **-S** blesbok
BLATHER	*v* **-ED, -ING, -S** to talk foolishly	**BLESS**	*v* **BLESSED** or **BLEST, BLESSING, BLESSES** to sanctify
BLATTED	past tense of blat		
BLATTER	*v* **-ED, -ING, -S** to chatter	**BLESSED**	*adj* **-EDER, -EDEST** holy
BLATTING	present participle of blat	**BLESSER**	*n* pl. **-S** one that blesses
BLAUBOK	*n* pl. **-S** an extinct antelope	**BLESSING**	*n* pl. **-S** a prayer
BLAW	*v* **BLAWED, BLAWN, BLAWING, BLAWS** to blow	**BLEST**	a past tense of bless
		BLET	*n* pl. **-S** a decay of fruit
BLAZE	*v* **BLAZED, BLAZING, BLAZES** to burn brightly	**BLETHER**	*v* **-ED, -ING, -S** to blather
		BLEW	past tense of blow
BLAZER	*n* pl. **-S** a lightweight jacket **BLAZERED** *adj*	**BLIGHT**	*v* **-ED, -ING, -S** to cause decay
		BLIGHTER	*n* pl. **-S** one that blights
BLAZON	*v* **-ED, -ING, -S** to proclaim	**BLIGHTY**	*n* pl. **BLIGHTIES** a wound causing one to be sent home to England
BLAZONER	*n* pl. **-S** one that blazons		
BLAZONRY	*n* pl. **-RIES** a great display	**BLIMEY**	*interj* — used as an expression of surprise
BLEACH	*v* **-ED, -ING, -ES** to whiten		
BLEACHER	*n* pl. **-S** one that bleaches	**BLIMP**	*n* pl. **-S** a nonrigid aircraft **BLIMPISH** *adj*
BLEAK	*adj* **BLEAKER, BLEAKEST** dreary		
BLEAK	*n* pl. **-S** a freshwater fish	**BLIMY**	*interj* blimey
BLEAKISH	*adj* somewhat bleak	**BLIN**	*n* pl. **BLINI** or **BLINIS** a blintze
BLEAKLY	*adv* in a bleak manner	**BLIND**	*adj* **BLINDER, BLINDEST** sightless
BLEAR	*v* **-ED, -ING, -S** to dim		
BLEARY	*adj* **BLEARIER, BLEARIEST** dimmed **BLEARILY** *adv*	**BLIND**	*v* **-ED, -ING, -S** to make sightless
		BLINDAGE	*n* pl. **-S** a protective screen
BLEAT	*v* **-ED, -ING, -S** to utter the cry of a sheep	**BLINDER**	*n* pl. **-S** an obstruction to sight
		BLINDGUT	*n* pl. **-S** a cecum
BLEATER	*n* pl. **-S** one that bleats	**BLINDLY**	*adv* in a blind manner
BLEB	*n* pl. **-S** a blister **BLEBBY** *adj*	**BLINI**	a pl. of blin
BLEBBING	*n* pl. **-S** the forming of a blister	**BLINIS**	a pl. of blin

BLINK   v **-ED, -ING, -S** to open and shut the eyes

BLINKARD   n pl. **-S** one who habitually blinks

BLINKER   v **-ED, -ING, -S** to put blinders on

BLINTZ   n pl. **-ES** blintze

BLINTZE   n pl. **-S** a thin pancake

BLIP   v **BLIPPED, BLIPPING, BLIPS** to remove sound from a recording

BLISS   v **-ED, -ING, -ES** to experience or produce ecstasy

BLISSFUL   adj very happy

BLISTER   v **-ED, -ING, -S** to cause blisters (skin swellings)

BLISTERY   adj having blisters

BLITE   n pl. **-S** an annual herb

BLITHE   adj **BLITHER, BLITHEST** merry **BLITHELY** adv

BLITHER   v **-ED, -ING, -S** to blather

BLITZ   v **-ED, -ING, -ES** to subject to a sudden attack

BLITZER   n pl. **-S** one that blitzes

BLIZZARD   n pl. **-S** a heavy snowstorm

BLOAT   v **-ED, -ING, -S** to swell

BLOATER   n pl. **-S** a smoked herring

BLOB   v **BLOBBED, BLOBBING, BLOBS** to splotch

BLOC   n pl. **-S** a coalition

BLOCK   v **-ED, -ING, -S** to obstruct

BLOCKADE   v **-ADED, -ADING, -ADES** to block

BLOCKAGE   n pl. **-S** the act of blocking

BLOCKER   n pl. **-S** one that blocks

BLOCKISH   adj blocky

BLOCKY   adj **BLOCKIER, BLOCKIEST** short and stout

BLOG   n pl. **-S** a website containing a personal journal

BLOGGER   n pl. **-S** one who maintains a blog

BLOGGING   n pl. **-S** the act or practice of maintaining a blog

BLOKE   n pl. **-S** a fellow

BLOND   adj **BLONDER, BLONDEST** light-colored

BLOND   n pl. **-S** a person with blond hair

BLONDE   n pl. **-S** blond

BLONDINE   v **-INED, -INING, -INES** to bleach hair blond

BLONDISH   adj somewhat blond

BLOOD   v **-ED, -ING, -S** to stain with blood (the fluid circulated by the heart)

BLOODFIN   n pl. **-S** a freshwater fish

BLOODIED   past tense of bloody

BLOODIER   comparative of bloody

BLOODIES   present 3d person sing. of bloody

BLOODIEST   superlative of bloody

BLOODILY   adv in a bloody manner

BLOODING   n pl. **-S** a fox hunting ceremony

BLOODRED   adj of the color of blood

BLOODY   adj **BLOODIER, BLOODIEST** stained with blood

BLOODY   v **BLOODIED, BLOODYING, BLOODIES** to make bloody

BLOOEY   adj being out of order

BLOOIE   adj blooey

BLOOM   v **-ED, -ING, -S** to bear flowers

BLOOMER   n pl. **-S** a blooming plant

BLOOMERY   n pl. **-ERIES** a furnace for smelting iron

BLOOMY   adj **BLOOMIER, BLOOMIEST** covered with flowers

BLOOP   v **-ED, -ING, -S** to hit a short fly ball

BLOOPER   n pl. **-S** a public blunder

BLOSSOM   v **-ED, -ING, -S** to bloom

BLOSSOMY   adj having blossoms

BLOT   v **BLOTTED, BLOTTING, BLOTS** to spot or stain

BLOTCH   v **-ED, -ING, -ES** to mark with large spots

BLOTCHY   adj **BLOTCHIER, BLOTCHIEST** blotched

BLOTLESS   adj spotless

BLOTTED   past tense of blot

BLOTTER   n pl. **-S** a piece of ink-absorbing paper

BLOTTIER   comparative of blotty

BLOTTIEST   superlative of blotty

BLOTTING   present participle of blot

BLOTTO   adj drunk

BLOTTY   adj **-TIER, -TIEST** spotty

BLOUSE   v **BLOUSED, BLOUSING, BLOUSES** to hang loosely

BLOUSON   n pl. **-S** a woman's garment

BLOUSY   adj **BLOUSIER, BLOUSIEST** blowsy **BLOUSILY** adv

BLOVIATE   v **-ATED, -ATING, -ATES** to speak pompously

BLOW	*v* **BLEW, BLOWED, BLOWING, BLOWS** to damn
BLOW	*v* **BLEW, BLOWN, BLOWING, BLOWS** to drive or impel by a current of air
BLOWBACK	*n* pl. **-S** an escape of gases
BLOWBALL	*n* pl. **-S** a fluffy seed ball
BLOWBY	*n* pl. **-BYS** leakage of exhaust fumes
BLOWDOWN	*n* pl. **-S** a tree blown down by the wind
BLOWER	*n* pl. **-S** one that blows
BLOWFISH	*n* pl. **-ES** a marine fish
BLOWFLY	*n* pl. **-FLIES** a type of fly
BLOWGUN	*n* pl. **-S** a tube through which darts may be blown
BLOWHARD	*n* pl. **-S** a braggart
BLOWHOLE	*n* pl. **-S** an air or gas vent
BLOWIER	comparative of blowy
BLOWIEST	superlative of blowy
BLOWN	past participle of blow
BLOWOFF	*n* pl. **-S** the expelling of gas
BLOWOUT	*n* pl. **-S** a sudden rupture
BLOWPIPE	*n* pl. **-S** a blowgun
BLOWSED	*adj* blowsy
BLOWSY	*adj* **-SIER, -SIEST** slovenly **BLOWSILY** *adv*
BLOWTUBE	*n* pl. **-S** a blowgun
BLOWUP	*n* pl. **-S** an explosion
BLOWY	*adj* **BLOWIER, BLOWIEST** windy
BLOWZED	*adj* blowzy
BLOWZY	*adj* **-ZIER, -ZIEST** blowsy **BLOWZILY** *adv*
BLUB	*v* **BLUBBED, BLUBBING, BLUBS** to blubber
BLUBBER	*v* **-ED, -ING, -S** to weep noisily
BLUBBERY	*adj* fat; swollen
BLUCHER	*n* pl. **-S** a half boot
BLUDGE	*v* **BLUDGED, BLUDGING, BLUDGES** to avoid work
BLUDGEON	*v* **-ED, -ING, -S** to hit with a club
BLUDGER	*n* pl. **-S** a loafer or shirker
BLUE	*adj* **BLUER, BLUEST** having the color of the clear sky
BLUE	*v* **BLUED, BLUEING** or **BLUING, BLUES** to make blue
BLUEBALL	*n* pl. **-S** a medicinal herb
BLUEBEAT	*n* pl. **-S** ska
BLUEBELL	*n* pl. **-S** a flowering plant
BLUEBILL	*n* pl. **-S** the scaup duck
BLUEBIRD	*n* pl. **-S** a songbird
BLUEBOOK	*n* pl. **-S** an examination booklet
BLUECAP	*n* pl. **-S** a flowering plant
BLUECOAT	*n* pl. **-S** a police officer
BLUED	past tense of blue
BLUEFIN	*n* pl. **-S** a large tuna
BLUEFISH	*n* pl. **-ES** a marine fish
BLUEGILL	*n* pl. **-S** an edible sunfish
BLUEGUM	*n* pl. **-S** a timber tree
BLUEHEAD	*n* pl. **-S** a marine fish
BLUEING	*n* pl. **-S** bluing
BLUEISH	*adj* bluish
BLUEJACK	*n* pl. **-S** an oak tree
BLUEJAY	*n* pl. **-JAYS** a corvine bird
BLUELINE	*n* pl. **-S** a line that divides a hockey rink
BLUELY	*adv* in a blue manner
BLUENESS	*n* pl. **-ES** the state of being blue
BLUENOSE	*n* pl. **-S** a puritanical person
BLUER	comparative of blue
BLUESIER	comparative of bluesy
BLUESIEST	superlative of bluesy
BLUESMAN	*n* pl. **-MEN** one who plays the blues
BLUEST	superlative of blue
BLUESTEM	*n* pl. **-S** a prairie grass
BLUESY	*adj* **BLUESIER, BLUESIEST** resembling the blues (a musical form)
BLUET	*n* pl. **-S** a meadow flower
BLUETICK	*n* pl. **-S** a hunting dog
BLUEWEED	*n* pl. **-S** a bristly weed
BLUEWOOD	*n* pl. **-S** a shrub
BLUEY	*n* pl. **BLUEYS** a bag of clothing carried in travel
BLUFF	*adj* **BLUFFER, BLUFFEST** having a broad front **BLUFFLY** *adv*
BLUFF	*v* **-ED, -ING, -S** to mislead
BLUFFER	*n* pl. **-S** one that bluffs
BLUING	*n* pl. **-S** a fabric coloring
BLUISH	*adj* somewhat blue
BLUME	*v* **BLUMED, BLUMING, BLUMES** to blossom
BLUNDER	*v* **-ED, -ING, -S** to make a mistake

BLUNGE	*v* **BLUNGED, BLUNGING, BLUNGES** to mix clay with water	**BOATLIFT**	*v* **-ED, -ING, -S** to transport by boats
BLUNGER	*n* pl. **-S** one that blunges	**BOATLIKE**	*adj* resembling a boat
BLUNT	*adj* **BLUNTER, BLUNTEST** not sharp or pointed **BLUNTLY** *adv*	**BOATLOAD**	*n* pl. **-S** the amount that a boat holds
BLUNT	*v* **-ED, -ING, -S** to make blunt	**BOATMAN**	*n* pl. **-MEN** one who works on boats
BLUR	*v* **BLURRED, BLURRING, BLURS** to make unclear	**BOATNECK**	*n* pl. **-S** a wide neckline
BLURB	*v* **-ED, -ING, -S** to praise in a publicity notice	**BOATSMAN**	*n* pl. **-MEN** boatman
		BOATYARD	*n* pl. **-S** a marina
BLURBIST	*n* pl. **-S** one that blurbs	**BOB**	*v* **BOBBED, BOBBING, BOBS** to move up and down
BLURRY	*adj* **-RIER, -RIEST** unclear **BLURRILY** *adv*	**BOBBER**	*n* pl. **-S** one that bobs
BLURT	*v* **-ED, -ING, -S** to speak abruptly	**BOBBERY**	*n* pl. **-BERIES** a disturbance
BLURTER	*n* pl. **-S** one that blurts	**BOBBIES**	pl. of bobby
BLUSH	*v* **-ED, -ING, -ES** to become red	**BOBBIN**	*n* pl. **-S** a thread holder
BLUSHER	*n* pl. **-S** one that blushes	**BOBBINET**	*n* pl. **-S** a machine-made net
BLUSHFUL	*adj* of a red color	**BOBBING**	present participle of bob
BLUSTER	*v* **-ED, -ING, -S** to blow violently	**BOBBLE**	*v* **-BLED, -BLING, -BLES** to fumble
BLUSTERY	*adj* windy	**BOBBY**	*n* pl. **-BIES** a police officer
BLYPE	*n* pl. **-S** a shred	**BOBBYSOX**	*n/pl* girls' socks that reach above the ankle
BO	*n* pl. **BOS** a pal		
BOA	*n* pl. **-S** a large snake	**BOBCAT**	*n* pl. **-S** a lynx
BOAR	*n* pl. **-S** a male pig	**BOBECHE**	*n* pl. **-S** a glass collar on a candle holder
BOARD	*v* **-ED, -ING, -S** to take meals for a fixed price	**BOBOLINK**	*n* pl. **-S** a songbird
BOARDER	*n* pl. **-S** one that boards	**BOBSLED**	*v* **-SLEDDED, -SLEDDING, -SLEDS** to ride on a bobsled (a racing sled)
BOARDING	*n* pl. **-S** a surface of wooden boards		
BOARDMAN	*n* pl. **-MEN** a board member	**BOBSTAY**	*n* pl. **-STAYS** a steadying rope
BOARFISH	*n* pl. **-ES** a marine fish	**BOBTAIL**	*v* **-ED, -ING, -S** to cut short
BOARISH	*adj* swinish; coarse	**BOBWHITE**	*n* pl. **-S** a game bird
BOART	*n* pl. **-S** bort	**BOCACCIO**	*n* pl. **-CIOS** a rockfish
BOAST	*v* **-ED, -ING, -S** to brag	**BOCCE**	*n* pl. **-S** boccie
BOASTER	*n* pl. **-S** one that boasts	**BOCCI**	*n* pl. **-S** boccie
BOASTFUL	*adj* given to boasting	**BOCCIA**	*n* pl. **-S** boccie
BOAT	*v* **-ED, -ING, -S** to travel by boat (watercraft) **BOATABLE** *adj*	**BOCCIE**	*n* pl. **-S** an Italian bowling game
		BOCK	*n* pl. **-S** a dark beer
BOATBILL	*n* pl. **-S** a wading bird	**BOD**	*n* pl. **-S** a body
BOATEL	*n* pl. **-S** a waterside hotel	**BODE**	*v* **BODED, BODING, BODES** to be an omen of
BOATER	*n* pl. **-S** one that boats		
BOATFUL	*n* pl. **-S** as much as a boat can hold	**BODEGA**	*n* pl. **-S** a grocery store
		BODEMENT	*n* pl. **-S** an omen
BOATHOOK	*n* pl. **-S** a pole with a metal hook for use aboard a boat	**BODHRAN**	*n* pl. **-S** an Irish drum
		BODICE	*n* pl. **-S** a corset
BOATING	*n* pl. **-S** the sport of traveling by boat	**BODIED**	past tense of body
		BODIES	present 3d person sing. of body

BODILESS	*adj* lacking material form
BODILY	*adj* of the body
BODING	*n* pl. **-S** an omen
BODINGLY	*adv* ominously
BODKIN	*n* pl. **-S** a sharp instrument
BODY	*v* **BODIED, BODYING, BODIES** to give form to
BODYSUIT	*n* pl. **-S** a one-piece garment for the torso
BODYSURF	*v* **-ED, -ING, -S** to ride a wave without a surfboard
BODYWORK	*n* pl. **-S** a vehicle body
BOEHMITE	*n* pl. **-S** a mineral
BOFF	*n* pl. **-S** a hearty laugh
BOFFIN	*n* pl. **-S** a scientific expert
BOFFO	*n* pl. **-FOS** a boff
BOFFOLA	*n* pl. **-S** a boff
BOG	*v* **BOGGED, BOGGING, BOGS** to impede
BOGAN	*n* pl. **-S** a backwater or tributary
BOGART	*v* **-ED, -ING, -S** to use without sharing
BOGBEAN	*n* pl. **-S** a marsh plant
BOGEY	*v* **-GEYED, -GEYING, -GEYS** to shoot in one stroke over par in golf
BOGEYMAN	*n* pl. **-MEN** a terrifying creature
BOGGED	past tense of bog
BOGGIER	comparative of boggy
BOGGIEST	superlative of boggy
BOGGING	present participle of bog
BOGGISH	*adj* boggy
BOGGLE	*v* **-GLED, -GLING, -GLES** to hesitate
BOGGLER	*n* pl. **-S** one that causes another to boggle
BOGGY	*adj* **-GIER, -GIEST** marshy
BOGIE	*n* pl. **-S** bogy
BOGIES	pl. of bogy
BOGLE	*n* pl. **-S** a bogy
BOGUS	*adj* not genuine; fake **BOGUSLY** *adv*
BOGWOOD	*n* pl. **-S** preserved tree wood
BOGY	*n* pl. **-GIES** a goblin
BOGYISM	*n* pl. **-S** behavior characteristic of a bogy
BOGYMAN	*n* pl. **-MEN** bogeyman
BOHEA	*n* pl. **-S** a black tea
BOHEMIA	*n* pl. **-S** a community of bohemians
BOHEMIAN	*n* pl. **-S** an unconventional person
BOHO	*n* pl. **-HOS** a bohemian
BOHRIUM	*n* pl. **-S** a radioactive element
BOIL	*v* **-ED, -ING, -S** to vaporize liquid **BOILABLE** *adj*
BOILER	*n* pl. **-S** a vessel for boiling
BOILOFF	*n* pl. **-S** the vaporization of liquid
BOILOVER	*n* pl. **-S** an overflowing while boiling
BOING	*n* pl. **-S** the sound of reverberation or vibration
BOISERIE	*n* pl. **-S** wood paneling on a wall
BOITE	*n* pl. **-S** a nightclub
BOLA	*n* pl. **-S** a throwing weapon
BOLAR	*adj* pertaining to bole
BOLAS	*n* pl. **-ES** bola
BOLD	*adj* **BOLDER, BOLDEST** daring **BOLDLY** *adv*
BOLD	*n* pl. **-S** a thick type
BOLDFACE	*v* **-FACED, -FACING, -FACES** to print in thick type
BOLDNESS	*n* pl. **-ES** the quality of being bold
BOLE	*n* pl. **-S** a fine clay
BOLERO	*n* pl. **-ROS** a Spanish dance
BOLETE	*n* pl. **-S** boletus
BOLETUS	*n* pl. **-TUSES** or **-TI** a fungus
BOLIDE	*n* pl. **-S** an exploding meteor
BOLIVAR	*n* pl. **-S** or **-ES** a monetary unit of Venezuela
BOLIVIA	*n* pl. **-S** a soft fabric
BOLL	*v* **-ED, -ING, -S** to form pods
BOLLARD	*n* pl. **-S** a thick post on a ship or wharf
BOLLIX	*v* **-ED, -ING, -ES** to bungle
BOLLOX	*v* **-ED, -ING, -ES** to bollix
BOLLWORM	*n* pl. **-S** the larva of a certain moth
BOLO	*n* pl. **-LOS** a machete
BOLOGNA	*n* pl. **-S** a seasoned sausage
BOLONEY	*n* pl. **-NEYS** bologna
BOLSHIE	*n* pl. **-S** a Bolshevik
BOLSHY	*n* pl. **-SHIES** bolshie
BOLSON	*n* pl. **-S** a flat arid valley
BOLSTER	*v* **-ED, -ING, -S** to support
BOLT	*v* **-ED, -ING, -S** to sift
BOLTER	*n* pl. **-S** a sifting machine

BOLTHEAD *n* pl. **-S** a matrass

BOLTHOLE *n* pl. **-S** a place or way of escape

BOLTLESS *adj* having no bolt

BOLTLIKE *adj* resembling a bolt

BOLTONIA *n* pl. **-S** a perennial herb

BOLTROPE *n* pl. **-S** a rope sewn to a sail

BOLUS *n* pl. **-ES** a large pill

BOMB *v* **-ED, -ING, -S** to attack with bombs (explosive projectiles) **BOMBABLE** *adj*

BOMBARD *v* **-ED, -ING, -S** to bomb

BOMBAST *n* pl. **-S** pompous language

BOMBAX *adj* pertaining to a family of tropical trees

BOMBE *n* pl. **-S** a frozen dessert

BOMBER *n* pl. **-S** one that bombs

BOMBESIN *n* pl. **-S** a combination of amino acids

BOMBING *n* pl. **-S** an attack with bombs

BOMBLET *n* pl. **-S** a small bomb

BOMBLOAD *n* pl. **-S** the quantity of bombs being carried

BOMBYCID *n* pl. **-S** a moth

BOMBYX *n* pl. **-ES** a silkworm

BONACI *n* pl. **-S** an edible fish

BONANZA *n* pl. **-S** a rich mine

BONBON *n* pl. **-S** a sugared candy

BOND *v* **-ED, -ING, -S** to join together **BONDABLE** *adj*

BONDAGE *n* pl. **-S** slavery

BONDER *n* pl. **-S** one that bonds

BONDING *n* pl. **-S** the formation of a close personal relationship

BONDLESS *adj* having no bond

BONDMAID *n* pl. **-S** a female slave

BONDMAN *n* pl. **-MEN** a male slave

BONDSMAN *n* pl. **-MEN** bondman

BONDUC *n* pl. **-S** a prickly seed

BONE *v* **BONED, BONING, BONES** to debone

BONEFISH *n* pl. **-ES** a slender marine fish

BONEHEAD *n* pl. **-S** a stupid person

BONELESS *adj* having no bones (hard connective tissue)

BONEMEAL *n* pl. **-S** fertilizer or feed made from crushed bone

BONER *n* pl. **-S** a blunder

BONESET *n* pl. **-S** a perennial herb

BONEY *adj* **BONEYER, BONEYEST** bony

BONEYARD *n* pl. **-S** a junkyard

BONFIRE *n* pl. **-S** an open fire

BONG *v* **-ED, -ING, -S** to make a deep, ringing sound

BONGO *n* pl. **-GOS** or **-GOES** a small drum

BONGOIST *n* pl. **-S** a bongo player

BONHOMIE *n* pl. **-S** friendliness

BONIATO *n* pl. **-TOS** a sweet potato

BONIER comparative of bony

BONIEST superlative of bony

BONIFACE *n* pl. **-S** an innkeeper

BONINESS *n* pl. **-ES** the state of being bony

BONING present participle of bone

BONITA *n* pl. **-S** bonito

BONITO *n* pl. **-TOS** or **-TOES** a marine food fish

BONK *v* **-ED, -ING, -S** to hit on the head with a hollow blow

BONKERS *adj* crazy

BONNE *n* pl. **-S** a housemaid

BONNET *v* **-ED, -ING, -S** to provide with a bonnet (a type of hat)

BONNIE *adj* bonny

BONNOCK *n* pl. **-S** bannock

BONNY *adj* **-NIER, -NIEST** pretty **BONNILY** *adv*

BONOBO *n* pl. **-BOS** an anthropoid ape

BONSAI *n* pl. **BONSAI** a potted shrub that has been dwarfed

BONSPELL *n* pl. **-S** bonspiel

BONSPIEL *n* pl. **-S** a curling match or tournament

BONTEBOK *n* pl. **-S** an antelope

BONUS *n* pl. **-ES** an additional payment

BONY *adj* **BONIER, BONIEST** full of bones

BONZE *n* pl. **-S** a Buddhist monk

BONZER *adj* very good

BOO *v* **-ED, -ING, -S** to cry "boo"

BOOB *v* **-ED, -ING, -S** to make a foolish mistake

BOOBIRD *n* pl. **-S** a fan who boos players of the home team

BOOBISH *adj* doltish

BOOBOO *n* pl. **-BOOS** a mistake

BOOBY *n* pl. **-BIES** a dolt

BOOCOO *n* pl. **-COOS** beaucoup

BOODLE *v* **-DLED, -DLING, -DLES** to take bribes

BOODLER *n* pl. **-S** one that boodles

BOOGER *n* pl. **-S** a bogeyman

BOOGEY *v* **-GEYED, -GEYING, -GEYS** to boogie

BOOGIE *v* **-GIED, -GIEING, -GIES** to dance to rock music

BOOGY *v* **-GIED, -GYING, -GIES** to boogie

BOOGYMAN *n* pl. **-MEN** bogeyman

BOOHOO *v* **-ED, -ING, -S** to weep noisily

BOOJUM *n* pl. **-S** a spiny desert tree

BOOK *v* **-ED, -ING, -S** to engage services **BOOKABLE** *adj*

BOOKCASE *n* pl. **-S** a case which holds books (literary volumes)

BOOKEND *n* pl. **-S** a support for a row of books

BOOKER *n* pl. **-S** one that books

BOOKFUL *n* pl. **-S** as much as a book can hold

BOOKIE *n* pl. **-S** a bet taker

BOOKING *n* pl. **-S** an engagement

BOOKISH *adj* pertaining to books

BOOKLET *n* pl. **-S** a small book

BOOKLICE *n/pl* wingless insects that damage books

BOOKLORE *n* pl. **-S** book learning

BOOKMAN *n* pl. **-MEN** a scholar

BOOKMARK *v* **-ED, -ING, -S** to create a shortcut to a previously viewed website

BOOKOO *n* pl. **-KOOS** beaucoup

BOOKRACK *n* pl. **-S** a support for an open book

BOOKREST *n* pl. **-S** a bookrack

BOOKSHOP *n* pl. **-S** a store where books are sold

BOOKWORM *n* pl. **-S** an avid book reader

BOOM *v* **-ED, -ING, -S** to make a deep, resonant sound

BOOMBOX *n* pl. **-ES** a portable radio and tape or compact disc player

BOOMER *n* pl. **-S** one that booms

BOOMIER comparative of boomy

BOOMIEST superlative of boomy

BOOMKIN *n* pl. **-S** a bumkin

BOOMLET *n* pl. **-S** a small increase in prosperity

BOOMTOWN *n* pl. **-S** a prospering town

BOOMY *adj* **BOOMIER, BOOMIEST** prospering

BOON *n* pl. **-S** a timely benefit

BOONDOCK *adj* pertaining to a backwoods area

BOONIES *n/pl* a backwoods area

BOONLESS *adj* having no boon

BOOR *n* pl. **-S** a rude person

BOORISH *adj* rude

BOOST *v* **-ED, -ING, -S** to support

BOOSTER *n* pl. **-S** one that boosts

BOOT *v* **-ED, -ING, -S** to load a program into a computer **BOOTABLE** *adj*

BOOTEE *n* pl. **-S** a baby's sock

BOOTERY *n* pl. **-ERIES** a shoe store

BOOTH *n* pl. **-S** a small enclosure

BOOTIE *n* pl. **-S** bootee

BOOTIES pl. of booty

BOOTJACK *n* pl. **-S** a device for pulling off boots

BOOTLACE *n* pl. **-S** a shoelace

BOOTLEG *v* **-LEGGED, -LEGGING, -LEGS** to smuggle

BOOTLESS *adj* useless

BOOTLICK *v* **-ED, -ING, -S** to flatter servilely

BOOTY *n* pl. **-TIES** a rich gain or prize

BOOZE *v* **BOOZED, BOOZING, BOOZES** to drink liquor excessively

BOOZER *n* pl. **-S** one that boozes

BOOZY *adj* **BOOZIER, BOOZIEST** drunken **BOOZILY** *adv*

BOP *v* **BOPPED, BOPPING, BOPS** to hit or strike

BOPEEP *n* pl. **-S** a game of peekaboo

BOPPER *n* pl. **-S** a bebopper

BORA *n* pl. **-S** a cold wind

BORACES a pl. of borax

BORACIC *adj* boric

BORACITE *n* pl. **-S** a mineral

BORAGE *n* pl. **-S** a medicinal herb

BORAL *n* pl. **-S** a mixture of boron carbide and aluminum

BORANE *n* pl. **-S** a chemical compound

BORATE *v* **-RATED, -RATING, -RATES** to mix with borax or boric acid

BORAX	*n* pl. **-RAXES** or **-RACES** a white crystalline compound	**BOSCAGE**	*n* pl. **-S** a thicket
BORDEAUX	*n* pl. **BORDEAUX** a red or white wine	**BOSCHBOK**	*n* pl. **-S** bushbuck
		BOSH	*n* pl. **-ES** nonsense
BORDEL	*n* pl. **-S** a brothel	**BOSHBOK**	*n* pl. **-S** bushbuck
BORDELLO	*n* pl. **-LOS** a brothel	**BOSHVARK**	*n* pl. **-S** a wild hog
BORDER	*v* **-ED, -ING, -S** to put a border (an edge) on	**BOSK**	*n* pl. **-S** a small wooded area
BORDERER	*n* pl. **-S** one that borders	**BOSKAGE**	*n* pl. **-S** boscage
BORDURE	*n* pl. **-S** a border around a shield	**BOSKER**	*adj* fine; very good
BORE	*v* **BORED, BORING, BORES** to pierce with a rotary tool	**BOSKET**	*n* pl. **-S** a thicket
		BOSKY	*adj* **BOSKIER, BOSKIEST** wooded; bushy
BOREAL	*adj* pertaining to the north	**BOSOM**	*v* **-ED, -ING, -S** to embrace
BOREAS	*n* pl. **-ES** the north wind	**BOSOMY**	*adj* swelling outward
BORECOLE	*n* pl. **-S** kale	**BOSON**	*n* pl. **-S** a subatomic particle **BOSONIC** *adj*
BORED	past tense of bore		
BOREDOM	*n* pl. **-S** tedium	**BOSQUE**	*n* pl. **-S** bosk
BOREEN	*n* pl. **-S** a lane in Ireland	**BOSQUET**	*n* pl. **-S** bosket
BOREHOLE	*n* pl. **-S** a hole bored in the earth	**BOSS**	*v* **-ED, -ING, -ES** to supervise
BORER	*n* pl. **-S** one that bores	**BOSSDOM**	*n* pl. **-S** the domain of a political boss
BORESOME	*adj* tedious	**BOSSIES**	pl. of bossy
BORIC	*adj* pertaining to boron	**BOSSISM**	*n* pl. **-S** control by political bosses
BORIDE	*n* pl. **-S** a boron compound	**BOSSY**	*adj* **BOSSIER, BOSSIEST** domineering **BOSSILY** *adv*
BORING	*n* pl. **-S** an inner cavity		
BORINGLY	*adv* tediously	**BOSSY**	*n* pl. **BOSSIES** a cow
BORK	*v* **-ED, -ING, -S** to attack a candidate in the media	**BOSTON**	*n* pl. **-S** a card game
BORN	*adj* having particular qualities from birth	**BOSUN**	*n* pl. **-S** a boatswain
		BOT	*n* pl. **-S** the larva of a botfly
		BOTA	*n* pl. **-S** a leather bottle
BORNE	a past participle of bear	**BOTANIC**	*adj* pertaining to botany
BORNEOL	*n* pl. **-S** an alcohol	**BOTANICA**	*n* pl. **-S** a shop that sells herbs and magic charms
BORNITE	*n* pl. **-S** an ore of copper **BORNITIC** *adj*		
		BOTANIES	pl. of botany
BORON	*n* pl. **-S** a nonmetallic element **BORONIC** *adj*	**BOTANISE**	*v* **-NISED, -NISING, -NISES** to botanize
BOROUGH	*n* pl. **-S** an incorporated town	**BOTANIST**	*n* pl. **-S** one skilled in botany
BORRELIA	*n* pl. **-S** a coiled spirochete	**BOTANIZE**	*v* **-NIZED, -NIZING, -NIZES** to study plants
BORROW	*v* **-ED, -ING, -S** to take on loan		
BORROWER	*n* pl. **-S** one that borrows	**BOTANY**	*n* pl. **-NIES** the science of plants
BORSCH	*n* pl. **-ES** borscht	**BOTCH**	*v* **-ED, -ING, -ES** to bungle
BORSCHT	*n* pl. **-S** a beet soup	**BOTCHER**	*n* pl. **-S** one that botches
BORSHT	*n* pl. **-S** borscht	**BOTCHERY**	*n* pl. **-ERIES** something botched
BORSTAL	*n* pl. **-S** a reformatory	**BOTCHY**	*adj* **BOTCHIER, BOTCHIEST** badly done **BOTCHILY** *adv*
BORT	*n* pl. **-S** a low-quality diamond **BORTY** *adj*		
		BOTEL	*n* pl. **-S** boatel
BORTZ	*n* pl. **-ES** bort	**BOTFLY**	*n* pl. **-FLIES** a type of fly
BORZOI	*n* pl. **-S** a Russian hound	**BOTH**	*adj* being the two

BOTHER	*v* **-ED, -ING, -S** to annoy	**BOUNDEN**	*adj* obliged
BOTHRIUM	*n* pl. **-RIUMS** or **-RIA** a groove on a tapeworm	**BOUNDER**	*n* pl. **-S** one that bounds
BOTHY	*n* pl. **BOTHIES** a hut in Scotland	**BOUNTY**	*n* pl. **-TIES** a reward **BOUNTIED** *adj*
BOTONEE	*adj* having arms ending in a trefoil — used of a heraldic cross	**BOUQUET**	*n* pl. **-S** a bunch of flowers
BOTONNEE	*adj* botonee	**BOURBON**	*n* pl. **-S** a whiskey
BOTRYOID	*adj* resembling a cluster of grapes	**BOURDON**	*n* pl. **-S** a part of a bagpipe
BOTRYOSE	*adj* botryoid	**BOURG**	*n* pl. **-S** a medieval town
BOTRYTIS	*n* pl. **-TISES** a plant disease	**BOURGEON**	*v* **-ED, -ING, -S** to burgeon
BOTT	*n* pl. **-S** bot	**BOURN**	*n* pl. **-S** a stream
BOTTLE	*v* **-TLED, -TLING, -TLES** to put into a bottle (a rigid container)	**BOURNE**	*n* pl. **-S** bourn
BOTTLER	*n* pl. **-S** one that bottles	**BOURREE**	*n* pl. **-S** an old French dance
BOTTLING	*n* pl. **-S** a bottled beverage	**BOURRIDE**	*n* pl. **-S** a fish stew
BOTTOM	*v* **-ED, -ING, -S** to comprehend	**BOURSE**	*n* pl. **-S** a stock exchange
BOTTOMER	*n* pl. **-S** one that bottoms	**BOURTREE**	*n* pl. **-S** a European tree
BOTTOMRY	*n* pl. **-RIES** a maritime contract	**BOUSE**	*v* **BOUSED, BOUSING, BOUSES** to haul by means of a tackle
BOTULIN	*n* pl. **-S** a nerve poison	**BOUSOUKI**	*n* pl. **-KIS** or **-KIA** bouzouki
BOTULISM	*n* pl. **-S** botulin poisoning	**BOUSY**	*adj* boozy
BOUBOU	*n* pl. **-S** a long flowing garment	**BOUT**	*n* pl. **-S** a contest
BOUCHEE	*n* pl. **-S** a small patty shell	**BOUTIQUE**	*n* pl. **-S** a small shop
BOUCLE	*n* pl. **-S** a knitted fabric	**BOUTON**	*n* pl. **-S** an enlarged end of a nerve fiber
BOUDIN	*n* pl. **-S** a spicy Cajun sausage	**BOUVIER**	*n* pl. **-S** a large dog
BOUDOIR	*n* pl. **-S** a woman's bedroom	**BOUZOUKI**	*n* pl. **-KIS** or **-KIA** a stringed musical instrument
BOUFFANT	*n* pl. **-S** a woman's hairdo	**BOVID**	*n* pl. **-S** a bovine
BOUFFE	*n* pl. **-S** a comic opera	**BOVINE**	*n* pl. **-S** an ox-like animal
BOUGH	*n* pl. **-S** a tree branch **BOUGHED** *adj*	**BOVINELY**	*adv* stolidly
BOUGHPOT	*n* pl. **-S** a large vase	**BOVINITY**	*n* pl. **-TIES** the state of being a bovine
BOUGHT	past tense of buy	**BOW**	*v* **-ED, -ING, -S** to bend forward
BOUGHTEN	*adj* purchased	**BOWEL**	*v* **-ELED, -ELING, -ELS** or **-ELLED, -ELLING, -ELS** to disbowel
BOUGIE	*n* pl. **-S** a wax candle		
BOUILLON	*n* pl. **-S** a clear broth	**BOWER**	*v* **-ED, -ING, -S** to embower
BOULDER	*v* **-ED, -ING, -S** to climb up large rocks	**BOWERY**	*n* pl. **-ERIES** a colonial Dutch farm
BOULDERY	*adj* characterized by large rocks	**BOWFIN**	*n* pl. **-S** a freshwater fish
BOULE	*n* pl. **-S** buhl	**BOWFRONT**	*adj* having a curved front
BOULLE	*n* pl. **-S** buhl	**BOWHEAD**	*n* pl. **-S** an arctic whale
BOUNCE	*v* **BOUNCED, BOUNCING, BOUNCES** to spring back	**BOWING**	*n* pl. **-S** the technique of managing the bow of a stringed instrument
BOUNCER	*n* pl. **-S** one that bounces	**BOWINGLY**	*adv* in a bowing manner
BOUNCY	*adj* **BOUNCIER, BOUNCIEST** tending to bounce **BOUNCILY** *adv*	**BOWKNOT**	*n* pl. **-S** a type of knot
		BOWL	*v* **-ED, -ING, -S** to play at bowling
BOUND	*v* **-ED, -ING, -S** to leap	**BOWLDER**	*n* pl. **-S** boulder
BOUNDARY	*n* pl. **-ARIES** a dividing line	**BOWLEG**	*n* pl. **-S** an outwardly curved leg
		BOWLER	*n* pl. **-S** one that bowls

BOWLESS	*adj* being without an archery bow
BOWLFUL	*n* pl. **-S** as much as a bowl can hold
BOWLIKE	*adj* curved
BOWLINE	*n* pl. **-S** a type of knot
BOWLING	*n* pl. **-S** a game in which balls are rolled at objects
BOWLLIKE	*adj* concave
BOWMAN	*n* pl. **-MEN** an archer
BOWPOT	*n* pl. **-S** boughpot
BOWSE	*v* **BOWSED, BOWSING, BOWSES** to bouse
BOWSHOT	*n* pl. **-S** the distance an arrow is shot
BOWSPRIT	*n* pl. **-S** a ship's spar
BOWWOW	*v* **-ED, -ING, -S** to bark like a dog
BOWYER	*n* pl. **-S** a maker of archery bows
BOX	*v* **-ED, -ING, -ES** to put in a box (a rectangular container)
BOXBALL	*n* pl. **-S** a form of handball
BOXBERRY	*n* pl. **-RIES** an evergreen plant
BOXBOARD	*n* pl. **-S** stiff paperboard
BOXCAR	*n* pl. **-S** a roofed freight car
BOXER	*n* pl. **-S** one that packs boxes
BOXFISH	*n* pl. **-ES** a marine fish
BOXFUL	*n* pl. **-S** as much as a box can hold
BOXHAUL	*v* **-ED, -ING, -S** to veer a ship around
BOXIER	comparative of boxy
BOXIEST	superlative of boxy
BOXINESS	*n* pl. **-ES** the state of being boxy
BOXING	*n* pl. **-S** a casing
BOXLIKE	*adj* resembling a box
BOXTHORN	*n* pl. **-S** a thorny shrub
BOXWOOD	*n* pl. **-S** an evergreen shrub
BOXY	*adj* **BOXIER, BOXIEST** resembling a box **BOXILY** *adv*
BOY	*n* pl. **BOYS** a male child
BOYAR	*n* pl. **-S** a former Russian aristocrat
BOYARD	*n* pl. **-S** boyar
BOYARISM	*n* pl. **-S** the rule of boyars
BOYCHICK	*n* pl. **-S** boychik
BOYCHIK	*n* pl. **-S** a young man
BOYCOTT	*v* **-ED, -ING, -S** to refuse to buy
BOYHOOD	*n* pl. **-S** the state of being a boy
BOYISH	*adj* resembling a boy **BOYISHLY** *adv*
BOYLA	*n* pl. **-S** a witch doctor
BOYO	*n* pl. **BOYOS** a boy
BOZO	*n* pl. **-ZOS** a fellow
BRA	*n* pl. **-S** a brassiere
BRABBLE	*v* **-BLED, -BLING, -BLES** to quarrel noisily
BRABBLER	*n* pl. **-S** one that brabbles
BRACE	*v* **BRACED, BRACING, BRACES** to support
BRACELET	*n* pl. **-S** a wrist ornament
BRACER	*n* pl. **-S** one that braces
BRACERO	*n* pl. **-ROS** a Mexican laborer
BRACH	*n* pl. **-S** or **-ES** a hound bitch
BRACHET	*n* pl. **-S** a brach
BRACHIAL	*n* pl. **-S** a part of the arm
BRACHIUM	*n* pl. **-IA** the upper part of arm
BRACING	*n* pl. **-S** a brace or reinforcement
BRACIOLA	*n* pl. **-S** a thin slice of meat
BRACIOLE	*n* pl. **-S** braciola
BRACKEN	*n* pl. **-S** a large fern
BRACKET	*v* **-ED, -ING, -S** to classify
BRACKISH	*adj* salty
BRACONID	*n* pl. **-S** any of a family of flies
BRACT	*n* pl. **-S** a leaflike plant part **BRACTEAL, BRACTED** *adj*
BRACTLET	*n* pl. **-S** a small bract
BRAD	*v* **BRADDED, BRADDING, BRADS** to fasten with thin nails
BRADAWL	*n* pl. **-S** a type of awl
BRADOON	*n* pl. **-S** bridoon
BRAE	*n* pl. **-S** a hillside
BRAG	*adj* **BRAGGER, BRAGGEST** first-rate
BRAG	*v* **BRAGGED, BRAGGING, BRAGS** to speak vainly of one's deeds
BRAGGART	*n* pl. **-S** one who brags
BRAGGER	*n* pl. **-S** a braggart
BRAGGY	*adj* **-GIER, -GIEST** tending to brag
BRAHMA	*n* pl. **-S** a large domestic fowl
BRAID	*v* **-ED, -ING, -S** to weave together
BRAIDER	*n* pl. **-S** one that braids
BRAIDING	*n* pl. **-S** something made of braided material
BRAIL	*v* **-ED, -ING, -S** to haul in a sail
BRAILLE	*v* **BRAILLED, BRAILLING, BRAILLES** to write in braille (raised writing for the blind)

BRAILLER *n* pl. **-S** a machine for printing in braille

BRAIN *v* **-ED, -ING, -S** to hit on the head

BRAINIAC *n* pl. **-S** a very intelligent person

BRAINIER comparative of brainy

BRAINIEST superlative of brainy

BRAINILY *adv* in a brainy manner

BRAINISH *adj* impetuous

BRAINPAN *n* pl. **-S** the skull

BRAINY *adj* **BRAINIER, BRAINIEST** smart

BRAISE *v* **BRAISED, BRAISING, BRAISES** to cook in fat

BRAIZE *n* pl. **-S** a marine fish

BRAKE *v* **BRAKED, BRAKING, BRAKES** to slow down or stop

BRAKEAGE *n* pl. **-S** the act of braking

BRAKEMAN *n* pl. **-MEN** a trainman

BRAKING present participle of brake

BRAKY *adj* **BRAKIER, BRAKIEST** abounding in shrubs or ferns

BRALESS *adj* wearing no bra

BRAMBLE *v* **-BLED, -BLING, -BLES** to gather berries

BRAMBLY *adj* **-BLIER, -BLIEST** prickly

BRAN *v* **BRANNED, BRANNING, BRANS** to soak in water mixed with bran (the outer coat of cereals)

BRANCH *v* **-ED, -ING, -ES** to form branches (offshoots)

BRANCHIA *n* pl. **-CHIAE** a respiratory organ of aquatic animals

BRANCHY *adj* **BRANCHIER, BRANCHIEST** having many branches

BRAND *v* **-ED, -ING, -S** to mark with a hot iron

BRANDER *n* pl. **-S** one that brands

BRANDING *n* pl. **-S** the promoting of a product by associating it with a brand name

BRANDISH *v* **-ED, -ING, -ES** to wave menacingly

BRANDY *v* **-DIED, -DYING, -DIES** to mix with brandy (a liquor)

BRANK *n* pl. **-S** a device used to restrain the tongue

BRANNED past tense of bran

BRANNER *n* pl. **-S** one that brans

BRANNING present participle of bran

BRANNY *adj* **-NIER, -NIEST** containing bran

BRANT *n* pl. **-S** a wild goose

BRANTAIL *n* pl. **-S** a singing bird

BRASH *adj* **BRASHER, BRASHEST** rash; hasty **BRASHLY** *adv*

BRASH *n* pl. **-ES** a mass of fragments

BRASHY *adj* **BRASHIER, BRASHIEST** brash

BRASIER *n* pl. **-S** brazier

BRASIL *n* pl. **-S** brazil

BRASILIN *n* pl. **-S** brazilin

BRASS *v* **-ED, -ING, -ES** to coat with brass (an alloy of copper and zinc)

BRASSAGE *n* pl. **-S** a fee for coining money

BRASSARD *n* pl. **-S** an insignia

BRASSART *n* pl. **-S** brassard

BRASSICA *n* pl. **-S** a tall herb

BRASSIE *n* pl. **-S** a golf club

BRASSISH *adj* resembling brass

BRASSY *adj* **BRASSIER, BRASSIEST** resembling brass **BRASSILY** *adv*

BRAT *n* pl. **-S** a spoiled child **BRATTISH** *adj*

BRATTICE *v* **-TICED, -TICING, -TICES** to partition

BRATTLE *v* **-TLED, -TLING, -TLES** to clatter

BRATTY *adj* **-TIER, -TIEST** resembling a brat

BRAUNITE *n* pl. **-S** a mineral

BRAVA *n* pl. **-S** a shout of approval

BRAVADO *n* pl. **-DOS** or **-DOES** false bravery

BRAVE *adj* **BRAVER, BRAVEST** showing courage **BRAVELY** *adv*

BRAVE *v* **BRAVED, BRAVING, BRAVES** to face with courage

BRAVER *n* pl. **-S** one that braves

BRAVERY *n* pl. **-ERIES** courage

BRAVEST superlative of brave

BRAVI a pl. of bravo

BRAVING present participle of brave

BRAVO *n* pl. **-VOS** or **-VOES** or **-VI** a hired killer

BRAVO *v* **-ED, -ING, -ES** to applaud by shouting "bravo"

BRAVURA *n* pl. **-RAS** or **-RE** fine musical technique

BRAW *adj* **BRAWER, BRAWEST** splendid

BRAWL *v* **-ED, -ING, -S** to fight

BRAWLER	*n* pl. **-S** a fighter
BRAWLIE	*adv* splendidly
BRAWLY	*adj* **BRAWLIER, BRAWLIEST** inclined to brawl
BRAWN	*n* pl. **-S** muscular strength
BRAWNY	*adj* **BRAWNIER, BRAWNIEST** muscular **BRAWNILY** *adv*
BRAWS	*n/pl* fine clothes
BRAXY	*n* pl. **BRAXIES** a fever of sheep
BRAY	*v* **BRAYED, BRAYING, BRAYS** to utter a harsh cry
BRAYER	*n* pl. **-S** a roller used to spread ink
BRAZA	*n* pl. **-S** a Spanish unit of length
BRAZE	*v* **BRAZED, BRAZING, BRAZES** to solder together
BRAZEN	*v* **-ED, -ING, -S** to face boldly
BRAZENLY	*adv* boldly
BRAZER	*n* pl. **-S** one that brazes
BRAZIER	*n* pl. **-S** one who works in brass
BRAZIL	*n* pl. **-S** a dyewood
BRAZILIN	*n* pl. **-S** a chemical compound
BRAZING	present participle of braze
BREACH	*v* **-ED, -ING, -ES** to break through
BREACHER	*n* pl. **-S** one that breaches
BREAD	*v* **-ED, -ING, -S** to cover with crumbs of bread (a baked foodstuff made from flour)
BREADBOX	*n* pl. **-ES** a container for bread
BREADNUT	*n* pl. **-S** a tropical fruit
BREADTH	*n* pl. **-S** width
BREADY	*adj* resembling or characteristic of bread
BREAK	*v* **BROKE, BROKEN, BREAKING, BREAKS** to reduce to fragments
BREAKAGE	*n* pl. **-S** the act of breaking
BREAKER	*n* pl. **-S** one that breaks
BREAKING	*n* pl. **-S** the change of a pure vowel to a diphthong
BREAKOUT	*n* pl. **-S** an escape
BREAKUP	*n* pl. **-S** the act of breaking up
BREAM	*v* **-ED, -ING, -S** to clean a ship's bottom
BREAST	*v* **-ED, -ING, -S** to confront boldly
BREATH	*n* pl. **-S** air inhaled and exhaled
BREATHE	*v* **BREATHED, BREATHING, BREATHES** to inhale and exhale air
BREATHER	*n* pl. **-S** one that breathes
BREATHY	*adj* **BREATHIER, BREATHIEST** marked by loud breathing
BRECCIA	*n* pl. **-S** a type of rock **BRECCIAL** *adj*
BRECHAM	*n* pl. **-S** a collar for a horse
BRECHAN	*n* pl. **-S** brecham
BRED	past tense of breed
BREDE	*n* pl. **-S** a braid
BREE	*n* pl. **-S** broth
BREECH	*v* **-ED, -ING, -ES** to clothe with breeches (trousers)
BREED	*v* **BRED, BREEDING, BREEDS** to cause to give birth
BREEDER	*n* pl. **-S** one that breeds
BREEDING	*n* pl. **-S** upbringing
BREEKS	*n/pl* breeches
BREEZE	*v* **BREEZED, BREEZING, BREEZES** to move swiftly
BREEZY	*adj* **BREEZIER, BREEZIEST** windy **BREEZILY** *adv*
BREGMA	*n* pl. **-MATA** a junction point of the skull **BREGMATE** *adj*
BREN	*n* pl. **-S** a submachine gun
BRENT	*n* pl. **-S** brant
BRETHREN	a pl. of brother
BREVE	*n* pl. **-S** a symbol used to indicate a short vowel
BREVET	*v* **-VETED, -VETING, -VETS** or **-VETTED, -VETTING, -VETS** to confer an honorary rank upon
BREVETCY	*n* pl. **-CIES** an honorary rank
BREVIARY	*n* pl. **-RIES** a prayer book
BREVIER	*n* pl. **-S** a size of type
BREVITY	*n* pl. **-TIES** shortness of duration
BREW	*v* **-ED, -ING, -S** to make beer or the like
BREWAGE	*n* pl. **-S** a brewed beverage
BREWER	*n* pl. **-S** one that brews
BREWERY	*n* pl. **-ERIES** a place for brewing
BREWING	*n* pl. **-S** a quantity brewed at one time
BREWIS	*n* pl. **BREWISES** broth
BREWPUB	*n* pl. **-S** a restaurant that sells beverages brewed on the premises
BREWSKI	*n* pl. **-SKIES** or **-SKIS** a serving of beer
BRIAR	*n* pl. **-S** brier **BRIARY** *adj*
BRIARD	*n* pl. **-S** a large dog

BRIBE	v **BRIBED, BRIBING, BRIBES** to practice bribery **BRIBABLE** adj
BRIBEE	n pl. **-S** one that is bribed
BRIBER	n pl. **-S** one that bribes
BRIBERY	n pl. **-ERIES** an act of influencing corruptly
BRIBING	present participle of bribe
BRICK	v **-ED, -ING, -S** to build with bricks (blocks of clay)
BRICKBAT	n pl. **-S** a piece of brick
BRICKLE	n pl. **-S** a brittle candy
BRICKY	adj **BRICKIER, BRICKIEST** made of bricks
BRICOLE	n pl. **-S** a cushion shot in billiards
BRIDAL	n pl. **-S** a wedding
BRIDALLY	adv in a manner befitting a bride
BRIDE	n pl. **-S** a woman just married or about to be married
BRIDGE	v **BRIDGED, BRIDGING, BRIDGES** to connect
BRIDGING	n pl. **-S** a bracing
BRIDLE	v **-DLED, -DLING, -DLES** to control with a restraint
BRIDLER	n pl. **-S** one that bridles
BRIDOON	n pl. **-S** a device used to control a horse
BRIE	n pl. **-S** bree
BRIEF	adj **BRIEFER, BRIEFEST** short
BRIEF	v **-ED, -ING, -S** to summarize
BRIEFER	n pl. **-S** one that briefs
BRIEFING	n pl. **-S** a short lecture
BRIEFLY	adv in a brief manner
BRIER	n pl. **-S** a thorny shrub **BRIERY** adj
BRIG	n pl. **-S** a two-masted ship
BRIGADE	v **-GADED, -GADING, -GADES** to group together
BRIGAND	n pl. **-S** a bandit
BRIGHT	adj **BRIGHTER, BRIGHTEST** emitting much light **BRIGHTLY** adv
BRIGHT	n pl. **-S** a light-hued tobacco
BRIGHTEN	v **-ED, -ING, -S** to make bright
BRILL	n pl. **-S** an edible flatfish
BRIM	v **BRIMMED, BRIMMING, BRIMS** to fill to the top
BRIMFUL	adj ready to overflow
BRIMFULL	adj brimful
BRIMLESS	adj having no brim (an upper edge)
BRIMMED	past tense of brim
BRIMMER	n pl. **-S** a brimming cup or glass
BRIMMING	present participle of brim
BRIN	n pl. **-S** a rib of a fan
BRINDED	adj brindled
BRINDLE	n pl. **-S** a brindled color
BRINDLED	adj streaked
BRINE	v **BRINED, BRINING, BRINES** to treat with brine (salted water)
BRINER	n pl. **-S** one that brines
BRING	v **BROUGHT** or **BRUNG, BRINGING, BRINGS** to take with oneself to a place
BRINGER	n pl. **-S** one that brings
BRINIER	comparative of briny
BRINIES	pl. of briny
BRINIEST	superlative of briny
BRINING	present participle of brine
BRINISH	adj resembling brine
BRINK	n pl. **-S** an extreme edge
BRINY	adj **BRINIER, BRINIEST** salty
BRINY	n pl. **BRINIES** the sea
BRIO	n pl. **BRIOS** liveliness
BRIOCHE	n pl. **-S** a rich roll
BRIONY	n pl. **-NIES** bryony
BRIQUET	v **-QUETTED, -QUETTING, -QUETS** to mold into small bricks
BRIS	n pl. **-ES** a Jewish circumcision rite
BRISANCE	n pl. **-S** the shattering effect of an explosive **BRISANT** adj
BRISK	adj **BRISKER, BRISKEST** lively
BRISK	v **-ED, -ING, -S** to make brisk
BRISKET	n pl. **-S** the breast of an animal
BRISKLY	adv in a brisk manner
BRISLING	n pl. **-S** a small herring
BRISS	n pl. **-ES** bris
BRISTLE	v **-TLED, -TLING, -TLES** to rise stiffly
BRISTLY	adj **-TLIER, -TLIEST** stiffly erect
BRISTOL	n pl. **-S** a smooth cardboard
BRIT	n pl. **-S** a young herring
BRITCHES	n/pl breeches; trousers
BRITH	n pl. **-S** bris
BRITSKA	n pl. **-S** an open carriage
BRITT	n pl. **-S** brit
BRITTLE	adj **-TLER, -TLEST** likely to break

BRITTLE	v **-TLED, -TLING, -TLES** to become brittle	**BROMATE**	v **-MATED, -MATING, -MATES** to combine with bromine
BRITTLY	adv in a brittle manner	**BROME**	n pl. **-S** a tall grass
BRITZKA	n pl. **-S** britska	**BROMELIN**	n pl. **-S** an enzyme
BRITZSKA	n pl. **-S** britska	**BROMIC**	adj containing bromine
BRO	n pl. **BROS** a brother	**BROMID**	n pl. **-S** bromide
BROACH	v **-ED, -ING, -ES** to pierce so as to withdraw a liquid	**BROMIDE**	n pl. **-S** a bromine compound
		BROMIDIC	adj commonplace; trite
BROACHER	n pl. **-S** one that broaches	**BROMIN**	n pl. **-S** bromine
BROAD	adj **BROADER, BROADEST** wide	**BROMINE**	n pl. **-S** a volatile liquid element
BROAD	n pl. **-S** an expansion of a river	**BROMISM**	n pl. **-S** a diseased condition of the skin
BROADAX	n pl. **-ES** a broad-edged ax		
BROADAXE	n pl. **-S** broadax	**BROMIZE**	v **-MIZED, -MIZING, -MIZES** to treat with bromine or a bromide
BROADEN	v **-ED, -ING, -S** to make broad	**BROMO**	n pl. **-MOS** a medicinal compound
BROADISH	adj somewhat broad	**BRONC**	n pl. **-S** bronco
BROADLY	adv in a broad manner	**BRONCHI**	pl. of bronchus
BROCADE	v **-CADED, -CADING, -CADES** to weave with a raised design	**BRONCHIA**	n/pl the main air passages of the lungs
BROCATEL	n pl. **-S** a heavy fabric	**BRONCHO**	n pl. **-CHOS** bronco
BROCCOLI	n pl. **-S** a vegetable related to the cabbage	**BRONCHUS**	n pl. **-CHI** a tracheal branch
		BRONCO	n pl. **-COS** a wild horse
BROCHE	adj brocaded	**BRONZE**	v **BRONZED, BRONZING, BRONZES** to make brown or tan
BROCHURE	n pl. **-S** a pamphlet		
BROCK	n pl. **-S** a badger	**BRONZER**	n pl. **-S** one that bronzes
BROCKAGE	n pl. **-S** an imperfectly minted coin	**BRONZING**	n pl. **-S** a brownish coloring
BROCKET	n pl. **-S** a small, red deer	**BRONZY**	adj **BRONZIER, BRONZIEST** of a brownish color
BROCOLI	n pl. **-S** broccoli		
BROGAN	n pl. **-S** a heavy shoe	**BROO**	n pl. **BROOS** a bree
BROGUE	n pl. **-S** an Irish accent	**BROOCH**	n pl. **-ES** a decorative pin
BROGUERY	n pl. **-ERIES** the use of an Irish accent	**BROOD**	v **-ED, -ING, -S** to ponder deeply
		BROODER	n pl. **-S** one that broods
BROGUISH	adj resembling a brogue	**BROODY**	adj **BROODIER, BROODIEST** tending to brood **BROODILY** adv
BROIDER	v **-ED, -ING, -S** to adorn with needlework		
BROIDERY	n pl. **-DERIES** the act of broidering	**BROOK**	v **-ED, -ING, -S** to tolerate
BROIL	v **-ED, -ING, -S** to cook by direct heat	**BROOKIE**	n pl. **-S** a brook trout
		BROOKITE	n pl. **-S** a mineral
BROILER	n pl. **-S** a device for broiling	**BROOKLET**	n pl. **-S** a small brook or creek
BROKAGE	n pl. **-S** the business of a broker	**BROOM**	v **-ED, -ING, -S** to sweep
BROKE	past tense of break	**BROOMY**	adj **BROOMIER, BROOMIEST** abounding in broom (a type of shrub)
BROKEN	adj shattered **BROKENLY** adv		
BROKER	v **-ED, -ING, -S** to act as a broker (an agent who buys and sells stocks)	**BROS**	pl. of bro
		BROSE	n pl. **-S** a porridge
BROKING	n pl. **-S** the business of a broker	**BROSY**	adj smeared with brose
BROLLY	n pl. **-LIES** an umbrella	**BROTH**	n pl. **-S** a thin clear soup
BROMAL	n pl. **-S** a medicinal liquid	**BROTHEL**	n pl. **-S** a house of prostitution

BROTHER *n pl.* **-S** or **BRETHREN** a male sibling

BROTHER *v* **-ED, -ING, -S** to treat like a brother

BROTHY *adj* resembling broth

BROUGHAM *n pl.* **-S** a type of carriage

BROUGHT past tense of bring

BROUHAHA *n pl.* **-S** an uproar

BROW *n pl.* **-S** the forehead **BROWED** *adj*

BROWBAND *n pl.* **-S** a band designed to cross the forehead

BROWBEAT *v* **-BEAT, -BEATEN, -BEATING, -BEATS** to intimidate

BROWLESS *adj* lacking eyebrows

BROWN *adj* **BROWNER, BROWNEST** of a dark color

BROWN *v* **-ED, -ING, -S** to make brown

BROWNIE *n pl.* **-S** a small sprite

BROWNIER comparative of browny

BROWNIEST superlative of browny

BROWNISH *adj* somewhat brown

BROWNOUT *n pl.* **-S** a power reduction

BROWNY *adj* **BROWNIER, BROWNIEST** somewhat brown

BROWSE *v* **BROWSED, BROWSING, BROWSES** to look at casually

BROWSER *n pl.* **-S** one that browses

BRR *interj* brrr

BRRR *interj* — used to indicate that one feels cold

BRUCELLA *n pl.* **-LAS** or **-LAE** any of a genus of harmful bacteria

BRUCIN *n pl.* **-S** brucine

BRUCINE *n pl.* **-S** a poisonous alkaloid

BRUGH *n pl.* **-S** a borough

BRUIN *n pl.* **-S** a bear

BRUISE *v* **BRUISED, BRUISING, BRUISES** to injure without breaking the surface of the skin

BRUISER *n pl.* **-S** a big, husky man

BRUIT *v* **-ED, -ING, -S** to spread news of

BRUITER *n pl.* **-S** one that bruits

BRULOT *n pl.* **-S** a biting fly

BRULYIE *n pl.* **-S** a noisy quarrel

BRULZIE *n pl.* **-S** brulyie

BRUMAL *adj* wintry

BRUMBY *n pl.* **-BIES** a wild horse

BRUME *n pl.* **-S** fog **BRUMOUS** *adj*

BRUNCH *v* **-ED, -ING, -ES** to eat a late morning meal

BRUNCHER *n pl.* **-S** one that brunches

BRUNET *n pl.* **-S** a dark-haired male

BRUNETTE *n pl.* **-S** a dark-haired female

BRUNG a past tense of bring

BRUNIZEM *n pl.* **-S** a prairie soil

BRUNT *n pl.* **-S** the main impact

BRUSH *v* **-ED, -ING, -ES** to touch lightly

BRUSHER *n pl.* **-S** one that brushes

BRUSHIER comparative of brushy

BRUSHIEST superlative of brushy

BRUSHOFF *n pl.* **-S** an abrupt dismissal

BRUSHUP *n pl.* **-S** a quick review

BRUSHY *adj* **BRUSHIER, BRUSHIEST** shaggy; rough

BRUSK *adj* **BRUSKER, BRUSKEST** brusque

BRUSQUE *adj* **BRUSQUER, BRUSQUEST** abrupt in manner

BRUT *n pl.* **-S** a very dry champagne

BRUTAL *adj* cruel; savage **BRUTALLY** *adv*

BRUTE *v* **BRUTED, BRUTING, BRUTES** to shape a diamond by rubbing it with another diamond

BRUTELY *adv* in a brutal manner

BRUTIFY *v* **-FIED, -FYING, -FIES** to make brutal

BRUTISH *adj* brutal

BRUTISM *n pl.* **-S** the state of being brutal

BRUX *v* **-ED, -ING, -ES** to grind the teeth

BRUXISM *n pl.* **-S** a nervous grinding of the teeth

BRYOLOGY *n pl.* **-GIES** the study of mosses

BRYONY *n pl.* **-NIES** a climbing plant

BRYOZOAN *n pl.* **-S** a type of small aquatic animal

BUB *n pl.* **-S** young fellow

BUBAL *n pl.* **-S** a large antelope

BUBALE *n pl.* **-S** bubal

BUBALINE *adj* pertaining to the bubal

BUBALIS *n pl.* **-LISES** bubal

BUBBLE *v* **-BLED, -BLING, -BLES** to form bubbles (bodies of gas contained within a liquid)

BUBBLER *n pl.* **-S** a drinking fountain

BUBBLY *adj* **-BLIER, -BLIEST** full of bubbles

BUBBLY *n pl.* **-BLIES** champagne

BUBINGA *n pl.* **-S** an African tree

BUBKES *n/pl* the least amount

BUBO *n pl.* **-BOES** a swelling of a lymph gland **BUBOED** *adj*

BUBONIC *adj* pertaining to a bubo

BUBU *n pl.* **-S** boubou

BUCCAL *adj* pertaining to the cheek **BUCCALLY** *adv*

BUCK *v* **-ED, -ING, -S** to leap forward and upward suddenly

BUCKAROO *n pl.* **-ROOS** a cowboy

BUCKAYRO *n pl.* **-ROS** buckaroo

BUCKBEAN *n pl.* **-S** a marsh plant

BUCKEEN *n pl.* **-S** a poor man who acts as if wealthy

BUCKER *n pl.* **-S** a bucking horse

BUCKEROO *n pl.* **-ROOS** buckaroo

BUCKET *v* **-ED, -ING, -S** to hurry

BUCKEYE *n pl.* **-S** a nut-bearing tree

BUCKISH *adj* foppish

BUCKLE *v* **-LED, -LING, -LES** to bend under pressure

BUCKLER *v* **-ED, -ING, -S** to shield

BUCKO *n pl.* **BUCKOS** or **BUCKOES** a bully

BUCKRAM *v* **-ED, -ING, -S** to stiffen

BUCKSAW *n pl.* **-S** a wood-cutting saw

BUCKSHEE *n pl.* **-S** something extra obtained free

BUCKSHOT *n pl.* **BUCKSHOT** a large lead shot

BUCKSKIN *n pl.* **-S** the skin of a male deer

BUCKTAIL *n pl.* **-S** a fishing lure

BUCOLIC *n pl.* **-S** a pastoral poem

BUD *v* **BUDDED, BUDDING, BUDS** to put forth buds (undeveloped plant parts)

BUDDER *n pl.* **-S** one that buds

BUDDIED past tense of buddy

BUDDIES present 3d person sing. of buddy

BUDDING *n pl.* **-S** a type of asexual reproduction

BUDDLE *n pl.* **-S** an apparatus on which crushed ore is washed

BUDDLEIA *n pl.* **-S** a tropical shrub

BUDDY *v* **-DIED, -DYING, -DIES** to become close friends

BUDGE *v* **BUDGED, BUDGING, BUDGES** to move slightly

BUDGER *n pl.* **-S** one that budges

BUDGET *v* **-ED, -ING, -S** to estimate expenditures

BUDGETER *n pl.* **-S** one that budgets

BUDGIE *n pl.* **-S** a small parrot

BUDGING present participle of budge

BUDLESS *adj* being without buds

BUDLIKE *adj* resembling a bud

BUDWORM *n pl.* **-S** a caterpillar that eats buds

BUFF *adj* **BUFFER, BUFFEST** having a muscular physique

BUFF *v* **-ED, -ING, -S** to polish **BUFFABLE** *adj*

BUFFALO *n pl.* **-LOS** or **-LOES** an ox-like animal

BUFFALO *v* **-ED, -ING, -ES** to intimidate

BUFFER *v* **-ED, -ING, -S** to cushion

BUFFET *v* **-ED, -ING, -S** to hit sharply

BUFFETER *n pl.* **-S** one that buffets

BUFFI a pl. of buffo

BUFFIER comparative of buffy

BUFFIEST superlative of buffy

BUFFO *n pl.* **-FOS** or **-FI** an operatic clown

BUFFOON *n pl.* **-S** a clown

BUFFY *adj* **BUFFIER, BUFFIEST** of a yellowish-brown color

BUG *v* **BUGGED, BUGGING, BUGS** to annoy

BUGABOO *n pl.* **-BOOS** a bugbear

BUGBANE *n pl.* **-S** a perennial herb

BUGBEAR *n pl.* **-S** an object or source of dread

BUGEYE *n pl.* **-S** a small boat

BUGGED past tense of bug

BUGGER *v* **-ED, -ING, -S** to damn

BUGGERY *n pl.* **-GERIES** sodomy

BUGGING present participle of bug

BUGGY *adj* **-GIER, -GIEST** infested with bugs

BUGGY *n pl.* **-GIES** a light carriage

BUGHOUSE *n pl.* **-S** an insane asylum

BUGLE *v* **-GLED, -GLING, -GLES** to play a bugle (a brass wind instrument)

BUGLER *n pl.* **-S** one that plays a bugle

BUGLOSS *n pl.* **-ES** a coarse plant

BUGOUT	*n* pl. **-S** one that leaves hurriedly
BUGSEED	*n* pl. **-S** an annual herb
BUGSHA	*n* pl. **-S** buqsha
BUHL	*n* pl. **-S** a style of furniture decoration
BUHLWORK	*n* pl. **-S** buhl
BUHR	*n* pl. **-S** a heavy stone
BUILD	*v* **BUILT** or **BUILDED, BUILDING, BUILDS** to construct
BUILDER	*n* pl. **-S** one that builds
BUILDING	*n* pl. **-S** something that is built
BUILDUP	*n* pl. **-S** an accumulation
BUILT	a past tense of build
BUIRDLY	*adj* burly
BULB	*n* pl. **-S** an underground bud **BULBAR, BULBED** *adj*
BULBEL	*n* pl. **-S** bulbil
BULBIL	*n* pl. **-S** a small bulb
BULBLET	*n* pl. **-S** a small bulb
BULBOUS	*adj* bulb-shaped; bulging
BULBUL	*n* pl. **-S** a songbird
BULGE	*v* **BULGED, BULGING, BULGES** to swell out
BULGER	*n* pl. **-S** a golf club
BULGHUR	*n* pl. **-S** bulgur
BULGUR	*n* pl. **-S** crushed wheat
BULGY	*adj* **BULGIER, BULGIEST** bulging
BULIMIA	*n* pl. **-S** insatiable appetite **BULIMIAC** *adj*
BULIMIC	*n* pl. **-S** one who is affected with bulimia
BULK	*v* **-ED, -ING, -S** to gather into a mass
BULKAGE	*n* pl. **-S** a peristaltic stimulant
BULKHEAD	*n* pl. **-S** a partition in a ship
BULKY	*adj* **BULKIER, BULKIEST** massive **BULKILY** *adv*
BULL	*v* **-ED, -ING, -S** to push ahead
BULLA	*n* pl. **-LAE** a large blister
BULLACE	*n* pl. **-S** a purple plum
BULLATE	*adj* blistered in appearance
BULLBAT	*n* pl. **-S** a nocturnal bird
BULLDOG	*v* **-DOGGED, -DOGGING, -DOGS** to throw a steer
BULLDOZE	*v* **-DOZED, -DOZING, -DOZES** to bully
BULLET	*v* **-ED, -ING, -S** to move swiftly

BULLETIN	*v* **-ED, -ING, -S** to issue a news item
BULLFROG	*n* pl. **-S** a large frog
BULLHEAD	*n* pl. **-S** a freshwater catfish
BULLHORN	*n* pl. **-S** an electric megaphone
BULLIED	past tense of bully
BULLIER	comparative of bully
BULLIES	present 3d person sing. of bully
BULLIEST	superlative of bully
BULLION	*n* pl. **-S** uncoined gold or silver
BULLISH	*adj* stubborn
BULLNECK	*n* pl. **-S** a thick neck
BULLNOSE	*n* pl. **-S** a disease of swine
BULLOCK	*n* pl. **-S** a castrated bull **BULLOCKY** *adj*
BULLOUS	*adj* resembling bullae
BULLPEN	*n* pl. **-S** an enclosure for bulls
BULLPOUT	*n* pl. **-S** a bullhead
BULLRING	*n* pl. **-S** a bullfight arena
BULLRUSH	*n* pl. **-ES** bulrush
BULLSHOT	*n* pl. **-S** a drink made of vodka and bouillon
BULLWEED	*n* pl. **-S** knapweed
BULLWHIP	*v* **-WHIPPED, -WHIPPING, -WHIPS** to strike with a long whip
BULLY	*adj* **-LIER, -LIEST** wonderful
BULLY	*v* **-LIED, -LYING, -LIES** to treat abusively
BULLYBOY	*n* pl. **-BOYS** a ruffian
BULLYRAG	*v* **-RAGGED, -RAGGING, -RAGS** to bully
BULRUSH	*n* pl. **-ES** a tall marsh plant
BULWARK	*v* **-ED, -ING, -S** to fortify with a defensive wall
BUM	*adj* **BUMMER, BUMMEST** of little value; worthless
BUM	*v* **BUMMED, BUMMING, BUMS** to live idly
BUMBLE	*v* **-BLED, -BLING, -BLES** to bungle
BUMBLER	*n* pl. **-S** one that bumbles
BUMBLING	*n* pl. **-S** an instance of clumsiness
BUMBOAT	*n* pl. **-S** a boat used to peddle wares to larger ships
BUMELIA	*n* pl. **-S** a thorny tree
BUMF	*n* pl. **-S** paperwork
BUMKIN	*n* pl. **-S** a ship's spar
BUMMALO	*n* pl. **-LOS** a small Asian fish

BUMMED	past tense of bum	**BUNTING**	n pl. **-S** a fabric used for flags
BUMMER	n pl. **-S** one that bums	**BUNTLINE**	n pl. **-S** a rope used to haul up a sail
BUMMEST	superlative of bum		
BUMMING	present participle of bum	**BUNYA**	n pl. **-S** an evergreen tree
BUMP	v **-ED, -ING, -S** to knock against	**BUOY**	v **-ED, -ING, -S** to mark with a buoy (a warning float)
BUMPER	v **-ED, -ING, -S** to fill to the brim		
BUMPH	n pl. **-S** bumf	**BUOYAGE**	n pl. **-S** a group of buoys
BUMPKIN	n pl. **-S** an unsophisticated rustic	**BUOYANCE**	n pl. **-S** buoyancy
BUMPY	adj **BUMPIER, BUMPIEST** of uneven surface **BUMPILY** adv	**BUOYANCY**	n pl. **-CIES** the tendency to float
		BUOYANT	adj having buoyancy
BUN	n pl. **-S** a small bread roll	**BUPKES**	n/pl bubkes
BUNA	n pl. **-S** a synthetic rubber	**BUPKUS**	n/pl bubkes
BUNCH	v **-ED, -ING, -ES** to group together	**BUPPIE**	n pl. **-S** a black professional person working in a city
BUNCHY	adj **BUNCHIER, BUNCHIEST** clustered **BUNCHILY** adv	**BUPPY**	n pl. **-PIES** buppie
BUNCO	v **-ED, -ING, -S** to swindle	**BUQSHA**	n pl. **-S** a monetary unit of Yemen
BUNCOMBE	n pl. **-S** nonsense	**BUR**	v **BURRED, BURRING, BURS** to burr
BUND	n pl. **-S** a political association		
BUNDIST	n pl. **-S** a member of a bund	**BURA**	n pl. **-S** buran
BUNDLE	v **-DLED, -DLING, -DLES** to fasten a group of objects together	**BURAN**	n pl. **-S** a violent windstorm
		BURB	n pl. **-S** a suburb
BUNDLER	n pl. **-S** one that bundles	**BURBLE**	v **-BLED, -BLING, -BLES** to speak quickly and excitedly
BUNDLING	n pl. **-S** a former courtship custom		
BUNDT	n pl. **-S** a type of cake pan	**BURBLER**	n pl. **-S** one that burbles
BUNG	v **-ED, -ING, -S** to plug with a cork or stopper	**BURBLY**	adj **-BLIER, -BLIEST** burbling
		BURBOT	n pl. **-S** a freshwater fish
BUNGALOW	n pl. **-S** a small cottage	**BURD**	n pl. **-S** a maiden
BUNGEE	n pl. **-S** an elasticized cord	**BURDEN**	v **-ED, -ING, -S** to load heavily
BUNGHOLE	n pl. **-S** a hole in a keg or barrel	**BURDENER**	n pl. **-S** one that burdens
BUNGLE	v **-GLED, -GLING, -GLES** to work, make, or do clumsily	**BURDIE**	n pl. **-S** burd
		BURDOCK	n pl. **-S** a coarse weed
BUNGLER	n pl. **-S** one that bungles	**BUREAU**	n pl. **-REAUS** or **-REAUX** a chest of drawers
BUNGLING	n pl. **-S** something done clumsily		
BUNION	n pl. **-S** a painful swelling of the foot	**BURET**	n pl. **-S** burette
		BURETTE	n pl. **-S** a measuring tube
BUNK	v **-ED, -ING, -S** to go to bed	**BURG**	n pl. **-S** a city or town
BUNKER	v **-ED, -ING, -S** to store in a large bin	**BURGAGE**	n pl. **-S** a feudal tenure
		BURGEE	n pl. **-S** a small flag
BUNKMATE	n pl. **-S** a person with whom sleeping quarters are shared	**BURGEON**	v **-ED, -ING, -S** to develop rapidly
		BURGER	n pl. **-S** a hamburger
BUNKO	v **-ED, -ING, -S** to bunco	**BURGESS**	n pl. **-ES** a citizen of an English borough
BUNKUM	n pl. **-S** nonsense		
BUNN	n pl. **-S** bun	**BURGH**	n pl. **-S** a Scottish borough **BURGHAL** adj
BUNNY	n pl. **-NIES** a rabbit		
BUNRAKU	n pl. **-S** a Japanese puppet show	**BURGHER**	n pl. **-S** a citizen of a borough
BUNT	v **-ED, -ING, -S** to butt	**BURGLAR**	n pl. **-S** one who commits burglary
BUNTER	n pl. **-S** one that bunts		

BURGLARY	*n* pl. **-GLARIES** a felonious theft
BURGLE	*v* **-GLED, -GLING, -GLES** to commit burglary
BURGONET	*n* pl. **-S** an open helmet
BURGOO	*n* pl. **-GOOS** a thick oatmeal
BURGOUT	*n* pl. **-S** burgoo
BURGRAVE	*n* pl. **-S** a German nobleman
BURGUNDY	*n* pl. **-DIES** a red wine
BURIAL	*n* pl. **-S** the act of burying
BURIED	past tense of bury
BURIER	*n* pl. **-S** one that buries
BURIES	present 3d person sing. of bury
BURIN	*n* pl. **-S** an engraving tool
BURKA	*n* pl. **-S** a long loose outer garment worn by some Muslim women
BURKE	*v* **BURKED, BURKING, BURKES** to murder by suffocation
BURKER	*n* pl. **-S** one that burkes
BURKITE	*n* pl. **-S** a burker
BURL	*v* **-ED, -ING, -S** to finish cloth by removing lumps
BURLAP	*n* pl. **-S** a coarse fabric
BURLER	*n* pl. **-S** one that burls
BURLESK	*n* pl. **-S** a type of stage show
BURLEY	*n* pl. **-LEYS** a light tobacco
BURLY	*adj* **-LIER, -LIEST** heavy and muscular **BURLILY** *adv*
BURN	*v* **BURNED** or **BURNT, BURNING, BURNS** to destroy by fire
BURNABLE	*n* pl. **-S** something that can be burned
BURNER	*n* pl. **-S** one that burns
BURNET	*n* pl. **-S** a perennial herb
BURNIE	*n* pl. **-S** a brooklet
BURNING	*n* pl. **-S** the firing of ceramic materials
BURNISH	*v* **-ED, -ING, -ES** to polish
BURNOOSE	*n* pl. **-S** a hooded cloak
BURNOUS	*n* pl. **-ES** burnoose
BURNOUT	*n* pl. **-S** a destructive fire
BURNT	a past tense of burn
BURP	*v* **-ED, -ING, -S** to belch
BURQA	*n* pl. **-S** burka
BURR	*v* **-ED, -ING, -S** to remove a rough edge from
BURRED	past tense of bur
BURRER	*n* pl. **-S** one that burrs

BURRIER	comparative of burry
BURRIEST	superlative of burry
BURRING	present participle of bur
BURRITO	*n* pl. **-TOS** a tortilla rolled around a filling
BURRO	*n* pl. **-ROS** a small donkey
BURROW	*v* **-ED, -ING, -S** to dig a hole or tunnel in the ground
BURROWER	*n* pl. **-S** one that burrows
BURRY	*adj* **-RIER, -RIEST** prickly
BURSA	*n* pl. **-SAS** or **-SAE** a bodily pouch **BURSAL** *adj*
BURSAR	*n* pl. **-S** a college treasurer
BURSARY	*n* pl. **-RIES** a college treasury
BURSATE	*adj* pertaining to a bursa
BURSE	*n* pl. **-S** a small bag or pouch
BURSEED	*n* pl. **-S** a coarse weed
BURSERA	*adj* designating a family of shrubs and trees
BURSITIS	*n* pl. **-TISES** inflammation of a bursa
BURST	*v* **BURSTED** or **BURST, BURSTING, BURSTS** to break open suddenly or violently
BURSTER	*n* pl. **-S** one that bursts
BURSTONE	*n* pl. **-S** a heavy stone
BURTHEN	*v* **-ED, -ING, -S** to burden
BURTON	*n* pl. **-S** a hoisting tackle
BURWEED	*n* pl. **-S** a coarse weed
BURY	*v* **BURIED, BURYING, BURIES** to put in the ground and cover with earth
BUS	*v* **BUSED, BUSING, BUSES** or **BUSSED, BUSSING, BUSSES** to transport by bus (a large motor vehicle)
BUSBAR	*n* pl. **-S** a type of electrical conductor
BUSBOY	*n* pl. **-BOYS** a boy or man who is a server's assistant in a restaurant
BUSBY	*n* pl. **-BIES** a tall fur hat
BUSGIRL	*n* pl. **-S** a girl or woman who is a server's assistant in a restaurant
BUSH	*v* **-ED, -ING, -ES** to cover with bushes (shrubs)
BUSHBUCK	*n* pl. **-S** a small antelope
BUSHEL	*v* **-ELED, -ELING, -ELS** or **-ELLED, -ELLING, -ELS** to mend clothing
BUSHELER	*n* pl. **-S** one that bushels

BUSHER *n* pl. **-S** a minor league baseball player

BUSHFIRE *n* pl. **-S** a fire in a wooded area

BUSHGOAT *n* pl. **-S** a bushbuck

BUSHIDO *n* pl. **-DOS** the code of the samurai

BUSHIER comparative of bushy

BUSHIEST superlative of bushy

BUSHILY *adv* in a bushy manner

BUSHING *n* pl. **-S** a lining for a hole

BUSHLAND *n* pl. **-S** unsettled forest land

BUSHLESS *adj* having no bushes

BUSHLIKE *adj* resembling a bush

BUSHMAN *n* pl. **-MEN** a woodsman

BUSHPIG *n* pl. **-S** a wild African pig

BUSHTIT *n* pl. **-S** a titmouse

BUSHVELD *n* pl. **-S** a veld with shrubby vegetation

BUSHWA *n* pl. **-S** nonsense

BUSHWAH *n* pl. **-S** bushwa

BUSHY *adj* **BUSHIER, BUSHIEST** covered with bushes

BUSIED past tense of busy

BUSIER comparative of busy

BUSIES present 3d person sing. of busy

BUSIEST superlative of busy

BUSILY *adv* in a busy manner

BUSINESS *n* pl. **-ES** an occupation, profession, or trade

BUSING *n* pl. **-S** the act of transporting by bus

BUSK *v* **-ED, -ING, -S** to prepare

BUSKER *n* pl. **-S** a roaming entertainer

BUSKIN *n* pl. **-S** a high shoe **BUSKINED** *adj*

BUSLOAD *n* pl. **-S** a load that fills a bus

BUSMAN *n* pl. **-MEN** a bus operator

BUSS *v* **-ED, -ING, -ES** to kiss

BUSSED a past tense of bus

BUSSES a present 3d person sing. of bus

BUSSING *n* pl. **-S** busing

BUST *v* **-ED, -ING, -S** to burst

BUSTARD *n* pl. **-S** a game bird

BUSTER *n* pl. **-S** one that breaks up something

BUSTIC *n* pl. **-S** a tropical tree

BUSTIER *n* pl. **-S** a woman's undergarment

BUSTLE *v* **-TLED, -TLING, -TLES** to move energetically

BUSTLER *n* pl. **-S** one that bustles

BUSTLINE *n* pl. **-S** the distance around the bust (the upper torso of a woman)

BUSTY *adj* **BUSTIER, BUSTIEST** full-bosomed

BUSULFAN *n* pl. **-S** a medicine

BUSY *adj* **BUSIER, BUSIEST** occupied

BUSY *v* **BUSIED, BUSYING, BUSIES** to make busy

BUSYBODY *n* pl. **-BODIES** a nosy person

BUSYNESS *n* pl. **-ES** the state of being busy

BUSYWORK *n* pl. **-S** active but valueless work

BUT *n* pl. **-S** a flatfish

BUTANE *n* pl. **-S** a flammable gas

BUTANOL *n* pl. **-S** a flammable alcohol

BUTANONE *n* pl. **-S** a flammable ketone

BUTCH *n* pl. **-ES** a lesbian with mannish traits

BUTCHER *v* **-ED, -ING, -S** to slaughter

BUTCHERY *n* pl. **-ERIES** wanton or cruel killing

BUTE *n* pl. **-S** a drug for treating arthritis

BUTENE *n* pl. **-S** butylene

BUTEO *n* pl. **-TEOS** a hawk

BUTLE *v* **-LED, -LING, -LES** to serve as a butler

BUTLER *n* pl. **-S** a male servant

BUTLERY *n* pl. **-LERIES** a storage room

BUTLES present 3d person sing. of butle

BUTLING present participle of butle

BUTT *v* **-ED, -ING, -S** to hit with the head

BUTTALS *n/pl* boundary lines

BUTTE *n* pl. **-S** an isolated hill

BUTTER *v* **-ED, -ING, -S** to spread with butter (a milk product)

BUTTERY *adj* **-TERIER, -TERIEST** containing butter

BUTTERY *n* pl. **-TERIES** a wine cellar

BUTTHEAD *n* pl. **-S** a stupid person

BUTTIES pl. of butty

BUTTOCK *n* pl. **-S** either of the two rounded parts of the rump

BUTTON *v* **-ED, -ING, -S** to fasten with a button (a small disk)

BUTTONER *n* pl. **-S** one that buttons

BUTTONY *adj* resembling a button

BUTTRESS *v* **-ED, -ING, -ES** to prop up

BUTTY *n* pl. **-TIES** a fellow workman

BUTUT *n* pl. **-S** a monetary unit of Gambia

BUTYL *n* pl. **-S** a hydrocarbon radical

BUTYLATE *v* **-ATED, -ATING, -ATES** to add a butyl to

BUTYLENE *n* pl. **-S** a gaseous hydrocarbon

BUTYRAL *n* pl. **-S** a chemical compound

BUTYRATE *n* pl. **-S** a chemical salt

BUTYRIC *adj* derived from butter

BUTYRIN *n* pl. **-S** a chemical compound

BUTYROUS *adj* resembling butter

BUTYRYL *n* pl. **-S** a radical of butyric acid

BUXOM *adj* **-OMER, -OMEST** healthily plump **BUXOMLY** *adv*

BUY *v* **BOUGHT, BUYING, BUYS** to purchase **BUYABLE** *adj*

BUYBACK *n* pl. **-S** the repurchase by a corporation of its own stock

BUYER *n* pl. **-S** one that buys

BUYOFF *n* pl. **-S** a payment for a consideration

BUYOUT *n* pl. **-S** the purchase of a business

BUZUKI *n* pl. **-KIS** or **-KIA** bouzouki

BUZZ *v* **-ED, -ING, -ES** to make a vibrating sound

BUZZARD *n* pl. **-S** a large bird of prey

BUZZCUT *n* pl. **-S** a very short haircut

BUZZER *n* pl. **-S** a signaling device

BUZZWIG *n* pl. **-S** a large, thick wig

BUZZWORD *n* pl. **-S** a word used to impress someone

BWANA *n* pl. **-S** master; boss

BY *n* pl. **BYS** a pass in certain card games

BYCATCH *n* pl. **-ES** marine animals caught unintentionally

BYE *n* pl. **-S** a side issue

BYELAW *n* pl. **-S** bylaw

BYGONE *n* pl. **-S** a past occurrence

BYLAW *n* pl. **-S** a secondary law

BYLINE *v* **-LINED, -LINING, -LINES** to write under a byline (a line giving the author's name)

BYLINER *n* pl. **-S** one that writes under a byline

BYNAME *n* pl. **-S** a secondary name

BYPASS *v* **-ED, -ING, -ES** to avoid by going around

BYPAST *adj* past; gone by

BYPATH *n* pl. **-S** an indirect road

BYPLAY *n* pl. **-PLAYS** secondary action

BYRE *n* pl. **-S** a cowshed

BYRL *v* **-ED, -ING, -S** to birle

BYRNIE *n* pl. **-S** an armored shirt

BYROAD *n* pl. **-S** a side road

BYSSUS *n* pl. **BYSSUSES** or **BYSSI** a fine linen **BYSSAL** *adj*

BYSTREET *n* pl. **-S** a side street

BYTALK *n* pl. **-S** small talk

BYTE *n* pl. **-S** a group of adjacent binary digits

BYWAY *n* pl. **-WAYS** a side road

BYWORD *n* pl. **-S** a well-known saying

BYWORK *n* pl. **-S** work done during leisure time

BYZANT *n* pl. **-S** bezant

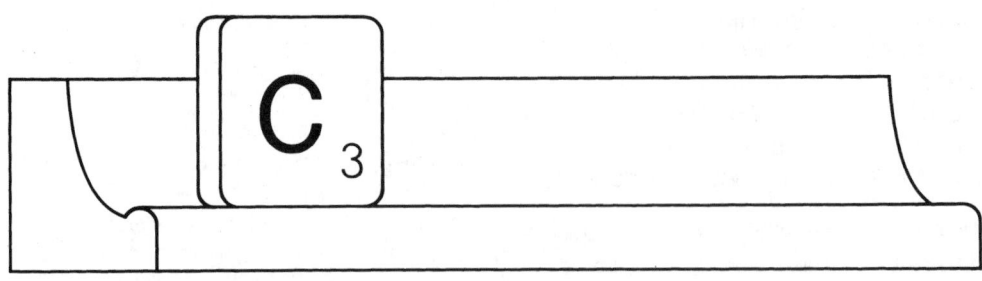

CAB	*v* **CABBED, CABBING, CABS** to take or drive a taxicab
CABAL	*v* **-BALLED, -BALLING, -BALS** to conspire
CABALA	*n* pl. **-S** an occult or secret doctrine
CABALISM	*n* pl. **-S** adherence to a cabala
CABALIST	*n* pl. **-S** one who practices cabalism
CABALLED	past tense of cabal
CABALLING	present participle of cabal
CABANA	*n* pl. **-S** a small cabin
CABARET	*n* pl. **-S** a music hall
CABBAGE	*v* **-BAGED, -BAGING, -BAGES** to steal
CABBAGEY	*adj* resembling a cabbage (a leafy vegetable)
CABBAGY	*adj* cabbagey
CABBALA	*n* pl. **-S** cabala
CABBALAH	*n* pl. **-S** cabala
CABBED	past tense of cab
CABBIE	*n* pl. **-S** cabby
CABBING	present participle of cab
CABBY	*n* pl. **-BIES** a driver of a cab
CABER	*n* pl. **-S** a heavy pole thrown as a trial of strength
CABERNET	*n* pl. **-S** a dry red wine
CABESTRO	*n* pl. **-TROS** a lasso
CABEZON	*n* pl. **-S** a large, edible fish
CABEZONE	*n* pl. **-S** cabezon
CABILDO	*n* pl. **-DOS** a town council
CABIN	*v* **-ED, -ING, -S** to live in a cabin (a roughly built house)
CABINET	*n* pl. **-S** a piece of furniture with shelves and drawers
CABLE	*v* **-BLED, -BLING, -BLES** to fasten with a cable (a heavy rope)
CABLER	*n* pl. **-S** one that supplies a cable
CABLET	*n* pl. **-S** a small cable
CABLEWAY	*n* pl. **-WAYS** a suspended cable
CABLING	present participle of cable
CABMAN	*n* pl. **-MEN** a driver of a cab
CABOB	*n* pl. **-S** kabob
CABOCHED	*adj* full-faced — used of an animal's head in heraldry
CABOCHON	*n* pl. **-S** a precious stone
CABOMBA	*n* pl. **-S** an aquatic plant
CABOODLE	*n* pl. **-S** a collection
CABOOSE	*n* pl. **-S** the last car of a freight train
CABOSHED	*adj* caboched
CABOTAGE	*n* pl. **-S** coastal trade
CABRESTA	*n* pl. **-S** cabestro
CABRESTO	*n* pl. **-TOS** cabestro
CABRETTA	*n* pl. **-S** a soft leather
CABRILLA	*n* pl. **-S** a sea bass
CABRIOLE	*n* pl. **-S** a curved furniture leg
CABSTAND	*n* pl. **-S** a place where cabs await hire
CACA	*n* pl. **-S** excrement
CACAO	*n* pl. **-CAOS** a tropical tree
CACHALOT	*n* pl. **-S** a large whale
CACHE	*v* **CACHED, CACHING, CACHES** to store in a hiding place
CACHEPOT	*n* pl. **-S** an ornamental container for a flowerpot
CACHET	*v* **-ED, -ING, -S** to print a design on an envelope
CACHEXIA	*n* pl. **-S** general ill health **CACHEXIC** *adj*
CACHEXY	*n* pl. **-CHEXIES** cachexia
CACHING	present participle of cache
CACHOU	*n* pl. **-S** catechu
CACHUCHA	*n* pl. **-S** a Spanish dance
CACIQUE	*n* pl. **-S** a tropical oriole

CACKLE   *v* **-LED, -LING, -LES** to make the sound of a hen

CACKLER   *n* pl. **-S** one that cackles

CACODYL   *n* pl. **-S** a poisonous liquid

CACOMIXL   *n* pl. **-S** a raccoon-like mammal

CACONYM   *n* pl. **-S** an erroneous name

CACONYMY   *n* pl. **-MIES** the state of having an erroneous name

CACTUS   *n* pl. **-TUSES** or **-TI** a plant native to arid regions **CACTOID** *adj*

CAD   *n* pl. **-S** an ungentlemanly man

CADASTER   *n* pl. **-S** a public record of land ownership

CADASTRE   *n* pl. **-S** cadaster

CADAVER   *n* pl. **-S** a corpse

CADDICE   *n* pl. **-S** caddis

CADDIE   *v* **-DIED, -DYING, -DIES** to serve as a golfer's assistant

CADDIS   *n* pl. **-DISES** a coarse woolen fabric **CADDISED** *adj*

CADDISH   *adj* resembling a cad

CADDY   *v* **-DIED, -DYING, -DIES** to caddie

CADE   *n* pl. **-S** a European shrub

CADELLE   *n* pl. **-S** a small, black beetle

CADENCE   *v* **-DENCED, -DENCING, -DENCES** to make rhythmic

CADENCY   *n* pl. **-CIES** a rhythm

CADENT   *adj* having rhythm

CADENZA   *n* pl. **-S** an elaborate musical passage

CADET   *n* pl. **-S** a student at a military school

CADGE   *v* **CADGED, CADGING, CADGES** to get by begging

CADGER   *n* pl. **-S** one that cadges

CADGY   *adj* cheerful

CADI   *n* pl. **-S** a Muslim judge

CADMIUM   *n* pl. **-S** a metallic element **CADMIC** *adj*

CADRE   *n* pl. **-S** a nucleus of trained personnel

CADUCEUS   *n* pl. **-CEI** a heraldic wand or staff **CADUCEAN** *adj*

CADUCITY   *n* pl. **-TIES** senility

CADUCOUS   *adj* transitory; perishable

CAECUM   *n* pl. **-CA** cecum **CAECAL** *adj* **CAECALLY** *adv*

CAEOMA   *n* pl. **-S** a spore-forming organ of a fungus

CAESAR   *n* pl. **-S** an emperor

CAESIUM   *n* pl. **-S** cesium

CAESTUS   *n* pl. **-ES** cestus

CAESURA   *n* pl. **-RAS** or **-RAE** a pause in a line of verse **CAESURAL, CAESURIC** *adj*

CAFE   *n* pl. **-S** a small restaurant

CAFF   *n* pl. **-S** a cafe

CAFFEIN   *n* pl. **-S** caffeine

CAFFEINE   *n* pl. **-S** a bitter alkaloid used as a stimulant

CAFTAN   *n* pl. **-S** a full-length tunic **CAFTANED** *adj*

CAGE   *v* **CAGED, CAGING, CAGES** to confine

CAGEFUL   *n* pl. **-S** the number held in a cage (an enclosure)

CAGELIKE   *adj* resembling a cage (an enclosure)

CAGELING   *n* pl. **-S** a caged bird

CAGER   *n* pl. **-S** a basketball player

CAGEY   *adj* **CAGIER, CAGIEST** shrewd

CAGIER   comparative of cagy

CAGIEST   superlative of cagy

CAGILY   *adv* in a cagey manner

CAGINESS   *n* pl. **-ES** the quality of being cagey

CAGING   present participle of cage

CAGY   *adj* **CAGIER, CAGIEST** cagey

CAHIER   *n* pl. **-S** a notebook

CAHOOT   *n* pl. **-S** partnership

CAHOW   *n* pl. **-S** a sea bird

CAID   *n* pl. **-S** a Muslim leader

CAIMAN   *n* pl. **-S** a tropical reptile

CAIN   *n* pl. **-S** kain

CAIQUE   *n* pl. **-S** a long, narrow rowboat

CAIRD   *n* pl. **-S** a gypsy

CAIRN   *n* pl. **-S** a mound of stones set up as a memorial **CAIRNED, CAIRNY** *adj*

CAISSON   *n* pl. **-S** a watertight chamber

CAITIFF   *n* pl. **-S** a despicable person

CAJAPUT   *n* pl. **-S** cajeput

CAJEPUT   *n* pl. **-S** an Australian tree

CAJOLE   *v* **-JOLED, -JOLING, -JOLES** to persuade by flattery

CAJOLER   *n* pl. **-S** one that cajoles

CAJOLERY   *n* pl. **-ERIES** persuasion by flattery

CAJON *n* pl. **-ES** a steep-sided canyon

CAJUPUT *n* pl. **-S** cajeput

CAKE *v* **CAKED, CAKING, CAKES** to form into a hardened mass

CAKEWALK *v* **-ED, -ING, -S** to step stylishly

CAKEY *adj* **CAKIER, CAKIEST** tending to form lumps

CAKINESS *n* pl. **-ES** the state of being cakey

CAKY *adj* **CAKIER, CAKIEST** cakey

CALABASH *n* pl. **-ES** a gourd

CALABAZA *n* pl. **-S** a large winter squash

CALADIUM *n* pl. **-S** a tropical plant

CALAMAR *n* pl. **-S** calamary

CALAMARI *n* pl. **-S** squid used as food

CALAMARY *n* pl. **-MARIES** a squid

CALAMATA *n* pl. **-S** kalamata

CALAMI pl. of calamus

CALAMINE *v* **-MINED, -MINING, -MINES** to apply an ointment for skin ailments

CALAMINT *n* pl. **-S** a perennial herb

CALAMITE *n* pl. **-S** an extinct treelike plant

CALAMITY *n* pl. **-TIES** a grievous misfortune

CALAMUS *n* pl. **-MI** a marsh plant

CALANDO *adj* gradually diminishing

CALASH *n* pl. **-ES** a light carriage

CALATHOS *n* pl. **-THI** a fruit basket

CALATHUS *n* pl. **-THI** calathos

CALCANEA *n/pl* calcanei

CALCANEI *n/pl* bones of the heel

CALCAR *n* pl. **-CARIA** an anatomical projection

CALCAR *n* pl. **-S** a type of oven

CALCEATE *adj* wearing shoes

CALCES a pl. of calx

CALCIC *adj* pertaining to lime or calcium

CALCIFIC *adj* containing salts of calcium

CALCIFY *v* **-FIED, -FYING, -FIES** to harden

CALCINE *v* **-CINED, -CINING, -CINES** to reduce to a calx by heat

CALCITE *n* pl. **-S** a mineral **CALCITIC** *adj*

CALCIUM *n* pl. **-S** a metallic element

CALCSPAR *n* pl. **-S** a calcite

CALCTUFA *n* pl. **-S** a mineral deposit

CALCTUFF *n* pl. **-S** calctufa

CALCULUS *n* pl. **-LUSES** or **-LI** a branch of mathematics

CALDARIA *n/pl* rooms for taking hot baths

CALDERA *n* pl. **-S** a large crater

CALDRON *n* pl. **-S** a large kettle or boiler

CALECHE *n* pl. **-S** calash

CALENDAL *adj* pertaining to calends

CALENDAR *v* **-ED, -ING, -S** to schedule

CALENDER *v* **-ED, -ING, -S** to smooth by pressing between rollers

CALENDS *n* pl. **CALENDS** the first day of the Roman month

CALESA *n* pl. **-S** a calash

CALF *n* pl. **CALVES** or **CALFS** a young cow or bull **CALFLIKE** *adj*

CALFSKIN *n* pl. **-S** the skin of a calf

CALIBER *n* pl. **-S** the diameter of a gun barrel

CALIBRE *n* pl. **-S** caliber **CALIBRED** *adj*

CALICES pl. of calix

CALICHE *n* pl. **-S** a mineral deposit

CALICLE *n* pl. **-S** a cup-shaped anatomical structure

CALICO *n* pl. **-COS** or **-COES** a cotton fabric

CALIF *n* pl. **-S** caliph

CALIFATE *n* pl. **-S** the domain of a calif

CALIPASH *n* pl. **-ES** an edible part of a turtle

CALIPEE *n* pl. **-S** an edible part of a turtle

CALIPER *v* **-ED, -ING, -S** to use a type of measuring device

CALIPH *n* pl. **-S** a Muslim leader **CALIPHAL** *adj*

CALISAYA *n* pl. **-S** the medicinal bark of the cinchona

CALIX *n* pl. **-LICES** a cup

CALK *v* **-ED, -ING, -S** to caulk

CALKER *n* pl. **-S** one that calks

CALKIN *n* pl. **-S** a gripping projection on a horseshoe

CALKING *n* pl. **-S** material used to calk

CALL *v* **-ED, -ING, -S** to summon **CALLABLE** *adj*

CALLA *n* pl. **-S** a tropical plant

CALLALOO *n* pl. **-LOOS** a crabmeat soup

CALLAN *n* pl. **-S** callant

CALLANT *n* pl. **-S** a lad

CALLBACK *n* pl. **-S** a recall of a defective product

CALLBOY *n* pl. **-BOYS** a bellboy

CALLEE *n* pl. **-S** one that is called

CALLER *n* pl. **-S** one that calls

CALLET *n* pl. **-S** a prostitute

CALLING *n* pl. **-S** a vocation or profession

CALLIOPE *n* pl. **-S** a keyboard musical instrument

CALLIPEE *n* pl. **-S** calipee

CALLIPER *v* **-ED, -ING, -S** to caliper

CALLOSE *n* pl. **-S** a part of a plant cell wall

CALLOUS *v* **-ED, -ING, -ES** to make or become hard

CALLOW *adj* **-LOWER, -LOWEST** immature

CALLUS *v* **-ED, -ING, -ES** to form a hard growth

CALM *adj* **CALMER, CALMEST** free from agitation **CALMLY** *adv*

CALM *v* **-ED, -ING, -S** to make calm

CALMNESS *n* pl. **-ES** the state of being calm

CALO *n* pl. **-LOS** a Spanish argot used by Chicano youths

CALOMEL *n* pl. **-S** a chemical compound used as a purgative

CALORIC *n* pl. **-S** heat

CALORIE *n* pl. **-S** a unit of heat

CALORIZE *v* **-RIZED, -RIZING, -RIZES** to coat steel with aluminum

CALORY *n* pl. **-RIES** calorie

CALOTTE *n* pl. **-S** a skullcap

CALOTYPE *n* pl. **-S** a kind of photograph

CALOYER *n* pl. **-S** a monk of the Eastern Church

CALPAC *n* pl. **-S** a sheepskin hat

CALPACK *n* pl. **-S** calpac

CALPAIN *n* pl. **-S** an enzyme for digesting proteins

CALQUE *v* **CALQUED, CALQUING, CALQUES** to model a word's meaning upon that of an analogous word in another language

CALTHROP *n* pl. **-S** caltrop

CALTRAP *n* pl. **-S** caltrop

CALTROP *n* pl. **-S** a spiny plant

CALUMET *n* pl. **-S** a ceremonial pipe

CALUMNY *n* pl. **-NIES** a false and malicious accusation

CALUTRON *n* pl. **-S** a device used for separating isotopes

CALVADOS *n* pl. **-ES** a dry apple brandy

CALVARIA *n* pl. **-S** the dome of the skull

CALVARY *n* pl. **-RIES** a representation of the Crucifixion

CALVE *v* **CALVED, CALVING, CALVES** to give birth to a calf

CALVES a pl. of calf

CALX *n* pl. **-ES** or **CALCES** a mineral residue

CALYCATE *adj* calycine

CALYCEAL *adj* calycine

CALYCES a pl. of calyx

CALYCINE *adj* pertaining to a calyx

CALYCLE *n* pl. **-S** an outer calyx

CALYCULI *n/pl* small, cup-shaped structures

CALYPSO *n* pl. **-SOS** or **-SOES** an improvised song

CALYPTER *n* pl. **-S** calyptra

CALYPTRA *n* pl. **-S** a hood-shaped organ of flowers

CALYX *n* pl. **-LYXES** or **-LYCES** the outer protective covering of a flower

CALZONE *n* pl. **-S** a turnover with a savory filling

CAM *n* pl. **-S** a rotating or sliding piece of machinery

CAMAIL *n* pl. **-S** a piece of armor for the neck **CAMAILED** *adj*

CAMAS *n* pl. **-ES** camass

CAMASS *n* pl. **-ES** a perennial herb

CAMBER *v* **-ED, -ING, -S** to arch slightly

CAMBIA a pl. of cambium

CAMBIAL *adj* pertaining to cambium

CAMBISM *n* pl. **-S** the theory and practice of exchange in commerce

CAMBIST *n* pl. **-S** a dealer in bills of exchange

CAMBIUM *n* pl. **-BIUMS** or **-BIA** a layer of plant tissue

CAMBOGIA *n* pl. **-S** a gum resin

CAMBRIC *n* pl. **-S** a fine linen

CAME *n* pl. **-S** a leaden window rod

CAMEL *n* pl. **-S** a large, humped mammal

CAMELEER *n* pl. **-S** a camel driver

CAMELIA *n* pl. **-S** camellia

CAMELID *n* pl. **-S** any of a family of 2-toed ruminant mammals

CAMELLIA *n* pl. **-S** a tropical shrub

CAMEO *v* **-ED, -ING, -S** to portray in sharp, delicate relief

CAMERA	*n* pl. **-ERAS** or **-ERAE** a judge's chamber **CAMERAL** *adj*
CAMION	*n* pl. **-S** a military truck
CAMISA	*n* pl. **-S** a shirt or chemise
CAMISADE	*n* pl. **-S** camisado
CAMISADO	*n* pl. **-DOS** or **-DOES** an attack made at night
CAMISE	*n* pl. **-S** a loose shirt or gown
CAMISIA	*n* pl. **-S** camise
CAMISOLE	*n* pl. **-S** a brief negligee
CAMLET	*n* pl. **-S** a durable fabric
CAMMIE	*n* pl. **-S** camouflage
CAMO	*n* pl. **CAMOS** a camouflage pattern
CAMOMILE	*n* pl. **-S** a medicinal herb
CAMORRA	*n* pl. **-S** an unscrupulous secret society
CAMP	*v* **-ED, -ING, -S** to live in the open
CAMPAGNA	*n* pl. **-PAGNE** a flat, open plain
CAMPAIGN	*v* **-ED, -ING, -S** to conduct a series of operations to reach a specific goal
CAMPER	*n* pl. **-S** one that camps
CAMPFIRE	*n* pl. **-S** an outdoor fire
CAMPHENE	*n* pl. **-S** camphine
CAMPHINE	*n* pl. **-S** an explosive liquid
CAMPHIRE	*n* pl. **-S** a flowering plant
CAMPHOL	*n* pl. **-S** borneol
CAMPHOR	*n* pl. **-S** a volatile compound
CAMPI	pl. of campo
CAMPIER	comparative of campy
CAMPIEST	superlative of campy
CAMPILY	*adv* in a campy manner
CAMPING	*n* pl. **-S** the act of living outdoors
CAMPION	*n* pl. **-S** an herb
CAMPO	*n* pl. **-PI** an open space in a town
CAMPO	*n* pl. **-POS** a level, grassy plain
CAMPONG	*n* pl. **-S** kampong
CAMPOREE	*n* pl. **-S** a gathering of Boy Scouts
CAMPOUT	*n* pl. **-S** a camping out by a group
CAMPSITE	*n* pl. **-S** an area suitable for camping
CAMPUS	*v* **-ED, -ING, -ES** to restrict a student to the school grounds
CAMPY	*adj* **CAMPIER, CAMPIEST** comically exaggerated
CAMSHAFT	*n* pl. **-S** a shaft fitted with cams
CAN	*v* **CANNED, CANNING, CANS** to put in a can (a cylindrical container)
CAN	*v* present sing. 2d person **CAN** or **CANST,** past sing. 2d person **COULD** or **COULDEST** or **COULDST** — used as an auxiliary to express ability
CANAILLE	*n* pl. **-S** the common people
CANAKIN	*n* pl. **-S** cannikin
CANAL	*v* **-NALLED, -NALLING, -NALS** or **-NALED, -NALING, -NALS** to dig an artificial waterway through
CANALISE	*v* **-ISED, -ISING, -ISES** to canalize
CANALIZE	*v* **-IZED, -IZING, -IZES** to canal
CANALLER	*n* pl. **-S** a freight boat
CANALLING	a present participle of canal
CANAPE	*n* pl. **-S** a food served before a meal
CANARD	*n* pl. **-S** a false story
CANARY	*n* pl. **-NARIES** a songbird
CANASTA	*n* pl. **-S** a card game
CANCAN	*n* pl. **-S** a dance marked by high kicking
CANCEL	*v* **-CELED, -CELING, -CELS** or **-CELLED, -CELLING, -CELS** to annul
CANCELER	*n* pl. **-S** one that cancels
CANCER	*n* pl. **-S** a malignant growth **CANCERED** *adj*
CANCHA	*n* pl. **-S** a jai alai court
CANCROID	*n* pl. **-S** a skin cancer
CANDELA	*n* pl. **-S** a unit of light intensity
CANDENT	*adj* glowing
CANDID	*adj* **-DIDER, -DIDEST** frank and sincere
CANDID	*n* pl. **-S** an unposed photograph
CANDIDA	*n* pl. **-S** a parasitic fungus **CANDIDAL** *adj*
CANDIDLY	*adv* in a candid manner
CANDIED	past tense of candy
CANDIES	present 3d person sing. of candy
CANDLE	*v* **-DLED, -DLING, -DLES** to examine eggs in front of a light
CANDLER	*n* pl. **-S** one that candles
CANDOR	*n* pl. **-S** frankness; sincerity
CANDOUR	*n* pl. **-S** candor
CANDY	*v* **-DIED, -DYING, -DIES** to coat with sugar

CANE	*v* **CANED, CANING, CANES** to weave or furnish with cane (hollow woody stems)
CANELLA	*n* pl. **-S** a medicinal tree bark
CANEPHOR	*n* pl. **-S** a Greek maiden bearing a basket on her head
CANER	*n* pl. **-S** one that canes
CANEWARE	*n* pl. **-S** a yellowish stoneware
CANFIELD	*n* pl. **-S** a card game
CANFUL	*n* pl. **CANFULS** or **CANSFUL** as much as a can holds
CANGUE	*n* pl. **-S** an ancient Chinese punishing device
CANID	*n* pl. **-S** a dog
CANIKIN	*n* pl. **-S** cannikin
CANINE	*n* pl. **-S** a dog
CANING	present participle of cane
CANINITY	*n* pl. **-TIES** the state of being a canine
CANISTEL	*n* pl. **-S** a tropical tree
CANISTER	*n* pl. **-S** a small, metal box
CANITIES	*n* pl. **CANITIES** the turning gray of the hair
CANKER	*v* **-ED, -ING, -S** to affect with ulcerous sores
CANNA	*n* pl. **-S** a tropical plant
CANNABIC	*adj* pertaining to cannabis
CANNABIN	*n* pl. **-S** a resin extracted from cannabis
CANNABIS	*n* pl. **-BISES** hemp
CANNED	past tense of can
CANNEL	*n* pl. **-S** an oily, compact coal
CANNELON	*n* pl. **-S** a stuffed roll
CANNER	*n* pl. **-S** one that cans food
CANNERY	*n* pl. **-NERIES** a place where food is canned
CANNIBAL	*n* pl. **-S** one who eats his own kind
CANNIE	*adj* **-NIER, -NIEST** canny
CANNIER	comparative of canny
CANNIEST	superlative of canny
CANNIKIN	*n* pl. **-S** a small can or cup
CANNILY	*adv* in a canny manner
CANNING	*n* pl. **-S** the business of preserving food in airtight containers
CANNOLI	*n* pl. **-S** a tube of pastry with a sweet filling
CANNON	*v* **-ED, -ING, -S** to fire a cannon (a heavy firearm)

CANNONRY	*n* pl. **-RIES** artillery
CANNOT	the negative form of can
CANNULA	*n* pl. **-LAS** or **-LAE** a tube inserted into a bodily cavity **CANNULAR** *adj*
CANNY	*adj* **-NIER, -NIEST** prudent
CANOE	*v* **-NOED, -NOEING, -NOES** to paddle a canoe (a light, slender boat)
CANOEIST	*n* pl. **-S** one who canoes
CANOER	*n* pl. **-S** one who canoes
CANOLA	*n* pl. **-S** an oil from the seeds of a kind of herb
CANON	*n* pl. **-S** a law decreed by a church council **CANONIC** *adj*
CANONESS	*n* pl. **-ES** a woman who lives according to a canon
CANONISE	*v* **-ISED, -ISING, -ISES** to canonize
CANONIST	*n* pl. **-S** a specialist in canon law
CANONIZE	*v* **-IZED, -IZING, -IZES** to declare to be a saint
CANONRY	*n* pl. **-RIES** a clerical office
CANOODLE	*v* **-DLED, -DLING, -DLES** to caress
CANOPIC	*adj* pertaining to an Egyptian jar
CANOPY	*v* **-PIED, -PYING, -PIES** to cover from above
CANOROUS	*adj* melodic
CANSFUL	a pl. of canful
CANSO	*n* pl. **-SOS** a love song
CANST	a present 2d person sing. of can
CANT	*v* **-ED, -ING, -S** to tilt or slant
CANTAL	*n* pl. **-S** a hard cheese of France
CANTALA	*n* pl. **-S** a tropical plant
CANTATA	*n* pl. **-S** a vocal composition
CANTDOG	*n* pl. **-S** a device used to move logs
CANTEEN	*n* pl. **-S** a small container for carrying water
CANTER	*v* **-ED, -ING, -S** to ride a horse at a moderate pace
CANTHUS	*n* pl. **-THI** a corner of the eye **CANTHAL** *adj*
CANTIC	*adj* slanted
CANTICLE	*n* pl. **-S** a hymn
CANTINA	*n* pl. **-S** a saloon
CANTLE	*n* pl. **-S** the rear part of a saddle
CANTO	*n* pl. **-TOS** a division of a long poem

CANTON   *v* **-ED, -ING, -S** to divide into cantons (districts)

CANTONAL   *adj* pertaining to a canton

CANTOR   *n* pl. **-S** a religious singer

CANTRAIP   *n* pl. **-S** cantrip

CANTRAP   *n* pl. **-S** cantrip

CANTRIP   *n* pl. **-S** a magic spell

CANTUS   *n* pl. **CANTUS** a style of church music

CANTY   *adj* cheerful

CANULA   *n* pl. **-LAS** or **-LAE** cannula **CANULAR** *adj*

CANULATE   *v* **-LATED, -LATING, -LATES** to insert a canula into

CANVAS   *v* **-ED, -ING, -ES** to canvass

CANVASER   *n* pl. **-S** one that canvases

CANVASS   *v* **-ED, -ING, -ES** to examine thoroughly

CANYON   *n* pl. **-S** a deep valley with steep sides

CANZONA   *n* pl. **-S** canzone

CANZONE   *n* pl. **-NES** or **-NI** a form of lyric poetry

CANZONET   *n* pl. **-S** a short song

CAP   *v* **CAPPED, CAPPING, CAPS** to provide with a cap (a type of head covering)

CAPABLE   *adj* **-BLER, -BLEST** having ability **CAPABLY** *adv*

CAPACITY   *n* pl. **-TIES** the ability to receive or contain

CAPE   *n* pl. **-S** a sleeveless garment **CAPED** *adj*

CAPELAN   *n* pl. **-S** capelin

CAPELET   *n* pl. **-S** a small cape

CAPELIN   *n* pl. **-S** a small, edible fish

CAPER   *v* **-ED, -ING, -S** to frolic

CAPERER   *n* pl. **-S** one that capers

CAPESKIN   *n* pl. **-S** a soft leather

CAPEWORK   *n* pl. **-S** a bullfighting technique

CAPFUL   *n* pl. **-S** as much as a cap can hold

CAPH   *n* pl. **-S** kaph

CAPIAS   *n* pl. **-ES** a judicial writ

CAPITA   pl. of caput

CAPITAL   *n* pl. **-S** the upper part of a column

CAPITATE   *adj* head-shaped

CAPITOL   *n* pl. **-S** a building occupied by a state legislature

CAPITULA   *n/pl* flower clusters

CAPIZ   *n* pl. **-ES** a bivalve mollusk

CAPLESS   *adj* being without a cap

CAPLET   *n* pl. **-S** a coated tablet

CAPLIN   *n* pl. **-S** capelin

CAPMAKER   *n* pl. **-S** one that makes caps

CAPO   *n* pl. **-POS** a pitch-raising device for fretted instruments

CAPOEIRA   *n* pl. **-S** a Brazilian dance

CAPON   *n* pl. **-S** a gelded rooster

CAPONATA   *n* pl. **-S** a relish made with eggplant

CAPONIER   *n* pl. **-S** a type of defense

CAPONIZE   *v* **-IZED, -IZING, -IZES** to geld a rooster

CAPORAL   *n* pl. **-S** a coarse tobacco

CAPOTE   *n* pl. **-S** a hooded cloak or overcoat

CAPOUCH   *n* pl. **-ES** capuche

CAPPED   past tense of cap

CAPPER   *n* pl. **-S** a capmaker

CAPPING   *n* pl. **-S** a wax covering in a honeycomb

CAPRIC   *adj* pertaining to a goat

CAPRICCI   *n/pl* caprices

CAPRICE   *n* pl. **-S** a whim

CAPRIFIG   *n* pl. **-S** a European tree

CAPRINE   *adj* capric

CAPRIOLE   *v* **-OLED, -OLING, -OLES** to leap

CAPRIS   *n/pl* pants for women

CAPROCK   *n* pl. **-S** an overlying rock layer

CAPSICIN   *n* pl. **-S** a liquid used as a flavoring

CAPSICUM   *n* pl. **-S** a tropical herb

CAPSID   *n* pl. **-S** the outer shell of a virus particle **CAPSIDAL** *adj*

CAPSIZE   *v* **-SIZED, -SIZING, -SIZES** to overturn

CAPSOMER   *n* pl. **-S** a protein forming the capsid

CAPSTAN   *n* pl. **-S** a machine used to hoist weights

CAPSTONE   *n* pl. **-S** the top stone of a structure

CAPSULAR   *adj* enclosed and compact

CAPSULE   *v* **-SULED, -SULING, -SULES** to condense into a brief form

CAPTAIN   *v* **-ED, -ING, -S** to lead or command

CAPTAN   *n* pl. **-S** a fungicide

CAPTION *v* **-ED, -ING, -S** to provide with a title

CAPTIOUS *adj* tending to find fault

CAPTIVE *n* pl. **-S** a prisoner

CAPTOR *n* pl. **-S** one who takes or holds a captive

CAPTURE *v* **-TURED, -TURING, -TURES** to take by force or cunning

CAPTURER *n* pl. **-S** one that captures

CAPUCHE *n* pl. **-S** a hood or cowl **CAPUCHED** *adj*

CAPUCHIN *n* pl. **-S** a long-tailed monkey

CAPUT *n* pl. **CAPITA** a head or head-like part

CAPYBARA *n* pl. **-S** a large rodent

CAR *n* pl. **-S** an automobile

CARABAO *n* pl. **-BAOS** a water buffalo

CARABID *n* pl. **-S** a predatory beetle

CARABIN *n* pl. **-S** carbine

CARABINE *n* pl. **-S** carbine

CARACAL *n* pl. **-S** an African lynx

CARACARA *n* pl. **-S** a large hawk

CARACK *n* pl. **-S** carrack

CARACOL *v* **-COLLED, -COLLING, -COLS** to caracole

CARACOLE *v* **-COLED, -COLING, -COLES** to perform a half turn on a horse

CARACUL *n* pl. **-S** karakul

CARAFE *n* pl. **-S** a glass bottle

CARAGANA *n* pl. **-S** an Asian shrub

CARAGEEN *n* pl. **-S** an edible seaweed

CARAMBA *interj* — used to express surprise or dismay

CARAMEL *n* pl. **-S** a chewy candy

CARANGID *n* pl. **-S** a marine fish

CARAPACE *n* pl. **-S** a hard, protective outer covering

CARAPAX *n* pl. **-ES** carapace

CARASSOW *n* pl. **-S** curassow

CARAT *n* pl. **-S** a unit of weight for gems

CARATE *n* pl. **-S** a tropical skin disease

CARAVAN *v* **-VANED, -VANING, -VANS** or **-VANNED, -VANNING, -VANS** to travel in a group

CARAVEL *n* pl. **-S** a small sailing ship

CARAWAY *n* pl. **-WAYS** an herb used in cooking

CARB *n* pl. **-S** a carburetor

CARBAMIC *adj* pertaining to a type of acid

CARBAMYL *n* pl. **-S** a chemical radical

CARBARN *n* pl. **-S** a garage for buses

CARBARYL *n* pl. **-S** an insecticide

CARBIDE *n* pl. **-S** a carbon compound

CARBINE *n* pl. **-S** a light rifle

CARBINOL *n* pl. **-S** an alcohol

CARBO *n* pl. **-BOS** a carbohydrate

CARBOLIC *n* pl. **-S** an acidic compound

CARBON *n* pl. **-S** a nonmetallic element **CARBONIC** *adj*

CARBONYL *n* pl. **-S** a chemical compound

CARBORA *n* pl. **-S** a wood-boring worm

CARBOXYL *n* pl. **-S** a univalent acid radical

CARBOY *n* pl. **-BOYS** a large bottle **CARBOYED** *adj*

CARBURET *v* **-RETED, -RETING, -RETS** or **-RETTED, -RETTING, -RETS** to combine chemically with carbon

CARCAJOU *n* pl. **-S** a carnivorous mammal

CARCANET *n* pl. **-S** a jeweled necklace

CARCASE *n* pl. **-S** carcass

CARCASS *n* pl. **-ES** the body of a dead animal

CARCEL *n* pl. **-S** a unit of illumination

CARCERAL *adj* pertaining to a prison

CARD *v* **-ED, -ING, -S** to provide with a card (a stiff piece of paper)

CARDAMOM *n* pl. **-S** a tropical herb

CARDAMON *n* pl. **-S** cardamom

CARDAMUM *n* pl. **-S** cardamom

CARDCASE *n* pl. **-S** a case for holding cards

CARDER *n* pl. **-S** one that does carding

CARDIA *n* pl. **-DIAS** or **-DIAE** an opening of the esophagus

CARDIAC *n* pl. **-S** a person with a heart disorder

CARDIGAN *n* pl. **-S** a type of sweater

CARDINAL *n* pl. **-S** a bright red bird

CARDING *n* pl. **-S** the process of combing and cleaning cotton fibers; cleaned and combed fibers

CARDIO *adj* pertaining to the heart and blood vessels

CARDIOID *n* pl. **-S** a heart-shaped curve

CARDITIS *n* pl. **-TISES** inflammation of the heart **CARDITIC** *adj*

CARDON *n* pl. **-S** cardoon

CARDOON *n* pl. **-S** a perennial plant

CARE *v* **CARED, CARING, CARES** to be concerned or interested

CAREEN *v* **-ED, -ING, -S** to lurch while moving

CAREENER *n* pl. **-S** one that careens

CAREER *v* **-ED, -ING, -S** to go at full speed

CAREERER *n* pl. **-S** one that careers

CAREFREE *adj* being without worry or anxiety

CAREFUL *adj* **-FULLER, -FULLEST** cautious

CARELESS *adj* inattentive; negligent

CARER *n* pl. **-S** one that cares

CARESS *v* **-ED, -ING, -ES** to touch lovingly

CARESSER *n* pl. **-S** one that caresses

CARET *n* pl. **-S** a proofreaders' symbol

CARETAKE *v* **-TOOK, -TAKEN, -TAKING, -TAKES** to take care of someone else's house or land

CAREWORN *adj* haggard

CAREX *n* pl. **CARICES** a marsh plant

CARFARE *n* pl. **-S** payment for a bus or car ride

CARFUL *n* pl. **-S** as much as a car can hold

CARGO *n* pl. **-GOS** or **-GOES** conveyed merchandise

CARHOP *v* **-HOPPED, -HOPPING, -HOPS** to serve customers at a drive-in restaurant

CARIBE *n* pl. **-S** the piranha

CARIBOU *n* pl. **-S** a large deer

CARICES pl. of carex

CARIES *n* pl. **CARIES** tooth decay **CARIED** *adj*

CARILLON *v* **-LONNED, -LONNING, -LONS** to play a set of bells

CARINA *n* pl. **-NAS** or **-NAE** a carinate anatomical part **CARINAL** *adj*

CARINATE *adj* shaped like the keel of a ship

CARING present participle of care

CARIOCA *n* pl. **-S** a South American dance

CARIOLE *n* pl. **-S** a small, open carriage

CARIOUS *adj* decayed

CARITAS *n* pl. **-ES** love for all people

CARJACK *v* **-ED, -ING, -S** to steal a vehicle from its driver by force

CARK *v* **-ED, -ING, -S** to worry

CARL *n* pl. **-S** a peasant

CARLE *n* pl. **-S** carl

CARLESS *adj* being without a car

CARLIN *n* pl. **-S** an old woman

CARLINE *n* pl. **-S** carling

CARLING *n* pl. **-S** a beam supporting a ship's deck

CARLISH *adj* resembling a carl

CARLOAD *n* pl. **-S** as much as a car can hold

CARMAKER *n* pl. **-S** an automobile manufacturer

CARMAN *n* pl. **-MEN** a streetcar driver

CARMINE *n* pl. **-S** a vivid red color

CARN *n* pl. **-S** cairn

CARNAGE *n* pl. **-S** great and bloody slaughter

CARNAL *adj* pertaining to bodily appetites **CARNALLY** *adv*

CARNAUBA *n* pl. **-S** a palm tree

CARNET *n* pl. **-S** an official permit

CARNEY *n* pl. **-NEYS** carny

CARNIE *n* pl. **-S** carny

CARNIES pl. of carny

CARNIFY *v* **-FIED, -FYING, -FIES** to form into flesh

CARNIVAL *n* pl. **-S** a traveling amusement show

CARNY *n* pl. **-NIES** a carnival

CAROACH *n* pl. **-ES** caroche

CAROB *n* pl. **-S** an evergreen tree

CAROCH *n* pl. **-ES** caroche

CAROCHE *n* pl. **-S** a stately carriage

CAROL *v* **-OLED, -OLING, -OLS** or **-OLLED, -OLLING, -OLS** to sing joyously

CAROLER *n* pl. **-S** one that carols

CAROLI a pl. of carolus

CAROLLER *n* pl. **-S** caroler

CAROLLING a present participle of carol

CAROLUS *n* pl. **-LUSES** or **-LI** an old English coin

CAROM *v* **-ED, -ING, -S** to collide with and rebound

CAROTENE *n* pl. **-S** a plant pigment

CAROTID *n* pl. **-S** an artery in the neck

CAROTIN *n* pl. **-S** carotene

CAROUSAL *n* pl. **-S** a boisterous drinking party

CAROUSE *v* **-ROUSED, -ROUSING, -ROUSES** to engage in a carousal

CAROUSEL *n* pl. **-S** an amusement park ride

CAROUSER *n* pl. **-S** one that carouses

CAROUSING present participle of carouse

CARP *v* **-ED, -ING, -S** to find fault unreasonably

CARPAL *n* pl. **-S** carpale

CARPALE *n* pl. **-LIA** a bone of the wrist

CARPEL *n* pl. **-S** a simple pistil

CARPER *n* pl. **-S** one that carps

CARPET *v* **-ED, -ING, -S** to cover a floor with a heavy fabric

CARPI pl. of carpus

CARPING *n* pl. **-S** the act of one who carps

CARPOOL *v* **-ED, -ING, -S** to take turns driving a group of commuters

CARPORT *n* pl. **-S** a shelter for a car

CARPUS *n* pl. **-PI** the wrist

CARR *n* pl. **-S** a marsh

CARRACK *n* pl. **-S** a type of merchant ship

CARREL *n* pl. **-S** a desk in a library stack for solitary study

CARRELL *n* pl. **-S** carrel

CARRIAGE *n* pl. **-S** a wheeled, horse-drawn vehicle

CARRIED past tense of carry

CARRIER *n* pl. **-S** one that carries

CARRIES present 3d person sing. of carry

CARRIOLE *n* pl. **-S** cariole

CARRION *n* pl. **-S** dead and putrefying flesh

CARRITCH *n* pl. **-ES** a religious handbook

CARROCH *n* pl. **-ES** caroche

CARROM *v* **-ED, -ING, -S** to carom

CARROT *n* pl. **-S** an edible orange root

CARROTIN *n* pl. **-S** carotene

CARROTY *adj* **-ROTIER, -ROTIEST** resembling a carrot in color

CARRY *v* **-RIED, -RYING, -RIES** to convey from one place to another

CARRYALL *n* pl. **-S** a light covered carriage

CARRYON *n* pl. **-S** a small piece of luggage

CARRYOUT *n* pl. **-S** a take-out order of food

CARSE *n* pl. **-S** low, fertile land along a river

CARSICK *adj* nauseated from riding in a car

CART *v* **-ED, -ING, -S** to convey in a cart (a two-wheeled vehicle) **CARTABLE** *adj*

CARTAGE *n* pl. **-S** the act of carting

CARTE *n* pl. **-S** a menu

CARTEL *n* pl. **-S** a business organization

CARTER *n* pl. **-S** one that carts

CARTLOAD *n* pl. **-S** as much as a cart can hold

CARTON *v* **-ED, -ING, -S** to pack in a cardboard box

CARTOON *v* **-ED, -ING, -S** to sketch a cartoon (a humorous representation) of

CARTOONY *adj* resembling a cartoon

CARTOP *adj* able to fit on top of a car

CARTOUCH *n* pl. **-ES** a scroll-like tablet

CARUNCLE *n* pl. **-S** a fleshy outgrowth

CARVE *v* **CARVED, CARVING, CARVES** to form by cutting

CARVEL *n* pl. **-S** caravel

CARVEN *adj* carved

CARVER *n* pl. **-S** one that carves

CARVING *n* pl. **-S** a carved figure or design

CARWASH *n* pl. **-ES** an establishment equipped to wash automobiles

CARYATIC *adj* resembling a caryatid

CARYATID *n* pl. **-S** or **-ES** a sculptured female figure used as a column

CARYOTIN *n* pl. **-S** karyotin

CASA *n* pl. **-S** a dwelling

CASABA *n* pl. **-S** a variety of melon

CASAVA *n* pl. **-S** cassava

CASBAH *n* pl. **-S** the old section of a North African city

CASCABEL *n* pl. **-S** the rear part of a cannon

CASCABLE *n* pl. **-S** cascabel

CASCADE *v* **-CADED, -CADING, -CADES** to fall like a waterfall

CASCARA *n* pl. **-S** a medicinal tree bark

CASE *v* **CASED, CASING, CASES** to put in a case (a container or receptacle)

CASEASE *n* pl. **-S** an enzyme

CASEATE *v* **-ATED, -ATING, -ATES** to become cheesy

CASEBOOK *n* pl. **-S** a law textbook

CASED past tense of case

CASEFY *v* **-FIED, -FYING, -FIES** to caseate

CASEIN *n* pl. **-S** a milk protein **CASEIC** *adj*

CASELOAD *n* pl. **-S** the number of cases being handled

CASEMATE *n* pl. **-S** a bombproof shelter

CASEMENT *n* pl. **-S** a type of window

CASEOSE *n* pl. **-S** a proteose

CASEOUS *adj* cheesy

CASERN *n* pl. **-S** a barracks for soldiers

CASERNE *n* pl. **-S** casern

CASETTE *n* pl. **-S** cassette

CASEWORK *n* pl. **-S** a form of social work

CASEWORM *n* pl. **-S** an insect larva

CASH *v* **-ED, -ING, -ES** to convert into cash (ready money) **CASHABLE** *adj*

CASHAW *n* pl. **-S** cushaw

CASHBOOK *n* pl. **-S** a book of monetary records

CASHBOX *n* pl. **-ES** a container for money

CASHEW *n* pl. **-S** a nut-bearing tree

CASHIER *v* **-ED, -ING, -S** to dismiss in disgrace

CASHLESS *adj* having no cash

CASHMERE *n* pl. **-S** a fine wool

CASHOO *n* pl. **-SHOOS** catechu

CASIMERE *n* pl. **-S** a woolen fabric

CASIMIRE *n* pl. **-S** casimere

CASING *n* pl. **-S** a protective outer covering

CASINO *n* pl. **-NOS** or **-NI** a gambling room

CASITA *n* pl. **-S** a small house

CASK *v* **-ED, -ING, -S** to store in a cask (a strong barrel)

CASKET *v* **-ED, -ING, -S** to place in a casket (a burial case)

CASKY *adj* resembling a cask

CASQUE *n* pl. **-S** a helmet **CASQUED** *adj*

CASSABA *n* pl. **-S** casaba

CASSATA *n* pl. **-S** an Italian ice cream

CASSAVA *n* pl. **-S** a tropical plant

CASSENA *n* pl. **-S** cassina

CASSENE *n* pl. **-S** cassina

CASSETTE *n* pl. **-S** a small case containing audiotape or videotape

CASSIA *n* pl. **-S** a variety of cinnamon

CASSINA *n* pl. **-S** an evergreen tree

CASSINE *n* pl. **-S** cassina

CASSINO *n* pl. **-NOS** a card game

CASSIS *n* pl. **-SISES** a European bush

CASSOCK *n* pl. **-S** a long garment worn by clergymen

CAST *v* **CAST, CASTING, CASTS** to throw with force **CASTABLE** *adj*

CASTANET *n* pl. **-S** a rhythm instrument

CASTAWAY *n* pl. **-WAYS** an outcast

CASTE *n* pl. **-S** a system of distinct social classes

CASTEISM *n* pl. **-S** the use of a caste system

CASTER *n* pl. **-S** a small, swiveling wheel

CASTING *n* pl. **-S** something made in a mold

CASTLE *v* **-TLED, -TLING, -TLES** to make a certain move in chess

CASTOFF *n* pl. **-S** a discarded person or thing

CASTOR *n* pl. **-S** caster

CASTRATE *v* **-TRATED, -TRATING, -TRATES** to remove the testes of

CASTRATO *n* pl. **-TOS** or **-TI** a singer castrated in boyhood

CASUAL *n* pl. **-S** one who works occasionally

CASUALLY *adv* informally

CASUALTY *n* pl. **-TIES** a victim of war or disaster

CASUIST *n* pl. **-S** one who resolves ethical problems

CASUS *n* pl. **CASUS** a legal occurrence or event

CAT *v* **CATTED, CATTING, CATS** to hoist an anchor to the cathead

CATACOMB *n* pl. **-S** an underground cemetery

CATALASE *n* pl. **-S** an enzyme

CATALO *n* pl. **-LOS** or **-LOES** a hybrid between a buffalo and a cow

CATALOG *v* **-ED, -ING, -S** to classify information descriptively

CATALPA *n* pl. **-S** a tree

CATALYST *n* pl. **-S** a substance that accelerates a chemical reaction

CATALYZE *v* **-LYZED, -LYZING, -LYZES** to act as a catalyst

CATAMITE *n* pl. **-S** a boy used in sodomy

CATAPULT *v* **-ED, -ING, -S** to hurl through the air

CATARACT *n* pl. **-S** a tremendous waterfall

CATARRH *n* pl. **-S** inflammation of a mucous membrane

CATAWBA *n* pl. **-S** a variety of fox grape

CATBIRD *n* pl. **-S** a songbird

CATBOAT *n* pl. **-S** a small sailboat

CATBRIER *n* pl. **-S** a thorny vine

CATCALL *v* **-ED, -ING, -S** to deride by making shrill sounds

CATCH   *v* **CAUGHT, CATCHING, CATCHES** to capture after pursuit

CATCHALL   *n* pl. **-S** a container for odds and ends

CATCHER   *n* pl. **-S** one that catches

CATCHFLY   *n* pl. **-FLIES** an insect-catching plant

CATCHUP   *n* pl. **-S** ketchup

CATCHY   *adj* **CATCHIER, CATCHIEST** pleasing and easily remembered

CATCLAW   *n* pl. **-S** a flowering shrub

CATE   *n* pl. **-S** a choice food

CATECHIN   *n* pl. **-S** a chemical used in dyeing

CATECHOL   *n* pl. **-S** a chemical used in photography

CATECHU   *n* pl. **-S** a resin used in tanning

CATEGORY   *n* pl. **-RIES** a division in any system of classification

CATENA   *n* pl. **-NAS** or **-NAE** a closely linked series

CATENARY   *n* pl. **-NARIES** a mathematical curve

CATENATE   *v* **-NATED, -NATING, -NATES** to link together

CATENOID   *n* pl. **-S** a geometric surface

CATER   *v* **-ED, -ING, -S** to provide food and service for

CATERAN   *n* pl. **-S** a brigand

CATERER   *n* pl. **-S** one that caters

CATERESS   *n* pl. **-ES** a woman who caters

CATFACE   *n* pl. **-S** a deformity of fruit

CATFALL   *n* pl. **-S** an anchor line

CATFIGHT   *n* pl. **-S** a fight between two women

CATFISH   *n* pl. **-ES** a scaleless, large-headed fish

CATGUT   *n* pl. **-S** a strong cord

CATHEAD   *n* pl. **-S** a beam projecting from a ship's bow

CATHECT   *v* **-ED, -ING, -S** to invest with psychic energy

CATHEDRA   *n* pl. **-DRAS** or **-DRAE** a bishop's throne

CATHETER   *n* pl. **-S** a medical instrument

CATHEXIS   *n* pl. **-THEXES** the concentration of psychic energy on a person or idea

CATHODE   *n* pl. **-S** a negatively charged electrode **CATHODAL, CATHODIC** *adj*

CATHOLIC   *n* pl. **-S** a member of the universal Christian church

CATHOUSE   *n* pl. **-S** a brothel

CATION   *n* pl. **-S** a positively charged ion **CATIONIC** *adj*

CATJANG   *n* pl. **-S** an African shrub

CATKIN   *n* pl. **-S** a flower cluster

CATLIKE   *adj* resembling a cat; stealthy; silent

CATLIN   *n* pl. **-S** catling

CATLING   *n* pl. **-S** a surgical knife

CATMINT   *n* pl. **-S** catnip

CATNAP   *v* **-NAPPED, -NAPPING, -NAPS** to doze

CATNAPER   *n* pl. **-S** one that steals cats

CATNIP   *n* pl. **-S** an aromatic herb

CATSPAW   *n* pl. **-S** a light wind

CATSUIT   *n* pl. **-S** a close-fitting one-piece garment

CATSUP   *n* pl. **-S** ketchup

CATTAIL   *n* pl. **-S** a marsh plant

CATTALO   *n* pl. **-LOS** or **-LOES** catalo

CATTED   past tense of cat

CATTERY   *n* pl. **-TERIES** an establishment for breeding cats

CATTIE   *n* pl. **-S** an Asian unit of weight

CATTIER   comparative of catty

CATTIEST   superlative of catty

CATTILY   *adv* in a catty manner

CATTING   present participle of cat

CATTISH   *adj* catty

CATTLE   *n/pl* domesticated bovines

CATTLEYA   *n* pl. **-S** a tropical orchid

CATTY   *adj* **-TIER, -TIEST** catlike; spiteful

CATWALK   *n* pl. **-S** a narrow walkway

CAUCUS   *v* **-CUSED, -CUSING, -CUSES** or **-CUSSED, -CUSSING, -CUSSES** to hold a political meeting

CAUDAD   *adv* toward the tail

CAUDAL   *adj* taillike **CAUDALLY** *adv*

CAUDATE   *n* pl. **-S** a basal ganglion of the brain

CAUDATED   *adj* having a tail

CAUDEX   *n* pl. **-DEXES** or **-DICES** the woody base of some plants

CAUDILLO   *n* pl. **-DILLOS** a military dictator

CAUDLE   *n* pl. **-S** a warm beverage

CAUGHT   past tense of catch

CAUL   *n* pl. **-S** a fetal membrane

CAULD	*n* pl. **-S** cold
CAULDRON	*n* pl. **-S** caldron
CAULES	pl. of caulis
CAULICLE	*n* pl. **-S** a small stem
CAULINE	*adj* pertaining to a stem
CAULIS	*n* pl. **-LES** a plant stem
CAULK	*v* **-ED, -ING, -S** to make the seams of a ship watertight
CAULKER	*n* pl. **-S** one that caulks
CAULKING	*n* pl. **-S** the material used to caulk
CAUSABLE	*adj* capable of being caused
CAUSAL	*n* pl. **-S** a word expressing cause or reason
CAUSALLY	*adv* by way of causing
CAUSE	*v* **CAUSED, CAUSING, CAUSES** to bring about
CAUSER	*n* pl. **-S** one that causes
CAUSERIE	*n* pl. **-S** an informal conversation
CAUSEWAY	*v* **-ED, -ING, -S** to build a causeway (a raised roadway) over
CAUSEY	*n* pl. **-SEYS** a paved road
CAUSING	present participle of cause
CAUSTIC	*n* pl. **-S** a corrosive substance
CAUTERY	*n* pl. **-TERIES** something used to destroy tissue
CAUTION	*v* **-ED, -ING, -S** to warn
CAUTIOUS	*adj* exercising prudence to avoid danger
CAVALERO	*n* pl. **-ROS** a horseman
CAVALIER	*v* **-ED, -ING, -S** to behave haughtily
CAVALLA	*n* pl. **-S** a large food fish
CAVALLY	*n* pl. **-LIES** cavalla
CAVALRY	*n* pl. **-RIES** a mobile army unit
CAVATINA	*n* pl. **-NAS** or **-NE** a simple song
CAVE	*v* **CAVED, CAVING, CAVES** to hollow out
CAVEAT	*v* **-ED, -ING, -S** to enter a type of legal notice
CAVEATOR	*n* pl. **-S** one that files a caveat
CAVED	past tense of cave
CAVEFISH	*n* pl. **-ES** a sightless fish
CAVELIKE	*adj* resembling a cave (an underground chamber)
CAVEMAN	*n* pl. **-MEN** a cave dweller
CAVER	*n* pl. **-S** one that caves
CAVERN	*v* **-ED, -ING, -S** to hollow out

CAVETTO	*n* pl. **-TOS** or **-TI** a concave molding
CAVIAR	*n* pl. **-S** the roe of sturgeon
CAVIARE	*n* pl. **-S** caviar
CAVICORN	*adj* having hollow horns
CAVIE	*n* pl. **-S** a hencoop
CAVIES	pl. of cavy
CAVIL	*v* **-ILED, -ILING, -ILS** or **-ILLED, -ILLING, -ILS** to carp
CAVILER	*n* pl. **-S** one that cavils
CAVILLER	*n* pl. **-S** caviler
CAVILLING	a present participle of cavil
CAVING	*n* pl. **-S** the sport of exploring caves
CAVITARY	*adj* pertaining to the formation of cavities in tissue
CAVITATE	*v* **-TATED, -TATING, -TATES** to form cavities
CAVITY	*n* pl. **-TIES** an unfilled space within a mass **CAVITIED** *adj*
CAVORT	*v* **-ED, -ING, -S** to frolic
CAVORTER	*n* pl. **-S** one that cavorts
CAVY	*n* pl. **-VIES** a short-tailed rodent
CAW	*v* **-ED, -ING, -S** to utter the sound of a crow
CAY	*n* pl. **CAYS** a small low island
CAYENNE	*n* pl. **-S** a hot seasoning **CAYENNED** *adj*
CAYMAN	*n* pl. **-S** caiman
CAYUSE	*n* pl. **-S** an Indian pony
CAZIQUE	*n* pl. **-S** cacique
CEASE	*v* **CEASED, CEASING, CEASES** to stop
CEBID	*n* pl. **-S** ceboid
CEBOID	*n* pl. **-S** one of a family of monkeys
CECITY	*n* pl. **-TIES** blindness
CECROPIA	*n* pl. **-S** a large North American moth
CECUM	*n* pl. **CECA** a bodily cavity with one opening **CECAL** *adj* **CECALLY** *adv*
CEDAR	*n* pl. **-S** an evergreen tree **CEDARN, CEDARY** *adj*
CEDE	*v* **CEDED, CEDING, CEDES** to yield
CEDER	*n* pl. **-S** one that cedes
CEDI	*n* pl. **-S** a monetary unit of Ghana
CEDILLA	*n* pl. **-S** a pronunciation mark
CEDING	present participle of cede

CEDULA	n pl. **-S** a Philippine tax
CEE	n pl. **-S** the letter C
CEIBA	n pl. **-S** a tropical tree
CEIL	v **-ED, -ING, -S** to furnish with a ceiling
CEILER	n pl. **-S** one that ceils
CEILI	n pl. **-S** ceilidh
CEILIDH	n pl. **-S** an Irish or Scottish party
CEILING	n pl. **-S** the overhead lining of a room
CEINTURE	n pl. **-S** a belt for the waist
CEL	n pl. **-S** a sheet of celluloid used in animation
CELADON	n pl. **-S** a pale green color
CELEB	n pl. **-S** a celebrity; a famous person
CELERIAC	n pl. **-S** a variety of celery
CELERITY	n pl. **-TIES** swiftness
CELERY	n pl. **-ERIES** a plant with edible stalks
CELESTA	n pl. **-S** a keyboard instrument
CELESTE	n pl. **-S** celesta
CELIAC	n pl. **-S** one that has a chronic nutritional disturbance
CELIBACY	n pl. **-CIES** abstention from sexual intercourse
CELIBATE	n pl. **-S** one who lives a life of celibacy
CELL	v **-ED, -ING, -S** to store in a honeycomb
CELLA	n pl. **-LAE** the interior of an ancient temple
CELLAR	v **-ED, -ING, -S** to store in an underground room
CELLARER	n pl. **-S** the steward of a monastery
CELLARET	n pl. **-S** a cabinet for wine bottles
CELLIST	n pl. **-S** one who plays the cello
CELLMATE	n pl. **-S** one of two or more prisoners sharing a cell
CELLO	n pl. **-LOS** or **-LI** a stringed musical instrument
CELLULAR	n pl. **-S** a cell phone
CELLULE	n pl. **-S** a small cell
CELOM	n pl. **-LOMS** or **-LOMATA** coelom
CELOSIA	n pl. **-S** a flowering plant
CELT	n pl. **-S** a primitive ax
CEMBALO	n pl. **-LOS** or **-LI** a harpsichord
CEMENT	v **-ED, -ING, -S** to bind firmly
CEMENTER	n pl. **-S** one that cements
CEMENTUM	n pl. **-TUMS** or **-TA** the hard tissue covering the roots of the teeth
CEMETERY	n pl. **-TERIES** a burial ground
CENACLE	n pl. **-S** a small dining room
CENOBITE	n pl. **-S** a member of a religious order
CENOTAPH	n pl. **-S** an empty tomb
CENOTE	n pl. **-S** a sinkhole in limestone
CENSE	v **CENSED, CENSING, CENSES** to perfume with incense
CENSER	n pl. **-S** a vessel for burning incense
CENSOR	v **-ED, -ING, -S** to delete an objectionable word or passage
CENSUAL	adj pertaining to the act of censusing
CENSURE	v **-SURED, -SURING, -SURES** to criticize severely
CENSURER	n pl. **-S** one that censures
CENSUS	v **-ED, -ING, -ES** to take an official count of
CENT	n pl. **-S** the 100th part of a dollar
CENTAL	n pl. **-S** a unit of weight
CENTARE	n pl. **-S** a measure of land area
CENTAS	n pl. **CENTAI** or **CENTU** a monetary unit of Lithuania
CENTAUR	n pl. **-S** a mythological creature
CENTAURY	n pl. **-RIES** a medicinal herb
CENTAVO	n pl. **-VOS** a coin of various Spanish-American nations
CENTER	v **-ED, -ING, -S** to place at the center (the midpoint)
CENTESIS	n pl. **-TESES** a surgical puncture
CENTIARE	n pl. **-S** centare
CENTILE	n pl. **-S** a value of a statistical variable
CENTIME	n pl. **-S** the 100th part of a franc
CENTIMO	n pl. **-MOS** any of various small coins
CENTNER	n pl. **-S** a unit of weight
CENTO	n pl. **-TOS** or **-TONES** a literary work made up of parts from other works
CENTRA	a pl. of centrum
CENTRAL	adj **-TRALER, -TRALEST** situated at, in, or near the center
CENTRAL	n pl. **-S** a telephone exchange
CENTRE	v **-TRED, -TRING, -TRES** to center

CENTRIC *adj* situated at the center

CENTRING *n* pl. **-S** a temporary framework for an arch

CENTRISM *n* pl. **-S** moderate political philosophy

CENTRIST *n* pl. **-S** an advocate of centrism

CENTROID *n* pl. **-S** the center of mass of an object

CENTRUM *n* pl. **-TRUMS** or **-TRA** the body of a vertebra

CENTU a pl. of centas

CENTUM *n* pl. **-S** one hundred

CENTUPLE *v* **-PLED, -PLING, -PLES** to increase a hundredfold

CENTURY *n* pl. **-RIES** a period of 100 years

CEORL *n* pl. **-S** a freeman of low birth **CEORLISH** *adj*

CEP *n* pl. **-S** cepe

CEPE *n* pl. **-S** a large mushroom

CEPHALAD *adv* toward the head

CEPHALIC *adj* pertaining to the head

CEPHALIN *n* pl. **-S** a bodily chemical

CEPHEID *n* pl. **-S** a giant star

CERAMAL *n* pl. **-S** a heat-resistant alloy

CERAMIC *n* pl. **-S** an item made of baked clay

CERAMIDE *n* pl. **-S** any of various lipids

CERAMIST *n* pl. **-S** one who makes ceramics

CERASTES *n* pl. **CERASTES** a venomous snake

CERATE *n* pl. **-S** a medicated ointment

CERATED *adj* covered with wax

CERATIN *n* pl. **-S** keratin

CERATOID *adj* hornlike

CERCARIA *n* pl. **-IAS** or **-IAE** a parasitic worm

CERCIS *n* pl. **-CISES** a shrub

CERCUS *n* pl. **CERCI** a sensory appendage of an insect **CERCAL** *adj*

CERE *v* **CERED, CERING, CERES** to wrap in a waxy cloth

CEREAL *n* pl. **-S** a food made from grain

CEREBRAL *n* pl. **-S** a kind of consonant

CEREBRUM *n* pl. **-BRUMS** or **-BRA** a part of the brain **CEREBRIC** *adj*

CERED past tense of cere

CEREMENT *n* pl. **-S** a waxy cloth

CEREMONY *n* pl. **-NIES** a formal observance

CEREUS *n* pl. **-ES** a tall cactus

CERIA *n* pl. **-S** a chemical compound

CERIC *adj* containing cerium

CERING present participle of cere

CERIPH *n* pl. **-S** serif

CERISE *n* pl. **-S** a red color

CERITE *n* pl. **-S** a mineral

CERIUM *n* pl. **-S** a metallic element

CERMET *n* pl. **-S** ceramal

CERNUOUS *adj* drooping or nodding

CERO *n* pl. **CEROS** a large food fish

CEROTIC *adj* pertaining to beeswax

CEROTYPE *n* pl. **-S** a process of engraving using wax

CEROUS *adj* pertaining to cerium

CERTAIN *adj* **-TAINER, -TAINEST** absolutely confident

CERTES *adv* in truth

CERTIFY *v* **-FIED, -FYING, -FIES** to confirm

CERULEAN *n* pl. **-S** a blue color

CERUMEN *n* pl. **-S** a waxy secretion of the ear

CERUSE *n* pl. **-S** a lead compound

CERUSITE *n* pl. **-S** a lead ore

CERVELAS *n* pl. **-ES** cervelat

CERVELAT *n* pl. **-S** a smoked sausage

CERVEZA *n* pl. **-S** beer

CERVICAL *adj* pertaining to the cervix

CERVID *adj* of the deer family

CERVINE *adj* pertaining to deer

CERVIX *n* pl. **-VIXES** or **-VICES** the neck

CESAREAN *n* pl. **-S** a method of child delivery

CESARIAN *n* pl. **-S** cesarean

CESIUM *n* pl. **-S** a metallic element

CESS *v* **-ED, -ING, -ES** to tax or assess

CESSION *n* pl. **-S** the act of ceding

CESSPIT *n* pl. **-S** a cesspool

CESSPOOL *n* pl. **-S** a covered well or pit for sewage

CESTA *n* pl. **-S** a basket used in jai alai

CESTI pl. of cestus

CESTODE *n* pl. **-S** a tapeworm

CESTOID *n* pl. **-S** cestode

CESTOS *n* pl. **-TOI** cestus

CESTUS *n* pl. **-ES** a hand covering for ancient Roman boxers

CESTUS *n* pl. **-TI** a belt or girdle

CESURA   *n* pl. **-RAS** or **-RAE** caesura

CETACEAN   *n* pl. **-S** an aquatic mammal

CETANE   *n* pl. **-S** a diesel fuel

CETE   *n* pl. **-S** a group of badgers

CETOLOGY   *n* pl. **-GIES** the study of whales

CEVICHE   *n* pl. **-S** seviche

CHABLIS   *n* pl. **CHABLIS** a dry white wine

CHABOUK   *n* pl. **-S** a type of whip

CHABUK   *n* pl. **-S** chabouk

CHACHKA   *n* pl. **-S** chatchka

CHACMA   *n* pl. **-S** a large baboon

CHACONNE   *n* pl. **-S** an ancient dance

CHAD   *n* pl. **-S** a scrap of paper **CHADLESS** *adj*

CHADAR   *n* pl. **-DARS** or **-DRI** chador

CHADARIM   a pl. of cheder

CHADOR   *n* pl. **-DORS** or **-DRI** a large shawl

CHAEBOL   *n* pl. **-S** a group of businesses in Korea owned by one family

CHAETA   *n* pl. **-TAE** a bristle or seta **CHAETAL** *adj*

CHAFE   *v* **CHAFED, CHAFING, CHAFES** to warm by rubbing

CHAFER   *n* pl. **-S** a large beetle

CHAFF   *v* **-ED, -ING, -S** to poke fun at

CHAFFER   *v* **-ED, -ING, -S** to bargain or haggle

CHAFFY   *adj* **CHAFFIER, CHAFFIEST** worthless

CHAFING   present participle of chafe

CHAGRIN   *v* **-GRINED, -GRINING, -GRINS** or **-GRINNED, -GRINNING, -GRINS** to humiliate

CHAI   *n* pl. **-S** spiced tea with honey and milk

CHAIN   *v* **-ED, -ING, -S** to bind with a chain (a series of connected rings)

CHAINE   *n* pl. **-S** a series of ballet turns

CHAINMAN   *n* pl. **-MEN** a surveyor's assistant who uses a measuring chain

CHAINSAW   *v* **-SAWED, -SAWING, -SAWS** to cut with a chain saw

CHAIR   *v* **-ED, -ING, -S** to install in office

CHAIRMAN   *n* pl. **-MEN** the presiding officer of a meeting

CHAIRMAN   *v* **-MANED, -MANING, -MANS** or **-MANNED, -MANNING, -MANS** to act as chairman of

CHAISE   *n* pl. **-S** a light carriage

CHAKRA   *n* pl. **-S** a body center in yoga

CHALAH   *n* pl. **-LAHS** or **-LOTH** or **-LOT** challah

CHALAZA   *n* pl. **-ZAS** or **-ZAE** a band of tissue in an egg **CHALAZAL** *adj*

CHALAZIA   *n/pl* tumors of the eyelid

CHALCID   *n* pl. **-S** a tiny fly

CHALDRON   *n* pl. **-S** a unit of dry measure

CHALEH   *n* pl. **-S** challah

CHALET   *n* pl. **-S** a Swiss cottage

CHALICE   *n* pl. **-S** a drinking cup **CHALICED** *adj*

CHALK   *v* **-ED, -ING, -S** to mark with chalk (a soft limestone)

CHALKY   *adj* **CHALKIER, CHALKIEST** resembling chalk

CHALLA   *n* pl. **-S** challah

CHALLAH   *n* pl. **-LAHS** or **-LOTH** or **-LOT** a kind of bread

CHALLIE   *n* pl. **-S** challis

CHALLIES   pl. of chally

CHALLIS   *n* pl. **-LISES** a light fabric

CHALLOT   a pl. of challah

CHALLOTH   a pl. of challah

CHALLY   *n* pl. **-LIES** challis

CHALONE   *n* pl. **-S** a hormone

CHALOT   a pl. of chalah

CHALOTH   a pl. of chalah

CHALUPA   *n* pl. **-S** a fried corn tortilla spread with a savory mixture

CHALUTZ   *n* pl. **-LUTZIM** halutz

CHAM   *n* pl. **-S** a khan

CHAMADE   *n* pl. **-S** a signal made with a drum

CHAMBER   *v* **-ED, -ING, -S** to put in a chamber (a room)

CHAMBRAY   *n* pl. **-BRAYS** a fine fabric

CHAMFER   *v* **-ED, -ING, -S** to groove

CHAMFRON   *n* pl. **-S** armor for a horse's head

CHAMISA   *n* pl. **-S** a saltbush of the Southwest

CHAMISE   *n* pl. **-S** chamiso

CHAMISO   *n* pl. **-SOS** a flowering shrub

CHAMMY   *v* **-MIED, -MYING, -MIES** to chamois

CHAMOIS   *n* pl. **-OIX** a soft leather

CHAMOIS   *v* **-ED, -ING, -ES** to prepare leather like chamois

CHAMP   *v* **-ED, -ING, -S** to chew noisily

CHAMPAC *n* pl. **-S** champak

CHAMPACA *n* pl. **-S** champak

CHAMPAK *n* pl. **-S** an East Indian tree

CHAMPER *n* pl. **-S** one that champs

CHAMPION *v* **-ED, -ING, -S** to defend or support

CHAMPY *adj* broken up by the trampling of beasts

CHANCE *v* **CHANCED, CHANCING, CHANCES** to risk

CHANCEL *n* pl. **-S** an area around a church altar

CHANCER *n* pl. **-S** an opportunist

CHANCERY *n* pl. **-CERIES** a court of public record

CHANCIER comparative of chancy

CHANCIEST superlative of chancy

CHANCILY *adv* in a chancy manner

CHANCING present participle of chance

CHANCRE *n* pl. **-S** a hard-based sore

CHANCY *adj* **CHANCIER, CHANCIEST** risky

CHANDLER *n* pl. **-S** a dealer in provisions

CHANFRON *n* pl. **-S** chamfron

CHANG *n* pl. **-S** a cattie

CHANGE *v* **CHANGED, CHANGING, CHANGES** to make different

CHANGER *n* pl. **-S** one that changes

CHANGEUP *n* pl. **-S** a slow pitch thrown like a fastball

CHANNEL *v* **-NELED, -NELING, -NELS** or **-NELLED, -NELLING, -NELS** to direct along some desired course

CHANOYU *n* pl. **-S** a Japanese tea ritual

CHANSON *n* pl. **-S** a song

CHANT *v* **-ED, -ING, -S** to sing

CHANTAGE *n* pl. **-S** blackmail

CHANTER *n* pl. **-S** one that chants

CHANTEY *n* pl. **-TEYS** a sailor's song

CHANTIES pl. of chanty

CHANTOR *n* pl. **-S** chanter

CHANTRY *n* pl. **-TRIES** an endowment given to a church

CHANTY *n* pl. **-TIES** chantey

CHAO *n* pl. **CHAO** a monetary unit of Vietnam

CHAOS *n* pl. **-ES** a state of total disorder; a confused mass **CHAOTIC** *adj*

CHAP *v* **CHAPPED** or **CHAPT, CHAPPING, CHAPS** to split, crack, or redden

CHAPATI *n* pl. **-S** an unleavened bread of India

CHAPATTI *n* pl. **-S** chapati

CHAPBOOK *n* pl. **-S** a small book of popular tales

CHAPE *n* pl. **-S** a part of a scabbard

CHAPEAU *n* pl. **-PEAUS** or **-PEAUX** a hat

CHAPEL *n* pl. **-S** a place of worship

CHAPERON *v* **-ED, -ING, -S** to accompany

CHAPITER *n* pl. **-S** the capital of a column

CHAPLAIN *n* pl. **-S** a clergyman for a chapel

CHAPLET *n* pl. **-S** a wreath for the head

CHAPMAN *n* pl. **-MEN** a peddler

CHAPPATI *n* pl. **-S** chapati

CHAPPED a past tense of chap

CHAPPIE *n* pl. **-S** a fellow

CHAPPING present participle of chap

CHAPT a past tense of chap

CHAPTER *v* **-ED, -ING, -S** to divide a book into chapters (main sections)

CHAQUETA *n* pl. **-S** a jacket worn by cowboys

CHAR *v* **CHARRED, CHARRING, CHARS** to burn slightly

CHARACID *n* pl. **-S** characin

CHARACIN *n* pl. **-S** a tropical fish

CHARADE *n* pl. **-S** a word represented by pantomime

CHARAS *n* pl. **-ES** hashish

CHARCOAL *v* **-ED, -ING, -S** to blacken with charcoal (a dark, porous carbon)

CHARD *n* pl. **-S** a variety of beet

CHARE *v* **CHARED, CHARING, CHARES** to do small jobs

CHARGE *v* **CHARGED, CHARGING, CHARGES** to accuse formally

CHARGER *n* pl. **-S** one that charges

CHARIER comparative of chary

CHARIEST superlative of chary

CHARILY *adv* in a chary manner

CHARING present participle of chare

CHARIOT *v* **-ED, -ING, -S** to ride in a chariot (a type of cart)

CHARISM *n* pl. **-S** charisma

CHARISMA *n* pl. **-MAS** or **-MATA** a special magnetic appeal

CHARITY   *n* pl. **-TIES** something given to the needy

CHARK   *v* **-ED, -ING, -S** to char

CHARKA   *n* pl. **-S** charkha

CHARKHA   *n* pl. **-S** a spinning wheel

CHARLADY   *n* pl. **-DIES** a cleaning woman

CHARLEY   *n* pl. **-LEYS** charlie

CHARLIE   *n* pl. **-LIES** a fool

CHARLOCK   *n* pl. **-S** a troublesome weed

CHARM   *v* **-ED, -ING, -S** to attract irresistibly

CHARMER   *n* pl. **-S** one that charms

CHARMING   *adj* **-INGER, -INGEST** pleasing

CHARNEL   *n* pl. **-S** a room where corpses are placed

CHARPAI   *n* pl. **-S** charpoy

CHARPOY   *n* pl. **-POYS** a bed used in India

CHARQUI   *n* pl. **-S** a type of meat **CHARQUID** *adj*

CHARR   *n* pl. **-S** a small-scaled trout

CHARRED   past tense of char

CHARRIER   comparative of charry

CHARRIEST   superlative of charry

CHARRING   present participle of char

CHARRO   *n* pl. **-ROS** a cowboy

CHARRY   *adj* **-RIER, -RIEST** resembling charcoal

CHART   *v* **-ED, -ING, -S** to map out

CHARTER   *v* **-ED, -ING, -S** to lease or hire

CHARTIST   *n* pl. **-S** a stock market specialist

CHARY   *adj* **CHARIER, CHARIEST** cautious

CHASE   *v* **CHASED, CHASING, CHASES** to pursue

CHASER   *n* pl. **-S** one that chases

CHASING   *n* pl. **-S** a design engraved on metal

CHASM   *n* pl. **-S** a deep cleft in the earth **CHASMAL, CHASMED, CHASMIC, CHASMY** *adj*

CHASSE   *v* **CHASSED, CHASSEING, CHASSES** to perform a dance movement

CHASSEUR   *n* pl. **-S** a cavalry soldier

CHASSIS   *n* pl. **CHASSIS** the frame of a car

CHASTE   *adj* **CHASTER, CHASTEST** morally pure **CHASTELY** *adv*

CHASTEN   *v* **-ED, -ING, -S** to chastise

CHASTISE   *v* **-TISED, -TISING, -TISES** to discipline by punishment

CHASTITY   *n* pl. **-TIES** moral purity

CHASUBLE   *n* pl. **-S** a sleeveless vestment

CHAT   *v* **CHATTED, CHATTING, CHATS** to converse informally

CHATCHKA   *n* pl. **-S** a knickknack

CHATCHKE   *n* pl. **-S** chatchka

CHATEAU   *n* pl. **-TEAUS** or **-TEAUX** a large country house

CHATROOM   *n* pl. **-S** a real-time online discussion group

CHATTED   past tense of chat

CHATTEL   *n* pl. **-S** a slave

CHATTER   *v* **-ED, -ING, -S** to talk rapidly and trivially **CHATTERY** *adj*

CHATTING   present participle of chat

CHATTY   *adj* **-TIER, -TIEST** talkative **CHATTILY** *adv*

CHAUFER   *n* pl. **-S** chauffer

CHAUFFER   *n* pl. **-S** a small furnace

CHAUNT   *v* **-ED, -ING, -S** to chant

CHAUNTER   *n* pl. **-S** one that chaunts

CHAUSSES   *n/pl* medieval armor

CHAW   *v* **-ED, -ING, -S** to chew

CHAWER   *n* pl. **-S** one that chaws

CHAY   *n* pl. **CHAYS** the root of an East Indian herb

CHAYOTE   *n* pl. **-S** a tropical vine

CHAZAN   *n* pl. **-ZANS** or **-ZANIM** a cantor

CHAZZAN   *n* pl. **-ZANS** or **-ZANIM** chazan

CHAZZEN   *n* pl. **-ZENS** or **-ZENIM** chazan

CHEAP   *adj* **CHEAPER, CHEAPEST** inexpensive

CHEAP   *n* pl. **-S** a market

CHEAPEN   *v* **-ED, -ING, -S** to make cheap

CHEAPIE   *n* pl. **-S** one that is cheap

CHEAPISH   *adj* somewhat cheap

CHEAPLY   *adv* in a cheap manner

CHEAPO   *n* pl. **CHEAPOS** a cheapie

CHEAT   *v* **-ED, -ING, -S** to defraud

CHEATER   *n* pl. **-S** one that cheats

CHEBEC   *n* pl. **-S** a small bird

CHECHAKO   *n* pl. **-KOS** a newcomer

CHECK   *v* **-ED, -ING, -S** to inspect

CHECKER   *v* **-ED, -ING, -S** to mark with squares

CHECKOFF *n* pl. **-S** a method of collecting union dues

CHECKOUT *n* pl. **-S** a test of a machine

CHECKROW *v* **-ED, -ING, -S** to plant in rows which divide the land into squares

CHECKSUM *n* pl. **-S** a sum derived from bits of computer data

CHECKUP *n* pl. **-S** an examination

CHEDDAR *n* pl. **-S** a type of cheese **CHEDDARY** *adj*

CHEDDITE *n* pl. **-S** chedite

CHEDER *n* pl. **CHEDERS** or **CHADARIM** heder

CHEDITE *n* pl. **-S** an explosive

CHEEK *v* **-ED, -ING, -S** to speak impudently to

CHEEKFUL *n* pl. **-S** the amount held in one's cheek

CHEEKY *adj* **CHEEKIER, CHEEKIEST** impudent **CHEEKILY** *adv*

CHEEP *v* **-ED, -ING, -S** to chirp

CHEEPER *n* pl. **-S** one that cheeps

CHEER *v* **-ED, -ING, -S** to applaud with shouts of approval

CHEERER *n* pl. **-S** one that cheers

CHEERFUL *adj* **-FULLER, -FULLEST** full of spirits

CHEERIER comparative of cheery

CHEERIEST superlative of cheery

CHEERILY *adv* in a cheery manner

CHEERIO *n* pl. **-IOS** a greeting

CHEERLED past tense of cheerlead

CHEERLY *adv* cheerily

CHEERO *n* pl. **CHEEROS** cheerio

CHEERY *adj* **CHEERIER, CHEERIEST** cheerful

CHEESE *v* **CHEESED, CHEESING, CHEESES** to stop

CHEESY *adj* **CHEESIER, CHEESIEST** resembling cheese (a food made from milk curds) **CHEESILY** *adv*

CHEETAH *n* pl. **-S** a swift-running wildcat

CHEF *v* **CHEFFED, CHEFFING, CHEFS** or **CHEFED, CHEFING, CHEFS** to work as a chef (a chief cook)

CHEFDOM *n* pl. **-S** the status of a chef

CHEGOE *n* pl. **-S** chigoe

CHELA *n* pl. **-LAE** a pincerlike claw

CHELA *n* pl. **-S** a pupil of a guru

CHELATE *v* **-LATED, -LATING, -LATES** to combine a metal ion with a compound

CHELATOR *n* pl. **-S** one that chelates

CHELIPED *n* pl. **-S** a claw-bearing leg

CHELOID *n* pl. **-S** keloid

CHEMIC *n* pl. **-S** a chemist

CHEMICAL *n* pl. **-S** a substance obtained by a process of chemistry

CHEMISE *n* pl. **-S** a loose dress

CHEMISM *n* pl. **-S** chemical attraction

CHEMIST *n* pl. **-S** one versed in chemistry

CHEMO *n* pl. **-S** treatment (as of disease) with chemical agents

CHEMURGY *n* pl. **-GIES** a branch of applied chemistry

CHENILLE *n* pl. **-S** a soft fabric

CHENOPOD *n* pl. **-S** a flowering plant

CHEQUE *n* pl. **-S** a written order directing a bank to pay money

CHEQUER *v* **-ED, -ING, -S** to checker

CHERISH *v* **-ED, -ING, -ES** to hold dear

CHEROOT *n* pl. **-S** a square-cut cigar

CHERRY *n* pl. **-RIES** a fruit

CHERT *n* pl. **-S** a compact rock

CHERTY *adj* **CHERTIER, CHERTIEST** resembling chert

CHERUB *n* pl. **-UBS** or **-UBIM** or **-UBIMS** an angel **CHERUBIC** *adj*

CHERVIL *n* pl. **-S** an aromatic herb

CHESHIRE *n* pl. **-S** a hard English cheese

CHESS *n* pl. **-ES** a weed

CHESSMAN *n* pl. **-MEN** one of the pieces used in chess (a board game for two players)

CHEST *n* pl. **-S** a part of the body **CHESTED** *adj*

CHESTFUL *n* pl. **-S** as much as a chest or box can hold

CHESTNUT *n* pl. **-S** an edible nut

CHESTY *adj* **CHESTIER, CHESTIEST** proud **CHESTILY** *adv*

CHETAH *n* pl. **-S** cheetah

CHETH *n* pl. **-S** heth

CHETRUM *n* pl. **-S** a monetary unit of Bhutan

CHEVALET *n* pl. **-S** a part of a stringed instrument

CHEVERON *n* pl. **-S** chevron

CHEVIED past tense of chevy

CHEVIES	present 3d person sing. of chevy
CHEVIOT	*n* pl. **-S** a coarse fabric
CHEVRE	*n* pl. **-S** a cheese made from goat's milk
CHEVRET	*n* pl. **-S** chevre
CHEVRON	*n* pl. **-S** a V-shaped pattern
CHEVY	*v* **CHEVIED, CHEVYING, CHEVIES** to chase about
CHEW	*v* **-ED, -ING, -S** to crush or grind with the teeth **CHEWABLE** *adj*
CHEWER	*n* pl. **-S** one that chews
CHEWINK	*n* pl. **-S** a common finch
CHEWY	*adj* **CHEWIER, CHEWIEST** not easily chewed
CHEZ	*prep* at the home of
CHI	*n* pl. **-S** a Greek letter
CHIA	*n* pl. **-S** a Mexican herb
CHIANTI	*n* pl. **-S** a dry red wine
CHIAO	*n* pl. **CHIAO** a monetary unit of China
CHIASM	*n* pl. **-S** chiasma
CHIASMA	*n* pl. **-MAS** or **-MATA** an anatomical junction **CHIASMAL, CHIASMIC** *adj*
CHIASMUS	*n* pl. **-MI** a reversal of word order between parallel phrases **CHIASTIC** *adj*
CHIAUS	*n* pl. **-ES** a Turkish messenger
CHIBOUK	*n* pl. **-S** a Turkish tobacco pipe
CHIC	*adj* **CHICER, CHICEST** smartly stylish
CHIC	*n* pl. **-S** elegance of dress or manner
CHICA	*n* pl. **-S** a girl or young woman
CHICANE	*v* **-CANED, -CANING, -CANES** to trick by a clever ruse
CHICANER	*n* pl. **-S** one that chicanes
CHICANO	*n* pl. **-NOS** an American of Mexican descent
CHICCORY	*n* pl. **-RIES** chicory
CHICHI	*adj* **CHICHIER, CHICHIEST** showily stylish
CHICHI	*n* pl. **-S** elaborate ornamentation
CHICK	*n* pl. **-S** a young bird
CHICKEE	*n* pl. **-S** a stilt house of the Seminole Indians
CHICKEN	*v* **-ED, -ING, -S** to lose one's nerve
CHICKORY	*n* pl. **-RIES** chicory
CHICKPEA	*n* pl. **-S** an Asian herb
CHICLE	*n* pl. **-S** a tree gum
CHICLY	*adv* in an elegant manner
CHICNESS	*n* pl. **-ES** elegance
CHICO	*n* pl. **-COS** a prickly shrub
CHICORY	*n* pl. **-RIES** a perennial herb
CHIDE	*v* **CHIDED** or **CHID, CHIDDEN, CHIDING, CHIDES** to scold
CHIDER	*n* pl. **-S** one that chides
CHIEF	*adj* **CHIEFER, CHIEFEST** highest in authority
CHIEF	*n* pl. **-S** the person highest in authority
CHIEFDOM	*n* pl. **-S** the domain of a chief
CHIEFLY	*adv* above all
CHIEL	*n* pl. **-S** chield
CHIELD	*n* pl. **-S** a young man
CHIFFON	*n* pl. **-S** a sheer fabric
CHIGETAI	*n* pl. **-S** a wild ass
CHIGGER	*n* pl. **-S** a parasitic mite
CHIGNON	*n* pl. **-S** a woman's hairdo
CHIGOE	*n* pl. **-S** a tropical flea
CHILD	*n* pl. **CHILDREN** a young person
CHILDBED	*n* pl. **-S** the state of a woman giving birth
CHILDE	*n* pl. **-S** a youth of noble birth
CHILDING	*adj* pregnant
CHILDISH	*adj* resembling a child
CHILDLY	*adj* **-LIER, -LIEST** resembling a child
CHILDREN	pl. of child
CHILE	*n* pl. **-S** chili
CHILI	*n* pl. **-S** or **-ES** a hot pepper
CHILIAD	*n* pl. **-S** a group of one thousand
CHILIASM	*n* pl. **-S** a religious doctrine
CHILIAST	*n* pl. **-S** a supporter of chiliasm
CHILIDOG	*n* pl. **-S** a hot dog topped with chili
CHILL	*adj* **CHILLER, CHILLEST** cool
CHILL	*v* **-ED, -ING, -S** to make cold
CHILLER	*n* pl. **-S** one that chills
CHILLI	*n* pl. **-ES** or **-S** chili
CHILLUM	*n* pl. **-S** a part of a water pipe
CHILLY	*adj* **CHILLIER, CHILLIEST** cool **CHILLILY** *adv*
CHILOPOD	*n* pl. **-S** a multi-legged insect
CHIMAERA	*n* pl. **-S** a marine fish

CHIMAR	*n* pl. **-S** chimere	**CHIPPER**	*v* **-ED, -ING, -S** to chirp
CHIMB	*n* pl. **-S** the rim of a cask	**CHIPPIE**	*n* pl. **-S** chippy
CHIMBLEY	*n* pl. **-BLEYS** chimley	**CHIPPING**	present participle of chip
CHIMBLY	*n* pl. **-BLIES** chimley	**CHIPPY**	*adj* **-PIER, -PIEST** belligerent
CHIME	*v* **CHIMED, CHIMING, CHIMES** to ring harmoniously	**CHIPPY**	*n* pl. **-PIES** a prostitute
CHIMER	*n* pl. **-S** one that chimes	**CHIRAL**	*adj* pertaining to an asymmetrical molecule
CHIMERA	*n* pl. **-S** an imaginary monster	**CHIRK**	*adj* **CHIRKER, CHIRKEST** cheerful
CHIMERE	*n* pl. **-S** a bishop's robe		
CHIMERIC	*adj* imaginary; unreal	**CHIRK**	*v* **-ED, -ING, -S** to make a shrill noise
CHIMING	present participle of chime		
CHIMLA	*n* pl. **-S** chimley	**CHIRM**	*v* **-ED, -ING, -S** to chirp
CHIMLEY	*n* pl. **-LEYS** a chimney	**CHIRO**	*n* pl. **-ROS** a marine fish
CHIMNEY	*n* pl. **-NEYS** a flue	**CHIRP**	*v* **-ED, -ING, -S** to utter a short, shrill sound
CHIMP	*n* pl. **-S** a chimpanzee		
CHIN	*v* **CHINNED, CHINNING, CHINS** to hold with the chin (the lower part of the face)	**CHIRPER**	*n* pl. **-S** one that chirps
		CHIRPY	*adj* **CHIRPIER, CHIRPIEST** cheerful **CHIRPILY** *adv*
CHINA	*n* pl. **-S** fine porcelain ware	**CHIRR**	*v* **-ED, -ING, -S** to make a harsh, vibrant sound
CHINBONE	*n* pl. **-S** the lower jaw		
CHINCH	*n* pl. **-ES** a bedbug	**CHIRRE**	*v* **CHIRRED, CHIRRING, CHIRRES** to chirr
CHINCHY	*adj* **CHINCHIER, CHINCHIEST** stingy		
		CHIRREN	*n/pl* children
CHINE	*v* **CHINED, CHINING, CHINES** to cut through the backbone of	**CHIRRUP**	*v* **-ED, -ING, -S** to chirp repeatedly **CHIRRUPY** *adj*
CHINK	*v* **-ED, -ING, -S** to fill cracks or fissures in	**CHIRU**	*n* pl. **-S** a Tibetan antelope
		CHISEL	*v* **-ELED, -ELING, -ELS** or **-ELLED, -ELLING, -ELS** to use a chisel (a cutting tool)
CHINKY	*adj* **CHINKIER, CHINKIEST** full of cracks		
CHINLESS	*adj* lacking a chin	**CHISELER**	*n* pl. **-S** one that chisels
CHINNED	past tense of chin	**CHIT**	*n* pl. **-S** a short letter
CHINNING	present participle of chin	**CHITAL**	*n* pl. **CHITAL** an Asian deer
CHINO	*n* pl. **-NOS** a strong fabric	**CHITCHAT**	*v* **-CHATTED, -CHATTING, -CHATS** to indulge in small talk
CHINONE	*n* pl. **-S** quinone		
CHINOOK	*n* pl. **-S** a warm wind	**CHITIN**	*n* pl. **-S** the main component of insect shells
CHINTS	*n* pl. **-ES** chintz		
CHINTZ	*n* pl. **-ES** a cotton fabric	**CHITLIN**	*n* pl. **-S** chitling
CHINTZY	*adj* **CHINTZIER, CHINTZIEST** gaudy; cheap	**CHITLING**	*n* pl. **-S** a part of the small intestine of swine
CHINWAG	*v* **-WAGGED, -WAGGING, -WAGS** to gossip	**CHITON**	*n* pl. **-S** a tunic worn in ancient Greece
CHIP	*v* **CHIPPED, CHIPPING, CHIPS** to break a small piece from	**CHITOSAN**	*n* pl. **-S** a compound derived from chitin
CHIPMUCK	*n* pl. **-S** a chipmunk	**CHITTER**	*v* **-ED, -ING, -S** to twitter
CHIPMUNK	*n* pl. **-S** a small rodent	**CHITTY**	*n* pl. **-TIES** a chit
CHIPOTLE	*n* pl. **-S** a smoked and dried jalapeno pepper	**CHIVALRY**	*n* pl. **-RIES** knightly behavior and skill
CHIPPED	past tense of chip	**CHIVAREE**	*v* **-REED, -REEING, -REES** to perform a mock serenade
		CHIVARI	*v* **-RIED, -RIING, -RIES** to chivaree

CHIVE *n* pl. **-S** an herb used as a seasoning

CHIVVY *v* **-VIED, -VYING, -VIES** to chevy

CHIVY *v* **CHIVIED, CHIVYING, CHIVIES** to chevy

CHLAMYS *n* pl. **-MYSES** or **-MYDES** a garment worn in ancient Greece

CHLOASMA *n* pl. **-MAS** or **-MATA** a skin discoloration

CHLORAL *n* pl. **-S** a chemical compound

CHLORATE *n* pl. **-S** a chemical salt

CHLORDAN *n* pl. **-S** a toxic compound of chlorine

CHLORIC *adj* pertaining to chlorine

CHLORID *n* pl. **-S** chloride

CHLORIDE *n* pl. **-S** a chlorine compound

CHLORIN *n* pl. **-S** chlorine

CHLORINE *n* pl. **-S** a gaseous element

CHLORITE *n* pl. **-S** a mineral group

CHLOROUS *adj* pertaining to chlorine

CHOANA *n* pl. **-NAE** a funnel-shaped opening

CHOCK *v* **-ED, -ING, -S** to secure with a wedge of wood or metal

CHOCKFUL *adj* full to the limit

CHOICE *adj* **CHOICER, CHOICEST** of fine quality **CHOICELY** *adv*

CHOICE *n* pl. **-S** one that is chosen

CHOIR *v* **-ED, -ING, -S** to sing in unison

CHOIRBOY *n* pl. **-BOYS** a boy who sings in a choir (a body of church singers)

CHOKE *v* **CHOKED, CHOKING, CHOKES** to impede the breathing of

CHOKER *n* pl. **-S** one that chokes

CHOKEY *adj* **CHOKIER, CHOKIEST** choky

CHOKY *adj* **CHOKIER, CHOKIEST** tending to cause choking

CHOLA *n* pl. **-S** a Mexican-American girl

CHOLATE *n* pl. **-S** a chemical salt

CHOLENT *n* pl. **-S** a traditional Jewish stew

CHOLER *n* pl. **-S** anger

CHOLERA *n* pl. **-S** an acute disease

CHOLERIC *adj* bad-tempered

CHOLINE *n* pl. **-S** a B vitamin

CHOLLA *n* pl. **-S** a treelike cactus

CHOLO *n* pl. **-LOS** a pachuco

CHOMP *v* **-ED, -ING, -S** to champ

CHOMPER *n* pl. **-S** one that chomps

CHON *n* pl. **CHON** a monetary unit of South Korea

CHOOK *n* pl. **-S** a chicken

CHOOSE *v* **CHOSE, CHOSEN, CHOOSING, CHOOSES** to take by preference

CHOOSER *n* pl. **-S** one that chooses

CHOOSEY *adj* **CHOOSIER, CHOOSIEST** choosy

CHOOSY *adj* **CHOOSIER, CHOOSIEST** hard to please

CHOP *v* **CHOPPED, CHOPPING, CHOPS** to sever with a sharp tool

CHOPIN *n* pl. **-S** chopine

CHOPINE *n* pl. **-S** a type of shoe

CHOPPED past tense of chop

CHOPPER *v* **-ED, -ING, -S** to travel by helicopter

CHOPPING present participle of chop

CHOPPY *adj* **CHOPPIER, CHOPPIEST** full of short, rough waves **CHOPPILY** *adv*

CHORAGUS *n* pl. **-GUSES** or **-GI** the leader of a chorus or choir **CHORAGIC** *adj*

CHORAL *n* pl. **-S** chorale

CHORALE *n* pl. **-S** a hymn that is sung in unison

CHORALLY *adv* harmoniously

CHORD *v* **-ED, -ING, -S** to play a chord (a combination of three or more musical tones)

CHORDAL *adj* pertaining to a chord

CHORDATE *n* pl. **-S** any of a large phylum of animals

CHORE *v* **CHORED, CHORING, CHORES** to do small jobs

CHOREA *n* pl. **-S** a nervous disorder **CHOREAL, CHOREIC** *adj*

CHOREGUS *n* pl. **-GUSES** or **-GI** choragus

CHOREMAN *n* pl. **-MEN** a menial worker

CHOREOID *adj* resembling chorea

CHORIAL *adj* pertaining to the chorion

CHORIAMB *n* pl. **-S** a type of metrical foot

CHORIC *adj* pertaining to a chorus

CHORINE *n* pl. **-S** a chorus girl

CHORING present participle of chore

CHORIOID *n* pl. **-S** choroid

CHORION *n* pl. **-S** an embryonic membrane

CHORIZO *n* pl. **-ZOS** a highly seasoned sausage

CHOROID	*n* pl. **-S** a membrane of the eye
CHORTEN	*n* pl. **-S** a Tibetan shrine
CHORTLE	*v* **-TLED, -TLING, -TLES** to chuckle with glee
CHORTLER	*n* pl. **-S** one that chortles
CHORUS	*v* **-RUSED, -RUSING, -RUSES** or **-RUSSED, -RUSSING, -RUSSES** to sing in unison
CHOSE	*n* pl. **-S** an item of personal property
CHOSEN	past participle of choose
CHOTT	*n* pl. **-S** a saline lake
CHOUGH	*n* pl. **-S** a crow-like bird
CHOUSE	*v* **CHOUSED, CHOUSING, CHOUSES** to swindle
CHOUSER	*n* pl. **-S** one that chouses
CHOUSH	*n* pl. **-ES** chiaus
CHOW	*v* **-ED, -ING, -S** to eat
CHOWCHOW	*n* pl. **-S** a relish of mixed pickles in mustard
CHOWDER	*v* **-ED, -ING, -S** to make a thick soup of
CHOWSE	*v* **CHOWSED, CHOWSING, CHOWSES** to chouse
CHOWTIME	*n* pl. **-S** mealtime
CHRESARD	*n* pl. **-S** the available water of the soil
CHRISM	*n* pl. **-S** a consecrated oil **CHRISMAL** *adj*
CHRISMON	*n* pl. **-MONS** or **-MA** a Christian monogram
CHRISOM	*n* pl. **-S** chrism
CHRISTEN	*v* **-ED, -ING, -S** to baptize
CHRISTIE	*n* pl. **-S** christy
CHRISTY	*n* pl. **-TIES** a skiing turn
CHROMA	*n* pl. **-S** the purity of a color
CHROMATE	*n* pl. **-S** a chemical salt
CHROME	*v* **CHROMED, CHROMING, CHROMES** to plate with chromium
CHROMIC	*adj* pertaining to chromium
CHROMIDE	*n* pl. **-S** a tropical fish
CHROMING	*n* pl. **-S** a chromium ore
CHROMITE	*n* pl. **-S** a chromium ore
CHROMIUM	*n* pl. **-S** a metallic element
CHROMIZE	*v* **-MIZED, -MIZING, -MIZES** to chrome
CHROMO	*n* pl. **-MOS** a type of color picture
CHROMOUS	*adj* pertaining to chromium
CHROMY	*adj* **CHROMIER, CHROMIEST** decorated with chrome
CHROMYL	*n* pl. **-S** a bivalent radical
CHRONAXY	*n* pl. **-AXIES** the time required to excite a nerve cell electrically
CHRONIC	*n* pl. **-S** one that suffers from a long-lasting disease
CHRONON	*n* pl. **-S** a hypothetical unit of time
CHTHONIC	*adj* pertaining to the gods of the underworld
CHUB	*n* pl. **-S** a freshwater fish
CHUBASCO	*n* pl. **-COS** a violent thunderstorm
CHUBBY	*adj* **-BIER, -BIEST** plump **CHUBBILY** *adv*
CHUCK	*v* **-ED, -ING, -S** to throw
CHUCKIES	pl. of chucky
CHUCKLE	*v* **-LED, -LING, -LES** to laugh quietly
CHUCKLER	*n* pl. **-S** one that chuckles
CHUCKY	*n* pl. **CHUCKIES** a little chick
CHUDDAH	*n* pl. **-S** chuddar
CHUDDAR	*n* pl. **-S** a large, square shawl
CHUDDER	*n* pl. **-S** chuddar
CHUFA	*n* pl. **-S** a European sedge
CHUFF	*adj* **CHUFFER, CHUFFEST** gruff
CHUFF	*v* **-ED, -ING, -S** to chug
CHUFFY	*adj* **-FIER, -FIEST** plump
CHUG	*v* **CHUGGED, CHUGGING, CHUGS** to move with a dull explosive sound
CHUGALUG	*v* **-LUGGED, -LUGGING, -LUGS** to drink without pause
CHUGGER	*n* pl. **-S** one that chugs
CHUKAR	*n* pl. **-S** a game bird
CHUKKA	*n* pl. **-S** a type of boot
CHUKKAR	*n* pl. **-S** a chukker
CHUKKER	*n* pl. **-S** a period of play in polo
CHUM	*v* **CHUMMED, CHUMMING, CHUMS** to be close friends with someone
CHUMMY	*adj* **-MIER, -MIEST** friendly **CHUMMILY** *adv*
CHUMP	*v* **-ED, -ING, -S** to munch
CHUMSHIP	*n* pl. **-S** friendship
CHUNK	*v* **-ED, -ING, -S** to make a dull explosive sound
CHUNKY	*adj* **CHUNKIER, CHUNKIEST** stocky **CHUNKILY** *adv*

CHUNNEL *n* pl. **-S** a tunnel under the English Channel

CHUNTER *v* **-ED, -ING, -S** to mutter

CHUPPA *n* pl. **-S** chuppah

CHUPPAH *n* pl. **-S** a canopy used at a Jewish wedding

CHURCH *v* **-ED, -ING, -ES** to bring to church (a building for Christian worship)

CHURCHLY *adj* **-LIER, -LIEST** pertaining to a church

CHURCHY *adj* **CHURCHIER, CHURCHIEST** churchly

CHURL *n* pl. **-S** a rude person **CHURLISH** *adj*

CHURN *v* **-ED, -ING, -S** to stir briskly in order to make butter

CHURNER *n* pl. **-S** one that churns

CHURNING *n* pl. **-S** the butter churned at one time

CHURR *v* **-ED, -ING, -S** to make a vibrant sound

CHURRO *n* pl. **-ROS** a Spanish and Mexican pastry

CHUTE *v* **CHUTED, CHUTING, CHUTES** to convey by chute (a vertical passage)

CHUTIST *n* pl. **-S** a parachutist

CHUTNEE *n* pl. **-S** chutney

CHUTNEY *n* pl. **-NEYS** a sweet and sour sauce

CHUTZPA *n* pl. **-S** chutzpah

CHUTZPAH *n* pl. **-S** supreme self-confidence

CHYLE *n* pl. **-S** a digestive fluid **CHYLOUS** *adj*

CHYME *n* pl. **-S** semi-digested food

CHYMIC *n* pl. **-S** chemic

CHYMIST *n* pl. **-S** chemist

CHYMOSIN *n* pl. **-S** rennin

CHYMOUS *adj* pertaining to chyme

CHYTRID *n* pl. **-S** an aquatic or soil fungus

CIAO *interj* — used as an expression of greeting and farewell

CIBOL *n* pl. **-S** a variety of onion

CIBORIUM *n* pl. **-RIA** a vessel for holding holy bread

CIBOULE *n* pl. **-S** cibol

CICADA *n* pl. **-DAS** or **-DAE** a winged insect

CICALA *n* pl. **-LAS** or **-LE** cicada

CICATRIX *n* pl. **-TRIXES** or **-TRICES** scar tissue

CICELY *n* pl. **-LIES** a fragrant herb

CICERO *n* pl. **-ROS** a unit of measure in printing

CICERONE *n* pl. **-NES** or **-NI** a tour guide

CICHLID *n* pl. **-LIDS** or **-LIDAE** a tropical fish

CICISBEO *n* pl. **-BEOS** or **-BEI** a lover of a married woman

CICOREE *n* pl. **-S** a perennial herb

CIDER *n* pl. **-S** the juice pressed from apples

CIG *n* pl. **-S** a cigarette

CIGAR *n* pl. **-S** a roll of tobacco leaf for smoking

CIGARET *n* pl. **-S** a narrow roll of finely cut tobacco for smoking

CILANTRO *n* pl. **-TROS** an herb used in cooking

CILIA pl. of cilium

CILIARY *adj* pertaining to cilia

CILIATE *n* pl. **-S** one of a class of ciliated protozoans

CILIATED *adj* having cilia

CILICE *n* pl. **-S** a coarse cloth

CILIUM *n* pl. **CILIA** a short, hairlike projection

CIMBALOM *n* pl. **-S** a Hungarian dulcimer

CIMEX *n* pl. **-MICES** a bedbug

CINCH *v* **-ED, -ING, -ES** to girth

CINCHONA *n* pl. **-S** a Peruvian tree

CINCTURE *v* **-TURED, -TURING, -TURES** to gird or encircle

CINDER *v* **-ED, -ING, -S** to reduce to cinders (ashes)

CINDERY *adj* containing cinders

CINE *n* pl. **-S** a motion picture

CINEAST *n* pl. **-S** a devotee of motion pictures

CINEASTE *n* pl. **-S** cineast

CINEMA *n* pl. **-S** a motion-picture theater

CINEOL *n* pl. **-S** a liquid used as an antiseptic

CINEOLE *n* pl. **-S** cineol

CINERARY *adj* used for cremated ashes

CINERIN *n* pl. **-S** a compound used in insecticides

CINGULUM *n pl.* **-LA** an anatomical band or girdle **CINGULAR** *adj*

CINNABAR *n pl.* **-S** the principal ore of mercury

CINNAMON *n pl.* **-S** a spice obtained from tree bark **CINNAMIC** *adj*

CINNAMYL *n pl.* **-S** a chemical used to make soap

CINQUAIN *n pl.* **-S** a stanza of five lines

CINQUE *n pl.* **-S** the number five

CION *n pl.* **-S** a cutting from a plant or tree

CIOPPINO *n pl.* **-NOS** a spicy fish stew

CIPHER *v* **-ED, -ING, -S** to solve problems in arithmetic

CIPHERER *n pl.* **-S** one that ciphers

CIPHONY *n pl.* **-NIES** the electronic scrambling of voice transmissions

CIPOLIN *n pl.* **-S** a type of marble

CIRCA *prep* about; around

CIRCLE *v* **-CLED, -CLING, -CLES** to move or revolve around

CIRCLER *n pl.* **-S** one that circles

CIRCLET *n pl.* **-S** a small ring or ring-shaped object

CIRCUIT *v* **-ED, -ING, -S** to move around

CIRCUITY *n pl.* **-ITIES** lack of straightforwardness

CIRCULAR *n pl.* **-S** a leaflet intended for wide distribution

CIRCUS *n pl.* **-ES** a public entertainment **CIRCUSY** *adj*

CIRE *n pl.* **-S** a highly glazed finish for fabrics

CIRQUE *n pl.* **-S** a deep, steep-walled basin on a mountain

CIRRATE *adj* having cirri

CIRRI *pl.* of cirrus

CIRRIPED *n pl.* **-S** any of an order of crustaceans

CIRROSE *adj* cirrous

CIRROUS *adj* having cirri

CIRRUS *n pl.* **-RI** a tendril or similar part

CIRSOID *adj* varicose

CIS *adj* having certain atoms on the same side of the molecule

CISCO *n pl.* **-COS** or **-COES** a freshwater fish

CISLUNAR *adj* situated between the earth and the moon

CISSOID *n pl.* **-S** a type of geometric curve

CISSY *n pl.* **-SIES** sissy

CIST *n pl.* **-S** a prehistoric stone coffin **CISTED** *adj*

CISTERN *n pl.* **-S** a water tank

CISTERNA *n pl.* **-NAE** a fluid-containing sac

CISTRON *n pl.* **-S** a segment of DNA

CISTUS *n pl.* **-ES** a flowering shrub

CITABLE *adj* citeable

CITADEL *n pl.* **-S** a fortress or stronghold

CITATION *n pl.* **-S** the act of citing **CITATORY** *adj*

CITATOR *n pl.* **-S** one that cites

CITE *v* **CITED, CITING, CITES** to quote as an authority or example

CITEABLE *adj* suitable for citation

CITER *n pl.* **-S** one that cites

CITHARA *n pl.* **-S** an ancient stringed instrument

CITHER *n pl.* **-S** cittern

CITHERN *n pl.* **-S** cittern

CITHREN *n pl.* **-S** cittern

CITIED *adj* having cities

CITIES *pl.* of city

CITIFY *v* **-FIED, -FYING, -FIES** to urbanize

CITING present participle of cite

CITIZEN *n pl.* **-S** a resident of a city or town

CITOLA *n pl.* **-S** a cittern

CITOLE *n pl.* **-S** citola

CITRAL *n pl.* **-S** a lemon flavoring

CITRATE *n pl.* **-S** a salt of citric acid **CITRATED** *adj*

CITREOUS *adj* having a lemonlike color

CITRIC *adj* derived from citrus fruits

CITRIN *n pl.* **-S** a citric vitamin

CITRINE *n pl.* **-S** a variety of quartz

CITRININ *n pl.* **-S** an antibiotic

CITRON *n pl.* **-S** a lemonlike fruit

CITROUS *adj* pertaining to a citrus tree

CITRUS *n pl.* **-ES** any of a genus of tropical, fruit-bearing trees **CITRUSY** *adj*

CITTERN *n pl.* **-S** a pear-shaped guitar

CITY *n pl.* **CITIES** a large town

CITYFIED *adj* having the customs and manners of city people

CITYWARD *adv* toward the city

CITYWIDE   *adj* including all parts of a city

CIVET   *n* pl. **-S** a catlike mammal

CIVIC   *adj* pertaining to a city

CIVICISM   *n* pl. **-S** a system of government based upon individual rights

CIVICS   *n/pl* the science of civic affairs

CIVIE   *n* pl. **-S** civvy

CIVIL   *adj* pertaining to citizens

CIVILIAN   *n* pl. **-S** a nonmilitary person

CIVILISE   *v* **-LISED, -LISING, -LISES** to civilize

CIVILITY   *n* pl. **-TIES** courtesy; politeness

CIVILIZE   *v* **-LIZED, -LIZING, -LIZES** to bring out of savagery

CIVILLY   *adv* politely

CIVISM   *n* pl. **-S** good citizenship

CIVVY   *n* pl. **-VIES** a civilian

CLABBER   *v* **-ED, -ING, -S** to curdle

CLACH   *n* pl. **-S** clachan

CLACHAN   *n* pl. **-S** a hamlet

CLACK   *v* **-ED, -ING, -S** to make an abrupt, dry sound

CLACKER   *n* pl. **-S** one that clacks

CLAD   *v* **CLADDED, CLADDING, CLADS** to coat one metal over another

CLADDAGH   *n* pl. **-S** a ring designed with two hands clasping

CLADDING   *n* pl. **-S** something that overlays

CLADE   *n* pl. **-S** a group of biological taxa

CLADISM   *n* pl. **-S** the method of a cladist

CLADIST   *n* pl. **-S** a taxonomist who uses clades in classifying life-forms

CLADODE   *n* pl. **-S** a leaflike part of a stem

CLAFOUTI   *n* pl. **-S** a dessert consisting of a layer of fruit topped with batter and baked

CLAG   *v* **CLAGGED, CLAGGING, CLAGS** to clog

CLAIM   *v* **-ED, -ING, -S** to demand as one's due

CLAIMANT   *n* pl. **-S** one that asserts a right or title

CLAIMER   *n* pl. **-S** one that claims

CLAM   *v* **CLAMMED, CLAMMING, CLAMS** to dig for clams (bivalve mollusks)

CLAMANT   *adj* noisy

CLAMBAKE   *n* pl. **-S** a beach picnic

CLAMBER   *v* **-ED, -ING, -S** to climb awkwardly

CLAMLIKE   *adj* resembling a clam

CLAMMED   past tense of clam

CLAMMER   *n* pl. **-S** one that clams

CLAMMING   present participle of clam

CLAMMY   *adj* **CLAMMIER, CLAMMIEST** cold and damp **CLAMMILY** *adv*

CLAMOR   *v* **-ED, -ING, -S** to make loud outcries

CLAMORER   *n* pl. **-S** one that clamors

CLAMOUR   *v* **-ED, -ING, -S** to clamor

CLAMP   *v* **-ED, -ING, -S** to fasten with a clamp (a securing device)

CLAMPER   *n* pl. **-S** a device worn on shoes to prevent slipping on ice

CLAMWORM   *n* pl. **-S** a marine worm

CLAN   *n* pl. **-S** a united group of families

CLANG   *v* **-ED, -ING, -S** to ring loudly

CLANGER   *n* pl. **-S** a blunder

CLANGOR   *v* **-ED, -ING, -S** to clang repeatedly

CLANGOUR   *v* **-ED, -ING, -S** to clangor

CLANK   *v* **-ED, -ING, -S** to make a sharp, metallic sound

CLANKY   *adj* **CLANKIER, CLANKIEST** making a sharp, metallic sound

CLANNISH   *adj* characteristic of a clan

CLANSMAN   *n* pl. **-MEN** a member of a clan

CLAP   *v* **CLAPPED** or **CLAPT, CLAPPING, CLAPS** to strike one palm against the other

CLAPPER   *n* pl. **-S** one that claps

CLAPTRAP   *n* pl. **-S** pretentious language

CLAQUE   *n* pl. **-S** a group of hired applauders

CLAQUER   *n* pl. **-S** claqueur

CLAQUEUR   *n* pl. **-S** a member of a claque

CLARENCE   *n* pl. **-S** a closed carriage

CLARET   *n* pl. **-S** a dry red wine

CLARIES   pl. of clary

CLARIFY   *v* **-FIED, -FYING, -FIES** to make clear

CLARINET   *n* pl. **-S** a woodwind instrument

CLARION   *v* **-ED, -ING, -S** to proclaim by blowing a medieval trumpet

CLARITY   *n* pl. **-TIES** the state of being clear

CLARKIA   *n* pl. **-S** an annual herb

CLARO   *n* pl. **-ROS** or **-ROES** a mild cigar

CLARY   *n* pl. **CLARIES** an aromatic herb

CLASH	v **-ED, -ING, -ES** to conflict or disagree
CLASHER	n pl. **-S** one that clashes
CLASP	v **CLASPED** or **CLASPT, CLASPING, CLASPS** to embrace tightly
CLASPER	n pl. **-S** one that clasps
CLASS	v **-ED, -ING, -ES** to classify
CLASSER	n pl. **-S** one that classes
CLASSES	pl. of classis
CLASSIC	n pl. **-S** a work of enduring excellence
CLASSICO	adj made from grapes grown in a certain part of Italy
CLASSIER	comparative of classy
CLASSIEST	superlative of classy
CLASSIFY	v **-FIED, -FYING, -FIES** to arrange according to characteristics
CLASSILY	adj in a classy manner
CLASSIS	n pl. **CLASSES** a governing body in certain churches
CLASSISM	n pl. **-S** discrimination based on social class
CLASSIST	n pl. **-S** an advocate of classism
CLASSON	n pl. **-S** a subatomic particle
CLASSY	adj **CLASSIER, CLASSIEST** stylish; elegant
CLAST	n pl. **-S** a fragment of rock
CLASTIC	n pl. **-S** a rock made up of other rocks
CLATTER	v **-ED, -ING, -S** to move with a rattling noise
CLATTERY	adj having a rattling noise
CLAUCHT	a past tense of cleek
CLAUGHT	v **-ED, -ING, -S** to clutch
CLAUSE	n pl. **-S** a distinct part of a composition **CLAUSAL** adj
CLAUSTRA	n/pl basal ganglia in the brain
CLAVATE	adj shaped like a club
CLAVE	n pl. **-S** one of a pair of percussion sticks
CLAVER	v **-ED, -ING, -S** to gossip
CLAVI	pl. of clavus
CLAVICLE	n pl. **-S** a bone of the shoulder
CLAVIER	n pl. **-S** a keyboard instrument
CLAVUS	n pl. **-VI** a horny thickening of the skin
CLAW	v **-ED, -ING, -S** to scratch with claws (sharp, curved toenails)
CLAWBACK	n pl. **-S** money taken back by taxation
CLAWER	n pl. **-S** one that claws
CLAWLESS	adj having no claws
CLAWLIKE	adj resembling a claw
CLAXON	n pl. **-S** klaxon
CLAY	v **-ED, -ING, -S** to treat with clay (a fine-grained, earthy material)
CLAYBANK	n pl. **-S** a yellow-brown color
CLAYEY	adj **CLAYIER, CLAYIEST** resembling clay
CLAYISH	adj resembling or containing clay
CLAYLIKE	adj resembling clay
CLAYMORE	n pl. **-S** a type of sword
CLAYPAN	n pl. **-S** a shallow natural depression
CLAYWARE	n pl. **-S** pottery
CLEAN	adj **CLEANER, CLEANEST** free from dirt or stain
CLEAN	v **-ED, -ING, -S** to rid of dirt or stain
CLEANER	n pl. **-S** one that cleans
CLEANLY	adj **-LIER, -LIEST** habitually clean
CLEANSE	v **CLEANSED, CLEANSING, CLEANSES** to clean
CLEANSER	n pl. **-S** one that cleanses
CLEANUP	n pl. **-S** an act of cleaning
CLEAR	adj **CLEARER, CLEAREST** clean and pure
CLEAR	v **-ED, -ING, -S** to remove obstructions
CLEARCUT	v **-CUT, -CUTTING, -CUTS** to cut a forest completely
CLEARER	n pl. **-S** one that clears
CLEARING	n pl. **-S** an open space
CLEARLY	adv in a clear manner
CLEAT	v **-ED, -ING, -S** to strengthen with a strip of wood or iron
CLEAVAGE	n pl. **-S** the act of cleaving
CLEAVE	v **CLEAVED, CLEFT, CLOVE** or **CLAVE, CLOVEN, CLEAVING, CLEAVES** to split or divide
CLEAVER	n pl. **-S** a heavy knife
CLEEK	v **CLAUCHT** or **CLEEKED, CLEEKING, CLEEKS** to clutch
CLEF	n pl. **-S** a musical symbol
CLEFT	v **-ED, -ING, -S** to insert a scion into the stock of a plant
CLEIDOIC	adj enclosed in a shell
CLEMATIS	n pl. **-TISES** a flowering vine

CLEMENCY *n pl.* **-CIES** mercy

CLEMENT *adj* merciful

CLENCH *v* **-ED, -ING, -ES** to grasp firmly

CLENCHER *n pl.* **-S** one that clenches

CLEOME *n pl.* **-S** a tropical plant

CLEPE *v* **CLEPED** or **CLEPT, CLEPING, CLEPES** to call by name

CLERGY *n pl.* **-GIES** the body of persons ordained for religious service

CLERIC *n pl.* **-S** a member of the clergy

CLERICAL *n pl.* **-S** a cleric

CLERID *n pl.* **-S** a predatory beetle

CLERIHEW *n pl.* **-S** a humorous poem

CLERISY *n pl.* **-SIES** the well-educated class

CLERK *v* **-ED, -ING, -S** to serve as a clerk (an office worker)

CLERKDOM *n pl.* **-S** the status or function of a clerk

CLERKISH *adj* resembling or suitable to a clerk

CLERKLY *adj* **-LIER, -LIEST** pertaining to a clerk

CLEVEITE *n pl.* **-S** a radioactive mineral

CLEVER *adj* **-ERER, -EREST** mentally keen **CLEVERLY** *adv*

CLEVIS *n pl.* **-ISES** a metal fastening device

CLEW *v* **-ED, -ING, -S** to roll into a ball

CLICHE *n pl.* **-S** a trite expression **CLICHED** *adj*

CLICK *v* **-ED, -ING, -S** to make a short, sharp sound

CLICKER *n pl.* **-S** one that clicks

CLIENT *n pl.* **-S** a customer **CLIENTAL** *adj*

CLIFF *n pl.* **-S** a high, steep face of rock

CLIFFY *adj* **CLIFFIER, CLIFFIEST** abounding in cliffs

CLIFT *n pl.* **-S** cliff

CLIMATE *n pl.* **-S** the weather conditions characteristic of an area **CLIMATAL, CLIMATIC** *adj*

CLIMAX *v* **-ED, -ING, -ES** to reach a high or dramatic point

CLIMB *v* **CLIMBED** or **CLOMB, CLIMBING, CLIMBS** to ascend

CLIMBER *n pl.* **-S** one that climbs

CLIME *n pl.* **-S** climate

CLINAL *adj* pertaining to a cline

CLINALLY *adv* in a clinal manner

CLINCH *v* **-ED, -ING, -ES** to settle a matter decisively

CLINCHER *n pl.* **-S** a decisive fact or remark

CLINE *n pl.* **-S** a series of changes within a species

CLING *v* **-ED, -ING, -S** to make a high-pitched ringing sound

CLING *v* **CLUNG, CLINGING, CLINGS** to adhere closely

CLINGER *n pl.* **-S** one that clings

CLINGY *adj* **CLINGIER, CLINGIEST** adhesive

CLINIC *n pl.* **-S** a medical facility **CLINICAL** *adj*

CLINK *v* **-ED, -ING, -S** to make a soft, sharp, ringing sound

CLINKER *v* **-ED, -ING, -S** to form fused residue in burning

CLIP *v* **CLIPPED** or **CLIPT, CLIPPING, CLIPS** to trim by cutting

CLIPPER *n pl.* **-S** one that clips

CLIPPING *n pl.* **-S** something that is clipped out or off

CLIPT a past participle of clip

CLIQUE *v* **CLIQUED, CLIQUING, CLIQUES** to form a clique (an exclusive group of persons)

CLIQUEY *adj* **CLIQUIER, CLIQUIEST** inclined to form cliques

CLIQUISH *adj* cliquey

CLIQUY *adj* **CLIQUIER, CLIQUIEST** cliquey

CLITELLA *n/pl* regions in the body walls of certain annelids

CLITIC *n pl.* **-S** a word pronounced as part of a neighboring word

CLITORIS *n pl.* **-RISES** or **-RIDES** a sex organ **CLITORAL, CLITORIC** *adj*

CLIVERS *n pl.* **CLIVERS** an annual herb

CLIVIA *n pl.* **-S** a flowering plant

CLOACA *n pl.* **-ACAS** or **-ACAE** a sewer **CLOACAL** *adj*

CLOAK *v* **-ED, -ING, -S** to conceal

CLOBBER *v* **-ED, -ING, -S** to trounce

CLOCHARD *n pl.* **-S** a vagrant

CLOCHE *n pl.* **-S** a bell-shaped hat

CLOCK *v* **-ED, -ING, -S** to time with a stopwatch

CLOCKER *n pl.* **-S** one that clocks

CLOD *n pl.* **-S** a dolt **CLODDISH** *adj*

CLODDY *adj* **-DIER, -DIEST** lumpy

CLODPATE *n* pl. **-S** a stupid person

CLODPOLE *n* pl. **-S** clodpate

CLODPOLL *n* pl. **-S** clodpate

CLOG *v* **CLOGGED, CLOGGING, CLOGS** to block up or obstruct

CLOGGER *n* pl. **-S** one that clogs

CLOGGY *adj* **-GIER, -GIEST** clogging or able to clog **CLOGGILY** *adv*

CLOISTER *v* **-ED, -ING, -S** to seclude

CLOMB a past tense of climb

CLOMP *v* **-ED, -ING, -S** to walk heavily and clumsily

CLON *n* pl. **-S** a group of asexually derived organisms **CLONAL** *adj* **CLONALLY** *adv*

CLONE *v* **CLONED, CLONING, CLONES** to reproduce by asexual means

CLONER *n* pl. **-S** one that clones

CLONIC *adj* pertaining to clonus

CLONING *n* pl. **-S** a technique for reproducing by asexual means

CLONISM *n* pl. **-S** the condition of having clonus

CLONK *v* **-ED, -ING, -S** to make a dull thumping sound

CLONUS *n* pl. **-ES** a form of muscular spasm

CLOOT *n* pl. **-S** a cloven hoof

CLOP *v* **CLOPPED, CLOPPING, CLOPS** to make the sound of a hoof striking pavement

CLOQUE *n* pl. **-S** a fabric with an embossed design

CLOSE *adj* **CLOSER, CLOSEST** near **CLOSELY** *adv*

CLOSE *v* **CLOSED, CLOSING, CLOSES** to block against entry or passage **CLOSABLE** *adj*

CLOSEOUT *n* pl. **-S** a clearance sale

CLOSER *n* pl. **-S** one that closes

CLOSEST superlative of close

CLOSET *v* **-ED, -ING, -S** to enclose in a private room

CLOSEUP *n* pl. **-S** a photograph taken at close range

CLOSING *n* pl. **-S** a concluding part

CLOSURE *v* **-SURED, -SURING, -SURES** to cloture

CLOT *v* **CLOTTED, CLOTTING, CLOTS** to form into a clot (a thick mass)

CLOTH *n* pl. **-S** fabric

CLOTHE *v* **CLOTHED** or **CLAD, CLOTHING, CLOTHES** to provide with clothing

CLOTHIER *n* pl. **-S** one who makes or sells clothing

CLOTHING *n* pl. **-S** wearing apparel

CLOTTED past tense of clot

CLOTTING present participle of clot

CLOTTY *adj* tending to clot

CLOTURE *v* **-TURED, -TURING, -TURES** to end a debate by calling for a vote

CLOUD *v* **-ED, -ING, -S** to cover with clouds (masses of visible vapor)

CLOUDLET *n* pl. **-S** a small cloud

CLOUDY *adj* **CLOUDIER, CLOUDIEST** overcast with clouds **CLOUDILY** *adv*

CLOUGH *n* pl. **-S** a ravine

CLOUR *v* **-ED, -ING, -S** to knock or bump

CLOUT *v* **-ED, -ING, -S** to hit with the hand

CLOUTER *n* pl. **-S** one that clouts

CLOVE *n* pl. **-S** a spice

CLOVEN *adj* split; divided

CLOVER *n* pl. **-S** a plant **CLOVERED, CLOVERY** *adj*

CLOWDER *n* pl. **-S** a group of cats

CLOWN *v* **-ED, -ING, -S** to act like a clown (a humorous performer)

CLOWNERY *n* pl. **-ERIES** clownish behavior

CLOWNISH *adj* resembling or befitting a clown

CLOY *v* **-ED, -ING, -S** to gratify beyond desire

CLOZE *n* pl. **-S** a test of reading comprehension

CLUB *v* **CLUBBED, CLUBBING, CLUBS** to form a club (an organized group of persons)

CLUBABLE *adj* sociable

CLUBBER *n* pl. **-S** a member of a club

CLUBBISH *adj* clubby

CLUBBY *adj* **-BIER, -BIEST** characteristic of a club

CLUBFACE *n* pl. **-S** the striking surface of a clubhead

CLUBFOOT *n* pl. **-FEET** a deformed foot

CLUBHAND *n* pl. **-S** a deformed hand

CLUBHAUL *v* **-ED, -ING, -S** to put a vessel about

CLUBHEAD *n* pl. **-S** the part of a golf club that strikes the ball

CLUBMAN *n* pl. **-MEN** a male member of a club

CLUBROOM *n* pl. **-S** a room for a club's meetings

CLUBROOT *n* pl. **-S** a plant disease

CLUCK *v* **-ED, -ING, -S** to make the sound of a hen

CLUE *v* **CLUED, CLUEING** or **CLUING, CLUES** to give guiding information

CLUELESS *adj* hopelessly confused or ignorant

CLUMBER *n* pl. **-S** a stocky spaniel

CLUMP *v* **-ED, -ING, -S** to form into a thick mass

CLUMPISH *adj* resembling a clump (a thick mass)

CLUMPY *adj* **CLUMPIER, CLUMPIEST** lumpy

CLUMSY *adj* **-SIER, -SIEST** awkward **CLUMSILY** *adv*

CLUNG past tense of cling

CLUNK *v* **-ED, -ING, -S** to thump

CLUNKER *n* pl. **-S** a jalopy

CLUNKY *adj* **CLUNKIER, CLUNKIEST** clumsy in style

CLUPEID *n* pl. **-S** a fish of the herring family

CLUPEOID *n* pl. **-S** a clupeid

CLUSTER *v* **-ED, -ING, -S** to form into a cluster (a group of similar objects)

CLUSTERY *adj* pertaining to a cluster

CLUTCH *v* **-ED, -ING, -ES** to grasp and hold tightly

CLUTCHY *adj* tending to clutch

CLUTTER *v* **-ED, -ING, -S** to pile in a disorderly state

CLUTTERY *adj* characterized by disorder

CLYPEUS *n* pl. **CLYPEI** a shield-like structure **CLYPEAL, CLYPEATE** *adj*

CLYSTER *n* pl. **-S** an enema

CNIDA *n* pl. **-DAE** a stinging organ in a jellyfish

COACH *v* **-ED, -ING, -ES** to tutor or train

COACHER *n* pl. **-S** one that coaches

COACHMAN *n* pl. **-MEN** one who drives a coach or carriage

COACT *v* **-ED, -ING, -S** to act together

COACTION *n* pl. **-S** joint action

COACTIVE *adj* mutually active

COACTOR *n* pl. **-S** a fellow actor in a production

COADMIRE *v* **-MIRED, -MIRING, -MIRES** to admire together

COADMIT *v* **-MITTED, -MITTING, -MITS** to admit several things equally

COAEVAL *n* pl. **-S** coeval

COAGENCY *n* pl. **-CIES** a joint agency

COAGENT *n* pl. **-S** a person, force, or other agent working together with another

COAGULUM *n* pl. **-LUMS** or **-LA** a clot

COAL *v* **-ED, -ING, -S** to supply with coal (a carbon fuel)

COALA *n* pl. **-S** koala

COALBIN *n* pl. **-S** a bin for storing coal

COALBOX *n* pl. **-ES** a box for storing coal

COALER *n* pl. **-S** one that supplies coal

COALESCE *v* **-ALESCED, -ALESCING, -ALESCES** to blend

COALFISH *n* pl. **-ES** a blackish fish

COALHOLE *n* pl. **-S** a compartment for storing coal

COALIER comparative of coaly

COALIEST superlative of coaly

COALIFY *v* **-FIED, -FYING, -FIES** to convert into coal

COALLESS *adj* lacking coal

COALPIT *n* pl. **-S** a pit from which coal is obtained

COALSACK *n* pl. **-S** a dark region of the Milky Way

COALSHED *n* pl. **-S** a shed for storing coal

COALY *adj* **COALIER, COALIEST** containing coal

COALYARD *n* pl. **-S** a yard for storing coal

COAMING *n* pl. **-S** a raised border

COANCHOR *v* **-ED, -ING, -S** to present televised news reports jointly

COANNEX *v* **-ED, -ING, -ES** to annex jointly

COAPPEAR *v* **-ED, -ING, -S** to appear together or at the same time

COAPT *v* **-ED, -ING, -S** to fit together and make fast

COARSE *adj* **COARSER, COARSEST** rough **COARSELY** *adv*

COARSEN *v* **-ED, -ING, -S** to make coarse

COASSIST *v* **-ED, -ING, -S** to assist jointly

COASSUME *v* **-SUMED, -SUMING, -SUMES** to assume together

COAST	v **-ED, -ING, -S** to slide down a hill
COASTAL	adj pertaining to or located near a seashore
COASTER	n pl. **-S** a sled
COASTING	n pl. **-S** coastal trade
COAT	v **-ED, -ING, -S** to cover with a coat (an outer garment)
COATEE	n pl. **-S** a small coat
COATER	n pl. **-S** one that coats
COATI	n pl. **-S** a tropical mammal
COATING	n pl. **-S** a covering layer
COATLESS	adj lacking a coat
COATRACK	n pl. **-S** a rack or stand for coats
COATROOM	n pl. **-S** a room for storing coats
COATTAIL	n pl. **-S** the back lower portion of a coat
COATTEND	v **-ED, -ING, -S** to attend together
COATTEST	v **-ED, -ING, -S** to attest jointly
COAUTHOR	v **-ED, -ING, -S** to write together
COAX	v **-ED, -ING, -ES** to cajole
COAXAL	adj coaxial
COAXER	n pl. **-S** one that coaxes
COAXIAL	adj having a common axis
COB	n pl. **-S** a corncob
COBALT	n pl. **-S** a metallic element **COBALTIC** adj
COBB	n pl. **-S** a sea gull
COBBER	n pl. **-S** a comrade
COBBIER	comparative of cobby
COBBIEST	superlative of cobby
COBBLE	v **-BLED, -BLING, -BLES** to mend
COBBLER	n pl. **-S** a mender of shoes
COBBY	adj **-BIER, -BIEST** stocky
COBIA	n pl. **-S** a large game fish
COBLE	n pl. **-S** a small fishing boat
COBNUT	n pl. **-S** an edible nut
COBRA	n pl. **-S** a venomous snake
COBWEB	v **-WEBBED, -WEBBING, -WEBS** to cover with cobwebs (spider webs)
COBWEBBY	adj **-BIER, -BIEST** covered with cobwebs
COCA	n pl. **-S** a South American shrub
COCAIN	n pl. **-S** cocaine
COCAINE	n pl. **-S** a narcotic alkaloid
COCCAL	adj pertaining to a coccus

COCCI	pl. of coccus
COCCIC	adj coccal
COCCID	n pl. **-S** an insect
COCCIDIA	n/pl parasitic protozoans
COCCOID	n pl. **-S** a spherical cell or body
COCCUS	n pl. **COCCI** a spherical bacterium **COCCOUS** adj
COCCYX	n pl. **-CYXES** or **-CYGES** a bone of the spine
COCHAIR	v **-ED, -ING, -S** to serve jointly as chairman of
COCHIN	n pl. **-S** a large domestic chicken
COCHLEA	n pl. **-CHLEAS** or **-CHLEAE** a part of the ear **COCHLEAR** adj
COCINERA	n pl. **-S** a cook
COCK	v **-ED, -ING, -S** to tilt to one side
COCKADE	n pl. **-S** an ornament worn on a hat **COCKADED** adj
COCKAPOO	n pl. **-POOS** a hybrid between a cocker spaniel and a poodle
COCKATOO	n pl. **-TOOS** a parrot
COCKBILL	v **-ED, -ING, -S** to raise the yardarm on a ship
COCKBOAT	n pl. **-S** a small boat
COCKCROW	n pl. **-S** daybreak
COCKER	v **-ED, -ING, -S** to pamper
COCKEREL	n pl. **-S** a young rooster
COCKEYE	n pl. **-S** a squinting eye **COCKEYED** adj
COCKIER	comparative of cocky
COCKIEST	superlative of cocky
COCKILY	adv in a cocky manner
COCKISH	adj cocky
COCKLE	v **-LED, -LING, -LES** to wrinkle or pucker
COCKLIKE	adj resembling a rooster
COCKLOFT	n pl. **-S** a small attic
COCKNEY	n pl. **-NEYS** a resident of the East End of London
COCKPIT	n pl. **-S** a pilot's compartment in certain airplanes
COCKSHUT	n pl. **-S** the close of day
COCKSHY	n pl. **-SHIES** a target in a throwing contest
COCKSPUR	n pl. **-S** a thorny plant
COCKSURE	adj certain
COCKTAIL	v **-ED, -ING, -S** to drink alcoholic beverages

COCKUP *n* pl. **-S** a turned-up part of something

COCKY *adj* **COCKIER, COCKIEST** arrogantly self-confident

COCO *n* pl. **-COS** a tall palm tree

COCOA *n* pl. **-S** chocolate

COCOANUT *n* pl. **-S** coconut

COCOBOLA *n* pl. **-S** cocobolo

COCOBOLO *n* pl. **-LOS** a tropical tree

COCOMAT *n* pl. **-S** a matting made from coir

COCONUT *n* pl. **-S** the fruit of the coco

COCOON *v* **-ED, -ING, -S** to wrap or envelop tightly

COCOPLUM *n* pl. **-S** an evergreen shrub

COCOTTE *n* pl. **-S** a prostitute

COCOYAM *n* pl. **-S** a tropical plant having edible rootstocks

COCREATE *v* **-ATED, -ATING, -ATES** to create together

COD *v* **CODDED, CODDING, CODS** to fool

CODA *n* pl. **-S** a passage at the end of a musical composition

CODABLE *adj* capable of being coded

CODDER *n* pl. **-S** a cod fisherman

CODDING present participle of cod

CODDLE *v* **-DLED, -DLING, -DLES** to pamper

CODDLER *n* pl. **-S** one that coddles

CODE *v* **CODED, CODING, CODES** to convert into symbols

CODEBOOK *n* pl. **-S** a book listing words and their coded equivalents

CODEBTOR *n* pl. **-S** one that shares a debt

CODEC *n* pl. **-S** an integrated circuit

CODED past tense of code

CODEIA *n* pl. **-S** codeine

CODEIN *n* pl. **-S** codeine

CODEINA *n* pl. **-S** codeine

CODEINE *n* pl. **-S** a narcotic alkaloid

CODELESS *adj* being without a set of laws

CODEN *n* pl. **-S** a coding classification

CODER *n* pl. **-S** one that codes

CODERIVE *v* **-RIVED, -RIVING, -RIVES** to derive jointly

CODESIGN *v* **-ED, -ING, -S** to design jointly

CODEX *n* pl. **-DICES** an ancient manuscript

CODFISH *n* pl. **-ES** a marine food fish

CODGER *n* pl. **-S** an old man

CODICES pl. of codex

CODICIL *n* pl. **-S** a supplement to a will

CODIFIER *n* pl. **-S** one that codifies

CODIFY *v* **-FIED, -FYING, -FIES** to arrange or systematize

CODING present participle of code

CODIRECT *v* **-ED, -ING, -S** to direct jointly

CODLIN *n* pl. **-S** codling

CODLING *n* pl. **-S** an unripe apple

CODON *n* pl. **-S** a triplet of nucleotides (basic components of DNA)

CODPIECE *n* pl. **-S** a cover for the crotch in men's breeches

CODRIVE *v* **-DROVE, -DRIVEN, -DRIVING, -DRIVES** to work as a codriver

CODRIVER *n* pl. **-S** one who takes turns driving a vehicle

COED *n* pl. **-S** a female student

COEDIT *v* **-ED, -ING, -S** to edit with another person

COEDITOR *n* pl. **-S** one that coedits

COEFFECT *n* pl. **-S** an accompanying effect

COELIAC *adj* celiac

COELOM *n* pl. **-LOMS** or **-LOMATA** a body cavity in some animals **COELOMIC** *adj*

COELOME *n* pl. **-S** coelom

COEMBODY *v* **-BODIED, -BODYING, -BODIES** to embody jointly

COEMPLOY *v* **-ED, -ING, -S** to employ together

COEMPT *v* **-ED, -ING, -S** to buy up the entire supply of a product

COENACT *v* **-ED, -ING, -S** to enact jointly or at the same time

COENAMOR *v* **-ED, -ING, -S** to inflame with mutual love

COENDURE *v* **-DURED, -DURING, -DURES** to endure together

COENURE *n* pl. **-S** coenurus

COENURUS *n* pl. **-RI** a tapeworm larva

COENZYME *n* pl. **-S** a substance necessary for the functioning of certain enzymes

COEQUAL *n* pl. **-S** one who is equal with another

COEQUATE *v* **-QUATED, -QUATING, -QUATES** to equate with something else

COERCE *v* **-ERCED, -ERCING, -ERCES** to compel by force or threat

COERCER *n* pl. **-S** one that coerces

COERCION *n* pl. **-S** the act of coercing

COERCIVE *adj* serving to coerce

COERECT *v* **-ED, -ING, -S** to erect together

COESITE *n* pl. **-S** a type of silica

COEVAL *n* pl. **-S** one of the same era or period as another

COEVALLY *adv* contemporarily

COEVOLVE *v* **-VOLVED, -VOLVING, -VOLVES** to evolve together

COEXERT *v* **-ED, -ING, -S** to exert jointly

COEXIST *v* **-ED, -ING, -S** to exist together

COEXTEND *v* **-ED, -ING, -S** to extend through the same space or time as another

COFACTOR *n* pl. **-S** a coenzyme

COFF *v* **COFT, COFFING, COFFS** to buy

COFFEE *n* pl. **-S** an aromatic, mildly stimulating beverage

COFFER *v* **-ED, -ING, -S** to put in a strongbox

COFFIN *v* **-ED, -ING, -S** to put in a coffin (a burial case)

COFFING present participle of coff

COFFLE *v* **-FLED, -FLING, -FLES** to chain slaves together

COFFRET *n* pl. **-S** a small strongbox

COFOUND *v* **-ED, -ING, -S** to found jointly

COFT past tense of coff

COG *v* **COGGED, COGGING, COGS** to cheat at dice

COGENCY *n* pl. **-CIES** the state of being cogent

COGENT *adj* convincing **COGENTLY** *adv*

COGITATE *v* **-TATED, -TATING, -TATES** to ponder

COGITO *n* pl. **-TOS** a philosophical principle

COGNAC *n* pl. **-S** a brandy

COGNATE *n* pl. **-S** one that is related to another

COGNISE *v* **-NISED, -NISING, -NISES** to cognize

COGNIZE *v* **-NIZED, -NIZING, -NIZES** to become aware of in one's mind

COGNIZER *n* pl. **-S** one that cognizes

COGNOMEN *n* pl. **-MENS** or **-MINA** a family name

COGNOVIT *n* pl. **-S** a written admission of liability

COGON *n* pl. **-S** a tall tropical grass

COGWAY *n* pl. **-WAYS** a railway operating on steep slopes

COGWHEEL *n* pl. **-S** a toothed wheel

COHABIT *v* **-ED, -ING, -S** to live together as man and wife while unmarried

COHEAD *v* **-ED, -ING, -S** to head jointly

COHEIR *n* pl. **-S** a joint heir

COHERE *v* **-HERED, -HERING, -HERES** to stick together

COHERENT *adj* sticking together

COHERER *n* pl. **-S** a device used to detect radio waves

COHESION *n* pl. **-S** the act or state of cohering **COHESIVE** *adj*

COHO *n* pl. **-HOS** a small salmon

COHOBATE *v* **-BATED, -BATING, -BATES** to distill again

COHOG *n* pl. **-S** a quahog

COHOLDER *n* pl. **-S** an athlete who holds a record with another

COHORT *n* pl. **-S** a companion or associate

COHOSH *n* pl. **-ES** a medicinal plant

COHOST *v* **-ED, -ING, -S** to host jointly

COHUNE *n* pl. **-S** a palm tree

COIF *v* **-ED, -ING, -S** to style the hair

COIFFE *v* **COIFFED, COIFFING, COIFFES** to coif

COIFFEUR *n* pl. **-S** a male hairdresser

COIFFURE *v* **-FURED, -FURING, -FURES** to coif

COIGN *v* **-ED, -ING, -S** to quoin

COIGNE *v* **COIGNED, COIGNING, COIGNES** to quoin

COIL *v* **-ED, -ING, -S** to wind in even rings

COILER *n* pl. **-S** one that coils

COIN *v* **-ED, -ING, -S** to make coins (metal currency) **COINABLE** *adj*

COINAGE *n* pl. **-S** the act of making coins

COINCIDE *v* **-CIDED, -CIDING, -CIDES** to be in the same place

COINER *n* pl. **-S** one that coins

COINFECT *v* **-ED, -ING, -S** to infect with two organisms

COINFER *v* **-FERRED, -FERRING, -FERS** to infer jointly

COINHERE *v* **-HERED, -HERING, -HERES** to inhere jointly

COINMATE   *n* pl. **-S** a fellow inmate

COINSURE   *v* **-SURED, -SURING, -SURES** to insure with another

COINTER   *v* **-TERRED, -TERRING, -TERS** to bury together

COINVENT   *v* **-ED, -ING, -S** to invent together

COIR   *n* pl. **-S** a fiber obtained from coconut husks

COISTREL   *n* pl. **-S** a knave

COISTRIL   *n* pl. **-S** coistrel

COITION   *n* pl. **-S** coitus

COITUS   *n* pl. **-ES** sexual intercourse **COITAL** *adj* **COITALLY** *adv*

COJOIN   *v* **-ED, -ING, -S** to join together

COKE   *v* **COKED, COKING, COKES** to change into a carbon fuel

COKEHEAD   *n* pl. **-S** a cocaine addict

COKELIKE   *adj* resembling coke (a carbon fuel)

COKY   *adj* cokelike

COL   *n* pl. **-S** a depression between two mountains

COLA   *n* pl. **-S** a carbonated beverage

COLANDER   *n* pl. **-S** a kitchen utensil for draining off liquids

COLBY   *n* pl. **-BYS** a mild cheese

COLD   *adj* **COLDER, COLDEST** having little or no warmth

COLD   *n* pl. **-S** the relative lack of heat; a chill

COLDCOCK   *v* **-ED, -ING, -S** to knock unconscious

COLDISH   *adj* somewhat cold

COLDLY   *adv* in a cold manner

COLDNESS   *n* pl. **-ES** the state of being cold

COLE   *n* pl. **-S** a plant of the cabbage family

COLEAD   *v* **-LED, -LEADING, -LEADS** to lead jointly

COLEADER   *n* pl. **-S** one that coleads

COLESEED   *n* pl. **-S** colza

COLESLAW   *n* pl. **-S** a salad made of shredded raw cabbage

COLESSEE   *n* pl. **-S** a joint lessee

COLESSOR   *n* pl. **-S** a joint lessor

COLEUS   *n* pl. **-ES** a tropical plant

COLEWORT   *n* pl. **-S** cole

COLIC   *n* pl. **-S** acute abdominal pain

COLICIN   *n* pl. **-S** an antibacterial substance

COLICINE   *n* pl. **-S** colicin

COLICKY   *adj* pertaining to or associated with colic

COLIES   pl. of coly

COLIFORM   *n* pl. **-S** a bacillus of the colon

COLIN   *n* pl. **-S** the bobwhite

COLINEAR   *adj* lying in the same straight line

COLISEUM   *n* pl. **-S** a large structure for public entertainment

COLISTIN   *n* pl. **-S** an antibiotic

COLITIS   *n* pl. **-TISES** inflammation of the colon **COLITIC** *adj*

COLLAGE   *v* **-LAGED, -LAGING, -LAGES** to arrange materials in a collage (a kind of artistic composition)

COLLAGEN   *n* pl. **-S** a protein

COLLAPSE   *v* **-LAPSED, -LAPSING, -LAPSES** to crumble suddenly

COLLAR   *v* **-ED, -ING, -S** to provide with a collar (something worn around the neck)

COLLARD   *n* pl. **-S** a variety of kale

COLLARET   *n* pl. **-S** a small collar

COLLATE   *v* **-LATED, -LATING, -LATES** to compare critically

COLLATOR   *n* pl. **-S** one that collates

COLLECT   *v* **-ED, -ING, -S** to bring together in a group

COLLEEN   *n* pl. **-S** an Irish girl

COLLEGE   *n* pl. **-S** a school of higher learning

COLLEGER   *n* pl. **-S** a student supported by funds from his college

COLLEGIA   *n/pl* soviet executive councils

COLLET   *v* **-ED, -ING, -S** to set a gem in a rim or ring

COLLIDE   *v* **-LIDED, -LIDING, -LIDES** to come together with violent impact

COLLIDER   *n* pl. **-S** a type of particle accelerator

COLLIE   *n* pl. **-S** a large dog

COLLIED   past tense of colly

COLLIER   *n* pl. **-S** a coal miner

COLLIERY   *n* pl. **-LIERIES** a coal mine

COLLIES   present 3d person sing. of colly

COLLINS   *n* pl. **-ES** an alcoholic beverage

COLLOGUE   *v* **-LOGUED, -LOGUING, -LOGUES** to conspire

COLLOID   *n* pl. **-S** a type of chemical suspension

COLLOP *n* pl. **-S** a small portion of meat

COLLOQUY *n* pl. **-QUIES** a conversation

COLLUDE *v* **-LUDED, -LUDING, -LUDES** to conspire

COLLUDER *n* pl. **-S** one that colludes

COLLUVIA *n/pl* rock debris

COLLY *v* **-LIED, -LYING, -LIES** to blacken with coal dust

COLLYRIA *n/pl* medicinal lotions

COLOBOMA *n* pl. **-MATA** a lesion of the eye

COLOBUS *n* pl. **-BUSES** or **-BI** a large African monkey

COLOCATE *v* **-CATED, -CATING, -CATES** to place two or more housing units in close proximity

COLOG *n* pl. **-S** the logarithm of the reciprocal of a number

COLOGNE *n* pl. **-S** a scented liquid **COLOGNED** *adj*

COLON *n* pl. **-ES** a monetary unit of Costa Rica

COLON *n* pl. **-S** a section of the large intestine

COLONE *n* pl. **-S** colon

COLONEL *n* pl. **-S** a military officer

COLONI pl. of colonus

COLONIAL *n* pl. **-S** a citizen of a colony

COLONIC *n* pl. **-S** irrigation of the colon

COLONIES pl. of colony

COLONISE *v* **-NISED, -NISING, -NISES** to colonize

COLONIST *n* pl. **-S** one who settles a colony

COLONIZE *v* **-NIZED, -NIZING, -NIZES** to establish a colony

COLONUS *n* pl. **-NI** a freeborn serf

COLONY *n* pl. **-NIES** a group of emigrants living in a new land

COLOPHON *n* pl. **-S** an inscription placed at the end of a book

COLOR *v* **-ED, -ING, -S** to give color (a visual attribute of objects) to

COLORADO *adj* of medium strength and color — used of cigars

COLORANT *n* pl. **-S** a pigment or dye

COLORED *adj* having color

COLORER *n* pl. **-S** one that colors

COLORFUL *adj* full of color

COLORING *n* pl. **-S** appearance in regard to color

COLORISM *n* pl. **-S** coloring

COLORIST *n* pl. **-S** a person skilled in the use of color

COLORIZE *v* **-IZED, -IZING, -IZES** to give color to a black-and-white film

COLORMAN *n* pl. **-MEN** a sportscaster who provides commentary during a game

COLORWAY *n* pl. **-WAYS** an arrangement of colors

COLOSSAL *adj* gigantic

COLOSSUS *n* pl. **-LOSSUSES** or **-LOSSI** a gigantic statue

COLOTOMY *n* pl. **-MIES** a surgical incision of the colon

COLOUR *v* **-ED, -ING, -S** to color

COLOURER *n* pl. **-S** colorer

COLPITIS *n* pl. **-TISES** a vaginal inflammation

COLT *n* pl. **-S** a young male horse **COLTISH** *adj*

COLTER *n* pl. **-S** a blade on a plow

COLUBRID *n* pl. **-S** any of a large family of snakes

COLUGO *n* pl. **-GOS** a small mammal

COLUMBIC *adj* pertaining to niobium

COLUMEL *n* pl. **-S** a small column-like anatomical part

COLUMN *n* pl. **-S** a vertical cylindrical support **COLUMNAL, COLUMNAR, COLUMNED** *adj*

COLUMNEA *n* pl. **-S** a bushy tropical plant

COLURE *n* pl. **-S** an astronomical circle

COLY *n* pl. **COLIES** an African bird

COLZA *n* pl. **-S** a plant of the cabbage family

COMA *n* pl. **-MAE** a tuft of silky hairs

COMA *n* pl. **-S** a condition of prolonged unconsciousness

COMAKE *v* **-MADE, -MAKING, -MAKES** to serve as comaker for another's loan

COMAKER *n* pl. **-S** one who assumes financial responsibility for another's default

COMAL *adj* comose

COMANAGE *v* **-AGED, -AGING, -AGES** to manage jointly

COMATE *n* pl. **-S** a companion

COMATIC *adj* having blurred vision as a result of coma

COMATIK *n* pl. **-S** komatik

COMATOSE *adj* affected with coma

COMATULA *n* pl. **-LAE** a marine animal

COMB *v* **-ED, -ING, -S** to arrange or clean with a comb (a toothed instrument)

COMBAT *v* **-BATED, -BATING, -BATS** or **-BATTED, -BATTING, -BATS** to fight against

COMBATER *n* pl. **-S** one that combats

COMBE *n* pl. **-S** a narrow valley

COMBER *n* pl. **-S** one that combs

COMBINE *v* **-BINED, -BINING, -BINES** to blend

COMBINED *n* pl. **-S** a skiing competition combining two events

COMBINER *n* pl. **-S** one that combines

COMBINGS *n/pl* hair removed by a comb

COMBINING present participle of combine

COMBLIKE *adj* resembling a comb

COMBO *n* pl. **-BOS** a small jazz band

COMBUST *v* **-ED, -ING, -S** to burn

COME *v* **CAME, COMING, COMES** or **COMETH** to move toward something or someone

COMEBACK *n* pl. **-S** a return to former prosperity

COMEDIAN *n* pl. **-S** a humorous entertainer

COMEDIC *adj* pertaining to comedy

COMEDIES pl. of comedy

COMEDO *n* pl. **-DOS** or **-DONES** a skin blemish

COMEDOWN *n* pl. **-S** a drop in status

COMEDY *n* pl. **-DIES** a humorous play, movie, or other work

COMELY *adj* **-LIER, -LIEST** pleasing to look at **COMELILY** *adv*

COMEMBER *n* pl. **-S** one that shares membership

COMER *n* pl. **-S** one showing great promise

COMET *n* pl. **-S** a celestial body **COMETARY** *adj*

COMETH a present 3d person sing. of come

COMETHER *n* pl. **-S** an affair or matter

COMETIC *adj* pertaining to a comet

COMFIER comparative of comfy

COMFIEST superlative of comfy

COMFIT *n* pl. **-S** a candy

COMFORT *v* **-ED, -ING, -S** to soothe in time of grief

COMFREY *n* pl. **-FREYS** a coarse herb

COMFY *adj* **-FIER, -FIEST** comfortable

COMIC *n* pl. **-S** a comedian

COMICAL *adj* funny

COMING *n* pl. **-S** arrival

COMINGLE *v* **-GLED, -GLING, -GLES** to blend thoroughly

COMITIA *n* pl. **COMITIA** a public assembly in ancient Rome **COMITIAL** *adj*

COMITY *n* pl. **-TIES** civility

COMIX *n/pl* comic books or strips

COMMA *n* pl. **-MAS** or **-MATA** a fragment of a few words or feet in ancient prosody

COMMAND *v* **-ED, -ING, -S** to direct with authority

COMMANDO *n* pl. **-DOS** or **-DOES** a military unit

COMMATA a pl. of comma

COMMENCE *v* **-MENCED, -MENCING, -MENCES** to begin

COMMEND *v* **-ED, -ING, -S** to praise

COMMENT *v* **-ED, -ING, -S** to remark

COMMERCE *v* **-MERCED, -MERCING, -MERCES** to commune

COMMIE *n* pl. **-S** a Communist

COMMIES pl. of commy

COMMIT *v* **-MITTED, -MITTING, -MITS** to do, perform, or perpetrate

COMMIX *v* **-MIXED** or **-MIXT, -MIXING, -MIXES** to mix together

COMMODE *n* pl. **-S** a cabinet

COMMON *adj* **-MONER, -MONEST** ordinary

COMMON *n* pl. **-S** a tract of publicly used land

COMMONER *n* pl. **-S** one of the common people

COMMONLY *adv* in a common manner

COMMOVE *v* **-MOVED, -MOVING, -MOVES** to move violently

COMMUNAL *adj* belonging to a community; public

COMMUNE *v* **-MUNED, -MUNING, -MUNES** to converse intimately

COMMUNER *n* pl. **-S** one that communes

COMMUTE *v* **-MUTED, -MUTING, -MUTES** to exchange

COMMUTER *n* pl. **-S** one that commutes

COMMY *n* pl. **-MIES** commie

COMORBID *adj* existing simultaneously with another medical condition

COMOSE *adj* bearing a tuft of silky hairs

COMOUS *adj* comose

COMP *v* **-ED, -ING, -S** to play a jazz accompaniment

COMPACT *adj* **-PACTER, -PACTEST** closely and firmly united

COMPACT *v* **-ED, -ING, -S** to pack closely together

COMPADRE *n* pl. **-S** a close friend

COMPANY *v* **-NIED, -NYING, -NIES** to associate with

COMPARE *v* **-PARED, -PARING, -PARES** to represent as similar

COMPARER *n* pl. **-S** one that compares

COMPART *v* **-ED, -ING, -S** to divide into parts

COMPAS *n* a popular music of Haiti

COMPASS *v* **-ED, -ING, -ES** to go around

COMPEER *v* **-ED, -ING, -S** to equal or match

COMPEL *v* **-PELLED, -PELLING, -PELS** to urge forcefully

COMPEND *n* pl. **-S** a brief summary

COMPERE *v* **-PERED, -PERING, -PERES** to act as master of ceremonies

COMPETE *v* **-PETED, -PETING, -PETES** to vie

COMPILE *v* **-PILED, -PILING, -PILES** to collect into a volume

COMPILER *n* pl. **-S** one that compiles

COMPLAIN *v* **-ED, -ING, -S** to express discontent

COMPLEAT *adj* highly skilled

COMPLECT *v* **-ED, -ING, -S** to weave together

COMPLETE *adj* **-PLETER, -PLETEST** having all necessary parts

COMPLETE *v* **-PLETED, -PLETING, -PLETES** to bring to an end

COMPLEX *adj* **-PLEXER, -PLEXEST** complicated

COMPLEX *v* **-ED, -ING, -ES** to make complex

COMPLICE *n* pl. **-S** an associate

COMPLIED past tense of comply

COMPLIER *n* pl. **-S** one that complies

COMPLIES present 3d person sing. of comply

COMPLIN *n* pl. **-S** compline

COMPLINE *n* pl. **-S** the last liturgical prayer of the day

COMPLOT *v* **-PLOTTED, -PLOTTING, -PLOTS** to conspire

COMPLY *v* **-PLIED, -PLYING, -PLIES** to obey

COMPO *n* pl. **-POS** a mixed substance

COMPONE *adj* compony

COMPONY *adj* composed of squares of alternating colors

COMPORT *v* **-ED, -ING, -S** to conduct oneself in a certain way

COMPOSE *v* **-POSED, -POSING, -POSES** to form the substance of

COMPOSER *n* pl. **-S** one that writes music

COMPOST *v* **-ED, -ING, -S** to fertilize

COMPOTE *n* pl. **-S** fruit stewed in syrup

COMPOUND *v* **-ED, -ING, -S** to add to

COMPRESS *v* **-ED, -ING, -ES** to compact

COMPRISE *v* **-PRISED, -PRISING, -PRISES** to include or contain

COMPRIZE *v* **-PRIZED, -PRIZING, -PRIZES** to comprise

COMPT *v* **-ED, -ING, -S** to count

COMPUTE *v* **-PUTED, -PUTING, -PUTES** to calculate

COMPUTER *n* pl. **-S** a machine that computes automatically

COMRADE *n* pl. **-S** a close friend

COMTE *n* pl. **-S** a French nobleman

CON *v* **CONNED, CONNING, CONS** to study carefully

CONATION *n* pl. **-S** the inclination to act purposefully **CONATIVE** *adj*

CONATUS *n* pl. **CONATUS** an effort

CONCAVE *v* **-CAVED, -CAVING, -CAVES** to make concave (curving inward)

CONCEAL *v* **-ED, -ING, -S** to keep from sight or discovery

CONCEDE *v* **-CEDED, -CEDING, -CEDES** to acknowledge as true

CONCEDER *n* pl. **-S** one that concedes

CONCEIT *v* **-ED, -ING, -S** to imagine

CONCEIVE *v* **-CEIVED, -CEIVING, -CEIVES** to understand

CONCENT *n* pl. **-S** harmony

CONCEPT *n* pl. **-S** a general idea

CONCEPTI *n/pl* fertilized eggs

CONCERN *v* **-ED, -ING, -S** to be of interest to

CONCERT *v* **-ED, -ING, -S** to plan

CONCERTO *n* pl. **-TOS** or **-TI** a musical composition

CONCH *n* pl. **-S** or **-ES** a marine mollusk

CONCHA *n* pl. **-S** an ornamental disk

CONCHA *n pl.* **-CHAE** an anatomical shell-like structure **CONCHAL** *adj*

CONCHIE *n pl.* **-S** conchy

CONCHO *n pl.* **-CHOS** concha (ornamental disk)

CONCHOID *n pl.* **-S** a type of geometric curve

CONCHY *n pl.* **-CHIES** a conscientious objector

CONCISE *adj* **-CISER, -CISEST** succinct

CONCLAVE *n pl.* **-S** a secret meeting

CONCLUDE *v* **-CLUDED, -CLUDING, -CLUDES** to finish

CONCOCT *v* **-ED, -ING, -S** to prepare by combining ingredients

CONCORD *n pl.* **-S** a state of agreement

CONCOURS *n pl.* **CONCOURS** a public competition

CONCRETE *v* **-CRETED, -CRETING, -CRETES** to solidify

CONCUR *v* **-CURRED, -CURRING, -CURS** to agree

CONCUSS *v* **-ED, -ING, -ES** to injure the brain by a violent blow

CONDEMN *v* **-ED, -ING, -S** to criticize severely

CONDENSE *v* **-DENSED, -DENSING, -DENSES** to compress

CONDIGN *adj* deserved; appropriate

CONDO *n pl.* **-DOS** or **-DOES** an individually owned unit in a multiunit structure

CONDOLE *v* **-DOLED, -DOLING, -DOLES** to mourn

CONDOLER *n pl.* **-S** one that condoles

CONDOM *n pl.* **-S** a prophylactic

CONDONE *v* **-DONED, -DONING, -DONES** to forgive or overlook

CONDONER *n pl.* **-S** one that condones

CONDOR *n pl.* **-S** or **-ES** a coin of Chile

CONDUCE *v* **-DUCED, -DUCING, -DUCES** to contribute to a result

CONDUCER *n pl.* **-S** one that conduces

CONDUCT *v* **-ED, -ING, -S** to lead or guide

CONDUIT *n pl.* **-S** a channel or pipe for conveying fluids

CONDYLE *n pl.* **-S** a protuberance on a bone **CONDYLAR** *adj*

CONE *v* **CONED, CONING, CONES** to shape like a cone (a geometric solid)

CONELRAD *n pl.* **-S** a system of defense in the event of air attack

CONENOSE *n pl.* **-S** a bloodsucking insect

CONEPATE *n pl.* **-S** a skunk

CONEPATL *n pl.* **-S** conepate

CONEY *n pl.* **-NEYS** cony

CONFAB *v* **-FABBED, -FABBING, -FABS** to chat

CONFECT *v* **-ED, -ING, -S** to prepare from various ingredients

CONFER *v* **-FERRED, -FERRING, -FERS** to bestow

CONFEREE *n pl.* **-S** one upon whom something is conferred

CONFERVA *n pl.* **-VAS** or **-VAE** a freshwater alga

CONFESS *v* **-ED, -ING, -ES** to acknowledge or disclose

CONFETTO *n pl.* **-TI** a bonbon

CONFIDE *v* **-FIDED, -FIDING, -FIDES** to reveal in trust or confidence

CONFIDER *n pl.* **-S** one that confides

CONFINE *v* **-FINED, -FINING, -FINES** to shut within an enclosure

CONFINER *n pl.* **-S** one that confines

CONFIRM *v* **-ED, -ING, -S** to assure the validity of

CONFIT *n pl.* **-S** meat cooked and preserved in its own fat

CONFLATE *v* **-FLATED, -FLATING, -FLATES** to blend

CONFLICT *v* **-ED, -ING, -S** to come into opposition

CONFLUX *n pl.* **-ES** a flowing together of streams

CONFOCAL *adj* having the same focus or foci

CONFORM *v* **-ED, -ING, -S** to become the same or similar

CONFOUND *v* **-ED, -ING, -S** to confuse

CONFRERE *n pl.* **-S** a colleague

CONFRONT *v* **-ED, -ING, -S** to face defiantly

CONFUSE *v* **-FUSED, -FUSING, -FUSES** to mix up mentally

CONFUTE *v* **-FUTED, -FUTING, -FUTES** to disprove

CONFUTER *n pl.* **-S** one that confutes

CONGA *v* **-ED, -ING, -S** to perform a conga (Latin-American dance)

CONGE *n pl.* **-S** permission to depart

CONGEAL *v* **-ED, -ING, -S** to change from a fluid to a solid

CONGEE	v **-GEED, -GEEING, -GEES** to bow politely
CONGENER	n pl. **-S** one of the same kind or class
CONGER	n pl. **-S** a marine eel
CONGEST	v **-ED, -ING, -S** to fill to excess
CONGIUS	n pl. **-GII** an ancient unit of measure
CONGLOBE	v **-GLOBED, -GLOBING, -GLOBES** to become a globule
CONGO	n pl. **-GOES** an eellike amphibian
CONGO	n pl. **-GOS** congou
CONGOU	n pl. **-S** a Chinese tea
CONGRATS	n/pl congratulations
CONGRESS	v **-ED, -ING, -ES** to assemble together
CONI	pl. of conus
CONIC	n pl. **-S** a geometric curve
CONICAL	adj shaped like a cone
CONICITY	n pl. **-TIES** the state of being conical
CONIDIUM	n pl. **-NIDIA** a fungus spore **CONIDIAL, CONIDIAN** adj
CONIES	pl. of cony
CONIFER	n pl. **-S** an evergreen tree
CONIINE	n pl. **-S** a poisonous alkaloid
CONIN	n pl. **-S** coniine
CONINE	n pl. **-S** coniine
CONING	present participle of cone
CONIOSIS	n pl. **-OSES** an infection caused by the inhalation of dust
CONIUM	n pl. **-S** a poisonous herb
CONJOIN	v **-ED, -ING, -S** to join together **CONJOINT** adj
CONJUGAL	adj pertaining to marriage
CONJUNCT	n pl. **-S** one that is joined with another
CONJUNTO	n pl. **-TOS** a style of dance music along the Mexican border
CONJURE	v **-JURED, -JURING, -JURES** to summon a spirit
CONJURER	n pl. **-S** a sorcerer
CONJUROR	n pl. **-S** conjurer
CONK	v **-ED, -ING, -S** to hit on the head
CONKER	n pl. **-S** a chestnut used in a British game
CONKY	adj full of a tree fungus
CONN	v **-ED, -ING, -S** to direct the steering of a ship
CONNATE	adj innate
CONNECT	v **-ED, -ING, -S** to join together
CONNED	past tense of con
CONNER	n pl. **-S** one that cons
CONNING	present participle of con
CONNIVE	v **-NIVED, -NIVING, -NIVES** to feign ignorance of wrongdoing
CONNIVER	n pl. **-S** one that connives
CONNOTE	v **-NOTED, -NOTING, -NOTES** to imply another meaning besides the literal one
CONODONT	n pl. **-S** a fossil
CONOID	n pl. **-S** a geometric solid **CONOIDAL** adj
CONQUER	v **-ED, -ING, -S** to overcome by force
CONQUEST	n pl. **-S** the act of conquering
CONQUIAN	n pl. **-S** a card game
CONSENT	v **-ED, -ING, -S** to permit or approve
CONSERVE	v **-SERVED, -SERVING, -SERVES** to protect from loss or depletion
CONSIDER	v **-ED, -ING, -S** to think about
CONSIGN	v **-ED, -ING, -S** to give over to another's care
CONSIST	v **-ED, -ING, -S** to be made up or composed
CONSOL	n pl. **-S** a government bond
CONSOLE	v **-SOLED, -SOLING, -SOLES** to comfort
CONSOLER	n pl. **-S** one that consoles
CONSOMME	n pl. **-S** a clear soup
CONSORT	v **-ED, -ING, -S** to keep company
CONSPIRE	v **-SPIRED, -SPIRING, -SPIRES** to plan secretly with another
CONSTANT	n pl. **-S** something that does not vary
CONSTRUE	v **-STRUED, -STRUING, -STRUES** to interpret
CONSUL	n pl. **-S** an official serving abroad **CONSULAR** adj
CONSULT	v **-ED, -ING, -S** to ask an opinion of
CONSUME	v **-SUMED, -SUMING, -SUMES** to use up
CONSUMER	n pl. **-S** one that consumes
CONTACT	v **-ED, -ING, -S** to communicate with
CONTAGIA	n/pl causative agents of infectious diseases
CONTAIN	v **-ED, -ING, -S** to hold within

CONTE	*n* pl. **-S** a short story	**CONVERSE**	*v* **-VERSED, -VERSING, -VERSES** to speak together
CONTEMN	*v* **-ED, -ING, -S** to scorn		
CONTEMPO	*adj* contemporary	**CONVERSO**	*n* pl. **-SOS** a Jew who converted to Christianity
CONTEMPT	*n* pl. **-S** the feeling of one who views something as mean, vile, or worthless	**CONVERT**	*v* **-ED, -ING, -S** to change into another form
CONTEND	*v* **-ED, -ING, -S** to vie	**CONVEX**	*n* pl. **-ES** a surface or body that is convex (curving outward)
CONTENT	*v* **-ED, -ING, -S** to satisfy		
CONTESSA	*n* pl. **-S** an Italian countess	**CONVEXLY**	*adv* in a convex manner
CONTEST	*v* **-ED, -ING, -S** to compete for	**CONVEY**	*v* **-ED, -ING, -S** to transport
CONTEXT	*n* pl. **-S** the part of a discourse in which a particular word or phrase appears	**CONVEYER**	*n* pl. **-S** one that conveys
		CONVEYOR	*n* pl. **-S** conveyer
CONTINUA	*n/pl* mathematical sets	**CONVICT**	*v* **-ED, -ING, -S** to prove guilty
CONTINUE	*v* **-UED, -UING, -UES** to go on with	**CONVINCE**	*v* **-VINCED, -VINCING, -VINCES** to cause to believe something
CONTINUO	*n* pl. **-UOS** a type of instrumental part	**CONVOKE**	*v* **-VOKED, -VOKING, -VOKES** to cause to assemble
CONTO	*n* pl. **-TOS** a Portuguese money of account	**CONVOKER**	*n* pl. **-S** one that convokes
CONTORT	*v* **-ED, -ING, -S** to twist out of shape	**CONVOLVE**	*v* **-VOLVED, -VOLVING, -VOLVES** to roll together
CONTOUR	*v* **-ED, -ING, -S** to make the outline of	**CONVOY**	*v* **-ED, -ING, -S** to escort
		CONVULSE	*v* **-VULSED, -VULSING, -VULSES** to shake violently
CONTRA	*n* pl. **-S** a Nicaraguan revolutionary		
CONTRACT	*v* **-ED, -ING, -S** to decrease in size or volume	**CONY**	*n* pl. **CONIES** a rabbit
		COO	*v* **-ED, -ING, -S** to make the sound of a dove
CONTRAIL	*n* pl. **-S** a visible trail of water vapor from an aircraft	**COOCH**	*n* pl. **-ES** a sinuous dance
CONTRARY	*n* pl. **-TRARIES** an opposite	**COOCOO**	*adj* crazy
CONTRAST	*v* **-ED, -ING, -S** to place in opposition to set off differences	**COOEE**	*v* **COOEED, COOEEING, COOEES** to cry out shrilly
CONTRITE	*adj* deeply sorry for one's sins	**COOER**	*n* pl. **-S** one that coos
CONTRIVE	*v* **-TRIVED, -TRIVING, -TRIVES** to devise	**COOEY**	*v* **-EYED, -EYING, -EYS** to cooee
		COOF	*n* pl. **-S** a dolt
CONTROL	*v* **-TROLLED, -TROLLING, -TROLS** to exercise authority over	**COOING**	present participle of coo
		COOINGLY	*adv* in the manner of cooing doves; affectionately
CONTUSE	*v* **-TUSED, -TUSING, -TUSES** to bruise	**COOK**	*v* **-ED, -ING, -S** to prepare food by heating **COOKABLE** *adj*
CONUS	*n* pl. **CONI** an anatomical part in mammals	**COOKBOOK**	*n* pl. **-S** a book of recipes
		COOKER	*n* pl. **-S** one that cooks
CONVECT	*v* **-ED, -ING, -S** to transfer heat by a process of circulation	**COOKERY**	*n* pl. **-ERIES** the art of cooking
CONVENE	*v* **-VENED, -VENING, -VENES** to assemble	**COOKEY**	*n* pl. **-EYS** cookie
		COOKIE	*n* pl. **-S** a small, flat cake
CONVENER	*n* pl. **-S** one that convenes	**COOKING**	*n* pl. **-S** the act of one that cooks
CONVENOR	*n* pl. **-S** convener	**COOKLESS**	*adj* having no person that cooks
CONVENT	*v* **-ED, -ING, -S** to convene	**COOKOFF**	*n* pl. **-S** a cooking contest
CONVERGE	*v* **-VERGED, -VERGING, -VERGES** to come together	**COOKOUT**	*n* pl. **-S** a meal eaten and prepared outdoors

COOKSHOP *n* pl. **-S** a shop that sells cooked food

COOKTOP *n* pl. **-S** a counter-top cooking apparatus

COOKWARE *n* pl. **-S** utensils used in cooking

COOKY *n* pl. **COOKIES** cookie

COOL *adj* **COOLER, COOLEST** moderately cold

COOL *v* **-ED, -ING, -S** to make less warm

COOLANT *n* pl. **-S** a fluid used to cool engines

COOLDOWN *n* pl. **-S** a gradual return of physiological functions to normal levels after strenuous exercise

COOLER *n* pl. **-S** something that cools

COOLIE *n* pl. **-S** a laborer in or from the Far East

COOLIES pl. of cooly

COOLISH *adj* somewhat cool

COOLLY *adv* in a cool manner

COOLNESS *n* pl. **-ES** the state of being cool

COOLTH *n* pl. **-S** coolness

COOLY *n* pl. **COOLIES** coolie

COOMB *n* pl. **-S** combe

COOMBE *n* pl. **-S** combe

COON *n* pl. **-S** a raccoon

COONCAN *n* pl. **-S** conquian

COONSKIN *n* pl. **-S** the pelt of a raccoon

COONTIE *n* pl. **-S** a tropical plant

COOP *v* **-ED, -ING, -S** to confine

COOPER *v* **-ED, -ING, -S** to make or mend barrels

COOPERY *n* pl. **-ERIES** the trade of coopering

COOPT *v* **-ED, -ING, -S** to elect or appoint

COOPTION *n* pl. **-S** the act of coopting

COOT *n* pl. **-S** an aquatic bird

COOTER *n* pl. **-S** a turtle

COOTIE *n* pl. **-S** a body louse

COP *v* **COPPED, COPPING, COPS** to steal

COPAIBA *n* pl. **-S** a resin

COPAL *n* pl. **-S** a resin

COPALM *n* pl. **-S** a hardwood tree

COPARENT *v* **-ED, -ING, -S** to share in the custody of one's child

COPASTOR *n* pl. **-S** one that shares the duties of a pastor

COPATRON *n* pl. **-S** a fellow patron

COPAY *n* pl. **-PAYS** a fee required by a health insurer to be paid by the patient

COPE *v* **COPED, COPING, COPES** to contend or strive

COPECK *n* pl. **-S** kopeck

COPEMATE *n* pl. **-S** an antagonist

COPEN *n* pl. **-S** a blue color

COPEPOD *n* pl. **-S** a minute crustacean

COPER *n* pl. **-S** a horse dealer

COPIED past tense of copy

COPIER *n* pl. **-S** one that copies

COPIES present 3d person sing. of copy

COPIHUE *n* pl. **-S** a climbing vine

COPILOT *n* pl. **-S** an assistant pilot

COPING *n* pl. **-S** the top part of a wall

COPIOUS *adj* abundant

COPLANAR *adj* lying in the same plane

COPLOT *v* **-PLOTTED, -PLOTTING, -PLOTS** to plot together

COPOUT *n* pl. **-S** a backing out of a responsibility

COPPED past tense of cop

COPPER *v* **-ED, -ING, -S** to cover with copper (a metallic element)

COPPERAH *n* pl. **-S** copra

COPPERAS *n* pl. **-ES** a compound used in making inks

COPPERY *adj* resembling copper

COPPICE *v* **-PICED, -PICING, -PICES** to cause to grow in the form of a coppice (a thicket)

COPPING present participle of cop

COPPRA *n* pl. **-S** copra

COPRA *n* pl. **-S** dried coconut meat

COPRAH *n* pl. **-S** copra

COPREMIA *n* pl. **-S** a form of blood poisoning **COPREMIC** *adj*

COPRINCE *n* pl. **-S** one of two princes ruling jointly

COPSE *n* pl. **-S** a coppice

COPTER *n* pl. **-S** a helicopter

COPULA *n* pl. **-LAS** or **-LAE** something that links **COPULAR** *adj*

COPULATE *v* **-LATED, -LATING, -LATES** to engage in coitus

COPURIFY   *v* **-FIED, -FYING, -FIES** to become purified with another substance

COPY   *v* **COPIED, COPYING, COPIES** to imitate **COPYABLE** *adj*

COPYBOOK   *n* pl. **-S** a book used in teaching penmanship

COPYBOY   *n* pl. **-BOYS** a boy who runs errands in a newspaper office

COPYCAT   *v* **-CATTED, -CATTING, -CATS** to imitate

COPYDESK   *n* pl. **-S** an editor's desk in a newspaper office

COPYEDIT   *v* **-ED, -ING, -S** to prepare copy for the printer

COPYGIRL   *n* pl. **-S** a girl who runs errands in a newspaper office

COPYHOLD   *n* pl. **-S** a type of ownership of land

COPYIST   *n* pl. **-S** an imitator

COPYLEFT   *n* pl. **-S** a license that allows use of copyrighted software free

COPYREAD   *v* **-READ, -READING, -READS** to copyedit

COQUET   *v* **-QUETTED, -QUETTING, -QUETS** to flirt

COQUETRY   *n* pl. **-TRIES** flirtatious behavior

COQUETTE   *v* **-QUETTED, -QUETTING, -QUETTES** to coquet

COQUILLE   *n* pl. **-S** a cooking utensil

COQUINA   *n* pl. **-S** a small marine clam

COQUITO   *n* pl. **-TOS** a palm tree

COR   *n* pl. **-S** an ancient unit of measure

CORACLE   *n* pl. **-S** a small boat

CORACOID   *n* pl. **-S** a bone of the shoulder girdle

CORAL   *n* pl. **-S** a mass of marine animal skeletons

CORANTO   *n* pl. **-TOS** or **-TOES** courante

CORBAN   *n* pl. **-S** an offering to God

CORBEIL   *n* pl. **-S** a sculptured fruit basket

CORBEL   *v* **-BELED, -BELING, -BELS** or **-BELLED, -BELLING, -BELS** to provide a wall with a bracket

CORBIE   *n* pl. **-S** a raven or crow

CORBINA   *n* pl. **-S** a food and game fish

CORBY   *n* pl. **CORBIES** corbie

CORD   *v* **-ED, -ING, -S** to fasten with a cord (a thin rope)

CORDAGE   *n* pl. **-S** the amount of wood in an area

CORDATE   *adj* heart-shaped

CORDELLE   *v* **-DELLED, -DELLING, -DELLES** to tow a boat with a cordelle (a towrope)

CORDER   *n* pl. **-S** one that cords

CORDIAL   *n* pl. **-S** a liqueur

CORDING   *n* pl. **-S** the ribbed surface of cloth

CORDITE   *n* pl. **-S** an explosive powder

CORDLESS   *n* pl. **-ES** an electrical device with its own power supply

CORDLIKE   *adj* resembling a cord

CORDOBA   *n* pl. **-S** a monetary unit of Nicaragua

CORDON   *v* **-ED, -ING, -S** to form a barrier around

CORDOVAN   *n* pl. **-S** a fine leather

CORDUROY   *v* **-ED, -ING, -S** to build a type of road

CORDWAIN   *n* pl. **-S** cordovan

CORDWOOD   *n* pl. **-S** wood used for fuel

CORE   *v* **CORED, CORING, CORES** to remove the core (the central part) of

COREDEEM   *v* **-ED, -ING, -S** to redeem jointly

COREIGN   *n* pl. **-S** a joint reign

CORELATE   *v* **-LATED, -LATING, -LATES** to place into mutual or reciprocal relation

CORELESS   *adj* having no core

COREMIUM   *n* pl. **-MIA** an organ of certain fungi

CORER   *n* pl. **-S** a utensil for coring apples

CORF   *n* pl. **CORVES** a wagon used in a mine

CORGI   *n* pl. **-S** a short-legged dog

CORING   present participle of core

CORIUM   *n* pl. **-RIA** a skin layer

CORK   *v* **-ED, -ING, -S** to stop up

CORKAGE   *n* pl. **-S** a charge for wine in a restaurant

CORKER   *n* pl. **-S** one that corks

CORKIER   comparative of corky

CORKIEST   superlative of corky

CORKLIKE   *adj* resembling cork (a porous tree bark)

CORKWOOD   *n* pl. **-S** a small tree

CORKY   *adj* **CORKIER, CORKIEST** corklike

CORM   *n* pl. **-S** a stem of certain plants **CORMLIKE, CORMOID, CORMOUS** *adj*

CORMEL   *n* pl. **-S** a small corm

CORN v **-ED, -ING, -S** to preserve with salt

CORNBALL n pl. **-S** a hick

CORNCAKE n pl. **-S** a cake made of cornmeal

CORNCOB n pl. **-S** the woody core of an ear of corn

CORNCRIB n pl. **-S** a building in which corn is stored

CORNEA n pl. **-S** a part of the eye **CORNEAL** adj

CORNEL n pl. **-S** a hardwood tree or shrub

CORNEOUS adj of a hornlike texture

CORNER v **-ED, -ING, -S** to gain control of

CORNET n pl. **-S** a trumpetlike instrument

CORNETCY n **-CIES** a rank in the British cavalry

CORNFED adj fed on corn

CORNHUSK n pl. **-S** the husk covering an ear of corn

CORNICE v **-NICED, -NICING, -NICES** to decorate with a molding

CORNICHE n pl. **-S** a road built along a cliff

CORNICLE n pl. **-S** a part of an aphid

CORNIER comparative of corny

CORNIEST superlative of corny

CORNIFY v **-FIED, -FYING, -FIES** to form keratin

CORNILY adv in a corny manner

CORNMEAL n pl. **-S** meal made from corn

CORNPONE n pl. **-S** a bread made with cornmeal

CORNROW v **-ED, -ING, -S** to braid hair tightly in rows close to the scalp

CORNU n pl. **-NUA** a hornlike bone formation **CORNUAL** adj

CORNUS n pl. **-ES** a cornel

CORNUTE adj horn-shaped

CORNUTED adj cornute

CORNUTO n pl. **-TOS** the husband of an unfaithful wife

CORNY adj **CORNIER, CORNIEST** trite

CORODY n pl. **-DIES** an allowance of food or clothes

COROLLA n pl. **-S** a protective covering of a flower

CORONA n pl. **-NAS** or **-NAE** a luminous circle around a celestial body

CORONACH n pl. **-S** a dirge

CORONAL n pl. **-S** a wreath worn on the head

CORONARY n pl. **-NARIES** an artery supplying blood to the heart

CORONATE v **-NATED, -NATING, -NATES** to crown

CORONEL n pl. **-S** coronal

CORONER n pl. **-S** an officer who investigates questionable deaths

CORONET n pl. **-S** a small crown

CORONOID adj crown-shaped

COROTATE v **-TATED, -TATING, -TATES** to rotate together

CORPORA a pl. of corpus

CORPORAL n pl. **-S** a military rank

CORPS n pl. **CORPS** a military unit

CORPSE n pl. **-S** a dead body

CORPSMAN n pl. **-MEN** an enlisted man trained in first aid

CORPUS n pl. **-PORA** or **-PUSES** a human or animal body

CORRADE v **-RADED, -RADING, -RADES** to erode

CORRAL v **-RALLED, -RALLING, -RALS** to place livestock in a corral (an enclosure)

CORRECT adj **-RECTER, -RECTEST** free from error

CORRECT v **-ED, -ING, -S** to make free from error

CORRIDA n pl. **-S** a bullfight

CORRIDOR n pl. **-S** a narrow hallway

CORRIE n pl. **-S** a cirque

CORRIVAL n pl. **-S** a rival or opponent

CORRODE v **-RODED, -RODING, -RODES** to eat away gradually

CORRODY n pl. **-DIES** corody

CORRUPT adj **-RUPTER, -RUPTEST** dishonest and venal

CORRUPT v **-ED, -ING, -S** to subvert the honesty or integrity of

CORSAC n pl. **-S** an Asian fox

CORSAGE n pl. **-S** a small bouquet of flowers

CORSAIR n pl. **-S** a pirate

CORSE n pl. **-S** a corpse

CORSELET n pl. **-S** a piece of body armor

CORSET v **-ED, -ING, -S** to fit with a corset (a supporting undergarment)

CORSETRY n pl. **-RIES** the work of making corsets

CORSLET n pl. **-S** corselet

CORTEGE n pl. **-S** a retinue

CORTEX n pl. **-TEXES** or **-TICES** the outer layer of an organ **CORTICAL** adj

CORTIN n pl. **-S** a hormone

CORTINA n pl. **-S** a membrane on some mushrooms

CORTISOL n pl. **-S** a hormone

CORULER n pl. **-S** one that rules jointly

CORUNDUM n pl. **-S** a hard mineral

CORVEE n pl. **-S** an obligation to perform feudal service

CORVES pl. of corf

CORVET n pl. **-S** corvette

CORVETTE n pl. **-S** a small, swift warship

CORVID n pl. **-S** any of a family of passerine birds

CORVINA n pl. **-S** corbina

CORVINE adj pertaining or belonging to the crow family of birds

CORY n pl. **CORY** a former monetary unit of Guinea

CORYBANT n pl. **-BANTS** or **-BANTES** a reveler

CORYMB n pl. **-S** a flower cluster **CORYMBED** adj

CORYPHEE n pl. **-S** a ballet dancer

CORYZA n pl. **-S** a head cold **CORYZAL** adj

COS n pl. **-ES** a variety of lettuce

COSCRIPT v **-ED, -ING, -S** to collaborate in preparing a script for

COSEC n pl. **-S** cosecant

COSECANT n pl. **-S** a trigonometric function of an angle

COSET n pl. **-S** a mathematical subset

COSEY n pl. **-SEYS** a cozy

COSH v **-ED, -ING, -ES** to bludgeon

COSHER v **-ED, -ING, -S** to coddle

COSIE n pl. **-S** a cozy

COSIED past tense of cosy

COSIER comparative of cosy

COSIES present 3d person sing. of cosy

COSIEST superlative of cosy

COSIGN v **-ED, -ING, -S** to sign jointly

COSIGNER n pl. **-S** one that cosigns

COSILY adv in a cosy manner

COSINE n pl. **-S** a trigonometric function of an angle

COSINESS n pl. **-ES** coziness

COSMETIC n pl. **-S** a beauty preparation

COSMIC adj pertaining to the cosmos

COSMICAL adj cosmic

COSMID n pl. **-S** a hybrid vector used in cloning

COSMISM n pl. **-S** a philosophical theory

COSMIST n pl. **-S** a supporter of cosmism

COSMOS n pl. **-ES** the universe regarded as an orderly system

COSS n pl. **COSS** kos

COSSACK n pl. **-S** a Russian cavalryman

COSSET v **-ED, -ING, -S** to fondle

COST v **COST** or **COSTED, COSTING, COSTS** to estimate a price for production of

COSTA n pl. **-TAE** a rib **COSTAL** adj **COSTALLY** adv

COSTAR v **-STARRED, -STARRING, -STARS** to star with another actor

COSTARD n pl. **-S** a large cooking apple

COSTATE adj having a rib or ribs

COSTER n pl. **-S** a hawker of fruit or vegetables

COSTIVE adj constipated

COSTLESS adj free of charge

COSTLY adj **-LIER, -LIEST** expensive

COSTMARY n pl. **-MARIES** an herb used in salads

COSTREL n pl. **-S** a flask

COSTUME v **-TUMED, -TUMING, -TUMES** to supply with a costume (a style of dress)

COSTUMER n pl. **-S** one that costumes

COSTUMEY adj of or pertaining to a costume

COSY adj **COSIER, COSIEST** cozy

COSY v **COSIED, COSYING, COSIES** to cozy

COT n pl. **-S** a light, narrow bed

COTAN n pl. **-S** a trigonometric function of an angle

COTE v **COTED, COTING, COTES** to pass by

COTEAU n pl. **-TEAUX** the higher ground of a region

COTENANT n pl. **-S** one who is a tenant with another in the same place

COTERIE n pl. **-S** a clique

COTHURN n pl. **-S** a buskin worn by ancient Roman actors

COTHURNI *n/pl* cothurns

COTIDAL *adj* indicating coincidence of the tides

COTILLON *n* pl. **-S** a ballroom dance

COTING present participle of cote

COTINGA *n* pl. **-S** a tropical bird

COTININE *n* pl. **-S** an alkaloid produced by nicotine in the body

COTQUEAN *n* pl. **-S** a vulgar woman

COTTA *n* pl. **-TAS** or **-TAE** a short surplice

COTTAGE *n* pl. **-S** a small house **COTTAGEY** *adj*

COTTAGER *n* pl. **-S** one that lives in a cottage

COTTAR *n* pl. **-S** a tenant farmer

COTTER *n* pl. **-S** a pin or wedge used for fastening parts together **COTTERED** *adj*

COTTIER *n* pl. **-S** cottar

COTTON *v* **-ED, -ING, -S** to take a liking

COTTONY *adj* resembling cotton (a soft, fibrous material)

COTURNIX *n* pl. **-ES** a small quail

COTYLOID *adj* cup-shaped

COTYPE *n* pl. **-S** a taxonomic type

COUCH *v* **-ED, -ING, -ES** to put into words

COUCHANT *adj* lying down

COUCHER *n* pl. **-S** one that couches

COUCHING *n* pl. **-S** a form of embroidery

COUDE *adj* pertaining to a type of telescope

COUGAR *n* pl. **-S** a mountain lion

COUGH *v* **-ED, -ING, -S** to expel air from the lungs noisily

COUGHER *n* pl. **-S** one that coughs

COULD past tense of can

COULDEST a past 2d person sing. of can

COULDST a past 2d person sing. of can

COULEE *n* pl. **-S** a small ravine

COULIS *n* pl. **COULIS** a thick sauce of pureed vegetable or fruit

COULISSE *n* pl. **-S** a side scene of a theatre stage

COULOIR *n* pl. **-S** a deep gorge or gully

COULOMB *n* pl. **-S** an electrical measure

COULTER *n* pl. **-S** colter

COUMARIN *n* pl. **-S** a chemical compound **COUMARIC** *adj*

COUMAROU *n* pl. **-S** the seed of a tropical tree

COUNCIL *n* pl. **-S** a group of persons appointed for a certain function

COUNSEL *v* **-SELED, -SELING, -SELS** or **-SELLED, -SELLING, -SELS** to advise

COUNT *v* **-ED, -ING, -S** to list or mention the units of one by one to ascertain the total

COUNTER *v* **-ED, -ING, -S** to oppose

COUNTESS *n* pl. **-ES** a noblewoman

COUNTIAN *n* pl. **-S** a resident of a county

COUNTRY *n* pl. **-TRIES** the territory of a nation

COUNTY *n* pl. **-TIES** an administrative division of a state

COUP *v* **-ED, -ING, -S** to overturn

COUPE *n* pl. **-S** an automobile with two doors

COUPLE *v* **-PLED, -PLING, -PLES** to unite in pairs

COUPLER *n* pl. **-S** one that couples

COUPLET *n* pl. **-S** a pair of successive lines of verse

COUPLING *n* pl. **-S** a joining device

COUPON *n* pl. **-S** a certificate entitling the holder to certain benefits

COURAGE *n* pl. **-S** the quality that enables one to face danger fearlessly; spirit

COURANT *n* pl. **-S** courante

COURANTE *n* pl. **-S** an old, lively dance

COURANTO *n* pl. **-TOS** or **-TOES** courante

COURIER *n* pl. **-S** a messenger

COURLAN *n* pl. **-S** a wading bird

COURSE *v* **COURSED, COURSING, COURSES** to cause hounds to chase game

COURSER *n* pl. **-S** one that courses

COURSING *n* pl. **-S** the pursuit of game by hounds

COURT *v* **-ED, -ING, -S** to woo

COURTER *n* pl. **-S** one that courts

COURTESY *v* **-SIED, -SYING, -SIES** to curtsy

COURTIER *n* pl. **-S** one who attends a royal court

COURTLY *adj* **-LIER, -LIEST** stately

COUSCOUS *n* pl. **-ES** a North African cereal

COUSIN *n* pl. **-S** a child of one's aunt or uncle **COUSINLY** *adj*

COUSINRY *n* pl. **-RIES** cousins collectively

COUTEAU *n* pl. **-TEAUX** a knife

COUTER *n* pl. **-S** a piece of armor for the elbow

COUTH *adj* **COUTHER, COUTHEST** sophisticated

COUTH *n* pl. **-S** refinement

COUTHIE *adj* **COUTHIER, COUTHIEST** friendly

COUTURE *n* pl. **-S** the business of dressmaking

COUVADE *n* pl. **-S** a primitive birth ritual

COVALENT *adj* sharing electron pairs

COVARY *v* **-VARIED, -VARYING, -VARIES** to exhibit variation of two or more variables

COVE *v* **COVED, COVING, COVES** to curve over or inward

COVEN *n* pl. **-S** a group of witches

COVENANT *v* **-ED, -ING, -S** to enter into a binding agreement

COVER *v* **-ED, -ING, -S** to place something over or upon

COVERAGE *n* pl. **-S** the extent to which something is covered

COVERALL *n* pl. **-S** a one-piece work garment

COVERER *n* pl. **-S** one that covers

COVERING *n* pl. **-S** something that covers

COVERLET *n* pl. **-S** a bed covering

COVERLID *n* pl. **-S** a coverlet

COVERT *n* pl. **-S** a hiding place

COVERTLY *adv* secretly

COVERUP *n* pl. **-S** something used to conceal improper activity

COVET *v* **-ED, -ING, -S** to desire greatly

COVETER *n* pl. **-S** one that covets

COVETOUS *adj* excessively desirous

COVEY *n* pl. **-EYS** a flock of birds

COVIN *n* pl. **-S** a conspiracy to defraud

COVING *n* pl. **-S** a concave molding

COW *v* **-ED, -ING, -S** to intimidate

COWAGE *n* pl. **-S** a tropical vine

COWARD *n* pl. **-S** one who lacks courage

COWARDLY *adj* lacking courage

COWBANE *n* pl. **-S** a poisonous plant

COWBELL *n* pl. **-S** a bell around a cow's neck

COWBERRY *n* pl. **-RIES** a pasture shrub

COWBIND *n* pl. **-S** a species of bryony

COWBIRD *n* pl. **-S** a blackbird

COWBOY *v* **-BOYED, -BOYING, -BOYS** to tend cattle or horses

COWEDLY *adv* in a cowed manner

COWER *v* **-ED, -ING, -S** to cringe

COWFISH *n* pl. **-ES** an aquatic mammal

COWFLAP *n* pl. **-S** cowflop

COWFLOP *n* pl. **-S** a cowpat

COWGIRL *n* pl. **-S** a female ranch worker

COWHAGE *n* pl. **-S** cowage

COWHAND *n* pl. **-S** a ranch worker

COWHERB *n* pl. **-S** an annual herb

COWHERD *n* pl. **-S** one who tends cattle

COWHIDE *v* **-HIDED, -HIDING, -HIDES** to flog with a leather whip

COWIER comparative of cowy

COWIEST superlative of cowy

COWINNER *n* pl. **-S** one of two or more winners

COWL *v* **-ED, -ING, -S** to cover with a hood

COWLICK *n* pl. **-S** a lock of unruly hair

COWLING *n* pl. **-S** a covering for an aircraft engine

COWMAN *n* pl. **-MEN** one who owns cattle

COWORKER *n* pl. **-S** a fellow worker

COWPAT *n* pl. **-S** a dropping of cow dung

COWPEA *n* pl. **-S** a black-eyed pea

COWPIE *n* pl. **-S** a cowpat

COWPLOP *n* pl. **-S** a cowpat

COWPOKE *n* pl. **-S** a cowhand

COWPOX *n* pl. **-ES** a cattle disease

COWRIE *n* pl. **-S** cowry

COWRITE *v* **-WROTE, -WRITTEN, -WRITING, -WRITES** to collaborate in writing

COWRITER *n* pl. **-S** one that cowrites

COWRY *n* pl. **-RIES** a glossy seashell

COWSHED *n* pl. **-S** a shelter for cows

COWSKIN *n* pl. **-S** the hide of a cow

COWSLIP *n* pl. **-S** a flowering plant

COWY *adj* **COWIER, COWIEST** suggestive of a cow

COX *v* **-ED, -ING, -ES** to coxswain

COXA *n* pl. **COXAE** the hip or hip joint **COXAL** *adj*

COXALGIA *n* pl. **-S** pain in the hip **COXALGIC** *adj*

COXALGY *n* pl. **-GIES** coxalgia

COXCOMB *n* pl. **-S** a conceited dandy

COXITIS	*n* pl. **COXITIDES** inflammation of the hip joint
COXLESS	*adj* having no coxswain (the director of the crew of a racing rowboat)
COXSWAIN	*v* **-ED, -ING, -S** to direct (a crew) as coxswain
COY	*adj* **COYER, COYEST** shy
COY	*v* **-ED, -ING, -S** to caress
COYDOG	*n* pl. **-S** a hybrid between a coyote and a wild dog
COYISH	*adj* somewhat coy
COYLY	*adv* in a coy manner
COYNESS	*n* pl. **-ES** the state of being coy
COYOTE	*n* pl. **-S** a small wolf
COYPOU	*n* pl. **-S** a coypu
COYPU	*n* pl. **-S** an aquatic rodent
COZ	*n* pl. **COZES** or **COZZES** a cousin
COZEN	*v* **-ED, -ING, -S** to deceive
COZENAGE	*n* pl. **-S** the practice of cozening
COZENER	*n* pl. **-S** one that cozens
COZEY	*n* pl. **-ZEYS** a cover for a teapot
COZIE	*n* pl. **-S** a cozey
COZIED	past tense of cozy
COZIER	comparative of cozy
COZIES	present 3d person sing. of cozy
COZINESS	*n* pl. **-ES** the state of being cozy
COZY	*adj* **COZIER, COZIEST** snug and comfortable **COZILY** *adv*
COZY	*v* **COZIED, COZYING, COZIES** to attempt to get on friendly terms
COZZES	a pl. of coz
CRAAL	*v* **-ED, -ING, -S** to kraal
CRAB	*v* **CRABBED, CRABBING, CRABS** to complain
CRABBER	*n* pl. **-S** one that crabs
CRABBY	*adj* **-BIER, -BIEST** grumpy **CRABBILY** *adv*
CRABLIKE	*adj* resembling a crab
CRABMEAT	*n* pl. **-S** the edible part of a crab
CRABWISE	*adv* sideways
CRACK	*v* **-ED, -ING, -S** to break without dividing into parts
CRACKER	*n* pl. **-S** a thin, crisp biscuit
CRACKING	*n* pl. **-S** a chemical process
CRACKLE	*v* **-LED, -LING, -LES** to make a succession of snapping sounds
CRACKLY	*adj* **-LIER, -LIEST** brittle
CRACKNEL	*n* pl. **-S** a hard, crisp biscuit
CRACKPOT	*n* pl. **-S** an eccentric person
CRACKUP	*n* pl. **-S** a collision
CRACKY	*interj* — used to express surprise
CRADLE	*v* **-DLED, -DLING, -DLES** to nurture during infancy
CRADLER	*n* pl. **-S** one that cradles
CRAFT	*v* **-ED, -ING, -S** to make by hand
CRAFTER	*n* pl. **-S** one that crafts
CRAFTY	*adj* **CRAFTIER, CRAFTIEST** skillful in deceiving **CRAFTILY** *adv*
CRAG	*n* pl. **-S** a large jagged rock **CRAGGED** *adj*
CRAGGY	*adj* **-GIER, -GIEST** full of crags **CRAGGILY** *adv*
CRAGSMAN	*n* pl. **-MEN** one who climbs crags
CRAKE	*n* pl. **-S** a small, harsh-voiced bird
CRAM	*v* **CRAMMED, CRAMMING, CRAMS** to fill or pack tightly
CRAMBE	*n* pl. **-S** an annual herb
CRAMBO	*n* pl. **-BOS** or **-BOES** a word game
CRAMMER	*n* pl. **-S** one that crams
CRAMMING	present participle of cram
CRAMOISY	*n* pl. **-SIES** crimson cloth
CRAMP	*v* **-ED, -ING, -S** to restrain or confine
CRAMPIT	*n* pl. **-S** a piece of equipment used in curling
CRAMPON	*n* pl. **-S** a device for raising heavy objects
CRAMPOON	*n* pl. **-S** crampon
CRAMPY	*adj* **CRAMPIER, CRAMPIEST** affected with a cramp
CRANCH	*v* **-ED, -ING, -ES** to craunch
CRANE	*v* **CRANED, CRANING, CRANES** to stretch out one's neck
CRANIA	a pl. of cranium
CRANIAL	*adj* pertaining to the skull
CRANIATE	*n* pl. **-S** one that has a skull
CRANING	present participle of crane
CRANIUM	*n* pl. **-NIUMS** or **-NIA** the skull
CRANK	*adj* **CRANKER, CRANKEST** lively
CRANK	*v* **-ED, -ING, -S** to start manually
CRANKIER	comparative of cranky
CRANKIEST	superlative of cranky
CRANKILY	*adv* in a cranky manner
CRANKISH	*adj* eccentric

CRANKLE *v* **-KLED, -KLING, -KLES** to crinkle

CRANKLY *adv* in a crank manner

CRANKOUS *adj* cranky

CRANKPIN *n pl.* **-S** the handle of a crank

CRANKY *adj* **CRANKIER, CRANKIEST** grumpy

CRANNIES pl. of cranny

CRANNOG *n pl.* **-S** an artificial island

CRANNOGE *n pl.* **-S** crannog

CRANNY *n pl.* **-NIES** a crevice **CRANNIED** *adj*

CRAP *v* **CRAPPED, CRAPPING, CRAPS** to throw a 2, 3, or 12 in a dice game

CRAPE *v* **CRAPED, CRAPING, CRAPES** to crepe

CRAPOLA *n pl.* **-S** nonsense, drivel

CRAPPIE *n pl.* **-S** an edible fish

CRAPPY *adj* **-PIER, -PIEST** markedly inferior in quality

CRASH *v* **-ED, -ING, -ES** to collide noisily

CRASHER *n pl.* **-S** one that crashes

CRASIS *n pl.* **CRASES** a vowel contraction

CRASS *adj* **CRASSER, CRASSEST** grossly vulgar or stupid **CRASSLY** *adv*

CRATCH *n pl.* **-ES** a manger

CRATE *v* **CRATED, CRATING, CRATES** to put in a packing box

CRATER *v* **-ED, -ING, -S** to form cavities in a surface

CRATON *n pl.* **-S** a part of the earth's crust **CRATONIC** *adj*

CRAUNCH *v* **-ED, -ING, -ES** to crunch

CRAVAT *n pl.* **-S** a necktie

CRAVE *v* **CRAVED, CRAVING, CRAVES** to desire greatly

CRAVEN *v* **-ED, -ING, -S** to make cowardly

CRAVENLY *adv* in a cowardly manner

CRAVER *n pl.* **-S** one that craves

CRAVING *n pl.* **-S** a great desire

CRAW *n pl.* **-S** the stomach of an animal

CRAWDAD *n pl.* **-S** a crayfish

CRAWFISH *v* **-ED, -ING, -ES** to back out or retreat

CRAWL *v* **-ED, -ING, -S** to move with the body on or near the ground

CRAWLER *n pl.* **-S** one that crawls

CRAWLWAY *n pl.* **-WAYS** a small, low tunnel

CRAWLY *adj* **CRAWLIER, CRAWLIEST** creepy

CRAYFISH *n pl.* **-ES** a crustacean

CRAYON *v* **-ED, -ING, -S** to use a drawing implement

CRAYONER *n pl.* **-S** one that crayons

CRAZE *v* **CRAZED, CRAZING, CRAZES** to make insane

CRAZY *adj* **-ZIER, -ZIEST** insane **CRAZILY** *adv*

CRAZY *n pl.* **-ZIES** a crazy person

CREAK *v* **-ED, -ING, -S** to squeak

CREAKY *adj* **CREAKIER, CREAKIEST** creaking **CREAKILY** *adv*

CREAM *v* **-ED, -ING, -S** to form cream (a part of milk)

CREAMER *n pl.* **-S** a cream pitcher

CREAMERY *n pl.* **-ERIES** a dairy

CREAMY *adj* **CREAMIER, CREAMIEST** rich in cream **CREAMILY** *adv*

CREASE *v* **CREASED, CREASING, CREASES** to make a fold or wrinkle in

CREASER *n pl.* **-S** one that creases

CREASY *adj* **CREASIER, CREASIEST** having folds or wrinkles

CREATE *v* **-ATED, -ATING, -ATES** to cause to exist

CREATIN *n pl.* **-S** creatine

CREATINE *n pl.* **-S** a chemical compound

CREATION *n pl.* **-S** something created

CREATIVE *n pl.* **-S** one who has the ability to create

CREATOR *n pl.* **-S** one that creates

CREATURE *n pl.* **-S** a living being

CRECHE *n pl.* **-S** a day nursery

CRED *n pl.* **-S** credibility

CREDAL *adj* pertaining to a creed

CREDENCE *n pl.* **-S** belief

CREDENDA *n/pl* articles of faith

CREDENT *adj* believing

CREDENZA *n pl.* **-S** a piece of furniture

CREDIBLE *adj* believable **CREDIBLY** *adv*

CREDIT *v* **-ED, -ING, -S** to accept as true

CREDITOR *n pl.* **-S** one to whom money is owed

CREDO *n pl.* **-DOS** a creed

CREED *n* pl. **-S** a statement of belief **CREEDAL** *adj*

CREEK *n* pl. **-S** a watercourse smaller than a river

CREEL *v* **-ED, -ING, -S** to put fish in a creel (a fish basket)

CREEP *v* **CREPT** or **CREEPED, CREEPING, CREEPS** to crawl

CREEPAGE *n* pl. **-S** gradual movement

CREEPER *n* pl. **-S** one that creeps

CREEPIE *n* pl. **-S** a low stool

CREEPING present participle of creep

CREEPY *adj* **CREEPIER, CREEPIEST** repugnant **CREEPILY** *adv*

CREESE *n* pl. **-S** kris

CREESH *v* **-ED, -ING, -ES** to grease

CREMAINS *n/pl* the ashes of a cremated body

CREMATE *v* **-MATED, -MATING, -MATES** to reduce to ashes by burning

CREMATOR *n* pl. **-S** one that cremates

CREME *n* pl. **-S** cream

CREMINI *n* pl. **-S** a brown mushroom

CRENATE *adj* having an edge with rounded projections

CRENATED *adj* crenate

CRENEL *v* **-ELED, -ELING, -ELS** or **-ELLED, -ELLING, -ELS** to provide with crenelles

CRENELLE *n* pl. **-S** a rounded projection

CRENSHAW *n* pl. **-S** a variety of honeydew melon

CREODONT *n* pl. **-S** an extinct carnivore

CREOLE *n* pl. **-S** a type of mixed language

CREOLISE *v* **-ISED, -ISING, -ISES** to creolize

CREOLIZE *v* **-IZED, -IZING, -IZES** to cause a language to become a creole

CREOSOL *n* pl. **-S** a chemical compound

CREOSOTE *v* **-SOTED, -SOTING, -SOTES** to treat with a wood preservative

CREPE *v* **CREPED, CREPING, CREPES** to frizz the hair

CREPEY *adj* **CREPIER, CREPIEST** crinkly

CREPON *n* pl. **-S** a crinkled fabric

CREPT past tense of creep

CREPY *adj* **CREPIER, CREPIEST** crepey

CRESCENT *n* pl. **-S** the figure of the moon in its first or last quarter

CRESCIVE *adj* increasing

CRESOL *n* pl. **-S** a chemical disinfectant

CRESS *n* pl. **-ES** a plant used in salads **CRESSY** *adj*

CRESSET *n* pl. **-S** a metal cup for burning oil

CREST *v* **-ED, -ING, -S** to reach a crest (a peak)

CRESTAL *adj* pertaining to a crest

CRESTING *n* pl. **-S** a decorative coping

CRESYL *n* pl. **-S** tolyl

CRESYLIC *adj* pertaining to cresol

CRETIC *n* pl. **-S** a type of metrical foot

CRETIN *n* pl. **-S** an idiot

CRETONNE *n* pl. **-S** a heavy fabric

CREVALLE *n* pl. **-S** a food and game fish

CREVASSE *v* **-VASSED, -VASSING, -VASSES** to fissure

CREVICE *n* pl. **-S** a cleft **CREVICED** *adj*

CREW *v* **-ED, -ING, -S** to serve aboard a ship

CREWCUT *n* pl. **-S** a short haircut

CREWEL *n* pl. **-S** a woolen yarn

CREWLESS *adj* being without any crewmen

CREWMAN *n* pl. **-MEN** one who serves on a ship

CREWMATE *n* pl. **-S** a fellow crewman

CREWNECK *n* pl. **-S** a sweater with a collarless neckline

CRIB *v* **CRIBBED, CRIBBING, CRIBS** to confine closely

CRIBBAGE *n* pl. **-S** a card game

CRIBBER *n* pl. **-S** one that cribs

CRIBBING *n* pl. **-S** a supporting framework

CRIBBLED *adj* covered with dots

CRIBROUS *adj* pierced with small holes

CRIBWORK *n* pl. **-S** a framework of logs

CRICETID *n* pl. **-S** a small rodent

CRICK *v* **-ED, -ING, -S** to cause a spasm of the neck

CRICKET *v* **-ED, -ING, -S** to play cricket (a ball game)

CRICKEY *interj* — used as a mild oath

CRICOID *n* pl. **-S** a cartilage of the larynx

CRIED past tense of cry

CRIER *n* pl. **-S** one that cries

CRIES present 3d person sing. of cry

CRIKEY *interj* — used as a mild oath

CRIME *n* pl. **-S** a violation of the law

CRIMINAL *n* pl. **-S** one who has committed a crime

CRIMINE *interj* —used to express surprise or anger

CRIMINI *n* pl. **-S** cremini

CRIMINY *interj* crimine

CRIMMER *n* pl. **-S** krimmer

CRIMP *v* **-ED, -ING, -S** to pleat

CRIMPER *n* pl. **-S** one that crimps

CRIMPLE *v* **-PLED, -PLING, -PLES** to wrinkle

CRIMPY *adj* **CRIMPIER, CRIMPIEST** wavy

CRIMSON *v* **-ED, -ING, -S** to make crimson (a red color)

CRINGE *v* **CRINGED, CRINGING, CRINGES** to shrink in fear

CRINGER *n* pl. **-S** one that cringes

CRINGLE *n* pl. **-S** a small loop of rope

CRINITE *n* pl. **-S** a fossil crinoid

CRINKLE *v* **-KLED, -KLING, -KLES** to wrinkle

CRINKLY *adj* **-KLIER, -KLIEST** crinkled

CRINOID *n* pl. **-S** a marine animal

CRINUM *n* pl. **-S** a tropical herb

CRIOLLO *n* pl. **-LOS** a person of Spanish ancestry

CRIPE *interj* — used as a mild oath

CRIPES *interj* — used as a mild oath

CRIPPLE *v* **-PLED, -PLING, -PLES** to disable or impair

CRIPPLER *n* pl. **-S** one that cripples

CRIS *n* pl. **-ES** kris

CRISIS *n* pl. **CRISES** a crucial turning point **CRISIC** *adj*

CRISP *adj* **CRISPER, CRISPEST** brittle

CRISP *v* **-ED, -ING, -S** to make crisp

CRISPATE *adj* curled

CRISPEN *v* **-ED, -ING, -S** to make crisp

CRISPER *n* pl. **-S** one that crisps

CRISPLY *adv* in a crisp manner

CRISPY *adj* **CRISPIER, CRISPIEST** crisp **CRISPILY** *adv*

CRISSUM *n* pl. **CRISSA** a region of feathers on a bird **CRISSAL** *adj*

CRISTA *n* pl. **-TAE** a cell part

CRISTATE *adj* having a projection on the head

CRIT *n* pl. **-S** criticism

CRITERIA *n/pl* standards of judgment

CRITIC *n* pl. **-S** one who judges the merits of something **CRITICAL** *adj*

CRITIQUE *v* **-TIQUED, -TIQUING, -TIQUES** to judge as a critic

CRITTER *n* pl. **-S** a creature

CRITTUR *n* pl. **-S** critter

CROAK *v* **-ED, -ING, -S** to utter a low, hoarse sound

CROAKER *n* pl. **-S** one that croaks

CROAKY *adj* **CROAKIER, CROAKIEST** low and hoarse **CROAKILY** *adv*

CROC *n* pl. **-S** a crocodile

CROCEIN *n* pl. **-S** a red dye

CROCEINE *n* pl. **-S** crocein

CROCHET *v* **-ED, -ING, -S** to do a type of needlework

CROCI a pl. of crocus

CROCINE *adj* pertaining to the crocus

CROCK *v* **-ED, -ING, -S** to soil

CROCKERY *n* pl. **-ERIES** pottery

CROCKET *n* pl. **-S** an architectural ornament

CROCKPOT *n* pl. **-S** an electric cooking pot

CROCOITE *n* pl. **-S** a mineral

CROCUS *n* pl. **-CUSES** or **-CI** a flowering plant

CROFT *n* pl. **-S** a small tenant farm

CROFTER *n* pl. **-S** a tenant farmer

CROJIK *n* pl. **-S** a triangular sail

CROMLECH *n* pl. **-S** a dolmen

CRONE *n* pl. **-S** a withered old woman **CRONISH** *adj*

CRONY *n* pl. **CRONIES** a close friend

CRONYISM *n* pl. **-S** a kind of political favoritism

CROOK *adj* **CROOKER, CROOKEST** sick

CROOK *v* **-ED, -ING, -S** to bend

CROOKED *adj* **-EDER, -EDEST** dishonest

CROOKERY *n* pl. **-ERIES** crooked activity

CROON *v* **-ED, -ING, -S** to sing softly

CROONER *n* pl. **-S** one that croons

CROP *v* **CROPPED, CROPPING, CROPS** to cut off short

CROPLAND *n* pl. **-S** farmland

CROPLESS *adj* being without crops (agricultural produce)

CROPPER *n* pl. **-S** one that crops

CROPPIE *n* pl. **-S** crappie

CROPPING present participle of crop

CROQUET   v **-ED, -ING, -S** to drive a ball away in a certain game

CROQUIS   n pl. **CROQUIS** a sketch

CRORE   n pl. **-S** a monetary unit of India

CROSIER   n pl. **-S** a bishop's staff

CROSS   adj **CROSSER, CROSSEST** ill-tempered

CROSS   v **-ED, -ING, -ES** to intersect

CROSSARM   n pl. **-S** a horizontal bar

CROSSBAR   v **-BARRED, -BARRING, -BARS** to fasten with crossarms

CROSSBOW   n pl. **-S** a kind of weapon

CROSSCUT   v **-CUT, -CUTTING, -CUTS** to cut across

CROSSE   n pl. **-S** a lacrosse stick

CROSSER   n pl. **-S** one that crosses

CROSSING   n pl. **-S** an intersection

CROSSLET   n pl. **-S** a heraldic symbol

CROSSLY   adv in a cross manner

CROSSTIE   n pl. **-S** a transverse beam

CROSSWAY   n pl. **-WAYS** a road that crosses another road

CROSTINO   n pl. **-NI** a small piece of toast topped with a spread

CROTCH   n pl. **-ES** an angle formed by two diverging parts **CROTCHED** adj

CROTCHET   n pl. **-S** a small hook

CROTON   n pl. **-S** a tropical plant

CROUCH   v **-ED, -ING, -ES** to stoop

CROUP   n pl. **-S** a disease of the throat

CROUPE   n pl. **-S** the rump of certain animals

CROUPIER   n pl. **-S** an attendant in a casino

CROUPOUS   adj pertaining to croup

CROUPY   adj **CROUPIER, CROUPIEST** affected with croup **CROUPILY** adv

CROUSE   adj lively **CROUSELY** adv

CROUTE   n pl. **-S** a pastry case

CROUTON   n pl. **-S** a small cube of toasted bread

CROW   v **-ED, -ING, -S** to boast

CROWBAR   v **-BARRED, -BARRING, -BARS** to use a steel bar as a lever

CROWD   v **-ED, -ING, -S** to press into an insufficient space

CROWDER   n pl. **-S** one that crowds

CROWDIE   n pl. **-S** crowdy

CROWDY   n pl. **-DIES** porridge

CROWER   n pl. **-S** one that crows

CROWFOOT   n pl. **-FOOTS** or **-FEET** a flowering plant

CROWN   v **-ED, -ING, -S** to supply with a crown (a royal headpiece)

CROWNER   n pl. **-S** a coroner

CROWNET   n pl. **-S** a coronet

CROWSTEP   n pl. **-S** a step on top of a wall

CROZE   n pl. **-S** a tool used in barrel-making

CROZER   n pl. **-S** a croze

CROZIER   n pl. **-S** crosier

CRU   n pl. **-S** a grade or class of wine

CRUCES   a pl. of crux

CRUCIAL   adj of supreme importance

CRUCIAN   n pl. **-S** a European fish

CRUCIATE   adj cross-shaped

CRUCIBLE   n pl. **-S** a heat-resistant vessel

CRUCIFER   n pl. **-S** one who carries a cross

CRUCIFIX   n pl. **-ES** a cross bearing an image of Christ

CRUCIFY   v **-FIED, -FYING, -FIES** to put to death on a cross

CRUCK   n pl. **-S** a curved roof timber

CRUD   v **CRUDDED, CRUDDING, CRUDS** to curd

CRUDDY   adj **-DIER, -DIEST** filthy; contemptible

CRUDE   adj **CRUDER, CRUDEST** unrefined **CRUDELY** adv

CRUDE   n pl. **-S** unrefined petroleum

CRUDITES   n/pl pieces of raw vegetables served with a dip

CRUDITY   n pl. **-TIES** the state of being crude

CRUEL   adj **CRUELER, CRUELEST** or **CRUELLER, CRUELLEST** indifferent to the pain of others **CRUELLY** adv

CRUELTY   n pl. **-TIES** a cruel act

CRUET   n pl. **-S** a glass bottle

CRUISE   v **CRUISED, CRUISING, CRUISES** to sail about touching at several ports

CRUISER   n pl. **-S** a boat that cruises

CRUISING   n pl. **-S** the act of driving around in search of fun

CRULLER   n pl. **-S** a small sweet cake

CRUMB   v **-ED, -ING, -S** to break into crumbs (small pieces)

CRUMBER *n* pl. **-S** one that crumbs

CRUMBIER comparative of crumby

CRUMBIEST superlative of crumby

CRUMBLE *v* **-BLED, -BLING, -BLES** to break into small pieces

CRUMBLY *adj* **-BLIER, -BLIEST** easily crumbled

CRUMBUM *n* pl. **-S** a despicable person

CRUMBY *adj* **CRUMBIER, CRUMBIEST** full of crumbs

CRUMHORN *n* pl. **-S** a double-reed woodwind instrument

CRUMMIE *n* pl. **-S** a cow with crooked horns

CRUMMY *adj* **-MIER, -MIEST** of little or no value

CRUMP *v* **-ED, -ING, -S** to crunch

CRUMPET *n* pl. **-S** a small cake cooked on a griddle

CRUMPLE *v* **-PLED, -PLING, -PLES** to wrinkle

CRUMPLY *adj* **-PLIER, -PLIEST** easily wrinkled

CRUNCH *v* **-ED, -ING, -ES** to chew with a crackling sound

CRUNCHER *n* pl. **-S** one that crunches

CRUNCHY *adj* **CRUNCHIER, CRUNCHIEST** crisp

CRUNODE *n* pl. **-S** a point at which a curve crosses itself **CRUNODAL** *adj*

CRUOR *n* pl. **-S** clotted blood

CRUPPER *n* pl. **-S** the rump of a horse

CRURAL *adj* pertaining to the thigh or leg

CRUS *n* pl. **CRURA** a part of the leg

CRUSADE *v* **-SADED, -SADING, -SADES** to engage in a holy war

CRUSADER *n* pl. **-S** one that crusades

CRUSADO *n* pl. **-DOS** or **-DOES** an old Portuguese coin

CRUSE *n* pl. **-S** a small bottle

CRUSET *n* pl. **-S** a melting pot

CRUSH *v* **-ED, -ING, -ES** to press or squeeze out of shape

CRUSHER *n* pl. **-S** one that crushes

CRUSILY *adj* covered with crosslets

CRUST *v* **-ED, -ING, -S** to form a crust (a hardened outer surface)

CRUSTAL *adj* pertaining to the earth's crust

CRUSTOSE *adj* forming a thin, brittle crust

CRUSTY *adj* **CRUSTIER, CRUSTIEST** surly **CRUSTILY** *adv*

CRUTCH *v* **-ED, -ING, -ES** to prop up or support

CRUX *n* pl. **CRUXES** or **CRUCES** a basic or decisive point

CRUZADO *n* pl. **-DOS** or **-DOES** crusado

CRUZEIRO *n* pl. **-ROS** a monetary unit of Brazil

CRWTH *n* pl. **-S** an ancient stringed musical instrument

CRY *v* **CRIED, CRYING, CRIES** to weep **CRYINGLY** *adv*

CRYBABY *n* pl. **-BIES** a person who cries easily

CRYOBANK *n* pl. **-S** a place for storing human tissue at very low temperatures

CRYOGEN *n* pl. **-S** a substance for producing low temperatures

CRYOGENY *n* pl. **-NIES** a branch of physics

CRYOLITE *n* pl. **-S** a mineral

CRYONICS *n/pl* the practice of freezing dead bodies for future revival **CRYONIC** *adj*

CRYOSTAT *n* pl. **-S** a refrigerating device

CRYOTRON *n* pl. **-S** an electronic device

CRYPT *n* pl. **-S** a burial vault **CRYPTAL** *adj*

CRYPTIC *adj* mysterious

CRYPTO *n* pl. **-TOS** one who belongs secretly to a group

CRYSTAL *n* pl. **-S** a transparent mineral

CTENIDIA *n/pl* comblike anatomical structures

CTENOID *adj* comblike

CUATRO *n* pl. **-ROS** a small guitar of Latin America

CUB *n* pl. **-S** the young of certain animals

CUBAGE *n* pl. **-S** cubature

CUBATURE *n* pl. **-S** cubical content

CUBBISH *adj* resembling a cub

CUBBY *n* pl. **-BIES** a small, enclosed space

CUBE *v* **CUBED, CUBING, CUBES** to form into a cube (a regular solid)

CUBEB *n* pl. **-S** a woody vine

CUBER *n* pl. **-S** one that cubes

CUBIC *n* pl. **-S** a mathematical equation or expression

CUBICAL *adj* shaped like a cube

CUBICITY *n* pl. **-TIES** the state of being cubical

CUBICLE *n* pl. **-S** a small chamber

CUBICLY *adv* in the form of a cube

CUBICULA *n/pl* burial chambers

CUBIFORM *adj* shaped like a cube

CUBING present participle of cube

CUBISM *n* pl. **-S** a style of art **CUBISTIC** *adj*

CUBIST *n* pl. **-S** an adherent of cubism

CUBIT *n* pl. **-S** an ancient measure of length **CUBITAL** *adj*

CUBITUS *n* pl. **-TI** the forearm

CUBOID *n* pl. **-S** a bone of the foot **CUBOIDAL** *adj*

CUCKOLD *v* **-ED, -ING, -S** to make a cuckold (a cornuto) of

CUCKOO *v* **-ED, -ING, -S** to repeat monotonously

CUCUMBER *n* pl. **-S** a garden vegetable

CUCURBIT *n* pl. **-S** a gourd

CUD *n* pl. **-S** a portion of food to be chewed again

CUDBEAR *n* pl. **-S** a red dye

CUDDIE *n* pl. **-S** cuddy

CUDDIES pl. of cuddy

CUDDLE *v* **-DLED, -DLING, -DLES** to hug tenderly

CUDDLER *n* pl. **-S** one that cuddles

CUDDLY *adj* **-DLIER, -DLIEST** fit for cuddling

CUDDY *n* pl. **-DIES** a donkey

CUDGEL *v* **-ELED, -ELING, -ELS** or **-ELLED, -ELLING, -ELS** to beat with a heavy club

CUDGELER *n* pl. **-S** one that cudgels

CUDWEED *n* pl. **-S** a perennial herb

CUE *v* **CUED, CUING** or **CUEING, CUES** to give a signal to an actor

CUESTA *n* pl. **-S** a type of land elevation

CUFF *v* **-ED, -ING, -S** to furnish with a cuff (a part of a sleeve)

CUFFLESS *adj* having no cuff

CUFFLINK *n* pl. **-S** a fastening for a shirt cuff

CUIF *n* pl. **-S** coof

CUING a present participle of cue

CUIRASS *v* **-ED, -ING, -ES** to cover with a type of armor

CUISH *n* pl. **-ES** cuisse

CUISINE *n* pl. **-S** a style of cooking

CUISSE *n* pl. **-S** a piece of armor for the thigh

CUITTLE *v* **-TLED, -TLING, -TLES** to coax

CUKE *n* pl. **-S** a cucumber

CULCH *n* pl. **-ES** an oyster bed

CULET *n* pl. **-S** a piece of armor for the lower back

CULEX *n* pl. **CULEXES** or **CULICES** a mosquito

CULICID *n* pl. **-S** a culicine

CULICINE *n* pl. **-S** a mosquito

CULINARY *adj* pertaining to cookery

CULL *v* **-ED, -ING, -S** to select from others

CULLAY *n* pl. **-LAYS** quillai

CULLER *n* pl. **-S** one that culls

CULLET *n* pl. **-S** broken glass gathered for remelting

CULLIED past tense of cully

CULLION *n* pl. **-S** a vile fellow

CULLIS *n* pl. **-LISES** a gutter in a roof

CULLY *v* **-LIED, -LYING, -LIES** to trick

CULM *v* **-ED, -ING, -S** to form a hollow stem

CULOTTE *n* pl. **-S** a divided skirt

CULPA *n* pl. **-PAE** negligence for which one is liable

CULPABLE *adj* deserving blame or censure **CULPABLY** *adv*

CULPRIT *n* pl. **-S** one that is guilty

CULT *n* pl. **-S** a group of zealous devotees

CULTCH *n* pl. **-ES** culch

CULTI a pl. of cultus

CULTIC *adj* pertaining to a cult

CULTIGEN *n* pl. **-S** a cultivar

CULTISH *adj* pertaining to a cult

CULTISM *n* pl. **-S** devotion to a cult

CULTIST *n* pl. **-S** a member of a cult

CULTIVAR *n* pl. **-S** a variety of plant originating under cultivation

CULTLIKE *adj* resembling a cult

CULTRATE *adj* sharp-edged and pointed

CULTURAL *adj* produced by breeding

CULTURE *v* **-TURED, -TURING, -TURES** to make fit for raising crops

CULTUS *n* pl. **-TUSES** or **-TI** a cult

CULVER *n* pl. **-S** a pigeon

CULVERIN	*n* pl. **-S** a medieval musket
CULVERT	*n* pl. **-S** a conduit
CUM	*prep* together with
CUMARIN	*n* pl. **-S** coumarin
CUMBER	*v* **-ED, -ING, -S** to hinder
CUMBERER	*n* pl. **-S** one that cumbers
CUMBIA	*n* pl. **-S** a Latin-American dance
CUMBROUS	*adj* unwieldy
CUMIN	*n* pl. **-S** a plant used in cooking
CUMMER	*n* pl. **-S** a godmother
CUMMIN	*n* pl. **-S** cumin
CUMQUAT	*n* pl. **-S** kumquat
CUMSHAW	*n* pl. **-S** a gift
CUMULATE	*v* **-LATED, -LATING, -LATES** to heap
CUMULUS	*n* pl. **-LI** a type of cloud **CUMULOUS** *adj*
CUNDUM	*n* pl. **-S** condom
CUNEAL	*adj* cuneate
CUNEATE	*adj* wedge-shaped; triangular
CUNEATED	*adj* cuneate
CUNEATIC	*adj* cuneate
CUNIFORM	*n* pl. **-S** wedge-shaped writing characters
CUNNER	*n* pl. **-S** a marine fish
CUNNING	*adj* **-NINGER, -NINGEST** crafty
CUNNING	*n* pl. **-S** skill in deception
CUP	*v* **CUPPED, CUPPING, CUPS** to place in a cup (a small, open container)
CUPBOARD	*n* pl. **-S** a cabinet
CUPCAKE	*n* pl. **-S** a small cake
CUPEL	*v* **-PELED, -PELING, -PELS** or **-PELLED, -PELLING, -PELS** to refine gold or silver in a cuplike vessel
CUPELER	*n* pl. **-S** cupeller
CUPELLER	*n* pl. **-S** one that cupels
CUPFUL	*n* pl. **CUPFULS** or **CUPSFUL** as much as a cup can hold
CUPID	*n* pl. **-S** a naked, winged representation of the Roman god of love
CUPIDITY	*n* pl. **-TIES** greed; lust
CUPLIKE	*adj* resembling a cup
CUPOLA	*v* **-ED, -ING, -S** to shape like a dome
CUPPA	*n* pl. **-S** a cup of tea
CUPPED	past tense of cup
CUPPER	*n* pl. **-S** one that performs cupping
CUPPING	*n* pl. **-S** an archaic medical process
CUPPY	*adj* **-PIER, -PIEST** cuplike
CUPREOUS	*adj* containing copper
CUPRIC	*adj* containing copper
CUPRITE	*n* pl. **-S** an ore of copper
CUPROUS	*adj* containing copper
CUPRUM	*n* pl. **-S** copper
CUPSFUL	a pl. of cupful
CUPULA	*n* pl. **-LAE** cupule
CUPULAR	*adj* cupulate
CUPULATE	*adj* cup-shaped
CUPULE	*n* pl. **-S** a cup-shaped anatomical structure
CUR	*n* pl. **-S** a mongrel dog
CURABLE	*adj* capable of being cured **CURABLY** *adv*
CURACAO	*n* pl. **-S** a type of liqueur
CURACOA	*n* pl. **-S** curacao
CURACY	*n* pl. **-CIES** the office of a curate
CURAGH	*n* pl. **-S** currach
CURARA	*n* pl. **-S** curare
CURARE	*n* pl. **-S** an arrow poison
CURARI	*n* pl. **-S** curare
CURARINE	*n* pl. **-S** a poisonous alkaloid
CURARIZE	*v* **-RIZED, -RIZING, -RIZES** to poison with curare
CURASSOW	*n* pl. **-S** a turkey-like bird
CURATE	*v* **-RATED, -RATING, -RATES** to act as curator of
CURATIVE	*n* pl. **-S** something that cures
CURATOR	*n* pl. **-S** a museum manager
CURB	*v* **-ED, -ING, -S** to restrain **CURBABLE** *adj*
CURBER	*n* pl. **-S** one that curbs
CURBING	*n* pl. **-S** a concrete border along a street
CURBSIDE	*n* pl. **-S** the side of a pavement bordered by a curbing
CURCH	*n* pl. **-ES** a kerchief
CURCULIO	*n* pl. **-LIOS** a weevil
CURCUMA	*n* pl. **-S** a tropical plant
CURD	*v* **-ED, -ING, -S** to curdle
CURDLE	*v* **-DLED, -DLING, -DLES** to congeal

CURDLER *n pl.* **-S** one that curdles

CURDY *adj* **CURDIER, CURDIEST** curdled

CURE *v* **CURED, CURING, CURES** to restore to health

CURELESS *adj* not curable

CURER *n pl.* **-S** one that cures

CURET *n pl.* **-S** a surgical instrument

CURETTE *v* **-RETTED, -RETTING, -RETTES** to treat with a curet

CURF *n pl.* **-S** an incision made by a cutting tool

CURFEW *n pl.* **-S** a regulation concerning the hours which one may keep

CURIA *n pl.* **-RIAE** a court of justice **CURIAL** *adj*

CURIE *n pl.* **-S** a unit of radioactivity

CURING present participle of cure

CURIO *n pl.* **-RIOS** an unusual art object

CURIOSA *n/pl* pornographic books

CURIOUS *adj* **-OUSER, -OUSEST** eager for information

CURITE *n pl.* **-S** a radioactive mineral

CURIUM *n pl.* **-S** a radioactive element

CURL *v* **-ED, -ING, -S** to form into ringlets

CURLER *n pl.* **-S** one that curls

CURLEW *n pl.* **-S** a shore bird

CURLICUE *v* **-CUED, -CUING, -CUES** to decorate with curlicues (fancy spiral figures)

CURLING *n pl.* **-S** a game played on ice

CURLY *adj* **CURLIER, CURLIEST** tending to curl **CURLILY** *adv*

CURLYCUE *n pl.* **-S** curlicue

CURN *n pl.* **-S** grain

CURR *v* **-ED, -ING, -S** to purr

CURRACH *n pl.* **-S** a coracle

CURRAGH *n pl.* **-S** currach

CURRAN *n pl.* **-S** curn

CURRANT *n pl.* **-S** an edible berry

CURRENCY *n pl.* **-CIES** money

CURRENT *n pl.* **-S** a continuous flow

CURRICLE *n pl.* **-S** a light carriage

CURRIE *v* **-RIED, -RYING, -RIES** to prepare food a certain way

CURRIED past tense of curry

CURRIER *n pl.* **-S** one that curries leather

CURRIERY *n pl.* **-ERIES** the shop of a currier

CURRISH *adj* resembling a cur

CURRY *v* **-RIED, -RYING, -RIES** to prepare leather for use or sale

CURRYING present participle of currie

CURSE *v* **CURSED** or **CURST, CURSING, CURSES** to wish evil upon

CURSED *adj* **CURSEDER, CURSEDEST** wicked **CURSEDLY** *adv*

CURSER *n pl.* **-S** one that curses

CURSING present participle of curse

CURSIVE *n pl.* **-S** a style of print

CURSOR *n pl.* **-S** a light indicator on a computer display

CURSORY *adj* hasty and superficial

CURST a past tense of curse

CURT *adj* **CURTER, CURTEST** abrupt

CURTAIL *v* **-ED, -ING, -S** to cut short

CURTAIN *v* **-ED, -ING, -S** to provide with a hanging piece of fabric

CURTAL *n pl.* **-S** an animal with a clipped tail

CURTALAX *n pl.* **-ES** a cutlass

CURTATE *adj* shortened

CURTESY *n pl.* **-SIES** a type of legal tenure

CURTLY *adv* in a curt manner

CURTNESS *n pl.* **-ES** the quality of being curt

CURTSEY *v* **-ED, -ING, -S** to curtsy

CURTSY *v* **-SIED, -SYING, -SIES** to bow politely

CURULE *adj* of the highest rank

CURVE *v* **CURVED, CURVING, CURVES** to deviate from straightness **CURVEDLY** *adv*

CURVET *v* **-VETED, -VETING, -VETS** or **-VETTED, -VETTING, -VETS** to prance

CURVEY *adj* **CURVIER, CURVIEST** curvy

CURVING present participle of curve

CURVY *adj* **CURVIER, CURVIEST** curved

CUSCUS *n pl.* **-ES** an arboreal mammal

CUSEC *n pl.* **-S** a volumetric unit of flow of liquids

CUSHAT *n pl.* **-S** a pigeon

CUSHAW *n pl.* **-S** a variety of squash

CUSHIER comparative of cushy

CUSHIEST superlative of cushy

CUSHILY *adv* in a cushy manner

CUSHION   *v* **-ED, -ING, -S** to pad with soft material

CUSHIONY   *adj* soft

CUSHY   *adj* **CUSHIER, CUSHIEST** easy

CUSK   *n* pl. **-S** a marine food fish

CUSP   *n* pl. **-S** a pointed end **CUSPAL, CUSPATE, CUSPATED, CUSPED** *adj*

CUSPID   *n* pl. **-S** a pointed tooth

CUSPIDAL   *adj* having a cusp

CUSPIDOR   *n* pl. **-S** a spittoon

CUSPIS   *n* pl. **-PIDES** a cusp

CUSS   *v* **-ED, -ING, -ES** to curse

CUSSEDLY   *adv* in a cranky manner

CUSSER   *n* pl. **-S** one that cusses

CUSSO   *n* pl. **-SOS** an Ethiopian tree

CUSSWORD   *n* pl. **-S** a profane or obscene word

CUSTARD   *n* pl. **-S** a thick, soft dessert **CUSTARDY** *adj*

CUSTODES   pl. of custos

CUSTODY   *n* pl. **-DIES** guardianship

CUSTOM   *n* pl. **-S** a habitual practice

CUSTOMER   *n* pl. **-S** one who buys something

CUSTOS   *n* pl. **-TODES** a guardian or keeper

CUSTUMAL   *n* pl. **-S** a written record of laws and customs

CUT   *v* **CUT, CUTTING, CUTS** to divide into parts with a sharp-edged instrument

CUTAWAY   *n* pl. **-AWAYS** a type of coat

CUTBACK   *n* pl. **-S** a reduction

CUTBANK   *n* pl. **-S** a steep stream bank

CUTCH   *n* pl. **-ES** catechu

CUTCHERY   *n* pl. **-CHERIES** a judicial office in India

CUTDOWN   *n* pl. **-S** a reduction

CUTE   *adj* **CUTER, CUTEST** pleasingly attractive **CUTELY** *adv*

CUTENESS   *n* pl. **-ES** the quality of being cute

CUTES   a pl. of cutis

CUTESIE   *adj* **-SIER, -SIEST** cutesy

CUTEST   superlative of cute

CUTESY   *adj* **-SIER, -SIEST** self-consciously cute

CUTEY   *n* pl. **-TEYS** cutie

CUTGRASS   *n* pl. **-ES** a swamp grass

CUTICLE   *n* pl. **-S** the epidermis

CUTICULA   *n* pl. **-LAE** the outer hard covering of an insect

CUTIE   *n* pl. **-S** a cute person

CUTIN   *n* pl. **-S** a waxy substance found on plants

CUTINISE   *v* **-ISED, -ISING, -ISES** to cutinize

CUTINIZE   *v* **-IZED, -IZING, -IZES** to become coated with cutin

CUTIS   *n* pl. **-TISES** or **-TES** the corium

CUTLAS   *n* pl. **-ES** cutlass

CUTLASS   *n* pl. **-ES** a short sword

CUTLER   *n* pl. **-S** one who sells and repairs cutting tools

CUTLERY   *n* pl. **-LERIES** the occupation of a cutler

CUTLET   *n* pl. **-S** a slice of meat

CUTLINE   *n* pl. **-S** a caption

CUTOFF   *n* pl. **-S** the point at which something terminates

CUTOUT   *n* pl. **-S** something cut out

CUTOVER   *n* pl. **-S** land cleared of trees

CUTPURSE   *n* pl. **-S** a pickpocket

CUTTABLE   *adj* capable of being cut

CUTTAGE   *n* pl. **-S** a means of plant propagation

CUTTER   *n* pl. **-S** one that cuts

CUTTIES   pl. of cutty

CUTTING   *n* pl. **-S** a section cut from a plant

CUTTLE   *v* **-TLED, -TLING, -TLES** to fold cloth in a particular fashion

CUTTY   *n* pl. **-TIES** a thickset girl

CUTUP   *n* pl. **-S** a mischievous person

CUTWATER   *n* pl. **-S** the front part of a ship's prow

CUTWORK   *n* pl. **-S** a type of embroidery

CUTWORM   *n* pl. **-S** a caterpillar

CUVEE   *n* pl. **-S** wine blended in casks

CUVETTE   *n* pl. **-S** a small tube or vessel

CWM   *n* pl. **-S** a cirque

CYAN   *n* pl. **-S** a blue color

CYANAMID   *n* pl. **-S** a chemical compound

CYANATE   *n* pl. **-S** a chemical salt

CYANIC   *adj* blue or bluish

CYANID   *n* pl. **-S** a compound of cyanogen

CYANIDE   *v* **-NIDED, -NIDING, -NIDES** to treat an ore with cyanid

CYANIN   *n* pl. **-S** cyanine

CYANINE   *n* pl. **-S** a blue dye

CYANITE   *n* pl. **-S** a mineral **CYANITIC** *adj*

CYANO   *adj* pertaining to cyanogen

CYANOGEN   *n* pl. **-S** a reactive compound of carbon and nitrogen

CYANOSIS   *n* pl. **-NOSES** bluish discoloration of the skin **CYANOSED, CYANOTIC** *adj*

CYBER   *adj* pertaining to computers

CYBERSEX   *n* pl. **-ES** an online sex-oriented conversation

CYBORG   *n* pl. **-S** a human linked to a mechanical device for life support

CYCAD   *n* pl. **-S** a tropical plant

CYCAS   *n* pl. **-ES** a tropical plant

CYCASIN   *n* pl. **-S** a sugar derivative

CYCLAMEN   *n* pl. **-S** a flowering plant

CYCLASE   *n* pl. **-S** an enzyme

CYCLE   *v* **-CLED, -CLING, -CLES** to ride a bicycle

CYCLECAR   *n* pl. **-S** a type of motor vehicle

CYCLER   *n* pl. **-S** a cyclist

CYCLERY   *n* pl. **-RIES** a bicycle shop

CYCLEWAY   *n* pl. **-WAYS** a bikeway

CYCLIC   *adj* moving in complete circles **CYCLICLY** *adv*

CYCLICAL   *n* pl. **-S** a stock whose earnings fluctuate widely with variations in the economy

CYCLIN   *n* pl. **-S** any of a group of proteins that control the cell cycle

CYCLING   *n* pl. **-S** the act of riding a bicycle

CYCLIST   *n* pl. **-S** one who rides a bicycle

CYCLITOL   *n* pl. **-S** a chemical compound

CYCLIZE   *v* **-CLIZED, -CLIZING, -CLIZES** to form one or more rings in a chemical compound

CYCLO   *n* pl. **-CLOS** a three-wheeled motor vehicle

CYCLOID   *n* pl. **-S** a geometric curve

CYCLONE   *n* pl. **-S** a rotating system of winds **CYCLONAL, CYCLONIC** *adj*

CYCLOPS   *n* pl. **CYCLOPS** a minute one-eyed crustacean

CYCLOSIS   *n* pl. **-CLOSES** the circulation of protoplasm within a cell

CYDER   *n* pl. **-S** cider

CYESIS   *n* pl. **CYESES** pregnancy

CYGNET   *n* pl. **-S** a young swan

CYLINDER   *v* **-ED, -ING, -S** to furnish with a cylinder (a chamber in an engine)

CYLIX   *n* pl. **CYLICES** kylix

CYMA   *n* pl. **-MAS** or **-MAE** a curved molding

CYMAR   *n* pl. **-S** simar

CYMATIUM   *n* pl. **-TIA** a cyma

CYMBAL   *n* pl. **-S** a percussion instrument

CYMBALER   *n* pl. **-S** one that plays the cymbals

CYMBALOM   *n* pl. **-S** cimbalom

CYMBIDIA   *n/pl* tropical orchids

CYMBLING   *n* pl. **-S** cymling

CYME   *n* pl. **-S** a flower cluster

CYMENE   *n* pl. **-S** a hydrocarbon

CYMLIN   *n* pl. **-S** cymling

CYMLING   *n* pl. **-S** a variety of squash

CYMOGENE   *n* pl. **-S** a volatile compound

CYMOID   *adj* resembling a cyma

CYMOL   *n* pl. **-S** cymene

CYMOSE   *adj* resembling a cyme **CYMOSELY** *adv*

CYMOUS   *adj* cymose

CYNIC   *n* pl. **-S** a cynical person

CYNICAL   *adj* distrusting the motives of others

CYNICISM   *n* pl. **-S** cynical quality

CYNOSURE   *n* pl. **-S** a center of attraction

CYPHER   *v* **-ED, -ING, -S** to cipher

CYPRES   *n* pl. **-ES** a legal doctrine

CYPRESS   *n* pl. **-ES** a thin fabric

CYPRIAN   *n* pl. **-S** a prostitute

CYPRINID   *n* pl. **-S** a small freshwater fish

CYPRUS   *n* pl. **-ES** cypress

CYPSELA   *n* pl. **-LAE** an achene in certain plants

CYST   *n* pl. **-S** a sac

CYSTEIN   *n* pl. **-S** cysteine

CYSTEINE   *n* pl. **-S** an amino acid

CYSTIC   *adj* pertaining to a cyst

CYSTINE   *n* pl. **-S** an amino acid

CYSTITIS   *n* pl. **-TITIDES** inflammation of the urinary bladder

CYSTOID   *n* pl. **-S** a cyst-like structure

CYTASTER   *n* pl. **-S** a structure formed in a cell during mitosis

CYTIDINE   *n* pl. **-S** a compound containing cytosine

CYTOGENY   *n* pl. **-NIES** the formation of cells

CYTOKINE   *n* pl. **-S** a kind of substance secreted by cells of the immune system

CYTOLOGY   *n* pl. **-GIES** a study of cells

CYTON   *n* pl. **-S** the body of a nerve cell

CYTOSINE   *n* pl. **-S** a component of DNA and RNA

CYTOSOL   *n* pl. **-S** the fluid portion of cell material

CZAR   *n* pl. **-S** an emperor or king

CZARDAS   *n* pl. **-ES** a Hungarian dance

CZARDOM   *n* pl. **-S** the domain of a czar

CZAREVNA   *n* pl. **-S** the daughter of a czar

CZARINA   *n* pl. **-S** the wife of a czar

CZARISM   *n* pl. **-S** autocratic government

CZARIST   *n* pl. **-S** a supporter of czarism

CZARITZA   *n* pl. **-S** a czarina

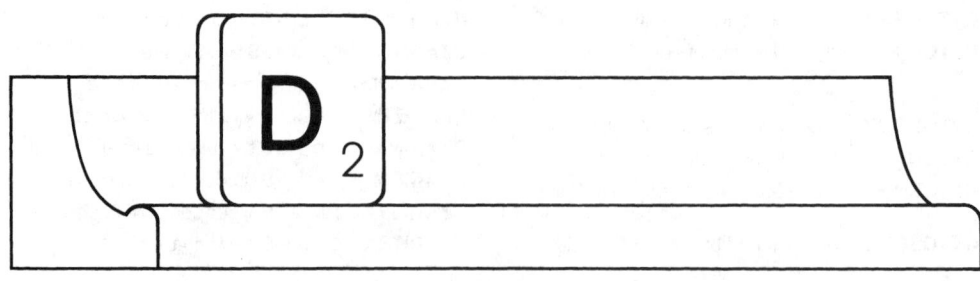

DAB   *v* **DABBED, DABBING, DABS** to touch lightly

DABBER   *n* pl. **-S** one that dabs

DABBLE   *v* **-BLED, -BLING, -BLES** to involve oneself in a superficial interest

DABBLER   *n* pl. **-S** one that dabbles

DABBLING   *n* pl. **-S** a superficial interest

DABCHICK   *n* pl. **-S** a small grebe

DABSTER   *n* pl. **-S** a dabbler

DACE   *n* pl. **-S** a freshwater fish

DACHA   *n* pl. **-S** a Russian cottage

DACITE   *n* pl. **-S** a light gray rock

DACKER   *v* **-ED, -ING, -S** to waver

DACOIT   *n* pl. **-S** a bandit in India

DACOITY   *n* pl. **-COITIES** robbery by dacoits

DACTYL   *n* pl. **-S** a type of metrical foot

DACTYLIC   *n* pl. **-S** a verse consisting of dactyls

DACTYLUS   *n* pl. **-LI** a leg joint of certain insects

DAD   *n* pl. **-S** father

DADA   *n* pl. **-S** an artistic and literary movement

DADAISM   *n* pl. **-S** the dada movement

DADAIST   *n* pl. **-S** a follower of dadaism

DADDLE   *v* **-DLED, -DLING, -DLES** to diddle

DADDY   *n* pl. **-DIES** father

DADGUM   *adj* — used as an intensive

DADO   *v* **-ED, -ING, -S** or **-ES** to set into a groove

DAEDAL   *adj* skillful

DAEMON   *n* pl. **-S** demon **DAEMONIC** *adj*

DAEMON   *n* pl. **-S** or **-ES** daimon

DAFF   *v* **-ED, -ING, -S** to thrust aside

DAFFODIL   *n* pl. **-S** a flowering plant

DAFFY   *adj* **-FIER, -FIEST** silly **DAFFILY** *adv*

DAFT   *adj* **DAFTER, DAFTEST** insane **DAFTLY** *adv*

DAFTNESS   *n* pl. **-ES** the quality of being daft

DAG   *n* pl. **-S** a hanging end or shred

DAGGA   *n* pl. **-S** marijuana

DAGGER   *v* **-ED, -ING, -S** to stab with a small knife

DAGGLE   *v* **-GLED, -GLING, -GLES** to drag in mud

DAGLOCK   *n* pl. **-S** a dirty or tangled lock of wool

DAGOBA   *n* pl. **-S** a Buddhist shrine

DAGWOOD   *n* pl. **-S** a large sandwich

DAH   *n* pl. **-S** a dash in Morse code

DAHABEAH   *n* pl. **-S** a large passenger boat

DAHABIAH   *n* pl. **-S** dahabeah

DAHABIEH   *n* pl. **-S** dahabeah

DAHABIYA   *n* pl. **-S** dahabeah

DAHL   *n* pl. **-S** dal

DAHLIA   *n* pl. **-S** a flowering plant

DAHOON   *n* pl. **-S** an evergreen tree

DAIDZEIN   *n* pl. **-S** a chemical found chiefly in soybeans

DAIKER   *v* **-ED, -ING, -S** to dacker

DAIKON   *n* pl. **-S** a Japanese radish

DAILY   *n* pl. **-LIES** a newspaper published every weekday

DAIMEN   *adj* occasional

DAIMIO   *n* pl. **-MIOS** a former Japanese nobleman

DAIMON   *n* pl. **-S** or **-ES** an attendant spirit **DAIMONIC** *adj*

DAIMYO   *n* pl. **-MYOS** daimio

DAINTY   *adj* **-TIER, -TIEST** delicately pretty **DAINTILY** *adv*

DAINTY   *n* pl. **-TIES** something delicious

DAIQUIRI	*n* pl. **-S** a cocktail
DAIRY	*n* pl. **DAIRIES** an establishment dealing in milk products
DAIRYING	*n* pl. **-S** the business of a dairy
DAIRYMAN	*n* pl. **-MEN** a man who works in or owns a dairy
DAIS	*n* pl. **-ISES** a raised platform
DAISHIKI	*n* pl. **-S** dashiki
DAISY	*n* pl. **-SIES** a flowering plant **DAISIED** *adj*
DAK	*n* pl. **-S** transportation by relays of men and horses
DAKERHEN	*n* pl. **-S** a European bird
DAKOIT	*n* pl. **-S** dacoit
DAKOITY	*n* pl. **-TIES** dacoity
DAL	*n* pl. **-S** a dish of lentils and spices in India
DALAPON	*n* pl. **-S** an herbicide used on unwanted grasses
DALASI	*n* pl. **-S** a unit of Gambian currency
DALE	*n* pl. **-S** a valley
DALEDH	*n* pl. **-S** daleth
DALESMAN	*n* pl. **-MEN** one living in a dale
DALETH	*n* pl. **-S** a Hebrew letter
DALLES	*n/pl* rapids
DALLIER	*n* pl. **-S** one that dallies
DALLY	*v* **-LIED, -LYING, -LIES** to waste time
DALMATIC	*n* pl. **-S** a wide-sleeved vestment
DALTON	*n* pl. **-S** a unit of atomic mass
DALTONIC	*adj* pertaining to a form of color blindness
DAM	*v* **DAMMED, DAMMING, DAMS** to build a barrier to obstruct the flow of water
DAMAGE	*v* **-AGED, -AGING, -AGES** to injure
DAMAGER	*n* pl. **-S** one that damages
DAMAN	*n* pl. **-S** a small mammal
DAMAR	*n* pl. **-S** dammar
DAMASK	*v* **-ED, -ING, -S** to weave with elaborate design
DAME	*n* pl. **-S** a matron
DAMEWORT	*n* pl. **-S** a flowering plant
DAMIANA	*n* pl. **-S** a tropical American shrub
DAMMAR	*n* pl. **-S** a hard resin
DAMMED	past tense of dam
DAMMER	*n* pl. **-S** dammar
DAMMING	present participle of dam
DAMMIT	*interj* —used to express anger
DAMN	*v* **-ED, -ING, -S** to curse
DAMNABLE	*adj* detestable **DAMNABLY** *adv*
DAMNDEST	*n* pl. **-S** utmost
DAMNED	*adj* **DAMNEDER, DAMNEDEST** or **DAMNDEST** damnable
DAMNER	*n* pl. **-S** one that damns
DAMNIFY	*v* **-FIED, -FYING, -FIES** to cause loss or damage to
DAMOSEL	*n* pl. **-S** damsel
DAMOZEL	*n* pl. **-S** damsel
DAMP	*adj* **DAMPER, DAMPEST** moist
DAMP	*v* **-ED, -ING, -S** to lessen in intensity
DAMPEN	*v* **-ED, -ING, -S** to moisten
DAMPENER	*n* pl. **-S** one that dampens
DAMPER	*n* pl. **-S** one that damps
DAMPING	*n* pl. **-S** the ability of a device to prevent instability
DAMPISH	*adj* somewhat damp
DAMPLY	*adv* in a damp manner
DAMPNESS	*n* pl. **-ES** the state of being damp
DAMSEL	*n* pl. **-S** a maiden
DAMSON	*n* pl. **-S** a small purple plum
DAN	*n* pl. **-S** a level of skill in martial arts
DANAZOL	*n* pl. **-S** a synthetic androgen
DANCE	*v* **DANCED, DANCING, DANCES** to move rhythmically to music
DANCER	*n* pl. **-S** one that dances
DANDER	*v* **-ED, -ING, -S** to stroll
DANDIER	comparative of dandy
DANDIES	pl. of dandy
DANDIEST	superlative of dandy
DANDIFY	*v* **-FIED, -FYING, -FIES** to cause to resemble a dandy
DANDILY	*adv* in a dandy manner
DANDLE	*v* **-DLED, -DLING, -DLES** to fondle
DANDLER	*n* pl. **-S** one that dandles
DANDRIFF	*n* pl. **-S** dandruff
DANDRUFF	*n* pl. **-S** a scurf that forms on the scalp
DANDY	*adj* **-DIER, -DIEST** fine
DANDY	*n* pl. **-DIES** a man who is overly concerned about his appearance
DANDYISH	*adj* suggestive of a dandy

DANDYISM	*n* pl. **-S** the style or conduct of a dandy
DANEGELD	*n* pl. **-S** an annual tax in medieval England
DANEGELT	*n* pl. **-S** danegeld
DANEWEED	*n* pl. **-S** a danewort
DANEWORT	*n* pl. **-S** a flowering plant
DANG	*v* **-ED, -ING, -S** to damn
DANGER	*v* **-ED, -ING, -S** to endanger
DANGLE	*v* **-GLED, -GLING, -GLES** to hang loosely
DANGLER	*n* pl. **-S** one that dangles
DANGLY	*adj* **-GLIER, -GLIEST** dangling
DANIO	*n* pl. **-NIOS** an aquarium fish
DANISH	*n* pl. **-ES** a pastry of raised dough
DANK	*adj* **DANKER, DANKEST** unpleasantly damp **DANKLY** *adv*
DANKNESS	*n* pl. **-ES** the state of being dank
DANSEUR	*n* pl. **-S** a male ballet dancer
DANSEUSE	*n* pl. **-S** a female ballet dancer
DAP	*v* **DAPPED, DAPPING, DAPS** to dip lightly or quickly into water
DAPHNE	*n* pl. **-S** a flowering shrub
DAPHNIA	*n* pl. **-S** a minute crustacean
DAPPER	*adj* **-PERER, -PEREST** looking neat and trim **DAPPERLY** *adv*
DAPPING	present participle of dap
DAPPLE	*v* **-PLED, -PLING, -PLES** to mark with spots
DAPSONE	*n* pl. **-S** a medicinal substance
DARB	*n* pl. **-S** something considered extraordinary
DARBAR	*n* pl. **-S** durbar
DARBIES	*n/pl* handcuffs
DARE	*v* **DARED** or **DURST, DARING, DARES** to have the necessary courage
DAREFUL	*adj* brave
DARER	*n* pl. **-S** one that dares
DARESAY	*v* to venture to say — DARESAY is the only form of this verb; it is not conjugated
DARIC	*n* pl. **-S** an ancient Persian coin
DARING	*n* pl. **-S** bravery
DARINGLY	*adv* in a brave manner
DARIOLE	*n* pl. **-S** a type of pastry filled with cream, custard, or jelly
DARK	*adj* **DARKER, DARKEST** having little or no light
DARK	*v* **-ED, -ING, -S** to darken
DARKEN	*v* **-ED, -ING, -S** to make dark
DARKENER	*n* pl. **-S** one that darkens
DARKISH	*adj* somewhat dark
DARKLE	*v* **-KLED, -KLING, -KLES** to become dark
DARKLING	*n* pl. **-S** the dark
DARKLY	*adv* **-LIER, -LIEST** in a dark manner
DARKNESS	*n* pl. **-ES** the state of being dark
DARKROOM	*n* pl. **-S** a room in which film is processed
DARKSOME	*adj* dark
DARLING	*n* pl. **-S** a much-loved person
DARN	*v* **-ED, -ING, -S** to mend with interlacing stitches
DARNDEST	*n* pl. **-S** damndest
DARNED	*adj* **DARNEDER, DARNEDEST** or **DARNDEST** damned
DARNEL	*n* pl. **-S** an annual grass
DARNER	*n* pl. **-S** one that darns
DARNING	*n* pl. **-S** things to be darned
DARSHAN	*n* pl. **-S** a Hindu blessing
DART	*v* **-ED, -ING, -S** to move suddenly or swiftly
DARTER	*n* pl. **-S** one that darts
DARTLE	*v* **-TLED, -TLING, -TLES** to dart repeatedly
DASH	*v* **-ED, -ING, -ES** to strike violently
DASHEEN	*n* pl. **-S** a tropical plant
DASHER	*n* pl. **-S** one that dashes
DASHI	*n* pl. **-S** a fish broth
DASHIER	comparative of dashy
DASHIEST	superlative of dashy
DASHIKI	*n* pl. **-S** an African tunic
DASHPOT	*n* pl. **-S** a shock absorber
DASHY	*adj* **DASHIER, DASHIEST** stylish
DASSIE	*n* pl. **-S** a hyrax
DASTARD	*n* pl. **-S** a base coward
DASYURE	*n* pl. **-S** a flesh-eating mammal
DATA	*a* pl. of datum
DATABANK	*n* pl. **-S** a database
DATABASE	*v* **-BASED, -BASING, -BASES** to put data into a database (a collection of data in a computer)
DATABLE	*adj* capable of being dated

DATARY *n* pl. **-RIES** a cardinal in the Roman Catholic Church

DATCHA *n* pl. **-S** dacha

DATE *v* **DATED, DATING, DATES** to determine or record the date of **DATEABLE** *adj*

DATEBOOK *n* pl. **-S** a notebook for listing appointments

DATEDLY *adv* in an old-fashioned manner

DATELESS *adj* having no date

DATELINE *v* **-LINED, -LINING, -LINES** to provide a news story with its date and place of origin

DATER *n* pl. **-S** one that dates

DATING present participle of date

DATIVE *n* pl. **-S** a grammatical case **DATIVAL** *adj* **DATIVELY** *adv*

DATO *n* pl. **-TOS** datto

DATTO *n* pl. **-TOS** a Philippine tribal chief

DATUM *n* pl. **-TUMS** or **-TA** something used as a basis for calculating

DATURA *n* pl. **-S** a flowering plant **DATURIC** *adj*

DAUB *v* **-ED, -ING, -S** to smear

DAUBE *n* pl. **-S** a braised meat stew

DAUBER *n* pl. **-S** one that daubs

DAUBERY *n* pl. **-ERIES** a bad or inexpert painting

DAUBRY *n* pl. **-RIES** daubery

DAUBY *adj* **DAUBIER, DAUBIEST** smeary

DAUGHTER *n* pl. **-S** a female child

DAUNDER *v* **-ED, -ING, -S** to dander

DAUNT *v* **-ED, -ING, -S** to intimidate

DAUNTER *n* pl. **-S** one that daunts

DAUPHIN *n* pl. **-S** the eldest son of a French king

DAUPHINE *n* pl. **-S** the wife of a dauphin

DAUT *v* **-ED, -ING, -S** to fondle

DAUTIE *n* pl. **-S** a small pet

DAVEN *v* **-ED, -ING, -S** to utter Jewish prayers

DAVIT *n* pl. **-S** a hoisting device on a ship

DAVY *n* pl. **-VIES** a safety lamp

DAW *v* **DAWED, DAWEN, DAWING, DAWS** to dawn

DAWDLE *v* **-DLED, -DLING, -DLES** to waste time

DAWDLER *n* pl. **-S** one that dawdles

DAWK *n* pl. **-S** dak

DAWN *v* **-ED, -ING, -S** to begin to grow light in the morning

DAWNLIKE *adj* suggestive of daybreak

DAWT *v* **-ED, -ING, -S** to daut

DAWTIE *n* pl. **-S** dautie

DAY *n* pl. **DAYS** the time between sunrise and sunset

DAYBED *n* pl. **-S** a couch that can be converted into a bed

DAYBOOK *n* pl. **-S** a diary

DAYBREAK *n* pl. **-S** the first appearance of light in the morning

DAYCARE *n* pl. **-S** care for children and disabled adults during the day

DAYDREAM *v* **-DREAMED** or **-DREAMT, -DREAMING, -DREAMS** to fantasize

DAYFLY *n* pl. **-FLIES** a mayfly

DAYGLOW *n* pl. **-S** airglow seen during the day

DAYLIGHT *v* **-LIGHTED** or **-LIT, -LIGHTING, -LIGHTS** to illuminate with the light of day

DAYLILY *n* pl. **-LILIES** a flowering plant

DAYLONG *adj* lasting all day

DAYMARE *n* pl. **-S** a nightmarish fantasy experienced while awake

DAYROOM *n* pl. **-S** a room for reading and recreation

DAYSIDE *n* pl. **-S** the sun side of a planet or the moon

DAYSMAN *n* pl. **-MEN** an arbiter

DAYSTAR *n* pl. **-S** a planet visible in the east just before sunrise

DAYTIME *n* pl. **-S** day

DAYWORK *n* pl. **-S** work done on a daily basis

DAZE *v* **DAZED, DAZING, DAZES** to stun **DAZEDLY** *adv*

DAZZLE *v* **-ZLED, -ZLING, -ZLES** to blind by bright light

DAZZLER *n* pl. **-S** one that dazzles

DE *prep* of; from — used in names

DEACON *v* **-ED, -ING, -S** to read a hymn aloud

DEACONRY *n* pl. **-RIES** a clerical office

DEAD *adj* **DEADER, DEADEST** deprived of life

DEAD *n* pl. **-S** the period of greatest intensity

DEADBEAT *n* pl. **-S** a loafer

DEADBOLT *n* pl. **-S** a lock for a door

DEADEN *v* **-ED, -ING, -S** to diminish the sensitivity or vigor of

DEADENER *n* pl. **-S** one that deadens

DEADEYE *n* pl. **-S** an expert marksman

DEADFALL *n* pl. **-S** a type of animal trap

DEADHEAD *v* **-ED, -ING, -S** to travel without freight

DEADLIER comparative of deadly

DEADLIEST superlative of deadly

DEADLIFT *v* **-ED, -ING, -S** to execute a type of lift in weight lifting

DEADLINE *v* **-LINED, -LINING, -LINES** to set a time limit on something

DEADLOCK *v* **-ED, -ING, -S** to come to a standstill

DEADLY *adj* **-LIER, -LIEST** fatal

DEADMAN *n* pl. **-MEN** an anchor for securing a rope in mountain climbing

DEADNESS *n* pl. **-ES** the state of being dead

DEADPAN *v* **-PANNED, -PANNING, -PANS** to act without emotion

DEADWOOD *n* pl. **-S** a reinforcement in a ship's keel

DEAERATE *v* **-ATED, -ATING, -ATES** to remove air or gas from

DEAF *adj* **DEAFER, DEAFEST** lacking the sense of hearing

DEAFEN *v* **-ED, -ING, -S** to make deaf

DEAFISH *adj* somewhat deaf

DEAFLY *adv* in a deaf manner

DEAFNESS *n* pl. **-ES** the state of being deaf

DEAIR *v* **-ED, -ING, -S** to remove air from

DEAL *v* **DEALT, DEALING, DEALS** to trade or do business

DEALATE *n* pl. **-S** an insect divested of its wings **DEALATED** *adj*

DEALER *n* pl. **-S** one that deals

DEALFISH *n* pl. **-ES** a marine fish

DEALING *n* pl. **-S** a business transaction

DEALT past tense of deal

DEAN *v* **-ED, -ING, -S** to serve as dean (the head of a faculty)

DEANERY *n* pl. **-ERIES** the office of a dean

DEANSHIP *n* pl. **-S** deanery

DEAR *adj* **DEARER, DEAREST** greatly loved

DEAR *n* pl. **-S** a loved one

DEARIE *n* pl. **-S** deary

DEARIES pl. of deary

DEARLY *adv* in a dear manner

DEARNESS *n* pl. **-ES** the state of being dear

DEARTH *n* pl. **-S** scarcity

DEARY *n* pl. **DEARIES** darling

DEASH *v* **-ED, -ING, -ES** to remove ash from

DEASIL *adv* clockwise

DEATH *n* pl. **-S** the end of life

DEATHBED *n* pl. **-S** the bed on which a person dies

DEATHCUP *n* pl. **-S** a poisonous mushroom

DEATHFUL *adj* fatal

DEATHLY *adj* fatal

DEATHY *adj* deathly

DEAVE *v* **DEAVED, DEAVING, DEAVES** to deafen

DEB *n* pl. **-S** a debutante

DEBACLE *n* pl. **-S** a sudden collapse

DEBAG *v* **-BAGGED, -BAGGING, -BAGS** to remove the pants from someone

DEBAR *v* **-BARRED, -BARRING, -BARS** to exclude

DEBARK *v* **-ED, -ING, -S** to unload from a ship

DEBARKER *n* pl. **-S** one that removes bark (the outer covering of woody plants)

DEBASE *v* **-BASED, -BASING, -BASES** to lower in character, quality, or value

DEBASER *n* pl. **-S** one that debases

DEBATE *v* **-BATED, -BATING, -BATES** to argue about

DEBATER *n* pl. **-S** one that debates

DEBAUCH *v* **-ED, -ING, -ES** to corrupt

DEBEAK *v* **-ED, -ING, -S** to remove the tip of the upper beak of

DEBEARD *v* **-ED, -ING, -S** to remove filaments from a mussel

DEBILITY *n* pl. **-TIES** weakness

DEBIT *v* **-ED, -ING, -S** to charge with a debt

DEBONAIR *adj* suave

DEBONE *v* **-BONED, -BONING, -BONES** to remove the bones from

DEBONER *n* pl. **-S** a bone remover

DEBOUCH *v* **-ED, -ING, -ES** to march into the open

DEBOUCHE *n* pl. **-S** an opening for the passage of troops

DEBRIDE   *v* **-BRIDED, -BRIDING, -BRIDES** to remove dead tissue surgically

DEBRIEF   *v* **-ED, -ING, -S** to question after a mission

DEBRIS   *n* pl. **DEBRIS** fragments or scattered remains

DEBRUISE   *v* **-BRUISED, -BRUISING, -BRUISES** to cross a coat of arms

DEBT   *n* pl. **-S** something that is owed **DEBTLESS** *adj*

DEBTOR   *n* pl. **-S** one who owes something to another

DEBUG   *v* **-BUGGED, -BUGGING, -BUGS** to remove bugs from

DEBUGGER   *n* pl. **-S** one that debugs

DEBUNK   *v* **-ED, -ING, -S** to expose the sham or falseness of

DEBUNKER   *n* pl. **-S** one that debunks

DEBUT   *v* **-ED, -ING, -S** to make one's first public appearance

DEBUTANT   *n* pl. **-S** one who is debuting

DEBYE   *n* pl. **-S** a unit of measure for electric dipole moments

DECADE   *n* pl. **-S** a period of ten years **DECADAL** *adj*

DECADENT   *n* pl. **-S** one in a state of mental or moral decay

DECAF   *n* pl. **-S** decaffeinated coffee

DECAGON   *n* pl. **-S** a ten-sided polygon

DECAGRAM   *n* pl. **-S** dekagram

DECAL   *n* pl. **-S** a picture or design made to be transferred from specially prepared paper

DECALOG   *n* pl. **-S** the Ten Commandments

DECAMP   *v* **-ED, -ING, -S** to depart from a camping ground

DECANAL   *adj* pertaining to a dean

DECANE   *n* pl. **-S** a hydrocarbon

DECANT   *v* **-ED, -ING, -S** to pour from one container into another

DECANTER   *n* pl. **-S** a decorative bottle

DECAPOD   *n* pl. **-S** a ten-legged crustacean

DECARE   *n* pl. **-S** dekare

DECAY   *v* **-ED, -ING, -S** to decompose

DECAYER   *n* pl. **-S** one that decays

DECEASE   *v* **-CEASED, -CEASING, -CEASES** to die

DECEDENT   *n* pl. **-S** a deceased person

DECEIT   *n* pl. **-S** the act of deceiving

DECEIVE   *v* **-CEIVED, -CEIVING, -CEIVES** to mislead by falsehood

DECEIVER   *n* pl. **-S** one that deceives

DECEMVIR   *n* pl. **-VIRS** or **-VIRI** one of a body of ten Roman magistrates

DECENARY   *n* pl. **-RIES** a tithing

DECENCY   *n* pl. **-CIES** the state of being decent

DECENNIA   *n/pl* decades

DECENT   *adj* **-CENTER, -CENTEST** conforming to recognized standards of propriety **DECENTLY** *adv*

DECENTER   *v* **-ED, -ING, -S** to put out of center

DECENTRE   *v* **-TRED, -TRING, -TRES** to decenter

DECERN   *v* **-ED, -ING, -S** to decree by judicial sentence

DECIARE   *n* pl. **-S** a metric unit of area

DECIBEL   *n* pl. **-S** a unit of sound intensity

DECIDE   *v* **-CIDED, -CIDING, -CIDES** to make a choice or judgment

DECIDER   *n* pl. **-S** one that decides

DECIDUA   *n* pl. **-UAS** or **-UAE** a mucous membrane of the uterus **DECIDUAL** *adj*

DECIGRAM   *n* pl. **-S** one tenth of a gram

DECILE   *n* pl. **-S** a statistical interval

DECIMAL   *n* pl. **-S** a fraction whose denominator is some power of ten

DECIMATE   *v* **-MATED, -MATING, -MATES** to destroy a large part of

DECIPHER   *v* **-ED, -ING, -S** to decode

DECISION   *v* **-ED, -ING, -S** to win a victory over a boxing opponent on points

DECISIVE   *adj* conclusive

DECK   *v* **-ED, -ING, -S** to adorn

DECKEL   *n* pl. **-S** deckle

DECKER   *n* pl. **-S** something having a specified number of levels, floors, or layers

DECKHAND   *n* pl. **-S** a seaman who performs manual duties

DECKING   *n* pl. **-S** material for a ship's deck

DECKLE   *n* pl. **-S** a frame used in making paper by hand

DECLAIM   *v* **-ED, -ING, -S** to speak formally

DECLARE   *v* **-CLARED, -CLARING, -CLARES** to make known clearly

DECLARER   *n* pl. **-S** one that declares

DECLASS	v **-ED, -ING, -ES** to lower in status
DECLASSE	adj lowered in status
DECLAW	v **-CLAWED, -CLAWING, -CLAWS** to surgically remove the claws of
DECLINE	v **-CLINED, -CLINING, -CLINES** to refuse
DECLINER	n pl. **-S** one that declines
DECO	n pl. **DECOS** a decorative style
DECOCT	v **-ED, -ING, -S** to extract the flavor of by boiling
DECODE	v **-CODED, -CODING, -CODES** to convert a coded message into plain language
DECODER	n pl. **-S** one that decodes
DECOLOR	v **-ED, -ING, -S** to deprive of color
DECOLOUR	v **-ED, -ING, -S** to decolor
DECOR	n pl. **-S** style or mode of decoration
DECORATE	v **-RATED, -RATING, -RATES** to adorn
DECOROUS	adj proper
DECORUM	n pl. **-S** conformity to social conventions
DECOUPLE	v **-PLED, -PLING, -PLES** to disconnect
DECOY	v **-ED, -ING, -S** to lure into a trap
DECOYER	n pl. **-S** one that decoys
DECREASE	v **-CREASED, -CREASING, -CREASES** to diminish
DECREE	v **-CREED, -CREEING, -CREES** to order or establish by law or edict
DECREER	n pl. **-S** one that decrees
DECREPIT	adj worn out by long use
DECRETAL	n pl. **-S** a papal edict
DECRIAL	n pl. **-S** the act of decrying
DECRIED	past tense of decry
DECRIER	n pl. **-S** one that decries
DECROWN	v **-ED, -ING, -S** to deprive of a crown; depose
DECRY	v **-CRIED, -CRYING, -CRIES** to denounce
DECRYPT	v **-ED, -ING, -S** to decode
DECUMAN	adj extremely large
DECUPLE	v **-PLED, -PLING, -PLES** to increase tenfold
DECURIES	pl. of decury
DECURION	n pl. **-S** a commander of a decury
DECURVE	v **-CURVED, -CURVING, -CURVES** to curve downward

DECURY	n pl. **-RIES** a group of ten soldiers in ancient Rome
DEDAL	adj daedal
DEDANS	n pl. **DEDANS** a gallery for tennis spectators
DEDICATE	v **-CATED, -CATING, -CATES** to set apart for some special use
DEDUCE	v **-DUCED, -DUCING, -DUCES** to infer
DEDUCT	v **-ED, -ING, -S** to subtract
DEE	n pl. **-S** the letter D
DEED	v **-ED, -ING, -S** to transfer by deed (a legal document)
DEEDLESS	adj being without deeds
DEEDY	adj **DEEDIER, DEEDIEST** industrious
DEEJAY	v **-JAYED, -JAYING, -JAYS** to work as a disc jockey
DEEM	v **-ED, -ING, -S** to hold as an opinion
DEEMSTER	n pl. **-S** a judicial officer of the Isle of Man
DEEP	adj **DEEPER, DEEPEST** extending far down from a surface
DEEP	n pl. **-S** a place or thing of great depth
DEEPEN	v **-ED, -ING, -S** to make deep
DEEPENER	n pl. **-S** one that deepens
DEEPLY	adv at or to a great depth
DEEPNESS	n pl. **-ES** the quality of being deep
DEER	n pl. **-S** a ruminant mammal **DEERLIKE** adj
DEERFLY	n pl. **-FLIES** a bloodsucking fly
DEERSKIN	n pl. **-S** the skin of a deer
DEERWEED	n pl. **-S** a bushlike herb
DEERYARD	n pl. **-S** an area where deer herd in winter
DEET	n pl. **-S** an insect repellent
DEEWAN	n pl. **-S** dewan
DEF	adj **DEFFER, DEFFEST** excellent
DEFACE	v **-FACED, -FACING, -FACES** to mar the appearance of
DEFACER	n pl. **-S** one that defaces
DEFAME	v **-FAMED, -FAMING, -FAMES** to attack the good name of
DEFAMER	n pl. **-S** one that defames
DEFANG	v **-ED, -ING, -S** to make harmless
DEFAT	v **-FATTED, -FATTING, -FATS** to remove fat from

DEFAULT	*v* **-ED, -ING, -S** to fail to do something required	**DEFLOWER**	*v* **-ED, -ING, -S** to deprive of flowers
DEFEAT	*v* **-ED, -ING, -S** to win victory over	**DEFOAM**	*v* **-ED, -ING, -S** to remove foam from
DEFEATER	*n* pl. **-S** one that defeats	**DEFOAMER**	*n* pl. **-S** one that defoams
DEFECATE	*v* **-CATED, -CATING, -CATES** to discharge feces	**DEFOCUS**	*v* **-CUSED, -CUSING, -CUSES** or **-CUSSED, -CUSSING, -CUSSES** to cause to go out of focus
DEFECT	*v* **-ED, -ING, -S** to desert an allegiance	**DEFOG**	*v* **-FOGGED, -FOGGING, -FOGS** to remove fog from
DEFECTOR	*n* pl. **-S** one that defects	**DEFOGGER**	*n* pl. **-S** one that defogs
DEFENCE	*v* **-FENCED, -FENCING, -FENCES** to defense	**DEFORCE**	*v* **-FORCED, -FORCING, -FORCES** to withhold by force
DEFEND	*v* **-ED, -ING, -S** to protect	**DEFORCER**	*n* pl. **-S** one that deforces
DEFENDER	*n* pl. **-S** one that defends	**DEFOREST**	*v* **-ED, -ING, -S** to clear of forests
DEFENSE	*v* **-FENSED, -FENSING, -FENSES** to guard against a specific attack	**DEFORM**	*v* **-ED, -ING, -S** to spoil the form of
DEFER	*v* **-FERRED, -FERRING, -FERS** to postpone	**DEFORMER**	*n* pl. **-S** one that deforms
DEFERENT	*n* pl. **-S** an imaginary circle around the earth	**DEFRAG**	*v* **-FRAGGED, -FRAGGING, -FRAGS** to eliminate fragmentation in a computer file
DEFERRAL	*n* pl. **-S** the act of deferring	**DEFRAUD**	*v* **-ED, -ING, -S** to swindle
DEFERRER	*n* pl. **-S** one that defers	**DEFRAY**	*v* **-ED, -ING, -S** to pay
DEFERRING	present participle of defer	**DEFRAYAL**	*n* pl. **-S** the act of defraying
DEFFER	comparative of def	**DEFRAYER**	*n* pl. **-S** one that defrays
DEFFEST	superlative of def	**DEFROCK**	*v* **-ED, -ING, -S** to unfrock
DEFI	*n* pl. **-S** a challenge	**DEFROST**	*v* **-ED, -ING, -S** to remove frost from
DEFIANCE	*n* pl. **-S** bold opposition	**DEFT**	*adj* **DEFTER, DEFTEST** skillful **DEFTLY** *adv*
DEFIANT	*adj* showing defiance		
DEFICIT	*n* pl. **-S** a shortage	**DEFTNESS**	*n* pl. **-ES** the quality of being deft
DEFIED	past tense of defy	**DEFUEL**	*v* **-ELED, -ELING, -ELS** or **-ELLED, -ELLING, -ELS** to remove fuel from
DEFIER	*n* pl. **-S** one that defies		
DEFIES	present 3d person sing. of defy	**DEFUNCT**	*adj* deceased
DEFILADE	*v* **-LADED, -LADING, -LADES** to shield from enemy fire	**DEFUND**	*v* **-ED, -ING, -S** to withdraw funding from
DEFILE	*v* **-FILED, -FILING, -FILES** to make dirty	**DEFUSE**	*v* **-FUSED, -FUSING, -FUSES** to remove the fuse from
DEFILER	*n* pl. **-S** one that defiles	**DEFUSER**	*n* pl. **-S** one that defuses
DEFINE	*v* **-FINED, -FINING, -FINES** to state the meaning of	**DEFUZE**	*v* **-FUZED, -FUZING, -FUZES** to defuse
DEFINER	*n* pl. **-S** one that defines	**DEFY**	*v* **-FIED, -FYING, -FIES** to resist openly and boldly
DEFINITE	*adj* known for certain		
DEFLATE	*v* **-FLATED, -FLATING, -FLATES** to release the air or gas from	**DEGAGE**	*adj* free and relaxed in manner
DEFLATER	*n* pl. **-S** one that deflates	**DEGAME**	*n* pl. **-S** a tropical tree
DEFLATOR	*n* pl. **-S** one that deflates	**DEGAMI**	*n* pl. **-S** degame
DEFLEA	*v* **-ED, -ING, -S** to rid of fleas	**DEGAS**	*v* **-GASSED, -GASSING, -GASES** or **-GASSES** to remove gas from
DEFLECT	*v* **-ED, -ING, -S** to turn aside	**DEGASSER**	*n* pl. **-S** one that degasses
DEFLEXED	*adj* bent downward	**DEGAUSS**	*v* **-ED, -ING, -ES** to demagnetize

DEGENDER *v* **-ED, -ING, -S** to remove references to a person's gender

DEGERM *v* **-ED, -ING, -S** to remove germs from

DEGLAZE *v* **-GLAZED, -GLAZING, -GLAZES** to remove the glaze from

DEGRADE *v* **-GRADED, -GRADING, -GRADES** to debase

DEGRADER *n* pl. **-S** one that degrades

DEGREASE *v* **-GREASED, -GREASING, -GREASES** to remove the grease from

DEGREE *n* pl. **-S** one of a series of stages **DEGREED** *adj*

DEGUM *v* **-GUMMED, -GUMMING, -GUMS** to free from gum

DEGUST *v* **-ED, -ING, -S** to taste with pleasure

DEHISCE *v* **-HISCED, -HISCING, -HISCES** to split open

DEHORN *v* **-ED, -ING, -S** to deprive of horns

DEHORNER *n* pl. **-S** one that dehorns

DEHORT *v* **-ED, -ING, -S** to try to dissuade

DEICE *v* **-ICED, -ICING, -ICES** to free from ice

DEICER *n* pl. **-S** one that deices

DEICIDE *n* pl. **-S** the killing of a god **DEICIDAL** *adj*

DEICTIC *n* pl. **-S** a word or phrase that specifies identity or location

DEIFIC *adj* godlike

DEIFICAL *adj* deific

DEIFIED past tense of deify

DEIFIER *n* pl. **-S** one that deifies

DEIFORM *adj* having the form of a god

DEIFY *v* **-FIED, -FYING, -FIES** to make a god of

DEIGN *v* **-ED, -ING, -S** to lower oneself to do something

DEIL *n* pl. **-S** the devil

DEIONIZE *v* **-IZED, -IZING, -IZES** to remove ions from

DEISM *n* pl. **-S** a religious philosophy

DEIST *n* pl. **-S** an adherent of deism **DEISTIC** *adj*

DEITY *n* pl. **-TIES** a god or goddess

DEIXIS *n* pl. **DEIXISES** the specifying function of some words

DEJECT *v* **-ED, -ING, -S** to depress

DEJECTA *n/pl* excrements

DEJEUNER *n* pl. **-S** a late breakfast

DEKAGRAM *n* pl. **-S** a measure equal to ten grams

DEKARE *n* pl. **-S** a measure equal to ten ares

DEKE *v* **DEKED, DEKING** or **DEKEING, DEKES** to fake an opponent out of position

DEKKO *n* pl. **-KOS** a look

DEL *n* pl. **-S** an operator in differential calculus

DELAINE *n* pl. **-S** a wool fabric

DELATE *v* **-LATED, -LATING, -LATES** to accuse

DELATION *n* pl. **-S** the act of delating

DELATOR *n* pl. **-S** one that delates

DELAY *v* **-ED, -ING, -S** to put off to a later time

DELAYER *n* pl. **-S** one that delays

DELE *v* **DELED, DELEING, DELES** to delete

DELEAD *v* **-ED, -ING, -S** to remove lead from

DELEAVE *v* **-LEAVED, -LEAVING, -LEAVES** to separate the copies of

DELEGACY *n* pl. **-CIES** the act of delegating

DELEGATE *v* **-GATED, -GATING, -GATES** to appoint as one's representative

DELETE *v* **-LETED, -LETING, -LETES** to remove written or printed matter

DELETION *n* pl. **-S** the act of deleting

DELF *n* pl. **-S** delft

DELFT *n* pl. **-S** an earthenware

DELI *n* pl. **DELIS** a delicatessen

DELICACY *n* pl. **-CIES** a choice food

DELICATE *n* pl. **-S** a delicacy

DELICT *n* pl. **-S** an offense against civil law

DELIGHT *v* **-ED, -ING, -S** to give great pleasure to

DELIME *v* **-LIMED, -LIMING, -LIMES** to free from lime

DELIMIT *v* **-ED, -ING, -S** to mark the boundaries of

DELIRIUM *n* pl. **-IUMS** or **-IA** wild frenzy

DELISH *adj* delicious

DELIST *v* **-ED, -ING, -S** to remove from a list

DELIVER *v* **-ED, -ING, -S** to take to the intended recipient

DELIVERY	*n* pl. **-ERIES** the act of delivering
DELL	*n* pl. **-S** a small, wooded valley
DELLY	*n* pl. **DELLIES** deli
DELOUSE	*v* **-LOUSED, -LOUSING, -LOUSES** to remove lice from
DELOUSER	*n* pl. **-S** one that gets rid of lice
DELPHIC	*adj* ambiguous
DELT	*n* pl. **-S** a deltoid
DELTA	*n* pl. **-S** an alluvial deposit at the mouth of a river **DELTAIC, DELTIC** *adj*
DELTOID	*n* pl. **-S** a shoulder muscle
DELUDE	*v* **-LUDED, -LUDING, -LUDES** to mislead the mind or judgment of
DELUDER	*n* pl. **-S** one that deludes
DELUGE	*v* **-UGED, -UGING, -UGES** to flood
DELUSION	*n* pl. **-S** the act of deluding
DELUSIVE	*adj* tending to delude
DELUSORY	*adj* delusive
DELUSTER	*v* **-ED, -ING, -S** to lessen the sheen of
DELUXE	*adj* of special elegance or luxury
DELVE	*v* **DELVED, DELVING, DELVES** to search in depth
DELVER	*n* pl. **-S** one that delves
DEMAGOG	*v* **-ED, -ING, -S** to behave like a demagog (a leader who appeals to emotions and prejudices)
DEMAGOGY	*n* pl. **-GOGIES** the rule of a demagog
DEMAND	*v* **-ED, -ING, -S** to ask for with authority
DEMANDER	*n* pl. **-S** one that demands
DEMARCHE	*n* pl. **-S** a procedure
DEMARK	*v* **-ED, -ING, -S** to delimit
DEMAST	*v* **-ED, -ING, -S** to strip masts from
DEME	*n* pl. **-S** a Greek district
DEMEAN	*v* **-ED, -ING, -S** to conduct oneself in a particular manner
DEMEANOR	*n* pl. **-S** the manner in which one conducts oneself
DEMENT	*v* **-ED, -ING, -S** to make insane
DEMENTIA	*n* pl. **-S** mental illness
DEMERARA	*n* pl. **-S** a coarse light-brown sugar
DEMERGE	*v* **-MERGED, -MERGING, -MERGES** to remove a division from a corporation
DEMERGER	*v* **-ED, -ING, -S** to demerge
DEMERIT	*v* **-ED, -ING, -S** to lower in rank or status
DEMERSAL	*adj* found at the bottom of the sea
DEMESNE	*n* pl. **-S** the legal possession of land as one's own
DEMETON	*n* pl. **-S** an insecticide
DEMIC	*adj* pertaining to a deme
DEMIES	pl. of demy
DEMIGOD	*n* pl. **-S** a lesser god
DEMIJOHN	*n* pl. **-S** a narrow-necked jug
DEMILUNE	*n* pl. **-S** a half-moon
DEMIREP	*n* pl. **-S** a prostitute
DEMISE	*v* **-MISED, -MISING, -MISES** to bequeath
DEMISTER	*n* pl. **-S** one that defogs
DEMIT	*v* **-MITTED, -MITTING, -MITS** to resign
DEMIURGE	*n* pl. **-S** a magistrate of ancient Greece
DEMIVOLT	*n* pl. **-S** a half turn made by a horse
DEMO	*v* **-ED, -ING, -S** to demonstrate
DEMOB	*v* **-MOBBED, -MOBBING, -MOBS** to discharge from military service
DEMOCRAT	*n* pl. **-S** one who believes in political and social equality
DEMODE	*adj* demoded
DEMODED	*adj* out-of-date
DEMOLISH	*v* **-ED, -ING, -ES** to destroy
DEMON	*n* pl. **-S** an evil spirit
DEMONESS	*n* pl. **-ES** a female demon
DEMONIAC	*n* pl. **-S** one regarded as possessed by a demon
DEMONIAN	*adj* demonic
DEMONIC	*adj* characteristic of a demon
DEMONISE	*v* **-ISED, -ISING, -ISES** to demonize
DEMONISM	*n* pl. **-S** belief in demons
DEMONIST	*n* pl. **-S** one who believes in demons
DEMONIZE	*v* **-IZED, -IZING, -IZES** to make a demon of
DEMOS	*n* pl. **-ES** the people of an ancient Greek state
DEMOTE	*v* **-MOTED, -MOTING, -MOTES** to lower in rank or grade
DEMOTIC	*adj* pertaining to a simplified form of ancient Egyptian writing
DEMOTICS	*n/pl* the study of people in society

DEMOTION *n* pl. **-S** the act of demoting

DEMOTIST *n* pl. **-S** a student of demotic writings

DEMOUNT *v* **-ED, -ING, -S** to remove from a mounting

DEMPSTER *n* pl. **-S** a deemster

DEMUR *v* **-MURRED, -MURRING, -MURS** to object

DEMURE *adj* **-MURER, -MUREST** shy and modest **DEMURELY** *adv*

DEMURRAL *n* pl. **-S** the act of demurring

DEMURRER *n* pl. **-S** one that demurs

DEMURRING present participle of demur

DEMY *n* pl. **-MIES** a size of paper

DEN *v* **DENNED, DENNING, DENS** to live in a lair

DENAR *n* pl. **-NARS** or **-NARI** a monetary unit of Macedonia

DENARIUS *n* pl. **DENARII** a coin of ancient Rome

DENARY *adj* containing ten

DENATURE *v* **-TURED, -TURING, -TURES** to deprive of natural qualities

DENAZIFY *v* **-FIED, -FYING, -FIES** to rid of Nazism

DENDRITE *n* pl. **-S** a branched part of a nerve cell

DENDROID *adj* shaped like a tree

DENDRON *n* pl. **-S** a dendrite

DENE *n* pl. **-S** a valley

DENGUE *n* pl. **-S** a tropical disease

DENI *n* pl. **DENI** a monetary unit of Macedonia

DENIABLE *adj* capable of being denied **DENIABLY** *adv*

DENIAL *n* pl. **-S** the act of denying

DENIED past tense of deny

DENIER *n* pl. **-S** one that denies

DENIES present 3d person sing. of deny

DENIM *n* pl. **-S** a durable fabric **DENIMED** *adj*

DENIZEN *v* **-ED, -ING, -S** to make a citizen of

DENNED past tense of den

DENNING present participle of den

DENOTE *v* **-NOTED, -NOTING, -NOTES** to indicate **DENOTIVE** *adj*

DENOUNCE *v* **-NOUNCED, -NOUNCING, -NOUNCES** to condemn openly

DENSE *adj* **DENSER, DENSEST** compact **DENSELY** *adv*

DENSIFY *v* **-FIED, -FYING, -FIES** to make denser

DENSITY *n* pl. **-TIES** the state of being dense

DENT *v* **-ED, -ING, -S** to make a depression in

DENTAL *n* pl. **-S** a dentally produced sound

DENTALIA *n/pl* mollusks with long, tapering shells

DENTALLY *adv* with the tip of the tongue against the upper front teeth

DENTATE *adj* having teeth

DENTATED *adj* dentate

DENTICLE *n* pl. **-S** a small tooth

DENTIL *n* pl. **-S** a small rectangular block **DENTILED** *adj*

DENTIN *n* pl. **-S** the hard substance forming the body of a tooth **DENTINAL** *adj*

DENTINE *n* pl. **-S** dentin

DENTIST *n* pl. **-S** one who treats the teeth

DENTOID *adj* resembling a tooth

DENTURE *n* pl. **-S** a set of teeth **DENTURAL** *adj*

DENUDATE *v* **-DATED, -DATING, -DATES** to denude

DENUDE *v* **-NUDED, -NUDING, -NUDES** to strip of all covering

DENUDER *n* pl. **-S** one that denudes

DENY *v* **-NIED, -NYING, -NIES** to declare to be untrue

DEODAND *n* pl. **-S** property forfeited to the crown under a former English law

DEODAR *n* pl. **-S** an East Indian cedar

DEODARA *n* pl. **-S** deodar

DEONTIC *adj* pertaining to moral obligation

DEORBIT *v* **-ED, -ING, -S** to come out of an orbit

DEOXY *adj* having less oxygen than the compound from which it is derived

DEPAINT *v* **-ED, -ING, -S** to depict

DEPART *v* **-ED, -ING, -S** to go away

DEPARTEE *n* pl. **-S** one that departs

DEPEND *v* **-ED, -ING, -S** to rely

DEPEOPLE *v* **-PLED, -PLING, -PLES** to reduce the population of

DEPERM *v* **-ED, -ING, -S** to demagnetize

DEPICT *v* **-ED, -ING, -S** to portray

DEPICTER *n* pl. **-S** one that depicts

DEPICTOR *n* pl. **-S** depicter

DEPILATE *v* **-LATED, -LATING, -LATES** to remove hair from

DEPLANE *v* **-PLANED, -PLANING, -PLANES** to get off an airplane

DEPLETE *v* **-PLETED, -PLETING, -PLETES** to lessen or exhaust the supply of

DEPLETER *n* pl. **-S** one that depletes

DEPLORE *v* **-PLORED, -PLORING, -PLORES** to regret strongly

DEPLORER *n* pl. **-S** one that deplores

DEPLOY *v* **-ED, -ING, -S** to position troops for battle

DEPLOYER *n* pl. **-S** one that deploys

DEPLUME *v* **-PLUMED, -PLUMING, -PLUMES** to deprive of feathers

DEPOLISH *v* **-ED, -ING, -ES** to remove the gloss or polish of

DEPONE *v* **-PONED, -PONING, -PONES** to testify under oath

DEPONENT *n* pl. **-S** one that depones

DEPORT *v* **-ED, -ING, -S** to expel from a country

DEPORTEE *n* pl. **-S** one who is deported

DEPORTER *n* pl. **-S** one that deports

DEPOSAL *n* pl. **-S** the act of deposing

DEPOSE *v* **-POSED, -POSING, -POSES** to remove from office

DEPOSER *n* pl. **-S** one that deposes

DEPOSIT *v* **-ED, -ING, -S** to place

DEPOT *n* pl. **-S** a railroad or bus station

DEPRAVE *v* **-PRAVED, -PRAVING, -PRAVES** to corrupt in morals

DEPRAVER *n* pl. **-S** one that depraves

DEPRENYL *n* pl. **-S** a drug for treating Parkinson's disease

DEPRESS *v* **-ED, -ING, -ES** to make sad

DEPRIVAL *n* pl. **-S** the act of depriving

DEPRIVE *v* **-PRIVED, -PRIVING, -PRIVES** to take something away from

DEPRIVER *n* pl. **-S** one that deprives

DEPSIDE *n* pl. **-S** an aromatic compound

DEPTH *n* pl. **-S** deepness

DEPURATE *v* **-RATED, -RATING, -RATES** to free from impurities

DEPUTE *v* **-PUTED, -PUTING, -PUTES** to delegate

DEPUTIZE *v* **-TIZED, -TIZING, -TIZES** to appoint as a deputy

DEPUTY *n* pl. **-TIES** one appointed to act for another

DERAIGN *v* **-ED, -ING, -S** to dispute a claim

DERAIL *v* **-ED, -ING, -S** to run off the rails of a track

DERANGE *v* **-RANGED, -RANGING, -RANGES** to disorder

DERANGER *n* pl. **-S** one that deranges

DERAT *v* **-RATTED, -RATTING, -RATS** to rid of rats

DERATE *v* **-RATED, -RATING, -RATES** to lower the rated capability of

DERAY *n* pl. **-RAYS** disorderly revelry

DERBY *n* pl. **-BIES** a type of hat

DERE *adj* dire

DERELICT *n* pl. **-S** something abandoned

DERIDE *v* **-RIDED, -RIDING, -RIDES** to ridicule

DERIDER *n* pl. **-S** one that derides

DERINGER *n* pl. **-S** a short-barreled pistol

DERISION *n* pl. **-S** the act of deriding

DERISIVE *adj* expressing derision

DERISORY *adj* derisive

DERIVATE *n* pl. **-S** something derived

DERIVE *v* **-RIVED, -RIVING, -RIVES** to obtain or receive from a source

DERIVER *n* pl. **-S** one that derives

DERM *n* pl. **-S** derma

DERMA *n* pl. **-S** a layer of the skin **DERMAL** *adj*

DERMIS *n* pl. **-MISES** derma **DERMIC** *adj*

DERMOID *n* pl. **-S** a cystic tumor

DERNIER *adj* last

DEROGATE *v* **-GATED, -GATING, -GATES** to detract

DERRICK *n* pl. **-S** a hoisting apparatus

DERRIERE *n* pl. **-S** the buttocks

DERRIS *n* pl. **-RISES** a climbing plant

DERRY *n* pl. **-RIES** a meaningless word used in the chorus of old songs

DERVISH *n* pl. **-ES** a member of a Muslim religious order

DESALT *v* **-ED, -ING, -S** to remove the salt from

DESALTER *n* pl. **-S** one that desalts

DESAND *v* **-ED, -ING, -S** to remove sand from

DESCANT *v* **-ED, -ING, -S** to sing a counterpoint to a melody

DESCEND *v* **-ED, -ING, -S** to come or go down

DESCENT *n* pl. **-S** the act of descending

DESCRIBE *v* **-SCRIBED, -SCRIBING, -SCRIBES** to give a verbal account of

DESCRIER *n* pl. **-S** one that descries

DESCRY *v* **-SCRIED, -SCRYING, -SCRIES** to discern

DESELECT *v* **-ED, -ING, -S** to dismiss from a training program

DESERT *v* **-ED, -ING, -S** to abandon

DESERTER *n* pl. **-S** one that deserts

DESERTIC *adj* arid and barren

DESERVE *v* **-SERVED, -SERVING, -SERVES** to be entitled to or worthy of

DESERVER *n* pl. **-S** one that deserves

DESEX *v* **-ED, -ING, -ES** to castrate or spay

DESIGN *v* **-ED, -ING, -S** to conceive and plan out

DESIGNEE *n* pl. **-S** one who is designated

DESIGNER *n* pl. **-S** one that designs

DESILVER *v* **-ED, -ING, -S** to remove the silver from

DESINENT *adj* terminating

DESIRE *v* **-SIRED, -SIRING, -SIRES** to wish for

DESIRER *n* pl. **-S** one that desires

DESIROUS *adj* desiring

DESIST *v* **-ED, -ING, -S** to cease doing something

DESK *n* pl. **-S** a writing table

DESKMAN *n* pl. **-MEN** one who works at a desk

DESKTOP *n* pl. **-S** the top of a desk

DESMAN *n* pl. **-S** an aquatic mammal

DESMID *n* pl. **-S** a freshwater alga

DESMOID *n* pl. **-S** a very hard tumor

DESOLATE *v* **-LATED, -LATING, -LATES** to lay waste

DESORB *v* **-ED, -ING, -S** to remove by the reverse of absorption

DESOXY *adj* deoxy

DESPAIR *v* **-ED, -ING, -S** to lose all hope

DESPATCH *v* **-ED, -ING, -ES** to dispatch

DESPISAL *n* pl. **-S** intense dislike

DESPISE *v* **-SPISED, -SPISING, -SPISES** to loathe

DESPISER *n* pl. **-S** one that despises

DESPITE *v* **-SPITED, -SPITING, -SPITES** to treat with contempt

DESPOIL *v* **-ED, -ING, -S** to plunder

DESPOND *v* **-ED, -ING, -S** to lose spirit or hope

DESPOT *n* pl. **-S** a tyrant **DESPOTIC** *adj*

DESSERT *n* pl. **-S** something served as the last course of a meal

DESTAIN *v* **-ED, -ING, -S** to remove stain from

DESTINE *v* **-TINED, -TINING, -TINES** to determine beforehand

DESTINY *n* pl. **-NIES** the fate or fortune to which one is destined

DESTRIER *n* pl. **-S** a war horse

DESTROY *v* **-ED, -ING, -S** to damage beyond repair or renewal

DESTRUCT *v* **-ED, -ING, -S** to destroy

DESUGAR *v* **-ED, -ING, -S** to remove sugar from

DESULFUR *v* **-ED, -ING, -S** to free from sulfur

DETACH *v* **-ED, -ING, -ES** to unfasten and separate

DETACHER *n* pl. **-S** one that detaches

DETAIL *v* **-ED, -ING, -S** to report with complete particulars

DETAILER *n* pl. **-S** one that details

DETAIN *v* **-ED, -ING, -S** to hold in custody

DETAINEE *n* pl. **-S** one who is detained

DETAINER *n* pl. **-S** the unlawful withholding of another's property

DETASSEL *v* **-SELED, -SELING, -SELS** or **-SELLED, -SELLING, -SELS** to remove tassels from

DETECT *v* **-ED, -ING, -S** to discover or perceive

DETECTER *n* pl. **-S** detector

DETECTOR *n* pl. **-S** one that detects

DETENT *n* pl. **-S** a locking or unlocking mechanism

DETENTE *n* pl. **-S** an easing of international tension

DETER *v* **-TERRED, -TERRING, -TERS** to stop from proceeding

DETERGE *v* **-TERGED, -TERGING, -TERGES** to cleanse

DETERGER *n* pl. **-S** one that deterges

DETERRER *n* pl. **-S** one that deters

DETERRING present participle of deter

DETEST *v* **-ED, -ING, -S** to dislike intensely

DETESTER *n* pl. **-S** one that detests

DETHATCH *v* **-ED, -ING, -ES** to remove thatch from

DETHRONE *v* **-THRONED, -THRONING, -THRONES** to remove from a throne

DETICK *v* **-ED, -ING, -S** to remove ticks from

DETICKER *n* pl. **-S** one that deticks

DETINUE *n* pl. **-S** an action to recover property wrongfully detained

DETONATE *v* **-NATED, -NATING, -NATES** to cause to explode

DETOUR *v* **-ED, -ING, -S** to take an indirect route

DETOX *v* **-ED, -ING, -ES** to detoxify

DETOXIFY *v* **-FIED, -FYING, -FIES** to remove a toxin from

DETRACT *v* **-ED, -ING, -S** to take away

DETRAIN *v* **-ED, -ING, -S** to get off a railroad train

DETRITUS *n* pl. **DETRITUS** particles of rock **DETRITAL** *adj*

DETRUDE *v* **-TRUDED, -TRUDING, -TRUDES** to thrust out

DEUCE *v* **DEUCED, DEUCING, DEUCES** to bring a tennis score to a tie

DEUCEDLY *adv* extremely

DEUTERIC *adj* pertaining to heavy hydrogen

DEUTERON *n* pl. **-S** an atomic particle

DEUTZIA *n* pl. **-S** an ornamental shrub

DEV *n* pl. **-S** deva

DEVA *n* pl. **-S** a Hindu god

DEVALUE *v* **-UED, -UING, -UES** to lessen the worth of

DEVEIN *v* **-ED, -ING, -S** to remove the dorsal vein from

DEVEL *v* **-ED, -ING, -S** to strike forcibly

DEVELOP *v* **-ED, -ING, -S** to bring to a more advanced or effective state

DEVELOPE *v* **-OPED, -OPING, -OPES** to develop

DEVERBAL *n* pl. **-S** a word derived from a verb

DEVEST *v* **-ED, -ING, -S** to divest

DEVIANCE *n* pl. **-S** the behavior of a deviant

DEVIANCY *n* pl. **-CIES** deviance

DEVIANT *n* pl. **-S** one that deviates from a norm

DEVIATE *v* **-ATED, -ATING, -ATES** to turn aside from a course or norm

DEVIATOR *n* pl. **-S** one that deviates

DEVICE *n* pl. **-S** something devised or constructed for a specific purpose

DEVIL *v* **-ILED, -ILING, -ILS** or **-ILLED, -ILLING, -ILS** to prepare food with pungent seasoning

DEVILISH *adj* fiendish

DEVILKIN *n* pl. **-S** a small demon

DEVILRY *n* pl. **-RIES** deviltry

DEVILTRY *n* pl. **-TRIES** mischief

DEVIOUS *adj* indirect

DEVISAL *n* pl. **-S** the act of devising

DEVISE *v* **-VISED, -VISING, -VISES** to form in the mind

DEVISEE *n* pl. **-S** one to whom a will is made

DEVISER *n* pl. **-S** one that devises

DEVISOR *n* pl. **-S** one who makes a will

DEVOICE *v* **-VOICED, -VOICING, -VOICES** to unvoice

DEVOID *adj* completely lacking

DEVOIR *n* pl. **-S** an act of civility or respect

DEVOLVE *v* **-VOLVED, -VOLVING, -VOLVES** to transfer from one person to another

DEVON *n* pl. **-S** one of a breed of small, hardy cattle

DEVOTE *v* **-VOTED, -VOTING, -VOTES** to give oneself wholly to

DEVOTEE *n* pl. **-S** an ardent follower or supporter

DEVOTION *n* pl. **-S** the act of devoting

DEVOUR *v* **-ED, -ING, -S** to eat up voraciously

DEVOURER *n* pl. **-S** one that devours

DEVOUT *adj* **-VOUTER, -VOUTEST** pious **DEVOUTLY** *adv*

DEW *v* **-ED, -ING, -S** to wet with dew (condensed moisture)

DEWAN *n* pl. **-S** an official in India

DEWAR *n* pl. **-S** a double-walled flask

DEWATER *v* **-ED, -ING, -S** to remove water from

DEWAX *v* **-ED, -ING, -ES** to remove wax from

DEWBERRY *n* pl. **-RIES** an edible berry

DEWCLAW *n* pl. **-S** a vestigial toe

DEWDROP *n* pl. **-S** a drop of dew

DEWFALL *n* pl. **-S** the formation of dew

DEWIER comparative of dewy

DEWIEST superlative of dewy

DEWILY *adv* in a dewy manner

DEWINESS *n* pl. **-ES** the state of being dewy

DEWLAP *n* pl. **-S** a fold of loose skin under the neck

DEWLESS *adj* having no dew

DEWOOL *v* **-ED, -ING, -S** to remove the wool from

DEWORM *v* **-ED, -ING, -S** to rid of worms

DEWORMER *n* pl. **-S** one that deworms

DEWY *adj* **DEWIER, DEWIEST** moist with dew

DEX *n* pl. **-ES** a sulfate used as a central nervous system stimulant

DEXIE *n* pl. **-S** a tablet of dex

DEXIES pl. of dexy

DEXTER *adj* situated on the right

DEXTRAL *adj* pertaining to the right

DEXTRAN *n* pl. **-S** a substance used as a blood plasma substitute

DEXTRIN *n* pl. **-S** a substance used as an adhesive

DEXTRINE *n* pl. **-S** dextrin

DEXTRO *adj* turning to the right

DEXTROSE *n* pl. **-S** a form of glucose

DEXTROUS *adj* adroit

DEXY *n* pl. **DEXIES** dexie

DEY *n* pl. **DEYS** a former North African ruler

DEZINC *v* **-ZINCKED, -ZINCKING, -ZINCS** or **-ZINCED, -ZINCING, -ZINCS** to remove zinc from

DHAK *n* pl. **-S** an Asian tree

DHAL *n* pl. **-S** dal

DHARMA *n* pl. **-S** conformity to Hindu law **DHARMIC** *adj*

DHARNA *n* pl. **-S** a form of protest in India

DHOBI *n* pl. **-S** a person who does laundry in India

DHOLE *n* pl. **-S** a wild dog of India

DHOOLY *n* pl. **-LIES** dooly

DHOORA *n* pl. **-S** durra

DHOOTI *n* pl. **-S** dhoti

DHOOTIE *n* pl. **-S** dhoti

DHOTI *n* pl. **-S** a loincloth worn by Hindu men

DHOURRA *n* pl. **-S** durra

DHOW *n* pl. **-S** an Arabian sailing vessel

DHURNA *n* pl. **-S** dharna

DHURRIE *n* pl. **-S** a cotton rug made in India

DHUTI *n* pl. **-S** dhoti

DIABASE *n* pl. **-S** an igneous rock **DIABASIC** *adj*

DIABETES *n* pl. **DIABETES** a metabolic disorder

DIABETIC *n* pl. **-S** one who has diabetes

DIABLERY *n* pl. **-RIES** sorcery

DIABOLIC *adj* devilish

DIABOLO *n* pl. **-LOS** a game requiring manual dexterity

DIACETYL *n* pl. **-S** biacetyl

DIACID *n* pl. **-S** a type of acid **DIACIDIC** *adj*

DIACONAL *adj* pertaining to a deacon

DIADEM *v* **-ED, -ING, -S** to adorn with a crown

DIAGNOSE *v* **-NOSED, -NOSING, -NOSES** to recognize a disease by its signs and symptoms

DIAGONAL *n* pl. **-S** an oblique line

DIAGRAM *v* **-GRAMED, -GRAMING, -GRAMS** or **-GRAMMED, -GRAMMING, -GRAMS** to illustrate by a diagram (a graphic design)

DIAGRAPH *n* pl. **-S** a drawing device

DIAL *v* **DIALED, DIALING, DIALS** or **DIALLED, DIALLING, DIALS** to manipulate a calibrated disk

DIALECT *n* pl. **-S** a regional variety of a language

DIALER *n* pl. **-S** one that dials

DIALING *n* pl. **-S** the measurement of time by sundials

DIALIST *n* pl. **-S** a dialer

DIALLAGE *n* pl. **-S** a mineral

DIALLED a past tense of dial

DIALLEL *adj* pertaining to a genetic crossing

DIALLER *n* pl. **-S** dialer

DIALLING *n* pl. **-S** dialing

DIALLIST *n* pl. **-S** dialist

DIALOG *v* **-ED, -ING, -S** to dialogue

DIALOGER *n* pl. **-S** one that dialogs

DIALOGIC   *adj* conversational

DIALOGUE   *v* **-LOGUED, -LOGUING, -LOGUES** to carry on a conversation

DIALYSE   *v* **-LYSED, -LYSING, -LYSES** to dialyze

DIALYSER   *n* pl. **-S** dialyzer

DIALYSIS   *n* pl. **-YSES** the separation of substances in a solution by diffusion through a membrane

DIALYTIC   *adj* pertaining to dialysis

DIALYZE   *v* **-LYZED, -LYZING, -LYZES** to subject to dialysis

DIALYZER   *n* pl. **-S** an apparatus used for dialysis

DIAMANTE   *n* pl. **-S** a sparkling decoration

DIAMETER   *n* pl. **-S** a straight line passing through the center of a circle and ending at the periphery

DIAMIDE   *n* pl. **-S** a chemical compound

DIAMIN   *n* pl. **-S** diamine

DIAMINE   *n* pl. **-S** a chemical compound

DIAMOND   *v* **-ED, -ING, -S** to adorn with diamonds (precious gems)

DIANTHUS   *n* pl. **-ES** an ornamental herb

DIAPASON   *n* pl. **-S** a burst of harmonious sound

DIAPAUSE   *v* **-PAUSED, -PAUSING, -PAUSES** to undergo dormancy

DIAPER   *v* **-ED, -ING, -S** to put a diaper (a baby's breechcloth) on

DIAPHONE   *n* pl. **-S** a low-pitched foghorn

DIAPHONY   *n* pl. **-NIES** organum

DIAPIR   *n* pl. **-S** a bend in a layer of rock **DIAPIRIC** *adj*

DIAPSID   *n* pl. **-S** a reptile with two pairs of temporal openings in the skull

DIARCHY   *n* pl. **-CHIES** a government with two rulers **DIARCHIC** *adj*

DIARIES   pl. of diary

DIARIST   *n* pl. **-S** one who keeps a diary

DIARRHEA   *n* pl. **-S** an intestinal disorder

DIARY   *n* pl. **-RIES** a personal journal

DIASPORA   *n* pl. **-S** migration

DIASPORE   *n* pl. **-S** a mineral

DIASTASE   *n* pl. **-S** an enzyme

DIASTEM   *n* pl. **-S** an interruption in the deposition of sediment

DIASTEMA   *n* pl. **-MAS** or **-MATA** a space between teeth

DIASTER   *n* pl. **-S** a stage in mitosis **DIASTRAL** *adj*

DIASTOLE   *n* pl. **-S** the normal rhythmical dilation of the heart

DIATOM   *n* pl. **-S** any of a class of algae

DIATOMIC   *adj* composed of two atoms

DIATONIC   *adj* pertaining to a type of musical scale

DIATRIBE   *n* pl. **-S** a bitter and abusive criticism

DIATRON   *n* pl. **-S** a circuitry design that uses diodes

DIAZEPAM   *n* pl. **-S** a tranquilizer

DIAZIN   *n* pl. **-S** diazine

DIAZINE   *n* pl. **-S** a chemical compound

DIAZINON   *n* pl. **-S** an insecticide

DIAZO   *adj* containing a certain chemical group

DIAZOLE   *n* pl. **-S** a chemical compound

DIB   *v* **DIBBED, DIBBING, DIBS** to fish by letting the bait bob lightly on the water

DIBASIC   *adj* having two replaceable hydrogen atoms

DIBBER   *n* pl. **-S** a planting implement

DIBBLE   *v* **-BLED, -BLING, -BLES** to dib

DIBBLER   *n* pl. **-S** one that dibbles

DIBBUK   *n* pl. **-BUKS** or **-BUKIM** dybbuk

DICAMBA   *n* pl. **-S** an herbicide

DICAST   *n* pl. **-S** a judge of ancient Athens **DICASTIC** *adj*

DICE   *v* **DICED, DICING, DICES** to cut into small cubes

DICENTRA   *n* pl. **-S** a perennial herb

DICER   *n* pl. **-S** a device that dices food

DICEY   *adj* **DICIER, DICIEST** dangerous

DICHASIA   *n/pl* flower clusters

DICHOTIC   *adj* affecting the two ears differently

DICHROIC   *adj* having two colors

DICIER   comparative of dicey

DICIEST   superlative of dicey

DICING   present participle of dice

DICK   *n* pl. **-S** a detective

DICKENS   *n* pl. **-ES** devil

DICKER   *v* **-ED, -ING, -S** to bargain

DICKEY   *n* pl. **-EYS** a blouse front

DICKIE   *n* pl. **-S** dickey

DICKY *adj* **DICKIER, DICKIEST** poor in condition

DICKY *n* pl. **DICKIES** dickey

DICLINY *n* pl. **-NIES** the state of having stamens and pistils in separate flowers

DICOT *n* pl. **-S** a plant with two seed leaves

DICOTYL *n* pl. **-S** dicot

DICROTAL *adj* dicrotic

DICROTIC *adj* having a double pulse beat

DICTA a pl. of dictum

DICTATE *v* **-TATED, -TATING, -TATES** to read aloud for recording

DICTATOR *n* pl. **-S** one that dictates

DICTION *n* pl. **-S** choice and use of words in speech or writing

DICTUM *n* pl. **-TUMS** or **-TA** an authoritative statement

DICTY *adj* **-TIER, -TIEST** snobbish

DICYCLIC *adj* having two maxima of population each year

DICYCLY *n* pl. **-CLIES** the state of being dicyclic

DID a past tense of do

DIDACT *n* pl. **-S** a didactic person

DIDACTIC *adj* instructive

DIDACTYL *adj* having two digits at the end of each limb

DIDAPPER *n* pl. **-S** a dabchick

DIDDLE *v* **-DLED, -DLING, -DLES** to swindle

DIDDLER *n* pl. **-S** one that diddles

DIDDLEY *n* pl. **-DLEYS** diddly

DIDDLY *n* pl. **-DLIES** the least amount

DIDIE *n* pl. **-S** didy

DIDIES pl. of didy

DIDO *n* pl. **-DOS** or **-DOES** a mischievous act

DIDST a past tense of do

DIDY *n* pl. **-DIES** a diaper

DIDYMIUM *n* pl. **-S** a mixture of rare-earth elements

DIDYMOUS *adj* occurring in pairs

DIDYNAMY *n* pl. **-MIES** the state of having four stamens in pairs of unequal length

DIE *v* **DIED, DIEING, DIES** to cut with a die (a device for shaping material)

DIE *v* **DIED, DYING, DIES** to cease living

DIEBACK *n* pl. **-S** a gradual dying of plant shoots

DIECIOUS *adj* dioicous

DIED past tense of die

DIEHARD *n* pl. **-S** a stubborn person

DIEL *adj* involving a full day

DIELDRIN *n* pl. **-S** an insecticide

DIEMAKER *n* pl. **-S** one that makes dies

DIENE *n* pl. **-S** a chemical compound

DIEOFF *n* pl. **-S** a sudden decline in a population

DIERESIS *n* pl. **DIERESES** the separation of two vowels into two syllables **DIERETIC** *adj*

DIESEL *v* **-ED, -ING, -S** to continue running after the ignition is turned off

DIESIS *n* pl. **DIESES** a reference mark in printing

DIESTER *n* pl. **-S** a type of chemical compound

DIESTOCK *n* pl. **-S** a frame for holding dies

DIESTRUM *n* pl. **-S** diestrus

DIESTRUS *n* pl. **-ES** a period of sexual inactivity

DIET *v* **-ED, -ING, -S** to regulate one's daily sustenance

DIETARY *n* pl. **-ETARIES** a system of dieting

DIETER *n* pl. **-S** one that diets

DIETETIC *adj* pertaining to diet

DIETHER *n* pl. **-S** a chemical compound

DIF *n* pl. **-S** diff

DIFF *n* pl. **-S** a difference

DIFFER *v* **-ED, -ING, -S** to be unlike

DIFFRACT *v* **-ED, -ING, -S** to separate into parts

DIFFUSE *v* **-FUSED, -FUSING, -FUSES** to spread widely or thinly

DIFFUSER *n* pl. **-S** one that diffuses

DIFFUSOR *n* pl. **-S** diffuser

DIG *v* **DUG** or **DIGGED, DIGGING, DIGS** to break up, turn over, or remove earth

DIGAMIES pl. of digamy

DIGAMIST *n* pl. **-S** one who practices digamy

DIGAMMA *n* pl. **-S** a Greek letter

DIGAMY *n* pl. **-MIES** a second legal marriage **DIGAMOUS** *adj*

DIGERATI *n/pl* persons skilled in the use of computers

DIGEST *v* **-ED, -ING, -S** to render food usable for the body

DIGESTER *n* pl. **-S** an apparatus in which substances are softened or decomposed

DIGESTIF *n* pl. **-S** an alcoholic drink taken after a meal

DIGESTOR *n* pl. **-S** digester

DIGGED a past tense of dig

DIGGER *n* pl. **-S** one that digs

DIGGING present participle of dig

DIGGINGS *n/pl* an excavation site

DIGHT *v* **-ED, -ING, -S** to adorn

DIGIT *n* pl. **-S** a finger or toe

DIGITAL *n* pl. **-S** a piano key

DIGITATE *adj* having digits

DIGITIZE *v* **-TIZED, -TIZING, -TIZES** to put data into digital notation

DIGLOT *n* pl. **-S** a bilingual book or edition

DIGNIFY *v* **-FIED, -FYING, -FIES** to add dignity to

DIGNITY *n* pl. **-TIES** stateliness and nobility of manner

DIGOXIN *n* pl. **-S** a drug to improve heart function

DIGRAPH *n* pl. **-S** a pair of letters representing a single speech sound

DIGRESS *v* **-ED, -ING, -ES** to stray from the main topic

DIHEDRAL *n* pl. **-S** a dihedron

DIHEDRON *n* pl. **-S** a figure formed by two intersecting planes

DIHYBRID *n* pl. **-S** an offspring of parents differing in two pairs of genes

DIHYDRIC *adj* containing two hydroxyl radicals

DIKDIK *n* pl. **-S** a small antelope

DIKE *v* **DIKED, DIKING, DIKES** to furnish with an embankment

DIKER *n* pl. **-S** one that dikes

DIKTAT *n* pl. **-S** a harsh settlement imposed on a defeated nation

DILATANT *n* pl. **-S** a dilator

DILATATE *adj* dilated

DILATE *v* **-LATED, -LATING, -LATES** to make wider or larger

DILATER *n* pl. **-S** dilator

DILATION *n* pl. **-S** the act of dilating

DILATIVE *adj* tending to dilate

DILATOR *n* pl. **-S** one that dilates

DILATORY *adj* tending to delay

DILDO *n* pl. **-DOS** an object used as a penis substitute

DILDOE *n* pl. **-S** dildo

DILEMMA *n* pl. **-S** a perplexing situation **DILEMMIC** *adj*

DILIGENT *adj* persevering

DILL *n* pl. **-S** an annual herb

DILLED *adj* flavored with dill

DILLY *n* pl. **DILLIES** something remarkable

DILUENT *n* pl. **-S** a diluting substance

DILUTE *v* **-LUTED, -LUTING, -LUTES** to thin or reduce the concentration of

DILUTER *n* pl. **-S** one that dilutes

DILUTION *n* pl. **-S** the act of diluting

DILUTIVE *adj* tending to dilute

DILUTOR *n* pl. **-S** diluter

DILUVIA a pl. of diluvium

DILUVIAL *adj* pertaining to a flood

DILUVIAN *adj* diluvial

DILUVION *n* pl. **-S** diluvium

DILUVIUM *n* pl. **-VIUMS** or **-VIA** coarse rock material deposited by glaciers

DIM *adj* **DIMMER, DIMMEST** obscure

DIM *v* **DIMMED, DIMMING, DIMS** to make dim

DIME *n* pl. **-S** a coin of the United States

DIMER *n* pl. **-S** a molecule composed of two identical molecules

DIMERIC *adj* dimerous

DIMERISM *n* pl. **-S** the state of being dimerous

DIMERIZE *v* **-IZED, -IZING, -IZES** to form a dimer

DIMEROUS *adj* composed of two parts

DIMETER *n* pl. **-S** a verse of two metrical feet

DIMETHYL *n* pl. **-S** ethane

DIMETRIC *adj* pertaining to a type of crystal system

DIMINISH *v* **-ED, -ING, -ES** to lessen

DIMITY *n* pl. **-TIES** a cotton fabric

DIMLY *adv* in a dim manner

DIMMABLE *adj* capable of being dimmed

DIMMED past tense of dim

DIMMER *n* pl. **-S** a device for varying the intensity of illumination

DIMMEST superlative of dim

DIMMING present participle of dim

DIMNESS *n* pl. **-ES** the state of being dim

DIMORPH *n* pl. **-S** either of two distinct forms

DIMOUT *n* pl. **-S** a condition of partial darkness

DIMPLE *v* **-PLED, -PLING, -PLES** to mark with indentations

DIMPLY *adj* **-PLIER, -PLIEST** dimpled

DIMWIT *n* pl. **-S** a dunce

DIN *v* **DINNED, DINNING, DINS** to make a loud noise

DINAR *n* pl. **-S** an ancient gold coin of Muslim areas

DINDLE *v* **-DLED, -DLING, -DLES** to tingle

DINE *v* **DINED, DINING, DINES** to eat dinner

DINER *n* pl. **-S** one that dines

DINERIC *adj* pertaining to the interface between two immiscible liquids

DINERO *n* pl. **-ROS** a former silver coin of Peru

DINETTE *n* pl. **-S** a small dining room

DING *v* **-ED, -ING, -S** to ring

DINGBAT *n* pl. **-S** a typographical ornament

DINGDONG *v* **-ED, -ING, -S** to make a ringing sound

DINGE *n* pl. **-S** the condition of being dingy

DINGER *n* pl. **-S** a home run

DINGEY *n* pl. **-GEYS** dinghy

DINGHY *n* pl. **-GHIES** a small boat

DINGIER comparative of dingy

DINGIES pl. of dingy

DINGIEST superlative of dingy

DINGILY *adv* in a dingy manner

DINGLE *n* pl. **-S** a dell

DINGO *n* pl. **-GOES** a wild dog of Australia

DINGUS *n* pl. **-ES** a doodad

DINGY *adj* **-GIER, -GIEST** grimy

DINGY *n* pl. **-GIES** dinghy

DINING present participle of dine

DINITRO *adj* containing two nitro groups

DINK *v* **-ED, -ING, -S** to adorn

DINKEY *n* pl. **-KEYS** a small locomotive

DINKIER comparative of dinky

DINKIES pl. of dinky

DINKIEST superlative of dinky

DINKLY *adv* neatly

DINKUM *n* pl. **-S** the truth

DINKY *adj* **-KIER, -KIEST** small

DINKY *n* pl. **-KIES** dinkey

DINNED past tense of din

DINNER *n* pl. **-S** the main meal of the day

DINNING present participle of din

DINO *n* pl. **-NOS** a dinosaur

DINOSAUR *n* pl. **-S** one of a group of extinct reptiles

DINT *v* **-ED, -ING, -S** to dent

DIOBOL *n* pl. **-S** a coin of ancient Greece

DIOBOLON *n* pl. **-S** diobol

DIOCESAN *n* pl. **-S** a bishop

DIOCESE *n* pl. **-S** an ecclesiastical district

DIODE *n* pl. **-S** a type of electron tube

DIOECISM *n* pl. **-S** the state of being dioicous

DIOECY *n* pl. **DIOECIES** dioecism

DIOICOUS *adj* unisexual

DIOL *n* pl. **-S** a chemical compound

DIOLEFIN *n* pl. **-S** a hydrocarbon

DIOPSIDE *n* pl. **-S** a mineral

DIOPTASE *n* pl. **-S** a mineral

DIOPTER *n* pl. **-S** a measure of refractive power **DIOPTRAL** *adj*

DIOPTRE *n* pl. **-S** diopter

DIOPTRIC *adj* aiding the vision by refraction

DIORAMA *n* pl. **-S** a three-dimensional exhibit **DIORAMIC** *adj*

DIORITE *n* pl. **-S** an igneous rock **DIORITIC** *adj*

DIOXAN *n* pl. **-S** dioxane

DIOXANE *n* pl. **-S** a flammable liquid

DIOXID *n* pl. **-S** dioxide

DIOXIDE *n* pl. **-S** a type of oxide

DIOXIN *n* pl. **-S** a toxic solid hydrocarbon

DIP *v* **DIPPED** or **DIPT, DIPPING, DIPS** to immerse briefly

DIPHASE *adj* having two phases

DIPHASIC *adj* diphase

DIPHENYL *n* pl. **-S** biphenyl

DIPLEGIA *n* pl. **-S** paralysis of the same part on both sides of the body **DIPLEGIC** *adj*

DIPLEX *adj* pertaining to the simultaneous transmission or reception of two radio signals

DIPLEXER *n* pl. **-S** a coupling device

DIPLOE *n* pl. **-S** a bony tissue of the cranium **DIPLOIC** *adj*

DIPLOID *n* pl. **-S** a cell having the basic chromosome number doubled

DIPLOIDY *n* pl. **-DIES** the condition of being a diploid

DIPLOMA *n* pl. **-MAS** or **-MATA** a certificate of an academic degree

DIPLOMA *v* **-ED, -ING, -S** to furnish with a diploma

DIPLOMAT *n* pl. **-S** a governmental official

DIPLONT *n* pl. **-S** an organism having a particular chromosomal structure

DIPLOPIA *n* pl. **-S** double vision **DIPLOPIC** *adj*

DIPLOPOD *n* pl. **-S** a multi-legged insect

DIPLOSIS *n* pl. **-LOSES** a method of chromosome formation

DIPNET *v* **-NETTED, -NETTING, -NETS** to scoop fish with a type of net

DIPNOAN *n* pl. **-S** a lungfish

DIPODY *n* pl. **-DIES** a dimeter **DIPODIC** *adj*

DIPOLE *n* pl. **-S** a pair of equal and opposite electric charges **DIPOLAR** *adj*

DIPPABLE *adj* capable of being dipped

DIPPED a past tense of dip

DIPPER *n* pl. **-S** one that dips

DIPPING present participle of dip

DIPPY *adj* **-PIER, -PIEST** foolish

DIPROTIC *adj* having two hydrogen ions to donate to bases

DIPSAS *n* pl. **DIPSADES** a fabled serpent

DIPSO *n* pl. **-SOS** a person who craves alcoholic liquors

DIPSTICK *n* pl. **-S** a measuring rod

DIPT a past tense of dip

DIPTERA pl. of dipteron

DIPTERAL *adj* having two rows or columns

DIPTERAN *n* pl. **-S** a two-winged fly

DIPTERON *n* pl. **-TERA** dipteran

DIPTYCA *n* pl. **-S** diptych

DIPTYCH *n* pl. **-S** an ancient writing tablet

DIQUAT *n* pl. **-S** an herbicide

DIRAM *n* pl. **-S** a monetary unit of Tajikistan

DIRDUM *n* pl. **-S** blame

DIRE *adj* **DIRER, DIREST** disastrous

DIRECT *adj* **-RECTER, -RECTEST** straightforward **DIRECTLY** *adv*

DIRECT *v* **-ED, -ING, -S** to control or conduct the affairs of

DIRECTOR *n* pl. **-S** one that directs

DIREFUL *adj* dreadful

DIRELY *adv* in a dire manner

DIRENESS *n* pl. **-ES** the state of being dire

DIRER comparative of dire

DIREST superlative of dire

DIRGE *n* pl. **-S** a funeral song **DIRGEFUL** *adj*

DIRHAM *n* pl. **-S** a monetary unit of Morocco

DIRIMENT *adj* nullifying

DIRK *v* **-ED, -ING, -S** to stab with a small knife

DIRL *v* **-ED, -ING, -S** to tremble

DIRNDL *n* pl. **-S** a woman's dress

DIRT *n* pl. **-S** earth or soil

DIRTBAG *n* pl. **-S** a dirty or contemptible person

DIRTY *adj* **DIRTIER, DIRTIEST** unclean **DIRTILY** *adv*

DIRTY *v* **DIRTIED, DIRTYING, DIRTIES** to make dirty

DIS *v* **DISSED, DISSING, DISSES** to insult or criticize

DISABLE *v* **-ABLED, -ABLING, -ABLES** to render incapable or unable

DISABLER *n* pl. **-S** one that disables

DISABUSE *v* **-ABUSED, -ABUSING, -ABUSES** to free from false or mistaken ideas

DISAGREE *v* **-AGREED, -AGREEING, -AGREES** to differ in opinion

DISALLOW *v* **-ED, -ING, -S** to refuse to allow

DISANNUL *v* **-NULLED, -NULLING, -NULS** to annul

DISARM *v* **-ED, -ING, -S** to deprive of weapons

DISARMER *n* pl. **-S** one that disarms

DISARRAY *v* **-ED, -ING, -S** to disorder

DISASTER *n* pl. **-S** a calamity

DISAVOW *v* **-ED, -ING, -S** to disclaim responsibility for

DISBAND   v **-ED, -ING, -S** to break up

DISBAR   v **-BARRED, -BARRING, -BARS** to expel from the legal profession

DISBOSOM   v **-ED, -ING, -S** to confess

DISBOUND   adj not having a binding

DISBOWEL   v **-ELED, -ELING, -ELS** or **-ELLED, -ELLING, -ELS** to remove the intestines of

DISBUD   v **-BUDDED, -BUDDING, -BUDS** to remove buds from

DISBURSE   v **-BURSED, -BURSING, -BURSES** to pay out

DISC   v **-ED, -ING, -S** to disk

DISCANT   v **-ED, -ING, -S** to descant

DISCARD   v **-ED, -ING, -S** to throw away

DISCASE   v **-CASED, -CASING, -CASES** to remove the case of

DISCEPT   v **-ED, -ING, -S** to debate

DISCERN   v **-ED, -ING, -S** to perceive

DISCI   a pl. of discus

DISCIPLE   v **-PLED, -PLING, -PLES** to cause to become a follower

DISCLAIM   v **-ED, -ING, -S** to renounce any claim to or connection with

DISCLIKE   adj disklike

DISCLOSE   v **-CLOSED, -CLOSING, -CLOSES** to reveal

DISCO   v **-ED, -ING, -S** to dance at a discotheque

DISCOID   n pl. **-S** a disk

DISCOLOR   v **-ED, -ING, -S** to alter the color of

DISCORD   v **-ED, -ING, -S** to disagree

DISCOUNT   v **-ED, -ING, -S** to reduce the price of

DISCOVER   v **-ED, -ING, -S** to gain sight or knowledge of

DISCREET   adj **-CREETER, -CREETEST** tactful

DISCRETE   adj separate

DISCROWN   v **-ED, -ING, -S** to deprive of a crown

DISCUS   n pl. **-CUSES** or **-CI** a disk hurled in athletic competition

DISCUSS   v **-ED, -ING, -ES** to talk over or write about

DISDAIN   v **-ED, -ING, -S** to scorn

DISEASE   v **-EASED, -EASING, -EASES** to make unhealthy

DISENDOW   v **-ED, -ING, -S** to deprive of endowment

DISEUR   n pl. **-S** a skilled reciter

DISEUSE   n pl. **-S** a female entertainer

DISFAVOR   v **-ED, -ING, -S** to regard with disapproval

DISFROCK   v **-ED, -ING, -S** to unfrock

DISGORGE   v **-GORGED, -GORGING, -GORGES** to vomit

DISGRACE   v **-GRACED, -GRACING, -GRACES** to bring shame or discredit upon

DISGUISE   v **-GUISED, -GUISING, -GUISES** to alter the appearance of

DISGUST   v **-ED, -ING, -S** to cause nausea or loathing in

DISH   v **-ED, -ING, -ES** to put into a dish (a concave vessel)

DISHELM   v **-ED, -ING, -S** to deprive of a helmet

DISHERIT   v **-ED, -ING, -S** to deprive of an inheritance

DISHEVEL   v **-ELED, -ELING, -ELS** or **-ELLED, -ELLING, -ELS** to make messy

DISHFUL   n pl. **-S** as much as a dish can hold

DISHIER   comparative of dishy

DISHIEST   superlative of dishy

DISHLIKE   adj resembling a dish

DISHONOR   v **-ED, -ING, -S** to deprive of honor

DISHPAN   n pl. **-S** a pan for washing dishes

DISHRAG   n pl. **-S** a cloth for washing dishes

DISHWARE   n pl. **-S** tableware used in serving food

DISHY   adj **DISHIER, DISHIEST** attractive

DISINTER   v **-TERRED, -TERRING, -TERS** to exhume

DISJECT   v **-ED, -ING, -S** to disperse

DISJOIN   v **-ED, -ING, -S** to separate

DISJOINT   v **-ED, -ING, -S** to put out of order

DISJUNCT   n pl. **-S** an alternative in a logical disjunction

DISK   v **-ED, -ING, -S** to break up land with a type of farm implement

DISKETTE   n pl. **-S** a floppy disk for a computer

DISKLIKE   adj resembling a disk (a flat, circular plate)

DISLIKE   v **-LIKED, -LIKING, -LIKES** to regard with aversion

DISLIKER   n pl. **-S** one that dislikes

DISLIMN   v **-ED, -ING, -S** to make dim

DISLODGE   *v* **-LODGED, -LODGING, -LODGES** to remove from a firm position

DISLOYAL   *adj* not loyal

DISMAL   *adj* **-MALER, -MALEST** cheerless and depressing **DISMALLY** *adv*

DISMAL   *n pl.* **-S** a track of swampy land

DISMAST   *v* **-ED, -ING, -S** to remove the mast of

DISMAY   *v* **-ED, -ING, -S** to deprive of courage or resolution

DISME   *n pl.* **-S** a former coin of the United States

DISMISS   *v* **-ED, -ING, -ES** to permit or cause to leave

DISMOUNT   *v* **-ED, -ING, -S** to get down from an elevated position

DISOBEY   *v* **-ED, -ING, -S** to fail to obey

DISOMIC   *adj* having a number of chromosomes duplicated

DISORDER   *v* **-ED, -ING, -S** to put out of order

DISOWN   *v* **-ED, -ING, -S** to deny the ownership of

DISPART   *v* **-ED, -ING, -S** to separate

DISPATCH   *v* **-ED, -ING, -ES** to send off with speed

DISPEL   *v* **-PELLED, -PELLING, -PELS** to drive off in various directions

DISPEND   *v* **-ED, -ING, -S** to squander

DISPENSE   *v* **-PENSED, -PENSING, -PENSES** to distribute

DISPERSE   *v* **-PERSED, -PERSING, -PERSES** to scatter

DISPIRIT   *v* **-ED, -ING, -S** to lower in spirit

DISPLACE   *v* **-PLACED, -PLACING, -PLACES** to remove from the usual or proper place

DISPLANT   *v* **-ED, -ING, -S** to dislodge

DISPLAY   *v* **-ED, -ING, -S** to make evident or obvious

DISPLODE   *v* **-PLODED, -PLODING, -PLODES** to explode

DISPLUME   *v* **-PLUMED, -PLUMING, -PLUMES** to deplume

DISPORT   *v* **-ED, -ING, -S** to amuse oneself

DISPOSAL   *n pl.* **-S** the act of disposing

DISPOSE   *v* **-POSED, -POSING, -POSES** to put in place

DISPOSER   *n pl.* **-S** one that disposes

DISPREAD   *v* **-SPREAD, -SPREADING, -SPREADS** to spread out

DISPRIZE   *v* **-PRIZED, -PRIZING, -PRIZES** to disdain

DISPROOF   *n pl.* **-S** the act of disproving

DISPROVE   *v* **-PROVED, -PROVEN, -PROVING, -PROVES** to refute

DISPUTE   *v* **-PUTED, -PUTING, -PUTES** to argue about

DISPUTER   *n pl.* **-S** one that disputes

DISQUIET   *v* **-ED, -ING, -S** to deprive of quiet, rest, or peace

DISRATE   *v* **-RATED, -RATING, -RATES** to lower in rating or rank

DISROBE   *v* **-ROBED, -ROBING, -ROBES** to undress

DISROBER   *n pl.* **-S** one that disrobes

DISROOT   *v* **-ED, -ING, -S** to uproot

DISRUPT   *v* **-ED, -ING, -S** to throw into confusion

DISS   *v* **-ED, -ING, -ES** to dis

DISSAVE   *v* **-SAVED, -SAVING, -SAVES** to use savings for current expenses

DISSEAT   *v* **-ED, -ING, -S** to unseat

DISSECT   *v* **-ED, -ING, -S** to cut apart for scientific examination

DISSED   past tense of dis

DISSEISE   *v* **-SEISED, -SEISING, -SEISES** to deprive

DISSEIZE   *v* **-SEIZED, -SEIZING, -SEIZES** to disseise

DISSENT   *v* **-ED, -ING, -S** to disagree

DISSERT   *v* **-ED, -ING, -S** to discuss in a learned or formal manner

DISSERVE   *v* **-SERVED, -SERVING, -SERVES** to treat badly

DISSES   present 3d person sing. of dis

DISSEVER   *v* **-ED, -ING, -S** to sever

DISSING   present participle of dis

DISSOLVE   *v* **-SOLVED, -SOLVING, -SOLVES** to make into a solution

DISSUADE   *v* **-SUADED, -SUADING, -SUADES** to persuade not to do something

DISTAFF   *n pl.* **-TAFFS** or **-TAVES** a type of staff

DISTAIN   *v* **-ED, -ING, -S** to stain

DISTAL   *adj* located far from the point of origin **DISTALLY** *adv*

DISTANCE   *v* **-TANCED, -TANCING, -TANCES** to leave behind

DISTANT   *adj* far off or apart

DISTASTE *v* **-TASTED, -TASTING, -TASTES** to dislike

DISTAVES a pl. of distaff

DISTEND *v* **-ED, -ING, -S** to swell

DISTENT *adj* distended

DISTICH *n* pl. **-S** a couplet

DISTIL *v* **-TILLED, -TILLING, -TILS** to distill

DISTILL *v* **-ED, -ING, -S** to extract by vaporization and condensation

DISTINCT *adj* **-TINCTER, -TINCTEST** clearly different

DISTOME *n* pl. **-S** a parasitic flatworm

DISTORT *v* **-ED, -ING, -S** to put out of shape

DISTRACT *v* **-ED, -ING, -S** to divert the attention of

DISTRAIN *v* **-ED, -ING, -S** to seize and hold property as security

DISTRAIT *adj* absentminded

DISTRESS *v* **-ED, -ING, -ES** to cause anxiety or suffering to

DISTRICT *v* **-ED, -ING, -S** to divide into localities

DISTRUST *v* **-ED, -ING, -S** to have no trust in

DISTURB *v* **-ED, -ING, -S** to interrupt the quiet, rest, or peace of

DISULFID *n* pl. **-S** a chemical compound

DISUNION *n* pl. **-S** the state of being disunited

DISUNITE *v* **-UNITED, -UNITING, -UNITES** to separate

DISUNITY *n* pl. **-TIES** lack of unity

DISUSE *v* **-USED, -USING, -USES** to stop using

DISVALUE *v* **-UED, -UING, -UES** to treat as of little value

DISYOKE *v* **-YOKED, -YOKING, -YOKES** to free from a yoke

DIT *n* pl. **-S** a dot in Morse code

DITA *n* pl. **-S** a Philippine tree

DITCH *v* **-ED, -ING, -ES** to dig a long, narrow excavation in the ground

DITCHER *n* pl. **-S** one that ditches

DITE *n* pl. **-S** a small amount

DITHEISM *n* pl. **-S** belief in two coequal gods

DITHEIST *n* pl. **-S** an adherent of ditheism

DITHER *v* **-ED, -ING, -S** to act nervously or indecisively

DITHERER *n* pl. **-S** one that dithers

DITHERY *adj* nervously excited

DITHIOL *adj* containing two chemical groups both of which include sulfur and hydrogen

DITSY *adj* **-SIER, -SIEST** silly, eccentric

DITTANY *n* pl. **-NIES** a perennial herb

DITTO *v* **-ED, -ING, -S** to repeat

DITTY *n* pl. **-TIES** a short, simple song

DITZ *n* pl. **-ES** a ditsy person

DITZY *adj* **-ZIER, -ZIEST** ditsy

DIURESIS *n* pl. **DIURESES** excessive discharge of urine

DIURETIC *n* pl. **-S** a drug which increases urinary discharge

DIURNAL *n* pl. **-S** a diary

DIURON *n* pl. **-S** an herbicide

DIVA *n* pl. **-S** a distinguished female operatic singer

DIVAGATE *v* **-GATED, -GATING, -GATES** to wander

DIVALENT *adj* having a valence of two

DIVAN *n* pl. **-S** a sofa or couch

DIVE *v* **DIVED** or **DOVE, DIVING, DIVES** to plunge headfirst into water

DIVEBOMB *v* **-ED, -ING, -S** to drop bombs on a target from a diving airplane

DIVER *n* pl. **-S** one that dives

DIVERGE *v* **-VERGED, -VERGING, -VERGES** to move in different directions from a common point

DIVERSE *adj* different

DIVERT *v* **-ED, -ING, -S** to turn aside

DIVERTER *n* pl. **-S** one that diverts

DIVEST *v* **-ED, -ING, -S** to strip or deprive of anything

DIVIDE *v* **-VIDED, -VIDING, -VIDES** to separate into parts, areas, or groups

DIVIDEND *n* pl. **-S** a quantity to be divided

DIVIDER *n* pl. **-S** one that divides

DIVIDING present participle of divide

DIVIDUAL *adj* capable of being divided

DIVINE *adj* **-VINER, -VINEST** pertaining to or characteristic of a god **DIVINELY** *adv*

DIVINE *v* **-VINED, -VINING, -VINES** to foretell by occult means

DIVINER *n* pl. **-S** one that divines

DIVING present participle of dive

DIVINING present participle of divine

DIVINISE *v* **-NISED, -NISING, -NISES** to divinize

DIVINITY *n* pl. **-TIES** the state of being divine

DIVINIZE *v* **-NIZED, -NIZING, -NIZES** to make divine

DIVISION *n* pl. **-S** the act of dividing

DIVISIVE *adj* causing disunity or dissension

DIVISOR *n* pl. **-S** a number by which a dividend is divided

DIVORCE *v* **-VORCED, -VORCING, -VORCES** to terminate the marriage contract between

DIVORCEE *n* pl. **-S** a divorced woman

DIVORCER *n* pl. **-S** one that divorces

DIVOT *n* pl. **-S** a piece of turf

DIVULGE *v* **-VULGED, -VULGING, -VULGES** to reveal

DIVULGER *n* pl. **-S** one that divulges

DIVULSE *v* **-VULSED, -VULSING, -VULSES** to tear away

DIVVY *v* **-VIED, -VYING, -VIES** to divide

DIWAN *n* pl. **-S** dewan

DIXIT *n* pl. **-S** a statement

DIZEN *v* **-ED, -ING, -S** to dress in fine clothes

DIZYGOUS *adj* developed from two fertilized ova

DIZZY *adj* **-ZIER, -ZIEST** having a sensation of whirling **DIZZILY** *adv*

DIZZY *v* **-ZIED, -ZYING, -ZIES** to make dizzy

DJEBEL *n* pl. **-S** jebel

DJELLABA *n* pl. **-S** a long hooded garment

DJIN *n* pl. **-S** jinni

DJINN *n* pl. **-S** jinni

DJINNI *n* pl. **DJINN** jinni

DJINNY *n* pl. **DJINN** jinni

DO *n* pl. **DOS** the first tone of the diatonic musical scale

DO *v* **DID** or **DIDST, DONE, DOING,** present sing. 2d person **DO** or **DOEST** or **DOST,** 3d person **DOES** or **DOETH** or **DOTH** to begin and carry through to completion

DOABLE *adj* able to be done

DOAT *v* **-ED, -ING, -S** to dote

DOBBER *n* pl. **-S** a float for a fishing line

DOBBIN *n* pl. **-S** a farm horse

DOBBY *n* pl. **-BIES** a fool

DOBIE *n* pl. **-S** adobe

DOBIES pl. of doby

DOBLA *n* pl. **-S** a former gold coin of Spain

DOBLON *n* pl. **-S** or **-ES** a former gold coin of Spain and Spanish America

DOBRA *n* pl. **-S** a former gold coin of Portugal

DOBSON *n* pl. **-S** an aquatic insect larva

DOBY *n* pl. **-BIES** dobie

DOC *n* pl. **-S** doctor

DOCENT *n* pl. **-S** a college or university lecturer

DOCETIC *adj* pertaining to a religious doctrine

DOCILE *adj* easily trained **DOCILELY** *adv*

DOCILITY *n* pl. **-TIES** the quality of being docile

DOCK *v* **-ED, -ING, -S** to bring into a dock (a wharf)

DOCKAGE *n* pl. **-S** a charge for the use of a dock

DOCKER *n* pl. **-S** a dock worker

DOCKET *v* **-ED, -ING, -S** to supply with an identifying statement

DOCKHAND *n* pl. **-S** a docker

DOCKLAND *n* pl. **-S** the part of a port occupied by docks

DOCKSIDE *n* pl. **-S** the area adjacent to a dock

DOCKYARD *n* pl. **-S** a shipyard

DOCTOR *v* **-ED, -ING, -S** to treat medically **DOCTORLY** *adj*

DOCTORAL *adj* pertaining to a doctor

DOCTRINE *n* pl. **-S** a belief or set of beliefs taught or advocated

DOCUMENT *v* **-ED, -ING, -S** to support by conclusive information or evidence

DODDER *v* **-ED, -ING, -S** to totter

DODDERER *n* pl. **-S** one that dodders

DODDERY *adj* feeble

DODGE *v* **DODGED, DODGING, DODGES** to evade

DODGEM *n* pl. **-S** an amusement park ride

DODGER *n* pl. **-S** one that dodges

DODGERY *n* pl. **-ERIES** evasion

DODGING present participle of dodge

DODGY *adj* **DODGIER, DODGIEST** evasive

DODO *n* pl. **-DOS** or **-DOES** an extinct flightless bird

DODOISM *n* pl. **-S** a stupid remark

DOE *n* pl. **-S** a female deer

DOER *n* pl. **-S** one that does something

DOES a present 3d person sing. of do

DOESKIN *n* pl. **-S** the skin of a doe

DOEST a present 2d person sing. of do

DOETH a present 3d person sing. of do

DOFF *v* **-ED, -ING, -S** to take off

DOFFER *n* pl. **-S** one that doffs

DOG *v* **DOGGED, DOGGING, DOGS** to follow after like a dog (a domesticated, carnivorous mammal)

DOGBANE *n* pl. **-S** a perennial herb

DOGBERRY *n* pl. **-RIES** a wild berry

DOGCART *n* pl. **-S** a one-horse carriage

DOGDOM *n* pl. **-S** the world of dogs

DOGE *n* pl. **-S** the chief magistrate in the former republics of Venice and Genoa

DOGEAR *v* **-ED, -ING, -S** to turn down a corner of a page

DOGEDOM *n* pl. **-S** the domain of a doge

DOGESHIP *n* pl. **-S** the office of a doge

DOGEY *n* pl. **-GEYS** dogie

DOGFACE *n* pl. **-S** a soldier in the U.S. Army

DOGFIGHT *v* **-FOUGHT, -FIGHTING, -FIGHTS** to engage in an aerial battle

DOGFISH *n* pl. **-ES** a small shark

DOGGED past tense of dog

DOGGEDLY *adv* stubbornly

DOGGER *n* pl. **-S** a fishing vessel

DOGGEREL *n* pl. **-S** trivial, awkwardly written verse

DOGGERY *n* pl. **-GERIES** surly behavior

DOGGIE *n* pl. **-S** doggy

DOGGIER comparative of doggy

DOGGIES pl. of doggy

DOGGIEST superlative of doggy

DOGGING present participle of dog

DOGGISH *adj* doglike

DOGGO *adv* in hiding

DOGGONE *adj* **-GONER, -GONEST** damned

DOGGONE *v* **-GONED, -GONING, -GONES** to damn

DOGGONED *adj* **-GONEDER, -GONEDEST** damned

DOGGREL *n* pl. **-S** doggerel

DOGGY *adj* **-GIER, -GIEST** resembling or suggestive of a dog

DOGGY *n* pl. **-GIES** a small dog

DOGHOUSE *n* pl. **-S** a shelter for a dog

DOGIE *n* pl. **-S** a stray calf

DOGIES pl. of dogy

DOGLEG *v* **-LEGGED, -LEGGING, -LEGS** to move along a bent course

DOGLIKE *adj* resembling a dog

DOGMA *n* pl. **-MAS** or **-MATA** a principle or belief put forth as authoritative **DOGMATIC** *adj*

DOGNAP *v* **-NAPED, -NAPING, -NAPS** or **-NAPPED, -NAPPING, -NAPS** to steal a dog

DOGNAPER *n* pl. **-S** one that dognaps

DOGSBODY *n* pl. **-BODIES** a menial worker

DOGSLED *v* **-SLEDDED, -SLEDDING, -SLEDS** to move on a sled drawn by dogs

DOGTOOTH *n* pl. **-TEETH** a cuspid

DOGTROT *v* **-TROTTED, -TROTTING, -TROTS** to move at a steady trot

DOGVANE *n* pl. **-S** a small vane

DOGWATCH *n* pl. **-ES** a short period of watch duty on a ship

DOGWOOD *n* pl. **-S** a tree

DOGY *n* pl. **-GIES** dogie

DOILED *adj* dazed

DOILY *n* pl. **-LIES** a small napkin

DOING *n* pl. **-S** an action

DOIT *n* pl. **-S** a former Dutch coin

DOITED *adj* old and feeble

DOJO *n* pl. **-JOS** a school that teaches judo or karate

DOL *n* pl. **-S** a unit of pain intensity

DOLCE *n* pl. **-CI** a soft-toned organ stop

DOLCETTO *n* pl. **-TOS** a red wine of Italy

DOLDRUMS *n/pl* a slump or slack period

DOLE *v* **DOLED, DOLING, DOLES** to distribute in small portions

DOLEFUL *adj* **-FULLER, -FULLEST** mournful

DOLERITE *n* pl. **-S** a variety of basalt

DOLESOME *adj* doleful

DOLING present participle of dole

DOLL *v* **-ED, -ING, -S** to dress stylishly

DOLLAR *n* pl. **-S** a monetary unit of the United States

DOLLIED past tense of dolly

DOLLIES present 3d person sing. of dolly

DOLLISH *adj* pretty

DOLLOP *v* **-ED, -ING, -S** to dispense in small amounts

DOLLY *v* **-LIED, -LYING, -LIES** to move on a wheeled platform

DOLMA *n* pl. **-MAS** or **-MADES** a stuffed grape leaf

DOLMAN *n* pl. **-S** a Turkish robe

DOLMEN *n* pl. **-S** a prehistoric monument **DOLMENIC** *adj*

DOLOMITE *n* pl. **-S** a mineral

DOLOR *n* pl. **-S** grief

DOLOROSO *adj* having a mournful musical quality

DOLOROUS *adj* mournful

DOLOUR *n* pl. **-S** dolor

DOLPHIN *n* pl. **-S** a marine mammal

DOLT *n* pl. **-S** a stupid person **DOLTISH** *adj*

DOM *n* pl. **-S** a title given to certain monks

DOMAIN *n* pl. **-S** an area of control

DOMAINE *n* pl. **-S** a vineyard in Burgundy

DOMAL *adj* domical

DOME *v* **DOMED, DOMING, DOMES** to cover with a dome (a rounded roof)

DOMELIKE *adj* resembling a dome

DOMESDAY *n* pl. **-DAYS** doomsday

DOMESTIC *n* pl. **-S** a household servant

DOMIC *adj* domical

DOMICAL *adj* shaped like a dome

DOMICIL *v* **-ED, -ING, -S** to domicile

DOMICILE *v* **-CILED, -CILING, -CILES** to establish in a residence

DOMINANT *n* pl. **-S** a controlling genetic character

DOMINATE *v* **-NATED, -NATING, -NATES** to control

DOMINE *n* pl. **-S** master

DOMINEER *v* **-ED, -ING, -S** to tyrannize

DOMING present participle of dome

DOMINICK *n* pl. **-S** one of an American breed of chickens

DOMINIE *n* pl. **-S** a clergyman

DOMINION *n* pl. **-S** supreme authority

DOMINIUM *n* pl. **-S** the right of ownership and control of property

DOMINO *n* pl. **-NOS** or **-NOES** a small mask

DON *v* **DONNED, DONNING, DONS** to put on

DONA *n* pl. **-S** a Spanish lady

DONATE *v* **-NATED, -NATING, -NATES** to contribute

DONATION *n* pl. **-S** something donated

DONATIVE *n* pl. **-S** a donation

DONATOR *n* pl. **-S** a donor

DONE past participle of do

DONEE *n* pl. **-S** a recipient of a gift

DONENESS *n* pl. **-ES** the state of being cooked enough

DONG *n* pl. **-S** a deep sound like that of a large bell

DONGA *n* pl. **-S** a gully in a veldt

DONGLE *n* pl. **-S** a device for a computer

DONGOLA *n* pl. **-S** a type of leather

DONJON *n* pl. **-S** the main tower of a castle

DONKEY *n* pl. **-KEYS** the domestic ass

DONNA *n* pl. **DONNAS** or **DONNE** an Italian lady

DONNED past tense of don

DONNEE *n* pl. **-S** the set of assumptions upon which a story proceeds

DONNERD *adj* donnered

DONNERED *adj* dazed

DONNERT *adj* donnered

DONNIKER *n* pl. **-S** a bathroom or privy

DONNING present participle of don

DONNISH *adj* scholarly

DONOR *n* pl. **-S** one that donates

DONSIE *adj* unlucky

DONSY *adj* donsie

DONUT *n* pl. **-S** doughnut

DONZEL *n* pl. **-S** a young squire

DOOBIE *n* pl. **-S** a marijuana cigarette

DOODAD *n* pl. **-S** an article whose name is unknown or forgotten

DOODLE *v* **-DLED, -DLING, -DLES** to draw or scribble aimlessly

DOODLER *n* pl. **-S** one that doodles

DOODOO *n* pl. **-DOOS** feces

DOODY *n* pl. **-DIES** feces

DOOFUS	*n* pl. **-ES** a stupid or foolish person
DOOLEE	*n* pl. **-S** a stretcher for the sick or wounded
DOOLIE	*n* pl. **-S** doolee
DOOLY	*n* pl. **-LIES** doolee
DOOM	*v* **-ED, -ING, -S** to destine to an unhappy fate
DOOMFUL	*adj* ominous
DOOMSDAY	*n* pl. **-DAYS** judgment day
DOOMSTER	*n* pl. **-S** a judge
DOOMY	*adj* **DOOMIER, DOOMIEST** doomful **DOOMILY** *adv*
DOOR	*n* pl. **-S** a movable barrier at an entranceway
DOORBELL	*n* pl. **-S** a bell at a door
DOORJAMB	*n* pl. **-S** a vertical piece at the side of a doorway
DOORKNOB	*n* pl. **-S** a handle for opening a door
DOORLESS	*adj* having no door
DOORMAN	*n* pl. **-MEN** the door attendant of a building
DOORMAT	*n* pl. **-S** a mat placed in front of a door
DOORNAIL	*n* pl. **-S** a large-headed nail
DOORPOST	*n* pl. **-S** a doorjamb
DOORSILL	*n* pl. **-S** the sill of a door
DOORSTEP	*n* pl. **-S** a step leading to a door
DOORSTOP	*n* pl. **-S** an object used for holding a door open
DOORWAY	*n* pl. **-WAYS** the entranceway to a room or building
DOORYARD	*n* pl. **-S** a yard in front of a house
DOOWOP	*n* pl. **-S** a singing style
DOOZER	*n* pl. **-S** an extraordinary one of its kind
DOOZIE	*n* pl. **-S** doozy
DOOZY	*n* pl. **-ZIES** doozer
DOPA	*n* pl. **-S** a drug to treat Parkinson's disease
DOPAMINE	*n* pl. **-S** a form of dopa used to stimulate the heart
DOPANT	*n* pl. **-S** an impurity added to a pure substance
DOPE	*v* **DOPED, DOPING, DOPES** to give a narcotic to
DOPEHEAD	*n* pl. **-S** a drug addict
DOPER	*n* pl. **-S** one that dopes
DOPESTER	*n* pl. **-S** one who predicts the outcomes of contests
DOPEY	*adj* **DOPIER, DOPIEST** lethargic; stupid **DOPILY** *adv*
DOPIER	comparative of dopy
DOPIEST	superlative of dopy
DOPINESS	*n* pl. **-ES** the state of being dopey
DOPING	*n* pl. **-S** the use of drugs by athletes
DOPY	*adj* **DOPIER, DOPIEST** dopey
DOR	*n* pl. **-S** a black European beetle
DORADO	*n* pl. **-DOS** a marine fish
DORBUG	*n* pl. **-S** a dor
DORE	*adj* gilded
DORHAWK	*n* pl. **-S** a nocturnal bird
DORIES	pl. of dory
DORK	*n* pl. **-S** a stupid or foolish person
DORKY	*adj* **DORKIER, DORKIEST** stupid, foolish
DORM	*n* pl. **-S** a dormitory
DORMANCY	*n* pl. **-CIES** the state of being dormant
DORMANT	*adj* lying asleep
DORMER	*n* pl. **-S** a type of window **DORMERED** *adj*
DORMICE	pl. of dormouse
DORMIE	*adj* being ahead by as many holes in golf as remain to be played
DORMIENT	*adj* dormant
DORMIN	*n* pl. **-S** a plant hormone
DORMOUSE	*n* pl. **-MICE** a small rodent
DORMY	*adj* dormie
DORNECK	*n* pl. **-S** dornick
DORNICK	*n* pl. **-S** a heavy linen fabric
DORNOCK	*n* pl. **-S** dornick
DORP	*n* pl. **-S** a village
DORPER	*n* pl. **-S** one of a breed of mutton-producing sheep
DORR	*n* pl. **-S** dor
DORSA	pl. of dorsum
DORSAD	*adv* dorsally
DORSAL	*n* pl. **-S** a dorsally located anatomical part
DORSALLY	*adv* toward the back
DORSEL	*n* pl. **-S** a dossal
DORSER	*n* pl. **-S** dosser

DORSUM *n* pl. **-SA** the back

DORTY *adj* sullen

DORY *n* pl. **-RIES** a flat-bottomed boat

DOSAGE *n* pl. **-S** the amount of medicine to be given

DOSE *v* **DOSED, DOSING, DOSES** to give a specified quantity of medicine to

DOSER *n* pl. **-S** one that doses

DOSS *v* **-ED, -ING, -ES** to sleep in any convenient place

DOSSAL *n* pl. **-S** an ornamental cloth hung behind an altar

DOSSEL *n* pl. **-S** dossal

DOSSER *n* pl. **-S** a basket carried on the back

DOSSERET *n* pl. **-S** a block resting on the capital of a column

DOSSIER *n* pl. **-S** a file of papers on a single subject

DOSSIL *n* pl. **-S** a cloth roll for wiping ink

DOST a present 2d person sing. of do

DOT *v* **DOTTED, DOTTING, DOTS** to cover with dots (tiny round marks)

DOTAGE *n* pl. **-S** a state of senility

DOTAL *adj* pertaining to a dowry

DOTARD *n* pl. **-S** a senile person **DOTARDLY** *adj*

DOTATION *n* pl. **-S** an endowment

DOTE *v* **DOTED, DOTING, DOTES** to show excessive affection

DOTER *n* pl. **-S** one that dotes

DOTH a present 3d person sing. of do

DOTIER comparative of doty

DOTIEST superlative of doty

DOTING present participle of dote

DOTINGLY *adv* in an excessively affectionate manner

DOTTED past tense of dot

DOTTEL *n* pl. **-S** dottle

DOTTER *n* pl. **-S** one that dots

DOTTEREL *n* pl. **-S** a shore bird

DOTTIER comparative of dotty

DOTTIEST superlative of dotty

DOTTILY *adv* in a dotty manner

DOTTING present participle of dot

DOTTLE *n* pl. **-S** a mass of half-burnt pipe tobacco

DOTTREL *n* pl. **-S** dotterel

DOTTY *adj* **-TIER, -TIEST** crazy

DOTY *adj* **DOTIER, DOTIEST** stained by decay

DOUBLE *v* **-BLED, -BLING, -BLES** to make twice as great

DOUBLER *n* pl. **-S** one that doubles

DOUBLET *n* pl. **-S** a close-fitting jacket

DOUBLING present participle of double

DOUBLOON *n* pl. **-S** a former Spanish gold coin

DOUBLURE *n* pl. **-S** the lining of a book cover

DOUBLY *adv* to twice the degree

DOUBT *v* **-ED, -ING, -S** to be uncertain about

DOUBTER *n* pl. **-S** one that doubts

DOUBTFUL *adj* uncertain

DOUCE *adj* sedate **DOUCELY** *adv*

DOUCEUR *n* pl. **-S** a gratuity

DOUCHE *v* **DOUCHED, DOUCHING, DOUCHES** to cleanse with a jet of water

DOUGH *n* pl. **-S** a flour mixture

DOUGHBOY *n* pl. **-BOYS** an infantryman

DOUGHIER comparative of doughy

DOUGHIEST superlative of doughy

DOUGHNUT *n* pl. **-S** a ring-shaped cake

DOUGHT a past tense of dow

DOUGHTY *adj* **-TIER, -TIEST** courageous

DOUGHY *adj* **DOUGHIER, DOUGHIEST** resembling dough

DOULA *n* pl. **-S** a woman who assists another woman during childbirth

DOUM *n* pl. **-S** an African palm tree

DOUMA *n* pl. **-S** duma

DOUPIONI *n* pl. **-S** a silk yarn

DOUR *adj* **DOURER, DOUREST** sullen

DOURA *n* pl. **-S** durra

DOURAH *n* pl. **-S** durra

DOURINE *n* pl. **-S** a disease of horses

DOURLY *adv* in a dour manner

DOURNESS *n* pl. **-ES** the state of being dour

DOUSE *v* **DOUSED, DOUSING, DOUSES** to plunge into water

DOUSER *n* pl. **-S** one that douses

DOUX *adj* very sweet — used of champagne

DOUZEPER *n* pl. **-S** one of twelve legendary knights

DOVE *n* pl. **-S** a bird of the pigeon family

DOVECOT *n* pl. **-S** dovecote

DOVECOTE *n* pl. **-S** a roost for domesticated pigeons

DOVEKEY *n* pl. **-KEYS** dovekie

DOVEKIE *n* pl. **-S** a seabird

DOVELIKE *adj* resembling or suggestive of a dove

DOVEN *v* **-ED, -ING, -S** to daven

DOVETAIL *v* **-ED, -ING, -S** to fit together closely

DOVISH *adj* not warlike

DOW *v* **DOWED** or **DOUGHT, DOWING, DOWS** to prosper

DOWABLE *adj* entitled to an endowment

DOWAGER *n* pl. **-S** a dignified elderly woman

DOWDY *adj* **DOWDIER, DOWDIEST** lacking in stylishness or neatness **DOWDILY** *adv* **DOWDYISH** *adj*

DOWDY *n* pl. **DOWDIES** a dowdy woman

DOWEL *v* **-ELED, -ELING, -ELS** or **-ELLED, -ELLING, -ELS** to fasten with wooden pins

DOWER *v* **-ED, -ING, -S** to provide with a dowry

DOWERY *n* pl. **-ERIES** dowry

DOWIE *adj* dreary

DOWN *v* **-ED, -ING, -S** to cause to fall

DOWNBEAT *n* pl. **-S** the first beat of a musical measure

DOWNBOW *n* pl. **-S** a type of stroke in playing a bowed instrument

DOWNCAST *n* pl. **-S** an overthrow or ruin

DOWNCOME *n* pl. **-S** downfall

DOWNER *n* pl. **-S** a depressant drug

DOWNFALL *n* pl. **-S** a sudden fall

DOWNHAUL *n* pl. **-S** a rope for hauling down sails

DOWNHILL *n* pl. **-S** a downward slope

DOWNIER comparative of downy

DOWNIEST superlative of downy

DOWNLAND *n* pl. **-S** a rolling treeless upland

DOWNLESS *adj* having no down (soft furry feathers)

DOWNLIKE *adj* resembling down

DOWNLINK *v* **-ED, -ING, -S** to transmit data from a satellite to earth

DOWNLOAD *v* **-ED, -ING, -S** to transfer data from a large computer to a smaller one

DOWNPIPE *n* pl. **-S** a pipe for draining water from a roof

DOWNPLAY *v* **-ED, -ING, -S** to de-emphasize

DOWNPOUR *n* pl. **-S** a heavy rain

DOWNSIDE *n* pl. **-S** a negative aspect

DOWNSIZE *v* **-SIZED, -SIZING, -SIZES** to produce in a smaller size

DOWNSPIN *n* pl. **-S** a spinning motion

DOWNTICK *n* pl. **-S** a stock market transaction

DOWNTIME *n* pl. **-S** the time when a machine or factory is inactive

DOWNTOWN *n* pl. **-S** the business district of a city

DOWNTROD *adj* oppressed

DOWNTURN *n* pl. **-S** a downward turn

DOWNWARD *adv* from a higher to a lower place

DOWNWASH *n* pl. **-ES** a downward deflection of air

DOWNWIND *adv* in the direction that the wind blows

DOWNY *adj* **DOWNIER, DOWNIEST** soft

DOWNZONE *v* **-ZONED, -ZONING, -ZONES** to reduce or limit the number of buildings permitted

DOWRY *n* pl. **-RIES** the money or property a wife brings to her husband at marriage

DOWSABEL *n* pl. **-S** a sweetheart

DOWSE *v* **DOWSED, DOWSING, DOWSES** to search for underground water with a divining rod

DOWSER *n* pl. **-S** one that dowses

DOXIE *n* pl. **-S** doxy

DOXOLOGY *n* pl. **-GIES** a hymn or verse of praise to God

DOXY *n* pl. **DOXIES** a doctrine

DOYEN *n* pl. **-S** the senior member of a group

DOYENNE *n* pl. **-S** a female doyen

DOYLEY *n* pl. **-LEYS** doily

DOYLY *n* pl. **-LIES** doily

DOZE *v* **DOZED, DOZING, DOZES** to sleep lightly

DOZEN *v* **-ED, -ING, -S** to stun

DOZENTH *n* pl. **-S** twelfth

DOZER *n* pl. **-S** one that dozes

DOZIER comparative of dozy

DOZIEST	superlative of dozy
DOZILY	*adv* in a dozy manner
DOZINESS	*n* pl. **-ES** the state of being dozy
DOZING	present participle of doze
DOZY	*adj* **DOZIER, DOZIEST** drowsy
DRAB	*adj* **DRABBER, DRABBEST** cheerless
DRAB	*v* **DRABBED, DRABBING, DRABS** to consort with prostitutes
DRABBET	*n* pl. **-S** a coarse linen fabric
DRABBLE	*v* **-BLED, -BLING, -BLES** to draggle
DRABLY	*adv* in a drab manner
DRABNESS	*n* pl. **-ES** the quality of being drab
DRACAENA	*n* pl. **-S** a tropical plant
DRACENA	*n* pl. **-S** dracaena
DRACHM	*n* pl. **-S** a unit of weight
DRACHMA	*n* pl. **-MAS, -MAE** or **-MAI** a former monetary unit of Greece
DRACONIC	*adj* pertaining to a dragon
DRAFF	*n* pl. **-S** the damp remains of malt after brewing
DRAFFISH	*adj* draffy
DRAFFY	*adj* **DRAFFIER, DRAFFIEST** worthless
DRAFT	*v* **-ED, -ING, -S** to conscript for military service
DRAFTEE	*n* pl. **-S** one that is drafted
DRAFTER	*n* pl. **-S** one that drafts
DRAFTING	*n* pl. **-S** mechanical drawing
DRAFTY	*adj* **DRAFTIER, DRAFTIEST** having or exposed to currents of air **DRAFTILY** *adv*
DRAG	*v* **DRAGGED, DRAGGING, DRAGS** to pull along the ground
DRAGEE	*n* pl. **-S** a sugarcoated candy
DRAGGER	*n* pl. **-S** one that drags
DRAGGIER	comparative of draggy
DRAGGIEST	superlative of draggy
DRAGGING	present participle of drag
DRAGGLE	*v* **-GLED, -GLING, -GLES** to make wet and dirty
DRAGGY	*adj* **-GIER, -GIEST** sluggish
DRAGLINE	*n* pl. **-S** a line used for dragging
DRAGNET	*n* pl. **-S** a net for trawling
DRAGOMAN	*n* pl. **-MANS** or **-MEN** an interpreter in Near Eastern countries
DRAGON	*n* pl. **-S** a mythical, serpentlike monster
DRAGONET	*n* pl. **-S** a marine fish
DRAGOON	*v* **-ED, -ING, -S** to harass by the use of troops
DRAGROPE	*n* pl. **-S** a rope used for dragging
DRAGSTER	*n* pl. **-S** a vehicle used in drag racing
DRAIL	*n* pl. **-S** a heavy fishhook
DRAIN	*v* **-ED, -ING, -S** to draw off a liquid
DRAINAGE	*n* pl. **-S** the act of draining
DRAINER	*n* pl. **-S** one that drains
DRAKE	*n* pl. **-S** a male duck
DRAM	*v* **DRAMMED, DRAMMING, DRAMS** to tipple
DRAMA	*n* pl. **-S** a composition written for theatrical performance
DRAMADY	*n* pl. **-DIES** dramedy
DRAMATIC	*adj* pertaining to drama
DRAMEDY	*n* pl. **-DIES** a sitcom having dramatic scenes
DRAMMED	past tense of dram
DRAMMING	present participle of dram
DRAMMOCK	*n* pl. **-S** raw oatmeal mixed with cold water
DRAMSHOP	*n* pl. **-S** a barroom
DRANK	past tense of drink
DRAPE	*v* **DRAPED, DRAPING, DRAPES** to arrange in graceful folds **DRAPABLE** *adj*
DRAPER	*n* pl. **-S** a dealer in cloth
DRAPERY	*n* pl. **-ERIES** cloth arranged in graceful folds
DRAPEY	*adj* characterized by graceful folds
DRAPING	present participle of drape
DRASTIC	*adj* extremely severe
DRAT	*v* **DRATTED, DRATTING, DRATS** to damn
DRAUGHT	*v* **-ED, -ING, -S** to draft
DRAUGHTY	*adj* **DRAUGHTIER, DRAUGHTIEST** drafty
DRAVE	a past tense of drive
DRAW	*v* **DREW, DRAWN, DRAWING, DRAWS** to move by pulling **DRAWABLE** *adj*
DRAWBACK	*n* pl. **-S** a hindrance
DRAWBAR	*n* pl. **-S** a railroad coupler
DRAWBORE	*n* pl. **-S** a hole for joining a mortise and tenon

DRAWDOWN *n* pl. **-S** a lowering of a water level

DRAWEE *n* pl. **-S** the person on whom a bill of exchange is drawn

DRAWER *n* pl. **-S** one that draws

DRAWING *n* pl. **-S** a portrayal in lines of a form or figure

DRAWL *v* **-ED, -ING, -S** to speak slowly with vowels greatly prolonged

DRAWLER *n* pl. **-S** one that drawls

DRAWLY *adj* **DRAWLIER, DRAWLIEST** marked by drawling

DRAWN past participle of draw

DRAWTUBE *n* pl. **-S** a tube that slides within another tube

DRAY *v* **-ED, -ING, -S** to transport by dray (a low, strong cart)

DRAYAGE *n* pl. **-S** transportation by dray

DRAYMAN *n* pl. **-MEN** one who drives a dray

DREAD *v* **-ED, -ING, -S** to fear greatly

DREADFUL *n* pl. **-S** a publication containing sensational material

DREAM *v* **DREAMED** or **DREAMT, DREAMING, DREAMS** to have a dream (a series of images occurring during sleep)

DREAMER *n* pl. **-S** one that dreams

DREAMFUL *adj* dreamy

DREAMY *adj* **DREAMIER, DREAMIEST** full of dreams **DREAMILY** *adv*

DREAR *n* pl. **-S** the state of being dreary

DREARY *adj* **DREARIER, DREARIEST** dismal **DREARILY** *adv*

DREARY *n* pl. **DREARIES** a dismal person

DRECK *n* pl. **-S** rubbish **DRECKY** *adj*

DREDGE *v* **DREDGED, DREDGING, DREDGES** to clear with a dredge (a machine for scooping mud)

DREDGER *n* pl. **-S** one that dredges

DREDGING *n* pl. **-S** matter that is dredged up

DREE *v* **DREED, DREEING, DREES** to suffer

DREG *n* pl. **-S** the sediment of liquors **DREGGISH** *adj*

DREGGY *adj* **-GIER, -GIEST** full of dregs

DREICH *adj* dreary

DREIDEL *n* pl. **-S** a spinning toy

DREIDL *n* pl. **-S** dreidel

DREIGH *adj* dreich

DREK *n* pl. **-S** dreck

DRENCH *v* **-ED, -ING, -ES** to wet thoroughly

DRENCHER *n* pl. **-S** one that drenches

DRESS *v* **DRESSED** or **DREST, DRESSING, DRESSES** to put clothes on

DRESSAGE *n* pl. **-S** the training of a horse in obedience and deportment

DRESSER *n* pl. **-S** one that dresses

DRESSING *n* pl. **-S** material applied to cover a wound

DRESSY *adj* **DRESSIER, DRESSIEST** stylish **DRESSILY** *adv*

DREST a past tense of dress

DREW past tense of draw

DRIB *v* **DRIBBED, DRIBBING, DRIBS** to drip

DRIBBLE *v* **-BLED, -BLING, -BLES** to drivel

DRIBBLER *n* pl. **-S** one that dribbles

DRIBBLET *n* pl. **-S** driblet

DRIBBLING present participle of dribble

DRIBBLY *adj* tending to dribble

DRIBLET *n* pl. **-S** a small drop of liquid

DRIED past tense of dry

DRIEGH *adj* dreary

DRIER *n* pl. **-S** one that dries

DRIES present 3d person sing. of dry

DRIEST a superlative of dry

DRIFT *v* **-ED, -ING, -S** to move along in a current

DRIFTAGE *n* pl. **-S** the act of drifting

DRIFTER *n* pl. **-S** one that drifts

DRIFTPIN *n* pl. **-S** a metal rod for securing timbers

DRIFTY *adj* **DRIFTIER, DRIFTIEST** full of drifts (masses of wind-driven snow)

DRILL *v* **-ED, -ING, -S** to bore a hole in

DRILLER *n* pl. **-S** one that drills

DRILLING *n* pl. **-S** a heavy twilled cotton fabric

DRILY *adv* dryly

DRINK *v* **DRANK, DRUNK, DRINKING, DRINKS** to swallow liquid

DRINKER *n* pl. **-S** one that drinks

DRINKING *n* pl. **-S** a habit of drinking alcoholic beverages

DRIP *v* **DRIPPED** or **DRIPT, DRIPPING, DRIPS** to fall in drops

DRIPLESS *adj* designed not to drip

DRIPPER *n* pl. **-S** something from which a liquid drips

DRIPPING *n* pl. **-S** juice drawn from meat during cooking

DRIPPY *adj* **-PIER, -PIEST** very wet **DRIPPILY** *adv*

DRIPT a past tense of drip

DRIVE *v* **DROVE** or **DRAVE, DRIVEN, DRIVING, DRIVES** to urge or propel forward **DRIVABLE** *adj*

DRIVEL *v* **-ELED, -ELING, -ELS** or **-ELLED, -ELLING, -ELS** to let saliva flow from the mouth

DRIVELER *n* pl. **-S** one that drivels

DRIVER *n* pl. **-S** one that drives

DRIVEWAY *n* pl. **-WAYS** a private road providing access to a building

DRIVING *n* pl. **-S** management of a motor vehicle

DRIZZLE *v* **-ZLED, -ZLING, -ZLES** to rain lightly

DRIZZLY *adj* **-ZLIER, -ZLIEST** characterized by light rain

DROGUE *n* pl. **-S** a sea anchor

DROID *n* pl. **-S** an android

DROIT *n* pl. **-S** a legal right

DROLL *adj* **DROLLER, DROLLEST** comical

DROLL *v* **-ED, -ING, -S** to jest

DROLLERY *n* pl. **-ERIES** something droll

DROLLY *adv* in a droll manner

DROMON *n* pl. **-S** dromond

DROMOND *n* pl. **-S** a large fast-sailing medieval galley

DRONE *v* **DRONED, DRONING, DRONES** to make a continuous low sound

DRONER *n* pl. **-S** one that drones

DRONGO *n* pl. **-GOS** a tropical bird

DRONISH *adj* habitually lazy

DROOL *v* **-ED, -ING, -S** to drivel

DROOLY *adj* **DROOLIER, DROOLIEST** drooling

DROOP *v* **-ED, -ING, -S** to hang downward

DROOPY *adj* **DROOPIER, DROOPIEST** drooping **DROOPILY** *adv*

DROP *v* **DROPPED** or **DROPT, DROPPING, DROPS** to fall in drops (globules)

DROPHEAD *n* pl. **-S** a convertible car

DROPKICK *n* pl. **-S** a type of kick in football

DROPLET *n* pl. **-S** a tiny drop

DROPOUT *n* pl. **-S** one who quits school prematurely

DROPPED a past tense of drop

DROPPER *n* pl. **-S** a tube for dispensing liquid in drops

DROPPING *n* pl. **-S** something that has been dropped

DROPSHOT *n* pl. **-S** a type of shot in tennis

DROPSY *n* pl. **-SIES** an excessive accumulation of serous fluid **DROPSIED** *adj*

DROPT a past tense of drop

DROPWORT *n* pl. **-S** a perennial herb

DROSERA *n* pl. **-S** a sundew

DROSHKY *n* pl. **-KIES** an open carriage

DROSKY *n* pl. **-KIES** droshky

DROSS *n* pl. **-ES** waste matter

DROSSY *adj* **DROSSIER, DROSSIEST** worthless

DROUGHT *n* pl. **-S** a dry period

DROUGHTY *adj* **DROUGHTIER, DROUGHTIEST** dry

DROUK *v* **-ED, -ING, -S** to drench

DROUTH *n* pl. **-S** drought

DROUTHY *adj* **DROUTHIER, DROUTHIEST** droughty

DROVE *v* **DROVED, DROVING, DROVES** to drive cattle or sheep

DROVER *n* pl. **-S** a driver of cattle or sheep

DROWN *v* **-ED, -ING, -S** to suffocate in water

DROWND *v* **-ED, -ING, -S** to drown

DROWNER *n* pl. **-S** one that drowns

DROWSE *v* **DROWSED, DROWSING, DROWSES** to doze

DROWSY *adj* **DROWSIER, DROWSIEST** sleepy **DROWSILY** *adv*

DRUB *v* **DRUBBED, DRUBBING, DRUBS** to beat severely

DRUBBER *n* pl. **-S** one that drubs

DRUBBING *n* pl. **-S** a severe beating

DRUDGE *v* **DRUDGED, DRUDGING, DRUDGES** to do hard, menial, or tedious work

DRUDGER *n* pl. **-S** one that drudges

DRUDGERY *n* pl. **-ERIES** hard, menial, or tedious work

DRUG	*v* **DRUGGED, DRUGGING, DRUGS** to affect with a drug (a medicinal substance)
DRUGGET	*n* pl. **-S** a coarse woolen fabric
DRUGGIE	*n* pl. **-S** a drug addict
DRUGGIST	*n* pl. **-S** a pharmacist
DRUGGY	*adj* **-GIER, -GIEST** affected by drugs
DRUID	*n* pl. **-S** one of an ancient Celtic order of priests **DRUIDIC** *adj*
DRUIDESS	*n* pl. **-ES** a female druid
DRUIDISM	*n* pl. **-S** the religious system of the druids
DRUM	*v* **DRUMMED, DRUMMING, DRUMS** to beat a drum (a percussion instrument)
DRUMBEAT	*n* pl. **-S** the sound of a drum
DRUMBLE	*v* **-BLED, -BLING, -BLES** to move slowly
DRUMFIRE	*n* pl. **-S** heavy, continuous gunfire
DRUMFISH	*n* pl. **-ES** a fish that makes a drumming sound
DRUMHEAD	*n* pl. **-S** the material stretched over the end of a drum
DRUMLIKE	*adj* resembling the head of a drum
DRUMLIN	*n* pl. **-S** a long hill of glacial drift
DRUMLY	*adj* **-LIER, -LIEST** dark and gloomy
DRUMMED	past tense of drum
DRUMMER	*n* pl. **-S** one that drums
DRUMMING	present participle of drum
DRUMROLL	*n* pl. **-S** a roll played on a drum
DRUNK	*adj* **DRUNKER, DRUNKEST** intoxicated
DRUNK	*n* pl. **-S** a drunken person
DRUNKARD	*n* pl. **-S** one who is habitually drunk
DRUNKEN	*adj* drunk
DRUPE	*n* pl. **-S** a fleshy fruit
DRUPELET	*n* pl. **-S** a small drupe
DRUSE	*n* pl. **-S** a crust of small crystals lining a rock cavity
DRUTHERS	*n/pl* one's preference
DRY	*adj* **DRIER, DRIEST** or **DRYER, DRYEST** having no moisture
DRY	*n* pl. **DRYS** a prohibitionist
DRY	*v* **DRIED, DRYING, DRIES** to make dry **DRYABLE** *adj*
DRYAD	*n* pl. **-S** or **-ES** a nymph of the woods **DRYADIC** *adj*
DRYER	*n* pl. **-S** drier
DRYISH	*adj* somewhat dry
DRYLAND	*adj* relating to an arid region
DRYLOT	*n* pl. **-S** an enclosure for livestock
DRYLY	*adv* in a dry manner
DRYNESS	*n* pl. **-ES** the state of being dry
DRYPOINT	*n* pl. **-S** a method of engraving
DRYSTONE	*adj* constructed of stone without mortar
DRYWALL	*v* **-ED, -ING, -S** to cover a wall with plasterboard
DRYWELL	*n* pl. **-S** a hole for receiving drainage from a roof
DUAD	*n* pl. **-S** a pair
DUAL	*n* pl. **-S** a linguistic form
DUALISM	*n* pl. **-S** a philosophical theory
DUALIST	*n* pl. **-S** an adherent of dualism
DUALITY	*n* pl. **-TIES** the state of being twofold
DUALIZE	*v* **-IZED, -IZING, -IZES** to make twofold
DUALLY	*adv* in two ways
DUB	*v* **DUBBED, DUBBING, DUBS** to confer knighthood on
DUBBER	*n* pl. **-S** one that dubs
DUBBIN	*n* pl. **-S** material for softening and waterproofing leather
DUBBING	*n* pl. **-S** dubbin
DUBIETY	*n* pl. **-ETIES** the state of being dubious
DUBIOUS	*adj* doubtful
DUBNIUM	*n* pl. **-S** a radioactive element
DUBONNET	*n* pl. **-S** a red color
DUCAL	*adj* pertaining to a duke (a high-ranking nobleman) **DUCALLY** *adv*
DUCAT	*n* pl. **-S** any of several gold coins formerly used in Europe
DUCE	*n* pl. **DUCES** or **DUCI** a leader
DUCHESS	*n* pl. **-ES** the wife or widow of a duke
DUCHY	*n* pl. **DUCHIES** the domain of a duke
DUCI	a pl. of duce
DUCK	*v* **-ED, -ING, -S** to lower quickly
DUCKBILL	*n* pl. **-S** a platypus
DUCKER	*n* pl. **-S** one that ducks

DUCKIE	*adj* ducky
DUCKIER	comparative of ducky
DUCKIES	pl. of ducky
DUCKIEST	superlative of ducky
DUCKLING	*n* pl. **-S** a young duck
DUCKPIN	*n* pl. **-S** a type of bowling pin
DUCKTAIL	*n* pl. **-S** a style of haircut
DUCKWALK	*v* **-ED, -ING, -S** to walk in a squatting position
DUCKWEED	*n* pl. **-S** an aquatic plant
DUCKY	*adj* **DUCKIER, DUCKIEST** excellent
DUCKY	*n* pl. **DUCKIES** a darling
DUCT	*v* **-ED, -ING, -S** to convey through a duct (a tubular passage)
DUCTAL	*adj* made up of ducts
DUCTILE	*adj* easily molded or shaped
DUCTING	*n* pl. **-S** a system of ducts
DUCTLESS	*adj* being without a duct
DUCTULE	*n* pl. **-S** a small duct
DUCTWORK	*n* pl. **-S** a system of ducts
DUD	*n* pl. **-S** a bomb that fails to explode
DUDDIE	*adj* ragged
DUDDY	*adj* duddie
DUDE	*v* **DUDED, DUDING, DUDES** to dress up in flashy clothes
DUDEEN	*n* pl. **-S** a short tobacco pipe
DUDGEON	*n* pl. **-S** a feeling of resentment
DUDING	present participle of dude
DUDISH	*adj* resembling a dude (a dandy)
DUDISHLY	*adv* in the manner of a dude
DUE	*n* pl. **-S** something that is owed
DUECENTO	*n* pl. **-TOS** the thirteenth century
DUEL	*v* **DUELED, DUELING, DUELS** or **DUELLED, DUELLING, DUELS** to fight formally
DUELER	*n* pl. **-S** one that duels
DUELIST	*n* pl. **-S** a dueler
DUELLER	*n* pl. **-S** dueler
DUELLI	a pl. of duello
DUELLING	a present participle of duel
DUELLIST	*n* pl. **-S** duelist
DUELLO	*n* pl. **-LOS** or **-LI** the art of dueling; a duel
DUENDE	*n* pl. **-S** charisma
DUENESS	*n* pl. **-ES** the state of being owed
DUENNA	*n* pl. **-S** a governess
DUET	*v* **DUETED, DUETING, DUETS** or **DUETTED, DUETTING, DUETS** to perform a duet (a musical composition for two)
DUETTIST	*n* pl. **-S** a participant in a duet
DUFF	*n* pl. **-S** a thick pudding
DUFFEL	*n* pl. **-S** a coarse woolen fabric
DUFFER	*n* pl. **-S** a clumsy person
DUFFLE	*n* pl. **-S** duffel
DUFUS	*n* pl. **-ES** doofus
DUG	*n* pl. **-S** the teat or udder of a female mammal
DUGONG	*n* pl. **-S** an aquatic mammal
DUGOUT	*n* pl. **-S** a canoe made by hollowing out a log
DUH	*interj* — used to indicate that something just stated is too obvious
DUI	a pl. of duo
DUIKER	*n* pl. **-S** a small antelope
DUIT	*n* pl. **-S** doit
DUKE	*v* **DUKED, DUKING, DUKES** to fight
DUKEDOM	*n* pl. **-S** a duchy
DULCET	*n* pl. **-S** a soft-toned organ stop
DULCETLY	*adv* melodiously
DULCIANA	*n* pl. **-S** a soft-toned organ stop
DULCIFY	*v* **-FIED, -FYING, -FIES** to sweeten
DULCIMER	*n* pl. **-S** a stringed instrument
DULCINEA	*n* pl. **-S** a sweetheart
DULIA	*n* pl. **-S** veneration of saints
DULL	*adj* **DULLER, DULLEST** mentally slow
DULL	*v* **-ED, -ING, -S** to make less sharp
DULLARD	*n* pl. **-S** a dolt
DULLISH	*adj* somewhat dull
DULLNESS	*n* pl. **-ES** the state of being dull
DULLY	*adv* in a dull manner
DULNESS	*n* pl. **-ES** dullness
DULSE	*n* pl. **-S** an edible seaweed
DULY	*adv* rightfully
DUMA	*n* pl. **-S** a Russian council
DUMB	*adj* **DUMBER, DUMBEST** incapable of speech
DUMB	*v* **-ED, -ING, -S** to make silent
DUMBBELL	*n* pl. **-S** a weight lifted for muscular exercise

DUMBCANE	*n* pl. **-S** a tropical plant
DUMBHEAD	*n* pl. **-S** a stupid person
DUMBLY	*adv* in a dumb manner
DUMBNESS	*n* pl. **-ES** the state of being dumb
DUMBO	*n* pl. **-BOS** a stupid person
DUMDUM	*n* pl. **-S** a type of bullet
DUMFOUND	*v* **-ED, -ING, -S** to astonish
DUMKA	*n* pl. **-KY** a Slavic folk ballad
DUMMKOPF	*n* pl. **-S** a dolt
DUMMY	*v* **-MIED, -MYING, -MIES** to make a representation of
DUMP	*v* **-ED, -ING, -S** to let fall heavily
DUMPCART	*n* pl. **-S** a type of cart
DUMPER	*n* pl. **-S** one that dumps
DUMPIER	comparative of dumpy
DUMPIEST	superlative of dumpy
DUMPILY	*adv* in a dumpy manner
DUMPING	*n* pl. **-S** the selling of large quantities of goods at below the market price
DUMPISH	*adj* sad
DUMPLING	*n* pl. **-S** a ball of dough cooked with stew or soup
DUMPSITE	*n* pl. **-S** a place for dumping rubbish
DUMPY	*adj* **DUMPIER, DUMPIEST** short and thick
DUN	*adj* **DUNNER, DUNNEST** of a dull brown color
DUN	*v* **DUNNED, DUNNING, DUNS** to make demands upon for payment of a debt
DUNAM	*n* pl. **-S** a unit of land measure in Israel
DUNCE	*n* pl. **-S** a stupid person **DUNCICAL, DUNCISH** *adj*
DUNCH	*n* pl. **-ES** a push
DUNE	*n* pl. **-S** a hill of sand **DUNELIKE** *adj*
DUNELAND	*n* pl. **-S** an area having many dunes
DUNG	*v* **-ED, -ING, -S** to fertilize with manure
DUNGAREE	*n* pl. **-S** a coarse cotton fabric
DUNGEON	*v* **-ED, -ING, -S** to confine in a dungeon (an underground prison)
DUNGHILL	*n* pl. **-S** a heap of manure
DUNGY	*adj* **DUNGIER, DUNGIEST** filthy

DUNITE	*n* pl. **-S** an igneous rock **DUNITIC** *adj*
DUNK	*v* **-ED, -ING, -S** to dip into liquid
DUNKER	*n* pl. **-S** one that dunks
DUNLIN	*n* pl. **-S** a wading bird
DUNNAGE	*n* pl. **-S** packing material used to protect cargo
DUNNED	past tense of dun
DUNNER	comparative of dun
DUNNESS	*n* pl. **-ES** the state of being dun
DUNNEST	superlative of dun
DUNNING	present participle of dun
DUNNITE	*n* pl. **-S** an explosive
DUNT	*v* **-ED, -ING, -S** to strike with a heavy blow
DUO	*n* pl. **DUOS** or **DUI** an instrumental duet
DUODENUM	*n* pl. **-DENUMS** or **-DENA** the first portion of the small intestine **DUODENAL** *adj*
DUOLOG	*n* pl. **-S** duologue
DUOLOGUE	*n* pl. **-S** a conversation between two persons
DUOMO	*n* pl. **-MOS** or **-MI** a cathedral
DUOPOLY	*n* pl. **-LIES** the market condition existing when there are two sellers only
DUOPSONY	*n* pl. **-NIES** the market condition existing when there are two buyers only
DUOTONE	*n* pl. **-S** an illustration in two tones
DUP	*v* **DUPPED, DUPPING, DUPS** to open
DUPE	*v* **DUPED, DUPING, DUPES** to deceive **DUPABLE** *adj*
DUPER	*n* pl. **-S** one that dupes
DUPERY	*n* pl. **-ERIES** the act of duping
DUPLE	*adj* having two parts or elements
DUPLEX	*v* **-ED, -ING, -ES** to make duple
DUPLEXER	*n* pl. **-S** an electronic switching device
DUPPED	past tense of dup
DUPPING	present participle of dup
DURA	*n* pl. **-S** durra
DURABLE	*adj* able to withstand wear or decay **DURABLY** *adv*
DURABLES	*n/pl* durable goods
DURAL	*adj* of the dura mater (a brain membrane)

DURAMEN	n pl. **-S** the central wood of a tree	**DUTCH**	adv with each person paying for himself
DURANCE	n pl. **-S** restraint by or as if by physical force	**DUTCHMAN**	n pl. **-MEN** something used to hide structural defects
DURATION	n pl. **-S** continuance in time	**DUTEOUS**	adj dutiful
DURATIVE	n pl. **-S** a type of verb	**DUTIABLE**	adj subject to import tax
DURBAR	n pl. **-S** the court of a native ruler in India	**DUTIFUL**	adj obedient
DURE	v **DURED, DURING, DURES** to endure	**DUTY**	n pl. **-TIES** a moral or legal obligation
DURESS	n pl. **-ES** compulsion by threat	**DUUMVIR**	n pl. **-VIRS** or **-VIRI** a magistrate of ancient Rome
DURIAN	n pl. **-S** an East Indian tree	**DUVET**	n pl. **-S** a down-filled bed covering
DURION	n pl. **-S** durian	**DUVETINE**	n pl. **-S** duvetyn
DURMAST	n pl. **-S** a European oak	**DUVETYN**	n pl. **-S** a soft fabric
DURN	v **-ED, -ING, -S** to damn	**DUVETYNE**	n pl. **-S** duvetyn
DURNED	adj **DURNEDER, DURNEDEST** or **DURNDEST** damned	**DUXELLES**	n pl. **DUXELLES** a garnish or sauce with minced mushrooms
DURO	n pl. **-ROS** a Spanish silver dollar	**DWARF**	adj **DWARFER, DWARFEST** extremely small
DUROC	n pl. **-S** a large red hog	**DWARF**	n pl. **DWARFS** or **DWARVES** an extremely small person
DURR	n pl. **-S** durra		
DURRA	n pl. **-S** a cereal grain	**DWARF**	v **-ED, -ING, -S** to cause to appear small
DURRIE	n pl. **-S** dhurrie	**DWARFISH**	adj resembling a dwarf
DURST	a past tense of dare	**DWARFISM**	n pl. **-S** a condition of stunted growth
DURUM	n pl. **-S** a kind of wheat		
DUSK	v **-ED, -ING, -S** to become dark	**DWARVES**	a pl. of dwarf
DUSKISH	adj dusky	**DWEEB**	n pl. **-S** an unattractive or inept person **DWEEBISH** adj
DUSKY	adj **DUSKIER, DUSKIEST** somewhat dark **DUSKILY** adv	**DWEEBY**	adj **DWEEBIER, DWEEBIEST** socially inept
DUST	v **-ED, -ING, -S** to make free of dust (minute particles of matter)	**DWELL**	v **DWELT** or **DWELLED, DWELLING, DWELLS** to reside
DUSTBIN	n pl. **-S** a trash can	**DWELLER**	n pl. **-S** one that dwells
DUSTER	n pl. **-S** one that dusts	**DWELLING**	n pl. **-S** a place of residence
DUSTHEAP	n pl. **-S** a pile of trash	**DWINDLE**	v **-DLED, -DLING, -DLES** to decrease steadily
DUSTIER	comparative of dusty		
DUSTIEST	superlative of dusty	**DWINE**	v **DWINED, DWINING, DWINES** to pine or waste away
DUSTILY	adv in a dusty manner		
DUSTING	n pl. **-S** a light sprinkling	**DYABLE**	adj dyeable
DUSTLESS	adj being without dust	**DYAD**	n pl. **-S** a pair of units
DUSTLIKE	adj resembling dust	**DYADIC**	n pl. **-S** a sum of mathematical dyads
DUSTMAN	n pl. **-MEN** a trashman		
DUSTOFF	n pl. **-S** a military helicopter for evacuating the wounded	**DYARCHY**	n pl. **-CHIES** diarchy **DYARCHIC** adj
DUSTPAN	n pl. **-S** a pan for holding swept dust	**DYBBUK**	n pl. **-BUKS** or **-BUKIM** a wandering soul in Jewish folklore
DUSTRAG	n pl. **-S** a rag used for dusting	**DYE**	v **DYED, DYEING, DYES** to treat with a dye (a coloring matter)
DUSTUP	n pl. **-S** an argument		
DUSTY	adj **DUSTIER, DUSTIEST** full of dust	**DYEABLE**	adj capable of being dyed

DYEING   *n* pl. **-S** something colored with a dye

DYER   *n* pl. **-S** one that dyes

DYESTUFF   *n* pl. **-S** a dye

DYEWEED   *n* pl. **-S** a shrub that yields a yellow dye

DYEWOOD   *n* pl. **-S** a wood from which a dye is extracted

DYING   *n* pl. **-S** a passing out of existence

DYKE   *v* **DYKED, DYKING, DYKES** to dike

DYNAMIC   *n* pl. **-S** a physical force

DYNAMISM   *n* pl. **-S** a theory that explains the universe in terms of force or energy

DYNAMIST   *n* pl. **-S** an adherent of dynamism

DYNAMITE   *v* **-MITED, -MITING, -MITES** to blow up with a powerful explosive

DYNAMO   *n* pl. **-MOS** a generator

DYNAST   *n* pl. **-S** a ruler

DYNASTY   *n* pl. **-TIES** a succession of rulers from the same line of descent **DYNASTIC** *adj*

DYNATRON   *n* pl. **-S** a type of electron tube

DYNE   *n* pl. **-S** a unit of force

DYNEIN   *n* pl. **-S** an enzyme involved in cell movement

DYNEL   *n* pl. **-S** a synthetic fiber

DYNODE   *n* pl. **-S** a type of electrode

DYSGENIC   *adj* causing the deterioration of hereditary qualities

DYSLEXIA   *n* pl. **-S** impairment of the ability to read

DYSLEXIC   *n* pl. **-S** one who is affected with dyslexia

DYSPEPSY   *n* pl. **-SIES** indigestion

DYSPNEA   *n* pl. **-S** labored breathing **DYSPNEAL, DYSPNEIC** *adj*

DYSPNOEA   *n* pl. **-S** dyspnea **DYSPNOIC** *adj*

DYSTAXIA   *n* pl. **-S** a form of muscular tremor

DYSTOCIA   *n* pl. **-S** difficult labor and delivery in childbirth

DYSTONIA   *n* pl. **-S** a condition of disordered tonicity of muscle tissue **DYSTONIC** *adj*

DYSTOPIA   *n* pl. **-S** a wretched place

DYSURIA   *n* pl. **-S** painful urination **DYSURIC** *adj*

DYVOUR   *n* pl. **-S** one who is bankrupt

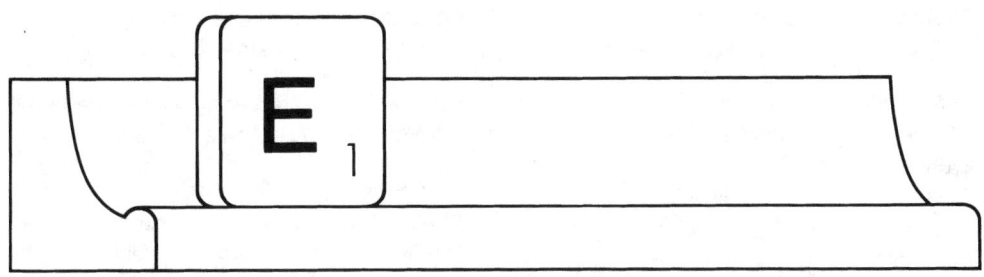

EACH   *adj* being one of two or more distinct individuals

EAGER   *adj* **-GERER, -GEREST** impatiently longing **EAGERLY** *adv*

EAGER   *n* pl. **-S** eagre

EAGLE   *v* **EAGLED, EAGLING, EAGLES** to score an eagle (two strokes under par) on a hole in golf

EAGLET   *n* pl. **-S** a young eagle

EAGRE   *n* pl. **-S** a tidal flood

EANLING   *n* pl. **-S** yeanling

EAR   *v* **-ED, -ING, -S** to form the fruiting head of a cereal

EARACHE   *n* pl. **-S** a pain in the ear (an organ of hearing)

EARBUD   *n* pl. **-S** a small earphone

EARDROP   *n* pl. **-S** an earring

EARDRUM   *n* pl. **-S** the tympanic membrane

EARED   *adj* having ears

EARFLAP   *n* pl. **-S** a part of a cap designed to cover the ears

EARFUL   *n* pl. **-S** a flow of information

EARING   *n* pl. **-S** a line on a ship

EARL   *n* pl. **-S** a British nobleman

EARLAP   *n* pl. **-S** an earflap

EARLDOM   *n* pl. **-S** the rank of an earl

EARLESS   *adj* lacking ears

EARLIER   comparative of early

EARLIEST   superlative of early

EARLOBE   *n* pl. **-S** a part of the ear

EARLOCK   *n* pl. **-S** a curl of hair by the ear

EARLSHIP   *n* pl. **-S** earldom

EARLY   *adv* **-LIER, -LIEST** near the beginning of a period of time or a series of events

EARMARK   *v* **-ED, -ING, -S** to designate for a specific use

EARMUFF   *n* pl. **-S** one of a pair of ear coverings

EARN   *v* **-ED, -ING, -S** to gain or deserve for one's labor or service

EARNER   *n* pl. **-S** one that earns

EARNEST   *n* pl. **-S** a down payment

EARNINGS   *n/pl* something earned

EARPHONE   *n* pl. **-S** a listening device worn over the ear

EARPIECE   *n* pl. **-S** an earphone

EARPLUG   *n* pl. **-S** a plug for the ear

EARRING   *n* pl. **-S** an ornament for the earlobe

EARSHOT   *n* pl. **-S** the range within which sound can be heard

EARSTONE   *n* pl. **-S** an otolith

EARTH   *v* **-ED, -ING, -S** to cover with earth (soil)

EARTHEN   *adj* made of earth

EARTHIER   comparative of earthy

EARTHIEST   superlative of earthy

EARTHILY   *adv* in an earthy manner

EARTHLY   *adj* **-LIER, -LIEST** worldly

EARTHMAN   *n* pl. **-MEN** a person from the planet earth

EARTHNUT   *n* pl. **-S** a European herb

EARTHPEA   *n* pl. **-S** a twining plant

EARTHSET   *n* pl. **-S** the setting of the earth as seen from the moon

EARTHY   *adj* **EARTHIER, EARTHIEST** composed of, resembling, or suggestive of earth

EARWAX   *n* pl. **-ES** cerumen

EARWIG   *v* **-WIGGED, -WIGGING, -WIGS** to insinuate against in secret

EARWORM   *n* pl. **-S** a bollworm

EASE   *v* **EASED, EASING, EASES** to give rest or relief to

EASEFUL	*adj* restful
EASEL	*n* pl. **-S** a three-legged frame **EASELED** *adj*
EASEMENT	*n* pl. **-S** relief
EASIER	comparative of easy
EASIES	pl. of easy
EASIEST	superlative of easy
EASILY	*adv* without difficulty
EASINESS	*n* pl. **-ES** the state of being easy
EASING	present participle of ease
EAST	*n* pl. **-S** a cardinal point of the compass
EASTER	*n* pl. **-S** a wind or storm from the east
EASTERLY	*n* pl. **-LIES** a wind from the east
EASTERN	*adj* being to, toward, or in the east
EASTING	*n* pl. **-S** a movement toward the east
EASTWARD	*n* pl. **-S** a direction toward the east
EASY	*adj* **EASIER, EASIEST** not difficult
EASY	*n* pl. **EASIES** a communications code word for the letter E
EAT	*v* **ATE** or **ET, EATEN, EATING, EATS** to consume food
EATABLE	*n* pl. **-S** an edible
EATER	*n* pl. **-S** one that eats
EATERY	*n* pl. **-ERIES** a lunchroom
EATH	*adj* easy
EATING	*n* pl. **-S** the act of consuming food
EAU	*n* pl. **EAUX** water (a transparent, tasteless, odorless liquid)
EAVE	*n* pl. **-S** the lower projecting edge of a roof **EAVED** *adj*
EBB	*v* **-ED, -ING, -S** to recede
EBBET	*n* pl. **-S** a common green newt
EBON	*n* pl. **-S** ebony
EBONICS	*n/pl* a dialect of English spoken by some African-Americans
EBONIES	pl. of ebony
EBONISE	*v* **-ISED, -ISING, -ISES** to ebonize
EBONITE	*n* pl. **-S** a hard rubber
EBONIZE	*v* **-IZED, -IZING, -IZES** to stain black in imitation of ebony
EBONY	*n* pl. **-NIES** a hard, heavy wood
EBOOK	*n* pl. **-S** a device for reading books in electronic format
ECARTE	*n* pl. **-S** a card game
ECAUDATE	*adj* having no tail
ECBOLIC	*n* pl. **-S** a type of drug
ECCLESIA	*n* pl. **-SIAE** an assembly in ancient Greece
ECCRINE	*adj* producing secretions externally
ECDYSIS	*n* pl. **-DYSES** the shedding of an outer layer of skin **ECDYSIAL** *adj*
ECDYSON	*n* pl. **-S** ecdysone
ECDYSONE	*n* pl. **-S** an insect hormone
ECESIS	*n* pl. **-SISES** the establishment of a plant or animal in a new environment **ECESIC** *adj*
ECHARD	*n* pl. **-S** the water in the soil not available to plants
ECHE	*v* **ECHED, ECHING, ECHES** to increase
ECHELLE	*n* pl. **-S** a device for spreading light into its component colors
ECHELON	*v* **-ED, -ING, -S** to group in a particular formation
ECHIDNA	*n* pl. **-NAS** or **-NAE** a spiny anteater
ECHINATE	*adj* spiny
ECHING	present participle of eche
ECHINOID	*n* pl. **-S** a spiny marine animal
ECHINUS	*n* pl. **-NI** echinoid
ECHO	*n* pl. **ECHOS** or **ECHOES** a repetition of sound by reflection of sound waves
ECHO	*v* **-ED, -ING, -ES** to produce an echo
ECHOER	*n* pl. **-S** one that echoes
ECHOEY	*adj* full of echoes
ECHOGRAM	*n* pl. **-S** a record produced by a device that uses ultrasonic waves
ECHOIC	*adj* resembling an echo
ECHOISM	*n* pl. **-S** the formation of words in imitation of sounds
ECHOLESS	*adj* producing no echo
ECHT	*adj* genuine
ECLAIR	*n* pl. **-S** a type of pastry
ECLAT	*n* pl. **-S** brilliance
ECLECTIC	*n* pl. **-S** one who draws his beliefs from various sources
ECLIPSE	*v* **ECLIPSED, ECLIPSING, ECLIPSES** to obscure
ECLIPSER	*n* pl. **-S** one that eclipses
ECLIPSIS	*n* pl. **ECLIPSISES** or **ECLIPSES** an ellipsis
ECLIPTIC	*n* pl. **-S** an astronomical plane
ECLOGITE	*n* pl. **-S** a type of rock

ECLOGUE   *n* pl. **-S** a pastoral poem

ECLOSION   *n* pl. **-S** the emergence of an insect larva from an egg

ECOCIDE   *n* pl. **-S** the destruction of the natural environment **ECOCIDAL** *adj*

ECOFREAK   *n* pl. **-S** a zealous environmentalist

ECOLOGY   *n* pl. **-GIES** an environmental science **ECOLOGIC** *adj*

ECONOBOX   *n* pl. **-ES** a small economical car

ECONOMIC   *adj* pertaining to financial matters

ECONOMY   *n* pl. **-MIES** thrift

ECOTAGE   *n* pl. **-S** obstructive action in defense of the natural environment

ECOTONE   *n* pl. **-S** a type of ecological zone **ECOTONAL** *adj*

ECOTOUR   *n* pl. **-S** a tour of a natural habitat

ECOTYPE   *n* pl. **-S** a subspecies adapted to specific environmental conditions **ECOTYPIC** *adj*

ECRASEUR   *n* pl. **-S** a surgical instrument

ECRU   *n* pl. **-S** a yellowish brown color

ECSTASY   *n* pl. **-SIES** a state of exaltation

ECSTATIC   *n* pl. **-S** one that is subject to ecstasies

ECTASIS   *n* pl. **-TASES** the lengthening of a usually short syllable **ECTATIC** *adj*

ECTHYMA   *n* pl. **-MATA** a virus disease

ECTODERM   *n* pl. **-S** the outermost germ layer of an embryo

ECTOMERE   *n* pl. **-S** a cell that develops into ectoderm

ECTOPIA   *n* pl. **-S** congenital displacement of parts or organs **ECTOPIC** *adj*

ECTOSARC   *n* pl. **-S** the outermost layer of protoplasm of certain protozoans

ECTOZOAN   *n* pl. **-S** ectozoon

ECTOZOON   *n* pl. **-ZOA** a parasite on the body of an animal

ECTYPE   *n* pl. **-S** a copy **ECTYPAL** *adj*

ECU   *n* pl. **-S** an old French coin

ECUMENIC   *adj* universal

ECZEMA   *n* pl. **-S** a skin disease

ED   *n* pl. **-S** education

EDACIOUS   *adj* voracious

EDACITY   *n* pl. **-TIES** gluttony

EDAPHIC   *adj* pertaining to the soil

EDDO   *n* pl. **-DOES** a tropical plant

EDDY   *v* **-DIED, -DYING, -DIES** to move against the main current

EDEMA   *n* pl. **-MAS** or **-MATA** an excessive accumulation of serous fluid

EDENIC   *adj* pertaining to a paradise

EDENTATE   *n* pl. **-S** a toothless mammal

EDGE   *v* **EDGED, EDGING, EDGES** to provide with an edge (a bounding or dividing line)

EDGELESS   *adj* lacking an edge

EDGER   *n* pl. **-S** a tool used to trim a lawn's edge

EDGEWAYS   *adv* edgewise

EDGEWISE   *adv* sideways

EDGIER   comparative of edgy

EDGIEST   superlative of edgy

EDGILY   *adv* in an edgy manner

EDGINESS   *n* pl. **-ES** the state of being edgy

EDGING   *n* pl. **-S** something that forms or serves as an edge

EDGY   *adj* **EDGIER, EDGIEST** tense, nervous, or irritable

EDH   *n* pl. **-S** an Old English letter

EDIBLE   *n* pl. **-S** something fit to be eaten

EDICT   *n* pl. **-S** an authoritative order having the force of law **EDICTAL** *adj*

EDIFICE   *n* pl. **-S** a building

EDIFIER   *n* pl. **-S** one that edifies

EDIFY   *v* **-FIED, -FYING, -FIES** to enlighten

EDILE   *n* pl. **-S** aedile

EDIT   *v* **-ED, -ING, -S** to correct and prepare for publication **EDITABLE** *adj*

EDITION   *n* pl. **-S** a particular series of printed material

EDITOR   *n* pl. **-S** one that edits

EDITRESS   *n* pl. **-ES** a female editor

EDITRIX   *n* pl. **-TRIXES** or **-TRICES** a female editor

EDUCABLE   *n* pl. **-S** a mildly retarded person

EDUCATE   *v* **-CATED, -CATING, -CATES** to teach

EDUCATOR   *n* pl. **-S** one that educates

EDUCE   *v* **EDUCED, EDUCING, EDUCES** to draw forth or bring out **EDUCIBLE** *adj*

EDUCT   *n* pl. **-S** something educed

EDUCTION   *n* pl. **-S** the act of educing
EDUCTIVE *adj*

EDUCTOR   *n* pl. **-S** one that educes

EEK   *interj* —used to express sudden fright

EEL   *n* pl. **-S** a snakelike fish

EELGRASS   *n* pl. **-ES** an aquatic plant

EELIER   comparative of eely

EELIEST   superlative of eely

EELLIKE   *adj* resembling an eel

EELPOUT   *n* pl. **-S** a marine fish

EELWORM   *n* pl. **-S** a small roundworm

EELY   *adj* **EELIER, EELIEST** resembling an eel

EERIE   *adj* **-RIER, -RIEST** weird **EERILY** *adv*

EERINESS   *n* pl. **-ES** the state of being eerie

EERY   *adj* **-RIER, -RIEST** eerie

EF   *n* pl. **-S** the letter F

EFF   *n* pl. **-S** ef

EFFABLE   *adj* capable of being uttered or expressed

EFFACE   *v* **-FACED, -FACING, -FACES** to rub or wipe out

EFFACER   *n* pl. **-S** one that effaces

EFFECT   *v* **-ED, -ING, -S** to bring about

EFFECTER   *n* pl. **-S** effector

EFFECTOR   *n* pl. **-S** a bodily organ that responds to a nerve impulse

EFFENDI   *n* pl. **-S** a Turkish title of respect

EFFERENT   *n* pl. **-S** an organ or part conveying nervous impulses to an effector

EFFETE   *adj* exhausted of vigor or energy **EFFETELY** *adv*

EFFICACY   *n* pl. **-CIES** effectiveness

EFFIGIAL   *adj* resembling an effigy

EFFIGY   *n* pl. **-GIES** a likeness or representation

EFFLUENT   *n* pl. **-S** an outflow

EFFLUVIA   *n/pl* byproducts in the form of waste

EFFLUX   *n* pl. **-ES** an outflow

EFFORT   *n* pl. **-S** a deliberate exertion

EFFULGE   *v* **-FULGED, -FULGING, -FULGES** to shine forth

EFFUSE   *v* **-FUSED, -FUSING, -FUSES** to pour forth

EFFUSION   *n* pl. **-S** an outpouring of emotion

EFFUSIVE   *adj* pouring forth

EFT   *n* pl. **-S** a newt

EFTSOON   *adv* soon afterward

EFTSOONS   *adv* eftsoon

EGAD   *interj* — used as a mild oath

EGADS   *interj* egad

EGAL   *adj* equal

EGALITE   *n* pl. **-S** equality

EGER   *n* pl. **-S** eagre

EGEST   *v* **-ED, -ING, -S** to discharge from the body

EGESTA   *n/pl* egested matter

EGESTION   *n* pl. **-S** the act of egesting **EGESTIVE** *adj*

EGG   *v* **-ED, -ING, -S** to incite or urge

EGGAR   *n* pl. **-S** egger

EGGCUP   *n* pl. **-S** a cup from which an egg is eaten

EGGER   *n* pl. **-S** a kind of moth

EGGFRUIT   *n* pl. **-S** a tropical tree

EGGHEAD   *n* pl. **-S** an intellectual

EGGLESS   *adj* lacking eggs

EGGNOG   *n* pl. **-S** a beverage

EGGPLANT   *n* pl. **-S** a perennial herb yielding edible fruit

EGGSHELL   *n* pl. **-S** the hard exterior of a bird's egg

EGGY   *adj* containing eggs

EGIS   *n* pl. **EGISES** aegis

EGLATERE   *n* pl. **-S** a wild rose

EGLOMISE   *adj* made of glass with a painted picture on the back

EGO   *n* pl. **EGOS** the conscious self

EGOISM   *n* pl. **-S** extreme devotion to self-interest

EGOIST   *n* pl. **-S** one who practices egoism **EGOISTIC** *adj*

EGOLESS   *adj* not characterized by egoism

EGOMANIA   *n* pl. **-S** extreme egotism

EGOTISM   *n* pl. **-S** self-conceit

EGOTIST   *n* pl. **-S** a conceited person

EGRESS   *v* **-ED, -ING, -ES** to go out

EGRET   *n* pl. **-S** a wading bird

EGYPTIAN   *n* pl. **-S** a typeface with squared serifs

EH   *interj* — used to express doubt or surprise

EIDE	pl. of eidos
EIDER	*n* pl. **-S** a large sea duck
EIDETIC	*adj* pertaining to vivid recall
EIDOLIC	*adj* pertaining to an eidolon
EIDOLON	*n* pl. **-LONS** or **-LA** a phantom
EIDOS	*n* pl. **EIDE** an essence
EIGHT	*n* pl. **-S** a number
EIGHTEEN	*n* pl. **-S** a number
EIGHTH	*n* pl. **-S** one of eight equal parts
EIGHTHLY	*adv* in the eighth place
EIGHTVO	*n* pl. **-VOS** octavo
EIGHTY	*n* pl. **EIGHTIES** a number
EIKON	*n* pl. **-S** or **-ES** icon
EINKORN	*n* pl. **-S** a variety of wheat
EINSTEIN	*n* pl. **-S** a very intelligent person
EIRENIC	*adj* irenic
EISWEIN	*n* pl. **-S** a sweet German wine
EITHER	*adj* being one or the other
EJECT	*v* **-ED, -ING, -S** to throw out forcibly
EJECTA	*n/pl* ejected material
EJECTION	*n* pl. **-S** the act of ejecting
EJECTIVE	*n* pl. **-S** a sound produced with air compressed above the closed glottis
EJECTOR	*n* pl. **-S** one that ejects
EKE	*v* **EKED, EKING, EKES** to supplement with great effort
EKISTICS	*n/pl* a science dealing with human habitats **EKISTIC** *adj*
EKPWELE	*n* pl. **-S** a former monetary unit of Equatorial Guinea
EKTEXINE	*n* pl. **-S** an outer layer of the exine
EKUELE	*n* pl. **EKUELE** ekpwele
EL	*n* pl. **-S** an elevated railroad or train
ELAIN	*n* pl. **-S** olein
ELAN	*n* pl. **-S** enthusiasm
ELAND	*n* pl. **-S** a large antelope
ELAPHINE	*adj* pertaining to a genus of deer
ELAPID	*n* pl. **-S** a venomous snake
ELAPINE	*adj* pertaining to a family of snakes
ELAPSE	*v* **ELAPSED, ELAPSING, ELAPSES** to pass away
ELASTASE	*n* pl. **-S** an enzyme
ELASTIC	*n* pl. **-S** a stretchable material
ELASTIN	*n* pl. **-S** a bodily protein
ELATE	*v* **ELATED, ELATING, ELATES** to raise the spirits of **ELATEDLY** *adv*
ELATER	*n* pl. **-S** a click beetle
ELATERID	*n* pl. **-S** an elater
ELATERIN	*n* pl. **-S** a chemical compound
ELATING	present participle of elate
ELATION	*n* pl. **-S** a feeling of great joy
ELATIVE	*n* pl. **-S** an adjectival form in some languages
ELBOW	*v* **-ED, -ING, -S** to jostle
ELD	*n* pl. **-S** old age
ELDER	*n* pl. **-S** an older person
ELDERLY	*n* pl. **-LIES** a rather old person
ELDEST	*adj* oldest
ELDRESS	*n* pl. **-ES** a female elder (a church officer)
ELDRICH	*adj* eldritch
ELDRITCH	*adj* weird
ELECT	*v* **-ED, -ING, -S** to select by vote for an office
ELECTEE	*n* pl. **-S** a person who has been elected
ELECTION	*n* pl. **-S** the act of electing
ELECTIVE	*n* pl. **-S** an optional course of study
ELECTOR	*n* pl. **-S** one that elects
ELECTRET	*n* pl. **-S** a type of nonconductor
ELECTRIC	*n* pl. **-S** something run by electricity
ELECTRO	*v* **-ED, -ING, -S** to make a metallic copy of a page of type for printing
ELECTRON	*n* pl. **-S** an elementary particle
ELECTRUM	*n* pl. **-S** an alloy of gold and silver
ELEGANCE	*n* pl. **-S** tasteful opulence
ELEGANCY	*n* pl. **-CIES** elegance
ELEGANT	*adj* tastefully opulent
ELEGIAC	*n* pl. **-S** a type of verse
ELEGIES	pl. of elegy
ELEGISE	*v* **-GISED, -GISING, -GISES** to elegize
ELEGIST	*n* pl. **-S** one that writes elegies
ELEGIT	*n* pl. **-S** a type of judicial writ
ELEGIZE	*v* **-GIZED, -GIZING, -GIZES** to write an elegy
ELEGY	*n* pl. **-GIES** a mournful poem for one who is dead
ELEMENT	*n* pl. **-S** a substance that cannot be separated into simpler substances by chemical means

ELEMI *n* pl. **-S** a fragrant resin

ELENCHUS *n* pl. **-CHI** a logical refutation **ELENCHIC, ELENCTIC** *adj*

ELEPHANT *n* pl. **-S** a large mammal

ELEVATE *v* **-VATED, -VATING, -VATES** to raise

ELEVATED *n* pl. **-S** a railway that operates on a raised structure

ELEVATOR *n* pl. **-S** one that elevates

ELEVEN *n* pl. **-S** a number

ELEVENTH *n* pl. **-S** one of eleven equal parts

ELEVON *n* pl. **-S** a type of airplane control surface

ELF *n* pl. **ELVES** a small, often mischievous fairy **ELFLIKE** *adj*

ELFIN *n* pl. **-S** an elf

ELFISH *adj* resembling an elf **ELFISHLY** *adv*

ELFLOCK *n* pl. **-S** a lock of tangled hair

ELHI *adj* pertaining to school grades 1 through 12

ELICIT *v* **-ED, -ING, -S** to educe

ELICITOR *n* pl. **-S** one that elicits

ELIDE *v* **ELIDED, ELIDING, ELIDES** to omit **ELIDIBLE** *adj*

ELIGIBLE *n* pl. **-S** one that is qualified to be chosen

ELIGIBLY *adv* in a qualified manner

ELINT *n* pl. **-S** the gathering of intelligence by electronic devices

ELISION *n* pl. **-S** the act of eliding

ELITE *n* pl. **-S** a socially superior group

ELITISM *n* pl. **-S** belief in rule by an elite

ELITIST *n* pl. **-S** an adherent of elitism

ELIXIR *n* pl. **-S** a medicinal beverage

ELK *n* pl. **-S** a large deer

ELKHOUND *n* pl. **-S** a hunting dog

ELL *n* pl. **-S** the letter L

ELLIPSE *n* pl. **-S** a type of plane curve

ELLIPSIS *n* pl. **-LIPSES** an omission of a word or words in a sentence

ELLIPTIC *adj* having the shape of an ellipse

ELM *n* pl. **-S** a deciduous tree

ELMY *adj* **-MIER, -MIEST** abounding in elms

ELODEA *n* pl. **-S** an aquatic herb

ELOIGN *v* **-ED, -ING, -S** to remove to a distant place

ELOIGNER *n* pl. **-S** one that eloigns

ELOIN *v* **-ED, -ING, -S** to eloign

ELOINER *n* pl. **-S** one that eloins

ELONGATE *v* **-GATED, -GATING, -GATES** to lengthen

ELOPE *v* **ELOPED, ELOPING, ELOPES** to run off secretly to be married

ELOPER *n* pl. **-S** one that elopes

ELOQUENT *adj* fluent and convincing in speech

ELSE *adv* in a different place, time, or way

ELUANT *n* pl. **-S** a solvent

ELUATE *n* pl. **-S** the material obtained by eluting

ELUDE *v* **ELUDED, ELUDING, ELUDES** to evade

ELUDER *n* pl. **-S** one that eludes

ELUENT *n* pl. **-S** eluant

ELUSION *n* pl. **-S** the act of eluding

ELUSIVE *adj* tending to elude

ELUSORY *adj* elusive

ELUTE *v* **ELUTED, ELUTING, ELUTES** to remove by means of a solvent

ELUTION *n* pl. **-S** the act of eluting

ELUVIA a pl. of eluvium

ELUVIAL *adj* pertaining to an eluvium

ELUVIATE *v* **-ATED, -ATING, -ATES** to undergo a transfer of materials in the soil

ELUVIUM *n* pl. **-VIUMS** or **-VIA** a soil deposit

ELVER *n* pl. **-S** a young eel

ELVES pl. of elf

ELVISH *adj* elfish **ELVISHLY** *adv*

ELYSIAN *adj* delightful

ELYTRON *n* pl. **-TRA** a hardened forewing of certain insects **ELYTROID, ELYTROUS** *adj*

ELYTRUM *n* pl. **-TRA** elytron

EM *n* pl. **-S** the letter M

EMACIATE *v* **-ATED, -ATING, -ATES** to make thin

EMAIL *v* **-ED, -ING, -S** to send a message to by computer

EMANANT *adj* issuing from a source

EMANATE *v* **-NATED, -NATING, -NATES** to send forth

EMANATOR *n* pl. **-S** one that emanates

EMBALM	*v* **-ED, -ING, -S** to treat so as to protect from decay	**EMBOSSER**	*n* pl. **-S** one that embosses
EMBALMER	*n* pl. **-S** one that embalms	**EMBOW**	*v* **-ED, -ING, -S** to arch
EMBANK	*v* **-ED, -ING, -S** to confine or protect with a raised structure	**EMBOWEL**	*v* **-ELED, -ELING, -ELS** or **-ELLED, -ELLING, -ELS** to disbowel
EMBAR	*v* **-BARRED, -BARRING, -BARS** to imprison	**EMBOWER**	*v* **-ED, -ING, -S** to surround with foliage
EMBARGO	*v* **-ED, -ING, -ES** to restrain trade by a governmental order	**EMBRACE**	*v* **-BRACED, -BRACING, -BRACES** to hug
EMBARK	*v* **-ED, -ING, -S** to make a start	**EMBRACER**	*n* pl. **-S** one that embraces
EMBASSY	*n* pl. **-SIES** the headquarters of an ambassador	**EMBROIL**	*v* **-ED, -ING, -S** to involve in conflict
		EMBROWN	*v* **-ED, -ING, -S** to make brown
EMBATTLE	*v* **-TLED, -TLING, -TLES** to prepare for battle	**EMBRUE**	*v* **-BRUED, -BRUING, -BRUES** to imbrue
EMBAY	*v* **-ED, -ING, -S** to enclose in a bay	**EMBRUTE**	*v* **-BRUTED, -BRUTING, -BRUTES** to imbrute
EMBED	*v* **-BEDDED, -BEDDING, -BEDS** to fix firmly into a surrounding mass	**EMBRYO**	*n* pl. **-BRYOS** an organism in its early stages of development
EMBER	*n* pl. **-S** a glowing fragment from a fire	**EMBRYOID**	*n* pl. **-S** a mass of tissue that resembles an embryo
EMBEZZLE	*v* **-ZLED, -ZLING, -ZLES** to appropriate fraudulently to one's own use	**EMBRYON**	*n* pl. **-S** an embryo
		EMCEE	*v* **-CEED, -CEEING, -CEES** to serve as master of ceremonies
EMBITTER	*v* **-ED, -ING, -S** to make bitter	**EMDASH**	*n* pl. **-ES** a mark in writing that indicates a break in thought or structure
EMBLAZE	*v* **-BLAZED, -BLAZING, -BLAZES** to set on fire		
EMBLAZER	*n* pl. **-S** one that emblazes	**EME**	*n* pl. **-S** an uncle
EMBLAZON	*v* **-ED, -ING, -S** to decorate with brilliant colors	**EMEER**	*n* pl. **-S** emir
		EMEERATE	*n* pl. **-S** emirate
EMBLEM	*v* **-ED, -ING, -S** to represent with an emblem (a graphical symbol)	**EMEND**	*v* **-ED, -ING, -S** to correct
EMBODIER	*n* pl. **-S** one that embodies	**EMENDATE**	*v* **-DATED, -DATING, -DATES** to emend
EMBODY	*v* **-BODIED, -BODYING, -BODIES** to provide with a body	**EMENDER**	*n* pl. **-S** one that emends
		EMERALD	*n* pl. **-S** a green gem
EMBOLDEN	*v* **-ED, -ING, -S** to instill with courage	**EMERGE**	*v* **EMERGED, EMERGING, EMERGES** to come out into view
EMBOLI	pl. of embolus		
EMBOLIES	pl. of emboly	**EMERGENT**	*n* pl. **-S** a type of aquatic plant
EMBOLISM	*n* pl. **-S** the obstruction of a blood vessel by an embolus **EMBOLIC** *adj*	**EMERIES**	pl. of emery
		EMERITA	*n* pl. **-TAS** or **-TAE** a retired woman who retains an honorary title
EMBOLUS	*n* pl. **-LI** an abnormal particle circulating in the blood	**EMERITUS**	*n* pl. **-TI** a retired person who retains an honorary title
EMBOLY	*n* pl. **-LIES** a phase of embryonic growth	**EMEROD**	*n* pl. **-S** a tumor
		EMEROID	*n* pl. **-S** emerod
EMBORDER	*v* **-ED, -ING, -S** to provide with a border	**EMERSED**	*adj* standing out of water
EMBOSK	*v* **-ED, -ING, -S** to conceal with foliage	**EMERSION**	*n* pl. **-S** the act of emerging
		EMERY	*n* pl. **-ERIES** a granular corundum
EMBOSOM	*v* **-ED, -ING, -S** to embrace	**EMESIS**	*n* pl. **EMESES** the act of vomiting
EMBOSS	*v* **-ED, -ING, -ES** to decorate with raised designs	**EMETIC**	*n* pl. **-S** a substance which induces vomiting

EMETIN *n* pl. **-S** emetine

EMETINE *n* pl. **-S** an alkaloid

EMEU *n* pl. **-S** emu

EMEUTE *n* pl. **-S** a riot

EMIC *adj* relating to a type of linguistic analysis

EMIGRANT *n* pl. **-S** one that emigrates

EMIGRATE *v* **-GRATED, -GRATING, -GRATES** to leave one country or region to settle in another

EMIGRE *n* pl. **-S** an emigrant

EMINENCE *n* pl. **-S** high station or rank

EMINENCY *n* pl. **-CIES** eminence

EMINENT *adj* of high station or rank

EMIR *n* pl. **-S** an Arab chieftain or prince

EMIRATE *n* pl. **-S** the rank of an emir

EMISSARY *n* pl. **-SARIES** a person sent on a mission

EMISSION *n* pl. **-S** the act of emitting **EMISSIVE** *adj*

EMIT *v* **EMITTED, EMITTING, EMITS** to send forth

EMITTER *n* pl. **-S** one that emits

EMMER *n* pl. **-S** a type of wheat

EMMET *n* pl. **-S** an ant

EMODIN *n* pl. **-S** a chemical compound

EMOTE *v* **EMOTED, EMOTING, EMOTES** to express emotion in an exaggerated manner

EMOTER *n* pl. **-S** one that emotes

EMOTICON *n* pl. **-S** a group of keyboard characters used to suggest a facial expression or an emotion

EMOTION *n* pl. **-S** an affective state of consciousness

EMOTIVE *adj* pertaining to emotion

EMPALE *v* **-PALED, -PALING, -PALES** to impale

EMPALER *n* pl. **-S** one that empales

EMPANADA *n* pl. **-S** a pastry turnover

EMPANEL *v* **-ELED, -ELING, -ELS** or **-ELLED, -ELLING, -ELS** to impanel

EMPATHY *n* pl. **-THIES** imaginative identification with another's thoughts and feelings **EMPATHIC** *adj*

EMPEROR *n* pl. **-S** the ruler of an empire

EMPERY *n* pl. **-PERIES** absolute dominion

EMPHASIS *n* pl. **-PHASES** special significance imparted to something

EMPHATIC *adj* strongly expressive

EMPIRE *n* pl. **-S** a major political unit

EMPIRIC *n* pl. **-S** one who relies on practical experience

EMPLACE *v* **-PLACED, -PLACING, -PLACES** to position

EMPLANE *v* **-PLANED, -PLANING, -PLANES** to enplane

EMPLOY *v* **-ED, -ING, -S** to hire

EMPLOYE *n* pl. **-S** employee

EMPLOYEE *n* pl. **-S** a person who is employed

EMPLOYER *n* pl. **-S** one that employs

EMPOISON *v* **-ED, -ING, -S** to embitter

EMPORIUM *n* pl. **-RIUMS** or **-RIA** a trading or market center

EMPOWER *v* **-ED, -ING, -S** to give legal power to

EMPRESS *n* pl. **-ES** a female ruler of an empire

EMPRISE *n* pl. **-S** an adventurous undertaking

EMPRIZE *n* pl. **-S** emprise

EMPTIED past tense of empty

EMPTIER *n* pl. **-S** one that empties

EMPTIES present 3d person sing. of empty

EMPTIEST superlative of empty

EMPTILY *adv* in an empty manner

EMPTINGS *n/pl* emptins

EMPTINS *n/pl* a liquid leavening

EMPTY *adj* **-TIER, -TIEST** containing nothing

EMPTY *v* **-TIED, -TYING, -TIES** to remove the contents of

EMPURPLE *v* **-PLED, -PLING, -PLES** to tinge with purple

EMPYEMA *n* pl. **-EMAS** or **-EMATA** a collection of pus in a body cavity **EMPYEMIC** *adj*

EMPYREAL *adj* pertaining to the sky

EMPYREAN *n* pl. **-S** the highest heaven

EMU *n* pl. **-S** a large, flightless bird

EMULATE *v* **-LATED, -LATING, -LATES** to try to equal or surpass

EMULATOR *n* pl. **-S** one that emulates

EMULOUS *adj* eager to equal or surpass another

EMULSIFY v **-FIED, -FYING, -FIES** to make into an emulsion

EMULSION n pl. **-S** a type of liquid mixture **EMULSIVE** adj

EMULSOID n pl. **-S** a liquid dispersed in another liquid

EMYD n pl. **-S** a freshwater tortoise

EMYDE n pl. **-S** emyd

EN n pl. **-S** the letter N

ENABLE v **-BLED, -BLING, -BLES** to make possible

ENABLER n pl. **-S** one that enables

ENACT v **-ED, -ING, -S** to make into a law

ENACTIVE adj having the power to enact

ENACTOR n pl. **-S** one that enacts

ENACTORY adj pertaining to the enactment of law

ENAMEL v **-ELED, -ELING, -ELS** or **-ELLED, -ELLING, -ELS** to cover with a hard, glossy surface

ENAMELER n pl. **-S** one that enamels

ENAMINE n pl. **-S** a type of amine

ENAMOR v **-ED, -ING, -S** to inspire with love

ENAMOUR v **-ED, -ING, -S** to enamor

ENATE n pl. **-S** a relative on the mother's side **ENATIC** adj

ENATION n pl. **-S** an outgrowth from the surface of an organ

ENCAENIA n/pl annual university ceremonies

ENCAGE v **-CAGED, -CAGING, -CAGES** to confine in a cage

ENCAMP v **-ED, -ING, -S** to set up a camp

ENCASE v **-CASED, -CASING, -CASES** to enclose in a case

ENCASH v **-ED, -ING, -ES** to cash

ENCEINTE n pl. **-S** an encircling fortification

ENCHAIN v **-ED, -ING, -S** to bind with chains

ENCHANT v **-ED, -ING, -S** to delight

ENCHASE v **-CHASED, -CHASING, -CHASES** to place in an ornamental setting

ENCHASER n pl. **-S** one that enchases

ENCHORIC adj belonging to a particular country

ENCINA n pl. **-S** an evergreen oak **ENCINAL** adj

ENCIPHER v **-ED, -ING, -S** to write in characters of hidden meaning

ENCIRCLE v **-CLED, -CLING, -CLES** to form a circle around

ENCLASP v **-ED, -ING, -S** to embrace

ENCLAVE v **-CLAVED, -CLAVING, -CLAVES** to enclose within a foreign territory

ENCLITIC n pl. **-S** a word pronounced as part of the preceding word

ENCLOSE v **-CLOSED, -CLOSING, -CLOSES** to close in on all sides

ENCLOSER n pl. **-S** one that encloses

ENCODE v **-CODED, -CODING, -CODES** to put into code

ENCODER n pl. **-S** one that encodes

ENCOMIUM n pl. **-MIUMS** or **-MIA** a eulogy

ENCORE v **-CORED, -CORING, -CORES** to call for the reappearance of a performer

ENCROACH v **-ED, -ING, -ES** to advance beyond the proper limits

ENCRUST v **-ED, -ING, -S** to cover with a crust

ENCRYPT v **-ED, -ING, -S** to encipher

ENCUMBER v **-ED, -ING, -S** to hinder in action or movement

ENCYCLIC n pl. **-S** a letter addressed by the pope to the bishops of the world

ENCYST v **-ED, -ING, -S** to enclose in a cyst

END v **-ED, -ING, -S** to terminate

ENDAMAGE v **-AGED, -AGING, -AGES** to damage

ENDAMEBA n pl. **-BAS** or **-BAE** a parasitic ameba

ENDANGER v **-ED, -ING, -S** to imperil

ENDARCH adj formed from the center outward

ENDARCHY n pl. **-CHIES** the condition of being endarch

ENDASH n pl. **-ES** a mark in writing used to connect elements of a compound

ENDBRAIN n pl. **-S** a part of the brain

ENDEAR v **-ED, -ING, -S** to make dear or beloved

ENDEAVOR v **-ED, -ING, -S** to make an effort

ENDEMIAL adj peculiar to a country or people

ENDEMIC n pl. **-S** an endemial disease

ENDEMISM n pl. **-S** the state of being endemial

ENDER n pl. **-S** one that ends something

ENDERMIC adj acting by absorption through the skin

ENDEXINE n pl. **-S** an inner layer of the exine

ENDGAME n pl. **-S** the last stage of a chess game

ENDING *n* pl. **-S** a termination

ENDITE *v* **-DITED, -DITING, -DITES** to indite

ENDIVE *n* pl. **-S** an herb cultivated as a salad plant

ENDLEAF *n* pl. **-LEAVES** or **-LEAFS** an endpaper

ENDLESS *adj* enduring forever

ENDLONG *adv* lengthwise

ENDMOST *adj* farthest

ENDNOTE *n* pl. **-S** a note placed at the end of the text

ENDOCARP *n* pl. **-S** the inner layer of a pericarp

ENDOCAST *n* pl. **-S** a cast of the cranial cavity

ENDODERM *n* pl. **-S** the innermost germ layer of an embryo

ENDOGAMY *n* pl. **-MIES** marriage within a particular group

ENDOGEN *n* pl. **-S** a type of plant

ENDOGENY *n* pl. **-NIES** growth from within

ENDOPOD *n* pl. **-S** a branch of a crustacean limb

ENDORSE *v* **-DORSED, -DORSING, -DORSES** to sign the back of a negotiable document

ENDORSEE *n* pl. **-S** one to whom a document is transferred by endorsement

ENDORSER *n* pl. **-S** one that endorses

ENDORSOR *n* pl. **-S** endorser

ENDOSARC *n* pl. **-S** a portion of a cell

ENDOSMOS *n* pl. **-ES** a form of osmosis

ENDOSOME *n* pl. **-S** a cellular particle

ENDOSTEA *n/pl* bone membranes

ENDOW *v* **-ED, -ING, -S** to provide with something

ENDOWER *n* pl. **-S** one that endows

ENDOZOIC *adj* involving passage through an animal

ENDPAPER *n* pl. **-S** a sheet of paper used in bookbinding

ENDPLATE *n* pl. **-S** a type of nerve terminal

ENDPLAY *v* **-ED, -ING, -S** to force (an opponent in bridge) to lead

ENDPOINT *n* pl. **-S** either of two points that mark the end of a line segment

ENDRIN *n* pl. **-S** an insecticide

ENDUE *v* **-DUED, -DUING, -DUES** to provide with some quality or gift

ENDURE *v* **-DURED, -DURING, -DURES** to last

ENDURER *n* pl. **-S** one that endures

ENDURO *n* pl. **-DUROS** a long race

ENDWAYS *adv* endwise

ENDWISE *adv* lengthwise

ENEMA *n* pl. **-MAS** or **-MATA** a liquid injected into the rectum

ENEMY *n* pl. **-MIES** one that is antagonistic toward another

ENERGID *n* pl. **-S** a nucleus and the body of cytoplasm with which it interacts

ENERGIES pl. of energy

ENERGISE *v* **-GISED, -GISING, -GISES** to energize

ENERGIZE *v* **-GIZED, -GIZING, -GIZES** to give energy to

ENERGY *n* **-GIES** the capacity for vigorous activity

ENERVATE *v* **-VATED, -VATING, -VATES** to deprive of strength or vitality

ENFACE *v* **-FACED, -FACING, -FACES** to write on the front of

ENFEEBLE *v* **-BLED, -BLING, -BLES** to make feeble

ENFEOFF *v* **-ED, -ING, -S** to invest with a feudal estate

ENFETTER *v* **-ED, -ING, -S** to enchain

ENFEVER *v* **-ED, -ING, -S** to fever

ENFILADE *v* **-LADED, -LADING, -LADES** to direct heavy gunfire along the length of

ENFLAME *v* **-FLAMED, -FLAMING, -FLAMES** to inflame

ENFOLD *v* **-ED, -ING, -S** to envelop

ENFOLDER *n* pl. **-S** one that enfolds

ENFORCE *v* **-FORCED, -FORCING, -FORCES** to compel obedience to

ENFORCER *n* pl. **-S** one that enforces

ENFRAME *v* **-FRAMED, -FRAMING, -FRAMES** to frame

ENG *n* pl. **-S** a phonetic symbol

ENGAGE *v* **-GAGED, -GAGING, -GAGES** to employ

ENGAGER *n* pl. **-S** one that engages

ENGENDER *v* **-ED, -ING, -S** to bring into existence

ENGILD *v* **-ED, -ING, -S** to brighten

ENGINE *v* **-GINED, -GINING, -GINES** to equip with machinery

ENGINEER *v* **-ED, -ING, -S** to carry through or manage by contrivance

ENGINERY *n* pl. **-RIES** machinery

ENGINING present participle of engine

ENGINOUS *adj* ingenious

ENGIRD *v* **-GIRT** or **-GIRDED, -GIRDING, -GIRDS** to gird

ENGIRDLE *v* **-DLED, -DLING, -DLES** to engird

ENGLISH *v* **-ED, -ING, -ES** to cause a billiard ball to spin around its vertical axis

ENGLUT *v* **-GLUTTED, -GLUTTING, -GLUTS** to gulp down

ENGORGE *v* **-GORGED, -GORGING, -GORGES** to fill with blood

ENGRAFT *v* **-ED, -ING, -S** to graft for propagation

ENGRAIL *v* **-ED, -ING, -S** to ornament the edge of with curved indentations

ENGRAIN *v* **-ED, -ING, -S** to ingrain

ENGRAM *n* pl. **-S** the durable mark caused by a stimulus upon protoplasm

ENGRAMME *n* pl. **-S** engram

ENGRAVE *v* **-GRAVED, -GRAVING, -GRAVES** to form by incision

ENGRAVER *n* pl. **-S** one that engraves

ENGROSS *v* **-ED, -ING, -ES** to occupy completely

ENGULF *v* **-ED, -ING, -S** to surround completely

ENHALO *v* **-ED, -ING, -S** or **-ES** to surround with a halo

ENHANCE *v* **-HANCED, -HANCING, -HANCES** to raise to a higher degree

ENHANCER *n* pl. **-S** one that enhances

ENIGMA *n* pl. **-MAS** or **-MATA** something that is hard to understand or explain

ENISLE *v* **-ISLED, -ISLING, -ISLES** to isolate

ENJAMBED *adj* marked by the continuation of a sentence from one line of a poem to the next

ENJOIN *v* **-ED, -ING, -S** to command

ENJOINER *n* pl. **-S** one that enjoins

ENJOY *v* **-ED, -ING, -S** to receive pleasure from

ENJOYER *n* pl. **-S** one that enjoys

ENKINDLE *v* **-DLED, -DLING, -DLES** to set on fire

ENLACE *v* **-LACED, -LACING, -LACES** to bind with laces

ENLARGE *v* **-LARGED, -LARGING, -LARGES** to make or become larger

ENLARGER *n* pl. **-S** a device used to enlarge photographs

ENLIST *v* **-ED, -ING, -S** to engage for military service

ENLISTEE *n* pl. **-S** one that is enlisted

ENLISTER *n* pl. **-S** one that enlists

ENLIVEN *v* **-ED, -ING, -S** to make lively

ENMESH *v* **-ED, -ING, -ES** to ensnare or entangle in a net

ENMITY *n* pl. **-TIES** hostility

ENNEAD *n* pl. **-S** a group of nine **ENNEADIC** *adj*

ENNEAGON *n* pl. **-S** a nonagon

ENNOBLE *v* **-BLED, -BLING, -BLES** to make noble

ENNOBLER *n* pl. **-S** one that ennobles

ENNUI *n* pl. **-S** a feeling of weariness and discontent

ENNUYE *adj* oppressed with ennui

ENNUYEE *adj* ennuye

ENOKI *n* pl. **-S** a small mushroom

ENOL *n* pl. **-S** a chemical compound **ENOLIC** *adj*

ENOLASE *n* pl. **-S** an enzyme

ENOLOGY *n* pl. **-GIES** oenology

ENOPHILE *n* pl. **-S** oenophile

ENORM *adj* enormous

ENORMITY *n* pl. **-TIES** great wickedness

ENORMOUS *adj* huge

ENOSIS *n* pl. **-SISES** union

ENOUGH *n* pl. **-S** a sufficient supply

ENOUNCE *v* **ENOUNCED, ENOUNCING, ENOUNCES** to announce

ENOW *n* pl. **-S** enough

ENPLANE *v* **-PLANED, -PLANING, -PLANES** to board an airplane

ENQUIRE *v* **-QUIRED, -QUIRING, -QUIRES** to inquire

ENQUIRY *n* pl. **-RIES** inquiry

ENRAGE *v* **-RAGED, -RAGING, -RAGES** to make very angry

ENRAPT *adj* rapt

ENRAVISH *v* **-ED, -ING, -ES** to delight greatly

ENRICH *v* **-ED, -ING, -ES** to add desirable elements to

ENRICHER *n* pl. **-S** one that enriches

ENROBE *v* **-ROBED, -ROBING, -ROBES** to dress

ENROBER *n* pl. **-S** one that enrobes

ENROL *v* **-ROLLED, -ROLLING, -ROLS** to enroll

ENROLL *v* **-ED, -ING, -S** to enter the name of in a register, record, or roll

ENROLLEE *n* pl. **-S** one that is enrolled

ENROLLER *n* pl. **-S** one that enrolls

ENROLLING present participle of enrol

ENROOT *v* **-ED, -ING, -S** to implant

ENS *n* pl. **ENTIA** an entity

ENSAMPLE *n* pl. **-S** an example

ENSCONCE *v* **-SCONCED, -SCONCING, -SCONCES** to settle securely or comfortably

ENSCROLL *v* **-ED, -ING, -S** to write on a scroll

ENSEMBLE *n* pl. **-S** a group of complementary parts

ENSERF *v* **-ED, -ING, -S** to make a serf of

ENSHEATH *v* **-ED, -ING, -S** to enclose in a sheath

ENSHRINE *v* **-SHRINED, -SHRINING, -SHRINES** to place in a shrine

ENSHROUD *v* **-ED, -ING, -S** to conceal

ENSIFORM *adj* sword-shaped

ENSIGN *n* pl. **-S** a navy officer

ENSIGNCY *n* pl. **-CIES** the rank of an ensign

ENSILAGE *v* **-LAGED, -LAGING, -LAGES** to ensile

ENSILE *v* **-SILED, -SILING, -SILES** to store in a silo

ENSKY *v* **-SKIED** or **-SKYED, -SKYING, -SKIES** to raise to the skies

ENSLAVE *v* **-SLAVED, -SLAVING, -SLAVES** to make a slave of

ENSLAVER *n* pl. **-S** one that enslaves

ENSNARE *v* **-SNARED, -SNARING, -SNARES** to trap

ENSNARER *n* pl. **-S** one that ensnares

ENSNARL *v* **-ED, -ING, -S** to tangle

ENSORCEL *v* **-ED, -ING, -S** to bewitch

ENSOUL *v* **-ED, -ING, -S** to endow with a soul

ENSPHERE *v* **-SPHERED, -SPHERING, -SPHERES** to enclose in a sphere

ENSUE *v* **-SUED, -SUING, -SUES** to occur afterward or as a result

ENSURE *v* **-SURED, -SURING, -SURES** to make certain

ENSURER *n* pl. **-S** one that ensures

ENSWATHE *v* **-SWATHED, -SWATHING, -SWATHES** to swathe

ENTAIL *v* **-ED, -ING, -S** to restrict the inheritance of to a specified line of heirs

ENTAILER *n* pl. **-S** one that entails

ENTAMEBA *n* pl. **-BAS** or **-BAE** endameba

ENTANGLE *v* **-TANGLED, -TANGLING, -TANGLES** to tangle

ENTASIA *n* pl. **-S** spasmodic contraction of a muscle

ENTASIS *n* pl. **-TASES** a slight convexity in a column **ENTASTIC** *adj*

ENTELLUS *n* pl. **-ES** a hanuman

ENTENTE *n* pl. **-S** an agreement between nations

ENTER *v* **-ED, -ING, -S** to come or go into

ENTERA a pl. of enteron

ENTERAL *adj* enteric

ENTERER *n* pl. **-S** one that enters

ENTERIC *adj* pertaining to the enteron

ENTERICS *n/pl* a family of bacteria

ENTERON *n* pl. **-TERONS** or **-TERA** the alimentary canal

ENTHALPY *n* pl. **-PIES** a thermodynamic measure of heat

ENTHETIC *adj* introduced from outside

ENTHRAL *v* **-THRALLED, -THRALLING, -THRALS** to enthrall

ENTHRALL *v* **-ED, -ING, -S** to charm

ENTHRONE *v* **-THRONED, -THRONING, -THRONES** to place on a throne

ENTHUSE *v* **-THUSED, -THUSING, -THUSES** to show enthusiasm

ENTIA pl. of ens

ENTICE *v* **-TICED, -TICING, -TICES** to allure

ENTICER *n* pl. **-S** one that entices

ENTIRE *n* pl. **-S** the whole of something

ENTIRELY *adv* completely

ENTIRETY *n* pl. **-TIES** completeness

ENTITLE *v* **-TLED, -TLING, -TLES** to give a title to

ENTITY *n* pl. **-TIES** something that has a real existence

ENTODERM	*n* pl. **-S** endoderm
ENTOIL	*v* **-ED, -ING, -S** to entrap
ENTOMB	*v* **-ED, -ING, -S** to place in a tomb
ENTOPIC	*adj* situated in the normal place
ENTOZOA	a pl. of entozoan and pl. of entozoon
ENTOZOAL	*adj* entozoic
ENTOZOAN	*n* pl. **-ZOANS** or **-ZOA** an entozoic parasite
ENTOZOIC	*adj* living within an animal
ENTOZOON	*n* pl. **-ZOA** entozoan
ENTRAILS	*n/pl* the internal organs
ENTRAIN	*v* **-ED, -ING, -S** to board a train
ENTRANCE	*v* **-TRANCED, -TRANCING, -TRANCES** to fill with delight or wonder
ENTRANT	*n* pl. **-S** one that enters
ENTRAP	*v* **-TRAPPED, -TRAPPING, -TRAPS** to trap
ENTREAT	*v* **-ED, -ING, -S** to ask for earnestly
ENTREATY	*n* pl. **-TREATIES** an earnest request
ENTREE	*n* pl. **-S** the principal dish of a meal
ENTRENCH	*v* **-ED, -ING, -ES** to establish firmly
ENTREPOT	*n* pl. **-S** a warehouse
ENTRESOL	*n* pl. **-S** a mezzanine
ENTRIES	pl. of entry
ENTROPY	*n* pl. **-PIES** a thermodynamic measure of disorder **ENTROPIC** *adj*
ENTRUST	*v* **-ED, -ING, -S** to give over for safekeeping
ENTRY	*n* pl. **-TRIES** a place of entrance
ENTRYWAY	*n* pl. **-WAYS** a passage serving as an entrance
ENTWINE	*v* **-TWINED, -TWINING, -TWINES** to twine around
ENTWIST	*v* **-ED, -ING, -S** to twist together
ENURE	*v* **-URED, -URING, -URES** to inure
ENURESIS	*n* pl. **-RESES** involuntary urination
ENURETIC	*n* pl. **-S** one who is affected with enuresis
ENVELOP	*v* **-ED, -ING, -S** to cover completely
ENVELOPE	*n* pl. **-S** a paper container
ENVENOM	*v* **-ED, -ING, -S** to put venom into
ENVIABLE	*adj* desirable **ENVIABLY** *adv*
ENVIED	past tense of envy
ENVIER	*n* pl. **-S** one that envies
ENVIES	present 3d person sing. of envy
ENVIOUS	*adj* resentful and desirous of another's possessions or qualities
ENVIRO	*n* pl. **-ROS** an advocate for the preservation of the natural environment
ENVIRON	*v* **-ED, -ING, -S** to encircle
ENVISAGE	*v* **-AGED, -AGING, -AGES** to form a mental image of
ENVISION	*v* **-ED, -ING, -S** to envisage
ENVOI	*n* pl. **-S** the closing of a poem or prose work
ENVOY	*n* pl. **-VOYS** a representative
ENVY	*v* **-VIED, -VYING, -VIES** to be envious of
ENWHEEL	*v* **-ED, -ING, -S** to encircle
ENWIND	*v* **-WOUND, -WINDING, -WINDS** to wind around
ENWOMB	*v* **-ED, -ING, -S** to enclose as if in a womb
ENWRAP	*v* **-WRAPPED, -WRAPPING, -WRAPS** to envelop
ENZOOTIC	*n* pl. **-S** a type of animal disease
ENZYM	*n* pl. **-S** enzyme
ENZYME	*n* pl. **-S** a complex protein **ENZYMIC** *adj*
EOBIONT	*n* pl. **-S** a type of basic organism
EOHIPPUS	*n* pl. **-ES** an extinct horse
EOLIAN	*adj* pertaining to the wind
EOLIPILE	*n* pl. **-S** a type of engine
EOLITH	*n* pl. **-S** a prehistoric stone tool **EOLITHIC** *adj*
EOLOPILE	*n* pl. **-S** eolipile
EON	*n* pl. **-S** an indefinitely long period of time
EONIAN	*adj* everlasting
EONISM	*n* pl. **-S** adoption of the dress and mannerisms of the opposite sex
EOSIN	*n* pl. **-S** a red dye **EOSINIC** *adj*
EOSINE	*n* pl. **-S** eosin
EPACT	*n* pl. **-S** the difference between the lengths of the solar and lunar years
EPARCH	*n* pl. **-S** the head of an eparchy
EPARCHY	*n* pl. **-CHIES** a district of modern Greece
EPAULET	*n* pl. **-S** a shoulder ornament
EPAZOTE	*n* pl. **-S** an herb of the goosefoot family
EPEE	*n* pl. **-S** a type of sword

EPEEIST   *n* pl. **-S** one who fences with an epee

EPEIRIC   *adj* pertaining to vertical movement of the earth's crust

EPENDYMA   *n* pl. **-S** a membrane lining certain body cavities

EPERGNE   *n* pl. **-S** an ornamental dish

EPHA   *n* pl. **-S** ephah

EPHAH   *n* pl. **-S** a Hebrew unit of dry measure

EPHEBE   *n* pl. **-S** ephebus **EPHEBIC** *adj*

EPHEBOS   *n* pl. **-BOI** ephebus

EPHEBUS   *n* pl. **-BI** a young man of ancient Greece

EPHEDRA   *n* pl. **-S** a desert shrub

EPHEDRIN   *n* pl. **-S** an alkaloid used to treat allergies

EPHEMERA   *n* pl. **-ERAS** or **-ERAE** something of very short life or duration

EPHOD   *n* pl. **-S** an ancient Hebrew vestment

EPHOR   *n* pl. **-ORS** or **-ORI** a magistrate of ancient Greece **EPHORAL** *adj*

EPHORATE   *n* pl. **-S** the office of ephor

EPIBLAST   *n* pl. **-S** the ectoderm

EPIBOLY   *n* pl. **-LIES** the growth of one part around another **EPIBOLIC** *adj*

EPIC   *n* pl. **-S** a long narrative poem **EPICAL** *adj* **EPICALLY** *adv*

EPICALYX   *n* pl. **-LYXES** or **-LYCES** a set of bracts close to and resembling a calyx

EPICARP   *n* pl. **-S** the outer layer of a pericarp

EPICEDIA   *n/pl* funeral songs

EPICENE   *n* pl. **-S** one having both male and female characteristics

EPICLIKE   *adj* resembling an epic

EPICOTYL   *n* pl. **-S** a part of a plant embryo

EPICURE   *n* pl. **-S** a gourmet

EPICYCLE   *n* pl. **-S** a circle that rolls on the circumference of another circle

EPIDEMIC   *n* pl. **-S** a rapid spread of a disease

EPIDERM   *n* pl. **-S** the outer layer of skin

EPIDOTE   *n* pl. **-S** a mineral **EPIDOTIC** *adj*

EPIDURAL   *n* pl. **-S** an injection to produce loss of sensation

EPIFAUNA   *n* pl. **-FAUNAS** or **-FAUNAE** fauna living on a hard sea floor

EPIFOCAL   *adj* pertaining to the point of origin of an earthquake

EPIGEAL   *adj* epigeous

EPIGEAN   *adj* epigeous

EPIGEIC   *adj* epigeous

EPIGENE   *adj* occurring near the surface of the earth

EPIGENIC   *adj* pertaining to change in the mineral character of a rock

EPIGEOUS   *adj* growing on or close to the ground

EPIGON   *n* pl. **-S** epigone

EPIGONE   *n* pl. **-S** an inferior imitator **EPIGONIC** *adj*

EPIGONUS   *n* pl. **-NI** epigone

EPIGRAM   *n* pl. **-S** a brief, witty remark

EPIGRAPH   *n* pl. **-S** an engraved inscription

EPIGYNY   *n* pl. **-NIES** the state of having floral organs near the top of the ovary

EPILATE   *v* **-LATED, -LATING, -LATES** to remove hair from

EPILATOR   *n* pl. **-S** an agent for removing hair

EPILEPSY   *n* pl. **-SIES** a disorder of the nervous system

EPILOG   *n* pl. **-S** a concluding section

EPILOGUE   *v* **-LOGUED, -LOGUING, -LOGUES** to provide with a concluding section

EPIMER   *n* pl. **-S** a type of sugar compound **EPIMERIC** *adj*

EPIMERE   *n* pl. **-S** a part of an embryo

EPIMYSIA   *n/pl* muscle sheaths

EPINAOS   *n* pl. **-NAOI** a rear vestibule

EPINASTY   *n* pl. **-TIES** a downward bending of plant parts

EPIPHANY   *n* pl. **-NIES** an appearance of a deity

EPIPHYTE   *n* pl. **-S** a plant growing upon another plant

EPISCIA   *n* pl. **-S** a tropical herb

EPISCOPE   *n* pl. **-S** a type of projector

EPISODE   *n* pl. **-S** an incident in the course of a continuous experience **EPISODIC** *adj*

EPISOME   *n* pl. **-S** a genetic determinant **EPISOMAL** *adj*

EPISTASY   *n* pl. **-SIES** a suppression of genetic effect

EPISTLE   *n* pl. **-S** a long or formal letter

EPISTLER *n* pl. **-S** one that writes epistles

EPISTOME *n* pl. **-S** a structure covering the mouth of various invertebrates

EPISTYLE *n* pl. **-S** a part of a classical building

EPITAPH *n* pl. **-S** an inscription on a tomb

EPITASIS *n* pl. **-ASES** the main part of a classical drama

EPITAXY *n* pl. **-TAXIES** a type of crystalline growth **EPITAXIC** *adj*

EPITHET *n* pl. **-S** a term used to characterize a person or thing

EPITOME *n* pl. **-S** a typical or ideal example **EPITOMIC** *adj*

EPITOPE *n* pl. **-S** a region on the surface of an antigen

EPIZOA pl. of epizoon

EPIZOIC *adj* living on the body of an animal

EPIZOISM *n* pl. **-S** the state of being epizoic

EPIZOITE *n* pl. **-S** an epizoic organism

EPIZOON *n* pl. **-ZOA** an epizoic parasite

EPIZOOTY *n* pl. **-TIES** a type of animal disease

EPOCH *n* pl. **-S** a particular period of time **EPOCHAL** *adj*

EPODE *n* pl. **-S** a type of poem

EPONYM *n* pl. **-S** the person for whom something is named **EPONYMIC** *adj*

EPONYMY *n* pl. **-MIES** the derivation of an eponymic name

EPOPEE *n* pl. **-S** an epic poem

EPOPOEIA *n* pl. **-S** epopee

EPOS *n* pl. **-ES** an epic poem

EPOXIDE *n* pl. **-S** an epoxy compound

EPOXY *v* **EPOXIED** or **EPOXYED, EPOXYING, EPOXIES** to glue with epoxy (a type of resin)

EPSILON *n* pl. **-S** a Greek letter

EQUABLE *adj* not changing or varying greatly **EQUABLY** *adv*

EQUAL *adj* having the same capability, quantity, or effect as another

EQUAL *v* **EQUALED, EQUALING, EQUALS** or **EQUALLED, EQUALLING, EQUALS** to be equal to

EQUALISE *v* **-ISED, -ISING, -ISES** to equalize

EQUALITY *n* pl. **-TIES** the state of being equal

EQUALIZE *v* **-IZED, -IZING, -IZES** to make equal

EQUALLED a past tense of equal

EQUALLING a past participle of equal

EQUALLY *adv* in an equal manner

EQUATE *v* **EQUATED, EQUATING, EQUATES** to make equal

EQUATION *n* pl. **-S** the act of equating

EQUATOR *n* pl. **-S** a great circle of spherical celestial bodies

EQUERRY *n* pl. **-RIES** an officer in charge of the care of horses

EQUID *n* pl. **-S** an animal of the horse family

EQUINE *n* pl. **-S** a horse

EQUINELY *adv* in a horselike manner

EQUINITY *n* pl. **-TIES** the state of being like a horse

EQUINOX *n* pl. **-ES** a point on the celestial sphere

EQUIP *v* **EQUIPPED, EQUIPPING, EQUIPS** to provide with whatever is needed

EQUIPAGE *n* pl. **-S** a carriage

EQUIPPER *n* pl. **-S** one that equips

EQUISETA *n/pl* rushlike plants

EQUITANT *adj* overlapping

EQUITES *n/pl* a privileged military class of ancient Rome

EQUITY *n* pl. **-TIES** fairness or impartiality

EQUIVOKE *n* pl. **-S** a play on words

ER *interj* — used to express hesitation

ERA *n* pl. **-S** an epoch

ERADIATE *v* **-ATED, -ATING, -ATES** to radiate

ERASE *v* **ERASED, ERASING, ERASES** to rub or scrape out **ERASABLE** *adj*

ERASER *n* pl. **-S** one that erases

ERASION *n* pl. **-S** an erasure

ERASURE *n* pl. **-S** the act of erasing

ERBIUM *n* pl. **-S** a metallic element

ERE *prep* previous to; before

ERECT *v* **-ED, -ING, -S** to build

ERECTER *n* pl. **-S** erector

ERECTILE *adj* capable of being raised upright

ERECTION *n* pl. **-S** the act of erecting

ERECTIVE *adj* tending to erect

ERECTLY *adv* in an upright manner

ERECTOR *n* pl. **-S** one that erects

ERELONG *adv* soon

EREMITE *n* pl. **-S** a hermit **EREMITIC** *adj*

EREMURUS *n* pl. **-URUSES** or **-URI** a perennial herb

ERENOW *adv* before this time

EREPSIN *n* pl. **-S** a mixture of enzymes in the small intestine

ERETHISM *n* pl. **-S** abnormal irritability **ERETHIC** *adj*

EREWHILE *adv* some time ago

ERG *n* pl. **-S** a unit of work or energy

ERGASTIC *adj* constituting the nonliving by-products of protoplasmic activity

ERGATE *n* pl. **-S** a worker ant

ERGATIVE *n* pl. **-S** a type of verb

ERGO *conj* therefore

ERGODIC *adj* pertaining to the probability that any state will recur

ERGOT *n* pl. **-S** a fungus **ERGOTIC** *adj*

ERGOTISM *n* pl. **-S** poisoning produced by eating ergot-infected grain

ERICA *n* pl. **-S** a shrub of the heath family

ERICOID *adj* resembling heath

ERIGERON *n* pl. **-S** an herb

ERINGO *n* pl. **-GOS** or **-GOES** eryngo

ERISTIC *n* pl. **-S** an expert in debate

ERLKING *n* pl. **-S** an evil spirit of Germanic folklore

ERMINE *n* pl. **-S** the fur of certain weasels **ERMINED** *adj*

ERN *n* pl. **-S** erne

ERNE *n* pl. **-S** a sea eagle

ERODABLE *adj* erosible

ERODE *v* **ERODED, ERODING, ERODES** to wear away by constant friction

ERODENT *adj* erosive

ERODIBLE *adj* erosible

EROGENIC *adj* arousing sexual desire

EROS *n* pl. **-ES** sexual desire

EROSE *adj* uneven **EROSELY** *adv*

EROSIBLE *adj* capable of being eroded

EROSION *n* pl. **-S** the act of eroding

EROSIVE *adj* causing erosion

EROTIC *n* pl. **-S** an amatory poem **EROTICAL** *adj*

EROTICA *n/pl* literature or art dealing with sexual love

EROTISM *n* pl. **-S** sexual excitement

EROTIZE *v* **-TIZED, -TIZING, -TIZES** to give a sexual meaning to

ERR *v* **-ED, -ING, -S** to make a mistake **ERRABLE** *adj*

ERRANCY *n* pl. **-CIES** an instance of erring

ERRAND *n* pl. **-S** a short trip made for a particular purpose

ERRANT *n* pl. **-S** a wanderer

ERRANTLY *adv* in a wandering manner

ERRANTRY *n* pl. **-RIES** the state of wandering

ERRATA *n* pl. **-S** a list of printing errors

ERRATIC *n* pl. **-S** an eccentric person

ERRATUM *n* pl. **-TA** a printing error

ERRHINE *n* pl. **-S** a substance that promotes nasal discharge

ERRINGLY *adv* in a mistaken manner

ERROR *n* pl. **-S** a mistake

ERS *n* pl. **-ES** ervil

ERSATZ *n* pl. **-ES** a substitute

ERST *adv* formerly

ERUCT *v* **-ED, -ING, -S** to belch

ERUCTATE *v* **-TATED, -TATING, -TATES** to eruct

ERUDITE *adj* scholarly

ERUGO *n* pl. **-GOS** aerugo

ERUMPENT *adj* bursting forth

ERUPT *v* **-ED, -ING, -S** to burst forth

ERUPTION *n* pl. **-S** the act of erupting

ERUPTIVE *n* pl. **-S** a type of rock

ERVIL *n* pl. **-S** a European vetch

ERYNGO *n* pl. **-GOS** or **-GOES** a medicinal herb

ERYTHEMA *n* pl. **-S** a redness of the skin

ERYTHRON *n* pl. **-S** a bodily organ consisting of the red blood cells

ES *n* pl. **ESES** ess

ESCALADE *v* **-LADED, -LADING, -LADES** to enter by means of ladders

ESCALATE *v* **-LATED, -LATING, -LATES** to increase

ESCALLOP *v* **-ED, -ING, -S** to scallop

ESCALOP *v* **-ED, -ING, -S** to escallop

ESCALOPE *n* pl. **-S** a thin slice of meat or fish

ESCAPADE *n* pl. **-S** a reckless adventure

ESCAPE *v* **-CAPED, -CAPING, -CAPES** to get away

ESCAPEE *n* pl. **-S** one that has escaped

ESCAPER *n* pl. **-S** one that escapes

ESCAPISM *n* pl. **-S** the avoidance of reality by diversion of the mind

ESCAPIST *n* pl. **-S** one given to escapism

ESCAR *n* pl. **-S** esker

ESCARGOT *n* pl. **-S** an edible snail

ESCAROLE *n* pl. **-S** a variety of endive

ESCARP *v* **-ED, -ING, -S** to cause to slope steeply

ESCHALOT *n* pl. **-S** a shallot

ESCHAR *n* pl. **-S** a hard, dry scab

ESCHEAT *v* **-ED, -ING, -S** to confiscate

ESCHEW *v* **-ED, -ING, -S** to avoid

ESCHEWAL *n* pl. **-S** the act of eschewing

ESCHEWER *n* pl. **-S** one that avoids something

ESCOLAR *n* pl. **-S** a food fish

ESCORT *v* **-ED, -ING, -S** to accompany

ESCOT *v* **-ED, -ING, -S** to provide support for

ESCROW *v* **-ED, -ING, -S** to place in the custody of a third party

ESCUAGE *n* pl. **-S** scutage

ESCUDO *n* pl. **-DOS** a former monetary unit of Portugal

ESCULENT *n* pl. **-S** something that is edible

ESERINE *n* pl. **-S** a toxic alkaloid

ESKAR *n* pl. **-S** esker

ESKER *n* pl. **-S** a narrow ridge of gravel and sand

ESNE *n* pl. **-S** a laborer in Anglo-Saxon England

ESOPHAGI *n/pl* tubes connecting the mouth to the stomach

ESOTERIC *adj* designed for a select few

ESPALIER *v* **-ED, -ING, -S** to furnish with a trellis

ESPANOL *n* pl. **-ES** a native of Spain

ESPARTO *n* pl. **-TOS** a perennial grass

ESPECIAL *adj* special

ESPIAL *n* pl. **-S** the act of espying

ESPIED past tense of espy

ESPIEGLE *adj* playful

ESPIES present 3d person sing. of espy

ESPOUSAL *n* pl. **-S** a marriage ceremony

ESPOUSE *v* **-POUSED, -POUSING, -POUSES** to marry

ESPOUSER *n* pl. **-S** one that espouses

ESPRESSO *n* pl. **-SOS** a strong coffee

ESPRIT *n* pl. **-S** spirit

ESPY *v* **-PIED, -PYING, -PIES** to catch sight of

ESQUIRE *v* **-QUIRED, -QUIRING, -QUIRES** to escort

ESS *n* pl. **-ES** the letter S

ESSAY *v* **-ED, -ING, -S** to try

ESSAYER *n* pl. **-S** one that essays

ESSAYIST *n* pl. **-S** a writer of essays (prose compositions)

ESSENCE *n* pl. **-S** a fundamental nature or quality

ESSOIN *n* pl. **-S** an excuse

ESSONITE *n* pl. **-S** a variety of garnet

ESTANCIA *n* pl. **-S** a cattle ranch

ESTATE *v* **-TATED, -TATING, -TATES** to provide with landed property

ESTEEM *v* **-ED, -ING, -S** to have a high opinion of

ESTER *n* pl. **-S** a type of chemical compound

ESTERASE *n* pl. **-S** a type of enzyme

ESTERIFY *v* **-FIED, -FYING, -FIES** to convert into an ester

ESTHESIA *n* pl. **-S** the ability to receive sensation

ESTHESIS *n* pl. **-THESISES** or **-THESES** esthesia

ESTHETE *n* pl. **-S** an esthetic person

ESTHETIC *n* pl. **-S** a conception of beauty

ESTIMATE *v* **-MATED, -MATING, -MATES** to make an approximate judgment of

ESTIVAL *adj* pertaining to summer

ESTIVATE *v* **-VATED, -VATING, -VATES** to spend the summer

ESTOP *v* **-TOPPED, -TOPPING, -TOPS** to impede by estoppel

ESTOPPEL *n* pl. **-S** a legal restraint preventing a person from contradicting his own previous statement

ESTOVERS *n/pl* necessities allowed by law

ESTRAGON *n* pl. **-S** tarragon

ESTRAL *adj* estrous

ESTRANGE *v* **-TRANGED, -TRANGING, -TRANGES** to alienate

ESTRAY *v* **-ED, -ING, -S** to stray

ESTREAT *v* **-ED, -ING, -S** to copy from court records for use in prosecution

ESTRIN *n* pl. **-S** estrone

ESTRIOL *n* pl. **-S** an estrogen

ESTROGEN *n* pl. **-S** a female sex hormone promoting or producing estrus

ESTRONE *n* pl. **-S** an estrogen

ESTROUS *adj* pertaining to estrus

ESTRUAL *adj* estrous

ESTRUM *n* pl. **-S** estrus

ESTRUS *n* pl. **-ES** the period of heat in female mammals

ESTUARY *n* pl. **-ARIES** an inlet of the sea at a river's lower end

ESURIENT *adj* greedy

ET a past tense of eat

ETA *n* pl. **-S** a Greek letter

ETAGERE *n* pl. **-S** an ornamental stand

ETALON *n* pl. **-S** an optical instrument

ETAMIN *n* pl. **-S** etamine

ETAMINE *n* pl. **-S** a loosely woven fabric

ETAPE *n* pl. **-S** a warehouse

ETATISM *n* pl. **-S** state socialism **ETATIST** *adj*

ETCETERA *n* pl. **-S** a number of additional items

ETCH *v* **-ED, -ING, -ES** to engrave with acid

ETCHANT *n* pl. **-S** a substance used in etching

ETCHER *n* pl. **-S** one that etches

ETCHING *n* pl. **-S** an etched design

ETERNAL *n* pl. **-S** something lasting forever

ETERNE *adj* everlasting

ETERNISE *v* **-NISED, -NISING, -NISES** to eternize

ETERNITY *n* pl. **-TIES** infinite time

ETERNIZE *v* **-NIZED, -NIZING, -NIZES** to make everlasting

ETESIAN *n* pl. **-S** an annually recurring wind

ETH *n* pl. **-S** edh

ETHANE *n* pl. **-S** a gaseous hydrocarbon

ETHANOL *n* pl. **-S** an alcohol

ETHENE *n* pl. **-S** ethylene

ETHEPHON *n* pl. **-S** a synthetic plant growth regulator

ETHER *n* pl. **-S** a volatile liquid used as an anesthetic **ETHERIC** *adj*

ETHEREAL *adj* airy

ETHERIFY *v* **-FIED, -FYING, -FIES** to convert into ether

ETHERISH *adj* resembling ether

ETHERIZE *v* **-IZED, -IZING, -IZES** to treat with ether

ETHIC *n* pl. **-S** a body of moral principles

ETHICAL *n* pl. **-S** a drug sold by prescription only

ETHICIAN *n* pl. **-S** an ethicist

ETHICIST *n* pl. **-S** a specialist in ethics

ETHICIZE *v* **-CIZED, -CIZING, -CIZES** to make ethical

ETHINYL *n* pl. **-S** ethynyl

ETHION *n* pl. **-S** a pesticide

ETHMOID *n* pl. **-S** a bone of the nasal cavity

ETHNARCH *n* pl. **-S** the ruler of a people or province

ETHNIC *n* pl. **-S** a member of a particular ethnos **ETHNICAL** *adj*

ETHNONYM *n* pl. **-S** the name of an ethnic group

ETHNOS *n* pl. **-ES** a group of people who share a common and distinctive culture

ETHOGRAM *n* pl. **-S** a list of the behavior patterns of a species

ETHOLOGY *n* pl. **-GIES** the study of animal behavior

ETHOS *n* pl. **-ES** the fundamental character of a culture

ETHOXY *n* pl. **-OXIES** ethoxyl

ETHOXYL *n* pl. **-S** a univalent chemical radical

ETHYL *n* pl. **-S** a univalent chemical radical

ETHYLATE *v* **-ATED, -ATING, -ATES** to introduce the ethyl group into

ETHYLENE *n* pl. **-S** a flammable gas

ETHYLIC *adj* pertaining to ethyl

ETHYNE *n* pl. **-S** a flammable gas

ETHYNYL *n* pl. **-S** a univalent chemical radical

ETIC *adj* relating to a type of linguistic analysis

ETIOLATE *v* **-LATED, -LATING, -LATES** to whiten

ETIOLOGY *n* pl. **-GIES** the study of the causes of diseases

ETNA *n* pl. **-S** a container for heating liquids

ETOILE *n* pl. **-S** a star

ETOUFFEE *n* pl. **-S** a Cajun stew

ETUDE *n* pl. **-S** a piece of music for the practice of a point of technique

ETUI *n* pl. **-S** a case for holding small articles

ETWEE *n* pl. **-S** etui

ETYMON *n* pl. **-MONS** or **-MA** the earliest known form of a word

EUCAINE *n* pl. **-S** an anesthetic

EUCALYPT *n* pl. **-S** an evergreen tree

EUCHARIS *n* pl. **-RISES** a flowering plant

EUCHRE *v* **-CHRED, -CHRING, -CHRES** to prevent from winning three tricks in euchre (a card game)

EUCLASE *n* pl. **-S** a mineral

EUCRITE *n* pl. **-S** a type of meteorite **EUCRITIC** *adj*

EUDAEMON *n* pl. **-S** eudemon

EUDAIMON *n* pl. **-S** eudemon

EUDEMON *n* pl. **-S** a good spirit

EUGENIA *n* pl. **-S** a tropical evergreen tree

EUGENICS *n/pl* the science of hereditary improvement **EUGENIC** *adj*

EUGENIST *n* pl. **-S** a student of eugenics

EUGENOL *n* pl. **-S** an aromatic liquid

EUGLENA *n* pl. **-S** a freshwater protozoan

EUGLENID *n* pl. **-S** a euglena

EULACHAN *n* pl. **-S** eulachon

EULACHON *n* pl. **-S** a marine food fish

EULOGIA *n* pl. **-GIAE** holy bread

EULOGIA *n* pl. **-S** a blessing

EULOGIES pl. of eulogy

EULOGISE *v* **-GISED, -GISING, -GISES** to eulogize

EULOGIST *n* pl. **-S** one that eulogizes

EULOGIUM *n* pl. **-GIUMS** or **-GIA** a eulogy

EULOGIZE *v* **-GIZED, -GIZING, -GIZES** to praise highly

EULOGY *n* pl. **-GIES** a formal expression of high praise

EUNUCH *n* pl. **-S** a castrated man

EUONYMUS *n* pl. **-ES** any of a genus of shrubs or small trees

EUPATRID *n* pl. **-RIDS** or **-RIDAE** an aristocrat of ancient Athens

EUPEPSIA *n* pl. **-S** good digestion **EUPEPTIC** *adj*

EUPEPSY *n* pl. **-SIES** eupepsia

EUPHENIC *adj* dealing with biological improvement

EUPHONY *n* pl. **-NIES** pleasant sound **EUPHONIC** *adj*

EUPHORIA *n* pl. **-S** a feeling of well-being **EUPHORIC** *adj*

EUPHOTIC *adj* pertaining to the upper layer of a body of water

EUPHRASY *n* pl. **-SIES** an annual herb

EUPHROE *n* pl. **-S** a device used to adjust a shipboard awning

EUPHUISM *n* pl. **-S** an artificially elegant style of speech or writing

EUPHUIST *n* pl. **-S** one given to euphuism

EUPLOID *n* pl. **-S** a cell having three or more identical genomes

EUPLOIDY *n* pl. **-DIES** the state of being a euploid

EUPNEA *n* pl. **-S** normal breathing **EUPNEIC** *adj*

EUPNOEA *n* pl. **-S** eupnea **EUPNOEIC** *adj*

EUREKA *interj* — used to express triumph upon discovering something

EURIPUS *n* pl. **-PI** a swift sea channel

EURO *n* pl. **EUROS** a large kangaroo

EUROKY *n* pl. **-KIES** the ability of an organism to live under variable conditions **EUROKOUS** *adj*

EUROPIUM *n* pl. **-S** a metallic element

EURYBATH *n* pl. **-S** an organism that can live in a wide range of water depths

EURYOKY *n* pl. **-KIES** euroky

EURYTHMY *n* pl. **-MIES** harmony of movement or structure

EUSOCIAL *adj* pertaining to an animal society marked by specialization of tasks

EUSTACY *n* pl. **-CIES** a worldwide change in sea level **EUSTATIC** *adj*

EUSTASY *n* pl. **-SIES** eustacy

EUSTELE *n* pl. **-S** a plant part

EUTAXY *n* pl. **-TAXIES** good order

EUTECTIC *n* pl. **-S** an alloy that has the lowest possible melting point

EUTROPHY *n* pl. **-PHIES** healthful nutrition

EUXENITE *n* pl. **-S** a mineral

EVACUANT *n* pl. **-S** a cathartic medicine

EVACUATE *v* **-ATED, -ATING, -ATES** to remove from a dangerous area

EVACUEE *n* pl. **-S** one that is evacuated

EVADE *v* **EVADED, EVADING, EVADES** to escape or avoid by cleverness or deceit **EVADABLE, EVADIBLE** *adj*

EVADER	*n* pl. **-S** one that evades
EVALUATE	*v* **-ATED, -ATING, -ATES** to determine the value of
EVANESCE	*v* **-NESCED, -NESCING, -NESCES** to fade away
EVANGEL	*n* pl. **-S** a preacher of the gospel
EVANISH	*v* **-ED, -ING, -ES** to vanish
EVASION	*n* pl. **-S** the act of evading
EVASIVE	*adj* tending to evade
EVE	*n* pl. **-S** evening
EVECTION	*n* pl. **-S** irregularity in the moon's motion
EVEN	*adj* **EVENER, EVENEST** flat and smooth
EVEN	*v* **-ED, -ING, -S** to make even
EVENER	*n* pl. **-S** one that evens
EVENFALL	*n* pl. **-S** twilight
EVENING	*n* pl. **-S** the latter part of the day and early part of the night
EVENLY	*adv* in an even manner
EVENNESS	*n* pl. **-ES** the state of being even
EVENSONG	*n* pl. **-S** an evening prayer service
EVENT	*n* pl. **-S** something that occurs
EVENTFUL	*adj* momentous
EVENTIDE	*n* pl. **-S** evening
EVENTUAL	*adj* occurring at a later time
EVER	*adv* at all times
EVERMORE	*adv* forever
EVERSION	*n* pl. **-S** the act of everting
EVERT	*v* **-ED, -ING, -S** to turn outward or inside out
EVERTOR	*n* pl. **-S** a muscle that turns a part outward
EVERY	*adj* each without exception
EVERYDAY	*n* pl. **-S** the routine day
EVERYMAN	*n* pl. **-MEN** the typical or ordinary man
EVERYONE	*pron* every person
EVERYWAY	*adv* in every way
EVICT	*v* **-ED, -ING, -S** to expel by legal process
EVICTEE	*n* pl. **-S** one that is evicted
EVICTION	*n* pl. **-S** the act of evicting
EVICTOR	*n* pl. **-S** one that evicts
EVIDENCE	*v* **-DENCED, -DENCING, -DENCES** to indicate clearly

EVIDENT	*adj* clear to the vision or understanding
EVIL	*adj* **EVILER, EVILEST** or **EVILLER, EVILLEST** morally bad
EVIL	*n* pl. **-S** something that is evil
EVILDOER	*n* pl. **-S** one that does evil
EVILLY	*adv* in an evil manner
EVILNESS	*n* pl. **-ES** the quality of being evil
EVINCE	*v* **EVINCED, EVINCING, EVINCES** to show clearly **EVINCIVE** *adj*
EVITE	*v* **EVITED, EVITING, EVITES** to avoid **EVITABLE** *adj*
EVOCABLE	*adj* capable of being evoked
EVOCATOR	*n* pl. **-S** one that evokes
EVOKE	*v* **EVOKED, EVOKING, EVOKES** to call forth
EVOKER	*n* pl. **-S** an evocator
EVOLUTE	*n* pl. **-S** a type of geometric curve
EVOLVE	*v* **EVOLVED, EVOLVING, EVOLVES** to develop
EVOLVER	*n* pl. **-S** one that evolves
EVONYMUS	*n* pl. **-ES** euonymus
EVULSE	*v* **EVULSED, EVULSING, EVULSES** to extract forcibly
EVULSION	*n* pl. **-S** the act of pulling out
EVZONE	*n* pl. **-S** a Greek soldier
EWE	*n* pl. **-S** a female sheep
EWER	*n* pl. **-S** a large pitcher
EX	*v* **-ED, -ING, -ES** to cross out
EXABYTE	*n* pl. **-S** one quintillion bytes
EXACT	*adj* **-ACTER, -ACTEST** precise
EXACT	*v* **-ED, -ING, -S** to force the payment or yielding of
EXACTA	*n* pl. **-S** a type of horse racing bet
EXACTER	*n* pl. **-S** one that exacts
EXACTION	*n* pl. **-S** the act of exacting
EXACTLY	*adv* in an exact manner
EXACTOR	*n* pl. **-S** exacter
EXAHERTZ	*n* pl. **EXAHERTZ** one quintillion hertz
EXALT	*v* **-ED, -ING, -S** to raise
EXALTER	*n* pl. **-S** one that exalts
EXAM	*n* pl. **-S** an examination
EXAMEN	*n* pl. **-S** a critical study
EXAMINE	*v* **-INED, -INING, -INES** to inspect
EXAMINEE	*n* pl. **-S** one that is taking an examination

EXAMINER _n_ pl. **-S** one that examines

EXAMPLE _v_ **-PLED, -PLING, -PLES** to show by representation

EXANTHEM _n_ pl. **-S** a skin eruption

EXAPTED _adj_ utililized for a function other than the one developed through natural selection

EXAPTIVE _adj_ pertaining to an exapted function

EXARCH _n_ pl. **-S** the ruler of a province in the Byzantine Empire **EXARCHAL** _adj_

EXARCHY _n_ pl. **-CHIES** the domain of an exarch

EXCAVATE _v_ **-VATED, -VATING, -VATES** to dig out

EXCEED _v_ **-ED, -ING, -S** to go beyond

EXCEEDER _n_ pl. **-S** one that exceeds

EXCEL _v_ **-CELLED, -CELLING, -CELS** to surpass others

EXCEPT _v_ **-ED, -ING, -S** to leave out

EXCERPT _v_ **-ED, -ING, -S** to pick out a passage from for quoting

EXCESS _v_ **-ED, -ING, -ES** to eliminate the position of

EXCHANGE _v_ **-CHANGED, -CHANGING, -CHANGES** to give and receive reciprocally

EXCIDE _v_ **-CIDED, -CIDING, -CIDES** to excise

EXCIMER _n_ pl. **-S** a dimer that exists in an excited state

EXCIPLE _n_ pl. **-S** a rim around the hymenium of various lichens

EXCISE _v_ **-CISED, -CISING, -CISES** to remove by cutting out

EXCISION _n_ pl. **-S** the act of excising

EXCITANT _n_ pl. **-S** a stimulant

EXCITE _v_ **-CITED, -CITING, -CITES** to arouse the emotions of

EXCITER _n_ pl. **-S** one that excites

EXCITON _n_ pl. **-S** a phenomenon occurring in an excited crystal

EXCITOR _n_ pl. **-S** exciter

EXCLAIM _v_ **-ED, -ING, -S** to cry out suddenly

EXCLAVE _n_ pl. **-S** a portion of a country which is isolated in foreign territory

EXCLUDE _v_ **-CLUDED, -CLUDING, -CLUDES** to shut out

EXCLUDER _n_ pl. **-S** one that excludes

EXCRETA _n/pl_ excreted matter **EXCRETAL** _adj_

EXCRETE _v_ **-CRETED, -CRETING, -CRETES** to separate and eliminate from an organic body

EXCRETER _n_ pl. **-S** one that excretes

EXCURSUS _n_ pl. **-ES** a long appended exposition of a topic

EXCUSE _v_ **-CUSED, -CUSING, -CUSES** to apologize for

EXCUSER _n_ pl. **-S** one that excuses

EXEC _n_ pl. **-S** an executive officer

EXECRATE _v_ **-CRATED, -CRATING, -CRATES** to curse

EXECUTE _v_ **-CUTED, -CUTING, -CUTES** to carry out

EXECUTER _n_ pl. **-S** executor

EXECUTOR _n_ pl. **-S** one that executes

EXEDRA _n_ pl. **-DRAS** or **-DRAE** a curved outdoor bench

EXEGESIS _n_ pl. **-GESES** critical explanation or analysis **EXEGETIC** _adj_

EXEGETE _n_ pl. **-S** one skilled in exegesis

EXEMPLAR _n_ pl. **-S** one that is worthy of being copied

EXEMPLUM _n_ pl. **-PLA** an example

EXEMPT _v_ **-ED, -ING, -S** to free from an obligation required of others

EXEQUY _n_ pl. **-QUIES** a funeral procession **EXEQUIAL** _adj_

EXERCISE _v_ **-CISED, -CISING, -CISES** to make use of

EXERGUE _n_ pl. **-S** a space on a coin **EXERGUAL** _adj_

EXERT _v_ **-ED, -ING, -S** to put into action

EXERTION _n_ pl. **-S** the act of exerting

EXERTIVE _adj_ tending to exert

EXEUNT _v_ they leave the stage — used as a stage direction

EXHALANT _n_ pl. **-S** something that exhales

EXHALE _v_ **-HALED, -HALING, -HALES** to expel air or vapor

EXHALENT _n_ pl. **-S** exhalant

EXHAUST _v_ **-ED, -ING, -S** to use up

EXHEDRA _n_ pl. **-DRAE** exedra

EXHIBIT _v_ **-ED, -ING, -S** to present for public viewing

EXHORT _v_ **-ED, -ING, -S** to advise urgently

EXHORTER _n_ pl. **-S** one that exhorts

EXHUME v **-HUMED, -HUMING, -HUMES** to dig out of the earth

EXHUMER n pl. **-S** one that exhumes

EXIGENCE n pl. **-S** exigency

EXIGENCY n pl. **-CIES** urgency

EXIGENT adj urgent

EXIGIBLE adj liable to be demanded

EXIGUITY n pl. **-ITIES** the state of being exiguous

EXIGUOUS adj meager

EXILE v **-ILED, -ILING, -ILES** to banish from one's own country **EXILABLE** adj

EXILER n pl. **-S** one that exiles

EXILIAN adj exilic

EXILIC adj pertaining to exile (banishment from one's own country)

EXILING present participle of exile

EXIMIOUS adj excellent

EXINE n pl. **-S** the outer layer of certain spores

EXIST v **-ED, -ING, -S** to be

EXISTENT n pl. **-S** something that exists

EXIT v **-ED, -ING, -S** to go out

EXITLESS adj lacking a way out

EXOCARP n pl. **-S** the epicarp

EXOCRINE n pl. **-S** an external secretion

EXOCYTIC adj pertaining to cellular excretion

EXODERM n pl. **-S** the ectoderm

EXODOS n pl. **-DOI** a concluding dramatic scene

EXODUS n pl. **-ES** a movement away

EXOERGIC adj releasing energy

EXOGAMY n pl. **-MIES** marriage outside of a particular group **EXOGAMIC** adj

EXOGEN n pl. **-S** a type of plant

EXON n pl. **-S** a sequence in the genetic code **EXONIC** adj

EXONUMIA n/pl collectible items other than coins or paper money

EXONYM n pl. **-S** a name for a people used by outsiders and not by the people themselves

EXORABLE adj persuadable

EXORCISE v **-CISED, -CISING, -CISES** to free of an evil spirit

EXORCISM n pl. **-S** the act of exorcising

EXORCIST n pl. **-S** one who practices exorcism

EXORCIZE v **-CIZED, -CIZING, -CIZES** to exorcise

EXORDIUM n pl. **-DIUMS** or **-DIA** a beginning **EXORDIAL** adj

EXOSMOSE n pl. **-S** a form of osmosis **EXOSMIC** adj

EXOSPORE n pl. **-S** the outer coat of a spore

EXOTERIC adj suitable for the public

EXOTIC n pl. **-S** something from another part of the world

EXOTICA n/pl things excitingly different or unusual

EXOTISM n pl. **-S** an exotic

EXOTOXIN n pl. **-S** an excreted toxin **EXOTOXIC** adj

EXPAND v **-ED, -ING, -S** to increase in size or volume

EXPANDER n pl. **-S** one that expands

EXPANDOR n pl. **-S** a type of transducer

EXPANSE n pl. **-S** a wide, continuous area

EXPAT n pl. **-S** an expatriate person

EXPECT v **-ED, -ING, -S** to anticipate

EXPECTER n pl. **-S** one that expects

EXPEDITE v **-DITED, -DITING, -DITES** to speed up the progress of

EXPEL v **-PELLED, -PELLING, -PELS** to force out

EXPELLEE n pl. **-S** a deportee

EXPELLER n pl. **-S** one that expels

EXPEND v **-ED, -ING, -S** to use up

EXPENDER n pl. **-S** one that expends

EXPENSE v **-PENSED, -PENSING, -PENSES** to charge with costs

EXPERT v **-ED, -ING, -S** to serve as an authority

EXPERTLY adv skillfully

EXPIABLE adj capable of being expiated

EXPIATE v **-ATED, -ATING, -ATES** to atone for

EXPIATOR n pl. **-S** one that expiates

EXPIRE v **-PIRED, -PIRING, -PIRES** to come to an end

EXPIRER n pl. **-S** one that expires

EXPIRY n pl. **-RIES** a termination

EXPLAIN v **-ED, -ING, -S** to make plain or understandable

EXPLANT v **-ED, -ING, -S** to remove from the natural site of growth and place in a medium

EXPLICIT *n* pl. **-S** a statement formerly used at the close of a book

EXPLODE *v* **-PLODED, -PLODING, -PLODES** to blow up

EXPLODER *n* pl. **-S** one that explodes

EXPLOIT *v* **-ED, -ING, -S** to take advantage of

EXPLORE *v* **-PLORED, -PLORING, -PLORES** to travel through for the purpose of discovery

EXPLORER *n* pl. **-S** one that explores

EXPO *n* pl. **-POS** a public exhibition

EXPONENT *n* pl. **-S** one who expounds

EXPORT *v* **-ED, -ING, -S** to send to other countries for commercial purposes

EXPORTER *n* pl. **-S** one that exports

EXPOSAL *n* pl. **-S** an exposure

EXPOSE *v* **-POSED, -POSING, -POSES** to lay open to view

EXPOSER *n* pl. **-S** one that exposes

EXPOSIT *v* **-ED, -ING, -S** to expound

EXPOSURE *n* pl. **-S** the act of exposing

EXPOUND *v* **-ED, -ING, -S** to explain in detail

EXPRESS *v* **-ED, -ING, -ES** to set forth in words

EXPRESSO *n* pl. **-SOS** espresso

EXPULSE *v* **-PULSED, -PULSING, -PULSES** to expel

EXPUNGE *v* **-PUNGED, -PUNGING, -PUNGES** to delete

EXPUNGER *n* pl. **-S** one that expunges

EXSCIND *v* **-ED, -ING, -S** to cut out

EXSECANT *n* pl. **-S** a trigonometric function of an angle

EXSECT *v* **-ED, -ING, -S** to cut out

EXSERT *v* **-ED, -ING, -S** to thrust out

EXTANT *adj* still in existence

EXTEND *v* **-ED, -ING, -S** to stretch out to full length

EXTENDER *n* pl. **-S** a substance added to another substance

EXTENSOR *n* pl. **-S** a muscle that extends a limb

EXTENT *n* pl. **-S** the range over which something extends

EXTERIOR *n* pl. **-S** a part or surface that is outside

EXTERN *n* pl. **-S** a nonresident of an institution

EXTERNAL *n* pl. **-S** an exterior

EXTERNE *n* pl. **-S** extern

EXTINCT *v* **-ED, -ING, -S** to extinguish

EXTOL *v* **-TOLLED, -TOLLING, -TOLS** to praise highly

EXTOLL *v* **-ED, -ING, -S** to extol

EXTOLLER *n* pl. **-S** one that extols

EXTORT *v* **-ED, -ING, -S** to obtain from a person by violence or intimidation

EXTORTER *n* pl. **-S** one that extorts

EXTRA *n* pl. **-S** something additional

EXTRACT *v* **-ED, -ING, -S** to pull or draw out

EXTRADOS *n* pl. **-ES** the outer curve of an arch

EXTRANET *n* pl. **-S** an intranet that permits limited access by outsiders

EXTREMA pl. of extremum

EXTREME *adj* **-TREMER, -TREMEST** existing in a very high degree

EXTREME *n* pl. **-S** the highest degree

EXTREMUM *n* pl. **-MA** a maximum or a minimum of a mathematical function

EXTRORSE *adj* facing outward

EXTRUDE *v* **-TRUDED, -TRUDING, -TRUDES** to force, thrust, or push out

EXTRUDER *n* pl. **-S** one that extrudes

EXTUBATE *v* **-BATED, -BATING, -BATES** to remove a tube from

EXUDATE *n* pl. **-S** an exuded substance

EXUDE *v* **-UDED, -UDING, -UDES** to ooze forth

EXULT *v* **-ED, -ING, -S** to rejoice greatly

EXULTANT *adj* exulting

EXURB *n* pl. **-S** a residential area lying beyond the suburbs of a city **EXURBAN** *adj*

EXURBIA *n* pl. **-S** an exurb

EXUVIATE *v* **-ATED, -ATING, -ATES** to molt

EXUVIUM *n* pl. **-VIAE** or **-VIA** the molted covering of an animal **EXUVIAL** *adj*

EYAS *n* pl. **-ES** a young hawk

EYASS *n* pl. **-ES** eyas

EYE *n* pl. **EYES, EYEN** or **EYNE** the organ of sight

EYE *v* **EYED, EYING** or **EYEING, EYES** to watch closely **EYEABLE** *adj*

EYEBALL *v* **-ED, -ING, -S** to eye

EYEBAR *n* pl. **-S** a metal bar with a loop at one or both ends

EYEBEAM *n* pl. **-S** a glance

EYEBLACK *n* pl. **-S** a dark pigment applied under the eyes

EYEBLINK *n* pl. **-S** an instant

EYEBOLT *n* pl. **-S** a type of bolt or screw

EYEBROW *n* pl. **-S** the ridge over the eye

EYECUP *n* pl. **-S** a cup used for applying lotions to the eyes

EYED past tense of eye

EYEDNESS *n* pl. **-ES** preference for the use of one eye over the other

EYEDROPS *n/pl* a medicated solution for the eyes applied in drops

EYEFOLD *n* pl. **-S** a fold of skin of the upper eyelid

EYEFUL *n* pl. **-S** a complete view

EYEGLASS *n* pl. **-ES** a lens used to aid vision

EYEHOLE *n* pl. **-S** a small opening

EYEHOOK *n* pl. **-S** a type of hook

EYELASH *n* pl. **-ES** a hair growing on the edge of an eyelid

EYELESS *adj* lacking eyes

EYELET *v* **-LETTED, -LETTING, -LETS** to make a small hole in

EYELID *n* pl. **-S** the lid of skin that can be closed over an eyeball

EYELIFT *n* pl. **-S** plastic surgery of the eyelid

EYELIKE *adj* resembling an eye

EYELINER *n* pl. **-S** makeup for the eyes

EYEN a pl. of eye

EYEPIECE *n* pl. **-S** the lens or lens group nearest the eye in an optical instrument

EYEPOINT *n* pl. **-S** the point at which an eye is placed in using an optical instrument

EYER *n* pl. **-S** one that eyes

EYESHADE *n* pl. **-S** a visor for shading the eyes

EYESHINE *n* pl. **-S** a reflection from the eyes of some animals

EYESHOT *n* pl. **-S** the range of vision

EYESIGHT *n* pl. **-S** the ability to see

EYESOME *adj* pleasant to look at

EYESORE *n* pl. **-S** something offensive to the sight

EYESPOT *n* pl. **-S** a simple visual organ of lower animals

EYESTALK *n* pl. **-S** a stalklike structure with an eye at its tip

EYESTONE *n* pl. **-S** a disk used to remove foreign matter from the eye

EYETOOTH *n* pl. **-TEETH** a cuspid

EYEWASH *n* pl. **-ES** an eye lotion

EYEWATER *n* pl. **-S** an eyewash

EYEWEAR *n* pl. **EYEWEAR** a device worn on or over the eyes

EYEWINK *n* pl. **-S** a wink of the eye

EYING a present participle of eye

EYNE a pl. of eye

EYRA *n* pl. **-S** a wild cat of tropical America

EYRE *n* pl. **-S** a journey

EYRIE *n* pl. **-S** aerie

EYRIR *n* pl. **AURAR** a monetary unit of Iceland

EYRY *n* pl. **-RIES** aerie

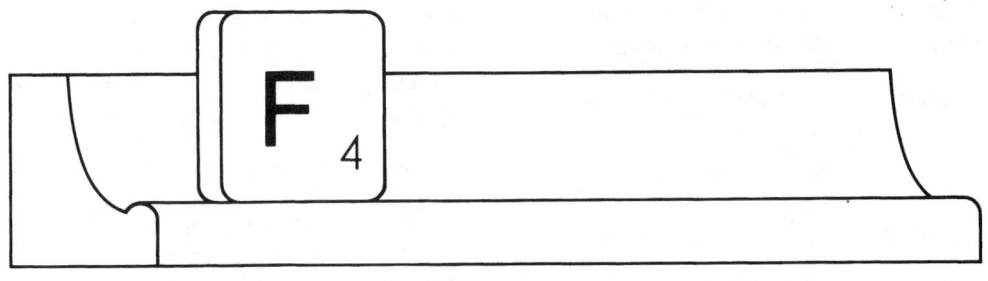

FA   *n* pl. **-S** the fourth tone of the diatonic musical scale

FAB   *n* pl. **-S** something created or constructed

FAB   *adj* **FABBER, FABBEST** fabulous

FABLE   *v* **-BLED, -BLING, -BLES** to compose or tell fictitious tales

FABLER   *n* pl. **-S** one that fables

FABLIAU   *n* pl. **-AUX** a short metrical tale popular in medieval France

FABLING   present participle of fable

FABRIC   *n* pl. **-S** a woven, felted, or knitted material

FABULAR   *adj* legendary

FABULATE   *v* **-LATED, -LATING, -LATES** to compose fables

FABULIST   *n* pl. **-S** a liar

FABULOUS   *adj* almost unbelievable

FACADE   *n* pl. **-S** the front of a building

FACE   *v* **FACED, FACING, FACES** to oppose or meet defiantly **FACEABLE** *adj*

FACEDOWN   *n* pl. **-S** a confrontation between opponents

FACELESS   *adj* lacking personal distinction or identity

FACELIFT   *v* **-ED, -ING, -S** to perform plastic surgery on the face

FACEMASK   *n* pl. **-S** a device to shield the face

FACER   *n* pl. **-S** one that faces

FACET   *v* **-ETED, -ETING, -ETS** or **-ETTED, -ETTING, -ETS** to cut small plane surfaces on

FACETE   *adj* witty **FACETELY** *adv*

FACETIAE   *n/pl* witty sayings or writings

FACEUP   *adv* with the front part up

FACIA   *n* pl. **-CIAE** or **-CIAS** fascia

FACIAL   *n* pl. **-S** a treatment for the face

FACIALLY   *adv* with respect to the face

FACIEND   *n* pl. **-S** a number to be multiplied by another

FACIES   *n* pl. **FACIES** general appearance

FACILE   *adj* easily achieved or performed **FACILELY** *adv*

FACILITY   *n* pl. **-TIES** the quality of being facile

FACING   *n* pl. **-S** a lining at the edge of a garment

FACT   *n* pl. **-S** something known with certainty **FACTFUL** *adj*

FACTION   *n* pl. **-S** a clique within a larger group

FACTIOUS   *adj* promoting dissension

FACTOID   *n* pl. **-S** a brief news item

FACTOR   *v* **-ED, -ING, -S** to express as a product of two or more quantities

FACTORY   *n* pl. **-RIES** a building or group of buildings in which goods are manufactured

FACTOTUM   *n* pl. **-S** a person employed to do many kinds of work

FACTUAL   *adj* pertaining to facts

FACTURE   *n* pl. **-S** the act of making something

FACULA   *n* pl. **-LAE** an unusually bright spot on the sun's surface **FACULAR** *adj*

FACULTY   *n* pl. **-TIES** an inherent power or ability

FAD   *n* pl. **-S** a practice or interest that enjoys brief popularity

FADABLE   *adj* capable of fading

FADDIER   comparative of faddy

FADDIEST   superlative of faddy

FADDISH   *adj* inclined to take up fads

FADDISM   *n* pl. **-S** inclination to take up fads

FADDIST   *n* pl. **-S** a faddish person

FADDY   *adj* **-DIER, -DIEST** faddish

FADE   *v* **FADED, FADING, FADES** to lose color or brightness **FADEDLY** *adv*

FADEAWAY   *n* pl. **-AWAYS** a type of pitch in baseball

FADEIN   *n* pl. **-S** a gradual increase in the brightness of an image

FADELESS   *adj* not fading

FADEOUT   *n* pl. **-S** a gradual disappearance of an image

FADER   *n* pl. **-S** one that fades

FADGE   *v* **FADGED, FADGING, FADGES** to succeed

FADING   *n* pl. **-S** an Irish dance

FADLIKE   *adj* resembling a fad

FADO   *n* pl. **-DOS** a Portuguese folk song

FAECES   *n/pl* feces **FAECAL** *adj*

FAENA   *n* pl. **-S** a series of passes made by a matador in a bullfight

FAERIE   *n* pl. **-S** a fairy

FAERY   *n* pl. **-ERIES** faerie

FAG   *v* **FAGGED, FAGGING, FAGS** to make weary by hard work

FAGGOT   *v* **-ED, -ING, -S** to fagot

FAGIN   *n* pl. **-S** a person who instructs others in crime

FAGOT   *v* **-ED, -ING, -S** to bind together into a bundle

FAGOTER   *n* pl. **-S** one that fagots

FAGOTING   *n* pl. **-S** a type of embroidery

FAHLBAND   *n* pl. **-S** a band or stratum of rock impregnated with metallic sulfides

FAIENCE   *n* pl. **-S** a variety of glazed pottery

FAIL   *v* **-ED, -ING, -S** to be unsuccessful in an attempt

FAILING   *n* pl. **-S** a minor fault or weakness

FAILLE   *n* pl. **-S** a woven fabric

FAILURE   *n* pl. **-S** the act of failing

FAIN   *adj* **FAINER, FAINEST** glad

FAINEANT   *n* pl. **-S** a lazy person

FAINT   *adj* **FAINTER, FAINTEST** lacking strength or vigor

FAINT   *v* **-ED, -ING, -S** to lose consciousness

FAINTER   *n* pl. **-S** one that faints

FAINTISH   *adj* somewhat faint

FAINTLY   *adv* in a faint manner

FAIR   *adj* **FAIRER, FAIREST** free from bias, dishonesty, or injustice

FAIR   *v* **-ED, -ING, -S** to make smooth

FAIRGOER   *n* pl. **-S** one who attends a fair

FAIRIES   pl. of fairy

FAIRING   *n* pl. **-S** a structure on an aircraft serving to reduce drag

FAIRISH   *adj* moderately good

FAIRLEAD   *n* pl. **-S** a device used to hold a ship's rigging in place

FAIRLY   *adv* in a fair manner

FAIRNESS   *n* pl. **-ES** the quality of being fair

FAIRWAY   *n* pl. **-WAYS** the mowed part of a golf course between tee and green

FAIRY   *n* pl. **FAIRIES** an imaginary supernatural being

FAIRYISM   *n* pl. **-S** the quality of being like a fairy

FAITH   *v* **-ED, -ING, -S** to believe or trust

FAITHFUL   *n* pl. **-S** a loyal follower or member

FAITOUR   *n* pl. **-S** an impostor

FAJITA   *n* pl. **-S** marinated and grilled beef, chicken, or shrimp served with a flour tortilla

FAKE   *v* **FAKED, FAKING, FAKES** to contrive and present as genuine

FAKEER   *n* pl. **-S** fakir

FAKER   *n* pl. **-S** one that fakes

FAKERY   *n* pl. **-ERIES** the practice of faking

FAKEY   *adj* not genuine; phony

FAKING   present participle of fake

FAKIR   *n* pl. **-S** a Hindu ascetic

FALAFEL   *n* pl. **-S** ground spiced vegetables formed into patties

FALBALA   *n* pl. **-S** a trimming for a woman's garment

FALCATE   *adj* curved and tapering to a point

FALCATED   *adj* falcate

FALCES   pl. of falx

FALCHION   *n* pl. **-S** a broad-bladed sword

FALCON   *n* pl. **-S** a bird of prey

FALCONER   *n* pl. **-S** one that hunts with hawks

FALCONET   *n* pl. **-S** a small falcon

FALCONRY   *n* pl. **-RIES** the sport of hunting with falcons

FALDERAL   *n* pl. **-S** nonsense

FALDEROL   *n* pl. **-S** falderal

FALL   *v* **FELL, FALLEN, FALLING, FALLS** to descend under the force of gravity

FALLACY *n* pl. **-CIES** a false idea

FALLAL *n* pl. **-S** a showy article of dress

FALLAWAY *n* pl. **-AWAYS** a shot in basketball

FALLBACK *n* pl. **-S** an act of retreating

FALLEN past participle of fall

FALLER *n* pl. **-S** one that falls

FALLFISH *n* pl. **-ES** a freshwater fish

FALLIBLE *adj* capable of erring **FALLIBLY** *adv*

FALLOFF *n* pl. **-S** a decline in quantity or quality

FALLOUT *n* pl. **-S** radioactive debris resulting from a nuclear explosion

FALLOW *v* **-ED, -ING, -S** to plow and leave unseeded

FALSE *adj* **FALSER, FALSEST** contrary to truth or fact **FALSELY** *adv*

FALSETTO *n* pl. **-TOS** an artificially high voice

FALSIE *n* pl. **-S** a pad worn within a brassiere

FALSIFY *v* **-FIED, -FYING, -FIES** to represent falsely

FALSITY *n* pl. **-TIES** something false

FALTBOAT *n* pl. **-S** a collapsible boat resembling a kayak

FALTER *v* **-ED, -ING, -S** to hesitate

FALTERER *n* pl. **-S** one that falters

FALX *n* pl. **FALCES** a sickle-shaped structure

FAME *v* **FAMED, FAMING, FAMES** to make famous

FAMELESS *adj* not famous

FAMILIAL *adj* pertaining to a family

FAMILIAR *n* pl. **-S** a close friend or associate

FAMILISM *n* pl. **-S** a social structure in which the family takes precedence over the individual

FAMILY *n* pl. **-LIES** a group of persons related by blood or marriage

FAMINE *n* pl. **-S** a widespread scarcity of food

FAMING present participle of fame

FAMISH *v* **-ED, -ING, -ES** to suffer extreme hunger

FAMOUS *adj* well-known **FAMOUSLY** *adv*

FAMULUS *n* pl. **-LI** a servant or attendant

FAN *v* **FANNED, FANNING, FANS** to cool or refresh with a fan (a device for putting air into motion)

FANATIC *n* pl. **-S** a zealot

FANCIED past tense of fancy

FANCIER *n* pl. **-S** one that has a special liking for something

FANCIES present 3d person sing. of fancy

FANCIFUL *adj* unrealistic

FANCIFY *v* **-FIED, -FYING, -FIES** to make fancy

FANCY *adj* **-CIER, -CIEST** ornamental **FANCILY** *adv*

FANCY *v* **-CIED, -CYING, -CIES** to take a liking to

FANDANGO *n* pl. **-GOS** a lively Spanish dance

FANDOM *n* pl. **-S** an aggregate of enthusiastic devotees

FANE *n* pl. **-S** a temple

FANEGA *n* pl. **-S** a Spanish unit of dry measure

FANEGADA *n* pl. **-S** a Spanish unit of area

FANFARE *n* pl. **-S** a short, lively musical flourish

FANFARON *n* pl. **-S** a braggart

FANFIC *n* pl. **-S** fiction written by fans of an admired work

FANFOLD *v* **-ED, -ING, -S** to fold paper like a fan

FANG *n* pl. **-S** a long, pointed tooth **FANGED, FANGLESS, FANGLIKE** *adj*

FANGA *n* pl. **-S** fanega

FANION *n* pl. **-S** a small flag

FANJET *n* pl. **-S** a type of jet engine

FANLIGHT *n* pl. **-S** a type of window

FANLIKE *adj* resembling a fan

FANNED past tense of fan

FANNER *n* pl. **-S** one that fans

FANNING present participle of fan

FANNY *n* pl. **-NIES** the buttocks

FANO *n* pl. **FANOS** a fanon

FANON *n* pl. **-S** a cape worn by the pope

FANTAIL *n* pl. **-S** a fan-shaped tail or end

FANTASIA *n* pl. **-S** a free-form musical composition

FANTASIE *n* pl. **-S** a fantasia

FANTASIED past tense of fantasy

FANTASM *n* pl. **-S** phantasm

FANTAST *n* pl. **-S** an impractical person

FANTASY *v* **-SIED, -SYING, -SIES** to imagine

FANTOD *n* pl. **-S** an emotional outburst

FANTOM *n* pl. **-S** phantom

FANUM *n* pl. **-S** fanon

FANWISE *adj* spread out like an open fan

FANWORT *n* pl. **-S** an aquatic plant

FANZINE *n* pl. **-S** a magazine written by and for enthusiastic devotees

FAQIR *n* pl. **-S** fakir

FAQUIR *n* pl. **-S** fakir

FAR *adv* **FARTHER, FARTHEST** or **FURTHER, FURTHEST** at or to a great distance

FARAD *n* pl. **-S** a unit of electrical capacitance

FARADAIC *adj* faradic

FARADAY *n* pl. **-DAYS** a unit of electricity

FARADIC *adj* pertaining to a type of electric current

FARADISE *v* **-DISED, -DISING, -DISES** to faradize

FARADISM *n* pl. **-S** the use of faradic current for therapeutic purposes

FARADIZE *v* **-DIZED, -DIZING, -DIZES** to treat by faradism

FARAWAY *adj* distant

FARCE *v* **FARCED, FARCING, FARCES** to fill out with witty material

FARCER *n* pl. **-S** farceur

FARCEUR *n* pl. **-S** a joker

FARCI *adj* stuffed with finely chopped meat

FARCICAL *adj* absurd

FARCIE *adj* farci

FARCING present participle of farce

FARCY *n* pl. **-CIES** a disease of horses

FARD *v* **-ED, -ING, -S** to apply cosmetics to

FARDEL *n* pl. **-S** a bundle

FARE *v* **FARED, FARING, FARES** to get along

FAREBOX *n* pl. **-ES** a receptacle for fares on a bus

FARER *n* pl. **-S** a traveler

FAREWELL *v* **-ED, -ING, -S** to say goodby

FARFAL *n* pl. **-S** farfel

FARFALLE *n* pl. **FARFALLE** pasta in the shape of bow ties

FARFEL *n* pl. **-S** noodles in the form of small pellets or granules

FARINA *n* pl. **-S** a fine meal made from cereal grain

FARING present participle of fare

FARINHA *n* pl. **-S** a meal made from the root of the cassava

FARINOSE *adj* resembling farina

FARL *n* pl. **-S** a thin oatmeal cake

FARLE *n* pl. **-S** farl

FARM *v* **-ED, -ING, -S** to manage and cultivate as a farm (a tract of land devoted to agriculture) **FARMABLE** *adj*

FARMER *n* pl. **-S** one that farms

FARMHAND *n* pl. **-S** a farm laborer

FARMING *n* pl. **-S** the business of operating a farm

FARMLAND *n* pl. **-S** cultivated land

FARMWIFE *n* pl. **-WIVES** a farmer's wife

FARMWORK *n* pl. **-S** labor done on a farm

FARMYARD *n* pl. **-S** an area surrounded by farm buildings

FARNESOL *n* pl. **-S** an alcohol used in perfumes

FARNESS *n* pl. **-ES** the state of being far off or apart

FARO *n* pl. **FAROS** a card game

FAROLITO *n* pl. **-TOS** a candle in a paper bag weighted with sand

FAROUCHE *adj* sullenly shy

FARRAGO *n* pl. **-GOES** a confused mixture

FARRIER *n* pl. **-S** one that shoes horses

FARRIERY *n* pl. **-ERIES** the trade of a farrier

FARROW *v* **-ED, -ING, -S** to give birth to a litter of pigs

FARSIDE *n* pl. **-S** the farther side

FARTHER a comparative of far

FARTHEST a superlative of far

FARTHING *n* pl. **-S** a former British coin

FARTLEK *n* pl. **-S** an athletic training technique

FASCES *n* pl. **FASCES** an ancient Roman symbol of power

FASCIA *n* pl. **-CIAS** or **-CIAE** a broad and distinct band of color **FASCIAL, FASCIATE** *adj*

FASCICLE *n* pl. **-S** a small bundle

FASCINE *n* pl. **-S** a bundle of sticks used in building fortifications

FASCISM *n* pl. **-S** an oppressive political system

FASCIST	*n* pl. **-S** an advocate of fascism
FASCITIS	*n* pl. **-TISES** inflammation of a connective tissue
FASH	*v* **-ED, -ING, -ES** to annoy
FASHION	*v* **-ED, -ING, -S** to give a particular shape or form to
FASHIOUS	*adj* annoying
FAST	*adj* **FASTER, FASTEST** moving or able to move quickly
FAST	*v* **-ED, -ING, -S** to abstain from eating
FASTBACK	*n* pl. **-S** a type of automobile roof
FASTBALL	*n* pl. **-S** a type of pitch in baseball
FASTEN	*v* **-ED, -ING, -S** to secure
FASTENER	*n* pl. **-S** one that fastens
FASTING	*n* pl. **-S** abstention from eating
FASTNESS	*n* pl. **-ES** the quality of being fast
FASTUOUS	*adj* arrogant
FAT	*adj* **FATTER, FATTEST** having an abundance of flesh
FAT	*v* **FATTED, FATTING, FATS** to make fat
FATAL	*adj* causing or capable of causing death
FATALISM	*n* pl. **-S** the doctrine that all events are predetermined
FATALIST	*n* pl. **-S** a believer in fatalism
FATALITY	*n* pl. **-TIES** a death resulting from an unexpected occurrence
FATALLY	*adv* in a fatal manner
FATBACK	*n* pl. **-S** a marine fish
FATBIRD	*n* pl. **-S** a wading bird
FATE	*v* **FATED, FATING, FATES** to destine
FATEFUL	*adj* decisively important
FATHEAD	*n* pl. **-S** a dolt
FATHER	*v* **-ED, -ING, -S** to cause to exist
FATHERLY	*adj* paternal
FATHOM	*v* **-ED, -ING, -S** to understand
FATHOMER	*n* pl. **-S** one that fathoms
FATIDIC	*adj* pertaining to prophecy
FATIGUE	*v* **-TIGUED, -TIGUING, -TIGUES** to weary
FATING	present participle of fate
FATLESS	*adj* having no fat
FATLIKE	*adj* resembling fat
FATLING	*n* pl. **-S** a young animal fattened for slaughter
FATLY	*adv* in the manner of one that is fat
FATNESS	*n* pl. **-ES** the state of being fat
FATSTOCK	*n* pl. **-S** livestock that is fat and ready for market
FATTED	past tense of fat
FATTEN	*v* **-ED, -ING, -S** to make fat
FATTENER	*n* pl. **-S** one that fattens
FATTER	comparative of fat
FATTEST	superlative of fat
FATTIER	comparative of fatty
FATTIES	pl. of fatty
FATTIEST	superlative of fatty
FATTILY	*adv* in a fatty manner
FATTING	present participle of fat
FATTISH	*adj* somewhat fat
FATTY	*adj* **-TIER, -TIEST** greasy; oily
FATTY	*n* pl. **-TIES** one that is fat
FATUITY	*n* pl. **-ITIES** something foolish or stupid
FATUOUS	*adj* smugly stupid
FATWA	*n* pl. **-S** an Islamic legal decree
FATWOOD	*n* pl. **-S** wood used for kindling
FAUBOURG	*n* pl. **-S** a suburb
FAUCAL	*n* pl. **-S** a sound produced in the fauces
FAUCES	*n/pl* the passage from the mouth to the pharynx
FAUCET	*n* pl. **-S** a device for controlling the flow of liquid from a pipe
FAUCIAL	*adj* pertaining to the fauces
FAUGH	*interj* — used to express disgust
FAULD	*n* pl. **-S** a piece of armor below the breastplate
FAULT	*v* **-ED, -ING, -S** to criticize
FAULTY	*adj* **FAULTIER, FAULTIEST** imperfect **FAULTILY** *adv*
FAUN	*n* pl. **-S** a woodland deity of Roman mythology **FAUNLIKE** *adj*
FAUNA	*n* pl. **-NAS** or **-NAE** the animal life of a particular region **FAUNAL** *adj* **FAUNALLY** *adv*
FAUTEUIL	*n* pl. **-S** an armchair
FAUVE	*n* pl. **-S** a fauvist
FAUVISM	*n* pl. **-S** a movement in painting
FAUVIST	*n* pl. **-S** an advocate of fauvism
FAUX	*adj* not genuine; fake
FAVA	*n* pl. **-S** the edible seed of a climbing vine

FAVE *n* pl. **-S** a favorite

FAVELA *n* pl. **-S** a slum area

FAVELLA *n* pl. **-S** favela

FAVISM *n* pl. **-S** an acute anemia

FAVONIAN *adj* pertaining to the west wind

FAVOR *v* **-ED, -ING, -S** to regard with approval

FAVORER *n* pl. **-S** one that favors

FAVORITE *n* pl. **-S** a person or thing preferred above all others

FAVOUR *v* **-ED, -ING, -S** to favor

FAVOURER *n* pl. **-S** favorer

FAVUS *n* pl. **-ES** a skin disease

FAWN *v* **-ED, -ING, -S** to seek notice or favor by servile demeanor

FAWNER *n* pl. **-S** one that fawns

FAWNLIKE *adj* resembling a young deer

FAWNY *adj* **FAWNIER, FAWNIEST** of a yellowish-brown color

FAX *v* **-ED, -ING, -ES** to transmit and reproduce by electronic means

FAY *v* **-ED, -ING, -S** to join closely

FAYALITE *n* pl. **-S** a mineral

FAZE *v* **FAZED, FAZING, FAZES** to disturb the composure of

FAZENDA *n* pl. **-S** a Brazilian plantation

FE *n* pl. **-S** a Hebrew letter

FEAL *adj* loyal

FEALTY *n* pl. **-TIES** loyalty

FEAR *v* **-ED, -ING, -S** to be afraid of

FEARER *n* pl. **-S** one that fears

FEARFUL *adj* **-FULLER, -FULLEST** afraid

FEARLESS *adj* unafraid

FEARSOME *adj* frightening

FEASANCE *n* pl. **-S** the performance of a condition, obligation, or duty

FEASE *v* **FEASED, FEASING, FEASES** to faze

FEASIBLE *adj* capable of being done **FEASIBLY** *adv*

FEAST *v* **-ED, -ING, -S** to eat sumptuously

FEASTER *n* pl. **-S** one that feasts

FEASTFUL *adj* festive

FEAT *adj* **FEATER, FEATEST** skillful

FEAT *n* pl. **-S** a notable act or achievement

FEATHER *v* **-ED, -ING, -S** to cover with feathers (horny structures that form the principal covering of birds)

FEATHERY *adj* **-ERIER, -ERIEST** resembling feathers

FEATLY *adj* **-LIER, -LIEST** graceful

FEATURE *v* **-TURED, -TURING, -TURES** to give special prominence to

FEAZE *v* **FEAZED, FEAZING, FEAZES** to faze

FEBRIFIC *adj* feverish

FEBRILE *adj* feverish

FECAL *adj* pertaining to feces

FECES *n/pl* bodily waste discharged through the anus

FECIAL *n* pl. **-S** fetial

FECK *n* pl. **-S** value

FECKLESS *adj* worthless

FECKLY *adv* almost

FECULA *n* pl. **-LAE** fecal matter

FECULENT *adj* foul with impurities

FECUND *adj* fruitful

FED *n* pl. **-S** a federal agent

FEDAYEE *n* pl. **-YEEN** an Arab commando

FEDERACY *n* pl. **-CIES** an alliance

FEDERAL *n* pl. **-S** a supporter of a type of central government

FEDERATE *v* **-ATED, -ATING, -ATES** to unite in an alliance

FEDEX *v* **-ED, -ING, -ES** to send by Federal Express

FEDORA *n* pl. **-S** a type of hat

FEE *v* **FEED, FEEING, FEES** to pay a fee (a fixed charge) to

FEEB *n* pl. **-S** a wimp (a weak or ineffective person)

FEEBLE *adj* **-BLER, -BLEST** weak **FEEBLY** *adv*

FEEBLISH *adj* somewhat feeble

FEED *v* **FED, FEEDING, FEEDS** to give food to **FEEDABLE** *adj*

FEEDBACK *n* pl. **-S** the return of a portion of the output to the input

FEEDBAG *n* pl. **-S** a bag for feeding horses

FEEDBOX *n* pl. **-ES** a box for animal feed

FEEDER *n* pl. **-S** one that feeds

FEEDHOLE *n* pl. **-S** one of a series of holes in paper tape

FEEDLOT *n* pl. **-S** a plot of land on which livestock is fattened

FEEDYARD	n pl. **-S** a feedlot	**FELLOW**	v **-ED, -ING, -S** to produce an equal to
FEEL	v **FELT, FEELING, FEELS** to perceive through the sense of touch	**FELLOWLY**	adj friendly
		FELLY	n pl. **-LIES** a felloe
FEELER	n pl. **-S** a tactile organ	**FELON**	n pl. **-S** a person who has committed a felony
FEELESS	adj requiring no fee		
FEELING	n pl. **-S** the function or power of perceiving by touch	**FELONRY**	n pl. **-RIES** the whole class of felons
FEET	pl. of foot	**FELONY**	n pl. **-NIES** a grave crime
FEETLESS	adj having no feet	**FELSIC**	adj consisting of feldspar and silicates
FEEZE	v **FEEZED, FEEZING, FEEZES** to faze	**FELSITE**	n pl. **-S** an igneous rock **FELSITIC** adj
FEH	n pl. **-S** peh		
FEIGN	v **-ED, -ING, -S** to pretend	**FELSPAR**	n pl. **-S** feldspar
FEIGNER	n pl. **-S** one that feigns	**FELSTONE**	n pl. **-S** felsite
FEIJOA	n pl. **-S** a green edible fruit	**FELT**	v **-ED, -ING, -S** to mat together
FEINT	v **-ED, -ING, -S** to make a deceptive movement	**FELTING**	n pl. **-S** felted material
		FELTLIKE	adj like a cloth made from wool
FEIRIE	adj nimble	**FELUCCA**	n pl. **-S** a swift sailing vessel
FEIST	n pl. **-S** a small dog of mixed breed	**FELWORT**	n pl. **-S** a flowering plant
		FEM	n pl. **-S** a passive homosexual
FEISTY	adj **FEISTIER, FEISTIEST** full of nervous energy **FEISTILY** adv	**FEMALE**	n pl. **-S** an individual that bears young or produces ova
FELAFEL	n pl. **-S** falafel	**FEME**	n pl. **-S** a wife
FELDSHER	n pl. **-S** a medical worker in Russia	**FEMINACY**	n pl. **-CIES** the state of being a female
FELDSPAR	n pl. **-S** a mineral		
FELICITY	n pl. **-TIES** happiness	**FEMINIE**	n/pl women collectively
FELID	n pl. **-S** a feline	**FEMININE**	n pl. **-S** a word or form having feminine gender
FELINE	n pl. **-S** an animal of the cat family		
FELINELY	adv in a catlike manner	**FEMINISE**	v **-NISED, -NISING, -NISES** to feminize
FELINITY	n pl. **-TIES** the quality of being catlike	**FEMINISM**	n pl. **-S** a doctrine advocating rights for women equal to those of men
FELL	adj **FELLER, FELLEST** cruel		
FELL	v **-ED, -ING, -S** to cause to fall	**FEMINIST**	n pl. **-S** a supporter of feminism
FELLA	n pl. **-S** a man or boy	**FEMINITY**	n pl. **-TIES** the quality of being womanly
FELLABLE	adj capable of being felled		
FELLAH	n pl. **-LAHS, -LAHIN** or **-LAHEEN** a peasant or laborer in Arab countries	**FEMINIZE**	v **-NIZED, -NIZING, -NIZES** to make womanly
		FEMME	n pl. **-S** a woman
FELLATE	v **-LATED, -LATING, -LATES** to perform fellatio	**FEMORAL**	adj pertaining to the femur
		FEMUR	n pl. **-MURS** or **-MORA** a bone of the leg
FELLATIO	n pl. **-TIOS** oral stimulation of the penis		
		FEN	n pl. **-S** a marsh
FELLATOR	n pl. **-S** one that fellates	**FENAGLE**	v **-GLED, -GLING, -GLES** to finagle
FELLER	n pl. **-S** one that fells		
FELLIES	pl. of felly	**FENCE**	v **FENCED, FENCING, FENCES** to practice the art of fencing
FELLNESS	n pl. **-ES** extreme cruelty		
FELLOE	n pl. **-S** the rim of a wheel	**FENCER**	n pl. **-S** one that fences

FENCEROW *n pl.* **-S** the land occupied by a fence

FENCIBLE *n pl.* **-S** a soldier enlisted for home service only

FENCING *n pl.* **-S** the art of using a sword in attack and defense

FEND *v* **-ED, -ING, -S** to ward off

FENDER *n pl.* **-S** a metal guard over the wheel of a motor vehicle **FENDERED** *adj*

FENESTRA *n pl.* **-TRAE** a small anatomical opening

FENLAND *n pl.* **-S** marshy ground

FENNEC *n pl.* **-S** an African fox

FENNEL *n pl.* **-S** a perennial herb

FENNY *adj* **-NIER, -NIEST** marshy

FENTANYL *n pl.* **-S** a narcotic opioid

FENTHION *n pl.* **-S** an insecticide

FENURON *n pl.* **-S** an herbicide

FEOD *n pl.* **-S** a fief

FEODARY *n pl.* **-RIES** a vassal

FEOFF *v* **-ED, -ING, -S** to grant a fief to

FEOFFEE *n pl.* **-S** one to whom a fief is granted

FEOFFER *n pl.* **-S** one that grants a fief to another

FEOFFOR *n pl.* **-S** feoffer

FER *prep* for

FERACITY *n pl.* **-TIES** the state of being fruitful

FERAL *n pl.* **-S** a wild beast

FERBAM *n pl.* **-S** a fungicide

FERE *n pl.* **-S** a companion

FERETORY *n pl.* **-RIES** a receptacle in which sacred relics are kept

FERIA *n pl.* **-RIAS** or **-RIAE** a weekday of a church calendar on which no feast is celebrated **FERIAL** *adj*

FERINE *adj* feral

FERITY *n pl.* **-TIES** wildness

FERLIE *n pl.* **-S** a strange sight

FERLY *n pl.* **-LIES** ferlie

FERMATA *n pl.* **-TAS** or **-TE** the sustaining of a musical note, chord, or rest beyond its written time value

FERMENT *v* **-ED, -ING, -S** to undergo a type of chemical reaction

FERMI *n pl.* **-S** a unit of length

FERMION *n pl.* **-S** a type of atomic particle

FERMIUM *n pl.* **-S** a radioactive element

FERN *n pl.* **-S** a flowerless vascular plant **FERNLESS, FERNLIKE** *adj*

FERNERY *n pl.* **-ERIES** a place in which ferns are grown

FERNINST *prep* near to

FERNY *adj* **FERNIER, FERNIEST** abounding in ferns

FEROCITY *n pl.* **-TIES** fierceness

FERRATE *n pl.* **-S** a chemical salt

FERREL *v* **-RELED, -RELING, -RELS** or **-RELLED, -RELLING, -RELS** to ferrule

FERREOUS *adj* containing iron

FERRET *v* **-ED, -ING, -S** to search out by careful investigation

FERRETER *n pl.* **-S** one that ferrets

FERRETY *adj* suggestive of a ferret (a polecat)

FERRIAGE *n pl.* **-S** transportation by ferry

FERRIC *adj* pertaining to iron

FERRIED past tense of ferry

FERRIES present 3d person sing. of ferry

FERRITE *n pl.* **-S** a magnetic substance **FERRITIC** *adj*

FERRITIN *n pl.* **-S** a protein that contains iron

FERROUS *adj* pertaining to iron

FERRULE *v* **-RULED, -RULING, -RULES** to furnish with a metal ring or cap to prevent splitting

FERRUM *n pl.* **-S** iron

FERRY *v* **-RIED, -RYING, -RIES** to transport by ferry (a type of boat)

FERRYMAN *n pl.* **-MEN** one who operates a ferry

FERTILE *adj* capable of reproducing

FERULA *n pl.* **-LAS** or **-LAE** a flat piece of wood

FERULE *v* **-ULED, -ULING, -ULES** to ferrule

FERVENCY *n pl.* **-CIES** fervor

FERVENT *adj* marked by fervor

FERVID *adj* fervent **FERVIDLY** *adv*

FERVOR *n pl.* **-S** great warmth or intensity

FERVOUR *n pl.* **-S** fervor

FESCUE *n pl.* **-S** a perennial grass

FESS *v* **-ED, -ING, -ES** to confess

FESSE *n pl.* **-S** a horizontal band across the middle of a heraldic shield

FESSWISE *adv* horizontally

FEST	*n* pl. **-S** a gathering for an activity
FESTAL	*adj* festive **FESTALLY** *adv*
FESTER	*v* **-ED, -ING, -S** to generate pus
FESTIVAL	*n* pl. **-S** a day or time of celebration
FESTIVE	*adj* of or befitting a festival
FESTOON	*v* **-ED, -ING, -S** to hang decorative chains or strips on
FET	*v* **FETTED, FETTING, FETS** to fetch
FETA	*n* pl. **-S** a Greek cheese
FETAL	*adj* pertaining to a fetus
FETATION	*n* pl. **-S** the development of a fetus
FETCH	*v* **-ED, -ING, -ES** to go after and bring back
FETCHER	*n* pl. **-S** one that fetches
FETE	*v* **FETED, FETING, FETES** to honor with a celebration
FETERITA	*n* pl. **-S** a cereal grass
FETIAL	*n* pl. **-S** a priest of ancient Rome
FETIALIS	*n* pl. **-LES** fetial
FETICH	*n* pl. **-ES** fetish
FETICIDE	*n* pl. **-S** the killing of a fetus
FETID	*adj* having an offensive odor **FETIDLY** *adv*
FETIDITY	*n* pl. **-TIES** the state of being fetid
FETING	present participle of fete
FETISH	*n* pl. **-ES** an object believed to have magical power
FETLOCK	*n* pl. **-S** a joint of a horse's leg
FETOLOGY	*n* pl. **-GIES** the branch of medicine dealing with the fetus
FETOR	*n* pl. **-S** an offensive odor
FETTED	past tense of fet
FETTER	*v* **-ED, -ING, -S** to shackle
FETTERER	*n* pl. **-S** one that fetters
FETTING	present participle of fet
FETTLE	*v* **-TLED, -TLING, -TLES** to cover the hearth of with fettling
FETTLING	*n* pl. **-S** loose material thrown on the hearth of a furnace to protect it
FETUS	*n* pl. **-ES** the unborn organism carried within the womb in the later stages of its development
FEU	*v* **-ED, -ING, -S** to grant land to under Scottish feudal law
FEUAR	*n* pl. **-S** one granted land under Scottish feudal law
FEUD	*v* **-ED, -ING, -S** to engage in a feud (a bitter, continuous hostility)
FEUDAL	*adj* pertaining to a political and economic system of medieval Europe **FEUDALLY** *adv*
FEUDARY	*n* pl. **-RIES** a vassal
FEUDIST	*n* pl. **-S** one that feuds
FEVER	*v* **-ED, -ING, -S** to affect with fever (abnormal elevation of the body temperature)
FEVERFEW	*n* pl. **-S** a perennial herb
FEVERISH	*adj* having a fever
FEVEROUS	*adj* feverish
FEW	*adj* **FEWER, FEWEST** amounting to or consisting of a small number
FEWNESS	*n* pl. **-ES** the state of being few
FEWTRILS	*n/pl* things of little value
FEY	*adj* **FEYER, FEYEST** crazy **FEYLY** *adv*
FEYNESS	*n* pl. **-ES** the state of being fey
FEZ	*n* pl. **FEZES** or **FEZZES** a brimless cap worn by men in the Near East **FEZZED, FEZZY** *adj*
FIACRE	*n* pl. **-S** a small carriage
FIANCE	*n* pl. **-S** a man engaged to be married
FIANCEE	*n* pl. **-S** a woman engaged to be married
FIAR	*n* pl. **-S** the holder of a type of absolute ownership of land under Scottish law
FIASCO	*n* pl. **-COES** or **-CHI** a wine bottle
FIASCO	*n* pl. **-COS** or **-COES** a complete failure
FIAT	*n* pl. **-S** an authoritative order
FIB	*v* **FIBBED, FIBBING, FIBS** to tell a trivial lie
FIBBER	*n* pl. **-S** one that fibs
FIBER	*n* pl. **-S** a thread or threadlike object or structure **FIBERED** *adj*
FIBERIZE	*v* **-IZED, -IZING, -IZES** to break into fibers
FIBRANNE	*n* pl. **-S** a fabric made of spun-rayon yarn
FIBRE	*n* pl. **-S** fiber
FIBRIL	*n* pl. **-S** a small fiber
FIBRILLA	*n* pl. **-LAE** a fibril
FIBRIN	*n* pl. **-S** an insoluble protein
FIBROID	*n* pl. **-S** a fibroma
FIBROIN	*n* pl. **-S** an insoluble protein
FIBROMA	*n* pl. **-MAS** or **-MATA** a benign tumor composed of fibrous tissue

FIBROSIS	*n* pl. **-BROSES** the development of excess fibrous tissue in a bodily organ **FIBROTIC** *adj*
FIBROUS	*adj* containing, consisting of, or resembling fibers
FIBSTER	*n* pl. **-S** one that fibs
FIBULA	*n* pl. **-LAS** or **-LAE** a bone of the leg **FIBULAR** *adj*
FICE	*n* pl. **-S** a feist
FICHE	*n* pl. **-S** a sheet of microfilm
FICHU	*n* pl. **-S** a woman's scarf
FICIN	*n* pl. **-S** an enzyme
FICKLE	*adj* **-LER, -LEST** not constant or loyal **FICKLY** *adv*
FICO	*n* pl. **-COES** something of little worth
FICTILE	*adj* moldable
FICTION	*n* pl. **-S** a literary work whose content is produced by the imagination
FICTIVE	*adj* imaginary
FICUS	*n* pl. **-ES** a tropical tree
FID	*n* pl. **-S** a square bar used as a support for a topmast
FIDDLE	*v* **-DLED, -DLING, -DLES** to play a violin
FIDDLER	*n* pl. **-S** one that fiddles
FIDDLY	*adj* intricately difficult to handle
FIDEISM	*n* pl. **-S** reliance on faith rather than reason
FIDEIST	*n* pl. **-S** a believer in fideism
FIDELITY	*n* pl. **-TIES** loyalty
FIDGE	*v* **FIDGED, FIDGING, FIDGES** to fidget
FIDGET	*v* **-ED, -ING, -S** to move nervously or restlessly
FIDGETER	*n* pl. **-S** one that fidgets
FIDGETY	*adj* nervously restless
FIDGING	present participle of fidge
FIDO	*n* pl. **-DOS** a defective coin
FIDUCIAL	*adj* based on faith or trust
FIE	*interj* — used to express disapproval
FIEF	*n* pl. **-S** a feudal estate
FIEFDOM	*n* pl. **-S** a fief
FIELD	*v* **-ED, -ING, -S** to play as a fielder
FIELDER	*n* pl. **-S** one that catches or picks up a ball in play
FIEND	*n* pl. **-S** a demon
FIENDISH	*adj* extremely wicked or cruel
FIERCE	*adj* **FIERCER, FIERCEST** violently hostile or aggressive **FIERCELY** *adv*
FIERY	*adj* **-ERIER, -ERIEST** intensely hot **FIERILY** *adv*
FIESTA	*n* pl. **-S** a festival
FIFE	*v* **FIFED, FIFING, FIFES** to play a fife (a high-pitched flute)
FIFER	*n* pl. **-S** one that plays a fife
FIFTEEN	*n* pl. **-S** a number
FIFTH	*n* pl. **-S** one of five equal parts
FIFTHLY	*adv* in the fifth place
FIFTIETH	*n* pl. **-S** one of fifty equal parts
FIFTY	*n* pl. **-TIES** a number
FIFTYISH	*adj* being about fifty years old
FIG	*v* **FIGGED, FIGGING, FIGS** to adorn
FIGEATER	*n* pl. **-S** a large beetle
FIGHT	*v* **FOUGHT, FIGHTING, FIGHTS** to attempt to defeat an adversary
FIGHTER	*n* pl. **-S** one that fights
FIGHTING	*n* pl. **-S** the act of one that fights
FIGMENT	*n* pl. **-S** a product of mental invention
FIGULINE	*n* pl. **-S** a piece of pottery
FIGURAL	*adj* consisting of human or animal form
FIGURANT	*n* pl. **-S** a ballet dancer who dances only in groups
FIGURATE	*adj* having a definite shape
FIGURE	*v* **-URED, -URING, -URES** to compute
FIGURER	*n* pl. **-S** one that figures
FIGURINE	*n* pl. **-S** a small statue
FIGWORT	*n* pl. **-S** a flowering plant
FIL	*n* pl. **-S** a coin of Iraq and Jordan
FILA	pl. of filum
FILAGREE	*v* **-GREED, -GREEING, -GREES** to filigree
FILAMENT	*n* pl. **-S** a very thin thread or threadlike structure
FILAR	*adj* pertaining to a thread
FILAREE	*n* pl. **-S** a European weed
FILARIA	*n* pl. **-IAE** a parasitic worm **FILARIAL, FILARIAN** *adj*
FILARIID	*n* pl. **-S** filaria
FILATURE	*n* pl. **-S** the reeling of silk from cocoons

FILBERT *n* pl. **-S** the edible nut of a European shrub

FILCH *v* **-ED, -ING, -ES** to steal

FILCHER *n* pl. **-S** one that filches

FILE *v* **FILED, FILING, FILES** to arrange in order for future reference **FILEABLE** *adj*

FILEFISH *n* pl. **-ES** a marine fish

FILEMOT *adj* of a brownish yellow color

FILENAME *n* pl. **-S** the name of a computer file

FILER *n* pl. **-S** one that files

FILET *v* **-ED, -ING, -S** to fillet

FILIAL *adj* pertaining to a son or daughter **FILIALLY** *adv*

FILIATE *v* **-ATED, -ATING, -ATES** to bring into close association

FILIBEG *n* pl. **-S** a pleated skirt worn by Scottish Highlanders

FILICIDE *n* pl. **-S** the killing of one's child

FILIFORM *adj* shaped like a filament

FILIGREE *v* **-GREED, -GREEING, -GREES** to adorn with intricate ornamental work

FILING *n* pl. **-S** a particle removed by a file

FILISTER *n* pl. **-S** a groove on a window frame

FILL *v* **-ED, -ING, -S** to put as much as can be held into **FILLABLE** *adj*

FILLE *n* pl. **-S** a girl

FILLER *n* pl. **-S** one that fills

FILLET *v* **-ED, -ING, -S** to cut boneless slices from

FILLIES pl. of filly

FILLING *n* pl. **-S** that which is used to fill something

FILLIP *v* **-ED, -ING, -S** to strike sharply

FILLO *n* pl. **-LOS** phyllo

FILLY *n* pl. **-LIES** a young female horse

FILM *v* **-ED, -ING, -S** to make a motion picture **FILMABLE** *adj*

FILMCARD *n* pl. **-S** a fiche

FILMDOM *n* pl. **-S** the motion-picture industry

FILMER *n* pl. **-S** one that films

FILMGOER *n* pl. **-S** one that goes to see motion pictures

FILMI *n* pl. **-S** music composed for Indian films

FILMIC *adj* pertaining to motion pictures

FILMIER comparative of filmy

FILMIEST superlative of filmy

FILMILY *adv* in a filmy manner

FILMLAND *n* pl. **-S** filmdom

FILMLESS *adj* having no film

FILMLIKE *adj* resembling film

FILMSET *v* **-SET, -SETTING, -SETS** to photoset

FILMY *adj* **FILMIER, FILMIEST** resembling or covered with film; hazy

FILO *n* pl. **-LOS** phyllo

FILOSE *adj* resembling a thread

FILS *n* pl. **FILS** son

FILTER *v* **-ED, -ING, -S** to pass through a filter (a device for removing suspended matter)

FILTERER *n* pl. **-S** one that filters

FILTH *n* pl. **-S** foul or dirty matter

FILTHY *adj* **FILTHIER, FILTHIEST** offensively dirty **FILTHILY** *adv*

FILTRATE *v* **-TRATED, -TRATING, -TRATES** to filter

FILUM *n* pl. **-LA** a threadlike anatomical structure

FIMBLE *n* pl. **-S** the male hemp plant

FIMBRIA *n* pl. **-BRIAE** a fringe or fringe-like structure **FIMBRIAL** *adj*

FIN *v* **FINNED, FINNING, FINS** to equip with fins (external paddle-like structures)

FINABLE *adj* subject to the payment of a fine

FINAGLE *v* **-GLED, -GLING, -GLES** to obtain by trickery

FINAGLER *n* pl. **-S** one that finagles

FINAL *n* pl. **-S** the last examination of an academic course

FINALE *n* pl. **-S** a close or termination of something

FINALIS *n* pl. **-LES** a type of tone in medieval music

FINALISE *v* **-ISED, -ISING, -ISES** finalize

FINALISM *n* pl. **-S** the doctrine that all events are determined by ultimate purposes

FINALIST *n* pl. **-S** a contestant who reaches the last part of a competition

FINALITY *n* pl. **-TIES** the state of being conclusive

FINALIZE *v* **-IZED, -IZING, -IZES** to put into finished form

FINALLY *adv* at the end

FINANCE	*v* **-NANCED, -NANCING, -NANCES** to supply the money for	**FINK**	*v* **-ED, -ING, -S** to inform to the police
FINBACK	*n* pl. **-S** the rorqual	**FINLESS**	*adj* having no fins
FINCA	*n* pl. **-S** an estate in Spanish America	**FINLIKE**	*adj* resembling a fin
FINCH	*n* pl. **-ES** a small bird	**FINMARK**	*n* pl. **-S** a monetary unit of Finland
FIND	*v* **FOUND, FINDING, FINDS** to come upon after a search **FINDABLE** *adj*	**FINNED**	past tense of fin
		FINNICKY	*adj* **-NICKIER, -NICKIEST** finicky
		FINNIER	comparative of finny
FINDER	*n* pl. **-S** one that finds	**FINNIEST**	superlative of finny
FINDING	*n* pl. **-S** something that is found	**FINNING**	present participle of fin
FINE	*adj* **FINER, FINEST** excellent	**FINNMARK**	*n* pl. **-S** finmark
FINE	*v* **FINED, FINING, FINES** to subject to a fine (a monetary penalty)	**FINNY**	*adj* **-NIER, -NIEST** having or characterized by fins
		FINO	*n* pl. **-NOS** a very dry sherry
FINEABLE	*adj* finable	**FINOCHIO**	*n* pl. **-CHIOS** a perennial herb
FINELY	*adv* in a fine manner	**FIORD**	*n* pl. **-S** fjord
FINENESS	*n* pl. **-ES** the quality of being fine	**FIPPLE**	*n* pl. **-S** a plug of wood at the mouth of certain wind instruments
FINER	comparative of fine		
FINERY	*n* pl. **-ERIES** elaborate adornment	**FIQUE**	*n* pl. **-S** a tropical plant
FINESPUN	*adj* developed with extreme care	**FIR**	*n* pl. **-S** an evergreen tree
FINESSE	*v* **-NESSED, -NESSING, -NESSES** to bring about by adroit maneuvering	**FIRE**	*v* **FIRED, FIRING, FIRES** to project by discharging from a gun **FIREABLE** *adj*
FINEST	superlative of fine	**FIREARM**	*n* pl. **-S** a weapon from which a shot is discharged by gunpowder
FINFISH	*n* pl. **-ES** a true fish		
FINFOOT	*n* pl. **-S** an aquatic bird	**FIREBACK**	*n* pl. **-S** a cast-iron plate along the back of a fireplace
FINGER	*v* **-ED, -ING, -S** to touch with the fingers (the terminating members of the hand)	**FIREBALL**	*n* pl. **-S** a luminous meteor
		FIREBASE	*n* pl. **-S** a military base from which fire is directed against the enemy
FINGERER	*n* pl. **-S** one that fingers	**FIREBIRD**	*n* pl. **-S** a brightly colored bird
FINIAL	*n* pl. **-S** a crowning ornament **FINIALED** *adj*	**FIREBOAT**	*n* pl. **-S** a boat equipped with fire-fighting apparatus
FINICAL	*adj* finicky	**FIREBOMB**	*v* **-ED, -ING, -S** to attack with incendiary bombs
FINICKIN	*adj* finicky		
FINICKY	*adj* **-ICKIER, -ICKIEST** difficult to please	**FIREBOX**	*n* pl. **-ES** a chamber in which fuel is burned
FINIKIN	*adj* finicky	**FIREBRAT**	*n* pl. **-S** a small, wingless insect
FINIKING	*adj* finicky	**FIREBUG**	*n* pl. **-S** an arsonist
FINING	*n* pl. **-S** the clarifying of wines	**FIRECLAY**	*n* pl. **-CLAYS** a heat-resistant clay
FINIS	*n* pl. **-NISES** the end	**FIRED**	past tense of fire
FINISH	*v* **-ED, -ING, -ES** to bring to an end	**FIREDAMP**	*n* pl. **-S** a combustible gas
FINISHER	*n* pl. **-S** one that finishes	**FIREDOG**	*n* pl. **-S** an andiron
FINITE	*n* pl. **-S** something that is finite (having definite limits)	**FIREFANG**	*v* **-ED, -ING, -S** to decompose by oxidation
FINITELY	*adv* to a finite extent	**FIREFLY**	*n* pl. **-FLIES** a luminous insect
FINITO	*adj* finished	**FIREHALL**	*n* pl. **-S** a fire station
FINITUDE	*n* pl. **-S** the state of being finite	**FIRELESS**	*adj* having no fire

FIRELIT *adj* lighted by firelight

FIRELOCK *n* pl. **-S** a type of gun

FIREMAN *n* pl. **-MEN** a man employed to extinguish fires

FIREPAN *n* pl. **-S** an open pan for holding live coals

FIREPINK *n* pl. **-S** a flowering plant

FIREPLUG *n* pl. **-S** a hydrant

FIREPOT *n* pl. **-S** a clay pot filled with burning items

FIRER *n* pl. **-S** one that fires

FIREROOM *n* pl. **-S** a room containing a ship's boilers

FIRESHIP *n* pl. **-S** a burning ship sent among the enemy's ships

FIRESIDE *n* pl. **-S** the area immediately surrounding a fireplace

FIRETRAP *n* pl. **-S** a building that is likely to catch on fire

FIREWALL *n* pl. **-S** a computer component that prevents unauthorized access to data

FIREWEED *n* pl. **-S** a perennial herb

FIREWOOD *n* pl. **-S** wood used as fuel

FIREWORK *n* pl. **-S** a device for producing a striking display of light or a loud noise

FIREWORM *n* pl. **-S** a glowworm

FIRING *n* pl. **-S** the process of maturing ceramic products by heat

FIRKIN *n* pl. **-S** a British unit of capacity

FIRM *adj* **FIRMER, FIRMEST** unyielding to pressure

FIRM *v* **-ED, -ING, -S** to make firm

FIRMAN *n* pl. **-S** an edict issued by a Middle Eastern sovereign

FIRMER *n* pl. **-S** a woodworking tool

FIRMLY *adv* in a firm manner

FIRMNESS *n* pl. **-ES** the state of being firm

FIRMWARE *n* pl. **-S** computer programs permanently stored on a microchip

FIRN *n* pl. **-S** neve

FIRRY *adj* **-RIER, -RIEST** abounding in firs

FIRST *n* pl. **-S** something that precedes all others

FIRSTLY *adv* before all others

FIRTH *n* pl. **-S** an inlet of the sea

FISC *n* pl. **-S** a state or royal treasury

FISCAL *n* pl. **-S** a public prosecutor

FISCALLY *adv* with regard to financial matters

FISH *v* **-ED, -ING, -ES** to catch or try to catch fish (cold-blooded aquatic vertebrates)

FISHABLE *adj* suitable for fishing

FISHBOLT *n* pl. **-S** a type of bolt

FISHBONE *n* pl. **-S** a bone of a fish

FISHBOWL *n* pl. **-S** a bowl in which live fish are kept

FISHER *n* pl. **-S** one that fishes

FISHERY *n* pl. **-ERIES** a place for catching fish

FISHEYE *n* pl. **-S** a suspicious stare

FISHGIG *n* pl. **-S** a pronged implement for spearing fish

FISHHOOK *n* pl. **-S** a barbed hook for catching fish

FISHIER comparative of fishy

FISHIEST superlative of fishy

FISHILY *adv* in a fishy manner

FISHING *n* pl. **-S** the occupation or pastime of catching fish

FISHKILL *n* pl. **-S** the sudden destruction of large numbers of fish

FISHLESS *adj* having no fish

FISHLIKE *adj* resembling a fish

FISHLINE *n* pl. **-S** a line used in fishing

FISHMEAL *n* pl. **-S** ground dried fish

FISHNET *n* pl. **-S** a net for catching fish

FISHPOLE *n* pl. **-S** a fishing rod

FISHPOND *n* pl. **-S** a pond abounding in edible fish

FISHTAIL *v* **-ED, -ING, -S** to have the rear end of a moving vehicle slide from side to side

FISHWAY *n* pl. **-WAYS** a device for enabling fish to pass around a dam

FISHWIFE *n* pl. **-WIVES** a woman who sells fish

FISHWORM *n* pl. **-S** a worm used as bait

FISHY *adj* **FISHIER, FISHIEST** of or resembling fish

FISSATE *adj* deeply split

FISSILE *adj* capable of being split

FISSION *v* **-ED, -ING, -S** to split into parts

FISSIPED *n* pl. **-S** a mammal that has separated toes

FISSURAL *adj* pertaining to a long narrow opening

FISSURE	*v* **-SURED, -SURING, -SURES** to split
FIST	*v* **-ED, -ING, -S** to strike with the fist (the hand closed tightly)
FISTFUL	*n* pl. **-S** a handful
FISTIC	*adj* pertaining to pugilism
FISTNOTE	*n* pl. **-S** a part of a text to which attention is drawn by an index mark
FISTULA	*n* pl. **-LAS** or **-LAE** a duct formed by the imperfect closing of a wound **FISTULAR** *adj*
FIT	*adj* **FITTER, FITTEST** healthy
FIT	*v* **FITTED, FITTING, FITS** to bring to a required form and size
FITCH	*n* pl. **-ES** a polecat
FITCHEE	*adj* fitchy
FITCHET	*n* pl. **-S** a fitch
FITCHEW	*n* pl. **-S** a fitch
FITCHY	*adj* having the arms ending in a point — used of a heraldic cross
FITFUL	*adj* recurring irregularly **FITFULLY** *adv*
FITLY	*adv* in a fit manner
FITMENT	*n* pl. **-S** equipment
FITNESS	*n* pl. **-ES** the state of being fit
FITTABLE	*adj* capable of being fitted
FITTED	past tense of fit
FITTER	*n* pl. **-S** one that fits
FITTEST	superlative of fit
FITTING	*n* pl. **-S** a small often standardized accessory part
FIVE	*n* pl. **-S** a number
FIVEFOLD	*adj* five times as great
FIVEPINS	*n/pl* a bowling game
FIVER	*n* pl. **-S** a five-dollar bill
FIX	*v* **FIXED** or **FIXT, FIXING, FIXES** to repair **FIXABLE** *adj*
FIXATE	*v* **-ATED, -ATING, -ATES** to make stable or stationary
FIXATIF	*n* pl. **-S** fixative
FIXATION	*n* pl. **-S** the act of fixating
FIXATIVE	*n* pl. **-S** a substance for preserving paintings or drawings
FIXEDLY	*adv* firmly
FIXER	*n* pl. **-S** one that fixes
FIXINGS	*n/pl* accompaniments to the main dish of a meal
FIXIT	*adj* involved with fixing things
FIXITY	*n* pl. **-TIES** stability
FIXT	a past tense of fix
FIXTURE	*n* pl. **-S** a permanent part or appendage of a house
FIXURE	*n* pl. **-S** firmness
FIZ	*n* pl. **FIZZES** a hissing or sputtering sound
FIZGIG	*n* pl. **-S** fishgig
FIZZ	*v* **-ED, -ING, -ES** to make a hissing or sputtering sound
FIZZER	*n* pl. **-S** one that fizzes
FIZZES	pl. of fiz
FIZZLE	*v* **-ZLED, -ZLING, -ZLES** to fizz
FIZZY	*adj* **FIZZIER, FIZZIEST** fizzing
FJELD	*n* pl. **-S** a high, barren plateau
FJORD	*n* pl. **-S** a narrow inlet of the sea between steep cliffs **FJORDIC** *adj*
FLAB	*n* pl. **-S** flabby body tissue
FLABBY	*adj* **-BIER, -BIEST** flaccid **FLABBILY** *adv*
FLABELLA	*n/pl* fan-shaped anatomical structures
FLACCID	*adj* lacking firmness
FLACK	*v* **-ED, -ING, -S** to work as a press agent
FLACKERY	*n* pl. **-ERIES** publicity
FLACON	*n* pl. **-S** a small stoppered bottle
FLAG	*v* **FLAGGED, FLAGGING, FLAGS** to mark with a flag (a piece of cloth used as a symbol)
FLAGELLA	*n/pl* long, slender plant shoots
FLAGGER	*n* pl. **-S** one that flags
FLAGGING	*n* pl. **-S** a type of pavement
FLAGGY	*adj* **-GIER, -GIEST** drooping
FLAGLESS	*adj* having no flag
FLAGMAN	*n* pl. **-MEN** one who carries a flag
FLAGON	*n* pl. **-S** a large bulging bottle
FLAGPOLE	*n* pl. **-S** a pole on which a flag is displayed
FLAGRANT	*adj* extremely conspicuous
FLAGSHIP	*n* pl. **-S** a ship bearing the flag of a fleet
FLAIL	*v* **-ED, -ING, -S** to swing freely
FLAIR	*n* pl. **-S** a natural aptitude
FLAK	*n* pl. **FLAK** antiaircraft fire
FLAKE	*v* **FLAKED, FLAKING, FLAKES** to peel off in flakes (flat, thin pieces)
FLAKER	*n* pl. **-S** one that flakes

FLAKEY *adj* **FLAKIER, FLAKIEST** flaky

FLAKY *adj* **FLAKIER, FLAKIEST** resembling flakes **FLAKILY** *adv*

FLAM *v* **FLAMMED, FLAMMING, FLAMS** to deceive

FLAMBE *v* **-BEED, -BEING, -BES** to douse with a liqueur and ignite

FLAMBEAU *n* pl. **-BEAUS** or **-BEAUX** a flaming torch

FLAMBEE *adj* flaming

FLAME *v* **FLAMED, FLAMING, FLAMES** to burn brightly

FLAMEN *n* pl. **-MENS** or **-MINES** a priest of ancient Rome

FLAMENCO *n* pl. **-COS** a strongly rhythmic style of dancing

FLAMEOUT *n* pl. **-S** a failure of a jet engine in flight

FLAMER *n* pl. **-S** one that flames

FLAMIER comparative of flamy

FLAMIEST superlative of flamy

FLAMINES a pl. of flamen

FLAMING present participle of flame

FLAMINGO *n* pl. **-GOS** or **-GOES** a wading bird

FLAMMED past tense of flam

FLAMMING present participle of flam

FLAMY *adj* **FLAMIER, FLAMIEST** flaming

FLAN *n* pl. **-S** or **-ES** a type of custard

FLANCARD *n* pl. **-S** a piece of armor for the side of a horse

FLANERIE *n* pl. **-S** idleness

FLANEUR *n* pl. **-S** an idler

FLANGE *v* **FLANGED, FLANGING, FLANGES** to provide with a protecting rim

FLANGER *n* pl. **-S** one that flanges

FLANK *v* **-ED, -ING, -S** to be located at the side of

FLANKEN *n/pl* beef cut from the sides that is boiled with vegetables

FLANKER *n* pl. **-S** one that flanks

FLANNEL *v* **-NELED, -NELING, -NELS** or **-NELLED, -NELLING, -NELS** to cover with flannel (a soft fabric)

FLAP *v* **FLAPPED, FLAPPING, FLAPS** to wave up and down

FLAPERON *n* pl. **-S** an airfoil that functions as a flap and an aileron

FLAPJACK *n* pl. **-S** a pancake

FLAPLESS *adj* having no flap (a flat appendage)

FLAPPED past tense of flap

FLAPPER *n* pl. **-S** one that flaps

FLAPPING present participle of flap

FLAPPY *adj* **-PIER, -PIEST** flapping

FLARE *v* **FLARED, FLARING, FLARES** to burn with a bright, wavering light

FLAREUP *n* pl. **-S** a sudden outbreak

FLASH *v* **-ED, -ING, -ES** to send forth a sudden burst of light

FLASHER *n* pl. **-S** one that flashes

FLASHGUN *n* pl. **-S** a photographic apparatus

FLASHING *n* pl. **-S** sheet metal used in waterproofing a roof

FLASHY *adj* **FLASHIER, FLASHIEST** gaudy **FLASHILY** *adv*

FLASK *n* pl. **-S** a narrow-necked container

FLASKET *n* pl. **-S** a small flask

FLAT *adj* **FLATTER, FLATTEST** having a smooth or even surface

FLAT *v* **FLATTED, FLATTING, FLATS** to flatten

FLATBED *n* pl. **-S** a type of truck or trailer

FLATBOAT *n* pl. **-S** a flat-bottomed boat

FLATCAP *n* pl. **-S** a type of hat

FLATCAR *n* pl. **-S** a railroad car without sides or roof

FLATFISH *n* pl. **-ES** any of an order of marine fishes

FLATFOOT *n* pl. **-FEET** a foot condition

FLATFOOT *v* **-ED, -ING, -S** to walk with a dragging gait

FLATHEAD *n* pl. **-S** a marine food fish

FLATIRON *n* pl. **-S** a device for pressing clothes

FLATLAND *n* pl. **-S** land lacking significant variation in elevation

FLATLET *n* pl. **-S** a type of apartment

FLATLINE *v* **-LINED, -LINING, -LINES** to register as having no brain waves or heartbeat

FLATLING *adv* with a flat side or edge

FLATLONG *adv* flatling

FLATLY *adv* in a flat manner

FLATMATE *n* pl. **-S** one with whom an apartment is shared

FLATNESS *n* pl. **-ES** the state of being flat

FLATTED past tense of flat

FLATTEN	*v* **-ED, -ING, -S** to make or become flat
FLATTER	*v* **-ED, -ING, -S** to praise excessively
FLATTERY	*n* pl. **-TERIES** the act of flattering
FLATTEST	superlative of flat
FLATTING	present participle of flat
FLATTISH	*adj* somewhat flat
FLATTOP	*n* pl. **-S** an aircraft carrier
FLATUS	*n* pl. **-ES** intestinal gas
FLATWARE	*n* pl. **-S** tableware that is fairly flat
FLATWASH	*n* pl. **-ES** flatwork
FLATWAYS	*adv* flatwise
FLATWISE	*adv* with the flat side in a particular position
FLATWORK	*n* pl. **-S** laundry that can be ironed mechanically
FLATWORM	*n* pl. **-S** a flat-bodied worm
FLAUNT	*v* **-ED, -ING, -S** to exhibit in a gaudy manner
FLAUNTER	*n* pl. **-S** one that flaunts
FLAUNTY	*adj* **FLAUNTIER, FLAUNTIEST** gaudy
FLAUTA	*n* pl. **-S** a tortilla rolled around a filling and fried
FLAUTIST	*n* pl. **-S** flutist
FLAVANOL	*n* pl. **-S** flavonol
FLAVIN	*n* pl. **-S** a yellow pigment
FLAVINE	*n* pl. **-S** flavin
FLAVONE	*n* pl. **-S** a chemical compound
FLAVONOL	*n* pl. **-S** a derivative of flavone
FLAVOR	*v* **-ED, -ING, -S** to give flavor (distinctive taste) to
FLAVORER	*n* pl. **-S** one that flavors
FLAVORY	*adj* full of flavor
FLAVOUR	*v* **-ED, -ING, -S** to flavor
FLAVOURY	*adj* flavory
FLAW	*v* **-ED, -ING, -S** to produce a flaw (an imperfection) in
FLAWLESS	*adj* having no flaw
FLAWY	*adj* **FLAWIER, FLAWIEST** full of flaws
FLAX	*n* pl. **-ES** an annual herb
FLAXEN	*adj* of a pale yellow color
FLAXSEED	*n* pl. **-S** the seed of flax
FLAXY	*adj* **FLAXIER, FLAXIEST** flaxen
FLAY	*v* **-ED, -ING, -S** to strip off the skin of
FLAYER	*n* pl. **-S** one that flays
FLEA	*n* pl. **-S** a parasitic insect
FLEABAG	*n* pl. **-S** an inferior hotel
FLEABANE	*n* pl. **-S** a flowering plant
FLEABITE	*n* pl. **-S** the bite of a flea
FLEAM	*n* pl. **-S** a surgical instrument
FLEAPIT	*n* pl. **-S** a run-down movie theater
FLEAWORT	*n* pl. **-S** a European herb
FLECHE	*n* pl. **-S** a steeple
FLECK	*v* **-ED, -ING, -S** to mark with flecks (tiny streaks or spots)
FLECKY	*adj* flecked
FLECTION	*n* pl. **-S** the act of bending
FLED	past tense of flee
FLEDGE	*v* **FLEDGED, FLEDGING, FLEDGES** to furnish with feathers
FLEDGY	*adj* **FLEDGIER, FLEDGIEST** covered with feathers
FLEE	*v* **FLED, FLEEING, FLEES** to run away
FLEECE	*v* **FLEECED, FLEECING, FLEECES** to remove the coat of wool from
FLEECER	*n* pl. **-S** one that fleeces
FLEECH	*v* **-ED, -ING, -ES** to coax
FLEECY	*adj* **FLEECIER, FLEECIEST** woolly **FLEECILY** *adv*
FLEER	*v* **-ED, -ING, -S** to deride
FLEET	*adj* **FLEETER, FLEETEST** swift **FLEETLY** *adv*
FLEET	*v* **-ED, -ING, -S** to move swiftly
FLEHMEN	*v* **-ED, -ING, -S** to inhale with the mouth open and upper lip curled
FLEISHIG	*adj* made of meat or meat products
FLEMISH	*v* **-ED, -ING, -ES** to coil rope in a certain manner
FLENCH	*v* **-ED, -ING, -ES** to flense
FLENSE	*v* **FLENSED, FLENSING, FLENSES** to strip the blubber or skin from
FLENSER	*n* pl. **-S** one that flenses
FLESH	*v* **-ED, -ING, -ES** to plunge into the flesh (soft body tissue)
FLESHER	*n* pl. **-S** one that removes flesh from animal hides
FLESHIER	comparative of fleshy
FLESHIEST	superlative of fleshy

FLESHING *n* pl. **-S** the distribution of the lean and fat on an animal

FLESHLY *adj* **-LIER, -LIEST** pertaining to the body

FLESHPOT *n* pl. **-S** a pot for cooking meat

FLESHY *adj* **FLESHIER, FLESHIEST** having much flesh **FLESHILY** *adv*

FLETCH *v* **-ED, -ING, -ES** to fledge

FLETCHER *n* pl. **-S** one that makes arrows

FLEURON *n* pl. **-S** a floral ornamnent

FLEURY *adj* having the arms terminating in three leaves — used of a heraldic cross

FLEW *n* pl. **-S** a fishing net

FLEX *v* **-ED, -ING, -ES** to bend

FLEXAGON *n* pl. **-S** a folded paper construction

FLEXIBLE *adj* capable of being bent **FLEXIBLY** *adv*

FLEXILE *adj* flexible

FLEXION *n* pl. **-S** flection

FLEXOR *n* pl. **-S** a muscle that serves to bend a bodily part

FLEXTIME *n* pl. **-S** a system that allows flexible working hours

FLEXUOSE *adj* flexuous

FLEXUOUS *adj* winding

FLEXURE *n* pl. **-S** the act of bending **FLEXURAL** *adj*

FLEY *v* **-ED, -ING, -S** to frighten

FLIC *n* pl. **-S** a Parisian policeman

FLICHTER *v* **-ED, -ING, -S** to flicker

FLICK *v* **-ED, -ING, -S** to strike with a quick, light blow

FLICKER *v* **-ED, -ING, -S** to move waveringly

FLICKERY *adj* flickering

FLIED a past tense of fly

FLIER *n* pl. **-S** one that flies

FLIES present 3d person sing. of fly

FLIEST superlative of fly

FLIGHT *v* **-ED, -ING, -S** to fly in a flock

FLIGHTY *adj* **FLIGHTIER, FLIGHTIEST** fickle

FLIMFLAM *v* **-FLAMMED, -FLAMMING, -FLAMS** to swindle

FLIMSY *adj* **-SIER, -SIEST** lacking solidity or strength **FLIMSILY** *adv*

FLIMSY *n* pl. **-SIES** a thin paper

FLINCH *v* **-ED, -ING, -ES** to shrink back involuntarily

FLINCHER *n* pl. **-S** one that flinches

FLINDER *n* pl. **-S** a small fragment

FLING *v* **FLUNG, FLINGING, FLINGS** to throw with force

FLINGER *n* pl. **-S** one that flings

FLINKITE *n* pl. **-S** a mineral

FLINT *v* **-ED, -ING, -S** to provide with flint (a spark-producing rock)

FLINTY *adj* **FLINTIER, FLINTIEST** resembling flint **FLINTILY** *adv*

FLIP *adj* **FLIPPER, FLIPPEST** flippant

FLIP *v* **FLIPPED, FLIPPING, FLIPS** to throw with a brisk motion

FLIPBOOK *n* pl. **-S** a book of a series of images that when flipped give the illusion of movement

FLIPFLOP *v* **-FLOPPED, -FLOPPING, -FLOPS** to perform a backward somersault

FLIPPANT *adj* impudent

FLIPPED past tense of flip

FLIPPER *n* pl. **-S** a broad, flat limb adapted for swimming

FLIPPEST superlative of flip

FLIPPING present participle of flip

FLIPPY *adj* flaring at the bottom

FLIR *n* pl. **-S** an electronic heat sensor

FLIRT *v* **-ED, -ING, -S** to behave amorously without serious intent

FLIRTER *n* pl. **-S** one that flirts

FLIRTY *adj* **FLIRTIER, FLIRTIEST** given to flirting

FLIT *v* **FLITTED, FLITTING, FLITS** to move lightly and swiftly

FLITCH *v* **-ED, -ING, -ES** to cut into strips

FLITE *v* **FLITED, FLITING, FLITES** to quarrel

FLITTED past tense of flit

FLITTER *v* **-ED, -ING, -S** to flutter

FLITTING present participle of flit

FLIVVER *n* pl. **-S** an old, battered car

FLOAT *v* **-ED, -ING, -S** to rest or remain on the surface of a liquid

FLOATAGE *n* pl. **-S** flotage

FLOATEL *n* pl. **-S** a houseboat used as a hotel

FLOATER *n* pl. **-S** one that floats

FLOATY *adj* **FLOATIER, FLOATIEST** tending to float

FLOC *v* **FLOCCED, FLOCCING, FLOCS** to aggregate into floccules

FLOCCI pl. of floccus

FLOCCOSE *adj* having woolly tufts

FLOCCULE *n* pl. **-S** a tuft-like mass

FLOCCULI *n/pl* small, loosely aggregated masses

FLOCCUS *n* pl. **FLOCCI** a floccule

FLOCK *v* **-ED, -ING, -S** to gather or move in a crowd

FLOCKING *n* pl. **-S** a velvety design in short fibers on cloth or paper

FLOCKY *adj* **FLOCKIER, FLOCKIEST** woolly

FLOE *n* pl. **-S** a large mass of floating ice

FLOG *v* **FLOGGED, FLOGGING, FLOGS** to beat with a whip or rod

FLOGGER *n* pl. **-S** one that flogs

FLOGGING *n* pl. **-S** a whipping

FLOKATI *n* pl. **-S** a Greek handwoven rug

FLONG *n* pl. **-S** a sheet of a certain type of paper

FLOOD *v* **-ED, -ING, -S** to inundate

FLOODER *n* pl. **-S** one that floods

FLOODLIT *adj* illuminated by floodlights

FLOODWAY *n* pl. **-WAYS** an overflow channel

FLOOEY *adj* awry

FLOOIE *adj* flooey

FLOOR *v* **-ED, -ING, -S** to provide with a floor (the level base of a room)

FLOORAGE *n* pl. **-S** floor space

FLOORER *n* pl. **-S** one that floors

FLOORING *n* pl. **-S** a floor

FLOOSIE *n* pl. **-S** floozy

FLOOSY *n* pl. **-SIES** floozy

FLOOZIE *n* pl. **-S** floozy

FLOOZY *n* pl. **-ZIES** a prostitute

FLOP *v* **FLOPPED, FLOPPING, FLOPS** to fall heavily and noisily

FLOPOVER *n* pl. **-S** a defect in television reception

FLOPPER *n* pl. **-S** one that flops

FLOPPING present participle of flop

FLOPPY *adj* **-PIER, -PIEST** soft and flexible **FLOPPILY** *adv*

FLOPPY *n* pl. **-PIES** a type of computer disk

FLOPS *n* pl. **FLOPS** a measure of computer speed

FLORA *n* pl. **-RAS** or **-RAE** the plant life of a particular region

FLORAL *n* pl. **-S** a design having flowers

FLORALLY *adv* in a manner like that of a flower

FLORENCE *n* pl. **-S** florin

FLORET *n* pl. **-S** a small flower

FLORID *adj* ruddy **FLORIDLY** *adv*

FLORIGEN *n* pl. **-S** a plant hormone

FLORIN *n* pl. **-S** a former gold coin of Europe

FLORIST *n* pl. **-S** a grower or seller of flowers

FLORUIT *n* pl. **-S** a period of flourishing

FLOSS *v* **-ED, -ING, -ES** to clean between the teeth with a thread

FLOSSER *n* pl. **-S** one that flosses

FLOSSIE *n* pl. **-S** a floozy

FLOSSY *adj* **FLOSSIER, FLOSSIEST** resembling floss (a soft, light fiber) **FLOSSILY** *adv*

FLOTA *n* pl. **-S** a fleet of Spanish ships

FLOTAGE *n* pl. **-S** the act of floating

FLOTILLA *n* pl. **-S** a fleet of ships

FLOTSAM *n* pl. **-S** floating wreckage of a ship or its cargo

FLOUNCE *v* **FLOUNCED, FLOUNCING, FLOUNCES** to move with exaggerated motions

FLOUNCY *adj* **FLOUNCIER, FLOUNCIEST** flouncing

FLOUNDER *v* **-ED, -ING, -S** to struggle clumsily

FLOUR *v* **-ED, -ING, -S** to cover with flour (a finely ground meal of grain)

FLOURISH *v* **-ED, -ING, -ES** to thrive

FLOURY *adj* resembling flour

FLOUT *v* **-ED, -ING, -S** to treat with contempt

FLOUTER *n* pl. **-S** one that flouts

FLOW *v* **-ED, -ING, -S** to move steadily and smoothly along

FLOWAGE *n* pl. **-S** the act of flowing

FLOWER *v* **-ED, -ING, -S** to put forth flowers (reproductive structures of seed-bearing plants)

FLOWERER *n* pl. **-S** a plant that flowers at a certain time

FLOWERET *n* pl. **-S** a floret

FLOWERY   *adj* **-ERIER, -ERIEST** abounding in flowers

FLOWN   a past participle of fly

FLU   *n* pl. **-S** a virus disease

FLUB   *v* **FLUBBED, FLUBBING, FLUBS** to bungle

FLUBBER   *n* pl. **-S** one that flubs

FLUBDUB   *n* pl. **-S** pretentious nonsense

FLUE   *n* pl. **-S** an enclosed passageway for directing a current **FLUED** *adj*

FLUENCY   *n* pl. **-CIES** the quality of being fluent

FLUENT   *adj* spoken or written with effortless ease **FLUENTLY** *adv*

FLUERICS   *n/pl* fluidics **FLUERIC** *adj*

FLUFF   *v* **-ED, -ING, -S** to make fluffy

FLUFFER   *n* pl. **-S** one that fluffs

FLUFFY   *adj* **FLUFFIER, FLUFFIEST** light and soft **FLUFFILY** *adv*

FLUID   *n* pl. **-S** a substance that tends to flow **FLUIDAL** *adj*

FLUIDICS   *n/pl* a branch of mechanical engineering **FLUIDIC** *adj*

FLUIDISE   *v* **-ISED, -ISING, -ISES** to fluidize

FLUIDITY   *n* pl. **-TIES** the quality of being able to flow

FLUIDIZE   *v* **-IZED, -IZING, -IZES** to cause to flow like a fluid

FLUIDLY   *adv* with fluidity

FLUIDRAM   *n* pl. **-S** a unit of liquid capacity

FLUISH   *adj* having symptoms like those of the flu

FLUKE   *v* **FLUKED, FLUKING, FLUKES** to obtain by chance

FLUKEY   *adj* **FLUKIER, FLUKIEST** fluky

FLUKY   *adj* **FLUKIER, FLUKIEST** happening by or depending on chance **FLUKILY** *adv*

FLUME   *v* **FLUMED, FLUMING, FLUMES** to convey by means of an artificial water channel

FLUMMERY   *n* pl. **-MERIES** a sweet dessert

FLUMMOX   *v* **-ED, -ING, -ES** to confuse

FLUMP   *v* **-ED, -ING, -S** to fall heavily

FLUNG   past tense of fling

FLUNK   *v* **-ED, -ING, -S** to fail an examination or course

FLUNKER   *n* pl. **-S** one that flunks

FLUNKEY   *n* pl. **-KEYS** flunky

FLUNKIE   *n* pl. **-S** flunky

FLUNKY   *n* pl. **-KIES** a servile follower

FLUOR   *n* pl. **-S** fluorite **FLUORIC** *adj*

FLUORENE   *n* pl. **-S** a chemical compound

FLUORID   *n* pl. **-S** fluoride

FLUORIDE   *n* pl. **-S** a compound of fluorine

FLUORIN   *n* pl. **-S** fluorine

FLUORINE   *n* pl. **-S** a gaseous element

FLUORITE   *n* pl. **-S** a mineral

FLURRY   *v* **-RIED, -RYING, -RIES** to confuse

FLUSH   *adj* **FLUSHER, FLUSHEST** ruddy

FLUSH   *v* **-ED, -ING, -ES** to blush

FLUSHER   *n* pl. **-S** one that flushes

FLUSTER   *v* **-ED, -ING, -S** to put into a state of nervous confusion

FLUTE   *v* **FLUTED, FLUTING, FLUTES** to play on a flute (a woodwind instrument)

FLUTER   *n* pl. **-S** a flutist

FLUTEY   *adj* **FLUTIER, FLUTIEST** fluty

FLUTIER   comparative of fluty

FLUTIEST   superlative of fluty

FLUTING   *n* pl. **-S** a series of parallel grooves

FLUTIST   *n* pl. **-S** one who plays the flute

FLUTTER   *v* **-ED, -ING, -S** to wave rapidly and irregularly

FLUTTERY   *adj* marked by fluttering

FLUTY   *adj* **FLUTIER, FLUTIEST** resembling a flute in sound

FLUVIAL   *adj* pertaining to a river

FLUX   *v* **-ED, -ING, -ES** to melt

FLUXGATE   *n* pl. **-S** a device to measure a magnetic field

FLUXION   *n* pl. **-S** the act of flowing

FLUYT   *n* pl. **-S** a type of ship

FLY   *adj* **FLIER, FLIEST** clever

FLY   *v* **FLEW, FLOWN, FLYING, FLIES** to move through the air

FLY   *v* **FLIED, FLYING, FLIES** to hit a ball high into the air in baseball

FLYABLE   *adj* suitable for flying

FLYAWAY   *n* pl. **-AWAYS** one that is elusive

FLYBELT   *n* pl. **-S** an area infested with tsetse flies

FLYBLOW   *v* **-BLEW, -BLOWN, -BLOWING, -BLOWS** to taint

FLYBOAT   *n* pl. **-S** a small, fast boat

FLYBOY   *n* pl. **-BOYS** a pilot in an air force

FLYBY   *n pl.* **-BYS** a flight of aircraft close to a specified place

FLYER   *n pl.* **-S** flier

FLYING   *n pl.* **-S** the operation of an aircraft

FLYLEAF   *n pl.* **-LEAVES** a blank leaf at the beginning or end of a book

FLYLESS   *adj* free of flies (winged insects)

FLYMAN   *n pl.* **-MEN** a stage worker in a theater

FLYOFF   *n pl.* **-S** a competitive testing of model aircraft

FLYOVER   *n pl.* **-S** a flight of aircraft over a specific location

FLYPAPER   *n pl.* **-S** paper designed to catch or kill flies

FLYPAST   *n pl.* **-S** a flyby

FLYSCH   *n pl.* **-ES** a sandstone deposit

FLYSHEET   *n pl.* **-S** a circular

FLYSPECK   *v* **-ED, -ING, -S** to mark with minute spots

FLYTE   *v* **FLYTED, FLYTING, FLYTES** to flite

FLYTIER   *n pl.* **-S** a maker of fishing flies

FLYTING   *n pl.* **-S** a dispute in verse form

FLYTRAP   *n pl.* **-S** a trap for catching flies

FLYWAY   *n pl.* **-WAYS** an established air route of migratory birds

FLYWHEEL   *n pl.* **-S** a heavy disk used in machinery

FOAL   *v* **-ED, -ING, -S** to give birth to a horse

FOAM   *v* **-ED, -ING, -S** to form foam (a light, bubbly, gas and liquid mass) **FOAMABLE** *adj*

FOAMER   *n pl.* **-S** one that foams

FOAMIER   comparative of foamy

FOAMIEST   superlative of foamy

FOAMILY   *adv* in a foamy manner

FOAMLESS   *adj* being without foam

FOAMLIKE   *adj* resembling foam

FOAMY   *adj* **FOAMIER, FOAMIEST** covered with foam

FOB   *v* **FOBBED, FOBBING, FOBS** to deceive

FOCACCIA   *n pl.* **-S** a flat Italian bread

FOCAL   *adj* pertaining to a focus

FOCALISE   *v* **-ISED, -ISING, -ISES** to focalize

FOCALIZE   *v* **-IZED, -IZING, -IZES** to focus

FOCALLY   *adv* with regard to focus

FOCUS   *n pl.* **-CUSES** or **-CI** a point at which rays converge or from which they diverge

FOCUS   *v* **-CUSED, -CUSING, -CUSES** or **-CUSSED, -CUSSING, -CUSSES** to bring to a focus

FOCUSER   *n pl.* **-S** one that focuses

FODDER   *v* **-ED, -ING, -S** to feed with coarse food

FODGEL   *adj* plump

FOE   *n pl.* **-S** an enemy

FOEHN   *n pl.* **-S** a warm, dry wind

FOEMAN   *n pl.* **-MEN** an enemy in war

FOETAL   *adj* fetal

FOETID   *adj* fetid

FOETOR   *n pl.* **-S** fetor

FOETUS   *n pl.* **-ES** fetus

FOG   *v* **FOGGED, FOGGING, FOGS** to cover with fog (condensed water vapor near the earth's surface)

FOGBOUND   *adj* surrounded by fog

FOGBOW   *n pl.* **-S** a nebulous arc of light sometimes seen in a fog

FOGDOG   *n pl.* **-S** a fogbow

FOGEY   *n pl.* **-GEYS** fogy **FOGEYISH** *adj*

FOGEYISM   *n pl.* **-S** fogyism

FOGFRUIT   *n pl.* **-S** a flowering plant

FOGGAGE   *n pl.* **-S** a second growth of grass

FOGGED   past tense of fog

FOGGER   *n pl.* **-S** one that fogs

FOGGING   present participle of fog

FOGGY   *adj* **-GIER, -GIEST** filled with fog **FOGGILY** *adv*

FOGHORN   *n pl.* **-S** a horn sounded in a fog

FOGIE   *n pl.* **-S** fogy

FOGLESS   *adj* having no fog

FOGY   *n pl.* **-GIES** an old-fashioned person **FOGYISH** *adj*

FOGYISM   *n pl.* **-S** old-fashioned behavior

FOH   *interj* faugh

FOHN   *n pl.* **-S** foehn

FOIBLE   *n pl.* **-S** a minor weakness

FOIL   *v* **-ED, -ING, -S** to prevent the success of **FOILABLE** *adj*

FOILSMAN   *n pl.* **-MEN** a fencer

FOIN   *v* **-ED, -ING, -S** to thrust with a pointed weapon

FOISON   *n pl.* **-S** strength

FOIST v **-ED, -ING, -S** to force upon slyly

FOLACIN n pl. **-S** a B vitamin

FOLATE n pl. **-S** folacin

FOLD v **-ED, -ING, -S** to lay one part over another part of **FOLDABLE** adj

FOLDAWAY n pl. **-S** an object designed to be folded out of the way

FOLDAWAY adj designed to fold out of the way

FOLDBOAT n pl. **-S** a faltboat

FOLDER n pl. **-S** one that folds

FOLDEROL n pl. **-S** falderal

FOLDOUT n pl. **-S** a gatefold

FOLDUP n pl. **-S** an object that folds up

FOLEY n pl. **-LEYS** a process for creating sounds for films

FOLIA a pl. of folium

FOLIAGE n pl. **-S** the growth of leaves of a plant **FOLIAGED** adj

FOLIAR adj pertaining to a leaf

FOLIATE v **-ATED, -ATING, -ATES** to hammer into thin plates

FOLIC adj derived from folic acid

FOLIO v **-ED, -ING, -S** to number the pages of

FOLIOSE adj having leaves

FOLIOUS adj foliose

FOLIUM n pl. **-LIUMS** or **-LIA** a thin layer

FOLK n pl. **-S** a people or tribe

FOLKIE adj **FOLKIER, FOLKIEST** being in the style of folk music

FOLKIE n pl. **-S** a performer of folk music

FOLKISH adj characteristic of the common people

FOLKLIFE n pl. **-LIVES** the traditions, skills, and products of a people

FOLKLIKE adj folkish

FOLKLORE n pl. **-S** the lore of a people

FOLKMOOT n pl. **-S** a general assembly of the people in early England

FOLKMOT n pl. **-S** folkmoot

FOLKMOTE n pl. **-S** folkmoot

FOLKSONG n pl. **-S** a song of the folk music of an area

FOLKSY adj **FOLKSIER, FOLKSIEST** friendly **FOLKSILY** adv

FOLKTALE n pl. **-S** a tale forming part of the oral tradition of a people

FOLKWAY n pl. **-WAYS** a traditional custom of a people

FOLKY adj **FOLKIER, FOLKIEST** folkie

FOLKY n pl. **FOLKIES** folkie

FOLLES pl. of follis

FOLLICLE n pl. **-S** a small bodily cavity

FOLLIES pl. of folly

FOLLIS n pl. **-LES** a coin of ancient Rome

FOLLOW v **-ED, -ING, -S** to come or go after

FOLLOWER n pl. **-S** one that follows

FOLLOWUP n pl. **-S** a news article that adds information to a previous article

FOLLY n pl. **-LIES** a foolish idea or action

FOMENT v **-ED, -ING, -S** to promote the development of

FOMENTER n pl. **-S** one that foments

FOMITE n pl. **-S** an inanimate object that serves to transmit infectious organisms

FON n pl. **-S** foehn

FOND adj **FONDER, FONDEST** having an affection

FOND v **-ED, -ING, -S** to display affection

FONDANT n pl. **-S** a soft, creamy candy

FONDLE v **-DLED, -DLING, -DLES** to caress

FONDLER n pl. **-S** one that fondles

FONDLING n pl. **-S** one that is fondled

FONDLY adv in a fond manner

FONDNESS n pl. **-ES** affection

FONDU n pl. **-S** a dish of melted cheese

FONDUE v **-DUED, -DUING** or **-DUEING, -DUES** to cook in a pot of melted cheese

FONT n pl. **-S** a receptacle for the water used in baptism **FONTAL** adj

FONTANEL n pl. **-S** a space in the fetal and infantile skull

FONTINA n pl. **-S** an Italian cheese

FOOD n pl. **-S** a substance taken into the body to maintain life and growth **FOODLESS** adj

FOODIE n pl. **-S** an enthusiast of foods and their preparation

FOODWAYS n/pl the eating habits of a people

FOOFARAW n pl. **-S** excessive ornamentation

FOOL v **-ED, -ING, -S** to deceive

FOOLERY n pl. **-ERIES** foolish behavior or speech

FOOLFISH n pl. **-ES** a marine fish

FOOLISH *adj* **-ISHER, -ISHEST** lacking good sense or judgment

FOOLSCAP *n* pl. **-S** a paper size

FOOSBALL *n* pl. **-S** a table game resembling soccer

FOOT *n* pl. **FEET** the terminal part of the leg on which the body stands and moves

FOOT *v* **-ED, -ING, -S** to walk

FOOTAGE *n* pl. **-S** a length or quantity expressed in feet

FOOTBAG *n* pl. **-S** a small bag filled with pellets that is kept aloft with the feet

FOOTBALL *n* pl. **-S** a type of ball

FOOTBATH *n* pl. **-S** a bath for the feet

FOOTBOY *n* pl. **-BOYS** a serving boy

FOOTER *n* pl. **-S** one that walks

FOOTFALL *n* pl. **-S** the sound of a footstep

FOOTGEAR *n* pl. **FOOTGEAR** footwear

FOOTHILL *n* pl. **-S** a low hill at the foot of higher hills

FOOTHOLD *n* pl. **-S** a secure support for the feet

FOOTIE *n* pl. **-S** footsie

FOOTIER comparative of footy

FOOTIEST superlative of footy

FOOTING *n* pl. **-S** a foothold

FOOTLE *v* **-TLED, -TLING, -TLES** to waste time

FOOTLER *n* pl. **-S** one that footles

FOOTLESS *adj* having no feet

FOOTLIKE *adj* resembling a foot

FOOTLING present participle of footle

FOOTMAN *n* pl. **-MEN** a male servant

FOOTMARK *n* pl. **-S** a mark left by the foot on a surface

FOOTNOTE *v* **-NOTED, -NOTING, -NOTES** to furnish with explanatory notes

FOOTPACE *n* pl. **-S** a walking pace

FOOTPAD *n* pl. **-S** one who robs a pedestrian

FOOTPATH *n* pl. **-S** a path for pedestrians

FOOTRACE *n* pl. **-S** a race run on foot

FOOTREST *n* pl. **-S** a support for the feet

FOOTROPE *n* pl. **-S** a rope used in sailing

FOOTSIE *n* pl. **-S** a flirting game played with the feet

FOOTSLOG *v* **-SLOGGED, -SLOGGING, -SLOGS** to march through mud

FOOTSORE *adj* having sore or tired feet

FOOTSTEP *n* pl. **-S** a step with the foot

FOOTSY *n* pl. **-SIES** footsie

FOOTWALL *n* pl. **-S** the layer of rock beneath a vein of ore

FOOTWAY *n* pl. **-WAYS** a footpath

FOOTWEAR *n* pl. **FOOTWEAR** wearing apparel for the feet

FOOTWORK *n* pl. **-S** the use of the feet

FOOTWORN *adj* footsore

FOOTY *adj* **-TIER, -TIEST** paltry

FOOZLE *v* **-ZLED, -ZLING, -ZLES** to bungle

FOOZLER *n* pl. **-S** one that foozles

FOP *v* **FOPPED, FOPPING, FOPS** to deceive

FOPPERY *n* pl. **-PERIES** foppish behavior

FOPPISH *adj* characteristic of a dandy

FOR *prep* directed or sent to

FORA a pl. of forum

FORAGE *v* **-AGED, -AGING, -AGES** to search about

FORAGER *n* pl. **-S** one that forages

FORAM *n* pl. **-S** a marine rhizopod

FORAMEN *n* pl. **-MENS** or **-MINA** a small anatomical opening

FORAY *v* **-ED, -ING, -S** to raid

FORAYER *n* pl. **-S** one that forays

FORB *n* pl. **-S** an herb other than grass

FORBEAR *v* **-BORE** or **-BARE, -BORNE, -BEARING, -BEARS** to refrain from

FORBID *v* **-BADE** or **-BAD, -BIDDEN, -BIDDING, -BIDS** to command not to do something

FORBIDAL *n* pl. **-S** the act of forbidding

FORBODE *v* **-BODED, -BODING, -BODES** to forebode

FORBORE past tense of forbear

FORBORNE past participle of forbear

FORBY *prep* close by

FORBYE *prep* forby

FORCE *v* **FORCED, FORCING, FORCES** to overcome resistance by the exertion of strength **FORCEDLY** *adv*

FORCEFUL *adj* strong

FORCEPS *n* pl. **-CIPES** an instrument for seizing and holding objects

FORCER *n* pl. **-S** one that forces**

FORCIBLE	*adj* effected by force **FORCIBLY** *adv*
FORCING	present participle of force
FORCIPES	pl. of forceps
FORD	*v* **-ED, -ING, -S** to cross by wading **FORDABLE** *adj*
FORDLESS	*adj* unable to be forded
FORDO	*v* **-DID, -DONE, -DOING, -DOES** to destroy
FORE	*n* pl. **-S** the front part of something
FOREARM	*v* **-ED, -ING, -S** to arm in advance
FOREBAY	*n* pl. **-BAYS** a reservoir from which water is taken to run equipment
FOREBEAR	*n* pl. **-S** an ancestor
FOREBODE	*v* **-BODED, -BODING, -BODES** to indicate in advance
FOREBODY	*n* pl. **-BODIES** the forward part of a ship
FOREBOOM	*n* pl. **-S** the boom of a ship's foremast
FOREBY	*prep* forby
FOREBYE	*prep* forby
FORECAST	*v* **-ED, -ING, -S** to estimate or calculate in advance
FOREDATE	*v* **-DATED, -DATING, -DATES** to antedate
FOREDECK	*n* pl. **-S** the forward part of a ship's deck
FOREDO	*v* **-DID, -DONE, -DOING, -DOES** to fordo
FOREDOOM	*v* **-ED, -ING, -S** to doom in advance
FOREFACE	*n* pl. **-S** the front part of the head of a quadruped
FOREFEEL	*v* **-FELT, -FEELING, -FEELS** to have a premonition of
FOREFEND	*v* **-ED, -ING, -S** to forfend
FOREFOOT	*n* pl. **-FEET** one of the front feet of an animal
FOREGO	*v* **-WENT, -GONE, -GOING, -GOES** to go before
FOREGOER	*n* pl. **-S** one that foregoes
FOREGUT	*n* pl. **-S** the front part of the embryonic alimentary canal
FOREHAND	*n* pl. **-S** a type of tennis stroke
FOREHEAD	*n* pl. **-S** the part of the face above the eyes
FOREHOOF	*n* pl. **-HOOFS** or **-HOOVES** the hoof of a forefoot
FOREIGN	*adj* situated outside a place or country
FOREKNOW	*v* **-KNEW, -KNOWN, -KNOWING, -KNOWS** to know in advance
FORELADY	*n* pl. **-DIES** a woman who supervises workers
FORELAND	*n* pl. **-S** a projecting mass of land
FORELEG	*n* pl. **-S** one of the front legs of an animal
FORELIMB	*n* pl. **-S** a foreleg
FORELOCK	*v* **-ED, -ING, -S** to fasten with a linchpin
FOREMAN	*n* pl. **-MEN** a man who supervises workers
FOREMAST	*n* pl. **-S** the forward mast of a ship
FOREMILK	*n* pl. **-S** the milk secreted immediately after childbirth
FOREMOST	*adj* first in position
FORENAME	*n* pl. **-S** a first name
FORENOON	*n* pl. **-S** the period of daylight before noon
FORENSIC	*n* pl. **-S** an argumentative exercise
FOREPART	*n* pl. **-S** the front part
FOREPAST	*adj* already in the past
FOREPAW	*n* pl. **-S** the paw of a foreleg
FOREPEAK	*n* pl. **-S** the forward part of a ship's hold
FOREPLAY	*n* pl. **-PLAYS** erotic stimulation preceding sexual intercourse
FORERANK	*n* pl. **-S** the first rank
FORERUN	*v* **-RAN, -RUNNING, -RUNS** to run in advance of
FORESAID	*adj* previously said
FORESAIL	*n* pl. **-S** the lowest sail on a foremast
FORESEE	*v* **-SAW, -SEEN, -SEEING, -SEES** to see in advance
FORESEER	*n* pl. **-S** one that foresees
FORESHOW	*v* **-SHOWED, -SHOWN, -SHOWING, -SHOWS** to show in advance
FORESIDE	*n* pl. **-S** the front side
FORESKIN	*n* pl. **-S** the prepuce
FOREST	*v* **-ED, -ING, -S** to convert into a forest (a densely wooded area)
FORESTAL	*adj* of or pertaining to a forest
FORESTAY	*n* pl. **-STAYS** a wire or rope used to support a foremast
FORESTER	*n* pl. **-S** one skilled in forestry
FORESTRY	*n* pl. **-RIES** the science of planting and managing forests

FORETELL   *v* **-TOLD, -TELLING, -TELLS** to tell of or about in advance

FORETIME   *n* pl. **-S** the past

FORETOP   *n* pl. **-S** a forelock

FOREVER   *n* pl. **-S** an indefinite length of time

FOREWARN   *v* **-ED, -ING, -S** to warn in advance

FOREWENT   past tense of forego

FOREWING   *n* pl. **-S** an anterior wing of an insect

FOREWORD   *n* pl. **-S** an introductory statement

FOREWORN   *adj* forworn

FOREYARD   *n* pl. **-S** the lowest yard on a foremast

FORFEIT   *v* **-ED, -ING, -S** to lose as a penalty

FORFEND   *v* **-ED, -ING, -S** to protect

FORGAT   a past tense of forget

FORGAVE   past tense of forgive

FORGE   *v* **FORGED, FORGING, FORGES** to fashion or reproduce for fraudulent purposes

FORGER   *n* pl. **-S** one that forges

FORGERY   *n* pl. **-ERIES** the act of forging

FORGET   *v* **-GOT** or **-GAT, -GOTTEN, -GETTING, -GETS** to fail to remember

FORGING   *n* pl. **-S** a forgery

FORGIVE   *v* **-GAVE, -GIVEN, -GIVING, -GIVES** to pardon

FORGIVER   *n* pl. **-S** one that forgives

FORGO   *v* **-WENT, -GONE, -GOING, -GOES** to refrain from

FORGOER   *n* pl. **-S** one that forgoes

FORGOT   a past tense of forget

FORGOTTEN   past participle of forget

FORINT   *n* pl. **-S** a monetary unit of Hungary

FORJUDGE   *v* **-JUDGED, -JUDGING, -JUDGES** to deprive by judgment of a court

FORK   *v* **-ED, -ING, -S** to work with a fork (a pronged implement) **FORKEDLY** *adv*

FORKBALL   *n* pl. **-S** a breaking pitch in baseball

FORKER   *n* pl. **-S** one that forks

FORKFUL   *n* pl. **FORKFULS** or **FORKSFUL** as much as a fork will hold

FORKIER   comparative of forky

FORKIEST   superlative of forky

FORKLESS   *adj* having no fork

FORKLIFT   *v* **-ED, -ING, -S** to raise or transport by means of a forklift (a machine with projecting prongs)

FORKLIKE   *adj* resembling a fork

FORKSFUL   a pl. of forkful

FORKY   *adj* **FORKIER, FORKIEST** resembling a fork

FORLORN   *adj* **-LORNER, -LORNEST** dreary

FORM   *v* **-ED, -ING, -S** to produce **FORMABLE** *adj* **FORMABLY** *adv*

FORMAL   *n* pl. **-S** a social event that requires evening dress

FORMALIN   *n* pl. **-S** an aqueous solution of formaldehyde

FORMALLY   *adv* in a prescribed or customary manner

FORMANT   *n* pl. **-S** a characteristic component of the quality of a speech sound

FORMAT   *v* **-MATTED, -MATTING, -MATS** to produce in a specified style

FORMATE   *n* pl. **-S** a chemical salt

FORME   *n* pl. **-S** an assemblage of printing type secured in a metal frame

FORMEE   *adj* having the arms narrow at the center and expanding toward the ends — used of a heraldic cross

FORMER   *n* pl. **-S** one that forms

FORMERLY   *adv* previously

FORMFUL   *adj* exhibiting good form

FORMIC   *adj* pertaining to ants

FORMLESS   *adj* lacking structure

FORMOL   *n* pl. **-S** formalin

FORMULA   *n* pl. **-LAS** or **-LAE** an exact method for doing something

FORMWORK   *n* pl. **-S** a set of forms to hold concrete until it sets

FORMYL   *n* pl. **-S** a univalent chemical radical

FORNENT   *prep* near to

FORNIX   *n* pl. **-NICES** an arched anatomical structure **FORNICAL** *adj*

FORRADER   *adv* further ahead

FORRIT   *adv* toward the front

FORSAKE   *v* **-SOOK, -SAKEN, -SAKING, -SAKES** to quit or leave entirely

FORSAKER   *n* pl. **-S** one that forsakes

FORSOOTH   *adv* in truth

FORSPENT   *adj* worn out

FORSWEAR	*v* **-SWORE, -SWORN, -SWEARING, -SWEARS** to deny under oath
FORT	*n* pl. **-S** a fortified enclosure or structure
FORTE	*n* pl. **-S** a strong point
FORTES	pl. of fortis
FORTH	*adv* onward in time, place, or order
FORTIES	pl. of forty
FORTIETH	*n* pl. **-S** one of forty equal parts
FORTIFY	*v* **-FIED, -FYING, -FIES** to strengthen against attack
FORTIS	*n* pl. **-TES** a consonant pronounced with relatively strong release of breath
FORTRESS	*v* **-ED, -ING, -ES** to fortify
FORTUITY	*n* pl. **-ITIES** an accidental occurrence
FORTUNE	*v* **-TUNED, -TUNING, -TUNES** to endow with wealth
FORTY	*n* pl. **-TIES** a number
FORTYISH	*adj* being about forty years old
FORUM	*n* pl. **-RUMS** or **-RA** a public meeting place
FORWARD	*adj* **-WARDER, -WARDEST** being at a point in advance
FORWARD	*v* **-ED, -ING, -S** to help onward
FORWENT	past tense of forgo
FORWHY	*adv* for what reason
FORWORN	*adj* worn out
FORZANDO	*n* pl. **-DOS** or **-DI** sforzato
FOSS	*n* pl. **-ES** fosse
FOSSA	*n* pl. **-S** a catlike mammal
FOSSA	*n* pl. **-SAE** an anatomical depression **FOSSATE** *adj*
FOSSE	*n* pl. **-S** a ditch
FOSSETTE	*n* pl. **-S** a small fossa
FOSSICK	*v* **-ED, -ING, -S** to search for gold
FOSSIL	*n* pl. **-S** the remains of an animal or plant preserved in the earth's crust
FOSTER	*v* **-ED, -ING, -S** to promote the growth of
FOSTERER	*n* pl. **-S** one that fosters
FOU	*adj* drunk
FOUETTE	*n* pl. **-S** a movement in ballet
FOUGHT	past tense of fight
FOUGHTEN	*adj* exhausted especially from fighting
FOUL	*adj* **FOULER, FOULEST** offensive to the senses
FOUL	*v* **-ED, -ING, -S** to make foul
FOULARD	*n* pl. **-S** a soft fabric
FOULING	*n* pl. **-S** a deposit or crust
FOULLY	*adv* in a foul manner
FOULNESS	*n* pl. **-ES** the state of being foul
FOUND	*v* **-ED, -ING, -S** to establish
FOUNDER	*v* **-ED, -ING, -S** to become disabled
FOUNDRY	*n* pl. **-RIES** an establishment in which metal is cast
FOUNT	*n* pl. **-S** a fountain
FOUNTAIN	*v* **-ED, -ING, -S** to flow like a fountain (a spring of water)
FOUR	*n* pl. **-S** a number
FOURCHEE	*adj* having the end of each arm forked — used of a heraldic cross
FOUREYED	*adj* wearing eyeglasses
FOURFOLD	*adj* four times as great
FOURGON	*n* pl. **-S** a wagon for carrying baggage
FOURPLEX	*n* pl. **-ES** quadplex
FOURSOME	*n* pl. **-S** a group of four
FOURTEEN	*n* pl. **-S** a number
FOURTH	*n* pl. **-S** one of four equal parts
FOURTHLY	*adv* in the fourth place
FOVEA	*n* pl. **-VEAS** or **-VEAE** a shallow anatomical depression **FOVEAL, FOVEATE, FOVEATED** *adj*
FOVEOLA	*n* pl. **-LAS** or **-LAE** a small fovea **FOVEOLAR** *adj*
FOVEOLE	*n* pl. **-S** a foveola
FOVEOLET	*n* pl. **-S** a foveola
FOWL	*v* **-ED, -ING, -S** to hunt birds
FOWLER	*n* pl. **-S** one that fowls
FOWLING	*n* pl. **-S** the hunting of birds
FOWLPOX	*n* pl. **-ES** a virus disease of poultry
FOX	*v* **-ED, -ING, -ES** to outwit
FOXFIRE	*n* pl. **-S** a glow produced by certain fungi on decaying wood
FOXFISH	*n* pl. **-ES** a large shark
FOXGLOVE	*n* pl. **-S** a flowering plant
FOXHOLE	*n* pl. **-S** a small pit used for cover in a battle area
FOXHOUND	*n* pl. **-S** a hunting dog
FOXHUNT	*v* **-ED, -ING, -S** to hunt with hounds for a fox

FOXIER	comparative of foxy
FOXIEST	superlative of foxy
FOXILY	*adv* in a foxy manner
FOXINESS	*n* pl. **-ES** the state of being foxy
FOXING	*n* pl. **-S** a piece of material used to cover the upper portion of a shoe
FOXLIKE	*adj* resembling a fox (a carnivorous mammal)
FOXSKIN	*n* pl. **-S** the skin of a fox
FOXTAIL	*n* pl. **-S** the tail of a fox
FOXTROT	*v* **-TROTTED, -TROTTING, -TROTS** to dance the fox trot (a dance for couples)
FOXY	*adj* **FOXIER, FOXIEST** crafty
FOY	*n* pl. **FOYS** a farewell feast or gift
FOYER	*n* pl. **-S** an entrance room or hall
FOZINESS	*n* pl. **-ES** the state of being fozy
FOZY	*adj* **-ZIER, -ZIEST** too ripe
FRABJOUS	*adj* splendid
FRACAS	*n* pl. **-ES** a brawl
FRACTAL	*n* pl. **-S** a complex geometric curve
FRACTED	*adj* broken
FRACTI	pl. of fractus
FRACTION	*v* **-ED, -ING, -S** to divide into portions
FRACTUR	*n* pl. **-S** fraktur
FRACTURE	*v* **-TURED, -TURING, -TURES** to break
FRACTUS	*n* pl. **-TI** a ragged cloud
FRAE	*prep* from
FRAENUM	*n* pl. **-NUMS** or **-NA** frenum
FRAG	*v* **FRAGGED, FRAGGING, FRAGS** to injure with a type of grenade
FRAGGING	*n* pl. **-S** the act of one that frags
FRAGILE	*adj* easily broken or damaged
FRAGMENT	*v* **-ED, -ING, -S** to break into pieces
FRAGRANT	*adj* having a pleasant odor
FRAIL	*adj* **FRAILER, FRAILEST** fragile **FRAILLY** *adv*
FRAIL	*n* pl. **-S** a basket for holding dried fruits
FRAILTY	*n* pl. **-TIES** a weakness of character
FRAISE	*n* pl. **-S** a barrier of pointed stakes
FRAKTUR	*n* pl. **-S** a style of type
FRAME	*v* **FRAMED, FRAMING, FRAMES** to construct by putting together the various parts **FRAMABLE** *adj*
FRAMER	*n* pl. **-S** one that frames
FRAMING	*n* pl. **-S** framework
FRANC	*n* pl. **-S** a former monetary unit of France
FRANCIUM	*n* pl. **-S** a radioactive element
FRANCIZE	*v* **-CIZED, -CIZING, -CIZES** to force to adopt French customs and language
FRANK	*adj* **FRANKER, FRANKEST** honest and unreserved in speech
FRANK	*v* **-ED, -ING, -S** to mark (a piece of mail) for free delivery
FRANKER	*n* pl. **-S** one that franks
FRANKLIN	*n* pl. **-S** a medieval English landowner
FRANKLY	*adv* in a frank manner
FRANTIC	*adj* wildly excited
FRAP	*v* **FRAPPED, FRAPPING, FRAPS** to bind firmly
FRAPPE	*n* pl. **-S** a partly frozen drink
FRASS	*n* pl. **-ES** debris made by insects
FRAT	*n* pl. **-S** a college fraternity
FRATER	*n* pl. **-S** a comrade
FRAUD	*n* pl. **-S** trickery
FRAUGHT	*v* **-ED, -ING, -S** to load down
FRAULEIN	*n* pl. **-S** a German governess
FRAY	*v* **-ED, -ING, -S** to wear off by rubbing
FRAYING	*n* pl. **-S** something worn off by rubbing
FRAZIL	*n* pl. **-S** tiny ice crystals formed in supercooled waters
FRAZZLE	*v* **-ZLED, -ZLING, -ZLES** to fray
FREAK	*v* **-ED, -ING, -S** to streak with color
FREAKIER	comparative of freaky
FREAKIEST	superlative of freaky
FREAKILY	*adv* in a freaky manner
FREAKISH	*adj* unusual
FREAKOUT	*n* pl. **-S** an event marked by wild excitement
FREAKY	*adj* **FREAKIER, FREAKIEST** freakish
FRECKLE	*v* **-LED, -LING, -LES** to mark with freckles (small, brownish spots)
FRECKLY	*adj* **-LIER, -LIEST** marked with freckles
FREE	*adj* **FREER, FREEST** not subject to restriction or control

FREE   *v* **FREED, FREEING, FREES** to make free

FREEBASE   *v* **-BASED, -BASING, -BASES** to use a form of cocaine that is inhaled

FREEBEE   *n* pl. **-S** freebie

FREEBIE   *n* pl. **-S** something given or received without charge

FREEBOOT   *v* **-ED, -ING, -S** to plunder

FREEBORN   *adj* born free

FREED   past tense of free

FREEDMAN   *n* pl. **-MEN** a man who has been freed from slavery

FREEDOM   *n* pl. **-S** the state of being free

FREEFORM   *adj* having a free flowing design or shape

FREEHAND   *adj* drawn by hand without mechanical aids

FREEHOLD   *n* pl. **-S** a form of tenure of real property

FREELOAD   *v* **-ED, -ING, -S** to live at the expense of others

FREELY   *adv* in a free manner

FREEMAN   *n* pl. **-MEN** one who is free

FREENESS   *n* pl. **-ES** freedom

FREER   *n* pl. **-S** one that frees

FREESIA   *n* pl. **-S** an African herb

FREEST   superlative of free

FREEWARE   *n* pl. **-S** software distributed without charge

FREEWAY   *n* pl. **-WAYS** an express highway

FREEWILL   *adj* voluntary

FREEZE   *v* **FROZE, FROZEN, FREEZING, FREEZES** to become hardened into a solid body by loss of heat

FREEZER   *n* pl. **-S** an apparatus for freezing food

FREIGHT   *v* **-ED, -ING, -S** to load with goods for transportation

FREMD   *adj* strange

FREMITUS   *n* pl. **-ES** a palpable vibration

FRENA   a pl. of frenum

FRENCH   *v* **-ED, -ING, -ES** to cut into thin strips before cooking

FRENETIC   *n* pl. **-S** a frantic person

FRENULUM   *n* pl. **-LUMS** or **-LA** a frenum **FRENULAR** *adj*

FRENUM   *n* pl. **-NUMS** or **-NA** a connecting fold of membrane

FRENZILY   *adv* in a frantic manner

FRENZY   *v* **-ZIED, -ZYING, -ZIES** to make frantic

FREQUENT   *adj* **-QUENTER, -QUENTEST** occurring again and again

FREQUENT   *v* **-ED, -ING, -S** to be in or at often

FRERE   *n* pl. **-S** brother

FRESCO   *v* **-ED, -ING, -S** or **-ES** to paint on a surface of plaster

FRESCOER   *n* pl. **-S** one that frescoes

FRESH   *adj* **FRESHER, FRESHEST** new

FRESH   *v* **-ED, -ING, -ES** to freshen

FRESHEN   *v* **-ED, -ING, -S** to make or become fresh

FRESHET   *n* pl. **-S** a sudden overflow of a stream

FRESHLY   *adv* in a fresh manner

FRESHMAN   *n* pl. **-MEN** a first-year student

FRESNEL   *n* pl. **-S** a unit of frequency

FRET   *v* **FRETTED, FRETTING, FRETS** to worry

FRETFUL   *adj* inclined to fret

FRETLESS   *adj* having no fretwork

FRETSAW   *n* pl. **-S** a narrow-bladed saw

FRETSOME   *adj* fretful

FRETTED   past tense of fret

FRETTER   *n* pl. **-S** one that frets

FRETTING   present participle of fret

FRETTY   *adj* **-TIER, -TIEST** fretful

FRETWORK   *n* pl. **-S** ornamental work consisting of interlacing parts

FRIABLE   *adj* easily crumbled

FRIAR   *n* pl. **-S** a member of a religious order **FRIARLY** *adj*

FRIARY   *n* pl. **-ARIES** a monastery of friars

FRIBBLE   *v* **-BLED, -BLING, -BLES** to act foolishly

FRIBBLER   *n* pl. **-S** one that fribbles

FRICANDO   *n* pl. **-DOES** a roasted loin of veal

FRICTION   *n* pl. **-S** the rubbing of one body against another

FRIDGE   *n* pl. **-S** a refrigerator

FRIED   past tense of fry

FRIEND   *v* **-ED, -ING, -S** to enter into a warm association with

FRIENDLY   *adj* **-LIER, -LIEST** inclined to approve, help, or support

FRIENDLY   *n* pl. **-LIES** one who is friendly

FRIER   *n* pl. **-S** fryer

FRIES	present 3d person sing. of fry
FRIEZE	*n* pl. **-S** a coarse woolen fabric
FRIG	*n* pl. **-ES** a refrigerator
FRIG	*v* **FRIGGED, FRIGGING, FRIGS** to cheat or trick
FRIGATE	*n* pl. **-S** a sailing vessel
FRIGHT	*v* **-ED, -ING, -S** to frighten
FRIGHTEN	*v* **-ED, -ING, -S** to make afraid
FRIGID	*adj* very cold **FRIGIDLY** *adv*
FRIJOL	*n* pl. **-ES** a bean used as food
FRIJOLE	*n* pl. **-S** frijol
FRILL	*v* **-ED, -ING, -S** to provide with a frill (an ornamental ruffled edge)
FRILLER	*n* pl. **-S** one that frills
FRILLING	*n* pl. **-S** an arrangement of frills
FRILLY	*adj* **FRILLIER, FRILLIEST** having frills
FRINGE	*v* **FRINGED, FRINGING, FRINGES** to provide with a fringe (an ornamental border)
FRINGY	*adj* **FRINGIER, FRINGIEST** resembling a fringe
FRIPPERY	*n* pl. **-PERIES** excessive ornamentation
FRISE	*n* pl. **-S** frieze
FRISEE	*n* pl. **-S** curly leaves of endive
FRISETTE	*n* pl. **-S** frizette
FRISEUR	*n* pl. **-S** a hairdresser
FRISK	*v* **-ED, -ING, -S** to move or leap about playfully
FRISKER	*n* pl. **-S** one that frisks
FRISKET	*n* pl. **-S** a frame used to protect paper in a printing press
FRISKY	*adj* **FRISKIER, FRISKIEST** lively and playful **FRISKILY** *adv*
FRISSON	*n* pl. **-S** a shudder
FRIT	*v* **FRITTED, FRITTING, FRITS** to fuse into a vitreous substance
FRITES	*n/pl* french fries
FRITH	*n* pl. **-S** firth
FRITT	*v* **-ED, -ING, -S** to frit
FRITTATA	*n* pl. **-S** an unfolded omelet with chopped vegetables or meat
FRITTED	past tense of frit
FRITTER	*v* **-ED, -ING, -S** to squander little by little
FRITTING	present participle of frit
FRITZ	*n* pl. **-ES** a nonfunctioning state
FRIVOL	*v* **-OLED, -OLING, -OLS** or **-OLLED, -OLLING, -OLS** to behave playfully
FRIVOLER	*n* pl. **-S** one that frivols
FRIZ	*v* **-ED, -ING, -ES** to frizz
FRIZER	*n* pl. **-S** frizzer
FRIZETTE	*n* pl. **-S** a frizzed fringe of hair
FRIZZ	*v* **-ED, -ING, -ES** to form into small, tight curls
FRIZZER	*n* pl. **-S** one that frizzes
FRIZZIER	comparative of frizzy
FRIZZIES	*n/pl* frizzy hair
FRIZZIEST	superlative of frizzy
FRIZZILY	*adv* in a frizzy manner
FRIZZLE	*v* **-ZLED, -ZLING, -ZLES** to frizz
FRIZZLER	*n* pl. **-S** one that frizzles
FRIZZLY	*adj* **-ZLIER, -ZLIEST** frizzy
FRIZZY	*adj* **FRIZZIER, FRIZZIEST** tightly curled
FRO	*adv* away
FROCK	*v* **-ED, -ING, -S** to clothe in a long, loose outer garment
FROE	*n* pl. **-S** a cleaving tool
FROG	*v* **FROGGED, FROGGING, FROGS** to hunt frogs (web-footed, tailless amphibians)
FROGEYE	*n* pl. **-S** a plant disease **FROGEYED** *adj*
FROGFISH	*n* pl. **-ES** a marine fish
FROGGED	past tense of frog
FROGGING	present participle of frog
FROGGY	*adj* **-GIER, -GIEST** abounding in frogs
FROGLET	*n* pl. **-S** a young frog
FROGLIKE	*adj* resembling a frog
FROGMAN	*n* pl. **-MEN** a person equipped for extended periods of underwater swimming
FROLIC	*v* **-ICKED, -ICKING, -ICS** to play and run about merrily **FROLICKY** *adj*
FROM	*prep* starting at
FROMAGE	*n* pl. **-S** cheese
FROMENTY	*n* pl. **-TIES** frumenty
FROND	*n* pl. **-S** a type of leaf **FRONDED, FRONDOSE** *adj*
FRONDEUR	*n* pl. **-S** a rebel
FRONS	*n* pl. **FRONTES** the upper anterior portion of an insect's head
FRONT	*adj* **FRONTER** articulated at the front of the oral passage

FRONT v **-ED, -ING, -S** to provide with a front (a forward part)

FRONTAGE n pl. **-S** the front of a building or lot

FRONTAL n pl. **-S** a bone of the skull

FRONTES pl. of frons

FRONTIER n pl. **-S** a border between two countries

FRONTLET n pl. **-S** a decorative band worn across the forehead

FRONTMAN n pl. **-MEN** the most prominent member of a group of musicians

FRONTON n pl. **-S** a jai alai arena

FRORE adj frozen

FROSH n pl. **FROSH** a freshman

FROST v **-ED, -ING, -S** to cover with frost (a deposit of minute ice crystals)

FROSTBIT adj injured by extreme cold

FROSTED n pl. **-S** a type of milk shake

FROSTING n pl. **-S** icing

FROSTNIP n pl. **-S** the freezing of outer skin layers

FROSTY adj **FROSTIER, FROSTIEST** covered with frost **FROSTILY** adv

FROTH v **-ED, -ING, -S** to foam

FROTHER n pl. **-S** one that froths

FROTHY adj **FROTHIER, FROTHIEST** foamy **FROTHILY** adv

FROTTAGE n pl. **-S** masturbation by rubbing against another person

FROTTEUR n pl. **-S** one who practices frottage

FROUFROU n pl. **-S** a rustling sound

FROUNCE v **FROUNCED, FROUNCING, FROUNCES** to pleat

FROUZY adj **-ZIER, -ZIEST** frowzy

FROW n pl. **-S** froe

FROWARD adj disobedient

FROWN v **-ED, -ING, -S** to contract the brow in displeasure

FROWNER n pl. **-S** one that frowns

FROWST v **-ED, -ING, -S** to lounge in a stuffy room

FROWSTY adj **-TIER, -TIEST** musty

FROWSY adj **-SIER, -SIEST** frowzy

FROWZY adj **-ZIER, -ZIEST** unkempt **FROWZILY** adv

FROZE past tense of freeze

FROZEN adj very cold **FROZENLY** adv

FRUCTIFY v **-FIED, -FYING, -FIES** to bear fruit

FRUCTOSE n pl. **-S** a sugar found in various fruits

FRUG v **FRUGGED, FRUGGING, FRUGS** to perform a type of vigorous dance

FRUGAL adj thrifty **FRUGALLY** adv

FRUIT v **-ED, -ING, -S** to bear fruit (usually edible reproductive bodies of a seed plant)

FRUITAGE n pl. **-S** the process of bearing fruit

FRUITER n pl. **-S** one that grows or sells fruit

FRUITFUL adj **-FULLER, -FULLEST** producing abundantly

FRUITIER comparative of fruity

FRUITIEST superlative of fruity

FRUITION n pl. **-S** the accomplishment of something desired

FRUITLET n pl. **-S** a small fruit

FRUITY adj **FRUITIER, FRUITIEST** suggestive of fruit **FRUITILY** adv

FRUMENTY n pl. **-TIES** a dish of wheat boiled in milk and sweetened with sugar

FRUMP n pl. **-S** a dowdy woman **FRUMPISH** adj

FRUMPY adj **FRUMPIER, FRUMPIEST** dowdy **FRUMPILY** adv

FRUSTULE n pl. **-S** the shell of a diatom

FRUSTUM n pl. **-TUMS** or **-TA** a part of a conical solid

FRY v **FRIED, FRYING, FRIES** to cook over direct heat in hot fat or oil **FRYABLE** adj

FRYBREAD n pl. **-S** a fried bread

FRYER n pl. **-S** one that fries

FRYPAN n pl. **-S** a pan for frying food

FUB v **FUBBED, FUBBING, FUBS** to fob

FUBSY adj **FUBSIER, FUBSIEST** chubby and somewhat squat

FUCHSIA n pl. **-S** a flowering shrub

FUCHSIN n pl. **-S** a red dye

FUCHSINE n pl. **-S** fuchsin

FUCI a pl. of fucus

FUCOID n pl. **-S** a brown seaweed **FUCOIDAL** adj

FUCOSE n pl. **-S** a type of sugar

FUCOUS adj of or pertaining to fucoids

FUCUS n pl. **-CUSES** or **-CI** any of a genus of brown algae

FUD n pl. **-S** an old-fashioned person

FUDDLE   *v* **-DLED, -DLING, -DLES** to confuse

FUDDY   *n* pl. **-DIES** a fussy person

FUDGE   *v* **FUDGED, FUDGING, FUDGES** to falsify

FUEHRER   *n* pl. **-S** fuhrer

FUEL   *v* **-ELED, -ELING, -ELS** or **-ELLED, -ELLING, -ELS** to provide with fuel (material used to produce energy)

FUELER   *n* pl. **-S** one that fuels

FUELLER   *n* pl. **-S** fueler

FUELWOOD   *n* pl. **-S** firewood

FUG   *v* **FUGGED, FUGGING, FUGS** to make stuffy and odorous

FUGACITY   *n* pl. **-TIES** lack of enduring qualities

FUGAL   *adj* being in the style of a fugue **FUGALLY** *adv*

FUGATO   *n* pl. **-TOS** a fugal composition

FUGGED   past tense of fug

FUGGING   present participle of fug

FUGGY   *adj* **-GIER, -GIEST** stuffy and odorous **FUGGILY** *adv*

FUGIO   *n* pl. **-GIOS** a former coin of the United States

FUGITIVE   *n* pl. **-S** one who flees

FUGLE   *v* **-GLED, -GLING, -GLES** to lead

FUGLEMAN   *n* pl. **-MEN** a leader

FUGU   *n* pl. **-S** a toxin-containing fish

FUGUE   *v* **FUGUED, FUGUING, FUGUES** to compose a fugue (a type of musical composition)

FUGUIST   *n* pl. **-S** one who composes fugues

FUHRER   *n* pl. **-S** a leader

FUJI   *n* pl. **-S** a silk fabric

FULCRUM   *n* pl. **-CRUMS** or **-CRA** a support for a lever

FULFIL   *v* **-FILLED, -FILLING, -FILS** to fulfill

FULFILL   *v* **-ED, -ING, -S** to bring about the accomplishment of

FULGENT   *adj* shining brightly

FULGID   *adj* fulgent

FULHAM   *n* pl. **-S** a loaded die

FULL   *adj* **FULLER, FULLEST** filled completely

FULL   *v* **-ED, -ING, -S** to shrink and thicken, as cloth

FULLAM   *n* pl. **-S** fulham

FULLBACK   *n* pl. **-S** an offensive back in football

FULLER   *v* **-ED, -ING, -S** to groove with a type of hammer

FULLERY   *n* pl. **-ERIES** a place for fulling cloth

FULLFACE   *n* pl. **-S** a heavy-faced type

FULLNESS   *n* pl. **-ES** the state of being full

FULLY   *adv* in a full manner

FULMAR   *n* pl. **-S** an arctic seabird

FULMINE   *v* **-MINED, -MINING, -MINES** to explode loudly

FULMINIC   *adj* highly explosive

FULNESS   *n* pl. **-ES** fullness

FULSOME   *adj* repulsive

FULVOUS   *adj* of a brownish yellow color

FUMARASE   *n* pl. **-S** an enzyme

FUMARATE   *n* pl. **-S** a chemical salt

FUMARIC   *adj* pertaining to a certain acid

FUMAROLE   *n* pl. **-S** a hole from which volcanic vapors issue

FUMATORY   *n* pl. **-RIES** a fumigation chamber

FUMBLE   *v* **-BLED, -BLING, -BLES** to handle clumsily

FUMBLER   *n* pl. **-S** one that fumbles

FUME   *v* **FUMED, FUMING, FUMES** to give off fumes (gaseous exhalations)

FUMELESS   *adj* having no fumes

FUMELIKE   *adj* resembling fumes

FUMER   *n* pl. **-S** one that fumes

FUMET   *n* pl. **-S** the odor of meat while cooking

FUMETTE   *n* pl. **-S** fumet

FUMIER   comparative of fumy

FUMIEST   superlative of fumy

FUMIGANT   *n* pl. **-S** a substance used in fumigating

FUMIGATE   *v* **-GATED, -GATING, -GATES** to subject to fumes in order to destroy pests

FUMING   present participle of fume

FUMINGLY   *adv* angrily

FUMITORY   *n* pl. **-RIES** a climbing plant

FUMULUS   *n* pl. **-LI** a thin cloud

FUMY   *adj* **FUMIER, FUMIEST** producing or full of fumes

FUN   *adj* **FUNNER, FUNNEST** providing enjoyment

FUN	*v* **FUNNED, FUNNING, FUNS** to act playfully
FUNCTION	*v* **-ED, -ING, -S** to be in action
FUNCTOR	*n* pl. **-S** one that functions
FUND	*v* **-ED, -ING, -S** to provide money for
FUNDER	*n* pl. **-S** a provider of money
FUNDUS	*n* pl. **-DI** the inner basal surface of a bodily organ **FUNDIC** *adj*
FUNERAL	*n* pl. **-S** a ceremony held for a dead person
FUNERARY	*adj* pertaining to a funeral
FUNEREAL	*adj* funerary
FUNEST	*adj* portending death or evil
FUNFAIR	*n* pl. **-S** an amusement park
FUNFEST	*n* pl. **-S** a party for fun
FUNGAL	*n* pl. **-S** a fungus
FUNGI	a pl. of fungus
FUNGIBLE	*n* pl. **-S** something that may be exchanged for an equivalent unit of the same class
FUNGIC	*adj* fungous
FUNGO	*n* pl. **-GOES** a fly ball hit to a fielder for practice in baseball
FUNGOID	*n* pl. **-S** a growth resembling a fungus
FUNGOUS	*adj* pertaining to a fungus
FUNGUS	*n* pl. **-GUSES** or **-GI** any of a major group of lower plants
FUNHOUSE	*n* pl. **-S** an amusement park attraction
FUNICLE	*n* pl. **-S** a cordlike anatomical structure
FUNICULI	*n/pl* funicles
FUNK	*v* **-ED, -ING, -S** to shrink back in fear
FUNKER	*n* pl. **-S** one that funks
FUNKIA	*n* pl. **-S** a flowering plant
FUNKY	*adj* **FUNKIER, FUNKIEST** having an offensive odor **FUNKILY** *adv*
FUNNED	past tense of fun
FUNNEL	*v* **-NELED, -NELING, -NELS** or **-NELLED, -NELLING, -NELS** to pass through a funnel (a cone-shaped utensil)
FUNNER	comparative of fun
FUNNEST	superlative of fun
FUNNING	present participle of fun
FUNNY	*adj* **-NIER, -NIEST** causing laughter or amusement **FUNNILY** *adv*
FUNNY	*n* pl. **-NIES** a comic strip
FUNNYMAN	*n* pl. **-MEN** a comedian
FUNPLEX	*n* pl. **-ES** a building with facilities for sports and games
FUR	*v* **FURRED, FURRING, FURS** to cover with fur (a dressed animal pelt)
FURAN	*n* pl. **-S** a flammable liquid
FURANE	*n* pl. **-S** furan
FURANOSE	*n* pl. **-S** a type of sugar
FURBELOW	*v* **-ED, -ING, -S** to decorate with ruffles
FURBISH	*v* **-ED, -ING, -ES** to polish
FURCATE	*v* **-CATED, -CATING, -CATES** to divide into branches
FURCRAEA	*n* pl. **-S** a tropical plant
FURCULA	*n* pl. **-LAE** a forked bone **FURCULAR** *adj*
FURCULUM	*n* pl. **-LA** a furcula
FURFUR	*n* pl. **-ES** dandruff
FURFURAL	*n* pl. **-S** a chemical compound
FURFURAN	*n* pl. **-S** furan
FURIBUND	*adj* furious
FURIES	pl. of fury
FURIOSO	*adv* with great force — used as a musical direction
FURIOUS	*adj* extremely angry
FURL	*v* **-ED, -ING, -S** to roll up **FURLABLE** *adj*
FURLER	*n* pl. **-S** one that furls
FURLESS	*adj* having no fur
FURLONG	*n* pl. **-S** a unit of distance
FURLOUGH	*v* **-ED, -ING, -S** to grant a leave of absence to
FURMENTY	*n* pl. **-TIES** frumenty
FURMETY	*n* pl. **-TIES** frumenty
FURMITY	*n* pl. **-TIES** frumenty
FURNACE	*v* **-NACED, -NACING, -NACES** to subject to heat
FURNISH	*v* **-ED, -ING, -ES** to equip
FUROR	*n* pl. **-S** an uproar
FURORE	*n* pl. **-S** furor
FURRED	past tense of fur
FURRIER	*n* pl. **-S** one that deals in furs
FURRIERY	*n* pl. **-ERIES** the business of a furrier

FURRIEST superlative of furry

FURRILY *adv* in a furry manner

FURRINER *n* pl. **-S** a foreigner

FURRING *n* pl. **-S** a trimming or lining of fur

FURROW *v* **-ED, -ING, -S** to make furrows (narrow depressions) in

FURROWER *n* pl. **-S** one that furrows

FURROWY *adj* marked by furrows

FURRY *adj* **-RIER, -RIEST** covered with fur

FURTHER *v* **-ED, -ING, -S** to help forward

FURTHEST a superlative of far

FURTIVE *adj* stealthy

FURUNCLE *n* pl. **-S** a painful swelling of the skin

FURY *n* pl. **-RIES** violent anger

FURZE *n* pl. **-S** a spiny shrub

FURZY *adj* **FURZIER, FURZIEST** abounding in furze

FUSAIN *n* pl. **-S** a fine charcoal used in drawing

FUSARIUM *n* pl. **-SARIA** a disease-causing fungus

FUSCOUS *adj* of a dusky color

FUSE *v* **FUSED, FUSING, FUSES** to equip with a fuse (a detonating device)

FUSEE *n* pl. **-S** a large-headed friction match

FUSEL *n* pl. **-S** an oily liquid

FUSELAGE *n* pl. **-S** the body of an airplane

FUSELESS *adj* lacking a fuse

FUSELIKE *adj* resmbling a fuse

FUSIBLE *adj* capable of being melted **FUSIBLY** *adv*

FUSIFORM *adj* tapering toward each end

FUSIL *n* pl. **-S** a type of musket

FUSILE *adj* formed by melting

FUSILEER *n* pl. **-S** fusilier

FUSILIER *n* pl. **-S** a soldier armed with a fusil

FUSILLI *n* pl. **-S** spiral-shaped pasta

FUSING present participle of fuse

FUSION *n* pl. **-S** the act of melting together **FUSIONAL** *adj*

FUSS *v* **-ED, -ING, -ES** to be overly concerned with small details

FUSSER *n* pl. **-S** one that fusses

FUSSPOT *n* pl. **-S** a fusser

FUSSY *adj* **FUSSIER, FUSSIEST** overly concerned with small details **FUSSILY** *adv*

FUSTIAN *n* pl. **-S** a cotton fabric

FUSTIC *n* pl. **-S** a tropical tree

FUSTY *adj* **-TIER, -TIEST** musty **FUSTILY** *adv*

FUSUMA *n* pl. **FUSUMA** a sliding partitiion in a Japanese house

FUTHARC *n* pl. **-S** futhark

FUTHARK *n* pl. **-S** an ancient alphabet

FUTHORC *n* pl. **-S** futhark

FUTHORK *n* pl. **-S** futhark

FUTILE *adj* having no useful result **FUTILELY** *adv*

FUTILITY *n* pl. **-TIES** the quality of being futile

FUTON *n* pl. **-S** a cotton filled mattress for use as a bed

FUTTOCK *n* pl. **-S** a curved timber in the frame of a wooden ship

FUTURE *n* pl. **-S** the time yet to come **FUTURAL** *adj*

FUTURISM *n* pl. **-S** an artistic and literary movement

FUTURIST *n* pl. **-S** an advocate of futurism

FUTURITY *n* pl. **-TIES** the future

FUTZ *v* **-ED, -ING, -ES** to spend time aimlessly

FUZE *v* **FUZED, FUZING, FUZES** to fuse

FUZEE *n* pl. **-S** fusee

FUZIL *n* pl. **-S** fusil

FUZING present participle of fuze

FUZZ *v* **-ED, -ING, -ES** to become fuzzy

FUZZTONE *n* pl. **-S** a blurred audio effect

FUZZY *adj* **FUZZIER, FUZZIEST** blurry **FUZZILY** *adv*

FYCE *n* pl. **-S** feist

FYKE *n* pl. **-S** a bag-shaped fishnet

FYLFOT *n* pl. **-S** a swastika

FYNBOS *n* pl. **FYNBOS** a type of biome in South Africa

FYTTE *n* pl. **-S** a division of a poem or song

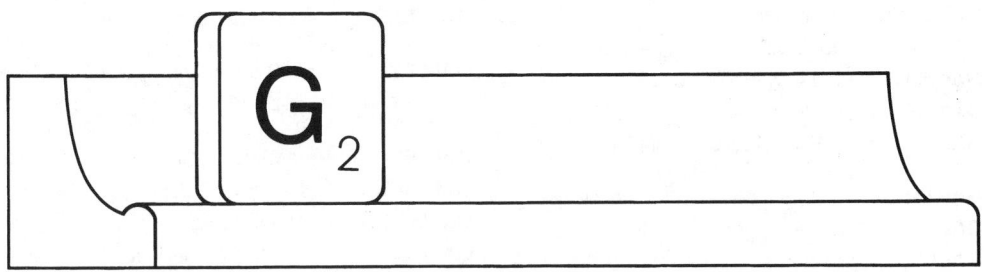

GAB	v **GABBED, GABBING, GABS** to chatter
GABBARD	n pl. **-S** a barge
GABBART	n pl. **-S** gabbard
GABBED	past tense of gab
GABBER	n pl. **-S** one that gabs
GABBIER	comparative of gabby
GABBIEST	superlative of gabby
GABBING	present participle of gab
GABBLE	v **-BLED, -BLING, -BLES** to jabber
GABBLER	n pl. **-S** one that gabbles
GABBRO	n pl. **-BROS** a type of rock **GABBROIC, GABBROID** adj
GABBY	adj **-BIER, -BIEST** talkative
GABELLE	n pl. **-S** a tax on salt **GABELLED** adj
GABFEST	n pl. **-S** an informal gathering for general talk
GABIES	pl. of gaby
GABION	n pl. **-S** a type of basket
GABLE	v **-BLED, -BLING, -BLES** to form a triangular section of a wall
GABOON	n pl. **-S** a spittoon
GABY	n pl. **-BIES** a dolt
GAD	v **GADDED, GADDING, GADS** to roam about restlessly
GADABOUT	n pl. **-S** one that gads about
GADARENE	adj headlong
GADDED	past tense of gad
GADDER	n pl. **-S** one that gads about
GADDI	n pl. **-S** a hassock
GADDING	present participle of gad
GADFLY	n pl. **-FLIES** a biting fly
GADGET	n pl. **-S** a mechanical device **GADGETY** adj
GADGETRY	n pl. **-RIES** the devising or constructing of gadgets
GADI	n pl. **-S** gaddi
GADID	n pl. **-S** gadoid
GADOID	n pl. **-S** a type of fish
GADROON	v **-ED, -ING, -S** to decorate with bands of fluted or reeded molding
GADWALL	n pl. **-S** a wild duck
GADZOOKS	interj —used as a mild oath
GAE	v **GAED, GANE** or **GAEN, GAEING** or **GAUN, GAES** to go
GAFF	v **-ED, -ING, -S** to catch a fish with a sharp hook
GAFFE	n pl. **-S** a social blunder
GAFFER	n pl. **-S** an old man
GAG	v **GAGGED, GAGGING, GAGS** to stop up the mouth
GAGA	adj crazy
GAGAKU	n pl. **-S** ancient court music of Japan
GAGE	v **GAGED, GAGING, GAGES** to pledge as security
GAGER	n pl. **-S** gauger
GAGGED	past tense of gag
GAGGER	n pl. **-S** one that gags
GAGGING	present participle of gag
GAGGLE	v **-GLED, -GLING, -GLES** to cackle
GAGING	present participle of gage
GAGMAN	n pl. **-MEN** one who writes jokes
GAGSTER	n pl. **-S** a gagman
GAHNITE	n pl. **-S** a mineral
GAIETY	n pl. **-ETIES** festive activity
GAIJIN	n pl. **GAIJIN** a foreigner in Japan
GAILY	adv in a gay manner
GAIN	v **-ED, -ING, -S** to acquire **GAINABLE** adj
GAINER	n pl. **-S** one that gains
GAINFUL	adj profitable

GAINLESS *adj* profitless

GAINLY *adj* **-LIER, -LIEST** graceful

GAINSAY *v* **-SAID, -SAYING, -SAYS** to deny

GAINST *prep* against

GAIT *v* **-ED, -ING, -S** to train a horse to move in a particular way

GAITER *n pl.* **-S** a covering for the lower leg

GAL *n pl.* **-S** a girl

GALA *n pl.* **-S** a celebration

GALABIA *n pl.* **-S** djellaba

GALABIEH *n pl.* **-S** djellaba

GALABIYA *n pl.* **-S** djellaba

GALACTIC *adj* pertaining to a galaxy

GALAGO *n pl.* **-GOS** a small primate

GALAH *n pl.* **-S** a cockatoo

GALANGA *n pl.* **-S** galangal

GALANGAL *n pl.* **-S** a medicinal plant

GALATEA *n pl.* **-S** a strong cotton fabric

GALAVANT *v* **-ED, -ING, -S** to gad about

GALAX *n pl.* **-ES** an evergreen herb

GALAXY *n pl.* **-AXIES** a large system of celestial bodies

GALBANUM *n pl.* **-S** a gum resin

GALE *n pl.* **-S** a strong wind

GALEA *n pl.* **-LEAS** or **-LEAE** a helmet-shaped anatomical part **GALEATE, GALEATED** *adj*

GALENA *n pl.* **-S** the principal ore of lead **GALENIC** *adj*

GALENITE *n pl.* **-S** galena

GALERE *n pl.* **-S** a group of people having a common quality

GALETTE *n pl.* **-S** a flat round cake

GALILEE *n pl.* **-S** a type of porch

GALIOT *n pl.* **-S** galliot

GALIPOT *n pl.* **-S** a type of turpentine

GALIVANT *v* **-ED, -ING, -S** to gad about

GALL *v* **-ED, -ING, -S** to vex or irritate

GALLANT *v* **-ED, -ING, -S** to court a woman

GALLATE *n pl.* **-S** a chemical salt

GALLEASS *n pl.* **-ES** a large war galley

GALLEIN *n pl.* **-S** a green dye

GALLEON *n pl.* **-S** a large sailing vessel

GALLERIA *n pl.* **-S** a roofed promenade or court

GALLERY *v* **-LERIED, -LERYING, -LERIES** to provide with a long covered area

GALLET *v* **-ED, -ING, -S** to fill in mortar joints with stone chips

GALLETA *n pl.* **-S** a perennial grass

GALLEY *n pl.* **-LEYS** a long, low medieval ship

GALLFLY *n pl.* **-FLIES** a small insect

GALLIARD *n pl.* **-S** a lively dance

GALLIASS *n pl.* **-ES** galleass

GALLIC *adj* containing gallium

GALLICA *n pl.* **-S** a European rose

GALLICAN *adj* pertaining to a French religious movement

GALLIED past tense of gally

GALLIES present 3d person sing. of gally

GALLIOT *n pl.* **-S** a small galley

GALLIPOT *n pl.* **-S** a small earthen jar

GALLIUM *n pl.* **-S** a metallic element

GALLNUT *n pl.* **-S** an abnormal swelling of plant tissue

GALLON *n pl.* **-S** a unit of liquid measure

GALLOON *n pl.* **-S** an ornamental braid

GALLOOT *n pl.* **-S** galoot

GALLOP *v* **-ED, -ING, -S** to ride a horse at full speed

GALLOPER *n pl.* **-S** one that gallops

GALLOUS *adj* containing gallium

GALLOWS *n pl.* **-ES** a structure used for hanging a condemned person

GALLUS *n pl.* **-ES** a suspender for trousers **GALLUSED** *adj*

GALLY *v* **-LIED, -LYING, -LIES** to frighten

GALOOT *n pl.* **-S** an awkward or uncouth person

GALOP *v* **-ED, -ING, -S** to dance a galop (a lively round dance)

GALOPADE *n pl.* **-S** a lively round dance

GALORE *n pl.* **-S** abundance

GALOSH *n pl.* **-ES** an overshoe **GALOSHED** *adj*

GALOSHE *n pl.* **-S** galosh

GALUMPH *v* **-ED, -ING, -S** to move clumsily

GALVANIC *adj* pertaining to a direct electric current

GALYAC *n pl.* **-S** galyak

GALYAK *n pl.* **-S** a fur made from lambskin

GAM *v* **GAMMED, GAMMING, GAMS** to visit socially

GAMA *n pl.* **-S** a pasture grass

GAMASHES *n/pl* boots worn by horseback riders

GAMAY *n* pl. **-MAYS** a red grape

GAMB *n* pl. **-S** a leg

GAMBA *n* pl. **-S** a bass viol

GAMBADE *n* pl. **-S** a gambado

GAMBADO *n* pl. **-DOS** or **-DOES** a leap made by a horse

GAMBE *n* pl. **-S** gamb

GAMBESON *n* pl. **-S** a medieval coat

GAMBIA *n* pl. **-S** gambier

GAMBIER *n* pl. **-S** an extract obtained from an Asian vine

GAMBIR *n* pl. **-S** gambier

GAMBIT *n* pl. **-S** a type of chess opening

GAMBLE *v* **-BLED, -BLING, -BLES** to play a game of chance for money or valuables

GAMBLER *n* pl. **-S** one that gambles

GAMBOGE *n* pl. **-S** a gum resin

GAMBOL *v* **-BOLED, -BOLING, -BOLS** or **-BOLLED, -BOLLING, -BOLS** to leap about playfully

GAMBREL *n* pl. **-S** a part of a horse's leg

GAMBUSIA *n* pl. **-S** a small fish

GAME *adj* **GAMER, GAMEST** plucky

GAME *v* **GAMED, GAMING, GAMES** to gamble

GAMECOCK *n* pl. **-S** a rooster trained for fighting

GAMELAN *n* pl. **-S** a type of orchestra

GAMELIKE *adj* similar to a game (a contest governed by a set of rules)

GAMELY *adv* in a game manner

GAMENESS *n* pl. **-ES** the quality of being game

GAMER *n* pl. **-S** an avid game player

GAMESMAN *n* pl. **-MEN** one who plays games

GAMESOME *adj* playful

GAMEST superlative of game

GAMESTER *n* pl. **-S** a gambler

GAMETE *n* pl. **-S** a mature reproductive cell **GAMETAL, GAMETIC** *adj*

GAMEY *adj* **GAMIER, GAMIEST** gamy

GAMIC *adj* requiring fertilization

GAMIER comparative of gamy

GAMIEST superlative of gamy

GAMILY *adv* in a game manner

GAMIN *n* pl. **-S** an urchin

GAMINE *n* pl. **-S** a tomboy

GAMINESS *n* pl. **-ES** the quality of being gamy

GAMING *n* pl. **-S** the practice of gambling

GAMMA *n* pl. **-S** a Greek letter

GAMMADIA *n/pl* Greek ornamental designs

GAMMED past tense of gam

GAMMER *n* pl. **-S** an old woman

GAMMIER comparative of gammy

GAMMIEST superlative of gammy

GAMMING present participle of gam

GAMMON *v* **-ED, -ING, -S** to mislead by deceptive talk

GAMMONER *n* pl. **-S** one that gammons

GAMMY *adj* **-MIER, -MIEST** lame

GAMODEME *n* pl. **-S** a somewhat isolated breeding community of organisms

GAMP *n* pl. **-S** a large umbrella

GAMUT *n* pl. **-S** an entire range

GAMY *adj* **GAMIER, GAMIEST** plucky

GAN past tense of gin

GANACHE *n* pl. **-S** creamy chocolate mixture

GANDER *v* **-ED, -ING, -S** to wander

GANE a past participle of gae

GANEF *n* pl. **-S** a thief

GANEV *n* pl. **-S** ganef

GANG *v* **-ED, -ING, -S** to form into a gang (a group)

GANGBANG *v* **-ED, -ING, -S** to participate in gang-related activities

GANGER *n* pl. **-S** a foreman of a gang of laborers

GANGLAND *n* pl. **-S** the criminal underworld

GANGLIA a pl. of ganglion

GANGLIAL *adj* gangliar

GANGLIAR *adj* pertaining to a ganglion

GANGLIER comparative of gangly

GANGLIEST superlative of gangly

GANGLING *adj* awkwardly tall and lanky

GANGLION *n* pl. **-GLIONS** or **-GLIA** a group of nerve cells

GANGLY *adj* **-GLIER, -GLIEST** gangling

GANGPLOW *n* pl. **-S** an agricultural implement

GANGREL *n* pl. **-S** a vagabond

GANGRENE *v* **-GRENED, -GRENING, -GRENES** to suffer the loss of tissue in part of the body

GANGSTA *n* pl. **-S** a member of a street gang

GANGSTER *n* pl. **-S** a member of a criminal gang

GANGUE *n* pl. **-S** the worthless rock in which valuable minerals are found

GANGWAY *n* pl. **-WAYS** a passageway

GANISTER *n* pl. **-S** a type of rock

GANJA *n* pl. **-S** cannabis used for smoking

GANJAH *n* pl. **-S** ganja

GANNET *n* pl. **-S** a large seabird

GANOF *n* pl. **-S** ganef

GANOID *n* pl. **-S** a type of fish

GANTLET *v* **-ED, -ING, -S** to overlap railroad tracks

GANTLINE *n* pl. **-S** a rope on a ship

GANTLOPE *n* pl. **-S** a former military punishment

GANTRY *n* pl. **-TRIES** a structure for supporting railroad signals

GANYMEDE *n* pl. **-S** a youth who serves liquors

GAOL *v* **-ED, -ING, -S** to jail

GAOLER *n* pl. **-S** jailer

GAP *v* **GAPPED, GAPPING, GAPS** to make an opening in

GAPE *v* **GAPED, GAPING, GAPES** to stare with open mouth

GAPER *n* pl. **-S** one that gapes

GAPESEED *n* pl. **-S** something that causes wonder

GAPEWORM *n* pl. **-S** a worm that causes a disease of young birds

GAPING present participle of gape

GAPINGLY *adv* in a gaping manner

GAPLESS *adj* having no gap

GAPOSIS *n* pl. **-SISES** a gap in a row of buttons or snaps

GAPPED past tense of gap

GAPPING present participle of gap

GAPPY *adj* **-PIER, -PIEST** having openings

GAPY *adj* infested with gapeworms

GAR *v* **GARRED, GARRING, GARS** to cause or compel

GARAGE *v* **-RAGED, -RAGING, -RAGES** to put in a garage (a car shelter)

GARB *v* **-ED, -ING, -S** to clothe

GARBAGE *n* pl. **-S** food waste **GARBAGEY, GARBAGY** *adj*

GARBANZO *n* pl. **-ZOS** a chickpea

GARBLE *v* **-BLED, -BLING, -BLES** to distort the meaning of

GARBLER *n* pl. **-S** one that garbles

GARBLESS *adj* being without clothing

GARBOARD *n* pl. **-S** a plank on a ship's bottom

GARBOIL *n* pl. **-S** turmoil

GARCON *n* pl. **-S** a waiter

GARDA *n* pl. **-DAI** a police officer in Ireland

GARDANT *adj* turned directly toward the observer — used of a heraldic animal

GARDEN *v* **-ED, -ING, -S** to cultivate a plot of ground

GARDENER *n* pl. **-S** one that gardens

GARDENIA *n* pl. **-S** a tropical shrub or tree

GARDYLOO *interj* — used as a warning cry

GARFISH *n* pl. **-ES** a freshwater fish

GARGANEY *n* pl. **-NEYS** a small duck

GARGET *n* pl. **-S** mastitis of domestic animals **GARGETY** *adj*

GARGLE *v* **-GLED, -GLING, -GLES** to rinse the mouth or throat

GARGLER *n* pl. **-S** one that gargles

GARGOYLE *n* pl. **-S** an ornamental figure

GARIGUE *n* pl. **-S** a low scrubland

GARISH *adj* gaudy **GARISHLY** *adv*

GARLAND *v* **-ED, -ING, -S** to deck with wreaths of flowers

GARLIC *v* **-LICKED, -LICKING, -LICS** to season with garlic (an herb used in cooking)

GARLICKY *adj* **-LICKIER, -LICKIEST** smelling or tasting of garlic

GARMENT *v* **-ED, -ING, -S** to clothe

GARNER *v* **-ED, -ING, -S** to gather and store

GARNET *n* pl. **-S** a mineral

GARNI *adj* garnished

GARNISH *v* **-ED, -ING, -ES** to decorate

GAROTE *v* **-ROTED, -ROTING, -ROTES** to garrote

GAROTTE *v* **-ROTTED, -ROTTING, -ROTTES** to garrote

GAROTTER *n* pl. **-S** one that garottes

GARPIKE *n* pl. **-S** a garfish

GARRED past tense of gar

GARRET *n* pl. **-S** an attic **GARRETED** *adj*

GARRING present participle of gar

GARRISON   v **-ED, -ING, -S** to assign to a military post

GARRON   n pl. **-S** a small, sturdy horse

GARROTE   v **-ROTED, -ROTING, -ROTES** to execute by strangling

GARROTER   n pl. **-S** one that garrotes

GARROTTE   v **-ROTTED, -ROTTING, -ROTTES** to garrote

GARTER   v **-ED, -ING, -S** to fasten with an elastic band

GARTH   n pl. **-S** a yard or garden

GARVEY   n pl. **-VEYS** a small scow

GAS   v **GASSED, GASSING, GASES** or **GASSES** to supply with gas (a substance capable of indefinite expansion)

GASALIER   n pl. **-S** gaselier

GASBAG   n pl. **-S** a bag for holding gas

GASCON   n pl. **-S** a boaster

GASEITY   n pl. **-TIES** the state of being a gas

GASELIER   n pl. **-S** a gaslight chandelier

GASEOUS   adj pertaining to gas

GASH   adj **GASHER, GASHEST** knowing

GASH   v **-ED, -ING, -ES** to make a long deep cut in

GASHOUSE   n pl. **-S** a gasworks

GASIFIED   past tense of gasify

GASIFIER   n pl. **-S** one that gasifies

GASIFORM   adj having the form of gas

GASIFY   v **-IFIED, -IFYING, -IFIES** to convert into gas

GASKET   n pl. **-S** packing for making something fluid-tight

GASKIN   n pl. **-S** a part of a horse's leg

GASKING   n pl. **-S** a gasket

GASLESS   adj having no gas

GASLIGHT   n pl. **-S** light made by burning gas

GASLIT   adj illuminated by gaslight

GASMAN   n pl. **-MEN** an employee of a gas company

GASOGENE   n pl. **-S** gazogene

GASOHOL   n pl. **-S** a fuel mixture of gasoline and ethyl alcohol

GASOLENE   n pl. **-S** gasoline

GASOLIER   n pl. **-S** gaselier

GASOLINE   n pl. **-S** a liquid fuel

GASP   v **-ED, -ING, -S** to breathe convulsively

GASPER   n pl. **-S** a cigarette

GASSED   past tense of gas

GASSER   n pl. **-S** one that gasses

GASSES   a present 3d person sing. of gas

GASSING   n pl. **-S** a poisoning by noxious gas

GASSY   adj **-SIER, -SIEST** containing gas **GASSILY** adv

GAST   v **-ED, -ING, -S** to scare

GASTER   n pl. **-S** the enlarged part of the abdomen in some insects

GASTIGHT   adj not allowing gas to escape or enter

GASTNESS   n pl. **-ES** fright

GASTRAEA   n pl. **-S** a type of metazoan

GASTRAL   adj pertaining to the stomach

GASTREA   n pl. **-S** gastraea

GASTRIC   adj pertaining to the stomach

GASTRIN   n pl. **-S** a hormone

GASTRULA   n pl. **-LAS** or **-LAE** a metazoan embryo

GASWORKS   n pl. **GASWORKS** a factory where gas is produced

GAT   n pl. **-S** a pistol

GATE   v **GATED, GATING, GATES** to supply with a gate (a movable barrier)

GATEAU   n pl. **-TEAUS** or **-TEAUX** a fancy cake

GATEFOLD   n pl. **-S** a folded insert in a book or magazine

GATELESS   adj lacking a gate

GATELIKE   adj resembling a gate

GATEMAN   n pl. **-MEN** a person in charge of a gate

GATEPOST   n pl. **-S** a post from which a gate is hung

GATER   n pl. **-S** gator

GATEWAY   n pl. **-WAYS** a passage that may be closed by a gate

GATHER   v **-ED, -ING, -S** to bring together into one place or group

GATHERER   n pl. **-S** one that gathers

GATING   n pl. **-S** the process of opening and closing a channel

GATOR   n pl. **-S** an alligator

GAUCHE   adj **GAUCHER, GAUCHEST** lacking social grace **GAUCHELY** adv

GAUCHO *n* pl. **-CHOS** a cowboy of the South American pampas

GAUD *n* pl. **-S** a showy ornament

GAUDERY *n* pl. **-ERIES** finery

GAUDY *adj* **GAUDIER, GAUDIEST** tastelessly showy **GAUDILY** *adv*

GAUDY *n* pl. **-DIES** a festival

GAUFFER *v* **-ED, -ING, -S** to goffer

GAUGE *v* **GAUGED, GAUGING, GAUGES** to measure precisely

GAUGER *n* pl. **-S** one that gauges

GAULT *n* pl. **-S** a heavy, thick clay soil

GAUM *v* **-ED, -ING, -S** to smear

GAUN present participle of gae

GAUNT *adj* **GAUNTER, GAUNTEST** emaciated **GAUNTLY** *adv*

GAUNTLET *v* **-ED, -ING, -S** to gantlet

GAUNTRY *n* pl. **-TRIES** gantry

GAUR *n* pl. **-S** a wild ox

GAUSS *n* pl. **-ES** a unit of magnetic induction

GAUZE *n* pl. **-S** a transparent fabric

GAUZY *adj* **GAUZIER, GAUZIEST** resembling gauze **GAUZILY** *adv*

GAVAGE *n* pl. **-S** introduction of material into the stomach by a tube

GAVE past tense of give

GAVEL *v* **-ELED, -ELING, -ELS** or **-ELLED, -ELLING, -ELS** to signal for attention or order by use of a gavel (a small mallet)

GAVELOCK *n* pl. **-S** a crowbar

GAVIAL *n* pl. **-S** a large reptile

GAVOT *n* pl. **-S** a French dance

GAVOTTE *v* **-VOTTED, -VOTTING, -VOTTES** to dance a gavot

GAWK *v* **-ED, -ING, -S** to stare stupidly

GAWKER *n* pl. **-S** one that gawks

GAWKIER comparative of gawky

GAWKIES pl. of gawky

GAWKISH *adj* gawky

GAWKY *adj* **GAWKIER, GAWKIEST** awkward **GAWKILY** *adv*

GAWKY *n* pl. **GAWKIES** an awkward person

GAWP *v* **-ED, -ING, -S** to stare stupidly

GAWPER *n* pl. **-S** one that gawps

GAWSIE *adj* well-fed and healthy looking

GAWSY *adj* gawsie

GAY *adj* **GAYER, GAYEST** merry

GAY *n* pl. **GAYS** a homosexual

GAYAL *n* pl. **-S** a domesticated ox

GAYDAR *n* pl. **-S** the ability to recognize that a person is homosexual

GAYETY *n* pl. **-ETIES** gaiety

GAYLY *adv* in a gay manner

GAYNESS *n* pl. **-ES** gaiety

GAYWINGS *n* pl. **GAYWINGS** a perennial herb

GAZABO *n* pl. **-BOS** or **-BOES** a fellow

GAZANIA *n* pl. **-S** a South African herb

GAZAR *n* pl. **-S** silky sheer fabric

GAZE *v* **GAZED, GAZING, GAZES** to look intently

GAZEBO *n* pl. **-BOS** or **-BOES** a roofed structure open on the sides

GAZELLE *n* pl. **-S** a small antelope

GAZER *n* pl. **-S** one that gazes

GAZETTE *v* **-ZETTED, -ZETTING, -ZETTES** to announce in an official journal

GAZING present participle of gaze

GAZOGENE *n* pl. **-S** an apparatus for carbonating liquids

GAZPACHO *n* pl. **-CHOS** a cold, spicy soup

GAZUMP *v* **-ED, -ING, -S** to cheat by raising the price originally agreed upon

GAZUMPER *n* pl. **-S** one that gazumps

GEAR *v* **-ED, -ING, -S** to provide with gears (toothed machine parts)

GEARBOX *n* pl. **-ES** an automotive transmission

GEARCASE *n* pl. **-S** a casing for gears

GEARHEAD *n* pl. **-S** a mechanically inclined person

GEARING *n* pl. **-S** a system of gears

GEARLESS *adj* being without gears

GECK *v* **-ED, -ING, -S** to mock

GECKO *n* pl. **GECKOS** or **GECKOES** a small lizard

GED *n* pl. **-S** a food fish

GEE *v* **GEED, GEEING, GEES** to turn to the right

GEEGAW *n* pl. **-S** gewgaw

GEEK *n* pl. **-S** a single-minded enthusiast or expert

GEEKDOM *n* pl. **-S** the world of geeks

GEEKED	*adj* filled with enthusiasm		**GEMMED**	past tense of gem
GEEKY	*adj* **GEEKIER, GEEKIEST** socially awkward or unappealing		**GEMMIER**	comparative of gemmy
			GEMMIEST	superlative of gemmy
GEEPOUND	*n* pl. **-S** a unit of mass		**GEMMILY**	*adv* in a manner suggesting a gem
GEESE	pl. of goose		**GEMMING**	present participle of gem
GEEST	*n* pl. **-S** old alluvial matter		**GEMMULE**	*n* pl. **-S** a small gemma
GEEZ	*interj* jeez		**GEMMY**	*adj* **-MIER, -MIEST** resembling a gem
GEEZER	*n* pl. **-S** an eccentric man		**GEMOLOGY**	*n* pl. **-GIES** the science of gems
GEISHA	*n* pl. **-S** a Japanese girl trained to entertain		**GEMOT**	*n* pl. **-S** a public meeting in Anglo-Saxon England
GEL	*v* **GELLED, GELLING, GELS** to become like jelly **GELABLE** *adj*		**GEMOTE**	*n* pl. **-S** gemot
GELADA	*n* pl. **-S** a baboon		**GEMSBOK**	*n* pl. **-S** a large antelope
GELANT	*n* pl. **-S** gellant		**GEMSBUCK**	*n* pl. **-S** gemsbok
GELATE	*v* **-ATED, -ATING, -ATES** to gel		**GEMSTONE**	*n* pl. **-S** a precious stone
GELATI	*n* pl. **-S** gelato		**GEN**	*n* pl. **-S** information obtained from study
GELATIN	*n* pl. **-S** a glutinous substance		**GENDARME**	*n* pl. **-S** a policeman
GELATINE	*n* pl. **-S** gelatin		**GENDER**	*v* **-ED, -ING, -S** to engender
GELATING	present participle of gelate		**GENE**	*n* pl. **-S** a hereditary unit
GELATION	*n* pl. **-S** the process of gelling		**GENERA**	a pl. of genus
GELATO	*n* pl. **-TOS** or **-TI** Italian ice cream		**GENERAL**	*n* pl. **-S** a military officer
GELCAP	*n* pl. **-S** a tablet coated with gelatin		**GENERATE**	*v* **-ATED, -ATING, -ATES** to bring into existence
GELD	*v* **-ED, -ING, -S** to castrate		**GENERIC**	*n* pl. **-S** a type of drug
GELDER	*n* pl. **-S** one that gelds		**GENEROUS**	*adj* willing to give
GELDING	*n* pl. **-S** a castrated animal		**GENESIS**	*n* pl. **GENESES** an origin
GELEE	*n* pl. **-S** a cosmetic gel		**GENET**	*n* pl. **-S** a carnivorous mammal
GELID	*adj* icy **GELIDLY** *adv*		**GENETIC**	*adj* pertaining to genetics
GELIDITY	*n* pl. **-TIES** iciness		**GENETICS**	*n/pl* the science of heredity
GELLANT	*n* pl. **-S** a substance used to produce gelling		**GENETTE**	*n* pl. **-S** genet
GELLED	past tense of gel		**GENEVA**	*n* pl. **-S** a liquor
GELLING	present participle of gel		**GENIAL**	*adj* having a pleasant or friendly manner **GENIALLY** *adv*
GELSEMIA	*n/pl* medicinal plant roots		**GENIC**	*adj* pertaining to genes
GELT	*n* pl. **-S** money		**GENIE**	*n* pl. **-S** jinni
GEM	*v* **GEMMED, GEMMING, GEMS** to adorn with gems (precious stones)		**GENII**	a pl. of genius
GEMATRIA	*n* pl. **-S** a cabalistic method of interpreting the Scriptures		**GENIP**	*n* pl. **-S** a tropical tree
GEMINAL	*adj* of or pertaining to two substituents on the same atom		**GENIPAP**	*n* pl. **-S** a tropical tree
GEMINATE	*v* **-NATED, -NATING, -NATES** to arrange in pairs		**GENITAL**	*adj* pertaining to reproduction
			GENITALS	*n/pl* the sexual organs
GEMLIKE	*adj* resembling a gem		**GENITIVE**	*n* pl. **-S** a grammatical case
GEMMA	*n* pl. **-MAE** an asexual reproductive structure		**GENITOR**	*n* pl. **-S** a male parent
			GENITURE	*n* pl. **-S** birth
GEMMATE	*v* **-MATED, -MATING, -MATES** to produce gemmae		**GENIUS**	*n* pl. **GENIUSES** or **GENII** an exceptional natural aptitude

GENNAKER *n pl.* **-S** a spinnaker sail

GENOA *n pl.* **-S** a triangular sail

GENOCIDE *n pl.* **-S** the deliberate extermination of a national or racial group

GENOGRAM *n pl.* **-S** a diagram of the history of behavior patterns of a family

GENOISE *n pl.* **-S** a rich sponge cake

GENOM *n pl.* **-S** genome

GENOME *n pl.* **-S** a haploid set of chromosomes **GENOMIC** *adj*

GENOMICS *n/pl* the study of genomes

GENOTYPE *n pl.* **-S** the genetic constitution of an organism

GENRE *n pl.* **-S** a type or kind

GENRO *n pl.* **-ROS** a group of elder statesmen in Japan

GENS *n pl.* **GENTES** a type of clan

GENSENG *n pl.* **-S** ginseng

GENT *n pl.* **-S** a gentleman

GENTEEL *adj* **-TEELER, -TEELEST** well-bred or refined

GENTES pl. of gens

GENTIAN *n pl.* **-S** a flowering plant

GENTIL *adj* kind

GENTILE *n pl.* **-S** a non-Jewish person

GENTLE *adj* **-TLER, -TLEST** mild **GENTLY** *adv*

GENTLE *v* **-TLED, -TLING, -TLES** to tame

GENTOO *n pl.* **-TOOS** a gray-backed penguin

GENTRICE *n pl.* **-S** good breeding

GENTRIFY *v* **-FIED, -FYING, -FIES** to renew a decayed urban area so as to attract middle-class residents

GENTRY *n pl.* **-TRIES** people of high social class

GENTS *n/pl* a public men's room

GENU *n pl.* **GENUA** the knee

GENUINE *adj* authentic

GENUS *n pl.* **GENUSES** or **GENERA** a kind, sort, or class

GEODE *n pl.* **-S** a type of rock

GEODESIC *n pl.* **-S** a geometric line

GEODESY *n pl.* **-SIES** geographical surveying

GEODETIC *adj* pertaining to geodesy

GEODIC *adj* of or pertaining to a geode

GEODUCK *n pl.* **-S** a large, edible clam

GEOGNOSY *n pl.* **-SIES** a branch of geology

GEOID *n pl.* **-S** a hypothetical surface of the earth **GEOIDAL** *adj*

GEOLOGER *n pl.* **-S** a specialist in geology

GEOLOGY *n pl.* **-GIES** the science that deals with the origin and structure of the earth **GEOLOGIC** *adj*

GEOMANCY *n pl.* **-CIES** a method of foretelling the future by geographical features

GEOMETER *n pl.* **-S** a specialist in geometry

GEOMETRY *n pl.* **-TRIES** a branch of mathematics

GEOPHAGY *n pl.* **-GIES** the practice of eating earthy substances

GEOPHONE *n pl.* **-S** a device that detects vibrations in the earth

GEOPHYTE *n pl.* **-S** a plant having underground buds

GEOPONIC *adj* pertaining to farming

GEOPROBE *n pl.* **-S** a spacecraft for exploring space near the earth

GEORGIC *n pl.* **-S** a poem about farming

GEOTAXIS *n pl.* **-TAXES** the movement of an organism in response to gravity

GERAH *n pl.* **-S** a Hebrew unit of weight

GERANIAL *n pl.* **-S** citral

GERANIOL *n pl.* **-S** an alcohol used in perfumes

GERANIUM *n pl.* **-S** a flowering plant

GERARDIA *n pl.* **-S** an herb

GERBERA *n pl.* **-S** an herb

GERBIL *n pl.* **-S** a burrowing rodent

GERBILLE *n pl.* **-S** gerbil

GERENT *n pl.* **-S** a ruler or manager

GERENUK *n pl.* **-S** a long-necked antelope

GERM *n pl.* **-S** a microorganism that causes disease

GERMAN *n pl.* **-S** an elaborate dance

GERMANE *adj* relevant

GERMANIC *adj* containing germanium (a metallic element)

GERMEN *n pl.* **-MENS** or **-MINA** something that serves as an origin

GERMFREE *adj* free from germs

GERMIER comparative of germy

GERMIEST superlative of germy

GERMINA a pl. of germen

GERMINAL *adj* being in the earliest stage of development

GERMLIKE	*adj* resembling a germ
GERMY	*adj* **GERMIER, GERMIEST** full of germs
GERONTIC	*adj* pertaining to old age
GERUND	*n* pl. **-S** a verbal noun
GESNERIA	*adj* designating a type of flowering plant
GESSO	*n* pl. **-SOES** a plaster mixture
GESSOED	*adj* having gesso as a coating
GEST	*n* pl. **-S** a feat
GESTALT	*n* pl. **-STALTS** or **-STALTEN** a unified whole
GESTAPO	*n* pl. **-POS** a secret-police organization
GESTATE	*v* **-TATED, -TATING, -TATES** to carry in the uterus during pregnancy
GESTE	*n* pl. **-S** gest
GESTIC	*adj* pertaining to bodily motion
GESTICAL	*adj* gestic
GESTURAL	*adj* pertaining to or consisting of gestures (expressive bodily motions)
GESTURE	*v* **-TURED, -TURING, -TURES** to express by bodily motion
GESTURER	*n* pl. **-S** one that gestures
GET	*n* pl. **GITTIN** a divorce by Jewish law
GET	*v* **GOT, GOTTEN, GETTING, GETS** to obtain or acquire **GETABLE, GETTABLE** *adj*
GETA	*n* pl. **-S** a Japanese wooden clog
GETAWAY	*n* pl. **-AWAYS** an escape
GETTER	*v* **-ED, -ING, -S** to purify with a chemically active substance
GETTING	present participle of get
GETUP	*n* pl. **-S** a costume
GEUM	*n* pl. **-S** a perennial herb
GEWGAW	*n* pl. **-S** a showy trinket **GEWGAWED** *adj*
GEY	*adv* very
GEYSER	*n* pl. **-S** a spring that ejects jets of hot water and steam
GHARIAL	*n* pl. **-S** a large reptile
GHARRI	*n* pl. **-S** gharry
GHARRY	*n* pl. **-RIES** a carriage used in India
GHAST	*adj* ghastly
GHASTFUL	*adj* frightful
GHASTLY	*adj* **-LIER, -LIEST** terrifying
GHAT	*n* pl. **-S** a passage to a river
GHAUT	*n* pl. **-S** ghat
GHAZI	*n* pl. **-S** or **-ES** a Muslim war hero
GHEE	*n* pl. **-S** a kind of liquid butter
GHERAO	*v* **-ED, -ING, -ES** to coerce by physical means
GHERKIN	*n* pl. **-S** a small cucumber
GHETTO	*v* **-ED, -ING, -S** or **-ES** to isolate in a slum
GHI	*n* pl. **-S** ghee
GHIBLI	*n* pl. **-S** a hot desert wind
GHILLIE	*n* pl. **-S** a type of shoe
GHOST	*v* **-ED, -ING, -S** to haunt
GHOSTING	*n* pl. **-S** a false image on a television screen
GHOSTLY	*adj* **-LIER, -LIEST** spectral
GHOSTY	*adj* **GHOSTIER, GHOSTIEST** ghostly
GHOUL	*n* pl. **-S** a demon **GHOULISH** *adj*
GHOULIE	*n* pl. **-S** a ghoul
GHYLL	*n* pl. **-S** a ravine
GIANT	*n* pl. **-S** a person or thing of great size
GIANTESS	*n* pl. **-ES** a female giant
GIANTISM	*n* pl. **-S** the condition of being a giant
GIAOUR	*n* pl. **-S** a non-Muslim
GIARDIA	*n* pl. **-S** a protozoan inhabiting the intestines
GIB	*v* **GIBBED, GIBBING, GIBS** to fasten with a wedge of wood or metal
GIBBER	*v* **-ED, -ING, -S** to jabber
GIBBET	*v* **-BETED, -BETING, -BETS** or **-BETTED, -BETTING, -BETS** to execute by hanging
GIBBON	*n* pl. **-S** an arboreal ape
GIBBOSE	*adj* gibbous
GIBBOUS	*adj* irregularly rounded
GIBBSITE	*n* pl. **-S** a mineral
GIBE	*v* **GIBED, GIBING, GIBES** to jeer **GIBINGLY** *adv*
GIBER	*n* pl. **-S** one that gibes
GIBLET	*n* pl. **-S** an edible part of a fowl
GIBSON	*n* pl. **-S** a martini served with a tiny onion
GID	*n* pl. **-S** a disease of sheep

GIDDAP *interj* — used as a command to a horse to go faster

GIDDY *adj* **-DIER, -DIEST** dizzy **GIDDILY** *adv*

GIDDY *v* **-DIED, -DYING, -DIES** to make giddy

GIDDYAP *interj* giddap

GIDDYUP *interj* giddap

GIE *v* **GIED, GIEN, GIEING, GIES** to give

GIFT *v* **-ED, -ING, -S** to present with a gift (something given without charge)

GIFTABLE *n* pl. **-S** something appropriate for a gift

GIFTEDLY *adv* in a talented manner

GIFTEE *n* pl. **-S** one that receives a gift

GIFTLESS *adj* being without a gift

GIFTWARE *n* pl. **-S** wares suitable for gifts

GIFTWRAP *v* **-WRAPPED, -WRAPPING, -WRAPS** to wrap with decorative paper

GIG *v* **GIGGED, GIGGING, GIGS** to catch fish with a pronged spear

GIGA *n* pl. **GIGHE** a gigue

GIGABIT *n* pl. **-S** a unit of information

GIGABYTE *n* pl. **-S** 1,073,741,824 bytes

GIGAFLOP *n* pl. **-S** a measure of computing speed

GIGANTIC *adj* huge

GIGAS *adj* pertaining to variations in plant development

GIGATON *n* pl. **-S** a unit of weight

GIGAWATT *n* pl. **-S** a unit of power

GIGGED past tense of gig

GIGGING present participle of gig

GIGGLE *v* **-GLED, -GLING, -GLES** to laugh in a silly manner

GIGGLER *n* pl. **-S** one that giggles

GIGGLY *adj* **-GLIER, -GLIEST** tending to giggle

GIGHE pl. of giga

GIGLET *n* pl. **-S** a playful girl

GIGLOT *n* pl. **-S** giglet

GIGOLO *n* pl. **-LOS** a man supported financially by a woman

GIGOT *n* pl. **-S** a leg of lamb

GIGUE *n* pl. **-S** a lively dance

GILBERT *n* pl. **-S** a unit of magnetomotive force

GILD *v* **GILDED** or **GILT, GILDING, GILDS** to cover with a thin layer of gold

GILDER *n* pl. **-S** one that gilds

GILDHALL *n* pl. **-S** a town hall

GILDING *n* pl. **-S** the application of gilt

GILL *v* **-ED, -ING, -S** to catch fish with a type of net

GILLER *n* pl. **-S** one that gills

GILLIE *n* pl. **-S** ghillie

GILLNET *v* **-NETTED, -NETTING, -NETS** to gill

GILLY *v* **-LIED, -LYING, -LIES** to transport on a type of wagon

GILT *n* pl. **-S** the gold with which something is gilded

GILTHEAD *n* pl. **-S** a marine fish

GIMBAL *v* **-BALED, -BALING, -BALS** or **-BALLED, -BALLING, -BALS** to support on a set of rings

GIMCRACK *n* pl. **-S** a gewgaw

GIMEL *n* pl. **-S** a Hebrew letter

GIMLET *v* **-ED, -ING, -S** to pierce with a boring tool

GIMMAL *n* pl. **-S** a pair of interlocked rings

GIMME *n* pl. **-S** something easily won

GIMMICK *v* **-ED, -ING, -S** to provide with a gimmick (a novel or tricky feature)

GIMMICKY *adj* having or being like a gimmick

GIMMIE *n* pl. **-MIES** an easy golf putt conceded to an opponent

GIMP *v* **-ED, -ING, -S** to limp

GIMPIER comparative of gimpy

GIMPIEST superlative of gimpy

GIMPY *adj* **GIMPIER, GIMPIEST** limping

GIN *v* **GAN, GUNNEN, GINNING, GINS** to begin

GIN *v* **GINNED, GINNING, GINS** to remove seeds from cotton

GINGAL *n* pl. **-S** jingal

GINGALL *n* pl. **-S** jingal

GINGELEY *n* pl. **-LEYS** gingelly

GINGELI *n* pl. **-S** gingelly

GINGELIES pl. of gingely

GINGELLI *n* pl. **-S** gingelly

GINGELLY *n* pl. **-LIES** the sesame seed or its oil

GINGELY   *n* pl. **-LIES** gingelly

GINGER   *v* **-ED, -ING, -S** to flavor with ginger (a pungent spice)

GINGERLY   *adv* in a careful manner

GINGERY   *adj* having the characteristics of ginger

GINGHAM   *n* pl. **-S** a cotton fabric

GINGILI   *n* pl. **-LIS** gingelly

GINGILLI   *n* pl. **-S** gingelly

GINGIVA   *n* pl. **-VAE** the fleshy tissue that surrounds the teeth **GINGIVAL** *adj*

GINGKO   *n* pl. **-KOS** or **-KOES** ginkgo

GINK   *n* pl. **-S** a fellow

GINKGO   *n* pl. **-GOS** or **-GOES** an ornamental tree

GINNED   past tense of gin

GINNER   *n* pl. **-S** one that gins cotton

GINNING   *n* pl. **-S** cotton as it comes from a gin

GINNY   *adj* **GINNIER, GINNIEST** affected with gin (a strong liquor)

GINSENG   *n* pl. **-S** a perennial herb

GIP   *v* **GIPPED, GIPPING, GIPS** to gyp

GIPON   *n* pl. **-S** jupon

GIPPER   *n* pl. **-S** one that gips

GIPSY   *v* **-SIED, -SYING, -SIES** to gypsy

GIRAFFE   *n* pl. **-S** a long-necked mammal

GIRASOL   *n* pl. **-S** a variety of opal

GIRASOLE   *n* pl. **-S** girasol

GIRD   *v* **GIRDED** or **GIRT, GIRDING, GIRDS** to surround

GIRDER   *n* pl. **-S** a horizontal support

GIRDLE   *v* **-DLED, -DLING, -DLES** to encircle with a belt

GIRDLER   *n* pl. **-S** one that girdles

GIRL   *n* pl. **-S** a female child

GIRLHOOD   *n* pl. **-S** the state of being a girl

GIRLIE   *adj* **GIRLIER, GIRLIEST** girlish

GIRLISH   *adj* of, pertaining to, or having the characteristics of a girl

GIRLY   *adj* **GIRLIER, GIRLIEST** girlie

GIRN   *v* **-ED, -ING, -S** to snarl

GIRO   *n* pl. **-ROS** an autogiro

GIROLLE   *n* pl. **-S** an edible mushroom

GIRON   *n* pl. **-S** gyron

GIROSOL   *n* pl. **-S** girasol

GIRSH   *n* pl. **-ES** qursh

GIRT   *v* **-ED, -ING, -S** to gird

GIRTH   *v* **-ED, -ING, -S** to encircle

GISARME   *n* pl. **-S** a medieval weapon

GISMO   *n* pl. **-MOS** a gadget

GIST   *n* pl. **-S** the main point

GIT   *v* **GITTED, GITTING, GITS** to get

GITANO   *n* pl. **-NOS** a Spanish gypsy

GITE   *n* pl. **-S** a vacation retreat in France

GITTED   past tense of git

GITTERN   *n* pl. **-S** a medieval guitar

GITTIN   pl. of get

GITTING   present participle of git

GIVE   *v* **GAVE, GIVEN, GIVING, GIVES** to transfer freely to another's possession **GIVEABLE** *adj*

GIVEAWAY   *n* pl. **-AWAYS** something given away free of charge

GIVEBACK   *n* pl. **-S** a worker's benefit given back to management

GIVEN   *n* pl. **-S** something assigned as a basis for a calculation

GIVER   *n* pl. **-S** one that gives

GIVING   present participle of give

GIZMO   *n* pl. **-MOS** gismo

GIZZARD   *n* pl. **-S** a digestive organ

GJETOST   *n* pl. **-S** a hard brown cheese

GLABELLA   *n* pl. **-BELLAE** the smooth area between the eyebrows

GLABRATE   *adj* glabrous

GLABROUS   *adj* smooth

GLACE   *v* **-CEED, -CEING, -CES** to cover with icing

GLACIAL   *adj* of or pertaining to glaciers

GLACIATE   *v* **-ATED, -ATING, -ATES** to cover with glaciers

GLACIER   *n* pl. **-S** a huge mass of ice

GLACIS   *n* pl. **-CISES** a slope

GLAD   *adj* **GLADDER, GLADDEST** feeling pleasure

GLAD   *v* **GLADDED, GLADDING, GLADS** to gladden

GLADDEN   *v* **-ED, -ING, -S** to make glad

GLADDER   comparative of glad

GLADDEST   superlative of glad

GLADDING   present participle of glad

GLADE   *n* pl. **-S** an open space in a forest

GLADIATE   adj shaped like a sword

GLADIER   comparative of glady

GLADIEST   superlative of glady

GLADIOLA   n pl. **-S** a flowering plant

GLADIOLI   n/pl segments of the sternum

GLADLY   adv **-LIER, -LIEST** in a glad manner

GLADNESS   n pl. **-ES** the state of being glad

GLADSOME   adj **-SOMER, -SOMEST** glad

GLADY   adj **GLADIER, GLADIEST** having glades

GLAIKET   adj glaikit

GLAIKIT   adj foolish

GLAIR   v **-ED, -ING, -S** to coat with egg white

GLAIRE   v **GLAIRED, GLAIRING, GLAIRES** to glair

GLAIRY   adj **GLAIRIER, GLAIRIEST** resembling egg white

GLAIVE   n pl. **-S** a sword **GLAIVED** adj

GLAM   n pl. **-S** glitzy attractiveness

GLAMOR   n pl. **-S** alluring attractiveness

GLAMOUR   v **-ED, -ING, -S** to bewitch

GLANCE   v **GLANCED, GLANCING, GLANCES** to look quickly

GLANCER   n pl. **-S** one that glances

GLAND   n pl. **-S** a secreting organ

GLANDERS   n/pl a disease of horses

GLANDULE   n pl. **-S** a small gland

GLANS   n pl. **GLANDES** the tip of the penis or clitoris

GLARE   v **GLARED, GLARING, GLARES** to shine with a harshly brilliant light

GLARY   adj **GLARIER, GLARIEST** glaring

GLASNOST   n pl. **-S** a Soviet policy of open political discussion

GLASS   v **-ED, -ING, -ES** to encase in glass (a transparent substance)

GLASSFUL   n pl. **-FULS** as much as a drinking glass will hold

GLASSIE   n pl. **-S** a type of playing marble

GLASSIER   comparative of glassy

GLASSIEST   superlative of glassy

GLASSILY   adv in a glassy manner

GLASSINE   n pl. **-S** a type of paper

GLASSMAN   n pl. **-MEN** a glazier

GLASSY   adj **GLASSIER, GLASSIEST** resembling glass

GLAUCOMA   n pl. **-S** a disease of the eye

GLAUCOUS   adj bluish green

GLAZE   v **GLAZED, GLAZING, GLAZES** to fit windows with glass panes

GLAZER   n pl. **-S** a glazier

GLAZIER   n pl. **-S** one that glazes

GLAZIERY   n pl. **-ZIERIES** the work of a glazier

GLAZING   n pl. **-S** glaziery

GLAZY   adj **GLAZIER, GLAZIEST** covered with a smooth, glossy coating **GLAZILY** adv

GLEAM   v **-ED, -ING, -S** to shine with a soft radiance

GLEAMER   n pl. **-S** one that gleams

GLEAMY   adj **GLEAMIER, GLEAMIEST** gleaming

GLEAN   v **-ED, -ING, -S** to gather little by little

GLEANER   n pl. **-S** one that gleans

GLEANING   n pl. **-S** something that is gleaned

GLEBA   n pl. **-BAE** a spore-bearing mass of some fungi

GLEBE   n pl. **-S** the soil or earth

GLED   n pl. **-S** glede

GLEDE   n pl. **-S** a bird of prey

GLEE   n pl. **-S** an unaccompanied song

GLEED   n pl. **-S** a glowing coal

GLEEFUL   adj merry

GLEEK   v **-ED, -ING, -S** to gibe

GLEEMAN   n pl. **-MEN** a minstrel

GLEESOME   adj gleeful

GLEET   v **-ED, -ING, -S** to discharge mucus from the urethra

GLEETY   adj **GLEETIER, GLEETIEST** resembling mucus

GLEG   adj alert **GLEGLY** adv

GLEGNESS   n pl. **-ES** alertness

GLEN   n pl. **-S** a small valley **GLENLIKE** adj

GLENOID   adj having the shallow or slightly cupped form of a bone socket

GLEY   n pl. **GLEYS** a clay soil layer **GLEYED** adj

GLEYING   n pl. **-S** development of gley

GLIA   n pl. **-S** supporting tissue that binds nerve tissue

GLIADIN   n pl. **-S** a simple protein

GLIADINE   n pl. **-S** gliadin

GLIAL   *adj* pertaining to the supporting tissue of the central nervous system

GLIB   *adj* **GLIBBER, GLIBBEST** fluent **GLIBLY** *adv*

GLIBNESS   *n* pl. **-ES** the quality of being glib

GLIDE   *v* **GLIDED, GLIDING, GLIDES** to move effortlessly

GLIDER   *n* pl. **-S** a type of aircraft

GLIFF   *n* pl. **-S** a brief moment

GLIM   *n* pl. **-S** a light or lamp

GLIME   *v* **GLIMED, GLIMING, GLIMES** to glance slyly

GLIMMER   *v* **-ED, -ING, -S** to shine faintly or unsteadily

GLIMPSE   *v* **GLIMPSED, GLIMPSING, GLIMPSES** to see for an instant

GLIMPSER   *n* pl. **-S** one that glimpses

GLINT   *v* **-ED, -ING, -S** to glitter

GLINTY   *adj* **GLINTIER, GLINTIEST** glittering

GLIOMA   *n* pl. **-MAS** or **-MATA** a type of tumor

GLISSADE   *v* **-SADED, -SADING, -SADES** to perform a gliding dance step

GLISTEN   *v* **-ED, -ING, -S** to shine by reflection

GLISTER   *v* **-ED, -ING, -S** to glisten

GLITCH   *n* pl. **-ES** a malfunction

GLITCHY   *adj* **GLITCHIER, GLITCHIEST** characterized by glitches

GLITTER   *v* **-ED, -ING, -S** to sparkle

GLITTERY   *adj* glittering

GLITZ   *v* **-ED, -ING, -ES** to make flashy in appearance

GLITZY   *adj* **GLITZIER, GLITZIEST** showy

GLOAM   *n* pl. **-S** twilight

GLOAMING   *n* pl. **-S** twilight

GLOAT   *v* **-ED, -ING, -S** to regard with great or excessive satisfaction

GLOATER   *n* pl. **-S** one that gloats

GLOB   *n* pl. **-S** a rounded mass

GLOBAL   *adj* spherical **GLOBALLY** *adv*

GLOBATE   *adj* spherical

GLOBATED   *adj* spherical

GLOBBY   *adj* **-BIER, -BIEST** full of globs

GLOBE   *v* **GLOBED, GLOBING, GLOBES** to form into a perfectly round body

GLOBIN   *n* pl. **-S** a simple protein

GLOBOID   *n* pl. **-S** a spheroid

GLOBOSE   *adj* spherical

GLOBOUS   *adj* spherical

GLOBULAR   *n* pl. **-S** a spherical cluster of stars

GLOBULE   *n* pl. **-S** a small spherical mass

GLOBULIN   *n* pl. **-S** a simple protein

GLOCHID   *n* pl. **-S** a barbed hair on some plants

GLOGG   *n* pl. **-S** an alcoholic beverage

GLOM   *v* **GLOMMED, GLOMMING, GLOMS** to steal

GLOMUS   *n* pl. **-MERA** a type of vascular tuft

GLONOIN   *n* pl. **-S** nitroglycerin

GLOOM   *v* **-ED, -ING, -S** to become dark

GLOOMFUL   *adj* gloomy

GLOOMING   *n* pl. **-S** gloaming

GLOOMY   *adj* **GLOOMIER, GLOOMIEST** dismally dark **GLOOMILY** *adv*

GLOP   *v* **GLOPPED, GLOPPING, GLOPS** to cover with glop (a messy mass or mixture)

GLOPPY   *adj* **-PIER, -PIEST** resembling glop

GLORIA   *n* pl. **-S** a halo

GLORIED   past tense of glory

GLORIES   present 3d person sing. of glory

GLORIFY   *v* **-FIED, -FYING, -FIES** to bestow honor or praise on

GLORIOLE   *n* pl. **-S** a halo

GLORIOUS   *adj* magnificent

GLORY   *v* **-RIED, -RYING, -RIES** to rejoice proudly

GLOSS   *v* **-ED, -ING, -ES** to make lustrous

GLOSSA   *n* pl. **-SAS** or **-SAE** the tongue **GLOSSAL** *adj*

GLOSSARY   *n* pl. **-RIES** a list of terms and their definitions

GLOSSEME   *n* pl. **-S** the smallest linguistic unit that signals a meaning

GLOSSER   *n* pl. **-S** one that glosses

GLOSSIES   pl. of glossy

GLOSSINA   *n* pl. **-S** a tsetse fly

GLOSSY   *adj* **GLOSSIER, GLOSSIEST** lustrous **GLOSSILY** *adv*

GLOSSY   *n* pl. **GLOSSIES** a type of photograph

GLOST   *n* pl. **-S** pottery that has been coated with a glassy surface

GLOTTIS *n* pl. **-TISES** or **-TIDES** the opening between the vocal cords **GLOTTAL, GLOTTIC** *adj*

GLOUT *v* **-ED, -ING, -S** to scowl

GLOVE *v* **GLOVED, GLOVING, GLOVES** to furnish with gloves (hand coverings)

GLOVER *n* pl. **-S** a maker or seller of gloves

GLOW *v* **-ED, -ING, -S** to emit light and heat

GLOWER *v* **-ED, -ING, -S** to scowl

GLOWFLY *n* pl. **-FLIES** a firefly

GLOWWORM *n* pl. **-S** a luminous insect

GLOXINIA *n* pl. **-S** a tropical plant

GLOZE *v* **GLOZED, GLOZING, GLOZES** to explain away

GLUCAGON *n* pl. **-S** a hormone

GLUCAN *n* pl. **-S** a polymer of glucose

GLUCINUM *n* pl. **-S** a metallic element **GLUCINIC** *adj*

GLUCOSE *n* pl. **-S** a sugar **GLUCOSIC** *adj*

GLUE *v* **GLUED, GLUING** or **GLUEING, GLUES** to fasten with glue (an adhesive substance)

GLUELIKE *adj* resembling glue

GLUEPOT *n* pl. **-S** a pot for melting glue

GLUER *n* pl. **-S** one that glues

GLUEY *adj* **GLUIER, GLUIEST** resembling glue **GLUILY** *adv*

GLUG *v* **GLUGGED, GLUGGING, GLUGS** to make a gurgling sound

GLUHWEIN *n* pl. **-S** wine flavored with spices

GLUINESS *n* pl. **-ES** the state of being gluey

GLUING present participle of glue

GLUM *n* pl. **-S** glumness

GLUM *adj* **GLUMMER, GLUMMEST** being in low spirits **GLUMLY** *adv*

GLUME *n* pl. **-S** a bract on grassy plants

GLUMNESS *n* pl. **-ES** the state of being glum

GLUMPY *adj* **GLUMPIER, GLUMPIEST** glum **GLUMPILY** *adv*

GLUNCH *v* **-ED, -ING, -ES** to frown

GLUON *n* pl. **-S** a hypothetical massless particle binding quarks together

GLUT *v* **GLUTTED, GLUTTING, GLUTS** to feed or fill to excess

GLUTE *n* pl. **-S** a gluteus

GLUTEAL *adj* of or pertaining to the buttock muscles

GLUTEI pl. of gluteus

GLUTELIN *n* pl. **-S** any of a group of proteins occurring in cereal grains

GLUTEN *n* pl. **-S** a sticky component of grain flours that contains glutenin

GLUTENIN *n* pl. **-S** a protein of cereal grains that gives adhesiveness to bread dough

GLUTEUS *n* pl. **-TEI** a buttock muscle

GLUTTED past tense of glut

GLUTTING present participle of glut

GLUTTON *n* pl. **-S** a person who eats to excess

GLUTTONY *n* pl. **-TONIES** excessive eating

GLYCAN *n* pl. **-S** a carbohydrate

GLYCERIN *n* pl. **-S** a glycerol **GLYCERIC** *adj*

GLYCEROL *n* pl. **-S** a syrupy alcohol

GLYCERYL *n* pl. **-S** a radical derived from glycerol

GLYCIN *n* pl. **-S** a compound used in photography

GLYCINE *n* pl. **-S** an amino acid

GLYCOGEN *n* pl. **-S** a carbohydrate

GLYCOL *n* pl. **-S** an alcohol **GLYCOLIC** *adj*

GLYCONIC *n* pl. **-S** a type of verse line

GLYCOSYL *n* pl. **-S** a radical derived from glucose

GLYCYL *n* pl. **-S** a radical derived from glycine

GLYPH *n* pl. **-S** an ornamental groove **GLYPHIC** *adj*

GLYPTIC *n* pl. **-S** the art or process of engraving on gems

GNAR *v* **GNARRED, GNARRING, GNARS** to snarl

GNARL *v* **-ED, -ING, -S** to twist into a state of deformity

GNARLY *adj* **GNARLIER, GNARLIEST** gnarled

GNARR *v* **-ED, -ING, -S** to gnar

GNARRED past tense of gnar

GNARRING present participle of gnar

GNASH *v* **-ED, -ING, -ES** to grind the teeth together

GNAT *n* pl. **-S** a small winged insect

GNATHAL *adj* gnathic

GNATHIC *adj* of or pertaining to the jaw

GNATHION *n* pl. **-S** the tip of the chin

GNATHITE *n* pl. **-S** a jawlike appendage of an insect

GNATLIKE *adj* resembling a gnat

GNATTY *adj* **-TIER, -TIEST** infested with gnats

GNAW *v* **GNAWED, GNAWN, GNAWING, GNAWS** to wear away by persistent biting **GNAWABLE** *adj*

GNAWER *n* pl. **-S** one that gnaws

GNAWING *n* pl. **-S** a persistent dull pain

GNEISS *n* pl. **-ES** a type of rock **GNEISSIC** *adj*

GNOCCHI *n/pl* dumplings made of pasta

GNOME *n* pl. **-S** a dwarf

GNOMIC *adj* resembling or containing aphorisms

GNOMICAL *adj* gnomic

GNOMISH *adj* resembling a gnome

GNOMIST *n* pl. **-S** a writer of aphorisms

GNOMON *n* pl. **-S** a part of a sundial **GNOMONIC** *adj*

GNOSIS *n* pl. **GNOSES** mystical knowledge

GNOSTIC *n* pl. **-S** an adherent of gnosticism

GNU *n* pl. **-S** a large antelope

GO *v* **WENT, GONE, GOING** or **GWINE, GOES** to move along

GO *n* pl. **GOS** a Japanese board game

GOA *n* pl. **-S** an Asian gazelle

GOAD *v* **-ED, -ING, -S** to drive animals with a goad (a pointed stick)

GOADLIKE *adj* resembling a goad

GOAL *v* **-ED, -ING, -S** to score a goal (a point-scoring play in some games)

GOALIE *n* pl. **-S** a player who defends against goals

GOALLESS *adj* having no goal

GOALPOST *n* pl. **-S** a post that marks a boundary of the scoring area in some games

GOALWARD *adv* toward a goal (a point-scoring area)

GOANNA *n* pl. **-S** a large monitor lizard

GOAT *n* pl. **-S** a horned mammal

GOATEE *n* pl. **-S** a small pointed beard **GOATEED** *adj*

GOATFISH *n* pl. **-ES** a tropical fish

GOATHERD *n* pl. **-S** one who tends goats

GOATISH *adj* resembling a goat

GOATLIKE *adj* goatish

GOATSKIN *n* pl. **-S** the hide of a goat

GOB *v* **GOBBED, GOBBING, GOBS** to fill a mine pit with waste material

GOBAN *n* pl. **-S** gobang

GOBANG *n* pl. **-S** a Japanese game

GOBBED past tense of gob

GOBBET *n* pl. **-S** a piece of raw meat

GOBBING present participle of gob

GOBBLE *v* **-BLED, -BLING, -BLES** to eat hastily

GOBBLER *n* pl. **-S** a male turkey

GOBIES pl. of goby

GOBIOID *n* pl. **-S** a fish of the goby family

GOBLET *n* pl. **-S** a drinking vessel

GOBLIN *n* pl. **-S** an evil or mischievous creature

GOBO *n* pl. **-BOS** or **-BOES** a device used to shield a microphone from extraneous sounds

GOBONEE *adj* gobony

GOBONY *adj* compony

GOBSHITE *n* pl. **-S** a contemptible person

GOBY *n* pl. **GOBIES** a small fish

GOD *v* **GODDED, GODDING, GODS** to treat as a god (a supernatural being)

GODCHILD *n* pl. **-CHILDREN** one whom a person sponsors at baptism

GODDED past tense of god

GODDESS *n* pl. **-ES** a female god

GODDING present participle of god

GODET *n* pl. **-S** insert of cloth in a seam

GODETIA *n* pl. **-S** a showy annual herb

GODHEAD *n* pl. **-S** godhood

GODHOOD *n* pl. **-S** the state of being a god

GODLESS *adj* worshiping no god

GODLIKE *adj* divine

GODLING *n* pl. **-S** a lesser god

GODLY *adj* **-LIER, -LIEST** pious **GODLILY** *adv*

GODOWN *n* pl. **-S** an Asian warehouse

GODROON *n* pl. **-S** gadroon

GODSEND *n* pl. **-S** an unexpected boon

GODSHIP *n* pl. **-S** the rank of a god

GODSON *n* pl. **-S** a male godchild

GODWIT *n* pl. **-S** a wading bird

GOER *n* pl. **-S** one that goes

GOETHITE *n* pl. **-S** an ore of iron

GOFER *n* pl. **-S** an employee who runs errands

GOFFER *v* **-ED, -ING, -S** to press ridges or pleats into

GOGGLE *v* **-GLED, -GLING, -GLES** to stare with wide eyes

GOGGLER *n* pl. **-S** one that goggles

GOGGLY *adj* **-GLIER, -GLIEST** wide-eyed

GOGLET *n* pl. **-S** a long-necked jar

GOGO *n* pl. **-GOS** a discotheque

GOING *n* pl. **-S** an advance toward an objective

GOITER *n* pl. **-S** an enlargement of the thyroid gland **GOITROUS** *adj*

GOITRE *n* pl. **-S** goiter

GOLCONDA *n* pl. **-S** a source of great wealth

GOLD *adj* **GOLDER, GOLDEST** golden

GOLD *n* pl. **-S** a precious metallic element

GOLDARN *n* pl. **-S** an expression of anger

GOLDBUG *n* pl. **-S** a gold beetle

GOLDEN *adj* **-ENER, -ENEST** of the color of gold **GOLDENLY** *adv*

GOLDEYE *n* pl. **-S** a freshwater fish

GOLDFISH *n* pl. **-ES** a freshwater fish

GOLDTONE *adj* made to resemble gold

GOLDURN *n* pl. **-S** goldarn

GOLEM *n* pl. **-S** a legendary creature

GOLF *v* **-ED, -ING, -S** to play golf (a type of ball game)

GOLFER *n* pl. **-S** one that golfs

GOLFING *n* pl. **-S** the game of golf

GOLGOTHA *n* pl. **-S** a place of burial

GOLIARD *n* pl. **-S** a wandering student

GOLIATH *n* pl. **-S** a person considered to be a giant

GOLLIWOG *n* pl. **-S** a grotesque doll

GOLLY *interj* — used as a mild oath

GOLLYWOG *n* pl. **-S** golliwog

GOLOSH *n* pl. **-ES** galosh

GOLOSHE *n* pl. **-S** galosh

GOMBEEN *n* pl. **-S** usury

GOMBO *n* pl. **-BOS** gumbo

GOMBROON *n* pl. **-S** a kind of Persian pottery

GOMER *n* pl. **-S** an undesirable hospital patient

GOMERAL *n* pl. **-S** a fool

GOMEREL *n* pl. **-S** gomeral

GOMERIL *n* pl. **-S** gomeral

GOMUTI *n* pl. **-S** a palm tree

GONAD *n* pl. **-S** a sex gland **GONADAL, GONADIAL, GONADIC** *adj*

GONDOLA *n* pl. **-S** a long, narrow boat

GONE *adj* departed

GONEF *n* pl. **-S** ganef

GONENESS *n* pl. **-ES** a state of exhaustion

GONER *n* pl. **-S** one who is in a hopeless situation

GONFALON *n* pl. **-S** a banner

GONFANON *n* pl. **-S** gonfalon

GONG *v* **-ED, -ING, -S** to make the sound of a gong (a disk-shaped percussion instrument)

GONGLIKE *adj* resembling a gong

GONIA pl. of gonion and of gonium

GONIDIUM *n* pl. **-IA** an asexual reproductive cell **GONIDIAL, GONIDIC** *adj*

GONIF *n* pl. **-S** ganef

GONIFF *n* pl. **-S** ganef

GONION *n* pl. **-NIA** a part of the lower jaw

GONIUM *n* pl. **-NIA** an immature reproductive cell

GONOCYTE *n* pl. **-S** a cell that produces gametes

GONOF *n* pl. **-S** ganef

GONOPH *n* pl. **-S** ganef

GONOPORE *n* pl. **-S** a genital pore

GONZO *adj* bizarre

GOO *n* pl. **GOOS** a sticky or viscid substance

GOOBER *n* pl. **-S** a peanut

GOOD *adj* **BETTER, BEST** having positive or desirable qualities

GOOD *n* pl. **-S** something that is good

GOODBY *n* pl. **-BYS** goodbye

GOODBYE *n* pl. **-S** a concluding remark or gesture at parting

GOODIE *n* pl. **-S** goody

GOODIES pl. of goody

GOODISH *adj* somewhat good

GOODLY *adj* **-LIER, -LIEST** of pleasing appearance

GOODMAN *n* pl. **-MEN** the master of a household

GOODNESS	*n* pl. **-ES** the state of being good
GOODWIFE	*n* pl. **-WIVES** the mistress of a household
GOODWILL	*n* pl. **-S** an attitude of friendliness
GOODY	*n* pl. **GOODIES** a desirable food
GOOEY	*adj* **GOOIER, GOOIEST** sticky or viscid
GOOF	*v* **-ED, -ING, -S** to blunder
GOOFBALL	*n* pl. **-S** a sleeping pill
GOOFY	*adj* **GOOFIER, GOOFIEST** silly **GOOFILY** *adv*
GOOGLY	*n* pl. **-GLIES** a type of bowled ball in cricket
GOOGOL	*n* pl. **-S** an enormous number
GOOIER	comparative of gooey
GOOIEST	superlative of gooey
GOOK	*n* pl. **-S** goo **GOOKY** *adj*
GOOMBAH	*n* pl. **-S** an older man who is a friend
GOOMBAY	*n* pl. **-BAYS** calypso music of the Bahamas
GOON	*n* pl. **-S** a hired thug
GOONEY	*n* pl. **-NEYS** an albatross
GOONIE	*n* pl. **-S** gooney
GOONY	*n* pl. **-NIES** gooney
GOONY	*adj* **GOONIER, GOONIEST** stupid
GOOP	*n* pl. **-S** goo, gunk
GOOPY	*adj* **GOOPIER, GOOPIEST** sticky, gooey
GOORAL	*n* pl. **-S** goral
GOOSE	*n* pl. **GEESE** a swimming bird
GOOSE	*v* **GOOSED, GOOSING, GOOSES** to poke between the buttocks
GOOSEY	*adj* **GOOSIER, GOOSIEST** goosy
GOOSY	*adj* **GOOSIER, GOOSIEST** resembling a goose
GOPHER	*n* pl. **-S** a burrowing rodent
GOPIK	*n* pl. **GOPIK** a monetary unit of Azerbaijan
GOR	*interj* — used as a mild oath
GORAL	*n* pl. **-S** a goat antelope
GORBELLY	*n* pl. **-LIES** a potbelly
GORBLIMY	*interj* blimey
GORCOCK	*n* pl. **-S** the male red grouse
GORDITA	*n* pl. **-S** a stuffed and fried pocket of cornmeal dough
GORE	*v* **GORED, GORING, GORES** to pierce with a horn or tusk
GORGE	*v* **GORGED, GORGING, GORGES** to stuff with food **GORGEDLY** *adv*
GORGEOUS	*adj* beautiful
GORGER	*n* pl. **-S** one that gorges
GORGERIN	*n* pl. **-S** a part of a column
GORGET	*n* pl. **-S** a piece of armor for the throat **GORGETED** *adj*
GORGING	present participle of gorge
GORGON	*n* pl. **-S** an ugly woman
GORHEN	*n* pl. **-S** the female red grouse
GORIER	comparative of gory
GORIEST	superlative of gory
GORILLA	*n* pl. **-S** a large ape
GORILY	*adv* in a gory manner
GORINESS	*n* pl. **-ES** the state of being gory
GORING	present participle of gore
GORM	*v* **-ED, -ING, -S** to gaum
GORMAND	*n* pl. **-S** gourmand
GORMLESS	*adj* stupid
GORP	*n* pl. **-S** a snack for quick energy
GORSE	*n* pl. **-S** furze
GORSY	*adj* **GORSIER, GORSIEST** abounding in gorse
GORY	*adj* **GORIER, GORIEST** bloody
GOSH	*interj* — used as an exclamation of surprise
GOSHAWK	*n* pl. **-S** a large hawk
GOSLING	*n* pl. **-S** a young goose
GOSPEL	*n* pl. **-S** the message concerning Christ, the kingdom of God, and salvation
GOSPELER	*n* pl. **-S** one that teaches the gospel
GOSPELLY	*adj* having characteristics of gospel music
GOSPORT	*n* pl. **-S** a communication device in an airplane
GOSSAMER	*n* pl. **-S** a fine film of cobwebs
GOSSAN	*n* pl. **-S** a type of decomposed rock
GOSSIP	*v* **-SIPED, -SIPING, -SIPS** or **-SIPPED, -SIPPING, -SIPS** to talk idly about the affairs of others
GOSSIPER	*n* pl. **-S** one that gossips
GOSSIPRY	*n* pl. **-RIES** the practice of gossiping
GOSSIPY	*adj* inclined to gossip
GOSSOON	*n* pl. **-S** a boy

GOSSYPOL *n* pl. **-S** a toxic pigment

GOT past tense of get

GOTCHA *n* pl. **-S** an instance of catching a person out in a deceit or wrongdoing

GOTH *n* pl. **-S** a morbid style of rock music

GOTHIC *n* pl. **-S** a style of printing

GOTHITE *n* pl. **-S** goethite

GOTTEN past participle of get

GOUACHE *n* pl. **-S** a method of painting

GOUGE *v* **GOUGED, GOUGING, GOUGES** to cut or scoop out

GOUGER *n* pl. **-S** one that gouges

GOULASH *n* pl. **-ES** a beef stew

GOURAMI *n* pl. **-S** or **-ES** a food fish

GOURD *n* pl. **-S** a hard-shelled fruit

GOURDE *n* pl. **-S** a monetary unit of Haiti

GOURMAND *n* pl. **-S** one who loves to eat

GOURMET *n* pl. **-S** a connoisseur of fine food and drink

GOUT *n* pl. **-S** a metabolic disease

GOUTY *adj* **GOUTIER, GOUTIEST** affected with gout **GOUTILY** *adv*

GOVERN *v* **-ED, -ING, -S** to rule or direct

GOVERNOR *n* pl. **-S** one that governs

GOWAN *n* pl. **-S** a daisy **GOWANED, GOWANY** *adj*

GOWD *n* pl. **-S** gold

GOWK *n* pl. **-S** a fool

GOWN *v* **-ED, -ING, -S** to dress in a gown (a long, loose outer garment)

GOWNSMAN *n* pl. **-MEN** a professional or academic person

GOX *n* pl. **-ES** gaseous oxygen

GRAAL *n* pl. **-S** grail

GRAB *v* **GRABBED, GRABBING, GRABS** to grasp suddenly

GRABBER *n* pl. **-S** one that grabs

GRABBIER comparative of grabby

GRABBIEST superlative of grabby

GRABBING present participle of grab

GRABBLE *v* **-BLED, -BLING, -BLES** to grope

GRABBLER *n* pl. **-S** one that grabbles

GRABBY *adj* **-BIER, -BIEST** tending to grab

GRABEN *n* pl. **-S** a depression of the earth's crust

GRACE *v* **GRACED, GRACING, GRACES** to give beauty to

GRACEFUL *adj* **-FULLER, -FULLEST** having beauty of form or movement

GRACILE *adj* gracefully slender

GRACILIS *n* pl. **-LES** a thigh muscle

GRACING present participle of grace

GRACIOSO *n* pl. **-SOS** a clown in Spanish comedy

GRACIOUS *adj* marked by kindness and courtesy

GRACKLE *n* pl. **-S** a blackbird

GRAD *n* pl. **-S** a graduate

GRADATE *v* **-DATED, -DATING, -DATES** to change by degrees

GRADE *v* **GRADED, GRADING, GRADES** to arrange in steps or degrees **GRADABLE** *adj*

GRADER *n* pl. **-S** one that grades

GRADIENT *n* pl. **-S** a rate of inclination

GRADIN *n* pl. **-S** gradine

GRADINE *n* pl. **-S** one of a series of steps

GRADING present participle of grade

GRADUAL *n* pl. **-S** a hymn sung in alternate parts

GRADUAND *n* pl. **-S** one who is about to graduate

GRADUATE *v* **-ATED, -ATING, -ATES** to receive an academic degree or diploma

GRADUS *n* pl. **-ES** a dictionary of prosody

GRAECIZE *v* **-CIZED, -CIZING, -CIZES** to grecize

GRAFFITI *v* **-TIED, -TIING** or **-TING, -TIS** to draw graffiti on

GRAFFITO *n* pl. **-TI** an inscription or drawing made on a rock or wall

GRAFT *v* **-ED, -ING, -S** to unite with a growing plant by insertion

GRAFTAGE *n* pl. **-S** the process of grafting

GRAFTER *n* pl. **-S** one that grafts

GRAHAM *n* pl. **-S** whole-wheat flour

GRAIL *n* pl. **-S** the object of a long quest

GRAIN *v* **-ED, -ING, -S** to form into small particles

GRAINER *n* pl. **-S** one that grains

GRAINY *adj* **GRAINIER, GRAINIEST** granular

GRAM *n* pl. **-S** a unit of mass and weight

GRAMA *n* pl. **-S** a pasture grass

GRAMARY *n* pl. **-RIES** gramarye

GRAMARYE *n* pl. **-S** occult learning; magic

GRAMERCY *n* pl. **-CIES** an expression of gratitude

GRAMMA *n* pl. **-S** grama

GRAMMAR *n* pl. **-S** the study of the formal features of a language

GRAMME *n* pl. **-S** gram

GRAMP *n* pl. **-S** grandfather

GRAMPA *n* pl. **-S** a grandfather

GRAMPUS *n* pl. **-ES** a marine mammal

GRAN *n* pl. **-S** a grandmother

GRANA pl. of granum

GRANARY *n* pl. **-RIES** a storehouse for grain

GRAND *adj* **GRANDER, GRANDEST** large and impressive

GRAND *n* pl. **-S** a type of piano

GRANDAD *n* pl. **-S** granddad

GRANDAM *n* pl. **-S** a grandmother

GRANDAME *n* pl. **-S** grandam

GRANDDAD *n* pl. **-S** a grandfather

GRANDDAM *n* pl. **-S** the female parent of an animal with offspring

GRANDEE *n* pl. **-S** man of high social position

GRANDEUR *n* pl. **-S** the state of being grand

GRANDKID *n* pl. **-S** the child of one's son or daughter

GRANDLY *adv* in a grand manner

GRANDMA *n* pl. **-S** a grandmother

GRANDPA *n* pl. **-S** a grandfather

GRANDSIR *n* pl. **-S** a grandfather

GRANDSON *n* pl. **-S** a son of one's son or daughter

GRANGE *n* pl. **-S** a farm

GRANGER *n* pl. **-S** a farmer

GRANITA *n* pl. **-S** an iced dessert

GRANITE *n* pl. **-S** a type of rock **GRANITIC** *adj*

GRANNIE *n* pl. **-S** granny

GRANNY *n* pl. **-NIES** a grandmother

GRANOLA *n* pl. **-S** a breakfast cereal

GRANT *v* **-ED, -ING, -S** to bestow upon

GRANTEE *n* pl. **-S** one to whom something is granted

GRANTER *n* pl. **-S** one that grants

GRANTOR *n* pl. **-S** granter

GRANULAR *adj* composed of granules

GRANULE *n* pl. **-S** a small particle

GRANUM *n* pl. **GRANA** a part of a plant chloroplast

GRAPE *n* pl. **-S** an edible berry

GRAPERY *n* pl. **-ERIES** a vinery

GRAPEY *adj* **GRAPIER, GRAPIEST** grapy

GRAPH *v* **-ED, -ING, -S** to represent by means of a diagram

GRAPHEME *n* pl. **-S** a unit of a writing system

GRAPHIC *n* pl. **-S** a product of the art of representation

GRAPHITE *n* pl. **-S** a variety of carbon

GRAPIER comparative of grapy

GRAPIEST superlative of grapy

GRAPLIN *n* pl. **-S** a grapnel

GRAPLINE *n* pl. **-S** graplin

GRAPNEL *n* pl. **-S** a type of anchor

GRAPPA *n* pl. **-S** an Italian brandy

GRAPPLE *v* **-PLED, -PLING, -PLES** to struggle or contend

GRAPPLER *n* pl. **-S** one that grapples

GRAPY *adj* **GRAPIER, GRAPIEST** resembling grapes

GRASP *v* **-ED, -ING, -S** to seize firmly with the hand

GRASPER *n* pl. **-S** one that grasps

GRASS *v* **-ED, -ING, -ES** to cover with grass (herbaceous plants)

GRASSY *adj* **GRASSIER, GRASSIEST** of, resembling, or pertaining to grass **GRASSILY** *adv*

GRAT past tense of greet (to weep)

GRATE *v* **GRATED, GRATING, GRATES** to reduce to shreds by rubbing

GRATEFUL *adj* **-FULLER, -FULLEST** deeply thankful

GRATER *n* pl. **-S** one that grates

GRATIFY *v* **-FIED, -FYING, -FIES** to satisfy

GRATIN *n* pl. **-S** a type of food crust

GRATINE *adj* covered with a crust

GRATINEE *v* **-NEED, -NEEING, -NEES** to cook food that is covered with a crust

GRATING *n* pl. **-S** a network of bars covering an opening

GRATIS *adj* free of charge

GRATUITY *n* pl. **-ITIES** a gift of money

GRAUPEL *n* pl. **-S** granular snow pellets

GRAVAMEN *n* pl. **-MENS** or **-MINA** the most serious part of an accusation

GRAVE *adj* **GRAVER, GRAVEST** extremely serious

GRAVE *v* **GRAVED, GRAVEN, GRAVING, GRAVES** to engrave

GRAVEL *v* **-ELED, -ELING, -ELS** or **-ELLED, -ELLING, -ELS** to pave with gravel (a mixture of rock fragments)

GRAVELLY *adj* containing gravel

GRAVELY *adv* in a grave manner

GRAVEN past participle of grave

GRAVER *n* pl. **-S** an engraver

GRAVEST superlative of grave

GRAVID *adj* pregnant **GRAVIDLY** *adv*

GRAVIDA *n* pl. **-DAS** or **-DAE** a pregnant woman

GRAVIES pl. of gravy

GRAVING present participle of grave

GRAVITAS *n* pl. **-ES** reserved, dignified behavior

GRAVITON *n* pl. **-S** a hypothetical particle

GRAVITY *n* pl. **-TIES** the force of attraction toward the earth's center

GRAVLAKS *n* pl. **GRAVLAKS** gravlax

GRAVLAX *n* pl. **GRAVLAX** cured salmon

GRAVURE *n* pl. **-S** a printing process

GRAVY *n* pl. **-VIES** a sauce of the fat and juices from cooked meat

GRAY *adj* **GRAYER, GRAYEST** of a color between white and black

GRAY *v* **-ED, -ING, -S** to make gray

GRAYBACK *n* pl. **-S** a gray bird

GRAYFISH *n* pl. **-ES** a dogfish

GRAYISH *adj* somewhat gray

GRAYLAG *n* pl. **-S** a wild goose

GRAYLING *n* pl. **-S** a food fish

GRAYLY *v* in a gray manner

GRAYMAIL *n* pl. **-S** pressure on an official to reveal sensitive information

GRAYNESS *n* pl. **-ES** the state of being gray

GRAYOUT *n* pl. **-S** a temporary blurring of vision

GRAZE *v* **GRAZED, GRAZING, GRAZES** to feed on growing grass **GRAZABLE** *adj*

GRAZER *n* pl. **-S** one that grazes

GRAZIER *n* pl. **-S** one that grazes cattle

GRAZING *n* pl. **-S** land used for the feeding of animals

GRAZIOSO *adj* graceful in style

GREASE *v* **GREASED, GREASING, GREASES** to smear with grease (a lubricating substance)

GREASER *n* pl. **-S** one that greases

GREASY *adj* **GREASIER, GREASIEST** containing or resembling grease **GREASILY** *adv*

GREAT *adj* **GREATER, GREATEST** large

GREAT *n* pl. **-S** a distinguished or outstanding person

GREATEN *v* **-ED, -ING, -S** to make greater

GREATLY *adv* in a great manner

GREAVE *n* pl. **-S** a piece of armor for the leg **GREAVED** *adj*

GREBE *n* pl. **-S** a diving bird

GRECIZE *v* **-CIZED, -CIZING, -CIZES** to provide with a Greek style

GREE *v* **GREED, GREEING, GREES** to agree

GREED *n* pl. **-S** excessive desire for gain or wealth

GREEDY *adj* **GREEDIER, GREEDIEST** marked by greed **GREEDILY** *adv*

GREEGREE *n* pl. **-S** grigri

GREEK *n* pl. **GREEK** something unintelligible

GREEN *adj* **GREENER, GREENEST** of the color of growing foliage

GREEN *v* **-ED, -ING, -S** to become green

GREENBUG *n* pl. **-S** a green aphid

GREENERY *n* pl. **-ERIES** green vegetation

GREENFLY *n* pl. **-FLIES** a green aphid

GREENIE *n* pl. **-S** an amphetamine pill

GREENIER comparative of greeny

GREENIEST superlative of greeny

GREENING *n* pl. **-S** a variety of apple

GREENISH *adj* somewhat green

GREENLET *n* pl. **-S** a vireo

GREENLIT a past tense of greenlight (to give approval for)

GREENLY *adv* in a green manner

GREENTH *n* pl. **-S** verdure

GREENWAY *n* pl. **-WAYS** piece of undeveloped land in a city

GREENY *adj* **GREENIER, GREENIEST** somewhat green

GREET *v* **-ED, -ING, -S** to address in a friendly and courteous way

GREET *v* **GRAT, GRUTTEN, GREETING, GREETS** to weep

GREETER	*n* pl. **-S** one that greets
GREETING	*n* pl. **-S** a salutation
GREGO	*n* pl. **-GOS** a hooded coat
GREIGE	*n* pl. **-S** fabric in a gray state
GREISEN	*n* pl. **-S** a type of rock
GREMIAL	*n* pl. **-S** a lap cloth used by a bishop during a service
GREMLIN	*n* pl. **-S** a mischievous creature
GREMMIE	*n* pl. **-S** an inexperienced surfer
GREMMY	*n* pl. **-MIES** gremmie
GRENADE	*n* pl. **-S** an explosive device
GREW	past tense of grow
GREWSOME	*adj* **-SOMER, -SOMEST** gruesome
GREY	*adj* **GREYER, GREYEST** gray
GREY	*v* **-ED, -ING, -S** to gray
GREYHEN	*n* pl. **-S** the female black grouse
GREYISH	*adj* grayish
GREYLAG	*n* pl. **-S** graylag
GREYLY	*adv* grayly
GREYNESS	*n* pl. **-ES** grayness
GRIBBLE	*n* pl. **-S** a marine isopod
GRID	*n* pl. **-S** a grating **GRIDDED** *adj*
GRIDDER	*n* pl. **-S** a football player
GRIDDLE	*v* **-DLED, -DLING, -DLES** to cook on a flat pan
GRIDE	*v* **GRIDED, GRIDING, GRIDES** to scrape harshly
GRIDIRON	*v* **-ED, -ING, -S** to mark off into squares
GRIDLOCK	*v* **-ED, -ING, -S** to bring to a standstill
GRIEF	*n* pl. **-S** intense mental distress
GRIEVANT	*n* pl. **-S** one that submits a complaint for arbitration
GRIEVE	*v* **GRIEVED, GRIEVING, GRIEVES** to feel grief
GRIEVER	*n* pl. **-S** one that grieves
GRIEVOUS	*adj* causing grief
GRIFF	*n* pl. **-S** griffe
GRIFFE	*n* pl. **-S** the offspring of a black person and a mulatto
GRIFFIN	*n* pl. **-S** a mythological creature
GRIFFON	*n* pl. **-S** griffin
GRIFT	*v* **-ED, -ING, -S** to swindle
GRIFTER	*n* pl. **-S** a swindler
GRIG	*n* pl. **-S** a lively person
GRIGRI	*n* pl. **-S** a fetish or amulet
GRILL	*v* **-ED, -ING, -S** to broil on a gridiron
GRILLADE	*n* pl. **-S** a dish of grilled meat
GRILLAGE	*n* pl. **-S** a framework of timber
GRILLE	*n* pl. **-S** a grating
GRILLER	*n* pl. **-S** one that grills
GRILLERY	*n* pl. **-ERIES** a place where grilled foods are served
GRILSE	*n* pl. **-S** a young salmon
GRIM	*adj* **GRIMMER, GRIMMEST** stern and unrelenting
GRIMACE	*v* **-MACED, -MACING, -MACES** to contort the facial features
GRIMACER	*n* pl. **-S** one that grimaces
GRIME	*v* **GRIMED, GRIMING, GRIMES** to make dirty
GRIMIER	comparative of grimy
GRIMIEST	superlative of grimy
GRIMILY	*adv* in a grimy manner
GRIMING	present participle of grime
GRIMLY	*adv* in a grim manner
GRIMMER	comparative of grim
GRIMMEST	superlative of grim
GRIMNESS	*n* pl. **-ES** the quality of being grim
GRIMY	*adj* **GRIMIER, GRIMIEST** dirty
GRIN	*v* **GRINNED, GRINNING, GRINS** to smile broadly
GRINCH	*n* pl. **-ES** one who spoils the fun of others
GRIND	*v* **GROUND** or **GRINDED, GRINDING, GRINDS** to wear, smooth, or sharpen by friction
GRINDER	*n* pl. **-S** one that grinds
GRINDERY	*n* pl. **-ERIES** a place where tools are ground
GRINNED	past tense of grin
GRINNER	*n* pl. **-S** one that grins
GRINNING	present participle of grin
GRIOT	*n* pl. **-S** a tribal entertainer in West Africa
GRIP	*v* **GRIPPED** or **GRIPT, GRIPPING, GRIPS** to grasp
GRIPE	*v* **GRIPED, GRIPING, GRIPES** to grasp
GRIPER	*n* pl. **-S** one that gripes
GRIPEY	*adj* **GRIPIER, GRIPIEST** gripy
GRIPIER	comparative of gripy
GRIPIEST	superlative of gripy

GRIPING present participle of gripe

GRIPMAN n pl. **-MEN** a cable car operator

GRIPPE n pl. **-S** a virus disease

GRIPPED a past tense of grip

GRIPPER n pl. **-S** one that grips

GRIPPING present participle of grip

GRIPPLE adj greedy

GRIPPY adj **GRIPPIER, GRIPPIEST** affected with the grippe

GRIPSACK n pl. **-S** a valise

GRIPT a past tense of grip

GRIPY adj **GRIPIER, GRIPIEST** causing sharp pains in the bowels

GRISEOUS adj grayish

GRISETTE n pl. **-S** a young French working-class girl

GRISKIN n pl. **-S** the lean part of a loin of pork

GRISLY adj **-LIER, -LIEST** horrifying

GRISON n pl. **-S** a carnivorous mammal

GRIST n pl. **-S** grain for grinding

GRISTER n pl. **-S** one that grinds grain

GRISTLE n pl. **-S** the tough part of meat

GRISTLY adj **-TLIER, -TLIEST** containing gristle

GRIT v **GRITTED, GRITTING, GRITS** to press the teeth together

GRITH n pl. **-S** sanctuary for a limited period of time

GRITTER n pl. **-S** one that grits

GRITTY adj **-TIER, -TIEST** plucky **GRITTILY** adv

GRIVET n pl. **-S** a small monkey

GRIZZLE v **-ZLED, -ZLING, -ZLES** to complain

GRIZZLER n pl. **-S** one that grizzles

GRIZZLY adj **-ZLIER, -ZLIEST** grayish

GRIZZLY n pl. **-ZLIES** a large bear

GROAN v **-ED, -ING, -S** to utter a low, mournful sound

GROANER n pl. **-S** one that groans

GROAT n pl. **-S** an old English coin

GROCER n pl. **-S** a dealer in foodstuffs and household supplies

GROCERY n pl. **-CERIES** a grocer's store

GRODY adj **GRODIER, GRODIEST** sleazy

GROG n pl. **-S** a mixture of liquor and water

GROGGERY n pl. **-GERIES** a barroom

GROGGY adj **-GIER, -GIEST** dazed **GROGGILY** adv

GROGRAM n pl. **-S** a coarse silk fabric

GROGSHOP n pl. **-S** a groggery

GROIN v **-ED, -ING, -S** to build with intersecting arches

GROK v **GROKKED, GROKKING, GROKS** to understand intuitively

GROMMET v **-ED, -ING, -S** to fasten with a reinforcing ring of metal

GROMWELL n pl. **-S** an herb

GROOM v **-ED, -ING, -S** to clean and care for

GROOMER n pl. **-S** one that grooms

GROOVE v **GROOVED, GROOVING, GROOVES** to form a groove (a long, narrow depression)

GROOVER n pl. **-S** one that grooves

GROOVY adj **GROOVIER, GROOVIEST** marvelous

GROPE v **GROPED, GROPING, GROPES** to feel about with the hands

GROPER n pl. **-S** one that gropes

GROSBEAK n pl. **-S** a finch

GROSCHEN n pl. **GROSCHEN** a formerly used Austrian coin

GROSS adj **GROSSER, GROSSEST** flagrant

GROSS v **-ED, -ING, -ES** to earn exclusive of deductions

GROSSER n pl. **-S** a product yielding a large volume of business

GROSSLY adv in a gross manner

GROSZ n pl. **GROSZY** a Polish coin

GROSZE n pl. **GROSZY** grosz

GROT n pl. **-S** a grotto

GROTTO n pl. **-TOS** or **-TOES** a cave **GROTTOED** adj

GROTTY adj **-TIER, -TIEST** wretched

GROUCH v **-ED, -ING, -ES** to complain

GROUCHY adj **GROUCHIER, GROUCHIEST** ill-tempered

GROUND v **-ED, -ING, -S** to place on a foundation

GROUNDER n pl. **-S** a type of batted baseball

GROUP v **-ED, -ING, -S** to arrange in a group (an assemblage of persons or things)

GROUPER n pl. **-S** a food fish

GROUPIE	*n* pl. **-S** a follower of rock groups
GROUPING	*n* pl. **-S** a set of objects
GROUPOID	*n* pl. **-S** a type of mathematical set
GROUSE	*v* **GROUSED, GROUSING, GROUSES** to complain
GROUSER	*n* pl. **-S** one that grouses
GROUT	*v* **-ED, -ING, -S** to fill with a thin mortar
GROUTER	*n* pl. **-S** one that grouts
GROUTY	*adj* **GROUTIER, GROUTIEST** surly
GROVE	*n* pl. **-S** a small forested area **GROVED** *adj*
GROVEL	*v* **-ELED, -ELING, -ELS** or **-ELLED, -ELLING, -ELS** to crawl in an abject manner
GROVELER	*n* pl. **-S** one that grovels
GROW	*v* **GREW, GROWN, GROWING, GROWS** to cultivate **GROWABLE** *adj*
GROWER	*n* pl. **-S** one that grows
GROWL	*v* **-ED, -ING, -S** to utter a deep, harsh sound
GROWLER	*n* pl. **-S** one that growls
GROWLY	*adj* **GROWLIER, GROWLIEST** deep and harsh in speech
GROWN	*adj* mature
GROWNUP	*n* pl. **-S** a mature person
GROWTH	*n* pl. **-S** development
GROWTHY	*adj* **GROWTHIER, GROWTHIEST** fast-growing
GROYNE	*n* pl. **-S** a structure built to protect a shore from erosion
GRUB	*v* **GRUBBED, GRUBBING, GRUBS** to dig
GRUBBER	*n* pl. **-S** one that grubs
GRUBBY	*adj* **-BIER, -BIEST** dirty **GRUBBILY** *adv*
GRUBWORM	*n* pl. **-S** the larva of some insects
GRUDGE	*v* **GRUDGED, GRUDGING, GRUDGES** to be unwilling to give or admit
GRUDGER	*n* pl. **-S** one that grudges
GRUE	*n* pl. **-S** a shudder of fear
GRUEL	*v* **-ELED, -ELING, -ELS** or **-ELLED, -ELLING, -ELS** to disable by hard work
GRUELER	*n* pl. **-S** one that gruels
GRUELING	*n* pl. **-S** an exhausting experience
GRUELLED	a past tense of gruel
GRUELLER	*n* pl. **-S** grueler
GRUELLING	present participle of gruel
GRUESOME	*adj* **-SOMER, -SOMEST** repugnant
GRUFF	*adj* **GRUFFER, GRUFFEST** low and harsh in speech
GRUFF	*v* **-ED, -ING, -S** to utter in a gruff voice
GRUFFIER	comparative of gruffy
GRUFFIEST	superlative of gruffy
GRUFFILY	*adv* in a gruffy manner
GRUFFISH	*adj* somewhat gruff
GRUFFLY	*adv* in a gruff manner
GRUFFY	*adj* **GRUFFIER, GRUFFIEST** gruff
GRUGRU	*n* pl. **-S** a palm tree
GRUIFORM	*adj* designating an order of birds
GRUM	*adj* **GRUMMER, GRUMMEST** morose
GRUMBLE	*v* **-BLED, -BLING, -BLES** to mutter in discontent **GRUMBLY** *adj*
GRUMBLER	*n* pl. **-S** one that grumbles
GRUME	*n* pl. **-S** a thick, viscid substance
GRUMMER	comparative of grum
GRUMMEST	superlative of grum
GRUMMET	*v* **-ED, -ING, -S** to grommet
GRUMOSE	*adj* grumous
GRUMOUS	*adj* consisting of clustered grains
GRUMP	*v* **-ED, -ING, -S** to complain
GRUMPHIE	*n* pl. **-S** a pig
GRUMPHY	*n* pl. **GRUMPHIES** grumphie
GRUMPISH	*adj* grumpy
GRUMPY	*adj* **GRUMPIER, GRUMPIEST** ill-tempered **GRUMPILY** *adv*
GRUNGE	*n* pl. **-S** dirt
GRUNGER	*n* pl. **-S** a fan of a style of rock music and associated fashions
GRUNGY	*adj* **-GIER, -GIEST** dirty
GRUNION	*n* pl. **-S** a small food fish
GRUNT	*v* **-ED, -ING, -S** to utter a deep, guttural sound
GRUNTER	*n* pl. **-S** one that grunts
GRUNTLE	*v* **-TLED, -TLING, -TLES** to put in a good humor
GRUSHIE	*adj* thriving
GRUTCH	*v* **-ED, -ING, -ES** to grudge
GRUTTEN	past participle of greet (to weep)
GRUYERE	*n* pl. **-S** a Swiss cheese
GRYPHON	*n* pl. **-S** griffin

GUACHARO *n* pl. **-ROS** or **-ROES** a tropical bird

GUACO *n* pl. **-COS** a tropical plant

GUAIAC *n* pl. **-S** guaiacum

GUAIACOL *n* pl. **-S** a chemical compound

GUAIACUM *n* pl. **-S** a medicinal resin

GUAIOCUM *n* pl. **-S** guaiacum

GUAN *n* pl. **-S** a large bird

GUANACO *n* pl. **-COS** a South American mammal

GUANASE *n* pl. **-S** an enzyme

GUANAY *n* pl. **-NAYS** a Peruvian cormorant

GUANIDIN *n* pl. **-S** a chemical compound

GUANIN *n* pl. **-S** guanine

GUANINE *n* pl. **-S** a chemical compound

GUANO *n* pl. **-NOS** the accumulated excrement of sea birds

GUAR *n* pl. **-S** a drought-tolerant legume

GUARANA *n* pl. **-S** a South American shrub

GUARANI *n* pl. **-NIS** or **-NIES** a monetary unit of Paraguay

GUARANTY *v* **-TIED, -TYING, -TIES** to assume responsibility for the quality of

GUARD *v* **-ED, -ING, -S** to protect

GUARDANT *n* pl. **-S** a guardian

GUARDDOG *n* pl. **-S** a dog trained to guard persons or property

GUARDER *n* pl. **-S** one that guards

GUARDIAN *n* pl. **-S** one that guards

GUAVA *n* pl. **-S** a tropical shrub

GUAYULE *n* pl. **-S** a shrub that is a source of rubber

GUCK *n* pl. **-S** a messy substance

GUDE *n* pl. **-S** good

GUDGEON *v* **-ED, -ING, -S** to dupe

GUENON *n* pl. **-S** a long-tailed monkey

GUERDON *v* **-ED, -ING, -S** to reward

GUERIDON *n* pl. **-S** a small stand or table

GUERILLA *n* pl. **-S** a member of a small independent band of soldiers

GUERNSEY *n* pl. **-SEYS** a woolen shirt

GUESS *v* **-ED, -ING, -ES** to form an opinion from little or no evidence

GUESSER *n* pl. **-S** one that guesses

GUEST *v* **-ED, -ING, -S** to appear as a visitor

GUFF *n* pl. **-S** foolish talk

GUFFAW *v* **-ED, -ING, -S** to laugh loudly

GUGGLE *v* **-GLED, -GLING, -GLES** to gurgle

GUGLET *n* pl. **-S** goglet

GUID *n* pl. **-S** good

GUIDANCE *n* pl. **-S** advice

GUIDE *v* **GUIDED, GUIDING, GUIDES** to show the way to **GUIDABLE** *adj*

GUIDER *n* pl. **-S** one that guides

GUIDEWAY *n* pl. **-WAYS** a track for controlling the line of motion of something

GUIDON *n* pl. **-S** a small flag

GUILD *n* pl. **-S** an association of people of the same trade

GUILDER *n* pl. **-S** a monetary unit of the Netherlands

GUILE *v* **GUILED, GUILING, GUILES** to beguile

GUILEFUL *adj* cunning

GUILT *n* pl. **-S** the fact of having committed an offense

GUILTY *adj* **GUILTIER, GUILTIEST** worthy of blame for an offense **GUILTILY** *adv*

GUIMPE *n* pl. **-S** a short blouse

GUINEA *n* pl. **-S** a formerly used British coin

GUIPURE *n* pl. **-S** a type of lace

GUIRO *n* pl. **-ROS** a percussion instrument

GUISARD *n* pl. **-S** a masker

GUISE *v* **GUISED, GUISING, GUISES** to disguise

GUITAR *n* pl. **-S** a stringed musical instrument

GUITGUIT *n* pl. **-S** a tropical American bird

GUL *n* pl. **-S** a design in oriental carpets

GULAG *n* pl. **-S** a forced-labor camp

GULAR *adj* of or pertaining to the throat

GULCH *n* pl. **-ES** a deep, narrow ravine

GULDEN *n* pl. **-S** a guilder

GULES *n* pl. **GULES** the color red

GULF *v* **-ED, -ING, -S** to swallow up

GULFIER comparative of gulfy

GULFIEST superlative of gulfy

GULFLIKE *adj* resembling a deep chasm

GULFWEED *n* pl. **-S** a brownish seaweed

GULFY *adj* **GULFIER, GULFIEST** full of whirlpools

GULL *v* **-ED, -ING, -S** to deceive

GULLABLE *adj* gullible **GULLABLY** *adv*

GULLET	*n* pl. **-S** the throat
GULLEY	*n* pl. **-LEYS** a ravine
GULLIBLE	*adj* easily deceived **GULLIBLY** *adv*
GULLWING	*adj* hinged at the top to swing upward
GULLY	*v* **-LIED, -LYING, -LIES** to form ravines by the action of water
GULOSITY	*n* pl. **-TIES** gluttony
GULP	*v* **-ED, -ING, -S** to swallow rapidly
GULPER	*n* pl. **-S** one that gulps
GULPY	*adj* **GULPIER, GULPIEST** marked by gulping
GUM	*v* **GUMMED, GUMMING, GUMS** to smear, seal, or clog with gum (a sticky, viscid substance)
GUMBALL	*n* pl. **-S** a small ball of chewing gum
GUMBO	*n* pl. **-BOS** the okra plant
GUMBOIL	*n* pl. **-S** an abscess in the gum
GUMBOOT	*n* pl. **-S** a rubber boot
GUMBOTIL	*n* pl. **-S** a sticky clay
GUMDROP	*n* pl. **-S** a chewy candy
GUMLESS	*adj* having no gum
GUMLIKE	*adj* resembling gum
GUMLINE	*n* pl. **-S** the edge of the gums meeting the teeth
GUMMA	*n* pl. **-MAS** or **-MATA** a soft tumor
GUMMED	past tense of gum
GUMMER	*n* pl. **-S** one that gums
GUMMIER	comparative of gummy
GUMMIEST	superlative of gummy
GUMMING	present participle of gum
GUMMITE	*n* pl. **-S** a mixture of various minerals
GUMMOSE	*adj* gummy
GUMMOSIS	*n* pl. **-MOSES** a disease of plants
GUMMOUS	*adj* gummy
GUMMY	*adj* **-MIER, -MIEST** resembling gum
GUMPTION	*n* pl. **-S** shrewdness
GUMSHOE	*v* **-SHOED, -SHOEING, -SHOES** to investigate stealthily
GUMTREE	*n* pl. **-S** a tree that yields gum
GUMWEED	*n* pl. **-S** a plant covered with a gummy substance
GUMWOOD	*n* pl. **-S** the wood of a gumtree

GUN	*v* **GUNNED, GUNNING, GUNS** to shoot with a gun (a portable firearm)
GUNBOAT	*n* pl. **-S** an armed vessel
GUNDOG	*n* pl. **-S** a hunting dog
GUNFIGHT	*v* **-FOUGHT, -FIGHTING, -FIGHTS** to fight with guns
GUNFIRE	*n* pl. **-S** the firing of guns
GUNFLINT	*n* pl. **-S** the flint in a flintlock
GUNITE	*n* pl. **-S** a mixture of cement, sand, and water
GUNK	*n* pl. **-S** filthy, sticky, or greasy matter
GUNKHOLE	*v* **-HOLED, -HOLING, -HOLES** to make a series of short boat trips
GUNKY	*adj* **GUNKIER, GUNKIEST** filthy, sticky, or greasy
GUNLESS	*adj* having no gun
GUNLOCK	*n* pl. **-S** the mechanism which ignites the charge of a gun
GUNMAN	*n* pl. **-MEN** one who is armed with a gun
GUNMETAL	*n* pl. **-S** a dark gray color
GUNNED	past tense of gun
GUNNEL	*n* pl. **-S** a marine fish
GUNNEN	past participle of gin
GUNNER	*n* pl. **-S** one that operates a gun
GUNNERY	*n* pl. **-NERIES** the use of guns
GUNNING	*n* pl. **-S** the sport of hunting with a gun
GUNNY	*n* pl. **-NIES** a coarse fabric
GUNNYBAG	*n* pl. **-S** a bag made of gunny
GUNPAPER	*n* pl. **-S** a type of explosive paper
GUNPLAY	*n* pl. **-PLAYS** the shooting of guns
GUNPOINT	*n* pl. **-S** the point or aim of a gun
GUNROOM	*n* pl. **-S** a room on a British warship
GUNSEL	*n* pl. **-S** a gunman
GUNSHIP	*n* pl. **-S** an armed helicopter
GUNSHOT	*n* pl. **-S** a projectile fired from a gun
GUNSMITH	*n* pl. **-S** one who makes or repairs firearms
GUNSTOCK	*n* pl. **-S** the rear wooden part of a rifle
GUNWALE	*n* pl. **-S** the upper edge of a ship's side
GUPPY	*n* pl. **-PIES** a small, tropical fish
GURGE	*v* **GURGED, GURGING, GURGES** to swirl

GURGLE	v **-GLED, -GLING, -GLES** to flow unevenly	**GUTTLE**	v **-TLED, -TLING, -TLES** to eat rapidly
GURGLET	n pl. **-S** goglet	**GUTTLER**	n pl. **-S** one that guttles
GURNARD	n pl. **-S** a marine fish	**GUTTURAL**	n pl. **-S** a throaty sound
GURNET	n pl. **-S** a gurnard	**GUTTY**	adj **-TIER, -TIEST** marked by courage
GURNEY	n pl. **-NEYS** a wheeled cot		
GURRY	n pl. **-RIES** fish offal	**GUV**	n pl. **-S** a governor
GURSH	n pl. **-ES** qursh	**GUY**	v **-ED, -ING, -S** to ridicule
GURU	n pl. **-S** a Hindu spiritual teacher	**GUYLINE**	n pl. **-S** a rope, chain, or wire used as a brace
GURUSHIP	n pl. **-S** the office of a guru		
GUSH	v **-ED, -ING, -ES** to flow forth forcefully	**GUYOT**	n pl. **-S** a flat-topped seamount
		GUZZLE	v **-ZLED, -ZLING, -ZLES** to drink rapidly
GUSHER	n pl. **-S** a gushing oil well		
GUSHY	adj **GUSHIER, GUSHIEST** overly sentimental **GUSHILY** adv	**GUZZLER**	n pl. **-S** one that guzzles
		GWEDUC	n pl. **-S** geoduck
GUSSET	v **-ED, -ING, -S** to furnish with a reinforcing piece of material	**GWEDUCK**	n pl. **-S** geoduck
		GWINE	a present participle of go
GUSSIE	v **-SIED, -SYING, -SIES** to gussy	**GYBE**	v **GYBED, GYBING, GYBES** to shift from side to side while sailing
GUSSY	v **-SIED, -SYING, -SIES** to dress up in fine or showy clothes		
		GYM	n pl. **-S** a room for athletic activities
GUST	v **-ED, -ING, -S** to blow in gusts (sudden blasts of wind)	**GYMKHANA**	n pl. **-S** an athletic meet
		GYMNASIA	n/pl gyms
GUSTABLE	n pl. **-S** a savory food	**GYMNAST**	n pl. **-S** one who is skilled in physical exercises
GUSTIER	comparative of gusty		
GUSTIEST	superlative of gusty	**GYNAECEA**	n/pl gynecia
GUSTILY	adv in a gusty manner	**GYNAECIA**	n/pl gynecia
GUSTLESS	adj having no gusts	**GYNANDRY**	n pl. **-DRIES** the condition of having both male and female sexual organs
GUSTO	n pl. **-TOES** vigorous enjoyment		
GUSTY	adj **GUSTIER, GUSTIEST** blowing in gusts		
		GYNARCHY	n pl. **-CHIES** government by women
GUT	v **GUTTED, GUTTING, GUTS** to remove the guts (intestines) of		
		GYNECIC	adj pertaining to women
GUTLESS	adj lacking courage	**GYNECIUM**	n pl. **-CIA** the pistil of a flower
GUTLIKE	adj resembling guts	**GYNECOID**	adj resembling a woman
GUTSILY	adv in a gutsy manner	**GYNIATRY**	n pl. **-TRIES** the treatment of women's diseases
GUTSY	adj **GUTSIER, GUTSIEST** brave		
GUTTA	n pl. **-TAE** a drop of liquid	**GYNOECIA**	n/pl gynecia
GUTTATE	adj resembling a drop	**GYOZA**	n pl. **-S** a stuffed and fried pocket of dough
GUTTATED	adj guttate		
GUTTED	past tense of gut	**GYP**	v **GYPPED, GYPPING, GYPS** to swindle
GUTTER	v **-ED, -ING, -S** to form channels for draining off water		
		GYPLURE	n pl. **-S** a synthetic attractant to trap gypsy moths
GUTTERY	adj marked by extreme vulgarity or indecency		
		GYPPER	n pl. **-S** one that gyps
GUTTIER	comparative of gutty	**GYPSEIAN**	adj of or pertaining to gypsies
GUTTIEST	superlative of gutty	**GYPSEOUS**	adj containing gypsum
GUTTING	present participle of gut	**GYPSTER**	n pl. **-S** one that gyps
		GYPSUM	n pl. **-S** a mineral

GYPSY   *v* **-SIED, -SYING, -SIES** to live like a gypsy (a wanderer)

GYPSYDOM   *n* pl. **-S** the realm of gypsies

GYPSYISH   *adj* resembling a gypsy

GYPSYISM   *n* pl. **-S** the mode of life of gypsies

GYRAL   *adj* gyratory **GYRALLY** *adv*

GYRASE   *n* pl. **-S** an enzyme

GYRATE   *v* **-RATED, -RATING, -RATES** to revolve or rotate

GYRATION   *n* pl. **-S** the act of gyrating

GYRATOR   *n* pl. **-S** one that gyrates

GYRATORY   *adj* moving in a circle or spiral

GYRE   *v* **GYRED, GYRING, GYRES** to move in a circle or spiral

GYRENE   *n* pl. **-S** a marine

GYRI   pl. of gyrus

GYRO   *n* pl. **-ROS** a gyroscope

GYROIDAL   *adj* spiral in arrangement

GYRON   *n* pl. **-S** a heraldic design

GYROSE   *adj* marked with wavy lines

GYROSTAT   *n* pl. **-S** a type of stabilizing device

GYRUS   *n* pl. **-RI** a ridge in the brain

GYTTJA   *n* pl. **-S** an organically rich mud

GYVE   *v* **GYVED, GYVING, GYVES** to shackle

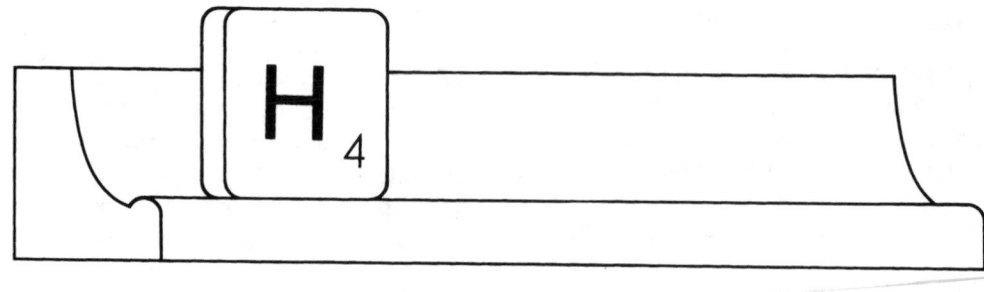

HA	*n* pl. **-S** a sound of surprise	**HACKNEY**	*v* **-NEYED, -NEYING, -NEYS** to make common
HAAF	*n* pl. **-S** a deep-sea fishing ground		
HAAR	*n* pl. **-S** a fog	**HACKSAW**	*v* **-SAWED, -SAWN, -SAWING, -SAWS** to use a saw having a fine-toothed blade
HABANERA	*n* pl. **-S** a Cuban dance		
HABANERO	*n* pl. **-ROS** a hot chili pepper	**HACKWORK**	*n* pl. **-S** artistic work done according to formula
HABDALAH	*n* pl. **-S** a Jewish ceremony	**HAD**	a past tense of have
HABILE	*adj* skillful	**HADAL**	*adj* pertaining to deep parts of the ocean
HABIT	*v* **-ED, -ING, -S** to clothe or dress		
HABITAN	*n* pl. **-S** a French settler	**HADARIM**	a pl. of heder
HABITANT	*n* pl. **-S** an inhabitant	**HADDEST**	a past 2d person sing. of have
HABITAT	*n* pl. **-S** the natural environment of an organism	**HADDOCK**	*n* pl. **-S** a food fish
		HADE	*v* **HADED, HADING, HADES** to incline
HABITUAL	*adj* occurring frequently or constantly		
		HADITH	*n* pl. **HADITH** or **HADITHS** a record of the sayings of Muhammed
HABITUDE	*n* pl. **-S** a usual course of action		
HABITUE	*n* pl. **-S** a frequent customer	**HADJ**	*n* pl. **-ES** a pilgrimage to Mecca
HABITUS	*n* pl. **HABITUS** bodily build and constitution	**HADJEE**	*n* pl. **-S** hadji
		HADJI	*n* pl. **-S** one who has made a hadj
HABOOB	*n* pl. **-S** a violent sandstorm	**HADRON**	*n* pl. **-S** an elementary particle **HADRONIC** *adj*
HABU	*n* pl. **-S** a poisonous snake		
HACEK	*n* pl. **-S** a mark placed over a letter to modify it	**HADST**	a past 2d person sing. of have
		HAE	*v* **HAED, HAEN, HAEING, HAES** to have
HACHURE	*v* **-CHURED, -CHURING, -CHURES** to make a hatching on a map		
		HAEM	*n* pl. **-S** heme
HACIENDA	*n* pl. **-S** an estate	**HAEMAL**	*adj* hemal
HACK	*v* **-ED, -ING, -S** to cut or chop roughly **HACKABLE** *adj*	**HAEMATAL**	*adj* hemal
		HAEMATIC	*n* pl. **-S** hematic
HACKBUT	*n* pl. **-S** a type of gun	**HAEMATIN**	*n* pl. **-S** hematin
HACKEE	*n* pl. **-S** a chipmunk	**HAEMIC**	*adj* hemic
HACKER	*n* pl. **-S** one that hacks	**HAEMIN**	*n* pl. **-S** hemin
HACKIE	*n* pl. **-S** a taxicab driver	**HAEMOID**	*adj* hemoid
HACKLE	*v* **-LED, -LING, -LES** to hack	**HAEN**	past participle of hae
HACKLER	*n* pl. **-S** one that hackles	**HAERES**	*n* pl. **-REDES** heres
HACKLY	*adj* **-LIER, -LIEST** jagged	**HAET**	*n* pl. **-S** a small amount
HACKMAN	*n* pl. **-MEN** a hackie	**HAFFET**	*n* pl. **-S** the cheekbone and temple

HAFFIT	*n* pl. **-S** haffet	**HAIR**	*n* pl. **-S** a threadlike growth
HAFIZ	*n* pl. **-ES** a Muslim who knows the Koran by heart	**HAIRBALL**	*n* pl. **-S** a ball of hair
		HAIRBAND	*n* pl. **-S** a headband
HAFNIUM	*n* pl. **-S** a metallic element	**HAIRCAP**	*n* pl. **-S** a hat
HAFT	*v* **-ED, -ING, -S** to supply with a handle	**HAIRCUT**	*n* pl. **-S** a cutting of the hair
HAFTARA	*n* pl. **-RAS, -ROT** or **-ROTH** haphtara	**HAIRDO**	*n* pl. **-DOS** a style of wearing the hair
HAFTARAH	*n* pl. **-RAHS, -ROS, -ROT** or **-ROTH** haphtara	**HAIRED**	*adj* having hair
		HAIRIER	comparative of hairy
HAFTER	*n* pl. **-S** one that hafts	**HAIRIEST**	superlative of hairy
HAFTORAH	*n* pl. **-RAHS, -ROT** or **-ROTH** haphtara	**HAIRLESS**	*adj* having no hair
		HAIRLIKE	*adj* resembling a hair
HAG	*v* **HAGGED, HAGGING, HAGS** to hack	**HAIRLINE**	*n* pl. **-S** a very thin line
		HAIRLOCK	*n* pl. **-S** a lock of hair
HAGADIC	*adj* haggadic	**HAIRNET**	*n* pl. **-S** a net worn to keep the hair in place
HAGADIST	*n* pl. **-S** a haggadic scholar		
HAGBERRY	*n* pl. **-RIES** a small cherry	**HAIRPIN**	*n* pl. **-S** a hair fastener
HAGBORN	*adj* born of a witch	**HAIRWORK**	*n* pl. **-S** the making of articles from hair
HAGBUSH	*n* pl. **-ES** a large tree		
HAGBUT	*n* pl. **-S** hackbut	**HAIRWORM**	*n* pl. **-S** a parasitic worm
HAGDON	*n* pl. **-S** a seabird	**HAIRY**	*adj* **HAIRIER, HAIRIEST** covered with hair
HAGFISH	*n* pl. **-ES** an eellike fish		
HAGGADA	*n* pl. **-DAS, -DOT** or **-DOTH** haggadah	**HAJ**	*n* pl. **-ES** hadj
		HAJI	*n* pl. **-S** hadji
HAGGADAH	*n* pl. **-DAHS, -DOT** or **-DOTH** a biblical narrative **HAGGADIC** *adj*	**HAJJ**	*n* pl. **-ES** hadj
		HAJJI	*n* pl. **-S** hadji
HAGGARD	*n* pl. **-S** an adult hawk	**HAKE**	*n* pl. **-S** a marine fish
HAGGED	past tense of hag	**HAKEEM**	*n* pl. **-S** hakim
HAGGING	present participle of hag	**HAKIM**	*n* pl. **-S** a Muslim physician
HAGGIS	*n* pl. **-GISES** a Scottish dish	**HAKU**	*n* pl. **-S** a crown of flowers
HAGGISH	*adj* resembling a hag	**HALACHA**	*n* pl. **-CHAS** or **-CHOT** or **-CHOTH** the legal part of the Talmud **HALACHIC** *adj*
HAGGLE	*v* **-GLED, -GLING, -GLES** to bargain		
HAGGLER	*n* pl. **-S** one that haggles	**HALAKAH**	*n* pl. **-KAHS** or **-KOTH** halacha **HALAKIC** *adj*
HAGRIDE	*v* **-RODE, -RIDDEN, -RIDING, -RIDES** to harass	**HALAKHA**	*n* pl. **-KHAS** or **-KHOT** halacha **HALAKHIC** *adj*
HAGRIDER	*n* pl. **-S** one that hagrides	**HALAKHAH**	*n* pl. **-KHAHS** or **-KHOTH** or **-KHOT** halacha **HALAKHIC** *adj*
HAH	*n* pl. **-S** ha		
HAHA	*n* pl. **-S** a fence set in a ditch	**HALAKIST**	*n* pl. **-S** a halakic writer
HAHNIUM	*n* pl. **-S** a radioactive element	**HALAKOTH**	a pl. of halakah
HAIK	*n* pl. **HAIKS** or **HAIKA** an outer garment worn by Arabs	**HALAL**	*n* pl. **-S** meat prepared in accordance with Islamic law
HAIKU	*n* pl. **-S** a Japanese poem	**HALALA**	*n* pl. **-S** a Saudi Arabian coin
HAIL	*v* **-ED, -ING, -S** to welcome	**HALALAH**	*n* pl. **-S** halala
HAILER	*n* pl. **-S** one that hails	**HALATION**	*n* pl. **-S** a blurring of light in photographs
HAIMISH	*adj* homey, unpretentious		
HAINT	*n* pl. **-S** a ghost	**HALAVAH**	*n* pl. **-S** halvah

HALAZONE *n* pl. **-S** a disinfectant for drinking water

HALBERD *n* pl. **-S** an axlike weapon of the 15th and 16th centuries

HALBERT *n* pl. **-S** halberd

HALCYON *n* pl. **-S** a mythical bird

HALE *adj* **HALER, HALEST** healthy

HALE *v* **HALED, HALING, HALES** to compel to go

HALENESS *n* pl. **-ES** the state of being hale

HALER *n* pl. **-LERS** or **-LERU** a coin of the Czech Republic

HALEST superlative of hale

HALF *n* pl. **HALVES** one of two equal parts

HALFBACK *n* pl. **-S** a football player

HALFBEAK *n* pl. **-S** a marine fish

HALFLIFE *n* pl. **-LIVES** a measure of radioactive decay

HALFNESS *n* pl. **-ES** the state of being half

HALFPIPE *n* pl. **-S** a U-shaped course used for skateboarding

HALFTIME *n* pl. **-S** an intermission in a football game

HALFTONE *n* pl. **-S** a shade between light and dark

HALFWAY *adj* being in the middle

HALIBUT *n* pl. **-S** a flatfish

HALID *n* pl. **-S** halide

HALIDE *n* pl. **-S** a chemical compound

HALIDOM *n* pl. **-S** something holy

HALIDOME *n* pl. **-S** halidom

HALING present participle of hale

HALITE *n* pl. **-S** a mineral

HALITUS *n* pl. **-ES** an exhalation

HALL *n* pl. **-S** a large room for assembly

HALLAH *n* pl. **-LAHS, -LOTH** or **-LOT** challah

HALLAL *adj* prepared according to Islamic law

HALLEL *n* pl. **-S** a chant of praise

HALLIARD *n* pl. **-S** halyard

HALLMARK *v* **-ED, -ING, -S** to mark with an official stamp

HALLO *v* **-ED, -ING, -S** or **-ES** to shout

HALLOA *v* **-ED, -ING, -S** to hallo

HALLOO *v* **-ED, -ING, -S** to hallo

HALLOT a pl. of hallah

HALLOTH a pl. of hallah

HALLOW *v* **-ED, -ING, -S** to make holy

HALLOWER *n* pl. **-S** one that hallows

HALLUX *n* pl. **-LUCES** the big toe **HALLUCAL** *adj*

HALLWAY *n* pl. **-WAYS** a hall

HALM *n* pl. **-S** haulm

HALMA *n* pl. **-S** a board game

HALO *v* **-ED, -ING, -S** or **-ES** to form a halo (a ring of light)

HALOGEN *n* pl. **-S** a nonmetallic element

HALOID *n* pl. **-S** a chemical salt

HALOLIKE *adj* resembling a halo

HALON *n* pl. **-S** a compound of carbon and bromine

HALT *v* **-ED, -ING, -S** to stop

HALTER *v* **-ED, -ING, -S** to put restraint upon

HALTERE *n* pl. **-S** a pair of wings of an insect

HALTLESS *adj* not hesitant

HALUTZ *n* pl. **-LUTZIM** an Israeli farmer

HALVA *n* pl. **-S** halvah

HALVAH *n* pl. **-S** a Turkish confection

HALVE *v* **HALVED, HALVING, HALVES** to divide into two equal parts

HALVERS *n* pl. **HALVERS** half shares

HALVES pl. of half

HALYARD *n* pl. **-S** a line used to hoist a sail

HAM *v* **HAMMED, HAMMING, HAMS** to overact

HAMADA *n* pl. **-S** hammada

HAMAL *n* pl. **-S** a porter in eastern countries

HAMARTIA *n* pl. **-S** a defect of character

HAMATE *n* pl. **-S** a wrist bone

HAMAUL *n* pl. **-S** hamal

HAMBONE *v* **-BONED, -BONING, -BONES** to overact

HAMBURG *n* pl. **-S** a patty of ground beef

HAME *n* pl. **-S** a part of a horse collar

HAMLET *n* pl. **-S** a small town

HAMMADA *n* pl. **-S** a desert plateau of bedrock

HAMMAL *n* pl. **-S** hamal

HAMMAM *n* pl. **-S** a Turkish bath

HAMMED past tense of ham

HAMMER *v* **-ED, -ING, -S** to strike repeatedly

HAMMERER *n* pl. **-S** one that hammers

HAMMIER	comparative of hammy
HAMMIEST	superlative of hammy
HAMMILY	*adv* in a hammy manner
HAMMING	present participle of ham
HAMMOCK	*n* pl. **-S** a hanging cot
HAMMY	*adj* **-MIER, -MIEST** overly theatrical
HAMPER	*v* **-ED, -ING, -S** to hinder
HAMPERER	*n* pl. **-S** one that hampers
HAMSTER	*n* pl. **-S** a burrowing rodent
HAMULUS	*n* pl. **-LI** a small hook **HAMULAR, HAMULATE, HAMULOSE, HAMULOUS** *adj*
HAMZA	*n* pl. **-S** an Arabic diacritical mark
HAMZAH	*n* pl. **-S** hamza
HANAPER	*n* pl. **-S** a wicker receptacle
HANCE	*n* pl. **-S** a side of an arch
HAND	*v* **-ED, -ING, -S** to present with the hand (the end of the forearm)
HANDAX	*n* pl. **-ES** a short-handled ax
HANDBAG	*n* pl. **-S** a small carrying bag
HANDBALL	*n* pl. **-S** a small rubber ball
HANDBELL	*n* pl. **-S** a small bell with a handle
HANDBILL	*n* pl. **-S** a circular
HANDBOOK	*n* pl. **-S** a manual
HANDCAR	*n* pl. **-S** a hand-operated railroad car
HANDCART	*n* pl. **-S** a cart pushed by hand
HANDCLAP	*n* pl. **-S** a striking together of the palms of the hands
HANDCUFF	*v* **-ED, -ING, -S** to fetter with restraining cuffs
HANDER	*n* pl. **-S** one that hands
HANDFAST	*v* **-ED, -ING, -S** to grip securely
HANDFUL	*n* pl. **HANDFULS** or **HANDSFUL** as much as the hand can hold
HANDGRIP	*n* pl. **-S** a grip by the hand or hands
HANDGUN	*n* pl. **-S** a small firearm
HANDHELD	*n* pl. **-S** something held in the hand
HANDHOLD	*n* pl. **-S** a handgrip
HANDICAP	*v* **-CAPPED, -CAPPING, -CAPS** to hinder
HANDIER	comparative of handy
HANDIEST	superlative of handy
HANDILY	*adv* in a handy manner
HANDLE	*v* **-DLED, -DLING, -DLES** to touch with the hands

HANDLER	*n* pl. **-S** one that handles
HANDLESS	*adj* having no hands
HANDLIKE	*adj* resembling a hand
HANDLING	*n* pl. **-S** the manner in which something is handled
HANDLIST	*n* pl. **-S** a reference list
HANDLOOM	*n* pl. **-S** a manually operated loom
HANDMADE	*adj* made by hand
HANDMAID	*n* pl. **-S** a female servant
HANDOFF	*n* pl. **-S** a play in football
HANDOUT	*n* pl. **-S** something given out free
HANDOVER	*n* pl. **-S** an instance of giving up control
HANDPICK	*v* **-ED, -ING, -S** to choose carefully
HANDRAIL	*n* pl. **-S** a railing used for support
HANDSAW	*n* pl. **-S** a saw used manually
HANDSEL	*v* **-SELED, -SELING, -SELS** or **-SELLED, -SELLING, -SELS** to give a gift to
HANDSET	*n* pl. **-S** a type of telephone
HANDSEWN	*adj* sewn by hand
HANDSFUL	a pl. of handful
HANDSOME	*adj* **-SOMER, -SOMEST** attractive
HANDWORK	*n* pl. **-S** manual labor
HANDWRIT	*adj* written by hand
HANDY	*adj* **HANDIER, HANDIEST** convenient for handling
HANDYMAN	*n* pl. **-MEN** a man who does odd jobs
HANG	*v* **HUNG** or **HANGED, HANGING, HANGS** to attach from above only **HANGABLE** *adj*
HANGAR	*v* **-ED, -ING, -S** to place in an aircraft shelter
HANGBIRD	*n* pl. **-S** a type of bird
HANGDOG	*n* pl. **-S** a sneaky person
HANGER	*n* pl. **-S** one that hangs
HANGFIRE	*n* pl. **-S** a delay in detonation
HANGING	*n* pl. **-S** an execution by strangling with a suspended noose
HANGMAN	*n* pl. **-MEN** an executioner
HANGNAIL	*n* pl. **-S** an agnail
HANGNEST	*n* pl. **-S** a hangbird
HANGOUT	*n* pl. **-S** a place often visited
HANGOVER	*n* pl. **-S** the physical effects following a drinking binge
HANGTAG	*n* pl. **-S** a type of tag used commercially

HANGUL	*n* the Korean alphabetic script
HANGUP	*n* pl. **-S** an inhibition or obsession
HANIWA	*n/pl* Japanese clay sculptures
HANK	*v* **-ED, -ING, -S** to fasten a sail
HANKER	*v* **-ED, -ING, -S** to long for
HANKERER	*n* pl. **-S** one that hankers
HANKIE	*n* pl. **-S** hanky
HANKY	*n* pl. **-KIES** a handkerchief
HANSA	*n* pl. **-S** hanse
HANSE	*n* pl. **-S** a guild of merchants
HANSEL	*v* **-SELED, -SELING, -SELS** or **-SELLED, -SELLING, -SELS** to handsel
HANSOM	*n* pl. **-S** a light carriage
HANT	*v* **-ED, -ING, -S** to haunt
HANTLE	*n* pl. **-S** a large amount
HANUMAN	*n* pl. **-S** an East Indian monkey
HAO	*n* pl. **HAO** a monetary unit of Vietnam
HAP	*v* **HAPPED, HAPPING, HAPS** to happen
HAPAX	*n* pl. **-ES** a word that occurs only once
HAPHTARA	*n* pl. **-RAS, -ROT** or **-ROTH** a biblical selection
HAPKIDO	*n* pl. **-DOS** a Korean martial art
HAPLESS	*adj* luckless
HAPLITE	*n* pl. **-S** aplite
HAPLOID	*n* pl. **-S** a cell having only one set of chromosomes
HAPLOIDY	*n* pl. **-DIES** the state of being a haploid
HAPLONT	*n* pl. **-S** an organism having a particular chromosomal structure
HAPLOPIA	*n* pl. **-S** normal vision
HAPLOSIS	*n* pl. **-LOSES** the halving of the chromosome number
HAPLY	*adv* by chance
HAPPED	past tense of hap
HAPPEN	*v* **-ED, -ING, -S** to occur
HAPPING	present participle of hap
HAPPY	*adj* **-PIER, -PIEST** marked by joy **HAPPILY** *adv*
HAPTEN	*n* pl. **-S** a substance similar to an antigen **HAPTENIC** *adj*
HAPTENE	*n* pl. **-S** hapten
HAPTIC	*adj* pertaining to the sense of touch
HAPTICAL	*adj* haptic
HARANGUE	*v* **-RANGUED, -RANGUING, -RANGUES** to deliver a tirade to
HARASS	*v* **-ED, -ING, -ES** to bother persistently
HARASSER	*n* pl. **-S** one that harasses
HARBOR	*v* **-ED, -ING, -S** to shelter
HARBORER	*n* pl. **-S** one that harbors
HARBOUR	*v* **-ED, -ING, -S** to harbor
HARD	*adj* **HARDER, HARDEST** firm and unyielding
HARDBACK	*n* pl. **-S** a hardcover book
HARDBALL	*n* pl. **-S** baseball
HARDBOOT	*n* pl. **-S** a horseman
HARDCASE	*adj* tough
HARDCORE	*n* pl. **-S** hard material used in foundations
HARDEDGE	*n* pl. **-S** a geometric painting
HARDEN	*v* **-ED, -ING, -S** to make hard
HARDENER	*n* pl. **-S** one that hardens
HARDHACK	*n* pl. **-S** a woody plant
HARDHAT	*n* pl. **-S** a conservative
HARDHEAD	*n* pl. **-S** a practical person
HARDIER	comparative of hardy
HARDIES	pl. of hardy
HARDIEST	superlative of hardy
HARDILY	*adv* in a hardy manner
HARDLINE	*adj* unyielding
HARDLY	*adv* scarcely
HARDNESS	*n* pl. **-ES** the state of being hard
HARDNOSE	*n* pl. **-S** a stubborn person
HARDPACK	*n* pl. **-S** compacted snow
HARDPAN	*n* pl. **-S** a layer of hard subsoil
HARDS	*n/pl* the coarse refuse of flax
HARDSET	*adj* rigid
HARDSHIP	*n* pl. **-S** a difficult, painful condition
HARDTACK	*n* pl. **-S** a hard biscuit
HARDTOP	*n* pl. **-S** a type of car
HARDWARE	*n* pl. **-S** metal goods
HARDWIRE	*v* **-WIRED, -WIRING, -WIRES** to permanently connect electronic components
HARDWOOD	*n* pl. **-S** the hard, compact wood of various trees
HARDY	*adj* **-DIER, -DIEST** very sturdy
HARDY	*n* pl. **-DIES** a blacksmith's chisel

HARE	*v* **HARED, HARING, HARES** to run
HAREBELL	*n* pl. **-S** a perennial herb
HAREEM	*n* pl. **-S** harem
HARELIKE	*adj* resembling a hare (a long-eared mammal)
HARELIP	*n* pl. **-S** a deformity of the upper lip
HAREM	*n* pl. **-S** the section of a Muslim household reserved for women
HARIANA	*n* pl. **-S** a breed of cattle
HARICOT	*n* pl. **-S** the seed of various string beans
HARIJAN	*n* pl. **-S** an outcaste in India
HARING	present participle of hare
HARISSA	*n* pl. **-S** a spicy North African sauce
HARK	*v* **-ED, -ING, -S** to listen to
HARKEN	*v* **-ED, -ING, -S** to hearken
HARKENER	*n* pl. **-S** one that harkens
HARL	*n* pl. **-S** a herl
HARLOT	*n* pl. **-S** a prostitute
HARLOTRY	*n* pl. **-RIES** prostitution
HARM	*v* **-ED, -ING, -S** to injure
HARMER	*n* pl. **-S** one that harms
HARMFUL	*adj* capable of harming
HARMIN	*n* pl. **-S** harmine
HARMINE	*n* pl. **-S** an alkaloid used as a stimulant
HARMLESS	*adj* not harmful
HARMONIC	*n* pl. **-S** an overtone
HARMONY	*n* pl. **-NIES** agreement
HARNESS	*v* **-ED, -ING, -ES** to put tackle on a draft animal
HARP	*v* **-ED, -ING, -S** to play on a harp (a type of stringed musical instrument)
HARPER	*n* pl. **-S** a harpist
HARPIES	pl. of harpy
HARPIN	*n* pl. **-S** harping
HARPING	*n* pl. **-S** a wooden plank used in shipbuilding
HARPIST	*n* pl. **-S** one that plays the harp
HARPOON	*v* **-ED, -ING, -S** to strike with a harpoon
HARPY	*n* pl. **-PIES** a shrewish person
HARRIDAN	*n* pl. **-S** a haggard woman
HARRIED	past tense of harry
HARRIER	*n* pl. **-S** a hunting dog
HARRIES	present 3d person sing. of harry
HARROW	*v* **-ED, -ING, -S** to break up and level soil
HARROWER	*n* pl. **-S** one that harrows
HARRUMPH	*v* **-ED, -ING, -S** to make a guttural sound
HARRY	*v* **-RIED, -RYING, -RIES** to pillage
HARSH	*adj* **HARSHER, HARSHEST** severe **HARSHLY** *adv*
HARSHEN	*v* **-ED, -ING, -S** to make harsh
HARSLET	*n* pl. **-S** haslet
HART	*n* pl. **-S** a male deer
HARTAL	*n* pl. **-S** a stoppage of work
HARUMPH	*v* **-ED, -ING, -S** to harrumph
HARUSPEX	*n* pl. **-PICES** a soothsayer of ancient Rome
HARVEST	*v* **-ED, -ING, -S** to gather a crop
HAS	a present 3d person sing. of have
HASH	*v* **-ED, -ING, -ES** to mince
HASHEESH	*n* pl. **-ES** hashish
HASHHEAD	*n* pl. **-S** a hashish addict
HASHISH	*n* pl. **-ES** a mild narcotic
HASLET	*n* pl. **-S** the edible viscera of an animal
HASP	*v* **-ED, -ING, -S** to fasten with a clasp
HASSEL	*n* pl. **-S** an argument
HASSIUM	*n* pl. **-S** a radioactive element
HASSLE	*v* **-SLED, -SLING, -SLES** to argue
HASSOCK	*n* pl. **-S** a footstool
HAST	a present 2d person sing. of have
HASTATE	*adj* triangular
HASTE	*v* **HASTED, HASTING, HASTES** to hasten
HASTEFUL	*adj* hasty
HASTEN	*v* **-ED, -ING, -S** to hurry
HASTENER	*n* pl. **-S** one that hastens
HASTING	present participle of haste
HASTY	*adj* **HASTIER, HASTIEST** speedy **HASTILY** *adv*
HAT	*v* **HATTED, HATTING, HATS** to provide with a hat (a covering for the head)
HATABLE	*adj* hateable
HATBAND	*n* pl. **-S** a band worn on a hat
HATBOX	*n* pl. **-ES** a box for a hat
HATCH	*v* **-ED, -ING, -ES** to bring forth young from an egg

HATCHECK *n* pl. **-S** a room for the temporary keeping of hats

HATCHEL *v* **-ELED, -ELING, -ELS** or **-ELLED, -ELLING, -ELS** to separate flax fibers with a comb

HATCHER *n* pl. **-S** one that hatches

HATCHERY *n* pl. **-ERIES** a place for hatching eggs

HATCHET *n* pl. **-S** a small ax

HATCHING *n* pl. **-S** a series of lines used to show shading

HATCHWAY *n* pl. **-WAYS** an opening in the deck of a ship

HATE *v* **HATED, HATING, HATES** to despise

HATEABLE *adj* meriting hatred

HATEFUL *adj* detestable

HATER *n* pl. **-S** one that hates

HATFUL *n* pl. **HATFULS** or **HATSFUL** as much as a hat can hold

HATH a present 3d person sing. of have

HATING present participle of hate

HATLESS *adj* lacking a hat

HATLIKE *adj* resembling a hat

HATMAKER *n* pl. **-S** one that makes hats

HATPIN *n* pl. **-S** a pin for securing a hat

HATRACK *n* pl. **-S** a rack for hats

HATRED *n* pl. **-S** intense dislike or aversion

HATSFUL a pl. of hatful

HATTED past tense of hat

HATTER *n* pl. **-S** a hatmaker

HATTERIA *n* pl. **-S** a reptile

HATTING present participle of hat

HAUBERK *n* pl. **-S** a coat of armor

HAUGH *n* pl. **-S** a low-lying meadow

HAUGHTY *adj* **-TIER, -TIEST** arrogant

HAUL *v* **-ED, -ING, -S** to pull with force

HAULAGE *n* pl. **-S** the act of hauling

HAULER *n* pl. **-S** one that hauls

HAULIER *n* pl. **-S** hauler

HAULM *n* pl. **-S** a plant stem

HAULMY *adj* **HAULMIER, HAULMIEST** having haulms

HAULYARD *n* pl. **-S** halyard

HAUNCH *n* pl. **-ES** the hindquarter **HAUNCHED** *adj*

HAUNT *v* **-ED, -ING, -S** to visit frequently

HAUNTER *n* pl. **-S** one that haunts

HAUSEN *n* pl. **-S** a Russian sturgeon

HAUSFRAU *n* pl. **-FRAUS** or **-FRAUEN** a housewife

HAUT *adj* haute

HAUTBOIS *n* pl. **HAUTBOIS** hautboy

HAUTBOY *n* pl. **-BOYS** an oboe

HAUTE *adj* high-class

HAUTEUR *n* pl. **-S** haughty manner or spirit

HAVARTI *n* pl. **-S** a Danish cheese

HAVDALAH *n* pl. **-S** habdalah

HAVE *n* pl. **-S** a wealthy person

HAVELOCK *n* pl. **-S** a covering for a cap

HAVEN *v* **-ED, -ING, -S** to shelter

HAVER *v* **-ED, -ING, -S** to hem and haw

HAVEREL *n* pl. **-S** a fool

HAVING present participle of have

HAVIOR *n* pl. **-S** behavior

HAVIOUR *n* pl. **-S** havior

HAVOC *v* **-OCKED, -OCKING, -OCS** to destroy

HAVOCKER *n* pl. **-S** one that havocs

HAW *v* **-ED, -ING, -S** to turn left

HAWALA *n* pl. **-S** a type of financial arrangement in Islamic societies

HAWFINCH *n* pl. **-ES** a Eurasian finch

HAWK *v* **-ED, -ING, -S** to peddle

HAWKBILL *n* pl. **-S** a sea turtle

HAWKER *n* pl. **-S** one that hawks

HAWKEY *n* pl. **-EYS** a hawkie

HAWKEYED *adj* having keen sight

HAWKIE *n* pl. **-S** a white-faced cow

HAWKING *n* pl. **-S** falconry

HAWKISH *adj* warlike

HAWKLIKE *adj* resembling a hawk (a bird of prey)

HAWKMOTH *n* pl. **-S** a large moth

HAWKNOSE *n* pl. **-S** a large, curved nose

HAWKSHAW *n* pl. **-S** a detective

HAWKWEED *n* pl. **-S** a weedlike herb

HAWSE *n* pl. **-S** a part of a ship's bow

HAWSER *n* pl. **-S** a mooring rope

HAWTHORN *n* pl. **-S** a thorny shrub

HAY *v* **-ED, -ING, -S** to convert into hay (grass, cut and dried for fodder)

HAYCOCK *n* pl. **-S** a pile of hay

HAYER *n* pl. **-S** one that hays

HAYEY *adj* resembling hay

HAYFIELD *n* pl. **-S** a field where grasses for hay are grown

HAYFORK *n* pl. **-S** a tool for pitching hay

HAYING *n* pl. **-S** the season for harvesting hay

HAYLAGE *n* pl. **-S** a type of hay

HAYLOFT *n* pl. **-S** a loft for hay storage

HAYMAKER *n* pl. **-S** one that makes hay

HAYMOW *n* pl. **-S** a hayloft

HAYRACK *n* pl. **-S** a frame used in hauling hay

HAYRICK *n* pl. **-S** a haystack

HAYRIDE *n* pl. **-S** a wagon ride

HAYSEED *n* pl. **-S** a bumpkin

HAYSTACK *n* pl. **-S** a pile of hay

HAYWARD *n* pl. **-S** an officer who tends cattle

HAYWIRE *n* pl. **-S** wire used in baling hay

HAZAN *n* pl. **-ZANS** or **-ZANIM** a cantor

HAZARD *v* **-ED, -ING, -S** to venture

HAZARDER *n* pl. **-S** one that hazards

HAZE *v* **HAZED, HAZING, HAZES** to subject to a humiliating initiation

HAZEL *n* pl. **-S** a shrub

HAZELHEN *n* pl. **-S** a European grouse

HAZELLY *adj* yellowish brown

HAZELNUT *n* pl. **-S** an edible nut

HAZER *n* pl. **-S** one that hazes

HAZIER comparative of hazy

HAZIEST superlative of hazy

HAZILY *adv* in a hazy manner

HAZINESS *n* pl. **-ES** the state of being hazy

HAZING *n* pl. **-S** an attempt to embarrass or ridicule

HAZMAT *n* pl. **-S** hazardous material

HAZY *adj* **HAZIER, HAZIEST** unclear

HAZZAN *n* pl. **HAZZANS** or **HAZZANIM** hazan

HE *n* pl. **-S** a male person

HEAD *v* **-ED, -ING, -S** to be chief of

HEADACHE *n* pl. **-S** a pain inside the head

HEADACHY *adj* **-ACHIER, -ACHIEST** having a headache

HEADBAND *n* pl. **-S** a band worn on the head

HEADEND *n* pl. **-S** a facility that receives and distributes communications signals

HEADER *n* pl. **-S** a grain harvester

HEADFISH *n* pl. **-ES** a marine fish

HEADFUL *n* pl. **-S** a great amount of knowledge

HEADGATE *n* pl. **-S** a gate to control the flow of water

HEADGEAR *n* pl. **HEADGEAR** a covering for the head

HEADHUNT *v* **-ED, -ING, -S** to seek out, decapitate, and preserve the heads of enemies

HEADIER comparative of heady

HEADIEST superlative of heady

HEADILY *adv* in a heady manner

HEADING *n* pl. **-S** a title

HEADLAMP *n* pl. **-S** a light on the front of a car

HEADLAND *n* pl. **-S** a cliff

HEADLESS *adj* lacking a head

HEADLINE *v* **-LINED, -LINING, -LINES** to provide with a title

HEADLOCK *n* pl. **-S** a wrestling hold

HEADLONG *adj* rash; impetuous

HEADMAN *n* pl. **-MEN** a foreman

HEADMOST *adj* foremost

HEADNOTE *n* pl. **-S** a prefixed note

HEADPIN *n* pl. **-S** a bowling pin

HEADRACE *n* pl. **-S** a water channel

HEADREST *n* pl. **-S** a support for the head

HEADROOM *n* pl. **-S** clear vertical space

HEADSAIL *n* pl. **-S** a type of sail

HEADSET *n* pl. **-S** a pair of earphones

HEADSHIP *n* pl. **-S** the position of a leader

HEADSMAN *n* pl. **-MEN** an executioner

HEADSTAY *n* pl. **-STAYS** a support for a ship's foremast

HEADWAY *n* pl. **-WAYS** forward movement

HEADWIND *n* pl. **-S** an oncoming wind

HEADWORD *n* pl. **-S** a word put at the beginning

HEADWORK *n* pl. **-S** mental work

HEADY *adj* **HEADIER, HEADIEST** intoxicating

HEAL *v* **-ED, -ING, -S** to make sound or whole **HEALABLE** *adj*

HEALER *n* pl. **-S** one that heals

HEALTH *n* pl. **-S** the physical condition of an organism

HEALTHY	*adj* **HEALTHIER, HEALTHIEST** having good health
HEAP	*v* **-ED, -ING, -S** to pile up
HEAPER	*n* pl. **-S** one that heaps
HEAPY	*adj* resembling a heap (a group of things piled one on another)
HEAR	*v* **HEARD, HEARING, HEARS** to perceive by the ear **HEARABLE** *adj*
HEARER	*n* pl. **-S** one that hears
HEARING	*n* pl. **-S** a preliminary examination
HEARKEN	*v* **-ED, -ING, -S** to listen to
HEARSAY	*n* pl. **-SAYS** secondhand information
HEARSE	*v* **HEARSED, HEARSING, HEARSES** to transport in a hearse (a vehicle for conveying corpses)
HEART	*v* **-ED, -ING, -S** to hearten
HEARTEN	*v* **-ED, -ING, -S** to give courage to
HEARTH	*n* pl. **-S** the floor of a fireplace
HEARTY	*adj* **HEARTIER, HEARTIEST** very friendly **HEARTILY** *adv*
HEARTY	*n* pl. **HEARTIES** a comrade
HEAT	*v* **HEATED** or **HET, HEATING, HEATS** to make hot **HEATABLE** *adj*
HEATEDLY	*adv* in an inflamed or excited manner
HEATER	*n* pl. **-S** an apparatus for heating
HEATH	*n* pl. **-S** an evergreen shrub
HEATHEN	*n* pl. **-S** an uncivilized person
HEATHER	*n* pl. **-S** an evergreen shrub **HEATHERY** *adj*
HEATHY	*adj* **HEATHIER, HEATHIEST** abounding in heath
HEATLESS	*adj* having no warmth
HEAUME	*n* pl. **-S** a medieval helmet
HEAVE	*v* **HEAVED** or **HOVE, HEAVING, HEAVES** to lift forcefully
HEAVEN	*n* pl. **-S** the sky
HEAVENLY	*adj* **-LIER, -LIEST** full of beauty and peace
HEAVER	*n* pl. **-S** one that heaves
HEAVIER	comparative of heavy
HEAVIES	pl. of heavy
HEAVING	present participle of heave
HEAVY	*adj* **HEAVIER, HEAVIEST** having much weight **HEAVILY** *adv*
HEAVY	*n* pl. **HEAVIES** a villain
HEAVYSET	*adj* solidly built; stocky
HEBDOMAD	*n* pl. **-S** the number seven
HEBETATE	*v* **-TATED, -TATING, -TATES** to make dull
HEBETIC	*adj* pertaining to puberty
HEBETUDE	*n* pl. **-S** mental dullness
HEBRAIZE	*v* **-IZED, -IZING, -IZES** to make Hebrew
HECATOMB	*n* pl. **-S** a great sacrifice or slaughter
HECK	*n* pl. **-S** hell (a place or state of misery)
HECKLE	*v* **-LED, -LING, -LES** to harass a speaker
HECKLER	*n* pl. **-S** one that heckles
HECTARE	*n* pl. **-S** a unit of area
HECTIC	*adj* filled with turmoil **HECTICLY** *adv*
HECTICAL	*adj* hectic
HECTOR	*v* **-ED, -ING, -S** to bully
HEDDLE	*n* pl. **-S** a part of a loom
HEDER	*n* pl. **HEDERS** or **HADARIM** a Jewish school
HEDGE	*v* **HEDGED, HEDGING, HEDGES** to surround with a hedge (a dense row of shrubs)
HEDGEHOG	*n* pl. **-S** a small mammal
HEDGEHOP	*v* **-HOPPED, -HOPPING, -HOPS** to fly near the ground
HEDGEPIG	*n* pl. **-S** a hedgehog
HEDGER	*n* pl. **-S** one that hedges
HEDGEROW	*n* pl. **-S** a row of bushes
HEDGING	present participle of hedge
HEDGY	*adj* **HEDGIER, HEDGIEST** abounding in hedges
HEDONIC	*adj* pertaining to pleasure
HEDONICS	*n/pl* a branch of psychology
HEDONISM	*n* pl. **-S** the pursuit of pleasure
HEDONIST	*n* pl. **-S** a follower of hedonism
HEED	*v* **-ED, -ING, -S** to pay attention to
HEEDER	*n* pl. **-S** one that heeds
HEEDFUL	*adj* paying close attention
HEEDLESS	*adj* paying little or no attention
HEEHAW	*v* **-ED, -ING, -S** to guffaw
HEEL	*v* **-ED, -ING, -S** to supply with a heel (the raised part of a shoe)
HEELBALL	*n* pl. **-S** a composition used for polishing

HEELER	*n* pl. **-S** one that puts heels on shoes
HEELING	*n* pl. **-S** the act of inclining laterally
HEELLESS	*adj* lacking heels
HEELPOST	*n* pl. **-S** a post fitted to the end of something
HEELTAP	*n* pl. **-S** material put on the heel of a shoe
HEEZE	*v* **HEEZED, HEEZING, HEEZES** to hoist
HEFT	*v* **-ED, -ING, -S** to lift up
HEFTER	*n* pl. **-S** one that hefts
HEFTY	*adj* **HEFTIER, HEFTIEST** heavy **HEFTILY** *adv*
HEGARI	*n* pl. **-S** a grain
HEGEMON	*n* pl. **-S** a political state having hegemony
HEGEMONY	*n* pl. **-NIES** great authority
HEGIRA	*n* pl. **-S** an exodus
HEGUMEN	*n* pl. **-S** the head of a monastery
HEGUMENE	*n* pl. **-S** the head of a nunnery
HEGUMENY	*n* pl. **-NIES** the office of a hegumen
HEH	*n* pl. **-S** a Hebrew letter
HEIFER	*n* pl. **-S** a young cow
HEIGH	*interj* — used to attract attention
HEIGHT	*n* pl. **-S** the highest point
HEIGHTEN	*v* **-ED, -ING, -S** to raise
HEIGHTH	*n* pl. **-S** height
HEIL	*v* **-ED, -ING, -S** to salute
HEIMISH	*adj* haimish
HEINIE	*n* pl. **-S** the buttocks
HEINOUS	*adj* very wicked
HEIR	*v* **-ED, -ING, -S** to inherit
HEIRDOM	*n* pl. **-S** heirship
HEIRESS	*n* pl. **-ES** a female inheritor
HEIRLESS	*adj* having no inheritors
HEIRLOOM	*n* pl. **-S** an inherited possession
HEIRSHIP	*n* pl. **-S** the right to inheritance
HEISHI	*n/pl* tiny beads made from shells
HEIST	*v* **-ED, -ING, -S** to steal
HEISTER	*n* pl. **-S** one that heists
HEJIRA	*n* pl. **-S** hegira
HEKTARE	*n* pl. **-S** hectare
HELD	past tense of hold
HELIAC	*adj* heliacal
HELIACAL	*adj* pertaining to the sun
HELIAST	*n* pl. **-S** an Athenian judge
HELICAL	*adj* shaped like a helix
HELICES	a pl. of helix
HELICITY	*n* pl. **-TIES** a component of a particle's spin
HELICOID	*n* pl. **-S** a type of geometrical surface
HELICON	*n* pl. **-S** a large bass tuba
HELICOPT	*v* **-ED, -ING, -S** to travel by helicopter
HELILIFT	*v* **-ED, -ING, -S** to transport by helicopter
HELIO	*n* pl. **-LIOS** a signaling mirror
HELIPAD	*n* pl. **-S** a heliport
HELIPORT	*n* pl. **-S** an airport for helicopters
HELISTOP	*n* pl. **-S** a heliport
HELIUM	*n* pl. **-S** a gaseous element
HELIX	*n* pl. **-LIXES** or **-LICES** something spiral in form
HELL	*v* **-ED, -ING, -S** to behave raucously
HELLBENT	*adj* stubbornly determined
HELLBOX	*n* pl. **-ES** a printer's receptacle
HELLCAT	*n* pl. **-S** a shrewish person
HELLER	*n* pl. **-S** a hellion
HELLERI	*n* pl. **-S** or **-ES** a tropical fish
HELLERY	*n* pl. **-LERIES** rough play
HELLFIRE	*n* pl. **-S** the torment of hell
HELLHOLE	*n* pl. **-S** a horrible place
HELLION	*n* pl. **-S** a troublesome person
HELLISH	*adj* horrible
HELLKITE	*n* pl. **-S** a cruel person
HELLO	*v* **-ED, -ING, -S** or **-ES** to greet
HELLUVA	*adj* disagreeable
HELM	*v* **-ED, -ING, -S** to steer a ship
HELMET	*v* **-ED, -ING, -S** to supply with a helmet (a protective covering for the head)
HELMINTH	*n* pl. **-S** a worm
HELMLESS	*adj* lacking a helm (a steering system)
HELMSMAN	*n* pl. **-MEN** one that steers a ship
HELO	*n* pl. **HELOS** a helicopter
HELOT	*n* pl. **-S** a slave or serf
HELOTAGE	*n* pl. **-S** helotism
HELOTISM	*n* pl. **-S** slavery or serfdom
HELOTRY	*n* pl. **-RIES** helotism

HELP	*v* **HELPED** or **HOLP, HELPED** or **HOLPEN, HELPING, HELPS** to give assistance to **HELPABLE** *adj*
HELPER	*n* pl. **-S** one that helps
HELPFUL	*adj* being of service or assistance
HELPING	*n* pl. **-S** a portion of food
HELPLESS	*adj* defenseless
HELPMATE	*n* pl. **-S** a helpful companion
HELPMEET	*n* pl. **-S** a helpmate
HELVE	*v* **HELVED, HELVING, HELVES** to provide with a handle
HEM	*v* **HEMMED, HEMMING, HEMS** to provide with an edge
HEMAGOG	*n* pl. **-S** an agent that promotes blood flow
HEMAL	*adj* pertaining to the blood
HEMATAL	*adj* hemal
HEMATEIN	*n* pl. **-S** a chemical compound
HEMATIC	*n* pl. **-S** a medicine for a blood disease
HEMATIN	*n* pl. **-S** heme
HEMATINE	*n* pl. **-S** hematin
HEMATITE	*n* pl. **-S** an ore of iron
HEMATOID	*adj* resembling blood
HEMATOMA	*n* pl. **-MAS** or **-MATA** a swelling filled with blood
HEME	*n* pl. **-S** a component of hemoglobin
HEMIC	*adj* hemal
HEMIN	*n* pl. **-S** a chloride of heme
HEMIOLA	*n* pl. **-S** a rhythmic alteration in music
HEMIOLIA	*n* pl. **-S** hemiola
HEMIPTER	*n* pl. **-S** an insect
HEMLINE	*n* pl. **-S** the bottom edge of a garment
HEMLOCK	*n* pl. **-S** a poisonous herb
HEMMED	past tense of hem
HEMMER	*n* pl. **-S** one that hems
HEMMING	present participle of hem
HEMOCOEL	*n* pl. **-S** a body cavity
HEMOCYTE	*n* pl. **-S** a blood cell
HEMOID	*adj* hemal
HEMOLYZE	*v* **-LYZED, -LYZING, -LYZES** to break down red blood cells
HEMOSTAT	*n* pl. **-S** an instrument for reducing bleeding
HEMP	*n* pl. **-S** a tall herb
HEMPEN	*adj* made of hemp
HEMPIE	*adj* **HEMPIER, HEMPIEST** hempy
HEMPIER	comparative of hempy
HEMPIEST	superlative of hempy
HEMPLIKE	*adj* resembling hemp
HEMPSEED	*n* pl. **-S** the seed of hemp
HEMPWEED	*n* pl. **-S** a climbing plant
HEMPY	*adj* **HEMPIER, HEMPIEST** mischievous
HEN	*n* pl. **-S** a female chicken
HENBANE	*n* pl. **-S** a poisonous herb
HENBIT	*n* pl. **-S** a perennial herb
HENCE	*adv* consequently
HENCHMAN	*n* pl. **-MEN** an unscrupulous supporter
HENCOOP	*n* pl. **-S** a cage for hens
HENEQUEN	*n* pl. **-S** a fiber used to make ropes
HENEQUIN	*n* pl. **-S** henequen
HENGE	*n* pl. **-S** a circular Bronze Age structure in England
HENHOUSE	*n* pl. **-S** a shelter for poultry
HENIQUEN	*n* pl. **-S** henequen
HENLEY	*n* pl. **-LEYS** a type of knit shirt
HENLIKE	*adj* resembling a hen
HENNA	*v* **-ED, -ING, -S** to dye with a reddish coloring
HENNERY	*n* pl. **-NERIES** a poultry farm
HENNISH	*adj* resembling a hen
HENPECK	*v* **-ED, -ING, -S** to dominate by nagging
HENRY	*n* pl. **-RYS** or **-RIES** a unit of inductance
HENT	*v* **-ED, -ING, -S** to grasp
HEP	*adj* **HEPPER, HEPPEST** hip
HEPARIN	*n* pl. **-S** a biochemical
HEPATIC	*n* pl. **-S** a drug acting on the liver
HEPATICA	*n* pl. **-CAS** or **-CAE** a perennial herb
HEPATIZE	*v* **-TIZED, -TIZING, -TIZES** to convert tissue into a firm mass
HEPATOMA	*n* pl. **-MAS** or **-MATA** a tumor of the liver
HEPCAT	*n* pl. **-S** a jazz enthusiast
HEPTAD	*n* pl. **-S** a group of seven
HEPTAGON	*n* pl. **-S** a seven-sided polygon
HEPTANE	*n* pl. **-S** a hydrocarbon used as a solvent

HEPTARCH *n* pl. **-S** one of a group of seven rulers

HEPTOSE *n* pl. **-S** a chemical compound

HER *pron* the objective or possessive case of the pronoun she

HERALD *v* **-ED, -ING, -S** to proclaim

HERALDIC *adj* pertaining to heraldry

HERALDRY *n* pl. **-RIES** the art or science of armorial bearings

HERB *n* pl. **-S** a flowering plant with a nonwoody stem

HERBAGE *n* pl. **-S** nonwoody plant life **HERBAGED** *adj*

HERBAL *n* pl. **-S** a book about herbs and plants

HERBARIA *n/pl* collections of dried plants

HERBED *adj* flavored with herbs

HERBLESS *adj* lacking herbs

HERBLIKE *adj* resembling an herb

HERBY *adj* **HERBIER, HERBIEST** abounding in herbs

HERCULES *n* pl. **-LESES** any man of great size and strength

HERD *v* **-ED, -ING, -S** to bring together in a herd (a group of animals)

HERDER *n* pl. **-S** one who tends a herd

HERDIC *n* pl. **-S** a type of carriage

HERDLIKE *adj* resembling a herd

HERDMAN *n* pl. **-MEN** herdsman

HERDSMAN *n* pl. **-MEN** a herder

HERE *n* pl. **-S** this place

HEREAT *adv* at this time

HEREAWAY *adv* in this vicinity

HEREBY *adv* by this means

HEREDES pl. of heres

HEREDITY *n* pl. **-TIES** the genetic transmission of characteristics

HEREIN *adv* in this

HEREINTO *adv* into this place

HEREOF *adv* of this

HEREON *adv* on this

HERES *n* pl. **HEREDES** an heir

HERESY *n* pl. **-SIES** a belief contrary to a church doctrine

HERETIC *n* pl. **-S** one that upholds heresy

HERETO *adv* to this matter

HERETRIX *n* pl. **-TRIXES** or **-TRICES** heritrix

HEREUNTO *adv* hereto

HEREUPON *adv* immediately following this

HEREWITH *adv* along with this

HERIOT *n* pl. **-S** a feudal tribute or payment

HERITAGE *n* pl. **-S** something that is inherited

HERITOR *n* pl. **-S** one that inherits

HERITRIX *n* pl. **-TRIXES** or **-TRICES** a female heritor

HERL *n* pl. **-S** a feathered fishing lure

HERM *n* pl. **-S** a type of statue

HERMA *n* pl. **-MAE** or **-MAI** a herm **HERMAEAN** *adj*

HERMETIC *adj* airtight

HERMIT *n* pl. **-S** a recluse **HERMITIC** *adj*

HERMITRY *n* pl. **-RIES** the state of being a hermit

HERN *n* pl. **-S** a heron

HERNIA *n* pl. **-NIAS** or **-NIAE** the protrusion of an organ through its surrounding wall **HERNIAL** *adj*

HERNIATE *v* **-ATED, -ATING, -ATES** to protrude through an abnormal bodily opening

HERO *n* pl. **-ROS** or **-ROES** a hoagie

HEROIC *n* pl. **-S** an epic verse

HEROICAL *adj* courageous; noble

HEROIN *n* pl. **-S** an addictive narcotic

HEROINE *n* pl. **-S** a brave woman

HEROISM *n* pl. **-S** heroic behavior

HEROIZE *v* **-IZED, -IZING, -IZES** to make heroic

HERON *n* pl. **-S** a wading bird

HERONRY *n* pl. **-RIES** a place where herons breed

HERPES *n* pl. **HERPES** a skin infection **HERPETIC** *adj*

HERRING *n* pl. **-S** a food fish

HERRY *v* **-RIED, -RYING, -RIES** to harry

HERS *pron* the possessive case of the pronoun she

HERSELF *pron* a form of the 3d person sing. feminine pronoun

HERSTORY *n* pl. **-RIES** history with a feminist viewpoint

HERTZ *n* pl. **HERTZ** a unit of frequency

HESITANT *adj* tending to hesitate

HESITATE *v* **-TATED, -TATING, -TATES** to hold back in uncertainty

HESSIAN *n* pl. **-S** a coarse cloth

HESSITE *n* pl. **-S** a mineral

HEST *n* pl. **-S** a command

HET *n* pl. **-S** heth

HETAERA *n* pl. **-RAS** or **-RAE** a concubine **HETAERIC** *adj*

HETAIRA *n* pl. **-RAS** or **-RAI** hetaera

HETERO *n* pl. **-EROS** a heterosexual

HETH *n* pl. **-S** a Hebrew letter

HETMAN *n* pl. **-S** a cossack leader

HEUCH *n* pl. **-S** heugh

HEUGH *n* pl. **-S** a steep cliff

HEW *v* **HEWED, HEWN, HEWING, HEWS** to cut with an ax **HEWABLE** *adj*

HEWER *n* pl. **-S** one that hews

HEX *v* **-ED, -ING, -ES** to cast an evil spell upon

HEXAD *n* pl. **-S** a group of six **HEXADIC** *adj*

HEXADE *n* pl. **-S** hexad

HEXAGON *n* pl. **-S** a polygon having six sides

HEXAGRAM *n* pl. **-S** a six-pointed star

HEXAMINE *n* pl. **-S** a chemical compound

HEXANE *n* pl. **-S** a volatile liquid

HEXAPLA *n* pl. **-S** an edition in which six texts are set in parallel columns **HEXAPLAR** *adj*

HEXAPOD *n* pl. **-S** a six-legged insect

HEXAPODY *n* pl. **-DIES** a line of verse with six feet

HEXARCHY *n* pl. **-CHIES** a group of six separate states

HEXER *n* pl. **-S** one that hexes

HEXEREI *n* pl. **-S** witchcraft

HEXONE *n* pl. **-S** a hydrocarbon solvent

HEXOSAN *n* pl. **-S** a carbohydrate

HEXOSE *n* pl. **-S** a simple sugar

HEXYL *n* pl. **-S** a hydrocarbon radical **HEXYLIC** *adj*

HEY *interj* — used to attract attention

HEYDAY *n* pl. **-DAYS** the period of one's greatest success

HEYDEY *n* pl. **-DEYS** heyday

HI *interj* — used as a greeting

HIATUS *n* pl. **-ES** a gap or missing section **HIATAL** *adj*

HIBACHI *n* pl. **-S** a cooking device

HIBERNAL *adj* pertaining to winter

HIBISCUS *n* pl. **-ES** a tropical plant

HIC *interj* — used to represent a hiccup

HICCOUGH *v* **-ED, -ING, -S** to hiccup

HICCUP *v* **-CUPED, -CUPING, -CUPS** or **-CUPPED, -CUPPING, -CUPS** to make a peculiar-sounding, spasmodic inhalation

HICK *n* pl. **-S** a rural person **HICKISH** *adj*

HICKEY *n* pl. **HICKEYS** or **HICKIES** a gadget

HICKIE *n* pl. **-S** hickey

HICKORY *n* pl. **-RIES** a hardwood tree

HID a past tense of hide

HIDABLE *adj* able to be hidden

HIDALGO *n* pl. **-GOS** a minor Spanish nobleman

HIDDEN *adj* concealed; obscure **HIDDENLY** *adv*

HIDE *v* **HID, HIDDEN, HIDING, HIDES** to conceal

HIDE *v* **HIDED, HIDING, HIDES** to flog

HIDEAWAY *n* pl. **-AWAYS** a hideout

HIDELESS *adj* lacking a skin

HIDEOUS *adj* very ugly

HIDEOUT *n* pl. **-S** a place of refuge

HIDER *n* pl. **-S** one that hides

HIDING *n* pl. **-S** a beating

HIDROSIS *n* pl. **-DROSES** abnormal perspiration

HIDROTIC *n* pl. **-S** a drug that induces perspiration

HIE *v* **HIED, HIEING** or **HYING, HIES** to hurry

HIEMAL *adj* pertaining to winter

HIERARCH *n* pl. **-S** a religious leader

HIERATIC *adj* pertaining to priests

HIERURGY *n* pl. **-GIES** a rite of worship

HIGGLE *v* **-GLED, -GLING, -GLES** to haggle

HIGGLER *n* pl. **-S** one that higgles

HIGH *adj* **HIGHER, HIGHEST** reaching far upward

HIGH *n* pl. **-S** a high level

HIGHBALL *v* **-ED, -ING, -S** to go at full speed

HIGHBORN *adj* of noble birth

HIGHBOY *n* pl. **-BOYS** a tall chest of drawers

HIGHBRED *adj* highborn

HIGHBROW *n* pl. **-S** a person who has superior tastes

HIGHBUSH	*adj* forming a tall bush	**HILT**	*v* **-ED, -ING, -S** to provide with a hilt (a handle for a weapon)
HIGHJACK	*v* **-ED, -ING, -S** to hijack	**HILTLESS**	*adj* having no hilt
HIGHLAND	*n* pl. **-S** an elevated region	**HILUM**	*n* pl. **HILA** a small opening in a bodily organ
HIGHLIFE	*n* pl. **-S** the lifestyle of fashionable society	**HILUS**	*n* pl. **HILI** hilum
HIGHLY	*adv* to a high degree	**HIM**	*n* pl. **-S** a male
HIGHNESS	*n* pl. **-ES** the state of being high	**HIMATION**	*n* pl. **-MATIONS** or **-MATIA** a loose outer garment
HIGHRISE	*n* pl. **-S** a building with many stories (horizontal divisions)	**HIMSELF**	*pron* a form of the 3d person sing. masculine pronoun
HIGHROAD	*n* pl. **-S** a highway	**HIN**	*n* pl. **-S** a Hebrew unit of liquid measure
HIGHSPOT	*n* pl. **-S** an event of major importance	**HIND**	*n* pl. **-S** a female red deer
HIGHT	*v* **-ED, -ING, -S** to command	**HINDER**	*v* **-ED, -ING, -S** to impede
HIGHTAIL	*v* **-ED, -ING, -S** to retreat rapidly	**HINDERER**	*n* pl. **-S** one that hinders
HIGHTH	*n* pl. **-S** height	**HINDGUT**	*n* pl. **-S** the rear part of the alimentary canal
HIGHTOP	*n* pl. **-S** a sports shoe extending over the ankle	**HINDMOST**	*adj* farthest to the rear
HIGHWAY	*n* pl. **-WAYS** a main road	**HINGE**	*v* **HINGED, HINGING, HINGES** to attach a jointed device
HIJAB	*n* pl. **-S** a head covering worn by Muslim women	**HINGER**	*n* pl. **-S** one that hinges
HIJACK	*v* **-ED, -ING, -S** to seize a vehicle while in transit	**HINKY**	*adj* **HINKIER, HINKIEST** suspicious
HIJACKER	*n* pl. **-S** one that hijacks	**HINNY**	*v* **-NIED, -NYING, -NIES** to whinny
HIJINKS	*n/pl* mischievous fun	**HINT**	*v* **-ED, -ING, -S** to suggest indirectly
HIJRA	*n* pl. **-S** hegira	**HINTER**	*n* pl. **-S** one that hints
HIJRAH	*n* pl. **-S** hegira	**HIP**	*adj* **HIPPER, HIPPEST** aware of the most current styles and trends
HIKE	*v* **HIKED, HIKING, HIKES** to walk a long distance	**HIP**	*v* **HIPPED, HIPPING, HIPS** to build a type of roof
HIKER	*n* pl. **-S** one that hikes	**HIPBONE**	*n* pl. **-S** a pelvic bone
HILA	pl. of hilum	**HIPLESS**	*adj* lacking a hip (the pelvic joint)
HILAR	*adj* pertaining to a hilum	**HIPLIKE**	*adj* suggestive of a hip
HILARITY	*n* pl. **-TIES** noisy merriment	**HIPLINE**	*n* pl. **-S** the distance around the hips
HILDING	*n* pl. **-S** a vile person	**HIPLY**	*adv* in a hip manner
HILI	pl. of hilus	**HIPNESS**	*n* pl. **-ES** the state of being hip
HILL	*v* **-ED, -ING, -S** to form into a hill (a rounded elevation)	**HIPPARCH**	*n* pl. **-S** a cavalry commander in ancient Greece
HILLER	*n* pl. **-S** one that hills	**HIPPED**	past tense of hip
HILLIER	comparative of hilly	**HIPPER**	comparative of hip
HILLIEST	superlative of hilly	**HIPPEST**	superlative of hip
HILLO	*v* **-ED, -ING, -S** or **-ES** to hallo	**HIPPIE**	*n* pl. **-S** a nonconformist
HILLOA	*v* **-ED, -ING, -S** to hallo	**HIPPIER**	comparative of hippy
HILLOCK	*n* pl. **-S** a small hill **HILLOCKY** *adj*	**HIPPIEST**	superlative of hippy
HILLSIDE	*n* pl. **-S** the side of a hill	**HIPPING**	present participle of hip
HILLTOP	*n* pl. **-S** the top of a hill		
HILLY	*adj* **HILLIER, HILLIEST** abounding in hills		

HIPPISH *adj* depressed; sad

HIPPO *n* pl. **-POS** a hippopotamus

HIPPY *adj* **-PIER, -PIEST** having big hips

HIPSHOT *adj* lame; awkward

HIPSTER *n* pl. **-S** one that is hip

HIRABLE *adj* available for hire

HIRAGANA *n* pl. **-S** a Japanese cursive script

HIRCINE *adj* pertaining to a goat

HIRE *v* **HIRED, HIRING, HIRES** to engage the services of for payment **HIREABLE** *adj*

HIREE *n* pl. **-S** one that is hired

HIRELING *n* pl. **-S** one that works for money only

HIRER *n* pl. **-S** one that hires

HIRPLE *v* **-PLED, -PLING, -PLES** to limp

HIRSEL *v* **-SELED, -SELING, -SELS** or **-SELLED, -SELLING, -SELS** to herd sheep

HIRSLE *v* **-SLED, -SLING, -SLES** to slide along

HIRSUTE *adj* hairy

HIRUDIN *n* pl. **-S** an anticoagulant

HIS *pron* the possessive form of the pronoun he

HISN *pron* his

HISPID *adj* covered with stiff hairs

HISS *v* **-ED, -ING, -ES** to make a sibilant sound

HISSELF *pron* himself

HISSER *n* pl. **-S** one that hisses

HISSING *n* pl. **-S** an object of scorn

HISSY *adj* **HISSIER, HISSIEST** characterized by a hissing sound

HISSY *n* pl. **HISSIES** a tantrum

HIST *v* **-ED, -ING, -S** to hoist

HISTAMIN *n* pl. **-S** an amine released in allergic reactions

HISTIDIN *n* pl. **-S** an amino acid

HISTOGEN *n* pl. **-S** interior plant tissue

HISTOID *adj* pertaining to connective tissue

HISTONE *n* pl. **-S** a simple protein

HISTORIC *adj* important in history

HISTORY *n* pl. **-RIES** a chronological record of past events

HIT *v* **HIT, HITTING, HITS** to strike forcibly

HITCH *v* **-ED, -ING, -ES** to fasten with a knot or hook

HITCHER *n* pl. **-S** one that hitches

HITHER *adv* toward this place

HITHERTO *adv* up to now

HITLESS *adj* being without a hit

HITMAN *n* pl. **-MEN** a professional killer

HITTABLE *adj* capable of being hit

HITTER *n* pl. **-S** one that hits

HITTING present participle of hit

HIVE *v* **HIVED, HIVING, HIVES** to cause to enter a hive (a bee's nest)

HIVELESS *adj* lacking a hive

HIZZONER *n* pl. **-S** — used as a title for a mayor

HM *interj* hmm

HMM *interj* — used to express thoughtful consideration

HO *interj* — used to express surprise

HOACTZIN *n* pl. **-S** or **-ES** hoatzin

HOAGIE *n* pl. **-S** a long sandwich

HOAGY *n* pl. **-GIES** hoagie

HOAR *n* pl. **-S** a white coating

HOARD *v* **-ED, -ING, -S** to gather and store away

HOARDER *n* pl. **-S** one that hoards

HOARDING *n* pl. **-S** something hoarded

HOARIER comparative of hoary

HOARIEST superlative of hoary

HOARILY *adv* in a hoary manner

HOARSE *adj* **HOARSER, HOARSEST** low and rough in sound **HOARSELY** *adv*

HOARSEN *v* **-ED, -ING, -S** to make hoarse

HOARY *adj* **HOARIER, HOARIEST** white with age

HOATZIN *n* pl. **-S** or **-ES** a tropical bird

HOAX *v* **-ED, -ING, -ES** to deceive

HOAXER *n* pl. **-S** one that hoaxes

HOB *v* **HOBBED, HOBBING, HOBS** to furnish with hobnails

HOBBER *n* pl. **-S** one that hobs

HOBBIES pl. of hobby

HOBBIT *n* pl. **-S** a fictitious creature that lives underground

HOBBLE *v* **-BLED, -BLING, -BLES** to limp

HOBBLER *n* pl. **-S** one that hobbles

HOBBY	*n* pl. **-BIES** a recreational pastime
HOBBYIST	*n* pl. **-S** one that pursues a hobby
HOBLIKE	*adj* suggestive of an elf
HOBNAIL	*v* **-ED, -ING, -S** to put hobnails (short nails with a broad head) on a shoe sole
HOBNOB	*v* **-NOBBED, -NOBBING, -NOBS** to associate in a friendly way
HOBO	*v* **-ED, -ING, -S** or **-ES** to live like a hobo (a vagrant or tramp)
HOBOISM	*n* pl. **-S** the state of being a hobo
HOCK	*v* **-ED, -ING, -S** to pawn
HOCKER	*n* pl. **-S** one that hocks
HOCKEY	*n* pl. **-EYS** a game played on ice
HOCKSHOP	*n* pl. **-S** a pawnshop
HOCUS	*v* **-CUSED, -CUSING, -CUSES** or **-CUSSED, -CUSSING, -CUSSES** to deceive or cheat
HOD	*n* pl. **-S** a portable trough
HODAD	*n* pl. **-S** a nonsurfer
HODADDY	*n* pl. **-DIES** hodad
HODDEN	*n* pl. **-S** a coarse cloth
HODDIN	*n* pl. **-S** hodden
HOE	*v* **HOED, HOEING, HOES** to use a hoe (a gardening tool)
HOECAKE	*n* pl. **-S** a cornmeal cake
HOEDOWN	*n* pl. **-S** a square dance
HOELIKE	*adj* resembling a hoe
HOER	*n* pl. **-S** one that hoes
HOG	*v* **HOGGED, HOGGING, HOGS** to take more than one's share
HOGAN	*n* pl. **-S** a Navaho Indian dwelling
HOGBACK	*n* pl. **-S** a sharp ridge
HOGFISH	*n* pl. **-ES** a tropical fish
HOGG	*n* pl. **-S** a young sheep
HOGGED	past tense of hog
HOGGER	*n* pl. **-S** one that hogs
HOGGET	*n* pl. **-S** a young unshorn sheep
HOGGING	present participle of hog
HOGGISH	*adj* coarsely selfish
HOGLIKE	*adj* hoggish
HOGMANAY	*n* pl. **-NAYS** a Scottish celebration
HOGMANE	*n* pl. **-S** hogmanay
HOGMENAY	*n* pl. **-NAYS** hogmanay
HOGNOSE	*n* pl. **-S** a nonvenomous snake
HOGNUT	*n* pl. **-S** a hickory nut
HOGSHEAD	*n* pl. **-S** a large cask
HOGTIE	*v* **-TIED, -TIEING** or **-TYING, -TIES** to tie together the legs of
HOGWASH	*n* pl. **-ES** meaningless talk
HOGWEED	*n* pl. **-S** a coarse plant
HOICK	*v* **-ED, -ING, -S** to change directions abruptly
HOIDEN	*v* **-ED, -ING, -S** to hoyden
HOISE	*v* **HOISED, HOISING, HOISES** to hoist
HOIST	*v* **-ED, -ING, -S** to haul up by some mechanical means
HOISTER	*n* pl. **-S** one that hoists
HOKE	*v* **HOKED, HOKING, HOKES** to give false value to
HOKEY	*adj* **HOKIER, HOKIEST** false; contrived **HOKILY** *adv*
HOKINESS	*n* pl. **-ES** the state of being hokey
HOKKU	*n* pl. **HOKKU** haiku
HOKUM	*n* pl. **-S** nonsense
HOKYPOKY	*n* pl. **-KIES** trickery
HOLARD	*n* pl. **-S** the total quantity of water in the soil
HOLD	*v* **HELD, HOLDEN, HOLDING, HOLDS** to maintain possession of **HOLDABLE** *adj*
HOLDALL	*n* pl. **-S** a carrying case
HOLDBACK	*n* pl. **-S** a restraining device
HOLDDOWN	*n* pl. **-S** a clamp for holding an object in place
HOLDEN	a past participle of hold
HOLDER	*n* pl. **-S** one that holds
HOLDFAST	*n* pl. **-S** a fastening device
HOLDING	*n* pl. **-S** something held
HOLDOUT	*n* pl. **-S** one who delays signing a contract
HOLDOVER	*n* pl. **-S** something left over
HOLDUP	*n* pl. **-S** a delay
HOLE	*v* **HOLED, HOLING, HOLES** to make a hole (a cavity in a solid)
HOLELESS	*adj* lacking a hole
HOLEY	*adj* full of holes
HOLIBUT	*n* pl. **-S** halibut
HOLIDAY	*v* **-ED, -ING, -S** to take a vacation
HOLIER	comparative of holy
HOLIES	pl. of holy
HOLIEST	superlative of holy
HOLILY	*adv* in a holy manner
HOLINESS	*n* pl. **-ES** the state of being holy

HOLING	present participle of hole
HOLISM	n pl. **-S** a philosophical theory
HOLIST	n pl. **-S** one who adheres to the theory of holism **HOLISTIC** adj
HOLK	v **-ED, -ING, -S** to howk
HOLLA	v **-ED, -ING, -S** to hallo
HOLLAND	n pl. **-S** a cotton fabric
HOLLER	v **-ED, -ING, -S** to yell
HOLLIES	pl. of holly
HOLLO	v **-ED, -ING, -S** or **-ES** to hallo
HOLLOA	v **-ED, -ING, -S** to hallo
HOLLOO	v **-ED, -ING, -S** to hallo
HOLLOW	adj **-LOWER, -LOWEST** not solid **HOLLOWLY** adv
HOLLOW	v **-ED, -ING, -S** to make hollow
HOLLY	n pl. **-LIES** a tree
HOLM	n pl. **-S** an island in a river
HOLMIUM	n pl. **-S** a metallic element **HOLMIC** adj
HOLOGAMY	n pl. **-MIES** the state of having gametes of the same size and form as other cells
HOLOGRAM	n pl. **-S** a three-dimensional photograph
HOLOGYNY	n pl. **-NIES** a trait transmitted solely in the female line
HOLOTYPE	n pl. **-S** an animal or plant specimen
HOLOZOIC	adj eating solid foods
HOLP	a past tense of help
HOLPEN	a past participle of help
HOLS	n/pl a vacation
HOLSTEIN	n pl. **-S** a breed of cattle
HOLSTER	v **-ED, -ING, -S** to put in a holster (a case for a pistol)
HOLT	n pl. **-S** a grove
HOLY	adj **-LIER, -LIEST** having a divine nature or origin
HOLY	n pl. **-LIES** a holy place
HOLYDAY	n pl. **-DAYS** a religious holiday
HOLYTIDE	n pl. **-S** a time of religious observance
HOMAGE	v **-AGED, -AGING, -AGES** to pay tribute to
HOMAGER	n pl. **-S** a feudal vassal
HOMBRE	n pl. **-S** a fellow
HOMBURG	n pl. **-S** a felt hat
HOME	v **HOMED, HOMING, HOMES** to return to one's home (place of residence)
HOMEBODY	n pl. **-BODIES** one who likes to stay at home
HOMEBOY	n pl. **-BOYS** a boy or man from one's neighborhood
HOMEBRED	n pl. **-S** a native athlete
HOMEBREW	n pl. **-S** an alcoholic beverage made at home
HOMED	past tense of home
HOMEGIRL	n pl. **-S** a girl or woman from one's neighborhood
HOMELAND	n pl. **-S** one's native land
HOMELESS	adj lacking a home
HOMELIKE	adj suggestive of a home
HOMELY	adj **-LIER, -LIEST** unattractive
HOMEMADE	adj made at home
HOMEOBOX	n pl. **-ES** a short DNA sequence
HOMEOTIC	adj being a gene producing a shift in development
HOMEPAGE	n pl. **-S** the main page of a website
HOMEPORT	v **-ED, -ING, -S** to assign a ship to a port
HOMER	v **-ED, -ING, -S** to hit a home run
HOMERIC	adj having a large or grand quality
HOMEROOM	n pl. **-S** the classroom where pupils report before classes begin
HOMESICK	adj longing for home
HOMESITE	n pl. **-S** a location for a house
HOMESPUN	n pl. **-S** a loosely woven fabric
HOMESTAY	n pl. **-STAYS** a period during which a visitor in a foreign country lives with a local family
HOMETOWN	n pl. **-S** the town of one's birth or residence
HOMEWARD	adv toward home
HOMEWORK	n pl. **-S** work done at home
HOMEY	adj **HOMIER, HOMIEST** homelike
HOMEY	n pl. **HOMEYS** a person from one's neighborhood
HOMICIDE	n pl. **-S** the killing of one person by another
HOMIE	n pl. **-S** homey
HOMIER	comparative of homy
HOMIEST	superlative of homy
HOMILIST	n pl. **-S** one that delivers a homily
HOMILY	n pl. **-LIES** a sermon
HOMINES	a pl. of homo

HOMINESS *n* pl. **-ES** the quality of being homey

HOMING present participle of home

HOMINIAN *n* pl. **-S** a hominid

HOMINID *n* pl. **-S** a manlike creature

HOMINIES pl. of hominy

HOMININE *adj* characteristic of man

HOMINIZE *v* **-NIZED, -NIZING, -NIZES** to alter the environment to conform with evolving man

HOMINOID *n* pl. **-S** a manlike animal

HOMINY *n* pl. **-NIES** hulled, dried corn

HOMMOCK *n* pl. **-S** a ridge in an ice field

HOMMOS *n* pl. **-ES** hummus

HOMO *n* pl. **HOMOS** or **HOMINES** a member of the genus that includes modern man

HOMOGAMY *n* pl. **-MIES** the bearing of sexually similar flowers

HOMOGENY *n* pl. **-NIES** correspondence in form or structure

HOMOGONY *n* pl. **-NIES** the condition of having flowers with uniform stamens and pistils

HOMOLOG *n* pl. **-S** something that exhibits homology

HOMOLOGY *n* pl. **-GIES** similarity in structure

HOMONYM *n* pl. **-S** a namesake

HOMONYMY *n* pl. **-MIES** the condition of having the same name

HOMOSEX *n* pl. **-ES** homosexuality

HOMY *adj* **HOMIER, HOMIEST** homey

HON *n* pl. **-S** a honeybun

HONAN *n* pl. **-S** a fine silk

HONCHO *v* **-ED, -ING, -S** to take charge of

HONDA *n* pl. **-S** a part of a lariat

HONDLE *v* **-DLED, -DLING, -DLES** to haggle

HONE *v* **HONED, HONING, HONES** to sharpen

HONER *n* pl. **-S** one that hones

HONEST *adj* **-ESTER, -ESTEST** truthful **HONESTLY** *adv*

HONESTY *n* pl. **-TIES** truthfulness

HONEWORT *n* pl. **-S** a perennial herb

HONEY *v* **HONEYED** or **HONIED, HONEYING, HONEYS** to sweeten with honey (a sweet, viscid fluid)

HONEYBEE *n* pl. **-S** a type of bee

HONEYBUN *n* pl. **-S** a sweetheart

HONEYDEW *n* pl. **-S** a sweet fluid

HONEYFUL *adj* containing much honey

HONEYPOT *n* pl. **-S** one that is attractive or desirable

HONG *n* pl. **-S** a Chinese factory

HONGI *v* **-GIED, -GIING, -GIES** to greet another by pressing noses together

HONIED a past tense of honey

HONING present participle of hone

HONK *v* **-ED, -ING, -S** to emit a cry like that of a goose

HONKER *n* pl. **-S** one that honks

HONOR *v* **-ED, -ING, -S** to respect

HONORAND *n* pl. **-S** an honoree

HONORARY *n* pl. **-ARIES** an honor society

HONOREE *n* pl. **-S** one that receives an honor

HONORER *n* pl. **-S** one that honors

HONOUR *v* **-ED, -ING, -S** to honor

HONOURER *n* pl. **-S** honorer

HOOCH *n* pl. **-ES** cheap whiskey

HOOCHIE *n* pl. **-S** a promiscuous young woman

HOOD *v* **-ED, -ING, -S** to furnish with a hood (a covering for the head)

HOODIE *n* pl. **-S** a gray crow of Europe

HOODIER comparative of hoody

HOODIEST superlative of hoody

HOODLESS *adj* lacking a hood

HOODLIKE *adj* resembling a hood

HOODLUM *n* pl. **-S** a thug

HOODMOLD *n* pl. **-S** a protective projection on a cornice

HOODOO *v* **-ED, -ING, -S** to jinx

HOODWINK *v* **-ED, -ING, -S** to trick

HOODY *adj* **HOODIER, HOODIEST** resembling a hoodlum

HOOEY *n* pl. **-EYS** nonsense

HOOF *n* pl. **HOOVES** or **HOOFS** the hard covering on the feet of certain animals

HOOF *v* **-ED, -ING, -S** to dance

HOOFBEAT *n* pl. **-S** the sound of hooves striking the ground

HOOFER *n* pl. **-S** a professional dancer

HOOFLESS *adj* lacking hooves

HOOFLIKE *adj* resembling a hoof

HOOK	*v* **-ED, -ING, -S** to catch with a hook (a bent piece of metal)
HOOKA	*n* pl. **-S** hookah
HOOKAH	*n* pl. **-S** a water pipe
HOOKER	*n* pl. **-S** a prostitute
HOOKEY	*n* pl. **-EYS** hooky
HOOKIER	comparative of hooky
HOOKIES	pl. of hooky
HOOKIEST	superlative of hooky
HOOKLESS	*adj* lacking a hook
HOOKLET	*n* pl. **-S** a small hook
HOOKLIKE	*adj* resembling a hook
HOOKNOSE	*n* pl. **-S** an aquiline nose
HOOKUP	*n* pl. **-S** an electrical assemblage
HOOKWORM	*n* pl. **-S** a parasitic worm
HOOKY	*adj* **HOOKIER, HOOKIEST** full of hooks
HOOKY	*n* pl. **HOOKIES** truancy
HOOLIE	*adj* easy; slow
HOOLIGAN	*n* pl. **-S** a hoodlum
HOOLY	*adj* hoolie
HOOP	*v* **-ED, -ING, -S** to fasten with a hoop (a circular band of metal)
HOOPER	*n* pl. **-S** one that hoops
HOOPLA	*n* pl. **-S** commotion
HOOPLESS	*adj* lacking a hoop
HOOPLIKE	*adj* suggestive of a hoop
HOOPOE	*n* pl. **-S** a European bird
HOOPOO	*n* pl. **-POOS** hoopoe
HOOPSTER	*n* pl. **-S** a basketball player
HOORAH	*v* **-ED, -ING, -S** to hurrah
HOORAY	*v* **-ED, -ING, -S** to hurrah
HOOSEGOW	*n* pl. **-S** a jail
HOOSGOW	*n* pl. **-S** hoosegow
HOOT	*v* **-ED, -ING, -S** to cry like an owl
HOOTCH	*n* pl. **-ES** hooch
HOOTER	*n* pl. **-S** one that hoots
HOOTY	*adj* **HOOTIER, HOOTIEST** sounding like the cry of an owl
HOOVED	*adj* having hooves
HOOVER	*v* **-ED, -ING, -S** to clean with a vacuum cleaner
HOOVES	a pl. of hoof
HOP	*v* **HOPPED, HOPPING, HOPS** to move by jumping on one foot
HOPE	*v* **HOPED, HOPING, HOPES** to have a desire or expectation
HOPEFUL	*n* pl. **-S** one that aspires
HOPELESS	*adj* despairing
HOPER	*n* pl. **-S** one that hopes
HOPHEAD	*n* pl. **-S** a drug addict
HOPING	present participle of hope
HOPINGLY	*adv* in a hopeful manner
HOPLITE	*n* pl. **-S** a foot soldier of ancient Greece **HOPLITIC** *adj*
HOPPED	past tense of hop
HOPPER	*n* pl. **-S** one that hops
HOPPING	*n* pl. **-S** a going from one place to another of the same kind
HOPPLE	*v* **-PLED, -PLING, -PLES** to hobble
HOPPY	*adj* **-PIER, -PIEST** having the taste of hops (catkins of a particular vine)
HOPSACK	*n* pl. **-S** a coarse fabric
HOPTOAD	*n* pl. **-S** a toad
HORA	*n* pl. **-S** an Israeli dance
HORAH	*n* pl. **-S** hora
HORAL	*adj* hourly
HORARY	*adj* hourly
HORDE	*v* **HORDED, HORDING, HORDES** to gather in a large group
HORDEIN	*n* pl. **-S** a simple protein
HORDEOLA	*n/pl* swellings of the eyelid
HORIZON	*n* pl. **-S** the line where the sky seems to meet the earth
HORMONE	*n* pl. **-S** a secretion of the endocrine organs **HORMONAL, HORMONIC** *adj*
HORN	*v* **-ED, -ING, -S** to form a horn (a hard, bonelike projection of the head)
HORNBEAM	*n* pl. **-S** a small tree
HORNBILL	*n* pl. **-S** a large-billed bird
HORNBOOK	*n* pl. **-S** a primer
HORNET	*n* pl. **-S** a stinging insect
HORNFELS	*n* pl. **HORNFELS** a silicate rock
HORNIER	comparative of horny
HORNIEST	superlative of horny
HORNILY	*adv* in a horny manner
HORNING	*n* pl. **-S** a mock serenade for newlyweds
HORNIST	*n* pl. **-S** a French horn player

HORNITO *n pl.* **-TOS** a mound of volcanic matter

HORNLESS *adj* lacking a horn

HORNLIKE *adj* resembling a horn

HORNPIPE *n pl.* **-S** a musical instrument

HORNPOUT *n pl.* **-S** a catfish

HORNTAIL *n pl.* **-S** a wasplike insect

HORNWORM *n pl.* **-S** the larva of a hawkmoth

HORNWORT *n pl.* **-S** an aquatic herb

HORNY *adj* **HORNIER, HORNIEST** hornlike in hardness

HOROLOGE *n pl.* **-S** a timepiece

HOROLOGY *n pl.* **-GIES** the science of measuring time

HORRENT *adj* bristling; standing erect

HORRIBLE *n pl.* **-S** something that causes horror

HORRIBLY *adv* dreadfully

HORRID *adj* **-RIDER, -RIDEST** repulsive **HORRIDLY** *adv*

HORRIFIC *adj* causing horror

HORRIFY *v* **-FIED, -FYING, -FIES** to cause to feel horror

HORROR *n pl.* **-S** a feeling of intense fear or repugnance

HORSE *v* **HORSED, HORSING, HORSES** to provide with a horse (a large, hoofed mammal)

HORSECAR *n pl.* **-S** a streetcar drawn by a horse

HORSEFLY *n pl.* **-FLIES** a large fly

HORSEMAN *n pl.* **-MEN** one who rides a horse

HORSEPOX *n pl.* **-ES** a skin disease of horses

HORSEY *adj* **HORSIER, HORSIEST** horsy

HORSIER comparative of horsy

HORSIEST superlative of horsy

HORSILY *adv* in a horsy manner

HORSING present participle of horse

HORST *n pl.* **-S** a portion of the earth's crust

HORSTE *n pl.* **-S** horst

HORSY *adj* **HORSIER, HORSIEST** resembling a horse

HOSANNA *v* **-ED, -ING, -S** to praise

HOSANNAH *n pl.* **-S** a shout of fervent praise

HOSE *n pl.* **HOSEN** stockings or socks

HOSE *v* **HOSED, HOSING, HOSES** to spray with water

HOSEL *n pl.* **-S** a part of a golf club

HOSELIKE *adj* resembling a hose

HOSEPIPE *n pl.* **-S** a flexible tube for conveying fluids

HOSER *n pl.* **-S** an uncouth man

HOSEY *v* **-SEYED, -SEYING, -SEYS** to choose sides for a children's game

HOSIER *n pl.* **-S** one that makes hose

HOSIERY *n pl.* **-SIERIES** hose

HOSING present participle of hose

HOSPICE *n pl.* **-S** a shelter

HOSPITAL *n pl.* **-S** a medical institution

HOSPITIA *n/pl* places of shelter

HOSPODAR *n pl.* **-S** a governor of a region under Turkish rule

HOST *v* **-ED, -ING, -S** to entertain socially

HOSTA *n pl.* **-S** a plantain lily

HOSTAGE *n pl.* **-S** a person held as security

HOSTEL *v* **-TELED, -TELING, -TELS** or **-TELLED, -TELLING, -TELS** to stay at inns overnight while traveling

HOSTELER *n pl.* **-S** an innkeeper

HOSTELRY *n pl.* **-RIES** an inn

HOSTESS *v* **-ED, -ING, -ES** to act as a hostess (a woman who entertains socially)

HOSTILE *n pl.* **-S** an unfriendly person

HOSTLER *n pl.* **-S** a person who tends horses or mules

HOSTLY *adj* pertaining to one who hosts

HOT *adj* **HOTTER, HOTTEST** having a high temperature

HOT *v* **HOTTED, HOTTING, HOTS** to heat

HOTBED *n pl.* **-S** a bed of rich soil

HOTBLOOD *n pl.* **-S** a thoroughbred horse

HOTBOX *n pl.* **-ES** an overheated bearing of a railroad car

HOTCAKE *n pl.* **-S** a pancake

HOTCH *v* **-ED, -ING, -ES** to wiggle

HOTCHPOT *n pl.* **-S** the combining of properties in order to divide them equally among heirs

HOTDOG *v* **-DOGGED, -DOGGING, -DOGS** to perform showily

HOTEL *n pl.* **-S** a public lodging

HOTELDOM *n pl.* **-S** hotels and hotel workers

HOTELIER *n pl.* **-S** a hotel manager

HOTELMAN	*n* pl. **-MEN** a hotelier
HOTFOOT	*v* **-FOOTED, -FOOTING, -FOOTS** to hurry
HOTHEAD	*n* pl. **-S** a quick-tempered person
HOTHOUSE	*v* **-HOUSED, -HOUSING, -HOUSES** to grow in a hothouse (a heated greenhouse)
HOTLINE	*n* pl. **-S** a direct communications system for immediate contact
HOTLINK	*n* pl. **-S** a connection between two computer files
HOTLY	*adv* in a hot manner
HOTNESS	*n* pl. **-ES** the state of being hot
HOTPRESS	*v* **-ED, -ING, -ES** to subject to heat and pressure
HOTROD	*n* pl. **-S** a car modified for high speeds
HOTSHOT	*n* pl. **-S** a showily skillful person
HOTSPOT	*n* pl. **-S** an area known for violence or unrest
HOTSPUR	*n* pl. **-S** a hothead
HOTTED	past tense of hot
HOTTER	comparative of hot
HOTTEST	superlative of hot
HOTTIE	*n* pl. **-S** an attractive person
HOTTING	present participle of hot
HOTTISH	*adj* somewhat hot
HOUDAH	*n* pl. **-S** howdah
HOUND	*v* **-ED, -ING, -S** to pursue relentlessly
HOUNDER	*n* pl. **-S** one that hounds
HOUR	*n* pl. **-S** a period of sixty minutes
HOURI	*n* pl. **-S** a beautiful maiden in Muslim belief
HOURLONG	*adj* lasting an hour
HOURLY	*n* pl. **-LIES** a worker paid by the hour
HOUSE	*v* **HOUSED, HOUSING, HOUSES** to lodge in a house (a building in which people live)
HOUSEBOY	*n* pl. **-BOYS** a male servant
HOUSEFLY	*n* pl. **-FLIES** a common fly
HOUSEFUL	*n* pl. **-S** as much as a house will hold
HOUSEL	*v* **-SELED, -SELING, -SELS** or **-SELLED, -SELLING, -SELS** to administer the Eucharist to
HOUSEMAN	*n* pl. **-MEN** a male servant
HOUSER	*n* pl. **-S** one who organizes housing projects
HOUSESIT	*v* **-SAT, -SITTING, -SITS** to occupy a dwelling while the tenants are away
HOUSETOP	*n* pl. **-S** the roof of a house
HOUSING	*n* pl. **-S** any dwelling place
HOVE	a past tense of heave
HOVEL	*v* **-ELED, -ELING, -ELS** or **-ELLED, -ELLING, -ELS** to live in a small, miserable dwelling
HOVER	*v* **-ED, -ING, -S** to hang suspended in the air
HOVERER	*n* pl. **-S** something that hovers
HOVERFLY	*n* pl. **-FLIES** a fly noted for hovering
HOW	*n* pl. **-S** a method of doing something
HOWBEIT	*adv* nevertheless
HOWDAH	*n* pl. **-S** a seat on an elephant or camel for riders
HOWDIE	*n* pl. **-S** a midwife
HOWDY	*v* **-DIED, -DYING, -DIES** to greet with the words "how do you do"
HOWE	*n* pl. **-S** a valley
HOWEVER	*adv* nevertheless
HOWF	*n* pl. **-S** a place frequently visited
HOWFF	*n* pl. **-S** howf
HOWITZER	*n* pl. **-S** a short cannon
HOWK	*v* **-ED, -ING, -S** to dig
HOWL	*v* **-ED, -ING, -S** to cry like a dog
HOWLER	*n* pl. **-S** one that howls
HOWLET	*n* pl. **-S** an owl
HOY	*n* pl. **HOYS** a heavy barge or scow
HOYA	*n* pl. **-S** a flowering plant
HOYDEN	*v* **-ED, -ING, -S** to act like a tomboy
HOYLE	*n* pl. **-S** a rule book
HRYVNA	*n* pl. **-S** hryvnia
HRYVNIA	*n* pl. **-S** a monetary unit of Ukraine
HUARACHE	*n* pl. **-S** a flat-heeled sandal
HUARACHO	*n* pl. **-CHOS** huarache
HUB	*n* pl. **-S** the center of a wheel
HUBBLY	*adj* having an uneven surface
HUBBUB	*n* pl. **-S** an uproar
HUBBY	*n* pl. **-BIES** a husband
HUBCAP	*n* pl. **-S** a covering for the hub of a wheel
HUBRIS	*n* pl. **-BRISES** arrogance
HUCK	*n* pl. **-S** a durable fabric

HUCKLE	*n* pl. **-S** the hip
HUCKSTER	*v* **-ED, -ING, -S** to peddle
HUDDLE	*v* **-DLED, -DLING, -DLES** to crowd together
HUDDLER	*n* pl. **-S** one that huddles
HUE	*n* pl. **-S** color **HUED, HUELESS** *adj*
HUFF	*v* **-ED, -ING, -S** to breathe heavily
HUFFISH	*adj* sulky
HUFFY	*adj* **HUFFIER, HUFFIEST** easily offended **HUFFILY** *adv*
HUG	*v* **HUGGED, HUGGING, HUGS** to clasp tightly in the arms
HUGE	*adj* **HUGER, HUGEST** very large **HUGELY** *adv*
HUGENESS	*n* pl. **-ES** the quality of being huge
HUGEOUS	*adj* huge
HUGGABLE	*adj* cuddlesome
HUGGED	past tense of hug
HUGGER	*n* pl. **-S** one that hugs
HUGGING	present participle of hug
HUH	*interj* — used to express surprise
HUIC	*interj* — used to encourage hunting hounds
HUIPIL	*n* pl. **-S** or **-ES** an embroidered blouse or dress of Mexico
HUISACHE	*n* pl. **-S** a flowering plant
HULA	*n* pl. **-S** a Hawaiian dance
HULK	*v* **-ED, -ING, -S** to appear impressively large
HULKY	*adj* **HULKIER, HULKIEST** massive
HULL	*v* **-ED, -ING, -S** to remove the shell from a seed
HULLER	*n* pl. **-S** one that hulls
HULLO	*v* **-ED, -ING, -S** or **-ES** to hallo
HULLOA	*v* **-ED, -ING, -S** to hallo
HULLOO	*v* **-ED, -ING, -S** to hallo
HUM	*v* **HUMMED, HUMMING, HUMS** to sing without opening the lips or saying words
HUMAN	*n* pl. **-S** a person
HUMANE	*adj* **-MANER, -MANEST** compassionate **HUMANELY** *adv*
HUMANISE	*v* **-ISED, -ISING, -ISES** to humanize
HUMANISM	*n* pl. **-S** the quality of being human
HUMANIST	*n* pl. **-S** one who studies human nature
HUMANITY	*n* pl. **-TIES** the human race
HUMANIZE	*v* **-IZED, -IZING, -IZES** to make human
HUMANLY	*adv* in a human manner
HUMANOID	*n* pl. **-S** something having human form
HUMATE	*n* pl. **-S** a chemical salt
HUMBLE	*adj* **-BLER, -BLEST** modest
HUMBLE	*v* **-BLED, -BLING, -BLES** to reduce the pride of
HUMBLER	*n* pl. **-S** one that humbles
HUMBLEST	superlative of humble
HUMBLING	present participle of humble
HUMBLY	*adv* in a humble manner
HUMBUG	*v* **-BUGGED, -BUGGING, -BUGS** to deceive
HUMDRUM	*n* pl. **-S** a dull, boring person
HUMERAL	*n* pl. **-S** a bone of the shoulder
HUMERUS	*n* pl. **-MERI** the large bone of the upper arm
HUMIC	*adj* derived from humus
HUMID	*adj* having much humidity
HUMIDEX	*n* pl. **-ES** an index of discomfort
HUMIDIFY	*v* **-FIED, -FYING, -FIES** to make humid
HUMIDITY	*n* pl. **-TIES** moisture of the air
HUMIDLY	*adv* in a humid manner
HUMIDOR	*n* pl. **-S** a cigar case
HUMIFIED	*adj* converted into humus
HUMILITY	*n* pl. **-TIES** the quality of being humble
HUMITURE	*n* pl. **-S** a combined measurement of temperature and humidity
HUMMABLE	*adj* capable of being hummed
HUMMED	past tense of hum
HUMMER	*n* pl. **-S** one that hums
HUMMING	present participle of hum
HUMMOCK	*v* **-ED, -ING, -S** to form into hummocks (small rounded hills)
HUMMOCKY	*adj* abounding in hummocks
HUMMUS	*n* pl. **-ES** a paste of pureed chickpeas and tahini
HUMOR	*v* **-ED, -ING, -S** to indulge
HUMORAL	*adj* pertaining to bodily fluids
HUMORFUL	*adj* humorous
HUMORIST	*n* pl. **-S** a humorous writer or entertainer
HUMOROUS	*adj* funny; witty
HUMOUR	*v* **-ED, -ING, -S** to humor

HUMP *v* **-ED, -ING, -S** to arch into a hump (a rounded protuberance)

HUMPBACK *n* pl. **-S** a humped back

HUMPER *n* pl. **-S** one that humps

HUMPH *v* **-ED, -ING, -S** to utter a grunt

HUMPLESS *adj* lacking a hump

HUMPY *adj* **HUMPIER, HUMPIEST** full of humps

HUMUS *n* pl. **-ES** decomposed organic matter

HUMVEE *n* pl. **-S** a type of motor vehicle

HUN *n* pl. **-S** a barbarous, destructive person

HUNCH *v* **-ED, -ING, -ES** to arch forward

HUNDRED *n* pl. **-S** a number

HUNG a past tense of hang

HUNGER *v* **-ED, -ING, -S** to crave

HUNGOVER *adj* suffering from a hangover

HUNGRY *adj* **-GRIER, -GRIEST** wanting food **HUNGRILY** *adv*

HUNH *interj* — used to ask for a repetition of an utterance

HUNK *n* pl. **-S** a large piece

HUNKER *v* **-ED, -ING, -S** to squat

HUNKY *adj* **HUNKIER, HUNKIEST** muscular and attractive

HUNNISH *adj* resembling a hun

HUNT *v* **-ED, -ING, -S** to pursue for food or sport **HUNTABLE** *adj* **HUNTEDLY** *adv*

HUNTER *n* pl. **-S** one that hunts

HUNTING *n* pl. **-S** an instance of searching

HUNTRESS *n* pl. **-ES** a female hunter

HUNTSMAN *n* pl. **-MEN** a hunter

HUP *interj* — used to mark a marching cadence

HUPPAH *n* pl. **-S** chuppah

HURDIES *n/pl* the buttocks

HURDLE *v* **-DLED, -DLING, -DLES** to jump over

HURDLER *n* pl. **-S** one that hurdles

HURDS *n/pl* hards

HURL *v* **-ED, -ING, -S** to throw with great force

HURLER *n* pl. **-S** one that hurls

HURLEY *n* pl. **-LEYS** hurling

HURLING *n* pl. **-S** an Irish game

HURLY *n* pl. **-LIES** commotion

HURRAH *v* **-ED, -ING, -S** to cheer

HURRAY *v* **-ED, -ING, -S** to hurrah

HURRIER *n* pl. **-S** one that hurries

HURRY *v* **-RIED, -RYING, -RIES** to move swiftly

HURST *n* pl. **-S** a small hill

HURT *v* **HURT, HURTING, HURTS** to injure

HURTER *n* pl. **-S** one that hurts

HURTFUL *adj* causing injury

HURTLE *v* **-TLED, -TLING, -TLES** to rush violently

HURTLESS *adj* harmless

HUSBAND *v* **-ED, -ING, -S** to spend wisely

HUSH *v* **-ED, -ING, -ES** to quiet **HUSHEDLY** *adv*

HUSHABY *v* go to sleep — used imperatively to soothe a child

HUSHFUL *adj* quiet

HUSK *v* **-ED, -ING, -S** to remove the husk (the outer covering) from

HUSKER *n* pl. **-S** one that husks

HUSKIER comparative of husky

HUSKIES pl. of husky

HUSKIEST superlative of husky

HUSKILY *adv* in a husky manner

HUSKING *n* pl. **-S** a gathering of families to husk corn

HUSKLIKE *adj* resembling a husk

HUSKY *adj* **-KIER, -KIEST** hoarse

HUSKY *n* pl. **-KIES** an Eskimo dog

HUSSAR *n* pl. **-S** a cavalry soldier

HUSSY *n* pl. **-SIES** a lewd woman

HUSTINGS *n* pl. **HUSTINGS** a British court

HUSTLE *v* **-TLED, -TLING, -TLES** to hurry

HUSTLER *n* pl. **-S** one that hustles

HUSWIFE *n* pl. **-WIVES** or **-WIFES** a sewing kit

HUT *v* **HUTTED, HUTTING, HUTS** to live in a hut (a simple shelter)

HUTCH *v* **-ED, -ING, -ES** to store away

HUTLIKE *adj* resembling a hut

HUTMENT *n* pl. **-S** a group of huts

HUTTED past tense of hut

HUTTING present participle of hut

HUTZPA *n* pl. **-S** chutzpah

HUTZPAH *n* pl. **-S** chutzpah

HUZZA   *v* **-ED, -ING, -S** to cheer

HUZZAH   *v* **-ED, -ING, -S** to huzza

HWAN   *n* pl. **HWAN** a monetary unit of South Korea

HYACINTH   *n* pl. **-S** a flowering plant

HYAENA   *n* pl. **-S** hyena **HYAENIC** *adj*

HYALIN   *n* pl. **-S** hyaline

HYALINE   *n* pl. **-S** a transparent substance

HYALITE   *n* pl. **-S** a colorless opal

HYALOGEN   *n* pl. **-S** a substance found in animal cells

HYALOID   *n* pl. **-S** a membrane of the eye

HYBRID   *n* pl. **-S** the offspring of genetically dissimilar parents

HYBRIS   *n* pl. **-BRISES** hubris

HYDATID   *n* pl. **-S** a cyst caused by a tapeworm

HYDRA   *n* pl. **-DRAS** or **-DRAE** a freshwater polyp

HYDRACID   *n* pl. **-S** an acid

HYDRAGOG   *n* pl. **-S** a purgative causing watery discharges

HYDRANT   *n* pl. **-S** an outlet from a water main

HYDRANTH   *n* pl. **-S** the oral opening of a hydra

HYDRASE   *n* pl. **-S** an enzyme

HYDRATE   *v* **-DRATED, -DRATING, -DRATES** to combine with water

HYDRATOR   *n* pl. **-S** one that hydrates

HYDRIA   *n* pl. **-DRIAE** a water jar

HYDRIC   *adj* pertaining to moisture

HYDRID   *n* pl. **-S** hydride

HYDRIDE   *n* pl. **-S** a chemical compound

HYDRILLA   *n* pl. **-S** an aquatic Asian plant

HYDRO   *n* pl. **-DROS** electricity produced by waterpower

HYDROGEL   *n* pl. **-S** a colloid

HYDROGEN   *n* pl. **-S** a gaseous element

HYDROID   *n* pl. **-S** a polyp

HYDROMEL   *n* pl. **-S** a mixture of honey and water

HYDRONIC   *adj* pertaining to heating and cooling by water

HYDROPIC   *adj* affected with hydropsy

HYDROPS   *n* pl. **-ES** hydropsy

HYDROPSY   *n* pl. **-SIES** dropsy

HYDROSKI   *n* pl. **-S** a plate attached to a seaplane to facilitate takeoffs and landings

HYDROSOL   *n* pl. **-S** an aqueous solution of a colloid

HYDROUS   *adj* containing water

HYDROXY   *adj* containing hydroxyl

HYDROXYL   *n* pl. **-S** the radical or group containing oxygen and hydrogen

HYENA   *n* pl. **-S** a wolflike mammal **HYENIC, HYENINE, HYENOID** *adj*

HYETAL   *adj* pertaining to rain

HYGEIST   *n* pl. **-S** an expert in hygiene

HYGIEIST   *n* pl. **-S** hygeist

HYGIENE   *n* pl. **-S** the science of health **HYGIENIC** *adj*

HYING   present participle of hie

HYLA   *n* pl. **-S** a tree frog

HYLOZOIC   *adj* pertaining to the doctrine that life and matter are inseparable

HYMEN   *n* pl. **-S** a vaginal membrane **HYMENAL** *adj*

HYMENEAL   *n* pl. **-S** a wedding song or poem

HYMENIUM   *n* pl. **-NIUMS** or **-NIA** a layer in certain fungi **HYMENIAL** *adj*

HYMN   *v* **-ED, -ING, -S** to sing a hymn (a song of praise to God)

HYMNAL   *n* pl. **-S** a book of hymns

HYMNARY   *n* pl. **-RIES** a hymnal

HYMNBOOK   *n* pl. **-S** a hymnal

HYMNIST   *n* pl. **-S** one who composes hymns

HYMNLESS   *adj* lacking a hymn

HYMNLIKE   *adj* resembling a hymn

HYMNODY   *n* pl. **-DIES** the singing of hymns

HYOID   *n* pl. **-S** a bone of the tongue **HYOIDAL, HYOIDEAN** *adj*

HYOSCINE   *n* pl. **-S** a sedative

HYP   *n* pl. **-S** hypochondria

HYPE   *v* **HYPED, HYPING, HYPES** to promote extravagantly

HYPER   *n* pl. **-S** one that hypes

HYPERGOL   *n* pl. **-S** a rocket fuel

HYPERON   *n* pl. **-S** an atomic particle

HYPEROPE   *n* pl. **-S** a farsighted person

HYPHA   *n* pl. **-PHAE** a threadlike element of a fungus **HYPHAL** *adj*

HYPHEMIA   *n* pl. **-S** deficiency of blood

HYPHEN   *v* **-ED, -ING, -S** to connect words or syllables with a hyphen (a mark of punctuation) **HYPHENIC** *adj*

HYPING   present participle of hype

HYPNIC   *adj* pertaining to sleep

HYPNOID   *adj* pertaining to hypnosis or sleep

HYPNOSIS   *n* pl. **-NOSES** an artificially induced state resembling sleep

HYPNOTIC   *n* pl. **-S** a sleep-inducing drug

HYPO   *v* **-ED, -ING, -S** to inject with a hypodermic needle

HYPOACID   *adj* having a lower than normal degree of acidity

HYPODERM   *n* pl. **-S** a skin layer

HYPOGEA   pl. of hypogeum

HYPOGEAL   *adj* underground

HYPOGEAN   *adj* hypogeal

HYPOGENE   *adj* formed underground

HYPOGEUM   *n* pl. **-GEA** an underground chamber

HYPOGYNY   *n* pl. **-NIES** the condition of having flowers with organs situated below the ovary

HYPONEA   *n* pl. **-S** hyponoia

HYPONOIA   *n* pl. **-S** dulled mental activity

HYPONYM   *n* pl. **-S** a word that denotes a subcategory

HYPONYMY   *n* pl. **-MIES** the state of being a hyponym

HYPOPNEA   *n* pl. **-S** abnormally shallow breathing

HYPOPYON   *n* pl. **-S** an accumulation of pus in the eye

HYPOTHEC   *n* pl. **-S** a type of mortgage

HYPOXIA   *n* pl. **-S** a deficiency of oxygen in body tissue **HYPOXIC** *adj*

HYRACOID   *n* pl. **-S** a hyrax

HYRAX   *n* pl. **-RAXES** or **-RACES** a small, harelike mammal

HYSON   *n* pl. **-S** a Chinese tea

HYSSOP   *n* pl. **-S** a medicinal herb

HYSTERIA   *n* pl. **-S** uncontrollable excitement or fear

HYSTERIC   *n* pl. **-S** one who is subject to fits of hysteria

HYTE   *adj* insane

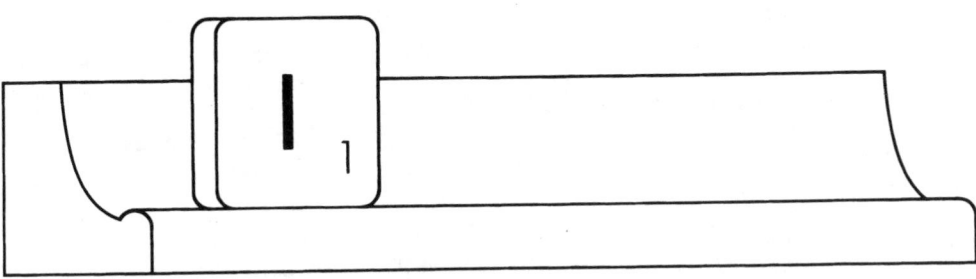

IAMB	*n* pl. **-S** a type of metrical foot	**ICIER**	comparative of icy
IAMBIC	*n* pl. **-S** an iamb	**ICIEST**	superlative of icy
IAMBUS	*n* pl. **-BUSES** or **-BI** an iamb	**ICILY**	*adv* in an icy manner
IATRIC	*adj* pertaining to medicine	**ICINESS**	*n* pl. **-ES** the state of being icy
IATRICAL	*adj* iatric	**ICING**	*n* pl. **-S** a sweet mixture for covering cakes
IBEX	*n* pl. **IBEXES** or **IBICES** a wild goat	**ICK**	*interj* — used to express disgust
IBIDEM	*adv* in the same place	**ICKER**	*n* pl. **-S** a head of grain
IBIS	*n* pl. **IBISES** a wading bird	**ICKINESS**	*n* pl. **-ES** the state of being icky
IBOGAINE	*n* pl. **-S** an alkaloid used as an antidepressant	**ICKY**	*adj* **ICKIER, ICKIEST** repulsive **ICKILY** *adv*
ICE	*v* **ICED, ICING, ICES** to cover with ice (frozen water)	**ICON**	*n* pl. **-S** or **-ES** a representation **ICONIC, ICONICAL** *adj*
ICEBERG	*n* pl. **-S** a large floating body of ice	**ICTERIC**	*n* pl. **-S** a remedy for icterus
ICEBLINK	*n* pl. **-S** a glare over an ice field	**ICTERUS**	*n* pl. **-ES** a diseased condition of the liver
ICEBOAT	*n* pl. **-S** a vehicle that sails on ice		
ICEBOUND	*adj* surrounded by ice	**ICTUS**	*n* pl. **-ES** a recurring stress or beat in a poetical form **ICTIC** *adj*
ICEBOX	*n* pl. **-ES** a cabinet for cooling food	**ICY**	*adj* **ICIER, ICIEST** covered with ice
ICECAP	*n* pl. **-S** a covering of ice and snow	**ID**	*n* pl. **-S** a part of the psyche
ICED	past tense of ice	**IDEA**	*n* pl. **-S** a conception existing in the mind **IDEALESS** *adj*
ICEFALL	*n* pl. **-S** a kind of frozen waterfall	**IDEAL**	*n* pl. **-S** a standard of perfection
ICEHOUSE	*n* pl. **-S** a building for storing ice	**IDEALISE**	*v* **-ISED, -ISING, -ISES** to idealize
ICEKHANA	*n* pl. **-S** an automotive event held on a frozen lake	**IDEALISM**	*n* pl. **-S** the pursuit of noble goals
ICELESS	*adj* having no ice	**IDEALIST**	*n* pl. **-S** an adherent of idealism
ICELIKE	*adj* resembling ice	**IDEALITY**	*n* pl. **-TIES** the state of being perfect; something idealized
ICEMAKER	*n* pl. **-S** an appliance that makes ice	**IDEALIZE**	*v* **-IZED, -IZING, -IZES** to regard as perfect
ICEMAN	*n* pl. **-MEN** a man who supplies ice		
ICH	*n* pl. **ICHS** a disease of certain fishes	**IDEALLY**	*adv* perfectly
		IDEALOGY	*n* pl. **-GIES** ideology
ICHNITE	*n* pl. **-S** a fossil footprint	**IDEATE**	*v* **-ATED, -ATING, -ATES** to form an idea
ICHOR	*n* pl. **-S** a watery discharge from a wound **ICHOROUS** *adj*		
		IDEATION	*n* pl. **-S** the act of ideating
ICHTHYIC	*adj* pertaining to fishes	**IDEATIVE**	*adj* pertaining to ideation
ICICLE	*n* pl. **-S** a hanging spike of ice **ICICLED** *adj*	**IDEM**	*adj* the same

IDENTIC	*adj* identical
IDENTIFY	*v* **-FIED, -FYING, -FIES** to establish the identity of
IDENTITY	*n* pl. **-TIES** the essential character of a person or thing
IDEOGRAM	*n* pl. **-S** a type of written symbol
IDEOLOGY	*n* pl. **-GIES** a systematic body of ideas
IDES	*n* pl. **IDES** a certain day in the ancient Roman calendar
IDIOCY	*n* pl. **-CIES** the condition of being an idiot
IDIOLECT	*n* pl. **-S** one's speech pattern
IDIOM	*n* pl. **-S** an expression peculiar to a language
IDIOT	*n* pl. **-S** a mentally deficient person **IDIOTIC** *adj*
IDIOTISM	*n* pl. **-S** idiocy
IDIOTYPE	*n* pl. **-S** a structure of an antibody
IDLE	*adj* **IDLER, IDLEST** inactive
IDLE	*v* **IDLED, IDLING, IDLES** to pass time idly
IDLENESS	*n* pl. **-ES** the state of being idle
IDLER	*n* pl. **-S** one that idles
IDLESSE	*n* pl. **-S** idleness
IDLEST	superlative of idle
IDLING	present participle of idle
IDLY	*adv* in an idle manner
IDOCRASE	*n* pl. **-S** a mineral
IDOL	*n* pl. **-S** an object of worship
IDOLATER	*n* pl. **-S** one that worships idols
IDOLATOR	*n* pl. **-S** idolater
IDOLATRY	*n* pl. **-TRIES** the worship of idols
IDOLISE	*v* **-ISED, -ISING, -ISES** to idolize
IDOLISER	*n* pl. **-S** one that idolises
IDOLISM	*n* pl. **-S** idolatry
IDOLIZE	*v* **-IZED, -IZING, -IZES** to worship
IDOLIZER	*n* pl. **-S** one that idolizes
IDONEITY	*n* pl. **-TIES** the state of being idoneous
IDONEOUS	*adj* suitable
IDYL	*n* pl. **-S** a poem or prose work depicting scenes of rural simplicity
IDYLIST	*n* pl. **-S** a writer of idyls
IDYLL	*n* pl. **-S** idyl **IDYLLIC** *adj*
IDYLLIST	*n* pl. **-S** idylist
IF	*n* pl. **-S** a possibility

IFF	*conj* if and only if
IFFINESS	*n* pl. **-ES** the state of being iffy
IFFY	*adj* **IFFIER, IFFIEST** full of uncertainty
IGG	*v* **-ED, -ING, -S** to ignore
IGLOO	*n* pl. **-LOOS** an Eskimo dwelling
IGLU	*n* pl. **-S** igloo
IGNATIA	*n* pl. **-S** a medicinal seed
IGNEOUS	*adj* pertaining to fire
IGNIFY	*v* **-FIED, -FYING, -FIES** to burn
IGNITE	*v* **-NITED, -NITING, -NITES** to set on fire
IGNITER	*n* pl. **-S** one that ignites
IGNITION	*n* pl. **-S** the act of igniting
IGNITOR	*n* pl. **-S** igniter
IGNITRON	*n* pl. **-S** a type of rectifier tube
IGNOBLE	*adj* of low character **IGNOBLY** *adv*
IGNOMINY	*n* pl. **-NIES** disgrace or dishonor
IGNORAMI	*n/pl* utterly ignorant persons
IGNORANT	*adj* having no knowledge
IGNORE	*v* **-NORED, -NORING, -NORES** to refuse to notice
IGNORER	*n* pl. **-S** one that ignores
IGUANA	*n* pl. **-S** a tropical lizard
IGUANIAN	*n* pl. **-S** a lizard related to the iguana
IGUANID	*n* pl. **-S** a long-tailed lizard
IHRAM	*n* pl. **-S** the garb worn by Muslim pilgrims
IKAT	*n* pl. **-S** a fabric of tie-dyed yarns
IKEBANA	*n* pl. **-S** the Japanese art of flower arranging
IKON	*n* pl. **-S** icon
ILEA	pl. of ileum
ILEAC	*adj* pertaining to the ileum
ILEAL	*adj* ileac
ILEITIS	*n* pl. **ILEITIDES** inflammation of the ileum
ILEUM	*n* pl. **ILEA** a part of the small intestine
ILEUS	*n* pl. **-ES** intestinal obstruction
ILEX	*n* pl. **-ES** a holly
ILIA	pl. of ilium
ILIAC	*adj* pertaining to the ilium
ILIAD	*n* pl. **-S** a long poem
ILIAL	*adj* iliac
ILIUM	*n* pl. **ILIA** a bone of the pelvis

ILK	*n* pl. **-S** a class or kind	**IMAUM**	*n* pl. **-S** imam
ILKA	*adj* each	**IMBALM**	*v* **-ED, -ING, -S** to embalm
ILL	*adj* **ILLER, ILLEST** not well	**IMBALMER**	*n* pl. **-S** embalmer
ILL	*n* pl. **-S** an evil	**IMBARK**	*v* **-ED, -ING, -S** to embark
ILLATION	*n* pl. **-S** the act of inferring	**IMBECILE**	*n* pl. **-S** a mentally deficient person
ILLATIVE	*n* pl. **-S** a word or phrase introducing an inference	**IMBED**	*v* **-BEDDED, -BEDDING, -BEDS** to embed
ILLEGAL	*n* pl. **-S** a person who enters a country without authorization	**IMBIBE**	*v* **-BIBED, -BIBING, -BIBES** to drink
ILLICIT	*adj* not permitted	**IMBIBER**	*n* pl. **-S** one that imbibes
ILLINIUM	*n* pl. **-S** a radioactive element	**IMBITTER**	*v* **-ED, -ING, -S** to embitter
ILLIQUID	*adj* not being cash	**IMBLAZE**	*v* **-BLAZED, -BLAZING, -BLAZES** to emblaze
ILLITE	*n* pl. **-S** a group of minerals **ILLITIC** *adj*	**IMBODY**	*v* **-BODIED, -BODYING, -BODIES** to embody
ILLNESS	*n* pl. **-ES** sickness	**IMBOLDEN**	*v* **-ED, -ING, -S** to embolden
ILLOGIC	*n* pl. **-S** absence of logic	**IMBOSOM**	*v* **-ED, -ING, -S** to embosom
ILLUDE	*v* **-LUDED, -LUDING, -LUDES** to deceive	**IMBOWER**	*v* **-ED, -ING, -S** to embower
ILLUME	*v* **-LUMED, -LUMING, -LUMES** to illuminate	**IMBROWN**	*v* **-ED, -ING, -S** to embrown
		IMBRUE	*v* **-BRUED, -BRUING, -BRUES** to stain
ILLUMINE	*v* **-MINED, -MINING, -MINES** to illuminate	**IMBRUTE**	*v* **-BRUTED, -BRUTING, -BRUTES** to make brutal
ILLUSION	*n* pl. **-S** a false perception		
ILLUSIVE	*adj* illusory	**IMBUE**	*v* **-BUED, -BUING, -BUES** to make thoroughly wet
ILLUSORY	*adj* based on illusion		
ILLUVIUM	*n* pl. **-VIUMS** or **-VIA** a type of material accumulated in soil **ILLUVIAL** *adj*	**IMID**	*n* pl. **-S** imide
		IMIDE	*n* pl. **-S** a chemical compound **IMIDIC** *adj*
ILLY	*adv* badly	**IMIDO**	*adj* containing an imide
ILMENITE	*n* pl. **-S** a mineral	**IMINE**	*n* pl. **-S** a chemical compound
IMAGE	*v* **-AGED, -AGING, -AGES** to imagine	**IMINO**	*adj* containing an imine
		IMITABLE	*adj* capable of being imitated
IMAGER	*n* pl. **-S** one that images	**IMITATE**	*v* **-TATED, -TATING, -TATES** to behave in the same way as
IMAGERY	*n* pl. **-ERIES** mental pictures		
IMAGINAL	*adj* pertaining to an imago	**IMITATOR**	*n* pl. **-S** one that imitates
IMAGINE	*v* **-INED, -INING, -INES** to form a mental picture of	**IMMANE**	*adj* great in size
		IMMANENT	*adj* existing within
IMAGINER	*n* pl. **-S** one that imagines	**IMMATURE**	*n* pl. **-S** an individual that is not fully grown or developed
IMAGING	*n* pl. **-S** the action of producing a visible representation		
		IMMENSE	*adj* **-MENSER, -MENSEST** great in size
IMAGINING	present participle of imagine		
IMAGISM	*n* pl. **-S** a movement in poetry	**IMMERGE**	*v* **-MERGED, -MERGING, -MERGES** to immerse
IMAGIST	*n* pl. **-S** an adherent of imagism		
IMAGO	*n* pl. **-GOS** or **-GOES** an adult insect	**IMMERSE**	*v* **-MERSED, -MERSING, -MERSES** to plunge into a liquid
IMAM	*n* pl. **-S** a Muslim priest	**IMMESH**	*v* **-ED, -ING, -ES** to enmesh
IMAMATE	*n* pl. **-S** the office of an imam	**IMMIES**	pl. of immy
IMARET	*n* pl. **-S** a Turkish inn	**IMMINENT**	*adj* ready to take place

IMMINGLE v **-GLED, -GLING, -GLES** to blend

IMMIX v **-ED, -ING, -ES** to mix in

IMMOBILE adj incapable of being moved

IMMODEST adj not modest

IMMOLATE v **-LATED, -LATING, -LATES** to kill as a sacrifice

IMMORAL adj contrary to established morality

IMMORTAL n pl. **-S** one who is not subject to death

IMMOTILE adj lacking mobility

IMMUNE n pl. **-S** one who is protected from a disease

IMMUNISE v **-NISED, -NISING, -NISES** to immunize

IMMUNITY n pl. **-TIES** the state of being protected from a disease

IMMUNIZE v **-NIZED, -NIZING, -NIZES** to protect from a disease

IMMURE v **-MURED, -MURING, -MURES** to imprison

IMMY n pl. **-MIES** a type of playing marble

IMP v **-ED, -ING, -S** to graft feathers onto a bird's wing

IMPACT v **-ED, -ING, -S** to pack firmly together

IMPACTER n pl. **-S** one that impacts

IMPACTOR n pl. **-S** impacter

IMPAINT v **-ED, -ING, -S** to paint or depict

IMPAIR v **-ED, -ING, -S** to make worse

IMPAIRER n pl. **-S** one that impairs

IMPALA n pl. **-S** an African antelope

IMPALE v **-PALED, -PALING, -PALES** to pierce with a pointed object

IMPALER n pl. **-S** one that impales

IMPANEL v **-ELED, -ELING, -ELS** or **-ELLED, -ELLING, -ELS** to enter on a list for jury duty

IMPARITY n pl. **-TIES** lack of equality

IMPARK v **-ED, -ING, -S** to confine in a park

IMPART v **-ED, -ING, -S** to make known

IMPARTER n pl. **-S** one that imparts

IMPASSE n pl. **-S** a road or passage having no exit

IMPASTE v **-PASTED, -PASTING, -PASTES** to make into a paste

IMPASTO n pl. **-TOS** a painting technique

IMPAVID adj brave

IMPAWN v **-ED, -ING, -S** to pawn

IMPEACH v **-ED, -ING, -ES** to charge with misconduct in office

IMPEARL v **-ED, -ING, -S** to make pearly

IMPEDE v **-PEDED, -PEDING, -PEDES** to obstruct the progress of

IMPEDER n pl. **-S** one that impedes

IMPEL v **-PELLED, -PELLING, -PELS** to force into action

IMPELLER n pl. **-S** one that impels

IMPELLOR n pl. **-S** impeller

IMPEND v **-ED, -ING, -S** to be imminent

IMPERIA a pl. of imperium

IMPERIAL n pl. **-S** an emperor or empress

IMPERIL v **-ILED, -ILING, -ILS** or **-ILLED, -ILLING, -ILS** to place in jeopardy

IMPERIUM n pl. **-RIUMS** or **-RIA** absolute power

IMPETIGO n pl. **-GOS** a skin disease

IMPETUS n pl. **-ES** an impelling force

IMPHEE n pl. **-S** an African grass

IMPI n pl. **-S** a body of warriors

IMPIETY n pl. **-TIES** lack of piety

IMPING n pl. **-S** the process of grafting

IMPINGE v **-PINGED, -PINGING, -PINGES** to collide

IMPINGER n pl. **-S** one that impinges

IMPIOUS adj not pious

IMPISH adj mischievous **IMPISHLY** adv

IMPLANT v **-ED, -ING, -S** to set securely

IMPLEAD v **-PLEADED** or **-PLED, -PLEADING, -PLEADS** to sue in a court of law

IMPLEDGE v **-PLEDGED, -PLEDGING, -PLEDGES** to pawn

IMPLICIT adj implied

IMPLIED past tense of imply

IMPLIES present 3d person sing. of imply

IMPLODE v **-PLODED, -PLODING, -PLODES** to collapse inward

IMPLORE v **-PLORED, -PLORING, -PLORES** to beg for urgently

IMPLORER n pl. **-S** one that implores

IMPLY v **-PLIED, -PLYING, -PLIES** to indicate or suggest indirectly

IMPOLICY n pl. **-CIES** an unwise course of action

IMPOLITE adj not polite

IMPONE v **-PONED, -PONING, -PONES** to wager

IMPOROUS *adj* extremely dense

IMPORT *v* **-ED, -ING, -S** to bring into a country from abroad

IMPORTER *n* pl. **-S** one that imports

IMPOSE *v* **-POSED, -POSING, -POSES** to establish as compulsory

IMPOSER *n* pl. **-S** one that imposes

IMPOST *v* **-ED, -ING, -S** to determine customs duties

IMPOSTER *n* pl. **-S** impostor

IMPOSTOR *n* pl. **-S** one that poses as another for deceptive purposes

IMPOTENT *n* pl. **-S** one that is powerless

IMPOUND *v* **-ED, -ING, -S** to seize and retain in legal custody

IMPOWER *v* **-ED, -ING, -S** to empower

IMPREGN *v* **-ED, -ING, -S** to make pregnant

IMPRESA *n* pl. **-S** a type of emblem

IMPRESE *n* pl. **-S** impresa

IMPRESS *v* **-ED, -ING, -ES** to affect strongly

IMPREST *n* pl. **-S** a loan or advance of money

IMPRIMIS *adv* in the first place

IMPRINT *v* **-ED, -ING, -S** to produce a mark by pressure

IMPRISON *v* **-ED, -ING, -S** to confine

IMPROPER *adj* not proper

IMPROV *n* pl. **-S** improvisation

IMPROVE *v* **-PROVED, -PROVING, -PROVES** to make better

IMPROVER *n* pl. **-S** one that improves

IMPUDENT *adj* offensively bold or disrespectful

IMPUGN *v* **-ED, -ING, -S** to make insinuations against

IMPUGNER *n* pl. **-S** one that impugns

IMPULSE *v* **-PULSED, -PULSING, -PULSES** to give impetus to

IMPUNITY *n* pl. **-TIES** exemption from penalty

IMPURE *adj* **-PURER, -PUREST** not pure

IMPURE *adj* not pure **IMPURELY** *adv*

IMPURITY *n* pl. **-TIES** something that is impure

IMPUTE *v* **-PUTED, -PUTING, -PUTES** to credit to a person or a cause

IMPUTER *n* pl. **-S** one that imputes

IN *v* **INNED, INNING, INS** to harvest

INACTION *n* pl. **-S** lack of action

INACTIVE *adj* not active

INANE *adj* **INANER, INANEST** nonsensical **INANELY** *adv*

INANE *n* pl. **-S** empty space

INANITY *n* pl. **-TIES** something that is inane

INAPT *adj* not apt **INAPTLY** *adv*

INARABLE *adj* not arable

INARCH *v* **-ED, -ING, -ES** to graft with in a certain way

INARM *v* **-ED, -ING, -S** to encircle with the arms

INBEING *n* pl. **-S** the state of being inherent

INBOARD *n* pl. **-S** a type of boat motor

INBORN *adj* existing in one from birth

INBOUND *v* **-ED, -ING, -S** to put a basketball in play from out of bounds

INBOUNDS *adj* being within certain boundaries

INBRED *n* pl. **-S** a product of inbreeding

INBREED *v* **-BRED, -BREEDING, -BREEDS** to breed closely related stock

INBUILT *adj* forming an integral part of a structure

INBURST *n* pl. **-S** the act of bursting inward

INBY *adv* inward

INBYE *adv* inby

INCAGE *v* **-CAGED, -CAGING, -CAGES** to encage

INCANT *v* **-ED, -ING, -S** to utter ritually

INCASE *v* **-CASED, -CASING, -CASES** to encase

INCENSE *v* **-CENSED, -CENSING, -CENSES** to make angry

INCENT *v* **-ED, -ING, -S** to provide with an incentive

INCENTER *n* pl. **-S** the point where the three lines bisecting the angles of a triangle meet

INCEPT *v* **-ED, -ING, -S** to take in

INCEPTOR *n* pl. **-S** one that incepts

INCEST *n* pl. **-S** sexual intercourse between closely related persons

INCH *v* **-ED, -ING, -ES** to move very slowly

INCHER *n* pl. **-S** something having a specified number of inches

INCHMEAL *adv* little by little

INCHOATE *adj* being in an early stage

INCHWORM *n* pl. **-S** a type of worm

INCIDENT *n* pl. **-S** an event

INCIPIT *n* pl. **-S** the opening words of a text

INCISAL *adj* being the cutting edge of a tooth

INCISE *v* **-CISED, -CISING, -CISES** to cut into

INCISION *n* pl. **-S** the act of incising

INCISIVE *adj* penetrating

INCISOR *n* pl. **-S** a cutting tooth

INCISORY *adj* adapted for cutting

INCISURE *n* pl. **-S** a notch or cleft of a body part

INCITANT *n* pl. **-S** something that incites

INCITE *v* **-CITED, -CITING, -CITES** to arouse to action

INCITER *n* pl. **-S** one that incites

INCIVIL *adj* discourteous

INCLASP *v* **-ED, -ING, -S** to enclasp

INCLINE *v* **-CLINED, -CLINING, -CLINES** to slant

INCLINER *n* pl. **-S** one that inclines

INCLIP *v* **-CLIPPED, -CLIPPING, -CLIPS** to clasp

INCLOSE *v* **-CLOSED, -CLOSING, -CLOSES** to enclose

INCLOSER *n* pl. **-S** one that incloses

INCLUDE *v* **-CLUDED, -CLUDING, -CLUDES** to have as a part

INCOG *n* pl. **-S** a disguised person

INCOME *n* pl. **-S** a sum of money earned regularly

INCOMER *n* pl. **-S** one that comes in

INCOMING *n* pl. **-S** an arrival

INCONNU *n* pl. **-S** a large food fish

INCONY *adj* pretty

INCORPSE *v* **-CORPSED, -CORPSING, -CORPSES** to become combined with

INCREASE *v* **-CREASED, -CREASING, -CREASES** to make or become greater

INCREATE *adj* not created

INCROSS *v* **-ED, -ING, -ES** to inbreed

INCRUST *v* **-ED, -ING, -S** to encrust

INCUBATE *v* **-BATED, -BATING, -BATES** to warm eggs for hatching

INCUBUS *n* pl. **-BUSES** or **-BI** a demon

INCUDAL *adj* pertaining to the incus

INCUDATE *adj* incudal

INCUDES pl. of incus

INCULT *adj* uncultivated

INCUMBER *v* **-ED, -ING, -S** to encumber

INCUR *v* **-CURRED, -CURRING, -CURS** to bring upon oneself

INCURVE *v* **-CURVED, -CURVING, -CURVES** to curve inward

INCUS *n* pl. **INCUDES** a bone in the middle ear

INCUSE *v* **-CUSED, -CUSING, -CUSES** to mark by stamping

INDABA *n* pl. **-S** a meeting of South African tribes

INDAGATE *v* **-GATED, -GATING, -GATES** to investigate

INDAMIN *n* pl. **-S** indamine

INDAMINE *n* pl. **-S** a chemical compound

INDEBTED *adj* beholden

INDECENT *adj* **-CENTER, -CENTEST** not decent

INDEED *adv* in truth

INDENE *n* pl. **-S** a hydrocarbon

INDENT *v* **-ED, -ING, -S** to cut or tear irregularly

INDENTER *n* pl. **-S** one that indents

INDENTOR *n* pl. **-S** indenter

INDEVOUT *adj* not devout

INDEX *n* pl. **INDEXES** or **INDICES** a type of reference guide at the end of a book

INDEX *v* **-ED, -ING, -ES** to provide with an index

INDEXER *n* pl. **-S** one that indexes

INDEXING *n* pl. **-S** the linking of wages and prices to cost-of-living levels

INDICAN *n* pl. **-S** a chemical compound

INDICANT *n* pl. **-S** something that indicates

INDICATE *v* **-CATED, -CATING, -CATES** to point out

INDICES a pl. of index

INDICIA *n* pl. **-S** a distinctive mark

INDICIUM *n* pl. **-S** an indicia

INDICT *v* **-ED, -ING, -S** to charge with a crime

INDICTEE *n* pl. **-S** one that is indicted

INDICTER *n* pl. **-S** one that indicts

INDICTOR *n* pl. **-S** indicter

INDIE *n* pl. **-S** a person who is independent

INDIGEN *n* pl. **-S** indigene

INDIGENE	*n* pl. **-S** a native
INDIGENT	*n* pl. **-S** a needy person
INDIGN	*adj* disgraceful **INDIGNLY** *adv*
INDIGO	*n* pl. **-GOS** or **-GOES** a blue dye
INDIGOID	*n* pl. **-S** a blue dye
INDIRECT	*adj* not direct
INDITE	*v* **-DITED, -DITING, -DITES** to write or compose
INDITER	*n* pl. **-S** one that indites
INDIUM	*n* pl. **-S** a metallic element
INDOCILE	*adj* not docile
INDOL	*n* pl. **-S** indole
INDOLE	*n* pl. **-S** a chemical compound
INDOLENT	*adj* lazy
INDOOR	*adj* pertaining to the interior of a building
INDOORS	*adv* in or into a house
INDORSE	*v* **-DORSED, -DORSING, -DORSES** to endorse
INDORSEE	*n* pl. **-S** endorsee
INDORSER	*n* pl. **-S** endorser
INDORSING	present participle of indorse
INDORSOR	*n* pl. **-S** endorsor
INDOW	*v* **-ED, -ING, -S** to endow
INDOXYL	*n* pl. **-S** a chemical compound
INDRAFT	*n* pl. **-S** an inward flow or current
INDRAWN	*adj* drawn in
INDRI	*n* pl. **-S** a short-tailed lemur
INDUCE	*v* **-DUCED, -DUCING, -DUCES** to influence into doing something
INDUCER	*n* pl. **-S** one that induces
INDUCT	*v* **-ED, -ING, -S** to bring into military service
INDUCTEE	*n* pl. **-S** one that is inducted
INDUCTOR	*n* pl. **-S** one that inducts
INDUE	*v* **-DUED, -DUING, -DUES** to endue
INDULGE	*v* **-DULGED, -DULGING, -DULGES** to yield to the desire of
INDULGER	*n* pl. **-S** one that indulges
INDULIN	*n* pl. **-S** induline
INDULINE	*n* pl. **-S** a blue dye
INDULT	*n* pl. **-S** a privilege granted by the pope
INDURATE	*v* **-RATED, -RATING, -RATES** to make hard

INDUSIUM	*n* pl. **-SIA** an enclosing membrane **INDUSIAL** *adj*
INDUSTRY	*n* pl. **-TRIES** a group of productive enterprises
INDWELL	*v* **-DWELT, -DWELLING, -DWELLS** to live within
INEARTH	*v* **-ED, -ING, -S** to bury
INEDIBLE	*adj* not fit to be eaten **INEDIBLY** *adv*
INEDITA	*n/pl* unpublished literary works
INEDITED	*adj* not published
INEPT	*adj* not suitable **INEPTLY** *adv*
INEQUITY	*n* pl. **-TIES** unfairness
INERRANT	*adj* free from error
INERT	*n* pl. **-S** something that lacks active properties
INERTIA	*n* pl. **-TIAS** or **-TIAE** the tendency of a body to resist acceleration **INERTIAL** *adj*
INERTLY	*adv* inactively
INEXACT	*adj* not exact
INEXPERT	*n* pl. **-S** a novice
INFALL	*n* pl. **-S** movement under the influence of gravity toward a celestial object
INFAMOUS	*adj* having a vile reputation
INFAMY	*n* pl. **-MIES** the state of being infamous
INFANCY	*n* pl. **-CIES** the state of being an infant
INFANT	*n* pl. **-S** a child in the earliest stages of life
INFANTA	*n* pl. **-S** a daughter of a Spanish or Portuguese monarch
INFANTE	*n* pl. **-S** a younger son of a Spanish or Portuguese monarch
INFANTRY	*n* pl. **-TRIES** a branch of the army composed of foot soldiers
INFARCT	*n* pl. **-S** an area of dead or dying tissue
INFARE	*n* pl. **-S** a reception for newlyweds
INFAUNA	*n* pl. **-NAS** or **-NAE** fauna living on a soft sea floor **INFAUNAL** *adj*
INFECT	*v* **-ED, -ING, -S** to contaminate with disease-producing germs
INFECTER	*n* pl. **-S** one that infects
INFECTOR	*n* pl. **-S** infecter
INFECUND	*adj* barren
INFEOFF	*v* **-ED, -ING, -S** to enfeoff

INFER *v* **-FERRED, -FERRING, -FERS** to reach or derive by reasoning

INFERIOR *n* pl. **-S** one of lesser rank

INFERNAL *adj* pertaining to hell

INFERNO *n* pl. **-NOS** a place that resembles or suggests hell

INFERRED past tense of infer

INFERRER *n* pl. **-S** one that infers

INFERRING present participle of infer

INFEST *v* **-ED, -ING, -S** to overrun in large numbers

INFESTER *n* pl. **-S** one that infests

INFIDEL *n* pl. **-S** one who has no religious faith

INFIELD *n* pl. **-S** a part of a baseball field

INFIGHT *v* **-FOUGHT, -FIGHTING, -FIGHTS** to contend with others within the same group

INFILL *adj* pertaining to the filling in of vacant land

INFINITE *n* pl. **-S** something that has no limits

INFINITY *n* pl. **-TIES** the state of having no limits

INFIRM *v* **-ED, -ING, -S** to weaken or destroy the validity of

INFIRMLY *adv* in a feeble manner

INFIX *v* **-ED, -ING, -ES** to implant

INFIXION *n* pl. **-S** the act of infixing

INFLAME *v* **-FLAMED, -FLAMING, -FLAMES** to set on fire

INFLAMER *n* pl. **-S** one that inflames

INFLATE *v* **-FLATED, -FLATING, -FLATES** to cause to expand by filling with gas or air

INFLATER *n* pl. **-S** one that inflates

INFLATOR *n* pl. **-S** inflater

INFLECT *v* **-ED, -ING, -S** to bend

INFLEXED *adj* bent inward

INFLICT *v* **-ED, -ING, -S** to cause to be endured; impose

INFLIGHT *adj* done during an air voyage

INFLOW *n* pl. **-S** the act of flowing in

INFLUENT *n* pl. **-S** a tributary

INFLUX *n* pl. **-ES** a flowing in

INFO *n* pl. **-FOS** information

INFOBAHN *n* pl. **-S** an electronic communications network

INFOLD *v* **-ED, -ING, -S** to fold inward

INFOLDER *n* pl. **-S** one that infolds

INFORM *v* **-ED, -ING, -S** to supply with information

INFORMAL *adj* marked by the absence of formality or ceremony

INFORMER *n* pl. **-S** one that informs

INFOUGHT past tense of infight

INFRA *adv* below

INFRACT *v* **-ED, -ING, -S** to break a legal rule

INFRARED *n* pl. **-S** a part of the invisible spectrum

INFRINGE *v* **-FRINGED, -FRINGING, -FRINGES** to violate an oath or a law

INFRUGAL *adj* not frugal

INFUSE *v* **-FUSED, -FUSING, -FUSES** to permeate with something

INFUSER *n* pl. **-S** one that infuses

INFUSION *n* pl. **-S** the act of infusing

INFUSIVE *adj* capable of infusing

INGATE *n* pl. **-S** a channel by which molten metal enters a mold

INGATHER *v* **-ED, -ING, -S** to gather in

INGENUE *n* pl. **-S** a naive young woman

INGEST *v* **-ED, -ING, -S** to take into the body

INGESTA *n/pl* ingested material

INGLE *n* pl. **-S** a fire

INGOING *adj* entering

INGOT *v* **-ED, -ING, -S** to shape into a convenient form for storage

INGRAFT *v* **-ED, -ING, -S** to engraft

INGRAIN *v* **-ED, -ING, -S** to impress firmly on the mind

INGRATE *n* pl. **-S** an ungrateful person

INGRESS *n* pl. **-ES** the act of entering

INGROUND *adj* built into the ground

INGROUP *n* pl. **-S** a group with which one feels a sense of solidarity

INGROWN *adj* grown into the flesh

INGROWTH *n* pl. **-S** growth inward

INGUINAL *adj* pertaining to the groin

INGULF *v* **-ED, -ING, -S** to engulf

INHABIT *v* **-ED, -ING, -S** to live in

INHALANT *n* pl. **-S** something that is inhaled

INHALE *v* **-HALED, -HALING, -HALES** to take into the lungs

INHALER *n* pl. **-S** one that inhales

INHAUL *n* pl. **-S** a line for bringing in a sail

INHAULER *n* pl. **-S** an inhaul

INHERE *v* **-HERED, -HERING, -HERES** to be inherent

INHERENT *adj* existing in something as an essential characteristic

INHERIT *v* **-ED, -ING, -S** to receive by legal succession

INHESION *n* pl. **-S** the state of inhering

INHIBIN *n* pl. **-S** a human hormone

INHIBIT *v* **-ED, -ING, -S** to restrain or hold back

INHOLDER *n* pl. **-S** one that owns a tract of land within a national park

INHUMAN *adj* lacking desirable human qualities

INHUMANE *adj* not humane

INHUME *v* **-HUMED, -HUMING, -HUMES** to bury

INHUMER *n* pl. **-S** one that inhumes

INIMICAL *adj* unfriendly

INION *n* pl. **INIA** a part of the skull

INIQUITY *n* pl. **-TIES** a gross injustice

INITIAL *v* **-TIALED, -TIALING, -TIALS** or **-TIALLED, -TIALLING, -TIALS** to mark with the first letters of one's name

INITIATE *v* **-ATED, -ATING, -ATES** to originate

INJECT *v* **-ED, -ING, -S** to force a fluid into

INJECTOR *n* pl. **-S** one that injects

INJURE *v* **-JURED, -JURING, -JURES** to do or cause injury to

INJURER *n* pl. **-S** one that injures

INJURY *n* pl. **-RIES** harm inflicted or suffered

INK *v* **-ED, -ING, -S** to mark with ink (a colored fluid used for writing)

INKBERRY *n* pl. **-RIES** a small shrub

INKBLOT *n* pl. **-S** a blotted pattern of spilled ink

INKER *n* pl. **-S** one that inks

INKHORN *n* pl. **-S** a small container for ink

INKIER comparative of inky

INKIEST superlative of inky

INKINESS *n* pl. **-ES** the state of being inky

INKJET *adj* being a high-speed printing process using jets of ink

INKLE *n* pl. **-S** a tape used for trimming

INKLESS *adj* being without ink

INKLIKE *adj* resembling ink

INKLING *n* pl. **-S** a slight suggestion

INKPOT *n* pl. **-S** an inkwell

INKSTAND *n* pl. **-S** an inkwell

INKSTONE *n* pl. **-S** a stone on which dry ink and water are mixed

INKWELL *n* pl. **-S** a small container for ink

INKWOOD *n* pl. **-S** an evergreen tree

INKY *adj* **INKIER, INKIEST** resembling ink

INLACE *v* **-LACED, -LACING, -LACES** to enlace

INLAID past tense of inlay

INLAND *n* pl. **-S** the interior of a region

INLANDER *n* pl. **-S** one living in the interior of a region

INLAY *v* **-LAID, -LAYING, -LAYS** to set into a surface

INLAYER *n* pl. **-S** one that inlays

INLET *v* **-LET, -LETTING, -LETS** to insert

INLIER *n* pl. **-S** a type of rock formation

INLY *adv* inwardly

INLYING *adj* located farther in

INMATE *n* pl. **-S** one who is confined to an institution

INMESH *v* **-ED, -ING, -ES** to enmesh

INMOST *adj* farthest within

INN *v* **-ED, -ING, -S** to put up at an inn (a public lodging house)

INNAGE *n* pl. **-S** the quantity of goods remaining in a container after shipment

INNARDS *n/pl* the internal organs

INNATE *adj* inborn **INNATELY** *adv*

INNED past tense of in

INNER *n* pl. **-S** something that is within

INNERLY *adv* inwardly

INNERVE *v* **-NERVED, -NERVING, -NERVES** to stimulate

INNING *n* pl. **-S** a division of a baseball game

INNLESS *adj* having no inns

INNOCENT *adj* **-CENTER, -CENTEST** free from guilt or sin

INNOCENT *n* pl. **-S** an innocent person

INNOVATE   *v* **-VATED, -VATING, -VATES** to introduce something new

INNUENDO   *v* **-ED, -ING, -S** or **-ES** to make a derogatory implication

INOCULUM   *n* pl. **-LUMS** or **-LA** the material used in an inoculation

INOSINE   *n* pl. **-S** a compound of hypoxanthine and ribose

INOSITE   *n* pl. **-S** inositol

INOSITOL   *n* pl. **-S** an alcohol found in plant and animal tissue

INPHASE   *adj* having matching electrical phases

INPOUR   *v* **-ED, -ING, -S** to pour in

INPUT   *v* **-PUTTED, -PUTTING, -PUTS** to enter data into a computer

INPUTTER   *n* pl. **-S** one that inputs

INQUEST   *n* pl. **-S** a legal inquiry

INQUIET   *v* **-ED, -ING, -S** to disturb

INQUIRE   *v* **-QUIRED, -QUIRING, -QUIRES** to ask about

INQUIRER   *n* pl. **-S** one that inquires

INQUIRY   *n* pl. **-RIES** a question

INRO   *n* pl. **INRO** a Japanese ornamental container

INROAD   *n* pl. **-S** a hostile invasion

INRUN   *n* pl. **-S** the approach ramp of a ski jump

INRUSH   *n* pl. **-ES** a rushing in

INSANE   *adj* **-SANER, -SANEST** mentally unsound **INSANELY** *adv*

INSANITY   *n* pl. **-TIES** the state of being insane; something utterly foolish

INSCAPE   *n* pl. **-S** the inner essential quality of something

INSCRIBE   *v* **-SCRIBED, -SCRIBING, -SCRIBES** to write or engrave as a lasting record

INSCROLL   *v* **-ED, -ING, -S** to enscroll

INSCULP   *v* **-ED, -ING, -S** to engrave

INSEAM   *n* pl. **-S** an inner seam

INSECT   *n* pl. **-S** any of a class of small invertebrate animals

INSECTAN   *adj* pertaining to insects

INSECURE   *adj* unsafe

INSERT   *v* **-ED, -ING, -S** to put in

INSERTER   *n* pl. **-S** one that inserts

INSET   *v* **-SETTED, -SETTING, -SETS** to insert

INSETTER   *n* pl. **-S** one that inserts

INSHEATH   *v* **-ED, -ING, -S** to ensheath

INSHORE   *adj* near the shore

INSHRINE   *v* **-SHRINED, -SHRINING, -SHRINES** to enshrine

INSIDE   *n* pl. **-S** something that lies within

INSIDER   *n* pl. **-S** an accepted member of a clique

INSIGHT   *n* pl. **-S** a perception of the inner nature of things

INSIGNE   *n* pl. **INSIGNIA** an insignia

INSIGNIA   *n* pl. **-S** an emblem of authority or honor

INSIPID   *adj* dull and uninteresting

INSIST   *v* **-ED, -ING, -S** to be resolute on some matter

INSISTER   *n* pl. **-S** one that insists

INSNARE   *v* **-SNARED, -SNARING, -SNARES** to ensnare

INSNARER   *n* pl. **-S** ensnarer

INSOFAR   *adv* to such an extent

INSOLATE   *v* **-LATED, -LATING, -LATES** to expose to sunlight

INSOLE   *n* pl. **-S** the inner sole of a boot or shoe

INSOLENT   *n* pl. **-S** an extremely rude person

INSOMNIA   *n* pl. **-S** chronic inability to sleep

INSOMUCH   *adv* to such a degree

INSOUL   *v* **-ED, -ING, -S** to ensoul

INSPAN   *v* **-SPANNED, -SPANNING, -SPANS** to harness or yoke to a vehicle

INSPECT   *v* **-ED, -ING, -S** to look carefully at or over

INSPHERE   *v* **-SPHERED, -SPHERING, -SPHERES** to ensphere

INSPIRE   *v* **-SPIRED, -SPIRING, -SPIRES** to animate the mind or emotions of

INSPIRER   *n* pl. **-S** one that inspires

INSPIRIT   *v* **-ED, -ING, -S** to fill with spirit or life

INSTABLE   *adj* unstable

INSTAL   *v* **-STALLED, -STALLING, -STALS** to install

INSTALL   *v* **-ED, -ING, -S** to place in position for use

INSTANCE   *v* **-STANCED, -STANCING, -STANCES** to cite as an example

INSTANCY   *n* pl. **-CIES** urgency

INSTANT   *n* pl. **-S** a very short time

INSTAR *v* **-STARRED, -STARRING, -STARS** to adorn with stars

INSTATE *v* **-STATED, -STATING, -STATES** to place in office

INSTEAD *adv* as a substitute or equivalent

INSTEP *n* pl. **-S** a part of the foot

INSTIL *v* **-STILLED, -STILLING, -STILS** to instill

INSTILL *v* **-ED, -ING, -S** to infuse slowly

INSTINCT *n* pl. **-S** an inborn behavioral pattern

INSTROKE *n* pl. **-S** an inward stroke

INSTRUCT *v* **-ED, -ING, -S** to supply with knowledge

INSULANT *n* pl. **-S** an insulating material

INSULAR *n* pl. **-S** an islander

INSULATE *v* **-LATED, -LATING, -LATES** to separate with nonconducting material

INSULIN *n* pl. **-S** a hormone

INSULT *v* **-ED, -ING, -S** to treat offensively

INSULTER *n* pl. **-S** one that insults

INSURANT *n* pl. **-S** one who is insured

INSURE *v* **-SURED, -SURING, -SURES** to guarantee against loss

INSURED *n* pl. **-S** one who is insured

INSURER *n* pl. **-S** one that insures

INSURING present participle of insure

INSWATHE *v* **-SWATHED, -SWATHING, -SWATHES** to enswathe

INSWEPT *adj* narrowed in front

INTACT *adj* not damaged in any way **INTACTLY** *adv*

INTAGLIO *n* pl. **-GLIOS** or **-GLI** an incised or sunken design

INTAGLIO *v* **-ED, -ING, -S** to engrave in intaglio

INTAKE *n* pl. **-S** the act of taking in

INTARSIA *n* pl. **-S** a decorative technique

INTEGER *n* pl. **-S** a whole number

INTEGRAL *n* pl. **-S** a total unit

INTEND *v* **-ED, -ING, -S** to have as a specific aim or purpose

INTENDED *n* pl. **-S** one's spouse to-be

INTENDER *n* pl. **-S** one that intends

INTENSE *adj* **-TENSER, -TENSEST** existing in an extreme degree

INTENT *n* pl. **-S** a purpose

INTENTLY *adv* in an unwavering manner

INTER *v* **-TERRED, -TERRING, -TERS** to bury

INTERACT *v* **-ED, -ING, -S** to act on each other

INTERAGE *adj* including persons of various ages

INTERBED *v* **-BEDDED, -BEDDING, -BEDS** to insert between other layers

INTERCOM *n* pl. **-S** a type of communication system

INTERCUT *v* **-CUT, -CUTTING, -CUTS** to alternate camera shots

INTEREST *v* **-ED, -ING, -S** to engage the attention of

INTERIM *n* pl. **-S** an interval

INTERIOR *n* pl. **-S** the inside

INTERLAP *v* **-LAPPED, -LAPPING, -LAPS** to lap one over another

INTERLAY *v* **-LAID, -LAYING, -LAYS** to place between

INTERMAT *v* **-MATTED, -MATTING, -MATS** to mat fibers together

INTERMIT *v* **-MITTED, -MITTING, -MITS** to stop temporarily

INTERMIX *v* **-ED, -ING, -ES** to mix together

INTERN *v* **-ED, -ING, -S** to confine during a war

INTERNAL *n* pl. **-S** an inner attribute

INTERNE *n* pl. **-S** a recent medical school graduate on a hospital staff

INTERNEE *n* pl. **-S** one who has been interned

INTERRED past tense of inter

INTERREX *n* pl. **-REGES** a type of sovereign

INTERRING present participle of inter

INTERROW *adj* existing between rows

INTERSEX *n* pl. **-ES** a person having characteristics of both sexes

INTERTIE *n* pl. **-S** a type of electrical connection

INTERVAL *n* pl. **-S** a space of time between periods or events

INTERWAR *adj* happening between wars

INTHRAL *v* **-THRALLED, -THRALLING, -THRALS** to enthrall

INTHRALL *v* **-ED, -ING, -S** to enthrall

INTHRONE *v* **-THRONED, -THRONING, -THRONES** to enthrone

INTI *n* pl. **-S** a monetary unit of Peru

INTIFADA *n* pl. **-S** an uprising of Palestinians against Israelis

INTIMA *n* pl. **-MAS** or **-MAE** the innermost layer of an organ **INTIMAL** *adj*

INTIMACY *n* pl. **-CIES** the state of being closely associated

INTIMATE *v* **-MATED, -MATING, -MATES** to make known indirectly

INTIME *adj* cozy

INTIMIST *n* pl. **-S** a writer or artist who deals with deep personal experiences

INTINE *n* pl. **-S** the inner wall of a spore

INTITLE *v* **-TLED, -TLING, -TLES** to entitle

INTITULE *v* **-ULED, -ULING, -ULES** to entitle

INTO *prep* to the inside of

INTOMB *v* **-ED, -ING, -S** to entomb

INTONATE *v* **-NATED, -NATING, -NATES** to intone

INTONE *v* **-TONED, -TONING, -TONES** to speak in a singing voice

INTONER *n* pl. **-S** one that intones

INTORT *v* **-ED, -ING, -S** to twist inward

INTOWN *adj* located in the center of a city

INTRADAY *adj* occurring within a single day

INTRADOS *n* pl. **-ES** the inner curve of an arch

INTRANET *n* pl. **-S** a computer network with restricted access

INTRANT *n* pl. **-S** an entrant

INTREAT *v* **-ED, -ING, -S** to entreat

INTRENCH *v* **-ED, -ING, -ES** to entrench

INTREPID *adj* fearless

INTRIGUE *v* **-TRIGUED, -TRIGUING, -TRIGUES** to arouse the curiosity of

INTRO *n* pl. **-TROS** an introduction

INTROFY *v* **-FIED, -FYING, -FIES** to increase the wetting properties of

INTROIT *n* pl. **-S** music sung at the beginning of a worship service

INTROMIT *v* **-MITTED, -MITTING, -MITS** to put in

INTRON *n* pl. **-S** an intervening sequence in the genetic code

INTRORSE *adj* facing inward

INTRUDE *v* **-TRUDED, -TRUDING, -TRUDES** to thrust or force oneself in

INTRUDER *n* pl. **-S** one that intrudes

INTRUST *v* **-ED, -ING, -S** to entrust

INTUBATE *v* **-BATED, -BATING, -BATES** to insert a tube into

INTUIT *v* **-ED, -ING, -S** to know without conscious reasoning

INTURN *n* pl. **-S** a turning inward **INTURNED** *adj*

INTWINE *v* **-TWINED, -TWINING, -TWINES** to entwine

INTWIST *v* **-ED, -ING, -S** to entwist

INULASE *n* pl. **-S** an enzyme

INULIN *n* pl. **-S** a chemical compound

INUNDANT *adj* inundating

INUNDATE *v* **-DATED, -DATING, -DATES** to overwhelm with water

INURBANE *adj* not urbane

INURE *v* **-URED, -URING, -URES** to accustom to accept something undesirable

INURN *v* **-ED, -ING, -S** to put in an urn

INUTILE *adj* useless

INVADE *v* **-VADED, -VADING, -VADES** to enter for conquest or plunder

INVADER *n* pl. **-S** one that invades

INVALID *v* **-ED, -ING, -S** to disable physically

INVAR *n* pl. **-S** an iron-nickel alloy

INVASION *n* pl. **-S** the act of invading **INVASIVE** *adj*

INVECTED *adj* edged by convex curves

INVEIGH *v* **-ED, -ING, -S** to protest angrily

INVEIGLE *v* **-GLED, -GLING, -GLES** to induce by guile or flattery

INVENT *v* **-ED, -ING, -S** to devise originally

INVENTER *n* pl. **-S** inventor

INVENTOR *n* pl. **-S** one that invents

INVERITY *n* pl. **-TIES** lack of truth

INVERSE *v* **-VERSED, -VERSING, -VERSES** to reverse

INVERT *v* **-ED, -ING, -S** to turn upside down

INVERTER *n* pl. **-S** one that inverts

INVERTIN *n* pl. **-S** an enzyme

INVERTOR *n* pl. **-S** a type of electrical device

INVEST *v* **-ED, -ING, -S** to commit something of value for future profit

INVESTOR *n* pl. **-S** one that invests

INVIABLE *adj* not viable **INVIABLY** *adv*

INVIRILE *adj* not virile

INVISCID *adj* not viscid

INVITAL	*adj* not vital
INVITE	*v* **-VITED, -VITING, -VITES** to request the presence of
INVITEE	*n* pl. **-S** one that is invited
INVITER	*n* pl. **-S** one that invites
INVITING	present participle of invite
INVOCATE	*v* **-CATED, -CATING, -CATES** to invoke
INVOICE	*v* **-VOICED, -VOICING, -VOICES** to bill
INVOKE	*v* **-VOKED, -VOKING, -VOKES** to appeal to for aid
INVOKER	*n* pl. **-S** one that invokes
INVOLUTE	*v* **-LUTED, -LUTING, -LUTES** to roll or curl up
INVOLVE	*v* **-VOLVED, -VOLVING, -VOLVES** to contain or include as a part
INVOLVER	*n* pl. **-S** one that involves
INWALL	*v* **-ED, -ING, -S** to surround with a wall
INWARD	*adv* toward the inside
INWARDLY	*adv* on the inside
INWARDS	*adv* inward
INWEAVE	*v* **-WOVE** or **-WEAVED, -WOVEN, -WEAVING, -WEAVES** to weave together
INWIND	*v* **-WOUND, -WINDING, -WINDS** to enwind
INWRAP	*v* **-WRAPPED, -WRAPPING, -WRAPS** to enwrap
IODATE	*v* **-DATED, -DATING, -DATES** to iodize
IODATION	*n* pl. **-S** the act of iodating
IODIC	*adj* pertaining to iodine
IODID	*n* pl. **-S** iodide
IODIDE	*n* pl. **-S** a compound of iodine
IODIN	*n* pl. **-S** iodine
IODINATE	*v* **-ATED, -ATING, -ATES** to iodize
IODINE	*n* pl. **-S** a nonmetallic element
IODISE	*v* **-DISED, -DISING, -DISES** to iodize
IODISM	*n* pl. **-S** iodine poisoning
IODIZE	*v* **-DIZED, -DIZING, -DIZES** to treat with iodine
IODIZER	*n* pl. **-S** one that iodizes
IODOFORM	*n* pl. **-S** an iodine compound
IODOPHOR	*n* pl. **-S** an iodine compound
IODOPSIN	*n* pl. **-S** a pigment in the retina
IODOUS	*adj* pertaining to iodine
IOLITE	*n* pl. **-S** a mineral
ION	*n* pl. **-S** an electrically charged atom
IONIC	*n* pl. **-S** a style of type
IONICITY	*n* pl. **-TIES** the state of existing as or like an ion
IONISE	*v* **-ISED, -ISING, -ISES** to ionize
IONIUM	*n* pl. **-S** an isotope of thorium
IONIZE	*v* **-IZED, -IZING, -IZES** to convert into ions
IONIZER	*n* pl. **-S** one that ionizes
IONOGEN	*n* pl. **-S** a compound capable of forming ions
IONOMER	*n* pl. **-S** a type of plastic
IONONE	*n* pl. **-S** a chemical compound
IOTA	*n* pl. **-S** a Greek letter
IOTACISM	*n* pl. **-S** excessive use of the letter iota
IPECAC	*n* pl. **-S** a medicinal plant
IPOMOEA	*n* pl. **-S** a flowering plant
IRACUND	*adj* easily angered
IRADE	*n* pl. **-S** a decree of a Muslim ruler
IRATE	*adj* **IRATER, IRATEST** angry **IRATELY** *adv*
IRE	*v* **IRED, IRING, IRES** to anger
IREFUL	*adj* angry **IREFULLY** *adv*
IRELESS	*adj* not angry
IRENIC	*adj* peaceful in purpose
IRENICAL	*adj* irenic
IRENICS	*n/pl* a branch of theology
IRID	*n* pl. **-S** a plant of the iris family
IRIDES	a pl. of iris
IRIDIC	*adj* pertaining to iridium
IRIDIUM	*n* pl. **-S** a metallic element
IRING	present participle of ire
IRIS	*n* pl. **IRISES** or **IRIDES** a part of the eye
IRIS	*v* **-ED, -ING, -ES** to give the form of a rainbow to
IRITIS	*n* pl. **-TISES** inflammation of the iris **IRITIC** *adj*
IRK	*v* **-ED, -ING, -S** to annoy or weary
IRKSOME	*adj* tending to irk
IROKO	*n* pl. **-KOS** a large African tree
IRON	*v* **-ED, -ING, -S** to furnish with iron (a metallic element)
IRONBARK	*n* pl. **-S** a timber tree

IRONCLAD	*n* pl. **-S** an armored warship
IRONE	*n* pl. **-S** an aromatic oil
IRONER	*n* pl. **-S** a machine for pressing clothes
IRONIC	*adj* pertaining to irony
IRONICAL	*adj* ironic
IRONIES	pl. of irony
IRONING	*n* pl. **-S** clothes pressed or to be pressed
IRONIST	*n* pl. **-S** one who uses irony
IRONIZE	*v* **-NIZED, -NIZING, -NIZES** to mix with nutritional iron
IRONLIKE	*adj* resembling iron
IRONMAN	*n* pl. **-MEN** a man of great strength and stamina
IRONNESS	*n* pl. **-ES** the state of being iron
IRONSIDE	*n* pl. **-S** a man of great strength
IRONWARE	*n* pl. **-S** articles made of iron
IRONWEED	*n* pl. **-S** a shrub
IRONWOOD	*n* pl. **-S** a hardwood tree
IRONWORK	*n* pl. **-S** objects made of iron
IRONY	*n* pl. **-NIES** the use of words to express the opposite of what is literally said
IRREAL	*adj* not real
IRRIGATE	*v* **-GATED, -GATING, -GATES** to supply with water by artificial means
IRRITANT	*n* pl. **-S** something that irritates
IRRITATE	*v* **-TATED, -TATING, -TATES** to excite to impatience or anger
IRRUPT	*v* **-ED, -ING, -S** to rush in forcibly
IS	present 3d person sing. of be
ISAGOGE	*n* pl. **-S** a type of introduction to a branch of study
ISAGOGIC	*n* pl. **-S** a branch of theology
ISARITHM	*n* pl. **-S** an isopleth
ISATIN	*n* pl. **-S** a chemical compound **ISATINIC** *adj*
ISATINE	*n* pl. **-S** isatin
ISBA	*n* pl. **-S** a Russian log hut
ISCHEMIA	*n* pl. **-S** a type of anemia **ISCHEMIC** *adj*
ISCHIUM	*n* pl. **-CHIA** a pelvic bone **ISCHIAL** *adj*
ISLAND	*v* **-ED, -ING, -S** to make into an island (a land area entirely surrounded by water)
ISLANDER	*n* pl. **-S** one that lives on an island
ISLE	*v* **ISLED, ISLING, ISLES** to place on an isle (a small island)
ISLELESS	*adj* lacking an isle
ISLET	*n* pl. **-S** a small island **ISLETED** *adj*
ISM	*n* pl. **-S** a distinctive theory or doctrine
ISOBAR	*n* pl. **-S** a type of atom **ISOBARIC** *adj*
ISOBARE	*n* pl. **-S** isobar
ISOBATH	*n* pl. **-S** a line on a map connecting points of equal water depth
ISOBUTYL	*n* pl. **-S** a hydrocarbon radical
ISOCHEIM	*n* pl. **-S** a type of isotherm
ISOCHIME	*n* pl. **-S** isocheim
ISOCHOR	*n* pl. **-S** isochore
ISOCHORE	*n* pl. **-S** a curve used to show a relationship between pressure and temperature
ISOCHRON	*n* pl. **-S** a line on a chart connecting points representing the same time
ISOCLINE	*n* pl. **-S** a type of rock formation
ISOCRACY	*n* pl. **-CIES** a form of government
ISODOSE	*adj* pertaining to zones that receive equal doses of radiation
ISOFORM	*n* pl. **-S** one of two or more proteins having a similar form
ISOGAMY	*n* pl. **-MIES** the fusion of two similar gametes
ISOGENIC	*adj* genetically similar
ISOGENY	*n* pl. **-NIES** the state of being of similar origin
ISOGLOSS	*n* pl. **-ES** a line on a map between linguistically varied areas
ISOGON	*n* pl. **-S** a polygon having equal angles
ISOGONAL	*n* pl. **-S** isogone
ISOGONE	*n* pl. **-S** a line on a map used to show characteristics of the earth's magnetic field
ISOGONIC	*n* pl. **-S** isogone
ISOGONY	*n* pl. **-NIES** an equivalent relative growth of parts
ISOGRAFT	*v* **-ED, -ING, -S** to transplant from one individual to another of the same species
ISOGRAM	*n* pl. **-S** a line on a map connecting points of equal value

ISOGRAPH *n* pl. **-S** a line on a map indicating areas that are linguistically similar

ISOGRIV *n* pl. **-S** a line drawn on a map such that all points have equal grid variation

ISOHEL *n* pl. **-S** a line on a map connecting points receiving equal sunshine

ISOHYET *n* pl. **-S** a line on a map connecting points having equal rainfall

ISOLABLE *adj* capable of being isolated

ISOLATE *v* **-LATED, -LATING, -LATES** to set apart from others

ISOLATOR *n* pl. **-S** one that isolates

ISOLEAD *n* pl. **-S** a line on a ballistic graph

ISOLINE *n* pl. **-S** an isogram

ISOLOG *n* pl. **-S** isologue

ISOLOGUE *n* pl. **-S** a type of chemical compound

ISOMER *n* pl. **-S** a type of chemical compound **ISOMERIC** *adj*

ISOMETRY *n* pl. **-TRIES** equality of measure

ISOMORPH *n* pl. **-S** something similar to something else in form

ISONOMY *n* pl. **-MIES** equality of civil rights **ISONOMIC** *adj*

ISOPACH *n* pl. **-S** an isogram connecting points of equal thickness

ISOPHOTE *n* pl. **-S** a curve on a chart joining points of equal light intensity

ISOPLETH *n* pl. **-S** a type of isogram

ISOPOD *n* pl. **-S** a kind of crustacean

ISOPODAN *n* pl. **-S** an isopod

ISOPRENE *n* pl. **-S** a volatile liquid

ISOSPIN *n* pl. **-S** a type of quantum number

ISOSPORY *n* pl. **-RIES** the condition of producing sexual or asexual spores of but one kind

ISOSTACY *n* pl. **-CIES** isostasy

ISOSTASY *n* pl. **-SIES** the state of balance in the earth's crust

ISOTACH *n* pl. **-S** a line on a map connecting points of equal wind velocity

ISOTHERE *n* pl. **-S** a type of isotherm

ISOTHERM *n* pl. **-S** a line on a map connecting points of equal mean temperature

ISOTONE *n* pl. **-S** a type of atom

ISOTONIC *adj* of equal tension

ISOTOPE *n* pl. **-S** a form of an element **ISOTOPIC** *adj*

ISOTOPY *n* pl. **-PIES** the state of being an isotope

ISOTROPY *n* pl. **-PIES** the state of being identical in all directions

ISOTYPE *n* pl. **-S** a type of diagram **ISOTYPIC** *adj*

ISOZYME *n* pl. **-S** a type of enzyme **ISOZYMIC** *adj*

ISSEI *n* pl. **-S** a Japanese immigrant to the United States

ISSUABLE *adj* authorized for issuing **ISSUABLY** *adv*

ISSUANCE *n* pl. **-S** the act of issuing

ISSUANT *adj* coming forth

ISSUE *v* **-SUED, -SUING, -SUES** to come forth

ISSUER *n* pl. **-S** one that issues

ISTHMI a pl. of isthmus

ISTHMIAN *n* pl. **-S** a native of an isthmus

ISTHMIC *adj* pertaining to an isthmus

ISTHMOID *adj* isthmic

ISTHMUS *n* pl. **-MUSES** or **-MI** a strip of land connecting two larger land masses

ISTLE *n* pl. **-S** a strong fiber

IT *pron* the 3d person sing. neuter pronoun

ITALIC *n* pl. **-S** a style of print

ITCH *v* **-ED, -ING, -ES** to have an uneasy or tingling skin sensation

ITCHING *n* pl. **-S** an uneasy or tingling skin sensation

ITCHY *adj* **ITCHIER, ITCHIEST** causing an itching sensation **ITCHILY** *adv*

ITEM *v* **-ED, -ING, -S** to itemize

ITEMISE *v* **-ISED, -ISING, -ISES** to itemize

ITEMIZE *v* **-IZED, -IZING, -IZES** to set down the particulars of

ITEMIZER *n* pl. **-S** one that itemizes

ITERANCE *n* pl. **-S** repetition

ITERANT *adj* repeating

ITERATE *v* **-ATED, -ATING, -ATES** to repeat

ITERUM *adv* again; once more

ITHER *adj* other

ITS *pron* the possessive form of the pronoun it

ITSELF *pron* a reflexive form of the pronoun it

IVIED *adj* covered with ivy

IVORY   *n* pl. **-RIES** a hard white substance found in elephant tusks

IVY   *n* pl. **IVIES** a climbing vine **IVYLIKE** *adj*

IWIS   *adv* certainly

IXIA   *n* pl. **-S** a flowering plant

IXODID   *n* pl. **-S** a bloodsucking insect

IXORA   *n* pl. **-S** a flowering plant

IXTLE   *n* pl. **-S** istle

IZAR   *n* pl. **-S** an outer garment worn by Muslim women

IZZARD   *n* pl. **-S** the letter Z

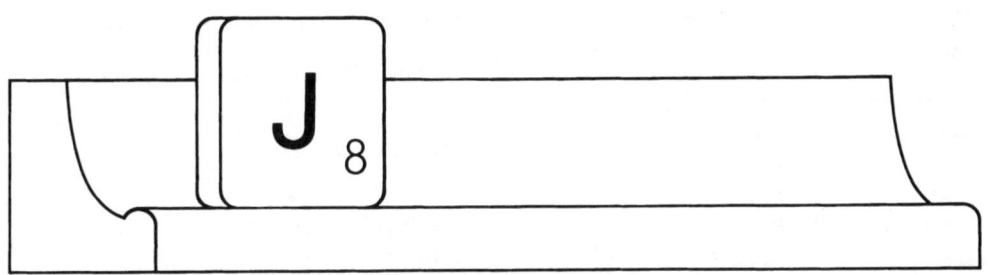

JAB   *v* **JABBED, JABBING, JABS** to poke sharply

JABBER   *v* **-ED, -ING, -S** to talk rapidly

JABBERER   *n* pl. **-S** one that jabbers

JABIRU   *n* pl. **-S** a wading bird

JABOT   *n* pl. **-S** a decoration on a shirt

JACAL   *n* pl. **-S** or **-ES** a hut

JACAMAR   *n* pl. **-S** a tropical bird

JACANA   *n* pl. **-S** a wading bird

JACINTH   *n* pl. **-S** a variety of zircon

JACINTHE   *n* pl. **-S** an orange color

JACK   *v* **-ED, -ING, -S** to raise with a type of lever

JACKAL   *n* pl. **-S** a doglike mammal

JACKAROO   *n* pl. **-ROOS** jackeroo

JACKASS   *n* pl. **-ES** a male donkey

JACKBOOT   *n* pl. **-S** a heavy boot

JACKDAW   *n* pl. **-S** a crowlike bird

JACKER   *n* pl. **-S** one that jacks

JACKEROO   *n* pl. **-ROOS** an inexperienced ranch hand

JACKET   *v* **-ED, -ING, -S** to provide with a jacket (a short coat)

JACKFISH   *n* pl. **-ES** a food fish

JACKIES   pl. of jacky

JACKLEG   *n* pl. **-S** an unskilled worker

JACKPOT   *n* pl. **-S** a top prize or reward

JACKROLL   *v* **-ED, -ING, -S** to rob a drunken or sleeping person

JACKSTAY   *n* pl. **-STAYS** a rope on a ship

JACKY   *n* pl. **JACKIES** a sailor

JACOBIN   *n* pl. **-S** a pigeon

JACOBUS   *n* pl. **-ES** an old English coin

JACONET   *n* pl. **-S** a cotton cloth

JACQUARD   *n* pl. **-S** a fabric of intricate weave

JACULATE   *v* **-LATED, -LATING, -LATES** to throw

JADE   *v* **JADED, JADING, JADES** to weary **JADEDLY** *adv*

JADEITE   *n* pl. **-S** a mineral **JADITIC** *adj*

JADELIKE   *adj* resembling jade (a green gemstone)

JADISH   *adj* worn-out **JADISHLY** *adv*

JAEGER   *n* pl. **-S** a hunter

JAG   *v* **JAGGED, JAGGING, JAGS** to cut unevenly

JAGER   *n* pl. **-S** jaeger

JAGG   *v* **-ED, -ING, -S** to jag

JAGGARY   *n* pl. **-RIES** jaggery

JAGGED   *adj* **-GEDER, -GEDEST** having a sharply uneven edge or surface **JAGGEDLY** *adv*

JAGGER   *n* pl. **-S** one that jags

JAGGERY   *n* pl. **-GERIES** a coarse, dark sugar

JAGGHERY   *n* pl. **-GHERIES** jaggery

JAGGIES   *n/pl* a jagged effect on a curved line

JAGGING   present participle of jag

JAGGY   *adj* **-GIER, -GIEST** jagged

JAGLESS   *adj* smooth and even

JAGRA   *n* pl. **-S** jaggery

JAGUAR   *n* pl. **-S** a large feline animal

JAIL   *v* **-ED, -ING, -S** to put in jail (a place of confinement) **JAILABLE** *adj*

JAILBAIT   *n* pl. **JAILBAIT** a girl under the age of consent with whom sexual intercourse constitutes statutory rape

JAILBIRD   *n* pl. **-S** a prisoner

JAILER   *n* pl. **-S** a keeper of a jail

JAILOR   *n* pl. **-S** jailer

JAKE   *adj* all right; fine

JAKES   *n/pl* an outhouse

JALAP   *n* pl. **-S** a Mexican plant **JALAPIC** *adj*

JALAPENO   *n* pl. **-NOS** a hot pepper

JALAPIN   *n* pl. **-S** a medicinal substance contained in jalap

JALOP   *n* pl. **-S** jalap

JALOPPY   *n* pl. **-PIES** jalopy

JALOPY   *n* pl. **-LOPIES** a decrepit car

JALOUSIE   *n* pl. **-S** a type of window

JAM   *v* **JAMMED, JAMMING, JAMS** to force together tightly **JAMMABLE** *adj*

JAMB   *v* **-ED, -ING, -S** to jam

JAMBE   *n* pl. **-S** a jambeau

JAMBEAU   *n* pl. **-BEAUX** a piece of armor for the leg

JAMBOREE   *n* pl. **-S** a noisy celebration

JAMLIKE   *adj* resembling jam

JAMMED   past tense of jam

JAMMER   *n* pl. **-S** one that jams

JAMMIES   *n/pl* pajamas

JAMMING   present participle of jam

JAMMY   *adj* **-MIER, -MIEST** sticky with jam (boiled fruit and sugar)

JANE   *n* pl. **-S** a girl or woman

JANGLE   *v* **-GLED, -GLING, -GLES** to make a harsh, metallic sound

JANGLER   *n* pl. **-S** one that jangles

JANGLY   *adj* **-GLIER, -GLIEST** jangling

JANIFORM   *adj* hypocritical

JANISARY   *n* pl. **-SARIES** janizary

JANITOR   *n* pl. **-S** a maintenance man

JANIZARY   *n* pl. **-ZARIES** a Turkish soldier

JANTY   *adj* jaunty

JAPAN   *v* **-PANNED, -PANNING, -PANS** to coat with a glossy, black lacquer

JAPANIZE   *v* **-NIZED, -NIZING, -NIZES** to make Japanese

JAPANNER   *n* pl. **-S** one that japans

JAPE   *v* **JAPED, JAPING, JAPES** to mock

JAPER   *n* pl. **-S** one that japes

JAPERY   *n* pl. **-ERIES** mockery

JAPING   present participle of jape

JAPINGLY   *adv* in a japing manner

JAPONICA   *n* pl. **-S** an Asian shrub

JAR   *v* **JARRED, JARRING, JARS** to cause to shake

JARFUL   *n* pl. **JARFULS** or **JARSFUL** the quantity held by a jar (a cylindrical container)

JARGON   *v* **-ED, -ING, -S** to speak or write an obscure and often pretentious kind of language

JARGONEL   *n* pl. **-S** a variety of pear

JARGONY   *adj* characterized by the use of obscure language

JARGOON   *n* pl. **-S** a variety of zircon

JARHEAD   *n* pl. **-S** a marine soldier

JARINA   *n* pl. **-S** the hard seed of a palm tree

JARL   *n* pl. **-S** a Scandinavian nobleman

JARLDOM   *n* pl. **-S** the domain of a jarl

JAROSITE   *n* pl. **-S** a mineral

JAROVIZE   *v* **-VIZED, -VIZING, -VIZES** to hasten the flowering of a plant

JARRAH   *n* pl. **-S** an evergreen tree

JARRED   past tense of jar

JARRING   present participle of jar

JARSFUL   a pl. of jarful

JARVEY   *n* pl. **-VEYS** the driver of a carriage for hire

JASMIN   *n* pl. **-S** jasmine

JASMINE   *n* pl. **-S** a climbing shrub

JASPER   *n* pl. **-S** a variety of quartz **JASPERY** *adj*

JASSID   *n* pl. **-S** any of a family of plant pests

JATO   *n* pl. **-TOS** a takeoff aided by jet propulsion

JAUK   *v* **-ED, -ING, -S** to dawdle

JAUNCE   *v* **JAUNCED, JAUNCING, JAUNCES** to prance

JAUNDICE   *v* **-DICED, -DICING, -DICES** to prejudice unfavorably

JAUNT   *v* **-ED, -ING, -S** to make a pleasure trip

JAUNTY   *adj* **-TIER, -TIEST** having a lively and self-confident manner **JAUNTILY** *adv*

JAUP   *v* **-ED, -ING, -S** to splash

JAVA   *n* pl. **-S** coffee

JAVELIN   *v* **-ED, -ING, -S** to pierce with a javelin (a light spear)

JAVELINA   *n* pl. **-S** a peccary

JAW   *v* **-ED, -ING, -S** to jabber

JAWAN	*n* pl. **-S** a soldier of India
JAWBONE	*v* **-BONED, -BONING, -BONES** to attempt to convince
JAWBONER	*n* pl. **-S** one that jawbones
JAWLESS	*adj* having no jaw (a bony structure bordering the mouth)
JAWLIKE	*adj* resembling the jaw (the framework of the mouth)
JAWLINE	*n* pl. **-S** the outline of the lower jaw
JAY	*n* pl. **JAYS** a corvine bird
JAYBIRD	*n* pl. **-S** a jay
JAYGEE	*n* pl. **-S** a military officer
JAYVEE	*n* pl. **-S** a junior varsity player
JAYWALK	*v* **-ED, -ING, -S** to cross a street recklessly
JAZZ	*v* **-ED, -ING, -ES** to enliven
JAZZBO	*n* pl. **-BOS** a devotee of jazz (a style of lively syncopated music)
JAZZER	*n* pl. **-S** one that jazzes
JAZZLIKE	*adj* resembling a type of music
JAZZMAN	*n* pl. **-MEN** a type of musician
JAZZY	*adj* **JAZZIER, JAZZIEST** lively **JAZZILY** *adv*
JEALOUS	*adj* resentful of another's advantages
JEALOUSY	*n* pl. **-SIES** a jealous feeling
JEAN	*n* pl. **-S** a durable cotton fabric **JEANED** *adj*
JEBEL	*n* pl. **-S** a mountain
JEE	*v* **JEED, JEEING, JEES** to gee
JEEP	*v* **-ED, -ING, -S** to travel by a small type of motor vehicle
JEEPERS	*interj* — used as a mild oath
JEEPNEY	*n* pl. **-NEYS** a Philippine jitney
JEER	*v* **-ED, -ING, -S** to mock
JEERER	*n* pl. **-S** one that jeers
JEEZ	*interj* — used as a mild oath
JEFE	*n* pl. **-S** a chief
JEHAD	*n* pl. **-S** jihad
JEHU	*n* pl. **-S** a fast driver
JEJUNA	pl. of jejunum
JEJUNAL	*adj* pertaining to the jejunum
JEJUNE	*adj* uninteresting; childish **JEJUNELY** *adv*
JEJUNITY	*n* pl. **-TIES** something that is jejune
JEJUNUM	*n* pl. **-NA** a part of the small intestine
JELL	*v* **-ED, -ING, -S** to congeal
JELLABA	*n* pl. **-S** djellaba
JELLIFY	*v* **-FIED, -FYING, -FIES** to jelly
JELLY	*v* **-LIED, -LYING, -LIES** to make into a jelly (a soft, semisolid substance)
JELUTONG	*n* pl. **-S** a tropical tree
JEMADAR	*n* pl. **-S** an officer in the army of India
JEMIDAR	*n* pl. **-S** jemadar
JEMMY	*v* **-MIED, -MYING, -MIES** to jimmy
JENNET	*n* pl. **-S** a small horse
JENNY	*n* pl. **-NIES** a female donkey
JEON	*n* pl. **JEON** a monetary unit of South Korea
JEOPARD	*v* **-ED, -ING, -S** to imperil
JEOPARDY	*n* pl. **-DIES** risk of loss or injury
JERBOA	*n* pl. **-S** a small rodent
JEREED	*n* pl. **-S** a wooden javelin
JEREMIAD	*n* pl. **-S** a tale of woe
JERID	*n* pl. **-S** jereed
JERK	*v* **-ED, -ING, -S** to move with a sharp, sudden motion
JERKER	*n* pl. **-S** one that jerks
JERKIES	pl. of jerky
JERKIN	*n* pl. **-S** a sleeveless jacket
JERKY	*adj* **JERKIER, JERKIEST** characterized by jerking movements **JERKILY** *adv*
JERKY	*n* pl. **-KIES** dried meat
JEROBOAM	*n* pl. **-S** a wine bottle
JERREED	*n* pl. **-S** jereed
JERRICAN	*n* pl. **-S** jerrycan
JERRID	*n* pl. **-S** jereed
JERRY	*n* pl. **-RIES** a German soldier
JERRYCAN	*n* pl. **-S** a fuel container
JERSEY	*n* pl. **-SEYS** a close-fitting knitted shirt **JERSEYED** *adj*
JESS	*v* **-ED, -ING, -ES** to fasten straps around the legs of a hawk
JESSANT	*adj* shooting forth
JESSE	*v* **JESSED, JESSING, JESSES** to jess
JEST	*v* **-ED, -ING, -S** to joke
JESTER	*n* pl. **-S** one that jests
JESTFUL	*adj* tending to jest
JESTING	*n* pl. **-S** the act of one who jests
JET	*v* **JETTED, JETTING, JETS** to spurt forth in a stream

JETBEAD *n* pl. **-S** an ornamental shrub

JETE *n* pl. **-S** a ballet leap

JETFOIL *n* pl. **-S** a jet-powered hydrofoil (a boat with winglike structures for lifting the hull above the water)

JETLAG *n* pl. **-S** the disruption of body rhythms after a flight through several time zones

JETLIKE *adj* resembling a jet airplane

JETLINER *n* pl. **-S** a type of aircraft

JETON *n* pl. **-S** jetton

JETPORT *n* pl. **-S** a type of airport

JETSAM *n* pl. **-S** goods cast overboard

JETSOM *n* pl. **-S** jetsam

JETTED past tense of jet

JETTIED past tense of jetty

JETTIER comparative of jetty

JETTIES present 3d person sing. of jetty

JETTIEST superlative of jetty

JETTING present participle of jet

JETTISON *v* **-ED, -ING, -S** to cast overboard

JETTON *n* pl. **-S** a piece used in counting

JETTY *adj* **-TIER, -TIEST** having the color jet black

JETTY *v* **-TIED, -TYING, -TIES** to jut

JEU *n* pl. **JEUX** a game

JEWEL *v* **-ELED, -ELING, -ELS** or **-ELLED, -ELLING, -ELS** to adorn or equip with jewels (precious stones)

JEWELER *n* pl. **-S** a dealer or maker of jewelry

JEWELLER *n* pl. **-S** jeweler

JEWELRY *n* pl. **-RIES** an article or articles for personal adornment

JEWFISH *n* pl. **-ES** a large marine fish

JEZAIL *n* pl. **-S** a type of firearm

JEZEBEL *n* pl. **-S** a scheming, wicked woman

JIAO *n* pl. **JIAO** chiao

JIB *v* **JIBBED, JIBBING, JIBS** to refuse to proceed further

JIBB *v* **-ED, -ING, -S** to shift from side to side while sailing

JIBBER *n* pl. **-S** a horse that jibs

JIBBOOM *n* pl. **-S** a ship's spar

JIBE *v* **JIBED, JIBING, JIBES** to gibe **JIBINGLY** *adv*

JIBER *n* pl. **-S** one that jibes

JICAMA *n* pl. **-S** a tropical plant with edible roots

JIFF *n* pl. **-S** jiffy

JIFFY *n* pl. **-FIES** a short time

JIG *v* **JIGGED, JIGGING, JIGS** to bob

JIGGER *v* **-ED, -ING, -S** to jerk up and down

JIGGERED *adj* damned

JIGGIER comparative of jiggy

JIGGIEST superlative of jiggy

JIGGISH *adj* suitable for a jig (a livley dance)

JIGGLE *v* **-GLED, -GLING, -GLES** to shake lightly

JIGGLY *adj* **-GLIER, -GLIEST** unsteady

JIGGY *adj* **-GIER, -GIEST** pleasurably excited

JIGLIKE *adj* resembling a jig

JIGSAW *v* **-SAWED, -SAWN, -SAWING, -SAWS** to cut with a type of saw

JIHAD *n* pl. **-S** a Muslim holy war

JILL *n* pl. **-S** a unit of liquid measure

JILLION *n* pl. **-S** a very large number

JILT *v* **-ED, -ING, -S** to reject a lover

JILTER *n* pl. **-S** one that jilts

JIMINY *interj* — used to express surprise

JIMJAMS *n/pl* violent delirium

JIMMIE *n* pl. **-S** a tiny bit of candy for decorating ice cream

JIMMINY *interj* jiminy

JIMMY *v* **-MIED, -MYING, -MIES** to pry open with a crowbar

JIMP *adj* **JIMPER, JIMPEST** natty **JIMPLY** *adv*

JIMPY *adj* jimp

JIN *n* pl. **-S** jinn

JINGAL *n* pl. **-S** a heavy musket

JINGALL *n* pl. **-S** jingal

JINGKO *n* pl. **-KOES** ginkgo

JINGLE *v* **-GLED, -GLING, -GLES** to make a tinkling sound

JINGLER *n* pl. **-S** one that jingles

JINGLY *adj* **-GLIER, -GLIEST** jingling

JINGO *n* pl. **-GOES** a zealous patriot **JINGOISH** *adj*

JINGOISM *n* pl. **-S** the spirit or policy of jingoes

JINGOIST *n* pl. **-S** a jingo

JINK   *v* **-ED, -ING, -S** to move quickly out of the way

JINKER   *n* pl. **-S** one that jinks

JINN   *n* pl. **-S** a supernatural being in Muslim mythology

JINNEE   *n* pl. **JINN** jinn

JINNI   *n* pl. **-S** jinn

JINX   *v* **-ED, -ING, -ES** to bring bad luck to

JIPIJAPA   *n* pl. **-S** a tropical plant

JITNEY   *n* pl. **-NEYS** a small bus

JITTER   *v* **-ED, -ING, -S** to fidget

JITTERY   *adj* **-TERIER, -TERIEST** extremely nervous

JIUJITSU   *n* pl. **-S** jujitsu

JIUJUTSU   *n* pl. **-S** jujitsu

JIVE   *v* **JIVED, JIVING, JIVES** to play jazz or swing music

JIVEASS   *adj* insincere, phony

JIVER   *n* pl. **-S** one that jives

JIVEY   *adj* **JIVIER, JIVIEST** jazzy, lively

JIVING   present participle of jive

JIVY   *adj* jivey

JNANA   *n* pl. **-S** knowledge acquired through meditation

JO   *n* pl. **JOES** a sweetheart

JOANNES   *n* pl. **JOANNES** johannes

JOB   *v* **JOBBED, JOBBING, JOBS** to work by the piece

JOBBER   *n* pl. **-S** a pieceworker

JOBBERY   *n* pl. **-BERIES** corruption in public office

JOBLESS   *adj* having no job

JOBNAME   *n* pl. **-S** a computer code for a job instruction

JOCK   *n* pl. **-S** an athletic supporter

JOCKETTE   *n* pl. **-S** a woman who rides horses in races

JOCKEY   *v* **-EYED, -EYING, -EYS** to maneuver for an advantage

JOCKO   *n* pl. **JOCKOS** a monkey

JOCOSE   *adj* humorous **JOCOSELY** *adv*

JOCOSITY   *n* pl. **-TIES** the state of being jocose

JOCULAR   *adj* given to joking

JOCUND   *adj* cheerful **JOCUNDLY** *adv*

JODHPUR   *n* pl. **-S** a type of boot

JOE   *n* pl. **-S** a fellow

JOEY   *n* pl. **-EYS** a young kangaroo

JOG   *v* **JOGGED, JOGGING, JOGS** to run at a slow, steady pace

JOGGER   *n* pl. **-S** one that jogs

JOGGING   *n* pl. **-S** the practice of running at a slow, steady pace

JOGGLE   *v* **-GLED, -GLING, -GLES** to shake slightly

JOGGLER   *n* pl. **-S** one that joggles

JOHANNES   *n* pl. **JOHANNES** a Portuguese coin

JOHN   *n* pl. **-S** a toilet

JOHNBOAT   *n* pl. **-S** a narrow square-ended boat

JOHNNIE   *n* pl. **-S** johnny

JOHNNY   *n* pl. **-NIES** a sleeveless hospital gown

JOIN   *v* **-ED, -ING, -S** to unite **JOINABLE** *adj*

JOINDER   *n* pl. **-S** a joining of parties in a lawsuit

JOINER   *n* pl. **-S** a carpenter

JOINERY   *n* pl. **-ERIES** the trade of a joiner

JOINING   *n* pl. **-S** a juncture

JOINT   *v* **-ED, -ING, -S** to fit together by means of a junction

JOINTER   *n* pl. **-S** one that joints

JOINTLY   *adv* together

JOINTURE   *v* **-TURED, -TURING, -TURES** to set aside property as an inheritance

JOIST   *v* **-ED, -ING, -S** to support with horizontal beams

JOJOBA   *n* pl. **-S** a small tree

JOKE   *v* **JOKED, JOKING, JOKES** to say something amusing

JOKER   *n* pl. **-S** one that jokes

JOKESTER   *n* pl. **-S** a practical joker

JOKEY   *adj* **JOKIER, JOKIEST** amusing **JOKILY** *adv*

JOKIER   comparative of joky

JOKIEST   superlative of joky

JOKINESS   *n* pl. **-ES** the state of being jokey

JOKING   present participle of joke

JOKINGLY   *adv* in a joking manner

JOKY   *adj* **JOKIER, JOKIEST** jokey

JOLE   *n* pl. **-S** jowl

JOLLIED   past tense of jolly

JOLLIER *n* pl. **-S** one who puts others in good humor

JOLLIES present 3d person sing. of jolly

JOLLIEST superlative of jolly

JOLLIFY *v* **-FIED, -FYING, -FIES** to make jolly

JOLLITY *n* pl. **-TIES** mirth

JOLLY *adj* **-LIER, -LIEST** cheerful **JOLLILY** *adv*

JOLLY *v* **-LIED, -LYING, -LIES** to put in a good humor for one's own purposes

JOLT *v* **-ED, -ING, -S** to jar or shake roughly

JOLTER *n* pl. **-S** one that jolts

JOLTY *adj* **JOLTIER, JOLTIEST** marked by a jolting motion **JOLTILY** *adv*

JOMON *adj* pertaining to a Japanese cultural period

JONES *v* **-ED, -ING, -ES** to have a strong craving for something

JONGLEUR *n* pl. **-S** a minstrel

JONQUIL *n* pl. **-S** a perennial herb

JORAM *n* pl. **-S** jorum

JORDAN *n* pl. **-S** a type of container

JORUM *n* pl. **-S** a large drinking bowl

JOSEPH *n* pl. **-S** a woman's long cloak

JOSH *v* **-ED, -ING, -ES** to tease

JOSHER *n* pl. **-S** one that joshes

JOSS *n* pl. **-ES** a Chinese idol

JOSTLE *v* **-TLED, -TLING, -TLES** to bump or push roughly

JOSTLER *n* pl. **-S** one that jostles

JOT *v* **JOTTED, JOTTING, JOTS** to write down quickly

JOTA *n* pl. **-S** a Spanish dance

JOTTER *n* pl. **-S** one that jots

JOTTING *n* pl. **-S** a brief note

JOTTY *adj* written down quickly

JOUAL *n* pl. **-S** a dialect of Canadian French

JOUK *v* **-ED, -ING, -S** to dodge

JOULE *n* pl. **-S** a unit of energy

JOUNCE *v* **JOUNCED, JOUNCING, JOUNCES** to move roughly up and down

JOUNCY *adj* **JOUNCIER, JOUNCIEST** marked by a jouncing motion

JOURNAL *v* **-ED, -ING, -S** to enter in a daily record

JOURNEY *v* **-ED, -ING, -S** to travel

JOURNO *n* pl. **-NOS** a writer for a news medium

JOUST *v* **-ED, -ING, -S** to engage in personal combat

JOUSTER *n* pl. **-S** one that jousts

JOVIAL *adj* good-humored **JOVIALLY** *adv*

JOVIALTY *n* pl. **-TIES** the quality or state of being jovial

JOW *v* **-ED, -ING, -S** to toll

JOWAR *n* pl. **-S** a durra grown in India

JOWL *n* pl. **-S** the fleshy part under the lower jaw **JOWLED** *adj*

JOWLY *adj* **JOWLIER, JOWLIEST** having prominent jowls

JOY *v* **-ED, -ING, -S** to rejoice

JOYANCE *n* pl. **-S** gladness

JOYFUL *adj* **-FULLER, -FULLEST** happy **JOYFULLY** *adv*

JOYLESS *adj* being without gladness

JOYOUS *adj* joyful **JOYOUSLY** *adv*

JOYPOP *v* **-POPPED, -POPPING, -POPS** to use habit-forming drugs occasionally

JOYRIDE *v* **-RODE, -RIDDEN, -RIDING, -RIDES** to take an automobile ride for pleasure

JOYRIDER *n* pl. **-S** one that joyrides

JOYSTICK *n* pl. **-S** the control stick in an airplane

JUBA *n* pl. **-S** a lively dance

JUBBAH *n* pl. **-S** a loose outer garment

JUBE *n* pl. **-S** a platform in a church

JUBHAH *n* pl. **-S** jubbah

JUBILANT *adj* exultant

JUBILATE *v* **-LATED, -LATING, -LATES** to exult

JUBILE *n* pl. **-S** jubilee

JUBILEE *n* pl. **-S** a celebration

JUCO *n* pl. **-COS** a junior college

JUDAS *n* pl. **-ES** a peephole

JUDDER *v* **-ED, -ING, -S** to vibrate

JUDGE *v* **JUDGED, JUDGING, JUDGES** to decide on critically

JUDGER *n* pl. **-S** one that judges

JUDGMENT *n* pl. **-S** an authoritative opinion

JUDICIAL *adj* pertaining to courts of law

JUDO	*n* pl. **-DOS** a form of jujitsu
JUDOIST	*n* pl. **-S** one skilled in judo
JUDOKA	*n* pl. **-S** a judoist
JUG	*v* **JUGGED, JUGGING, JUGS** to put into a jug (a large, deep container with a narrow mouth and a handle)
JUGA	a pl. of jugum
JUGAL	*adj* pertaining to the cheek or cheekbone
JUGATE	*adj* occurring in pairs
JUGFUL	*n* pl. **JUGFULS** or **JUGSFUL** as much as a jug will hold
JUGGED	past tense of jug
JUGGING	present participle of jug
JUGGLE	*v* **-GLED, -GLING, -GLES** to perform feats of manual dexterity
JUGGLER	*n* pl. **-S** one that juggles
JUGGLERY	*n* pl. **-GLERIES** the art of a juggler
JUGGLING	*n* pl. **-S** jugglery
JUGHEAD	*n* pl. **-S** a dolt
JUGSFUL	a pl. of jugful
JUGULA	pl. of jugulum
JUGULAR	*n* pl. **-S** a vein of the neck
JUGULATE	*v* **-LATED, -LATING, -LATES** to suppress a disease by extreme measures
JUGULUM	*n* pl. **-LA** a part of a bird's neck
JUGUM	*n* pl. **-GUMS** or **-GA** a pair of the opposite leaflets of a pinnate leaf
JUICE	*v* **JUICED, JUICING, JUICES** to extract the juice (the liquid part of a fruit or vegetable) from
JUICER	*n* pl. **-S** a juice extractor
JUICY	*adj* **JUICIER, JUICIEST** full of juice **JUICILY** *adv*
JUJITSU	*n* pl. **-S** a Japanese art of self-defense
JUJU	*n* pl. **-S** an object regarded as having magical power
JUJUBE	*n* pl. **-S** a fruit-flavored candy
JUJUISM	*n* pl. **-S** the system of beliefs connected with jujus
JUJUIST	*n* pl. **-S** a follower of jujuism
JUJUTSU	*n* pl. **-S** jujitsu
JUKE	*v* **JUKED, JUKING, JUKES** to fake out of position
JUKEBOX	*n* pl. **-ES** a coin-operated phonograph
JUKU	*n* pl. **-S** an additional school in Japan for preparing students for college
JULEP	*n* pl. **-S** a sweet drink
JULIENNE	*v* **-ENNED, -ENNING, -ENNES** to cut food into long thin strips
JUMBAL	*n* pl. **-S** a ring-shaped cookie
JUMBLE	*v* **-BLED, -BLING, -BLES** to mix in a disordered manner
JUMBLER	*n* pl. **-S** one that jumbles
JUMBO	*n* pl. **-BOS** a very large specimen of its kind
JUMBUCK	*n* pl. **-S** a sheep
JUMP	*v* **-ED, -ING, -S** to spring off the ground **JUMPABLE** *adj*
JUMPER	*n* pl. **-S** one that jumps
JUMPOFF	*n* pl. **-S** a starting point
JUMPSUIT	*n* pl. **-S** a one-piece garment
JUMPY	*adj* **JUMPIER, JUMPIEST** nervous **JUMPILY** *adv*
JUN	*n* pl. **JUN** a coin of North Korea
JUNCO	*n* pl. **-COS** or **-COES** a small finch
JUNCTION	*n* pl. **-S** a place where things join
JUNCTURE	*n* pl. **-S** the act of joining
JUNGLE	*n* pl. **-S** land covered with dense tropical vegetation **JUNGLED** *adj*
JUNGLY	*adj* **-GLIER, -GLIEST** resembling a jungle
JUNIOR	*n* pl. **-S** a person who is younger than another
JUNIPER	*n* pl. **-S** an evergreen tree
JUNK	*v* **-ED, -ING, -S** to discard as trash
JUNKER	*n* pl. **-S** something ready for junking
JUNKET	*v* **-ED, -ING, -S** to banquet
JUNKETER	*n* pl. **-S** one that junkets
JUNKIE	*n* pl. **-S** a drug addict
JUNKMAN	*n* pl. **-MEN** one who buys and sells junk
JUNKY	*adj* **JUNKIER, JUNKIEST** worthless
JUNKYARD	*n* pl. **-S** a place where junk is stored
JUNTA	*n* pl. **-S** a political or governmental council
JUNTO	*n* pl. **-TOS** a political faction
JUPE	*n* pl. **-S** a woman's jacket
JUPON	*n* pl. **-S** a tunic
JURA	pl. of jus

JURAL   *adj* pertaining to law **JURALLY** *adv*

JURANT   *n* pl. **-S** one that takes an oath

JURAT   *n* pl. **-S** a statement on an affidavit

JURATORY   *adj* pertaining to an oath

JUREL   *n* pl. **-S** a food fish

JURIDIC   *adj* pertaining to the law

JURIST   *n* pl. **-S** one versed in the law **JURISTIC** *adj*

JUROR   *n* pl. **-S** a member of a jury

JURY   *v* **-RIED, -RYING, -RIES** to select material for exhibition

JURYLESS   *adj* being without a jury

JURYMAN   *n* pl. **-MEN** a juror

JUS   *n* pl. **JURA** a legal right

JUSSIVE   *n* pl. **-S** a word used to express command

JUST   *adj* **JUSTER, JUSTEST** acting in conformity with what is morally good

JUST   *v* **-ED, -ING, -S** to joust

JUSTER   *n* pl. **-S** jouster

JUSTICE   *n* pl. **-S** a judge

JUSTIFY   *v* **-FIED, -FYING, -FIES** to show to be just, right, or valid

JUSTLE   *v* **-TLED, -TLING, -TLES** to jostle

JUSTLY   *adv* in a just manner

JUSTNESS   *n* pl. **-ES** the quality of being just

JUT   *v* **JUTTED, JUTTING, JUTS** to protrude

JUTE   *n* pl. **-S** a strong, coarse fiber

JUTELIKE   *adj* resembling jute

JUTTY   *v* **-TIED, -TYING, -TIES** to jut

JUVENAL   *n* pl. **-S** a young bird's plumage

JUVENILE   *n* pl. **-S** a young person

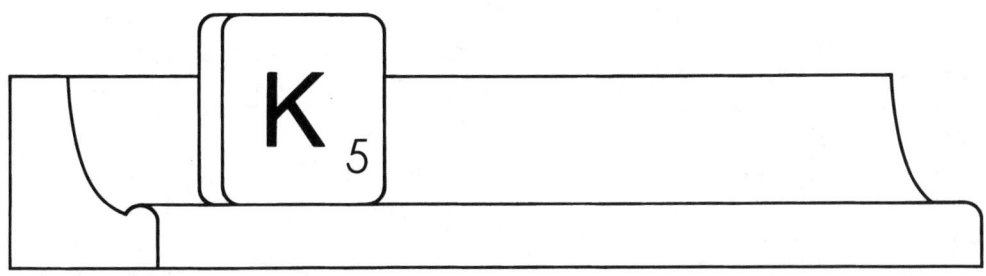

KA *n* pl. **-S** the spiritual self of a human being in Egyptian religion

KAAS *n* pl. **KAAS** kas

KAB *n* pl. **-S** an ancient Hebrew unit of measure

KABAB *n* pl. **-S** kabob

KABAKA *n* pl. **-S** a Ugandan emperor

KABALA *n* pl. **-S** cabala

KABALISM *n* pl. **-S** cabalism

KABALIST *n* pl. **-S** cabalist

KABAR *n* pl. **-S** caber

KABAYA *n* pl. **-S** a cotton jacket

KABBALA *n* pl. **-S** cabala

KABBALAH *n* pl. **-S** cabala

KABELJOU *n* pl. **-S** a large food fish

KABIKI *n* pl. **-S** a tropical tree

KABOB *n* pl. **-S** cubes of meat cooked on a skewer

KABUKI *n* pl. **-S** a form of Japanese theater

KACHINA *n* pl. **-S** an ancestral spirit

KADDISH *n* pl. **-DISHES** or **-DISHIM** a Jewish prayer

KADI *n* pl. **-S** cadi

KAE *n* pl. **-S** a bird resembling a crow

KAF *n* pl. **-S** kaph

KAFFIR *n* pl. **-S** kafir

KAFFIYAH *n* pl. **-S** kaffiyeh

KAFFIYEH *n* pl. **-S** a large, square kerchief

KAFIR *n* pl. **-S** a cereal grass

KAFTAN *n* pl. **-S** caftan

KAGU *n* pl. **-S** a flightless bird

KAHUNA *n* pl. **-S** a medicine man

KAIAK *n* pl. **-S** kayak

KAIF *n* pl. **-S** kef

KAIL *n* pl. **-S** kale

KAILYARD *n* pl. **-S** kaleyard

KAIN *n* pl. **-S** a tax paid in produce or livestock

KAINIT *n* pl. **-S** kainite

KAINITE *n* pl. **-S** a mineral salt

KAISER *n* pl. **-S** an emperor

KAISERIN *n* pl. **-S** a kaiser's wife

KAJEPUT *n* pl. **-S** cajuput

KAKA *n* pl. **-S** a parrot

KAKAPO *n* pl. **-POS** a flightless parrot

KAKEMONO *n* pl. **-NOS** a Japanese scroll

KAKI *n* pl. **-S** a Japanese tree

KAKIEMON *n* pl. **-S** a Japanese porcelain

KALAM *n* pl. **-S** a type of Muslim theology

KALAMATA *n* pl. **-S** a black olive grown in Greece

KALE *n* pl. **-S** a variety of cabbage

KALENDS *n* pl. **KALENDS** calends

KALEWIFE *n* pl. **-WIVES** a female vegetable vendor

KALEYARD *n* pl. **-S** a kitchen garden

KALIAN *n* pl. **-S** a hookah

KALIF *n* pl. **-S** caliph

KALIFATE *n* pl. **-S** califate

KALIMBA *n* pl. **-S** an African musical instrument

KALIPH *n* pl. **-S** caliph

KALIUM *n* pl. **-S** potassium

KALLIDIN *n* pl. **-S** a hormone

KALMIA *n* pl. **-S** an evergreen shrub

KALONG *n* pl. **-S** a fruit-eating bat

KALPA *n* pl. **-S** a period of time in Hindu religion

KALPAC *n* pl. **-S** calpac

KALPAK *n* pl. **-S** calpac

KALYPTRA *n* pl. **-S** a thin veil

KAMAAINA *n* pl. **-S** a longtime resident of Hawaii

KAMACITE *n* pl. **-S** an alloy of nickel and iron

KAMALA *n* pl. **-S** an Asian tree

KAME *n* pl. **-S** a mound of detrital material

KAMI *n* pl. **KAMI** a sacred power or force

KAMIK *n* pl. **-S** a type of boot

KAMIKAZE *n* pl. **-S** a plane to be flown in a suicide crash on a target

KAMPONG *n* pl. **-S** a small village

KAMSEEN *n* pl. **-S** khamsin

KAMSIN *n* pl. **-S** khamsin

KANA *n* pl. **-S** the Japanese syllabic script

KANBAN *n* pl. **-S** a manufacturing strategy wherein parts are delivered only as needed

KANE *n* pl. **-S** kain

KANGAROO *n* pl. **-ROOS** an Australian mammal

KANJI *n* pl. **-S** a system of Japanese writing

KANTAR *n* pl. **-S** a unit of weight

KANTELE *n* pl. **-S** a type of harp

KANZU *n* pl. **-S** a long white garment worn in Africa

KAOLIANG *n* pl. **-S** an Asian sorghum

KAOLIN *n* pl. **-S** a fine white clay **KAOLINIC** *adj*

KAOLINE *n* pl. **-S** kaolin

KAON *n* pl. **-S** a type of meson **KAONIC** *adj*

KAPA *n* pl. **-S** a coarse cloth

KAPH *n* pl. **-S** a Hebrew letter

KAPOK *n* pl. **-S** a mass of silky fibers

KAPPA *n* pl. **-S** a Greek letter

KAPUT *adj* ruined

KAPUTT *adj* kaput

KARAKUL *n* pl. **-S** an Asian sheep

KARAOKE *n* pl. **-S** a musical device to which a user sings along

KARAT *n* pl. **-S** a unit of quality for gold

KARATE *n* pl. **-S** a Japanese art of self-defense

KARMA *n* pl. **-S** the force generated by a person's actions **KARMIC** *adj*

KARN *n* pl. **-S** cairn

KAROO *n* pl. **-ROOS** karroo

KAROSS *n* pl. **-ES** an African garment

KARROO *n* pl. **-ROOS** a dry plateau

KARST *n* pl. **-S** a limestone region **KARSTIC** *adj*

KART *n* pl. **-S** a small motor vehicle

KARTING *n* pl. **-S** the sport of racing karts

KARYOTIN *n* pl. **-S** the nuclear material of a cell

KAS *n* pl. **KAS** a large cupboard

KASBAH *n* pl. **-S** casbah

KASHA *n* pl. **-S** a cooked cereal

KASHER *v* **-ED, -ING, -S** to kosher

KASHMIR *n* pl. **-S** cashmere

KASHRUT *n* pl. **-S** kashruth

KASHRUTH *n* pl. **-S** the Jewish dietary laws

KAT *n* pl. **-S** an evergreen shrub

KATA *n* pl. **-S** an exercise of set movements

KATAKANA *n* pl. **-S** a Japanese syllabic symbol

KATCHINA *n* pl. **-S** kachina

KATCINA *n* pl. **-S** kachina

KATHODE *n* pl. **-S** cathode **KATHODAL, KATHODIC** *adj*

KATION *n* pl. **-S** cation

KATSURA *n* pl. **-S** a deciduous tree of Japan and China

KATYDID *n* pl. **-S** a grasshopper

KAURI *n* pl. **-S** a timber tree

KAURY *n* pl. **-RIES** kauri

KAVA *n* pl. **-S** a tropical shrub

KAVAKAVA *n* pl. **-S** kava

KAVASS *n* pl. **-ES** a Turkish policeman

KAY *n* pl. **KAYS** the letter K

KAYAK *v* **-ED, -ING, -S** to travel in a kayak (an Eskimo canoe)

KAYAKER *n* pl. **-S** one that rides in a kayak

KAYAKING *n* pl. **-S** the act or skill of managing a kayak

KAYLES *n/pl* a British game

KAYO *v* **-ED, -ING, -S** or **-ES** to knock out

KAZACHOK *n* pl. **-ZACHKI** a Russian folk dance

KAZATSKI *n* pl. **-ES** kazachok

KAZATSKY *n* pl. **-SKIES** kazachok

KAZOO	*n* pl. **-ZOOS** a toy musical instrument	**KEEVE**	*n* pl. **-S** a tub or vat
KBAR	*n* pl. **-S** a kilobar	**KEF**	*n* pl. **-S** hemp smoked to produce euphoria
KEA	*n* pl. **-S** a parrot	**KEFFIYAH**	*n* pl. **-S** kaffiyeh
KEBAB	*n* pl. **-S** kabob	**KEFFIYEH**	*n* pl. **-S** kaffiyeh
KEBAR	*n* pl. **-S** caber	**KEFIR**	*n* pl. **-S** a fermented beverage made from cow's milk
KEBBIE	*n* pl. **-S** a rough walking stick		
KEBBOCK	*n* pl. **-S** kebbuck	**KEG**	*v* **KEGGED, KEGGING, KEGS** to store in a keg (a small barrel)
KEBBUCK	*n* pl. **-S** a whole cheese		
KEBLAH	*n* pl. **-S** kiblah	**KEGELER**	*n* pl. **-S** kegler
KEBOB	*n* pl. **-S** kabob	**KEGGER**	*n* pl. **-S** a party having one or more kegs of beer
KECK	*v* **-ED, -ING, -S** to retch		
KECKLE	*v* **-LED, -LING, -LES** to wind with rope to prevent chafing	**KEGLER**	*n* pl. **-S** a bowler
		KEGLING	*n* pl. **-S** bowling
KEDDAH	*n* pl. **-S** an enclosure for elephants	**KEIR**	*n* pl. **-S** kier
KEDGE	*v* **KEDGED, KEDGING, KEDGES** to move a vessel with the use of an anchor	**KEIRETSU**	*n* pl. **-S** a coalition of business groups in Japan
		KEISTER	*n* pl. **-S** the buttocks
KEDGEREE	*n* pl. **-S** a food in India	**KEITLOA**	*n* pl. **-S** a rhinoceros
KEEF	*n* pl. **-S** kef	**KELEP**	*n* pl. **-S** a stinging ant
KEEK	*v* **-ED, -ING, -S** to peep	**KELIM**	*n* pl. **-S** kilim
KEEL	*v* **-ED, -ING, -S** to capsize	**KELLY**	*n* pl. **-LIES** a bright green color
KEELAGE	*n* pl. **-S** the amount paid to keep a boat in a harbor	**KELOID**	*n* pl. **-S** a scar caused by excessive growth of fibrous tissue **KELOIDAL** *adj*
KEELBOAT	*n* pl. **-S** a freight boat		
KEELHALE	*v* **-HALED, -HALING, -HALES** to keelhaul	**KELP**	*v* **-ED, -ING, -S** to burn a type of seaweed
KEELHAUL	*v* **-ED, -ING, -S** to rebuke severely	**KELPIE**	*n* pl. **-S** a water sprite
KEELLESS	*adj* having no keel (the main structural part of a ship)	**KELPY**	*n* pl. **-PIES** kelpie
		KELSON	*n* pl. **-S** keelson
KEELSON	*n* pl. **-S** a beam in a ship	**KELT**	*n* pl. **-S** a salmon that has spawned
KEEN	*adj* **KEENER, KEENEST** enthusiastic		
		KELTER	*n* pl. **-S** kilter
KEEN	*v* **-ED, -ING, -S** to wail loudly over the dead	**KELVIN**	*n* pl. **-S** a unit of temperature
		KEMP	*n* pl. **-S** a champion
KEENER	*n* pl. **-S** one that keens	**KEMPT**	*adj* neatly kept
KEENLY	*adv* in a keen manner	**KEN**	*v* **KENNED** or **KENT, KENNING, KENS** to know
KEENNESS	*n* pl. **-ES** sharpness		
KEEP	*v* **KEPT, KEEPING, KEEPS** to continue to possess **KEEPABLE** *adj*	**KENAF**	*n* pl. **-S** an East Indian plant
		KENCH	*n* pl. **-ES** a bin for salting fish
KEEPER	*n* pl. **-S** one that keeps	**KENDO**	*n* pl. **-DOS** a Japanese sport
KEEPING	*n* pl. **-S** custody	**KENNED**	a past tense of ken
KEEPSAKE	*n* pl. **-S** a memento	**KENNEL**	*v* **-NELED, -NELING, -NELS** or **-NELLED, -NELLING, -NELS** to keep in a shelter for dogs
KEESHOND	*n* pl. **-HONDS** or **-HONDEN** a small, heavy-coated dog		
KEESTER	*n* pl. **-S** keister	**KENNING**	*n* pl. **-S** a metaphorical compound word or phrase
KEET	*n* pl. **-S** a young guinea fowl	**KENO**	*n* pl. **-NOS** a game of chance

KENOSIS — *n* pl. **-SISES** the incarnation of Christ **KENOTIC** *adj*

KENOTRON — *n* pl. **-S** a type of diode

KENT — a past tense of ken

KENTE — *n* pl. **-S** a colorful fabric made in Ghana

KEP — *v* **KEPPED, KEPPEN** or **KIPPEN, KEPPING, KEPS** to catch

KEPHALIN — *n* pl. **-S** cephalin

KEPI — *n* pl. **-S** a type of cap

KEPT — past tense of keep

KERAMIC — *n* pl. **-S** ceramic

KERATIN — *n* pl. **-S** a fibrous protein

KERATOID — *adj* horny

KERATOMA — *n* pl. **-MAS** or **-MATA** a skin disease

KERATOSE — *adj* of or resembling horny tissue

KERB — *v* **-ED, -ING, -S** to provide with curbing

KERCHIEF — *n* pl. **-CHIEFS** or **-CHIEVES** a cloth worn as a head covering

KERCHOO — *interj* ahchoo

KERF — *v* **-ED, -ING, -S** to make an incision with a cutting tool

KERMES — *n* pl. **KERMES** a red dye

KERMESS — *n* pl. **-ES** kermis

KERMESSE — *n* pl. **-S** kermis

KERMIS — *n* pl. **-MISES** a festival

KERN — *v* **-ED, -ING, -S** to be formed with a projecting typeface

KERNE — *n* pl. **-S** a medieval foot soldier

KERNEL — *v* **-NELED, -NELING, -NELS** or **-NELLED, -NELLING, -NELS** to envelop as a kernel (the inner part of a nut)

KERNELLY — *adj* resembling kernels

KERNITE — *n* pl. **-S** a mineral

KEROGEN — *n* pl. **-S** a substance found in shale

KEROSENE — *n* pl. **-S** a fuel oil

KEROSINE — *n* pl. **-S** kerosene

KERPLUNK — *v* **-ED, -ING, -S** to fall or drop with a heavy sound

KERRIA — *n* pl. **-S** a Chinese shrub

KERRY — *n* pl. **-RIES** one of an Irish breed of cattle

KERSEY — *n* pl. **-SEYS** a woolen cloth

KERYGMA — *n* pl. **-MAS** or **-MATA** the preaching of the gospel

KESTREL — *n* pl. **-S** a small falcon

KETAMINE — *n* pl. **-S** a general anesthetic

KETCH — *n* pl. **-ES** a sailing vessel

KETCHUP — *n* pl. **-S** a spicy tomato sauce

KETENE — *n* pl. **-S** a toxic gas

KETO — *adj* of or pertaining to ketone

KETOL — *n* pl. **-S** a chemical compound

KETONE — *n* pl. **-S** a type of chemical compound **KETONIC** *adj*

KETOSE — *n* pl. **-S** a simple sugar

KETOSIS — *n* pl. **-TOSES** a buildup of ketones in the body **KETOTIC** *adj*

KETTLE — *n* pl. **-S** a vessel for boiling liquids

KEVEL — *n* pl. **-S** a belaying cleat or peg

KEVIL — *n* pl. **-S** kevel

KEX — *n* pl. **-ES** a dry, hollow stalk

KEY — *v* **-ED, -ING, -S** to provide with a key (a device used to turn the bolt in a lock)

KEYBOARD — *v* **-ED, -ING, -S** to operate a machine by means of a keyset

KEYCARD — *n* pl. **-S** a coded card for operating a device

KEYHOLE — *n* pl. **-S** a hole for a key

KEYLESS — *adj* being without a key

KEYNOTE — *v* **-NOTED, -NOTING, -NOTES** to deliver the main speech at a function

KEYNOTER — *n* pl. **-S** one that keynotes

KEYPAD — *n* pl. **-S** a small keyboard

KEYPAL — *n* pl. **-S** a person with whom one corresponds by email

KEYPUNCH — *v* **-ED, -ING, -ES** to perforate with a machine

KEYSET — *n* pl. **-S** a system of finger levers

KEYSTER — *n* pl. **-S** keister

KEYSTONE — *n* pl. **-S** the central stone of an arch

KEYWAY — *n* pl. **-WAYS** a slot for a key

KEYWORD — *n* pl. **-S** a significant word

KHADDAR — *n* pl. **-S** a cotton cloth

KHADI — *n* pl. **-S** khaddar

KHAF — *n* pl. **-S** kaph

KHAKI — *n* pl. **-S** a durable cloth

KHALIF — *n* pl. **-S** caliph

KHALIFA — *n* pl. **-S** caliph

KHAMSEEN — *n* pl. **-S** khamsin

KHAMSIN — *n* pl. **-S** a hot, dry wind

KHAN — *n* pl. **-S** an Asian ruler

KHANATE *n* pl. **-S** the domain of a khan

KHAPH *n* pl. **-S** kaph

KHAT *n* pl. **-S** kat

KHAZEN *n* pl. **-ZENS** or **-ZENIM** hazzan

KHEDA *n* pl. **-S** keddah

KHEDAH *n* pl. **-S** keddah

KHEDIVE *n* pl. **-S** a Turkish viceroy **KHEDIVAL** *adj*

KHET *n* pl. **-S** heth

KHETH *n* pl. **-S** heth

KHI *n* pl. **-S** chi

KHIRKAH *n* pl. **-S** a patchwork garment

KHOUM *n* pl. **-S** a monetary unit of Mauritania

KI *n* pl. **KIS** the vital force in Chinese thought

KIANG *n* pl. **-S** a wild ass

KIAUGH *n* pl. **-S** trouble; worry

KIBBE *n* pl. **-S** a Near Eastern dish of ground lamb and bulgur

KIBBEH *n* pl. **-S** kibbe

KIBBI *n* pl. **-S** kibbe

KIBBITZ *v* **-ED, -ING, -ES** to kibitz

KIBBLE *v* **-BLED, -BLING, -BLES** to grind coarsely

KIBBUTZ *n* pl. **-BUTZIM** a collective farm in Israel

KIBE *n* pl. **-S** a sore caused by exposure to cold

KIBEI *n* pl. **-S** one born in America of immigrant Japanese parents and educated in Japan

KIBITZ *v* **-ED, -ING, -ES** to meddle

KIBITZER *n* pl. **-S** one that kibitzes

KIBLA *n* pl. **-S** kiblah

KIBLAH *n* pl. **-S** the direction toward which Muslims face while praying

KIBOSH *v* **-ED, -ING, -ES** to stop

KICK *v* **-ED, -ING, -S** to strike out with the foot or feet **KICKABLE** *adj*

KICKBACK *n* pl. **-S** a strong reaction

KICKBALL *n* pl. **-S** baseball using an inflated ball that is kicked

KICKBOX *v* **-ED, -ING, -ES** to box in a style that allows kicking

KICKER *n* pl. **-S** one that kicks

KICKIER comparative of kicky

KICKIEST superlative of kicky

KICKOFF *n* pl. **-S** the kick that begins play in football

KICKSHAW *n* pl. **-S** a trifle or trinket

KICKUP *n* pl. **-S** a noisy argument

KICKY *adj* **KICKIER, KICKIEST** exciting

KID *v* **KIDDED, KIDDING, KIDS** to tease

KIDDER *n* pl. **-S** one that kids

KIDDIE *n* pl. **-S** a small child

KIDDIES pl. of kiddy

KIDDING present participle of kid

KIDDISH *adj* childish

KIDDO *n* pl. **-DOS** or **-DOES** — used as a form of familiar address

KIDDUSH *n* pl. **-ES** a Jewish prayer

KIDDY *n* pl. **-DIES** kiddie

KIDLIKE *adj* resembling a child

KIDNAP *v* **-NAPED, -NAPING, -NAPS** or **-NAPPED, -NAPPING, -NAPS** to take a person by force and often for ransom

KIDNAPEE *n* pl. **-S** one that is kidnaped

KIDNAPER *n* pl. **-S** one that kidnaps

KIDNAPPER *n* pl. **-S** kidnaper

KIDNAPPING present participle of kidnap

KIDNEY *n* pl. **-NEYS** a bodily organ

KIDSKIN *n* pl. **-S** a type of leather

KIDVID *n* pl. **-S** television programs for children

KIEF *n* pl. **-S** kef

KIELBASA *n* pl. **-BASAS, -BASI** or **-BASY** a smoked sausage

KIER *n* pl. **-S** a vat for boiling and dyeing fabrics

KIESTER *n* pl. **-S** keister

KIF *n* pl. **-S** kef

KILIM *n* pl. **-S** an oriental tapestry

KILL *v* **-ED, -ING, -S** to cause to die **KILLABLE** *adj*

KILLDEE *n* pl. **-S** killdeer

KILLDEER *n* pl. **-S** a wading bird

KILLER *n* pl. **-S** one that kills

KILLICK *n* pl. **-S** a small anchor

KILLIE *n* pl. **-S** a freshwater fish

KILLING *n* pl. **-S** a sudden notable success

KILLJOY *n* pl. **-JOYS** one who spoils the fun of others

KILLOCK *n* pl. **-S** killick

KILN v **-ED, -ING, -S** to bake in a type of oven

KILO n pl. **KILOS** a kilogram or kilometer

KILOBAR n pl. **-S** a unit of atmospheric pressure

KILOBASE n pl. **-S** unit of measure of a nucleic-acid chain

KILOBAUD n pl. **-S** a unit of data transmission speed

KILOBIT n pl. **-S** a unit of computer information

KILOBYTE n pl. **-S** 1,024 bytes

KILOGRAM n pl. **-S** a unit of mass and weight

KILOMOLE n pl. **-S** one thousand moles

KILORAD n pl. **-S** a unit of nuclear radiation

KILOTON n pl. **-S** a unit of weight

KILOVOLT n pl. **-S** a unit of electromotive force

KILOWATT n pl. **-S** a unit of power

KILT v **-ED, -ING, -S** to make creases or pleats in

KILTER n pl. **-S** good condition

KILTIE n pl. **-S** one who wears a kilt (a type of skirt)

KILTING n pl. **-S** an arrangement of kilt pleats

KILTLIKE adj resembling a kilt

KILTY n pl. **KILTIES** kiltie

KIMCHEE n pl. **-S** kimchi

KIMCHI n pl. **-S** a spicy Korean dish of pickled cabbage

KIMONO n pl. **-NOS** a loose robe **KIMONOED** adj

KIN n pl. **-S** a group of persons of common ancestry

KINA n pl. **-S** a monetary unit of Papua New Guinea

KINARA n pl. **-S** a candelabra with seven candlesticks

KINASE n pl. **-S** an enzyme

KIND adj **KINDER, KINDEST** having a gentle, giving nature

KIND n pl. **-S** a class of similar or related objects or individuals

KINDLE v **-DLED, -DLING, -DLES** to cause to burn

KINDLER n pl. **-S** one that kindles

KINDLESS adj lacking kindness

KINDLING n pl. **-S** material that is easily ignited

KINDLY adj **-LIER, -LIEST** kind

KINDNESS n pl. **-ES** the quality of being kind

KINDRED n pl. **-S** a natural grouping

KINE n pl. **-S** a type of television tube

KINEMA n pl. **-S** cinema

KINESIC adj pertaining to kinesics

KINESICS n/pl the study of body motion in relation to communication

KINESIS n pl. **-NESES** a type of movement

KINETIC adj pertaining to motion

KINETICS n/pl a branch of science dealing with motion

KINETIN n pl. **-S** a substance that increases plant growth

KINFOLK n/pl relatives

KINFOLKS n/pl kinfolk

KING v **-ED, -ING, -S** to reign as king (a male monarch)

KINGBIRD n pl. **-S** an American bird

KINGBOLT n pl. **-S** a kingpin

KINGCUP n pl. **-S** a marsh plant

KINGDOM n pl. **-S** the area ruled by a king

KINGFISH n pl. **-ES** a marine food fish

KINGHOOD n pl. **-S** the office of a king

KINGLESS adj having no king

KINGLET n pl. **-S** a king who rules over a small area

KINGLIKE adj resembling a king

KINGLY adj **-LIER, -LIEST** of or befitting a king

KINGPIN n pl. **-S** a central bolt connecting an axle to a vehicle

KINGPOST n pl. **-S** a supporting structure of a roof

KINGSHIP n pl. **-S** the power or position of a king

KINGSIDE n pl. **-S** a part of a chessboard

KINGWOOD n pl. **-S** a hardwood tree

KININ n pl. **-S** a hormone

KINK v **-ED, -ING, -S** to form a tight curl or bend in

KINKAJOU n pl. **-S** an arboreal mammal

KINKY adj **KINKIER, KINKIEST** tightly curled **KINKILY** adv

KINLESS adj having no kin

KINO n pl. **-NOS** a gum resin

KINSFOLK n/pl kinfolk

KINSHIP n pl. **-S** relationship

KINSMAN — *n* pl. **-MEN** a male relative

KIOSK — *n* pl. **-S** an open booth

KIP — *v* **KIPPED, KIPPING, KIPS** to sleep

KIPPEN — a past participle of kep

KIPPER — *v* **-ED, -ING, -S** to cure fish by salting and smoking

KIPPERER — *n* pl. **-S** one that kippers

KIPPING — present participle of kip

KIPSKIN — *n* pl. **-S** an animal hide that has not been tanned

KIR — *n* pl. **-S** an alcoholic beverage

KIRIGAMI — *n* pl. **-S** the Japanese art of folding paper

KIRK — *n* pl. **-S** a church

KIRKMAN — *n* pl. **-MEN** a member of a church

KIRMESS — *n* pl. **-ES** kermis

KIRN — *v* **-ED, -ING, -S** to churn

KIRSCH — *n* pl. **-ES** a kind of brandy

KIRTLE — *n* pl. **-S** a man's tunic or coat **KIRTLED** *adj*

KISHKA — *n* pl. **-S** kishke

KISHKE — *n* pl. **-S** a sausage

KISMAT — *n* pl. **-S** kismet

KISMET — *n* pl. **-S** destiny **KISMETIC** *adj*

KISS — *v* **-ED, -ING, -ES** to touch with the lips as a sign of affection **KISSABLE** *adj* **KISSABLY** *adv*

KISSER — *n* pl. **-S** one that kisses

KISSY — *adj* inclined to kiss

KIST — *n* pl. **-S** a chest, box, or coffin

KISTFUL — *n* pl. **-S** as much as a kist can hold

KIT — *v* **KITTED, KITTING, KITS** to equip

KITBAG — *n* pl. **-S** a knapsack

KITCHEN — *n* pl. **-S** a room where food is cooked

KITE — *v* **KITED, KITING, KITES** to obtain money or credit fraudulently

KITELIKE — *adj* resembling a kite (a light, covered frame flown in the wind)

KITER — *n* pl. **-S** one that kites

KITH — *n* pl. **-S** one's friends and neighbors

KITHARA — *n* pl. **-S** cithara

KITHE — *v* **KITHED, KITHING, KITHES** to make known

KITING — present participle of kite

KITLING — *n* pl. **-S** a young animal

KITSCH — *n* pl. **-ES** faddish art or literature **KITSCHY** *adj*

KITTED — past tense of kit

KITTEL — *n* pl. **KITTEL** a Jewish ceremonial robe

KITTEN — *v* **-ED, -ING, -S** to bear kittens (young cats)

KITTIES — pl. of kitty

KITTING — present participle of kit

KITTLE — *adj* **-TLER, -TLEST** ticklish

KITTLE — *v* **-TLED, -TLING, -TLES** to tickle

KITTY — *n* pl. **-TIES** a kitten or cat

KIVA — *n* pl. **-S** an underground ceremonial chamber

KIWI — *n* pl. **-S** a flightless bird

KLATCH — *n* pl. **-ES** a social gathering

KLATSCH — *n* pl. **-ES** klatch

KLAVERN — *n* pl. **-S** a local branch of the Ku Klux Klan

KLAXON — *n* pl. **-S** a low-pitched horn

KLEAGLE — *n* pl. **-S** an official in the Ku Klux Klan

KLEPHT — *n* pl. **-S** a Greek guerrilla **KLEPHTIC** *adj*

KLEPTO — *n* pl. **-TOS** one that steals impulsively

KLEZMER — *n* pl. **-MERS** or **-MORIM** a Jewish folk musician

KLICK — *n* pl. **-S** a kilometer

KLIK — *n* pl. **-S** klick

KLISTER — *n* pl. **-S** a wax for skis

KLONDIKE — *n* pl. **-S** a card game

KLONG — *n* pl. **-S** a canal

KLOOF — *n* pl. **-S** a ravine

KLUDGE — *v* **KLUDGED, KLUDGING, KLUDGES** to put together from ill-fitting components

KLUDGEY — *adj* **KLUDGIER, KLUDGIEST** kludgy

KLUDGY — *adj* **KLUDGIER, KLUDGIEST** involving or put together with ill-fitting components

KLUGE — *v* **KLUGED, KLUGING, KLUGES** to kludge

KLUTZ — *n* pl. **-ES** a clumsy person

KLUTZY — *adj* **KLUTZIER, KLUTZIEST** clumsy

KLYSTRON — *n* pl. **-S** a type of electron tube

KNACK — *v* **-ED, -ING, -S** to strike sharply

KNACKER *n* pl. **-S** one that buys old livestock

KNACKERY *n* pl. **-ERIES** the place of business of a knacker

KNAP *v* **KNAPPED, KNAPPING, KNAPS** to strike sharply

KNAPPER *n* pl. **-S** one that knaps

KNAPSACK *n* pl. **-S** a bag carried on the back

KNAPWEED *n* pl. **-S** a meadow plant

KNAR *n* pl. **-S** a bump on a tree **KNARRED, KNARRY** *adj*

KNAUR *n* pl. **-S** knar

KNAVE *n* pl. **-S** a dishonest person **KNAVISH** *adj*

KNAVERY *n* pl. **-ERIES** trickery

KNAWE *n* pl. **-S** knawel

KNAWEL *n* pl. **-S** a Eurasian plant

KNEAD *v* **-ED, -ING, -S** to work into a uniform mixture with the hands

KNEADER *n* pl. **-S** one that kneads

KNEE *v* **KNEED, KNEEING, KNEES** to strike with the knee (a joint of the leg)

KNEECAP *v* **-CAPPED, -CAPPING, -CAPS** to maim by shooting in the kneecap (a bone at the front of the knee)

KNEEHOLE *n* pl. **-S** a space for the knees

KNEEL *v* **KNELT** or **KNEELED, KNEELING, KNEELS** to rest on the knees

KNEELER *n* pl. **-S** one that kneels

KNEEPAD *n* pl. **-S** a covering for a knee

KNEEPAN *n* pl. **-S** the kneecap

KNEESIES *n/pl* the pressing of one's knees against another person's knees

KNEESOCK *n* pl. **-S** a sock reaching up to the knee

KNELL *v* **-ED, -ING, -S** to sound a bell

KNELT a past tense of kneel

KNESSET *n* pl. **-S** the Israeli parliament

KNEW past tense of know

KNICKERS *n/pl* loose-fitting pants gathered at the knee

KNIFE *n* pl. **KNIVES** a sharp-edged instrument used for cutting

KNIFE *v* **KNIFED, KNIFING, KNIFES** to cut with a knife

KNIFER *n* pl. **-S** one that knifes

KNIGHT *v* **-ED, -ING, -S** to make a knight (a medieval gentleman-soldier) of

KNIGHTLY *adj* of or befitting a knight

KNISH *n* pl. **-ES** dough stuffed with filling and fried

KNIT *v* **KNITTED, KNITTING, KNITS** to make a fabric or garment by joining loops of yarn

KNITTER *n* pl. **-S** one that knits

KNITTING *n* pl. **-S** work done by a knitter

KNITWEAR *n* pl. **KNITWEAR** knitted clothing

KNIVES pl. of knife

KNOB *n* pl. **-S** a rounded protuberance **KNOBBED, KNOBLIKE** *adj*

KNOBBLY *adj* **-BLIER, -BLIEST** having very small knobs

KNOBBY *adj* **-BIER, -BIEST** full of knobs

KNOCK *v* **-ED, -ING, -S** to strike sharply

KNOCKER *n* pl. **-S** one that knocks

KNOCKOFF *n* pl. **-S** a copy that sells for less than the original

KNOCKOUT *n* pl. **-S** a blow that induces unconsciousness

KNOLL *v* **-ED, -ING, -S** to knell

KNOLLER *n* pl. **-S** one that knolls

KNOLLY *adj* hilly

KNOP *n* pl. **-S** a knob **KNOPPED** *adj*

KNOSP *n* pl. **-S** a knob

KNOT *v* **KNOTTED, KNOTTING, KNOTS** to tie in a knot (a closed loop)

KNOTHOLE *n* pl. **-S** a hole in a plank

KNOTLESS *adj* having no knots

KNOTLIKE *adj* resembling a knot

KNOTTED past tense of knot

KNOTTER *n* pl. **-S** one that knots

KNOTTING *n* pl. **-S** a fringe made of knotted threads

KNOTTY *adj* **-TIER, -TIEST** full of knots **KNOTTILY** *adv*

KNOTWEED *n* pl. **-S** a common weed

KNOUT *v* **-ED, -ING, -S** to flog with a leather whip

KNOW *v* **KNEW, KNOWN, KNOWING, KNOWS** to have a true understanding of **KNOWABLE** *adj*

KNOWER *n* pl. **-S** one that knows

KNOWING *adj* **-INGER, -INGEST** astute

KNOWING *n* pl. **-S** knowledge

KNOWN *n* pl. **-S** a mathematical quantity whose value is given

KNUBBY *adj* **-BIER, -BIEST** nubby

KNUCKLE *v* **-LED, -LING, -LES** to hit with the knuckles (the joints of the fingers)

KNUCKLER *n* pl. **-S** a type of baseball pitch

KNUCKLY *adj* **-LIER, -LIEST** having prominent knuckles

KNUR *n* pl. **-S** a bump on a tree

KNURL *v* **-ED, -ING, -S** to make grooves or ridges in

KNURLY *adj* **KNURLIER, KNURLIEST** gnarly

KOA *n* pl. **-S** a timber tree

KOALA *n* pl. **-S** an Australian mammal

KOAN *n* pl. **-S** a paradox meditated on by Buddhist monks

KOB *n* pl. **-S** a reddish brown antelope

KOBO *n* pl. **-BOS** a monetary unit of Nigeria

KOBOLD *n* pl. **-S** an elf

KOEL *n* pl. **-S** an Australian bird

KOHL *n* pl. **-S** a type of eye makeup

KOHLRABI *n* pl. **-ES** a variety of cabbage

KOI *n* pl. **-S** a large and colorful fish

KOINE *n* pl. **-S** a type of dialect

KOJI *n* pl. **-S** a fungus used to start fermentation

KOKANEE *n* pl. **-S** a food fish

KOLA *n* pl. **-S** cola

KOLACKY *n* pl. **KOLACKY** a kind of pastry

KOLBASI *n* pl. **-S** kielbasa

KOLBASSI *n* pl. **-S** kielbasa

KOLHOZ *n* pl. **-HOZES** or **-HOZY** kolkhoz

KOLINSKI *n* pl. **-ES** kolinsky

KOLINSKY *n* pl. **-SKIES** an Asian mink

KOLKHOS *n* pl. **-KHOSES** or **-KHOSY** kolkhoz

KOLKHOZ *n* pl. **-KHOZES** or **-KHOZY** a collective farm in Russia

KOLKOZ *n* pl. **-KOZES** or **-KOZY** kolkhoz

KOLO *n* pl. **-LOS** a European folk dance

KOMATIK *n* pl. **-S** an Eskimo sledge

KOMBU *n* pl. **-S** kelp used in Japanese cooking

KOMONDOR *n* pl. **-DORS, -DOROK** or **-DOROCK** a large, shaggy-coated dog

KONK *v* **-ED, -ING, -S** to conk

KOODOO *n* pl. **-DOOS** kudu

KOOK *n* pl. **-S** an eccentric person

KOOKIE *adj* **KOOKIER, KOOKIEST** kooky

KOOKY *adj* **KOOKIER, KOOKIEST** eccentric

KOP *n* pl. **-S** a hill

KOPECK *n* pl. **-S** a Russian coin

KOPEK *n* pl. **-S** kopeck

KOPH *n* pl. **-S** a Hebrew letter

KOPIYKA *n* pl. **-S** a monetary unit of Ukraine

KOPJE *n* pl. **-S** a small hill

KOPPA *n* pl. **-S** a Greek letter

KOPPIE *n* pl. **-S** kopje

KOR *n* pl. **-S** a Hebrew unit of measure

KORA *n* pl. **-S** a stringed African musical instrument

KORAT *n* pl. **-S** a cat having a silver-blue coat

KORE *n* pl. **-RAI** an ancient Greek statue of a young woman

KORMA *n* pl. **-S** an Indian dish of meat or vegetables with spices

KORUNA *n* pl. **KORUNAS, KORUNY** or **KORUN** a monetary unit of the Czech Republic

KOS *n* pl. **KOS** a land measure in India

KOSHER *v* **-ED, -ING, -S** to make fit to be eaten according to Jewish dietary laws

KOSS *n* pl. **KOSS** kos

KOTO *n* pl. **-TOS** a musical instrument

KOTOW *v* **-ED, -ING, -S** to kowtow

KOTOWER *n* pl. **-S** one that kotows

KOUMIS *n* pl. **-MISES** koumiss

KOUMISS *n* pl. **-ES** a beverage made from camel's milk

KOUMYS *n* pl. **-ES** koumiss

KOUMYSS *n* pl. **-ES** koumiss

KOUPREY *n* pl. **-PREYS** a short-haired ox

KOUROS *n* pl. **-ROI** an ancient Greek statue of a young man

KOUSSO   *n* pl. **-SOS** cusso

KOWTOW   *v* **-ED, -ING, -S** to behave in a servile manner

KOWTOWER   *n* pl. **-S** one that kowtows

KRAAL   *v* **-ED, -ING, -S** to pen in a type of enclosure

KRAFT   *n* pl. **-S** a strong paper

KRAIT   *n* pl. **-S** a venomous snake

KRAKEN   *n* pl. **-S** a legendary sea monster

KRATER   *n* pl. **-S** a type of vase

KRAUT   *n* pl. **-S** sauerkraut

KREEP   *n* pl. **-S** a basaltic lunar rock

KREMLIN   *n* pl. **-S** a Russian citadel

KREPLACH   *n* pl. **KREPLACH** dumplings filled with ground meat or cheese

KREPLECH   *n* pl. **KREPLECH** kreplach

KREUTZER   *n* pl. **-S** a former monetary unit of Austria

KREUZER   *n* pl. **-S** kreutzer

KREWE   *n* pl. **-S** a private group participating in the New Orleans Mardi Gras

KRILL   *n* pl. **-S** an aggregate of small marine crustaceans

KRIMMER   *n* pl. **-S** a kind of fur

KRIS   *n* pl. **-ES** a short sword

KRONA   *n* pl. **KRONOR** a monetary unit of Sweden

KRONA   *n* pl. **KRONUR** a monetary unit of Iceland

KRONE   *n* pl. **KRONEN** a former monetary unit of Austria

KRONE   *n* pl. **KRONER** a monetary unit of Denmark

KRONOR   pl. of krona

KRONUR   pl. of krona

KROON   *n* pl. **KROONS** or **KROONI** a former monetary unit of Estonia

KRUBI   *n* pl. **-S** a tropical plant

KRUBUT   *n* pl. **-S** krubi

KRULLER   *n* pl. **-S** cruller

KRUMHORN   *n* pl. **-S** crumhorn

KRUMKAKE   *n* pl. **-S** a large thin cookie

KRYOLITE   *n* pl. **-S** cryolite

KRYOLITH   *n* pl. **-S** cryolite

KRYPTON   *n* pl. **-S** a gaseous element

KUCHEN   *n* pl. **-S** a coffee cake

KUDO   *n* pl. **-DOS** award; honor

KUDU   *n* pl. **-S** a large antelope

KUDZU   *n* pl. **-S** an Asian vine

KUE   *n* pl. **-S** the letter Q

KUFI   *n* pl. **-S** a brimless hat

KUGEL   *n* pl. **-S** a baked pudding of potatoes or noodles

KUKRI   *n* pl. **-S** a long, curved knife of Nepal

KULAK   *n* pl. **-LAKS** or **-LAKI** a rich Russian peasant

KULTUR   *n* pl. **-S** culture; civilization

KUMISS   *n* pl. **-ES** koumiss

KUMMEL   *n* pl. **-S** a type of liqueur

KUMQUAT   *n* pl. **-S** a citrus fruit

KUMYS   *n* pl. **-ES** koumiss

KUNA   *n* pl. **KUNE** a monetary unit of Croatia

KUNZITE   *n* pl. **-S** a mineral

KURBASH   *v* **-ED, -ING, -ES** to flog with a leather whip

KURGAN   *n* pl. **-S** a mound of earth over a grave

KURTA   *n* pl. **-S** a shirt worn in India

KURTOSIS   *n* pl. **-TOSES** the relative degree of curvature in a statistical curve

KURU   *n* pl. **-S** a disease of the nervous system

KUSSO   *n* pl. **-SOS** cusso

KUVASZ   *n* pl. **-VASZOK** a large dog having a white coat

KVAS   *n* pl. **-ES** kvass

KVASS   *n* pl. **-ES** a Russian beer

KVELL   *v* **-ED, -ING, -S** to exclaim joyfully

KVETCH   *v* **-ED, -ING, -ES** to complain

KVETCHER   *n* pl. **-S** one that kvetches

KVETCHY   *adj* **KVETCHIER, KVETCHIEST** habitually complaining

KWACHA   *n* pl. **-S** a monetary unit of Malawi and Zambia

KWANZA   *n* pl. **-S** a monetary unit of Angola

KYACK   *n* pl. **-S** a packsack

KYAK   *n* pl. **-S** a kayak (an Eskimo canoe)

KYANISE   *v* **-ISED, -ISING, -ISES** to kyanize

KYANITE   *n* pl. **-S** cyanite

KYANIZE   *v* **-IZED, -IZING, -IZES** to treat wood with a type of preservative

KYAR   *n* pl. **-S** coir

KYAT   *n* pl. **-S** a monetary unit of Myanmar (Burma)

KYBOSH   *v* **-ED, -ING, -ES** to kibosh

KYE   *n* pl. **-S** a private Korean-American banking club

KYLIX   *n* pl. **-LIKES** a drinking vessel

KYMOGRAM   *n* pl. **-S** a record of fluid pressure

KYPHOSIS   *n* pl. **-PHOSES** abnormal curvature of the spine **KYPHOTIC** *adj*

KYRIE   *n* pl. **-S** a religious petition for mercy

KYTE   *n* pl. **-S** the stomach

KYTHE   *v* **KYTHED, KYTHING, KYTHES** to kithe

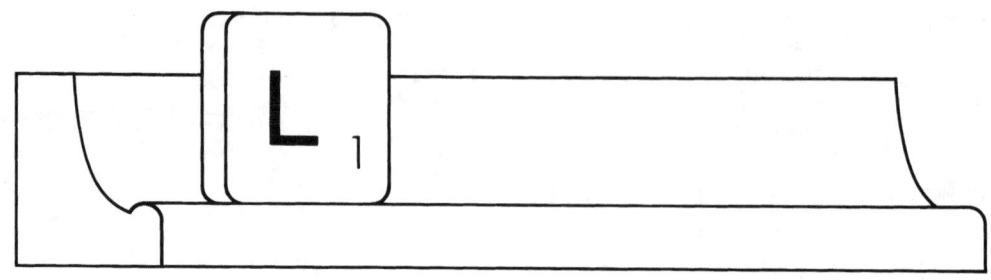

LA	*n* pl. **-S** the sixth tone of the diatonic musical scale	**LABROID**	*n* pl. **-S** a marine fish
LAAGER	*v* **-ED, -ING, -S** to form a defensive encampment	**LABRUM**	*n* pl. **-BRUMS** or **-BRA** a lip or liplike structure
LAARI	*n* pl. **LAARI** a monetary unit of the Maldives	**LABRUSCA**	*adj* designating a fox grape
		LABURNUM	*n* pl. **-S** an ornamental tree
LAB	*n* pl. **-S** a laboratory	**LAC**	*n* pl. **-S** a resinous substance secreted by certain insects
LABARUM	*n* pl. **-RUMS** or **-RA** an ecclesiastical banner	**LACE**	*v* **LACED, LACING, LACES** to fasten by means of a lace (a cord for drawing together two edges)
LABDANUM	*n* pl. **-S** a fragrant resin		
LABEL	*v* **-BELED, -BELING, -BELS** or **-BELLED, -BELLING, -BELS** to describe or designate	**LACELESS**	*adj* lacking lace
		LACELIKE	*adj* resembling lace
LABELER	*n* pl. **-S** one that labels	**LACER**	*n* pl. **-S** one that laces
LABELLA	pl. of labellum	**LACERATE**	*v* **-ATED, -ATING, -ATES** to tear roughly
LABELLER	*n* pl. **-S** labeler		
LABELLING	a present participle of label	**LACERTID**	*n* pl. **-S** a type of lizard
LABELLUM	*n* pl. **-LA** the lower petal of an orchid	**LACEWING**	*n* pl. **-S** a winged insect
		LACEWOOD	*n* pl. **-S** an Australian tree
LABIA	pl. of labium	**LACEWORK**	*n* pl. **-S** a delicate openwork fabric
LABIAL	*n* pl. **-S** a labially produced sound	**LACEY**	*adj* **LACIER, LACIEST** lacy
LABIALLY	*adv* by means of the lips	**LACHES**	*n* pl. **LACHES** undue delay in asserting a legal right
LABIATE	*n* pl. **-S** a labiated plant		
LABIATED	*adj* having corollas that are divided into two liplike parts	**LACIER**	comparative of lacy
		LACIEST	superlative of lacy
LABILE	*adj* likely to change	**LACILY**	*adv* in a lacy manner
LABILITY	*n* pl. **-TIES** the state of being labile	**LACINESS**	*n* pl. **-ES** the quality of being lacy
LABIUM	*n* pl. **-BIA** a fold of the vulva	**LACING**	*n* pl. **-S** a contrasting marginal band of color
LABOR	*v* **-ED, -ING, -S** to work		
LABORER	*n* pl. **-S** one that labors	**LACK**	*v* **-ED, -ING, -S** to be without
LABORITE	*n* pl. **-S** a supporter of labor interests	**LACKADAY**	*interj* — used to express regret
		LACKER	*v* **-ED, -ING, -S** to lacquer
LABOUR	*v* **-ED, -ING, -S** to labor	**LACKEY**	*v* **-ED, -ING, -S** to act in a servile manner
LABOURER	*n* pl. **-S** laborer		
LABRA	a pl. of labrum	**LACONIC**	*adj* using a minimum of words
LABRADOR	*n* pl. **-S** a hunting dog	**LACONISM**	*n* pl. **-S** brevity of expression
LABRET	*n* pl. **-S** an ornament worn in a perforation of the lip	**LACQUER**	*v* **-ED, -ING, -S** to coat with a glossy substance

LACQUEY *v* **-ED, -ING, -S** to lackey

LACRIMAL *n* pl. **-S** a type of vase

LACROSSE *n* pl. **-S** a type of ball game

LACTAM *n* pl. **-S** a chemical compound

LACTARY *adj* pertaining to milk

LACTASE *n* pl. **-S** an enzyme

LACTATE *v* **-TATED, -TATING, -TATES** to secrete milk

LACTEAL *n* pl. **-S** a lymphatic vessel

LACTEAN *adj* lacteous

LACTEOUS *adj* resembling milk

LACTIC *adj* derived from milk

LACTONE *n* pl. **-S** any of a group of esters **LACTONIC** *adj*

LACTOSE *n* pl. **-S** a lactic sugar

LACUNA *n* pl. **-NAS** or **-NAE** an empty space or missing part **LACUNAL, LACUNARY, LACUNATE** *adj*

LACUNAR *n* pl. **-NARS** or **-NARIA** a ceiling with recessed panels

LACUNE *n* pl. **-S** lacuna

LACUNOSE *adj* marked by shallow depressions

LACY *adj* **LACIER, LACIEST** resembling lacework

LAD *n* pl. **-S** a boy or youth **LADDISH** *adj*

LADANUM *n* pl. **-S** labdanum

LADDER *v* **-ED, -ING, -S** to cause a run in a stocking

LADDIE *n* pl. **-S** a lad

LADE *v* **LADED, LADEN, LADING, LADES** to load with a cargo

LADEN *v* **-ED, -ING, -S** to lade

LADER *n* pl. **-S** one that lades

LADHOOD *n* pl. **-S** the state of being a lad

LADIES pl. of lady

LADING *n* pl. **-S** cargo; freight

LADINO *n* pl. **-NOS** a fast-growing clover

LADLE *v* **-DLED, -DLING, -DLES** to lift out with a ladle (a type of spoon)

LADLEFUL *n* pl. **-S** as much as a ladle will hold

LADLER *n* pl. **-S** one that ladles

LADLING present participle of ladle

LADRON *n* pl. **-S** ladrone

LADRONE *n* pl. **-S** a thief

LADY *n* pl. **-DIES** a woman of refinement and gentle manners

LADYBIRD *n* pl. **-S** a ladybug

LADYBUG *n* pl. **-S** a small beetle

LADYFISH *n* pl. **-ES** a bonefish

LADYHOOD *n* pl. **-S** the state of being a lady

LADYISH *adj* somewhat ladylike

LADYKIN *n* pl. **-S** a small lady

LADYLIKE *adj* resembling or suitable to a lady

LADYLOVE *n* pl. **-S** a sweetheart

LADYPALM *n* pl. **-S** a palm tree

LADYSHIP *n* pl. **-S** the condition of being a lady

LAETRILE *n* pl. **-S** a drug derived from apricot pits

LAEVO *adj* levo

LAG *v* **LAGGED, LAGGING, LAGS** to stay or fall behind

LAGAN *n* pl. **-S** goods thrown into the sea with a buoy attached to enable recovery

LAGEND *n* pl. **-S** lagan

LAGER *v* **-ED, -ING, -S** to laager

LAGGARD *n* pl. **-S** one that lags

LAGGED past tense of lag

LAGGER *n* pl. **-S** a laggard

LAGGING *n* pl. **-S** an insulating material

LAGNAPPE *n* pl. **-S** a small gift given to a customer with his purchase

LAGOON *n* pl. **-S** a shallow body of water **LAGOONAL** *adj*

LAGUNA *n* pl. **-S** lagoon

LAGUNE *n* pl. **-S** lagoon

LAHAR *n* pl. **-S** a flowing mass of volcanic debris

LAIC *n* pl. **-S** a layman **LAICAL** *adj* **LAICALLY** *adv*

LAICH *n* pl. **-S** laigh

LAICISE *v* **-ICISED, -ICISING, -ICISES** to laicize

LAICISM *n* pl. **-S** a political system free from clerical control

LAICIZE *v* **-ICIZED, -ICIZING, -ICIZES** to free from clerical control

LAID a past tense of lay

LAIGH *n* pl. **-S** a lowland

LAIN past participle of lie

LAIR   *v* **-ED, -ING, -S** to live in a lair (a wild animal's resting or dwelling place)

LAIRD   *n* pl. **-S** the owner of a landed estate **LAIRDLY** *adj*

LAITANCE   *n* pl. **-S** a milky deposit on the surface of fresh concrete

LAITH   *adj* loath **LAITHLY** *adv*

LAITY   *n* pl. **-ITIES** the nonclerical membership of a religious faith

LAKE   *n* pl. **-S** a sizable inland body of water **LAKELIKE** *adj*

LAKEBED   *n* pl. **-S** the floor of a lake

LAKED   *adj* subjected to the process of laking

LAKEPORT   *n* pl. **-S** a city located on the shore of a lake

LAKER   *n* pl. **-S** a lake fish

LAKESIDE   *n* pl. **-S** the land along the edge of a lake

LAKH   *n* pl. **-S** the sum of one hundred thousand

LAKING   *n* pl. **-S** the reddening of blood plasma by the release of hemoglobin from the red corpuscles

LAKY   *adj* **LAKIER, LAKIEST** of the color of blood

LALIQUE   *n* pl. **-S** a style of cut glass or crystal

LALL   *v* **-ED, -ING, -S** to articulate the letter *r* as *l*

LALLAN   *n* pl. **-S** a lowland

LALLAND   *n* pl. **-S** a lowland

LALLYGAG   *v* **-GAGGED, -GAGGING, -GAGS** to dawdle

LAM   *v* **LAMMED, LAMMING, LAMS** to flee hastily

LAMA   *n* pl. **-S** a Buddhist monk

LAMASERY   *n* pl. **-SERIES** a monastery of lamas

LAMB   *v* **-ED, -ING, -S** to give birth to a lamb (a young sheep)

LAMBADA   *n* pl. **-S** a Brazilian dance

LAMBAST   *v* **-ED, -ING, -S** to lambaste

LAMBASTE   *v* **-BASTED, -BASTING, -BASTES** to beat severely

LAMBDA   *n* pl. **-S** a Greek letter **LAMBDOID** *adj*

LAMBENCY   *n* pl. **-CIES** the quality or an instance of being lambent

LAMBENT   *adj* flickering lightly and gently over a surface

LAMBER   *n* pl. **-S** a ewe that is lambing

LAMBERT   *n* pl. **-S** a unit of brightness

LAMBIE   *n* pl. **-S** a lambkin

LAMBIER   comparative of lamby

LAMBIEST   superlative of lamby

LAMBKILL   *n* pl. **-S** an evergreen shrub

LAMBKIN   *n* pl. **-S** a small lamb

LAMBLIKE   *adj* resembling a lamb

LAMBSKIN   *n* pl. **-S** the skin of a lamb

LAMBY   *adj* **LAMBIER, LAMBIEST** resembling a lamb

LAME   *adj* **LAMER, LAMEST** physically disabled

LAME   *v* **LAMED, LAMING, LAMES** to make lame

LAMED   *n* pl. **-S** a Hebrew letter

LAMEDH   *n* pl. **-S** lamed

LAMELLA   *n* pl. **-LAS** or **-LAE** a thin plate, scale, or membrane **LAMELLAR** *adj*

LAMELY   *adv* in a lame manner

LAMENESS   *n* pl. **-ES** the state of being lame

LAMENT   *v* **-ED, -ING, -S** to express sorrow or regret for

LAMENTER   *n* pl. **-S** one that laments

LAMER   comparative of lame

LAMEST   superlative of lame

LAMIA   *n* pl. **-MIAS** or **-MIAE** a female demon

LAMINA   *n* pl. **-NAS** or **-NAE** a thin plate, scale, or layer **LAMINAR, LAMINARY** *adj*

LAMINAL   *n* pl. **-S** a speech sound articulated with the blade of the tongue

LAMINATE   *v* **-NATED, -NATING, -NATES** to compress into a thin plate

LAMING   present participle of lame

LAMININ   *n* pl. **-S** a glycoprotein

LAMINOSE   *adj* composed of laminae

LAMINOUS   *adj* laminose

LAMISTER   *n* pl. **-S** lamster

LAMMED   past tense of lam

LAMMING   present participle of lam

LAMP   *v* **-ED, -ING, -S** to look at

LAMPAD   *n* pl. **-S** a candlestick

LAMPAS *n* pl. **-ES** inflammation of the roof of a horse's mouth

LAMPERS *n* pl. **-ES** lampas

LAMPION *n* pl. **-S** a type of light-generating device

LAMPOON *v* **-ED, -ING, -S** to ridicule in a satirical composition

LAMPPOST *n* pl. **-S** a post supporting a streetlight

LAMPREY *n* pl. **-PREYS** an eellike fish

LAMPYRID *n* pl. **-S** any of a family of beetles

LAMSTER *n* pl. **-S** a fugitive

LANAI *n* pl. **-S** a veranda

LANATE *adj* covered with wool

LANATED *adj* lanate

LANCE *v* **LANCED, LANCING, LANCES** to pierce with a lance (a spearlike weapon)

LANCELET *n* pl. **-S** a small marine organism

LANCER *n* pl. **-S** a cavalryman armed with a lance

LANCET *n* pl. **-S** a narrow, pointed arch **LANCETED** *adj*

LANCIERS *n* pl. **LANCIERS** a French dance

LANCING present participle of lance

LAND *v* **-ED, -ING, -S** to set down upon land (solid ground)

LANDAU *n* pl. **-S** a type of carriage

LANDER *n* pl. **-S** one that lands

LANDFALL *n* pl. **-S** a sighting or approach to land

LANDFILL *v* **-ED, -ING, -S** to build up an area by burying refuse

LANDFORM *n* pl. **-S** a natural feature of the earth's surface

LANDGRAB *n* pl. **-S** a swift and often fraudulent seizure of land

LANDING *n* pl. **-S** a place for discharging or taking on passengers or cargo

LANDLADY *n* pl. **-DIES** a female landlord

LANDLER *n* pl. **-S** a slow Austrian dance

LANDLESS *adj* owning no land

LANDLINE *n* pl. **-S** a line of communication on land

LANDLORD *n* pl. **-S** one who owns and rents out real estate

LANDMAN *n* pl. **-MEN** one who lives and works on land

LANDMARK *v* **-ED, -ING, -S** to designate a building or site as a place of historical or aesthetic importance

LANDMASS *n* pl. **-ES** a large area of land

LANDMEN pl. of landman

LANDSIDE *n* pl. **-S** a part of a plow

LANDSKIP *n* pl. **-S** landscape

LANDSLID past tense of landslide (to win an election by an overwhelming majority)

LANDSLIP *n* pl. **-S** the fall of a mass of earth

LANDSMAN *n* pl. **-MEN** landman

LANDSMAN *n* pl. **LANDSLEIT** a fellow Jew coming from one's own section of Eastern Europe

LANDWARD *adv* toward the land

LANE *n* pl. **-S** a narrow passageway

LANELY *adj* lonely

LANEWAY *n* pl. **-WAYS** a lane

LANG *adj* long

LANGLAUF *n* pl. **-S** a cross-country ski run

LANGLEY *n* pl. **-LEYS** a unit of illumination

LANGRAGE *n* pl. **-S** a shot formerly used in naval warfare

LANGREL *n* pl. **-S** langrage

LANGSHAN *n* pl. **-S** any of a breed of large domestic fowl

LANGSYNE *n* pl. **-S** time long past

LANGUAGE *n* pl. **-S** a body of words and systems serving as a means of communication

LANGUE *n* pl. **-S** a type of language

LANGUET *n* pl. **-S** a tonguelike part

LANGUID *adj* lacking in vigor or vitality

LANGUISH *v* **-ED, -ING, -ES** to lose vigor or vitality

LANGUOR *n* pl. **-S** the state of being languid

LANGUR *n* pl. **-S** an Asian monkey

LANIARD *n* pl. **-S** lanyard

LANIARY *n* pl. **-ARIES** a cuspid

LANITAL *n* pl. **-S** a woollike fiber

LANK *adj* **LANKER, LANKEST** long and slender **LANKLY** *adv*

LANKNESS *n* pl. **-ES** the state of being lank

LANKY *adj* **LANKIER, LANKIEST** ungracefully tall and thin **LANKILY** *adv*

LANNER *n* pl. **-S** a falcon of Europe and Asia

LANNERET *n* pl. **-S** a male lanner

LANOLIN *n* pl. **-S** a fatty substance obtained from wool

LANOLINE *n* pl. **-S** lanolin

LANOSE *adj* lanate

LANOSITY *n* pl. **-TIES** the state of being lanose

LANTANA *n* pl. **-S** a tropical shrub

LANTERN *n* pl. **-S** a protective case for a light

LANTHORN *n* pl. **-S** a lantern

LANUGO *n* pl. **-GOS** fine, soft hair

LANYARD *n* pl. **-S** a fastening rope on a ship

LAOGAI *n* pl. **-S** the system of forced-labor camps in China

LAP *v* **LAPPED, LAPPING, LAPS** to fold over or around something

LAPBOARD *n* pl. **-S** a flat board used as a table or desk

LAPDOG *n* pl. **-S** a small dog

LAPEL *n* pl. **-S** an extension of the collar of a garment **LAPELED, LAPELLED** *adj*

LAPFUL *n* pl. **-S** as much as the lap can hold

LAPIDARY *n* pl. **-DARIES** one who works with precious stones

LAPIDATE *v* **-DATED, -DATING, -DATES** to hurl stones at

LAPIDIFY *v* **-FIED, -FYING, -FIES** to turn to stone

LAPIDIST *n* pl. **-S** a lapidary

LAPILLUS *n* pl. **-LI** a small fragment of lava

LAPIN *n* pl. **-S** a rabbit

LAPIS *n* pl. **-PISES** or **-PIDES** a semiprecious stone

LAPPED past tense of lap

LAPPER *v* **-ED, -ING, -S** to lopper

LAPPET *n* pl. **-S** a decorative flap on a garment **LAPPETED** *adj*

LAPPING present participle of lap

LAPSE *v* **LAPSED, LAPSING, LAPSES** to fall from a previous standard **LAPSABLE, LAPSIBLE** *adj*

LAPSER *n* pl. **-S** one that lapses

LAPSUS *n* pl. **LAPSUS** a mistake

LAPTOP *n* pl. **-S** a small computer for use on one's lap

LAPWING *n* pl. **-S** a shore bird

LAR *n* pl. **-S** or **-ES** a tutelary god or spirit of an ancient Roman household

LARBOARD *n* pl. **-S** the left-hand side of a ship

LARCENER *n* pl. **-S** one that commits larceny

LARCENY *n* pl. **-NIES** the felonious taking and removal of another's personal goods

LARCH *n* pl. **-ES** a coniferous tree **LARCHEN** *adj*

LARD *v* **-ED, -ING, -S** to coat with lard (the melted fat of hogs)

LARDER *n* pl. **-S** a place where food is stored

LARDIER comparative of lardy

LARDIEST superlative of lardy

LARDLIKE *adj* resembling lard

LARDON *n* pl. **-S** a thin slice of bacon or pork

LARDOON *n* pl. **-S** lardon

LARDY *adj* **LARDIER, LARDIEST** resembling lard

LAREE *n* pl. **-S** lari

LARES a pl. of lar

LARGANDO *adj* becoming gradually slower — used as a musical direction

LARGE *adj* **LARGER, LARGEST** of considerable size or quantity **LARGELY** *adv*

LARGE *n* pl. **-S** generosity

LARGESS *n* pl. **-ES** generosity

LARGESSE *n* pl. **-S** largess

LARGEST superlative of large

LARGISH *adj* somewhat large

LARGO *n* pl. **-GOS** a slow musical movement

LARI *n* pl. **-S** a monetary unit of Maldives

LARIAT *v* **-ED, -ING, -S** to lasso

LARINE *adj* resembling a gull

LARK *v* **-ED, -ING, -S** to behave playfully

LARKER *n* pl. **-S** one that larks

LARKIER comparative of larky

LARKIEST superlative of larky

LARKISH *adj* playful

LARKSOME *adj* playful

LARKSPUR *n* pl. **-S** a flowering plant

LARKY *adj* **LARKIER, LARKIEST** playful

LARRIGAN *n* pl. **-S** a type of moccasin

LARRIKIN *n* pl. **-S** a rowdy

LARRUP *v* **-ED, -ING, -S** to beat or thrash

LARRUPER *n* pl. **-S** one that larrups

LARUM *n* pl. **-S** an alarm

LARVA *n* pl. **-VAS** or **-VAE** the immature form of various insects and animals when newly hatched **LARVAL** *adj*

LARYNGAL *n* pl. **-S** a speech sound articulated in the larynx

LARYNX *n* pl. **LARYNXES** or **LARYNGES** an organ of the respiratory tract

LASAGNA *n* pl. **-S** an Italian baked dish

LASAGNE *n* pl. **-S** lasagna

LASCAR *n* pl. **-S** an East Indian sailor

LASE *v* **LASED, LASING, LASES** to function as a laser

LASER *n* pl. **-S** a device that amplifies light waves

LASH *v* **-ED, -ING, -ES** to strike with a whip

LASHER *n* pl. **-S** one that lashes

LASHING *n* pl. **-S** a flogging

LASHINS *n/pl* an abundance

LASHKAR *n* pl. **-S** lascar

LASING present participle of lase

LASS *n* pl. **-ES** a young woman

LASSI *n* pl. **-S** a beverage of yogurt, water, and flavorings

LASSIE *n* pl. **-S** a lass

LASSO *v* **-ED, -ING, -S** or **-ES** to catch with a lasso (a long rope with a running noose)

LASSOER *n* pl. **-S** one that lassos

LAST *v* **-ED, -ING, -S** to continue in existence

LASTBORN *n* pl. **-S** a child born last in a family

LASTER *n* pl. **-S** one that lasts

LASTING *n* pl. **-S** a durable fabric

LASTLY *adv* in conclusion

LAT *n* pl. **-S** a muscle of the back

LATAKIA *n* pl. **-S** a variety of Turkish tobacco

LATCH *v* **-ED, -ING, -ES** to close with a type of fastening device

LATCHET *n* pl. **-S** a thong used to fasten a shoe

LATCHKEY *n* pl. **-KEYS** a key for opening a latched door

LATE *adj* **LATER, LATEST** coming or occurring after the expected time

LATED *adj* belated

LATEEN *n* pl. **-S** a sailing vessel

LATEENER *n* pl. **-S** a lateen

LATELY *adv* not long ago

LATEN *v* **-ED, -ING, -S** to become late

LATENCY *n* pl. **-CIES** the state of being present but not manifest

LATENESS *n* pl. **-ES** the state of being late

LATENT *n* pl. **-S** a barely visible fingerprint that can be developed for study

LATENTLY *adv* dormantly

LATER comparative of late

LATERAD *adv* toward the side

LATERAL *v* **-ALED, -ALING, -ALS** or **-ALLED, -ALLING, -ALS** to execute a type of pass in football

LATERITE *n* pl. **-S** a type of soil

LATERIZE *v* **-IZED, -IZING, -IZES** to convert to laterite

LATEST *n* pl. **-S** the most recent development

LATEWOOD *n* pl. **-S** a part of an annual ring of wood

LATEX *n* pl. **LATEXES** or **LATICES** a milky liquid of certain plants

LATH *v* **-ED, -ING, -S** to cover with laths (thin strips of wood)

LATHE *v* **LATHED, LATHING, LATHES** to cut or shape on a type of machine

LATHER *v* **-ED, -ING, -S** to cover with lather (a light foam)

LATHERER *n* pl. **-S** one that lathers

LATHERY *adj* covered with lather

LATHI *n* pl. **-S** a heavy stick of bamboo and iron in India

LATHING *n* pl. **-S** work made of or using laths

LATHWORK *n* pl. **-S** lathing

LATHY *adj* **LATHIER, LATHIEST** long and slender

LATI a pl. of lats

LATICES a pl. of latex

LATIGO *n* pl. **-GOS** or **-GOES** a strap used to fasten a saddle

LATILLA *n* pl. **-S** a peeled limb used in ceilings

LATINA *n* pl. **-S** a Latin-American woman or girl

LATINITY *n* pl. **-TIES** a manner of writing or speaking Latin

LATINIZE   *v* **-IZED, -IZING, -IZES** to translate into Latin

LATINO   *n* pl. **-NOS** a Latin American

LATISH   *adj* somewhat late

LATITUDE   *n* pl. **-S** freedom from narrow restrictions

LATKE   *n* pl. **-S** a potato pancake

LATOSOL   *n* pl. **-S** a tropical soil

LATRIA   *n* pl. **-S** the supreme worship given to God only, in Roman Catholicism

LATRINE   *n* pl. **-S** a type of toilet

LATS   *n* pl. **LATI** or **LATU** a monetary unit of Latvia

LATTE   *n* pl. **-S** espresso coffee with milk

LATTEN   *n* pl. **-S** a brass-like alloy

LATTER   *adj* being the second mentioned of two

LATTERLY   *adv* lately

LATTICE   *v* **-TICED, -TICING, -TICES** to form a structure consisting of interlaced strips of material

LATTIN   *n* pl. **-S** latten

LATU   a pl. of lats

LAUAN   *n* pl. **-S** a Philippine timber

LAUD   *v* **-ED, -ING, -S** to praise

LAUDABLE   *adj* worthy of praise **LAUDABLY** *adv*

LAUDANUM   *n* pl. **-S** a type of opium preparation

LAUDATOR   *n* pl. **-S** a lauder

LAUDER   *n* pl. **-S** one that lauds

LAUGH   *v* **-ED, -ING, -S** to express emotion, typically mirth, by a series of inarticulate sounds

LAUGHER   *n* pl. **-S** one that laughs

LAUGHING   *n* pl. **-S** laughter

LAUGHTER   *n* pl. **-S** the act or sound of one that laughs

LAUNCE   *n* pl. **-S** a marine fish

LAUNCH   *v* **-ED, -ING, -ES** to set in motion

LAUNCHER   *n* pl. **-S** a launching device

LAUNDER   *v* **-ED, -ING, -S** to wash clothes

LAUNDRY   *n* pl. **-DRIES** a collection of clothes to be washed

LAURA   *n* pl. **-RAS** or **-RAE** a type of monastery

LAUREATE   *v* **-ATED, -ATING, -ATES** to laurel

LAUREL   *v* **-RELED, -RELING, -RELS** or **-RELLED, -RELLING, -RELS** to crown with a wreath of evergreen leaves

LAUWINE   *n* pl. **-S** an avalanche

LAV   *n* pl. **-S** a lavatory

LAVA   *n* pl. **-S** molten rock that issues from a volcano

LAVABO   *n* pl. **-BOS** or **-BOES** a ceremonial washing in certain Christian churches

LAVAGE   *n* pl. **-S** a washing

LAVALAVA   *n* pl. **-S** a Polynesian garment

LAVALIER   *n* pl. **-S** a pendant worn on a chain around the neck

LAVALIKE   *adj* resembling lava

LAVASH   *n* pl. **-ES** a thin flat bread of Armenian origin

LAVATION   *n* pl. **-S** the acting of washing

LAVATORY   *n* pl. **-RIES** a room equipped with washing and toilet facilities

LAVE   *v* **LAVED, LAVING, LAVES** to wash

LAVEER   *v* **-ED, -ING, -S** to sail against the wind

LAVENDER   *v* **-ED, -ING, -S** to sprinkle with a type of perfume

LAVER   *n* pl. **-S** a vessel used for ancient Hebrew ceremonial washings

LAVEROCK   *n* pl. **-S** a songbird

LAVING   present participle of lave

LAVISH   *adj* **-ISHER, -ISHEST** expending or giving in great amounts **LAVISHLY** *adv*

LAVISH   *v* **-ED, -ING, -ES** to expend or give in great amounts

LAVISHER   *n* pl. **-S** one that lavishes

LAVROCK   *n* pl. **-S** laverock

LAW   *v* **-ED, -ING, -S** to take a complaint to court for settlement

LAWBOOK   *n* pl. **-S** a book containing or dealing with laws

LAWFUL   *adj* allowed by law (the body of rules governing the affairs of a community) **LAWFULLY** *adv*

LAWGIVER   *n* pl. **-S** one who institutes a legal system

LAWINE   *n* pl. **-S** lauwine

LAWING   *n* pl. **-S** a bill for food or drink in a tavern

LAWLESS   *adj* having no system of laws

LAWLIKE *adj* being like the law

LAWMAKER *n* pl. **-S** a legislator

LAWMAN *n* pl. **-MEN** a law-enforcement officer

LAWN *n* pl. **-S** an area of grass-covered land **LAWNY** *adj*

LAWSUIT *n* pl. **-S** a legal action

LAWYER *v* **-ED, -ING, -S** to work as a member of the legal profession

LAWYERLY *adj* befitting a member of the legal profession

LAX *adj* **LAXER, LAXEST** not strict or stringent

LAX *n* pl. **-ES** a vowel articulated with relatively relaxed muscles

LAXATION *n* pl. **-S** the act of relaxing

LAXATIVE *n* pl. **-S** a drug that stimulates evacuation of the bowels

LAXITY *n* pl. **-ITIES** the state of being lax

LAXLY *adv* in a lax manner

LAXNESS *n* pl. **-ES** laxity

LAY *v* **LAID** or **LAYED, LAYING, LAYS** to deposit as a wager

LAYABOUT *n* pl. **-S** a lazy person

LAYAWAY *n* pl. **-AWAYS** an item that has been reserved with a down payment

LAYER *v* **-ED, -ING, -S** to form a layer (a single thickness, coating, or covering)

LAYERAGE *n* pl. **-S** a method of plant propagation

LAYERING *n* pl. **-S** layerage

LAYETTE *n* pl. **-S** an outfit of clothing and equipment for a newborn child

LAYIN *n* pl. **-S** a type of shot in basketball

LAYMAN *n* pl. **-MEN** a member of the laity

LAYOFF *n* pl. **-S** the suspension or dismissal of employees

LAYOUT *n* pl. **-S** an arrangement or plan

LAYOVER *n* pl. **-S** a stopover

LAYUP *n* pl. **-S** a shot in basketball

LAYWOMAN *n* pl. **-WOMEN** a female member of the laity

LAZAR *n* pl. **-S** a beggar afflicted with a loathsome disease

LAZARET *n* pl. **-S** a hospital treating contagious diseases

LAZE *v* **LAZED, LAZING, LAZES** to pass time lazily

LAZIED past tense of lazy

LAZIER comparative of lazy

LAZIES present 3d person sing. of lazy

LAZIEST superlative of lazy

LAZILY *adv* in a lazy manner

LAZINESS *n* pl. **-ES** the state of being lazy

LAZING present participle of laze

LAZULI *n* pl. **-S** a mineral

LAZULITE *n* pl. **-S** a mineral

LAZURITE *n* pl. **-S** a mineral

LAZY *adj* **LAZIER, LAZIEST** disinclined toward work or exertion

LAZY *v* **LAZIED, LAZYING, LAZIES** to move or lie lazily

LAZYISH *adj* somewhat lazy

LEA *n* pl. **-S** a meadow

LEACH *v* **-ED, -ING, -ES** to subject to the filtering action of a liquid

LEACHATE *n* pl. **-S** a solution obtained by leaching

LEACHER *n* pl. **-S** one that leaches

LEACHY *adj* **LEACHIER, LEACHIEST** porous

LEAD *v* **-ED, -ING, -S** to cover with lead (a heavy metallic element)

LEAD *v* **LED, LEADING, LEADS** to show the way to by going in advance

LEADEN *v* **-ED, -ING, -S** to make dull or slugggish **LEADENLY** *adv*

LEADER *n* pl. **-S** one that leads or guides

LEADIER comparative of leady

LEADIEST superlative of leady

LEADING *n* pl. **-S** a covering or border of lead

LEADLESS *adj* having no lead

LEADMAN *n* pl. **-MEN** a worker in charge of other workers

LEADOFF *n* pl. **-S** an opening play or move

LEADSMAN *n* pl. **-MEN** a seaman who measures the depth of water

LEADWORK *n* pl. **-S** something made of lead

LEADWORT *n* pl. **-S** a tropical plant

LEADY *adj* **LEADIER, LEADIEST** resembling lead

LEAF *n* pl. **LEAVES** a usually green, flattened organ of vascular plants

LEAF *v* **-ED, -ING, -S** to turn pages rapidly

LEAFAGE *n* pl. **-S** foliage

LEAFIER comparative of leafy

LEAFIEST superlative of leafy

LEAFLESS *adj* having no leaves

LEAFLET *v* **-LETED, -LETING, -LETS** or **-LETTED, -LETTING, -LETS** to distribute printed sheets of paper

LEAFLIKE *adj* resembling a leaf

LEAFWORM *n* pl. **-S** a moth larva that feeds on leaves

LEAFY *adj* **LEAFIER, LEAFIEST** covered with leaves

LEAGUE *v* **LEAGUED, LEAGUING, LEAGUES** to come together for a common purpose

LEAGUER *v* **-ED, -ING, -S** to besiege

LEAK *v* **-ED, -ING, -S** to permit the escape of something through a breach or flaw

LEAKAGE *n* pl. **-S** the act or an instance of leaking

LEAKER *n* pl. **-S** one that leaks

LEAKLESS *adj* designed not to leak

LEAKY *adj* **LEAKIER, LEAKIEST** tending to leak **LEAKILY** *adv*

LEAL *adj* loyal **LEALLY** *adv*

LEALTY *n* pl. **-TIES** loyalty

LEAN *adj* **LEANER, LEANEST** having little fat **LEANLY** *adv*

LEAN *v* **LEANED** or **LEANT, LEANING, LEANS** to deviate from a vertical position

LEANER *n* pl. **-S** one that leans

LEANING *n* pl. **-S** a tendency

LEANNESS *n* pl. **-ES** the state of being lean

LEANT a past tense of lean

LEAP *v* **LEAPED** or **LEAPT** or **LEPT, LEAPING, LEAPS** to spring off the ground

LEAPER *n* pl. **-S** one that leaps

LEAPFROG *v* **-FROGGED, -FROGGING, -FROGS** to jump over with the legs wide apart

LEAR *n* pl. **-S** learning

LEARIER comparative of leary

LEARIEST superlative of leary

LEARN *v* **LEARNED** or **LEARNT, LEARNING, LEARNS** to gain knowledge by experience, instruction, or study

LEARNER *n* pl. **-S** one that learns

LEARNING *n* pl. **-S** acquired knowledge

LEARY *adj* **LEARIER, LEARIEST** leery

LEASE *v* **LEASED, LEASING, LEASES** to grant temporary use of in exchange for rent **LEASABLE** *adj*

LEASER *n* pl. **-S** one that leases

LEASH *v* **-ED, -ING, -ES** to restrain an animal with a line or thong

LEASING *n* pl. **-S** a falsehood

LEAST *n* pl. **-S** something that is smallest in size or degree

LEATHER *v* **-ED, -ING, -S** to cover with leather (the dressed or tanned hide of an animal)

LEATHERN *adj* made of leather

LEATHERY *adj* resembling leather

LEAVE *v* **LEFT, LEAVING, LEAVES** to go away from

LEAVED *adj* having a leaf or leaves

LEAVEN *v* **-ED, -ING, -S** to produce fermentation in

LEAVER *n* pl. **-S** one that leaves

LEAVES pl. of leaf

LEAVING *n* pl. **-S** a leftover

LEAVY *adj* **LEAVIER, LEAVIEST** leafy

LEBEN *n* pl. **-S** a type of liquid food

LECH *v* **-ED, -ING, -ES** to engage in lechery

LECHAYIM *n* pl. **-S** lehayim

LECHER *v* **-ED, -ING, -S** to engage in lechery

LECHERY *n* pl. **-ERIES** excessive sexual indulgence

LECHWE *n* pl. **-S** an African antelope

LECITHIN *n* pl. **-S** any of a group of fatty substances found in plant and animal tissues

LECTERN *n* pl. **-S** a reading desk

LECTIN *n* pl. **-S** a protein that binds to a sugar molecule

LECTION *n* pl. **-S** a portion of sacred writing read in a church service

LECTOR *n* pl. **-S** a reader of the lessons in a church service

LECTURE *v* **-TURED, -TURING, -TURES** to expound on a specific subject

LECTURER *n* pl. **-S** one that lectures

LECYTHIS *adj* designating a family of tropical shrubs

LECYTHUS *n* pl. **-THI** lekythos

LED past tense of lead

LEDGE   *n* pl. **-S** a narrow, shelflike projection

LEDGER   *n* pl. **-S** an account book of final entry

LEDGY   *adj* **LEDGIER, LEDGIEST** abounding in ledges

LEE   *n* pl. **-S** shelter from the wind

LEEBOARD   *n* pl. **-S** a board attached to a sailing vessel to prevent leeway

LEECH   *v* **-ED, -ING, -ES** to cling to and feed upon or drain

LEEK   *n* pl. **-S** an herb used in cookery

LEER   *v* **-ED, -ING, -S** to look with a sideways glance

LEERY   *adj* **LEERIER, LEERIEST** suspicious **LEERILY** *adv*

LEET   *n* pl. **-S** a former English court for petty offenses

LEEWARD   *n* pl. **-S** the direction toward which the wind is blowing

LEEWAY   *n* pl. **-WAYS** the lateral drift of a ship

LEFT   *adj* **LEFTER, LEFTEST** pertaining to the side of the body to the north when one faces east

LEFT   *n* pl. **-S** the left side or hand

LEFTIES   pl. of lefty

LEFTISH   *adj* inclined to be a leftist

LEFTISM   *n* pl. **-S** a liberal political philosophy

LEFTIST   *n* pl. **-S** an advocate of leftism

LEFTMOST   *adj* farthest on the left

LEFTOVER   *n* pl. **-S** an unused or unconsumed portion

LEFTWARD   *adv* toward the left

LEFTWING   *adj* favoring leftism

LEFTY   *n* pl. **LEFTIES** a left-handed person

LEG   *v* **LEGGED, LEGGING, LEGS** to move with the legs (appendages that serve as a means of support and locomotion)

LEGACY   *n* pl. **-CIES** something bequeathed

LEGAL   *n* pl. **-S** an authorized investment that may be made by investors such as savings banks

LEGALESE   *n* pl. **-S** the specialized language of lawyers

LEGALISE   *v* **-ISED, -ISING, -ISES** to legalize

LEGALISM   *n* pl. **-S** strict conformity to the law

LEGALIST   *n* pl. **-S** an adherent of legalism

LEGALITY   *n* pl. **-TIES** the condition of being lawful

LEGALIZE   *v* **-IZED, -IZING, -IZES** to make lawful

LEGALLY   *adv* in a lawful manner

LEGATE   *v* **-GATED, -GATING, -GATES** to bequeath

LEGATEE   *n* pl. **-S** the inheritor of a legacy

LEGATINE   *adj* pertaining to an official envoy

LEGATING   present participle of legate

LEGATION   *n* pl. **-S** the sending of an official envoy

LEGATO   *n* pl. **-TOS** a smooth and flowing musical style

LEGATOR   *n* pl. **-S** one that legates

LEGEND   *n* pl. **-S** an unverified story from earlier times

LEGENDRY   *n* pl. **-RIES** a collection of legends

LEGER   *n* pl. **-S** fishing bait made to lie on the bottom

LEGERITY   *n* pl. **-TIES** quickness of the mind or body

LEGES   pl. of lex

LEGGED   past tense of leg

LEGGIER   comparative of leggy

LEGGIERO   *adv* in a light or graceful manner — used as a musical direction

LEGGIEST   superlative of leggy

LEGGIN   *n* pl. **-S** legging

LEGGING   *n* pl. **-S** a covering for the leg

LEGGY   *adj* **-GIER, -GIEST** having long legs

LEGHORN   *n* pl. **-S** a smooth, plaited straw

LEGIBLE   *adj* capable of being read **LEGIBLY** *adv*

LEGION   *n* pl. **-S** a large military force

LEGIST   *n* pl. **-S** one learned or skilled in the law

LEGIT   *n* pl. **-S** legitimate drama

LEGLESS   *adj* having no legs

LEGLIKE   *adj* resembling a leg

LEGMAN   *n* pl. **-MEN** a newspaperman assigned to gather information

LEGONG   *n* pl. **-S** a Balinese dance

LEGROOM   *n* pl. **-S** space in which to extend the legs

LEGUME   *n* pl. **-S** a type of plant

LEGUMIN   *n* pl. **-S** a plant protein

LEGWORK *n* pl. **-S** work that involves extensive walking

LEHAYIM *n* pl. **-S** a traditional Jewish toast

LEHR *n* pl. **-S** a type of oven

LEHUA *n* pl. **-S** a tropical tree

LEI *n* pl. **-S** a wreath of flowers

LEISTER *v* **-ED, -ING, -S** to spear with a three-pronged fishing implement

LEISURE *n* pl. **-S** freedom from the demands of work or duty **LEISURED** *adj*

LEK *n* pl. **LEKS** or **LEKE** or **LEKU** a monetary unit of Albania

LEK *v* **LEKKED, LEKKING, LEKS** to assemble for competitive displays during the mating season

LEKVAR *n* pl. **-S** a prune butter

LEKYTHOS *n* pl. **-THOI** an oil jar used in ancient Greece

LEKYTHUS *n* pl. **-THI** lekythos

LEMAN *n* pl. **-S** a lover

LEMMA *n* pl. **-MAS** or **-MATA** a type of proposition in logic

LEMMING *n* pl. **-S** a mouselike rodent

LEMNISCI *n/pl* bands of nerve fibers

LEMON *n* pl. **-S** a citrus fruit **LEMONISH, LEMONY** *adj*

LEMONADE *n* pl. **-S** a beverage

LEMPIRA *n* pl. **-S** a monetary unit of Honduras

LEMUR *n* pl. **-S** an arboreal mammal related to the monkeys

LEMURES *n/pl* the ghosts of the dead in ancient Roman religion

LEMURINE *adj* pertaining to a lemur

LEMUROID *n* pl. **-S** a lemur

LEND *v* **LENT, LENDING, LENDS** to give the temporary use of **LENDABLE** *adj*

LENDER *n* pl. **-S** one that lends

LENES pl. of lenis

LENGTH *n* pl. **-S** the longer or longest dimension of an object

LENGTHEN *v* **-ED, -ING, -S** to make or become longer

LENGTHY *adj* **LENGTHIER, LENGTHIEST** very long

LENIENCE *n* pl. **-S** leniency

LENIENCY *n* pl. **-CIES** the quality of being lenient

LENIENT *adj* gently tolerant

LENIS *n* pl. **LENES** a speech sound pronounced with little or no aspiration

LENITE *v* **-NITED, -NITING, -NITES** to articulate a lenis

LENITION *n* pl. **-S** a change in articulation

LENITIVE *n* pl. **-S** a soothing medicine

LENITY *n* pl. **-TIES** leniency

LENO *n* pl. **-NOS** a style of weaving

LENS *n* pl. **-ES** a piece of transparent material used in changing the convergence of light rays **LENSLESS** *adj*

LENS *v* **-ED, -ING, -ES** to make a film of

LENSE *n* pl. **-S** lens

LENSMAN *n* pl. **-MEN** a photographer

LENT past tense of lend

LENTANDO *adv* becoming slower — used as a musical direction

LENTEN *adj* meager

LENTIC *adj* pertaining to still water

LENTICEL *n* pl. **-S** a mass of cells on a plant stem

LENTIGO *n* pl. **-TIGINES** a freckle

LENTIL *n* pl. **-S** a Eurasian annual plant

LENTISK *n* pl. **-S** an evergreen tree

LENTO *n* pl. **-TOS** a slow musical movement

LENTOID *n* pl. **-S** an object shaped like a lens

LEONE *n* pl. **-S** a monetary unit of Sierra Leone

LEONINE *adj* pertaining to a lion

LEOPARD *n* pl. **-S** a large, carnivorous feline mammal

LEOTARD *n* pl. **-S** a close-fitting garment

LEPER *n* pl. **-S** one affected with leprosy

LEPIDOTE *n* pl. **-S** a flowering shrub

LEPORID *n* pl. **-RIDS** or **-RIDAE** a gnawing mammal

LEPORINE *adj* resembling a rabbit or hare

LEPROSE *adj* leprous

LEPROSY *n* pl. **-SIES** a chronic disease characterized by skin lesions and deformities

LEPROTIC *adj* leprous

LEPROUS *adj* affected with leprosy

LEPT a past tense of leap

LEPTIN   *n* pl. **-S** a hormone released by fat cells

LEPTON   *n* pl. **-S** a subatomic particle **LEPTONIC** *adj*

LEPTON   *n* pl. **-TA** a former monetary unit of Greece

LESBIAN   *n* pl. **-S** a female homosexual

LESION   *v* **-ED, -ING, -S** to cause an abnormal change in the structure of an organ

LESS   *adj* **LESSER, LEAST** not as great in quantity or degree

LESSEE   *n* pl. **-S** one to whom a lease is granted

LESSEN   *v* **-ED, -ING, -S** to make or become less

LESSER   *adj* not as large or important

LESSON   *v* **-ED, -ING, -S** to instruct

LESSOR   *n* pl. **-S** one that grants a lease

LEST   *conj* for fear that

LET   *v* **LETTED, LETTING, LETS** to hinder

LETCH   *v* **-ED, -ING, -ES** to lech

LETDOWN   *n* pl. **-S** a decrease

LETHAL   *n* pl. **-S** a death-causing genetic defect

LETHALLY   *adv* in a deadly manner

LETHARGY   *n* pl. **-GIES** drowsiness; sluggishness

LETHE   *n* pl. **-S** forgetfulness **LETHEAN** *adj*

LETTED   past tense of let

LETTER   *v* **-ED, -ING, -S** to mark with letters (written symbols representing speech sounds)

LETTERER   *n* pl. **-S** one that letters

LETTING   present participle of let

LETTUCE   *n* pl. **-S** an herb cultivated as a salad plant

LETUP   *n* pl. **-S** a lessening or relaxation

LEU   *n* pl. **LEI** a monetary unit of Romania

LEUCEMIA   *n* pl. **-S** leukemia **LEUCEMIC** *adj*

LEUCIN   *n* pl. **-S** leucine

LEUCINE   *n* pl. **-S** an amino acid

LEUCITE   *n* pl. **-S** a mineral **LEUCITIC** *adj*

LEUCOMA   *n* pl. **-S** leukoma

LEUD   *n* pl. **-S** or **-ES** a feudal vassal

LEUKEMIA   *n* pl. **-S** a disease of the blood-forming organs

LEUKEMIC   *n* pl. **-S** one affected with leukemia

LEUKOMA   *n* pl. **-S** an opacity of the cornea

LEUKON   *n* pl. **-S** a bodily organ consisting of the white blood cells

LEUKOSIS   *n* pl. **-KOSES** leukemia **LEUKOTIC** *adj*

LEV   *n* pl. **LEVA** a monetary unit of Bulgaria

LEVANT   *v* **-ED, -ING, -S** to avoid a debt

LEVANTER   *n* pl. **-S** an easterly Mediterranean wind

LEVATOR   *n* pl. **-S** or **-ES** a muscle that raises an organ or part

LEVEE   *v* **LEVEED, LEVEEING, LEVEES** to provide with an embankment

LEVEL   *v* **-ELED, -ELING, -ELS** or **-ELLED, -ELLING, -ELS** to make even

LEVELER   *n* pl. **-S** one that levels

LEVELLER   *n* pl. **-S** leveler

LEVELLING   a present participle of level

LEVELLY   *adv* in an even manner

LEVER   *v* **-ED, -ING, -S** to move with a lever (a rigid body used to lift weight)

LEVERAGE   *v* **-AGED, -AGING, -AGES** to provide with a type of economic advantage

LEVERET   *n* pl. **-S** a young hare

LEVIABLE   *adj* liable to be levied

LEVIED   past tense of levy

LEVIER   *n* pl. **-S** one that levies

LEVIES   present 3d person sing. of levy

LEVIGATE   *v* **-GATED, -GATING, -GATES** to reduce to a fine powder

LEVIN   *n* pl. **-S** lightning

LEVIRATE   *n* pl. **-S** the custom of marrying the widow of one's brother

LEVITATE   *v* **-TATED, -TATING, -TATES** to rise and float in the air

LEVITY   *n* pl. **-TIES** conduct characterized by a lack of seriousness

LEVO   *adj* turning toward the left

LEVODOPA   *n* pl. **-S** a form of dopa

LEVOGYRE   *adj* turning toward the left

LEVULIN   *n* pl. **-S** a chemical compound

LEVULOSE   *n* pl. **-S** a very sweet sugar

LEVY   *v* **LEVIED, LEVYING, LEVIES** to impose or collect by legal authority

LEWD   *adj* **LEWDER, LEWDEST** obscene **LEWDLY** *adv*

LEWDNESS *n* pl. **-ES** the state of being lewd

LEWIS *n* pl. **-ISES** a hoisting device

LEWISITE *n* pl. **-S** a vesicant liquid

LEWISSON *n* pl. **-S** lewis

LEX *n* pl. **LEGES** law

LEXEME *n* pl. **-S** a linguistic unit **LEXEMIC** *adj*

LEXICAL *adj* pertaining to the words of a language

LEXICON *n* pl. **-CONS** or **-CA** a dictionary

LEXIS *n* pl. **LEXES** the vocabulary of a language, a group, or a subject field

LEY *n* pl. **LEYS** lea

LI *n* pl. **-S** a Chinese unit of distance

LIABLE *adj* subject or susceptible to something possible or likely

LIAISE *v* **LIAISED, LIAISING, LIAISES** to establish liaison

LIAISON *n* pl. **-S** a means for maintaining communication

LIANA *n* pl. **-S** a tropical vine

LIANE *n* pl. **-S** liana

LIANG *n* pl. **-S** a Chinese unit of weight

LIANOID *adj* pertaining to a liana

LIAR *n* pl. **-S** one that speaks falsely

LIARD *n* pl. **-S** a former silver coin of France

LIB *n* pl. **-S** liberation

LIBATION *n* pl. **-S** a ceremonial pouring of a liquid

LIBECCIO *n* pl. **-CIOS** a southwest wind

LIBEL *v* **-BELED, -BELING, -BELS** or **-BELLED, -BELLING, -BELS** to make or publish a defamatory statement about

LIBELANT *n* pl. **-S** a plaintiff in a type of lawsuit

LIBELEE *n* pl. **-S** a defendant in a type of lawsuit

LIBELER *n* pl. **-S** one that libels

LIBELIST *n* pl. **-S** a libeler

LIBELLED a past tense of libel

LIBELLEE *n* pl. **-S** libelee

LIBELLER *n* pl. **-S** libeler

LIBELLING a present participle of libel

LIBELOUS *adj* defamatory

LIBER *n* pl. **LIBERS** or **LIBRI** a book of public records

LIBERAL *n* pl. **-S** a person favorable to progress or reform

LIBERATE *v* **-ATED, -ATING, -ATES** to set free

LIBERTY *n* pl. **-TIES** the state of being free

LIBIDO *n* pl. **-DOS** the energy derived from instinctual biological drives

LIBLAB *n* pl. **-S** a person supporting a coalition of liberal and labor groups

LIBRA *n* pl. **-BRAE** an ancient Roman unit of weight

LIBRA *n* pl. **-S** a former gold coin of Peru

LIBRARY *n* pl. **-BRARIES** a place where literary materials are kept for reading and reference

LIBRATE *v* **-BRATED, -BRATING, -BRATES** to move from side to side

LIBRETTO *n* pl. **-TOS** or **-TI** the text of an opera

LIBRI a pl. of liber

LICE pl. of louse

LICENCE *v* **-CENCED, -CENCING, -CENCES** to license

LICENCEE *n* pl. **-S** licensee

LICENCER *n* pl. **-S** licenser

LICENSE *v* **-CENSED, -CENSING, -CENSES** to issue or grant authoritative permission to

LICENSEE *n* pl. **-S** one that is licensed

LICENSER *n* pl. **-S** one that licenses

LICENSOR *n* pl. **-S** licenser

LICENTE a pl. of sente

LICH *n* pl. **-ES** a corpse

LICHEE *n* pl. **-S** litchi

LICHEN *v* **-ED, -ING, -S** to cover with lichens (flowerless plants)

LICHENIN *n* pl. **-S** a chemical compound

LICHI *n* pl. **-S** litchi

LICHT *v* **-ED, -ING, -S** to light

LICHTLY *adv* lightly

LICIT *adj* lawful **LICITLY** *adv*

LICK *v* **-ED, -ING, -S** to pass the tongue over the surface of

LICKER *n* pl. **-S** one that licks

LICKING *n* pl. **-S** a thrashing or beating

LICKSPIT *n* pl. **-S** a fawning person

LICORICE *n* pl. **-S** a perennial herb

LICTOR *n* pl. **-S** a magistrate's attendant in ancient Rome

LID   *v* **LIDDED, LIDDING, LIDS** to provide with a lid (a movable cover)

LIDAR   *n* pl. **-S** an electronic locating device

LIDLESS   *adj* having no lid

LIDO   *n* pl. **-DOS** a fashionable beach resort

LIE   *v* **LAY, LAIN, LYING, LIES** to be in or get into a horizontal position

LIE   *v* **LIED, LYING, LIES** to speak falsely

LIED   *n* pl. **LIEDER** a German song

LIEF   *adj* **LIEFER, LIEFEST** willing **LIEFLY** *adv*

LIEGE   *n* pl. **-S** a feudal lord

LIEGEMAN   *n* pl. **-MEN** a feudal vassal

LIEN   *n* pl. **-S** a legal right to hold or sell a debtor's property

LIENABLE   *adj* capable of being subjected to a lien

LIENAL   *adj* pertaining to the spleen

LIENTERY   *n* pl. **-TERIES** a form of diarrhea

LIER   *n* pl. **-S** one that lies or reclines

LIERNE   *n* pl. **-S** a connecting part in Gothic vaulting

LIEU   *n* pl. **-S** place; stead

LIEVE   *adv* **LIEVER, LIEVEST** gladly

LIFE   *n* pl. **LIVES** the quality that distinguishes animals and plants from inanimate matter

LIFEBOAT   *n* pl. **-S** a small rescue boat

LIFECARE   *n* pl. **-S** housing and health services for the elderly

LIFEFUL   *adj* full of life

LIFELESS   *adj* having no life

LIFELIKE   *adj* resembling a living thing

LIFELINE   *n* pl. **-S** a rope used to aid a person in distress

LIFELONG   *adj* lasting for a lifetime

LIFER   *n* pl. **-S** a prisoner serving a life sentence

LIFESPAN   *n* pl. **-S** a lifetime

LIFETIME   *n* pl. **-S** the period of living existence

LIFEWAY   *n* pl. **-WAYS** a way of living

LIFEWORK   *n* pl. **-S** the major work of one's lifetime

LIFT   *v* **-ED, -ING, -S** to move to a higher position **LIFTABLE** *adj*

LIFTER   *n* pl. **-S** one that lifts

LIFTGATE   *n* pl. **-S** a rear panel on a station wagon that opens upward

LIFTMAN   *n* pl. **-MEN** an elevator operator

LIFTOFF   *n* pl. **-S** the vertical takeoff of a rocket

LIGAMENT   *n* pl. **-S** a band of firm, fibrous tissue

LIGAN   *n* pl. **-S** lagan

LIGAND   *n* pl. **-S** a type of ion or molecule

LIGASE   *n* pl. **-S** an enzyme

LIGATE   *v* **-GATED, -GATING, -GATES** to bind

LIGATION   *n* pl. **-S** the act of ligating **LIGATIVE** *adj*

LIGATURE   *v* **-TURED, -TURING, -TURES** to ligate

LIGER   *n* pl. **-S** the offspring of a male lion and a female tiger

LIGHT   *adj* **LIGHTER, LIGHTEST** having little weight

LIGHT   *v* **LIGHTED** or **LIT, LIGHTING, LIGHTS** to illuminate

LIGHTEN   *v* **-ED, -ING, -S** to reduce the weight of

LIGHTER   *v* **-ED, -ING, -S** to convey in a type of barge

LIGHTFUL   *adj* brightly illuminated

LIGHTING   *n* pl. **-S** illumination

LIGHTISH   *adj* somewhat light

LIGHTLY   *adv* to a moderate degree

LIGNAN   *n* pl. **-S** a type of polymer

LIGNEOUS   *adj* of or resembling wood

LIGNIFY   *v* **-FIED, -FYING, -FIES** to convert into wood

LIGNIN   *n* pl. **-S** an essential part of woody tissue

LIGNITE   *n* pl. **-S** a type of coal **LIGNITIC** *adj*

LIGROIN   *n* pl. **-S** a flammable liquid

LIGROINE   *n* pl. **-S** ligroin

LIGULA   *n* pl. **-LAS** or **-LAE** a strap-shaped organ or part **LIGULAR, LIGULATE, LIGULOID** *adj*

LIGULE   *n* pl. **-S** a strap-shaped plant part

LIGURE   *n* pl. **-S** a precious stone

LIKABLE   *adj* pleasant

LIKE   *adj* **LIKER, LIKEST** possessing the same or almost the same characteristics

LIKE *v* **LIKED, LIKING, LIKES** to find pleasant

LIKEABLE *adj* likable

LIKED past tense of like

LIKELY *adj* **-LIER, -LIEST** probable

LIKEN *v* **-ED, -ING, -S** to represent as similar

LIKENESS *n* pl. **-ES** a pictorial representation

LIKER *n* pl. **-S** one that likes

LIKEST superlative of like

LIKEWISE *adv* in a similar manner

LIKING *n* pl. **-S** a feeling of attraction or affection

LIKUTA *n* pl. **MAKUTA** a former monetary unit of Zaire

LILAC *n* pl. **-S** a flowering shrub

LILIED *adj* covered with lilies

LILIES pl. of lily

LILLIPUT *n* pl. **-S** a very small person

LILT *v* **-ED, -ING, -S** to sing or speak rhythmically

LILY *n* pl. **LILIES** a flowering plant **LILYLIKE** *adj*

LIMA *n* pl. **-S** the edible seed of a tropical American plant

LIMACINE *adj* resembling a type of mollusk

LIMACON *n* pl. **-S** a type of geometric curve

LIMAN *n* pl. **-S** a lagoon

LIMB *v* **-ED, -ING, -S** to cut off the arms or legs of

LIMBA *n* pl. **-S** an African tree

LIMBATE *adj* having an edge of a different color

LIMBECK *n* pl. **-S** alembic

LIMBER *adj* **-BERER, -BEREST** flexible **LIMBERLY** *adv*

LIMBER *v* **-ED, -ING, -S** to make flexible

LIMBI a pl. of limbus

LIMBIC *adj* pertaining to a system of the brain

LIMBIER comparative of limby

LIMBIEST superlative of limby

LIMBLESS *adj* having no arms or legs

LIMBO *n* pl. **-BOS** a condition of oblivion or neglect

LIMBUS *n* pl. **-BUSES** or **-BI** a distinctive border

LIMBY *adj* **LIMBIER, LIMBIEST** having many large branches

LIME *v* **LIMED, LIMING, LIMES** to treat with lime (a calcium compound)

LIMEADE *n* pl. **-S** a beverage

LIMEKILN *n* pl. **-S** a furnace in which shells are burned to produce lime

LIMELESS *adj* having no lime

LIMEN *n* pl. **-MENS** or **-MINA** a sensory threshold

LIMERICK *n* pl. **-S** a humorous verse

LIMES *n* pl. **LIMITES** a fortified boundary

LIMEY *n* pl. **-EYS** a British sailor

LIMIER comparative of limy

LIMIEST superlative of limy

LIMINA a pl. of limen

LIMINAL *adj* pertaining to the limen

LIMINESS *n* pl. **-ES** the state of being limy

LIMING present participle of lime

LIMIT *v* **-ED, -ING, -S** to restrict

LIMITARY *adj* limiting

LIMITED *n* pl. **-S** a train or bus making few stops

LIMITER *n* pl. **-S** one that limits

LIMITES pl. of limes

LIMMER *n* pl. **-S** a scoundrel

LIMN *v* **-ED, -ING, -S** to depict by painting or drawing

LIMNER *n* pl. **-S** one that limns

LIMNETIC *adj* pertaining to the open water of a lake or pond

LIMNIC *adj* limnetic

LIMO *n* pl. **LIMOS** a limousine

LIMONENE *n* pl. **-S** a chemical compound

LIMONITE *n* pl. **-S** a major ore of iron

LIMP *adj* **LIMPER, LIMPEST** lacking rigidity

LIMP *v* **-ED, -ING, -S** to walk lamely

LIMPA *n* pl. **-S** rye bread made with molasses

LIMPER *n* pl. **-S** one that limps

LIMPET *n* pl. **-S** a type of mollusk

LIMPID *adj* transparent **LIMPIDLY** *adv*

LIMPKIN *n* pl. **-S** a wading bird

LIMPLY *adv* in a limp manner

LIMPNESS *n* pl. **-ES** the state of being limp

LIMPSEY *adj* **-SIER, -SIEST** limpsy

LIMPSY *adj* **-SIER, -SIEST** lacking strength or vigor

LIMULOID	*n* pl. **-S** a horseshoe crab
LIMULUS	*n* pl. **-LI** a horseshoe crab
LIMY	*adj* **LIMIER, LIMIEST** resembling or containing lime
LIN	*n* pl. **-S** linn
LINABLE	*adj* lineable
LINAC	*n* pl. **-S** a device for imparting high velocities to charged particles
LINAGE	*n* pl. **-S** the number of lines of printed material
LINALOL	*n* pl. **-S** linalool
LINALOOL	*n* pl. **-S** a fragrant alcohol
LINCHPIN	*n* pl. **-S** a locking pin inserted in the end of a shaft
LINDANE	*n* pl. **-S** an insecticide
LINDEN	*n* pl. **-S** a tall forest tree
LINDY	*n* pl. **-DIES** a lively dance
LINE	*v* **LINED, LINING, LINES** to mark with lines (slender, continuous marks)
LINEABLE	*adj* lying in a straight line
LINEAGE	*n* pl. **-S** direct descent from an ancestor
LINEAL	*adj* being directly descended from an ancestor **LINEALLY** *adv*
LINEAR	*adj* of or resembling a straight line **LINEARLY** *adv*
LINEATE	*adj* marked with lines
LINEATED	*adj* lineate
LINEBRED	*adj* produced by interbreeding within a particular line of descent
LINECUT	*n* pl. **-S** a type of printing plate
LINED	past tense of line
LINELESS	*adj* having no lines
LINELIKE	*adj* resembling a line
LINEMAN	*n* pl. **-MEN** one who installs or repairs telephone wires
LINEN	*n* pl. **-S** a fabric woven from the fibers of flax **LINENY** *adj*
LINER	*n* pl. **-S** a commercial ship or airplane
LINESMAN	*n* pl. **-MEN** a football official
LINEUP	*n* pl. **-S** a row of persons
LINEY	*adj* **LINIER, LINIEST** liny
LING	*n* pl. **-S** a heath plant
LINGA	*n* pl. **-S** lingam
LINGAM	*n* pl. **-S** a Hindu phallic symbol
LINGCOD	*n* pl. **-S** a marine food fish

LINGER	*v* **-ED, -ING, -S** to delay leaving
LINGERER	*n* pl. **-S** one that lingers
LINGERIE	*n* pl. **-S** women's underwear
LINGIER	comparative of lingy
LINGIEST	superlative of lingy
LINGO	*n* pl. **-GOES** strange or incomprehensible language
LINGUA	*n* pl. **-GUAE** the tongue or a tonguelike part
LINGUAL	*n* pl. **-S** a sound articulated with the tongue
LINGUICA	*n* pl. **-S** a spicy Portuguese sausage
LINGUINE	*n* pl. **-S** linguini
LINGUINI	*n* pl. **-S** a type of pasta
LINGUISA	*n* pl. **-S** linguica
LINGUIST	*n* pl. **-S** a person skilled in several languages
LINGULA	*n* pl. **-LAE** an organ or process shaped like a tongue **LINGULAR** *adj*
LINGY	*adj* **LINGIER, LINGIEST** covered with heaths
LINIER	comparative of liney and liny
LINIEST	superlative of liney and liny
LINIMENT	*n* pl. **-S** a medicinal liquid
LININ	*n* pl. **-S** a substance in the nucleus of a cell
LINING	*n* pl. **-S** an inner layer
LINK	*v* **-ED, -ING, -S** to connect **LINKABLE** *adj*
LINKAGE	*n* pl. **-S** the act of linking
LINKBOY	*n* pl. **-BOYS** a man or boy hired to carry a torch to light the way along dark streets
LINKER	*n* pl. **-S** one that links
LINKMAN	*n* pl. **-MEN** a linkboy
LINKSMAN	*n* pl. **-MEN** a golfer
LINKUP	*n* pl. **-S** something that serves as a linking device
LINKWORK	*n* pl. **-S** something composed of interlocking rings
LINKY	*adj* full of interlocking rings
LINN	*n* pl. **-S** a waterfall
LINNET	*n* pl. **-S** a European songbird
LINO	*n* pl. **-NOS** linoleum
LINOCUT	*n* pl. **-S** a print made from a design cut into linoleum

LINOLEUM	*n* pl. **-S** a durable material used as a floor covering	**LIPOMA**	*n* pl. **-MAS** or **-MATA** a tumor of fatty tissue
LINOTYPE	*v* **-TYPED, -TYPING, -TYPES** to set type with a machine	**LIPOSOME**	*n* pl. **-S** a microscopic globule composed of lipids
LINSANG	*n* pl. **-S** a carnivorous mammal	**LIPPED**	past tense of lip
LINSEED	*n* pl. **-S** flaxseed	**LIPPEN**	*v* **-ED, -ING, -S** to trust
LINSEY	*n* pl. **-SEYS** a coarse fabric	**LIPPER**	*v* **-ED, -ING, -S** to ripple
LINSTOCK	*n* pl. **-S** a stick having one end divided to hold a match	**LIPPING**	*n* pl. **-S** a liplike outgrowth of bone
		LIPPY	*adj* **-PIER, -PIEST** impudent
LINT	*v* **-ED, -ING, -S** to give off lint (bits of fiber or fluff)	**LIPREAD**	*n* pl. **-READ, -READING, -READS** to understand spoken words by interpreting the lip movements of a speaker
LINTEL	*n* pl. **-S** a horizontal supporting beam		
LINTER	*n* pl. **-S** a machine for removing fibers from cotton seeds	**LIPSTICK**	*n* pl. **-S** a cosmetic used to color the lips
LINTIER	comparative of linty	**LIQUATE**	*v* **-QUATED, -QUATING, -QUATES** to purify metal by heating
LINTIEST	superlative of linty		
LINTLESS	*adj* free from lint	**LIQUEFY**	*v* **-FIED, -FYING, -FIES** to make or become liquid
LINTOL	*n* pl. **-S** lintel		
LINTY	*adj* **LINTIER, LINTIEST** covered with lint	**LIQUEUR**	*n* pl. **-S** a sweetened alcoholic beverage
LINUM	*n* pl. **-S** a plant of the flax family	**LIQUID**	*n* pl. **-S** a substance that flows freely
LINURON	*n* pl. **-S** a herbicide	**LIQUIDLY**	*adv* in a free-flowing manner
LINY	*adj* **LINIER, LINIEST** resembling a line	**LIQUIFY**	*v* **-FIED, -FYING, -FIES** to liquefy
LION	*n* pl. **-S** a large, carnivorous feline mammal	**LIQUOR**	*v* **-ED, -ING, -S** to intoxicate with liquor (an alcoholic beverage)
LIONESS	*n* pl. **-ES** a female lion	**LIRA**	*n* pl. **LIRAS** or **LIRE** a former monetary unit of Italy
LIONFISH	*n* pl. **-ES** a tropical fish	**LIRA**	*n* pl. **LIRI** a monetary unit of Malta
LIONISE	*v* **-ISED, -ISING, -ISES** to lionize	**LIRA**	*n* pl. **LIROTH** or **LIROT** a former monetary unit of Israel
LIONISER	*n* pl. **-S** one that lionises		
LIONIZE	*v* **-IZED, -IZING, -IZES** to treat or regard as a celebrity	**LIRIOPE**	*n* pl. **-S** a stemless Asian herb
		LIRIPIPE	*n* pl. **-S** a long scarf
LIONIZER	*n* pl. **-S** one that lionizes	**LISENTE**	a pl. of sente
LIONLIKE	*adj* resembling a lion	**LISLE**	*n* pl. **-S** a fine, tightly twisted cotton thread
LIP	*v* **LIPPED, LIPPING, LIPS** to touch with the lips (the folds of flesh around the mouth)		
		LISP	*v* **-ED, -ING, -S** to pronounce the letters *s* and *z* imperfectly
LIPA	*n* pl. **LIPE** a monetary unit of Croatia	**LISPER**	*n* pl. **-S** one that lisps
		LISSOM	*adj* lissome **LISSOMLY** *adv*
LIPASE	*n* pl. **-S** an enzyme	**LISSOME**	*adj* lithe
LIPID	*n* pl. **-S** any of a class of fatty substances **LIPIDIC** *adj*	**LIST**	*v* **-ED, -ING, -S** to write down in a particular order **LISTABLE** *adj*
LIPIDE	*n* pl. **-S** lipid	**LISTEE**	*n* pl. **-S** one that is on a list
LIPIN	*n* pl. **-S** a lipid	**LISTEL**	*n* pl. **-S** a narrow molding
LIPLESS	*adj* having no lips	**LISTEN**	*v* **-ED, -ING, -S** to make conscious use of the sense of hearing
LIPLIKE	*adj* resembling a lip		
LIPOCYTE	*n* pl. **-S** a fat-producing cell	**LISTENER**	*n* pl. **-S** one that listens
LIPOID	*n* pl. **-S** a lipid **LIPOIDAL** *adj*	**LISTER**	*n* pl. **-S** a type of plow

LISTERIA *n* pl. **-S** a rod-shaped bacterium

LISTING *n* pl. **-S** something that is listed

LISTLESS *adj* languid

LIT *n* pl. **-S** the litas

LITANY *n* pl. **-NIES** a ceremonial form of prayer

LITAS *n* pl. **LITAI** or **LITU** a former monetary unit of Lithuania

LITCHI *n* pl. **-S** the edible fruit of a Chinese tree

LITE *adj* lower in calories or having less of some ingredient

LITENESS *n* pl. **-ES** the state of being lite

LITER *n* pl. **-S** a unit of capacity

LITERACY *n* pl. **-CIES** the ability to read and write

LITERAL *n* pl. **-S** a small error in printing or writing

LITERARY *adj* of, pertaining to, or having the characteristics of books and writings

LITERATE *n* pl. **-S** one who can read and write

LITERATI *n/pl* scholars collectively

LITHARGE *n* pl. **-S** a monoxide of lead

LITHE *adj* **LITHER, LITHEST** bending easily **LITHELY** *adv*

LITHEMIA *n* pl. **-S** an excess of uric acid in the blood **LITHEMIC** *adj*

LITHIA *n* pl. **-S** an oxide of lithium

LITHIC *adj* pertaining to lithium

LITHIFY *v* **-FIED, -FYING, -FIES** to petrify

LITHIUM *n* pl. **-S** a metallic element

LITHO *v* **-ED, -ING, -S** to make prints by lithography

LITHOID *adj* resembling stone

LITHOPS *n* pl. **LITHOPS** a succulent African plant

LITHOSOL *n* pl. **-S** a type of soil

LITIGANT *n* pl. **-S** one who is engaged in a lawsuit

LITIGATE *v* **-GATED, -GATING, -GATES** to subject to legal proceedings

LITMUS *n* pl. **-ES** a blue coloring matter

LITORAL *adj* pertaining to a coastal region

LITOTES *n* pl. **LITOTES** a figure of speech in which an assertion is made by the negation of its opposite **LITOTIC** *adj*

LITRE *n* pl. **-S** liter

LITTEN *adj* lighted

LITTER *v* **-ED, -ING, -S** to scatter rubbish about

LITTERER *n* pl. **-S** one that litters

LITTERY *adj* covered with rubbish

LITTLE *adj* **-TLER, -TLEST** small

LITTLE *n* pl. **-S** a small amount

LITTLISH *adj* somewhat little

LITTORAL *n* pl. **-S** a coastal region

LITU a pl. of litas

LITURGY *n* pl. **-GIES** a prescribed system of public worship **LITURGIC** *adj*

LIVABLE *adj* suitable for living in

LIVE *adj* **LIVER, LIVEST** having life

LIVE *v* **LIVED, LIVING, LIVES** to function as an animal or plant

LIVEABLE *adj* livable

LIVELONG *adj* long in passing

LIVELY *adj* **-LIER, -LIEST** full of energy **LIVELILY** *adv*

LIVEN *v* **-ED, -ING, -S** to make lively

LIVENER *n* pl. **-S** one that livens

LIVENESS *n* pl. **-ES** the state of being live

LIVER *v* **-ED, -ING, -S** to thicken or gel

LIVERIED *adj* wearing a livery

LIVERISH *adj* having a disorder of the liver (a bodily organ)

LIVERY *n* pl. **-ERIES** a uniform worn by servants

LIVES pl. of life

LIVEST superlative of live

LIVETRAP *v* **-TRAPPED, -TRAPPING, -TRAPS** to capture in a type of animal trap

LIVID *adj* having the skin abnormally discolored **LIVIDLY** *adv*

LIVIDITY *n* pl. **-TIES** the state of being livid

LIVIER *n* pl. **-S** livyer

LIVING *n* pl. **-S** a means of subsistence

LIVINGLY *adv* realistically

LIVRE *n* pl. **-S** a former monetary unit of France

LIVYER *n* pl. **-S** a permanent resident of Newfoundland

LIXIVIUM *n* pl. **-IUMS** or **-IA** a solution obtained by leaching **LIXIVIAL** *adj*

LIZARD *n* pl. **-S** any of a suborder of reptiles

LLAMA   *n* pl. **-S** a ruminant mammal

LLANO   *n* pl. **-NOS** an open, grassy plain

LO   *interj* — used to attract attention or to express surprise

LOACH   *n* pl. **-ES** a freshwater fish

LOAD   *v* **-ED, -ING, -S** to place in or on a means of conveyance

LOADER   *n* pl. **-S** one that loads

LOADING   *n* pl. **-S** a burden

LOADSTAR   *n* pl. **-S** lodestar

LOAF   *n* pl. **LOAVES** a shaped mass of bread

LOAF   *v* **-ED, -ING, -S** to pass time idly

LOAFER   *n* pl. **-S** one that loafs

LOAM   *v* **-ED, -ING, -S** to cover with loam (a type of soil)

LOAMLESS   *adj* having no loam

LOAMY   *adj* **LOAMIER, LOAMIEST** resembling loam

LOAN   *v* **-ED, -ING, -S** to lend **LOANABLE** *adj*

LOANER   *n* pl. **-S** one that loans

LOANING   *n* pl. **-S** a lane

LOANWORD   *n* pl. **-S** a word taken from another language

LOATH   *adj* unwilling

LOATHE   *v* **LOATHED, LOATHING, LOATHES** to detest greatly

LOATHER   *n* pl. **-S** one that loathes

LOATHFUL   *adj* repulsive

LOATHING   *n* pl. **-S** extreme dislike

LOATHLY   *adj* repulsive

LOAVES   pl. of loaf

LOB   *v* **LOBBED, LOBBING, LOBS** to throw or hit in a high arc

LOBAR   *adj* pertaining to a lobe

LOBATE   *adj* having lobes **LOBATELY** *adv*

LOBATED   *adj* lobate

LOBATION   *n* pl. **-S** the formation of lobes

LOBBED   past tense of lob

LOBBER   *n* pl. **-S** one that lobs

LOBBING   present participle of lob

LOBBY   *v* **-BIED, -BYING, -BIES** to attempt to influence legislators

LOBBYER   *n* pl. **-S** a lobbyist

LOBBYGOW   *n* pl. **-S** an errand boy

LOBBYISM   *n* pl. **-S** the practice of lobbying

LOBBYIST   *n* pl. **-S** one who lobbies

LOBE   *n* pl. **-S** a rounded, projecting anatomical part **LOBED** *adj*

LOBEFIN   *n* pl. **-S** a bony fish

LOBELIA   *n* pl. **-S** a flowering plant

LOBELINE   *n* pl. **-S** a poisonous alkaloid

LOBLOLLY   *n* pl. **-LIES** a pine tree

LOBO   *n* pl. **-BOS** the timber wolf

LOBOTOMY   *n* pl. **-MIES** a type of surgical operation

LOBSTER   *v* **-ED, -ING, -S** to fish for lobsters (marine crustaceans)

LOBSTICK   *n* pl. **-S** a tree with its lower branches trimmed

LOBULE   *n* pl. **-S** a small lobe **LOBULAR, LOBULATE, LOBULOSE** *adj*

LOBWORM   *n* pl. **-S** a lugworm

LOCA   a pl. of locus

LOCAL   *n* pl. **-S** a train or bus making all stops

LOCALE   *n* pl. **-S** a locality

LOCALISE   *v* **-ISED, -ISING, -ISES** to localize

LOCALISM   *n* pl. **-S** a custom or mannerism peculiar to a locality

LOCALIST   *n* pl. **-S** one who is strongly concerned with the matters of a locality

LOCALITE   *n* pl. **-S** a resident of a locality

LOCALITY   *n* pl. **-TIES** an area or neighborhood

LOCALIZE   *v* **-IZED, -IZING, -IZES** to confine to a particular area

LOCALLY   *adv* in a particular area

LOCATE   *v* **-CATED, -CATING, -CATES** to determine the position of

LOCATER   *n* pl. **-S** one that locates

LOCATION   *n* pl. **-S** the place where something is at a given moment

LOCATIVE   *n* pl. **-S** a type of grammatical case

LOCATOR   *n* pl. **-S** locater

LOCH   *n* pl. **-S** a lake

LOCHAN   *n* pl. **-S** a small lake

LOCHIA   *n* pl. **LOCHIA** a vaginal discharge following childbirth **LOCHIAL** *adj*

LOCI   a pl. of locus

LOCK   *v* **-ED, -ING, -S** to secure by means of a mechanical fastening device **LOCKABLE** *adj*

LOCKAGE   *n* pl. **-S** a toll on a ship passing through a canal

LOCKBOX *n* pl. **-ES** a box that locks

LOCKDOWN *n* pl. **-S** the confinement of prisoners to their cells

LOCKER *n* pl. **-S** an enclosure that may be locked

LOCKET *n* pl. **-S** a small ornamental case

LOCKJAW *n* pl. **-S** a form of tetanus

LOCKNUT *n* pl. **-S** a nut which keeps another from loosening

LOCKOUT *n* pl. **-S** a closing of a business to coerce employees to agree to terms

LOCKRAM *n* pl. **-S** a coarse, linen fabric

LOCKSET *n* pl. **-S** a set of hardware for locking a door

LOCKSTEP *n* pl. **-S** a mode of marching in close file

LOCKUP *n* pl. **-S** a jail

LOCO *n* pl. **-COS** or **-COES** locoweed

LOCO *v* **-ED, -ING, -S** to poison with locoweed

LOCOFOCO *n* pl. **-COS** a type of friction match

LOCOISM *n* pl. **-S** a disease of livestock

LOCOMOTE *v* **-MOTED, -MOTING, -MOTES** to move about

LOCOWEED *n* pl. **-S** a plant that causes poisoning when eaten by livestock

LOCULAR *adj* having or divided into loculi

LOCULATE *adj* locular

LOCULE *n* pl. **-S** loculus **LOCULED** *adj*

LOCULUS *n* pl. **-LI** a small, cell-like chamber

LOCUM *n* pl. **-S** a temporary substitute

LOCUS *n* pl. **LOCI** or **LOCA** a place

LOCUST *n* pl. **-S** a migratory grasshopper

LOCUSTA *n* pl. **-TAE** a spikelet **LOCUSTAL** *adj*

LOCUTION *n* pl. **-S** a particular form of expression

LOCUTORY *n* pl. **-RIES** a room in a monastery

LODE *n* pl. **-S** a deposit of ore

LODEN *n* pl. **-S** a thick, woolen fabric

LODESTAR *n* pl. **-S** a star used as a point of reference

LODGE *v* **LODGED, LODGING, LODGES** to furnish with temporary quarters

LODGER *n* pl. **-S** one that resides in rented quarters

LODGING *n* pl. **-S** a temporary place to live

LODGMENT *n* pl. **-S** a lodging

LODICULE *n* pl. **-S** a scale at the base of the ovary of a grass

LOESS *n* pl. **-ES** a soil deposit **LOESSAL, LOESSIAL** *adj*

LOFT *v* **-ED, -ING, -S** to store in a loft (an upper room)

LOFTER *n* pl. **-S** a type of golf club

LOFTIER comparative of lofty

LOFTIEST superlative of lofty

LOFTILY *adv* in a lofty manner

LOFTLESS *adj* having no loft

LOFTLIKE *adj* resembling a loft

LOFTY *adj* **LOFTIER, LOFTIEST** extending high in the air

LOG *v* **LOGGED, LOGGING, LOGS** to cut down trees for timber

LOGAN *n* pl. **-S** a stone balanced to permit easy movement

LOGANIA *adj* designating a family of flowering plants

LOGBOOK *n* pl. **-S** a record book of a ship or aircraft

LOGE *n* pl. **-S** a small compartment

LOGGATS *n/pl* loggets

LOGGED past tense of log

LOGGER *n* pl. **-S** one that logs

LOGGETS *n/pl* an old English throwing game

LOGGIA *n* pl. **-GIAS** or **-GIE** an open gallery

LOGGING *n* pl. **-S** the business of cutting down trees for timber

LOGGISH *adj* resembling a log

LOGGY *adj* **-GIER, -GIEST** logy

LOGIA a pl. of logion

LOGIC *n* pl. **-S** the science of reasoning

LOGICAL *adj* pertaining to logic

LOGICIAN *n* pl. **-S** one who is skilled in logic

LOGICISE *v* **-CISED, -CISING, -CISES** to logicize

LOGICIZE *v* **-CIZED, -CIZING, -CIZES** to reason

LOGIER comparative of logy

LOGIEST superlative of logy

LOGILY *adv* in a logy manner

LOGIN *n* pl. **-S** the process of identifying oneself to a computer

LOGINESS *n* pl. **-ES** the state of being logy

LOGION *n* pl. **-GIONS** or **-GIA** a saying attributed to Jesus

LOGISTIC *n* pl. **-S** symbolic logic

LOGJAM *v* **-JAMMED, -JAMMING, -JAMS** to cause to become tangled in a mass

LOGO *n* pl. **LOGOS** an identifying symbol

LOGOGRAM *n* pl. **-S** a symbol used to represent an entire word

LOGOMACH *n* pl. **-S** one given to arguing about words

LOGON *n* pl. **-S** login

LOGOS *n* pl. **LOGOI** the rational principle that governs the universe in ancient Greek philosophy

LOGOTYPE *n* pl. **-S** a piece of type bearing a syllable, word, or words

LOGOTYPY *n* pl. **-TYPIES** the use of logotypes

LOGROLL *v* **-ED, -ING, -S** to obtain passage of by exchanging political favors

LOGWAY *n* pl. **-WAYS** a ramp used in logging

LOGWOOD *n* pl. **-S** a tropical tree

LOGY *adj* **-GIER, -GIEST** sluggish

LOID *v* **-ED, -ING, -S** to open a spring lock by using a piece of celluloid

LOIN *n* pl. **-S** a part of the side and back between the ribs and the hipbone

LOITER *v* **-ED, -ING, -S** to stand idly about

LOITERER *n* pl. **-S** one that loiters

LOLL *v* **-ED, -ING, -S** to lounge

LOLLER *n* pl. **-S** one that lolls

LOLLIES pl. of lolly

LOLLIPOP *n* pl. **-S** a piece of candy on the end of a stick

LOLLOP *v* **-ED, -ING, -S** to loll

LOLLOPY *adj* characterized by a bobbing motion

LOLLY *n* pl. **-LIES** a lollipop

LOLLYGAG *v* **-GAGGED, -GAGGING, -GAGS** to lallygag

LOLLYPOP *n* pl. **-S** lollipop

LOMEIN *n* pl. **-S** a Chinese dish of noodles, meat, and vegetables

LOMENT *n* pl. **-S** a type of plant pod

LOMENTUM *n* pl. **-TUMS** or **-TA** loment

LONE *adj* having no companions

LONELY *adj* **-LIER, -LIEST** sad from lack of companionship **LONELILY** *adv*

LONENESS *n* pl. **-ES** the state of being lone

LONER *n* pl. **-S** one that avoids others

LONESOME *n* pl. **-S** self

LONG *adj* **LONGER, LONGEST** extending for a considerable distance

LONG *v* **-ED, -ING, -S** to desire strongly

LONGAN *n* pl. **-S** the edible fruit of a Chinese tree

LONGBOAT *n* pl. **-S** the largest boat carried by a sailing vessel

LONGBOW *n* pl. **-S** a type of archery bow

LONGE *v* **LONGED, LONGEING, LONGES** to guide a horse by means of a long rope

LONGER *n* pl. **-S** one that longs

LONGERON *n* pl. **-S** a longitudinal support of an airplane

LONGHAIR *n* pl. **-S** an intellectual

LONGHAND *n* pl. **-S** ordinary handwriting

LONGHEAD *n* pl. **-S** a person having a long skull

LONGHORN *n* pl. **-S** one of a breed of long-horned cattle

LONGIES *n/pl* long underwear

LONGING *n* pl. **-S** a strong desire

LONGISH *adj* somewhat long

LONGJUMP *v* **-ED, -ING, -S** to jump for distance from a running start

LONGLEAF *n* pl. **-LEAVES** an evergreen tree

LONGLINE *n* pl. **-S** a type of fishing line

LONGLY *adv* for a considerable distance

LONGNECK *n* pl. **-S** a beer bottle with a long neck

LONGNESS *n* pl. **-ES** the state of being long

LONGSHIP *n* pl. **-S** a medieval ship

LONGSOME *adj* tediously long

LONGSPUR *n* pl. **-S** a long-clawed finch

LONGTIME *adj* of long duration

LONGUEUR *n* pl. **-S** a dull and tedious section

LONGWAYS *adv* longwise

LONGWISE *adv* lengthwise

LOO *v* **-ED, -ING, -S** to subject to a forfeit at loo (a card game)

LOOBY *n* pl. **-BIES** a large, awkward person

LOOEY *n* pl. **-EYS** looie

LOOF *n* pl. **-S** the palm of the hand

LOOFA *n* pl. **-S** loofah

LOOFAH *n* pl. **-S** a tropical vine

LOOIE *n* pl. **-S** a lieutenant of the armed forces

LOOK *v* **-ED, -ING, -S** to use one's eyes in seeing

LOOKDOWN *n* pl. **-S** a marine fish

LOOKER *n* pl. **-S** one that looks

LOOKISM *n* pl. **-S** discrimination based on physical appearance

LOOKIST *n* pl. **-S** one that practices lookism

LOOKOUT *n* pl. **-S** one engaged in keeping watch

LOOKSISM *n* pl. **-S** lookism

LOOKUP *n* pl. **-S** the process of looking something up

LOOM *v* **-ED, -ING, -S** to appear in an enlarged and indistinct form

LOON *n* pl. **-S** a diving waterfowl

LOONEY *adj* **-NIER, -NIEST** loony

LOONEY *n* pl. **-EYS** loony

LOONIE *n* pl. **-S** a coin worth one Canadian dollar

LOONY *adj* **-NIER, -NIEST** crazy **LOONILY** *adv*

LOONY *n* pl. **-NIES** a loony person

LOOP *v* **-ED, -ING, -S** to form loops (circular or oval openings)

LOOPER *n* pl. **-S** one that loops

LOOPHOLE *v* **-HOLED, -HOLING, -HOLES** to make small openings in

LOOPY *adj* **LOOPIER, LOOPIEST** full of loops **LOOPILY** *adv*

LOOSE *adj* **LOOSER, LOOSEST** not firm, taut, or rigid **LOOSELY** *adv*

LOOSE *v* **LOOSED, LOOSING, LOOSES** to set free

LOOSEN *v* **-ED, -ING, -S** to make looser

LOOSENER *n* pl. **-S** one that loosens

LOOSER comparative of loose

LOOSEST superlative of loose

LOOSING present participle of loose

LOOT *v* **-ED, -ING, -S** to plunder

LOOTER *n* pl. **-S** one that loots

LOP *v* **LOPPED, LOPPING, LOPS** to cut off branches or twigs from

LOPE *v* **LOPED, LOPING, LOPES** to run with a steady, easy gait

LOPER *n* pl. **-S** one that lopes

LOPPED past tense of lop

LOPPER *v* **-ED, -ING, -S** to curdle

LOPPING present participle of lop

LOPPY *adj* **-PIER, -PIEST** hanging limply

LOPSIDED *adj* leaning to one side

LOPSTICK *n* pl. **-S** lobstick

LOQUAT *n* pl. **-S** a small yellow fruit

LORAL *adj* pertaining to the space between the eye and bill of a bird

LORAN *n* pl. **-S** a type of navigational system

LORD *v* **-ED, -ING, -S** to invest with the power of a lord (a person having dominion over others)

LORDING *n* pl. **-S** a lordling

LORDLESS *adj* having no lord

LORDLIER comparative of lordly

LORDLIEST superlative of lordly

LORDLIKE *adj* lordly

LORDLING *n* pl. **-S** a young or unimportant lord

LORDLY *adj* **-LIER, -LIEST** of or befitting a lord

LORDOMA *n* pl. **-S** lordosis

LORDOSIS *n* pl. **-DOSES** a curvature of the spinal column **LORDOTIC** *adj*

LORDSHIP *n* pl. **-S** the power of a lord

LORE *n* pl. **-S** traditional knowledge or belief

LOREAL *adj* loral

LORGNON *n* pl. **-S** a pair of eyeglasses with a handle

LORICA *n* pl. **-CAE** a protective covering or shell

LORICATE *n* pl. **-S** an animal having a lorica

LORIES pl. of lory

LORIKEET *n* pl. **-S** a small parrot

LORIMER *n* pl. **-S** a maker of implements for harnesses and saddles

LORINER *n* pl. **-S** lorimer

LORIS *n* pl. **-RISES** an Asian lemur

LORN *adj* abandoned

LORNNESS *n* pl. **-ES** the state of being lorn

LORRY *n* pl. **-RIES** a type of wagon or truck

LORY *n* pl. **-RIES** a small parrot

LOSE *v* **LOST, LOSING, LOSES** to come to be without and be unable to find **LOSABLE** *adj*

LOSEL *n* pl. **-S** a worthless person

LOSER _n_ pl. **-S** one that loses

LOSING _n_ pl. **-S** a loss

LOSINGLY _adv_ in a manner characterized by defeat

LOSS _n_ pl. **-ES** the act of one that loses

LOSSLESS _adj_ done or being without loss

LOSSY _adj_ causing dissipation of electrical energy

LOST _adj_ not to be found or recovered

LOSTNESS _n_ pl. **-ES** the state of being lost

LOT _v_ **LOTTED, LOTTING, LOTS** to distribute proportionately

LOTA _n_ pl. **-S** lotah

LOTAH _n_ pl. **-S** a small water vessel used in India

LOTH _adj_ loath

LOTHARIO _n_ pl. **-IOS** a seducer of women

LOTHSOME _adj_ repulsive

LOTI _n_ pl. **MALOTI** a monetary unit of Lesotho

LOTIC _adj_ pertaining to moving water

LOTION _n_ pl. **-S** a liquid preparation for external application

LOTOS _n_ pl. **-ES** lotus

LOTTE _n_ pl. **-S** a monkfish

LOTTED past tense of lot

LOTTER _n_ pl. **-S** one who assembles merchandise into salable lots

LOTTERY _n_ pl. **-TERIES** a type of gambling game

LOTTING present participle of lot

LOTTO _n_ pl. **-TOS** a game of chance

LOTUS _n_ pl. **-ES** an aquatic plant

LOUCHE _adj_ not reputable

LOUD _adj_ **LOUDER, LOUDEST** strongly audible

LOUDEN _v_ **-ED, -ING, -S** to make or become louder

LOUDISH _adj_ somewhat loud

LOUDLY _adv_ **-LIER, -LIEST** in a loud manner

LOUDNESS _n_ pl. **-ES** the quality of being loud

LOUGH _n_ pl. **-S** a lake

LOUIE _n_ pl. **-S** looie

LOUIS _n_ pl. **LOUIS** a former gold coin of France

LOUMA _n_ pl. **-S** luma

LOUNGE _v_ **LOUNGED, LOUNGING, LOUNGES** to recline or lean in a relaxed, lazy manner

LOUNGER _n_ pl. **-S** one that lounges

LOUNGY _adj_ suitable for lounging

LOUP _v_ **LOUPED, LOUPEN, LOUPING, LOUPS** to leap

LOUPE _n_ pl. **-S** a small magnifying glass

LOUR _v_ **-ED, -ING, -S** to lower

LOURY _adj_ lowery

LOUSE _n_ pl. **LICE** a parasitic insect

LOUSE _v_ **LOUSED, LOUSING, LOUSES** to spoil or bungle

LOUSY _adj_ **LOUSIER, LOUSIEST** mean or contemptible **LOUSILY** _adv_

LOUT _v_ **-ED, -ING, -S** to bow in respect

LOUTISH _adj_ clumsy

LOUVER _n_ pl. **-S** a type of window **LOUVERED** _adj_

LOUVRE _n_ pl. **-S** louver **LOUVRED** _adj_

LOVABLE _adj_ having qualities that attract love **LOVABLY** _adv_

LOVAGE _n_ pl. **-S** a perennial herb

LOVAT _n_ pl. **-S** a chiefly green color mixture in fabrics

LOVE _v_ **LOVED, LOVING, LOVES** to feel great affection for

LOVEABLE _adj_ lovable **LOVEABLY** _adv_

LOVEBIRD _n_ pl. **-S** a small parrot

LOVEBUG _n_ pl. **-S** a small black fly that swarms along highways

LOVED past tense of love

LOVEFEST _n_ pl. **-S** a gathering to promote good feeling

LOVELESS _adj_ feeling no love

LOVELIER comparative of lovely

LOVELIES pl. of lovely

LOVELIEST superlative of lovely

LOVELILY _adv_ in a lovely manner

LOVELOCK _n_ pl. **-S** a lock of hair hanging separately

LOVELORN _adj_ not loved

LOVELY _adj_ **-LIER, -LIEST** beautiful

LOVELY _n_ pl. **-LIES** a beautiful woman

LOVER _n_ pl. **-S** one that loves another **LOVERLY** _adj_

LOVESEAT _n_ pl. **-S** a small sofa for two persons

LOVESICK _adj_ languishing with love

LOVESOME	*adj* lovely	**LUBBER**	*n* pl. **-S** a clumsy person **LUBBERLY** *adj*
LOVEVINE	*n* pl. **-S** a twining herb	**LUBE**	*v* **LUBED, LUBING, LUBES** to lubricate
LOVING	*adj* affectionate	**LUBRIC**	*adj* slippery
LOVINGLY	*adv* in a loving manner	**LUBRICAL**	*adj* lubric
LOW	*adj* **LOWER, LOWEST** having relatively little upward extension	**LUCARNE**	*n* pl. **-S** a type of window
LOW	*v* **-ED, -ING, -S** to utter the sound characteristic of cattle	**LUCE**	*n* pl. **-S** a freshwater fish
		LUCENCE	*n* pl. **-S** lucency
LOWBALL	*v* **-ED, -ING, -S** to give a customer a deceptively low price	**LUCENCY**	*n* pl. **-CIES** the quality of being lucent
LOWBORN	*adj* of humble birth	**LUCENT**	*adj* giving off light **LUCENTLY** *adv*
LOWBOY	*n* pl. **-BOYS** a low chest of drawers	**LUCERN**	*n* pl. **-S** lucerne
LOWBRED	*adj* lowborn	**LUCERNE**	*n* pl. **-S** alfalfa
LOWBROW	*n* pl. **-S** an uncultivated person	**LUCES**	a pl. of lux
LOWDOWN	*n* pl. **-S** the whole truth	**LUCID**	*adj* easily understood **LUCIDLY** *adv*
LOWE	*v* **LOWED, LOWING, LOWES** to blaze	**LUCIDITY**	*n* pl. **-TIES** the quality of being lucid
LOWER	*v* **-ED, -ING, -S** to appear dark and threatening	**LUCIFER**	*n* pl. **-S** a friction match
LOWERY	*adj* dark and threatening	**LUCK**	*v* **-ED, -ING, -S** to succeed by chance or good fortune
LOWING	*n* pl. **-S** the sound characteristic of cattle	**LUCKIE**	*n* pl. **-S** an old woman
LOWISH	*adj* somewhat low	**LUCKLESS**	*adj* unlucky
LOWLAND	*n* pl. **-S** an area of land lying lower than the adjacent country	**LUCKY**	*adj* **LUCKIER, LUCKIEST** having good fortune **LUCKILY** *adv*
LOWLIFE	*n* pl. **-LIFES** or **-LIVES** a despicable person	**LUCRE**	*n* pl. **-S** monetary gain
LOWLIFER	*n* pl. **-S** a lowlife	**LUCULENT**	*adj* lucid
LOWLIGHT	*n* pl. **-S** an unpleasant event, detail, or part	**LUDE**	*n* pl. **-S** a methaqualone pill
		LUDIC	*adj* aimlessly playful
LOWLY	*adj* **-LIER, -LIEST** low in position or rank **LOWLILY** *adv*	**LUES**	*n* pl. **LUES** syphilis
LOWN	*adj* peaceful	**LUETIC**	*n* pl. **-S** one infected with syphilis
LOWNESS	*n* pl. **-ES** the state of being low	**LUFF**	*v* **-ED, -ING, -S** to steer a sailing vessel nearer into the wind
LOWRIDER	*n* pl. **-S** a car having a lowered suspension	**LUFFA**	*n* pl. **-S** loofah
LOWSE	*adj* loose	**LUG**	*v* **LUGGED, LUGGING, LUGS** to carry or pull with effort
LOX	*v* **-ED, -ING, -ES** to supply with lox (liquid oxygen)	**LUGE**	*v* **LUGED, LUGEING** or **LUGING, LUGES** to race on a luge (a small sled)
LOYAL	*adj* **-ALER, -ALEST** faithful to one's allegiance		
LOYALISM	*n* pl. **-S** loyalty	**LUGER**	*n* pl. **-S** one that luges
LOYALIST	*n* pl. **-S** one who is loyal	**LUGGAGE**	*n* pl. **-S** articles containing a traveler's belongings
LOYALLY	*adv* in a loyal manner	**LUGGED**	past tense of lug
LOYALTY	*n* pl. **-TIES** the state of being loyal	**LUGGER**	*n* pl. **-S** a small sailing vessel
LOZENGE	*n* pl. **-S** a small, often medicated candy	**LUGGIE**	*n* pl. **-S** a small wooden dish or pail
		LUGGING	present participle of lug
LUAU	*n* pl. **-S** a Hawaiian feast	**LUGSAIL**	*n* pl. **-S** a type of sail

LUGWORM *n* pl. **-S** a burrowing marine worm

LUKEWARM *adj* moderately warm

LULL *v* **-ED, -ING, -S** to cause to sleep or rest

LULLABY *v* **-BIED, -BYING, -BIES** to lull with a soothing song

LULLER *n* pl. **-S** one that lulls

LULU *n* pl. **-S** something remarkable

LUM *n* pl. **-S** a chimney

LUMA *n* pl. **-S** a monetary unit of Armenia

LUMBAGO *n* pl. **-GOS** pain in the lower back

LUMBAR *n* pl. **-S** an anatomical part situated near the loins

LUMBER *v* **-ED, -ING, -S** to cut down and prepare timber for market

LUMBERER *n* pl. **-S** one that lumbers

LUMBERLY *adj* moving slowly with a heavy gait

LUMEN *n* pl. **-MENS** or **-MINA** the inner passage of a tubular organ **LUMENAL, LUMINAL** *adj*

LUMINARY *n* pl. **-NARIES** a body that gives light

LUMINISM *n* pl. **-S** a style of painting

LUMINIST *n* pl. **-S** a painter who uses the effects of light

LUMINOUS *adj* giving off light

LUMMOX *n* pl. **-ES** a clumsy person

LUMP *v* **-ED, -ING, -S** to make into lumps (shapeless masses)

LUMPEN *n* pl. **-S** an uprooted individual

LUMPER *n* pl. **-S** a laborer employed to load and unload ships

LUMPFISH *n* pl. **-ES** a marine fish

LUMPISH *adj* stupid

LUMPY *adj* **LUMPIER, LUMPIEST** full of lumps **LUMPILY** *adv*

LUNA *n* pl. **-S** an alchemical designation for silver

LUNACY *n* pl. **-CIES** insanity

LUNAR *n* pl. **-S** an observation of the moon taken for navigational purposes

LUNARIAN *n* pl. **-S** a supposed inhabitant of the moon

LUNATE *adj* crescent-shaped **LUNATELY** *adv*

LUNATED *adj* lunate

LUNATIC *n* pl. **-S** an insane person

LUNATION *n* pl. **-S** the interval between two successive new moons

LUNCH *v* **-ED, -ING, -ES** to eat a noonday meal

LUNCHBOX *n* pl. **-ES** a container for carrying meals to school or work

LUNCHEON *n* pl. **-S** a noonday meal

LUNCHER *n* pl. **-S** one that lunches

LUNE *n* pl. **-S** a crescent-shaped figure

LUNET *n* pl. **-S** lunette

LUNETTE *n* pl. **-S** a crescent-shaped object

LUNG *n* pl. **-S** a respiratory organ

LUNGAN *n* pl. **-S** longan

LUNGE *v* **LUNGED, LUNGING, LUNGES** to make a forceful forward movement

LUNGEE *n* pl. **-S** lungi

LUNGER *n* pl. **-S** one that lunges

LUNGFISH *n* pl. **-ES** a type of fish

LUNGFUL *n* pl. **-S** as much as the lungs can hold

LUNGI *n* pl. **-S** a loincloth worn by men in India

LUNGING present participle of lunge

LUNGWORM *n* pl. **-S** a parasitic worm

LUNGWORT *n* pl. **-S** a European herb

LUNGYI *n* pl. **-S** lungi

LUNIER comparative of luny

LUNIES pl. of luny

LUNIEST superlative of luny

LUNK *n* pl. **-S** a lunkhead

LUNKER *n* pl. **-S** a large game fish

LUNKHEAD *n* pl. **-S** a stupid person

LUNT *v* **-ED, -ING, -S** to emit smoke

LUNULA *n* pl. **-LAE** a small crescent-shaped structure **LUNULAR, LUNULATE** *adj*

LUNULE *n* pl. **-S** lunula

LUNY *adj* **-NIER, -NIEST** loony

LUNY *n* pl. **-NIES** a loony

LUPANAR *n* pl. **-S** a brothel

LUPIN *n* pl. **-S** lupine

LUPINE *n* pl. **-S** a flowering plant

LUPOUS *adj* pertaining to lupus

LUPULIN *n* pl. **-S** a medicinal powder obtained from the hop plant

LUPUS *n* pl. **-ES** a skin disease

LURCH *v* **-ED, -ING, -ES** to sway abruptly

LURCHER *n* pl. **-S** one that lurks or prowls

LURDAN *n* pl. **-S** a lazy or stupid person

LURDANE *n* pl. **-S** lurdan

LURE *v* **LURED, LURING, LURES** to attract with something desirable

LURER *n* pl. **-S** one that lures

LURID *adj* causing shock or horror **LURIDLY** *adv*

LURINGLY *adv* in an enticing manner

LURK *v* **-ED, -ING, -S** to wait in concealment

LURKER *n* pl. **-S** one that lurks

LUSCIOUS *adj* having a very pleasing taste or smell

LUSH *adj* **LUSHER, LUSHEST** abounding in vegetation **LUSHLY** *adv*

LUSH *v* **-ED, -ING, -ES** to drink to excess

LUSHNESS *n* pl. **-ES** the state of being lush

LUST *v* **-ED, -ING, -S** to have an intense desire

LUSTER *v* **-ED, -ING, -S** to make or become lustrous

LUSTFUL *adj* marked by excessive sexual desire

LUSTIER comparative of lusty

LUSTIEST superlative of lusty

LUSTILY *adv* in a lusty manner

LUSTRA a pl. of lustrum

LUSTRAL *adj* pertaining to a lustrum

LUSTRATE *v* **-TRATED, -TRATING, -TRATES** to purify ceremonially

LUSTRE *v* **-TRED, -TRING, -TRES** to luster

LUSTRING *n* pl. **-S** a glossy silk fabric

LUSTROUS *adj* reflecting light evenly and efficiently

LUSTRUM *n* pl. **-TRUMS** or **-TRA** a ceremonial purification of the population in ancient Rome

LUSTY *adj* **LUSTIER, LUSTIEST** full of vigor

LUSUS *n* pl. **-ES** an abnormality

LUTANIST *n* pl. **-S** one who plays the lute

LUTE *v* **LUTED, LUTING, LUTES** to play a lute (a stringed musical instrument)

LUTEA pl. of luteum

LUTEAL *adj* pertaining to the luteum

LUTECIUM *n* pl. **-S** lutetium

LUTED past tense of lute

LUTEFISK *n* pl. **-S** dried codfish

LUTEIN *n* pl. **-S** a yellow pigment

LUTENIST *n* pl. **-S** lutanist

LUTEOLIN *n* pl. **-S** a yellow pigment

LUTEOUS *adj* light to moderate greenish yellow in color

LUTETIUM *n* pl. **-S** a metallic element

LUTEUM *n* pl. **-TEA** a hormone-secreting body

LUTFISK *n* pl. **-S** lutefisk

LUTHERN *n* pl. **-S** a type of window

LUTHIER *n* pl. **-S** one who makes stringed instruments

LUTING *n* pl. **-S** a substance used as a sealant

LUTIST *n* pl. **-S** a lutanist

LUTZ *n* pl. **-ES** a jump in figure skating

LUV *n* pl. **-S** a sweetheart

LUX *n* pl. **LUXES** or **LUCES** a unit of illumination

LUXATE *v* **-ATED, -ATING, -ATES** to put out of joint

LUXATION *n* pl. **-S** the act of luxating

LUXE *n* pl. **-S** luxury

LUXURY *n* pl. **-RIES** free indulgence in that which affords pleasure or comfort

LWEI *n* pl. **-S** a monetary unit of Angola

LYARD *adj* streaked with gray

LYART *adj* lyard

LYASE *n* pl. **-S** an enzyme

LYCEE *n* pl. **-S** a French secondary school

LYCEUM *n* pl. **-CEUMS** or **-CEA** a hall for public lectures or discussions

LYCH *n* pl. **-ES** lich

LYCHEE *n* pl. **-S** litchi

LYCHNIS *n* pl. **-NISES** a flowering plant

LYCOPENE *n* pl. **-S** a red pigment

LYCOPOD *n* pl. **-S** an evergreen plant

LYDDITE *n* pl. **-S** an explosive

LYE *n* pl. **-S** a solution used in making soap

LYING *n* pl. **-S** the act of telling lies

LYINGLY *adv* falsely

LYMPH *n* pl. **-S** a body fluid containing white blood cells **LYMPHOID** *adj*

LYMPHOMA *n* pl. **-MAS** or **-MATA** a type of tumor

LYNCEAN *adj* of or resembling a lynx

LYNCH   *v* **-ED, -ING, -ES** to put to death without legal sanction

LYNCHER   *n* pl. **-S** one that lynches

LYNCHING   *n* pl. **-S** the act of one who lynches

LYNCHPIN   *n* pl. **-S** linchpin

LYNX   *n* pl. **-ES** a short-tailed wildcat

LYOPHILE   *adj* pertaining to a type of colloid

LYRATE   *adj* having the shape of a lyre **LYRATELY** *adv*

LYRATED   *adj* lyrate

LYRE   *n* pl. **-S** an ancient harp-like instrument

LYREBIRD   *n* pl. **-S** an Australian bird

LYRIC   *n* pl. **-S** a lyrical poem

LYRICAL   *adj* having the form of a song

LYRICISE   *v* **-CISED, -CISING, -CISES** to lyricize

LYRICISM   *n* pl. **-S** the quality of being lyrics

LYRICIST   *n* pl. **-S** one who writes the words for songs

LYRICIZE   *v* **-CIZED, -CIZING, -CIZES** to write lyrics

LYRICON   *n* pl. **-S** an electronic wind instrument

LYRIFORM   *adj* lyrate

LYRISM   *n* pl. **-S** lyricism

LYRIST   *n* pl. **-S** one who plays the lyre

LYSATE   *n* pl. **-S** a product of lysis

LYSE   *v* **LYSED, LYSING, LYSES** to cause to undergo lysis

LYSIN   *n* pl. **-S** a substance capable of disintegrating blood cells or bacteria

LYSINE   *n* pl. **-S** an amino acid

LYSING   present participle of lyse

LYSIS   *n* pl. **LYSES** the disintegration of cells by lysins

LYSOGEN   *n* pl. **-S** a type of antigen

LYSOGENY   *n* pl. **-NIES** the state of being like a lysogen

LYSOSOME   *n* pl. **-S** a saclike part of a cell

LYSOZYME   *n* pl. **-S** an enzyme

LYSSA   *n* pl. **-S** rabies

LYTIC   *adj* pertaining to lysis

LYTTA   *n* pl. **-TAS** or **-TAE** a fibrous band in the tongue of certain carnivorous mammals

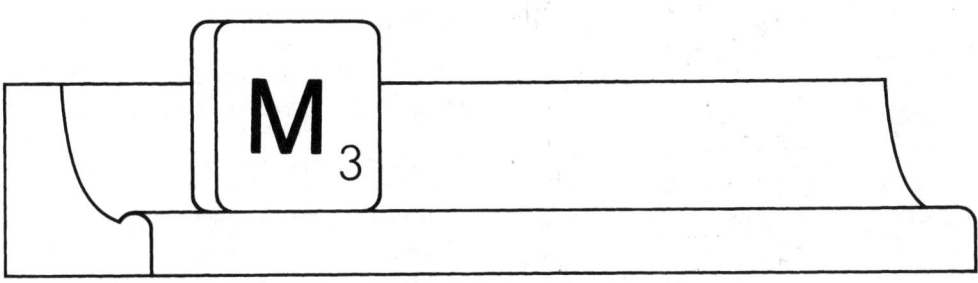

MA	*n* pl. **-S** mother
MAAR	*n* pl. **-S** a volcanic crater
MABE	*n* pl. **-S** a cultured pearl
MAC	*n* pl. **-S** a raincoat
MACABER	*adj* macabre
MACABRE	*adj* gruesome
MACACO	*n* pl. **-COS** a lemur
MACADAM	*n* pl. **-S** a type of pavement
MACAQUE	*n* pl. **-S** a short-tailed monkey
MACARONI	*n* pl. **-NIS** or **-NIES** a tubular pasta
MACAROON	*n* pl. **-S** a type of cookie
MACAW	*n* pl. **-S** a large parrot
MACCABAW	*n* pl. **-S** maccaboy
MACCABOY	*n* pl. **-BOYS** a type of snuff
MACCHIA	*n* pl. **-CHIE** a dense growth of small trees and shrubs
MACCOBOY	*n* pl. **-BOYS** maccaboy
MACE	*v* **MACED, MACING, MACES** to attack with a clublike weapon
MACER	*n* pl. **-S** an official who carries a ceremonial staff
MACERATE	*v* **-ATED, -ATING, -ATES** to soften by soaking in liquid
MACH	*n* pl. **-S** a number indicating the ratio of the speed of a body to the speed of sound
MACHE	*n* pl. **-S** a European herb
MACHETE	*n* pl. **-S** a large, heavy knife
MACHINE	*v* **-CHINED, -CHINING, -CHINES** to process by machine (a mechanical device)
MACHISMO	*n* pl. **-MOS** strong masculinity
MACHO	*n* pl. **-CHOS** a person who exhibits machismo
MACHOISM	*n* pl. **-S** machismo
MACHREE	*n* pl. **-S** dear
MACHZOR	*n* pl. **-ZORS** or **-ZORIM** mahzor
MACING	present participle of mace
MACK	*n* pl. **-S** mac
MACKEREL	*n* pl. **-S** a marine food fish
MACKINAW	*n* pl. **-S** a woolen fabric
MACKLE	*v* **-LED, -LING, -LES** to blur in printing
MACLE	*n* pl. **-S** a spot or discoloration in a mineral **MACLED** *adj*
MACON	*n* pl. **-S** a red or white French wine
MACRAME	*n* pl. **-S** a trimming of knotted thread or cord
MACRO	*n* pl. **-ROS** a type of computer instruction
MACRON	*n* pl. **-S** a symbol placed over a vowel to show that it has a long sound
MACRURAL	*adj* pertaining to macruran
MACRURAN	*n* pl. **-S** any of a suborder of crustaceans
MACULA	*n* pl. **-LAS** or **-LAE** a spot **MACULAR** *adj*
MACULATE	*v* **-LATED, -LATING, -LATES** to mark with spots
MACULE	*v* **-ULED, -ULING, -ULES** to mackle
MACUMBA	*n* pl. **-S** a religion practiced in Brazil
MAD	*adj* **MADDER, MADDEST** insane
MAD	*v* **MADDED, MADDING, MADS** to madden
MADAM	*n* pl. **-S** a woman who manages a brothel
MADAME	*n* pl. **-S** madam
MADAME	*n* pl. **MESDAMES** the French title of respect for a married woman
MADCAP	*n* pl. **-S** an impulsive person
MADDED	past tense of mad
MADDEN	*v* **-ED, -ING, -S** to make or become mad

MADDER *n* pl. **-S** a perennial herb

MADDEST superlative of mad

MADDING present participle of mad

MADDISH *adj* somewhat mad

MADE past tense of make

MADEIRA *n* pl. **-S** a white wine

MADERIZE *v* **-IZED, -IZING, -IZES** to turn brown — used of white wine

MADHOUSE *n* pl. **-S** an insane asylum

MADLY *adv* in a mad manner

MADMAN *n* pl. **-MEN** a man who is insane

MADNESS *n* pl. **-ES** the state of being mad

MADONNA *n* pl. **-S** a former Italian title of respect for a woman

MADRAS *n* pl. **-ES** a cotton fabric

MADRASA *n* pl. **-S** madrassa

MADRASAH *n* pl. **-S** madrassa

MADRASSA *n* pl. **-S** a Muslim school

MADRE *n* pl. **-S** mother

MADRIGAL *n* pl. **-S** a short lyric poem

MADRONA *n* pl. **-S** an evergreen tree

MADRONE *n* pl. **-S** madrona

MADRONO *n* pl. **-NOS** madrona

MADTOM *n* pl. **-S** a North American catfish

MADURO *n* pl. **-ROS** a dark-colored, relatively strong cigar

MADWOMAN *n* pl. **-WOMEN** a woman who is insane

MADWORT *n* pl. **-S** a flowering plant

MADZOON *n* pl. **-S** matzoon

MAE *n* pl. **-S** more

MAENAD *n* pl. **-S** or **-ES** a female participant in ancient Greek orgies **MAENADIC** *adj*

MAESTOSO *n* pl. **-SOS** a stately musical passage

MAESTRO *n* pl. **-STROS** or **-STRI** a master of an art

MAFFIA *n* pl. **-S** mafia

MAFFICK *v* **-ED, -ING, -S** to celebrate boisterously

MAFIA *n* pl. **-S** a secret criminal organization

MAFIC *adj* pertaining to minerals rich in magnesium and iron

MAFIOSO *n* pl. **-SOS** or **-SI** a member of the mafia

MAFTIR *n* pl. **-S** the concluding section of a parashah

MAG *n* pl. **-S** a magazine

MAGALOG *n* pl. **-S** a sales catalog resembling a magazine

MAGAZINE *n* pl. **-S** a type of periodical publication

MAGDALEN *n* pl. **-S** a reformed prostitute

MAGE *n* pl. **-S** a magician

MAGENTA *n* pl. **-S** a purplish red dye

MAGGOT *n* pl. **-S** the legless larva of certain insects **MAGGOTY** *adj*

MAGI pl. of magus

MAGIAN *n* pl. **-S** a magus

MAGIC *v* **-ICKED, -ICKING, -ICS** to affect by magic (sorcery)

MAGICAL *adj* resembling magic

MAGICIAN *n* pl. **-S** one skilled in magic

MAGICKED past tense of magic

MAGICKING present participle of magic

MAGILP *n* pl. **-S** megilp

MAGISTER *n* pl. **-S** a master or teacher

MAGLEV *n* pl. **-S** a train using magnets to move above the tracks

MAGMA *n* pl. **-MAS** or **-MATA** the molten matter from which igneous rock is formed **MAGMATIC** *adj*

MAGNATE *n* pl. **-S** a powerful or influential person

MAGNESIA *n* pl. **-S** a medicinal compound **MAGNESIC** *adj*

MAGNET *n* pl. **-S** a body that possesses the property of attracting iron

MAGNETIC *n* pl. **-S** a magnet

MAGNETO *n* pl. **-TOS** a type of electric generator

MAGNETON *n* pl. **-S** a unit of magnetic moment

MAGNIFIC *adj* magnificent

MAGNIFY *v* **-FIED, -FYING, -FIES** to increase the perceived size of

MAGNOLIA *n* pl. **-S** a flowering shrub or tree

MAGNUM *n* pl. **-S** a large wine bottle

MAGOT *n* pl. **-S** a tailless ape

MAGPIE *n* pl. **-S** a corvine bird

MAGUEY *n* pl. **-GUEYS** a tropical plant

MAGUS *n* pl. **-GI** a magician

MAHARAJA *n* pl. **-S** a king or prince in India

MAHARANI *n* pl. **-S** the wife of a maharaja

MAHATMA *n* pl. **-S** a Hindu sage

MAHIMAHI *n* pl. **-S** a food fish in Hawaii

MAHJONG *n* pl. **-S** a game of Chinese origin

MAHJONGG *n* pl. **-S** mahjong

MAHOE *n* pl. **-S** a tropical tree

MAHOGANY *n* pl. **-NIES** a tropical tree

MAHONIA *n* pl. **-S** a flowering shrub

MAHOUT *n* pl. **-S** the keeper and driver of an elephant

MAHUANG *n* pl. **-S** an Asian plant

MAHZOR *n* pl. **-ZORS** or **-ZORIM** a Jewish prayer book

MAIASAUR *n* pl. **-S** an herbivorous dinosaur

MAID *n* pl. **-S** a maiden **MAIDISH** *adj*

MAIDEN *n* pl. **-S** a young unmarried woman **MAIDENLY** *adj*

MAIDHOOD *n* pl. **-S** the state of being a maiden

MAIEUTIC *adj* pertaining to a method of eliciting knowledge

MAIGRE *adj* containing neither flesh nor its juices

MAIHEM *n* pl. **-S** mayhem

MAIL *v* **-ED, -ING, -S** to send by a governmental postal system **MAILABLE** *adj*

MAILBAG *n* pl. **-S** a bag for carrying mail (postal material)

MAILBOX *n* pl. **-ES** a box for depositing mail

MAILE *n* pl. **-S** a Pacific island vine

MAILER *n* pl. **-S** one that mails

MAILING *n* pl. **-S** a rented farm

MAILL *n* pl. **-S** a payment

MAILLESS *adj* having no armor

MAILLOT *n* pl. **-S** a woman's one-piece bathing suit

MAILMAN *n* pl. **-MEN** a man who carries and delivers mail

MAILROOM *n* pl. **-S** a room for processing mail

MAIM *v* **-ED, -ING, -S** to injure so as to cause lasting damage

MAIMER *n* pl. **-S** one that maims

MAIN *n* pl. **-S** the principal part

MAINLAND *n* pl. **-S** a principal land mass

MAINLINE *v* **-LINED, -LINING, -LINES** to inject a narcotic into a major vein

MAINLY *adv* for the most part

MAINMAST *n* pl. **-S** the principal mast of a vessel

MAINSAIL *n* pl. **-S** the principal sail of a vessel

MAINSTAY *n* pl. **-STAYS** a principal support

MAINTAIN *v* **-ED, -ING, -S** to keep in proper condition

MAINTOP *n* pl. **-S** a platform at the head of a mainmast

MAIOLICA *n* pl. **-S** majolica

MAIR *n* pl. **-S** more

MAIST *n* pl. **-S** most

MAIZE *n* pl. **-S** an American cereal grass

MAJAGUA *n* pl. **-S** a tropical tree

MAJESTIC *adj* having majesty

MAJESTY *n* pl. **-TIES** regal dignity

MAJOLICA *n* pl. **-S** a type of pottery

MAJOR *v* **-ED, -ING, -S** to pursue a specific principal course of study

MAJORITY *n* pl. **-TIES** the greater number or part

MAJORLY *adv* mainly

MAKAR *n* pl. **-S** a poet

MAKE *v* **MADE, MAKING, MAKES** to cause to exist **MAKABLE, MAKEABLE** *adj*

MAKEBATE *n* pl. **-S** one that encourages quarrels

MAKEFAST *n* pl. **-S** an object to which a boat is tied

MAKEOVER *n* pl. **-S** a changing of appearance

MAKER *n* pl. **-S** one that makes

MAKEUP *n* pl. **-S** the way in which the parts or ingredients of something are put together

MAKIMONO *n* pl. **-NOS** a Japanese ornamental scroll

MAKING *n* pl. **-S** material from which something can be developed

MAKO *n* pl. **-KOS** a large shark

MAKUTA pl. of likuta

MALACCA *n* pl. **-S** the cane of an Asian rattan palm

MALADY *n* pl. **-DIES** an illness

MALAISE *n* pl. **-S** a feeling of vague discomfort

MALAMUTE *n* pl. **-S** an Alaskan sled dog

MALANGA *n* pl. **-S** a yautia

MALAPERT *n* pl. **-S** an impudent person

MALAPROP *n* pl. **-S** a humorous misuse of a word

MALAR *n* pl. **-S** the cheekbone

MALARIA *n* pl. **-S** an infectious disease **MALARIAL, MALARIAN** *adj*

MALARKEY *n* pl. **-KEYS** nonsense

MALARKY *n* pl. **-KIES** malarkey

MALAROMA *n* pl. **-S** a malodor

MALATE *n* pl. **-S** a chemical salt

MALE *n* pl. **-S** an individual that begets young by fertilizing the female

MALEATE *n* pl. **-S** a chemical salt

MALEDICT *v* **-ED, -ING, -S** to curse

MALEFIC *adj* producing or causing evil

MALEMIUT *n* pl. **-S** malamute

MALEMUTE *n* pl. **-S** malamute

MALENESS *n* pl. **-ES** the quality of being a male

MALFED *adj* badly fed

MALGRE *prep* in spite of

MALIC *adj* pertaining to apples

MALICE *n* pl. **-S** a desire to injure another

MALIGN *v* **-ED, -ING, -S** to speak evil of

MALIGNER *n* pl. **-S** one that maligns

MALIGNLY *adv* in an evil manner

MALIHINI *n* pl. **-S** a newcomer to Hawaii

MALINE *n* pl. **-S** a delicate net used for veils

MALINGER *v* **-ED, -ING, -S** to feign illness in order to avoid duty or work

MALISON *n* pl. **-S** a curse

MALKIN *n* pl. **-S** an untidy woman

MALL *v* **-ED, -ING, -S** to maul

MALLARD *n* pl. **-S** a wild duck

MALLEE *n* pl. **-S** an evergreen tree

MALLEI pl. of malleus

MALLEOLI *n/pl* bony protuberances of the ankle

MALLET *n* pl. **-S** a type of hammer

MALLEUS *n* pl. **-LEI** a bone of the middle ear

MALLING *n* pl. **-S** the practice of shopping at malls (large buildings with many shops)

MALLOW *n* pl. **-S** a flowering plant

MALM *n* pl. **-S** a soft, friable limestone

MALMSEY *n* pl. **-SEYS** a white wine

MALMY *adj* **MALMIER, MALMIEST** resembling malm

MALODOR *n* pl. **-S** an offensive odor

MALOTI pl. of loti

MALPOSED *adj* being in the wrong position

MALT *v* **-ED, -ING, -S** to treat or combine with malt (germinated grain)

MALTASE *n* pl. **-S** an enzyme

MALTED *n* pl. **-S** a sweet beverage

MALTHA *n* pl. **-S** a natural tar

MALTIER comparative of malty

MALTIEST superlative of malty

MALTOL *n* pl. **-S** a chemical compound

MALTOSE *n* pl. **-S** a type of sugar

MALTREAT *v* **-ED, -ING, -S** to treat badly

MALTSTER *n* pl. **-S** one that makes malt

MALTY *adj* **MALTIER, MALTIEST** resembling malt

MALVASIA *n* pl. **-S** malmsey

MAMA *n* pl. **-S** mother

MAMALIGA *n* pl. **-S** a cornmeal porridge

MAMBA *n* pl. **-S** a venomous snake

MAMBO *v* **-ED, -ING, -ES** or **-S** to perform a ballroom dance

MAMELUKE *n* pl. **-S** a slave in Muslim countries

MAMEY *n* pl. **-MEYS** or **-MEYES** a tropical tree

MAMIE *n* pl. **-S** mamey

MAMLUK *n* pl. **-S** mameluke

MAMMA *n* pl. **-MAE** a milk-secreting organ

MAMMA *n* pl. **-S** mama

MAMMAL *n* pl. **-S** any of a class of warm-blooded vertebrates

MAMMARY *adj* pertaining to the mammae

MAMMATE *adj* having mammae

MAMMATUS *n* pl. **-TI** a type of cloud

MAMMEE *n* pl. **-S** mamey

MAMMER *v* **-ED, -ING, -S** to hesitate

MAMMET *n* pl. **-S** maumet

MAMMEY *n* pl. **-MEYS** mamey

MAMMIE *n* pl. **-S** mammy

MAMMIES pl. of mammy

MAMMILLA *n* pl. **-LAE** a nipple

MAMMITIS *n* pl. **-MITIDES** mastitis

MAMMOCK *v* **-ED, -ING, -S** to shred

MAMMON *n* pl. **-S** material wealth

MAMMOTH *n* pl. **-S** an extinct elephant

MAMMY *n* pl. **-MIES** mother

MAMZER *n* pl. **-S** a bastard**

MAN	*n* pl. **MEN** an adult human male
MAN	*v* **MANNED, MANNING, MANS** to supply with men
MANA	*n* pl. **-S** a supernatural force in certain Pacific island religions
MANACLE	*v* **-CLED, -CLING, -CLES** to handcuff
MANAGE	*v* **-AGED, -AGING, -AGES** to control or direct
MANAGER	*n* pl. **-S** one that manages
MANAKIN	*n* pl. **-S** a tropical bird
MANANA	*n* pl. **-S** tomorrow
MANAT	*n* pl. **-S** a monetary unit of Azerbaijan
MANATEE	*n* pl. **-S** an aquatic mammal **MANATOID** *adj*
MANCHE	*n* pl. **-S** a heraldic design
MANCHET	*n* pl. **-S** a small loaf of fine white bread
MANCIPLE	*n* pl. **-S** an officer authorized to purchase provisions
MANDALA	*n* pl. **-S** a Hindu or Buddhist graphic symbol of the universe **MANDALIC** *adj*
MANDAMUS	*v* **-ED, -ING, -ES** to command by means of writ issued by a superior court
MANDARIN	*n* pl. **-S** a citrus fruit
MANDATE	*v* **-DATED, -DATING, -DATES** to authorize or decree
MANDATOR	*n* pl. **-S** one that mandates
MANDIBLE	*n* pl. **-S** the bone of the lower jaw
MANDIOCA	*n* pl. **-S** manioc
MANDOLA	*n* pl. **-S** an ancient lute
MANDOLIN	*n* pl. **-S** a stringed musical instrument
MANDRAKE	*n* pl. **-S** a European herb
MANDREL	*n* pl. **-S** a shaft on which a tool is mounted
MANDRIL	*n* pl. **-S** mandrel
MANDRILL	*n* pl. **-S** a large baboon
MANE	*n* pl. **-S** the long hair growing on and about the neck of some animals **MANED, MANELESS** *adj*
MANEGE	*n* pl. **-S** the art of training and riding horses
MANEUVER	*v* **-ED, -ING, -S** to change the position of for a specific purpose
MANFUL	*adj* courageous **MANFULLY** *adv*
MANGA	*n* pl. **-S** a Japanese graphic novel
MANGABEY	*n* pl. **-BEYS** a long-tailed monkey
MANGABY	*n* pl. **-BIES** mangabey
MANGANIC	*adj* containing manganese (a metallic element)
MANGANIN	*n* pl. **-S** an alloy of copper, manganese, and nickel
MANGE	*n* pl. **-S** a skin disease of domestic animals
MANGEL	*n* pl. **-S** a variety of beet
MANGER	*n* pl. **-S** a trough or box from which horses or cattle eat
MANGEY	*adj* **MANGIER, MANGIEST** mangy
MANGIER	comparative of mangy
MANGIEST	superlative of mangy
MANGILY	*adv* in a mangy manner
MANGLE	*v* **-GLED, -GLING, -GLES** to cut, slash, or crush so as to disfigure
MANGLER	*n* pl. **-S** one that mangles
MANGO	*n* pl. **-GOS** or **-GOES** an edible tropical fruit
MANGOLD	*n* pl. **-S** mangel
MANGONEL	*n* pl. **-S** a medieval military device for hurling stones
MANGROVE	*n* pl. **-S** a tropical tree or shrub
MANGY	*adj* **MANGIER, MANGIEST** affected with mange
MANHOLE	*n* pl. **-S** a hole providing entrance to an underground or enclosed structure
MANHOOD	*n* pl. **-S** the state of being a man
MANHUNT	*n* pl. **-S** an intensive search for a person
MANIA	*n* pl. **-S** an excessive interest or enthusiasm
MANIAC	*n* pl. **-S** an insane person **MANIACAL** *adj*
MANIC	*n* pl. **-S** one that is affected with mania
MANICURE	*v* **-CURED, -CURING, -CURES** to trim and polish the fingernails of
MANIFEST	*v* **-ED, -ING, -S** to show clearly
MANIFOLD	*v* **-ED, -ING, -S** to make several copies of
MANIHOT	*n* pl. **-S** a tropical plant
MANIKIN	*n* pl. **-S** an anatomical model of the human body
MANILA	*n* pl. **-S** a strong paper
MANILLA	*n* pl. **-S** manila
MANILLE	*n* pl. **-S** the second highest trump in certain card games

MANIOC	*n* pl. **-S** a tropical plant
MANIOCA	*n* pl. **-S** manioc
MANIPLE	*n* pl. **-S** a silk band worn on the left arm as a vestment
MANITO	*n* pl. **-TOS** manitou
MANITOU	*n* pl. **-S** an Algonquian Indian deity
MANITU	*n* pl. **-S** manitou
MANKIND	*n* pl. **MANKIND** the human race
MANLESS	*adj* destitute of men
MANLIKE	*adj* resembling a man
MANLY	*adj* **-LIER, -LIEST** having the qualities of a man **MANLILY** *adv*
MANMADE	*adj* made by man
MANNA	*n* pl. **-S** divinely supplied food
MANNAN	*n* pl. **-S** a type of sugar
MANNED	past tense of man
MANNER	*n* pl. **-S** a way of acting **MANNERED** *adj*
MANNERLY	*adj* polite
MANNIKIN	*n* pl. **-S** manikin
MANNING	present participle of man
MANNISH	*adj* resembling or characteristic of a man
MANNITE	*n* pl. **-S** mannitol **MANNITIC** *adj*
MANNITOL	*n* pl. **-S** an alcohol
MANNOSE	*n* pl. **-S** a type of sugar
MANO	*n* pl. **-NOS** a stone used for grinding foods
MANOR	*n* pl. **-S** a landed estate or territorial unit **MANORIAL** *adj*
MANPACK	*adj* designed to be carried by one person
MANPOWER	*n* pl. **-S** the number of men available for service
MANQUE	*adj* frustrated in the fulfillment of one's aspirations
MANROPE	*n* pl. **-S** a rope used as a handrail
MANSARD	*n* pl. **-S** a type of roof
MANSE	*n* pl. **-S** a clergyman's house
MANSION	*n* pl. **-S** a large, impressive house
MANTA	*n* pl. **-S** a cotton fabric
MANTEAU	*n* pl. **-TEAUS** or **-TEAUX** a loose cloak
MANTEL	*n* pl. **-S** a shelf above a fireplace
MANTELET	*n* pl. **-S** a mobile screen used to protect soldiers
MANTES	a pl. of mantis
MANTIC	*adj* having powers of prophecy
MANTID	*n* pl. **-S** mantis
MANTILLA	*n* pl. **-S** a woman's scarf
MANTIS	*n* pl. **-TISES** or **-TES** a predatory insect
MANTISSA	*n* pl. **-S** the decimal part of a logarithm
MANTLE	*v* **-TLED, -TLING, -TLES** to cloak
MANTLET	*n* pl. **-S** mantelet
MANTLING	*n* pl. **-S** an ornamental cloth
MANTRA	*n* pl. **-S** a mystical formula of prayer or incantation in Hinduism **MANTRIC** *adj*
MANTRAM	*n* pl. **-S** mantra
MANTRAP	*n* pl. **-S** a trap for catching men
MANTUA	*n* pl. **-S** a woman's gown
MANUAL	*n* pl. **-S** a small reference book
MANUALLY	*adv* by means of the hands
MANUARY	*adj* involving the hands
MANUBRIA	*n/pl* handle-shaped anatomical parts
MANUMIT	*v* **-MITTED, -MITTING, -MITS** to free from slavery
MANURE	*v* **-NURED, -NURING, -NURES** to fertilize with manure (animal excrement)
MANURER	*n* pl. **-S** one that manures
MANURIAL	*adj* of or pertaining to manure
MANURING	present participle of manure
MANUS	*n* pl. **MANUS** the end of the forelimb in vertebrates
MANWARD	*adv* toward man
MANWARDS	*adv* manward
MANWISE	*adv* in a manner characteristic of man
MANY	*adj* **MORE, MOST** consisting of or amounting to a large number
MANYFOLD	*adv* by many times
MAP	*v* **MAPPED, MAPPING, MAPS** to delineate on a map (a representation of a region)
MAPLE	*n* pl. **-S** a hardwood tree
MAPLIKE	*adj* resembling a map
MAPMAKER	*n* pl. **-S** one that makes maps
MAPPABLE	*adj* capable of being mapped
MAPPED	past tense of map
MAPPER	*n* pl. **-S** one that maps
MAPPING	*n* pl. **-S** a mathematical correspondence
MAQUETTE	*n* pl. **-S** a small preliminary model

MAQUI   *n* pl. **-S** maquis

MAQUILA   *n* pl. **-S** a foreign-owned assembly factory in Mexico

MAQUIS   *n* pl. **MAQUIS** a thick underbrush

MAR   *v* **MARRED, MARRING, MARS** to detract from the perfection or wholeness of

MARA   *n* pl. **-S** a cavy of Argentina

MARABOU   *n* pl. **-S** an African stork

MARABOUT   *n* pl. **-S** a marabou

MARACA   *n* pl. **-S** a percussion instrument

MARANTA   *n* pl. **-S** a tropical plant

MARASCA   *n* pl. **-S** a wild cherry

MARASMUS   *n* pl. **-ES** a wasting away of the body **MARASMIC** *adj*

MARATHON   *n* pl. **-S** a long-distance race

MARAUD   *v* **-ED, -ING, -S** to rove in search of booty

MARAUDER   *n* pl. **-S** one that marauds

MARAVEDI   *n* pl. **-S** a former coin of Spain

MARBLE   *v* **-BLED, -BLING, -BLES** to give a mottled appearance to

MARBLER   *n* pl. **-S** one that marbles

MARBLING   *n* pl. **-S** an intermixture of fat and lean in meat

MARBLY   *adj* **-BLIER, -BLIEST** mottled

MARC   *n* pl. **-S** the residue remaining after a fruit has been pressed

MARCATO   *n* pl. **-TOS** a musical passage played with strong accentuation

MARCEL   *v* **-CELLED, -CELLING, -CELS** to make a deep, soft wave in the hair

MARCH   *v* **-ED, -ING, -ES** to walk in a formal military manner

MARCHEN   *n* pl. **MARCHEN** a folktale

MARCHER   *n* pl. **-S** one that marches

MARCHESA   *n* pl. **-CHESE** the wife or widow of a marchese

MARCHESE   *n* pl. **-CHESI** an Italian nobleman

MARE   *n* pl. **-RIA** a dark area on the surface of the moon or Mars

MARE   *n* pl. **-S** a mature female horse

MAREMMA   *n* pl. **-REMME** a marshy coastal region

MARENGO   *adj* served with a sauce of mushrooms, tomatoes, oil, and wine

MARGARIC   *adj* pearly

MARGARIN   *n* pl. **-S** a butter substitute

MARGAY   *n* pl. **-GAYS** a small American wildcat

MARGE   *n* pl. **-S** a margin

MARGENT   *v* **-ED, -ING, -S** to margin

MARGIN   *v* **-ED, -ING, -S** to provide with a margin (a border)

MARGINAL   *n* pl. **-S** one considered to be at a lower or outer limit

MARGRAVE   *n* pl. **-S** the military governor of a medieval German border province

MARIA   pl. of mare

MARIACHI   *n* pl. **-S** a Mexican musical band

MARIGOLD   *n* pl. **-S** a flowering plant

MARIMBA   *n* pl. **-S** a percussion instrument

MARINA   *n* pl. **-S** a docking area for small boats

MARINADE   *v* **-NADED, -NADING, -NADES** to marinate

MARINARA   *n* pl. **-S** a seasoned tomato sauce

MARINATE   *v* **-NATED, -NATING, -NATES** to soak in a seasoned liquid before cooking

MARINE   *n* pl. **-S** a soldier trained for service at sea and on land

MARINER   *n* pl. **-S** a sailor

MARIPOSA   *n* pl. **-S** a flowering plant

MARISH   *n* pl. **-ES** a marsh

MARITAL   *adj* pertaining to marriage

MARITIME   *adj* pertaining to navigation or commerce on the sea

MARJORAM   *n* pl. **-S** fragrant herb

MARK   *v* **-ED, -ING, -S** to make a visible impression on

MARKA   *n* pl. **-S** a monetary unit of Bosnia and Herzegovina

MARKDOWN   *n* pl. **-S** a reduction in price

MARKEDLY   *adv* in an evident manner

MARKER   *n* pl. **-S** one that marks

MARKET   *v* **-ED, -ING, -S** to offer for sale

MARKETER   *n* pl. **-S** one that markets

MARKHOOR   *n* pl. **-S** markhor

MARKHOR   *n* pl. **-S** a wild goat

MARKING   *n* pl. **-S** a pattern of marks

MARKKA   *n* pl. **-KAS** or **-KAA** a former monetary unit of Finland

MARKSMAN   *n* pl. **-MEN** a person skillful at hitting a target

MARKUP   *n* pl. **-S** an increase in price

MARL   *v* **-ED, -ING, -S** to fertilize with marl (an earthy deposit containing lime, clay, and sand)

MARLIER   comparative of marly

MARLIEST   superlative of marly

MARLIN   *n* pl. **-S** a marine game fish

MARLINE   *n* pl. **-S** a rope used on a ship

MARLING   *n* pl. **-S** marline

MARLITE   *n* pl. **-S** a type of marl **MARLITIC** *adj*

MARLY   *adj* **MARLIER, MARLIEST** abounding with marl

MARMITE   *n* pl. **-S** a large soup kettle

MARMOSET   *n* pl. **-S** a small monkey

MARMOT   *n* pl. **-S** a burrowing rodent

MAROCAIN   *n* pl. **-S** a light crinkled fabric

MAROON   *v* **-ED, -ING, -S** to abandon in an isolated place

MARPLOT   *n* pl. **-S** one that ruins a plan by meddling

MARQUE   *n* pl. **-S** reprisal

MARQUEE   *n* pl. **-S** a rooflike structure projecting over an entrance

MARQUESS   *n* pl. **-ES** marquis

MARQUIS   *n* pl. **-ES** a European nobleman

MARQUISE   *n* pl. **-S** the wife or widow of a marquis

MARRAM   *n* pl. **-S** a beach grass

MARRANO   *n* pl. **-NOS** a Jew in Spain who professed Christianity to avoid persecution

MARRED   past tense of mar

MARRER   *n* pl. **-S** one that mars

MARRIAGE   *n* pl. **-S** the legal union of a man and woman

MARRIED   *n* pl. **-S** one who has entered into marriage

MARRIER   *n* pl. **-S** one that marries

MARRIES   present 3d person sing. of marry

MARRING   present participle of mar

MARRON   *n* pl. **-S** a variety of chestnut

MARROW   *v* **-ED, -ING, -S** to marry

MARROWY   *adj* pithy

MARRY   *v* **-RIED, -RYING, -RIES** to enter into marriage

MARSALA   *n* pl. **-S** a Sicilian wine

MARSE   *n* pl. **-S** master

MARSH   *n* pl. **-ES** a tract of low, wet land

MARSHAL   *v* **-ED, -ING, -S** to put in proper order

MARSHALL   *v* **-ED, -ING, -S** to marshal

MARSHY   *adj* **MARSHIER, MARSHIEST** resembling a marsh

MARSUPIA   *n/pl* abdominal pouches of certain mammals

MART   *v* **-ED, -ING, -S** to market

MARTAGON   *n* pl. **-S** a flowering plant

MARTELLO   *n* pl. **-LOS** a circular fort

MARTEN   *n* pl. **-S** a carnivorous mammal

MARTIAL   *adj* pertaining to war

MARTIAN   *n* pl. **-S** a supposed inhabitant of the planet Mars

MARTIN   *n* pl. **-S** a small bird

MARTINET   *n* pl. **-S** one who demands rigid adherence to rules

MARTINI   *n* pl. **-S** an alcoholic beverage

MARTLET   *n* pl. **-S** a martin

MARTYR   *v* **-ED, -ING, -S** to put to death for adhering to a belief

MARTYRLY   *adj* resembling a martyr

MARTYRY   *n* pl. **-TYRIES** a shrine erected in honor of a martyred person

MARVEL   *v* **-VELED, -VELING, -VELS** or **-VELLED, -VELLING, -VELS** to be filled with wonder or astonishment

MARVY   *adj* marvelous

MARYJANE   *n* pl. **-S** marijuana

MARZIPAN   *n* pl. **-S** an almond candy

MASA   *n* pl. **-S** dough made of dried corn

MASALA   *n* pl. **-S** a blend of spices used in Indian cooking

MASCARA   *v* **-ED, -ING, -S** to color the eyelashes or eyebrows with a cosmetic

MASCON   *n* pl. **-S** a concentration of dense mass beneath the moon's surface

MASCOT   *n* pl. **-S** a person, animal, or object believed to bring good luck

MASER   *n* pl. **-S** a device for amplifying electrical impulses

MASH   *v* **-ED, -ING, -ES** to reduce to a pulpy mass

MASHER   *n* pl. **-S** one that mashes

MASHGIAH   *n* pl. **-GIHIM** an inspector of kosher establishments

MASHIE   *n* pl. **-S** a golf club

MASHY   *n* pl. **MASHIES** mashie

MASJID   *n* pl. **-S** a mosque

MASK *v* **-ED, -ING, -S** to cover with a mask (a covering used to disguise the face) **MASKABLE** *adj*

MASKEG *n* pl. **-S** muskeg

MASKER *n* pl. **-S** one that wears a mask

MASKING *n* pl. **-S** a piece of scenery used to conceal parts of a stage from the audience

MASKLIKE *adj* suggestive of a mask

MASON *v* **-ED, -ING, -S** to build with stone or brick

MASONIC *adj* pertaining to masonry

MASONRY *n* pl. **-RIES** a structure built of stone or brick

MASQUE *n* pl. **-S** a dramatic entertainment formerly popular in England

MASQUER *n* pl. **-S** masker

MASS *v* **-ED, -ING, -ES** to assemble in a mass (a body of coherent matter)

MASSA *n* pl. **-S** master

MASSACRE *v* **-CRED, -CRING, -CRES** to kill indiscriminately

MASSAGE *v* **-SAGED, -SAGING, -SAGES** to manipulate parts of the body for remedial or hygienic purposes

MASSAGER *n* pl. **-S** one that massages

MASSCULT *n* pl. **-S** culture as popularized by the mass media

MASSE *n* pl. **-S** a type of shot in billiards

MASSEDLY *adv* in a massed manner

MASSETER *n* pl. **-S** a muscle that raises the lower jaw

MASSEUR *n* pl. **-S** a man who massages

MASSEUSE *n* pl. **-S** a woman who massages

MASSICOT *n* pl. **-S** a yellow pigment

MASSIER comparative of massy

MASSIEST superlative of massy

MASSIF *n* pl. **-S** a principal mountain mass

MASSIVE *adj* of considerable size

MASSLESS *adj* having no mass

MASSY *adj* **MASSIER, MASSIEST** massive

MAST *v* **-ED, -ING, -S** to provide with a mast (a long pole on a ship that supports the sails and rigging)

MASTABA *n* pl. **-S** an ancient Egyptian tomb

MASTABAH *n* pl. **-S** mastaba

MASTER *v* **-ED, -ING, -S** to become skilled in

MASTERLY *adj* very skillful

MASTERY *n* pl. **-TERIES** superior knowledge or skill

MASTHEAD *v* **-ED, -ING, -S** to raise to the top of a mast

MASTIC *n* pl. **-S** an aromatic resin

MASTICHE *n* pl. **-S** mastic

MASTIFF *n* pl. **-S** a large, short-haired dog

MASTITIS *n* pl. **-TITIDES** inflammation of the breast **MASTITIC** *adj*

MASTIX *n* pl. **-ES** mastic

MASTLESS *adj* having no mast

MASTLIKE *adj* resembling a mast

MASTODON *n* pl. **-S** an extinct elephant-like mammal

MASTOID *n* pl. **-S** the rear portion of the temporal bone

MASURIUM *n* pl. **-S** a metallic element

MAT *v* **MATTED, MATTING, MATS** to pack down into a dense mass

MATADOR *n* pl. **-S** the bullfighter who kills the bull in a bullfight

MATAMBALA a pl. of tambala

MATCH *v* **-ED, -ING, -ES** to set in competition or opposition

MATCHBOX *n* pl. **-ES** a small box

MATCHER *n* pl. **-S** one that matches

MATCHUP *n* pl. **-S** a setting of two players against each other

MATE *v* **MATED, MATING, MATES** to join as mates (partners in a union)

MATELESS *adj* having no mate

MATELOT *n* pl. **-S** a sailor

MATELOTE *n* pl. **-S** a fish stew

MATER *n* pl. **-TERS** or **-TRES** mother

MATERIAL *n* pl. **-S** the substance of which anything is or may be composed

MATERIEL *n* pl. **-S** the aggregate of equipment and supplies used by an organization

MATERNAL *adj* pertaining to a mother

MATESHIP *n* pl. **-S** the state of being a mate

MATEY *n* pl. **-EYS** a friend

MATEY *adj* **MATIER, MATIEST** companionable

MATH *n* pl. **-S** mathematics

MATILDA *n* pl. **-S** a hobo's bundle

MATIN *n* pl. **-S** a morning song, as of birds

MATINAL *adj* pertaining to the morning

MATINEE	*n* pl. **-S** a daytime performance
MATINESS	*n* pl. **-ES** friendliness
MATING	*n* pl. **-S** the period during which a seasonal-breeding animal can mate
MATLESS	*adj* having no mats (small floor coverings)
MATRASS	*n* pl. **-ES** a long-necked glass vessel
MATRES	a pl. of mater
MATRIX	*n* pl. **-TRIXES** or **-TRICES** something within which something else originates or develops
MATRON	*n* pl. **-S** a married woman of established social position **MATRONAL, MATRONLY** *adj*
MATSAH	*n* pl. **-S** matzo
MATT	*v* **-ED, -ING, -S** to matte
MATTE	*v* **MATTED, MATTING, MATTES** to produce a dull finish on
MATTED	past tense of mat, matt, and matte
MATTEDLY	*adv* in a tangled manner
MATTER	*v* **-ED, -ING, -S** to be of importance
MATTERY	*adj* producing pus
MATTIN	*n* pl. **-S** matin
MATTING	*n* pl. **-S** a woven fabric used as a floor covering
MATTOCK	*n* pl. **-S** a digging tool
MATTOID	*n* pl. **-S** a mentally unbalanced person
MATTRASS	*n* pl. **-ES** matrass
MATTRESS	*n* pl. **-ES** a large pad filled with resilient material used on or as a bed
MATURATE	*v* **-RATED, -RATING, -RATES** to mature
MATURE	*adj* **-TURER, -TUREST** fully developed **MATURELY** *adv*
MATURE	*v* **-TURED, -TURING, -TURES** to make or become mature
MATURER	*n* pl. **-S** one that brings something to maturity
MATURITY	*n* pl. **-TIES** the state of being mature
MATZA	*n* pl. **-S** matzo
MATZAH	*n* pl. **-S** matzo
MATZO	*n* pl. **-ZOS** or **-ZOT** or **-ZOTH** an unleavened bread
MATZOH	*n* pl. **-S** matzo
MATZOON	*n* pl. **-S** a food made from milk

MAUD	*n* pl. **-S** a Scottish gray and black plaid
MAUDLIN	*adj* excessively emotional
MAUGER	*prep* maugre
MAUGRE	*prep* in spite of
MAUL	*v* **-ED, -ING, -S** to injure by beating
MAULER	*n* pl. **-S** one that mauls
MAUMET	*n* pl. **-S** an idol
MAUMETRY	*n* pl. **-RIES** idolatry
MAUN	*v* must — MAUN is the only form of this verb; it cannot be conjugated
MAUND	*n* pl. **-S** an Asian unit of weight
MAUNDER	*v* **-ED, -ING, -S** to talk incoherently
MAUNDY	*n* pl. **-DIES** the religious ceremony of washing the feet of the poor
MAUSOLEA	*n/pl* large, stately tombs
MAUT	*n* pl. **-S** malt
MAUVE	*n* pl. **-S** a purple color
MAVEN	*n* pl. **-S** mavin
MAVERICK	*n* pl. **-S** an unbranded range animal
MAVIE	*n* pl. **-S** mavis
MAVIN	*n* pl. **-S** an expert
MAVIS	*n* pl. **-VISES** a songbird
MAW	*v* **MAWED, MAWN, MAWING, MAWS** to mow
MAWKISH	*adj* offensively sentimental
MAX	*v* **-ED, -ING, -ES** to reach the upper limit
MAXI	*n* pl. **-S** a long skirt or coat
MAXICOAT	*n* pl. **-S** a long coat
MAXILLA	*n* pl. **-LAS** or **-LAE** the upper jaw or jawbone
MAXIM	*n* pl. **-S** a brief statement of a general truth or principle
MAXIMA	a pl. of maximum
MAXIMAL	*n* pl. **-S** an element of a mathematical set that is followed by no other
MAXIMIN	*n* pl. **-S** the maximum of a set of minima
MAXIMISE	*v* **-MISED, -MISING, -MISES** to maximize
MAXIMITE	*n* pl. **-S** a powerful explosive
MAXIMIZE	*v* **-MIZED, -MIZING, -MIZES** to make as great as possible
MAXIMUM	*n* pl. **-MUMS** or **-MA** the greatest possible amount, quantity, or degree

MAXIXE *n* pl. **-S** a Brazilian dance

MAXWELL *n* pl. **-S** a unit of magnetic flux

MAY *v* **-ED, -ING, -S** to gather flowers in the spring

MAYA *n* pl. **-S** the power to produce illusions, in Hindu philosophy **MAYAN** *adj*

MAYAPPLE *n* pl. **-S** a perennial herb

MAYBE *n* pl. **-S** an uncertainty

MAYBIRD *n* pl. **-S** a bobolink

MAYBUSH *n* pl. **-ES** a flowering shrub

MAYDAY *n* pl. **-DAYS** a radio distress call

MAYEST a present 2d person sing. of may

MAYFLY *n* pl. **-FLIES** a winged insect

MAYHAP *adv* maybe

MAYHEM *n* pl. **-S** the offense of willfully maiming a person

MAYING *n* pl. **-S** the gathering of spring flowers

MAYO *n* pl. **-YOS** mayonnaise

MAYOR *n* pl. **-S** the chief executive official of a city or borough **MAYORAL** *adj*

MAYORESS *n* pl. **-ES** a female mayor

MAYPOLE *n* pl. **-S** a decorated pole used in a spring celebration

MAYPOP *n* pl. **-S** a flowering vine

MAYST a present 2d person sing. of may

MAYVIN *n* pl. **-S** mavin

MAYWEED *n* pl. **-S** a malodorous weed

MAZAEDIA *n/pl* spore-producing organs of certain lichens

MAZARD *n* pl. **-S** the head or face

MAZE *v* **MAZED, MAZING, MAZES** to bewilder **MAZEDLY** *adv*

MAZELIKE *adj* mazy

MAZELTOV *interj* — used to express congratulations

MAZER *n* pl. **-S** a large drinking bowl

MAZIER comparative of mazy

MAZIEST superlative of mazy

MAZILY *adv* in a mazy manner

MAZINESS *n* pl. **-ES** the quality of being mazy

MAZING present participle of maze

MAZOURKA *n* pl. **-S** mazurka

MAZUMA *n* pl. **-S** money

MAZURKA *n* pl. **-S** a Polish dance

MAZY *adj* **MAZIER, MAZIEST** full of confusing turns and passages

MAZZARD *n* pl. **-S** a wild cherry

MBAQANGA *n* pl. **-S** a South African dance music

MBIRA *n* pl. **-S** an African musical instrument

ME *pron* the objective case of the pronoun I

MEAD *n* pl. **-S** an alcoholic beverage

MEADOW *n* pl. **-S** a tract of grassland **MEADOWY** *adj*

MEAGER *adj* deficient in quantity or quality **MEAGERLY** *adv*

MEAGRE *adj* meager **MEAGRELY** *adv*

MEAL *n* pl. **-S** the food served and eaten in one sitting

MEALIE *n* pl. **-S** an ear of corn

MEALIER comparative of mealy

MEALIEST superlative of mealy

MEALLESS *adj* lacking a meal

MEALTIME *n* pl. **-S** the usual time for a meal

MEALWORM *n* pl. **-S** the destructive larva of certain beetles

MEALY *adj* **MEALIER, MEALIEST** soft, dry, and friable

MEALYBUG *n* pl. **-S** a destructive insect

MEAN *adj* **MEANER, MEANEST** inferior in grade, quality, or character

MEAN *v* **MEANT, MEANING, MEANS** to intend

MEANDER *v* **-ED, -ING, -S** to wander

MEANER *n* pl. **-S** one that means

MEANIE *n* pl. **-S** a nasty person

MEANIES pl. of meany

MEANING *n* pl. **-S** something that one intends to convey by language

MEANLY *adv* in a mean manner

MEANNESS *n* pl. **-ES** the state of being mean

MEANT past tense of mean

MEANTIME *n* pl. **-S** the intervening time

MEANY *n* pl. **MEANIES** meanie

MEASLE *n* pl. **-S** a tapeworm larva **MEASLED** *adj*

MEASLY *adj* **-SLIER, -SLIEST** meager

MEASURE *v* **-SURED, -SURING, -SURES** to ascertain the dimensions, quantity, or capacity of

MEASURER *n* pl. **-S** one that measures

MEAT *n* pl. **-S** animal flesh used as food **MEATED** *adj*

MEATAL *adj* pertaining to a meatus

MEATBALL *n pl.* **-S** a small ball of chopped meat

MEATHEAD *n pl.* **-S** a dolt

MEATIER comparative of meaty

MEATIEST superlative of meaty

MEATILY *adv* in a meaty manner

MEATLESS *adj* having no meat

MEATLOAF *n pl.* **-LOAVES** a baked loaf of ground meat

MEATMAN *n pl.* **-MEN** a vendor of meat

MEATUS *n pl.* **-ES** a natural body passage

MEATY *adj* **MEATIER, MEATIEST** full of meat

MECCA *n pl.* **-S** a place visited by many people

MECHANIC *n pl.* **-S** a person who works with machines

MECHITZA *n pl.* **-TZAS** or **-TZOT** a partition separating men and women in a synagogue

MECONIUM *n pl.* **-S** the first fecal excretion of a newborn child

MED *n pl.* **-S** medication

MEDAKA *n pl.* **-S** a Japanese fish

MEDAL *v* **-ALED, -ALING, -ALS** or **-ALLED, -ALLING, -ALS** to honor with a medal (a commemorative piece of metal)

MEDALIST *n pl.* **-S** a person to whom a medal has been awarded

MEDALLIC *adj* of or pertaining to a medal

MEDALLING a present participle of medal

MEDDLE *v* **-DLED, -DLING, -DLES** to interest oneself in what is not one's concern

MEDDLER *n pl.* **-S** one that meddles

MEDEVAC *v* **-VACED, -VACING, -VACS** or **-VACKED, -VACKING, -VACS** to evacuate the wounded from a battlefield by helicopter

MEDFLY *n pl.* **-FLIES** a Mediterranean fruit fly

MEDIA *n pl.* **-DIAE** the middle layer of a blood or lymph vessel

MEDIA *n pl.* **-S** a channel of communication

MEDIACY *n pl.* **-CIES** the act of mediating

MEDIAD *adv* toward the middle of a body or part

MEDIAE pl. of media

MEDIAL *n pl.* **-S** a sound, syllable, or letter in the middle of a word

MEDIALLY *adv* in a central manner

MEDIAN *n pl.* **-S** a central part

MEDIANLY *adv* medially

MEDIANT *n pl.* **-S** a type of musical tone

MEDIATE *v* **-ATED, -ATING, -ATES** to act between disputing parties in order to bring about a settlement

MEDIATOR *n pl.* **-S** one that mediates

MEDIC *n pl.* **-S** one engaged in medical work

MEDICAID *n pl.* **-S** a type of governmental health program

MEDICAL *n pl.* **-S** a physical examination

MEDICANT *n pl.* **-S** a healing substance

MEDICARE *n pl.* **-S** a type of governmental health program

MEDICATE *v* **-CATED, -CATING, -CATES** to treat with medicine

MEDICIDE *n pl.* **-S** a medically assisted suicide

MEDICINE *v* **-CINED, -CINING, -CINES** to administer medicine (a substance used in the treatment of disease) to

MEDICK *n pl.* **-S** a flowering plant

MEDICO *n pl.* **-COS** a doctor or medical student

MEDIEVAL *n pl.* **-S** a person belonging to the Middle Ages

MEDIGAP *n pl.* **-S** a supplemental health insurance

MEDII pl. of medius

MEDINA *n pl.* **-S** the native quarter of a North African city

MEDIOCRE *adj* neither good nor bad

MEDITATE *v* **-TATED, -TATING, -TATES** to ponder

MEDIUM *n pl.* **-DIUMS** or **-DIA** a surrounding environment in which something functions and thrives

MEDIUS *n pl.* **-DII** the middle finger

MEDIVAC *v* **-VACED, -VACING, -VACS** or **-VACKED, -VACKING, -VACS** medevac

MEDLAR *n pl.* **-S** a Eurasian tree

MEDLEY *n pl.* **-LEYS** a mixture

MEDULLA *n pl.* **-LAS** or **-LAE** the central tissue in the stems of certain plants **MEDULLAR** *adj*

MEDUSA   *n* pl. **-SAS** or **-SAE** a jellyfish **MEDUSAL** *adj*

MEDUSAN   *n* pl. **-S** medusa

MEDUSOID   *n* pl. **-S** medusa

MEED   *n* pl. **-S** a deserved reward

MEEK   *adj* **MEEKER, MEEKEST** lacking in spirit and courage **MEEKLY** *adv*

MEEKNESS   *n* pl. **-ES** the quality of being meek

MEERKAT   *n* pl. **-S** an African mongoose

MEET   *v* **MET, MEETING, MEETS** to come into the company or presence of

MEETER   *n* pl. **-S** one that meets

MEETING   *n* pl. **-S** an assembly for a common purpose

MEETLY   *adv* suitably

MEETNESS   *n* pl. **-ES** suitability

MEG   *n* pl. **-S** a megabyte

MEGA   *adj* great in size or importance

MEGABAR   *n* pl. **-S** a unit of pressure

MEGABIT   *n* pl. **-S** a unit of computer information

MEGABUCK   *n* pl. **-S** one million dollars

MEGABYTE   *n* pl. **-S** 1,048,576 bytes

MEGACITY   *n* pl. **-CITIES** a very large city

MEGADEAL   *n* pl. **-S** a business deal involving a lot of money

MEGADOSE   *n* pl. **-S** an abnormally large dose

MEGADYNE   *n* pl. **-S** a unit of force

MEGAFLOP   *n* pl. **-S** a measure of computing speed

MEGAHIT   *n* pl. **-S** something extremely successful

MEGALITH   *n* pl. **-S** a huge stone used in prehistoric monuments

MEGALOPS   *n* pl. **-LOPSES** a larval stage of most crabs

MEGAPLEX   *n* pl. **-ES** a large building having many movie theaters

MEGAPOD   *n* pl. **-S** megapode

MEGAPODE   *n* pl. **-S** a large-footed bird

MEGARON   *n* pl. **-ARA** the great central hall of an ancient Greek house

MEGASS   *n* pl. **-ES** a bagasse

MEGASSE   *n* pl. **-S** megass

MEGASTAR   *n* pl. **-S** an extremely successful performer

MEGATON   *n* pl. **-S** a unit of explosive force

MEGAVOLT   *n* pl. **-S** a unit of electromotive force

MEGAWATT   *n* pl. **-S** a unit of power

MEGILLA   *n* pl. **-S** megillah

MEGILLAH   *n* pl. **-S** a long, involved story

MEGILP   *n* pl. **-S** a substance with which pigments are mixed in painting

MEGILPH   *n* pl. **-S** megilp

MEGOHM   *n* pl. **-S** a unit of electrical resistance

MEGRIM   *n* pl. **-S** a migraine

MEHNDI   *n* pl. **-S** the art of painting patterns on the skin with henna

MEIKLE   *adj* large

MEINIE   *n* pl. **-S** meiny

MEINY   *n* pl. **-NIES** a retinue

MEIOSIS   *n* pl. **-OSES** a type of cell division **MEIOTIC** *adj*

MEISTER   *n* pl. **-S** one who is knowledgeable about something specified

MEL   *n* pl. **-S** honey

MELAMED   *n* pl. **-LAMDIM** a teacher in a Jewish school

MELAMINE   *n* pl. **-S** a chemical compound

MELANGE   *n* pl. **-S** a mixture

MELANIAN   *adj* pertaining to dark pigmentation

MELANIC   *n* pl. **-S** one who is affected with melanism

MELANIN   *n* pl. **-S** a dark pigment

MELANISM   *n* pl. **-S** abnormally dark pigmentation of the skin

MELANIST   *n* pl. **-S** a melanic

MELANITE   *n* pl. **-S** a black variety of garnet

MELANIZE   *v* **-NIZED, -NIZING, -NIZES** to make dark

MELANOID   *n* pl. **-S** a dark pigment

MELANOMA   *n* pl. **-MAS** or **-MATA** a darkly pigmented tumor

MELANOUS   *adj* having dark skin and hair

MELD   *v* **-ED, -ING, -S** to blend

MELDER   *n* pl. **-S** the amount of grain ground at one time

MELEE   *n* pl. **-S** a confused struggle

MELENA   *n* pl. **-S** a condition marked by black tarry stool

MELIC   *adj* pertaining to song

MELILITE   *n* pl. **-S** a mineral group

MELILOT   *n* pl. **-S** a flowering plant

MELINITE   *n* pl. **-S** a powerful explosive

MELISMA *n* pl. **-MAS** or **-MATA** melodic embellishment

MELL *v* **-ED, -ING, -S** to mix

MELLIFIC *adj* producing honey

MELLOW *adj* **-LOWER, -LOWEST** soft and full-flavored from ripeness **MELLOWLY** *adv*

MELLOW *v* **-ED, -ING, -S** to make or become mellow

MELODEON *n* pl. **-S** a musical instrument

MELODIA *n* pl. **-S** a type of organ stop

MELODIC *adj* pertaining to melody

MELODICA *n* pl. **-S** a harmonica with a small keyboard at one end

MELODIES pl. of melody

MELODISE *v* **-DISED, -DISING, -DISES** to melodize

MELODIST *n* pl. **-S** a composer of melodies

MELODIZE *v* **-DIZED, -DIZING, -DIZES** to compose a melody

MELODY *n* pl. **-DIES** an agreeable succession of musical sounds

MELOID *n* pl. **-S** a type of beetle

MELON *n* pl. **-S** any of various gourds

MELT *v* **-ED, -ING, -S** to change from a solid to a liquid state by heat **MELTABLE** *adj*

MELTAGE *n* pl. **-S** the process of melting

MELTDOWN *n* pl. **-S** the melting of the core of a nuclear reactor

MELTER *n* pl. **-S** one that melts

MELTON *n* pl. **-S** a heavy woolen fabric

MELTY *adj* resembling a melted solid

MEM *n* pl. **-S** a Hebrew letter

MEMBER *n* pl. **-S** a distinct part of a whole **MEMBERED** *adj*

MEMBRANE *n* pl. **-S** a thin, pliable layer of tissue

MEME *n* pl. **-S** an idea or practice that spreads from person to person

MEMENTO *n* pl. **-TOS** or **-TOES** something that serves as a reminder of the past

MEMETICS *n/pl* the study of memes and their effects

MEMO *n* pl. **MEMOS** a note designating something to be remembered

MEMOIR *n* pl. **-S** a biography

MEMORIAL *n* pl. **-S** something that serves as a remembrance of a person or event

MEMORISE *v* **-ISED, -ISING, -ISES** to memorize

MEMORIZE *v* **-RIZED, -RIZING, -RIZES** to commit to memory

MEMORY *n* pl. **-RIES** the mental faculty of retaining and recalling past experience

MEMSAHIB *n* pl. **-S** a European woman living in colonial India

MEN pl. of man

MENACE *v* **-ACED, -ACING, -ACES** to threaten

MENACER *n* pl. **-S** one that menaces

MENAD *n* pl. **-S** maenad

MENAGE *n* pl. **-S** a household

MENARCHE *n* pl. **-S** the first occurrence of menstruation

MENAZON *n* pl. **-S** an insecticide

MEND *v* **-ED, -ING, -S** to repair **MENDABLE** *adj*

MENDER *n* pl. **-S** one that mends

MENDIGO *n* pl. **-GOS** a freshwater fish

MENDING *n* pl. **-S** an accumulation of articles to be mended

MENFOLK *n/pl* the men of a family or community

MENFOLKS *n/pl* menfolk

MENHADEN *n* pl. **-S** a marine fish

MENHIR *n* pl. **-S** a prehistoric monument

MENIAL *n* pl. **-S** a domestic servant

MENIALLY *adv* in a servile manner

MENINX *n* pl. **-NINGES** any of the membranes enclosing the brain and spinal cord

MENISCUS *n* pl. **-CUSES** or **-CI** a crescent-shaped body **MENISCAL** *adj*

MENO *adv* less — used as a musical direction

MENOLOGY *n* pl. **-GIES** an ecclesiastical calendar

MENORAH *n* pl. **-S** a candleholder used in Jewish worship

MENSA *n* pl. **-SAS** or **-SAE** the grinding surface of a tooth

MENSAL *adj* pertaining to or used at the table

MENSCH *n* pl. **MENSCHES** or **MENSCHEN** an admirable person **MENSCHY** *adj*

MENSE *v* **MENSED, MENSING, MENSES** to do honor to

MENSEFUL *adj* proper

MENSH	*n* pl. **MENSHES** or **MENSHEN** mensch
MENSTRUA	*n/pl* solvents
MENSURAL	*adj* pertaining to measure
MENSWEAR	*n* pl. **MENSWEAR** clothing for men
MENTA	pl. of mentum
MENTAL	*adj* pertaining to the mind **MENTALLY** *adv*
MENTEE	*n* pl. **-S** one who is being mentored
MENTHENE	*n* pl. **-S** a liquid hydrocarbon
MENTHOL	*n* pl. **-S** an alcohol
MENTION	*v* **-ED, -ING, -S** to refer to in a casual manner
MENTOR	*v* **-ED, -ING, -S** to serve as a friend and teacher to
MENTUM	*n* pl. **-TA** the chin
MENU	*n* pl. **-S** a list of the dishes available in a restaurant
MENUDO	*n* pl. **-DOS** a tripe stew with chili peppers
MEOU	*v* **-ED, -ING, -S** to meow
MEOW	*v* **-ED, -ING, -S** to make the crying sound of a cat
MEPHITIS	*n* pl. **-TISES** an offensive odor **MEPHITIC** *adj*
MERC	*n* pl. **-S** or **-ES** a mercenary
MERCAPTO	*adj* containing a particular chemical group
MERCER	*n* pl. **-S** a dealer in textiles
MERCERY	*n* pl. **-CERIES** a mercer's shop
MERCH	*n* pl. **-ES** merchandise
MERCHANT	*v* **-ED, -ING, -S** to buy and sell goods for profit
MERCIES	pl. of mercy
MERCIFUL	*adj* full of mercy
MERCURY	*n* pl. **-RIES** a metallic element **MERCURIC** *adj*
MERCY	*n* pl. **-CIES** compassion shown to an offender or enemy
MERE	*adj* **MERER, MEREST** being nothing more than **MERELY** *adv*
MERE	*n* pl. **-S** a pond or lake
MERENGUE	*n* pl. **-S** a ballroom dance
MERGE	*v* **MERGED, MERGING, MERGES** to combine
MERGEE	*n* pl. **-S** a company acquired by a merger
MERGENCE	*n* pl. **-S** the act of merging
MERGER	*n* pl. **-S** the union of two or more businesses into a single enterprise
MERGING	present participle of merge
MERIDIAN	*n* pl. **-S** a circle around the earth passing through both poles
MERINGUE	*n* pl. **-S** a topping for pastries
MERINO	*n* pl. **-NOS** a fine wool
MERISIS	*n* pl. **MERISES** growth
MERISTEM	*n* pl. **-S** formative plant tissue
MERISTIC	*adj* made up of segments
MERIT	*v* **-ED, -ING, -S** to earn
MERK	*n* pl. **-S** a former coin of Scotland
MERL	*n* pl. **-S** merle
MERLE	*n* pl. **-S** a blackbird
MERLIN	*n* pl. **-S** a European falcon
MERLON	*n* pl. **-S** the solid part of an indented parapet
MERLOT	*n* pl. **-S** a dry red wine
MERMAID	*n* pl. **-S** a legendary marine creature
MERMAN	*n* pl. **-MEN** a legendary marine creature
MEROPIA	*n* pl. **-S** partial blindness **MEROPIC** *adj*
MERRY	*adj* **-RIER, -RIEST** cheerful **MERRILY** *adv*
MESA	*n* pl. **-S** a land formation having a flat top and steep sides
MESALLY	*adv* medially
MESARCH	*adj* originating in a mesic habitat
MESCAL	*n* pl. **-S** a cactus
MESCLUN	*n* pl. **-S** a mixture of young tender green herbs
MESDAMES	pl. of madame
MESEEMS	*v* past tense **MESEEMED,** present 3d person sing. **MESEEMETH** it seems to me — MESEEMS is an impersonal verb and is used only in the 3d person sing.
MESH	*v* **-ED, -ING, -ES** to entangle
MESHIER	comparative of meshy
MESHIEST	superlative of meshy
MESHUGA	*adj* crazy
MESHUGAH	*adj* meshuga
MESHUGGA	*adj* meshuga
MESHUGGE	*adj* meshuga
MESHWORK	*n* pl. **-S** a network
MESHY	*adj* **MESHIER, MESHIEST** netty

MESIAL *adj* situated in the middle **MESIALLY** *adv*

MESIAN *adj* mesial

MESIC *adj* characterized by a medium supply of moisture

MESMERIC *adj* pertaining to hypnotism

MESNALTY *n pl.* **-TIES** a type of feudal estate

MESNE *n pl.* **-S** a feudal lord holding land from a superior

MESOCARP *n pl.* **-S** the middle layer of a pericarp

MESODERM *n pl.* **-S** the middle germ layer of an embryo

MESOGLEA *n pl.* **-S** a gelatinous material in sponges

MESOMERE *n pl.* **-S** an embryonic segment

MESON *n pl.* **-S** a subatomic particle **MESONIC** *adj*

MESOPHYL *n pl.* **-S** the soft tissue of a leaf

MESOSOME *n pl.* **-S** a specialized cellular part

MESOTRON *n pl.* **-S** a meson

MESOZOAN *n pl.* **-S** any of a phylum of wormlike organisms

MESQUIT *n pl.* **-S** mesquite

MESQUITE *n pl.* **-S** a spiny tree or shrub

MESS *v* **-ED, -ING, -ES** to make dirty or untidy

MESSAGE *v* **-SAGED, -SAGING, -SAGES** to send as a message (an oral, written, or signaled communication)

MESSAN *n pl.* **-S** a lapdog

MESSIAH *n pl.* **-S** an expected liberator

MESSIER comparative of messy

MESSIEST superlative of messy

MESSIEURS pl. of monsieur

MESSILY *adv* in a messy manner

MESSMAN *n pl.* **-MEN** a serviceman who works in a dining facility

MESSMATE *n pl.* **-S** a person with whom one eats regularly

MESSUAGE *n pl.* **-S** a dwelling house with its adjacent buildings and land

MESSY *adj* **MESSIER, MESSIEST** dirty or untidy

MESTEE *n pl.* **-S** mustee

MESTESO *n pl.* **-SOS** or **-SOES** mestizo

MESTINO *n pl.* **-NOS** or **-NOES** mestizo

MESTIZA *n pl.* **-S** a female mestizo

MESTIZO *n pl.* **-ZOS** or **-ZOES** a person of mixed ancestry

MET past tense of meet

META *adj* pertaining to positions in a benzene ring separated by one carbon atom

METAGE *n pl.* **-S** an official measurement of weight or contents

METAL *v* **-ALED, -ALING, -ALS** or **-ALLED, -ALLING, -ALS** to cover with metal (any of various ductile, fusible, and lustrous substances)

METALISE *v* **-ISED, -ISING, -ISES** to metalize

METALIST *n pl.* **-S** one who works with metals

METALIZE *v* **-IZED, -IZING, -IZES** to treat with metal

METALLED a past tense of metal

METALLIC *n pl.* **-S** a fabric or yarn made of or coated with metal

METALLING a present participle of metal

METAMER *n pl.* **-S** a type of chemical compound

METAMERE *n pl.* **-S** a somite

METAPHOR *n pl.* **-S** a type of figure of speech

METATAG *n pl.* **-S** an HTML tag having information about a webpage

METATE *n pl.* **-S** a stone used for grinding grains

METAZOAN *n pl.* **-S** any of a major division of multicellular animals **METAZOAL, METAZOIC** *adj*

METAZOON *n pl.* **-ZOA** a metazoan

METE *v* **METED, METING, METES** to distribute by measure

METEOR *n pl.* **-S** a small celestial body that enters the earth's atmosphere **METEORIC** *adj*

METEPA *n pl.* **-S** a chemical compound

METER *v* **-ED, -ING, -S** to measure by mechanical means

METERAGE *n pl.* **-S** the process of metering

METH *n pl.* **-S** a stimulant drug

METHADON *n pl.* **-S** a narcotic drug

METHANE *n pl.* **-S** a flammable gas

METHANOL *n pl.* **-S** a toxic alcohol

METHINKS *v* past tense **METHOUGHT** it seems to me — METHINKS is an impersonal verb and is used only in the 3d person sing.

METHOD *n pl.* **-S** a means of procedure

METHODIC *adj* systematic

METHOXY	*adj* containing a certain chemical group
METHOXYL	*adj* methoxy
METHYL	*n* pl. **-S** a univalent radical **METHYLIC** *adj*
METHYLAL	*n* pl. **-S** a flammable liquid
METICAL	*n* pl. **-CALS** or **-CAIS** a monetary unit of Mozambique
METIER	*n* pl. **-S** a vocation
METING	present participle of mete
METIS	*n* pl. **METIS** a person of mixed ancestry
METISSE	*n* pl. **-S** a female metis
METOL	*n* pl. **-S** a powder used as a photographic developer
METONYM	*n* pl. **-S** a word used in metonymy
METONYMY	*n* pl. **-MIES** a type of figure of speech
METOPE	*n* pl. **-PES** or **-PAE** a space between two triglyphs
METOPIC	*adj* pertaining to the forehead
METOPON	*n* pl. **-S** a narcotic drug
METRAZOL	*n* pl. **-S** a powder used as a stimulant
METRE	*v* **-TRED, -TRING, -TRES** to meter
METRIC	*n* pl. **-S** a standard of measurement
METRICAL	*adj* pertaining to or composed in a system of arranged and measured rhythm
METRIFY	*v* **-FIED, -FYING, -FIES** to compose in metrical form
METRING	present participle of metre
METRIST	*n* pl. **-S** one who metrifies
METRITIS	*n* pl. **-TISES** inflammation of the uterus
METRO	*n* pl. **-ROS** a subway
METTLE	*n* pl. **-S** quality of character **METTLED** *adj*
METUMP	*n* pl. **-S** a tumpline
MEUNIERE	*adj* cooked in browned butter
MEW	*v* **-ED, -ING, -S** to confine
MEWL	*v* **-ED, -ING, -S** to whimper
MEWLER	*n* pl. **-S** one that mewls
MEZCAL	*n* pl. **-S** mescal
MEZE	*n* pl. **-S** a Greek or Middle Eastern appetizer
MEZEREON	*n* pl. **-S** a flowering shrub
MEZEREUM	*n* pl. **-S** mezereon

MEZQUIT	*n* pl. **-S** mesquite
MEZQUITE	*n* pl. **-S** mesquite
MEZUZA	*n* pl. **-S** mezuzah
MEZUZAH	*n* pl. **-ZAHS, -ZOT** or **-ZOTH** a Judaic scroll
MEZZO	*n* pl. **-ZOS** a female voice of a full, deep quality
MHO	*n* pl. **MHOS** a unit of electrical conductance
MI	*n* pl. **-S** the third tone of the diatonic musical scale
MIAOU	*v* **-ED, -ING, -S** to meow
MIAOW	*v* **-ED, -ING, -S** to meow
MIASM	*n* pl. **-S** miasma
MIASMA	*n* pl. **-MAS** or **-MATA** a noxious vapor **MIASMAL, MIASMIC** *adj*
MIAUL	*v* **-ED, -ING, -S** to meow
MIB	*n* pl. **-S** a type of playing marble
MIC	*n* pl. **-S** a microphone
MICA	*n* pl. **-S** a mineral
MICAWBER	*n* pl. **-S** a person who remains hopeful despite adversity
MICE	pl. of mouse
MICELL	*n* pl. **-S** micelle
MICELLA	*n* pl. **-LAE** micelle
MICELLE	*n* pl. **-S** a coherent strand or structure in a fiber **MICELLAR** *adj*
MICHE	*v* **MICHED, MICHING, MICHES** to skulk
MICKEY	*n* pl. **-EYS** a drugged drink
MICKLE	*adj* **-LER, -LEST** large
MICKLE	*n* pl. **-S** a large amount
MICRA	a pl. of micron
MICRIFY	*v* **-FIED, -FYING, -FIES** to make small
MICRO	*n* pl. **-CROS** a very small computer
MICROBAR	*n* pl. **-S** a unit of atmospheric pressure
MICROBE	*n* pl. **-S** a minute life form **MICROBIC** *adj*
MICROBUS	*n* pl. **-BUSES** or **-BUSSES** a small bus
MICROCAP	*adj* of or pertaining to a company whose retained earnings are very small
MICRODOT	*n* pl. **-S** a copy of printed matter reduced to the size of a dot
MICROHM	*n* pl. **-S** a unit of electrical resistance

MICROLUX *n* pl. **-LUXES** or **-LUCES** a unit of illumination

MICROMHO *n* pl. **-S** a unit of electrical conductance

MICRON *n* pl. **-CRONS** or **-CRA** a unit of length

MICRURGY *n* pl. **-GIES** the use of minute tools under high magnification

MID *n* pl. **-S** the middle

MIDAIR *n* pl. **-S** a region in the middle of the air

MIDBRAIN *n* pl. **-S** the middle region of the brain

MIDCAP *adj* of or pertaining to a corporation whose retained earnings are between those of a small company and a large corporation

MIDCULT *n* pl. **-S** middle-class culture

MIDDAY *n* pl. **-DAYS** the middle of the day

MIDDEN *n* pl. **-S** a dunghill

MIDDIES pl. of middy

MIDDLE *v* **-DLED, -DLING, -DLES** to place in the middle (the area or point equidistant from extremes or limits)

MIDDLER *n* pl. **-S** a student in an intermediate grade

MIDDLING *n* pl. **-S** a cut of pork

MIDDY *n* pl. **-DIES** a loosely fitting blouse

MIDFIELD *n* pl. **-S** the middle portion of a playing field

MIDGE *n* pl. **-S** a small winged insect

MIDGET *n* pl. **-S** a very small person

MIDGUT *n* pl. **-S** the middle part of the embryonic digestive tract

MIDI *n* pl. **-S** a skirt or coat that extends to the middle of the calf

MIDIRON *n* pl. **-S** a golf club

MIDLAND *n* pl. **-S** the middle part of a country

MIDLEG *n* pl. **-S** the middle of the leg

MIDLIFE *n* pl. **-LIVES** middle age

MIDLIFER *n* pl. **-S** a middle-aged person

MIDLINE *n* pl. **-S** a median line

MIDLIST *n* pl. **-S** a section of a publisher's list of current titles

MIDMONTH *n* pl. **-S** the middle of the month

MIDMOST *n* pl. **-S** a part exactly in the middle

MIDNIGHT *n* pl. **-S** the middle of the night

MIDNOON *n* pl. **-S** midday

MIDPOINT *n* pl. **-S** a point at the middle

MIDRANGE *n* pl. **-S** the middle of a range

MIDRASH *n* pl. **-RASHIM** or **-RASHOTH** or **-RASHOT** an early Jewish interpretation of a biblical text

MIDRIB *n* pl. **-S** the central vein of a leaf

MIDRIFF *n* pl. **-S** the middle part of the body

MIDSHIP *adj* pertaining to the middle of a ship

MIDSHIPS *adv* toward the middle of a ship

MIDSIZE *adj* of intermediate size

MIDSIZED *adj* midsize

MIDSOLE *n* pl. **-S** a middle layer of the sole of a shoe

MIDSPACE *n* pl. **-S** the middle of a space

MIDST *n* pl. **-S** the middle

MIDSTORY *n* pl. **-RIES** the middle of a story

MIDTERM *n* pl. **-S** an examination given in the middle of an academic semester

MIDTOWN *n* pl. **-S** the central part of a city

MIDWATCH *n* pl. **-ES** a watch on a ship between midnight and 4 A.M.

MIDWAY *n* pl. **-WAYS** an avenue at a fair or carnival for concessions and amusements

MIDWEEK *n* pl. **-S** the middle of the week

MIDWIFE *v* **-WIFED, -WIFING, -WIFES** or **-WIVED, -WIVING, -WIVES** to assist a woman in childbirth

MIDYEAR *n* pl. **-S** the middle of the year

MIEN *n* pl. **-S** demeanor

MIFF *v* **-ED, -ING, -S** to annoy

MIFFY *adj* **MIFFIER, MIFFIEST** easily annoyed

MIG *n* pl. **-S** a type of playing marble

MIGG *n* pl. **-S** mig

MIGGLE *n* pl. **-S** a mig

MIGHT *n* pl. **-S** strength

MIGHTY *adj* **MIGHTIER, MIGHTIEST** strong **MIGHTILY** *adv*

MIGNON *n* pl. **-S** a cut of beef

MIGNONNE *adj* daintily small

MIGRAINE *n* pl. **-S** a severe headache

MIGRANT *n* pl. **-S** one that migrates

MIGRATE *v* **-GRATED, -GRATING, -GRATES** to move from one region to another

MIGRATOR *n* pl. **-S** a migrant

MIHRAB *n* pl. **-S** a niche in a mosque

MIJNHEER *n* pl. **-S** mynheer

MIKADO *n* pl. **-DOS** an emperor of Japan

MIKE *v* **MIKED, MIKING, MIKES** to amplify or record by use of a microphone

MIKRON *n* pl. **-KRONS** or **-KRA** micron

MIKVAH *n* pl. **-VAHS** or **-VOTH** or **-VOT** or **-VOS** a place for ritual bathing by Orthodox Jews

MIKVEH *n* pl. **-S** mikvah

MIL *n* pl. **-S** a unit of length

MILADI *n* pl. **-S** milady

MILADY *n* pl. **-DIES** an English gentlewoman

MILAGE *n* pl. **-S** mileage

MILCH *adj* giving milk

MILCHIG *adj* made of or derived from milk

MILD *v* **-ED, -ING, -S** to diminish

MILD *adj* **MILDER, MILDEST** not harsh or rough

MILDEN *v* **-ED, -ING, -S** to make or become mild

MILDEW *v* **-ED, -ING, -S** to affect with mildew (a whitish growth produced by fungi)

MILDEWY *adj* affected with or resembling mildew

MILDLY *adv* in a mild manner

MILDNESS *n* pl. **-ES** the quality of being mild

MILE *n* pl. **-S** a unit of distance

MILEAGE *n* pl. **-S** total distance expressed in miles

MILEPOST *n* pl. **-S** a post indicating distance in miles

MILER *n* pl. **-S** one that runs a mile race

MILESIAN *adj* pertaining to the the native people of Ireland

MILESIMO *n* pl. **-MOS** a former monetary unit of Chile

MILFOIL *n* pl. **-S** a perennial herb

MILIA pl. of milium

MILIARIA *n* pl. **-S** a skin disease

MILIARY *adj* made up of many small projections

MILIEU *n* pl. **-LIEUS** or **-LIEUX** environment

MILITANT *n* pl. **-S** a person who is aggressively engaged in a cause

MILITARY *n* pl. **-TARIES** armed forces

MILITATE *v* **-TATED, -TATING, -TATES** to have influence or effect

MILITIA *n* pl. **-S** a citizen army

MILIUM *n* pl. **-IA** a small, whitish lump in the skin

MILK *v* **-ED, -ING, -S** to draw milk (a whitish, nutritious liquid) from the udder of

MILKER *n* pl. **-S** one that milks

MILKFISH *n* pl. **-ES** a marine food fish

MILKIER comparative of milky

MILKIEST superlative of milky

MILKILY *adv* in a milky manner

MILKLESS *adj* lacking milk

MILKMAID *n* pl. **-S** a woman who milks cows

MILKMAN *n* pl. **-MEN** a man who sells or delivers milk

MILKSHED *n* pl. **-S** a region supplying milk to a particular community

MILKSOP *n* pl. **-S** an effeminate man

MILKWEED *n* pl. **-S** a plant that secretes a milky juice

MILKWOOD *n* pl. **-S** a tropical tree

MILKWORT *n* pl. **-S** a flowering plant

MILKY *adj* **MILKIER, MILKIEST** resembling or suggestive of milk

MILL *v* **-ED, -ING, -S** to grind by mechanical means **MILLABLE** *adj*

MILLAGE *n* pl. **-S** a type of monetary rate

MILLCAKE *n* pl. **-S** a residue from pressed linseed

MILLDAM *n* pl. **-S** a dam built to form a millpond

MILLE *n* pl. **-S** a thousand

MILLEPED *n* pl. **-S** milliped

MILLER *n* pl. **-S** one that mills

MILLET *n* pl. **-S** a cereal grass

MILLIARD *n* pl. **-S** a billion

MILLIARE *n* pl. **-S** a unit of area

MILLIARY *n* pl. **-ARIES** an ancient Roman milestone

MILLIBAR *n* pl. **-S** a unit of atmospheric pressure

MILLIEME *n* pl. **-S** unit of value of Egypt and Sudan

MILLIER *n* pl. **-S** a unit of weight

MILLIGAL *n* pl. **-S** a unit of acceleration

MILLILUX *n* pl. **-LUXES** or **-LUCES** a unit of illumination

MILLIME	*n* pl. **-S** a coin of Tunisia
MILLIMHO	*n* pl. **-MHOS** a unit of electrical conductance
MILLINE	*n* pl. **-S** a unit of advertising space
MILLINER	*n* pl. **-S** one who makes or sells women's hats
MILLING	*n* pl. **-S** a corrugated edge on a coin
MILLIOHM	*n* pl. **-S** a unit of electrical resistance
MILLION	*n* pl. **-S** a number
MILLIPED	*n* pl. **-S** a multi-legged arthropod
MILLIREM	*n* pl. **-S** a quantity of ionizing radiation
MILLPOND	*n* pl. **-S** a pond for supplying water to run a mill wheel (a type of waterwheel)
MILLRACE	*n* pl. **-S** the current of water that drives a mill wheel
MILLRUN	*n* pl. **-S** a millrace
MILLWORK	*n* pl. **-S** woodwork produced by milling
MILNEB	*n* pl. **-S** a fungicide
MILO	*n* pl. **-LOS** a cereal grass
MILORD	*n* pl. **-S** an English gentleman
MILPA	*n* pl. **-S** a field that is cleared from a jungle for farming purposes
MILREIS	*n* pl. **MILREIS** a former monetary unit of Portugal
MILT	*v* **-ED, -ING, -S** to impregnate with milt (fish sperm)
MILTER	*n* pl. **-S** a male fish at breeding time
MILTY	*adj* **MILTIER, MILTIEST** full of milt
MIM	*adj* primly demure
MIMBAR	*n* pl. **-S** a pulpit in a mosque
MIME	*v* **MIMED, MIMING, MIMES** to mimic
MIMEO	*v* **-ED, -ING, -S** to make copies of by use of a mimeograph
MIMER	*n* pl. **-S** one that mimes
MIMESIS	*n* pl. **-MESISES** or **-MESES** mimicry **MIMETIC** *adj*
MIMETITE	*n* pl. **-S** an ore of lead
MIMIC	*v* **-ICKED, -ICKING, -ICS** to imitate closely
MIMICAL	*adj* of the nature of mimicry
MIMICKER	*n* pl. **-S** one that mimics
MIMICKING	present participle of mimic

MIMICRY	*n* pl. **-RIES** an instance of mimicking
MIMING	present participle of mime
MIMOSA	*n* pl. **-S** a tropical plant
MINA	*n* pl. **-NAS** or **-NAE** an ancient unit of weight and value
MINABLE	*adj* capable of being mined
MINACITY	*n* pl. **-TIES** the state of being threatening
MINAE	a pl. of mina
MINARET	*n* pl. **-S** a slender tower attached to a mosque
MINATORY	*adj* threatening
MINCE	*v* **MINCED, MINCING, MINCES** to cut into very small pieces
MINCER	*n* pl. **-S** one that minces
MINCY	*adj* **MINCIER, MINCIEST** affectedly dainty
MIND	*v* **-ED, -ING, -S** to heed
MINDER	*n* pl. **-S** one that minds
MINDFUL	*adj* heedful
MINDLESS	*adj* lacking intelligence
MINDSET	*n* pl. **-S** a fixed mental attitude
MINE	*v* **MINED, MINING, MINES** to dig into for valuable materials
MINEABLE	*adj* minable
MINER	*n* pl. **-S** one that mines
MINERAL	*n* pl. **-S** a naturally occurring inorganic substance having a characteristic set of physical properties
MINGIER	comparative of mingy
MINGIEST	superlative of mingy
MINGLE	*v* **-GLED, -GLING, -GLES** to mix together
MINGLER	*n* pl. **-S** one that mingles
MINGY	*adj* **-GIER, -GIEST** mean and stingy
MINI	*n* pl. **-S** something distinctively smaller than others of its kind
MINIBAR	*n* pl. **-S** a small refrigerator stocked with beverages
MINIBIKE	*n* pl. **-S** a small motorcycle
MINIBUS	*n* pl. **-BUSES** or **-BUSSES** a small bus
MINICAB	*n* pl. **-S** a small taxicab
MINICAM	*n* pl. **-S** a small portable television camera
MINICAMP	*n* pl. **-S** a short training camp for football players

MINICAR	*n* pl. **-S** a small automobile
MINIDISC	*n* pl. **-S** a miniature compact disc
MINIFY	*v* **-FIED, -FYING, -FIES** to make small or smaller
MINIKIN	*n* pl. **-S** a small or dainty creature
MINILAB	*n* pl. **-S** a retail outlet offering rapid on-site film development
MINIM	*n* pl. **-S** a unit of liquid measure
MINIMA	a pl. of minimum
MINIMAL	*n* pl. **-S** an element of a mathematical set that precedes all others
MINIMAX	*n* pl. **-ES** the minimum of a set of maxima
MINIMILL	*n* pl. **-S** a small-scale steel mill
MINIMISE	*v* **-MISED, -MISING, -MISES** to minimize
MINIMIZE	*v* **-MIZED, -MIZING, -MIZES** to make as small as possible
MINIMUM	*n* pl. **-MUMS** or **-MA** the least possible amount, quantity, or degree
MINING	*n* pl. **-S** the process or business of working mines (excavations in the earth)
MINION	*n* pl. **-S** a servile follower
MINIPARK	*n* pl. **-S** a small city park
MINIPILL	*n* pl. **-S** a birth control pill containing no estrogen
MINISH	*v* **-ED, -ING, -ES** to diminish
MINISKI	*n* pl. **-S** a short ski
MINISTER	*v* **-ED, -ING, -S** to give aid or service
MINISTRY	*n* pl. **-TRIES** the act of ministering
MINIUM	*n* pl. **-S** a red pigment
MINIVAN	*n* pl. **-S** a small van
MINIVER	*n* pl. **-S** a white fur
MINK	*n* pl. **-S** a carnivorous mammal
MINKE	*n* pl. **-S** a small whale
MINNOW	*n* pl. **-S** a small fish
MINNY	*n* pl. **-NIES** minnow
MINOR	*v* **-ED, -ING, -S** to pursue a specific subordinate course of study
MINORCA	*n* pl. **-S** any of a breed of large domestic fowls
MINORITY	*n* pl. **-TIES** the smaller number or part
MINSTER	*n* pl. **-S** a large or important church
MINSTREL	*n* pl. **-S** a medieval musician

MINT	*v* **-ED, -ING, -S** to produce by stamping metal, as coins
MINTAGE	*n* pl. **-S** the act of minting
MINTER	*n* pl. **-S** one that mints
MINTY	*adj* **MINTIER, MINTIEST** having the flavor mint (an aromatic herb)
MINUEND	*n* pl. **-S** a number from which another is to be subtracted
MINUET	*n* pl. **-S** a slow, stately dance
MINUS	*n* pl. **-ES** a negative quantity
MINUTE	*adj* **-NUTER, -NUTEST** very small **MINUTELY** *adv*
MINUTE	*v* **-UTED, -UTING, -UTES** to make a brief note of
MINUTIA	*n* pl. **-TIAE** a small detail **MINUTIAL** *adj*
MINX	*n* pl. **-ES** a pert girl **MINXISH** *adj*
MINYAN	*n* pl. **-YANS** or **-YANIM** the minimum number required to be present for the conduct of a Jewish service
MIOSIS	*n* pl. **-OSES** excessive contraction of the pupil of the eye
MIOTIC	*n* pl. **-S** an agent that causes miosis
MIQUELET	*n* pl. **-S** a former Spanish or French soldier
MIR	*n* pl. **MIRS** or **MIRI** a Russian peasant commune
MIRACLE	*n* pl. **-S** an event ascribed to supernatural or divine origin
MIRADOR	*n* pl. **-S** an architectural feature designed to afford an extensive view
MIRAGE	*n* pl. **-S** a type of optical illusion
MIRE	*v* **MIRED, MIRING, MIRES** to cause to stick in swampy ground
MIREPOIX	*n* pl. **MIREPOIX** a sauteed mixture of diced vegetables
MIREX	*n* pl. **-ES** an insecticide
MIRI	a pl. of mir
MIRIER	comparative of miry
MIRIEST	superlative of miry
MIRIN	*n* pl. **-S** a sweet Japanese cooking wine
MIRINESS	*n* pl. **-ES** the state of being miry
MIRING	present participle of mire
MIRK	*adj* **MIRKER, MIRKEST** murk
MIRK	*n* pl. **-S** murk
MIRKY	*adj* **MIRKIER, MIRKIEST** murky **MIRKILY** *adv*

MIRLITON	*n* pl. **-S** a chayote
MIRROR	*v* **-ED, -ING, -S** to reflect an image of
MIRTH	*n* pl. **-S** spirited gaiety **MIRTHFUL** *adj*
MIRY	*adj* **MIRIER, MIRIEST** swampy
MIRZA	*n* pl. **-S** a Persian title of honor
MISACT	*v* **-ED, -ING, -S** to act badly
MISADAPT	*v* **-ED, -ING, -S** to adapt wrongly
MISADD	*v* **-ED, -ING, -S** to add incorrectly
MISAGENT	*n* pl. **-S** a bad agent
MISAIM	*v* **-ED, -ING, -S** to aim badly
MISALIGN	*v* **-ED, -ING, -S** to align improperly
MISALLOT	*v* **-LOTTED, -LOTTING, -LOTS** to allot wrongly
MISALLY	*v* **-LIED, -LYING, -LIES** to ally badly
MISALTER	*v* **-ED, -ING, -S** to alter wrongly
MISANDRY	*n* pl. **-DRIES** hatred of men
MISAPPLY	*v* **-PLIED, -PLYING, -PLIES** to apply wrongly
MISASSAY	*v* **-ED, -ING, -S** to attempt unsuccessfully
MISATE	past tense of miseat
MISATONE	*v* **-ATONED, -ATONING, -ATONES** to atone wrongly
MISAVER	*v* **-AVERRED, -AVERRING, -AVERS** to speak erroneously
MISAWARD	*v* **-ED, -ING, -S** to award wrongly
MISBEGIN	*v* **-GAN, -GUN, -GINNING, -GINS** to begin wrongly
MISBEGOT	*adj* born out of wedlock
MISBIAS	*v* **-ASED, -ASING, -ASES** or **-ASSED, -ASSING, -ASSES** to bias wrongly
MISBILL	*v* **-ED, -ING, -S** to bill wrongly
MISBIND	*v* **-BOUND, -BINDING, -BINDS** to bind imperfectly
MISBRAND	*v* **-ED, -ING, -S** to brand incorrectly
MISBUILD	*v* **-BUILT, -BUILDING, -BUILDS** to build imperfectly
MISCALL	*v* **-ED, -ING, -S** to call by a wrong name
MISCARRY	*v* **-RIED, -RYING, -RIES** to be unsuccessful
MISCAST	*v* **-CAST, -CASTING, -CASTS** to cast in an unsuitable role
MISCHIEF	*n* pl. **-S** action that causes irritation, harm, or trouble
MISCHOSE	past tense of mischoose (to select improperly)
MISCIBLE	*adj* capable of being mixed
MISCITE	*v* **-CITED, -CITING, -CITES** to misquote
MISCLAIM	*v* **-ED, -ING, -S** to claim wrongfully
MISCLASS	*v* **-ED, -ING, -ES** to put in the wrong class
MISCODE	*v* **-CODED, -CODING, -CODES** to code wrongly
MISCOIN	*v* **-ED, -ING, -S** to coin improperly
MISCOLOR	*v* **-ED, -ING, -S** to color incorrectly
MISCOOK	*v* **-ED, -ING, -S** to cook badly
MISCOPY	*v* **-COPIED, -COPYING, -COPIES** to copy incorrectly
MISCOUNT	*v* **-ED, -ING, -S** to count incorrectly
MISCUE	*v* **-CUED, -CUING, -CUES** to make a faulty stroke in billiards
MISCUT	*v* **-CUT, -CUTTING, -CUTS** to cut incorrectly
MISDATE	*v* **-DATED, -DATING, -DATES** to date incorrectly
MISDEAL	*v* **-DEALT, -DEALING, -DEALS** to deal cards incorrectly
MISDEED	*n* pl. **-S** an evil act
MISDEEM	*v* **-ED, -ING, -S** to judge unfavorably
MISDIAL	*v* **-DIALED, -DIALING, -DIALS** or **-DIALLED, -DIALLING, -DIALS** to dial wrongly
MISDO	*v* **-DID, -DONE, -DOING, -DOES** to do wrongly
MISDOER	*n* pl. **-S** one that misdoes
MISDOING	*n* pl. **-S** an instance of doing wrong
MISDONE	past participle of misdo
MISDOUBT	*v* **-ED, -ING, -S** to doubt
MISDRAW	*v* **-DREW, -DRAWN, -DRAWING, -DRAWS** to draw incorrectly
MISDRIVE	*v* **-DROVE, -DRIVEN, -DRIVING, -DRIVES** to drive wrongly or improperly
MISE	*n* pl. **-S** an agreement or settlement
MISEASE	*n* pl. **-S** discomfort
MISEAT	*v* **-ATE, -EATEN, -EATING, -EATS** to eat improperly
MISEDIT	*v* **-ED, -ING, -S** to edit incorrectly
MISENROL	*v* **-ROLLED, -ROLLING, -ROLS** to enroll improperly
MISENTER	*v* **-ED, -ING, -S** to enter erroneously
MISENTRY	*n* pl. **-TRIES** an erroneous entry

MISER   *n* pl. **-S** one who hoards money greedily

MISERERE   *n* pl. **-S** a part of a church seat

MISERLY   *adj* characteristic of a miser

MISERY   *n* pl. **-ERIES** a state of great suffering

MISEVENT   *n* pl. **-S** a mishap

MISFAITH   *n* pl. **-S** lack of faith; disbelief

MISFEED   *v* **-FED, -FEEDING, -FEEDS** to feed wrongly

MISFIELD   *v* **-ED, -ING, -S** to field badly

MISFILE   *v* **-FILED, -FILING, -FILES** to file in the wrong place

MISFIRE   *v* **-FIRED, -FIRING, -FIRES** to fail to fire

MISFIT   *v* **-FITTED, -FITTING, -FITS** to fit badly

MISFOCUS   *v* **-CUSED, -CUSING, -CUSES** or **-CUSSED, -CUSSING, -CUSSES** to focus badly

MISFORM   *v* **-ED, -ING, -S** to misshape

MISFRAME   *v* **-FRAMED, -FRAMING, -FRAMES** to frame badly

MISGAUGE   *v* **-GAUGED, -GAUGING, -GAUGES** to gauge wrongly or inaccurately

MISGIVE   *v* **-GAVE, -GIVEN, -GIVING, -GIVES** to make doubtful or fearful

MISGRADE   *v* **-GRADED, -GRADING, -GRADES** to grade incorrectly

MISGRAFT   *v* **-ED, -ING, -S** to graft wrongly

MISGROW   *v* **-GREW, -GROWN, -GROWING, -GROWS** to grow abnormally

MISGUESS   *v* **-ED, -ING, -ES** to guess wrongly

MISGUIDE   *v* **-GUIDED, -GUIDING, -GUIDES** to guide wrongly

MISHAP   *n* pl. **-S** an unfortunate accident

MISHEAR   *v* **-HEARD, -HEARING, -HEARS** to hear incorrectly

MISHIT   *v* **-HIT, -HITTING, -HITS** to hit poorly

MISHMASH   *n* pl. **-ES** a confused mixture

MISHMOSH   *n* pl. **-ES** mishmash

MISINFER   *v* **-FERRED, -FERRING, -FERS** to infer wrongly

MISINTER   *v* **-TERRED, -TERRING, -TERS** to inter improperly

MISJOIN   *v* **-ED, -ING, -S** to join improperly

MISJUDGE   *v* **-JUDGED, -JUDGING, -JUDGES** to judge wrongly

MISKAL   *n* pl. **-S** an Oriental unit of weight

MISKEEP   *v* **-KEPT, -KEEPING, -KEEPS** to keep wrongly

MISKICK   *v* **-ED, -ING, -S** to kick badly

MISKNOW   *v* **-KNEW, -KNOWN, -KNOWING, -KNOWS** to fail to understand or recognize

MISLABEL   *v* **-BELED, -BELING, -BELS** or **-BELLED, -BELLING, -BELS** to label incorrectly or falsely

MISLABOR   *v* **-ED, -ING, -S** to labor badly

MISLAIN   past participle of mislie

MISLAY   *v* **-LAID, -LAYING, -LAYS** to put in a forgotten place

MISLAYER   *n* pl. **-S** one that mislays

MISLEAD   *v* **-LED, -LEADING, -LEADS** to lead astray

MISLEARN   *v* **-LEARNED** or **-LEARNT, -LEARNING, -LEARNS** to learn wrongly

MISLIE   *v* **-LAY, -LAIN, -LYING, -LIES** to lie in a wrong position

MISLIGHT   *v* **-LIGHTED** or **-LIT, -LIGHTING, -LIGHTS** to lead astray by its light

MISLIKE   *v* **-LIKED, -LIKING, -LIKES** to dislike

MISLIKER   *n* pl. **-S** one that mislikes

MISLIT   a past tense of mislight

MISLIVE   *v* **-LIVED, -LIVING, -LIVES** to live a bad life

MISLODGE   *v* **-LODGED, -LODGING, -LODGES** to lodge in a wrong place

MISLYING   present participle of mislie

MISMAKE   *v* **-MADE, -MAKING, -MAKES** to make incorrectly

MISMARK   *v* **-ED, -ING, -S** to mark wrongly

MISMATCH   *v* **-ED, -ING, -ES** to match badly

MISMATE   *v* **-MATED, -MATING, -MATES** to mate unsuitably

MISMEET   *v* **-MET, -MEETING, -MEETS** to meet under unfortunate circumstances

MISMOVE   *v* **-MOVED, -MOVING, -MOVES** to move wrongly

MISNAME   *v* **-NAMED, -NAMING, -NAMES** to call by a wrong name

MISNOMER   *n* pl. **-S** a name wrongly used

MISO   *n* pl. **-SOS** a type of food paste

MISOGAMY   *n* pl. **-MIES** a hatred of marriage

MISOGYNY   *n* pl. **-NIES** a hatred of women

MISOLOGY *n pl.* **-GIES** a hatred of debate or reasoning

MISORDER *v* **-ED, -ING, -S** to order incorrectly

MISPAGE *v* **-PAGED, -PAGING, -PAGES** to page incorrectly

MISPAINT *v* **-ED, -ING, -S** to paint wrongly

MISPARSE *v* **-PARSED, -PARSING, -PARSES** to parse incorrectly

MISPART *v* **-ED, -ING, -S** to part badly

MISPATCH *v* **-ED, -ING, -ES** to patch badly

MISPEN *v* **-PENNED, -PENNING, -PENS** to write incorrectly

MISPLACE *v* **-PLACED, -PLACING, -PLACES** to put in a wrong place

MISPLAN *v* **-PLANNED, -PLANNING, -PLANS** to plan badly

MISPLANT *v* **-ED, -ING, -S** to plant wrongly

MISPLAY *v* **-ED, -ING, -S** to make a bad play in a game

MISPLEAD *v* **-PLEADED** or **-PLED, -PLEADING, -PLEADS** to plead wrongly or falsely

MISPOINT *v* **-ED, -ING, -S** to point improperly

MISPOISE *v* **-POISED, -POISING, -POISES** to poise incorrectly

MISPRICE *v* **-PRICED, -PRICING, -PRICES** to price incorrectly

MISPRINT *v* **-ED, -ING, -S** to print incorrectly

MISPRIZE *v* **-PRIZED, -PRIZING, -PRIZES** to despise

MISQUOTE *v* **-QUOTED, -QUOTING, -QUOTES** to quote incorrectly

MISRAISE *v* **-RAISED, -RAISING, -RAISES** to raise wrongly

MISRATE *v* **-RATED, -RATING, -RATES** to rate incorrectly

MISREAD *v* **-READ, -READING, -READS** to read incorrectly

MISREFER *v* **-FERRED, -FERRING, -FERS** to refer incorrectly

MISRELY *v* **-LIED, -LYING, -LIES** to rely wrongly

MISROUTE *v* **-ROUTED, -ROUTING, -ROUTES** to route incorrectly

MISRULE *v* **-RULED, -RULING, -RULES** to rule unwisely or unjustly

MISS *v* **-ED, -ING, -ES** to fail to make contact with

MISSABLE *adj* able to be missed

MISSAL *n pl.* **-S** a prayer book

MISSAY *v* **-SAID, -SAYING, -SAYS** to say incorrectly

MISSEAT *v* **-ED, -ING, -S** to seat wrongly

MISSEL *n pl.* **-S** a European thrush

MISSEND *v* **-SENT, -SENDING, -SENDS** to send incorrectly

MISSENSE *n pl.* **-S** a form of genetic mutation

MISSET *v* **-SET, -SETTING, -SETS** to set incorrectly

MISSHAPE *v* **-SHAPED, -SHAPEN, -SHAPING, -SHAPES** to shape badly

MISSHOD *adj* improperly shod

MISSIES pl. of missy

MISSILE *n pl.* **-S** an object or weapon that is thrown or projected

MISSILRY *n pl.* **-RIES** the science of designing and operating guided missiles

MISSION *v* **-ED, -ING, -S** to send to perform a specific task

MISSIS *n pl.* **-SISES** a wife

MISSIVE *n pl.* **-S** a written communication

MISSORT *v* **-ED, -ING, -S** to sort badly or improperly

MISSOUND *v* **-ED, -ING, -S** to sound wrongly

MISSOUT *n pl.* **-S** a losing throw of dice

MISSPACE *v* **-SPACED, -SPACING, -SPACES** to space incorrectly

MISSPEAK *v* **-SPOKE, -SPOKEN, -SPEAKING, -SPEAKS** to speak incorrectly

MISSPELL *v* **-SPELLED** or **-SPELT, -SPELLING, -SPELLS** to spell incorrectly

MISSPEND *v* **-SPENT, -SPENDING, -SPENDS** to spend wrongly

MISSPOKE past tense of misspeak

MISSPOKEN past participle of misspeak

MISSTAMP *v* **-ED, -ING, -S** to stamp wrongly

MISSTART *v* **-ED, -ING, -S** to start off badly

MISSTATE *v* **-STATED, -STATING, -STATES** to state wrongly

MISSTEER *v* **-ED, -ING, -S** to steer wrongly

MISSTEP *v* **-STEPPED, -STEPPING, -STEPS** to step wrongly

MISSTOP *v* **-STOPPED, -STOPPING, -STOPS** to stop wrongly

MISSTYLE *v* **-STYLED, -STYLING, -STYLES** to style or call wrongly

MISSUIT *v* **-ED, -ING, -S** to suit badly

MISSUS	*n* pl. **-ES** missis
MISSY	*n* pl. **MISSIES** a young girl
MIST	*v* **-ED, -ING, -S** to become blurry
MISTAKE	*v* **-TOOK** or **-TEUK, -TAKEN, -TAKING, -TAKES** to interpret wrongly
MISTAKER	*n* pl. **-S** one that mistakes
MISTBOW	*n* pl. **-S** a fogbow
MISTEACH	*v* **-TAUGHT, -TEACHING, -TEACHES** to teach wrongly or badly
MISTEND	*v* **-ED, -ING, -S** to tend to improperly
MISTER	*n* pl. **-S** sir
MISTERM	*v* **-ED, -ING, -S** to call by a wrong name
MISTEUK	a past tense of mistake
MISTHINK	*v* **-THOUGHT, -THINKING, -THINKS** to think wrongly
MISTHROW	*v* **-THREW, -THROWN, -THROWING, -THROWS** to throw errantly
MISTIER	comparative of misty
MISTIEST	superlative of misty
MISTILY	*adv* in a misty manner
MISTIME	*v* **-TIMED, -TIMING, -TIMES** to time wrongly
MISTITLE	*v* **-TLED, -TLING, -TLES** to call by a wrong title
MISTOOK	a past tense of mistake
MISTOUCH	*v* **-ED, -ING, -ES** to touch improperly
MISTRACE	*v* **-TRACED, -TRACING, -TRACES** to trace wrongly
MISTRAIN	*v* **-ED, -ING, -S** to train improperly
MISTRAL	*n* pl. **-S** a cold, dry wind
MISTREAT	*v* **-ED, -ING, -S** to treat badly
MISTRESS	*n* pl. **-ES** a woman in a position of authority
MISTRIAL	*n* pl. **-S** a trial made invalid because of some error in procedure
MISTRUST	*v* **-ED, -ING, -S** to distrust
MISTRUTH	*n* pl. **-S** a lie
MISTRYST	*v* **-ED, -ING, -S** to fail to keep an appointment with
MISTUNE	*v* **-TUNED, -TUNING, -TUNES** to tune incorrectly
MISTUTOR	*v* **-ED, -ING, -S** to instruct or bring up badly
MISTY	*adj* **MISTIER, MISTIEST** blurry
MISTYPE	*v* **-TYPED, -TYPING, -TYPES** to type incorrectly
MISUNION	*n* pl. **-S** a bad union
MISUSAGE	*n* pl. **-S** incorrect use
MISUSE	*v* **-USED, -USING, -USES** to use incorrectly
MISUSER	*n* pl. **-S** one that misuses
MISVALUE	*v* **-UED, -UING, -UES** to value incorrectly
MISWORD	*v* **-ED, -ING, -S** to word wrongly
MISWRITE	*v* **-WROTE** or **-WRIT, -WRITTEN, -WRITING, -WRITES** to write incorrectly
MISYOKE	*v* **-YOKED, -YOKING, -YOKES** to yoke improperly
MITE	*n* pl. **-S** a small arachnid
MITER	*v* **-ED, -ING, -S** to raise to the rank of a bishop
MITERER	*n* pl. **-S** one that miters
MITHER	*n* pl. **-S** mother
MITICIDE	*n* pl. **-S** a substance used to kill mites
MITIER	comparative of mity
MITIEST	superlative of mity
MITIGATE	*v* **-GATED, -GATING, -GATES** to make less severe
MITIS	*n* pl. **-TISES** a type of wrought iron
MITOGEN	*n* pl. **-S** a substance that induces mitosis
MITOSIS	*n* pl. **-TOSES** a type of cell division **MITOTIC** *adj*
MITRAL	*adj* pertaining to a valve of the heart
MITRE	*v* **-TRED, -TRING, -TRES** to miter
MITSVAH	*n* pl. **-VAHS** or **-VOTH** mitzvah
MITT	*n* pl. **-S** a type of baseball glove
MITTEN	*n* pl. **-S** a type of covering for the hand **MITTENED** *adj*
MITTIMUS	*n* pl. **-ES** a warrant committing a person to prison
MITY	*adj* **MITIER, MITIEST** infested with mites
MITZVAH	*n* pl. **-VAHS** or **-VOTH** a commandment of Jewish law
MIX	*v* **MIXED** or **MIXT, MIXING, MIXES** to put together into one mass **MIXABLE, MIXIBLE** *adj* **MIXEDLY** *adv*
MIXER	*n* pl. **-S** one that mixes

MIXOLOGY *n* pl. **-GIES** the art of making mixed drinks

MIXTURE *n* pl. **-S** something produced by mixing

MIXUP *n* pl. **-S** a state of confusion

MIZEN *n* pl. **-S** mizzen

MIZUNA *n* pl. **-S** a Japanese mustard

MIZZEN *n* pl. **-S** a type of sail

MIZZLE *v* **-ZLED, -ZLING, -ZLES** to rain in fine droplets

MIZZLY *adj* characterized by a fine rain

MM *interj* — used to express assent or satisfaction

MNEMONIC *n* pl. **-S** a device to assist the memory

MO *n* pl. **MOS** a moment

MOA *n* pl. **-S** an extinct flightless bird

MOAN *v* **-ED, -ING, -S** to utter a low, mournful sound

MOANER *n* pl. **-S** one that moans

MOANFUL *adj* moaning

MOAT *v* **-ED, -ING, -S** to surround with a moat (a water-filled trench)

MOATLIKE *adj* suggestive of a moat

MOB *v* **MOBBED, MOBBING, MOBS** to crowd about

MOBBER *n* pl. **-S** one that mobs

MOBBISH *adj* characteristic of a mob (a disorderly crowd of people)

MOBBISM *n* pl. **-S** mobbish conduct

MOBCAP *n* pl. **-S** a woman's cap

MOBILE *n* pl. **-S** a form of sculpture

MOBILISE *v* **-LISED, -LISING, -LISES** to mobilize

MOBILITY *n* pl. **-TIES** the ability to move

MOBILIZE *v* **-LIZED, -LIZING, -LIZES** to put into movement

MOBLED *adj* wrapped in or as if in a hood

MOBOCRAT *n* pl. **-S** a supporter of mob rule

MOBSTER *n* pl. **-S** a gangster

MOC *n* pl. **-S** a moccasin

MOCCASIN *n* pl. **-S** a type of shoe

MOCHA *n* pl. **-S** a choice, pungent coffee

MOCHILA *n* pl. **-S** a leather covering for a saddle

MOCK *v* **-ED, -ING, -S** to ridicule **MOCKABLE** *adj*

MOCKER *n* pl. **-S** one that mocks

MOCKERY *n* pl. **-ERIES** the act of mocking

MOCKTAIL *n* pl. **-S** a cocktail with no alcohol

MOCKUP *n* pl. **-S** a full-sized model

MOD *n* pl. **-S** one who wears boldly stylish clothes

MODAL *n* pl. **-S** a verb used with other verbs to express mood or tense

MODALITY *n* pl. **-TIES** the state of being modal

MODALLY *adv* in a manner pertaining to a mode

MODE *n* pl. **-S** a method of doing or acting

MODEL *v* **-ELED, -ELING, -ELS** or **-ELLED, -ELLING, -ELS** to plan or form after a pattern

MODELER *n* pl. **-S** one that models

MODELING *n* pl. **-S** the treatment of volume in sculpture

MODELIST *n* pl. **-S** one who makes models

MODELLED a past tense of model

MODELLER *n* pl. **-S** modeler

MODELLING a present participle of model

MODEM *v* **-ED, -ING, -S** to transmit by modem (a device for converting signals from one form to another)

MODERATE *v* **-ATED, -ATING, -ATES** to make less extreme

MODERATO *n* pl. **-TOS** a musical passage played at a medium tempo

MODERN *adj* **-ERNER, -ERNEST** pertaining to present or recent time **MODERNLY** *adv*

MODERN *n* pl. **-S** a person of modern times or views

MODERNE *n* pl. **-S** a design style of the 1920s and 1930s

MODEST *adj* **-ESTER, -ESTEST** having a moderate regard for oneself **MODESTLY** *adv*

MODESTY *n* pl. **-TIES** the quality of being modest

MODI pl. of modus

MODICUM *n* pl. **-CUMS** or **-CA** a small amount

MODIFIER *n* pl. **-S** one that modifies

MODIFY *v* **-FIED, -FYING, -FIES** to change in form or character

MODIOLUS *n* pl. **-LI** a bony shaft of the inner ear

MODISH   *adj* stylish **MODISHLY** *adv*

MODISTE   *n* pl. **-S** a dealer in stylish women's clothing

MODULAR   *n* pl. **-S** something built in self-contained units

MODULATE   *v* **-LATED, -LATING, -LATES** to adjust to a certain proportion

MODULE   *n* pl. **-S** a standard of measurement

MODULO   *adv* with respect to a modulus

MODULUS   *n* pl. **-LI** a number that produces the same remainder when divided into each of two numbers

MODUS   *n* pl. **-DI** a mode

MOFETTE   *n* pl. **-S** a noxious emanation from a fissure in the earth

MOFFETTE   *n* pl. **-S** mofette

MOG   *v* **MOGGED, MOGGING, MOGS** to move away

MOGGIE   *n* pl. **-S** moggy

MOGGY   *n* pl. **-GIES** a cat

MOGHUL   *n* pl. **-S** mogul

MOGUL   *n* pl. **-S** an important person

MOGULED   *adj* provided with bumps of hard snow

MOHAIR   *n* pl. **-S** the long, silky hair of the Angora goat

MOHAWK   *n* pl. **-S** a hairstyle marked by a stiff ridge of long hair from front to back

MOHEL   *n* pl. **-HELS** or **-HELIM** or **-HALIM** a person who performs Jewish ritual circumcisions

MOHUR   *n* pl. **-S** a former gold coin of India

MOIDORE   *n* pl. **-S** a former gold coin of Portugal

MOIETY   *n* pl. **-ETIES** a half

MOIL   *v* **-ED, -ING, -S** to work hard

MOILER   *n* pl. **-S** one that moils

MOIRA   *n* pl. **-RAI** fate or destiny, in ancient Greek religion

MOIRE   *n* pl. **-S** a fabric having a wavy pattern

MOIST   *adj* **MOISTER, MOISTEST** slightly wet

MOISTEN   *v* **-ED, -ING, -S** to make or become moist

MOISTFUL   *adj* moist

MOISTLY   *adv* in a moist manner

MOISTURE   *n* pl. **-S** condensed or diffused liquid

MOJARRA   *n* pl. **-S** a marine fish

MOJO   *n* pl. **-JOS** or **-JOES** a magic charm

MOKE   *n* pl. **-S** a donkey

MOL   *n* pl. **-S** mole

MOLA   *n* pl. **-S** a marine fish

MOLAL   *adj* pertaining to a mole

MOLALITY   *n* pl. **-TIES** the number of moles of solute per 1,000 grams of solvent

MOLAR   *n* pl. **-S** a grinding tooth

MOLARITY   *n* pl. **-TIES** the number of moles of solute per liter of solution

MOLASSES   *n* pl. **-LASSESES** a thick syrup

MOLD   *v* **-ED, -ING, -S** to work into a particular shape **MOLDABLE** *adj*

MOLDER   *v* **-ED, -ING, -S** to turn to dust by natural decay

MOLDIER   comparative of moldy

MOLDIEST   superlative of moldy

MOLDING   *n* pl. **-S** a long, narrow strip used to decorate a surface

MOLDWARP   *n* pl. **-S** a burrowing mammal

MOLDY   *adj* **MOLDIER, MOLDIEST** musty

MOLE   *n* pl. **-S** the quantity of a compound that has a weight equal to the compound's molecular weight

MOLECULE   *n* pl. **-S** the smallest physical unit of an element

MOLEHILL   *n* pl. **-S** a small mound of earth

MOLESKIN   *n* pl. **-S** a cotton fabric

MOLEST   *v* **-ED, -ING, -S** to disturb or annoy

MOLESTER   *n* pl. **-S** one that molests

MOLIES   pl. of moly

MOLINE   *adj* having arms forked and curved at the ends — used of a heraldic cross

MOLL   *n* pl. **-S** a gangster's girlfriend

MOLLAH   *n* pl. **-S** mullah

MOLLIE   *n* pl. **-S** a tropical fish

MOLLIES   pl. of molly

MOLLIFY   *v* **-FIED, -FYING, -FIES** to soothe

MOLLUSC   *n* pl. **-S** mollusk

MOLLUSCA   *n/pl* skin diseases

MOLLUSK   *n* pl. **-S** any of a phylum of soft-bodied invertebrates

MOLLY   *n* pl. **-LIES** mollie

MOLOCH   *n* pl. **-S** a spiny lizard

MOLT   *v* **-ED, -ING, -S** to cast off an outer covering

MOLTEN   *adj* made liquid by heat **MOLTENLY** *adv*

MOLTER   *n* pl. **-S** one that molts

MOLTO   *adv* very — used in musical directions

MOLY   *n* pl. **-LIES** a wild garlic

MOLYBDIC   *adj* pertaining to a certain metallic element

MOM   *n* pl. **-S** mother

MOME   *n* pl. **-S** a fool

MOMENT   *n* pl. **-S** a brief period of time

MOMENTA   a pl. of momentum

MOMENTLY   *adv* from moment to moment

MOMENTO   *n* pl. **-TOS** or **-TOES** memento

MOMENTUM   *n* pl. **-TUMS** or **-TA** force of movement

MOMI   a pl. of momus

MOMISM   *n* pl. **-S** an excessive dependence on mothers

MOMMA   *n* pl. **-S** mother

MOMMY   *n* pl. **-MIES** mother

MOMSER   *n* pl. **-S** a bastard

MOMUS   *n* pl. **-MUSES** or **-MI** a carping person

MOMZER   *n* pl. **-S** momser

MON   *n* pl. **MEN** man

MONACHAL   *adj* pertaining to monks

MONACID   *n* pl. **-S** monoacid

MONAD   *n* pl. **-S** a single-celled organism **MONADAL, MONADIC** *adj*

MONADES   pl. of monas

MONADISM   *n* pl. **-S** a philosophical doctrine

MONANDRY   *n* pl. **-DRIES** the condition of having one husband at a time

MONARCH   *n* pl. **-S** an absolute ruler

MONARCHY   *n* pl. **-CHIES** rule by a monarch

MONARDA   *n* pl. **-S** an aromatic herb

MONAS   *n* pl. **MONADES** a monad

MONASTIC   *n* pl. **-S** a monk

MONAURAL   *adj* pertaining to sound transmission, recording, or reproduction involving a single transmission path

MONAXIAL   *adj* having one axis

MONAXON   *n* pl. **-S** a straight spicule in sponges

MONAZITE   *n* pl. **-S** a mineral

MONDE   *n* pl. **-S** the world

MONDO   *n* pl. **-DOS** a rapid question and answer technique employed in Zen Buddhism

MONECIAN   *adj* having both male and female sex organs in the same individual

MONELLIN   *n* pl. **-S** a protein extracted from a West African red berry

MONERAN   *n* pl. **-S** a cellular organism that does not have a distinct nucleus

MONETARY   *adj* pertaining to money

MONETISE   *v* **-TISED, -TISING, -TISES** to monetize

MONETIZE   *v* **-TIZED, -TIZING, -TIZES** to coin into money

MONEY   *n* pl. **MONEYS** or **MONIES** an official medium of exchange and measure of value

MONEYBAG   *n* pl. **-S** a bag for holding money

MONEYED   *adj* having much money

MONEYER   *n* pl. **-S** one that coins money

MONEYMAN   *n* pl. **-MEN** a person who invests large sums of money

MONGEESE   a pl. of mongoose

MONGER   *v* **-ED, -ING, -S** to peddle

MONGO   *n* pl. **-GOS** mungo

MONGOE   *n* pl. **-S** mungo

MONGOL   *n* pl. **-S** a person affected with a form of mental deficiency

MONGOOSE   *n* pl. **-GOOSES** or **-GEESE** a carnivorous mammal

MONGREL   *n* pl. **-S** an animal or plant of mixed breed

MONGST   *prep* amongst

MONICKER   *n* pl. **-S** moniker

MONIE   *adj* many

MONIED   *adj* moneyed

MONIES   a pl. of money

MONIKER   *n* pl. **-S** a name

MONISH   *v* **-ED, -ING, -ES** to warn

MONISM   *n* pl. **-S** a philosophical theory

MONIST   *n* pl. **-S** an adherent of monism **MONISTIC** *adj*

MONITION   *n* pl. **-S** a warning

MONITIVE   *adj* giving warning

MONITOR   *v* **-ED, -ING, -S** to keep track of

MONITORY   *n* pl. **-RIES** a letter of warning

MONK   *n* pl. **-S** a man who is a member of a secluded religious order

MONKERY   *n* pl. **-ERIES** the mode of life of monks

MONKEY   *v* **-ED, -ING, -S** to mimic

MONKFISH   *n* pl. **-ES** a marine fish

MONKHOOD   *n* pl. **-S** the state of being a monk

MONKISH   *adj* pertaining to monks

MONO   *n* pl. **MONOS** an infectious disease

MONOACID   *n* pl. **-S** a type of acid

MONOCARP   *n* pl. **-S** a plant that yields fruit only once before dying

MONOCLE   *n* pl. **-S** an eyeglass for one eye **MONOCLED** *adj*

MONOCOT   *n* pl. **-S** a type of seed plant

MONOCRAT   *n* pl. **-S** an autocrat

MONOCYTE   *n* pl. **-S** a type of white blood cell

MONODIST   *n* pl. **-S** one who writes monodies

MONODY   *n* pl. **-DIES** an elegy performed by one person **MONODIC** *adj*

MONOECY   *n* pl. **-CIES** the condition of being monecian

MONOFIL   *n* pl. **-S** a single filament of synthetic fiber

MONOFUEL   *n* pl. **-S** a type of rocket propellant

MONOGAMY   *n* pl. **-MIES** marriage with one person at a time

MONOGENY   *n* pl. **-NIES** asexual reproduction

MONOGERM   *adj* being a fruit that produces a single plant

MONOGLOT   *n* pl. **-S** a person speaking or writing only one language

MONOGRAM   *v* **-GRAMED, -GRAMING, -GRAMS** or **-GRAMMED, -GRAMMING, -GRAMS** to mark with a design of one's initials

MONOGYNY   *n* pl. **-NIES** the condition of having one wife at a time

MONOHULL   *n* pl. **-S** a vessel with a single hull

MONOKINE   *n* pl. **-S** a substance secreted by white blood cells

MONOLITH   *n* pl. **-S** a large block of stone

MONOLOG   *v* **-LOGGED, -LOGGING, -LOGS** to deliver a monolog (a lengthy speech by one person)

MONOLOGY   *n* pl. **-GIES** the act of uttering a monolog

MONOMER   *n* pl. **-S** a type of chemical compound

MONOMIAL   *n* pl. **-S** an algebraic expression consisting of a single term

MONOPOD   *n* pl. **-S** a one-legged support for a camera

MONOPODE   *n* pl. **-S** a creature having one foot

MONOPODY   *n* pl. **-DIES** a measure consisting of a single metrical foot

MONOPOLE   *n* pl. **-S** a type of radio antenna

MONOPOLY   *n* pl. **-LIES** exclusive control of a commodity or service in a particular market

MONORAIL   *n* pl. **-S** a single rail serving as a track for a wheeled vehicle

MONOSOME   *n* pl. **-S** an unpaired chromosome

MONOSOMY   *n* pl. **-MIES** a condition of having one unpaired chromosome

MONOTINT   *n* pl. **-S** a painting done in different shades of one color

MONOTONE   *n* pl. **-S** a vocal utterance in one unvaried tone

MONOTONY   *n* pl. **-NIES** tedious sameness

MONOTYPE   *n* pl. **-S** the only representative of its group

MONOXIDE   *n* pl. **-S** a type of oxide

MONS   *n* pl. **MONTES** a protuberance of the body

MONSIEUR   *n* pl. **MESSIEURS** a French title of courtesy for a man

MONSOON   *n* pl. **-S** a seasonal wind

MONSTER   *n* pl. **-S** a strange or terrifying creature

MONSTERA   *n* pl. **-S** a tropical American plant

MONTAGE   *v* **-TAGED, -TAGING, -TAGES** to combine into a composite picture

MONTANE   *n* pl. **-S** the lower vegetation belt of a mountain

MONTE   *n* pl. **-S** a card game

MONTEITH   *n* pl. **-S** a large punch bowl

MONTERO   *n* pl. **-ROS** a type of cap

MONTES   pl. of mons

MONTH   *n* pl. **-S** a period of approximately 30 days

MONTHLY   *n* pl. **-LIES** a publication issued once a month

MONUMENT   *n* pl. **-S** a structure built as a memorial

MONURON   *n* pl. **-S** an herbicide

MONY   *adj* many

MOO   *v* **-ED, -ING, -S** to make the deep, moaning sound of a cow

MOOCH   *v* **-ED, -ING, -ES** to obtain without paying

MOOCHER   *n* pl. **-S** one that mooches

MOOD   *n* pl. **-S** a person's emotional state at a particular moment

MOODY   *adj* **MOODIER, MOODIEST** given to changing moods **MOODILY** *adv*

MOOL   *n* pl. **-S** soft soil

MOOLA   *n* pl. **-S** moolah

MOOLAH   *n* pl. **-S** money

MOOLEY   *n* pl. **-EYS** muley

MOON   *v* **-ED, -ING, -S** to spend time idly

MOONBEAM   *n* pl. **-S** a ray of light from the moon (the earth's natural satellite)

MOONBOW   *n* pl. **-S** a rainbow formed by light from the moon

MOONCALF   *n* pl. **-CALVES** a foolish person

MOONDUST   *n* pl. **-S** dust on the moon

MOONER   *n* pl. **-S** one that moons

MOONEYE   *n* pl. **-S** a freshwater fish

MOONFISH   *n* pl. **-ES** a marine fish

MOONIER   comparative of moony

MOONIEST   superlative of moony

MOONILY   *adv* in a moony manner

MOONISH   *adj* fickle

MOONLESS   *adj* lacking the light of the moon

MOONLET   *n* pl. **-S** a small satellite

MOONLIKE   *adj* resembling the moon

MOONLIT   *adj* lighted by the moon

MOONPORT   *n* pl. **-S** a facility for launching spacecraft to the moon

MOONRISE   *n* pl. **-S** the rising of the moon above the horizon

MOONROOF   *n* pl. **-S** a glass panel in an automobile roof

MOONSAIL   *n* pl. **-S** a light, square sail

MOONSEED   *n* pl. **-S** a climbing plant

MOONSET   *n* pl. **-S** the setting of the moon below the horizon

MOONSHOT   *n* pl. **-S** the launching of a spacecraft to the moon

MOONWALK   *v* **-ED, -ING, -S** to walk on the moon

MOONWARD   *adv* toward the moon

MOONWORT   *n* pl. **-S** a flowering plant

MOONY   *adj* **MOONIER, MOONIEST** resembling the moon

MOOR   *v* **-ED, -ING, -S** to secure a vessel by means of cables

MOORAGE   *n* pl. **-S** the act of mooring

MOORCOCK   *n* pl. **-S** the male moorfowl

MOORFOWL   *n* pl. **-S** a game bird

MOORHEN   *n* pl. **-S** the female moorfowl

MOORIER   comparative of moory

MOORIEST   superlative of moory

MOORING   *n* pl. **-S** a place where a vessel may be moored

MOORISH   *adj* marshy

MOORLAND   *n* pl. **-S** a tract of marshy land

MOORWORT   *n* pl. **-S** a marsh plant

MOORY   *adj* **MOORIER, MOORIEST** marshy

MOOSE   *n* pl. **MOOSE** a ruminant mammal

MOOT   *v* **-ED, -ING, -S** to bring up for discussion

MOOTER   *n* pl. **-S** one that moots

MOOTNESS   *n* pl. **-ES** the state of being without legal significance

MOP   *v* **MOPPED, MOPPING, MOPS** to wipe with a mop (an implement for cleaning floors)

MOPBOARD   *n* pl. **-S** a board at the base of a wall

MOPE   *v* **MOPED, MOPING, MOPES** to act in a dejected or gloomy manner

MOPED   *n* pl. **-S** a type of motorbike

MOPER   *n* pl. **-S** one that mopes

MOPERY   *n* pl. **-PERIES** an act of dawdling

MOPEY   *adj* **MOPIER, MOPIEST** dejected

MOPIER   comparative of mopy

MOPIEST   superlative of mopy

MOPINESS   *n* pl. **-ES** the state of being mopey

MOPING   present participle of mope

MOPINGLY   *adv* in a moping manner

MOPISH   *adj* given to moping **MOPISHLY** *adv*

MOPOKE   *n* pl. **-S** an Australian bird

MOPPED   past tense of mop

MOPPER   *n* pl. **-S** one that mops

MOPPET   *n* pl. **-S** a child

MOPPING   present participle of mop

MOPY   *adj* **MOPIER, MOPIEST** mopey

MOQUETTE   *n* pl. **-S** a woolen fabric

MOR   *n* pl. **-S** a forest humus

MORA   *n* pl. **-RAS** or **-RAE** a unit of metrical time in prosody

MORAINE   *n* pl. **-S** an accumulation of debris deposited by a glacier **MORAINAL, MORAINIC** *adj*

MORAL   *adj* pertaining to principles of right and wrong

MORALE   *n* pl. **-S** the state of the spirits of an individual or group

MORALISE   *v* **-ISED, -ISING, -ISES** to moralize

MORALISM   *n* pl. **-S** the practice of moralizing

MORALIST   *n* pl. **-S** a teacher of morality

MORALITY   *n* pl. **-TIES** conformity to the rules of right conduct

MORALIZE   *v* **-IZED, -IZING, -IZES** to explain in a moral sense

MORALLY   *adv* in a moral manner

MORALS   *n/pl* rules of conduct with respect to right and wrong

MORASS   *n* pl. **-ES** a marsh **MORASSY** *adj*

MORATORY   *adj* authorizing delay of payment

MORAY   *n* pl. **-RAYS** a tropical eel

MORBID   *adj* gruesome **MORBIDLY** *adv*

MORBIFIC   *adj* causing disease

MORBILLI   *n/pl* a virus disease

MORCEAU   *n* pl. **-CEAUX** a short literary or musical composition

MORDANCY   *n* pl. **-CIES** a sarcastic quality

MORDANT   *v* **-ED, -ING, -S** to treat with a caustic substance

MORDENT   *n* pl. **-S** a melodic embellishment

MORE   *adj* greater, additional

MOREEN   *n* pl. **-S** a heavy fabric

MOREL   *n* pl. **-S** an edible mushroom

MORELLE   *n* pl. **-S** a flowering plant

MORELLO   *n* pl. **-LOS** a variety of sour cherry

MORENESS   *n* pl. **-ES** the state of being more

MOREOVER   *adv* in addition

MORES   *n/pl* the customs of a particular group

MORESQUE   *n* pl. **-S** an ancient decorative style

MORGAN   *n* pl. **-S** a unit of distance between genes

MORGEN   *n* pl. **-S** a Dutch unit of land area

MORGUE   *n* pl. **-S** a place where dead bodies are kept for identification

MORIBUND   *adj* being about to die

MORION   *n* pl. **-S** a type of helmet

MORN   *n* pl. **-S** morning

MORNING   *n* pl. **-S** the early part of the day

MOROCCO   *n* pl. **-COS** a soft leather

MORON   *n* pl. **-S** a mentally deficient person **MORONIC** *adj*

MORONISM   *n* pl. **-S** the condition of being a moron

MORONITY   *n* pl. **-TIES** moronism

MOROSE   *adj* sullen **MOROSELY** *adv*

MOROSITY   *n* pl. **-TIES** the state of being morose

MORPH   *v* **-ED, -ING, -S** to be transformed

MORPHEME   *n* pl. **-S** a linguistic unit

MORPHIA   *n* pl. **-S** morphine

MORPHIC   *adj* pertaining to form

MORPHIN   *n* pl. **-S** morphine

MORPHINE   *n* pl. **-S** a narcotic alkaloid

MORPHING   *n* pl. **-S** the transformation of one form into another

MORPHO   *n* pl. **-PHOS** a tropical butterfly

MORRION   *n* pl. **-S** morion

MORRIS   *n* pl. **-RISES** an English folk dance

MORRO   *n* pl. **-ROS** a rounded elevation

MORROW   *n* pl. **-S** the next day

MORSE   *adj* designating a code used in telegraphy

MORSEL   *v* **-SELED, -SELING, -SELS** or **-SELLED, -SELLING, -SELS** to divide into small pieces

MORT   *n* pl. **-S** a note sounded on a hunting horn to announce the killing of an animal

MORTAL   *n* pl. **-S** a human being

MORTALLY   *adv* fatally

MORTAR   *v* **-ED, -ING, -S** to secure with mortar (a type of cement)

MORTARY   *adj* containing or resembling mortar

MORTGAGE   *v* **-GAGED, -GAGING, -GAGES** to pledge to a creditor as security

MORTICE   *v* **-TICED, -TICING, -TICES** to mortise

MORTIFY   *v* **-FIED, -FYING, -FIES** to humiliate

MORTISE   *v* **-TISED, -TISING, -TISES** to join or fasten securely

MORTISER   *n* pl. **-S** one that mortises

MORTMAIN   *n* pl. **-S** perpetual ownership of land

MORTUARY   *n* pl. **-ARIES** a place where dead bodies are kept until burial

MORULA   *n* pl. **-LAS** or **-LAE** an embryonic mass of cells **MORULAR** *adj*

MOSAIC	*v* **-ICKED, -ICKING, -ICS** to form into a mosaic (a type of inlaid surface decoration)	**MOTIF**	*n* pl. **-S** a recurring thematic element in an artistic work **MOTIFIC** *adj*
MOSASAUR	*n* pl. **-S** an extinct lizard	**MOTILE**	*n* pl. **-S** one whose mental imagery consists chiefly of inner feelings of action
MOSCHATE	*adj* musky		
MOSEY	*v* **-ED, -ING, -S** to saunter		
MOSH	*v* **-ED, -ING, -ES** to engage in frenzied dancing with others at a rock concert	**MOTILITY**	*n* pl. **-TIES** the ability to move
		MOTION	*v* **-ED, -ING, -S** to signal by a bodily movement
MOSHAV	*n* pl. **-SHAVIM** a cooperative settlement of small farms in Israel	**MOTIONAL**	*adj* pertaining to movement
		MOTIONER	*n* pl. **-S** one that motions
MOSHER	*n* pl. **-S** one that moshes	**MOTIVATE**	*v* **-VATED, -VATING, -VATES** to provide with an incentive
MOSHING	*n* pl. **-S** frenzied dancing at a rock concert	**MOTIVE**	*v* **-TIVED, -TIVING, -TIVES** to motivate
MOSK	*n* pl. **-S** mosque		
MOSQUE	*n* pl. **-S** a Muslim house of worship	**MOTIVIC**	*adj* pertaining to a musical motif
MOSQUITO	*n* pl. **-TOS** or **-TOES** a winged insect	**MOTIVITY**	*n* pl. **-TIES** the ability to move
		MOTLEY	*adj* **-LEYER, -LEYEST** or **-LIER, -LIEST** composed of diverse elements
MOSS	*v* **-ED, -ING, -ES** to cover with moss (a growth of small, leafy-stemmed plants)		
		MOTLEY	*n* pl. **-LEYS** a garment of various colors
MOSSBACK	*n* pl. **-S** a large, old fish	**MOTMOT**	*n* pl. **-S** a tropical bird
MOSSER	*n* pl. **-S** one that gathers or works with moss	**MOTOR**	*v* **-ED, -ING, -S** to travel by automobile
MOSSLIKE	*adj* resembling moss		
MOSSO	*adv* rapidly — used as a musical direction	**MOTORBUS**	*n* pl. **-BUSES** or **-BUSSES** a bus
		MOTORCAR	*n* pl. **-S** an automobile
MOSSY	*adj* **MOSSIER, MOSSIEST** covered with moss	**MOTORDOM**	*n* pl. **-S** the motor vehicle industry
		MOTORIC	*adj* pertaining to muscular movement
MOST	*n* pl. **-S** the greatest amount		
MOSTE	past tense of mote	**MOTORING**	*n* pl. **-S** the recreation of traveling by automobile
MOSTEST	*n* pl. **-S** most		
MOSTLY	*adv* mainly	**MOTORISE**	*v* **-ISED, -ISING, -ISES** to motorize
MOT	*n* pl. **-S** a witty saying	**MOTORIST**	*n* pl. **-S** one who travels by automobile
MOTE	*n* pl. **-S** a small particle		
MOTE	*v* past tense **MOSTE** may	**MOTORIZE**	*v* **-IZED, -IZING, -IZES** to equip with motor vehicles
MOTEL	*n* pl. **-S** a roadside hotel		
MOTET	*n* pl. **-S** a type of choral composition	**MOTORMAN**	*n* pl. **-MEN** one who operates an electric streetcar or subway train
MOTEY	*adj* full of motes	**MOTORWAY**	*n* pl. **-WAYS** a type of highway
MOTH	*n* pl. **-S** a winged insect	**MOTT**	*n* pl. **-S** motte
MOTHBALL	*v* **-ED, -ING, -S** to put into storage	**MOTTE**	*n* pl. **-S** a small growth of trees on a prairie
MOTHER	*v* **-ED, -ING, -S** to give birth to		
MOTHERLY	*adj* maternal	**MOTTLE**	*v* **-TLED, -TLING, -TLES** to mark with spots or streaks of different colors
MOTHERY	*adj* slimy		
MOTHLIKE	*adj* resembling a moth	**MOTTLER**	*n* pl. **-S** one that mottles
MOTHY	*adj* **MOTHIER, MOTHIEST** full of moths	**MOTTO**	*n* pl. **-TOS** or **-TOES** a short expression of a guiding principle
		MOUCH	*v* **-ED, -ING, -ES** to mooch
		MOUCHOIR	*n* pl. **-S** a small handkerchief

MOUE *n* pl. **-S** a pouting grimace

MOUFFLON *n* pl. **-S** mouflon

MOUFLON *n* pl. **-S** a wild sheep

MOUILLE *adj* pronounced with the front of the tongue against the palate

MOUJIK *n* pl. **-S** muzhik

MOULAGE *n* pl. **-S** the making of a cast or mold of a mark for use in a criminal investigation

MOULD *v* **-ED, -ING, -S** to mold

MOULDER *v* **-ED, -ING, -S** to molder

MOULDING *n* pl. **-S** molding

MOULDY *adj* **MOULDIER, MOULDIEST** moldy

MOULIN *n* pl. **-S** a vertical cavity in a glacier

MOULT *v* **-ED, -ING, -S** to molt

MOULTER *n* pl. **-S** molter

MOUND *v* **-ED, -ING, -S** to pile

MOUNT *v* **-ED, -ING, -S** to get up on

MOUNTAIN *n* pl. **-S** a large, natural elevation of the earth's surface

MOUNTER *n* pl. **-S** one that mounts

MOUNTING *n* pl. **-S** something that provides a backing or appropriate setting for something else

MOURN *v* **-ED, -ING, -S** to feel or express grief or sorrow

MOURNER *n* pl. **-S** one that mourns

MOURNFUL *adj* **-FULLER, -FULLEST** expressing grief or sorrow

MOURNING *n* pl. **-S** an outward sign of grief

MOUSAKA *n* pl. **-S** moussaka

MOUSE *n* pl. **MICE** a small rodent

MOUSE *v* **MOUSED, MOUSING, MOUSES** to catch mice

MOUSEPAD *n* pl. **-S** a flat pad on which a computer mouse is used

MOUSER *n* pl. **-S** an animal that catches mice

MOUSEY *adj* **MOUSIER, MOUSIEST** mousy

MOUSIER comparative of mousy

MOUSIEST superlative of mousy

MOUSILY *adv* in a mousy manner

MOUSING *n* pl. **-S** a wrapping around the shank end of a hook

MOUSSAKA *n* pl. **-S** a Middle Eastern dish of meat and eggplant

MOUSSE *v* **MOUSSED, MOUSSING, MOUSSES** to style with mousse (foamy preparation used in styling hair)

MOUSY *adj* **MOUSIER, MOUSIEST** resembling a mouse

MOUTH *v* **-ED, -ING, -S** to put into the mouth

MOUTHER *n* pl. **-S** a speaker

MOUTHFUL *n* pl. **-S** as much as the mouth can hold

MOUTHY *adj* **MOUTHIER, MOUTHIEST** very talkative **MOUTHILY** *adv*

MOUTON *n* pl. **-S** sheepskin processed to resemble seal or beaver

MOVABLE *n* pl. **-S** something that can be moved

MOVABLY *adv* so as to be capable of being moved

MOVE *v* **MOVED, MOVING, MOVES** to change from one position to another

MOVEABLE *n* pl. **-S** movable

MOVEABLY *adv* movably

MOVED past tense of move

MOVELESS *adj* incapable of movement

MOVEMENT *n* pl. **-S** the act of moving

MOVER *n* pl. **-S** one that moves

MOVIE *n* pl. **-S** a motion picture

MOVIEDOM *n* pl. **-S** filmdom

MOVIEOLA *n* pl. **-S** a device for viewing and editing film

MOVING present participle of move

MOVINGLY *adv* so as to affect the emotions

MOVIOLA *n* pl. **-S** movieola

MOW *v* **MOWED, MOWN, MOWING, MOWS** to cut down standing herbage

MOWER *n* pl. **-S** one that mows

MOWING *n* pl. **-S** the act of cutting down standing herbage

MOXA *n* pl. **-S** a Chinese plant

MOXIE *n* pl. **-S** spirit or courage

MOZETTA *n* pl. **-TAS** or **-TE** mozzetta

MOZO *n* pl. **-ZOS** a manual laborer

MOZZETTA *n* pl. **-TAS** or **-TE** a hooded cape worn by bishops

MRIDANGA *n* pl. **-S** a drum of India

MU *n* pl. **-S** a Greek letter

MUCH *n* pl. **-ES** a great amount

MUCHACHO	*n* pl. **-CHOS** a young man
MUCHLY	*adv* very much
MUCHNESS	*n* pl. **-ES** the quality of being great
MUCHO	*adj* much, many
MUCID	*adj* musty
MUCIDITY	*n* pl. **-TIES** the state of being mucid
MUCILAGE	*n* pl. **-S** an adhesive substance
MUCIN	*n* pl. **-S** a protein secreted by the mucous membranes **MUCINOID, MUCINOUS** *adj*
MUCK	*v* **-ED, -ING, -S** to fertilize with manure
MUCKER	*n* pl. **-S** a vulgar person
MUCKIER	comparative of mucky
MUCKIEST	superlative of mucky
MUCKILY	*adv* in a mucky manner
MUCKLE	*n* pl. **-S** a large amount
MUCKLUCK	*n* pl. **-S** mukluk
MUCKRAKE	*v* **-RAKED, -RAKING, -RAKES** to search for and expose corruption
MUCKWORM	*n* pl. **-S** a worm found in manure
MUCKY	*adj* **MUCKIER, MUCKIEST** filthy
MUCLUC	*n* pl. **-S** mukluk
MUCOID	*n* pl. **-S** a complex protein **MUCOIDAL** *adj*
MUCOR	*n* pl. **-S** a type of fungus
MUCOSA	*n* pl. **-SAS** or **-SAE** a mucous membrane **MUCOSAL** *adj*
MUCOSE	*adj* mucous
MUCOSITY	*n* pl. **-TIES** the state of being mucous
MUCOUS	*adj* secreting or containing mucus
MUCRO	*n* pl. **-CRONES** a sharp point at the end of certain plant and animal organs
MUCUS	*n* pl. **-ES** a viscid bodily fluid
MUD	*v* **MUDDED, MUDDING, MUDS** to cover with mud (soft, wet earth)
MUDBUG	*n* pl. **-S** a crayfish
MUDCAP	*v* **-CAPPED, -CAPPING, -CAPS** to cover an explosive with mud before detonating
MUDCAT	*n* pl. **-S** a type of catfish
MUDDER	*n* pl. **-S** a racehorse that runs well on a muddy track
MUDDIED	past tense of muddy
MUDDIER	comparative of muddy
MUDDIES	present 3d person sing. of muddy
MUDDIEST	superlative of muddy
MUDDILY	*adv* in a muddy manner
MUDDING	present participle of mud
MUDDLE	*v* **-DLED, -DLING, -DLES** to mix in a disordered manner
MUDDLER	*n* pl. **-S** one that muddles
MUDDLY	*adj* disordered
MUDDY	*adj* **-DIER, -DIEST** covered or filled with mud
MUDDY	*v* **-DIED, -DYING, -DIES** to make or become muddy
MUDFISH	*n* pl. **-ES** a fish found in mud or muddy water
MUDFLAP	*n* pl. **-S** a flap hung behind a rear wheel of a vehicle to prevent splashing
MUDFLAT	*n* pl. **-S** a level tract alternately covered and left bare by the tide
MUDFLOW	*n* pl. **-S** a moving mass of mud
MUDGUARD	*n* pl. **-S** a fender
MUDHEN	*n* pl. **-S** a bird that lives in marshes
MUDHOLE	*n* pl. **-S** a hole or hollow place full of mud
MUDLARK	*n* pl. **-S** a street urchin
MUDPACK	*n* pl. **-S** cosmetic paste for the face
MUDPUPPY	*n* pl. **-PIES** a large salamander
MUDRA	*n* pl. **-S** a hand gesture in East Indian classical dancing
MUDROCK	*n* pl. **-S** pelite
MUDROOM	*n* pl. **-S** a room for shedding muddy clothing or footwear
MUDSILL	*n* pl. **-S** the lowest supporting timber of a structure
MUDSLIDE	*n* pl. **-S** a mudflow down a slope
MUDSTONE	*n* pl. **-S** a type of rock
MUEDDIN	*n* pl. **-S** muezzin
MUENSTER	*n* pl. **-S** a mild cheese
MUESLI	*n* pl. **-S** a breakfast cereal
MUEZZIN	*n* pl. **-S** a Muslim crier who calls the faithful to prayer
MUFF	*v* **-ED, -ING, -S** to bungle
MUFFIN	*n* pl. **-S** a small, round bread
MUFFLE	*v* **-FLED, -FLING, -FLES** to wrap with something to deaden sound
MUFFLER	*n* pl. **-S** a device for deadening sound
MUFTI	*n* pl. **-S** a judge who interprets Muslim religious law

MUG   *v* **MUGGED, MUGGING, MUGS** to assault with intent to rob

MUGFUL   *n* pl. **-S** as much as a mug can hold

MUGG   *v* **-ED, -ING, -S** to make funny faces

MUGGAR   *n* pl. **-S** mugger

MUGGED   past tense of mug

MUGGEE   *n* pl. **-S** one who is mugged

MUGGER   *n* pl. **-S** a large Asian crocodile

MUGGIER   comparative of muggy

MUGGIEST   superlative of muggy

MUGGILY   *adv* in a muggy manner

MUGGING   *n* pl. **-S** a street assault or beating

MUGGINS   *n* pl. **MUGGINS** a card game

MUGGUR   *n* pl. **-S** mugger

MUGGY   *adj* **-GIER, -GIEST** warm and humid

MUGHAL   *n* pl. **-S** mogul

MUGWORT   *n* pl. **-S** a flowering plant

MUGWUMP   *n* pl. **-S** a political independent

MUHLY   *n* pl. **MUHLIES** a perennial grass

MUJIK   *n* pl. **-S** muzhik

MUKLUK   *n* pl. **-S** a soft boot worn by Eskimos

MUKTUK   *n* pl. **-S** whale skin used for food

MULATTO   *n* pl. **-TOS** or **-TOES** the offspring of one white and one black parent

MULBERRY   *n* pl. **-RIES** a tree bearing an edible, berrylike fruit

MULCH   *v* **-ED, -ING, -ES** to provide with a protective covering for the soil

MULCT   *v* **-ED, -ING, -S** to defraud

MULE   *v* **MULED, MULING, MULES** to strike from dies belonging to two different issues, as a coin

MULETA   *n* pl. **-S** a red cloth used by a matador

MULETEER   *n* pl. **-S** one who drives mules (hoofed work animals)

MULEY   *n* pl. **-LEYS** a hornless cow

MULING   present participle of mule

MULISH   *adj* stubborn **MULISHLY** *adv*

MULL   *v* **-ED, -ING, -S** to ponder

MULLA   *n* pl. **-S** mullah

MULLAH   *n* pl. **-S** a Muslim religious leader or teacher

MULLEIN   *n* pl. **-S** a Eurasian herb

MULLEN   *n* pl. **-S** mullein

MULLER   *n* pl. **-S** a grinding implement

MULLET   *n* pl. **-S** an edible fish

MULLEY   *n* pl. **-LEYS** muley

MULLIGAN   *n* pl. **-S** a stew of various meats and vegetables

MULLION   *v* **-ED, -ING, -S** to provide with vertical dividing strips

MULLITE   *n* pl. **-S** a mineral

MULLOCK   *n* pl. **-S** waste earth or rock from a mine **MULLOCKY** *adj*

MULTIAGE   *adj* including people of various ages

MULTICAR   *adj* owning or involving several cars

MULTIDAY   *adj* lasting or usable for many days

MULTIFID   *adj* divided into many parts

MULTIJET   *adj* having more than two jets

MULTIPED   *n* pl. **-S** an animal having many feet

MULTIPLE   *n* pl. **-S** the product of a quantity by an integer

MULTIPLY   *v* **-PLIED, -PLYING, -PLIES** to increase in number

MULTITON   *adj* weighing many tons

MULTIUSE   *adj* having many uses

MULTURE   *n* pl. **-S** a fee paid to a miller for grinding grain

MUM   *v* **MUMMED, MUMMING, MUMS** to act in a disguise

MUMBLE   *v* **-BLED, -BLING, -BLES** to speak unclearly

MUMBLER   *n* pl. **-S** one that mumbles

MUMBLY   *adj* given to mumbling

MUMM   *v* **-ED, -ING, -S** to mum

MUMMED   past tense of mum and mumm

MUMMER   *n* pl. **-S** one that mums

MUMMERY   *n* pl. **-MERIES** a performance by mummers

MUMMIED   past tense of mummy

MUMMIES   present 3d person sing. of mummy

MUMMIFY   *v* **-FIED, -FYING, -FIES** to preserve by embalming

MUMMING   present participle of mum

MUMMY   *v* **-MIED, -MYING, -MIES** to mummify

MUMP   *v* **-ED, -ING, -S** to beg

MUMPER   *n* pl. **-S** one that mumps

MUMU   *n* pl. **-S** muumuu

MUN *n* pl. **-S** man; fellow

MUNCH *v* **-ED, -ING, -ES** to chew with a crackling sound

MUNCHER *n* pl. **-S** one that munches

MUNCHIES *n/pl* hunger pangs

MUNCHKIN *n* pl. **-S** a small friendly person

MUNDANE *adj* ordinary

MUNDUNGO *n* pl. **-GOS** a foul-smelling tobacco

MUNGO *n* pl. **-GOS** or **-GOES** a low-quality wool

MUNGOOSE *n* pl. **-S** mongoose

MUNI *n* pl. **-S** a security issued by a state or local government

MUNIMENT *n* pl. **-S** a means of defense

MUNITION *v* **-ED, -ING, -S** to furnish with war materiel

MUNNION *n* pl. **-S** a muntin

MUNSTER *n* pl. **-S** muenster

MUNTIN *n* pl. **-S** a dividing strip for window panes

MUNTING *n* pl. **-S** muntin

MUNTJAC *n* pl. **-S** a small Asian deer

MUNTJAK *n* pl. **-S** muntjac

MUON *n* pl. **-S** a subatomic particle **MUONIC** *adj*

MUONIUM *n* pl. **-S** an electron and a positive muon bound together

MURA *n* pl. **-S** a Japanese village

MURAENID *n* pl. **-S** a moray

MURAL *n* pl. **-S** a painting applied directly to a wall or ceiling **MURALED, MURALLED** *adj*

MURALIST *n* pl. **-S** a painter of murals

MURDER *v* **-ED, -ING, -S** to kill unlawfully with premeditated malice

MURDEREE *n* pl. **-S** one that is murdered

MURDERER *n* pl. **-S** one that murders

MURE *v* **MURED, MURING, MURES** to immure

MUREIN *n* pl. **-S** a type of polymer

MUREX *n* pl. **-REXES** or **-RICES** a marine mollusk

MURIATE *n* pl. **-S** chloride

MURIATED *adj* pickled

MURICATE *adj* covered with short, sharp points

MURICES a pl. of murex

MURID *n* pl. **-S** a murine

MURINE *n* pl. **-S** any of a family of small rodents

MURING present participle of mure

MURK *adj* **MURKER, MURKEST** dark **MURKLY** *adv*

MURK *n* pl. **-S** darkness

MURKY *adj* **MURKIER, MURKIEST** dark **MURKILY** *adv*

MURMUR *v* **-ED, -ING, -S** to speak unclearly

MURMURER *n* pl. **-S** one that murmurs

MURPHY *n* pl. **-PHIES** a potato

MURR *n* pl. **-S** murre

MURRA *n* pl. **-S** a substance used to make fine vases and cups in ancient Rome

MURRAIN *n* pl. **-S** a disease of cattle

MURRE *n* pl. **-S** a diving bird

MURRELET *n* pl. **-S** a small diving bird

MURREY *n* pl. **-REYS** a dark purple color

MURRHA *n* pl. **-S** murra **MURRHINE** *adj*

MURRINE *adj* pertaining to murra

MURRY *n* pl. **-RIES** a moray

MURTHER *v* **-ED, -ING, -S** to murder

MUSCA *n* pl. **-CAE** any of a genus of flies

MUSCADEL *n* pl. **-S** muscatel

MUSCADET *n* pl. **-S** a dry white French wine

MUSCAT *n* pl. **-S** a sweet, white grape

MUSCATEL *n* pl. **-S** a wine made from muscat grapes

MUSCID *n* pl. **-S** musca

MUSCLE *v* **-CLED, -CLING, -CLES** to proceed by force

MUSCLY *adj* composed of muscle (tissue that produces bodily movement)

MUSCULAR *adj* pertaining to muscle

MUSE *v* **MUSED, MUSING, MUSES** to ponder

MUSEFUL *adj* pensive

MUSER *n* pl. **-S** one that muses

MUSETTE *n* pl. **-S** a small bagpipe

MUSEUM *n* pl. **-S** a place where objects of lasting interest or value are cared for and exhibited

MUSH *v* **-ED, -ING, -ES** to travel over snow with a dog sled

MUSHER *n* pl. **-S** one that mushes

MUSHROOM *v* **-ED, -ING, -S** to grow or spread rapidly

MUSHY *adj* **MUSHIER, MUSHIEST** pulpy **MUSHILY** *adv*

MUSIC *n* pl. **-S** vocal or instrumental sounds organized to produce a unified composition

MUSICAL *n* pl. **-S** a play in which dialogue is interspersed with songs and dances

MUSICALE *n* pl. **-S** a program of music performed at a social gathering

MUSICIAN *n* pl. **-S** one who performs or composes music

MUSICK *v* **-ED, -ING, -S** to compose music for

MUSING *n* pl. **-S** contemplation

MUSINGLY *adv* in a pensive manner

MUSJID *n* pl. **-S** a mosque

MUSK *n* pl. **-S** a strongly odorous substance secreted by certain animals

MUSKEG *n* pl. **-S** a marsh

MUSKET *n* pl. **-S** a type of firearm

MUSKETRY *n* pl. **-RIES** the technique of firing small arms

MUSKIE *n* pl. **-S** a freshwater fish

MUSKIER comparative of musky

MUSKIEST superlative of musky

MUSKILY *adv* in a musky manner

MUSKIT *n* pl. **-S** mesquite

MUSKOX *n* pl. **-OXEN** a large bovid of arctic regions

MUSKRAT *n* pl. **-S** an aquatic rodent

MUSKROOT *n* pl. **-S** a perennial herb

MUSKY *adj* **MUSKIER, MUSKIEST** resembling musk

MUSLIN *n* pl. **-S** a cotton fabric

MUSPIKE *n* pl. **-S** a freshwater fish

MUSQUASH *n* pl. **-ES** the muskrat

MUSS *v* **-ED, -ING, -ES** to mess

MUSSEL *n* pl. **-S** a bivalve mollusk

MUSSY *adj* **MUSSIER, MUSSIEST** messy **MUSSILY** *adv*

MUST *v* **-ED, -ING, -S** to become musty

MUSTACHE *n* pl. **-S** a growth of hair on the upper lip

MUSTANG *n* pl. **-S** a wild horse

MUSTARD *n* pl. **-S** a pungent seasoning

MUSTARDY *adj* resembling mustard

MUSTEE *n* pl. **-S** an octoroon

MUSTELID *n* pl. **-S** a mammal of the weasel family

MUSTER *v* **-ED, -ING, -S** to summon or assemble

MUSTH *n* pl. **-S** a state of frenzy occurring in male elephants

MUSTY *adj* **MUSTIER, MUSTIEST** having a stale odor **MUSTILY** *adv*

MUT *n* pl. **-S** mutt

MUTABLE *adj* capable of change **MUTABLY** *adv*

MUTAGEN *n* pl. **-S** a substance that causes biological mutation

MUTANT *n* pl. **-S** something that undergoes mutation

MUTASE *n* pl. **-S** an enzyme

MUTATE *v* **-TATED, -TATING, -TATES** to undergo mutation

MUTATION *n* pl. **-S** the act of changing **MUTATIVE** *adj*

MUTCH *n* pl. **-ES** a close-fitting cap

MUTCHKIN *n* pl. **-S** a Scottish unit of liquid measure

MUTE *adj* **MUTER, MUTEST** characterized by an absence of speech **MUTELY** *adv*

MUTE *v* **MUTED, MUTING, MUTES** to deaden the sound of **MUTEDLY** *adv*

MUTENESS *n* pl. **-ES** the state of being mute

MUTER comparative of mute

MUTEST superlative of mute

MUTICOUS *adj* lacking a point

MUTILATE *v* **-LATED, -LATING, -LATES** to deprive of a limb or other essential part

MUTINE *v* **-TINED, -TINING, -TINES** to mutiny

MUTINEER *v* **-ED, -ING, -S** to mutiny

MUTING present participle of mute

MUTINIED past tense of mutiny

MUTINIES present 3d person sing. of mutiny

MUTINING present participle of mutine

MUTINOUS *adj* disposed to mutiny

MUTINY *v* **-NIED, -NYING, -NIES** to revolt against constituted authority

MUTISM *n* pl. **-S** muteness

MUTON *n* pl. **-S** a unit of nucleic acid

MUTT *n* pl. **-S** a mongrel dog

MUTTER *v* **-ED, -ING, -S** to speak unclearly

MUTTERER *n* pl. **-S** one that mutters

MUTTON *n* pl. **-S** the flesh of sheep used as food **MUTTONY** *adj*

MUTUAL *n* pl. **-S** a mutual fund

MUTUALLY *adv* in a manner shared in common

MUTUEL *n* pl. **-S** a system of betting on races

MUTULE *n* pl. **-S** an ornamental block used in classical Greek architecture **MUTULAR** *adj*

MUUMUU *n* pl. **-S** a long, loose dress

MUZHIK *n* pl. **-S** a Russian peasant

MUZJIK *n* pl. **-S** muzhik

MUZZIER comparative of muzzy

MUZZIEST superlative of muzzy

MUZZILY *adv* in a muzzy manner

MUZZLE *v* **-ZLED, -ZLING, -ZLES** to put a covering over the mouth of to prevent biting or eating

MUZZLER *n* pl. **-S** one that muzzles

MUZZY *adj* **-ZIER, -ZIEST** confused

MY *pron* the possessive form of the pronoun I

MYALGIA *n* pl. **-S** muscular pain **MYALGIC** *adj*

MYASIS *n* pl. **MYASES** myiasis

MYC *n* pl. **-S** a gene that transforms a normal cell into a cancerous cell

MYCELE *n* pl. **-S** mycelium

MYCELIUM *n* pl. **-LIA** the vegetative portion of a fungus **MYCELIAL, MYCELIAN, MYCELOID** *adj*

MYCETOMA *n* pl. **-MAS** or **-MATA** a fungous infection

MYCOLOGY *n* pl. **-GIES** the branch of botany dealing with fungi

MYCOSIS *n* pl. **-COSES** a disease caused by a fungus **MYCOTIC** *adj*

MYELIN *n* pl. **-S** a fatty substance that encases certain nerve fibers **MYELINIC** *adj*

MYELINE *n* pl. **-S** myelin

MYELITIS *n* pl. **-LITIDES** inflammation of the bone marrow

MYELOID *adj* pertaining to bone marrow

MYELOMA *n* pl. **-MAS** or **-MATA** a tumor of the bone marrow

MYIASIS *n* pl. **MYIASES** infestation of human tissue by fly maggots

MYLONITE *n* pl. **-S** a type of rock

MYNA *n* pl. **-S** an Asian bird

MYNAH *n* pl. **-S** myna

MYNHEER *n* pl. **-S** a Dutch title of courtesy for a man

MYOBLAST *n* pl. **-S** a cell capable of giving rise to muscle cells

MYOGENIC *adj* originating in muscle tissue

MYOGRAPH *n* pl. **-S** an instrument for recording muscular contractions

MYOID *adj* resembling muscle

MYOLOGY *n* pl. **-GIES** the study of muscles **MYOLOGIC** *adj*

MYOMA *n* pl. **-MAS** or **-MATA** a tumor composed of muscle tissue

MYOPATHY *n* pl. **-THIES** a disorder of muscle tissue

MYOPE *n* pl. **-S** one who is affected with myopia

MYOPIA *n* pl. **-S** a visual defect **MYOPIC** *adj*

MYOPY *n* pl. **-PIES** myopia

MYOSCOPE *n* pl. **-S** an instrument for observing muscular contractions

MYOSIN *n* pl. **-S** a protein found in muscle tissue

MYOSIS *n* pl. **MYOSES** miosis

MYOSITIS *n* pl. **-TISES** muscular pain from infection

MYOSOTE *n* pl. **-S** myosotis

MYOSOTIS *n* pl. **-TISES** a flowering plant

MYOTIC *n* pl. **-S** miotic

MYOTOME *n* pl. **-S** a portion of an embryonic somite

MYOTONIA *n* pl. **-S** temporary muscular rigidity **MYOTONIC** *adj*

MYRIAD *n* pl. **-S** a very large number

MYRIAPOD *n* pl. **-S** a multi-legged arthropod

MYRICA *n* pl. **-S** a medicinal tree bark

MYRIOPOD *n* pl. **-S** myriapod

MYRMIDON *n* pl. **-S** or **-ES** a loyal follower

MYRRH *n* pl. **-S** an aromatic gum resin **MYRRHIC** *adj*

MYRTLE *n* pl. **-S** an evergreen shrub

MYSELF *pron* a form of the 1st person sing. pronoun

MYSID *n* pl. **-S** a small crustacean

MYSOST *n* pl. **-S** a mild cheese

MYSTAGOG *n* pl. **-S** a teacher of religious mysteries

MYSTERY   *n* pl. **-TERIES** something that is not or cannot be known, understood, or explained

MYSTIC   *n* pl. **-S** one who professes to have had mystical experiences

MYSTICAL   *adj* spiritually significant or symbolic

MYSTICLY   *adv* in a mystical manner

MYSTIFY   *v* **-FIED, -FYING, -FIES** to perplex

MYSTIQUE   *n* pl. **-S** an aura of mystery or mystical power surrounding a particular person or thing

MYTH   *n* pl. **-S** a type of traditional story

MYTHIC   *adj* mythical

MYTHICAL   *adj* based on or described in a myth

MYTHOS   *n* pl. **-THOI** a myth

MYTHY   *adj* **MYTHIER, MYTHIEST** resembling myth

MYXAMEBA   *n* pl. **-BAS** or **-BAE** a slime mold that resembles an amoeba

MYXEDEMA   *n* pl. **-S** a disease caused by decreased activity of the thyroid gland

MYXOCYTE   *n* pl. **-S** a large cell found in mucous tissue

MYXOID   *adj* containing mucus

MYXOMA   *n* pl. **-MAS** or **-MATA** a tumor composed of mucous tissue

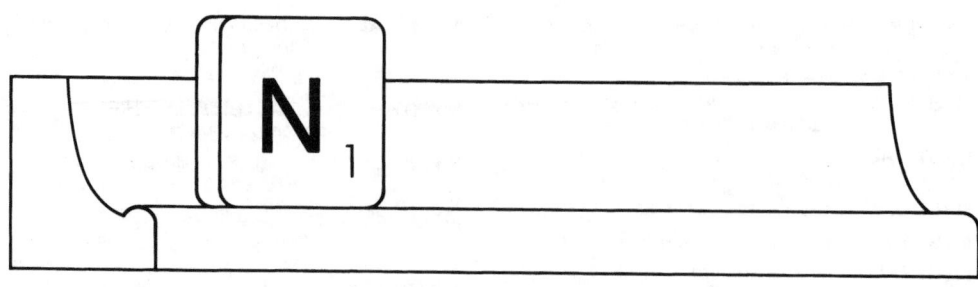

NA	*adv* no; not
NAAN	*n* pl. **-S** nan
NAB	*v* **NABBED, NABBING, NABS** to capture or arrest
NABBER	*n* pl. **-S** one that nabs
NABE	*n* pl. **-S** a neighborhood movie theater
NABIS	*n* pl. **NABIS** a group of French artists
NABOB	*n* pl. **-S** one who becomes rich and prominent **NABOBISH** *adj*
NABOBERY	*n* pl. **-ERIES** the state of being a nabob
NABOBESS	*n* pl. **-ES** a female nabob
NABOBISM	*n* pl. **-S** great wealth and luxury
NACELLE	*n* pl. **-S** a shelter on an aircraft
NACHAS	*n* pl. **NACHAS** pride in another's accomplishments
NACHES	*n* pl. **NACHES** nachas
NACHO	*n* pl. **-CHOS** a tortilla chip topped with cheese and a savory mixture and broiled
NACRE	*n* pl. **-S** the pearly internal layer of certain shells **NACRED, NACREOUS** *adj*
NADA	*n* pl. **-S** nothing
NADIR	*n* pl. **-S** a point on the celestial sphere **NADIRAL** *adj*
NAE	*adv* no; not
NAETHING	*n* pl. **-S** nothing
NAEVUS	*n* pl. **-VI** nevus **NAEVOID** *adj*
NAFF	*v* **-ED, -ING, -S** to fool around
NAG	*v* **NAGGED, NAGGING, NAGS** to find fault incessantly
NAGANA	*n* pl. **-S** a disease of horses in Africa
NAGGER	*n* pl. **-S** one that nags
NAGGY	*adj* **-GIER, -GIEST** given to nagging
NAH	*adv* no
NAIAD	*n* pl. **-S** or **-ES** a water nymph
NAIF	*n* pl. **-S** a naive person
NAIL	*v* **-ED, -ING, -S** to fasten with a nail (a slender piece of metal)
NAILER	*n* pl. **-S** one that nails
NAILFOLD	*n* pl. **-S** a fold of skin around the fingernail
NAILHEAD	*n* pl. **-S** the top of a nail
NAILSET	*n* pl. **-S** a steel rod for driving a nail into something
NAINSOOK	*n* pl. **-S** a cotton fabric
NAIRA	*n* pl. **-S** a monetary unit of Nigeria
NAIRU	*n* pl. **-S** the lowest rate of unemployment at which there is no inflation
NAIVE	*adj* **NAIVER, NAIVEST** lacking sophistication **NAIVELY** *adv*
NAIVE	*n* pl. **-S** a naive person
NAIVETE	*n* pl. **-S** the quality of being naive
NAIVETY	*n* pl. **-TIES** naivete
NAKED	*adj* **-KEDER, -KEDEST** being without clothing or covering **NAKEDLY** *adv*
NAKFA	*n* pl. **-S** a monetary unit of Eritrea
NALA	*n* pl. **-S** nullah
NALED	*n* pl. **-S** an insecticide
NALOXONE	*n* pl. **-S** a chemical compound
NAM	a past tense of nim
NAME	*v* **NAMED, NAMING, NAMES** to give a title to **NAMABLE, NAMEABLE** *adj*
NAMELESS	*adj* lacking distinction or fame
NAMELY	*adv* that is to say
NAMER	*n* pl. **-S** one that names
NAMESAKE	*n* pl. **-S** one who is named after another

NAMETAG — *n* pl. **-S** a tag bearing one's name worn for identification

NAMING — present participle of name

NAN — *n* pl. **-S** a round flat bread

NANA — *n* pl. **-S** a grandmother

NANDIN — *n* pl. **-S** an evergreen shrub

NANDINA — *n* pl. **-S** an Asian shrub

NANISM — *n* pl. **-S** abnormal smallness

NANKEEN — *n* pl. **-S** a cotton fabric

NANKIN — *n* pl. **-S** nankeen

NANNIE — *n* pl. **-S** nanny

NANNY — *n* pl. **-NIES** a children's nurse **NANNYISH** *adj*

NANOGRAM — *n* pl. **-S** a unit of mass and weight

NANOTECH — *n* pl. **-S** the technology of building electronic devices from individual atoms and molecules

NANOTUBE — *n* pl. **-S** a microscopic tube

NANOWATT — *n* pl. **-S** a unit of power

NAOS — *n* pl. **NAOI** an ancient temple

NAP — *v* **NAPPED, NAPPING, NAPS** to sleep briefly

NAPA — *n* pl. **-S** a soft leather

NAPALM — *v* **-ED, -ING, -S** to assault with a type of incendiary bomb

NAPE — *n* pl. **-S** the back of the neck

NAPERY — *n* pl. **-PERIES** table linen

NAPHTHA — *n* pl. **-S** a volatile liquid

NAPHTHOL — *n* pl. **-S** a chemical compound

NAPHTHYL — *n* pl. **-S** a radical derived from naphthalene

NAPHTOL — *n* pl. **-S** naphthol

NAPIFORM — *adj* shaped like a turnip

NAPKIN — *n* pl. **-S** a piece of material used to wipe the hands and mouth

NAPLESS — *adj* threadbare

NAPOLEON — *n* pl. **-S** a type of pastry

NAPPA — *n* pl. **-S** napa

NAPPE — *n* pl. **-S** a type of rock formation

NAPPED — past tense of nap

NAPPER — *n* pl. **-S** one that naps

NAPPIE — *n* pl. **-S** a diaper

NAPPING — present participle of nap

NAPPY — *adj* **-PIER, -PIEST** kinky

NAPROXEN — *n* pl. **-S** an anti-inflammatory drug

NARC — *n* pl. **-S** an undercover drug agent

NARCEIN — *n* pl. **-S** narceine

NARCEINE — *n* pl. **-S** an opium derivative

NARCISM — *n* pl. **-S** excessive love of oneself

NARCISSI — *n/pl* bulbous flowering plants

NARCIST — *n* pl. **-S** one given to narcism

NARCO — *n* pl. **-COS** narc

NARCOMA — *n* pl. **-MAS** or **-MATA** a stupor induced by a narcotic

NARCOSE — *adj* characterized by stupor

NARCOSIS — *n* pl. **-COSES** a drug-induced stupor

NARCOTIC — *n* pl. **-S** a drug that dulls the senses

NARD — *n* pl. **-S** a fragrant ointment **NARDINE** *adj*

NARES — pl. of naris

NARGHILE — *n* pl. **-S** a hookah

NARGILE — *n* pl. **-S** narghile

NARGILEH — *n* pl. **-S** narghile

NARIS — *n* pl. **NARES** a nostril **NARIAL, NARIC, NARINE** *adj*

NARK — *v* **-ED, -ING, -S** to spy or inform

NARKY — *adj* irritable

NARRATE — *v* **-RATED, -RATING, -RATES** to tell a story

NARRATER — *n* pl. **-S** narrator

NARRATOR — *n* pl. **-S** one that narrates

NARROW — *adj* **-ROWER, -ROWEST** of little width **NARROWLY** *adv*

NARROW — *v* **-ED, -ING, -S** to make narrow

NARTHEX — *n* pl. **-ES** a vestibule in a church

NARWAL — *n* pl. **-S** narwhal

NARWHAL — *n* pl. **-S** an arctic aquatic mammal

NARWHALE — *n* pl. **-S** narwhal

NARY — *adj* not one

NASAL — *n* pl. **-S** a sound uttered through the nose

NASALISE — *v* **-ISED, -ISING, -ISES** to nasalize

NASALISM — *n* pl. **-S** nasality

NASALITY — *n* pl. **-TIES** the quality or an instance of being produced nasally

NASALIZE — *v* **-IZED, -IZING, -IZES** to produce sounds nasally

NASALLY — *adv* through the nose

NASCENCE — *n* pl. **-S** nascency

NASCENCY — *n* pl. **-CIES** birth; origin

NASCENT — *adj* coming into existence

NASION	*n* pl. **-S** a point in the skull **NASIAL** *adj*
NASTIC	*adj* pertaining to an automatic response of plants
NASTY	*adj* **-TIER, -TIEST** offensive to the senses **NASTILY** *adv*
NASTY	*n* pl. **-TIES** something that is nasty
NATAL	*adj* pertaining to one's birth
NATALITY	*n* pl. **-TIES** birth rate
NATANT	*adj* floating or swimming **NATANTLY** *adv*
NATATION	*n* pl. **-S** the act of swimming
NATATORY	*adj* pertaining to swimming
NATCH	*adv* naturally
NATES	*n/pl* the buttocks
NATHLESS	*adv* nevertheless
NATION	*n* pl. **-S** a politically organized people who share a territory, customs, and history
NATIONAL	*n* pl. **-S** a citizen of a nation
NATIVE	*n* pl. **-S** an original inhabitant of an area
NATIVELY	*adv* in an inborn manner
NATIVISM	*n* pl. **-S** a policy of favoring the interests of native inhabitants
NATIVIST	*n* pl. **-S** an advocate of nativism
NATIVITY	*n* pl. **-TIES** the process of being born
NATRIUM	*n* pl. **-S** sodium
NATRON	*n* pl. **-S** a chemical compound
NATTER	*v* **-ED, -ING, -S** to chatter
NATTY	*adj* **-TIER, -TIEST** neatly dressed **NATTILY** *adv*
NATURAL	*n* pl. **-S** a type of musical note
NATURE	*n* pl. **-S** the essential qualities of a person or thing **NATURED** *adj*
NATURISM	*n* pl. **-S** nudism
NATURIST	*n* pl. **-S** a nudist
NAUGHT	*n* pl. **-S** a zero
NAUGHTY	*n* pl. **-TIES** one that is naughty
NAUGHTY	*adj* **-TIER, -TIEST** disobedient
NAUMACHY	*n* pl. **-CHIES** a mock sea battle
NAUPLIUS	*n* pl. **-PLII** a form of certain crustaceans **NAUPLIAL** *adj*
NAUSEA	*n* pl. **-S** a stomach disturbance
NAUSEANT	*n* pl. **-S** an agent that induces nausea
NAUSEATE	*v* **-ATED, -ATING, -ATES** to affect with nausea
NAUSEOUS	*adj* affected with nausea
NAUTCH	*n* pl. **-ES** a dancing exhibition in India
NAUTICAL	*adj* pertaining to ships
NAUTILUS	*n* pl. **-LUSES** or **-LI** a spiral-shelled mollusk
NAVAID	*n* pl. **-S** a navigational device
NAVAL	*adj* pertaining to ships **NAVALLY** *adv*
NAVAR	*n* pl. **-S** a system of air navigation
NAVE	*n* pl. **-S** the main part of a church
NAVEL	*n* pl. **-S** a depression in the abdomen
NAVETTE	*n* pl. **-S** a gem cut in a pointed oval form
NAVICERT	*n* pl. **-S** a document permitting a vessel passage through a naval blockade
NAVIES	pl. of navy
NAVIGATE	*v* **-GATED, -GATING, -GATES** to plan and control the course of
NAVVY	*n* pl. **-VIES** a manual laborer
NAVY	*n* pl. **-VIES** a nation's warships
NAW	*adv* no
NAWAB	*n* pl. **-S** a nabob
NAY	*n* pl. **NAYS** a negative vote
NAYSAY	*v* **-SAID, -SAYING, -SAYS** to oppose or deny
NAYSAYER	*n* pl. **-S** one that denies or opposes something
NAZI	*n* pl. **-S** a type of fascist
NAZIFY	*v* **-FIED, -FYING, -FIES** to cause to be like a nazi
NE	*adj* born with the name of
NEAP	*n* pl. **-S** a tide of lowest range
NEAR	*adj* **NEARER, NEAREST** situated within a short distance
NEAR	*v* **-ED, -ING, -S** to approach
NEARBY	*adj* near
NEARLY	*adv* **-LIER, -LIEST** with close approximation
NEARNESS	*n* pl. **-ES** the state of being near
NEARSIDE	*n* pl. **-S** the left side
NEAT	*adj* **NEATER, NEATEST** being in a state of cleanliness and order
NEAT	*n* pl. **-S** a bovine
NEATEN	*v* **-ED, -ING, -S** to make neat
NEATH	*prep* beneath
NEATHERD	*n* pl. **-S** a cowherd

NEATLY *adv* in a neat manner

NEATNESS *n* pl. **-ES** the state of being neat

NEATNIK *n* pl. **-S** a compulsively neat person

NEB *n* pl. **-S** the beak of a bird

NEBBISH *n* pl. **-ES** a meek person **NEBBISHY** *adj*

NEBULA *n* pl. **-LAS** or **-LAE** a cloud-like interstellar mass **NEBULAR** *adj*

NEBULE *adj* composed of successive short curves

NEBULISE *v* **-LISED, -LISING, -LISES** to nebulize

NEBULIZE *v* **-LIZED, -LIZING, -LIZES** to reduce to a fine spray

NEBULOSE *adj* nebulous

NEBULOUS *adj* unclear

NEBULY *adj* nebule

NECK *v* **-ED, -ING, -S** to kiss and caress in lovemaking

NECKBAND *n* pl. **-S** a band worn around the neck (the part of the body joining the head to the trunk)

NECKER *n* pl. **-S** one that necks

NECKING *n* pl. **-S** a small molding near the top of a column

NECKLACE *v* **-LACED, -LACING, -LACES** to kill by placing a tire around the neck and setting it on fire

NECKLESS *adj* having no neck

NECKLIKE *adj* resembling the neck

NECKLINE *n* pl. **-S** the line formed by the neck opening of a garment

NECKTIE *n* pl. **-S** a strip of fabric worn around the neck

NECKWEAR *n* pl. **NECKWEAR** something that is worn around the neck

NECROPSY *v* **-SIED, -SYING, -SIES** to perform an autopsy on

NECROSE *v* **-CROSED, -CROSING, -CROSES** to affect with necrosis

NECROSIS *n* pl. **-CROSES** the death of living tissue **NECROTIC** *adj*

NECTAR *n* pl. **-S** a delicious drink

NECTARY *n* pl. **-TARIES** a plant gland

NEDDY *n* pl. **-DIES** a donkey

NEE *adj* born with the name of

NEED *v* **-ED, -ING, -S** to have an urgent or essential use for

NEEDER *n* pl. **-S** one that needs

NEEDFUL *n* pl. **-S** something that is needed

NEEDIER comparative of needy

NEEDIEST superlative of needy

NEEDILY *adv* in a needy manner

NEEDLE *v* **-DLED, -DLING, -DLES** to sew with a slender, pointed instrument

NEEDLER *n* pl. **-S** one that needles

NEEDLESS *adj* not necessary

NEEDLING *n* pl. **-S** the act of one who needles

NEEDY *adj* **NEEDIER, NEEDIEST** in a state of poverty

NEEM *n* pl. **-S** an East Indian tree

NEEP *n* pl. **-S** a turnip

NEG *n* pl. **-S** a photographic negative

NEGATE *v* **-GATED, -GATING, -GATES** to nullify

NEGATER *n* pl. **-S** one that negates

NEGATION *n* pl. **-S** the act of negating

NEGATIVE *v* **-TIVED, -TIVING, -TIVES** to veto

NEGATON *n* pl. **-S** negatron

NEGATOR *n* pl. **-S** negater

NEGATRON *n* pl. **-S** an electron

NEGLECT *v* **-ED, -ING, -S** to fail to pay attention to

NEGLIGE *n* pl. **-S** negligee

NEGLIGEE *n* pl. **-S** a woman's dressing gown

NEGROID *n* pl. **-S** member of the black race

NEGRONI *n* pl. **-S** an alcoholic beverage

NEGUS *n* pl. **-ES** an alcoholic beverage

NEIF *n* pl. **-S** nieve

NEIGH *v* **-ED, -ING, -S** to utter the cry of a horse

NEIGHBOR *v* **-ED, -ING, -S** to live close to

NEIST *adj* next

NEITHER *adj* not one or the other

NEKTON *n* pl. **-S** free-swimming marine animals **NEKTONIC** *adj*

NELLIE *n* pl. **-S** an effeminate male

NELLY *n* pl. **-LIES** nellie

NELSON *n* pl. **-S** a wrestling hold

NELUMBO *n* pl. **-BOS** an aquatic herb

NEMA *n* pl. **-S** a nematode

NEMATIC *adj* pertaining to a phase of a liquid crystal

NEMATODE *n* pl. **-S** a kind of worm

NEMESIS *n* pl. **NEMESES** a formidable opponent

NENE *n* pl. **-S** a Hawaiian goose

NEOCON *n* pl. **-S** a neoconservative

NEOLITH *n* pl. **-S** an ancient stone implement

NEOLOGY *n* pl. **-GIES** a new word or phrase **NEOLOGIC** *adj*

NEOMORPH *n* pl. **-S** a type of biological structure

NEOMYCIN *n* pl. **-S** an antibiotic drug

NEON *n* pl. **-S** a gaseous element **NEONED** *adj*

NEONATE *n* pl. **-S** a newborn child **NEONATAL** *adj*

NEOPHYTE *n* pl. **-S** a novice

NEOPLASM *n* pl. **-S** a tumor

NEOPRENE *n* pl. **-S** a synthetic rubber

NEOTENY *n* pl. **-NIES** attainment of sexual maturity in the larval stage **NEOTENIC** *adj*

NEOTERIC *n* pl. **-S** a modern author

NEOTYPE *n* pl. **-S** a specimen of a species

NEPENTHE *n* pl. **-S** a drug that induces forgetfulness

NEPETA *n* pl. **-S** catnip

NEPHEW *n* pl. **-S** a son of one's brother or sister

NEPHRIC *adj* renal

NEPHRISM *n* pl. **-S** ill health caused by a kidney disease

NEPHRITE *n* pl. **-S** a mineral

NEPHRON *n* pl. **-S** an excretory unit of a kidney

NEPOTISM *n* pl. **-S** favoritism shown to a relative **NEPOTIC** *adj*

NEPOTIST *n* pl. **-S** one who practices nepotism

NERD *n* pl. **-S** a socially inept person **NERDISH** *adj*

NERDY *adj* **NERDIER, NERDIEST** socially inept

NEREID *n* pl. **-S** a sea nymph

NEREIS *n* pl. **-REIDES** a marine worm

NERITIC *adj* pertaining to shallow water

NEROL *n* pl. **-S** a fragrant alcohol

NEROLI *n* pl. **-S** a fragrant oil

NERTS *interj* — used to express defiance

NERTZ *interj* nerts

NERVATE *adj* having veins

NERVE *v* **NERVED, NERVING, NERVES** to give courage to

NERVIER comparative of nervy

NERVIEST superlative of nervy

NERVILY *adv* in a nervy manner

NERVINE *n* pl. **-S** a soothing medicine

NERVING *n* pl. **-S** a type of veterinary operation

NERVOUS *adj* easily excited

NERVULE *n* pl. **-S** nervure

NERVURE *n* pl. **-S** a vascular ridge on a leaf

NERVY *adj* **NERVIER, NERVIEST** impudent

NESCIENT *n* pl. **-S** one who is ignorant

NESS *n* pl. **-ES** a headland

NEST *v* **-ED, -ING, -S** to build a nest (a structure for holding bird eggs)

NESTABLE *adj* capable of being fitted closely within another container

NESTER *n* pl. **-S** one that nests

NESTLE *v* **-TLED, -TLING, -TLES** to lie snugly

NESTLER *n* pl. **-S** one that nestles

NESTLIKE *adj* resembling a nest

NESTLING *n* pl. **-S** a young bird

NESTOR *n* pl. **-S** a wise old man

NET *v* **NETTED, NETTING, NETS** to catch in a net (a type of openwork fabric)

NETHER *adj* situated below

NETIZEN *n* pl. **-S** a frequent user of the Internet

NETLESS *adj* having no net

NETLIKE *adj* resembling a net

NETOP *n* pl. **-S** friend; companion

NETSUKE *n* pl. **-S** a button-like fixture on Japanese clothing

NETT *v* **-ED, -ING, -S** to net

NETTABLE *adj* capable of being netted

NETTED past tense of net, nett

NETTER *n* pl. **-S** one that nets

NETTIER comparative of netty

NETTIEST superlative of netty

NETTING *n* pl. **-S** a net

NETTLE *v* **-TLED, -TLING, -TLES** to make angry

NETTLER *n* pl. **-S** one that nettles

NETTLY *adj* **-TLIER, -TLIEST** prickly

NETTY	*adj* **-TIER, -TIEST** resembling a net
NETWORK	*v* **-ED, -ING, -S** to cover with or as if with crossing lines
NEUK	*n* pl. **-S** nook
NEUM	*n* pl. **-S** neume
NEUME	*n* pl. **-S** a sign used in musical notation **NEUMATIC, NEUMIC** *adj*
NEURAL	*adj* pertaining to the nervous system **NEURALLY** *adv*
NEURAXON	*n* pl. **-S** a part of a neuron
NEURINE	*n* pl. **-S** a ptomaine poison
NEURITIC	*n* pl. **-S** one affected with neuritis
NEURITIS	*n* pl. **-RITISES** or **-RITIDES** inflammation of a nerve
NEUROID	*adj* resembling a nerve
NEUROMA	*n* pl. **-MAS** or **-MATA** a type of tumor
NEURON	*n* pl. **-S** the basic cellular unit of the nervous system **NEURONAL, NEURONIC** *adj*
NEURONE	*n* pl. **-S** neuron
NEUROSIS	*n* pl. **-ROSES** a type of emotional disturbance **NEUROSAL** *adj*
NEUROTIC	*n* pl. **-S** one affected with a neurosis
NEURULA	*n* pl. **-LAS** or **-LAE** a vertebrate embryo **NEURULAR** *adj*
NEUSTON	*n* pl. **-S** an aggregate of small aquatic organisms **NEUSTIC** *adj*
NEUTER	*v* **-ED, -ING, -S** to castrate
NEUTRAL	*n* pl. **-S** one that is impartial
NEUTRINO	*n* pl. **-NOS** a subatomic particle
NEUTRON	*n* pl. **-S** a subatomic particle
NEVE	*n* pl. **-S** a granular snow
NEVER	*adv* at no time
NEVUS	*n* pl. **-VI** a birthmark **NEVOID** *adj*
NEW	*adj* **NEWER, NEWEST** existing only a short time
NEW	*n* pl. **-S** something that is new
NEWBIE	*n* pl. **-S** a newcomer
NEWBORN	*n* pl. **-S** a recently born infant
NEWCOMER	*n* pl. **-S** one that has recently arrived
NEWEL	*n* pl. **-S** a staircase support
NEWFOUND	*adj* newly found
NEWIE	*n* pl. **-S** something new
NEWISH	*adj* somewhat new
NEWLY	*adv* recently
NEWLYWED	*n* pl. **-S** a person recently married
NEWMOWN	*adj* recently mown
NEWNESS	*n* pl. **-ES** the state of being new
NEWS	*n/pl* a report of recent events
NEWSBEAT	*n* pl. **-S** a news source that a reporter is assigned to cover
NEWSBOY	*n* pl. **-BOYS** a boy who delivers or sells newspapers
NEWSCAST	*n* pl. **-S** a news broadcast
NEWSDESK	*n* pl. **-S** the department that receives late-breaking news
NEWSGIRL	*n* pl. **-S** a girl who delivers or sells newspapers
NEWSHAWK	*n* pl. **-S** a newspaper reporter
NEWSIE	*n* pl. **-S** newsy
NEWSIER	comparative of newsy
NEWSIES	pl. of newsy
NEWSIEST	superlative of newsy
NEWSLESS	*adj* having no news
NEWSMAN	*n* pl. **-MEN** a news reporter
NEWSPEAK	*n* pl. **-S** a deliberately ambiguous language
NEWSREEL	*n* pl. **-S** a short movie presenting current events
NEWSROOM	*n* pl. **-S** a room where the news is gathered
NEWSWIRE	*n* pl. **-S** a news agency that transmits news copy to subscribers
NEWSY	*adj* **NEWSIER, NEWSIEST** full of news
NEWSY	*n* pl. **NEWSIES** a newsboy
NEWT	*n* pl. **-S** a small salamander
NEWTON	*n* pl. **-S** a unit of force
NEWWAVER	*n* pl. **-S** a member of a new-wave movement
NEXT	*adj* coming immediately after; adjoining
NEXTDOOR	*adj* located in the next building or room
NEXUS	*n* pl. **-ES** a connection or link
NGULTRUM	*n* pl. **-S** a monetary unit of Bhutan
NGWEE	*n* pl. **NGWEE** a monetary unit of Zambia
NIACIN	*n* pl. **-S** a B vitamin
NIB	*v* **NIBBED, NIBBING, NIBS** to provide with a penpoint
NIBBLE	*v* **-BLED, -BLING, -BLES** to eat with small bites

NIBBLER *n* pl. **-S** one that nibbles

NIBLICK *n* pl. **-S** a golf club

NIBLIKE *adj* resembling a penpoint

NICAD *n* pl. **-S** nickel cadmium

NICE *adj* **NICER, NICEST** pleasing to the senses **NICELY** *adv*

NICENESS *n* pl. **-ES** the quality of being nice

NICETY *n* pl. **-TIES** a fine point or distinction

NICHE *v* **NICHED, NICHING, NICHES** to place in a receding space or hollow

NICK *v* **-ED, -ING, -S** to make a shallow cut in

NICKEL *v* **-ELED, -ELING, -ELS** or **-ELLED, -ELLING, -ELS** to plate with nickel (a metallic element)

NICKELIC *adj* pertaining to or containing nickel

NICKER *v* **-ED, -ING, -S** to neigh

NICKLE *v* **-LED, -LING, -LES** to nickel

NICKNACK *n* pl. **-S** a trinket

NICKNAME *v* **-NAMED, -NAMING, -NAMES** to give an alternate name to

NICOISE *adj* served with black olives, tomatoes, olive oil, and often anchovies

NICOL *n* pl. **-S** a type of prism

NICOTIN *n* pl. **-S** nicotine

NICOTINE *n* pl. **-S** a poisonous alkaloid in tobacco

NICTATE *v* **-TATED, -TATING, -TATES** to wink

NIDAL *adj* pertaining to a nidus

NIDATE *v* **-DATED, -DATING, -DATES** to become implanted in the uterus

NIDATION *n* pl. **-S** the act of nidating

NIDE *v* **NIDED, NIDING, NIDES** to nest

NIDERING *n* pl. **-S** a coward

NIDGET *n* pl. **-S** an idiot

NIDI a pl. of nidus

NIDIFY *v* **-FIED, -FYING, -FIES** to nest

NIDING present participle of nide

NIDUS *n* pl. **NIDUSES** or **NIDI** a nest or breeding place

NIECE *n* pl. **-S** a daughter of one's brother or sister

NIELLIST *n* pl. **-S** one that niellos

NIELLO *n* pl. **-LOS** or **-LI** a black metallic substance

NIELLO *v* **-ED, -ING, -S** to decorate with niello

NIEVE *n* pl. **-S** the fist or hand

NIFFER *v* **-ED, -ING, -S** to barter

NIFTY *adj* **-TIER, -TIEST** stylish; pleasing **NIFTILY** *adv*

NIFTY *n* pl. **-TIES** something that is nifty

NIGELLA *n* pl. **-S** an annual herb

NIGGARD *v* **-ED, -ING, -S** to act stingily

NIGGLE *v* **-GLED, -GLING, -GLES** to worry over petty details

NIGGLER *n* pl. **-S** one that niggles

NIGGLING *n* pl. **-S** petty or meticulous work

NIGGLY *adj* **-GLIER, -GLIEST** petty

NIGH *adj* **NIGHER, NIGHEST** near

NIGH *v* **-ED, -ING, -S** to approach

NIGHNESS *n* pl. **-ES** the state of being nigh

NIGHT *n* pl. **-S** the period from sunset to sunrise

NIGHTCAP *n* pl. **-S** a cap worn to bed

NIGHTIE *n* pl. **-S** a nightgown

NIGHTJAR *n* pl. **-S** a nocturnal bird

NIGHTLY *adv* every night; at night

NIGHTY *n* pl. **NIGHTIES** nightie

NIGRIFY *v* **-FIED, -FYING, -FIES** to make black

NIGROSIN *n* pl. **-S** a type of dye

NIHIL *n* pl. **-S** nothing

NIHILISM *n* pl. **-S** a doctrine that denies traditional values

NIHILIST *n* pl. **-S** an adherent of nihilism

NIHILITY *n* pl. **-TIES** the state of being nothing

NIL *n* pl. **-S** nothing

NILGAI *n* pl. **-S** a large antelope

NILGAU *n* pl. **-S** nilgai

NILGHAI *n* pl. **-S** nilgai

NILGHAU *n* pl. **-S** nilgai

NILL *v* **-ED, -ING, -S** to be unwilling

NIM *v* **NIMMED** or **NAM, NIMMING, NIMS** to steal

NIMBLE *adj* **-BLER, -BLEST** agile **NIMBLY** *adv*

NIMBUS *n* pl. **-BUSES** or **-BI** a luminous cloud **NIMBUSED** *adj*

NIMIETY *n* pl. **-ETIES** excess **NIMIOUS** *adj*

NIMMED past tense of nim

NIMMING present participle of nim

NIMROD *n* pl. **-S** a hunter

NINE *n* pl. **-S** a number

NINEBARK *n* pl. **-S** a flowering shrub

NINEFOLD *adj* nine times as great

NINEPIN *n* pl. **-S** a wooden pin used in a bowling game

NINETEEN *n* pl. **-S** a number

NINETY *n* pl. **-TIES** a number

NINJA *n* pl. **-S** a feudal Japanese warrior

NINNY *n* pl. **-NIES** a fool **NINNYISH** *adj*

NINON *n* pl. **-S** a sheer fabric

NINTH *n* pl. **-S** one of nine equal parts

NINTHLY *adv* in the ninth place

NIOBATE *n* pl. **-S** a chemical salt

NIOBITE *n* pl. **-S** the mineral columbite

NIOBIUM *n* pl. **-S** a metallic element **NIOBIC, NIOBOUS** *adj*

NIP *v* **NIPPED, NIPPING, NIPS** to pinch

NIPA *n* pl. **-S** a palm tree

NIPPER *n* pl. **-S** one that nips

NIPPIER comparative of nippy

NIPPIEST superlative of nippy

NIPPILY *adv* in a nippy manner

NIPPING present participle of nip

NIPPLE *n* pl. **-S** a protuberance on the breast **NIPPLED** *adj*

NIPPY *adj* **-PIER, -PIEST** sharp or biting

NIRVANA *n* pl. **-S** a blessed state in Buddhism **NIRVANIC** *adj*

NISEI *n* pl. **-S** one born in America of immigrant Japanese parents

NISI *adj* not yet final

NISUS *n* pl. **NISUS** an effort

NIT *n* pl. **-S** the egg of a parasitic insect

NITE *n* pl. **-S** night

NITER *n* pl. **-S** a chemical salt

NITERIE *n* pl. **-S** nitery

NITERY *n* pl. **-ERIES** a nightclub

NITID *adj* bright

NITINOL *n* pl. **-S** an alloy of nickel and titanium

NITON *n* pl. **-S** radon

NITPICK *v* **-ED, -ING, -S** to fuss over petty details

NITPICKY *adj* **-PICKIER, -PICKIEST** tending to nitpick

NITRATE *v* **-TRATED, -TRATING, -TRATES** to treat with nitric acid

NITRATOR *n* pl. **-S** one that nitrates

NITRE *n* pl. **-S** niter

NITRIC *adj* containing nitrogen

NITRID *n* pl. **-S** nitride

NITRIDE *v* **-TRIDED, -TRIDING, -TRIDES** to convert into a nitride (a compound of nitrogen)

NITRIFY *v* **-FIED, -FYING, -FIES** to combine with nitrogen

NITRIL *n* pl. **-S** nitrile

NITRILE *n* pl. **-S** a chemical compound

NITRITE *n* pl. **-S** a salt of nitrous acid

NITRO *n* pl. **-TROS** a nitrated product

NITROGEN *n* pl. **-S** a gaseous element

NITROLIC *adj* pertaining to a class of acids

NITROSO *adj* containing nitrosyl

NITROSYL *n* pl. **-S** a univalent radical

NITROUS *adj* containing nitrogen

NITTY *adj* **-TIER, -TIEST** full of nits

NITWIT *n* pl. **-S** a stupid person

NIVAL *adj* pertaining to snow

NIVEOUS *adj* resembling snow

NIX *n* pl. **NIXES** or **NIXE** a water sprite

NIX *v* **-ED, -ING, -ES** to veto

NIXIE *n* pl. **-S** a female water sprite

NIXY *n* pl. **NIXIES** an undeliverable piece of mail

NIZAM *n* pl. **-S** a former sovereign of India

NIZAMATE *n* pl. **-S** the territory of a nizam

NO *n* pl. **NOS** or **NOES** a negative reply

NOB *n* pl. **-S** a wealthy person

NOBBIER comparative of nobby

NOBBIEST superlative of nobby

NOBBILY *adv* in a nobby manner

NOBBLE *v* **-BLED, -BLING, -BLES** to disable a racehorse

NOBBLER *n* pl. **-S** one that nobbles

NOBBY *adj* **-BIER, -BIEST** elegant

NOBELIUM *n* pl. **-S** a radioactive element

NOBILITY *n* pl. **-TIES** the social class composed of nobles

NOBLE	adj **-BLER, -BLEST** possessing qualities of excellence
NOBLE	n pl. **-S** a person of high birth, rank, or title
NOBLEMAN	n pl. **-MEN** a noble
NOBLER	comparative of noble
NOBLESSE	n pl. **-S** the nobility
NOBLEST	superlative of noble
NOBLY	adv in a noble manner
NOBODY	n pl. **-BODIES** an unimportant person
NOCENT	adj harmful
NOCK	v **-ED, -ING, -S** to notch a bow or arrow
NOCTUID	n pl. **-S** a night-flying moth **NOCTUOID** adj
NOCTULE	n pl. **-S** a large bat
NOCTURN	n pl. **-S** a religious service
NOCTURNE	n pl. **-S** a musical composition
NOCUOUS	adj harmful
NOD	v **NODDED, NODDING, NODS** to briefly lower the head forward
NODAL	adj of the nature of a node **NODALLY** adv
NODALITY	n pl. **-TIES** the state of being nodal
NODDED	past tense of nod
NODDER	n pl. **-S** one that nods
NODDIES	pl. of noddy
NODDING	present participle of nod
NODDLE	v **-DLED, -DLING, -DLES** to nod frequently
NODDY	n pl. **-DIES** a fool
NODE	n pl. **-S** a swollen enlargement
NODI	pl. of nodus
NODICAL	adj pertaining to an astronomical point
NODOSE	adj having nodes
NODOSITY	n pl. **-TIES** the state of being nodose
NODOUS	adj nodose
NODULE	n pl. **-S** a small node **NODULAR, NODULOSE, NODULOUS** adj
NODUS	n pl. **-DI** a difficulty
NOEL	n pl. **-S** a Christmas carol
NOES	a pl. of no
NOESIS	n pl. **-SISES** the process of reason
NOETIC	adj pertaining to reason

NOG	v **NOGGED, NOGGING, NOGS** to fill in a space in a wall with bricks
NOGG	n pl. **-S** a strong ale
NOGGIN	n pl. **-S** a small cup
NOGGING	n pl. **-S** a type of masonry
NOH	n pl. **NOH** the classical drama of Japan
NOHOW	adv in no manner
NOIL	n pl. **-S** a kind of short fiber **NOILY** adj
NOIR	n pl. **-S** a bleak type of crime fiction **NOIRISH** adj
NOISE	v **NOISED, NOISING, NOISES** to spread as a rumor or report
NOISETTE	n pl. **-S** a small round piece of meat
NOISOME	adj disgusting; harmful
NOISY	adj **NOISIER, NOISIEST** making loud sounds **NOISILY** adv
NOLO	n pl. **-LOS** a type of legal plea
NOM	n pl. **-S** a name
NOMA	n pl. **-S** a severe inflammation of the mouth
NOMAD	n pl. **-S** a wanderer **NOMADIC** adj
NOMADISM	n pl. **-S** the mode of life of a nomad
NOMARCH	n pl. **-S** the head of a nome
NOMARCHY	n pl. **-ARCHIES** a nome
NOMBLES	n/pl numbles
NOMBRIL	n pl. **-S** a point on a heraldic shield
NOME	n pl. **-S** a province of modern Greece
NOMEN	n pl. **-MINA** the second name of an ancient Roman
NOMINAL	n pl. **-S** a word used as a noun
NOMINATE	v **-NATED, -NATING, -NATES** to name as a candidate
NOMINEE	n pl. **-S** one that is nominated
NOMISM	n pl. **-S** strict adherence to moral law **NOMISTIC** adj
NOMOGRAM	n pl. **-S** a type of graph
NOMOLOGY	n pl. **-GIES** the science of law
NOMOS	n pl. **NOMOI** law
NONA	n pl. **-S** a virus disease
NONACID	n pl. **-S** a substance that is not an acid
NONACTOR	n pl. **-S** a person who is not an actor
NONADULT	n pl. **-S** a person who is not an adult

NONAGE *n* pl. **-S** a period of immaturity

NONAGON *n* pl. **-S** a nine-sided polygon

NONART *n* pl. **-S** something that is not art

NONBANK *n* pl. **-S** a business that is not a bank

NONBASIC *adj* not basic

NONBEING *n* pl. **-S** lack of being

NONBLACK *n* pl. **-S** one that is not black

NONBODY *n* pl. **-BODIES** a person's nonphysical nature

NONBOOK *n* pl. **-S** a book of little literary merit

NONBRAND *adj* lacking a brand name

NONCASH *adj* other than cash

NONCE *n* pl. **-S** the present occasion

NONCLASS *n* pl. **-ES** a lack of class

NONCLING *adj* not clinging

NONCOLA *n* pl. **-S** a beverage that is not a cola

NONCOLOR *n* pl. **-S** a lack of color

NONCOM *n* pl. **-S** a noncommissioned officer

NONCORE *adj* not being in or relating to a central part

NONCRIME *n* pl. **-S** something that is not a crime

NONDAIRY *adj* having no milk products

NONDANCE *n* pl. **-S** an unrhythmic dance

NONDRIP *adj* that does not drip

NONDRUG *adj* not involving drugs

NONE *n* pl. **-S** one of seven canonical daily periods for prayer and devotion

NONEGO *n* pl. **-GOS** all that is not part of the ego

NONELECT *adj* not chosen

NONELITE *adj* not belonging to an elite group

NONEMPTY *adj* not empty

NONENTRY *n* pl. **-TRIES** the fact of not entering

NONEQUAL *n* pl. **-S** one that is not equal

NONESUCH *n* pl. **-ES** a person or thing without an equal

NONET *n* pl. **-S** a composition for nine instruments or voices

NONEVENT *n* pl. **-S** an expected event that does not occur

NONFACT *n* pl. **-S** a statement not based on fact

NONFAN *n* pl. **-S** a person who is not a fan (an enthusiast)

NONFARM *adj* not pertaining to the farm

NONFAT *adj* having no fat solids

NONFATAL *adj* not fatal

NONFATTY *adj* not fatty

NONFINAL *adj* not being the last

NONFLUID *n* pl. **-S** a substance that is not a fluid

NONFOCAL *adj* not focal

NONFOOD *adj* pertaining to something other than food

NONFUEL *adj* not used as a fuel

NONGAME *adj* not hunted for food, sport, or fur

NONGAY *n* pl. **-S** a person who is not a homosexual

NONGLARE *n* pl. **-S** a lack of glare (harsh brilliant light)

NONGREEN *adj* not green

NONGUEST *n* pl. **-S** one who is not a guest

NONGUILT *n* pl. **-S** the absence of guilt

NONHARDY *adj* not hardy

NONHEME *adj* not containing iron that is bound like that of heme

NONHERO *n* pl. **-ROES** an antihero

NONHOME *adj* not taking place in the home

NONHUMAN *n* pl. **-S** one that is not a human

NONIDEAL *adj* not ideal

NONIMAGE *n* pl. **-S** one having no celebrity status

NONINERT *adj* not inactive

NONIONIC *adj* not ionic

NONIRON *adj* not needing to be ironed

NONISSUE *n* pl. **-S** a topic that is not controversial

NONJUROR *n* pl. **-S** one who refuses to take a required oath

NONJURY *n* pl. **-RIES** a case not involving a jury

NONLABOR *adj* not pertaining to labor

NONLEAFY *adj* not having leaves

NONLEGAL *adj* not legal

NONLEVEL *adj* not flat or even

NONLIFE *n* pl. **-LIVES** the absence of life

NONLOCAL *n* pl. **-S** one that is not local

NONLOYAL *adj* not loyal

NONLYRIC *adj* not lyrical

NONMAJOR *n* pl. **-S** a student who is not majoring in a specified subject

NONMAN _n_ pl. **-MEN** a being that is not a man

NONMEAT _adj_ not containing meat

NONMETAL _n_ pl. **-S** an element that lacks metallic properties

NONMETRO _adj_ not metropolitan

NONMODAL _adj_ not modal

NONMONEY _adj_ not involving money

NONMORAL _adj_ not pertaining to morals

NONMUSIC _n_ pl. **-S** inferior music

NONNASAL _adj_ not involving the nose

NONNAVAL _adj_ not naval

NONNEWS _adj_ not being news

NONNOBLE _adj_ not noble

NONNOVEL _n_ pl. **-S** a literary work that is not a novel

NONOBESE _adj_ not obese

NONOHMIC _adj_ not measured in ohms

NONOILY _adj_ not oily

NONORAL _adj_ not involving the mouth

NONOWNER _n_ pl. **-S** one who is not the owner

NONPAGAN _n_ pl. **-S** one who is not a pagan

NONPAID _adj_ not paid

NONPAPAL _adj_ not papal

NONPAR _adj_ being a stock that has no face value

NONPARTY _n_ pl. **-TIES** one not belonging to a party

NONPAST _n_ pl. **-S** a verb form that lacks an inflection for a past tense

NONPEAK _adj_ being a time when something is not at its highest level

NONPLAY _n_ pl. **-PLAYS** a theatrical work that is not a play

NONPLUS _v_ **-PLUSED, -PLUSING, -PLUSES** or **-PLUSSED, -PLUSSING, -PLUSSES** to baffle

NONPOINT _adj_ not occurring at a definite single site

NONPOLAR _adj_ not polar

NONPOOR _adj_ not being poor

NONPRINT _adj_ not involving printed material

NONPROS _v_ **-PROSSED, -PROSSING, -PROSSES** to enter a judgment against a plaintiff who fails to prosecute

NONQUOTA _adj_ not included in or subject to a quota

NONRATED _adj_ not rated

NONRIGID _adj_ not rigid

NONRIVAL _n_ pl. **-S** an unimportant rival

NONROYAL _adj_ not royal

NONRURAL _adj_ not rural

NONSELF _n_ pl. **-SELVES** foreign material in a body

NONSENSE _n_ pl. **-S** behavior or language that is meaningless or absurd

NONSKED _n_ pl. **-S** an airline without scheduled flying times

NONSKID _adj_ designed to inhibit skidding

NONSKIER _n_ pl. **-S** one that does not ski

NONSLIP _adj_ designed to prevent slipping

NONSOLAR _adj_ not solar

NONSOLID _n_ pl. **-S** a substance that is not a solid

NONSTICK _adj_ allowing of easy removal of cooked food particles

NONSTOP _n_ pl. **-S** a flight without a stop en route

NONSTORY _n_ pl. **-RIES** an insignificant news story

NONSTYLE _n_ pl. **-S** a style that is not identifiable

NONSUCH _n_ pl. **-ES** nonesuch

NONSUGAR _n_ pl. **-S** a substance that is not a sugar

NONSUIT _v_ **-ED, -ING, -S** to dismiss the lawsuit of

NONTAX _n_ pl. **-ES** a tax of little consequence

NONTIDAL _adj_ not tidal

NONTITLE _adj_ pertaining to an athletic contest in which a title is not at stake

NONTONAL _adj_ lacking tonality

NONTONIC _adj_ not based on the first tone of a scale

NONTOXIC _adj_ not toxic

NONTRUMP _adj_ not having a trump

NONTRUTH _n_ pl. **-S** something that is not true

NONUNION _n_ pl. **-S** failure of a broken bone to heal

NONUPLE _n_ pl. **-S** a number nine times as great as another

NONURBAN _adj_ not urban

NONUSE _n_ pl. **-S** failure to use

NONUSER _n_ pl. **-S** one that is not a user

NONUSING _adj_ not using

NONVALID *adj* not valid

NONVIRAL *adj* not viral

NONVITAL *adj* not vital

NONVOCAL *n* pl. **-S** one that does not involve the voice

NONVOTER *n* pl. **-S** one that does not vote

NONWAGE *adj* not including or involving wages (money paid for work or services)

NONWAR *n* pl. **-S** a war that is not officially declared

NONWHITE *n* pl. **-S** a person who is not of the white race

NONWOODY *adj* not woody

NONWOOL *adj* not made of wool

NONWORD *n* pl. **-S** a word that has no meaning

NONWORK *adj* not involving work

NONWOVEN *n* pl. **-S** a fabric not made by weaving

NONYL *n* pl. **-S** an alkyl radical

NONZERO *adj* having a value other than zero

NOO *adv* now

NOODGE *v* **NOODGED, NOODGING, NOODGES** to nag

NOODLE *v* **-DLED, -DLING, -DLES** to play idly on a musical instrument

NOOGIE *n* pl. **-S** a playful rubbing of one's knuckles on another's head

NOOK *n* pl. **-S** a corner, as in a room **NOOKLIKE** *adj*

NOON *n* pl. **-S** midday

NOONDAY *n* pl. **-DAYS** noon

NOONING *n* pl. **-S** a meal eaten at noon

NOONTIDE *n* pl. **-S** noon

NOONTIME *n* pl. **-S** noon

NOOSE *v* **NOOSED, NOOSING, NOOSES** to secure with a type of loop

NOOSER *n* pl. **-S** one that nooses

NOPAL *n* pl. **-S** or **-ES** a cactus of Mexico and Central America

NOPALITO *n* pl. **-TOS** the stem of the nopal used as food

NOPE *adv* no

NOPLACE *adv* not in or at any place

NOR *conj* and not

NORDIC *adj* pertaining to cross-country ski racing and ski jumping

NORI *n* pl. **-S** dried seaweed pressed into sheets

NORIA *n* pl. **-S** a type of waterwheel

NORITE *n* pl. **-S** a granular rock **NORITIC** *adj*

NORLAND *n* pl. **-S** a region in the north

NORM *n* pl. **-S** a standard regarded as typical for a specific group

NORMAL *n* pl. **-S** the usual or expected state or form

NORMALCY *n* pl. **-CIES** conformity with the norm

NORMALLY *adv* as a rule; usually

NORMANDE *adj* prepared with foods associated with Normandy

NORMED *adj* having a norm

NORMLESS *adj* having no norm

NORTH *n* pl. **-S** a point of the compass

NORTHER *n* pl. **-S** a wind or storm from the north

NORTHERN *n* pl. **-S** a person living in the north

NORTHING *n* pl. **-S** movement toward the north

NOSE *v* **NOSED, NOSING, NOSES** to sniff with the nose (the organ of smell)

NOSEBAG *n* pl. **-S** a feedbag

NOSEBAND *n* pl. **-S** a part of a horse's bridle

NOSEDIVE *v* **-DIVED** or **-DOVE, -DIVING, -DIVES** to go into a sudden steep drop

NOSEGAY *n* pl. **-GAYS** a bouquet

NOSELESS *adj* having no nose

NOSELIKE *adj* resembling a nose

NOSEY *adj* **NOSIER, NOSIEST** nosy

NOSH *v* **-ED, -ING, -ES** to eat snacks between meals

NOSHER *n* pl. **-S** one that noshes

NOSIER comparative of nosy

NOSIEST superlative of nosy

NOSILY *adv* in a nosy manner

NOSINESS *n* pl. **-ES** the quality of being nosy

NOSING *n* pl. **-S** a projecting edge

NOSOLOGY *n* pl. **-GIES** a classification of diseases

NOSTOC *n* pl. **-S** a freshwater alga

NOSTRIL *n* pl. **-S** an external opening of the nose

NOSTRUM *n* pl. **-S** a medicine of one's own invention

NOSY	*adj* **NOSIER, NOSIEST** unduly curious
NOT	*adv* in no way
NOTA	pl. of notum
NOTABLE	*n* pl. **-S** a person of distinction
NOTABLY	*adv* in a distinguished manner
NOTAL	*adj* pertaining to a notum
NOTARIAL	*adj* pertaining to a notary
NOTARIZE	*v* **-RIZED, -RIZING, -RIZES** to certify through a notary
NOTARY	*n* pl. **-RIES** a public officer who certifies documents
NOTATE	*v* **-TATED, -TATING, -TATES** to put into notation
NOTATION	*n* pl. **-S** a system of symbols
NOTCH	*v* **-ED, -ING, -ES** to make an angular cut in
NOTCHER	*n* pl. **-S** one that notches
NOTE	*v* **NOTED, NOTING, NOTES** to write down
NOTEBOOK	*n* pl. **-S** a book in which to write
NOTECARD	*n* pl. **-S** a card used for sending short messages
NOTECASE	*n* pl. **-S** a billfold
NOTED	past tense of note
NOTEDLY	*adv* in a famous manner
NOTELESS	*adj* undistinguished
NOTEPAD	*n* pl. **-S** a number of sheets of paper glued together at one end
NOTER	*n* pl. **-S** one that notes
NOTHER	*adj* different
NOTHING	*n* pl. **-S** the absence of all quantity or magnitude
NOTICE	*v* **-TICED, -TICING, -TICES** to become aware of
NOTICER	*n* pl. **-S** one that notices
NOTIFIER	*n* pl. **-S** one that notifies
NOTIFY	*v* **-FIED, -FYING, -FIES** to inform
NOTING	present participle of note
NOTION	*n* pl. **-S** a general idea **NOTIONAL** *adj*
NOTORNIS	*n* pl. **NOTORNIS** a flightless bird
NOTTURNO	*n* pl. **-NI** a nocturne
NOTUM	*n* pl. **-TA** a part of the thorax of an insect
NOUGAT	*n* pl. **-S** a chewy candy
NOUGHT	*n* pl. **-S** naught
NOUMENON	*n* pl. **-MENA** an object of intellectual intuition **NOUMENAL** *adj*
NOUN	*n* pl. **-S** a word used to denote the name of something **NOUNAL, NOUNLESS** *adj* **NOUNALLY** *adv*
NOURISH	*v* **-ED, -ING, -ES** to sustain with food
NOUS	*n* pl. **-ES** mind, reason, or intellect
NOUVEAU	*adj* newly arrived or developed
NOUVELLE	*n* pl. **-S** a style of French cooking
NOVA	*n* pl. **-VAS** or **-VAE** a type of star **NOVALIKE** *adj*
NOVATION	*n* pl. **-S** the substitution of a new legal obligation for an old one
NOVEL	*n* pl. **-S** a fictional prose narrative
NOVELISE	*v* **-ISED, -ISING, -ISES** to novelize
NOVELIST	*n* pl. **-S** a writer of novels
NOVELIZE	*v* **-IZED, -IZING, -IZES** to put into the form of a novel
NOVELLA	*n* pl. **-LAS** or **-LE** a short novel
NOVELLY	*adv* in a new or unusual manner
NOVELTY	*n* pl. **-TIES** something new or unusual
NOVENA	*n* pl. **-NAS** or **-NAE** a religious devotion lasting nine days
NOVERCAL	*adj* pertaining to a stepmother
NOVICE	*n* pl. **-S** a person new to any field or activity
NOW	*n* pl. **-S** the present time
NOWADAYS	*adv* in these times
NOWAY	*adv* in no way
NOWAYS	*adv* noway
NOWHERE	*n* pl. **-S** a nonexistent place
NOWISE	*adv* not at all
NOWNESS	*n* pl. **-ES** the state of existing at the present time
NOWT	*n* pl. **-S** naught
NOXIOUS	*adj* harmful to health
NOYADE	*n* pl. **-S** an execution by drowning
NOZZLE	*n* pl. **-S** a projecting spout
NTH	*adj* pertaining to an indefinitely large ordinal number
NU	*n* pl. **-S** a Greek letter
NUANCE	*n* pl. **-S** a slight variation **NUANCED** *adj*
NUB	*n* pl. **-S** a protuberance or knob
NUBBIER	comparative of nubby
NUBBIEST	superlative of nubby

NUBBIN	*n* pl. **-S** an undeveloped fruit
NUBBLE	*n* pl. **-S** a small nub
NUBBLY	*adj* **-BLIER, -BLIEST** having nubbles
NUBBY	*adj* **-BIER, -BIEST** having nubs
NUBIA	*n* pl. **-S** a woman's scarf
NUBILE	*adj* suitable for marriage
NUBILITY	*n* pl. **-TIES** the quality of being nubile
NUBILOSE	*adj* nubilous
NUBILOUS	*adj* cloudy
NUBUCK	*n* pl. **-S** soft sueded leather
NUCELLUS	*n* pl. **-LI** the essential part of a plant ovule **NUCELLAR** *adj*
NUCHA	*n* pl. **-CHAE** the nape of the neck
NUCHAL	*n* pl. **-S** an anatomical part lying in the region of the nape
NUCLEAL	*adj* nuclear
NUCLEAR	*adj* pertaining to a nucleus
NUCLEASE	*n* pl. **-S** an enzyme
NUCLEATE	*v* **-ATED, -ATING, -ATES** to form into a nucleus
NUCLEI	a pl. of nucleus
NUCLEIN	*n* pl. **-S** a protein found in nuclei
NUCLEOID	*n* pl. **-S** the DNA-containing area of certain cells
NUCLEOLE	*n* pl. **-S** a part of a nucleus
NUCLEOLI	*n/pl* nucleoles
NUCLEON	*n* pl. **-S** a subatomic particle
NUCLEUS	*n* pl. **-CLEUSES** or **-CLEI** an essential part of a cell
NUCLIDE	*n* pl. **-S** a species of atom **NUCLIDIC** *adj*
NUDE	*adj* **NUDER, NUDEST** being without clothing or covering **NUDELY** *adv*
NUDE	*n* pl. **-S** a nude figure
NUDENESS	*n* pl. **-ES** nudity
NUDGE	*v* **NUDGED, NUDGING, NUDGES** to push gently
NUDGER	*n* pl. **-S** one that nudges
NUDICAUL	*adj* having leafless stems
NUDIE	*n* pl. **-S** a movie featuring nude performers
NUDISM	*n* pl. **-S** the practice of going nude
NUDIST	*n* pl. **-S** an advocate of nudism
NUDITY	*n* pl. **-TIES** the state of being nude
NUDNICK	*n* pl. **-S** nudnik
NUDNIK	*n* pl. **-S** an annoying person
NUDZH	*v* **-ED, -ING, -ES** to noodge
NUGATORY	*adj* having no power
NUGGET	*n* pl. **-S** a mass of solid matter **NUGGETY** *adj*
NUISANCE	*n* pl. **-S** a source of annoyance
NUKE	*v* **NUKED, NUKING, NUKES** to attack with nuclear weapons
NULL	*v* **-ED, -ING, -S** to reduce to nothing
NULLAH	*n* pl. **-S** a ravine
NULLIFY	*v* **-FIED, -FYING, -FIES** to make useless or ineffective
NULLITY	*n* pl. **-TIES** something of no legal force
NUMB	*adj* **NUMBER, NUMBEST** lacking sensation
NUMB	*v* **-ED, -ING, -S** to make numb
NUMBAT	*n* pl. **-S** a small Australian mammal
NUMBER	*v* **-ED, -ING, -S** to count
NUMBERER	*n* pl. **-S** one that numbers
NUMBFISH	*n* pl. **-ES** a fish capable of emitting electric shocks
NUMBLES	*n/pl* animal entrails
NUMBLY	*adv* in a numb manner
NUMBNESS	*n* pl. **-ES** the state of being numb
NUMCHUCK	*n* pl. **-S** nunchaku
NUMEN	*n* pl. **-MINA** a deity
NUMERACY	*n* pl. **-CIES** the ability to understand basic mathematics
NUMERAL	*n* pl. **-S** a symbol that expresses a number
NUMERARY	*adj* pertaining to numbers
NUMERATE	*v* **-ATED, -ATING, -ATES** to count
NUMERIC	*n* pl. **-S** a numeral
NUMEROUS	*adj* many
NUMINA	pl. of numen
NUMINOUS	*adj* supernatural
NUMMARY	*adj* pertaining to coins
NUMMULAR	*adj* shaped like a coin
NUMSKULL	*n* pl. **-S** a dunce
NUN	*n* pl. **-S** a woman belonging to a religious order
NUNATAK	*n* pl. **-S** a mountain peak completely surrounded by glacial ice
NUNCHAKU	*n* pl. **-S** a Japanese weapon

NUNCIO — *n* pl. **-CIOS** an ambassador from the pope

NUNCLE — *n* pl. **-S** an uncle

NUNLIKE — *adj* resembling a nun

NUNNERY — *n* pl. **-NERIES** a religious house for nuns

NUNNISH — *adj* of, pertaining to, or characteristic of a nun

NUPTIAL — *n* pl. **-S** a wedding

NURD — *n* pl. **-S** nerd

NURL — *v* **-ED, -ING, -S** to knurl

NURSE — *v* **NURSED, NURSING, NURSES** to care for the sick or infirm

NURSER — *n* pl. **-S** a baby's bottle

NURSERY — *n* pl. **-ERIES** a room for young children

NURSING — *n* pl. **-S** the profession of one who nurses

NURSLING — *n* pl. **-S** an infant

NURTURAL — *adj* pertaining to the process of nurturing

NURTURE — *v* **-TURED, -TURING, -TURES** to nourish

NURTURER — *n* pl. **-S** one that nurtures

NUT — *v* **NUTTED, NUTTING, NUTS** to gather nuts (hard-shelled dry fruits)

NUTANT — *adj* drooping

NUTATE — *v* **-TATED, -TATING, -TATES** to exhibit nutation

NUTATION — *n* pl. **-S** an oscillatory movement of the axis of a rotating body

NUTBROWN — *adj* of a dark brown

NUTCASE — *n* pl. **-S** a crazy person

NUTGALL — *n* pl. **-S** a gallnut

NUTGRASS — *n* pl. **-ES** a perennial herb

NUTHATCH — *n* pl. **-ES** a small bird

NUTHOUSE — *n* pl. **-S** an insane asylum

NUTLET — *n* pl. **-S** a small nut

NUTLIKE — *adj* resembling a nut

NUTMEAT — *n* pl. **-S** the edible kernel of a nut

NUTMEG — *n* pl. **-S** an aromatic seed used as a spice

NUTPICK — *n* pl. **-S** a device for extracting the kernels from nuts

NUTRIA — *n* pl. **-S** the coypu

NUTRIENT — *n* pl. **-S** a nourishing substance

NUTSEDGE — *n* pl. **-S** nutgrass

NUTSHELL — *n* pl. **-S** the shell of a nut

NUTSY — *adj* **NUTSIER, NUTSIEST** crazy

NUTTED — past tense of nut

NUTTER — *n* pl. **-S** one that gathers nuts

NUTTING — *n* pl. **-S** the act of gathering nuts

NUTTY — *adj* **-TIER, -TIEST** silly; crazy **NUTTILY** *adv*

NUTWOOD — *n* pl. **-S** a nut-bearing tree

NUZZLE — *v* **-ZLED, -ZLING, -ZLES** to push with the nose

NUZZLER — *n* pl. **-S** one that nuzzles

NYALA — *n* pl. **-S** an antelope

NYLGHAI — *n* pl. **-S** nilgai

NYLGHAU — *n* pl. **-S** nilgai

NYLON — *n* pl. **-S** a synthetic material

NYMPH — *n* pl. **-S** a female spirit **NYMPHAL, NYMPHEAN** *adj*

NYMPHA — *n* pl. **-PHAE** a fold of the vulva

NYMPHET — *n* pl. **-S** a young nymph

NYMPHO — *n* pl. **-PHOS** a woman obsessed by sexual desire

NYSTATIN — *n* pl. **-S** an antibiotic

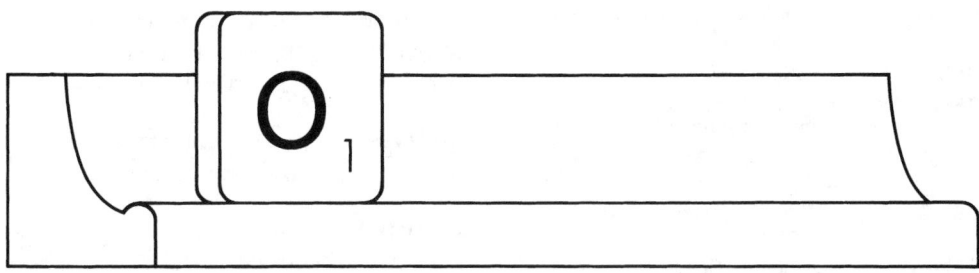

OAF   *n* pl. **OAFS** or **OAVES** a clumsy, stupid person **OAFISH** *adj* **OAFISHLY** *adv*

OAK   *n* pl. **-S** a hardwood tree or shrub **OAKEN, OAKLIKE** *adj*

OAKMOSS   *n* pl. **-ES** a lichen that grows on oak trees

OAKUM   *n* pl. **-S** loosely twisted hemp fiber

OAKY   *adj* **OAKIER, OAKIEST** tasting of oak sap

OAR   *v* **-ED, -ING, -S** to propel with oars (long, broad-bladed poles)

OARFISH   *n* pl. **-ES** a marine fish

OARLESS   *adj* having no oars

OARLIKE   *adj* resembling an oar

OARLOCK   *n* pl. **-S** a device for holding an oar in place

OARSMAN   *n* pl. **-MEN** a person who rows a boat

OASIS   *n* pl. **OASES** a green area in a desert region

OAST   *n* pl. **-S** a type of kiln

OAT   *n* pl. **-S** a cereal grass

OATCAKE   *n* pl. **-S** a cake made of oatmeal

OATEN   *adj* pertaining to oats

OATER   *n* pl. **-S** a cowboy movie

OATH   *n* pl. **-S** a formal declaration or promise to fulfill a pledge

OATLIKE   *adj* resembling oats

OATMEAL   *n* pl. **-S** meal made from oats

OAVES   a pl. of oaf

OBA   *n* pl. **-S** a hereditary chief in Benin and Nigeria

OBCONIC   *adj* conical with the apex below

OBDURACY   *n* pl. **-CIES** the quality or an instance of being obdurate

OBDURATE   *adj* stubborn

OBE   *n* pl. **-S** obeah

OBEAH   *n* pl. **-S** a form of sorcery of African origin

OBEAHISM   *n* pl. **-S** the use of obeah

OBEDIENT   *adj* obeying or willing to obey

OBEISANT   *adj* showing reverence or respect

OBELI   pl. of obelus

OBELIA   *n* pl. **-S** a marine hydroid

OBELISE   *v* **-LISED, -LISING, -LISES** to obelize

OBELISK   *n* pl. **-S** a four-sided shaft of stone with a pyramidal top

OBELISM   *n* pl. **-S** the act of obelizing

OBELIZE   *v* **-LIZED, -LIZING, -LIZES** to mark with an obelus

OBELUS   *n* pl. **-LI** a symbol used in ancient manuscripts to indicate a doubtful passage

OBENTO   *n* pl. **-TOS** a Japanese meal packed in a box

OBESE   *adj* very fat **OBESELY** *adv*

OBESITY   *n* pl. **-TIES** the state or condition of being obese

OBEY   *v* **-ED, -ING, -S** to follow the commands or guidance of **OBEYABLE** *adj*

OBEYER   *n* pl. **-S** one that obeys

OBI   *n* pl. **-S** obeah

OBIA   *n* pl. **-S** obeah

OBIISM   *n* pl. **-S** obeahism

OBIT   *n* pl. **-S** an obituary

OBITUARY   *n* pl. **-ARIES** a published notice of a death

OBJECT   *v* **-ED, -ING, -S** to argue in opposition

OBJECTOR   *n* pl. **-S** one that objects

OBJET   *n* pl. **-S** an article of artistic value

OBLAST   *n* pl. **-LASTS** or **-LASTI** an administrative division of Russia

OBLATE	*n* pl. **-S** a layman residing in a monastery
OBLATELY	*adv* elliptically
OBLATION	*n* pl. **-S** the act of making a religious offering **OBLATORY** *adj*
OBLIGATE	*v* **-GATED, -GATING, -GATES** to oblige
OBLIGATO	*n* pl. **-TOS** or **-TI** an important musical part
OBLIGE	*v* **OBLIGED, OBLIGING, OBLIGES** to put in one's debt by a favor or service
OBLIGEE	*n* pl. **-S** one that is obliged
OBLIGER	*n* pl. **-S** one that obliges
OBLIGING	present participle of oblige
OBLIGOR	*n* pl. **-S** one who places himself under a legal obligation
OBLIQUE	*v* **OBLIQUED, OBLIQUING, OBLIQUES** to slant
OBLIVION	*n* pl. **-S** the state of being forgotten; the act of forgetting
OBLONG	*n* pl. **-S** something that is oblong (elongated)
OBLONGLY	*adv* in an oblong manner
OBLOQUY	*n* pl. **-QUIES** abusive language
OBOE	*n* pl. **-S** a woodwind instrument
OBOIST	*n* pl. **-S** one who plays the oboe
OBOL	*n* pl. **-S** a coin of ancient Greece
OBOLE	*n* pl. **-S** a coin of medieval France
OBOLUS	*n* pl. **-LI** an obol
OBOVATE	*adj* ovate with the narrow end at the base
OBOVOID	*adj* ovoid with the narrow end at the base
OBSCENE	*adj* **-SCENER, -SCENEST** indecent
OBSCURE	*adj* **-SCURER, -SCUREST** dark or indistinct
OBSCURE	*v* **-SCURED, -SCURING, -SCURES** to make obscure
OBSEQUY	*n* pl. **-QUIES** a funeral rite
OBSERVE	*v* **-SERVED, -SERVING, -SERVES** to look attentively
OBSERVER	*n* pl. **-S** one that observes
OBSESS	*v* **-ED, -ING, -ES** to dominate the thoughts of
OBSESSOR	*n* pl. **-S** something that obsesses
OBSIDIAN	*n* pl. **-S** a volcanic glass
OBSOLETE	*v* **-LETED, -LETING, -LETES** to make out-of-date
OBSTACLE	*n* pl. **-S** something that obstructs
OBSTRUCT	*v* **-ED, -ING, -S** to get in the way of
OBTAIN	*v* **-ED, -ING, -S** to gain possession of
OBTAINER	*n* pl. **-S** one that obtains
OBTECT	*adj* covered by a hardened secretion
OBTECTED	*adj* obtect
OBTEST	*v* **-ED, -ING, -S** to beseech
OBTRUDE	*v* **-TRUDED, -TRUDING, -TRUDES** to thrust forward
OBTRUDER	*n* pl. **-S** one that obtrudes
OBTUND	*v* **-ED, -ING, -S** to deaden
OBTURATE	*v* **-RATED, -RATING, -RATES** to close or stop up
OBTUSE	*adj* **-TUSER, -TUSEST** dull **OBTUSELY** *adv*
OBTUSITY	*n* pl. **-TIES** the state of being obtuse
OBVERSE	*n* pl. **-S** the side of a coin bearing the main design
OBVERT	*v* **-ED, -ING, -S** to turn so as to show a different surface
OBVIATE	*v* **-ATED, -ATING, -ATES** to prevent or eliminate by effective measures **OBVIABLE** *adj*
OBVIATOR	*n* pl. **-S** one that obviates
OBVIOUS	*adj* easily perceived or understood
OBVOLUTE	*adj* rolled or turned in
OCA	*n* pl. **-S** a South American herb
OCARINA	*n* pl. **-S** a wind instrument
OCCASION	*v* **-ED, -ING, -S** to cause
OCCIDENT	*n* pl. **-S** the west
OCCIPUT	*n* pl. **-PUTS** or **-PITA** the back part of the skull
OCCLUDE	*v* **-CLUDED, -CLUDING, -CLUDES** to close or stop up
OCCLUSAL	*adj* pertaining to the biting surface of a tooth
OCCULT	*v* **-ED, -ING, -S** to conceal
OCCULTER	*n* pl. **-S** one that occults
OCCULTLY	*adv* secretly
OCCUPANT	*n* pl. **-S** a resident
OCCUPIER	*n* pl. **-S** one who occupies
OCCUPY	*v* **-PIED, -PYING, -PIES** to engage the attention or energies of
OCCUR	*v* **-CURRED, -CURRING, -CURS** to take place

OCEAN	*n* pl. **-S** the vast body of salt water that covers most of the earth's surface **OCEANIC** *adj*
OCEANAUT	*n* pl. **-S** an aquanaut
OCELLAR	*adj* pertaining to an ocellus
OCELLATE	*adj* having ocelli
OCELLUS	*n* pl. **-LI** a minute simple eye
OCELOT	*n* pl. **-S** an American wildcat **OCELOID** *adj*
OCHER	*v* **-ED, -ING, -S** to color with ocher (a red or yellow iron ore used as a pigment)
OCHEROUS	*adj* containing or resembling ocher
OCHERY	*adj* ocherous
OCHONE	*interj* — used to express grief
OCHRE	*v* **OCHRED, OCHRING, OCHRES** to ocher
OCHREA	*n* pl. **-REAE** ocrea
OCHREOUS	*adj* ocherous
OCHRING	present participle of ochre
OCHROID	*adj* ocherous
OCHROUS	*adj* ocherous
OCHRY	*adj* ochery
OCICAT	*n* pl. **-S** a domestic cat having a short spotted coat
OCKER	*n* pl. **-S** a boorish person
OCOTILLO	*n* pl. **-LOS** a Mexican shrub
OCREA	*n* pl. **-REAE** a sheathing plant part
OCREATE	*adj* having ocreae
OCTAD	*n* pl. **-S** a group of eight **OCTADIC** *adj*
OCTAGON	*n* pl. **-S** an eight-sided polygon
OCTAL	*adj* pertaining to a number system with a base of eight
OCTAN	*n* pl. **-S** a fever recurring every eighth day
OCTANE	*n* pl. **-S** a liquid hydrocarbon
OCTANGLE	*n* pl. **-S** an octagon
OCTANOL	*n* pl. **-S** an alcohol
OCTANT	*n* pl. **-S** an eighth of a circle **OCTANTAL** *adj*
OCTARCHY	*n* pl. **-TARCHIES** a government by eight persons
OCTAVE	*n* pl. **-S** a type of musical interval **OCTAVAL** *adj*
OCTAVO	*n* pl. **-VOS** a page size
OCTET	*n* pl. **-S** a group of eight
OCTETTE	*n* pl. **-S** octet

OCTONARY	*n* pl. **-NARIES** a stanza of eight lines
OCTOPOD	*n* pl. **-S** any of an order of eight-armed mollusks
OCTOPUS	*n* pl. **-PUSES** or **-PI** or **-PODES** a nocturnal octopod
OCTOROON	*n* pl. **-S** a person of one-eighth black ancestry
OCTROI	*n* pl. **-S** a tax on certain articles brought into a city
OCTUPLE	*v* **-PLED, -PLING, -PLES** to multiply by eight
OCTUPLET	*n* pl. **-S** a group of eight related items
OCTUPLEX	*adj* being eight times as great
OCTUPLING	present participle of octuple
OCTUPLY	*adv* to eight times the degree
OCTYL	*n* pl. **-S** a univalent radical
OCULAR	*n* pl. **-S** an eyepiece
OCULARLY	*adv* by means of the eyes or sight
OCULIST	*n* pl. **-S** a physician who treats diseases of the eye
OCULUS	*n* pl. **-LI** a circular window
OD	*n* pl. **-S** a hypothetical force of natural power
ODA	*n* pl. **-S** a room in a harem
ODAH	*n* pl. **-S** oda
ODALISK	*n* pl. **-S** a female slave in a harem
ODD	*adj* **ODDER, ODDEST** unusual
ODD	*n* pl. **-S** one that is odd
ODDBALL	*n* pl. **-S** an eccentric person
ODDISH	*adj* somewhat odd
ODDITY	*n* pl. **-TIES** one that is odd
ODDLY	*adv* in an odd manner
ODDMENT	*n* pl. **-S** a remnant
ODDNESS	*n* pl. **-ES** the state of being odd
ODE	*n* pl. **-S** a lyric poem
ODEON	*n* pl. **-S** odeum
ODEUM	*n* pl. **ODEUMS** or **ODEA** a theater or concert hall
ODIC	*adj* pertaining to an ode
ODIOUS	*adj* deserving or causing hatred **ODIOUSLY** *adv*
ODIST	*n* pl. **-S** one who writes odes
ODIUM	*n* pl. **-S** hatred
ODOGRAPH	*n* pl. **-S** an odometer
ODOMETER	*n* pl. **-S** a device for measuring distance traveled

ODOMETRY *n* pl. **-TRIES** the process of using an odometer

ODONATE *n* pl. **-S** any of an order of predacious insects

ODONTOID *n* pl. **-S** a toothlike vertebral projection

ODOR *n* pl. **-S** the property of a substance that affects the sense of smell **ODORED, ODORFUL** *adj*

ODORANT *n* pl. **-S** an odorous substance

ODORIZE *v* **-IZED, -IZING, -IZES** to make odorous

ODORLESS *adj* having no odor

ODOROUS *adj* having an odor

ODOUR *n* pl. **-S** odor **ODOURFUL** *adj*

ODYL *n* pl. **-S** an od

ODYLE *n* pl. **-S** odyl

ODYSSEY *n* pl. **-SEYS** a long, wandering journey

OE *n* pl. **-S** a whirlwind off the Faeroe islands

OECOLOGY *n* pl. **-GIES** ecology

OEDEMA *n* pl. **-MAS** or **-MATA** edema

OEDIPAL *adj* pertaining to the libidinal feelings in a child toward the parent of the opposite sex

OEDIPEAN *adj* oedipal

OEILLADE *n* pl. **-S** an amorous look

OENOLOGY *n* pl. **-GIES** the study of wines

OENOMEL *n* pl. **-S** an ancient Greek beverage of wine and honey

OERSTED *n* pl. **-S** a unit of magnetic intensity

OESTRIN *n* pl. **-S** estrin

OESTRIOL *n* pl. **-S** estriol

OESTRONE *n* pl. **-S** estrone

OESTROUS *adj* estrous

OESTRUM *n* pl. **-S** estrum

OESTRUS *n* pl. **-ES** estrus

OEUVRE *n* pl. **-S** a work of art

OF *prep* coming from

OFF *v* **-ED, -ING, -S** to go away

OFFAL *n* pl. **-S** waste material

OFFBEAT *n* pl. **-S** an unaccented beat in a musical measure

OFFCAST *n* pl. **-S** a castoff

OFFCUT *n* pl. **-S** something that is cut off

OFFENCE *n* pl. **-S** offense

OFFEND *v* **-ED, -ING, -S** to commit an offense

OFFENDER *n* pl. **-S** one that offends

OFFENSE *n* pl. **-S** a violation of a moral or social code

OFFER *v* **-ED, -ING, -S** to present for acceptance or rejection

OFFERER *n* pl. **-S** one that offers

OFFERING *n* pl. **-S** a contribution

OFFEROR *n* pl. **-S** offerer

OFFHAND *adv* without preparation

OFFICE *n* pl. **-S** a position of authority

OFFICER *v* **-ED, -ING, -S** to furnish with officers (persons holding positions of authority)

OFFICIAL *n* pl. **-S** one that holds a position of authority

OFFING *n* pl. **-S** the near future

OFFISH *adj* aloof **OFFISHLY** *adv*

OFFKEY *adj* pitched higher or lower than the correct musical tone

OFFLINE *adj* not connected to a computer network

OFFLOAD *v* **-ED, -ING, -S** to unload

OFFPRINT *v* **-ED, -ING, -S** to reprint an excerpt

OFFRAMP *n* pl. **-S** a road leading off an expressway

OFFSET *v* **-SET, -SETTING, -SETS** to compensate for

OFFSHOOT *n* pl. **-S** a lateral shoot from a main stem

OFFSHORE *n* pl. **-S** an area of submerged land out from the shore

OFFSIDE *n* pl. **-S** an improper football play

OFFSTAGE *n* pl. **-S** a part of a stage not visible to the audience

OFFTRACK *adj* away from a racetrack

OFT *adv* **OFTER, OFTEST** often

OFTEN *adv* **-ENER, -ENEST** frequently

OFTTIMES *adv* often

OGAM *n* pl. **-S** ogham

OGDOAD *n* pl. **-S** a group of eight

OGEE *n* pl. **-S** an S-shaped molding

OGHAM *n* pl. **-S** an Old Irish alphabet **OGHAMIC** *adj*

OGHAMIST *n* pl. **-S** one who writes in ogham

OGIVE *n* pl. **-S** a pointed arch **OGIVAL** *adj*

OGLE *v* **OGLED, OGLING, OGLES** to stare at

OGLER	*n* pl. **-S** one that ogles
OGRE	*n* pl. **-S** a monster
OGREISH	*adj* resembling an ogre
OGREISM	*n* pl. **-S** the state of being ogreish
OGRESS	*n* pl. **-ES** a female ogre
OGRISH	*adj* ogreish **OGRISHLY** *adv*
OGRISM	*n* pl. **-S** ogreism
OH	*v* **-ED, -ING, -S** to exclaim in surprise, pain, or desire
OHIA	*n* pl. **-S** lehua
OHM	*n* pl. **-S** a unit of electrical resistance **OHMIC** *adj*
OHMAGE	*n* pl. **-S** electrical resistance expressed in ohms
OHMMETER	*n* pl. **-S** an instrument for measuring ohmage
OHO	*interj* — used to express surprise or exultation
OI	*interj* oy
OIDIUM	*n* pl. **OIDIA** a type of fungus **OIDIOID** *adj*
OIL	*v* **-ED, -ING, -S** to supply with oil (a greasy liquid used for lubrication, fuel, or illumination)
OILBIRD	*n* pl. **-S** a tropical bird
OILCAMP	*n* pl. **-S** a living area for workers at an oil well
OILCAN	*n* pl. **-S** a can for applying lubricating oil
OILCLOTH	*n* pl. **-S** a waterproof fabric
OILCUP	*n* pl. **-S** a closed cup for supplying lubricant
OILER	*n* pl. **-S** one that oils
OILHOLE	*n* pl. **-S** a hole through which lubricating oil is injected
OILIER	comparative of oily
OILIEST	superlative of oily
OILILY	*adv* in an oily manner
OILINESS	*n* pl. **-ES** the state of being oily
OILMAN	*n* pl. **-MEN** one who owns or operates oil wells
OILPAPER	*n* pl. **-S** a water-resistant paper
OILPROOF	*adj* impervious to oil
OILSEED	*n* pl. **-S** a seed from which oil is pressed out
OILSKIN	*n* pl. **-S** a waterproof fabric
OILSTONE	*n* pl. **-S** a stone for sharpening tools
OILTIGHT	*adj* being so tight as to prevent the passage of oil
OILWAY	*n* pl. **-WAYS** a channel for the passage of oil
OILY	*adj* **OILIER, OILIEST** covered or soaked with oil
OINK	*v* **-ED, -ING, -S** to utter the natural grunt of a hog
OINOLOGY	*n* pl. **-GIES** oenology
OINOMEL	*n* pl. **-S** oenomel
OINTMENT	*n* pl. **-S** a viscous preparation applied to the skin as a medicine or cosmetic
OITICICA	*n* pl. **-S** a South American tree
OKA	*n* pl. **-S** a Turkish unit of weight
OKAPI	*n* pl. **-S** an African ruminant mammal
OKAY	*v* **-ED, -ING, -S** to approve
OKE	*n* pl. **-S** oka
OKEH	*n* pl. **-S** approval
OKEYDOKE	*adj* perfectly all right
OKRA	*n* pl. **-S** a tall annual herb
OLD	*adj* **OLDER, OLDEST** or **ELDER, ELDEST** living or existing for a relatively long time
OLD	*n* pl. **-S** an individual of a specified age
OLDEN	*adj* pertaining to a bygone era
OLDIE	*n* pl. **-S** a popular song of an earlier day
OLDISH	*adj* somewhat old
OLDNESS	*n* pl. **-ES** the state of being old
OLDSQUAW	*n* pl. **-S** a sea duck
OLDSTER	*n* pl. **-S** an old person
OLDSTYLE	*n* pl. **-S** a style of printing type
OLDWIFE	*n* pl. **-WIVES** a marine fish
OLDY	*n* pl. **OLDIES** oldie
OLE	*n* pl. **-S** a shout of approval
OLEA	pl. of oleum
OLEANDER	*n* pl. **-S** a flowering shrub
OLEASTER	*n* pl. **-S** a flowering shrub
OLEATE	*n* pl. **-S** a chemical salt
OLEFIN	*n* pl. **-S** an alkene **OLEFINIC** *adj*
OLEFINE	*n* pl. **-S** olefin
OLEIC	*adj* pertaining to oil
OLEIN	*n* pl. **-S** the liquid portion of a fat
OLEINE	*n* pl. **-S** olein
OLEO	*n* pl. **OLEOS** margarine

OLESTRA _n_ pl. **-S** a noncaloric fat substitute

OLEUM _n_ pl. **-S** a corrosive liquid

OLEUM _n_ pl. **OLEA** oil

OLIBANUM _n_ pl. **-S** a fragrant resin

OLICOOK _n_ pl. **-S** a doughnut

OLIGARCH _n_ pl. **-S** a ruler in a government by the few

OLIGOMER _n_ pl. **-S** a type of polymer

OLIGURIA _n_ pl. **-S** reduced excretion of urine

OLINGO _n_ pl. **-GOS** a small mammal of Central and South America

OLIO _n_ pl. **OLIOS** a miscellaneous collection

OLIVARY _adj_ shaped like an olive

OLIVE _n_ pl. **-S** the small oval fruit of a Mediterranean tree

OLIVINE _n_ pl. **-S** a mineral **OLIVINIC** _adj_

OLLA _n_ pl. **-S** a wide-mouthed pot or jar

OLOGIST _n_ pl. **-S** an expert in a particular ology

OLOGY _n_ pl. **-GIES** a branch of knowledge

OLOROSO _n_ pl. **-SOS** a dark sherry

OLYMPIAD _n_ pl. **-S** a celebration of the Olympic Games

OM _n_ pl. **-S** a mantra used in contemplation of ultimate reality

OMASUM _n_ pl. **-SA** the third stomach of a ruminant

OMBER _n_ pl. **-S** ombre

OMBRE _n_ pl. **-S** a card game

OMEGA _n_ pl. **-S** a Greek letter

OMELET _n_ pl. **-S** a dish of beaten eggs cooked and folded around a filling

OMELETTE _n_ pl. **-S** omelet

OMEN _v_ **-ED, -ING, -S** to be an omen (a prophetic sign) of

OMENTUM _n_ pl. **-TUMS** or **-TA** a fold in an abdominal membrane **OMENTAL** _adj_

OMER _n_ pl. **-S** a Hebrew unit of dry measure

OMICRON _n_ pl. **-S** a Greek letter

OMIKRON _n_ pl. **-S** omicron

OMINOUS _adj_ portending evil

OMISSION _n_ pl. **-S** something left undone

OMISSIVE _adj_ marked by omission

OMIT _v_ **OMITTED, OMITTING, OMITS** to leave out

OMITTER _n_ pl. **-S** one that omits

OMNIARCH _n_ pl. **-S** an almighty ruler

OMNIBUS _n_ pl. **-BUSES** or **-BUSSES** a bus

OMNIFIC _adj_ unlimited in creative power

OMNIFORM _adj_ of all forms

OMNIMODE _adj_ of all modes

OMNIVORA _n/pl_ omnivores

OMNIVORE _n_ pl. **-S** an animal that eats all kinds of food

OMOPHAGY _n_ pl. **-GIES** the eating of raw flesh

OMPHALOS _n_ pl. **-LI** a central point

ON _n_ pl. **-S** the side of the wicket where a batsman stands in cricket

ONAGER _n_ pl. **-GERS** or **-GRI** a wild ass of central Asia

ONANISM _n_ pl. **-S** coitus deliberately interrupted to prevent insemination

ONANIST _n_ pl. **-S** one who practices onanism

ONBOARD _adj_ carried aboard a vehicle

ONCE _adv_ one single time

ONCET _adv_ once

ONCIDIUM _n_ pl. **-S** a tropical orchid

ONCOGENE _n_ pl. **-S** a gene that causes a cell to become cancerous

ONCOLOGY _n_ pl. **-GIES** the science of tumors

ONCOMING _n_ pl. **-S** an approach

ONDOGRAM _n_ pl. **-S** a graph of electric wave forms

ONE _n_ pl. **-S** a number

ONEFOLD _adj_ constituting a single, undivided whole

ONEIRIC _adj_ pertaining to dreams

ONENESS _n_ pl. **-ES** unity

ONEROUS _adj_ burdensome or oppressive

ONERY _adj_ **-ERIER, -ERIEST** ornery

ONESELF _pron_ a person's self

ONETIME _adj_ former

ONGOING _adj_ continuing without interruption

ONION _n_ pl. **-S** the edible bulb of a cultivated herb **ONIONY** _adj_

ONIUM _adj_ characterized by a complex cation

ONLAY _n_ pl. **-S** something laid over something else

ONLINE _adj_ connected to a computer network

ONLOAD _v_ **-ED, -ING, -S** to load a vehicle or container

ONLOOKER _n_ pl. **-S** a spectator

ONLY	*adv* with nothing or no one else
ONO	*n* pl. **ONOS** a large mackerel
ONRUSH	*n* pl. **-ES** a forward rush or flow
ONSCREEN	*adj* shown on a movie, television, or display screen
ONSET	*n* pl. **-S** a beginning
ONSHORE	*adv* toward the shore
ONSIDE	*adj* not offside
ONSTAGE	*adj* being on a part of the stage visible to the audience
ONSTREAM	*adv* in or into production
ONTIC	*adj* having real being or existence
ONTO	*prep* to a position upon
ONTOGENY	*n* pl. **-NIES** the development of an individual organism
ONTOLOGY	*n* pl. **-GIES** the branch of philosophy that deals with being
ONUS	*n* pl. **-ES** a burden or responsibility
ONWARD	*adv* toward a point ahead or in front
ONWARDS	*adv* onward
ONYX	*n* pl. **-ES** a variety of quartz
OOCYST	*n* pl. **-S** a zygote
OOCYTE	*n* pl. **-S** an egg before maturation
OODLES	*n* pl. **OODLES** a large amount
OODLINS	*n* pl. **OODLINS** oodles
OOGAMETE	*n* pl. **-S** a female gamete of certain protozoa
OOGAMOUS	*adj* having structurally dissimilar gametes
OOGAMY	*n* pl. **-MIES** the state of being oogamous
OOGENY	*n* pl. **-NIES** the development of ova
OOGONIUM	*n* pl. **-NIUMS** or **-NIA** a female sexual organ in certain algae and fungi **OOGONIAL** *adj*
OOH	*v* **-ED, -ING, -S** to exclaim in amazement, joy, or surprise
OOLACHAN	*n* pl. **-S** eulachon
OOLITE	*n* pl. **-S** a variety of limestone **OOLITIC** *adj*
OOLITH	*n* pl. **-S** oolite
OOLOGIST	*n* pl. **-S** an expert in oology
OOLOGY	*n* pl. **-GIES** the study of birds' eggs **OOLOGIC** *adj*
OOLONG	*n* pl. **-S** a dark Chinese tea
OOMIAC	*n* pl. **-S** umiak
OOMIACK	*n* pl. **-S** umiak

OOMIAK	*n* pl. **-S** umiak
OOMPAH	*v* **-ED, -ING, -S** to play a repeated rhythmic bass accompaniment
OOMPH	*n* pl. **-S** spirited vigor
OOPHYTE	*n* pl. **-S** a stage of development in certain plants **OOPHYTIC** *adj*
OOPS	*interj* — used to express mild apology, surprise, or dismay
OORALI	*n* pl. **-S** curare
OORIE	*adj* ourie
OOSPERM	*n* pl. **-S** a fertilized egg
OOSPHERE	*n* pl. **-S** an unfertilized egg within an oogonium
OOSPORE	*n* pl. **-S** a fertilized egg within an oogonium **OOSPORIC** *adj*
OOT	*n* pl. **-S** out
OOTHECA	*n* pl. **-CAE** an egg case of certain insects **OOTHECAL** *adj*
OOTID	*n* pl. **-S** one of the four sections into which a mature ovum divides
OOZE	*v* **OOZED, OOZING, OOZES** to flow or leak out slowly
OOZINESS	*n* pl. **-ES** the state of being oozy
OOZY	*adj* **OOZIER, OOZIEST** containing or resembling soft mud or slime **OOZILY** *adv*
OP	*n* pl. **-S** a style of abstract art
OPACIFY	*v* **-FIED, -FYING, -FIES** to make opaque
OPACITY	*n* pl. **-TIES** something that is opaque
OPAH	*n* pl. **-S** a marine fish
OPAL	*n* pl. **-S** a mineral
OPALESCE	*v* **-ESCED, -ESCING, -ESCES** to emit an iridescent shimmer of colors
OPALINE	*n* pl. **-S** an opaque white glass
OPAQUE	*adj* **OPAQUER, OPAQUEST** impervious to light **OPAQUELY** *adv*
OPAQUE	*v* **OPAQUED, OPAQUING, OPAQUES** to make opaque
OPE	*v* **OPED, OPING, OPES** to open
OPEN	*adj* **OPENER, OPENEST** affording unobstructed access, passage, or view
OPEN	*v* **-ED, -ING, -S** to cause to become open **OPENABLE** *adj*
OPENCAST	*adj* worked from a surface open to the air
OPENER	*n* pl. **-S** one that opens

OPENING   *n* pl. **-S** a vacant or unobstructed space

OPENLY   *adv* in an open manner

OPENNESS   *n* pl. **-ES** the state of being open

OPENWORK   *n* pl. **-S** ornamental or structural work containing numerous openings

OPERA   *n* pl. **-S** a form of musical drama

OPERABLE   *adj* usable **OPERABLY** *adv*

OPERAND   *n* pl. **-S** a quantity on which a mathematical operation is performed

OPERANT   *n* pl. **-S** one that operates

OPERATE   *v* **-ATED, -ATING, -ATES** to perform a function

OPERATIC   *n* pl. **-S** the technique of staging operas

OPERATOR   *n* pl. **-S** a symbol that represents a mathematical function

OPERCELE   *n* pl. **-S** opercule

OPERCULA   *n/pl* opercules

OPERCULE   *n* pl. **-S** an anatomical part that serves as a lid or cover

OPERETTA   *n* pl. **-S** a light musical drama with spoken dialogue

OPERON   *n* pl. **-S** a type of gene cluster

OPEROSE   *adj* involving great labor

OPHIDIAN   *n* pl. **-S** a snake

OPHITE   *n* pl. **-S** a green mottled igneous rock **OPHITIC** *adj*

OPIATE   *v* **-ATED, -ATING, -ATES** to treat with opium

OPINE   *v* **OPINED, OPINING, OPINES** to hold or state as an opinion

OPING   present participle of ope

OPINION   *n* pl. **-S** a conclusion or judgment one holds to be true

OPIOID   *n* pl. **-S** a peptide that acts like opium

OPIUM   *n* pl. **-S** an addictive narcotic

OPIUMISM   *n* pl. **-S** opium addiction

OPOSSUM   *n* pl. **-S** an arboreal mammal

OPPIDAN   *n* pl. **-S** a townsman

OPPILATE   *v* **-LATED, -LATING, -LATES** to obstruct **OPPILANT** *adj*

OPPONENT   *n* pl. **-S** one that opposes another

OPPOSE   *v* **-POSED, -POSING, -POSES** to be in contention or conflict with

OPPOSER   *n* pl. **-S** one that opposes

OPPOSITE   *n* pl. **-S** one that is radically different from another in some related way

OPPRESS   *v* **-ED, -ING, -ES** to burden by abuse of power or authority

OPPUGN   *v* **-ED, -ING, -S** to assail with argument

OPPUGNER   *n* pl. **-S** one that oppugns

OPSIN   *n* pl. **-S** a type of protein

OPSONIC   *adj* pertaining to opsonin

OPSONIFY   *v* **-FIED, -FYING, -FIES** to opsonize

OPSONIN   *n* pl. **-S** an antibody of blood serum

OPSONIZE   *v* **-NIZED, -NIZING, -NIZES** to form opsonins in

OPT   *v* **-ED, -ING, -S** to choose

OPTATIVE   *n* pl. **-S** a mood of verbs that expresses a wish or desire

OPTIC   *n* pl. **-S** an eye

OPTICAL   *adj* pertaining to sight

OPTICIAN   *n* pl. **-S** one who makes or deals in optical goods

OPTICIST   *n* pl. **-S** one engaged in the study of light and vision

OPTIMA   a pl. of optimum

OPTIMAL   *adj* most desirable

OPTIME   *n* pl. **-S** an honor student in mathematics at Cambridge University

OPTIMISE   *v* **-MISED, -MISING, -MISES** to optimize

OPTIMISM   *n* pl. **-S** a disposition to look on the favorable side of things

OPTIMIST   *n* pl. **-S** one who exhibits optimism

OPTIMIZE   *v* **-MIZED, -MIZING, -MIZES** to make as perfect, useful, or effective as possible

OPTIMUM   *n* pl. **-MUMS** or **-MA** the most favorable condition for obtaining a given result

OPTION   *v* **-ED, -ING, -S** to grant an option (a right to buy or sell something at a specified price within a specified time) on

OPTIONAL   *n* pl. **-S** an elective course of study

OPTIONEE   *n* pl. **-S** one who holds a legal option

OPULENCE   *n* pl. **-S** wealth

OPULENCY   *n* pl. **-CIES** opulence

OPULENT   *adj* wealthy

OPUNTIA	*n* pl. **-S** an American cactus
OPUS	*n* pl. **OPUSES** or **OPERA** a literary or musical work
OPUSCULA	*n/pl* opuscules
OPUSCULE	*n* pl. **-S** a minor work
OQUASSA	*n* pl. **-S** a small lake trout
OR	*n* pl. **-S** the heraldic color gold
ORA	pl. of os
ORACH	*n* pl. **-ES** a cultivated plant
ORACHE	*n* pl. **-S** orach
ORACLE	*n* pl. **-S** a person through whom a deity is believed to speak **ORACULAR** *adj*
ORAD	*adv* toward the mouth
ORAL	*n* pl. **-S** an examination requiring spoken answers
ORALISM	*n* pl. **-S** the use of oral methods of teaching the deaf
ORALIST	*n* pl. **-S** an advocate of oralism
ORALITY	*n* pl. **-TIES** the state of being produced orally
ORALLY	*adv* through the mouth
ORANG	*n* pl. **-S** a large ape
ORANGE	*n* pl. **-S** a citrus fruit
ORANGERY	*n* pl. **-RIES** a place where orange trees are cultivated
ORANGEY	*adj* **-ANGIER, -ANGIEST** orangy
ORANGISH	*adj* of a somewhat orange color
ORANGY	*adj* **-ANGIER, -ANGIEST** resembling or suggestive of an orange
ORATE	*v* **ORATED, ORATING, ORATES** to speak formally
ORATION	*n* pl. **-S** a formal speech
ORATOR	*n* pl. **-S** one that orates
ORATORIO	*n* pl. **-RIOS** a type of musical composition
ORATORY	*n* pl. **-RIES** the art of public speaking
ORATRESS	*n* pl. **-ES** oratrix
ORATRIX	*n* pl. **-TRICES** a female orator
ORB	*v* **-ED, -ING, -S** to form into a circle or sphere
ORBIER	comparative of orby
ORBIEST	superlative of orby
ORBIT	*v* **-ED, -ING, -S** to move or revolve around
ORBITAL	*n* pl. **-S** a subdivision of a nuclear shell
ORBITER	*n* pl. **-S** one that orbits
ORBLESS	*adj* lacking an orb
ORBY	*adj* **ORBIER, ORBIEST** resembling a circle or sphere
ORC	*n* pl. **-S** a marine mammal
ORCA	*n* pl. **-S** orc
ORCEIN	*n* pl. **-S** a reddish brown dye
ORCHARD	*n* pl. **-S** an area for the cultivation of fruit trees
ORCHID	*n* pl. **-S** a flowering plant
ORCHIL	*n* pl. **-S** a purple dye
ORCHIS	*n* pl. **-CHISES** an orchid
ORCHITIS	*n* pl. **-TISES** inflammation of the testicle **ORCHITIC** *adj*
ORCIN	*n* pl. **-S** orcinol
ORCINOL	*n* pl. **-S** a chemical compound
ORDAIN	*v* **-ED, -ING, -S** to invest with holy authority
ORDAINER	*n* pl. **-S** one that ordains
ORDEAL	*n* pl. **-S** a severely difficult or painful experience
ORDER	*v* **-ED, -ING, -S** to give a command or instruction to
ORDERER	*n* pl. **-S** one that orders
ORDERLY	*n* pl. **-LIES** a male attendant
ORDINAL	*n* pl. **-S** a number designating position in a series
ORDINAND	*n* pl. **-S** a person about to be ordained
ORDINARY	*adj* **-NARIER, -NARIEST** of a kind to be expected in the normal order of events
ORDINARY	*n* pl. **-NARIES** something that is ordinary
ORDINATE	*n* pl. **-S** a particular geometric coordinate
ORDNANCE	*n* pl. **-S** artillery; a cannon
ORDO	*n* pl. **-DOS** or **-DINES** a calendar of religious directions
ORDURE	*n* pl. **-S** manure **ORDUROUS** *adj*
ORE	*n* pl. **-S** a mineral or rock containing a valuable metal
OREAD	*n* pl. **-S** a mountain nymph in Greek mythology
ORECTIC	*adj* pertaining to appetites or desires
ORECTIVE	*adj* orectic
OREGANO	*n* pl. **-NOS** an aromatic herb used as a seasoning
OREIDE	*n* pl. **-S** oroide

OREODONT *n* pl. **-S** an extinct sheep-sized mammal

ORFRAY *n* pl. **-FRAYS** orphrey

ORGAN *n* pl. **-S** a differentiated part of an organism performing a specific function

ORGANA a pl. of organon and organum

ORGANDIE *n* pl. **-S** organdy

ORGANDY *n* pl. **-DIES** a cotton fabric

ORGANIC *n* pl. **-S** a substance of animal or vegetable origin

ORGANISE *v* **-NISED, -NISING, -NISES** to organize

ORGANISM *n* pl. **-S** any form of animal or plant life

ORGANIST *n* pl. **-S** one who plays the organ (a keyboard musical instrument)

ORGANIZE *v* **-NIZED, -NIZING, -NIZES** to form into an orderly whole

ORGANON *n* pl. **-GANONS** or **-GANA** a system of rules for scientific investigation

ORGANUM *n* pl. **-GANUMS** or **-GANA** organon

ORGANZA *n* pl. **-S** a sheer fabric

ORGASM *v* **-ED, -ING, -S** to experience an orgasm (the climax of sexual excitement) **ORGASMIC, ORGASTIC** *adj*

ORGEAT *n* pl. **-S** an almond-flavored syrup

ORGIAC *adj* of the nature of an orgy

ORGIAST *n* pl. **-S** one who participates in an orgy

ORGIC *adj* orgiac

ORGONE *n* pl. **-S** a postulated energy pervading the universe

ORGULOUS *adj* proud

ORGY *n* pl. **-GIES** a party marked by unrestrained sexual indulgence

ORIBATID *n* pl. **-S** any of a family of eyeless mites

ORIBI *n* pl. **-S** an African antelope

ORIEL *n* pl. **-S** a type of projecting window

ORIENT *v* **-ED, -ING, -S** to adjust in relation to something else

ORIENTAL *n* pl. **-S** an inhabitant of an eastern country

ORIENTER *n* pl. **-S** one who helps another to adjust to surroundings

ORIFICE *n* pl. **-S** a mouth or mouthlike opening

ORIGAMI *n* pl. **-S** the Japanese art of paper folding

ORIGAN *n* pl. **-S** marjoram

ORIGANUM *n* pl. **-S** an aromatic herb

ORIGIN *n* pl. **-S** a coming into being

ORIGINAL *n* pl. **-S** the first form of something

ORINASAL *n* pl. **-S** a sound pronounced through both the mouth and nose

ORIOLE *n* pl. **-S** an American songbird

ORISHA *n* pl. **-S** a Yoruba deity

ORISON *n* pl. **-S** a prayer

ORLE *n* pl. **-S** a heraldic border

ORLOP *n* pl. **-S** the lowest deck of a ship

ORMER *n* pl. **-S** an abalone

ORMOLU *n* pl. **-S** an alloy used to imitate gold

ORNAMENT *v* **-ED, -ING, -S** to decorate

ORNATE *adj* elaborately or excessively ornamented **ORNATELY** *adv*

ORNERY *adj* **-NERIER, -NERIEST** stubborn and mean-spirited

ORNIS *n* pl. **ORNITHES** avifauna

ORNITHIC *adj* pertaining to birds

OROGENY *n* pl. **-NIES** the process of mountain formation **OROGENIC** *adj*

OROIDE *n* pl. **-S** an alloy used to imitate gold

OROLOGY *n* pl. **-GIES** the study of mountains

OROMETER *n* pl. **-S** a type of barometer

OROTUND *adj* full and clear in sound

ORPHAN *v* **-ED, -ING, -S** to deprive of both parents

ORPHIC *adj* mystical

ORPHICAL *adj* orphic

ORPHISM *n* pl. **-S** a style of art

ORPHREY *n* pl. **-PHREYS** an ornamental band or border

ORPIMENT *n* pl. **-S** a yellow dye

ORPIN *n* pl. **-S** orpine

ORPINE *n* pl. **-S** a perennial herb

ORRA *adj* occasional

ORRERY *n* pl. **-RERIES** a mechanical model of the solar system

ORRICE *n* pl. **-S** orris

ORRIS *n* pl. **-RISES** a flowering plant

ORT *n* pl. **-S** a scrap of food

ORTHICON *n* pl. **-S** a type of television camera tube

ORTHO *adj* pertaining to reproduction in a photograph of the full range of colors in nature

ORTHODOX *n* pl. **-ES** one holding traditional beliefs

ORTHOEPY *n* pl. **-EPIES** the study of correct pronunciation

ORTHOSIS *n* pl. **-THOSES** an orthotic

ORTHOTIC *n* pl. **-S** a brace for weak joints or muscles

ORTOLAN *n* pl. **-S** a European bird

ORYX *n* pl. **-ES** an African antelope

ORZO *n* pl. **-ZOS** rice-shaped pasta

OS *n* pl. **ORA** an orifice

OS *n* pl. **OSAR** an esker

OS *n* pl. **OSSA** a bone

OSCINE *n* pl. **-S** any of a family of songbirds **OSCININE** *adj*

OSCITANT *adj* yawning

OSCULA pl. of osculum

OSCULANT *adj* adhering closely

OSCULAR *adj* pertaining to the mouth

OSCULATE *v* **-LATED, -LATING, -LATES** to kiss

OSCULE *n* pl. **-S** osculum

OSCULUM *n* pl. **-LA** an opening in a sponge

OSE *n* pl. **-S** an esker

OSETRA *n* pl. **-S** a golden or brownish caviar

OSIER *n* pl. **-S** a European tree **OSIERED** *adj*

OSMATIC *adj* depending mainly on the sense of smell

OSMICS *n/pl* the study of the sense of smell

OSMIUM *n* pl. **-S** a metallic element **OSMIC, OSMIOUS** *adj*

OSMOL *n* pl. **-S** a unit of osmotic pressure **OSMOLAL** *adj*

OSMOLAR *adj* osmotic

OSMOLE *n* pl. **-S** osmol

OSMOSE *v* **-MOSED, -MOSING, -MOSES** to undergo osmosis

OSMOSIS *n* pl. **-MOSES** a form of diffusion of a fluid through a membrane

OSMOTIC *adj* pertaining to osmosis

OSMOUS *adj* containing osmium

OSMUND *n* pl. **-S** any of a genus of large ferns

OSMUNDA *n* pl. **-S** osmund

OSNABURG *n* pl. **-S** a cotton fabric

OSPREY *n* pl. **-PREYS** an American hawk

OSSA pl. of os

OSSATURE *n* pl. **-S** a framework

OSSEIN *n* pl. **-S** a protein substance in bone

OSSEOUS *adj* resembling bone

OSSETRA *n* pl. **-S** osetra

OSSIA *conj* or else — used as a musical direction

OSSICLE *n* pl. **-S** a small bone

OSSIFIC *adj* pertaining to the formation of bone

OSSIFIER *n* pl. **-S** one that ossifies

OSSIFY *v* **-FIED, -FYING, -FIES** to convert into bone

OSSUARY *n* pl. **-ARIES** a receptacle for the bones of the dead

OSTEAL *adj* osseous

OSTEITIS *n* pl. **-ITIDES** inflammation of bone **OSTEITIC** *adj*

OSTEOID *n* pl. **-S** uncalcified bone matrix

OSTEOMA *n* pl. **-MAS** or **-MATA** a tumor of bone tissue

OSTEOSIS *n* pl. **-OSISES** or **-OSES** the formation of bone

OSTIA pl. of ostium

OSTIARY *n* pl. **-ARIES** a doorkeeper at a church

OSTINATO *n* pl. **-TOS** or **-TI** a constantly recurring musical phrase

OSTIOLE *n* pl. **-S** a small bodily opening **OSTIOLAR** *adj*

OSTIUM *n* pl. **OSTIA** an opening in a bodily organ

OSTLER *n* pl. **-S** hostler

OSTMARK *n* pl. **-S** a former East German monetary unit

OSTOMATE *n* pl. **-S** one who has had an ostomy

OSTOMY *n* pl. **-MIES** a type of surgical operation

OSTOSIS *n* pl. **-TOSISES** or **-TOSES** the formation of bone

OSTRACOD *n* pl. **-S** a minute freshwater crustacean

OSTRACON *n* pl. **-CA** a fragment containing an inscription

OSTRAKON *n* pl. **-KA** ostracon

OSTRICH *n* pl. **-ES** a large, flightless bird

OTALGIA *n* pl. **-S** pain in the ear **OTALGIC** *adj*

OTALGY *n* pl. **-GIES** otalgia

OTHER *n* pl. **-S** one that remains of two or more

OTIC *adj* pertaining to the ear

OTIOSE *adj* lazy **OTIOSELY** *adv*

OTIOSITY *n* pl. **-TIES** the state of being otiose

OTITIS *n* pl. **OTITISES** or **OTITIDES** inflammation of the ear **OTITIC** *adj*

OTOCYST *n* pl. **-S** an organ of balance in many invertebrates

OTOLITH *n* pl. **-S** a hard mass that forms in the inner ear

OTOLOGY *n* pl. **-GIES** the science of the ear

OTOSCOPE *n* pl. **-S** an instrument for examining the ear

OTOSCOPY *n* pl. **-PIES** the use of an otoscope

OTOTOXIC *adj* adversely affecting hearing or balance

OTTAR *n* pl. **-S** attar

OTTAVA *n* pl. **-S** an octave

OTTER *n* pl. **-S** a carnivorous mammal

OTTO *n* pl. **-TOS** attar

OTTOMAN *n* pl. **-S** a type of sofa

OUABAIN *n* pl. **-S** a cardiac stimulant

OUCH *v* **-ED, -ING, -ES** to ornament with ouches (settings for precious stones)

OUD *n* pl. **-S** a stringed instrument of northern Africa

OUGHT *v* **-ED, -ING, -S** to owe

OUGUIYA *n* pl. **-S** a monetary unit of Mauritania

OUISTITI *n* pl. **-S** a South American monkey

OUNCE *n* pl. **-S** a unit of weight

OUPH *n* pl. **-S** ouphe

OUPHE *n* pl. **-S** an elf

OUR *pron* a possessive form of the pronoun we

OURANG *n* pl. **-S** orang

OURARI *n* pl. **-S** curare

OUREBI *n* pl. **-S** oribi

OURIE *adj* shivering with cold

OURS *pron* a possessive form of the pronoun we

OURSELF *pron* myself — used in formal or regal contexts

OUSEL *n* pl. **-S** ouzel

OUST *v* **-ED, -ING, -S** to expel or remove from a position or place

OUSTER *n* pl. **-S** the act of ousting

OUT *v* **-ED, -ING, -S** to be revealed

OUTACT *v* **-ED, -ING, -S** to surpass in acting

OUTADD *v* **-ED, -ING, -S** to surpass in adding

OUTAGE *n* pl. **-S** a failure or interruption in use or functioning

OUTARGUE *v* **-GUED, -GUING, -GUES** to get the better of by arguing

OUTASK *v* **-ED, -ING, -S** to surpass in asking

OUTATE past tense of outeat

OUTBACK *n* pl. **-S** isolated rural country

OUTBAKE *v* **-BAKED, -BAKING, -BAKES** to surpass in baking

OUTBARK *v* **-ED, -ING, -S** to surpass in barking

OUTBAWL *v* **-ED, -ING, -S** to surpass in bawling

OUTBEAM *v* **-ED, -ING, -S** to surpass in beaming

OUTBEG *v* **-BEGGED, -BEGGING, -BEGS** to surpass in begging

OUTBID *v* **-BID, -BIDDEN, -BIDDING, -BIDS** to bid higher than

OUTBITCH *v* **-ED, -ING, -ES** to surpass in bitching

OUTBLAZE *v* **-BLAZED, -BLAZING, -BLAZES** to surpass in brilliance of light

OUTBLEAT *v* **-ED, -ING, -S** to surpass in bleating

OUTBLESS *v* **-ED, -ING, -ES** to surpass in blessing

OUTBLOOM *v* **-ED, -ING, -S** to surpass in blooming

OUTBLUFF *v* **-ED, -ING, -S** to surpass in bluffing

OUTBLUSH *v* **-ED, -ING, -ES** to surpass in blushing

OUTBOARD *n* pl. **-S** a type of motor

OUTBOAST *v* **-ED, -ING, -S** to surpass in boasting

OUTBOUGHT past tense of outbuy

OUTBOUND *adj* outward bound

OUTBOX   *v* **-ED, -ING, -ES** to surpass in boxing

OUTBRAG   *v* **-BRAGGED, -BRAGGING, -BRAGS** to surpass in bragging

OUTBRAVE   *v* **-BRAVED, -BRAVING, -BRAVES** to surpass in courage

OUTBRAWL   *v* **-ED, -ING, -S** to surpass in brawling

OUTBREAK   *n* pl. **-S** a sudden eruption

OUTBREED   *v* **-BRED, -BREEDING, -BREEDS** to interbreed relatively unrelated stocks

OUTBRIBE   *v* **-BRIBED, -BRIBING, -BRIBES** to surpass in bribing

OUTBUILD   *v* **-BUILT, -BUILDING, -BUILDS** to surpass in building

OUTBULGE   *v* **-BULGED, -BULGING, -BULGES** to surpass in size

OUTBULK   *v* **-ED, -ING, -S** to surpass in bulking

OUTBULLY   *v* **-LIED, -LYING, -LIES** to surpass in bullying

OUTBURN   *v* **-BURNED** or **-BURNT, -BURNING, -BURNS** to burn longer than

OUTBURST   *n* pl. **-S** a sudden and violent outpouring

OUTBUY   *v* **-BOUGHT, -BUYING, -BUYS** to surpass in buying

OUTBY   *adv* outdoors

OUTBYE   *adv* outby

OUTCALL   *n* pl. **-S** a house call by a professional person

OUTCAPER   *v* **-ED, -ING, -S** to surpass in capering

OUTCAST   *n* pl. **-S** one that is cast out

OUTCASTE   *n* pl. **-S** a Hindu who has been expelled from his caste

OUTCATCH   *v* **-CAUGHT, -CATCHING, -CATCHES** to surpass in catching

OUTCAVIL   *v* **-ILED, -ILING, -ILS** or **-ILLED, -ILLING, -ILS** to surpass in caviling

OUTCHARM   *v* **-ED, -ING, -S** to surpass in charming

OUTCHEAT   *v* **-ED, -ING, -S** to surpass in cheating

OUTCHIDE   *v* **-CHIDED** or **-CHID, -CHIDDEN, -CHIDING, -CHIDES** to surpass in chiding

OUTCITY   *n* pl. **-TIES** a city on the outskirts of a larger city

OUTCLASS   *v* **-ED, -ING, -ES** to surpass so decisively as to appear of a higher class

OUTCLIMB   *v* **-CLIMBED** or **-CLOMB, -CLIMBING, -CLIMBS** to surpass in climbing

OUTCOACH   *v* **-ED, -ING, -ES** to surpass in coaching

OUTCOME   *n* pl. **-S** a result

OUTCOOK   *v* **-ED, -ING, -S** to surpass in cooking

OUTCOUNT   *v* **-ED, -ING, -S** to surpass in counting

OUTCRAWL   *v* **-ED, -ING, -S** to surpass in crawling

OUTCRIED   past tense of outcry

OUTCRIES   present 3d person sing. of outcry

OUTCROP   *v* **-CROPPED, -CROPPING, -CROPS** to protrude above the soil

OUTCROSS   *v* **-ED, -ING, -ES** to cross with a relatively unrelated individual

OUTCROW   *v* **-ED, -ING, -S** to surpass in crowing

OUTCROWD   *v* **-ED, -ING, -S** to cause to be too crowded

OUTCRY   *v* **-CRIED, -CRYING, -CRIES** to cry louder than

OUTCURSE   *v* **-CURSED, -CURSING, -CURSES** to surpass in cursing

OUTCURVE   *n* pl. **-S** a type of pitch in baseball

OUTDANCE   *v* **-DANCED, -DANCING, -DANCES** to surpass in dancing

OUTDARE   *v* **-DARED, -DARING, -DARES** to surpass in daring

OUTDATE   *v* **-DATED, -DATING, -DATES** to make out-of-date

OUTDO   *v* **-DID, -DONE, -DOING, -DOES** to exceed in performance

OUTDODGE   *v* **-DODGED, -DODGING, -DODGES** to surpass in dodging

OUTDOER   *n* pl. **-S** one that outdoes

OUTDOOR   *adj* pertaining to the open air

OUTDOORS   *adv* in the open air

OUTDRAG   *v* **-DRAGGED, -DRAGGING, -DRAGS** to surpass in drag racing

OUTDRANK   past tense of outdrink

OUTDRAW   *v* **-DREW, -DRAWN, -DRAWING, -DRAWS** to attract a larger audience than

OUTDREAM   *v* **-DREAMED** or **-DREAMT, -DREAMING, -DREAMS** to surpass in dreaming

OUTDRESS v **-ED, -ING, -ES** to surpass in dressing

OUTDRINK v **-DRANK, -DRUNK, -DRINKING, -DRINKS** to surpass in drinking

OUTDRIVE v **-DROVE, -DRIVEN, -DRIVING, -DRIVES** to drive a golf ball farther than

OUTDROP v **-DROPPED, -DROPPING, -DROPS** to surpass in dropping

OUTDUEL v **-DUELED, -DUELING, -DUELS** or **-DUELLED, -DUELLING, -DUELS** to surpass in dueling

OUTEARN v **-ED, -ING, -S** to surpass in earning

OUTEAT v **-ATE, -EATEN, -EATING, -EATS** to surpass in eating

OUTECHO v **-ED, -ING, -ES** to surpass in echoing

OUTER n pl. **-S** a part of a target

OUTFABLE v **-BLED, -BLING, -BLES** to surpass in fabling

OUTFACE v **-FACED, -FACING, -FACES** to confront unflinchingly

OUTFALL n pl. **-S** the outlet of a body of water

OUTFAST v **-ED, -ING, -S** to surpass in fasting

OUTFAWN v **-ED, -ING, -S** to surpass in fawning

OUTFEAST v **-ED, -ING, -S** to surpass in feasting

OUTFEEL v **-FELT, -FEELING, -FEELS** to surpass in feeling

OUTFENCE v **-FENCED, -FENCING, -FENCES** to surpass in fencing

OUTFIELD n pl. **-S** a part of a baseball field

OUTFIGHT v **-FOUGHT, -FIGHTING, -FIGHTS** to defeat

OUTFIND v **-FOUND, -FINDING, -FINDS** to surpass in finding

OUTFIRE v **-FIRED, -FIRING, -FIRES** to surpass in firing

OUTFISH v **-ED, -ING, -ES** to surpass in fishing

OUTFIT v **-FITTED, -FITTING, -FITS** to equip

OUTFLANK v **-ED, -ING, -S** to gain a tactical advantage over

OUTFLOAT v **-ED, -ING, -S** to float longer than

OUTFLOW v **-ED, -ING, -S** to flow out

OUTFLY v **-FLEW, -FLOWN, -FLYING, -FLIES** to surpass in speed of flight

OUTFOOL v **-ED, -ING, -S** to surpass in fooling

OUTFOOT v **-ED, -ING, -S** to surpass in speed

OUTFOUGHT past tense of outfight

OUTFOUND past tense of outfind

OUTFOX v **-ED, -ING, -ES** to outwit

OUTFROWN v **-ED, -ING, -S** to frown more than

OUTGAIN v **-ED, -ING, -S** to gain more than

OUTGAS v **-GASSED, -GASSING, -GASSES** to remove gas from

OUTGAZE v **-GAZED, -GAZING, -GAZES** to surpass in gazing

OUTGIVE v **-GAVE, -GIVEN, -GIVING, -GIVES** to give more than

OUTGLARE v **-GLARED, -GLARING, -GLARES** to surpass in glaring

OUTGLEAM v **-ED, -ING, -S** to surpass in gleaming

OUTGLOW v **-ED, -ING, -S** to surpass in glowing

OUTGNAW v **-GNAWED, -GNAWN, -GNAWING, -GNAWS** to surpass in gnawing

OUTGO v **-WENT, -GONE, -GOING, -GOES** to go beyond

OUTGOING n pl. **-S** a departure

OUTGREW past tense of outgrow

OUTGRIN v **-GRINNED, -GRINNING, -GRINS** to surpass in grinning

OUTGROSS v **-ED, -ING, -ES** to surpass in gross earnings

OUTGROUP n pl. **-S** a group of people outside one's own group

OUTGROW v **-GREW, -GROWN, -GROWING, -GROWS** to grow too large for

OUTGUESS v **-ED, -ING, -ES** to anticipate the actions of

OUTGUIDE v **-GUIDED, -GUIDING, -GUIDES** to surpass in guiding

OUTGUN v **-GUNNED, -GUNNING, -GUNS** to surpass in firepower

OUTGUSH v **-ED, -ING, -ES** to surpass in gushing

OUTHAUL n pl. **-S** a rope for extending a sail along a spar

OUTHEAR v **-HEARD, -HEARING, -HEARS** to surpass in hearing

OUTHIT v **-HIT, -HITTING, -HITS** to get more hits than

OUTHOMER v **-ED, -ING, -S** to surpass in hitting home runs

OUTHOUSE *n* pl. **-S** a toilet housed in a small structure

OUTHOWL *v* **-ED, -ING, -S** to surpass in howling

OUTHUMOR *v* **-ED, -ING, -S** to surpass in humoring

OUTHUNT *v* **-ED, -ING, -S** to surpass in hunting

OUTING *n* pl. **-S** a short pleasure trip

OUTJINX *v* **-ED, -ING, -ES** to surpass in jinxing

OUTJUMP *v* **-ED, -ING, -S** to surpass in jumping

OUTJUT *v* **-JUTTED, -JUTTING, -JUTS** to stick out

OUTKEEP *v* **-KEPT, -KEEPING, -KEEPS** to surpass in keeping

OUTKICK *v* **-ED, -ING, -S** to surpass in kicking

OUTKILL *v* **-ED, -ING, -S** to surpass in killing

OUTKISS *v* **-ED, -ING, -ES** to surpass in kissing

OUTLAID past tense of outlay

OUTLAIN past participle of outlie

OUTLAND *n* pl. **-S** a foreign land

OUTLAST *v* **-ED, -ING, -S** to last longer than

OUTLAUGH *v* **-ED, -ING, -S** to surpass in laughing

OUTLAW *v* **-ED, -ING, -S** to prohibit

OUTLAWRY *n* pl. **-RIES** habitual defiance of the law

OUTLAY *v* **-LAID, -LAYING, -LAYS** to pay out

OUTLEAD *v* **-LED, -LEADING, -LEADS** to surpass in leading

OUTLEAP *v* **-LEAPED** or **-LEAPT, -LEAPING, -LEAPS** to surpass in leaping

OUTLEARN *v* **-LEARNED** or **-LEARNT, -LEARNING, -LEARNS** to surpass in learning

OUTLET *n* pl. **-S** a passage for escape or discharge

OUTLIE *v* **-LAY, -LAIN, -LYING, -LIES** to lie beyond

OUTLIER *n* pl. **-S** an outlying area or portion

OUTLINE *v* **-LINED, -LINING, -LINES** to indicate the main features or different parts of

OUTLINER *n* pl. **-S** one that outlines

OUTLIVE *v* **-LIVED, -LIVING, -LIVES** to live longer than

OUTLIVER *n* pl. **-S** one that outlives

OUTLOOK *n* pl. **-S** a point of view

OUTLOVE *v* **-LOVED, -LOVING, -LOVES** to surpass in loving

OUTLYING present participle of outlie

OUTMAN *v* **-MANNED, -MANNING, -MANS** to surpass in manpower

OUTMARCH *v* **-ED, -ING, -ES** to surpass in marching

OUTMATCH *v* **-ED, -ING, -ES** to outdo

OUTMODE *v* **-MODED, -MODING, -MODES** to outdate

OUTMOST *adj* farthest out

OUTMOVE *v* **-MOVED, -MOVING, -MOVES** to move faster or farther than

OUTPACE *v* **-PACED, -PACING, -PACES** to surpass in speed

OUTPAINT *v* **-ED, -ING, -S** to surpass in painting

OUTPASS *v* **-ED, -ING, -ES** to excel in passing a football

OUTPITCH *v* **-ED, -ING, -ES** to surpass in pitching

OUTPITY *v* **-PITIED, -PITYING, -PITIES** to surpass in pitying

OUTPLACE *v* **-PLACED, -PLACING, -PLACES** to discontinue the employment of

OUTPLAN *v* **-PLANNED, -PLANNING, -PLANS** to surpass in planning

OUTPLAY *v* **-ED, -ING, -S** to excel or defeat in a game

OUTPLOD *v* **-PLODDED, -PLODDING, -PLODS** to surpass in plodding

OUTPLOT *v* **-PLOTTED, -PLOTTING, -PLOTS** to surpass in plotting

OUTPOINT *v* **-ED, -ING, -S** to score more points than

OUTPOLL *v* **-ED, -ING, -S** to get more votes than

OUTPORT *n* pl. **-S** a port of export or departure

OUTPOST *n* pl. **-S** a body of troops stationed at a distance from the main body

OUTPOUR *v* **-ED, -ING, -S** to pour out

OUTPOWER *v* **-ED, -ING, -S** to surpass in power

OUTPRAY *v* **-ED, -ING, -S** to surpass in praying

OUTPREEN *v* **-ED, -ING, -S** to surpass in preening

OUTPRESS *v* **-ED, -ING, -ES** to surpass in pressing

OUTPRICE   *v* **-PRICED, -PRICING, -PRICES** to surpass in pricing

OUTPULL   *v* **-ED, -ING, -S** to attract a larger audience or following than

OUTPUNCH   *v* **-ED, -ING, -ES** to surpass in punching

OUTPUPIL   *n* **-S** a pupil who lives off campus

OUTPUSH   *v* **-ED, -ING, -ES** to surpass in pushing

OUTPUT   *v* **-PUTTED, -PUTTING, -PUTS** to produce

OUTQUOTE   *v* **-QUOTED, -QUOTING, -QUOTES** to surpass in quoting

OUTRACE   *v* **-RACED, -RACING, -RACES** to run faster or farther than

OUTRAGE   *v* **-RAGED, -RAGING, -RAGES** to arouse anger or resentment in

OUTRAISE   *v* **-RAISED, -RAISING, -RAISES** to surpass in raising

OUTRAN   past tense of outrun

OUTRANCE   *n* pl. **-S** the last extremity

OUTRANG   past tense of outring

OUTRANGE   *v* **-RANGED, -RANGING, -RANGES** to surpass in range

OUTRANK   *v* **-ED, -ING, -S** to rank higher than

OUTRATE   *v* **-RATED, -RATING, -RATES** to surpass in a rating

OUTRAVE   *v* **-RAVED, -RAVING, -RAVES** to surpass in raving

OUTRE   *adj* deviating from what is usual or proper

OUTREACH   *v* **-ED, -ING, -ES** to reach beyond

OUTREAD   *v* **-READ, -READING, -READS** to surpass in reading

OUTRIDE   *v* **-RODE, -RIDDEN, -RIDING, -RIDES** to ride faster or better than

OUTRIDER   *n* pl. **-S** a mounted attendant who rides before or beside a carriage

OUTRIG   *v* **-RIGGED, -RIGGING, -RIGS** to equip (a boat) with outriggers (projections having floats)

OUTRIGHT   *adj* being without limit or reservation

OUTRING   *v* **-RANG, -RUNG, -RINGING, -RINGS** to ring louder than

OUTRIVAL   *v* **-VALED, -VALING, -VALS** or **-VALLED, -VALLING, -VALS** to outdo in a competition or rivalry

OUTROAR   *v* **-ED, -ING, -S** to roar louder than

OUTROCK   *v* **-ED, -ING, -S** to surpass in rocking

OUTRODE   past tense of outride

OUTROLL   *v* **-ED, -ING, -S** to roll out

OUTROOT   *v* **-ED, -ING, -S** to pull up by the roots

OUTROW   *v* **-ED, -ING, -S** to surpass in rowing

OUTRUN   *v* **-RAN, -RUNNING, -RUNS** to run faster than

OUTRUNG   past participle of outring

OUTRUSH   *v* **-ED, -ING, -ES** to surpass in rushing

OUTSAID   past tense of outsay

OUTSAIL   *v* **-ED, -ING, -S** to sail faster than

OUTSANG   past tense of outsing

OUTSAT   past tense of outsit

OUTSAVOR   *v* **-ED, -ING, -S** to surpass in a distinctive taste or smell

OUTSAW   past tense of outsee

OUTSAY   *v* **-SAID, -SAYING, -SAYS** to surpass in saying

OUTSCOLD   *v* **-ED, -ING, -S** to surpass in scolding

OUTSCOOP   *v* **-ED, -ING, -S** to surpass in scooping

OUTSCORE   *v* **-SCORED, -SCORING, -SCORES** to score more points than

OUTSCORN   *v* **-ED, -ING, -S** to surpass in scorning

OUTSEE   *v* **-SAW, -SEEN, -SEEING, -SEES** to see beyond

OUTSELL   *v* **-SOLD, -SELLING, -SELLS** to sell more than

OUTSERT   *n* pl. **-S** a folded sheet placed around a folded section of printed matter

OUTSERVE   *v* **-SERVED, -SERVING, -SERVES** to surpass in serving

OUTSET   *n* pl. **-S** a beginning

OUTSHAME   *v* **-SHAMED, -SHAMING, -SHAMES** to surpass in shaming

OUTSHINE   *v* **-SHONE** or **-SHINED, -SHINING, -SHINES** to shine brighter than

OUTSHOOT   *v* **-SHOT, -SHOOTING, -SHOOTS** to shoot better than

OUTSHOUT   *v* **-ED, -ING, -S** to shout louder than

OUTSIDE   *n* pl. **-S** the outer side, surface, or part

OUTSIDER   *n* pl. **-S** one that does not belong to a particular group

OUTSIGHT   *n* pl. **-S** the power of perceiving external things

OUTSIN _v_ **-SINNED, -SINNING, -SINS** to surpass in sinning

OUTSING _v_ **-SANG, -SUNG, -SINGING, -SINGS** to surpass in singing

OUTSIT _v_ **-SAT, -SITTING, -SITS** to remain sitting or in session longer than

OUTSIZE _n_ pl. **-S** an unusual size **OUTSIZED** _adj_

OUTSKATE _v_ **-SKATED, -SKATING, -SKATES** to surpass in skating

OUTSKIRT _n_ pl. **-S** an outlying area

OUTSLEEP _v_ **-SLEPT, -SLEEPING, -SLEEPS** to sleep later than

OUTSLICK _v_ **-ED, -ING, -S** to get the better of by trickery or cunning

OUTSMART _v_ **-ED, -ING, -S** to outwit

OUTSMELL _v_ **-SMELLED** or **-SMELT, -SMELLING, -SMELLS** to surpass in smelling

OUTSMILE _v_ **-SMILED, -SMILING, -SMILES** to surpass in smiling

OUTSMOKE _v_ **-SMOKED, -SMOKING, -SMOKES** to surpass in smoking

OUTSNORE _v_ **-SNORED, -SNORING, -SNORES** to surpass in snoring

OUTSOAR _v_ **-ED, -ING, -S** to soar beyond

OUTSOLD past tense of outsell

OUTSOLE _n_ pl. **-S** the outer sole of a boot or shoe

OUTSPAN _v_ **-SPANNED, -SPANNING, -SPANS** to unharness a draft animal

OUTSPEAK _v_ **-SPOKE, -SPOKEN, -SPEAKING, -SPEAKS** to outdo in speaking

OUTSPEED _v_ **-SPED** or **-SPEEDED, -SPEEDING, -SPEEDS** to go faster than

OUTSPELL _v_ **-SPELLED** or **-SPELT, -SPELLING, -SPELLS** to surpass in spelling

OUTSPEND _v_ **-SPENT, -SPENDING, -SPENDS** to exceed the limits of in spending

OUTSPOKE past tense of outspeak

OUTSPOKEN past participle of outspeak

OUTSTAND _v_ **-STOOD, -STANDING, -STANDS** to endure beyond

OUTSTARE _v_ **-STARED, -STARING, -STARES** to outface

OUTSTART _v_ **-ED, -ING, -S** to get ahead of at the start

OUTSTATE _v_ **-STATED, -STATING, -STATES** to surpass in stating

OUTSTAY _v_ **-ED, -ING, -S** to surpass in staying power

OUTSTEER _v_ **-ED, -ING, -S** to surpass in steering

OUTSTOOD past tense of outstand

OUTSTRIP _v_ **-STRIPPED, -STRIPPING, -STRIPS** to go faster or farther than

OUTSTUDY _v_ **-STUDIED, -STUDYING, -STUDIES** to surpass in studying

OUTSTUNT _v_ **-ED, -ING, -S** to surpass in stunting

OUTSULK _v_ **-ED, -ING, -S** to surpass in sulking

OUTSUNG past participle of outsing

OUTSWEAR _v_ **-SWORE** or **-SWARE, -SWORN, -SWEARING, -SWEARS** to surpass in swearing

OUTSWEEP _v_ **-SWEPT, -SWEEPING, -SWEEPS** to surpass in sweeping

OUTSWIM _v_ **-SWAM, -SWUM, -SWIMMING, -SWIMS** to swim faster or farther than

OUTSWING _v_ **-SWUNG, -SWINGING, -SWINGS** to surpass in swinging

OUTTAKE _n_ pl. **-S** a passage outwards

OUTTALK _v_ **-ED, -ING, -S** to surpass in talking

OUTTASK _v_ **-ED, -ING, -S** to surpass in tasking

OUTTELL _v_ **-TOLD, -TELLING, -TELLS** to say openly

OUTTHANK _v_ **-ED, -ING, -S** to surpass in thanking

OUTTHINK _v_ **-THOUGHT, -THINKING, -THINKS** to get the better of by thinking

OUTTHROB _v_ **-THROBBED, -THROBBING, -THROBS** to surpass in throbbing

OUTTHROW _v_ **-THREW, -THROWN, -THROWING, -THROWS** to throw farther or more accurately than

OUTTOLD past tense of outtell

OUTTOWER _v_ **-ED, -ING, -S** to tower above

OUTTRADE _v_ **-TRADED, -TRADING, -TRADES** to get the better of in a trade

OUTTRICK _v_ **-ED, -ING, -S** to get the better of by trickery

OUTTROT _v_ **-TROTTED, -TROTTING, -TROTS** to surpass in trotting

OUTTRUMP _v_ **-ED, -ING, -S** to outplay

OUTTURN _n_ pl. **-S** a quantity produced

OUTVALUE	*v* **-UED, -UING, -UES** to be worth more than
OUTVAUNT	*v* **-ED, -ING, -S** to surpass in vaunting
OUTVIE	*v* **-VIED, -VYING, -VIES** to surpass in a competition
OUTVOICE	*v* **-VOICED, -VOICING, -VOICES** to surpass in loudness of voice
OUTVOTE	*v* **-VOTED, -VOTING, -VOTES** to defeat by a majority of votes
OUTWAIT	*v* **-ED, -ING, -S** to exceed in patience
OUTWALK	*v* **-ED, -ING, -S** to surpass in walking
OUTWAR	*v* **-WARRED, -WARRING, -WARS** to surpass in warring
OUTWARD	*adv* toward the outside
OUTWARDS	*adv* outward
OUTWASH	*n* pl. **-ES** detritus washed from a glacier
OUTWASTE	*v* **-WASTED, -WASTING, -WASTES** to surpass in wasting
OUTWATCH	*v* **-ED, -ING, -ES** to watch longer than
OUTWEAR	*v* **-WORE, -WORN, -WEARING, -WEARS** to last longer than
OUTWEARY	*v* **-RIED, -RYING, -RIES** to surpass in wearying
OUTWEEP	*v* **-WEPT, -WEEPING, -WEEPS** to weep more than
OUTWEIGH	*v* **-ED, -ING, -S** to weigh more than
OUTWENT	past tense of outgo
OUTWHIRL	*v* **-ED, -ING, -S** to surpass in whirling
OUTWILE	*v* **-WILED, -WILING, -WILES** to surpass in wiling
OUTWILL	*v* **-ED, -ING, -S** to surpass in willpower
OUTWIND	*v* **-ED, -ING, -S** to cause to be out of breath
OUTWISH	*v* **-ED, -ING, -ES** to surpass in wishing
OUTWIT	*v* **-WITTED, -WITTING, -WITS** to get the better of by superior cleverness
OUTWITH	*prep* beyond the limits of
OUTWORE	past tense of outwear
OUTWORK	*v* **-WORKED** or **-WROUGHT, -WORKING, -WORKS** to work faster or better than
OUTWORN	past participle of outwear

OUTWRITE	*v* **-WROTE** or **-WRIT, -WRITTEN, -WRITING, -WRITES** to write better than
OUTYELL	*v* **-ED, -ING, -S** to yell louder than
OUTYELP	*v* **-ED, -ING, -S** to surpass in yelping
OUTYIELD	*v* **-ED, -ING, -S** to surpass in yield
OUZEL	*n* pl. **-S** a European bird
OUZO	*n* pl. **-ZOS** a Greek liqueur
OVA	pl. of ovum
OVAL	*n* pl. **-S** an oval (egg-shaped) figure or object
OVALITY	*n* pl. **-TIES** ovalness
OVALLY	*adv* in the shape of an oval
OVALNESS	*n* pl. **-ES** the state of being oval
OVARIAL	*adj* ovarian
OVARIAN	*adj* pertaining to an ovary
OVARIES	pl. of ovary
OVARIOLE	*n* pl. **-S** one of the tubes of which the ovaries of most insects are composed
OVARITIS	*n* pl. **-RITIDES** inflammation of an ovary
OVARY	*n* pl. **-RIES** a female reproductive gland
OVATE	*adj* egg-shaped **OVATELY** *adv*
OVATION	*n* pl. **-S** an expression or demonstration of popular acclaim
OVEN	*n* pl. **-S** an enclosed compartment in which substances are heated **OVENLIKE** *adj*
OVENBIRD	*n* pl. **-S** an American songbird
OVENWARE	*n* pl. **-S** heat-resistant dishes for baking and serving food
OVER	*v* **-ED, -ING, -S** to leap above and to the other side of
OVERABLE	*adj* excessively able
OVERACT	*v* **-ED, -ING, -S** to act with exaggeration
OVERAGE	*n* pl. **-S** an amount in excess
OVERAGED	*adj* too old to be useful
OVERALL	*n* pl. **-S** a loose outer garment
OVERAPT	*adj* excessively apt
OVERARCH	*v* **-ED, -ING, -ES** to form an arch over
OVERARM	*v* **-ED, -ING, -S** to supply with an excess of weaponry
OVERATE	past tense of overeat
OVERAWE	*v* **-AWED, -AWING, -AWES** to subdue by inspiring awe

OVERBAKE *v* **-BAKED, -BAKING, -BAKES** to bake too long

OVERBEAR *v* **-BORE, -BORNE** or **-BORN, -BEARING, -BEARS** to bring down by superior weight or force

OVERBEAT *v* **-BEAT, -BEATEN, -BEATING, -BEATS** to beat too much

OVERBED *adj* spanning a bed

OVERBET *v* **-BET** or **-BETTED, -BETTING, -BETS** to bet too much

OVERBID *v* **-BID, -BID** or **-BIDDEN, -BIDDING, -BIDS** to bid higher than

OVERBIG *adj* too big

OVERBILL *v* **-ED, -ING, -S** to bill too much

OVERBITE *n* pl. **-S** a faulty closure of the teeth

OVERBLOW *v* **-BLEW, -BLOWN, -BLOWING, -BLOWS** to give excessive importance to

OVERBOIL *v* **-ED, -ING, -S** to boil too long

OVERBOLD *adj* excessively bold or forward

OVERBOOK *v* **-ED, -ING, -S** to issue reservations in excess of the space available

OVERBORE past tense of overbear

OVERBORN a past participle of overbear

OVERBORNE a past participle of overbear

OVERBOUGHT past tense of overbuy

OVERBRED *adj* bred too finely or to excess

OVERBURN *v* **-BURNED** or **-BURNT, -BURNING, -BURNS** to burn too long

OVERBUSY *adj* too busy

OVERBUY *v* **-BOUGHT, -BUYING, -BUYS** to buy in quantities exceeding need or demand

OVERCALL *v* **-ED, -ING, -S** to overbid

OVERCAME past tense of overcome

OVERCAST *v* **-CAST** or **-CASTED, -CASTING, -CASTS** to become cloudy or dark

OVERCOAT *n* pl. **-S** a warm coat worn over indoor clothing

OVERCOLD *adj* too cold

OVERCOME *v* **-CAME, -COMING, -COMES** to get the better of

OVERCOOK *v* **-ED, -ING, -S** to cook too long

OVERCOOL *v* **-ED, -ING, -S** to make too cool

OVERCOY *adj* too coy

OVERCRAM *v* **-CRAMMED, -CRAMMING, -CRAMS** to stuff or cram to excess

OVERCROP *v* **-CROPPED, -CROPPING, -CROPS** to exhaust the fertility of by cultivating to excess

OVERCURE *v* **-CURED, -CURING, -CURES** to cure too long

OVERCUT *v* **-CUT, -CUTTING, -CUTS** to cut too much

OVERDARE *v* **-DARED, -DARING, -DARES** to become too daring

OVERDEAR *adj* too dear; too costly

OVERDECK *v* **-ED, -ING, -S** to adorn extravagantly

OVERDO *v* **-DID, -DONE, -DOING, -DOES** to do to excess

OVERDOER *n* pl. **-S** one that overdoes

OVERDOG *n* pl. **-S** one that is dominant or victorious

OVERDOSE *v* **-DOSED, -DOSING, -DOSES** to give an excessive dose to

OVERDRAW *v* **-DREW, -DRAWN, -DRAWING, -DRAWS** to draw checks on in excess of the balance

OVERDRY *v* **-DRIED, -DRYING, -DRIES** to dry too much

OVERDUB *v* **-DUBBED, -DUBBING, -DUBS** to add sound to an existing recording

OVERDUE *adj* not paid when due

OVERDYE *v* **-DYED, -DYEING, -DYES** to dye with too much color

OVERDYER *n* pl. **-S** one that overdyes

OVEREASY *adj* too easy

OVEREAT *v* **-ATE, -EATEN, -EATING, -EATS** to eat to excess

OVEREDIT *v* **-ED, -ING, -S** to edit more than necessary

OVERFAR *adj* too great in distance, extent, or degree

OVERFAST *adj* too fast

OVERFAT *adj* too fat

OVERFEAR *v* **-ED, -ING, -S** to fear too much

OVERFEED *v* **-FED, -FEEDING, -FEEDS** to feed too much

OVERFILL *v* **-ED, -ING, -S** to fill to overflowing

OVERFISH *v* **-ED, -ING, -ES** to deplete the supply of fish in an area by fishing to excess

OVERFIT *adj* fitted to excess

OVERFLOW *v* **-FLOWED, -FLOWN, -FLOWING, -FLOWS** to flow over the top of

OVERFLY *v* **-FLEW, -FLOWN, -FLYING, -FLIES** to fly over

OVERFOND	*adj* too fond or affectionate
OVERFOUL	*adj* too foul
OVERFREE	*adj* too free
OVERFULL	*adj* too full
OVERFUND	*v* **-ED, -ING, -S** to fund more than required
OVERGILD	*v* **-GILDED** or **-GILT, -GILDING, -GILDS** to gild over
OVERGIRD	*v* **-GIRDED** or **-GIRT, -GIRDING, -GIRDS** to gird to excess
OVERGLAD	*adj* too glad
OVERGOAD	*v* **-ED, -ING, -S** to goad too much
OVERGROW	*v* **-GREW, -GROWN, -GROWING, -GROWS** to grow over
OVERHAND	*v* **-ED, -ING, -S** to sew with short, vertical stitches
OVERHANG	*v* **-HUNG, -HANGING, -HANGS** to hang or project over
OVERHARD	*adj* too hard
OVERHATE	*v* **-HATED, -HATING, -HATES** to hate to excess
OVERHAUL	*v* **-ED, -ING, -S** to examine carefully for needed repairs
OVERHEAD	*n* pl. **-S** the general cost of running a business
OVERHEAP	*v* **-ED, -ING, -S** to heap up or accumulate to excess
OVERHEAR	*v* **-HEARD, -HEARING, -HEARS** to hear without the speaker's knowledge or intention
OVERHEAT	*v* **-ED, -ING, -S** to heat to excess
OVERHIGH	*adj* too high
OVERHOLD	*v* **-HELD, -HOLDING, -HOLDS** to rate too highly
OVERHOLY	*adj* too holy
OVERHOPE	*v* **-HOPED, -HOPING, -HOPES** to hope exceedingly
OVERHOT	*adj* too hot
OVERHUNG	past tense of overhang
OVERHUNT	*v* **-ED, -ING, -S** to deplete the supply of game in an area by hunting to excess
OVERHYPE	*v* **-HYPED, -HYPING, -HYPES** to hype to excess
OVERIDLE	*adj* too idle
OVERJOY	*v* **-ED, -ING, -S** to fill with great joy
OVERJUST	*adj* too just
OVERKEEN	*adj* too keen
OVERKILL	*v* **-ED, -ING, -S** to destroy with more nuclear force than required
OVERKIND	*adj* too kind
OVERLADE	*v* **-LADED, -LADEN, -LADING, -LADES** to load with too great a burden
OVERLAID	past tense of overlay
OVERLAIN	past participle of overlie
OVERLAND	*n* pl. **-S** a train or stagecoach that travels over land
OVERLAP	*v* **-LAPPED, -LAPPING, -LAPS** to extend over and cover a part of
OVERLATE	*adj* too late
OVERLAX	*adj* too lax
OVERLAY	*v* **-LAID, -LAYING, -LAYS** to lay over
OVERLEAF	*adv* on the other side of the page
OVERLEAP	*v* **-LEAPED** or **-LEAPT, -LEAPING, -LEAPS** to leap over
OVERLEND	*v* **-LENT, -LENDING, -LENDS** to lend too much
OVERLET	*v* **-LET, -LETTING, -LETS** to let to excess
OVERLEWD	*adj* too lewd
OVERLIE	*v* **-LAY, -LAIN, -LYING, -LIES** to lie over
OVERLIT	a past tense of overlight
OVERLIVE	*v* **-LIVED, -LIVING, -LIVES** to outlive
OVERLOAD	*v* **-ED, -ING, -S** to load to excess
OVERLONG	*adj* too long
OVERLOOK	*v* **-ED, -ING, -S** to fail to notice
OVERLORD	*v* **-ED, -ING, -S** to rule tyrannically
OVERLOUD	*adj* too loud
OVERLOVE	*v* **-LOVED, -LOVING, -LOVES** to love to excess
OVERLUSH	*adj* excessively lush
OVERLY	*adv* to an excessive degree
OVERLYING	present participle of overlie
OVERMAN	*n* pl. **-MEN** a foreman
OVERMAN	*v* **-MANNED, -MANNING, -MANS** to provide with more men than are needed
OVERMANY	*adj* too many
OVERMEEK	*adj* excessively meek
OVERMELT	*v* **-ED, -ING, -S** to melt too much
OVERMEN	pl. of overman
OVERMILD	*adj* too mild
OVERMILK	*v* **-ED, -ING, -S** to milk to excess
OVERMINE	*v* **-MINED, -MINING, -MINES** to mine to excess

OVERMIX *v* **-ED, -ING, -ES** to mix too much

OVERMUCH *n* pl. **-ES** an excess

OVERNEAR *adj* too near

OVERNEAT *adj* too neat

OVERNEW *adj* too new

OVERNICE *adj* excessively nice

OVERPACK *v* **-ED, -ING, -S** to pack to excess

OVERPASS *v* **-PASSED** or **-PAST, -PASSING, -PASSES** to pass over

OVERPAY *v* **-PAID, -PAYING, -PAYS** to pay too much

OVERPERT *adj* too pert

OVERPLAN *v* **-PLANNED, -PLANNING, -PLANS** to plan to excess

OVERPLAY *v* **-ED, -ING, -S** to exaggerate

OVERPLOT *v* **-PLOTTED, -PLOTTING, -PLOTS** to devise an overly complex plot for

OVERPLUS *n* pl. **-ES** a surplus

OVERPLY *v* **-PLIED, -PLYING, -PLIES** to ply to excess; overwork

OVERPUMP *v* **-ED, -ING, -S** to pump to excess

OVERRAN past tense of overrun

OVERRANK *adj* too luxuriant in growth

OVERRASH *adj* too rash

OVERRATE *v* **-RATED, -RATING, -RATES** to rate too highly

OVERRICH *adj* too rich

OVERRIDE *v* **-RODE, -RIDDEN, -RIDING, -RIDES** to ride over

OVERRIFE *adj* too rife

OVERRIPE *adj* too ripe

OVERRUDE *adj* excessively rude

OVERRUFF *v* **-ED, -ING, -S** to trump with a higher trump card than has already been played

OVERRULE *v* **-RULED, -RULING, -RULES** to disallow the arguments of

OVERRUN *v* **-RAN, -RUNNING, -RUNS** to spread or swarm over

OVERSAD *adj* excessively sad

OVERSALE *n* pl. **-S** the act of overselling

OVERSALT *v* **-ED, -ING, -S** to salt to excess

OVERSAVE *v* **-SAVED, -SAVING, -SAVES** to save too much

OVERSEA *adv* overseas

OVERSEAS *adv* beyond or across the sea

OVERSEE *v* **-SAW, -SEEN, -SEEING, -SEES** to watch over and direct

OVERSEED *v* **-ED, -ING, -S** to seed to excess

OVERSEER *n* pl. **-S** one that oversees

OVERSELL *v* **-SOLD, -SELLING, -SELLS** to sell more of than can be delivered

OVERSET *v* **-SET, -SETTING, -SETS** to turn or tip over

OVERSEW *v* **-SEWED, -SEWN, -SEWING, -SEWS** to overhand

OVERSHOE *n* pl. **-S** a protective outer shoe

OVERSHOT *n* pl. **-S** a type of fabric weave

OVERSICK *adj* too sick

OVERSIDE *n* pl. **-S** the other side of a phonograph record

OVERSIZE *n* pl. **-S** an unusually large size

OVERSLIP *v* **-SLIPPED** or **-SLIPT, -SLIPPING, -SLIPS** to leave out

OVERSLOW *adj* too slow

OVERSOAK *v* **-ED, -ING, -S** to soak too much

OVERSOFT *adj* too soft

OVERSOLD past tense of oversell

OVERSOON *adv* too soon

OVERSOUL *n* pl. **-S** a supreme reality or mind in transcendentalism

OVERSPIN *n* pl. **-S** a forward spin imparted to a ball

OVERSTAY *v* **-ED, -ING, -S** to stay beyond the limits or duration of

OVERSTEP *v* **-STEPPED, -STEPPING, -STEPS** to go beyond

OVERSTIR *v* **-STIRRED, -STIRRING, -STIRS** to stir too much

OVERSUDS *v* **-ED, -ING, -ES** to form an excessive amount of suds

OVERSUP *v* **-SUPPED, -SUPPING, -SUPS** to sup to excess

OVERSURE *adj* too sure

OVERT *adj* open to view

OVERTAKE *v* **-TOOK, -TAKEN, -TAKING, -TAKES** to catch up with

OVERTALK *v* **-ED, -ING, -S** to talk to excess

OVERTAME *adj* too tame

OVERTART *adj* too tart

OVERTASK *v* **-ED, -ING, -S** to task too severely

OVERTAX *v* **-ED, -ING, -ES** to tax too heavily

OVERTHIN *adj* too thin

OVERTIME *v* **-TIMED, -TIMING, -TIMES** to exceed the desired timing for

OVERTIP *v* **-TIPPED, -TIPPING, -TIPS** to tip more than what is customary

OVERTIRE *v* **-TIRED, -TIRING, -TIRES** to tire excessively

OVERTLY *adv* in an overt manner

OVERTOIL *v* **-ED, -ING, -S** to wear out or exhaust by excessive toil

OVERTONE *n* pl. **-S** a higher partial tone

OVERTOOK past tense of overtake

OVERTOP *v* **-TOPPED, -TOPPING, -TOPS** to rise above the top of

OVERTRIM *v* **-TRIMMED, -TRIMMING, -TRIMS** to trim too much

OVERTURE *v* **-TURED, -TURING, -TURES** to propose

OVERTURN *v* **-ED, -ING, -S** to turn over

OVERURGE *v* **-URGED, -URGING, -URGES** to urge too much

OVERUSE *v* **-USED, -USING, -USES** to use too much

OVERVIEW *n* pl. **-S** a summary

OVERVOTE *v* **-VOTED, -VOTING, -VOTES** to defeat by a majority of votes

OVERWARM *v* **-ED, -ING, -S** to warm too much

OVERWARY *adj* too wary

OVERWEAK *adj* too weak

OVERWEAR *v* **-WORE, -WORN, -WEARING, -WEARS** to wear out

OVERWEEN *v* **-ED, -ING, -S** to be arrogant

OVERWET *v* **-WETTED, -WETTING, -WETS** to wet too much

OVERWIDE *adj* too wide

OVERWILY *adj* too wily

OVERWIND *v* **-WOUND, -WINDING, -WINDS** to wind too much, as a watch

OVERWISE *adj* too wise

OVERWORD *n* pl. **-S** a word or phrase repeated at intervals in a song

OVERWORE past tense of overwear

OVERWORK *v* **-WORKED** or **-WROUGHT, -WORKING, -WORKS** to cause to work too hard

OVERWORN past participle of overwear

OVERWOUND past tense of overwind

OVERZEAL *n* pl. **-S** excess of zeal

OVIBOS *n* pl. **OVIBOS** a wild ox

OVICIDE *n* pl. **-S** an agent that kills eggs **OVICIDAL** *adj*

OVIDUCT *n* pl. **-S** a tube through which ova travel from an ovary **OVIDUCAL** *adj*

OVIFORM *adj* shaped like an egg

OVINE *n* pl. **-S** a sheep or a closely related animal

OVIPARA *n/pl* egg-laying animals

OVIPOSIT *v* **-ED, -ING, -S** to lay eggs

OVISAC *n* pl. **-S** a sac containing an ovum or ova

OVOID *n* pl. **-S** an egg-shaped body **OVOIDAL** *adj*

OVOLO *n* pl. **-LOS** or **-LI** a convex molding

OVONIC *n* pl. **-S** an electronic device

OVULATE *v* **-LATED, -LATING, -LATES** to produce ova

OVULE *n* pl. **-S** a rudimentary seed **OVULAR, OVULARY** *adj*

OVUM *n* pl. **OVA** the female reproductive cell of animals

OW *interj* — used to express sudden pain

OWE *v* **OWED, OWING, OWES** to be under obligation to pay or repay

OWL *n* pl. **-S** a nocturnal bird

OWLET *n* pl. **-S** a young owl

OWLISH *adj* resembling an owl **OWLISHLY** *adv*

OWLLIKE *adj* owlish

OWN *v* **-ED, -ING, -S** to have as a belonging **OWNABLE** *adj*

OWNER *n* pl. **-S** one that owns

OWSE *n* pl. **OWSEN** ox

OX *n* pl. **-ES** a clumsy person

OX *n* pl. **OXEN** a hoofed mammal

OXALATE *v* **-LATED, -LATING, -LATES** to treat with an oxalate (a chemical salt)

OXALIS *n* pl. **-ALISES** a flowering plant **OXALIC** *adj*

OXAZEPAM *n* pl. **-S** a tranquilizing drug

OXAZINE *n* pl. **-S** a chemical compound

OXBLOOD *n* pl. **-S** a deep red color

OXBOW *n* pl. **-S** a U-shaped piece of wood in an ox yoke

OXCART *n* pl. **-S** an ox-drawn cart

OXEN pl. of ox

OXEYE *n* pl. **-S** a flowering plant

OXFORD *n* pl. **-S** a type of shoe

OXHEART *n* pl. **-S** a variety of sweet cherry

OXID *n* pl. **-S** oxide

OXIDABLE *adj* capable of being oxidized

OXIDANT *n* pl. **-S** an oxidizing agent

OXIDASE   *n* pl. **-S** an oxidizing enzyme **OXIDASIC** *adj*

OXIDATE   *v* **-DATED, -DATING, -DATES** to oxidize

OXIDE   *n* pl. **-S** a binary compound of oxygen with another element or radical **OXIDIC** *adj*

OXIDISE   *v* **-DISED, -DISING, -DISES** to oxidize

OXIDISER   *n* pl. **-S** oxidizer

OXIDIZE   *v* **-DIZED, -DIZING, -DIZES** to combine with oxygen

OXIDIZER   *n* pl. **-S** an oxidant

OXIM   *n* pl. **-S** oxime

OXIME   *n* pl. **-S** a chemical compound

OXIMETER   *n* pl. **-S** an instrument for measuring the amount of oxygen in the blood

OXIMETRY   *n* pl. **-TRIES** the use of an oximeter

OXLIKE   *adj* resembling an ox

OXLIP   *n* pl. **-S** a flowering plant

OXO   *adj* containing oxygen

OXPECKER   *n* pl. **-S** an African bird

OXTAIL   *n* pl. **-S** the tail of an ox

OXTER   *n* pl. **-S** the armpit

OXTONGUE   *n* pl. **-S** a European herb

OXY   *adj* containing oxygen

OXYACID   *n* pl. **-S** an acid that contains oxygen

OXYGEN   *n* pl. **-S** a gaseous element **OXYGENIC** *adj*

OXYMORON   *n* pl. **-MORONS** or **-MORA** a combination of contradictory or incongruous words

OXYPHIL   *n* pl. **-S** oxyphile

OXYPHILE   *n* pl. **-S** an organism that thrives in a relatively acid environment

OXYSALT   *n* pl. **-S** a salt of an oxyacid

OXYSOME   *n* pl. **-S** a structural unit of cellular cristae

OXYTOCIC   *n* pl. **-S** a drug that hastens the process of childbirth

OXYTOCIN   *n* pl. **-S** a pituitary hormone

OXYTONE   *n* pl. **-S** a word having heavy stress on the last syllable

OY   *interj* — used to express dismay or pain

OYER   *n* pl. **-S** a type of legal writ

OYES   *n* pl. **OYESSES** oyez

OYEZ   *n* pl. **OYEZES** a cry used to introduce the opening of a court of law

OYSTER   *v* **-ED, -ING, -S** to gather oysters (edible mollusks)

OYSTERER   *n* pl. **-S** one that gathers or sells oysters

OZONATE   *v* **-ATED, -ATING, -ATES** to treat or combine with ozone

OZONE   *n* pl. **-S** a form of oxygen **OZONIC** *adj*

OZONIDE   *n* pl. **-S** a compound of ozone

OZONISE   *v* **-ISED, -ISING, -ISES** to ozonize

OZONIZE   *v* **-IZED, -IZING, -IZES** to convert into ozone

OZONIZER   *n* pl. **-S** a device for converting oxygen into ozone

OZONOUS   *adj* pertaining to ozone

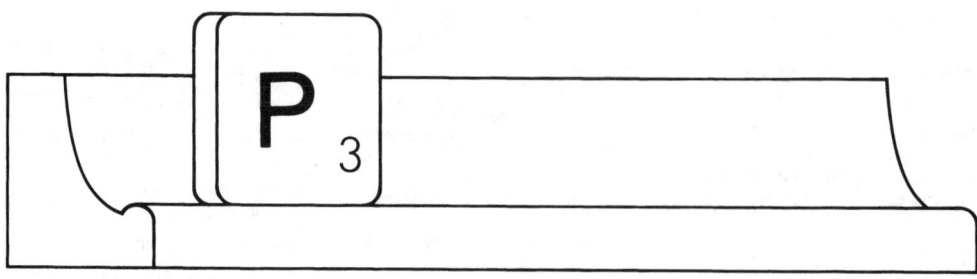

PA	*n* pl. **-S** a father
PABLUM	*n* pl. **-S** insipid writing or speech
PABULUM	*n* pl. **-S** food **PABULAR** *adj*
PAC	*n* pl. **-S** a shoe like a moccasin
PACA	*n* pl. **-S** a large rodent
PACE	*v* **PACED, PACING, PACES** to walk with a regular step
PACER	*n* pl. **-S** a horse whose gait is a pace
PACEY	*adj* **PACIER, PACIEST** keeping a fast pace (rate of speed)
PACHA	*n* pl. **-S** pasha
PACHADOM	*n* pl. **-S** pashadom
PACHALIC	*n* pl. **-S** pashalik
PACHINKO	*n* pl. **-KOS** a Japanese pinball game
PACHISI	*n* pl. **-S** a board game of India
PACHOULI	*n* pl. **-S** an East Indian herb
PACHUCO	*n* pl. **-COS** a flashy Mexican-American youth
PACIER	comparative of pacey and pacy
PACIEST	superlative of paceyand pacy
PACIFIC	*adj* peaceful
PACIFIED	past tense of pacify
PACIFIER	*n* pl. **-S** one that pacifies
PACIFISM	*n* pl. **-S** opposition to war or violence
PACIFIST	*n* pl. **-S** an advocate of pacifism
PACIFY	*v* **-FIED, -FYING, -FIES** to make peaceful
PACING	present participle of pace
PACK	*v* **-ED, -ING, -S** to put into a receptacle for transportation or storage **PACKABLE** *adj*
PACKAGE	*v* **-AGED, -AGING, -AGES** to make into a package (a wrapped or boxed object)
PACKAGER	*n* pl. **-S** one that packages
PACKER	*n* pl. **-S** one that packs
PACKET	*v* **-ED, -ING, -S** to make into a small package
PACKING	*n* pl. **-S** material used to pack
PACKLY	*adv* intimately
PACKMAN	*n* pl. **-MEN** a peddler
PACKNESS	*n* pl. **-ES** intimacy
PACKSACK	*n* pl. **-S** a carrying bag to be worn on the back
PACKWAX	*n* pl. **-ES** paxwax
PACT	*n* pl. **-S** an agreement
PACTION	*n* pl. **-S** a pact
PACY	*adj* **PACIER, PACIEST** pacey
PAD	*v* **PADDED, PADDING, PADS** to line or stuff with soft material
PADAUK	*n* pl. **-S** a tropical tree
PADDER	*n* pl. **-S** one that pads
PADDIES	pl. of paddy
PADDING	*n* pl. **-S** material with which to pad
PADDLE	*v* **-DLED, -DLING, -DLES** to propel with a broad-bladed implement
PADDLER	*n* pl. **-S** one that paddles
PADDLING	*n* pl. **-S** the act of one who paddles
PADDOCK	*v* **-ED, -ING, -S** to confine in an enclosure for horses
PADDY	*n* pl. **-DIES** a rice field
PADI	*n* pl. **-S** paddy
PADISHAH	*n* pl. **-S** a sovereign
PADLE	*n* pl. **-S** a hoe
PADLOCK	*v* **-ED, -ING, -S** to secure with a type of lock
PADNAG	*n* pl. **-S** a horse that moves along at an easy pace
PADOUK	*n* pl. **-S** padauk
PADRE	*n* pl. **-DRES** or **-DRI** a Christian clergyman
PADRONE	*n* pl. **-NES** or **-NI** a master

PADSHAH   *n* pl. **-S** padishah

PADUASOY   *n* pl. **-SOYS** a strong silk fabric

PAEAN   *n* pl. **-S** a song of joy

PAEANISM   *n* pl. **-S** the chanting of a paean

PAELLA   *n* pl. **-S** a saffron-flavored stew

PAEON   *n* pl. **-S** a metrical foot of four syllables

PAESAN   *n* pl. **-S** paesano

PAESANO   *n* pl. **-NOS** or **-NI** a fellow countryman

PAGAN   *n* pl. **-S** a follower of a polytheistic religion

PAGANDOM   *n* pl. **-S** the realm of pagans

PAGANISE   *v* **-ISED, -ISING, -ISES** to paganize

PAGANISH   *adj* resembling a pagan

PAGANISM   *n* pl. **-S** an irreligious attitude

PAGANIST   *n* pl. **-S** a pagan

PAGANIZE   *v* **-IZED, -IZING, -IZES** to make irreligious

PAGE   *v* **PAGED, PAGING, PAGES** to summon by calling out the name of

PAGEANT   *n* pl. **-S** an elaborate public spectacle

PAGEBOY   *n* pl. **-BOYS** a woman's hairstyle

PAGEFUL   *n* pl. **-S** as much as a page can hold

PAGER   *n* pl. **-S** a beeper

PAGINAL   *adj* pertaining to the pages of a book

PAGINATE   *v* **-NATED, -NATING, -NATES** to number the pages of

PAGING   *n* pl. **-S** a transfer of computer pages

PAGOD   *n* pl. **-S** pagoda

PAGODA   *n* pl. **-S** a Far Eastern temple

PAGURIAN   *n* pl. **-S** a hermit crab

PAGURID   *n* pl. **-S** pagurian

PAH   *interj* — used as an exclamation of disgust

PAHLAVI   *n* pl. **-S** a former coin of Iran

PAHOEHOE   *n* pl. **-S** smooth solidified lava

PAID   a past tense of pay

PAIK   *v* **-ED, -ING, -S** to beat or strike

PAIL   *n* pl. **-S** a watertight cylindrical container

PAILFUL   *n* pl. **PAILFULS** or **PAILSFUL** as much as a pail can hold

PAILLARD   *n* pl. **-S** a slice of meat pounded thin and grilled

PAIN   *v* **-ED, -ING, -S** to cause pain (suffering or distress)

PAINCH   *n* pl. **-ES** paunch

PAINFUL   *adj* **-FULLER, -FULLEST** causing pain

PAINLESS   *adj* not causing pain

PAINT   *v* **-ED, -ING, -S** to make a representation of with paints (coloring substances)

PAINTER   *n* pl. **-S** one that paints

PAINTING   *n* pl. **-S** a picture made with paints

PAINTY   *adj* **PAINTIER, PAINTIEST** covered with paint

PAIR   *v* **-ED, -ING, -S** to arrange in sets of two

PAIRING   *n* pl. **-S** a matching of two opponents in a tournament

PAISA   *n* pl. **PAISAS** or **PAISE** a coin of Pakistan

PAISAN   *n* pl. **-S** paisano

PAISANA   *n* pl. **-S** a female compatriot

PAISANO   *n* pl. **-NOS** a fellow countryman

PAISE   a pl. of paisa

PAISLEY   *n* pl. **-LEYS** a patterned wool fabric

PAJAMA   *n* pl. **-S** a garment for sleeping or lounging

PAJAMAED   *adj* wearing pajamas

PAKEHA   *n* pl. **-S** a person who is not of Maori descent

PAKORA   *n* pl. **-S** a small spicy cake of fried batter with vegetables or meat

PAL   *v* **PALLED, PALLING, PALS** to associate as friends

PALABRA   *n* pl. **-S** a word

PALACE   *n* pl. **-S** a royal residence **PALACED** *adj*

PALADIN   *n* pl. **-S** a knightly champion

PALAIS   *n* pl. **PALAIS** a palace

PALAPA   *n* pl. **-S** an open-sided dwelling with a roof of palm leaves

PALATAL   *n* pl. **-S** a bone of the palate

PALATE   *n* pl. **-S** the roof of the mouth

PALATIAL   *adj* resembling a palace

PALATINE   *n* pl. **-S** a high officer of an empire

PALAVER   *v* **-ED, -ING, -S** to chatter

PALAZZO   *n* pl. **-ZI** an impressive building

PALAZZOS   *n/pl* wide-legged pants for women

PALE	adj **PALER, PALEST** lacking intensity of color	**PALLIEST**	superlative of pally
PALE	v **PALED, PALING, PALES** to make or become pale	**PALLING**	present participle of pal
		PALLIUM	n pl. **-LIUMS** or **-LIA** a cloak worn in ancient Rome
PALEA	n pl. **-LEAE** a small bract **PALEAL** adj	**PALLOR**	n pl. **-S** paleness
PALEATE	adj covered with scales	**PALLY**	adj **-LIER, -LIEST** marked by close friendship
PALEFACE	n pl. **-S** a white person	**PALM**	v **-ED, -ING, -S** to touch with the palm (inner surface) of the hand
PALELY	adv in a pale manner		
PALENESS	n pl. **-ES** the quality of being pale	**PALMAR**	adj pertaining to the palm
PALEOSOL	n pl. **-S** a layer of ancient soil	**PALMARY**	adj worthy of praise
PALER	comparative of pale	**PALMATE**	adj resembling an open hand
PALEST	superlative of pale	**PALMATED**	adj palmate
PALESTRA	n pl. **-TRAS** or **-TRAE** a school for athletics in ancient Greece	**PALMER**	n pl. **-S** a religious pilgrim
		PALMETTE	n pl. **-S** a type of ornament
PALET	n pl. **-S** a palea	**PALMETTO**	n pl. **-TOS** or **-TOES** a tropical tree
PALETOT	n pl. **-S** a loose overcoat	**PALMFUL**	n pl. **-S** as much as a palm can hold
PALETTE	n pl. **-S** a board on which an artist mixes colors		
		PALMIER	comparative of palmy
PALEWAYS	adv palewise	**PALMIEST**	superlative of palmy
PALEWISE	adv vertically	**PALMIST**	n pl. **-S** a fortune-teller
PALFREY	n pl. **-FREYS** a riding horse	**PALMITIN**	n pl. **-S** a chemical compound
PALIER	comparative of paly	**PALMLIKE**	adj resembling a palm tree
PALIEST	superlative of paly	**PALMTOP**	n pl. **-S** a small computer that fits in the palm of the hand
PALIKAR	n pl. **-S** a Greek soldier		
PALIMONY	n pl. **-NIES** an allowance paid to one member of an unmarried couple who have separated	**PALMY**	adj **PALMIER, PALMIEST** marked by prosperity
		PALMYRA	n pl. **-S** a tropical tree
PALING	n pl. **-S** a picket fence	**PALOMINO**	n pl. **-NOS** a slender-legged horse
PALINODE	n pl. **-S** a formal retraction	**PALOOKA**	n pl. **-S** an inferior boxer
PALISADE	v **-SADED, -SADING, -SADES** to fortify with a heavy fence	**PALP**	v **-ED, -ING, -S** to touch
		PALPABLE	adj capable of being felt **PALPABLY** adv
PALISH	adj somewhat pale		
PALL	v **-ED, -ING, -S** to become insipid	**PALPAL**	adj pertaining to a palpus
PALLADIA	n/pl safeguards	**PALPATE**	v **-PATED, -PATING, -PATES** to examine by touch
PALLADIC	adj pertaining to the metallic element palladium		
		PALPATOR	n pl. **-S** one that palpates
PALLED	past tense of pal	**PALPEBRA**	n pl. **-BRAS** or **-BRAE** an eyelid
PALLET	v **-ED, -ING, -S** to place on platforms for storage or moving	**PALPUS**	n pl. **-PI** a sensory organ of an arthropod
PALLETTE	n pl. **-S** a piece of armor protecting the armpit		
		PALSHIP	n pl. **-S** the relation existing between close friends
PALLIA	a pl. of pallium		
PALLIAL	adj pertaining to a part of the brain	**PALSY**	v **-SIED, -SYING, -SIES** to paralyze
PALLIATE	v **-ATED, -ATING, -ATES** to conceal the seriousness of	**PALTER**	v **-ED, -ING, -S** to talk or act insincerely
PALLID	adj pale **PALLIDLY** adv	**PALTERER**	n pl. **-S** one that palters
PALLIER	comparative of pally	**PALTRY**	adj **-TRIER, -TRIEST** petty **PALTRILY** adv

PALUDAL	*adj* pertaining to a marsh
PALUDISM	*n* pl. **-S** malaria
PALY	*adj* **PALIER, PALIEST** somewhat pale
PAM	*n* pl. **-S** the jack of clubs in certain card games
PAMPA	*n* pl. **-S** a grassland of South America
PAMPEAN	*n* pl. **-S** a native of the pampas
PAMPER	*v* **-ED, -ING, -S** to treat with extreme or excessive indulgence
PAMPERER	*n* pl. **-S** one that pampers
PAMPERO	*n* pl. **-ROS** a cold, dry wind
PAMPHLET	*n* pl. **-S** a printed work with a paper cover
PAN	*v* **PANNED, PANNING, PANS** to criticize harshly
PANACEA	*n* pl. **-S** a remedy for all diseases or ills **PANACEAN** *adj*
PANACHE	*n* pl. **-S** an ornamental tuft of feathers
PANADA	*n* pl. **-S** a thick sauce
PANAMA	*n* pl. **-S** a lightweight hat
PANATELA	*n* pl. **-S** a long, slender cigar
PANBROIL	*v* **-ED, -ING, -S** to fry in a pan with little or no fat
PANCAKE	*v* **-CAKED, -CAKING, -CAKES** to land an airplane in a certain manner
PANCETTA	*n* pl. **-S** unsmoked Italian bacon
PANCHAX	*n* pl. **-ES** a tropical fish
PANCREAS	*n* pl. **-ES** a large gland
PANDA	*n* pl. **-S** an herbivorous mammal
PANDANUS	*n* pl. **-NUSES** or **-NI** a tropical plant
PANDECT	*n* pl. **-S** a complete body of laws
PANDEMIC	*n* pl. **-S** a widespread disease
PANDER	*v* **-ED, -ING, -S** to provide gratification for others' desires
PANDERER	*n* pl. **-S** one that panders
PANDIED	past tense of pandy
PANDIES	present 3d person sing. of pandy
PANDIT	*n* pl. **-S** a wise or learned man in India
PANDOOR	*n* pl. **-S** pandour
PANDORA	*n* pl. **-S** bandore
PANDORE	*n* pl. **-S** bandore
PANDOUR	*n* pl. **-S** a marauding soldier
PANDOWDY	*n* pl. **-DIES** an apple dessert
PANDURA	*n* pl. **-S** bandore
PANDY	*v* **-DIED, -DYING, -DIES** to punish by striking the hand
PANE	*n* pl. **-S** a sheet of glass for a window **PANED** *adj*
PANEL	*v* **-ELED, -ELING, -ELS** or **-ELLED, -ELLING, -ELS** to decorate with thin sheets of material
PANELESS	*adj* lacking panes
PANELING	*n* pl. **-S** material with which to panel
PANELIST	*n* pl. **-S** a member of a discussion or advisory group
PANELLED	a past tense of panel
PANELLING	a present participle of panel
PANETELA	*n* pl. **-S** panatela
PANFISH	*n* pl. **-ES** any small fish that can be fried whole
PANFRY	*v* **-FRIED, -FRYING, -FRIES** to fry in a frying pan
PANFUL	*n* pl. **-S** as much as a pan will hold
PANG	*v* **-ED, -ING, -S** to cause to have spasms of pain
PANGA	*n* pl. **-S** a large knife
PANGEN	*n* pl. **-S** a hypothetical heredity-controlling particle of protoplasm
PANGENE	*n* pl. **-S** pangen
PANGOLIN	*n* pl. **-S** a toothless mammal
PANGRAM	*n* pl. **-S** a sentence that includes all the letters of the alphabet
PANHUMAN	*adj* pertaining to all humanity
PANIC	*v* **-ICKED, -ICKING, -ICS** to be overwhelmed by fear
PANICKY	*adj* **-ICKIER, -ICKIEST** tending to panic
PANICLE	*n* pl. **-S** a loosely branched flower cluster **PANICLED** *adj*
PANICUM	*n* pl. **-S** a grass
PANIER	*n* pl. **-S** pannier
PANINO	*n* pl. **PANINI** a sandwich made with a small bread roll
PANMIXIA	*n* pl. **-S** random mating within a breeding population
PANMIXIS	*n* pl. **-MIXES** panmixia
PANNE	*n* pl. **-S** a lustrous velvet
PANNED	past tense of pan
PANNER	*n* pl. **-S** one that pans
PANNIER	*n* pl. **-S** a large basket
PANNIKIN	*n* pl. **-S** a small saucepan

PANNING	present participle of pan
PANOCHA	*n pl.* **-S** a coarse Mexican sugar
PANOCHE	*n pl.* **-S** panocha
PANOPLY	*n pl.* **-PLIES** a suit of armor
PANOPTIC	*adj* including everything visible in one view
PANORAMA	*n pl.* **-S** a complete view
PANPIPE	*n pl.* **-S** a musical instrument
PANSOPHY	*n pl.* **-PHIES** universal knowledge
PANSY	*n pl.* **-SIES** a flowering plant
PANT	*v* **-ED, -ING, -S** to breathe quickly and with difficulty
PANTALET	*n pl.* **-S** long underpants trimmed with ruffles
PANTHEON	*n pl.* **-S** a temple dedicated to all the gods
PANTHER	*n pl.* **-S** a leopard
PANTIE	*n pl.* **-S** a woman's or child's undergarment
PANTIES	pl. of panty
PANTILE	*n pl.* **-S** a roofing tile **PANTILED** *adj*
PANTO	*n pl.* **-TOS** a pantomime
PANTOFLE	*n pl.* **-S** a slipper
PANTOUM	*n pl.* **-S** a verse form
PANTRY	*n pl.* **-TRIES** a closet or room for storing kitchen utensils
PANTSUIT	*n pl.* **-S** a type of woman's suit
PANTY	*n pl.* **PANTIES** pantie
PANZER	*n pl.* **-S** an armored combat vehicle
PAP	*n pl.* **-S** a soft food for infants
PAPA	*n pl.* **-S** a father
PAPACY	*n pl.* **-CIES** the office of the pope
PAPADAM	*n pl.* **-S** papadum
PAPADOM	*n pl.* **-S** papadum
PAPADUM	*n pl.* **-S** a thin, crisp bread of India
PAPAIN	*n pl.* **-S** an enzyme
PAPAL	*adj* pertaining to the pope **PAPALLY** *adv*
PAPAW	*n pl.* **-S** a fleshy fruit
PAPAYA	*n pl.* **-S** a melon-like fruit **PAPAYAN** *adj*
PAPER	*v* **-ED, -ING, -S** to cover or wrap with paper (a thin sheet material made of cellulose pulp)
PAPERBOY	*n pl.* **-BOYS** a newsboy
PAPERER	*n pl.* **-S** one that papers

PAPERY	*adj* resembling paper
PAPHIAN	*n pl.* **-S** a prostitute
PAPILLA	*n pl.* **-LAE** a nipple-like projection **PAPILLAR** *adj*
PAPILLON	*n pl.* **-S** a small dog having large ears
PAPOOSE	*n pl.* **-S** an American Indian baby
PAPPADAM	*n pl.* **-S** papadum
PAPPI	a pl. of pappus
PAPPIER	comparative of pappy
PAPPIES	pl. of pappy
PAPPOOSE	*n pl.* **-S** papoose
PAPPUS	*n pl.* **-PI** a tuft of bristles on the achene of certain plants **PAPPOSE, PAPPOUS** *adj*
PAPPY	*adj* **-PIER, -PIEST** resembling pap
PAPPY	*n pl.* **-PIES** a father
PAPRICA	*n pl.* **-S** paprika
PAPRIKA	*n pl.* **-S** a seasoning made from red peppers
PAPULA	*n pl.* **-LAE** papule
PAPULE	*n pl.* **-S** a pimple **PAPULAR, PAPULOSE** *adj*
PAPYRUS	*n pl.* **-RUSES** or **-RI** a tall aquatic plant **PAPYRAL, PAPYRIAN, PAPYRINE** *adj*
PAR	*v* **PARRED, PARRING, PARS** to shoot in a standard number of strokes in golf
PARA	*n pl.* **PARAS** or **PARAE** a woman's status regarding the bearing of offspring
PARABLE	*n pl.* **-S** a simple story conveying a moral or religious lesson
PARABOLA	*n pl.* **-S** a conic section
PARACHOR	*n pl.* **-S** a mathematical constant that relates molecular volume to surface tension
PARADE	*v* **-RADED, -RADING, -RADES** to march in a public procession
PARADER	*n pl.* **-S** one that parades
PARADIGM	*n pl.* **-S** a pattern or example
PARADISE	*n pl.* **-S** a place of extreme beauty or delight
PARADOR	*n pl.* **-DORS** or **-DORES** an inn in Spain
PARADOS	*n pl.* **-ES** a protective embankment
PARADOX	*n pl.* **-ES** a statement seemingly contradictory or absurd yet perhaps true

PARADROP	*v* -**DROPPED, -DROPPING, -DROPS** to deliver by parachute
PARAFFIN	*v* -**ED, -ING, -S** to coat with a waxy substance
PARAFOIL	*n* pl. -**S** a fabric device that resembles a parachute
PARAFORM	*n* pl. -**S** a substance used as an antiseptic
PARAGOGE	*n* pl. -**S** the addition of a sound or sounds at the end of a word
PARAGON	*v* -**ED, -ING, -S** to compare with
PARAKEET	*n* pl. -**S** a small parrot
PARAKITE	*n* pl. -**S** a parachute kite for towing a person through the air by a motorboat
PARALLAX	*n* pl. -**ES** an apparent optical displacement of an object
PARALLEL	*v* -**LELED, -LELING, -LELS** or -**LELLED, -LELLING, -LELS** to be similar or analogous to
PARALYSE	*v* -**LYSED, -LYSING, -LYSES** to paralyze
PARALYZE	*v* -**LYZED, -LYZING, -LYZES** to render incapable of movement
PARAMENT	*n* pl. -**MENTS** or -**MENTA** an ornamental vestment
PARAMO	*n* pl. -**MOS** a plateau region of South America
PARAMOUR	*n* pl. -**S** an illicit lover
PARANG	*n* pl. -**S** a heavy knife
PARANOEA	*n* pl. -**S** paranoia
PARANOIA	*n* pl. -**S** a mental disorder
PARANOIC	*n* pl. -**S** a paranoid
PARANOID	*n* pl. -**S** one affected with paranoia
PARAPET	*n* pl. -**S** a protective wall
PARAPH	*n* pl. -**S** a flourish at the end of a signature
PARAQUAT	*n* pl. -**S** a weed killer
PARAQUET	*n* pl. -**S** parakeet
PARASAIL	*v* -**ED, -ING, -S** to soar while harnessed to a parachute towed by a car or boat
PARASANG	*n* pl. -**S** a Persian unit of distance
PARASHAH	*n* pl. -**SHAHS** or -**SHOTH** or -**SHOT** a portion of the Torah read on the Sabbath
PARASITE	*n* pl. -**S** an organism that lives and feeds on or in another organism
PARASOL	*n* pl. -**S** a small, light umbrella
PARAVANE	*n* pl. -**S** an underwater device used to cut cables

PARAWING	*n* pl. -**S** a winglike parachute
PARAZOAN	*n* pl. -**S** any of a major division of multicellular animals
PARBAKE	*v* -**BAKED, -BAKING, -BAKES** to bake partially
PARBOIL	*v* -**ED, -ING, -S** to cook partially by boiling for a short time
PARCEL	*v* -**CELED, -CELING, -CELS** or -**CELLED, -CELLING, -CELS** to divide into parts or shares
PARCENER	*n* pl. -**S** a joint heir
PARCH	*v* -**ED, -ING, -ES** to make very dry
PARCHESI	*n* pl. -**S** pachisi
PARCHISI	*n* pl. -**S** pachisi
PARCLOSE	*n* pl. -**S** a screen dividing areas in a church
PARD	*n* pl. -**S** a leopard
PARDAH	*n* pl. -**S** purdah
PARDEE	*interj* pardi
PARDI	*interj* — used as a mild oath
PARDIE	*interj* pardi
PARDINE	*adj* pertaining to a leopard
PARDNER	*n* pl. -**S** chum; friend
PARDON	*v* -**ED, -ING, -S** to release from liability for an offense
PARDONER	*n* pl. -**S** one that pardons
PARDY	*interj* pardi
PARE	*v* **PARED, PARING, PARES** to cut off the outer covering of
PARECISM	*n* pl. -**S** the state of having the male and female sexual organs beside or near each other
PAREIRA	*n* pl. -**S** a medicinal plant root
PARENT	*v* -**ED, -ING, -S** to exercise the functions of a parent (a father or mother)
PARENTAL	*adj* pertaining to a parent
PAREO	*n* pl. -**REOS** pareu
PARER	*n* pl. -**S** one that pares
PARERGON	*n* pl. -**GA** a composition derived from a larger work
PARESIS	*n* pl. -**RESES** partial loss of the ability to move
PARETIC	*n* pl. -**S** one affected with paresis
PAREU	*n* pl. -**S** a Polynesian garment
PAREVE	*adj* parve
PARFAIT	*n* pl. -**S** a frozen dessert
PARFLESH	*n* pl. -**ES** a rawhide soaked in lye to remove the hair and dried

PARFOCAL *adj* having lenses with the corresponding focal points in the same plane

PARGE *v* **PARGED, PARGING, PARGES** to parget

PARGET *v* **-GETED, -GETING, -GETS** or **-GETTED, -GETTING, -GETS** to cover with plaster

PARGING *n* pl. **-S** a thin coat of mortar or plaster for sealing masonry

PARGO *n* pl. **-GOS** a food fish

PARHELIA *n/pl* bright circular spots appearing on a solar halo

PARHELIC *adj* pertaining to parhelia

PARIAH *n* pl. **-S** a social outcast

PARIAN *n* pl. **-S** a hard, white porcelain

PARIES *n* pl. **PARIETES** the wall of an organ

PARIETAL *n* pl. **-S** a bone of the skull

PARING *n* pl. **-S** something pared off

PARIS *n* pl. **-ISES** a European herb

PARISH *n* pl. **-ES** an ecclesiastical district

PARITY *n* pl. **-TIES** equality

PARK *v* **-ED, -ING, -S** to leave a vehicle in a location for a time

PARKA *n* pl. **-S** a hooded garment

PARKADE *n* pl. **-S** a multilevel structure for parking vehicles

PARKER *n* pl. **-S** one that parks

PARKETTE *n* pl. **-S** a small public park

PARKING *n* pl. **-S** an area in which vehicles may be left

PARKLAND *n* pl. **-S** a grassland region with isolated or grouped trees

PARKLIKE *adj* resembling an outdoor recreational area

PARKWAY *n* pl. **-WAYS** a wide highway

PARLANCE *n* pl. **-S** a manner of speaking

PARLANDO *adj* sung in a manner suggestive of speech

PARLANTE *adj* parlando

PARLAY *v* **-ED, -ING, -S** to bet an original wager and its winnings on a subsequent event

PARLE *v* **PARLED, PARLING, PARLES** to parley

PARLEY *v* **-LEYED, -LEYING, -LEYS** to discuss terms with an enemy

PARLEYER *n* pl. **-S** one that parleys

PARLOR *n* pl. **-S** a room for the entertainment of visitors

PARLOUR *n* pl. **-S** parlor

PARLOUS *adj* dangerous

PARMESAN *n* pl. **-S** a hard, dry Italian cheese

PARODIC *adj* comically imitative

PARODIST *n* pl. **-S** one who parodies

PARODOS *n* pl. **-DOI** an ode sung in ancient Greek drama

PARODY *v* **-DIED, -DYING, -DIES** to imitate a serious literary work for comic effect

PAROL *n* pl. **-S** an utterance

PAROLE *v* **-ROLED, -ROLING, -ROLES** to release from prison before completion of the imposed sentence

PAROLEE *n* pl. **-S** one who is paroled

PARONYM *n* pl. **-S** a word having the same root as another

PAROQUET *n* pl. **-S** parakeet

PAROSMIA *n* pl. **-S** a distortion of the sense of smell

PAROTIC *adj* situated near the ear

PAROTID *n* pl. **-S** a salivary gland

PAROTOID *n* pl. **-S** a gland of certain toads and frogs

PAROUS *adj* having produced offspring

PAROXYSM *n* pl. **-S** a sudden fit or attack

PARQUET *v* **-ED, -ING, -S** to furnish with a floor of inlaid design

PARR *n* pl. **-S** a young salmon

PARRAL *n* pl. **-S** parrel

PARRED past tense of par

PARREL *n* pl. **-S** a sliding loop of rope or chain used on a ship

PARRIDGE *n* pl. **-S** porridge

PARRIED past tense of parry

PARRIER *n* pl. **-S** one that parries

PARRIES present 3d person sing. of parry

PARRING present participle of par

PARRITCH *n* pl. **-ES** porridge

PARROKET *n* pl. **-S** parakeet

PARROT *v* **-ED, -ING, -S** to repeat or imitate without thought or understanding

PARROTER *n* pl. **-S** one that parrots

PARROTY *adj* resembling a parrot (a hook-billed tropical bird)

PARRY	*v* **-RIED, -RYING, -RIES** to ward off a blow
PARSE	*v* **PARSED, PARSING, PARSES** to describe and analyze grammatically **PARSABLE** *adj*
PARSEC	*n* pl. **-S** a unit of astronomical distance
PARSER	*n* pl. **-S** one that parses
PARSLEY	*n* pl. **-LEYS** a cultivated herb **PARSLEYED, PARSLIED** *adj*
PARSNIP	*n* pl. **-S** a European herb
PARSON	*n* pl. **-S** a clergyman **PARSONIC** *adj*
PART	*v* **-ED, -ING, -S** to divide or break into separate pieces
PARTAKE	*v* **-TOOK, -TAKEN, -TAKING, -TAKES** to participate
PARTAKER	*n* pl. **-S** one that partakes
PARTAN	*n* pl. **-S** an edible crab
PARTERRE	*n* pl. **-S** a section of a theater
PARTIAL	*n* pl. **-S** a simple component of a complex tone
PARTIBLE	*adj* divisible
PARTICLE	*n* pl. **-S** a very small piece or part
PARTIED	past tense of party
PARTIER	*n* pl. **-S** partyer
PARTIES	present 3d person sing. of party
PARTING	*n* pl. **-S** a division or separation
PARTISAN	*n* pl. **-S** a firm supporter of a person, party, or cause
PARTITA	*n* pl. **-S** a set of related instrumental pieces
PARTITE	*adj* divided into parts
PARTIZAN	*n* pl. **-S** partisan
PARTLET	*n* pl. **-S** a woman's garment
PARTLY	*adv* in some measure or degree
PARTNER	*v* **-ED, -ING, -S** to associate with in some activity of common interest
PARTON	*n* pl. **-S** a hypothetical atomic particle
PARTOOK	past tense of partake
PARTWAY	*adv* to some extent
PARTY	*v* **-TIED, -TYING, -TIES** to attend a social gathering
PARTYER	*n* pl. **-S** one that parties
PARURA	*n* pl. **-S** parure
PARURE	*n* pl. **-S** a set of matched jewelry
PARVE	*adj* made without milk or meat
PARVENU	*n* pl. **-S** one who has suddenly risen above his class
PARVENUE	*n* pl. **-S** a woman who is a parvenu
PARVIS	*n* pl. **-VISES** an enclosed area in front of a church
PARVISE	*n* pl. **-S** parvis
PARVO	*n* pl. **-VOS** a contagious disease of dogs
PARVOLIN	*n* pl. **-S** an oily liquid obtained from fish
PAS	*n* pl. **PAS** a dance step
PASCAL	*n* pl. **-S** a unit of pressure
PASCHAL	*n* pl. **-S** a candle used in certain religious ceremonies
PASE	*n* pl. **-S** a movement of a matador's cape
PASEO	*n* pl. **-SEOS** a leisurely stroll
PASH	*v* **-ED, -ING, -ES** to strike violently
PASHA	*n* pl. **-S** a former Turkish high official
PASHADOM	*n* pl. **-S** the rank of a pasha
PASHALIC	*n* pl. **-S** pashalik
PASHALIK	*n* pl. **-S** the territory of a pasha
PASHMINA	*n* pl. **-S** wool obtained from Himalayan goats
PASQUIL	*n* pl. **-S** a satire or lampoon
PASS	*v* **-ED, -ING, -ES** to go by
PASSABLE	*adj* fairly good or acceptable **PASSABLY** *adv*
PASSADE	*n* pl. **-S** a turn of a horse backward or forward on the same ground
PASSADO	*n* pl. **-DOS** or **-DOES** a forward thrust in fencing
PASSAGE	*v* **-SAGED, -SAGING, -SAGES** to make a voyage
PASSANT	*adj* walking with the farther forepaw raised — used of a heraldic animal
PASSBAND	*n* pl. **-S** a frequency band that permits transmission with maximum efficiency
PASSBOOK	*n* pl. **-S** a bankbook
PASSE	*adj* outmoded
PASSEE	*adj* passe
PASSEL	*n* pl. **-S** a large quantity or number
PASSER	*n* pl. **-S** one that passes
PASSERBY	*n* pl. **PASSERSBY** one who passes by
PASSIBLE	*adj* capable of feeling or suffering
PASSIM	*adv* here and there

PASSING *n* pl. **-S** a death

PASSION *n* pl. **-S** an intense emotion

PASSIVE *n* pl. **-S** a verb form

PASSKEY *n* pl. **-KEYS** a key that opens several different locks

PASSLESS *adj* incapable of being traveled over or through

PASSOVER *n* pl. **-S** the lamb eaten at the feast of a Jewish holiday

PASSPORT *n* pl. **-S** a document allowing travel from one country to another

PASSUS *n* pl. **-ES** a section of a story or poem

PASSWORD *n* pl. **-S** a secret word that must be spoken to gain admission

PAST *n* pl. **-S** time gone by

PASTA *n* pl. **-S** a food made of dough

PASTE *v* **PASTED, PASTING, PASTES** to fasten with a sticky mixture

PASTEL *n* pl. **-S** a soft, delicate hue

PASTER *n* pl. **-S** one that pastes

PASTERN *n* pl. **-S** a part of a horse's foot

PASTEUP *n* pl. **-S** a finished copy to be photographed for making a printing plate

PASTICCI *n/pl* pastiches

PASTICHE *n* pl. **-S** an artistic work made of fragments from various sources

PASTIE *n* pl. **-S** pasty

PASTIER comparative of pasty

PASTIES pl. of pasty

PASTIEST superlative of pasty

PASTIL *n* pl. **-S** pastille

PASTILLE *n* pl. **-S** a lozenge

PASTIME *n* pl. **-S** a recreational activity

PASTINA *n* pl. **-S** a type of macaroni

PASTING present participle of paste

PASTIS *n* pl. **-TISES** a French liqueur

PASTITSO *n* pl. **-TSOS** a Greek dish of ground meat, pasta, white sauce, and cheese

PASTLESS *adj* having no past

PASTNESS *n* pl. **-ES** the state of being past or gone by

PASTOR *v* **-ED, -ING, -S** to serve as the spiritual overseer of

PASTORAL *n* pl. **-S** a literary or artistic work that depicts country life

PASTORLY *adj* befitting a pastor (a spiritual overseer)

PASTRAMI *n* pl. **-S** a highly seasoned smoked beef

PASTROMI *n* pl. **-S** pastrami

PASTRY *n* pl. **-TRIES** a sweet baked food

PASTURAL *adj* pertaining to a pasture

PASTURE *v* **-TURED, -TURING, -TURES** to put in a pasture (a grazing area)

PASTURER *n* pl. **-S** one that pastures livestock

PASTY *adj* **PASTIER, PASTIEST** pale and unhealthy in appearance

PASTY *n* pl. **PASTIES** a meat pie

PAT *v* **PATTED, PATTING, PATS** to touch lightly

PATACA *n* pl. **-S** a monetary unit of Macao

PATAGIAL *adj* pertaining to a patagium

PATAGIUM *n* pl. **-GIA** a wing membrane of a bat

PATAMAR *n* pl. **-S** a sailing vessel

PATCH *v* **-ED, -ING, -ES** to mend or cover a hole or weak spot in

PATCHER *n* pl. **-S** one that patches

PATCHY *adj* **PATCHIER, PATCHIEST** uneven in quality **PATCHILY** *adv*

PATE *n* pl. **-S** the top of the head **PATED** *adj*

PATELLA *n* pl. **-LAS** or **-LAE** the flat movable bone at the front of the knee **PATELLAR** *adj*

PATEN *n* pl. **-S** a plate

PATENCY *n* pl. **-CIES** the state of being obvious

PATENT *v* **-ED, -ING, -S** to obtain a patent (a government grant protecting the rights of an inventor) on

PATENTEE *n* pl. **-S** one that holds a patent

PATENTLY *adv* obviously

PATENTOR *n* pl. **-S** one that grants a patent

PATER *n* pl. **-S** a father

PATERNAL *adj* pertaining to a father

PATH *n* pl. **-S** a trodden way or track

PATHETIC *adj* arousing pity

PATHLESS *adj* having no path

PATHOGEN *n* pl. **-S** any disease-producing organism

PATHOS *n* pl. **-ES** a quality that arouses feelings of pity or compassion

PATHWAY *n* pl. **-WAYS** a path

PATIENCE	*n* pl. **-S** the quality of being patient
PATIENT	*adj* **-TIENTER, -TIENTEST** able to endure disagreeable circumstances without complaint
PATIENT	*n* pl. **-S** one who is under medical treatment
PATIN	*n* pl. **-S** paten
PATINA	*n* pl. **-NAS** or **-NAE** a green film that forms on bronze **PATINAED** *adj*
PATINATE	*v* **-NATED, -NATING, -NATES** to give a patina to
PATINE	*v* **-TINED, -TINING, -TINES** to cover with a patina
PATINIZE	*v* **-NIZED, -NIZING, -NIZES** to patinate
PATIO	*n* pl. **-TIOS** an outdoor paved area adjoining a house
PATLY	*adv* suitably
PATNESS	*n* pl. **-ES** suitability
PATOIS	*n* pl. **PATOIS** a dialect
PATOOTIE	*n* pl. **-S** the buttocks
PATRIATE	*v* **-ATED, -ATING, -ATES** to transfer (power of legislation) to an autonomous country
PATRIOT	*n* pl. **-S** one who loves his country
PATROL	*v* **-TROLLED, -TROLLING, -TROLS** to pass through an area for the purposes of observation or security
PATRON	*n* pl. **-S** a regular customer **PATRONAL, PATRONLY** *adj*
PATROON	*n* pl. **-S** a landowner granted manorial rights under old Dutch law
PATSY	*n* pl. **-SIES** a person who is easily fooled
PATTAMAR	*n* pl. **-S** patamar
PATTED	past tense of pat
PATTEE	*adj* paty
PATTEN	*n* pl. **-S** a shoe having a thick wooden sole **PATTENED** *adj*
PATTER	*v* **-ED, -ING, -S** to talk glibly or rapidly
PATTERER	*n* pl. **-S** one that patters
PATTERN	*v* **-ED, -ING, -S** to make according to a prescribed design
PATTIE	*n* pl. **-S** patty
PATTING	present participle of pat
PATTY	*n* pl. **-TIES** a small, flat cake of chopped food

PATTYPAN	*n* pl. **-S** a pan in which patties are baked
PATULENT	*adj* patulous
PATULOUS	*adj* spreading; open
PATY	*adj* formee
PATZER	*n* pl. **-S** an inept chess player
PAUCITY	*n* pl. **-TIES** smallness of number or quantity
PAUGHTY	*adj* arrogant
PAULDRON	*n* pl. **-S** a piece of armor for the shoulder
PAULIN	*n* pl. **-S** a sheet of waterproof material
PAUNCH	*n* pl. **-ES** the belly or abdomen **PAUNCHED** *adj*
PAUNCHY	*adj* **PAUNCHIER, PAUNCHIEST** having a protruding belly
PAUPER	*v* **-ED, -ING, -S** to reduce to poverty
PAUSAL	*adj* pertaining to a break or rest in speaking or writing
PAUSE	*v* **PAUSED, PAUSING, PAUSES** to stop temporarily
PAUSER	*n* pl. **-S** one that pauses
PAVAN	*n* pl. **-S** a slow, stately dance
PAVANE	*n* pl. **-S** pavan
PAVE	*v* **PAVED, PAVING, PAVES** to cover with material that forms a firm, level surface
PAVEED	*adj* set close together to conceal a metal base
PAVEMENT	*n* pl. **-S** a paved surface
PAVER	*n* pl. **-S** one that paves
PAVID	*adj* timid
PAVILION	*v* **-ED, -ING, -S** to cover with a large tent
PAVILLON	*n* pl. **-S** the bell of a wind instrument
PAVIN	*n* pl. **-S** pavan
PAVING	*n* pl. **-S** pavement
PAVIOR	*n* pl. **-S** a paver
PAVIOUR	*n* pl. **-S** a paver
PAVIS	*n* pl. **-ISES** a large medieval shield
PAVISE	*n* pl. **-S** pavis
PAVISER	*n* pl. **-S** a soldier carrying a pavis
PAVISSE	*n* pl. **-S** pavis
PAVLOVA	*n* pl. **-S** a meringue dessert
PAVONINE	*adj* resembling a peacock

PAW	*v* **-ED, -ING, -S** to strike or scrape with a beating motion
PAWER	*n* pl. **-S** one that paws
PAWKY	*adj* **PAWKIER, PAWKIEST** sly **PAWKILY** *adv*
PAWL	*n* pl. **-S** a hinged mechanical part
PAWN	*v* **-ED, -ING, -S** to give as security for something borrowed **PAWNABLE** *adj*
PAWNAGE	*n* pl. **-S** an act of pawning
PAWNEE	*n* pl. **-S** one to whom something is pawned
PAWNER	*n* pl. **-S** one that pawns something
PAWNOR	*n* pl. **-S** pawner
PAWNSHOP	*n* pl. **-S** a place where things are pawned
PAWPAW	*n* pl. **-S** papaw
PAX	*n* pl. **-ES** a ceremonial embrace given to signify Christian love and unity
PAXWAX	*n* pl. **-ES** the nuchal ligament of a quadruped
PAY	*v* **PAID** or **PAYED, PAYING, PAYS** to give money or something of value in exchange for goods or services
PAYABLE	*adj* profitable **PAYABLY** *adv*
PAYABLES	*n/pl* accounts payable
PAYBACK	*n* pl. **-S** a return on an investment equal to the original capital outlay
PAYCHECK	*n* pl. **-S** a check in payment of wages or salary
PAYDAY	*n* pl. **-DAYS** the day on which wages are paid
PAYEE	*n* pl. **-S** one to whom money is paid
PAYER	*n* pl. **-S** one that pays
PAYGRADE	*n* pl. **-S** the grade of military personnel according to a base pay scale
PAYLOAD	*n* pl. **-S** the part of a cargo producing income
PAYMENT	*n* pl. **-S** something that is paid
PAYNIM	*n* pl. **-S** a pagan
PAYOFF	*n* pl. **-S** the act of distributing gains
PAYOLA	*n* pl. **-S** a secret payment for favors
PAYOR	*n* pl. **-S** payer
PAYOUT	*n* pl. **-S** money that is paid out
PAYROLL	*n* pl. **-S** a list of employees entitled to payment
PAZAZZ	*n* pl. **-ES** pizazz

PE	*n* pl. **-S** a Hebrew letter
PEA	*n* pl. **-S** the edible seed of an annual herb
PEACE	*v* **PEACED, PEACING, PEACES** to be or become silent
PEACEFUL	*adj* **-FULLER, -FULLEST** undisturbed; calm
PEACENIK	*n* pl. **-S** one who demonstrates against a war
PEACH	*v* **-ED, -ING, -ES** to inform against someone
PEACHER	*n* pl. **-S** one that peaches
PEACHY	*adj* **PEACHIER, PEACHIEST** dandy
PEACING	present participle of peace
PEACOAT	*n* pl. **-S** a heavy woolen jacket
PEACOCK	*v* **-ED, -ING, -S** to strut vainly
PEACOCKY	*adj* **-COCKIER, -COCKIEST** flamboyant, showy
PEAFOWL	*n* pl. **-S** a large pheasant
PEAG	*n* pl. **-S** wampum
PEAGE	*n* pl. **-S** peag
PEAHEN	*n* pl. **-S** a female peafowl
PEAK	*v* **-ED, -ING, -S** to reach a maximum
PEAKIER	comparative of peaky
PEAKIEST	superlative of peaky
PEAKISH	*adj* somewhat sickly
PEAKLESS	*adj* having no peak (a pointed top)
PEAKLIKE	*adj* resembling a peak
PEAKY	*adj* **PEAKIER, PEAKIEST** sickly
PEAL	*v* **-ED, -ING, -S** to ring out
PEALIKE	*adj* resembling a pea
PEAN	*n* pl. **-S** paean
PEANUT	*n* pl. **-S** the nutlike seed or pod of an annual vine
PEAR	*n* pl. **-S** a fleshy fruit
PEARL	*v* **-ED, -ING, -S** to adorn with pearls (smooth, rounded masses formed in certain mollusks)
PEARLASH	*n* pl. **-ES** an alkaline compound
PEARLER	*n* pl. **-S** one that dives for pearls
PEARLITE	*n* pl. **-S** a cast-iron alloy
PEARLY	*adj* **PEARLIER, PEARLIEST** resembling a pearl
PEARMAIN	*n* pl. **-S** a variety of apple
PEART	*adj* **PEARTER, PEARTEST** lively **PEARTLY** *adv*

PEARWOOD *n* pl. **-S** the wood of the pear tree

PEASANT *n* pl. **-S** a person of inferior social rank

PEASCOD *n* pl. **-S** peasecod

PEASE *n* pl. **PEASES** or **PEASEN** a pea

PEASECOD *n* pl. **-S** a pea pod

PEAT *n* pl. **-S** a substance composed of partially decayed vegetable matter

PEATY *adj* **PEATIER, PEATIEST** resembling or containing peat

PEAVEY *n* pl. **-VEYS** a lever used to move logs

PEAVY *n* pl. **-VIES** peavey

PEBBLE *v* **-BLED, -BLING, -BLES** to cover with pebbles (small, rounded stones)

PEBBLY *adj* **-BLIER, -BLIEST** resembling pebbles

PEC *n* pl. **-S** a chest muscle

PECAN *n* pl. **-S** a nut-bearing tree

PECCABLE *adj* liable to sin

PECCANCY *n* pl. **-CIES** the state of being peccant

PECCANT *adj* sinful

PECCARY *n* pl. **-RIES** a piglike hoofed mammal

PECCAVI *n* pl. **-S** a confession of sin

PECH *v* **-ED, -ING, -S** to pant

PECHAN *n* pl. **-S** the stomach

PECK *v* **-ED, -ING, -S** to strike with the beak or something pointed

PECKER *n* pl. **-S** one that pecks

PECKISH *adj* irritable

PECKY *adj* **PECKIER, PECKIEST** marked by decay caused by fungi

PECORINO *n* pl. **-NOS** or **-NI** a hard cheese made from sheep's milk

PECTASE *n* pl. **-S** an enzyme

PECTATE *n* pl. **-S** a chemical salt

PECTEN *n* pl. **-TENS** or **-TINES** a comblike anatomical part

PECTIN *n* pl. **-S** a carbohydrate derivative **PECTIC** *adj*

PECTIZE *v* **-TIZED, -TIZING, -TIZES** to change into a jelly

PECTORAL *n* pl. **-S** something worn on the breast

PECULATE *v* **-LATED, -LATING, -LATES** to embezzle

PECULIAR *n* pl. **-S** something belonging exclusively to a person

PECULIUM *n* pl. **-LIA** private property

PED *n* pl. **-S** a natural soil aggregate

PEDAGOG *n* pl. **-S** a teacher

PEDAGOGY *n* pl. **-GIES** the work of a teacher

PEDAL *v* **-ALED, -ALING, -ALS** or **-ALLED, -ALLING, -ALS** to operate by means of foot levers

PEDALER *n* pl. **-S** one that pedals

PEDALFER *n* pl. **-S** a type of soil

PEDALIER *n* pl. **-S** the pedal keyboard of an organ

PEDALLER *n* pl. **-S** pedaler

PEDALO *n* pl. **-LOS** a paddleboat powered by pedals

PEDANT *n* pl. **-S** one who flaunts his knowledge **PEDANTIC** *adj*

PEDANTRY *n* pl. **-RIES** ostentatious display of knowledge

PEDATE *adj* resembling a foot **PEDATELY** *adv*

PEDDLE *v* **-DLED, -DLING, -DLES** to travel about selling wares

PEDDLER *n* pl. **-S** one that peddles

PEDDLERY *n* pl. **-RIES** the trade of a peddler

PEDERAST *n* pl. **-S** a man who engages in sexual activities with boys

PEDES pl. of pes

PEDESTAL *v* **-TALED, -TALING, -TALS** or **-TALLED, -TALLING, -TALS** to provide with an architectural support or base

PEDICAB *n* pl. **-S** a passenger vehicle that is pedaled

PEDICEL *n* pl. **-S** a slender basal part of an organism

PEDICLE *n* pl. **-S** pedicel **PEDICLED** *adj*

PEDICURE *v* **-CURED, -CURING, -CURES** to administer a cosmetic treatment to the feet and toenails

PEDIFORM *adj* shaped like a foot

PEDIGREE *n* pl. **-S** a line of ancestors

PEDIMENT *n* pl. **-S** a triangular architectural part

PEDIPALP *n* pl. **-S** an appendage of an arachnid

PEDLAR *n* pl. **-S** peddler

PEDLARY *n* pl. **-LARIES** peddlery

PEDLER *n* pl. **-S** peddler

PEDLERY *n pl.* **-LERIES** peddlery

PEDOCAL *n pl.* **-S** a type of soil

PEDOLOGY *n pl.* **-GIES** the scientific study of the behavior and development of children

PEDRO *n pl.* **-DROS** a card game

PEDUNCLE *n pl.* **-S** a flower stalk

PEE *n pl.* **-S** the letter P

PEEBEEN *n pl.* **-S** a large hardwood evergreen tree

PEEK *v* **-ED, -ING, -S** to look furtively or quickly

PEEKABOO *n pl.* **-BOOS** a children's game

PEEKAPOO *n pl.* **-POOS** a dog that is a cross between a Pekingese and a poodle

PEEL *v* **-ED, -ING, -S** to strip off an outer covering of **PEELABLE** *adj*

PEELER *n pl.* **-S** one that peels

PEELING *n pl.* **-S** a piece or strip that has been peeled off

PEEN *v* **-ED, -ING, -S** to beat with the non-flat end of a hammerhead

PEEP *v* **-ED, -ING, -S** to utter a short, shrill cry

PEEPER *n pl.* **-S** one that peeps

PEEPHOLE *n pl.* **-S** a small opening through which one may look

PEEPSHOW *n pl.* **-S** an exhibition viewed through a small opening

PEEPUL *n pl.* **-S** pipal

PEER *v* **-ED, -ING, -S** to look narrowly or searchingly

PEERAGE *n pl.* **-S** the rank of a nobleman

PEERESS *n pl.* **-ES** a noblewoman

PEERIE *n pl.* **-S** peery

PEERLESS *adj* having no equal

PEERY *n pl.* **PEERIES** a child's toy

PEESWEEP *n pl.* **-S** a lapwing

PEETWEET *n pl.* **-S** a wading bird

PEEVE *v* **PEEVED, PEEVING, PEEVES** to annoy

PEEVISH *adj* irritable

PEEWEE *n pl.* **-S** an unusually small person or thing

PEEWIT *n pl.* **-S** pewit

PEG *v* **PEGGED, PEGGING, PEGS** to fasten with a peg (a wooden pin)

PEGBOARD *n pl.* **-S** a board with holes for pegs

PEGBOX *n pl.* **-ES** a part of a stringed instrument

PEGLESS *adj* lacking a peg

PEGLIKE *adj* resembling a peg

PEH *n pl.* **-S** pe

PEIGNOIR *n pl.* **-S** a woman's gown

PEIN *v* **-ED, -ING, -S** to peen

PEISE *v* **PEISED, PEISING, PEISES** to weigh

PEKAN *n pl.* **-S** a carnivorous mammal

PEKE *n pl.* **-S** a small, long-haired dog

PEKEPOO *n pl.* **-POOS** peekapoo

PEKIN *n pl.* **-S** a silk fabric

PEKOE *n pl.* **-S** a black tea

PELAGE *n pl.* **-S** the coat or covering of a mammal **PELAGIAL** *adj*

PELAGIC *n pl.* **-S** an inhabitant of the ocean

PELE *n pl.* **-S** a medieval fortified tower

PELERINE *n pl.* **-S** a woman's cape

PELF *n pl.* **-S** money or wealth

PELICAN *n pl.* **-S** a large, web-footed bird

PELISSE *n pl.* **-S** a long outer garment

PELITE *n pl.* **-S** a rock composed of fine fragments **PELITIC** *adj*

PELLAGRA *n pl.* **-S** a niacin-deficiency disease

PELLET *v* **-ED, -ING, -S** to strike with pellets (small rounded masses)

PELLETAL *adj* resembling a pellet

PELLICLE *n pl.* **-S** a thin skin or film

PELLMELL *n pl.* **-S** a jumbled mass

PELLUCID *adj* transparent

PELMET *n pl.* **-S** a decorative cornice

PELON *adj* hairless

PELORIA *n pl.* **-S** abnormal regularity of a flower form **PELORIAN, PELORIC** *adj*

PELORUS *n pl.* **-ES** a navigational instrument

PELOTA *n pl.* **-S** a court game of Spanish origin

PELOTON *n pl.* **-S** the main body of riders in a bicycle race

PELT *v* **-ED, -ING, -S** to strike repeatedly with blows or missiles

PELTAST *n pl.* **-S** a soldier of ancient Greece

PELTATE *adj* shaped like a shield

PELTER *v* **-ED, -ING, -S** to pelt

PELTLESS *adj* lacking a pelt (the skin of an animal)

PELTRY	*n* pl. **-RIES** an animal skin
PELVIC	*n* pl. **-S** a bone of the pelvis
PELVIS	*n* pl. **-VISES** or **-VES** a part of the skeleton
PEMBINA	*n* pl. **-S** a variety of cranberry
PEMICAN	*n* pl. **-S** pemmican
PEMMICAN	*n* pl. **-S** a food prepared by North American Indians
PEMOLINE	*n* pl. **-S** a drug used as a stimulant
PEMPHIX	*n* pl. **-ES** a skin disease
PEN	*v* **PENNED, PENNING, PENS** to write with a pen (an instrument for writing with fluid ink)
PENAL	*adj* pertaining to punishment
PENALISE	*v* **-ISED, -ISING, -ISES** to penalize
PENALITY	*n* pl. **-TIES** liability to punishment
PENALIZE	*v* **-IZED, -IZING, -IZES** to subject to a penalty
PENALLY	*adv* in a penal manner
PENALTY	*n* pl. **-TIES** a punishment imposed for violation of a law, rule, or agreement
PENANCE	*v* **-ANCED, -ANCING, -ANCES** to impose a type of punishment upon
PENANG	*n* pl. **-S** a cotton fabric
PENATES	*n/pl* the Roman gods of the household
PENCE	a pl. of penny
PENCEL	*n* pl. **-S** a small flag
PENCHANT	*n* pl. **-S** a strong liking for something
PENCIL	*v* **-CILED, -CILING, -CILS** or **-CILLED, -CILLING, -CILS** to produce by using a pencil (a writing and drawing implement)
PENCILER	*n* pl. **-S** one that pencils
PEND	*v* **-ED, -ING, -S** to remain undecided or unsettled
PENDANT	*n* pl. **-S** a hanging ornament
PENDENCY	*n* pl. **-CIES** a pending state
PENDENT	*n* pl. **-S** pendant
PENDULUM	*n* pl. **-S** a type of free swinging body **PENDULAR** *adj*
PENES	a pl. of penis
PENGO	*n* pl. **-GOS** a former monetary unit of Hungary
PENGUIN	*n* pl. **-S** a flightless, aquatic bird
PENICIL	*n* pl. **-S** a small tuft of hairs
PENIS	*n* pl. **-NISES** or **-NES** the male organ of copulation **PENIAL, PENILE** *adj*
PENITENT	*n* pl. **-S** a person who repents his sins
PENKNIFE	*n* pl. **-KNIVES** a small pocketknife
PENLIGHT	*n* pl. **-S** a small flashlight
PENLITE	*n* pl. **-S** penlight
PENMAN	*n* pl. **-MEN** an author
PENNA	*n* pl. **-NAE** any of the feathers that determine a bird's shape
PENNAME	*n* pl. **-S** a name used by an author instead of his real name
PENNANT	*n* pl. **-S** a long, narrow flag
PENNATE	*adj* having wings or feathers
PENNATED	*adj* pennate
PENNE	*n* pl. **PENNE** short tubular pasta
PENNED	past tense of pen
PENNER	*n* pl. **-S** one that pens
PENNI	*n* pl. **-NIS** or **-NIA** a formerly used Finnish coin
PENNIES	a pl. of penny
PENNINE	*n* pl. **-S** a mineral
PENNING	present participle of pen
PENNON	*n* pl. **-S** a pennant **PENNONED** *adj*
PENNY	*n* pl. **PENNIES** or **PENCE** a coin of the United Kingdom
PENOCHE	*n* pl. **-S** penuche
PENOLOGY	*n* pl. **-GIES** the science of the punishment of crime
PENONCEL	*n* pl. **-S** a small pennon
PENPOINT	*n* pl. **-S** the point of a pen
PENSEE	*n* pl. **-S** a thought
PENSIL	*n* pl. **-S** pencel
PENSILE	*adj* hanging loosely
PENSION	*v* **-ED, -ING, -S** to grant a retirement allowance to
PENSIONE	*n* pl. **-S** a boarding house
PENSIVE	*adj* engaged in deep thought
PENSTER	*n* pl. **-S** a writer
PENSTOCK	*n* pl. **-S** a conduit for conveying water to a waterwheel
PENT	*adj* confined
PENTACLE	*n* pl. **-S** a five-pointed star
PENTAD	*n* pl. **-S** a group of five
PENTAGON	*n* pl. **-S** a five-sided polygon
PENTANE	*n* pl. **-S** a volatile liquid

PENTANOL *n* pl. **-S** an alcohol

PENTARCH *n* pl. **-S** one of five joint rulers

PENTENE *n* pl. **-S** a liquid hydrocarbon

PENTODE *n* pl. **-S** a type of electron tube

PENTOMIC *adj* made up of five battle groups

PENTOSAN *n* pl. **-S** a complex carbohydrate

PENTOSE *n* pl. **-S** a sugar having five carbon atoms per molecule

PENTYL *n* pl. **-S** amyl

PENUCHE *n* pl. **-S** a fudge-like candy

PENUCHI *n* pl. **-S** penuche

PENUCHLE *n* pl. **-S** pinochle

PENUCKLE *n* pl. **-S** pinochle

PENULT *n* pl. **-S** the next to last syllable in a word

PENUMBRA *n* pl. **-BRAS** or **-BRAE** a partial shadow

PENURY *n* pl. **-RIES** extreme poverty

PEON *n* pl. **-S** or **-ES** an unskilled laborer

PEONAGE *n* pl. **-S** the condition of being a peon

PEONISM *n* pl. **-S** peonage

PEONY *n* pl. **-NIES** a flowering plant

PEOPLE *v* **-PLED, -PLING, -PLES** to furnish with inhabitants

PEOPLER *n* pl. **-S** one that peoples

PEP *v* **PEPPED, PEPPING, PEPS** to fill with energy

PEPERONI *n* pl. **-S** a highly seasoned sausage

PEPINO *n* pl. **-NOS** a bushy perennial plant with edible fruit

PEPLOS *n* pl. **-ES** a garment worn by women in ancient Greece

PEPLUM *n* pl. **-LUMS** or **-LA** a short section attached to the waistline of a garment **PEPLUMED** *adj*

PEPLUS *n* pl. **-ES** peplos

PEPO *n* pl. **-POS** a fruit having a fleshy interior and a hard rind

PEPONIDA *n* pl. **-S** pepo

PEPONIUM *n* pl. **-S** pepo

PEPPED past tense of pep

PEPPER *v* **-ED, -ING, -S** to season with pepper (a pungent condiment)

PEPPERER *n* pl. **-S** one that peppers

PEPPERY *adj* resembling pepper

PEPPING present participle of pep

PEPPY *adj* **-PIER, -PIEST** full of energy **PEPPILY** *adv*

PEPSIN *n* pl. **-S** a digestive enzyme of the stomach

PEPSINE *n* pl. **-S** pepsin

PEPTALK *v* **-ED, -ING, -S** to inspire enthusiam in by an intense, emotional talk

PEPTIC *n* pl. **-S** a substance that promotes digestion

PEPTID *n* pl. **-S** peptide

PEPTIDE *n* pl. **-S** a combination of amino acids **PEPTIDIC** *adj*

PEPTIZE *v* **-TIZED, -TIZING, -TIZES** to increase the colloidal dispersion of

PEPTIZER *n* pl. **-S** one that peptizes

PEPTONE *n* pl. **-S** a protein compound **PEPTONIC** *adj*

PER *prep* for each

PERACID *n* pl. **-S** a type of acid

PERCALE *n* pl. **-S** a cotton fabric

PERCEIVE *v* **-CEIVED, -CEIVING, -CEIVES** to become aware of through the senses

PERCENT *n* pl. **-S** one part in a hundred

PERCEPT *n* pl. **-S** something that is perceived

PERCH *v* **-ED, -ING, -ES** to sit or rest on an elevated place

PERCHER *n* pl. **-S** one that perches

PERCOID *n* pl. **-S** a spiny-finned fish

PERCUSS *v* **-ED, -ING, -ES** to strike with force

PERDIE *interj* pardi

PERDU *n* pl. **-S** a soldier sent on a dangerous mission

PERDUE *n* pl. **-S** perdu

PERDURE *v* **-DURED, -DURING, -DURES** to continue to exist

PERDY *interj* pardi

PERE *n* pl. **-S** father

PEREGRIN *n* pl. **-S** a swift falcon much used in falconry

PEREION *n* pl. **-REIONS** or **-REIA** the thorax of some crustaceans

PEREON *n* pl. **-REONS** or **-REA** pereion

PEREOPOD *n* pl. **-S** an appendage of the pereion

PERFECT *adj* **-FECTER, -FECTEST** lacking fault or defect; of an extreme kind

PERFECT *v* **-ED, -ING, -S** to make perfect

PERFECTA *n* pl. **-S** a system of betting

PERFECTO *n* pl. **-TOS** a medium-sized cigar

PERFIDY *n* pl. **-DIES** deliberate breach of faith or trust

PERFORCE *adv* of necessity

PERFORM *v* **-ED, -ING, -S** to begin and carry through to completion

PERFUME *v* **-FUMED, -FUMING, -FUMES** to fill with a fragrant odor

PERFUMER *n* pl. **-S** one that perfumes

PERFUMY *adj* scented

PERFUSE *v* **-FUSED, -FUSING, -FUSES** to spread over or through something

PERGOLA *n* pl. **-S** a shaded shelter or passageway

PERHAPS *n* pl. **-ES** something open to doubt or conjecture

PERI *n* pl. **-S** a supernatural being of Persian mythology

PERIANTH *n* pl. **-S** an outer covering of a flower

PERIAPT *n* pl. **-S** an amulet

PERIBLEM *n* pl. **-S** a region of plant tissue

PERICARP *n* pl. **-S** the wall of a ripened plant ovary or fruit

PERICOPE *n* pl. **-PES** or **-PAE** a selection from a book

PERIDERM *n* pl. **-S** an outer layer of plant tissue

PERIDIUM *n* pl. **-IA** the covering of the spore-bearing organ in many fungi **PERIDIAL** *adj*

PERIDOT *n* pl. **-S** a mineral

PERIGEE *n* pl. **-S** the point in the orbit of a celestial body which is nearest to the earth **PERIGEAL, PERIGEAN** *adj*

PERIGON *n* pl. **-S** an angle equal to 360 degrees

PERIGYNY *n* pl. **-NIES** the state of being situated on a cuplike organ surrounding the pistil

PERIL *v* **-ILED, -ILING, -ILS** or **-ILLED, -ILLING, -ILS** to imperil

PERILLA *n* pl. **-S** an Asian herb

PERILOUS *adj* dangerous

PERILUNE *n* pl. **-S** the point in the orbit of a celestial body which is nearest to the moon

PERINEUM *n* pl. **-NEA** a region of the body at the lower end of the trunk **PERINEAL** *adj*

PERIOD *n* pl. **-S** a portion of time

PERIODIC *adj* recurring at regular intervals

PERIODID *n* pl. **-S** an iodide

PERIOTIC *adj* surrounding the ear

PERIPETY *n* pl. **-TIES** a sudden change in a course of events

PERIPTER *n* pl. **-S** a structure with a row of columns around all sides

PERIQUE *n* pl. **-S** a dark tobacco

PERISARC *n* pl. **-S** a protective covering of certain hydrozoans

PERISH *v* **-ED, -ING, -ES** to die

PERITUS *n* pl. **-TI** an expert theologian

PERIWIG *n* pl. **-S** a wig

PERJURE *v* **-JURED, -JURING, -JURES** to make a perjurer of

PERJURER *n* pl. **-S** one guilty of perjury

PERJURY *n* pl. **-RIES** the willful giving of false testimony under oath in a judicial proceeding

PERK *v* **-ED, -ING, -S** to prepare (coffee) in a percolator

PERKISH *adj* somewhat perky

PERKY *adj* **PERKIER, PERKIEST** jaunty **PERKILY** *adv*

PERLITE *n* pl. **-S** a volcanic glass **PERLITIC** *adj*

PERM *v* **-ED, -ING, -S** to give hair a permanent wave

PERMEANT *adj* that permeates

PERMEASE *n* pl. **-S** a catalyzing agent

PERMEATE *v* **-ATED, -ATING, -ATES** to spread through

PERMIT *v* **-MITTED, -MITTING, -MITS** to allow

PERMUTE *v* **-MUTED, -MUTING, -MUTES** to change the order of

PERNIO *n* pl. **-NIONES** an inflammation on the hands or feet caused by exposure to cold

PERONEAL *adj* pertaining to the fibula

PERORAL *adj* occurring through the mouth

PERORATE *v* **-RATED, -RATING, -RATES** to make a lengthy speech

PEROXID *n* pl. **-S** peroxide

PEROXIDE *v* **-IDED, -IDING, -IDES** to treat with peroxide (a bleaching agent)

PEROXY *adj* containing the bivalent group O_2

PERP *n* pl. **-S** a person who commits a crime

PERPEND *v* **-ED, -ING, -S** to ponder

PERPENT *n* pl. **-S** a large building stone

PERPLEX *v* **-ED, -ING, -ES** to make mentally uncertain

PERRON *n* pl. **-S** an outdoor stairway

PERRY *n* pl. **-RIES** a beverage of pear juice often fermented

PERSALT *n* pl. **-S** a chemical salt

PERSE *n* pl. **-S** a blue color

PERSIST *v* **-ED, -ING, -S** to continue resolutely in some activity

PERSON *n* pl. **-S** a human being

PERSONA *n* pl. **-NAE** a character in a literary work

PERSONA *n* pl. **-S** the public role that a person assumes

PERSONAL *n* pl. **-S** a brief, private notice in a newspaper

PERSPIRE *v* **-SPIRED, -SPIRING, -SPIRES** to give off moisture through the pores of the skin **PERSPIRY** *adj*

PERSUADE *v* **-SUADED, -SUADING, -SUADES** to cause to do something by means of argument, reasoning, or entreaty

PERT *adj* **PERTER, PERTEST** impudent **PERTLY** *adv*

PERTAIN *v* **-ED, -ING, -S** to have reference or relation

PERTNESS *n* pl. **-ES** the quality of being pert

PERTURB *v* **-ED, -ING, -S** to disturb greatly

PERUKE *n* pl. **-S** a wig **PERUKED** *adj*

PERUSAL *n* pl. **-S** the act of perusing

PERUSE *v* **-RUSED, -RUSING, -RUSES** to read

PERUSER *n* pl. **-S** one that peruses

PERV *n* pl. **-S** one who has been perverted

PERVADE *v* **-VADED, -VADING, -VADES** to spread through every part of

PERVADER *n* pl. **-S** one that pervades

PERVERSE *adj* willfully deviating from desired or expected conduct

PERVERT *v* **-ED, -ING, -S** to turn away from the right course of action

PERVIOUS *adj* capable of being penetrated

PES *n* pl. **PEDES** a foot or footlike part

PESADE *n* pl. **-S** the position of a horse when rearing

PESETA *n* pl. **-S** a monetary unit of Spain

PESEWA *n* pl. **-S** a monetary unit of Ghana

PESKY *adj* **-KIER, -KIEST** annoying **PESKILY** *adv*

PESO *n* pl. **-SOS** a monetary unit of various Spanish-speaking countries

PESSARY *n* pl. **-RIES** a contraceptive device worn in the vagina

PEST *n* pl. **-S** an annoying person or thing

PESTER *v* **-ED, -ING, -S** to bother

PESTERER *n* pl. **-S** one that pesters

PESTHOLE *n* pl. **-S** a place liable to epidemic disease

PESTLE *v* **-TLED, -TLING, -TLES** to crush with a club-shaped hand tool

PESTO *n* pl. **-TOS** a sauce of basil, garlic, and olive oil

PESTY *adj* **PESTIER, PESTIEST** annoying

PET *v* **PETTED, PETTING, PETS** to caress with the hand

PETABYTE *n* pl. **-S** one quadrillion bytes

PETAL *n* pl. **-S** a leaflike part of a corolla **PETALED, PETALLED** *adj*

PETALINE *adj* resembling a petal

PETALODY *n* pl. **-DIES** the metamorphosis of various floral organs into petals

PETALOID *adj* resembling a petal

PETALOUS *adj* having petals

PETARD *n* pl. **-S** an explosive device

PETASOS *n* pl. **-ES** petasus

PETASUS *n* pl. **-ES** a broad-brimmed hat worn in ancient Greece

PETCOCK *n* pl. **-S** a small valve or faucet

PETECHIA *n* pl. **-CHIAE** a small hemorrhagic spot on a body surface

PETER *v* **-ED, -ING, -S** to diminish gradually

PETIOLAR *adj* pertaining to a petiole

PETIOLE *n* pl. **-S** the stalk of a leaf **PETIOLED** *adj*

PETIT *adj* small; minor

PETITE *n* pl. **-S** a clothing size for short women

PETITION *v* **-ED, -ING, -S** to make a formal request

PETNAP *v* **-NAPPED, -NAPPING, -NAPS** to steal a pet for profit

PETNAPER *n* pl. **-S** one who steals a pet

PETRALE   *n* pl. **-S** a food fish

PETREL   *n* pl. **-S** a small seabird

PETRIFY   *v* **-FIED, -FYING, -FIES** to convert into stone

PETROL   *n* pl. **-S** gasoline

PETROLIC   *adj* derived from petroleum

PETRONEL   *n* pl. **-S** a portable firearm

PETROSAL   *adj* petrous

PETROUS   *adj* resembling stone in hardness

PETSAI   *n* pl. **-S** Chinese cabbage

PETTABLE   *adj* capable of being petted

PETTED   past tense of pet

PETTEDLY   *adv* peevishly

PETTER   *n* pl. **-S** one that pets

PETTI   pl. of petto

PETTIER   comparative of petty

PETTIEST   superlative of petty

PETTIFOG   *v* **-FOGGED, -FOGGING, -FOGS** to quibble

PETTILY   *adv* in a petty manner

PETTING   *n* pl. **-S** amorous caressing and kissing

PETTISH   *adj* peevish

PETTLE   *v* **-TLED, -TLING, -TLES** to caress

PETTO   *n* pl. **-TI** the breast

PETTY   *adj* **-TIER, -TIEST** insignificant

PETULANT   *adj* peevish

PETUNIA   *n* pl. **-S** a tropical herb

PETUNTSE   *n* pl. **-S** a mineral

PETUNTZE   *n* pl. **-S** petuntse

PEW   *n* pl. **-S** a bench in church

PEWEE   *n* pl. **-S** a small bird

PEWIT   *n* pl. **-S** the lapwing

PEWTER   *n* pl. **-S** a tin alloy

PEWTERER   *n* pl. **-S** one that makes articles of pewter

PEYOTE   *n* pl. **-S** a cactus

PEYOTL   *n* pl. **-S** peyote

PEYTRAL   *n* pl. **-S** a piece of armor for the breast of a horse

PEYTREL   *n* pl. **-S** peytral

PFENNIG   *n* pl. **-NIGS** or **-NIGE** a formerly used bronze coin of Germany

PFFT   *interj* — used to express a sudden ending

PFUI   *interj* phooey

PHAETON   *n* pl. **-S** a light carriage

PHAGE   *n* pl. **-S** an organism that destroys bacteria

PHALANGE   *n* pl. **-S** any bone of a finger or toe

PHALANX   *n* pl. **-ES** a formation of infantry in ancient Greece

PHALLI   a pl. of phallus

PHALLIC   *adj* pertaining to a phallus

PHALLISM   *n* pl. **-S** worship of the phallus as symbolic of nature's creative power

PHALLIST   *n* pl. **-S** one who practices phallism

PHALLUS   *n* pl. **-LUSES** or **-LI** the penis

PHANTASM   *n* pl. **-S** a creation of the imagination

PHANTAST   *n* pl. **-S** fantast

PHANTASY   *v* **-SIED, -SYING, -SIES** to fantasy

PHANTOM   *n* pl. **-S** something existing in appearance only

PHARAOH   *n* pl. **-S** a ruler of ancient Egypt

PHARISEE   *n* pl. **-S** a hypocritically self-righteous person

PHARMACY   *n* pl. **-CIES** a drugstore

PHARMING   *n* pl. **-S** the production of pharmaceuticals from genetically altered plants or animals

PHAROS   *n* pl. **-ES** a lighthouse or beacon to guide seamen

PHARYNX   *n* pl. **-YNXES** or **-YNGES** a section of the digestive tract

PHASE   *v* **PHASED, PHASING, PHASES** to plan or carry out by phases (distinct stages of development) **PHASEAL, PHASIC** *adj*

PHASEOUT   *n* pl. **-S** a gradual stopping of operations

PHASIS   *n* pl. **PHASES** a phase

PHASMID   *n* pl. **-S** a tropical insect

PHAT   *adj* **PHATTER, PHATTEST** excellent

PHATIC   *adj* sharing feelings rather than ideas

PHEASANT   *n* pl. **-S** a large, long-tailed bird

PHELLEM   *n* pl. **-S** a layer of plant cells

PHELONIA   *n/pl* liturgical vestments

PHENATE   *n* pl. **-S** a salt of carbolic acid

PHENAZIN   *n* pl. **-S** a chemical compound

PHENETIC   *adj* pertaining to a type of classificatory system

PHENETOL   *n* pl. **-S** a volatile liquid

PHENIX   *n* pl. **-ES** phoenix

PHENOL	*n* pl. **-S** a caustic compound	**PHONETIC**	*adj* pertaining to speech sounds
PHENOLIC	*n* pl. **-S** a synthetic resin	**PHONEY**	*adj* **-NIER, -NIEST** phony
PHENOM	*n* pl. **-S** a person of extraordinary ability or promise	**PHONEY**	*v* **-ED, -ING, -S** to phony
PHENOXY	*adj* containing a radical derived from phenol	**PHONIC**	*adj* pertaining to the nature of sound
PHENYL	*n* pl. **-S** a univalent chemical radical **PHENYLIC** *adj*	**PHONICS**	*n/pl* the science of sound
		PHONIED	past tense of phony
PHERESIS	*n* pl. **-RESES** withdrawal of blood from a donor, removing some components, and returning the remaining blood to the donor	**PHONIER**	comparative of phoney and phony
		PHONIES	present 3d person sing. of phony
		PHONIEST	superlative of phoney and phony
		PHONILY	*adv* in a phony manner
PHEW	*interj* — used to express relief, fatigue, or disgust	**PHONING**	present participle of phone
PHI	*n* pl. **-S** a Greek letter	**PHONO**	*n* pl. **-NOS** a record player
PHIAL	*n* pl. **-S** a vial	**PHONON**	*n* pl. **-S** a quantum of vibrational energy
PHILABEG	*n* pl. **-S** filibeg		
PHILIBEG	*n* pl. **-S** filibeg	**PHONY**	*adj* **-NIER, -NIEST** not genuine or real
PHILOMEL	*n* pl. **-S** a songbird		
PHILTER	*v* **-ED, -ING, -S** to put under the spell of a love potion	**PHONY**	*v* **-NIED, -NYING, -NIES** to alter so as to make appear genuine
PHILTRE	*v* **-TRED, -TRING, -TRES** to philter	**PHOOEY**	*interj* — used as an exclamation of disgust or contempt
PHILTRUM	*n* pl. **-TRA** the indentation between the upper lip and the nose	**PHORATE**	*n* pl. **-S** an insecticide
PHIMOSIS	*n* pl. **-MOSES** the abnormal constriction of the opening of the prepuce **PHIMOTIC** *adj*	**PHORESY**	*n* pl. **-SIES** a symbiotic relationship between some arthropods and fishes
PHIZ	*n* pl. **-ES** a face or facial expression	**PHORONID**	*n* pl. **-S** a wormlike marine animal
		PHOSGENE	*n* pl. **-S** a poisonous gas
PHLEGM	*n* pl. **-S** a thick mucus secreted in the air passages	**PHOSPHID**	*n* pl. **-S** a chemical compound
		PHOSPHIN	*n* pl. **-S** a poisonous gas
PHLEGMY	*adj* **PHLEGMIER, PHLEGMIEST** resembling phlegm	**PHOSPHOR**	*n* pl. **-S** a substance that will emit light when exposed to radiation
PHLOEM	*n* pl. **-S** a complex plant tissue	**PHOT**	*n* pl. **-S** a unit of illumination
PHLOX	*n* pl. **-ES** a flowering plant	**PHOTIC**	*adj* pertaining to light
PHOBIA	*n* pl. **-S** an obsessive or irrational fear	**PHOTICS**	*n/pl* the science of light
PHOBIC	*n* pl. **-S** one affected with a phobia	**PHOTO**	*v* **-ED, -ING, -S** to photograph
PHOCINE	*adj* pertaining to seals	**PHOTOG**	*n* pl. **-S** one who takes photographs
PHOEBE	*n* pl. **-S** a small bird		
PHOEBUS	*n* pl. **-ES** the sun	**PHOTOMAP**	*v* **-MAPPED, -MAPPING, -MAPS** to map by means of aerial photography
PHOENIX	*n* pl. **-ES** a mythical bird		
PHON	*n* pl. **-S** a unit of loudness	**PHOTON**	*n* pl. **-S** an elementary particle **PHOTONIC** *adj*
PHONAL	*adj* pertaining to speech sounds		
PHONATE	*v* **-NATED, -NATING, -NATES** to produce speech sounds	**PHOTOPIA**	*n* pl. **-S** vision in bright light **PHOTOPIC** *adj*
PHONE	*v* **PHONED, PHONING, PHONES** to telephone	**PHOTOSET**	*v* **-SET, -SETTING, -SETS** to prepare for printing by photographic means
PHONEME	*n* pl. **-S** a unit of speech **PHONEMIC** *adj*	**PHPHT**	*interj* pht

PHRASAL	*adj* pertaining to a group of two or more associated words
PHRASE	*v* **PHRASED, PHRASING, PHRASES** to express in words
PHRASING	*n* pl. **-S** manner or style of verbal expression
PHRATRY	*n* pl. **-TRIES** a tribal unit among primitive peoples **PHRATRAL, PHRATRIC** *adj*
PHREAK	*v* **-ED, -ING, -S** to gain illegal access to a long-distance telephone service to avoid tolls
PHREAKER	*n* pl. **-S** one that phreaks
PHREATIC	*adj* pertaining to underground waters
PHRENIC	*adj* pertaining to the mind
PHRENSY	*v* **-SIED, -SYING, -SIES** to frenzy
PHT	*interj* — used as an expression of mild anger or annoyance
PHTHALIC	*adj* pertaining to a certain acid
PHTHALIN	*n* pl. **-S** a chemical compound
PHTHISIC	*n* pl. **-S** phthisis
PHTHISIS	*n* pl. **PHTHISES** a disease of the lungs
PHUT	*n* pl. **-S** a dull, abrupt sound
PHYLA	pl. of phylon and phylum
PHYLAE	pl. of phyle
PHYLAR	*adj* pertaining to a phylum
PHYLAXIS	*n* pl. **-AXISES** an inhibiting of infection by the body
PHYLE	*n* pl. **-LAE** a political subdivision in ancient Greece **PHYLIC** *adj*
PHYLESIS	*n* pl. **-LESISES** or **-LESES** the course of evolutionary development **PHYLETIC** *adj*
PHYLLARY	*n* pl. **-RIES** a bract of certain plants
PHYLLITE	*n* pl. **-S** a foliated rock
PHYLLO	*n* pl. **-LOS** very thin pastry dough
PHYLLODE	*n* pl. **-S** a flattened petiole that serves as a leaf
PHYLLOID	*n* pl. **-S** a leaflike plant part
PHYLLOME	*n* pl. **-S** a leaf of a plant
PHYLON	*n* pl. **-LA** a genetically related group
PHYLUM	*n* pl. **-LA** a taxonomic division
PHYSED	*n* pl. **-S** physical education
PHYSES	pl. of physis
PHYSIC	*v* **-ICKED, -ICKING, -ICS** to treat with medicine
PHYSICAL	*n* pl. **-S** a medical examination of the body
PHYSIQUE	*n* pl. **-S** the form or structure of the body
PHYSIS	*n* pl. **PHYSES** the principle of growth or change in nature
PHYTANE	*n* pl. **-S** a chemical compound
PHYTIN	*n* pl. **-S** a calcium-magnesium salt
PHYTOID	*adj* resembling a plant
PHYTOL	*n* pl. **-S** an alcohol
PHYTON	*n* pl. **-S** a structural unit of a plant **PHYTONIC** *adj*
PI	*n* pl. **-S** a Greek letter
PI	*v* **PIED, PIEING** or **PIING, PIES** to jumble or disorder
PIA	*n* pl. **-S** a membrane of the brain
PIACULAR	*adj* atoning
PIAFFE	*v* **PIAFFED, PIAFFING, PIAFFES** to perform a piaffer
PIAFFER	*n* pl. **-S** a movement in horsemanship
PIAL	*adj* pertaining to a pia
PIAN	*n* pl. **-S** a tropical disease **PIANIC** *adj*
PIANISM	*n* pl. **-S** performance on the piano
PIANIST	*n* pl. **-S** one who plays the piano
PIANO	*n* pl. **-NOS** a musical instrument
PIASABA	*n* pl. **-S** piassava
PIASAVA	*n* pl. **-S** piassava
PIASSABA	*n* pl. **-S** piassava
PIASSAVA	*n* pl. **-S** a coarse, stiff fiber
PIASTER	*n* pl. **-S** a monetary unit of several Arab countries
PIASTRE	*n* pl. **-S** piaster
PIAZZA	*n* pl. **-ZAS** or **-ZE** a public square in an Italian town
PIBAL	*n* pl. **-S** a small balloon for determining the direction and speed of the wind
PIBROCH	*n* pl. **-S** a musical piece played on the bagpipe
PIC	*n* pl. **-S** a photograph
PICA	*n* pl. **-S** a craving for unnatural food
PICACHO	*n* pl. **-CHOS** an isolated peak of a hill
PICADOR	*n* pl. **-S** or **-ES** a horseman in a bullfight
PICAL	*adj* resembling a pica

PICANTE	*adj* prepared with a spicy sauce	**PICOT**	*v* **-ED, -ING, -S** to edge with ornamental loops
PICARA	*n* pl. **-S** a female picaro		
PICARO	*n* pl. **-ROS** a vagabond	**PICOTEE**	*n* pl. **-S** a variety of carnation
PICAROON	*v* **-ED, -ING, -S** to act as a pirate	**PICOWAVE**	*v* **-WAVED, -WAVING, -WAVES** to irradiate (food) with gamma rays
PICAYUNE	*n* pl. **-S** a former Spanish-American coin	**PICQUET**	*n* pl. **-S** piquet
PICCATA	*adj* prepared with a sauce of lemon, white wine, and butter	**PICRATE**	*n* pl. **-S** a chemical salt **PICRATED** *adj*
PICCOLO	*n* pl. **-LOS** a small flute	**PICRIC**	*adj* having a very bitter taste
PICE	*n* pl. **PICE** a former coin of India and Pakistan	**PICRITE**	*n* pl. **-S** an igneous rock **PICRITIC** *adj*
PICEOUS	*adj* glossy-black in color	**PICTURE**	*v* **-TURED, -TURING, -TURES** to make a visual representation of
PICIFORM	*adj* pertaining to an order of birds	**PICUL**	*n* pl. **-S** an Asian unit of weight
PICK	*v* **-ED, -ING, -S** to select	**PIDDLE**	*v* **-DLED, -DLING, -DLES** to waste time
PICKADIL	*n* pl. **-S** a type of collar		
PICKAX	*v* **-ED, -ING, -ES** to use a pickax (a tool for breaking hard surfaces)	**PIDDLER**	*n* pl. **-S** one that piddles
		PIDDLY	*adj* insignificant
PICKAXE	*v* **-AXED, -AXING, -AXES** to pickax	**PIDDOCK**	*n* pl. **-S** a bivalve mollusk
PICKEER	*v* **-ED, -ING, -S** to skirmish in advance of an army	**PIDGIN**	*n* pl. **-S** a mixed language
		PIE	*v* **PIED, PIEING, PIES** to pi
PICKER	*n* pl. **-S** one that picks	**PIEBALD**	*n* pl. **-S** a spotted animal
PICKEREL	*n* pl. **-S** a freshwater fish	**PIECE**	*v* **PIECED, PIECING, PIECES** to join into a whole
PICKET	*v* **-ED, -ING, -S** to stand outside of some location, as a business, to publicize one's grievances against it	**PIECER**	*n* pl. **-S** one that pieces
		PIECING	*n* pl. **-S** material to be sewn together
PICKETER	*n* pl. **-S** one who pickets	**PIECRUST**	*n* pl. **-S** the crust of a pie
PICKIER	comparative of picky	**PIED**	past tense of pie
PICKIEST	superlative of picky	**PIEDFORT**	*n* pl. **-S** piefort
PICKING	*n* pl. **-S** the act of one that picks	**PIEDMONT**	*n* pl. **-S** an area lying at the foot of a mountain
PICKLE	*v* **-LED, -LING, -LES** to preserve or flavor in a solution of brine or vinegar	**PIEFORT**	*n* pl. **-S** an unusually thick coin
		PIEHOLE	*n* pl. **-S** a mouth
PICKLOCK	*n* pl. **-S** a tool for opening locks	**PIEING**	a present participle of pi and pie
PICKOFF	*n* pl. **-S** a play in baseball	**PIEPLANT**	*n* pl. **-S** a rhubarb
PICKUP	*n* pl. **-S** a small truck	**PIER**	*n* pl. **-S** a structure extending from land out over water
PICKWICK	*n* pl. **-S** a device for raising wicks in oil lamps	**PIERCE**	*v* **PIERCED, PIERCING, PIERCES** to cut or pass into or through
PICKY	*adj* **PICKIER, PICKIEST** fussy		
PICLORAM	*n* pl. **-S** an herbicide	**PIERCER**	*n* pl. **-S** one that pierces
PICNIC	*v* **-NICKED, -NICKING, -NICS** to go on a picnic (an outdoor excursion with food)	**PIERCING**	*n* pl. **-S** a piece of jewelry attached to pierced flesh
		PIEROGI	*n* pl. **-ES** a small dumpling with a filling
PICNICKY	*adj* pertaining to a picnic		
PICOGRAM	*n* pl. **-S** one trillionth of a gram	**PIERROT**	*n* pl. **-S** a clown
PICOLIN	*n* pl. **-S** picoline	**PIETA**	*n* pl. **-S** a representation of the Virgin Mary mourning over the body of Christ
PICOLINE	*n* pl. **-S** a chemical compound		
PICOMOLE	*n* pl. **-S** one trillionth of a mole		

PIETIES   pl. of piety

PIETISM   *n* pl. **-S** piety

PIETIST   *n* pl. **-S** a pious person

PIETY   *n* pl. **-TIES** the quality or state of being pious

PIFFLE   *v* **-FLED, -FLING, -FLES** to babble

PIG   *v* **PIGGED, PIGGING, PIGS** to bear pigs (cloven-hoofed mammals)

PIGBOAT   *n* pl. **-S** a submarine

PIGEON   *n* pl. **-S** a short-legged bird

PIGFISH   *n* pl. **-ES** a marine fish

PIGGED   past tense of pig

PIGGERY   *n* pl. **-GERIES** a pigpen

PIGGIE   *n* pl. **-S** piggy

PIGGIER   comparative of piggy

PIGGIES   pl. of piggy

PIGGIEST   superlative of piggy

PIGGIN   *n* pl. **-S** a small wooden pail

PIGGING   present participle of pig

PIGGISH   *adj* greedy or dirty

PIGGY   *adj* **-GIER, -GIEST** piggish

PIGGY   *n* pl. **-GIES** a small pig

PIGLET   *n* pl. **-S** a small pig

PIGLIKE   *adj* resembling a pig

PIGMENT   *v* **-ED, -ING, -S** to add a coloring matter to

PIGMY   *n* pl. **-MIES** pygmy

PIGNOLI   *n* pl. **-S** pignolia

PIGNOLIA   *n* pl. **-S** the edible seed of nut pines

PIGNUS   *n* pl. **-NORA** property held as security for a debt

PIGNUT   *n* pl. **-S** a hickory nut

PIGOUT   *n* pl. **-S** an instance of eating to excess

PIGPEN   *n* pl. **-S** a place where pigs are kept

PIGSKIN   *n* pl. **-S** the skin of a pig

PIGSNEY   *n* pl. **-NEYS** a darling

PIGSTICK   *v* **-ED, -ING, -S** to hunt for wild boar

PIGSTY   *n* pl. **-STIES** a pigpen

PIGTAIL   *n* pl. **-S** a tight braid of hair

PIGWEED   *n* pl. **-S** a weedy plant

PIING   a present participle of pi

PIKA   *n* pl. **-S** a small mammal

PIKAKE   *n* pl. **-S** an East Indian vine

PIKE   *v* **PIKED, PIKING, PIKES** to pierce with a pike (a long spear)

PIKEMAN   *n* pl. **-MEN** a soldier armed with a pike

PIKER   *n* pl. **-S** a stingy person

PIKI   *n* pl. **-S** thin blue cornmeal bread

PIKING   present participle of pike

PILAF   *n* pl. **-S** a dish made of seasoned rice and often meat

PILAFF   *n* pl. **-S** pilaf

PILAR   *adj* pertaining to hair

PILASTER   *n* pl. **-S** a rectangular column

PILAU   *n* pl. **-S** pilaf

PILAW   *n* pl. **-S** pilaf

PILCHARD   *n* pl. **-S** a small marine fish

PILE   *v* **PILED, PILING, PILES** to lay one upon the other

PILEA   pl. of pileum

PILEATE   *adj* having a pileus

PILEATED   *adj* pileate

PILED   past tense of pile

PILEI   pl. of pileus

PILELESS   *adj* not having a raised surface of yarn

PILEOUS   *adj* pilose

PILEUM   *n* pl. **-LEA** the top of a bird's head

PILEUP   *n* pl. **-S** a collision involving several motor vehicles

PILEUS   *n* pl. **-LEI** the umbrella-shaped portion of a mushroom

PILEWORT   *n* pl. **-S** a medicinal plant

PILFER   *v* **-ED, -ING, -S** to steal

PILFERER   *n* pl. **-S** one that pilfers

PILGRIM   *n* pl. **-S** a traveler or wanderer

PILI   *n* pl. **-S** a Philippine tree

PILIFORM   *adj* resembling a hair

PILING   *n* pl. **-S** a structure of building supports

PILL   *v* **-ED, -ING, -S** to dose with pills (small, rounded masses of medicine)

PILLAGE   *v* **-LAGED, -LAGING, -LAGES** to plunder

PILLAGER   *n* pl. **-S** one that pillages

PILLAR   *v* **-ED, -ING, -S** to provide with vertical building supports

PILLBOX   *n* pl. **-ES** a small box for pills

PILLION n pl. **-S** a pad or cushion for an extra rider on a horse or motorcycle

PILLORY v **-RIED, -RYING, -RIES** to expose to public ridicule or abuse

PILLOW v **-ED, -ING, -S** to rest on a pillow (a cushion for the head)

PILLOWY adj resembling a pillow

PILOSE adj covered with hair

PILOSITY n pl. **-TIES** the state of being pilose

PILOT v **-ED, -ING, -S** to control the course of

PILOTAGE n pl. **-S** the act of piloting

PILOTING n pl. **-S** a branch of navigation

PILOUS adj pilose

PILSENER n pl. **-S** pilsner

PILSNER n pl. **-S** a light beer

PILULE n pl. **-S** a small pill **PILULAR** adj

PILUS n pl. **-LI** a hair or hairlike structure

PILY adj divided into a number of wedge-shaped heraldic designs

PIMA n pl. **-S** a strong, high-grade cotton

PIMENTO n pl. **-TOS** pimiento

PIMIENTO n pl. **-TOS** a sweet pepper

PIMP v **-ED, -ING, -S** to solicit clients for a prostitute

PIMPLE n pl. **-S** an inflamed swelling of the skin **PIMPLED** adj

PIMPLY adj **-PLIER, -PLIEST** covered with pimples

PIN v **PINNED, PINNING, PINS** to fasten with a pin (a slender, pointed piece of metal)

PINA n pl. **-S** a pineapple

PINAFORE n pl. **-S** a child's apron

PINANG n pl. **-S** a palm tree

PINASTER n pl. **-S** a pine tree

PINATA n pl. **-S** a pottery jar used in a Mexican game

PINBALL v **-ED, -ING, -S** to move abruptly from one place to another

PINBONE n pl. **-S** the hipbone

PINCER n pl. **-S** one of the two pivoted parts of a grasping tool

PINCH v **-ED, -ING, -ES** to squeeze between two edges or surfaces

PINCHBUG n pl. **-S** a large beetle

PINCHECK n pl. **-S** a fabric design

PINCHER n pl. **-S** one that pinches

PINDER n pl. **-S** an official who formerly impounded stray animals

PINDLING adj puny or sickly

PINE v **PINED, PINING, PINES** to yearn intensely

PINEAL n pl. **-S** a gland in the brain

PINECONE n pl. **-S** a cone-shaped fruit of a pine tree

PINED past tense of pine

PINELAND n pl. **-S** land forested with pine

PINELIKE adj resembling a pine (an evergreen tree)

PINENE n pl. **-S** the main constituent of turpentine

PINERY n pl. **-ERIES** an area where pineapples are grown

PINESAP n pl. **-S** a fragrant herb

PINETUM n pl. **-TA** a plantation of pine trees

PINEWOOD n pl. **-S** the wood of a pine tree

PINEY adj **PINIER, PINIEST** piny

PINFISH n pl. **-ES** a small marine fish

PINFOLD v **-ED, -ING, -S** to confine in an enclosure for stray animals

PING v **-ED, -ING, -S** to produce a brief, high-pitched sound

PINGER n pl. **-S** a device for producing pulses of sound

PINGO n pl. **-GOS** or **-GOES** a low mound of earth formed by expansion of underlying frost

PINGRASS n pl. **-ES** a European weed

PINGUID adj greasy

PINHEAD n pl. **-S** the head of a pin

PINHOLE n pl. **-S** a small hole made by a pin

PINIER comparative of piney and piny

PINIEST superlative of piney and piny

PINING present participle of pine

PINION v **-ED, -ING, -S** to remove or bind the wing feathers of to prevent flight

PINITE n pl. **-S** a mineral

PINITOL n pl. **-S** an alcohol

PINK adj **PINKER, PINKEST** of a pale reddish hue

PINK v **-ED, -ING, -S** to cut a saw-toothed edge on cloth

PINKEN v **-ED, -ING, -S** to become pink

PINKER n pl. **-S** one that pinks

PINKEY _n_ pl. **-EYS** a ship with a narrow overhanging stern

PINKEYE _n_ pl. **-S** an inflammation of the eye

PINKIE _n_ pl. **-S** the little finger

PINKIES pl. of pinky

PINKING _n_ pl. **-S** a method of cutting or decorating

PINKISH _adj_ somewhat pink

PINKLY _adv_ with a pink hue

PINKNESS _n_ pl. **-ES** the state of being pink

PINKO _n_ pl. **PINKOS** or **PINKOES** a person who holds somewhat radical political views

PINKROOT _n_ pl. **-S** a medicinal plant root

PINKY _n_ pl. **PINKIES** pinkie

PINNA _n_ pl. **-NAS** or **-NAE** a feather, wing, or winglike part

PINNACE _n_ pl. **-S** a small sailing ship

PINNACLE _v_ **-CLED, -CLING, -CLES** to place on a summit

PINNAL _adj_ pertaining to a pinna

PINNATE _adj_ resembling a feather

PINNATED _adj_ pinnate

PINNED past tense of pin

PINNER _n_ pl. **-S** one that pins

PINNIES pl. of pinny

PINNING present participle of pin

PINNIPED _n_ pl. **-S** a mammal with limbs modified into flippers

PINNULA _n_ pl. **-LAE** pinnule **PINNULAR** _adj_

PINNULE _n_ pl. **-S** a pinnate part or organ

PINNY _n_ pl. **-NIES** a pinafore

PINOCHLE _n_ pl. **-S** a card game

PINOCLE _n_ pl. **-S** pinochle

PINOLE _n_ pl. **-S** a finely ground flour

PINON _n_ pl. **-S** or **-ES** a pine tree

PINOT _n_ pl. **-S** a red or white grape

PINPOINT _v_ **-ED, -ING, -S** to locate precisely

PINPRICK _v_ **-ED, -ING, -S** to puncture with a pin

PINSCHER _n_ pl. **-S** a large, short-haired dog

PINT _n_ pl. **-S** a liquid and dry measure of capacity

PINTA _n_ pl. **-S** a skin disease

PINTADA _n_ pl. **-S** pintado

PINTADO _n_ pl. **-DOS** or **-DOES** a large food fish

PINTAIL _n_ pl. **-S** a river duck

PINTANO _n_ pl. **-NOS** a tropical fish

PINTLE _n_ pl. **-S** a pin on which something turns

PINTO _n_ pl. **-TOS** or **-TOES** a spotted horse

PINTSIZE _adj_ small

PINUP _n_ pl. **-S** a picture that may be pinned up on a wall

PINWALE _n_ pl. **-S** a type of fabric

PINWEED _n_ pl. **-S** a perennial herb

PINWHEEL _v_ **-ED, -ING, -S** to revolve at the end of a stick

PINWORK _n_ pl. **-S** a type of embroidery

PINWORM _n_ pl. **-S** a parasitic worm

PINY _adj_ **PINIER, PINIEST** suggestive of or covered with pine trees

PINYIN _n_ a system for romanizing Chinese ideograms

PINYON _n_ pl. **-S** pinon

PIOLET _n_ pl. **-S** an ice ax

PION _n_ pl. **-S** a subatomic particle **PIONIC** _adj_

PIONEER _v_ **-ED, -ING, -S** to take part in the beginnings of

PIOSITY _n_ pl. **-TIES** an excessive show of piety

PIOUS _adj_ marked by religious reverence **PIOUSLY** _adv_

PIP _v_ **PIPPED, PIPPING, PIPS** to break through the shell of an egg

PIPAGE _n_ pl. **-S** a system of pipes

PIPAL _n_ pl. **-S** a fig tree of India

PIPE _v_ **PIPED, PIPING, PIPES** to convey by means of a pipe (a hollow cylinder)

PIPEAGE _n_ pl. **-S** pipage

PIPEFISH _n_ pl. **-ES** a slender fish

PIPEFUL _n_ pl. **-S** a quantity sufficient to fill a tobacco pipe

PIPELESS _adj_ having no pipe

PIPELIKE _adj_ resembling a pipe

PIPELINE _v_ **-LINED, -LINING, -LINES** to convey by a line of pipe

PIPER _n_ pl. **-S** one that plays on a tubular musical instrument

PIPERINE _n_ pl. **-S** a chemical compound

PIPESTEM _n_ pl. **-S** the stem of a tobacco pipe

PIPET _v_ **-PETTED, -PETTING, -PETS** to pipette

PIPETTE — *v* **-PETTED, -PETTING, -PETTES** to measure liquid with a calibrated tube

PIPIER — comparative of pipy

PIPIEST — superlative of pipy

PIPINESS — *n* pl. **-ES** the quality of being pipy

PIPING — *n* pl. **-S** a system of pipes

PIPINGLY — *adv* shrilly

PIPIT — *n* pl. **-S** a songbird

PIPKIN — *n* pl. **-S** a small pot

PIPPED — past tense of pip

PIPPIN — *n* pl. **-S** any of several varieties of apple

PIPPING — present participle of pip

PIPY — *adj* **PIPIER, PIPIEST** shrill

PIQUANCE — *n* pl. **-S** piquancy

PIQUANCY — *n* pl. **-CIES** the quality of being piquant

PIQUANT — *adj* agreeably sharp in taste

PIQUE — *v* **PIQUED, PIQUING, PIQUES** to arouse anger or resentment in

PIQUET — *n* pl. **-S** a card game

PIRACY — *n* pl. **-CIES** robbery on the high seas

PIRAGUA — *n* pl. **-S** a dugout canoe

PIRANA — *n* pl. **-S** piranha

PIRANHA — *n* pl. **-S** a voracious fish

PIRARUCU — *n* pl. **-S** a large food fish

PIRATE — *v* **-RATED, -RATING, -RATES** to commit piracy

PIRATIC — *adj* pertaining to piracy

PIRAYA — *n* pl. **-S** piranha

PIRIFORM — *adj* pyriform

PIRN — *n* pl. **-S** a spinning-wheel bobbin

PIROG — *n* pl. **-ROGEN** or **-ROGHI** or **-ROGI** a large Russian pastry

PIROGI — *n* pl. **-ES** pierogi

PIROGUE — *n* pl. **-S** piragua

PIROQUE — *n* pl. **-S** piragua

PIROZHOK — *n* pl. **-ROZHKI, -ROSHKI** or **-ROJKI** a small Russian pastry

PISCARY — *n* pl. **-RIES** a place for fishing

PISCATOR — *n* pl. **-S** a fisherman

PISCINA — *n* pl. **-NAS** or **-NAE** a basin used in certain church ceremonies **PISCINAL** *adj*

PISCINE — *adj* pertaining to fish

PISCO — *n* pl. **-COS** a Peruvian brandy

PISH — *v* **-ED, -ING, -ES** to express contempt

PISHER — *n* pl. **-S** a young or inexperienced person

PISHOGE — *n* pl. **-S** pishogue

PISHOGUE — *n* pl. **-S** an evil spell

PISIFORM — *n* pl. **-S** a small bone of the wrist

PISMIRE — *n* pl. **-S** an ant

PISO — *n* pl. **-SOS** the Philippine peso

PISOLITE — *n* pl. **-S** a limestone

PISOLITH — *n* pl. **-S** a small rounded concretion of limestone

PISSOIR — *n* pl. **-S** a public urinal

PISTACHE — *n* pl. **-S** a shade of green

PISTE — *n* pl. **-S** a downhill ski trail

PISTIL — *n* pl. **-S** the seed-bearing organ of flowering plants

PISTOL — *v* **-TOLED, -TOLING, -TOLS** or **-TOLLED, -TOLLING, -TOLS** to shoot with a small firearm

PISTOLE — *n* pl. **-S** a formerly used European gold coin

PISTON — *n* pl. **-S** a part of an engine

PISTOU — *n* pl. **-S** a sauce made of olive oil, garlic, basil, and often cheese

PIT — *v* **PITTED, PITTING, PITS** to mark with cavities or depressions

PITA — *n* pl. **-S** a strong fiber

PITAHAYA — *n* pl. **-S** a cactus of southwestern U.S. and Mexico

PITAPAT — *v* **-PATTED, -PATTING, -PATS** to make a repeated tapping sound

PITAYA — *n* pl. **-S** pitahaya

PITCH — *v* **-ED, -ING, -ES** to throw

PITCHER — *n* pl. **-S** a container for holding and pouring liquids

PITCHIER — comparative of pitchy

PITCHIEST — superlative of pitchy

PITCHILY — *adv* in a very dark manner

PITCHMAN — *n* pl. **-MEN** a salesman of small wares

PITCHOUT — *n* pl. **-S** a type of pitch in baseball

PITCHY — *adj* **PITCHIER, PITCHIEST** tarry

PITEOUS — *adj* pitiful

PITFALL — *n* pl. **-S** a hidden danger or difficulty

PITH — *v* **-ED, -ING, -S** to sever the spinal cord of

PITHEAD — *n* pl. **-S** a mine entrance

PITHLESS	*adj* lacking force
PITHY	*adj* **PITHIER, PITHIEST** concise **PITHILY** *adv*
PITIABLE	*adj* pitiful **PITIABLY** *adv*
PITIED	past tense of pity
PITIER	*n* pl. **-S** one that pities
PITIES	present 3d person sing. of pity
PITIFUL	*adj* **-FULLER, -FULLEST** arousing pity
PITILESS	*adj* having no pity
PITMAN	*n* pl. **-MEN** a mine worker
PITMAN	*n* pl. **-S** a connecting rod
PITON	*n* pl. **-S** a metal spike used in mountain climbing
PITSAW	*n* pl. **-S** a large saw for cutting logs
PITTA	*n* pl. **-S** a perching bird of Asia, Australia, and Africa
PITTANCE	*n* pl. **-S** a small allowance of money
PITTED	past tense of pit
PITTING	*n* pl. **-S** an arrangement of cavities or depressions
PITY	*v* **PITIED, PITYING, PITIES** to feel pity (sorrow aroused by another's misfortune)
PIU	*adv* more — used as a musical direction
PIVOT	*v* **-ED, -ING, -S** to turn on a shaft or rod
PIVOTAL	*adj* critically important
PIVOTMAN	*n* pl. **-MEN** a center on a basketball team
PIX	*n* pl. **-ES** pyx
PIXEL	*n* pl. **-S** a basic unit of a video image
PIXIE	*n* pl. **-S** pixy **PIXIEISH** *adj*
PIXINESS	*n* pl. **-ES** the state of being playfully mischievous
PIXY	*n* pl. **PIXIES** a playfully mischievous fairy or elf **PIXYISH** *adj*
PIZAZZ	*n* pl. **-ES** the quality of being exciting or attractive
PIZAZZY	*adj* having pizazz
PIZZA	*n* pl. **-S** an Italian open pie
PIZZAZ	*n* pl. **-ES** pizazz
PIZZELLE	*n* pl. **-S** a thin, crisp Italian cookie
PIZZERIA	*n* pl. **-S** a place where pizzas are made and sold
PIZZLE	*n* pl. **-S** the penis of an animal

PLACABLE	*adj* capable of being placated **PLACABLY** *adv*
PLACARD	*v* **-ED, -ING, -S** to publicize by means of posters
PLACATE	*v* **-CATED, -CATING, -CATES** to soothe or mollify
PLACATER	*n* pl. **-S** one that placates
PLACE	*v* **PLACED, PLACING, PLACES** to set in a particular position
PLACEBO	*n* pl. **-BOS** or **-BOES** a substance containing no medication that is given for its psychological effect
PLACEMAN	*n* pl. **-MEN** a political appointee to a public office
PLACENTA	*n* pl. **-TAS** or **-TAE** a vascular organ in most mammals
PLACER	*n* pl. **-S** one that places
PLACET	*n* pl. **-S** a vote of assent
PLACID	*adj* calm or peaceful **PLACIDLY** *adv*
PLACING	present participle of place
PLACK	*n* pl. **-S** a former coin of Scotland
PLACKET	*n* pl. **-S** a slit in a garment
PLACOID	*n* pl. **-S** a fish having platelike scales
PLAFOND	*n* pl. **-S** an elaborately decorated ceiling
PLAGAL	*adj* designating a medieval musical mode
PLAGE	*n* pl. **-S** a bright region on the sun
PLAGIARY	*n* pl. **-RIES** the act of passing off another's work as one's own
PLAGUE	*v* **PLAGUED, PLAGUING, PLAGUES** to harass or torment
PLAGUER	*n* pl. **-S** one that plagues
PLAGUEY	*adj* plaguy
PLAGUY	*adj* troublesome **PLAGUILY** *adv*
PLAICE	*n* pl. **-S** a European flatfish
PLAID	*n* pl. **-S** a woolen scarf of a checkered pattern **PLAIDED** *adj*
PLAIN	*adj* **PLAINER, PLAINEST** evident **PLAINLY** *adv*
PLAIN	*v* **-ED, -ING, -S** to complain
PLAINT	*n* pl. **-S** a complaint
PLAISTER	*v* **-ED, -ING, -S** to plaster
PLAIT	*v* **-ED, -ING, -S** to braid
PLAITER	*n* pl. **-S** one that plaits
PLAITING	*n* pl. **-S** something that is plaited

PLAN	*v* **PLANNED, PLANNING, PLANS** to formulate a plan (a method for achieving an end)
PLANAR	*adj* flat
PLANARIA	*n* pl. **-S** an aquatic flatworm
PLANATE	*adj* having a flat surface
PLANCH	*n* pl. **-ES** a plank
PLANCHE	*n* pl. **-S** planch
PLANCHET	*n* pl. **-S** a flat piece of metal for stamping into a coin
PLANE	*v* **PLANED, PLANING, PLANES** to make smooth or even
PLANER	*n* pl. **-S** one that planes
PLANET	*n* pl. **-S** a celestial body
PLANFORM	*n* pl. **-S** the contour of an object as viewed from above
PLANGENT	*adj* resounding loudly
PLANING	present participle of plane
PLANISH	*v* **-ED, -ING, -ES** to toughen and smooth by hammering lightly
PLANK	*v* **-ED, -ING, -S** to cover with planks (long, flat pieces of lumber)
PLANKING	*n* pl. **-S** covering made of planks
PLANKTER	*n* pl. **-S** any organism that is an element of plankton
PLANKTON	*n* pl. **-S** the minute animal and plant life of a body of water
PLANLESS	*adj* having no plan
PLANNED	past tense of plan
PLANNER	*n* pl. **-S** one that plans
PLANNING	*n* pl. **-S** the establishment of goals or policies
PLANOSOL	*n* pl. **-S** a type of soil
PLANT	*v* **-ED, -ING, -S** to place in the ground for growing
PLANTAIN	*n* pl. **-S** a short-stemmed herb
PLANTAR	*adj* pertaining to the sole of the foot
PLANTER	*n* pl. **-S** one that plants
PLANTING	*n* pl. **-S** an area where plants are grown
PLANTLET	*n* pl. **-S** a small plant
PLANULA	*n* pl. **-LAE** the free-swimming larva of certain organisms **PLANULAR** *adj*
PLAQUE	*n* pl. **-S** an ornamental plate or disk
PLASH	*v* **-ED, -ING, -ES** to weave together
PLASHER	*n* pl. **-S** one that plashes
PLASHY	*adj* **PLASHIER, PLASHIEST** marshy
PLASM	*n* pl. **-S** plasma
PLASMA	*n* pl. **-S** the liquid part of blood **PLASMIC** *adj*
PLASMID	*n* pl. **-S** a hereditary structure of a cell
PLASMIN	*n* pl. **-S** an enzyme
PLASMOID	*n* pl. **-S** a type of high energy particle
PLASMON	*n* pl. **-S** a determinant of inheritance believed to exist in cells
PLASTER	*v* **-ED, -ING, -S** to cover with plaster (a mixture of lime, sand, and water)
PLASTERY	*adj* resembling plaster
PLASTIC	*n* pl. **-S** any of a group of synthetic or natural moldable materials
PLASTID	*n* pl. **-S** a structure in plant cells
PLASTRON	*n* pl. **-S** a part of the shell of a turtle **PLASTRAL** *adj*
PLASTRUM	*n* pl. **-S** plastron
PLAT	*v* **PLATTED, PLATTING, PLATS** to plait
PLATAN	*n* pl. **-S** a large tree
PLATANE	*n* pl. **-S** platan
PLATE	*v* **PLATED, PLATING, PLATES** to coat with a thin layer of metal
PLATEAU	*n* pl. **-TEAUS** or **-TEAUX** a level stretch of elevated land
PLATEAU	*v* **-ED, -ING, -S** to reach a period or condition of stability
PLATEFUL	*n* pl. **PLATEFULS** or **PLATESFUL** the quantity that fills a plate (a shallow dish)
PLATELET	*n* pl. **-S** a small, flattened body
PLATEN	*n* pl. **-S** the roller of a typewriter
PLATER	*n* pl. **-S** one that plates
PLATESFUL	a pl. of plateful
PLATFORM	*n* pl. **-S** a raised floor or flat surface
PLATIER	comparative of platy
PLATIES	a pl. of platy
PLATIEST	superlative of platy
PLATINA	*n* pl. **-S** platinum
PLATING	*n* pl. **-S** a thin layer of metal
PLATINIC	*adj* pertaining to platinum
PLATINUM	*n* pl. **-S** a metallic element
PLATONIC	*adj* purely spiritual and free from sensual desire

PLATOON   v **-ED, -ING, -S** to alternate with another player at the same position

PLATTED   past tense of plat

PLATTER   n pl. **-S** a large, shallow dish

PLATTING   present participle of plat

PLATY   adj **PLATIER, PLATIEST** split into thin, flat pieces

PLATY   n pl. **PLATYS** or **PLATIES** a small tropical fish

PLATYPUS   n pl. **-PUSES** or **-PI** an aquatic mammal

PLAUDIT   n pl. **-S** an expression of praise

PLAUSIVE   adj expressing praise

PLAY   v **-ED, -ING, -S** to engage in amusement or sport **PLAYABLE** adj

PLAYA   n pl. **-S** the bottom of a desert basin

PLAYACT   v **-ED, -ING, -S** to take part in a theatrical performance

PLAYBACK   n pl. **-S** the act of replaying a newly made recording

PLAYBILL   n pl. **-S** a program for a theatrical performance

PLAYBOOK   n pl. **-S** a book containing one or more literary works for the stage

PLAYBOY   n pl. **-BOYS** a man devoted to pleasurable activities

PLAYDATE   n pl. **-S** the scheduled date for showing a theatrical production

PLAYDAY   n pl. **-DAYS** a holiday

PLAYDOWN   n pl. **-S** a playoff

PLAYER   n pl. **-S** one that plays

PLAYFUL   adj frolicsome

PLAYGIRL   n pl. **-S** a woman devoted to pleasurable activities

PLAYGOER   n pl. **-S** one who attends the theater

PLAYLAND   n pl. **-S** a recreational area

PLAYLESS   adj lacking playfulness

PLAYLET   n pl. **-S** a short theatrical performance

PLAYLIKE   adj resembling a theatrical performance

PLAYLIST   n pl. **-S** a list of recordings to be played on the air

PLAYMATE   n pl. **-S** a companion in play

PLAYOFF   n pl. **-S** a series of games played to determine a championship

PLAYPEN   n pl. **-S** an enclosure in which a young child may play

PLAYROOM   n pl. **-S** a recreation room

PLAYSUIT   n pl. **-S** a sports outfit for women and children

PLAYTIME   n pl. **-S** a time for play or amusement

PLAYWEAR   n pl. **PLAYWEAR** clothing worn for leisure activities

PLAZA   n pl. **-S** a public square

PLEA   n pl. **-S** an entreaty

PLEACH   v **-ED, -ING, -ES** to weave together

PLEAD   v **PLEADED** or **PLED, PLEADING, PLEADS** to ask for earnestly

PLEADER   n pl. **-S** one that pleads

PLEADING   n pl. **-S** an allegation in a legal action

PLEASANT   adj **-ANTER, -ANTEST** pleasing

PLEASE   v **PLEASED, PLEASING, PLEASES** to give enjoyment or satisfaction to

PLEASER   n pl. **-S** one that pleases

PLEASURE   v **-SURED, -SURING, -SURES** to please

PLEAT   v **-ED, -ING, -S** to fold in an even manner

PLEATER   n pl. **-S** one that pleats

PLEATHER   n pl. **-S** a plastic fabric made to look like leather

PLEB   n pl. **-S** a commoner

PLEBE   n pl. **-S** a freshman at a military or naval academy

PLEBEIAN   n pl. **-S** a commoner

PLECTRON   n pl. **-TRONS** or **-TRA** plectrum

PLECTRUM   n pl. **-TRUMS** or **-TRA** an implement used to pluck the strings of a stringed instrument

PLED   a past tense of plead

PLEDGE   v **PLEDGED, PLEDGING, PLEDGES** to give as security for something borrowed

PLEDGEE   n pl. **-S** one to whom something is pledged

PLEDGEOR   n pl. **-S** pledger

PLEDGER   n pl. **-S** one that pledges something

PLEDGET   n pl. **-S** a pad of absorbent cotton

PLEDGING   present participle of pledge

PLEDGOR   n pl. **-S** pledger

PLEIAD   n pl. **-S** or **-ES** a group of seven illustrious persons

PLENA   a pl. of plenum

PLENARY	*n* pl. **-RIES** a session attended by all members
PLENCH	*n* pl. **-ES** a tool serving as pliers and a wrench
PLENISH	*v* **-ED, -ING, -ES** to fill up
PLENISM	*n* pl. **-S** the doctrine that space is fully occupied by matter
PLENIST	*n* pl. **-S** an advocate of plenism
PLENTY	*n* pl. **-TIES** a sufficient or abundant amount
PLENUM	*n* pl. **-NUMS** or **-NA** space considered as fully occupied by matter
PLEON	*n* pl. **-S** the abdomen of a crustacean **PLEONAL, PLEONIC** *adj*
PLEONASM	*n* pl. **-S** the use of needless words
PLEOPOD	*n* pl. **-S** an appendage of crustaceans
PLESSOR	*n* pl. **-S** plexor
PLETHORA	*n* pl. **-S** an excess
PLEURA	*n* pl. **-RAS** or **-RAE** a membrane that envelops the lungs **PLEURAL** *adj*
PLEURISY	*n* pl. **-SIES** inflammation of the pleura
PLEURON	*n* pl. **-RA** a part of a thoracic segment of an insect
PLEUSTON	*n* pl. **-S** aquatic vegetation
PLEW	*n* pl. **-S** a beaver skin
PLEX	*n* pl. **-ES** a multiplex
PLEXAL	*adj* pertaining to a plexus
PLEXOR	*n* pl. **-S** a small, hammer-like medical instrument
PLEXUS	*n* pl. **-ES** an interlacing of parts
PLIABLE	*adj* easily bent **PLIABLY** *adv*
PLIANCY	*n* pl. **-CIES** the quality of being pliant
PLIANT	*adj* easily bent **PLIANTLY** *adv*
PLICA	*n* pl. **-CAE** a fold of skin **PLICAL** *adj*
PLICATE	*adj* pleated
PLICATED	*adj* plicate
PLIE	*n* pl. **-S** a movement in ballet
PLIED	past tense of ply
PLIER	*n* pl. **-S** one that plies
PLIES	present 3d person sing. of ply
PLIGHT	*v* **-ED, -ING, -S** to promise or bind by a solemn pledge
PLIGHTER	*n* pl. **-S** one that plights

PLIMSOL	*n* pl. **-S** plimsoll
PLIMSOLE	*n* pl. **-S** plimsoll
PLIMSOLL	*n* pl. **-S** a rubber-soled cloth shoe
PLINK	*v* **-ED, -ING, -S** to shoot at random targets
PLINKER	*n* pl. **-S** one that plinks
PLINTH	*n* pl. **-S** a stone or slab upon which a column or pedestal rests
PLIOFILM	*n* pl. **-S** a transparent sheet of chlorinated rubber used in packaging
PLIOTRON	*n* pl. **-S** a type of vacuum tube
PLISKIE	*n* pl. **-S** a practical joke
PLISKY	*n* pl. **-KIES** pliskie
PLISSE	*n* pl. **-S** a puckered texture of cloth
PLOD	*v* **PLODDED, PLODDING, PLODS** to walk heavily
PLODDER	*n* pl. **-S** one that plods
PLOIDY	*n* pl. **-DIES** the extent of repetition of the basic number of chromosomes
PLONK	*v* **-ED, -ING, -S** to plunk
PLOP	*v* **PLOPPED, PLOPPING, PLOPS** to drop or fall heavily
PLOSION	*n* pl. **-S** a release of breath after the articulation of certain consonants
PLOSIVE	*n* pl. **-S** a sound produced by plosion
PLOT	*v* **PLOTTED, PLOTTING, PLOTS** to plan secretly
PLOTLESS	*adj* planless
PLOTLINE	*n* pl. **-S** the main story of a book
PLOTTAGE	*n* pl. **-S** an area of land
PLOTTED	past tense of plot
PLOTTER	*n* pl. **-S** one that plots
PLOTTING	present participle of plot
PLOTTY	*adj* **-TIER, -TIEST** full of intrigue, as a novel
PLOTTY	*n* pl. **-TIES** a hot, spiced beverage
PLOTZ	*v* **-ED, -ING, -ES** to be overwhelmed by an emotion
PLOUGH	*v* **-ED, -ING, -S** to plow
PLOUGHER	*n* pl. **-S** one that ploughs
PLOVER	*n* pl. **-S** a shore bird
PLOW	*v* **-ED, -ING, -S** to turn up land with a plow (a farm implement) **PLOWABLE** *adj*
PLOWBACK	*n* pl. **-S** a reinvestment of profits in a business

PLOWBOY	n pl. **-BOYS** a boy who leads a plow team	**PLUMMET**	v **-ED, -ING, -S** to drop straight down
PLOWER	n pl. **-S** one that plows	**PLUMMY**	adj **-MIER, -MIEST** full of plums
PLOWHEAD	n pl. **-S** the clevis of a plow	**PLUMOSE**	adj having feathers
PLOWLAND	n pl. **-S** land suitable for cultivation	**PLUMP**	adj **PLUMPER, PLUMPEST** well-rounded and full in form
PLOWMAN	n pl. **-MEN** a man who plows	**PLUMP**	v **-ED, -ING, -S** to make plump
PLOY	v **-ED, -ING, -S** to move from a line into column	**PLUMPEN**	v **-ED, -ING, -S** to plump
PLUCK	v **-ED, -ING, -S** to pull out or off	**PLUMPER**	n pl. **-S** a heavy fall
PLUCKER	n pl. **-S** one that plucks	**PLUMPISH**	adj somewhat plump
PLUCKY	adj **PLUCKIER, PLUCKIEST** brave and spirited **PLUCKILY** adv	**PLUMPLY**	adv in a plump way
PLUG	v **PLUGGED, PLUGGING, PLUGS** to seal or close with a plug (a piece of material used to fill a hole)	**PLUMULE**	n pl. **-S** the primary bud of a plant embryo **PLUMULAR** adj
		PLUMY	adj **PLUMIER, PLUMIEST** covered with feathers
PLUGGER	n pl. **-S** one that plugs	**PLUNDER**	v **-ED, -ING, -S** to rob of goods by force
PLUGLESS	adj having no plug		
PLUGOLA	n pl. **-S** free incidental advertising on radio or television	**PLUNGE**	v **PLUNGED, PLUNGING, PLUNGES** to throw or thrust suddenly or forcibly into something
PLUGUGLY	n pl. **-LIES** a hoodlum		
PLUM	n pl. **-S** a fleshy fruit	**PLUNGER**	n pl. **-S** one that plunges
PLUM	adj **PLUMMER, PLUMMEST** highly desirable	**PLUNK**	v **-ED, -ING, -S** to fall or drop heavily
PLUMAGE	n pl. **-S** the feathers of a bird **PLUMAGED** adj	**PLUNKER**	n pl. **-S** one that plunks
PLUMATE	adj resembling a feather	**PLUNKY**	adj **PLUNKIER, PLUNKIEST** marked by a quick, hollow, metallic sound
PLUMB	v **-ED, -ING, -S** to determine the depth of		
PLUMBAGO	n pl. **-GOS** graphite	**PLURAL**	n pl. **-S** a word that expresses more than one
PLUMBER	n pl. **-S** one who installs and repairs plumbing	**PLURALLY**	adv in a manner or form that expresses more than one
PLUMBERY	n pl. **-ERIES** the work of a plumber	**PLUS**	n pl. **PLUSES** or **PLUSSES** an additional quantity
PLUMBIC	adj containing lead		
PLUMBING	n pl. **-S** the pipe system of a building	**PLUSH**	adj **PLUSHER, PLUSHEST** luxurious **PLUSHLY** adv
PLUMBISM	n pl. **-S** lead poisoning	**PLUSH**	n pl. **-ES** a fabric with a long pile
PLUMBOUS	adj containing lead	**PLUSHY**	adj **PLUSHIER, PLUSHIEST** luxurious **PLUSHILY** adv
PLUMBUM	n pl. **-S** lead		
PLUME	v **PLUMED, PLUMING, PLUMES** to cover with feathers	**PLUSSAGE**	n pl. **-S** an amount over and above another
PLUMELET	n pl. **-S** a small feather	**PLUSSES**	a pl. of plus
PLUMERIA	n pl. **-S** a flowering shrub	**PLUTEUS**	n pl. **-TEI** the larva of a sea urchin
PLUMIER	comparative of plumy	**PLUTON**	n pl. **-S** a formation of igneous rock **PLUTONIC** adj
PLUMIEST	superlative of plumy		
PLUMING	present participle of plume	**PLUVIAL**	n pl. **-S** a prolonged period of wet climate
PLUMIPED	n pl. **-S** a bird having feathered feet		
		PLUVIAN	adj characterized by much rain
PLUMLIKE	adj resembling a plum	**PLUVIOSE**	adj pluvious
		PLUVIOUS	adj pertaining to rain

PLY   *v* **PLIED, PLYING, PLIES** to supply with or offer repeatedly **PLYINGLY** *adv*

PLYER   *n* pl. **-S** plier

PLYWOOD   *n* pl. **-S** a building material

PNEUMA   *n* pl. **-S** the soul or spirit

POACEOUS   *adj* pertaining to plants of the grass family

POACH   *v* **-ED, -ING, -ES** to trespass for the purpose of taking game or fish

POACHER   *n* pl. **-S** one that poaches

POACHY   *adj* **POACHIER, POACHIEST** swampy

POBLANO   *n* pl. **-NOS** a mild, dark-green chili pepper

POBOY   *n* pl. **-S** a large sandwich on a long split roll

POCHARD   *n* pl. **-S** a sea duck

POCK   *v* **-ED, -ING, -S** to mark with pocks (pustules caused by an eruptive disease)

POCKET   *v* **-ED, -ING, -S** to place in a pouch sewed into a garment

POCKETER   *n* pl. **-S** one that pockets

POCKMARK   *v* **-ED, -ING, -S** to mark with scars caused by an eruptive disease

POCKY   *adj* **POCKIER, POCKIEST** covered with pocks **POCKILY** *adv*

POCO   *adv* a little — used as a musical direction

POCOSEN   *n* pl. **-S** pocosin

POCOSIN   *n* pl. **-S** an upland swamp

POCOSON   *n* pl. **-S** pocosin

POD   *v* **PODDED, PODDING, PODS** to produce seed vessels

PODAGRA   *n* pl. **-S** gout in the foot **PODAGRAL, PODAGRIC** *adj*

PODESTA   *n* pl. **-S** an Italian magistrate

PODGY   *adj* **PODGIER, PODGIEST** pudgy **PODGILY** *adv*

PODIA   a pl. of podium

PODIATRY   *n* pl. **-TRIES** the study and treatment of the human foot

PODITE   *n* pl. **-S** a limb segment of an arthropod **PODITIC** *adj*

PODIUM   *n* pl. **-DIUMS** or **-DIA** a small platform

PODLIKE   *adj* resembling a pod (a seed vessel)

PODOCARP   *adj* designating a family of evergreen trees

PODOMERE   *n* pl. **-S** a podite

PODSOL   *n* pl. **-S** podzol **PODSOLIC** *adj*

PODZOL   *n* pl. **-S** an infertile soil **PODZOLIC** *adj*

POECHORE   *n* pl. **-S** a semiarid region

POEM   *n* pl. **-S** a composition in verse

POESY   *n* pl. **-ESIES** poetry

POET   *n* pl. **-S** one who writes poems

POETESS   *n* pl. **-ES** a female poet

POETIC   *adj* pertaining to poetry

POETICAL   *adj* poetic

POETICS   *n/pl* poetic theory or practice

POETISE   *v* **-ISED, -ISING, -ISES** to poetize

POETISER   *n* pl. **-S** poetizer

POETIZE   *v* **-IZED, -IZING, -IZES** to write poetry

POETIZER   *n* pl. **-S** one that poetizes

POETLESS   *adj* lacking a poet

POETLIKE   *adj* resembling a poet

POETRY   *n* pl. **-RIES** literary work in metrical form

POGEY   *n* pl. **-GEYS** any form of government relief

POGIES   pl. of pogy

POGONIA   *n* pl. **-S** a small orchid

POGONIP   *n* pl. **-S** a dense fog of suspended ice particles

POGROM   *v* **-ED, -ING, -S** to massacre systematically

POGY   *n* pl. **-GIES** a marine fish

POH   *interj* — used to express disgust

POI   *n* pl. **-S** a Hawaiian food

POIGNANT   *adj* emotionally distressing

POILU   *n* pl. **-S** a French soldier

POIND   *v* **-ED, -ING, -S** to seize and sell the property of to satisfy a debt

POINT   *v* **-ED, -ING, -S** to indicate direction with the finger

POINTE   *n* pl. **-S** a ballet position

POINTER   *n* pl. **-S** one that points

POINTMAN   *n* pl. **-MEN** a certain player in hockey

POINTY   *adj* **POINTIER, POINTIEST** coming to a sharp, tapering end

POISE   *v* **POISED, POISING, POISES** to hold in a state of equilibrium

POISER   *n* pl. **-S** one that poises

POISHA *n pl.* **POISHA** the paisa of Bangladesh

POISON *v* **-ED, -ING, -S** to administer a harmful substance to

POISONER *n pl.* **-S** one that poisons

POITREL *n pl.* **-S** peytral

POKE *v* **POKED, POKING, POKES** to push or prod **POKABLE** *adj*

POKER *n pl.* **-S** one that pokes

POKEROOT *n pl.* **-S** pokeweed

POKEWEED *n pl.* **-S** a perennial herb

POKEY *n pl.* **-KEYS** poky

POKIER comparative of poky

POKIES pl. of poky

POKIEST superlative of poky

POKILY *adv* in a poky manner

POKINESS *n pl.* **-ES** the state of being poky

POKING present participle of poke

POKY *adj* **POKIER, POKIEST** slow

POKY *n pl.* **POKIES** a jail

POL *n pl.* **-S** a politician

POLAR *n pl.* **-S** a straight line related to a point

POLARISE *v* **-ISED, -ISING, -ISES** to polarize

POLARITY *n pl.* **-TIES** the possession of two opposite qualities

POLARIZE *v* **-IZED, -IZING, -IZES** to give polarity to

POLARON *n pl.* **-S** a type of electron

POLDER *n pl.* **-S** a tract of low land reclaimed from a body of water

POLE *v* **POLED, POLING, POLES** to propel with a pole (a long, thin piece of wood or metal)

POLEAX *v* **-ED, -ING, -ES** to strike with an axlike weapon

POLEAXE *v* **-AXED, -AXING, -AXES** to poleax

POLECAT *n pl.* **-S** a carnivorous mammal

POLED past tense of pole

POLEIS pl. of polis

POLELESS *adj* having no pole

POLEMIC *n pl.* **-S** a controversial argument

POLEMIST *n pl.* **-S** one who engages in polemics

POLEMIZE *v* **-MIZED, -MIZING, -MIZES** to engage in polemics

POLENTA *n pl.* **-S** a thick mush of cornmeal

POLER *n pl.* **-S** one that poles

POLESTAR *n pl.* **-S** a guiding principle

POLEWARD *adv* in the direction of either extremity of the earth's axis

POLEYN *n pl.* **-S** a protective piece of leather for the knee

POLICE *v* **-LICED, -LICING, -LICES** to make clean or orderly

POLICER *n pl.* **-S** one that polices

POLICY *n pl.* **-CIES** an action or a procedure considered with reference to prudence or expediency

POLING present participle of pole

POLIO *n pl.* **-LIOS** an infectious virus disease

POLIS *n pl.* **-LEIS** an ancient Greek city-state

POLISH *v* **-ED, -ING, -ES** to make smooth and lustrous by rubbing

POLISHER *n pl.* **-S** one that polishes

POLITE *adj* **-LITER, -LITEST** showing consideration for others **POLITELY** *adv*

POLITIC *adj* shrewd

POLITICK *v* **-ED, -ING, -S** to engage in politics

POLITICO *n pl.* **-COS** or **-COES** one who politicks

POLITICS *n/pl* the art or science of government

POLITY *n pl.* **-TIES** a form or system of government

POLKA *v* **-ED, -ING, -S** to perform a lively dance

POLL *v* **-ED, -ING, -S** to question for the purpose of surveying public opinion

POLLACK *n pl.* **-S** a marine food fish

POLLARD *v* **-ED, -ING, -S** to cut the top branches of a tree back to the trunk

POLLEE *n pl.* **-S** one who is polled

POLLEN *v* **-ED, -ING, -S** to convey pollen (the fertilizing element in a seed plant) to

POLLER *n pl.* **-S** one that polls

POLLEX *n pl.* **-LICES** the innermost digit of the forelimb **POLLICAL** *adj*

POLLINIA *n/pl* masses of pollen grains

POLLINIC *adj* pertaining to pollen

POLLIST *n pl.* **-S** a poller

POLLIWOG *n* pl. **-S** a tadpole

POLLOCK *n* pl. **-S** pollack

POLLSTER *n* pl. **-S** a poller

POLLUTE *v* **-LUTED, -LUTING, -LUTES** to make unclean or impure

POLLUTER *n* pl. **-S** one that pollutes

POLLYWOG *n* pl. **-S** polliwog

POLO *n* pl. **-LOS** a game played on horseback

POLOIST *n* pl. **-S** a polo player

POLONIUM *n* pl. **-S** a radioactive element

POLTROON *n* pl. **-S** a base coward

POLY *n* pl. **POLYS** a type of white blood cell

POLY *n* pl. **POLIES** a garment made of polyester

POLYBRID *n* pl. **-S** a type of hybrid plant

POLYCOT *n* pl. **-S** a type of plant

POLYENE *n* pl. **-S** a chemical compound **POLYENIC** *adj*

POLYGALA *n* pl. **-S** a flowering plant

POLYGAMY *n* pl. **-MIES** the condition of having more than one spouse at the same time

POLYGENE *n* pl. **-S** a type of gene

POLYGLOT *n* pl. **-S** one that speaks or writes several languages

POLYGON *n* pl. **-S** a closed plane figure bounded by straight lines

POLYGONY *n* pl. **-NIES** an herb

POLYGYNY *n* pl. **-NIES** the condition of having more than one wife at the same time

POLYMATH *n* pl. **-S** a person of great and varied learning

POLYMER *n* pl. **-S** a complex chemical compound

POLYNYA *n* pl. **-YAS** or **-YI** an area of open water surrounded by sea ice

POLYOL *n* pl. **-S** an alcohol containing three or more hydroxyl groups

POLYOMA *n* pl. **-S** a type of virus

POLYP *n* pl. **-S** an invertebrate

POLYPARY *n* pl. **-ARIES** the common supporting structure of a polyp colony

POLYPED *n* pl. **-S** something having many legs

POLYPI a pl. of polypus

POLYPIDE *n* pl. **-S** a polyp

POLYPNEA *n* pl. **-S** rapid breathing

POLYPOD *n* pl. **-S** a many-footed organism

POLYPODY *n* pl. **-DIES** a fern

POLYPOID *adj* resembling a polyp

POLYPORE *n* pl. **-S** a type of fungus

POLYPOUS *adj* pertaining to a polyp

POLYPUS *n* pl. **-PUSES** or **-PI** a growth protruding from the mucous lining of an organ

POLYSEMY *n* pl. **-MIES** diversity of meanings

POLYSOME *n* pl. **-S** a cluster of protein particles

POLYTENE *adj* having chromosomes of a certain type

POLYTENY *n* pl. **-NIES** the state of being polytene

POLYTYPE *n* pl. **-S** a crystal structure

POLYURIA *n* pl. **-S** excessive urination **POLYURIC** *adj*

POLYZOAN *n* pl. **-S** a bryozoan

POLYZOIC *adj* composed of many zooids

POMACE *n* pl. **-S** the pulpy residue of crushed fruits

POMADE *v* **-MADED, -MADING, -MADES** to apply a perfumed hair dressing to

POMANDER *n* pl. **-S** a mixture of aromatic substances

POMATUM *n* pl. **-S** a perfumed hair dressing

POME *n* pl. **-S** a fleshy fruit with a core

POMELO *n* pl. **-LOS** a grapefruit

POMFRET *n* pl. **-S** a marine fish

POMMEE *adj* having arms with knoblike ends — used of a heraldic cross

POMMEL *v* **-MELED, -MELING, -MELS** or **-MELLED, -MELLING, -MELS** to strike with the fists

POMO *n* pl. **-MOS** the postmodern movement

POMOLOGY *n* pl. **-GIES** the study of fruits

POMP *n* pl. **-S** stately or splendid display

POMPANO *n* pl. **-NOS** a marine food fish

POMPOM *n* pl. **-S** an antiaircraft cannon

POMPON *n* pl. **-S** an ornamental tuft or ball

POMPOUS *adj* marked by exaggerated self-importance

PONCE *v* **PONCED, PONCING, PONCES** to pimp

PONCHO *n* pl. **-CHOS** a type of cloak **PONCHOED** *adj*

POND   *v* **-ED, -ING, -S** to collect into a pond (a small body of water)

PONDER   *v* **-ED, -ING, -S** to consider something deeply and thoroughly

PONDERER   *n* pl. **-S** one that ponders

PONDWEED   *n* pl. **-S** an aquatic plant

PONE   *n* pl. **-S** a corn bread

PONENT   *adj* affirmative

PONG   *v* **-ED, -ING, -S** to stink

PONGEE   *n* pl. **-S** a type of silk

PONGID   *n* pl. **-S** an anthropoid ape

PONIARD   *v* **-ED, -ING, -S** to stab with a dagger

PONIED   past tense of pony

PONIES   present 3d person sing. of pony

PONS   *n* pl. **PONTES** a band of nerve fibers in the brain

PONTIFEX   *n* pl. **-FICES** an ancient Roman priest

PONTIFF   *n* pl. **-S** a pope or bishop

PONTIFIC   *adj* pertaining to a pope or bishop

PONTIFICES   pl. of pontifex

PONTIL   *n* pl. **-S** a punty

PONTINE   *adj* pertaining to bridges

PONTON   *n* pl. **-S** pontoon

PONTOON   *n* pl. **-S** a flat-bottomed boat

PONY   *v* **-NIED, -NYING, -NIES** to prepare lessons with the aid of a literal translation

PONYTAIL   *n* pl. **-S** a hairstyle

POOCH   *v* **-ED, -ING, -ES** to bulge

POOD   *n* pl. **-S** a Russian unit of weight

POODLE   *n* pl. **-S** a heavy-coated dog

POOF   *interj* — used to indicate an instantaneous occurrence

POOH   *v* **-ED, -ING, -S** to express contempt for

POOL   *v* **-ED, -ING, -S** to combine in a common fund

POOLER   *n* pl. **-S** one that pools

POOLHALL   *n* pl. **-S** a poolroom

POOLROOM   *n* pl. **-S** an establishment for the playing of billiards

POOLSIDE   *n* pl. **-S** the area surrounding a swimming pool

POON   *n* pl. **-S** an East Indian tree

POOP   *v* **-ED, -ING, -S** to tire out

POOR   *adj* **POORER, POOREST** lacking the means of support

POORI   *n* pl. **-S** a light, flat wheat cake

POORISH   *adj* somewhat poor

POORLY   *adv* in a poor manner

POORNESS   *n* pl. **-ES** the state of being poor

POORTITH   *n* pl. **-S** poverty

POP   *v* **POPPED, POPPING, POPS** to make a sharp, explosive sound

POPCORN   *n* pl. **-S** a variety of corn

POPE   *n* pl. **-S** the head of the Roman Catholic Church **POPELESS, POPELIKE** *adj*

POPEDOM   *n* pl. **-S** the office of a pope

POPEYED   *adj* having bulging eyes

POPGUN   *n* pl. **-S** a toy gun

POPINJAY   *n* pl. **-JAYS** a vain person

POPLAR   *n* pl. **-S** a fast-growing tree

POPLIN   *n* pl. **-S** a durable fabric

POPLITEI   *n/pl* muscles at the back of knees

POPLITIC   *adj* pertaining to the part of the leg behind the knee

POPOVER   *n* pl. **-S** a very light egg muffin

POPPA   *n* pl. **-S** papa

POPPADOM   *n* pl. **-S** papadum

POPPADUM   *n* pl. **-S** papadum

POPPED   past tense of pop

POPPER   *n* pl. **-S** one that pops

POPPET   *n* pl. **-S** a mechanical valve

POPPIED   *adj* covered with poppies

POPPIES   pl. of poppy

POPPING   present participle of pop

POPPLE   *v* **-PLED, -PLING, -PLES** to move in a bubbling or rippling manner

POPPY   *n* pl. **-PIES** a flowering plant

POPSIE   *n* pl. **-S** popsy

POPSY   *n* pl. **-SIES** a girlfriend

POPULACE   *n* pl. **-S** the common people

POPULAR   *adj* liked by many people

POPULATE   *v* **-LATED, -LATING, -LATES** to inhabit

POPULISM   *n* pl. **-S** populists' doctrines

POPULIST   *n* pl. **-S** a member of a party which represents the common people

POPULOUS   *adj* containing many inhabitants

PORCH   *n* pl. **-ES** a covered structure at the entrance to a building

PORCINE *adj* pertaining to swine

PORCINI *n* pl. **-S** an edible mushroom

PORCINO *n* pl. **-NI** porcini

PORE *v* **PORED, PORING, PORES** to gaze intently

PORGY *n* pl. **-GIES** a marine food fish

PORISM *n* pl. **-S** a type of mathematical proposition

PORK *v* **-ED, -ING, -S** to eat ravenously

PORKER *n* pl. **-S** a pig

PORKIER comparative of porky

PORKIES pl. of porky

PORKIEST superlative of porky

PORKPIE *n* pl. **-S** a man's hat

PORKWOOD *n* pl. **-S** a tropical tree

PORKY *adj* **PORKIER, PORKIEST** resembling pork

PORKY *n* pl. **-KIES** a porcupine

PORN *n* pl. **-S** pornography

PORNO *n* pl. **-NOS** pornography

PORNY *adj* **PORNIER, PORNIEST** pornographic

POROSE *adj* porous

POROSITY *n* pl. **-TIES** the state of being porous

POROUS *adj* having minute openings **POROUSLY** *adv*

PORPHYRY *n* pl. **-RIES** an igneous rock

PORPOISE *v* **-POISED, -POISING, -POISES** to move forward with rising and falling motions

PORRECT *adj* extended forward

PORRIDGE *n* pl. **-S** a soft food **PORRIDGY** *adj*

PORT *v* **-ED, -ING, -S** to shift to the left side

PORTABLE *n* pl. **-S** something that can be carried

PORTABLY *adv* so as to be capable of being carried

PORTAGE *v* **-TAGED, -TAGING, -TAGES** to transport from one navigable waterway to another

PORTAL *n* pl. **-S** a door, gate, or entrance **PORTALED** *adj*

PORTANCE *n* pl. **-S** demeanor

PORTAPAK *n* pl. **-S** a portable combined video recorder and camera

PORTEND *v* **-ED, -ING, -S** to serve as an omen of

PORTENT *n* pl. **-S** an omen

PORTER *v* **-ED, -ING, -S** to carry luggage for pay

PORTHOLE *n* pl. **-S** a small window in a ship's side

PORTICO *n* pl. **-COS** or **-COES** a type of porch

PORTIERE *n* pl. **-S** a curtain for a doorway

PORTION *v* **-ED, -ING, -S** to divide into shares for distribution

PORTLESS *adj* having no place for ships to load or unload

PORTLY *adj* **-LIER, -LIEST** rather heavy or fat

PORTRAIT *n* pl. **-S** a likeness of a person

PORTRAY *v* **-ED, -ING, -S** to represent pictorially

PORTRESS *n* pl. **-ES** a female doorkeeper

PORTSIDE *adv* on the left side of a ship facing forward

POSADA *n* pl. **-S** an inn

POSE *v* **POSED, POSING, POSES** to assume a fixed position **POSABLE** *adj*

POSER *n* pl. **-S** one that poses

POSEUR *n* pl. **-S** an affected or insincere person

POSH *adj* **POSHER, POSHEST** stylish or elegant **POSHLY** *adv*

POSHNESS *n* pl. **-ES** the quality of being posh

POSIES pl. of posy

POSING present participle of pose

POSINGLY *adv* in a posing manner

POSIT *v* **-ED, -ING, -S** to place

POSITION *v* **-ED, -ING, -S** to put in a particular location

POSITIVE *adj* **-TIVER, -TIVEST** certain

POSITIVE *n* pl. **-S** a quantity greater than zero

POSITRON *n* pl. **-S** a subatomic particle

POSOLE *n* pl. **-S** a thick soup made of pork, corn, garlic, and chili

POSOLOGY *n* pl. **-GIES** a branch of medicine that deals with drug dosages

POSSE *n* pl. **-S** a body of men summoned to aid a peace officer

POSSESS *v* **-ED, -ING, -ES** to have as property

POSSET *n* pl. **-S** a hot, spiced drink

POSSIBLE *adj* **-BLER, -BLEST** capable of happening or proving true **POSSIBLY** *adv*

POSSUM *n* pl. **-S** opossum

POST *v* **-ED, -ING, -S** to affix in a public place

POSTAGE *n* pl. **-S** the charge for mailing an item

POSTAL *n* pl. **-S** a postcard

POSTALLY *adv* in a manner pertaining to the mails

POSTANAL *adj* situated behind the anus

POSTBAG *n* pl. **-S** a mailbag

POSTBASE *adj* following a base word

POSTBOX *n* pl. **-ES** a mailbox

POSTBOY *n* pl. **-BOYS** a boy who carries mail

POSTBURN *adj* following a burn

POSTCARD *n* pl. **-S** a card for use in the mail

POSTCAVA *n* pl. **-VAE** a vein in higher vertebrates

POSTCODE *n* pl. **-S** a code of numbers and letters used in a mailing address

POSTCOUP *adj* following a coup

POSTDATE *v* **-DATED, -DATING, -DATES** to give a date later than the actual date to

POSTDIVE *adj* following a dive

POSTDOC *n* pl. **-S** one engaged in postdoctoral study

POSTDRUG *adj* following the taking of a drug

POSTEEN *n* pl. **-S** an Afghan outer garment

POSTER *n* pl. **-S** a printed or written notice for posting

POSTERN *n* pl. **-S** a rear door or gate

POSTFACE *n* pl. **-S** a brief note placed at the end of a publication

POSTFIRE *adj* following a fire

POSTFIX *v* **-ED, -ING, -ES** to affix at the end of something

POSTFORM *v* **-ED, -ING, -S** to shape subsequently

POSTGAME *adj* following a game

POSTGRAD *n* pl. **-S** a student continuing formal education after graduation

POSTHEAT *n* pl. **-S** heat applied to a metal after welding

POSTHOLE *n* pl. **-S** a hole for a fence post

POSTICHE *n* pl. **-S** an imitation

POSTIE *n* pl. **-TIES** a letter carrier

POSTIN *n* pl. **-S** posteen

POSTING *n* pl. **-S** the act of transferring to a ledger

POSTIQUE *n* pl. **-S** postiche

POSTLUDE *n* pl. **-S** a closing musical piece

POSTMAN *n* pl. **-MEN** a mailman

POSTMARK *v* **-ED, -ING, -S** to stamp mail with an official mark

POSTOP *n* pl. **-S** a patient after undergoing a surgical operation

POSTORAL *adj* situated behind the mouth

POSTPAID *adv* with the postage prepaid

POSTPONE *v* **-PONED, -PONING, -PONES** to put off to a future time

POSTPOSE *v* **-POSED, -POSING, -POSES** to place (a word or phrase) after a grammatically related word

POSTPUNK *adj* pertaining to music coming after punk rock

POSTRACE *adj* following a race

POSTRIOT *adj* following a riot

POSTSHOW *adj* following a show

POSTSYNC *v* **-ED, -ING, -S** to add sound to a film after a scene has been photographed

POSTTAX *adj* remaining after taxes

POSTTEEN *n* pl. **-S** a person older than 19 years

POSTTEST *n* pl. **-S** a test given after an instructional program

POSTURAL *adj* pertaining to the position of the body

POSTURE *v* **-TURED, -TURING, -TURES** to assume a particular position

POSTURER *n* pl. **-S** one that postures

POSTWAR *adj* occurring or existing after a war

POSY *n* pl. **-SIES** a flower or bouquet

POT *v* **POTTED, POTTING, POTS** to put in a pot (a round, fairly deep container)

POTABLE *n* pl. **-S** a liquid suitable for drinking

POTAGE *n* pl. **-S** a thick soup

POTAMIC *adj* pertaining to rivers

POTASH *n* pl. **-ES** an alkaline compound

POTASSIC *adj* pertaining to potassium (a metallic element)

POTATION *n* pl. **-S** the act of drinking

POTATO *n* pl. **-TOES** the edible tuber of a cultivated plant

POTATORY *adj* pertaining to drinking

POTBELLY *n* pl. **-LIES** a protruding abdominal region

POTBOIL *v* **-ED, -ING, -S** to produce inferior literary or artistic work

POTBOUND *adj* having grown too large for its container

POTBOY *n* pl. **-BOYS** a boy who serves customers in a tavern

POTEEN *n* pl. **-S** Irish whiskey that is distilled unlawfully

POTENCE *n* pl. **-S** potency

POTENCY *n* pl. **-CIES** the quality of being potent

POTENT *adj* powerful **POTENTLY** *adv*

POTFUL *n* pl. **-S** as much as a pot can hold

POTHEAD *n* pl. **-S** one who smokes marijuana

POTHEEN *n* pl. **-S** poteen

POTHER *v* **-ED, -ING, -S** to trouble

POTHERB *n* pl. **-S** any herb used as a food or seasoning

POTHOLE *n* pl. **-S** a deep hole in a road **POTHOLED** *adj*

POTHOOK *n* pl. **-S** a hook for lifting or hanging pots

POTHOS *n* pl. **POTHOS** a climbing plant with glossy variegated leaves

POTHOUSE *n* pl. **-S** a tavern

POTICHE *n* pl. **-S** a type of vase

POTION *n* pl. **-S** a magical or medicinal drink

POTLACH *n* pl. **-ES** a ceremonial feast

POTLACHE *n* pl. **-S** potlach

POTLATCH *v* **-ED, -ING, -ES** to hold a ceremonial feast for

POTLIKE *adj* resembling a pot

POTLINE *n* pl. **-S** a row of electrolytic cells

POTLUCK *n* pl. **-S** food which is incidentally available

POTMAN *n* pl. **-MEN** a man who serves customers in a tavern

POTPIE *n* pl. **-S** a deep-dish pie containing meat and vegetables

POTSHARD *n* pl. **-S** potsherd

POTSHERD *n* pl. **-S** a fragment of broken pottery

POTSHOT *v* **-SHOT, -SHOTTING, -SHOTS** to shoot randomly at

POTSIE *n* pl. **-S** potsy

POTSTONE *n* pl. **-S** a variety of steatite

POTSY *n* pl. **-SIES** a children's game

POTTAGE *n* pl. **-S** a thick soup

POTTED past tense of pot

POTTEEN *n* pl. **-S** poteen

POTTER *v* **-ED, -ING, -S** to putter

POTTERER *n* pl. **-S** one that potters

POTTERY *n* pl. **-TERIES** ware molded from clay and hardened by heat

POTTIER comparative of potty

POTTIES pl. of potty

POTTIEST superlative of potty

POTTING present participle of pot

POTTLE *n* pl. **-S** a drinking vessel

POTTO *n* pl. **-TOS** a lemur of tropical Africa

POTTY *adj* **-TIER, -TIEST** of little importance

POTTY *n* pl. **-TIES** a small toilet seat

POTZER *n* pl. **-S** patzer

POUCH *v* **-ED, -ING, -ES** to put in a pouch (a small, flexible receptacle)

POUCHY *adj* **POUCHIER, POUCHIEST** resembling a pouch

POUF *n* pl. **-S** a loose roll of hair **POUFED, POUFFY** *adj*

POUFF *n* pl. **-S** pouf **POUFFED** *adj*

POUFFE *n* pl. **-S** pouf

POULARD *n* pl. **-S** a spayed hen

POULARDE *n* pl. **-S** poulard

POULT *n* pl. **-S** a young domestic fowl

POULTER *n* pl. **-S** one that deals in poultry

POULTICE *v* **-TICED, -TICING, -TICES** to apply a healing substance to

POULTRY *n* pl. **-TRIES** domestic fowls kept for eggs or meat

POUNCE *v* **POUNCED, POUNCING, POUNCES** to make a sudden assault or approach

POUNCER *n* pl. **-S** one that pounces

POUND *v* **-ED, -ING, -S** to strike heavily and repeatedly

POUNDAGE *n* pl. **-S** the act of impounding

POUNDAL *n* pl. **-S** a unit of force

POUNDER *n* pl. **-S** one that pounds

POUR *v* **-ED, -ING, -S** to cause to flow **POURABLE** *adj*

POURER	*n* pl. **-S** one that pours	**PRAISE**	*v* **PRAISED, PRAISING, PRAISES** to express approval or admiration of
POUSSIE	*n* pl. **-S** pussy		
POUT	*v* **-ED, -ING, -S** to protrude the lips in ill humor	**PRAISER**	*n* pl. **-S** one that praises
POUTER	*n* pl. **-S** one that pouts	**PRAJNA**	*n* pl. **-S** ultimate knowledge in Buddhism and Hinduism
POUTFUL	*adj* pouty	**PRALINE**	*n* pl. **-S** a confection made of nuts cooked in sugar
POUTINE	*n* pl. **-S** a dish of french fries and cheese curds topped with gravy	**PRAM**	*n* pl. **-S** a flat-bottomed boat
POUTY	*adj* **POUTIER, POUTIEST** tending to pout	**PRANCE**	*v* **PRANCED, PRANCING, PRANCES** to spring forward on the hind legs
POVERTY	*n* pl. **-TIES** the state of being poor	**PRANCER**	*n* pl. **-S** one that prances
POW	*n* pl. **-S** an explosive sound	**PRANDIAL**	*adj* pertaining to a meal
POWDER	*v* **-ED, -ING, -S** to reduce to powder (matter in a finely divided state)	**PRANG**	*v* **-ED, -ING, -S** to cause to crash
		PRANK	*v* **-ED, -ING, -S** to adorn gaudily
POWDERER	*n* pl. **-S** one that powders	**PRANKISH**	*adj* mischievous
POWDERY	*adj* resembling powder	**PRAO**	*n* pl. **PRAOS** prau
POWER	*v* **-ED, -ING, -S** to provide with means of propulsion	**PRASE**	*n* pl. **-S** a mineral
		PRAT	*n* pl. **-S** the buttocks
POWERFUL	*adj* possessing great force	**PRATE**	*v* **PRATED, PRATING, PRATES** to chatter
POWTER	*n* pl. **-S** a domestic pigeon		
POWWOW	*v* **-ED, -ING, -S** to hold a conference	**PRATER**	*n* pl. **-S** one that prates
		PRATFALL	*n* pl. **-S** a fall on the buttocks
POX	*v* **-ED, -ING, -ES** to infect with a pox (a disease marked by skin eruptions)	**PRATIQUE**	*n* pl. **-S** clearance given a ship by the health authority of a port
		PRATTLE	*v* **-TLED, -TLING, -TLES** to babble
POXVIRUS	*n* pl. **-ES** a type of virus	**PRATTLER**	*n* pl. **-S** one that prattles
POXY	*adj* **POXIER, POXIEST** afflicted with a pox	**PRAU**	*n* pl. **-S** a swift Malaysian sailing vessel
POYOU	*n* pl. **-S** an armadillo of Argentina	**PRAWN**	*v* **-ED, -ING, -S** to fish for prawns (edible shellfish)
POZOLE	*n* pl. **-S** posole		
POZZOLAN	*n* pl. **-S** a finely divided material used to make cement	**PRAWNER**	*n* pl. **-S** one that prawns
		PRAXIS	*n* pl. **PRAXISES** or **PRAXES** practical use of a theory
PRAAM	*n* pl. **-S** pram		
PRACTIC	*adj* practical	**PRAY**	*v* **-ED, -ING, -S** to address prayers to
PRACTICE	*v* **-TICED, -TICING, -TICES** to perform often so as to acquire skill	**PRAYER**	*n* pl. **-S** a devout petition to a deity
PRACTISE	*v* **-TISED, -TISING, -TISES** to practice	**PREACH**	*v* **-ED, -ING, -ES** to advocate or recommend urgently
PRAECIPE	*n* pl. **-S** a legal writ	**PREACHER**	*n* pl. **-S** one that preaches
PRAEDIAL	*adj* pertaining to land	**PREACHY**	*adj* **PREACHIER, PREACHIEST** tending to preach
PRAEFECT	*n* pl. **-S** prefect		
PRAELECT	*v* **-ED, -ING, -S** to prelect	**PREACT**	*v* **-ED, -ING, -S** to act beforehand
PRAETOR	*n* pl. **-S** an ancient Roman magistrate	**PREADAPT**	*v* **-ED, -ING, -S** to adapt beforehand
PRAHU	*n* pl. **-S** prau	**PREADMIT**	*v* **-MITTED, -MITTING, -MITS** to admit beforehand
PRAIRIE	*n* pl. **-S** a tract of grassland	**PREADOPT**	*v* **-ED, -ING, -S** to adopt beforehand

PREADULT *n* pl. **-S** a person not yet an adult

PREAGED *adj* previously aged

PREALLOT *v* **-LOTTED, -LOTTING, -LOTS** to allot beforehand

PREALTER *v* **-ED, -ING, -S** to alter beforehand

PREAMBLE *n* pl. **-S** an introductory statement

PREAMP *n* pl. **-S** an amplifier

PREANAL *adj* situated in front of the anus

PREAPPLY *v* **-PLIED, -PLYING, -PLIES** to apply beforehand

PREARM *v* **-ED, -ING, -S** to arm beforehand

PREAUDIT *n* pl. **-S** an audit made prior to a final settlement of a transaction

PREAVER *v* **-VERRED, -VERRING, -VERS** to aver or assert beforehand

PREAXIAL *adj* situated in front of an axis

PREBAKE *v* **-BAKED, -BAKING, -BAKES** to bake beforehand

PREBASAL *adj* situated in front of a base

PREBEND *n* pl. **-S** a clergyman's stipend

PREBID *v* **-BADE, -BIDDEN, -BIDDING, -BIDS** to bid beforehand

PREBILL *v* **-ED, -ING, -S** to bill beforehand

PREBIND *v* **-BOUND, -BINDING, -BINDS** to bind beforehand

PREBIRTH *n* pl. **-S** the period preceding a child's birth

PREBLESS *v* **-ED, -ING, -ES** to bless beforehand

PREBOARD *v* **-ED, -ING, -S** to board before the regular time

PREBOIL *v* **-ED, -ING, -S** to boil beforehand

PREBOOK *v* **-ED, -ING, -S** to book beforehand

PREBOOM *adj* preceding a sudden expansion of business

PREBOUND past tense of prebind

PREBUILD *v* **-BUILT, -BUILDING, -BUILDS** to build beforehand

PREBUY *v* **-BOUGHT, -BUYING, -BUYS** to buy beforehand

PRECAST *v* **-CAST, -CASTING, -CASTS** to cast before placing into position

PRECAVA *n* pl. **-VAE** a vein in higher vertebrates **PRECAVAL** *adj*

PRECEDE *v* **-CEDED, -CEDING, -CEDES** to go before

PRECENT *v* **-ED, -ING, -S** to lead a church choir in singing

PRECEPT *n* pl. **-S** a rule of conduct

PRECESS *v* **-ED, -ING, -ES** to rotate with a complex motion

PRECHECK *v* **-ED, -ING, -S** to check beforehand

PRECHILL *v* **-ED, -ING, -S** to chill beforehand

PRECHOSE past tense of prechoose (to choose beforehand)

PRECIEUX *adj* excessively refined

PRECINCT *n* pl. **-S** a subdivision of a city or town

PRECIOUS *n* pl. **-ES** a darling

PRECIPE *n* pl. **-S** praecipe

PRECIS *v* **-ED, -ING, -ES** to make a concise summary of

PRECISE *adj* **-CISER, -CISEST** sharply and clearly defined or stated

PRECITED *adj* previously cited

PRECLEAN *v* **-ED, -ING, -S** to clean beforehand

PRECLEAR *v* **-ED, -ING, -S** to clear beforehand

PRECLUDE *v* **-CLUDED, -CLUDING, -CLUDES** to make impossible by previous action

PRECODE *v* **-CODED, -CODING, -CODES** to code beforehand

PRECOOK *v* **-ED, -ING, -S** to cook beforehand

PRECOOL *v* **-ED, -ING, -S** to cool beforehand

PRECOUP *adj* preceding a coup

PRECRASH *adj* preceding a crash

PRECURE *v* **-CURED, -CURING, -CURES** to cure beforehand

PRECUT *v* **-CUT, -CUTTING, -CUTS** to cut beforehand

PREDATE *v* **-DATED, -DATING, -DATES** to date before the actual or a specified time

PREDATOR *n* pl. **-S** one that plunders

PREDAWN *n* pl. **-S** the time just before dawn

PREDEATH *n* pl. **-S** the period preceding a person's death

PREDELLA *n* pl. **-S** the base of an altarpiece

PREDIAL *adj* praedial

PREDICT *v* **-ED, -ING, -S** to tell of or about in advance

PREDIVE *adj* preceding a dive

PREDRAFT *adj* preceding a draft (a system for selecting players for professional teams)

PREDRILL *v* **-ED, -ING, -S** to drill beforehand

PREDRY *v* **-DRIED, -DRYING, -DRIES** to dry beforehand

PREDUSK *n* pl. **-S** the time just before dusk

PREE *v* **PREED, PREEING, PREES** to test by tasting

PREEDIT *v* **-ED, -ING, -S** to edit beforehand

PREELECT *v* **-ED, -ING, -S** to elect or choose beforehand

PREEMIE *n pl.* **-S** an infant born prematurely

PREEMPT *v* **-ED, -ING, -S** to acquire by prior right

PREEN *v* **-ED, -ING, -S** to smooth or clean with the beak or tongue

PREENACT *v* **-ED, -ING, -S** to enact beforehand

PREENER *n pl.* **-S** one that preens

PREERECT *v* **-ED, -ING, -S** to erect beforehand

PREEXIST *v* **-ED, -ING, -S** to exist before

PREFAB *v* **-FABBED, -FABBING, -FABS** to construct beforehand

PREFACE *v* **-ACED, -ACING, -ACES** to provide with an introductory statement

PREFACER *n pl.* **-S** one that prefaces

PREFADE *v* **-FADED, -FADING, -FADES** to fade beforehand

PREFECT *n pl.* **-S** an ancient Roman official

PREFER *v* **-FERRED, -FERRING, -FERS** to hold in higher regard or esteem

PREFIGHT *adj* preceding a fight

PREFILE *v* **-FILED, -FILING, -FILES** to file beforehand

PREFIRE *v* **-FIRED, -FIRING, -FIRES** to fire beforehand

PREFIX *v* **-ED, -ING, -ES** to add as a prefix (a form affixed to the beginning of a root word)

PREFIXAL *adj* pertaining to or being a prefix

PREFLAME *adj* preceding a flame

PREFOCUS *v* **-CUSED, -CUSING, -CUSES** or **-CUSSED, -CUSSING, -CUSSES** to focus beforehand

PREFORM *v* **-ED, -ING, -S** to form beforehand

PREFRANK *v* **-ED, -ING, -S** to frank beforehand

PREFREEZE *v* **-FROZE, -FROZEN, -FREEZING, -FREEZES** to freeze beforehand

PREFUND *v* **-ED, -ING, -S** to fund beforehand

PREGAME *n pl.* **-S** the period preceding a game

PREGGERS *adj* pregnant

PREGNANT *adj* carrying a developing fetus in the uterus

PREGUIDE *v* **-GUIDED, -GUIDING, -GUIDES** to guide beforehand

PREHEAT *v* **-ED, -ING, -S** to heat beforehand

PREHUMAN *n pl.* **-S** a prototype of man

PREJUDGE *v* **-JUDGED, -JUDGING, -JUDGES** to judge beforehand

PRELACY *n pl.* **-CIES** the office of a prelate

PRELATE *n pl.* **-S** a high-ranking clergyman **PRELATIC** *adj*

PRELAW *adj* preceding the professional study of law

PRELECT *v* **-ED, -ING, -S** to lecture

PRELEGAL *adj* occurring before the commencement of studies in law

PRELIFE *n pl.* **-LIVES** a life conceived as lived before one's earthly life

PRELIM *n pl.* **-S** a preliminary match

PRELIMIT *v* **-ED, -ING, -S** to limit beforehand

PRELOAD *v* **-ED, -ING, -S** to load beforehand

PRELUDE *v* **-LUDED, -LUDING, -LUDES** to play a musical introduction

PRELUDER *n pl.* **-S** one that preludes

PRELUNCH *adj* preceding lunch

PREMADE *adj* made beforehand

PREMAN *n pl.* **-MEN** a hypothetical ancestor of man

PREMEAL *adj* preceding a meal

PREMED *n pl.* **-S** a student preparing for the study of medicine

PREMEDIC *n pl.* **-S** a premed

PREMEET *adj* preceding a meet

PREMEN pl. of preman

PREMIE *n pl.* **-S** preemie

PREMIER *n pl.* **-S** a prime minister

PREMIERE *v* **-MIERED, -MIERING, -MIERES** to present publicly for the first time

PREMISE *v* **-MISED, -MISING, -MISES** to state in advance

PREMISS *n pl.* **-ES** a proposition in logic

PREMIUM *n pl.* **-S** an additional payment

PREMIX *v* **-MIXED** or **-MIXT, -MIXING, -MIXES** to mix before use

PREMOLAR *n pl.* **-S** a tooth

PREMOLD *v* **-ED, -ING, -S** to mold beforehand

PREMOLT *adj* preceding a molt

PREMORAL *adj* preceding the development of a moral code

PREMORSE *adj* ending abruptly, as if bitten off

PREMUNE *adj* resistant to a disease

PRENAME *n pl.* **-S** a forename

PRENATAL *adj* prior to birth

PRENOMEN *n* pl. **-MENS** or **-MINA** the first name of an ancient Roman

PRENOON *adj* preceding noon

PRENTICE *v* **-TICED, -TICING, -TICES** to place with an employer for instruction in a trade

PREOP *n* pl. **-S** a patient being prepared for surgery

PREORAL *adj* situated in front of the mouth

PREORDER *v* **-ED, -ING, -S** to order beforehand

PREOWNED *adj* owned beforehand by someone else

PREP *v* **PREPPED, PREPPING, PREPS** to attend a preparatory school

PREPACK *v* **-ED, -ING, -S** to package before retail distribution

PREPAID past tense of prepay

PREPARE *v* **-PARED, -PARING, -PARES** to put in proper condition or readiness

PREPARER *n* pl. **-S** one that prepares

PREPASTE *v* **-PASTED, -PASTING, -PASTES** to paste beforehand

PREPAVE *v* **-PAVED, -PAVING, -PAVES** to pave beforehand

PREPAY *v* **-PAID, -PAYING, -PAYS** to pay in advance

PREPENSE *adj* planned in advance

PREPILL *adj* preceding the development of a contraceptive pill

PREPLACE *v* **-PLACED, -PLACING, -PLACES** to place beforehand

PREPLAN *v* **-PLANNED, -PLANNING, -PLANS** to plan in advance

PREPLANT *adj* occurring before planting

PREPPED past tense of prep

PREPPIE *n* pl. **-S** one who preps

PREPPING present participle of prep

PREPPY *adj* **-PIER, -PIEST** associated with the style and behavior of preparatory school students **PREPPILY** *adv*

PREPREG *n* pl. **-S** reinforcing material already impregnated with a synthetic resin

PREPRESS *adj* pertaining to the preparation of copy for printing

PREPRICE *v* **-PRICED, -PRICING, -PRICES** to price beforehand

PREPRINT *v* **-ED, -ING, -S** to print in advance

PREPUBIS *n* pl. **-PUBES** a bone situated in front of the pubic bones

PREPUCE *n* pl. **-S** a fold of skin covering the penis

PREPUNCH *v* **-ED, -ING, -ES** to punch in advance

PREPUPA *n* pl. **-PAS** or **-PAE** a stage preceding the pupa

PREPUPAL *adj* preceding the pupal stage

PREQUEL *n* pl. **-S** a book whose story precedes that of an earlier work

PRERACE *adj* preceding a race

PRERADIO *adj* preceding the development of radio

PRERENAL *adj* situated in front of the kidney

PRERINSE *v* **-RINSED, -RINSING, -RINSES** to rinse beforehand

PRERIOT *adj* preceding a riot

PREROCK *adj* preceding the development of rock music

PRESA *n* pl. **-SE** a musical symbol

PRESAGE *v* **-SAGED, -SAGING, -SAGES** to foretell

PRESAGER *n* pl. **-S** one that presages

PRESALE *n* pl. **-S** a sale in advance

PRESCIND *v* **-ED, -ING, -S** to consider separately

PRESCORE *v* **-SCORED, -SCORING, -SCORES** to record the sound of before filming

PRESE pl. of presa

PRESELL *v* **-SOLD, -SELLING, -SELLS** to promote a product not yet being sold to the public

PRESENCE *n* pl. **-S** close proximity

PRESENT *v* **-ED, -ING, -S** to bring into the presence of someone

PRESERVE *v* **-SERVED, -SERVING, -SERVES** to keep free from harm or danger

PRESET *v* **-SET, -SETTING, -SETS** to set beforehand

PRESHAPE *v* **-SHAPED, -SHAPING, -SHAPES** to shape beforehand

PRESHIP *v* **-SHIPPED, -SHIPPING, -SHIPS** to ship beforehand

PRESHOW *v* **-SHOWED, -SHOWN, -SHOWING, -SHOWS** to show beforehand

PRESIDE *v* **-SIDED, -SIDING, -SIDES** to occupy the position of authority

PRESIDER *n* pl. **-S** one that presides

PRESIDIA	*n/pl* Soviet executive committees
PRESIDIO	*n* pl. **-DIOS** a Spanish fort
PRESIFT	*v* **-ED, -ING, -S** to sift beforehand
PRESLEEP	*adj* preceding sleep
PRESLICE	*v* **-SLICED, -SLICING, -SLICES** to slice beforehand
PRESOAK	*v* **-ED, -ING, -S** to soak beforehand
PRESOLD	past tense of presell
PRESOLVE	*v* **-SOLVED, -SOLVING, -SOLVES** to solve beforehand
PRESONG	*adj* preceding a song
PRESORT	*v* **-ED, -ING, -S** to sort beforehand
PRESPLIT	*adj* preceding a split
PRESS	*v* **-ED, -ING, -ES** to act upon with steady force
PRESSER	*n* pl. **-S** one that presses
PRESSING	*n* pl. **-S** an instance of stamping with a press
PRESSMAN	*n* pl. **-MEN** a printing press operator
PRESSOR	*n* pl. **-S** a substance that raises blood pressure
PRESSRUN	*n* pl. **-S** a continuous operation of a printing press
PRESSURE	*v* **-SURED, -SURING, -SURES** to apply force to
PREST	*n* pl. **-S** a loan
PRESTAMP	*v* **-ED, -ING, -S** to stamp beforehand
PRESTER	*n* pl. **-S** a priest
PRESTIGE	*n* pl. **-S** distinction or reputation in the eyes of people
PRESTO	*n* pl. **-TOS** a musical passage played in rapid tempo
PRESTORE	*v* **-STORED, -STORING, -STORES** to store beforehand
PRESUME	*v* **-SUMED, -SUMING, -SUMES** to take for granted
PRESUMER	*n* pl. **-S** one that presumes
PRETAPE	*v* **-TAPED, -TAPING, -TAPES** to tape beforehand
PRETASTE	*v* **-TASTED, -TASTING, -TASTES** to taste beforehand
PRETAX	*adj* existing before provision for taxes
PRETEEN	*n* pl. **-S** a child under the age of thirteen
PRETELL	*v* **-TOLD, -TELLING, -TELLS** to tell beforehand
PRETENCE	*n* pl. **-S** pretense

PRETEND	*v* **-ED, -ING, -S** to assume or display a false appearance of
PRETENSE	*n* pl. **-S** the act of pretending
PRETERIT	*n* pl. **-S** a past tense in grammar
PRETERM	*n* pl. **-S** a child born prematurely
PRETEST	*v* **-ED, -ING, -S** to give a preliminary test to
PRETEXT	*v* **-ED, -ING, -S** to allege as an excuse
PRETOLD	past tense of pretell
PRETOR	*n* pl. **-S** praetor
PRETRAIN	*v* **-ED, -ING, -S** to train beforehand
PRETREAT	*v* **-ED, -ING, -S** to treat beforehand
PRETRIAL	*n* pl. **-S** a proceeding that precedes a trial
PRETRIM	*v* **-TRIMMED, -TRIMMING, -TRIMS** to trim beforehand
PRETTIFY	*v* **-FIED, -FYING, -FIES** to make pretty
PRETTY	*adj* **-TIER, -TIEST** pleasing to the eye **PRETTILY** *adv*
PRETTY	*v* **-TIED, -TYING, -TIES** to make pretty
PRETYPE	*v* **-TYPED, -TYPING, -TYPES** to type beforehand
PRETZEL	*n* pl. **-S** a glazed, salted cracker
PREUNION	*n* pl. **-S** a union beforehand
PREUNITE	*v* **-UNITED, -UNITING, -UNITES** to unite beforehand
PREVAIL	*v* **-ED, -ING, -S** to triumph
PREVALUE	*v* **-UED, -UING, -UES** to value beforehand
PREVENT	*v* **-ED, -ING, -S** to keep from happening
PREVERB	*n* pl. **-S** a prefix or particle preceding the root of a verb
PREVIEW	*v* **-ED, -ING, -S** to view or exhibit in advance
PREVIOUS	*adj* coming or occurring before in time or order
PREVISE	*v* **-VISED, -VISING, -VISES** to foresee
PREVISIT	*v* **-ED, -ING, -S** to visit beforehand
PREVISOR	*n* pl. **-S** one that previses
PREVUE	*v* **-VUED, -VUING, -VUES** to preview
PREWAR	*adj* occurring or existing before a war
PREWARM	*v* **-ED, -ING, -S** to warm beforehand

PREWARN	*v* **-ED, -ING, -S** to warn in advance
PREWASH	*v* **-ED, -ING, -ES** to wash beforehand
PREWEIGH	*v* **-ED, -ING, -S** to weigh beforehand
PREWIRE	*v* **-WIRED, -WIRING, -WIRES** to wire beforehand
PREWORK	*v* **-ED, -ING, -S** to work beforehand
PREWORN	*adj* previously worn by someone
PREWRAP	*v* **-WRAPPED, -WRAPPING, -WRAPS** to wrap beforehand
PREX	*n* pl. **-ES** prexy
PREXY	*n* pl. **PREXIES** a president
PREY	*v* **-ED, -ING, -S** to seize and devour animals for food
PREYER	*n* pl. **-S** one that preys
PREZ	*n* pl. **-ES** a president
PRIAPEAN	*adj* priapic
PRIAPI	a pl. of priapus
PRIAPIC	*adj* phallic
PRIAPISM	*n* pl. **-S** a persistent erection of the penis
PRIAPUS	*n* pl. **-PUSES** or **-PI** a representation of the phallus
PRICE	*v* **PRICED, PRICING, PRICES** to set a value on
PRICER	*n* pl. **-S** one that prices
PRICEY	*adj* **PRICIER, PRICIEST** expensive
PRICIER	comparative of pricy
PRICIEST	superlative of pricy
PRICILY	*adv* in a pricey manner
PRICING	present participle of price
PRICK	*v* **-ED, -ING, -S** to puncture slightly
PRICKER	*n* pl. **-S** one that pricks
PRICKET	*n* pl. **-S** a spike for holding a candle upright
PRICKIER	comparative of pricky
PRICKIEST	superlative of pricky
PRICKING	*n* pl. **-S** a prickly feeling
PRICKLE	*v* **-LED, -LING, -LES** to prick
PRICKLY	*adj* **-LIER, -LIEST** having many sharp points
PRICKY	*adj* **PRICKIER, PRICKIEST** prickly
PRICY	*adj* **PRICIER, PRICIEST** pricey **PRICILY** *adv*
PRIDE	*v* **PRIDED, PRIDING, PRIDES** to feel pride (a feeling of self-esteem)
PRIDEFUL	*adj* full of pride
PRIED	past tense of pry
PRIEDIEU	*n* pl. **-DIEUS** or **-DIEUX** a piece of furniture for kneeling on during prayer
PRIER	*n* pl. **-S** one that pries
PRIES	present 3d person sing. of pry
PRIEST	*v* **-ED, -ING, -S** to ordain as a priest (one authorized to perform religious rites)
PRIESTLY	*adj* **-LIER, -LIEST** characteristic of or befitting a priest
PRIG	*v* **PRIGGED, PRIGGING, PRIGS** to steal
PRIGGERY	*n* pl. **-GERIES** priggism
PRIGGISH	*adj* marked by priggism
PRIGGISM	*n* pl. **-S** prim adherence to convention
PRILL	*v* **-ED, -ING, -S** to convert into pellets
PRIM	*adj* **PRIMMER, PRIMMEST** formally precise or proper
PRIM	*v* **PRIMMED, PRIMMING, PRIMS** to give a prim expression to
PRIMA	*n* pl. **-S** primo
PRIMACY	*n* pl. **-CIES** the state of being first
PRIMAGE	*n* pl. **-S** an amount paid as an addition to freight charges
PRIMAL	*adj* being at the beginning or foundation
PRIMARY	*n* pl. **-RIES** a preliminary election
PRIMATAL	*n* pl. **-S** a primate
PRIMATE	*n* pl. **-S** any of an advanced order of mammals
PRIME	*v* **PRIMED, PRIMING, PRIMES** to make ready
PRIMELY	*adv* excellently
PRIMER	*n* pl. **-S** a book that covers the basics of a subject
PRIMERO	*n* pl. **-ROS** a card game
PRIMEVAL	*adj* pertaining to the earliest ages
PRIMI	a pl. of primo
PRIMINE	*n* pl. **-S** the outer covering of an ovule
PRIMING	*n* pl. **-S** the act of one that primes
PRIMLY	*adv* in a prim manner
PRIMMED	past tense of prim
PRIMMER	comparative of prim
PRIMMEST	superlative of prim
PRIMMING	present participle of prim

PRIMNESS   *n* pl. **-ES** the state of being prim

PRIMO   *n* pl. **-MOS** or **-MI** the main part in a musical piece

PRIMP   *v* **-ED, -ING, -S** to dress or adorn carefully

PRIMROSE   *n* pl. **-S** a perennial herb

PRIMSIE   *adj* prim

PRIMULA   *n* pl. **-S** primrose

PRIMUS   *n* pl. **-ES** the head bishop of Scotland

PRINCE   *n* pl. **-S** a non-reigning male member of a royal family

PRINCELY   *adj* **-LIER, -LIEST** of or befitting a prince

PRINCESS   *n* pl. **-ES** a non-reigning female member of a royal family

PRINCIPE   *n* pl. **-PI** a prince

PRINCOCK   *n* pl. **-S** a coxcomb

PRINCOX   *n* pl. **-ES** princock

PRINK   *v* **-ED, -ING, -S** to dress or adorn in a showy manner

PRINKER   *n* pl. **-S** one that prinks

PRINT   *v* **-ED, -ING, -S** to produce by pressed type on a surface

PRINTER   *n* pl. **-S** one that prints

PRINTERY   *n* pl. **-ERIES** a place where printing is done

PRINTING   *n* pl. **-S** a reproduction from a printing surface

PRINTOUT   *n* pl. **-S** the printed output of a computer

PRION   *n* pl. **-S** a protein particle

PRIOR   *n* pl. **-S** an officer in a monastery

PRIORATE   *n* pl. **-S** the office of a prior

PRIORESS   *n* pl. **-ES** a nun corresponding in rank to a prior

PRIORITY   *n* pl. **-TIES** precedence established by importance

PRIORLY   *adv* previously

PRIORY   *n* pl. **-RIES** a religious house

PRISE   *v* **PRISED, PRISING, PRISES** to raise or force with a lever

PRISERE   *n* pl. **-S** a succession of vegetational stages

PRISM   *n* pl. **-S** a solid which disperses light into a spectrum

PRISMOID   *n* pl. **-S** a geometric solid

PRISON   *v* **-ED, -ING, -S** to imprison

PRISONER   *n* pl. **-S** one that is imprisoned

PRISS   *v* **-ED, -ING, -ES** to act in a prissy manner

PRISSY   *adj* **-SIER, -SIEST** excessively or affectedly proper **PRISSILY** *adv*

PRISSY   *n* pl. **-SIES** one who is prissy

PRISTANE   *n* pl. **-S** a chemical compound

PRISTINE   *adj* pertaining to the earliest time or state

PRITHEE   *interj* — used to express a wish or request

PRIVACY   *n* pl. **-CIES** the state of being private

PRIVATE   *adj* **-VATER, -VATEST** not for public use or knowledge

PRIVATE   *n* pl. **-S** a soldier of lower rank

PRIVET   *n* pl. **-S** an ornamental shrub

PRIVITY   *n* pl. **-TIES** private knowledge

PRIVY   *adj* **PRIVIER, PRIVIEST** private **PRIVILY** *adv*

PRIVY   *n* pl. **PRIVIES** an outhouse

PRIZE   *v* **PRIZED, PRIZING, PRIZES** to value highly

PRIZER   *n* pl. **-S** one who vies for a reward

PRO   *n* pl. **PROS** an argument or vote in favor of something

PROA   *n* pl. **-S** prau

PROBABLE   *n* pl. **-S** something likely to occur or prove true

PROBABLY   *adv* without much doubt

PROBAND   *n* pl. **-S** one whose reactions or responses are studied

PROBANG   *n* pl. **-S** a surgical rod

PROBATE   *v* **-BATED, -BATING, -BATES** to establish the validity of

PROBE   *v* **PROBED, PROBING, PROBES** to investigate or examine thoroughly

PROBER   *n* pl. **-S** one that probes

PROBIT   *n* pl. **-S** a unit of statistical probability

PROBITY   *n* pl. **-TIES** complete and confirmed integrity

PROBLEM   *n* pl. **-S** a perplexing question or situation

PROCAINE   *n* pl. **-S** a compound used as a local anesthetic

PROCARP   *n* pl. **-S** a female sexual organ in certain algae

PROCEED   *v* **-ED, -ING, -S** to go forward or onward

PROCESS	*v* **-ED, -ING, -ES** to treat or prepare by a special method	**PROFOUND**	*n* pl. **-S** something that is very deep
PROCHAIN	*adj* prochein	**PROFUSE**	*adj* pouring forth generously
PROCHEIN	*adj* nearest in time, relation, or degree	**PROG**	*v* **PROGGED, PROGGING, PROGS** to prowl about for food or plunder
PROCLAIM	*v* **-ED, -ING, -S** to make known publicly or officially		
PROCTOR	*v* **-ED, -ING, -S** to supervise	**PROGENY**	*n* pl. **-NIES** a descendant or offspring
PROCURAL	*n* pl. **-S** the act of procuring	**PROGERIA**	*n* pl. **-S** premature aging
PROCURE	*v* **-CURED, -CURING, -CURES** to obtain by effort	**PROGGER**	*n* pl. **-S** one that progs
		PROGGING	present participle of prog
PROCURER	*n* pl. **-S** one that procures	**PROGNOSE**	*v* **-NOSED, -NOSING, -NOSES** to forecast the probable course of a disease
PROD	*v* **PRODDED, PRODDING, PRODS** to jab with something pointed		
PRODDER	*n* pl. **-S** one that prods	**PROGRADE**	*adj* pertaining to the orbital motion of a body
PRODIGAL	*n* pl. **-S** one who spends lavishly and foolishly	**PROGRAM**	*v* **-GRAMED, -GRAMING, -GRAMS** or **-GRAMMED, -GRAMMING, -GRAMS** to arrange in a plan of proceedings
PRODIGY	*n* pl. **-GIES** a child having exceptional talent or ability		
PRODROME	*n* pl. **-DROMES** or **-DROMATA** a sign of impending disease	**PROGRESS**	*v* **-ED, -ING, -ES** to move forward or onward
PRODRUG	*n* pl. **-S** an inactive chemical substance that becomes an active drug in the body	**PROGUN**	*adj* favoring the right to own guns without restrictions
		PROHIBIT	*v* **-ED, -ING, -S** to forbid by authority
PRODUCE	*v* **-DUCED, -DUCING, -DUCES** to bring into existence	**PROJECT**	*v* **-ED, -ING, -S** to extend outward
PRODUCER	*n* pl. **-S** one that produces	**PROJET**	*n* pl. **-S** a plan or outline
PRODUCT	*n* pl. **-S** something produced by labor or effort	**PROLABOR**	*adj* favoring organized labor
PROEM	*n* pl. **-S** an introductory statement **PROEMIAL** *adj*	**PROLAMIN**	*n* pl. **-S** a simple protein
		PROLAN	*n* pl. **-S** a sex hormone
PROETTE	*n* pl. **-S** a female professional athlete	**PROLAPSE**	*v* **-LAPSED, -LAPSING, -LAPSES** to fall or slip out of place
PROF	*n* pl. **-S** a professor	**PROLATE**	*adj* extended lengthwise
PROFANE	*v* **-FANED, -FANING, -FANES** to treat with irreverence or abuse	**PROLE**	*n* pl. **-S** a member of the working class
PROFANER	*n* pl. **-S** one that profanes	**PROLEG**	*n* pl. **-S** an abdominal leg of certain insect larvae
PROFESS	*v* **-ED, -ING, -ES** to affirm openly		
PROFFER	*v* **-ED, -ING, -S** to present for acceptance	**PROLIFIC**	*adj* producing abundantly
		PROLINE	*n* pl. **-S** an amino acid
PROFILE	*v* **-FILED, -FILING, -FILES** to draw an outline of	**PROLIX**	*adj* tediously long and wordy **PROLIXLY** *adv*
PROFILER	*n* pl. **-S** one that profiles	**PROLOG**	*v* **-ED, -ING, -S** to prologue
PROFIT	*v* **-ED, -ING, -S** to gain an advantage or benefit	**PROLOGUE**	*v* **-LOGUED, -LOGUING, -LOGUES** to preface
PROFITER	*n* pl. **-S** one that profits	**PROLONG**	*v* **-ED, -ING, -S** to lengthen in duration
PROFORMA	*adj* provided in advance of shipment and showing description and quantity	**PROLONGE**	*n* pl. **-S** a rope used for pulling a gun carriage
PROFOUND	*adj* **-FOUNDER, -FOUNDEST** intellectually deep and penetrating	**PROM**	*n* pl. **-S** a formal dance

PROMINE   *n* pl. **-S** a substance that promotes growth

PROMISE   *v* **-ISED, -ISING, -ISES** to make a declaration of assurance

PROMISEE   *n* pl. **-S** one who is promised something

PROMISER   *n* pl. **-S** promisor

PROMISOR   *n* pl. **-S** one that promises

PROMO   *n* pl. **-MOS** a promotional presentation

PROMO   *v* **-ED, -ING, -S** to promote

PROMOTE   *v* **-MOTED, -MOTING, -MOTES** to contribute to the progress of

PROMOTER   *n* pl. **-S** one that promotes

PROMPT   *adj* **PROMPTER, PROMPTEST** quick to act or respond

PROMPT   *v* **-ED, -ING, -S** to induce to action

PROMPTER   *n* pl. **-S** one that prompts

PROMPTLY   *adv* in a prompt manner

PROMULGE   *v* **-MULGED, -MULGING, -MULGES** to proclaim

PRONATE   *v* **-NATED, -NATING, -NATES** to turn the palm downward or backward

PRONATOR   *n* pl. **-S** or **-ES** a forearm or forelimb muscle

PRONE   *adj* lying with the front or face downward **PRONELY** *adv*

PRONG   *v* **-ED, -ING, -S** to pierce with a pointed projection

PRONOTUM   *n* pl. **-NOTA** a hard outer plate of an insect

PRONOUN   *n* pl. **-S** a word that may be used in place of a noun

PRONTO   *adv* quickly

PROOF   *v* **-ED, -ING, -S** to examine for errors

PROOFER   *n* pl. **-S** one that proofs

PROP   *v* **PROPPED, PROPPING, PROPS** to keep from falling

PROPANE   *n* pl. **-S** a flammable gas

PROPEL   *v* **-PELLED, -PELLING, -PELS** to cause to move forward or onward

PROPEND   *v* **-ED, -ING, -S** to have a tendency toward

PROPENE   *n* pl. **-S** a flammable gas

PROPENOL   *n* pl. **-S** a flammable liquid

PROPENSE   *adj* tending toward

PROPENYL   *adj* pertaining to a certain chemical group

PROPER   *adj* **-ERER, -EREST** suitable **PROPERLY** *adv*

PROPER   *n* pl. **-S** a portion of the Mass

PROPERTY   *n* pl. **-TIES** something owned

PROPHAGE   *n* pl. **-S** a form of virus

PROPHASE   *n* pl. **-S** the first stage in mitosis

PROPHECY   *n* pl. **-CIES** a prediction

PROPHESY   *v* **-SIED, -SYING, -SIES** to predict

PROPHET   *n* pl. **-S** one who predicts

PROPINE   *v* **-PINED, -PINING, -PINES** to offer as a gift

PROPJET   *n* pl. **-S** a type of airplane

PROPMAN   *n* pl. **-MEN** a man in charge of stage properties

PROPOLIS   *n* pl. **-LISES** a resinous substance used as a cement by bees

PROPONE   *v* **-PONED, -PONING, -PONES** to propose

PROPOSAL   *n* pl. **-S** something that is proposed

PROPOSE   *v* **-POSED, -POSING, -POSES** to put forward for consideration or acceptance

PROPOSER   *n* pl. **-S** one that proposes

PROPOUND   *v* **-ED, -ING, -S** to propose

PROPPED   past tense of prop

PROPPING   present participle of prop

PROPRIUM   *n* pl. **-PRIA** an attribute belonging inseparably to every member of a species

PROPYL   *n* pl. **-S** a univalent radical **PROPYLIC** *adj*

PROPYLON   *n* pl. **-LA** an entrance to a temple

PRORATE   *v* **-RATED, -RATING, -RATES** to divide proportionally

PROROGUE   *v* **-ROGUED, -ROGUING, -ROGUES** to discontinue a session of

PROSAIC   *adj* pertaining to prose

PROSAISM   *n* pl. **-S** a prosaic style

PROSAIST   *n* pl. **-S** a writer of prose

PROSE   *v* **PROSED, PROSING, PROSES** to write prose (writing without metrical structure)

PROSECT   *v* **-ED, -ING, -S** to dissect

PROSER   *n* pl. **-S** a prosaist

PROSIER   comparative of prosy

PROSIEST   superlative of prosy

PROSILY   *adv* in a prosy manner

PROSING   present participle of prose

PROSIT   *interj* — used as a drinking toast

PROSO   *n* pl. **-SOS** millet

PROSODY   *n* pl. **-DIES** the study of poetical forms **PROSODIC** *adj*

PROSOMA   *n* pl. **-MAS** or **-MATA** the anterior region of the body of some invertebrates **PROSOMAL** *adj*

PROSPECT   *v* **-ED, -ING, -S** to explore for mineral deposits

PROSPER   *v* **-ED, -ING, -S** to be successful or fortunate

PROSS   *n* pl. **-ES** a prostitute

PROSSIE   *n* pl. **-S** a prostitute

PROST   *interj* prosit

PROSTATE   *n* pl. **-S** a gland in male mammals

PROSTIE   *n* pl. **-S** a prostitute

PROSTYLE   *n* pl. **-S** a building having a row of columns across the front only

PROSY   *adj* **PROSIER, PROSIEST** prosaic

PROTAMIN   *n* pl. **-S** a simple protein

PROTASIS   *n* pl. **-ASES** the introductory part of a classical drama **PROTATIC** *adj*

PROTEA   *n* pl. **-S** an evergreen shrub

PROTEAN   *n* pl. **-S** a type of protein

PROTEASE   *n* pl. **-S** an enzyme

PROTECT   *v* **-ED, -ING, -S** to keep from harm, attack, or injury

PROTEGE   *n* pl. **-S** one whose career is promoted by an influential person

PROTEGEE   *n* pl. **-S** a female protege

PROTEI   pl. of proteus

PROTEID   *n* pl. **-S** protein

PROTEIDE   *n* pl. **-S** proteid

PROTEIN   *n* pl. **-S** a nitrogenous organic compound

PROTEND   *v* **-ED, -ING, -S** to extend

PROTEOME   *n* pl. **-S** the complement of proteins expressed by a genome

PROTEOSE   *n* pl. **-S** a water-soluble protein

PROTEST   *v* **-ED, -ING, -S** to express strong objection

PROTEUS   *n* pl. **-ES** one that readily changes his appearance or principles

PROTEUS   *n* pl. **-TEI** any of a genus of aerobic bacteria

PROTIST   *n* pl. **-S** any of a group of unicellular organisms

PROTIUM   *n* pl. **-S** an isotope of hydrogen

PROTOCOL   *v* **-COLED, -COLING, -COLS** or **-COLLED, -COLLING, -COLS** to form a preliminary draft of an official document

PROTON   *n* pl. **-S** a subatomic particle **PROTONIC** *adj*

PROTOPOD   *n* pl. **-S** a part of a crustacean appendage

PROTOXID   *n* pl. **-S** an oxide

PROTOZOA   *n/pl* unicellular microscopic organisms

PROTRACT   *v* **-ED, -ING, -S** to prolong

PROTRADE   *adj* favoring international trade

PROTRUDE   *v* **-TRUDED, -TRUDING, -TRUDES** to extend beyond the main portion

PROTYL   *n* pl. **-S** protyle

PROTYLE   *n* pl. **-S** a hypothetical substance from which all the elements are supposedly derived

PROUD   *adj* **PROUDER, PROUDEST** having or displaying pride **PROUDLY** *adv*

PROUDFUL   *adj* prideful

PROUNION   *adj* favoring labor unions

PROVE   *v* **PROVED, PROVEN, PROVING, PROVES** to establish the truth or validity of **PROVABLE** *adj* **PROVABLY** *adv*

PROVENLY   *adv* without doubt

PROVER   *n* pl. **-S** one that proves

PROVERB   *v* **-ED, -ING, -S** to make a byword of

PROVIDE   *v* **-VIDED, -VIDING, -VIDES** to supply

PROVIDER   *n* pl. **-S** one that provides

PROVINCE   *n* pl. **-S** an administrative division of a country

PROVING   present participle of prove

PROVIRUS   *n* pl. **-ES** a form of virus **PROVIRAL** *adj*

PROVISO   *n* pl. **-SOS** or **-SOES** a clause in a document introducing a condition or restriction

PROVOKE   *v* **-VOKED, -VOKING, -VOKES** to incite to anger or resentment

PROVOKER   *n* pl. **-S** one that provokes

PROVOST   *n* pl. **-S** a high-ranking university official

PROW   *adj* **PROWER, PROWEST** brave

PROW   *n* pl. **-S** the forward part of a ship

PROWAR   *adj* favoring war

PROWESS   *n* pl. **-ES** exceptional ability

PROWL   *v* **-ED, -ING, -S** to move about stealthily

PROWLER   *n* pl. **-S** one that prowls

PROXEMIC   *adj* pertaining to a branch of environmental study

PROXIMAL   *adj* located near the point of origin

PROXIMO   *adj* of or occurring in the following month

PROXY   *n* pl. **PROXIES** a person authorized to act for another

PRUDE   *n* pl. **-S** a prudish person

PRUDENCE   *n* pl. **-S** the quality of being prudent

PRUDENT   *adj* having, showing, or exercising good judgment

PRUDERY   *n* pl. **-ERIES** excessive regard for propriety, modesty, or morality

PRUDISH   *adj* marked by prudery

PRUINOSE   *adj* having a powdery covering

PRUNE   *v* **PRUNED, PRUNING, PRUNES** to cut off branches or parts from **PRUNABLE** *adj*

PRUNELLA   *n* pl. **-S** a strong woolen fabric

PRUNELLE   *n* pl. **-S** a plum-flavored liqueur

PRUNELLO   *n* pl. **-LOS** prunella

PRUNER   *n* pl. **-S** one that prunes

PRUNING   present participle of prune

PRUNUS   *n* pl. **-ES** a flowering tree

PRURIENT   *adj* having lustful thoughts or desires

PRURIGO   *n* pl. **-GOS** a skin disease

PRURITUS   *n* pl. **-ES** intense itching **PRURITIC** *adj*

PRUSSIC   *adj* pertaining to a type of acid

PRUTA   *n* pl. **PRUTOT** prutah

PRUTAH   *n* pl. **PRUTOTH** a former monetary unit of Israel

PRY   *v* **PRIED, PRYING, PRIES** to inquire impertinently into private matters **PRYINGLY** *adv*

PRYER   *n* pl. **-S** prier

PRYTHEE   *interj* prithee

PSALM   *v* **-ED, -ING, -S** to praise in psalms (sacred songs)

PSALMIC   *adj* of or pertaining to a psalm

PSALMIST   *n* pl. **-S** a writer of psalms

PSALMODY   *n* pl. **-DIES** the use of psalms in worship

PSALTER   *n* pl. **-S** a book of psalms

PSALTERY   *n* pl. **-TERIES** an ancient stringed musical instrument

PSALTRY   *n* pl. **-TRIES** psaltery

PSAMMITE   *n* pl. **-S** a fine-grained rock

PSAMMON   *n* pl. **-S** a group of microorganisms living in waterlogged sands

PSCHENT   *n* pl. **-S** a crown worn by ancient Egyptian kings

PSEPHITE   *n* pl. **-S** a rock composed of small pebbles

PSEUD   *n* pl. **-S** a person pretending to be an intellectual

PSEUDO   *n* pl. **PSEUDOS** a pseud

PSHAW   *v* **-ED, -ING, -S** to utter an expression of disapproval

PSI   *n* pl. **-S** a Greek letter

PSILOCIN   *n* pl. **-S** a hallucinogenic drug

PSILOSIS   *n* pl. **-LOSES** a tropical disease **PSILOTIC** *adj*

PSOAS   *n* pl. **PSOAI** or **PSOAE** a muscle of the loin **PSOATIC** *adj*

PSOCID   *n* pl. **-S** a minute winged insect

PSORALEA   *n* pl. **-S** a plant of the bean family

PSORALEN   *n* pl. **-S** a drug used to treat psoriasis

PSST   *interj* — used to attract someone's attention

PST   *interj* psst

PSYCH   *v* **-ED, -ING, -S** to put into the proper frame of mind

PSYCHE   *n* pl. **-S** the mental structure of a person

PSYCHIC   *n* pl. **-S** one sensitive to extrasensory phenomena

PSYCHO   *n* pl. **-CHOS** a mentally unstable person

PSYLLA   *n* pl. **-S** any of various plant lice

PSYLLID   *n* pl. **-S** psylla

PSYLLIUM   *n* pl. **-S** the seed of a fleawort

PSYOPS   *n/pl* noncombative military operations to influence the enemy's state of mind

PSYWAR   *n* pl. **-S** psychological warfare

PTERIN   *n* pl. **-S** a chemical compound

PTEROPOD   *n* pl. **-S** a type of mollusk

PTERYGIA   *n/pl* fleshy growths over the cornea

PTERYLA   *n* pl. **-LAE** a feathered area on the skin of a bird

PTISAN   *n* pl. **-S** a tea of herbs or barley

PTOMAIN *n* pl. **-S** ptomaine

PTOMAINE *n* pl. **-S** a compound produced by the decomposition of protein

PTOOEY *interj* ptui

PTOSIS *n* pl. **PTOSES** a drooping of the upper eyelid **PTOTIC** *adj*

PTUI *interj* — used to express the sound of spitting

PTYALIN *n* pl. **-S** a salivary enzyme

PTYALISM *n* pl. **-S** an excessive flow of saliva

PUB *n* pl. **-S** a tavern

PUBERTY *n* pl. **-TIES** a period of sexual maturation **PUBERAL, PUBERTAL** *adj*

PUBIC *adj* pertaining to the pubes or pubis

PUBIS *n* pl. **PUBES** the forward portion of either of the hipbones

PUBLIC *n* pl. **-S** the community or the people as a whole

PUBLICAN *n* pl. **-S** one who owns or manages a pub

PUBLICLY *adv* by the public

PUBLISH *v* **-ED, -ING, -ES** to print and issue to the public

PUCCOON *n* pl. **-S** an herb that yields a red dye

PUCE *n* pl. **-S** a dark red color

PUCK *n* pl. **-S** a rubber disk used in ice hockey

PUCKA *adj* pukka

PUCKER *v* **-ED, -ING, -S** to gather into small wrinkles or folds

PUCKERER *n* pl. **-S** one that puckers

PUCKERY *adj* **-ERIER, -ERIEST** having a tendency to pucker

PUCKISH *adj* impish

PUD *n* pl. **-S** pudding

PUDDING *n* pl. **-S** a thick, soft dessert

PUDDLE *v* **-DLED, -DLING, -DLES** to strew with puddles (small pools of water)

PUDDLER *n* pl. **-S** one who subjects iron to puddling

PUDDLING *n* pl. **-S** the process of converting pig iron to wrought iron

PUDDLY *adj* **-DLIER, -DLIEST** full of puddles

PUDENCY *n* pl. **-CIES** modesty

PUDENDUM *n* pl. **-DA** the external genital organs of a woman **PUDENDAL** *adj*

PUDGY *adj* **PUDGIER, PUDGIEST** short and fat **PUDGILY** *adv*

PUDIBUND *adj* prudish

PUDIC *adj* to the pudendum

PUEBLO *n* pl. **-LOS** a communal dwelling of certain Indian tribes

PUERILE *adj* childish

PUERPERA *n* pl. **-PERAE** a woman who has recently given birth to a child

PUFF *v* **-ED, -ING, -S** to blow in short gusts

PUFFBALL *n* pl. **-S** any of various globular fungi

PUFFER *n* pl. **-S** one that puffs

PUFFERY *n* pl. **-ERIES** excessive public praise

PUFFIN *n* pl. **-S** a sea bird

PUFFY *adj* **-FIER, -FIEST** swollen **PUFFILY** *adv*

PUG *v* **PUGGED, PUGGING, PUGS** to fill in with clay or mortar

PUGAREE *n* pl. **-S** pugree

PUGGAREE *n* pl. **-S** pugree

PUGGIER comparative of puggy

PUGGIEST superlative of puggy

PUGGING present participle of pug

PUGGISH *adj* somewhat stubby

PUGGREE *n* pl. **-S** pugree

PUGGRY *n* pl. **-GRIES** pugree

PUGGY *adj* **-GIER, -GIEST** puggish

PUGH *interj* — used to express disgust

PUGILISM *n* pl. **-S** the art or practice of fighting with the fists

PUGILIST *n* pl. **-S** one who fights with his fists

PUGMARK *n* pl. **-S** a footprint

PUGREE *n* pl. **-S** a cloth band wrapped around a hat

PUISNE *n* pl. **-S** one of lesser rank

PUISSANT *adj* powerful

PUJA *n* pl. **-S** a Hindu prayer ritual

PUJAH *n* pl. **-S** puja

PUKE *v* **PUKED, PUKING, PUKES** to vomit

PUKKA *adj* genuine

PUL *n* pl. **PULS** or **PULI** a coin of Afghanistan

PULA *n* pl. **PULA** a monetary unit of Botswana

PULE   *v* **PULED, PULING, PULES** to whine

PULER   *n* pl. **-S** one that pules

PULI   *n* pl. **-LIS** or **-LIK** a long-haired sheepdog

PULICENE   *adj* pertaining to fleas

PULICIDE   *n* pl. **-S** an agent used for destroying fleas

PULING   *n* pl. **-S** a plaintive cry

PULINGLY   *adv* in a whining manner

PULL   *v* **-ED, -ING, -S** to exert force in order to cause motion toward the force

PULLBACK   *n* pl. **-S** a restraint or drawback

PULLER   *n* pl. **-S** one that pulls

PULLET   *n* pl. **-S** a young hen

PULLEY   *n* pl. **-LEYS** a device used for lifting weight

PULLMAN   *n* pl. **-S** a railroad sleeping car

PULLOUT   *n* pl. **-S** a withdrawal

PULLOVER   *n* pl. **-S** a garment that is put on by being drawn over the head

PULLUP   *n* pl. **-S** the act of raising oneself while hanging by the hands

PULMONIC   *adj* pertaining to the lungs

PULMOTOR   *n* pl. **-S** a respiratory device

PULP   *v* **-ED, -ING, -S** to reduce to pulp (a soft, moist mass of matter)

PULPAL   *adj* pertaining to pulp **PULPALLY** *adv*

PULPER   *n* pl. **-S** one that pulps

PULPIER   comparative of pulpy

PULPIEST   superlative of pulpy

PULPILY   *adv* in a pulpy manner

PULPIT   *n* pl. **-S** a platform in a church **PULPITAL** *adj*

PULPLESS   *adj* having no pulp

PULPOUS   *adj* pulpy

PULPWOOD   *n* pl. **-S** soft wood used in making paper

PULPY   *adj* **PULPIER, PULPIEST** resembling pulp

PULQUE   *n* pl. **-S** a fermented Mexican beverage

PULSANT   *adj* pulsating

PULSAR   *n* pl. **-S** a celestial source of radio waves

PULSATE   *v* **-SATED, -SATING, -SATES** to expand and contract rhythmically

PULSATOR   *n* pl. **-S** something that pulsates

PULSE   *v* **PULSED, PULSING, PULSES** to pulsate

PULSEJET   *n* pl. **-S** a type of engine

PULSER   *n* pl. **-S** a device that causes pulsations

PULSING   present participle of pulse

PULSION   *n* pl. **-S** propulsion

PULSOJET   *n* pl. **-S** pulsejet

PULVILLI   *n/pl* pads between the claws of an insect's foot

PULVINUS   *n* pl. **-NI** a swelling at the base of a leaf **PULVINAR** *adj*

PUMA   *n* pl. **-S** a cougar

PUMELO   *n* pl. **-LOS** pomelo

PUMICE   *v* **-ICED, -ICING, -ICES** to polish with a porous volcanic rock

PUMICER   *n* pl. **-S** one that pumices

PUMICITE   *n* pl. **-S** a porous volcanic rock

PUMMEL   *v* **-MELED, -MELING, -MELS** or **-MELLED, -MELLING, -MELS** to pommel

PUMMELO   *n* pl. **-LOS** a shaddock

PUMP   *v* **-ED, -ING, -S** to cause to flow by means of a pump (a device for moving fluids)

PUMPER   *n* pl. **-S** one that pumps

PUMPKIN   *n* pl. **-S** a large, edible fruit

PUMPLESS   *adj* lacking a pump

PUMPLIKE   *adj* resembling a pump

PUN   *v* **PUNNED, PUNNING, PUNS** to make a pun (a play on words)

PUNA   *n* pl. **-S** a cold, arid plateau

PUNCH   *v* **-ED, -ING, -ES** to perforate with a type of tool

PUNCHEON   *n* pl. **-S** a vertical supporting timber

PUNCHER   *n* pl. **-S** one that punches

PUNCHY   *adj* **PUNCHIER, PUNCHIEST** dazed **PUNCHILY** *adv*

PUNCTATE   *adj* covered with dots

PUNCTUAL   *adj* being on time

PUNCTURE   *v* **-TURED, -TURING, -TURES** to pierce with a pointed object

PUNDIT   *n* pl. **-S** a Hindu scholar **PUNDITIC** *adj*

PUNDITRY   *n* pl. **-RIES** the learning of pundits

PUNG   *n* pl. **-S** a box-shaped sleigh

PUNGENCY	*n* pl. **-CIES** the state of being pungent	**PUNY**	*adj* **PUNIER, PUNIEST** of inferior size, strength, or significance
PUNGENT	*adj* sharply affecting the organs of taste or smell	**PUP**	*v* **PUPPED, PUPPING, PUPS** to give birth to puppies
PUNGLE	*v* **-GLED, -GLING, -GLES** to contribute	**PUPA**	*n* pl. **-PAS** or **-PAE** an intermediate stage of a metamorphic insect **PUPAL** *adj*
PUNIER	comparative of puny		
PUNIEST	superlative of puny	**PUPARIUM**	*n* pl. **-IA** a pupal shell **PUPARIAL** *adj*
PUNILY	*adv* in a puny manner		
PUNINESS	*n* pl. **-ES** the state of being puny	**PUPATE**	*v* **-PATED, -PATING, -PATES** to pass through the pupal stage
PUNISH	*v* **-ED, -ING, -ES** to impose a penalty on in requital for wrongdoing	**PUPATION**	*n* pl. **-S** the act of pupating
		PUPFISH	*n* pl. **-ES** a small, freshwater fish
PUNISHER	*n* pl. **-S** one that punishes	**PUPIL**	*n* pl. **-S** a student under the close supervision of a teacher
PUNITION	*n* pl. **-S** the act of punishing; punishment		
		PUPILAGE	*n* pl. **-S** the state of being a pupil
PUNITIVE	*adj* inflicting punishment	**PUPILAR**	*adj* pertaining to a part of the eye
PUNITORY	*adj* punitive	**PUPILARY**	*adj* pupilar
PUNJI	*n* pl. **-S** a sharp bamboo stake placed and concealed so as to impale an enemy	**PUPPED**	past tense of pup
		PUPPET	*n* pl. **-S** a small figure, as of a person or animal, manipulated by the hand
PUNK	*adj* **PUNKER, PUNKEST** of inferior quality		
		PUPPETRY	*n* pl. **-RIES** the art of making or manipulating puppets
PUNK	*n* pl. **-S** dry, decayed wood used as tinder	**PUPPING**	present participle of pup
PUNKA	*n* pl. **-S** a ceiling fan used in India	**PUPPY**	*n* pl. **-PIES** a young dog **PUPPYISH** *adj*
PUNKAH	*n* pl. **-S** punka		
PUNKER	*n* pl. **-S** a punk rock musician	**PUPPYDOM**	*n* pl. **-S** the world of puppies
PUNKEY	*n* pl. **-KEYS** punkie	**PUPU**	*n* pl. **-S** a dish of Asian foods served as an appetizer
PUNKIE	*n* pl. **-S** a biting gnat		
PUNKIN	*n* pl. **-S** pumpkin	**PUR**	*v* **PURRED, PURRING, PURS** to purr
PUNKISH	*adj* pertaining to a style inspired by punk rock		
		PURANA	*n* pl. **-S** a Hindu scripture **PURANIC** *adj*
PUNKY	*adj* **PUNKIER, PUNKIEST** resembling punk	**PURBLIND**	*adj* partially blind
PUNNED	past tense of pun	**PURCHASE**	*v* **-CHASED, -CHASING, -CHASES** to acquire by the payment of money
PUNNER	*n* pl. **-S** a punster		
PUNNET	*n* pl. **-S** a small basket		
PUNNING	present participle of pun	**PURDA**	*n* pl. **-S** purdah
PUNNY	*adj* **-NIER, -NIEST** being or involving a pun	**PURDAH**	*n* pl. **-S** a curtain used in India to seclude women
PUNSTER	*n* pl. **-S** one who is given to punning	**PURE**	*adj* **PURER, PUREST** free from anything different, inferior, or contaminating
PUNT	*v* **-ED, -ING, -S** to propel through water with a pole	**PUREBRED**	*n* pl. **-S** an animal of unmixed stock
PUNTER	*n* pl. **-S** one that punts	**PUREE**	*v* **-REED, -REEING, -REES** to reduce to a thick pulp by cooking and sieving
PUNTO	*n* pl. **-TOS** a hit or thrust in fencing		
		PURELY	*adv* in a pure manner
PUNTY	*n* pl. **-TIES** an iron rod used in glassmaking	**PURENESS**	*n* pl. **-ES** the quality of being pure
		PURER	comparative of pure

PUREST	superlative of pure	**PURRED**	past tense of pur
PURFLE	v **-FLED, -FLING, -FLES** to decorate the border of	**PURRING**	present participle of pur
		PURSE	v **PURSED, PURSING, PURSES** to pucker
PURFLER	n pl. **-S** one that purfles		
PURFLING	n pl. **-S** an ornamental border	**PURSER**	n pl. **-S** an officer in charge of a ship's accounts
PURGE	v **PURGED, PURGING, PURGES** to purify	**PURSIER**	comparative of pursy
PURGER	n pl. **-S** one that purges	**PURSIEST**	superlative of pursy
PURGING	n pl. **-S** the act of purifying	**PURSILY**	adv in a pursy manner
PURI	n pl. **-S** poori	**PURSING**	present participle of purse
PURIFIER	n pl. **-S** one that purifies	**PURSLANE**	n pl. **-S** a common garden herb
PURIFY	v **-FIED, -FYING, -FIES** to free from impurities	**PURSUANT**	adv in accordance
		PURSUE	v **-SUED, -SUING, -SUES** to follow in order to overtake or capture
PURIN	n pl. **-S** purine		
PURINE	n pl. **-S** a chemical compound	**PURSUER**	n pl. **-S** one that pursues
PURISM	n pl. **-S** strict adherence to traditional correctness	**PURSUIT**	n pl. **-S** the act of pursuing
		PURSY	adj **PURSIER, PURSIEST** short of breath
PURIST	n pl. **-S** one who practices purism **PURISTIC** adj		
		PURTY	adj **-TIER, -TIEST** pretty
PURITAN	n pl. **-S** a rigorously moral or religious person	**PURULENT**	adj secreting pus
		PURVEY	v **-ED, -ING, -S** to supply
PURITY	n pl. **-TIES** the quality of being pure	**PURVEYOR**	n pl. **-S** one that purveys
PURL	v **-ED, -ING, -S** to knit with a particular stitch	**PURVIEW**	n pl. **-S** the extent of operation, authority, or concern
PURLIEU	n pl. **-S** an outlying or neighboring area	**PUS**	n pl. **-ES** a viscous fluid formed in infected tissue
PURLIN	n pl. **-S** a horizontal supporting timber	**PUSH**	v **-ED, -ING, -ES** to exert force in order to cause motion away from the force
PURLINE	n pl. **-S** purlin		
PURLING	n pl. **-S** an inversion of stitches in knitting	**PUSHBALL**	n pl. **-S** a type of ball game
		PUSHCART	n pl. **-S** a light cart pushed by hand
PURLOIN	v **-ED, -ING, -S** to steal		
PURPLE	adj **-PLER, -PLEST** of a color intermediate between red and blue	**PUSHDOWN**	n pl. **-S** a store of computer data
		PUSHER	n pl. **-S** one that pushes
PURPLE	v **-PLED, -PLING, -PLES** to make purple	**PUSHFUL**	adj pushy
		PUSHIER	comparative of pushy
PURPLISH	adj somewhat purple	**PUSHIEST**	superlative of pushy
PURPLY	adj purplish	**PUSHILY**	adv in a pushy manner
PURPORT	v **-ED, -ING, -S** to profess or claim	**PUSHOVER**	n pl. **-S** an easily defeated person or team
PURPOSE	v **-POSED, -POSING, -POSES** to resolve to perform or accomplish	**PUSHPIN**	n pl. **-S** a large-headed pin
PURPURA	n pl. **-S** a disease characterized by purple spots on the skin	**PUSHROD**	n pl. **-S** a rod for operating the valves in an engine
PURPURE	n pl. **-S** the heraldic color purple	**PUSHUP**	n pl. **-S** a type of exercise
PURPURIC	adj pertaining to purpura	**PUSHY**	adj **PUSHIER, PUSHIEST** offensively aggressive
PURPURIN	n pl. **-S** a reddish dye		
		PUSLEY	n pl. **-LEYS** pusley
PURR	v **-ED, -ING, -S** to utter a low, vibrant sound	**PUSLIKE**	adj resembling pus

PUSS	*n* pl. **-ES** a cat
PUSSIER	comparative of pussy
PUSSIES	pl. of pussy
PUSSIEST	superlative of pussy
PUSSLEY	*n* pl. **-LEYS** purslane
PUSSLIKE	*adj* catlike
PUSSLY	*n* pl. **-LIES** pussley
PUSSY	*adj* **-SIER, -SIEST** full of pus
PUSSY	*n* pl. **PUSSIES** a cat
PUSSYCAT	*n* pl. **-S** a cat
PUSTULE	*n* pl. **-S** a small elevation of the skin containing pus **PUSTULAR, PUSTULED** *adj*
PUT	*v* **PUT, PUTTING, PUTS** to place in a particular position
PUTAMEN	*n* pl. **-MINA** the hard covering of the kernel of certain fruits
PUTATIVE	*adj* generally regarded as such
PUTDOWN	*n* pl. **-S** a disparaging or snubbing remark
PUTLOG	*n* pl. **-S** a horizontal supporting timber
PUTOFF	*n* pl. **-S** an excuse
PUTON	*n* pl. **-S** a hoax or deception
PUTOUT	*n* pl. **-S** an act of causing an out in baseball
PUTREFY	*v* **-FIED, -FYING, -FIES** to make or become putrid
PUTRID	*adj* being in a decomposed, foul-smelling state **PUTRIDLY** *adv*
PUTSCH	*n* pl. **-ES** a suddenly executed attempt to overthrow a government
PUTT	*v* **-ED, -ING, -S** to hit with a light stroke in golf
PUTTEE	*n* pl. **-S** a strip of cloth wound around the leg
PUTTER	*v* **-ED, -ING, -S** to occupy oneself in a leisurely or ineffective manner
PUTTERER	*n* pl. **-S** one that putters
PUTTI	pl. of putto
PUTTIE	*n* pl. **-S** puttee
PUTTIED	past tense of putty
PUTTIER	*n* pl. **-S** one that putties
PUTTING	present participle of put
PUTTO	*n* pl. **-TI** an infant boy in art
PUTTY	*v* **-TIED, -TYING, -TIES** to fill with a type of cement
PUTZ	*v* **-ED, -ING, -ES** to waste time
PUZZLE	*v* **-ZLED, -ZLING, -ZLES** to cause uncertainty and indecision in
PUZZLER	*n* pl. **-S** something that puzzles
PYA	*n* pl. **-S** a copper coin of Myanmar (Burma)
PYAEMIA	*n* pl. **-S** pyemia **PYAEMIC** *adj*
PYCNIDIA	*n/pl* spore-bearing organs of certain fungi
PYCNOSIS	*n* pl. **-NOSES** pyknosis
PYCNOTIC	*adj* pyknotic
PYE	*n* pl. **-S** a book of ecclesiastical rules in the pre-Reformation English church
PYELITIS	*n* pl. **-TISES** inflammation of the pelvis or the kidney **PYELITIC** *adj*
PYEMIA	*n* pl. **-S** the presence of pus in the blood **PYEMIC** *adj*
PYGIDIUM	*n* pl. **-IA** the posterior region of certain invertebrates **PYGIDIAL** *adj*
PYGMY	*n* pl. **-MIES** a small person **PYGMAEAN, PYGMEAN, PYGMOID, PYGMYISH** *adj*
PYGMYISM	*n* pl. **-S** a stunted or dwarfish condition
PYIC	*adj* pertaining to pus
PYIN	*n* pl. **-S** a protein compound contained in pus
PYJAMA	*n* pl. **-S** pajama
PYKNIC	*n* pl. **-S** a person having a broad, stocky build
PYKNOSIS	*n* pl. **-NOSES** a shrinking and thickening of a cell nucleus
PYKNOTIC	*adj* exhibiting pyknosis
PYLON	*n* pl. **-S** a tall structure marking an entrance or approach
PYLORUS	*n* pl. **-RUSES** or **-RI** the opening between the stomach and the duodenum **PYLORIC** *adj*
PYODERMA	*n* pl. **-S** a pus-causing skin disease
PYOGENIC	*adj* producing pus
PYOID	*adj* puslike
PYORRHEA	*n* pl. **-S** a discharge of pus
PYOSIS	*n* pl. **-OSES** the formation of pus
PYRALID	*n* pl. **-S** a long-legged moth
PYRAMID	*v* **-ED, -ING, -S** to raise or increase by adding amounts gradually
PYRAN	*n* pl. **-S** a chemical compound **PYRANOID** *adj*
PYRANOSE	*n* pl. **-S** a simple sugar
PYRE	*n* pl. **-S** a pile of combustible material

PYRENE	*n* pl. **-S** a putamen
PYRENOID	*n* pl. **-S** a protein body of certain lower organisms
PYRETIC	*adj* pertaining to fever
PYREXIA	*n* pl. **-S** fever **PYREXIAL, PYREXIC** *adj*
PYRIC	*adj* pertaining to burning
PYRIDINE	*n* pl. **-S** a flammable liquid **PYRIDIC** *adj*
PYRIFORM	*adj* pear-shaped
PYRITE	*n* pl. **-S** a metallic sulfide **PYRITIC, PYRITOUS** *adj*
PYRO	*n* pl. **-ROS** a person who has a compulsion to set fires
PYROGEN	*n* pl. **-S** a substance that produces fever
PYROLA	*n* pl. **-S** a perennial herb
PYROLIZE	*v* **-LIZED, -LIZING, -LIZES** to pyrolyze
PYROLOGY	*n* pl. **-GIES** the scientific examination of materials by heat
PYROLYZE	*v* **-LYZED, -LYZING, -LYZES** to affect compounds by the application of heat
PYRONE	*n* pl. **-S** a chemical compound
PYRONINE	*n* pl. **-S** a dye
PYROPE	*n* pl. **-S** a variety of garnet
PYROSIS	*n* pl. **-SISES** heartburn
PYROSTAT	*n* pl. **-S** a thermostat
PYROXENE	*n* pl. **-S** any of a group of minerals common in igneous rocks
PYRRHIC	*n* pl. **-S** a type of metrical foot
PYRROL	*n* pl. **-S** pyrrole
PYRROLE	*n* pl. **-S** a chemical compound **PYRROLIC** *adj*
PYRUVATE	*n* pl. **-S** a chemical salt
PYTHON	*n* pl. **-S** a large snake **PYTHONIC** *adj*
PYURIA	*n* pl. **-S** the presence of pus in the urine
PYX	*n* pl. **-ES** a container in which the eucharistic bread is kept
PYXIDIUM	*n* pl. **-IA** a type of seed vessel
PYXIE	*n* pl. **-S** an evergreen shrub
PYXIS	*n* pl. **PYXIDES** a pyxidium

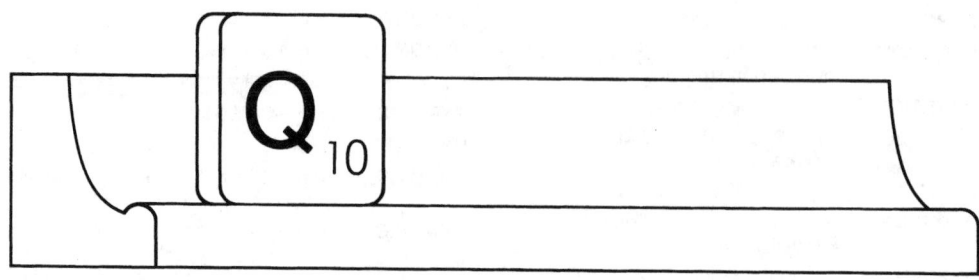

QABALA	*n* pl. **-S** cabala
QABALAH	*n* pl. **-S** cabala
QADI	*n* pl. **-S** cadi
QAID	*n* pl. **-S** caid
QANAT	*n* pl. **-S** a system of underground tunnels and wells in the Middle East
QAT	*n* pl. **-S** kat
QI	*n* pl. **-S** the vital force that in Chinese thought is inherent in all things
QINDAR	*n* pl. **-DARS** or **-DARKA** qintar
QINTAR	*n* pl. **-S** a monetary unit of Albania
QIVIUT	*n* pl. **-S** the wool of a musk-ox
QOPH	*n* pl. **-S** koph
QUA	*adv* in the capacity of
QUAALUDE	*n* pl. **-S** a sedative drug
QUACK	*v* **-ED, -ING, -S** to utter the characteristic cry of a duck
QUACKERY	*n* pl. **-ERIES** fraudulent practice
QUACKISH	*adj* fraudulent
QUACKISM	*n* pl. **-S** quackery
QUACKY	*adj* **QUACKIER, QUACKIEST** resembling the cry of a duck
QUAD	*v* **QUADDED, QUADDING, QUADS** to space out by means of quadrats
QUADPLEX	*n* pl. **-ES** a building having four units
QUADRANS	*n* pl. **-RANTES** an ancient Roman coin
QUADRANT	*n* pl. **-S** a quarter section of a circle
QUADRAT	*n* pl. **-S** a piece of type metal used for filling spaces
QUADRATE	*v* **-RATED, -RATING, -RATES** to correspond or agree
QUADRIC	*n* pl. **-S** a type of geometric surface
QUADRIGA	*n* pl. **-GAE** a chariot drawn by four horses
QUADROON	*n* pl. **-S** a person of one-quarter black ancestry
QUAERE	*n* pl. **-S** a question
QUAESTOR	*n* pl. **-S** an ancient Roman magistrate
QUAFF	*v* **-ED, -ING, -S** to drink deeply
QUAFFER	*n* pl. **-S** one that quaffs
QUAG	*n* pl. **-S** a quagmire
QUAGGA	*n* pl. **-S** an extinct zebralike mammal
QUAGGY	*adj* **-GIER, -GIEST** marshy
QUAGMIRE	*n* pl. **-S** an area of marshy ground
QUAGMIRY	*adj* **-MIRIER, -MIRIEST** marshy
QUAHAUG	*n* pl. **-S** quahog
QUAHOG	*n* pl. **-S** an edible clam
QUAI	*n* pl. **-S** quay
QUAICH	*n* pl. **-S** or **-ES** a small drinking vessel
QUAIGH	*n* pl. **-S** quaich
QUAIL	*v* **-ED, -ING, -S** to cower
QUAINT	*adj* **QUAINTER, QUAINTEST** pleasingly old-fashioned or unfamiliar **QUAINTLY** *adv*
QUAKE	*v* **QUAKED, QUAKING, QUAKES** to shake or vibrate
QUAKER	*n* pl. **-S** one that quakes
QUAKY	*adj* **QUAKIER, QUAKIEST** tending to quake **QUAKILY** *adv*
QUALE	*n* pl. **-LIA** a property considered apart from things having the property
QUALIFY	*v* **-FIED, -FYING, -FIES** to make suitable or capable
QUALITY	*n* pl. **-TIES** a characteristic or attribute
QUALM	*n* pl. **-S** a feeling of doubt or misgiving
QUALMISH	*adj* having qualms

QUALMY *adj* **QUALMIER, QUALMIEST** qualmish

QUAMASH *n* pl. **-ES** camass

QUANDANG *n* pl. **-S** quandong

QUANDARY *n* pl. **-RIES** a dilemma

QUANDONG *n* pl. **-S** an Australian tree

QUANGO *n* pl. **-GOS** a public administrative board

QUANT *v* **-ED, -ING, -S** to propel through water with a pole

QUANTA pl. of quantum

QUANTAL *adj* pertaining to a quantum

QUANTIC *n* pl. **-S** a type of mathematical function

QUANTIFY *v* **-FIED, -FYING, -FIES** to determine the quantity of

QUANTILE *n* pl. **-S** any of the values of a random variable that divides a frequency distribution

QUANTITY *n* pl. **-TIES** a specified or indefinite amount or number

QUANTIZE *v* **-TIZED, -TIZING, -TIZES** to limit the possible values of to a discrete set

QUANTONG *n* pl. **-S** quandong

QUANTUM *n* pl. **-TA** a fundamental unit of energy

QUARE *adj* queer

QUARK *n* pl. **-S** a hypothetical atomic particle

QUARREL *v* **-RELED, -RELING, -RELS** or **-RELLED, -RELLING, -RELS** to engage in an angry dispute

QUARRIER *n* pl. **-S** one that quarries

QUARRY *v* **-RIED, -RYING, -RIES** to dig stone from an excavation

QUART *n* pl. **-S** a liquid measure of capacity

QUARTAN *n* pl. **-S** a recurrent malarial fever

QUARTE *n* pl. **-S** a fencing thrust

QUARTER *v* **-ED, -ING, -S** to divide into four equal parts

QUARTERN *n* pl. **-S** one-fourth of something

QUARTET *n* pl. **-S** a group of four

QUARTIC *n* pl. **-S** a type of mathematical function

QUARTIER *n* pl. **-S** a district in a French city

QUARTILE *n* pl. **-S** a portion of a frequency distribution

QUARTO *n* pl. **-TOS** the size of a piece of paper cut four from a sheet

QUARTZ *n* pl. **-ES** a mineral

QUASAR *n* pl. **-S** a distant celestial object emitting strong radio waves

QUASH *v* **-ED, -ING, -ES** to suppress completely

QUASHER *n* pl. **-S** one that quashes

QUASI *adj* similar but not exactly the same

QUASS *n* pl. **-ES** kvass

QUASSIA *n* pl. **-S** a tropical tree

QUASSIN *n* pl. **-S** a medicinal compound obtained from the wood of a quassia

QUATE *adj* quiet

QUATORZE *n* pl. **-S** a set of four cards of the same denomination scoring fourteen points

QUATRAIN *n* pl. **-S** a stanza of four lines

QUATRE *n* pl. **-S** the four at cards or dice

QUAVER *v* **-ED, -ING, -S** to quiver

QUAVERER *n* pl. **-S** one that quavers

QUAVERY *adj* quivery

QUAY *n* pl. **QUAYS** a wharf **QUAYLIKE** *adj*

QUAYAGE *n* pl. **-S** a charge for the use of a quay

QUAYSIDE *n* pl. **-S** the area adjacent to a quay

QUBIT *n* pl. **-S** a quantum bit

QUBYTE *n* pl. **-S** a sequence of eight quantum bits

QUEAN *n* pl. **-S** a harlot

QUEASY *adj* **-SIER, -SIEST** easily nauseated **QUEASILY** *adv*

QUEAZY *adj* **-ZIER, -ZIEST** queasy

QUEEN *v* **-ED, -ING, -S** to make a queen (a female monarch) of

QUEENDOM *n* pl. **-S** the area ruled by a queen

QUEENLY *adj* **-LIER, -LIEST** of or befitting a queen

QUEER *adj* **QUEERER, QUEEREST** deviating from the expected or normal

QUEER *v* **-ED, -ING, -S** to spoil the effect or success of

QUEERISH *adj* somewhat queer

QUEERLY *adv* in a queer manner

QUELEA *n* pl. **-S** an African weaverbird

QUELL *v* **-ED, -ING, -S** to suppress

QUELLER *n* pl. **-S** one that quells

QUENCH	*v* **-ED, -ING, -ES** to put out or extinguish
QUENCHER	*n* pl. **-S** one that quenches
QUENELLE	*n* pl. **-S** a type of dumpling
QUERCINE	*adj* pertaining to oaks
QUERIDA	*n* pl. **-S** a female sweetheart
QUERIED	past tense of query
QUERIER	*n* pl. **-S** a querist
QUERIES	present 3d person sing. of query
QUERIST	*n* pl. **-S** one who queries
QUERN	*n* pl. **-S** a hand-turned grain mill
QUERY	*v* **-RIED, -RYING, -RIES** to question
QUEST	*v* **-ED, -ING, -S** to make a search
QUESTER	*n* pl. **-S** one that quests
QUESTION	*v* **-ED, -ING, -S** to put a question (an inquiry) to
QUESTOR	*n* pl. **-S** quaestor
QUETZAL	*n* pl. **-S** or **-ES** a tropical bird
QUEUE	*v* **QUEUED, QUEUING** or **QUEUEING, QUEUES** to line up
QUEUER	*n* pl. **-S** one that queues
QUEY	*n* pl. **QUEYS** a young cow
QUEZAL	*n* pl. **-S** or **-ES** quetzal
QUIBBLE	*v* **-BLED, -BLING, -BLES** to argue over trivialities
QUIBBLER	*n* pl. **-S** one that quibbles
QUICHE	*n* pl. **-S** a custard-filled pastry
QUICK	*adj* **QUICKER, QUICKEST** acting or capable of acting with speed
QUICK	*n* pl. **-S** a sensitive area of flesh
QUICKEN	*v* **-ED, -ING, -S** to speed up
QUICKIE	*n* pl. **-S** something done quickly
QUICKLY	*adv* in a quick manner
QUICKSET	*n* pl. **-S** a plant suitable for hedges
QUID	*n* pl. **-S** a portion of something to be chewed
QUIDDITY	*n* pl. **-TIES** the true nature of a thing
QUIDNUNC	*n* pl. **-S** a nosy person
QUIET	*adj* **-ETER, -ETEST** making little or no noise
QUIET	*v* **-ED, -ING, -S** to cause to be quiet
QUIETEN	*v* **-ED, -ING, -S** to quiet
QUIETER	*n* pl. **-S** one that quiets
QUIETISM	*n* pl. **-S** a form of religious mysticism
QUIETIST	*n* pl. **-S** an advocate of quietism
QUIETLY	*adv* in a quiet manner
QUIETUDE	*n* pl. **-S** a state of tranquillity
QUIETUS	*n* pl. **-ES** a final settlement
QUIFF	*n* pl. **-S** a forelock
QUILL	*v* **-ED, -ING, -S** to press small ridges in
QUILLAI	*n* pl. **-S** an evergreen tree
QUILLAIA	*n* pl. **-S** a quillai
QUILLAJA	*n* pl. **-S** a quillai
QUILLET	*n* pl. **-S** a trivial distinction
QUILLING	*n* pl. **-S** material that is quilled
QUILT	*v* **-ED, -ING, -S** to stitch together with padding in between
QUILTER	*n* pl. **-S** one that quilts
QUILTING	*n* pl. **-S** material that is used for making quilts
QUIN	*n* pl. **-S** a quintuplet
QUINARY	*n* pl. **-RIES** a group of five
QUINATE	*adj* arranged in groups of five
QUINCE	*n* pl. **-S** an apple-like fruit
QUINCUNX	*n* pl. **-ES** an arrangement of five objects
QUINELA	*n* pl. **-S** quinella
QUINELLA	*n* pl. **-S** a type of bet in horse racing
QUINIC	*adj* pertaining to quinine
QUINIELA	*n* pl. **-S** quinella
QUININ	*n* pl. **-S** quinine
QUININA	*n* pl. **-S** quinine
QUININE	*n* pl. **-S** a medicinal alkaloid
QUINNAT	*n* pl. **-S** a food fish
QUINOA	*n* pl. **-S** a weedy plant
QUINOID	*n* pl. **-S** a chemical compound
QUINOL	*n* pl. **-S** a chemical compound
QUINOLIN	*n* pl. **-S** a chemical compound
QUINONE	*n* pl. **-S** a chemical compound
QUINSY	*n* pl. **-SIES** an inflammation of the tonsils **QUINSIED** *adj*
QUINT	*n* pl. **-S** a group of five
QUINTA	*n* pl. **-S** a country estate in Portugal or Latin America
QUINTAIN	*n* pl. **-S** an object used as a target in a medieval sport
QUINTAL	*n* pl. **-S** a unit of weight
QUINTAN	*n* pl. **-S** a recurrent fever
QUINTAR	*n* pl. **-S** qintar

QUINTE *n* pl. **-S** a position in fencing

QUINTET *n* pl. **-S** a group of five

QUINTIC *n* pl. **-S** a type of mathematical function

QUINTILE *n* pl. **-S** a portion of a frequency distribution

QUINTIN *n* pl. **-S** a fine linen

QUIP *v* **QUIPPED, QUIPPING, QUIPS** to make witty remarks

QUIPPER *n* pl. **-S** one that quips

QUIPPISH *adj* witty

QUIPPU *n* pl. **-S** quipu

QUIPPY *adj* **-PIER, -PIEST** witty

QUIPSTER *n* pl. **-S** one that quips

QUIPU *n* pl. **-S** an ancient calculating device

QUIRE *v* **QUIRED, QUIRING, QUIRES** to arrange sheets of paper in sets of twenty-four

QUIRK *v* **-ED, -ING, -S** to twist

QUIRKISH *adj* quirky

QUIRKY *adj* **QUIRKIER, QUIRKIEST** peculiar **QUIRKILY** *adv*

QUIRT *v* **-ED, -ING, -S** to strike with a riding whip

QUISLING *n* pl. **-S** a traitor who aids the invaders of his country

QUIT *v* **QUITTED, QUITTING, QUITS** to end one's engagement in or occupation with

QUITCH *n* pl. **-ES** a perennial grass

QUITE *adv* to the fullest extent

QUITRENT *n* pl. **-S** a fixed rent due from a socage tenant

QUITTED past tense of quit

QUITTER *n* pl. **-S** one that quits

QUITTING present participle of quit

QUITTOR *n* pl. **-S** an inflammation of an animal's hoof

QUIVER *v* **-ED, -ING, -S** to shake with a slight but rapid motion

QUIVERER *n* pl. **-S** one that quivers

QUIVERY *adj* marked by quivering

QUIXOTE *n* pl. **-S** a quixotic person

QUIXOTIC *adj* extremely idealistic

QUIXOTRY *n* pl. **-TRIES** quixotic action or thought

QUIZ *v* **QUIZZED, QUIZZING, QUIZZES** to test the knowledge of by asking questions

QUIZZER *n* pl. **-S** one that quizzes

QUOD *n* pl. **-S** a prison

QUOHOG *n* pl. **-S** quahog

QUOIN *v* **-ED, -ING, -S** to secure with a type of wedge

QUOIT *v* **-ED, -ING, -S** to play a throwing game similar to ringtoss

QUOKKA *n* pl. **-S** a short-tailed wallaby

QUOLL *n* pl. **-S** a small spotted marsupial

QUOMODO *n* pl. **-DOS** a means or manner

QUONDAM *adj* that once was

QUORUM *n* pl. **-S** a particularly chosen group

QUOTA *n* pl. **-S** a proportional part or share

QUOTE *v* **QUOTED, QUOTING, QUOTES** to repeat the words of **QUOTABLE** *adj* **QUOTABLY** *adv*

QUOTER *n* pl. **-S** one that quotes

QUOTH *v* said — QUOTH is the only accepted form of this verb; it cannot be conjugated

QUOTHA *interj* — used to express surprise or sarcasm

QUOTIENT *n* pl. **-S** the number resulting from the division of one number by another

QUOTING present participle of quote

QURSH *n* pl. **-ES** a monetary unit of Saudi Arabia

QURUSH *n* pl. **-ES** qursh

QWERTY *n* pl. **-TYS** a standard keyboard

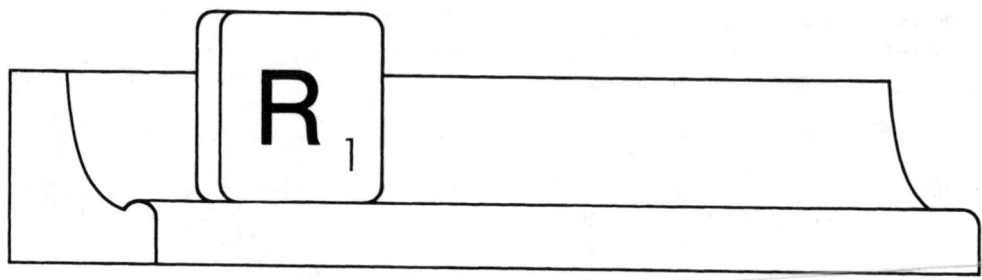

RABAT   *n* pl. **-S** a dickey attached to a clerical collar

RABATO   *n* pl. **-TOS** a wide, lace-edged collar

RABBET   *v* **-ED, -ING, -S** to cut a groove in

RABBI   *n* pl. **-S** or **-ES** a Jewish spiritual leader

RABBIN   *n* pl. **-S** rabbi

RABBINIC   *adj* pertaining to rabbis

RABBIT   *v* **-ED, -ING, -S** to hunt rabbits (rodent-like mammals)

RABBITER   *n* pl. **-S** one that rabbits

RABBITRY   *n* pl. **-RIES** a place where rabbits are kept

RABBITY   *adj* resembling a rabbit

RABBLE   *v* **-BLED, -BLING, -BLES** to mob

RABBLER   *n* pl. **-S** an iron bar used in puddling

RABBONI   *n* pl. **-S** master; teacher — used as a Jewish title of respect

RABIC   *adj* pertaining to rabies

RABID   *adj* affected with rabies **RABIDLY** *adv*

RABIDITY   *n* pl. **-TIES** the state of being rabid

RABIES   *n* pl. **RABIES** an infectious virus disease **RABIETIC** *adj*

RACCOON   *n* pl. **-S** a carnivorous mammal

RACE   *v* **RACED, RACING, RACES** to compete in a contest of speed

RACEMATE   *n* pl. **-S** a chemical salt

RACEME   *n* pl. **-S** a mode of arrangement of flowers along an axis **RACEMED** *adj*

RACEMIC   *adj* pertaining to a racemate

RACEMISM   *n* pl. **-S** the state of being racemic

RACEMIZE   *v* **-MIZED, -MIZING, -MIZES** to convert into a racemic compound

RACEMOID   *adj* pertaining to a raceme

RACEMOSE   *adj* having the form of a raceme

RACEMOUS   *adj* racemose

RACER   *n* pl. **-S** one that races

RACEWALK   *v* **-ED, -ING, -S** to walk for speed while maintaining foot contact with the ground and keeping the supporting leg straight

RACEWAY   *n* pl. **-WAYS** a channel for conducting water

RACHET   *v* **-ED, -ING, -S** ratchet

RACHILLA   *n* pl. **-LAE** the central stalk of a grass spikelet

RACHIS   *n* pl. **-CHISES** or **-CHIDES** the spinal column **RACHIAL** *adj*

RACHITIS   *n* pl. **-TIDES** rickets **RACHITIC** *adj*

RACIAL   *adj* pertaining to an ethnic group **RACIALLY** *adv*

RACIER   comparative of racy

RACIEST   superlative of racy

RACILY   *adv* in a racy manner

RACINESS   *n* pl. **-ES** the quality of being racy

RACING   *n* pl. **-S** the sport of engaging in contests of speed

RACISM   *n* pl. **-S** a doctrine of racial superiority

RACIST   *n* pl. **-S** an advocate of racism

RACK   *v* **-ED, -ING, -S** to place in a type of framework

RACKER   *n* pl. **-S** one that racks

RACKET   *v* **-ED, -ING, -S** to make a loud noise

RACKETY   *adj* **-ETIER, -ETIEST** noisy

RACKFUL   *n* pl. **-S** as much as a rack can hold

RACKLE   *adj* impetuous; rash

RACKWORK   *n* pl. **-S** a type of mechanism

RACLETTE   *n* pl. **-S** a cheese dish

RACON   *n* pl. **-S** a type of radar transmitter

RACOON   *n* pl. **-S** raccoon

RACQUET *n* pl. **-S** a lightweight implement used in various ball games

RACY *adj* **RACIER, RACIEST** bordering on impropriety or indecency

RAD *v* **RADDED, RADDING, RADS** to fear

RADAR *n* pl. **-S** an electronic locating device

RADDLE *v* **-DLED, -DLING, -DLES** to weave together

RADIABLE *adj* capable of radiating

RADIAL *n* pl. **-S** a part diverging from a center

RADIALE *n* pl. **-LIA** a bone of the carpus

RADIALLY *adv* in a diverging manner

RADIAN *n* pl. **-S** a unit of angular measure

RADIANCE *n* pl. **-S** brightness

RADIANCY *n* pl. **-CIES** radiance

RADIANT *n* pl. **-S** a point from which rays are emitted

RADIATE *v* **-ATED, -ATING, -ATES** to emit rays

RADIATOR *n* pl. **-S** a heating device

RADICAL *n* pl. **-S** a group of atoms that acts as a unit in chemical compounds

RADICAND *n* pl. **-S** a quantity in mathematics

RADICATE *v* **-CATED, -CATING, -CATES** to cause to take root

RADICEL *n* pl. **-S** a rootlet

RADICES a pl. of radix

RADICLE *n* pl. **-S** a part of a plant embryo

RADII a pl. of radius

RADIO *v* **-ED, -ING, -S** to transmit by radio (an apparatus for wireless communication)

RADIOMAN *n* pl. **-MEN** a radio operator or technician

RADISH *n* pl. **-ES** a pungent, edible root

RADIUM *n* pl. **-S** a radioactive element

RADIUS *n* pl. **-DIUSES** or **-DII** a straight line from the center of a circle to the circumference

RADIX *n* pl. **-DIXES** or **-DICES** the root of a plant

RADOME *n* pl. **-S** a domelike device used to shelter a radar antenna

RADON *n* pl. **-S** a radioactive element

RADULA *n* pl. **-LAS** or **-LAE** a tonguelike organ of mollusks **RADULAR** *adj*

RADWASTE *n* pl. **-S** radioactive waste

RAFF *n* pl. **-S** riffraff

RAFFIA *n* pl. **-S** a palm tree

RAFFISH *adj* tawdry

RAFFLE *v* **-FLED, -FLING, -FLES** to dispose of by a form of lottery

RAFFLER *n* pl. **-S** one that raffles

RAFT *v* **-ED, -ING, -S** to transport on a raft (a type of buoyant structure)

RAFTER *n* pl. **-S** a supporting beam

RAFTERED *adj* furnished with rafters

RAFTSMAN *n* pl. **-MEN** one who manages a raft

RAG *v* **RAGGED, RAGGING, RAGS** to scold

RAGA *n* pl. **-S** a Hindu musical form

RAGBAG *n* pl. **-S** a bag for storing scraps of cloth

RAGE *v* **RAGED, RAGING, RAGES** to act or speak with violent anger

RAGEE *n* pl. **-S** ragi

RAGG *n* pl. **-S** a wool fiber

RAGGED *adj* **-GEDER, -GEDEST** tattered **RAGGEDLY** *adv*

RAGGEDY *adj* **-GEDIER, -GEDIEST** somewhat ragged

RAGGEE *n* pl. **-S** ragi

RAGGIES pl. of raggy

RAGGING present participle of rag

RAGGLE *n* pl. **-S** a groove cut in masonry

RAGGY *n* pl. **-GIES** ragi

RAGI *n* pl. **-S** an East Indian cereal grass

RAGING present participle of rage

RAGINGLY *adv* in a furious manner

RAGLAN *n* pl. **-S** a type of overcoat

RAGMAN *n* pl. **-MEN** one who gathers and sells scraps of cloth

RAGOUT *v* **-ED, -ING, -S** to make into a highly seasoned stew

RAGTAG *n* pl. **-S** riffraff

RAGTIME *n* pl. **-S** a style of American dance music

RAGTOP *n* pl. **-S** a convertible automobile

RAGWEED *n* pl. **-S** a weedy herb

RAGWORT *n* pl. **-S** a flowering plant

RAH *interj* — used to cheer on a team or player

RAI *n* pl. **-S** a style of popular Algerian music

RAIA	*n* pl. **-S** rayah
RAID	*v* **-ED, -ING, -S** to make a sudden assault on
RAIDER	*n* pl. **-S** one that raids
RAIL	*v* **-ED, -ING, -S** to scold in abusive or insolent language
RAILBIRD	*n* pl. **-S** a racing enthusiast
RAILBUS	*n* pl. **-BUSES** or **-BUSSES** a passenger car equipped for operation on rails
RAILCAR	*n* pl. **-S** a railroad car
RAILER	*n* pl. **-S** one that rails
RAILHEAD	*n* pl. **-S** the end of a railroad line
RAILING	*n* pl. **-S** a fence-like barrier
RAILLERY	*n* pl. **-LERIES** good-natured teasing
RAILROAD	*v* **-ED, -ING, -S** to transport by railroad (a type of road on which locomotives are run)
RAILWAY	*n* pl. **-WAYS** a railroad
RAIMENT	*n* pl. **-S** clothing
RAIN	*v* **-ED, -ING, -S** to fall like rain (drops of water condensed from clouds)
RAINBAND	*n* pl. **-S** a dark band in the solar spectrum
RAINBIRD	*n* pl. **-S** a type of bird
RAINBOW	*n* pl. **-S** an arc of spectral colors formed in the sky
RAINCOAT	*n* pl. **-S** a waterproof coat
RAINDROP	*n* pl. **-S** a drop of rain
RAINFALL	*n* pl. **-S** a fall of rain
RAINIER	comparative of rainy
RAINIEST	superlative of rainy
RAINILY	*adv* in a rainy manner
RAINLESS	*adj* having no rain
RAINOUT	*n* pl. **-S** atomic fallout occurring in precipitation
RAINWASH	*v* **-ED, -ING, -ES** to wash material downhill by rain
RAINWEAR	*n* pl. **RAINWEAR** waterproof clothing
RAINY	*adj* **RAINIER, RAINIEST** marked by rain
RAISE	*v* **RAISED, RAISING, RAISES** to move to a higher position **RAISABLE** *adj*
RAISER	*n* pl. **-S** one that raises
RAISIN	*n* pl. **-S** a dried grape **RAISINY** *adj*
RAISING	*n* pl. **-S** an elevation

RAISONNE	*adj* arranged systematically
RAITA	*n* pl. **-S** an Indian salad made with yogurt and chopped vegetables or fruits
RAJ	*n* pl. **-ES** dominion; sovereignty
RAJA	*n* pl. **-S** rajah
RAJAH	*n* pl. **-S** a king or prince in India
RAKE	*v* **RAKED, RAKING, RAKES** to gather with a toothed implement
RAKEE	*n* pl. **-S** raki
RAKEHELL	*n* pl. **-S** a man lacking in moral restraint
RAKEOFF	*n* pl. **-S** a share of profits
RAKER	*n* pl. **-S** one that rakes
RAKI	*n* pl. **-S** a Turkish liqueur
RAKING	present participle of rake
RAKISH	*adj* dapper **RAKISHLY** *adv*
RAKU	*n* pl. **-S** a form of Japanese glazed pottery
RALE	*n* pl. **-S** an abnormal respiratory sound
RALLIER	*n* pl. **-S** one that rallies
RALLINE	*adj* pertaining to a family of marsh birds
RALLY	*v* **-LIED, -LYING, -LIES** to call together for a common purpose
RALLYE	*n* pl. **-S** a type of automobile race
RALLYING	*n* pl. **-S** the sport of driving in rallyes
RALLYIST	*n* pl. **-S** a participant in a rallye
RALPH	*v* **-ED, -ING, -S** to vomit
RAM	*v* **RAMMED, RAMMING, RAMS** to strike with great force
RAMADA	*n* pl. **-S** a roofed, open-sided shelter
RAMAL	*adj* pertaining to a ramus
RAMATE	*adj* having branches
RAMBLA	*n* pl. **-S** a dry ravine
RAMBLE	*v* **-BLED, -BLING, -BLES** to wander
RAMBLER	*n* pl. **-S** one that rambles
RAMBUTAN	*n* pl. **-S** the edible fruit of a Malayan tree
RAMEE	*n* pl. **-S** ramie
RAMEKIN	*n* pl. **-S** a cheese dish
RAMEN	*n* pl. **RAMEN** Japanese noodles in a broth with bits of meat and vegetables

RAMENTUM *n* pl. **-TA** a scale formed on the surface of leaves

RAMEQUIN *n* pl. **-S** ramekin

RAMET *n* pl. **-S** an independent member of a clone

RAMI pl. of ramus

RAMIE *n* pl. **-S** an Asian shrub

RAMIFORM *adj* shaped like a branch

RAMIFY *v* **-FIED, -FYING, -FIES** to divide into branches

RAMILIE *n* pl. **-S** ramillie

RAMILLIE *n* pl. **-S** a type of wig

RAMJET *n* pl. **-S** a type of engine

RAMMED past tense of ram

RAMMER *n* pl. **-S** one that rams

RAMMIER comparative of rammy

RAMMIEST superlative of rammy

RAMMING present participle of ram

RAMMISH *adj* resembling a ram (a male sheep)

RAMMY *adj* **-MIER, -MIEST** rammish

RAMONA *n* pl. **-S** a plant of the mint family

RAMOSE *adj* having many branches **RAMOSELY** *adv*

RAMOSITY *n* pl. **-TIES** the state of being ramose

RAMOUS *adj* ramose

RAMP *v* **-ED, -ING, -S** to rise or stand on the hind legs

RAMPAGE *v* **-PAGED, -PAGING, -PAGES** to move about wildly or violently

RAMPAGER *n* pl. **-S** one that rampages

RAMPANCY *n* pl. **-CIES** the state of being rampant

RAMPANT *adj* unrestrained

RAMPART *v* **-ED, -ING, -S** to furnish with a fortifying embankment

RAMPIKE *n* pl. **-S** a standing dead tree

RAMPION *n* pl. **-S** a European plant

RAMPOLE *n* pl. **-S** rampike

RAMROD *v* **-RODDED, -RODDING, -RODS** to supervise

RAMSHORN *n* pl. **-S** a snail used as an aquarium scavenger

RAMSON *n* pl. **-S** a broad-leaved garlic

RAMTIL *n* pl. **-S** a tropical plant

RAMTILLA *n* pl. **-S** ramtil

RAMULOSE *adj* having many small branches

RAMULOUS *adj* ramulose

RAMUS *n* pl. **-MI** a branch-like part of a structure

RAN past tense of run and rin

RANCE *n* pl. **-S** a variety of marble

RANCH *v* **-ED, -ING, -ES** to work on a ranch (an establishment for raising livestock)

RANCHER *n* pl. **-S** one that owns or works on a ranch

RANCHERO *n* pl. **-ROS** a rancher

RANCHMAN *n* pl. **-MEN** a rancher

RANCHO *n* pl. **-CHOS** a ranch

RANCID *adj* having an unpleasant odor or taste **RANCIDLY** *adv*

RANCOR *n* pl. **-S** bitter and vindictive enmity **RANCORED** *adj*

RANCOUR *n* pl. **-S** rancor

RAND *n* pl. **-S** a strip of leather at the heel of a shoe

RANDAN *n* pl. **-S** a boat rowed by three persons

RANDIER comparative of randy

RANDIES pl. of randy

RANDOM *n* pl. **-S** a haphazard course

RANDOMLY *adv* in a haphazard manner

RANDY *adj* **-DIER, -DIEST** lustful

RANDY *n* pl. **RANDIES** a rude person

RANEE *n* pl. **-S** rani

RANG past tense of ring

RANGE *v* **RANGED, RANGING, RANGES** to place in a particular order

RANGER *n* pl. **-S** an officer supervising the care of a forest

RANGY *adj* **RANGIER, RANGIEST** tall and slender

RANI *n* pl. **-S** the wife of a rajah

RANID *n* pl. **-S** any of a large family of frogs

RANK *adj* **RANKER, RANKEST** strong and disagreeable in odor or taste

RANK *v* **-ED, -ING, -S** to determine the relative position of

RANKER *n* pl. **-S** an enlisted soldier

RANKING *n* pl. **-S** a listing of ranked individuals

RANKISH *adj* somewhat rank

RANKLE *v* **-KLED, -KLING, -KLES** to cause irritation or resentment in

RANKLESS *adj* having no ranks

RANKLY *adv* in a rank manner

RANKNESS *n* pl. **-ES** the state of being rank

RANPIKE *n* pl. **-S** rampike

RANSACK *v* **-ED, -ING, -S** to search thoroughly

RANSOM *v* **-ED, -ING, -S** to obtain the release of by paying a demanded price

RANSOMER *n* pl. **-S** one that ransoms

RANT *v* **-ED, -ING, -S** to speak in a loud or vehement manner

RANTER *n* pl. **-S** one that rants

RANULA *n* pl. **-S** a cyst formed under the tongue **RANULAR** *adj*

RAP *v* **RAPPED, RAPPING, RAPS** to strike sharply

RAPACITY *n* pl. **-TIES** the quality of being ravenous

RAPE *v* **RAPED, RAPING, RAPES** to force to submit to sexual intercourse

RAPER *n* pl. **-S** a rapist

RAPESEED *n* pl. **-S** the seed of a European herb

RAPHE *n* pl. **RAPHES** or **RAPHAE** a seamlike ridge between two halves of an organ or part

RAPHIA *n* pl. **-S** raffia

RAPHIDE *n* pl. **-S** a needle-shaped crystal occurring in plant cells

RAPHIS *n* pl. **-PHIDES** raphide

RAPID *adj* **-IDER, -IDEST** fast-moving **RAPIDLY** *adv*

RAPID *n* pl. **-S** a fast-moving part of a river

RAPIDITY *n* pl. **-TIES** swiftness

RAPIER *n* pl. **-S** a long, slender sword **RAPIERED** *adj*

RAPINE *n* pl. **-S** the taking of property by force

RAPING present participle of rape

RAPINI *n/pl* rappini

RAPIST *n* pl. **-S** one who rapes

RAPPAREE *n* pl. **-S** a plunderer

RAPPED past tense of rap

RAPPEE *n* pl. **-S** a strong snuff

RAPPEL *v* **-PELED, -PELING, -PELS** or **-PELLED, -PELLING, -PELS** to descend from a steep height by means of a rope

RAPPEN *n* pl. **RAPPEN** a monetary unit of Switzerland

RAPPER *n* pl. **-S** one that raps

RAPPING present participle of rap

RAPPINI *n/pl* immature turnip plants

RAPPORT *n* pl. **-S** a harmonious relationship

RAPT *adj* deeply engrossed **RAPTLY** *adv*

RAPTNESS *n* pl. **-ES** the state of being rapt

RAPTOR *n* pl. **-S** a bird of prey

RAPTURE *v* **-TURED, -TURING, -TURES** to fill with great joy

RARE *adj* **RARER, RAREST** occurring infrequently

RARE *v* **RARED, RARING, RARES** to be enthusiastic

RAREBIT *n* pl. **-S** a cheese dish

RAREFIER *n* pl. **-S** one that rarefies

RAREFY *v* **-EFIED, -EFYING, -EFIES** to make less dense

RARELY *adv* not often

RARENESS *n* pl. **-ES** the quality of being rare

RARER comparative of rare

RARERIPE *n* pl. **-S** a fruit that ripens early

RAREST superlative of rare

RARIFY *v* **-FIED, -FYING, -FIES** to rarefy

RARING *adj* full of enthusiasm

RARITY *n* pl. **-TIES** rareness

RAS *n* pl. **-ES** an Ethiopian prince

RASBORA *n* pl. **-S** a tropical fish

RASCAL *n* pl. **-S** an unscrupulous or dishonest person

RASCALLY *adj* characteristic of a rascal

RASE *v* **RASED, RASING, RASES** to raze

RASER *n* pl. **-S** one that rases

RASH *adj* **RASHER, RASHEST** acting without due caution or forethought

RASH *n* pl. **-ES** a skin eruption **RASHLIKE** *adj*

RASHER *n* pl. **-S** a thin slice of meat

RASHLY *adv* in a rash manner

RASHNESS *n* pl. **-ES** the state of being rash

RASING present participle of rase

RASORIAL *adj* habitually scratching the ground for food

RASP *v* **-ED, -ING, -S** to rub with something rough

RASPER	*n* pl. **-S** one that rasps	**RATING**	*n* pl. **-S** relative estimate or evaluation
RASPING	*n* pl. **-S** a tiny piece of wood removed with a coarse file	**RATIO**	*n* pl. **-TIOS** a proportional relationship
RASPISH	*adj* irritable	**RATION**	*v* **-ED, -ING, -S** to distribute in fixed portions
RASPY	*adj* **RASPIER, RASPIEST** rough		
RASSLE	*v* **-SLED, -SLING, -SLES** to wrestle	**RATIONAL**	*n* pl. **-S** a number that can be expressed as a quotient of integers
RASTER	*n* pl. **-S** the area reproducing images on the picture tube of a television set	**RATITE**	*n* pl. **-S** a flightless bird
		RATLIKE	*adj* resembling a rat
RASURE	*n* pl. **-S** erasure	**RATLIN**	*n* pl. **-S** ratline
RAT	*v* **RATTED, RATTING, RATS** to hunt rats (long-tailed rodents)	**RATLINE**	*n* pl. **-S** one of the ropes forming the steps of a ship's rope ladder
RATABLE	*adj* capable of being rated **RATABLY** *adv*	**RATO**	*n* pl. **-TOS** a rocket-assisted airplane takeoff
RATABLES	*n/pl* taxable properties	**RATOON**	*v* **-ED, -ING, -S** to sprout from a root planted the previous year
RATAFEE	*n* pl. **-S** ratafia		
RATAFIA	*n* pl. **-S** an almond-flavored liqueur	**RATOONER**	*n* pl. **-S** a plant that ratoons
RATAL	*n* pl. **-S** an amount on which rates are assessed	**RATSBANE**	*n* pl. **-S** rat poison
		RATTAIL	*n* pl. **-S** a marine fish
RATAN	*n* pl. **-S** rattan	**RATTAN**	*n* pl. **-S** a palm tree
RATANY	*n* pl. **-NIES** rhatany	**RATTED**	past tense of rat
RATAPLAN	*v* **-PLANNED, -PLANNING, -PLANS** to make a rapidly repeating sound	**RATTEEN**	*n* pl. **-S** a coarse woolen fabric
		RATTEN	*v* **-ED, -ING, -S** to harass
RATATAT	*n* pl. **-S** a quick, sharp rapping sound	**RATTENER**	*n* pl. **-S** one that rattens
		RATTER	*n* pl. **-S** an animal used for catching rats
RATBAG	*n* pl. **-S** an eccentric or disagreeable person	**RATTIER**	comparative of ratty
RATCH	*n* pl. **-ES** a mechanism that allows motion in one direction only	**RATTIEST**	superlative of ratty
		RATTING	present participle of rat
RATCHET	*v* **-ED, -ING, -S** to increase or decrease by small amounts	**RATTISH**	*adj* ratlike
RATE	*v* **RATED, RATING, RATES** to estimate the value of	**RATTLE**	*v* **-TLED, -TLING, -TLES** to make a quick succession of short, sharp sounds
RATEABLE	*adj* ratable **RATEABLY** *adv*		
RATEL	*n* pl. **-S** a carnivorous mammal	**RATTLER**	*n* pl. **-S** one that rattles
RATER	*n* pl. **-S** one that rates	**RATTLING**	*n* pl. **-S** ratline
RATFINK	*n* pl. **-S** a contemptible person	**RATTLY**	*adj* tending to rattle
RATFISH	*n* pl. **-ES** a marine fish	**RATTON**	*n* pl. **-S** a rat
RATH	*adj* rathe	**RATTOON**	*v* **-ED, -ING, -S** to ratoon
RATHE	*adj* appearing or ripening early	**RATTRAP**	*n* pl. **-S** a trap for catching rats
RATHER	*adv* preferably	**RATTY**	*adj* **-TIER, -TIEST** infested with rats
RATHOLE	*n* pl. **-S** a hole made by a rat		
RATICIDE	*n* pl. **-S** a substance for killing rats	**RAUCITY**	*n* pl. **-TIES** the state of being raucous
RATIFIER	*n* pl. **-S** one that ratifies		
RATIFY	*v* **-FIED, -FYING, -FIES** to approve and sanction formally	**RAUCOUS**	*adj* loud and unruly
		RAUNCH	*n* pl. **-ES** vulgarity
RATINE	*n* pl. **-S** a heavy fabric woven loosely	**RAUNCHY**	*adj* **-CHIER, -CHIEST** slovenly

RAVAGE	v **-AGED, -AGING, -AGES** to destroy	**RAW**	adj **RAWER, RAWEST** uncooked
RAVAGER	n pl. **-S** one that ravages	**RAW**	n pl. **-S** a sore or irritated spot
RAVE	v **RAVED, RAVING, RAVES** to speak irrationally or incoherently	**RAWBONED**	adj having little flesh
		RAWHIDE	v **-HIDED, -HIDING, -HIDES** to beat with a type of whip
RAVEL	v **-ELED, -ELING, -ELS** or **-ELLED, -ELLING, -ELS** to separate the threads of	**RAWIN**	n pl. **-S** a wind measurement made by tracking a balloon with radar
RAVELER	n pl. **-S** one that ravels	**RAWISH**	adj somewhat raw
RAVELIN	n pl. **-S** a type of fortification	**RAWLY**	adv in a raw manner
RAVELING	n pl. **-S** a loose thread	**RAWNESS**	n pl. **-ES** the state of being raw
RAVELLED	a past tense of ravel	**RAX**	v **-ED, -ING, -ES** to stretch out
RAVELLER	n pl. **-S** raveler	**RAY**	v **-ED, -ING, -S** to emit rays (narrow beams of light)
RAVELLING	a present participle of ravel		
RAVELLY	adj tangled	**RAYA**	n pl. **-S** rayah
RAVEN	v **-ED, -ING, -S** to eat in a ravenous manner	**RAYAH**	n pl. **-S** a non-Muslim inhabitant of Turkey
RAVENER	n pl. **-S** one that ravens	**RAYGRASS**	n pl. **-ES** ryegrass
RAVENING	n pl. **-S** rapacity	**RAYLESS**	adj having no rays
RAVENOUS	adj extremely hungry	**RAYLIKE**	adj resembling a narrow beam of light
RAVER	n pl. **-S** one that raves		
RAVIGOTE	n pl. **-S** a spiced vinegar sauce	**RAYON**	n pl. **-S** a synthetic fiber
RAVIN	v **-ED, -ING, -S** to raven	**RAZE**	v **RAZED, RAZING, RAZES** to tear down or demolish
RAVINE	n pl. **-S** a narrow, steep-sided valley	**RAZEE**	v **-ZEED, -ZEEING, -ZEES** to make lower by removing the upper deck, as a ship
RAVING	n pl. **-S** irrational, incoherent speech		
RAVINGLY	adv in a delirious manner	**RAZER**	n pl. **-S** one that razes
RAVIOLI	n pl. **-S** an Italian pasta dish	**RAZOR**	v **-ED, -ING, -S** to shave or cut with a sharp-edged instrument
RAVISH	v **-ED, -ING, -ES** to seize and carry off by force	**RAZZ**	v **-ED, -ING, -ES** to deride
RAVISHER	n pl. **-S** one that ravishes	**RE**	n pl. **-S** the second tone of the diatonic musical scale

Following is a list of self-explanatory verbs containing the prefix RE- (again):

REABSORB	v **-ED, -ING, -S**	**REAFFIRM**	v **-ED, -ING, -S**	**REAROUSE**	v **-AROUSED, -AROUSING, -AROUSES**
REACCEDE	v **-CEDED, -CEDING, -CEDES**	**REAFFIX**	v **-ED, -ING, -ES**		
		REALIGN	v **-ED, -ING, -S**		
REACCENT	v **-ED, -ING, -S**	**REALLOT**	v **-LOTTED, -LOTTING, -LOTS**	**REARREST**	v **-ED, -ING, -S**
REACCEPT	v **-ED, -ING, -S**			**REASCEND**	v **-ED, -ING, -S**
REACCUSE	v **-CUSED, -CUSING, -CUSES**			**REASSAIL**	v **-ED, -ING, -S**
		REALTER	v **-ED, -ING, -S**	**REASSERT**	v **-ED, -ING, -S**
READAPT	v **-ED, -ING, -S**	**REANNEX**	v **-ED, -ING, -ES**	**REASSESS**	v **-ED, -ING, -ES**
READD	v **-ED, -ING, -S**	**REANOINT**	v **-ED, -ING, -S**	**REASSIGN**	v **-ED, -ING, -S**
READDICT	v **-ED, -ING, -S**	**REAPPEAR**	v **-ED, -ING, -S**	**REASSORT**	v **-ED, -ING, -S**
READJUST	v **-ED, -ING, -S**	**REAPPLY**	v **-PLIED, -PLYING, -PLIES**	**REASSUME**	v **-SUMED, -SUMING, -SUMES**
READMIT	v **-MITTED, -MITTING, -MITS**				
		REARGUE	v **-GUED, -GUING, -GUES**		
READOPT	v **-ED, -ING, -S**			**REASSURE**	v **-SURED, -SURING, -SURES**
READORN	v **-ED, -ING, -S**	**REARM**	v **-ED, -ING, -S**		

REACH *v* **-ED, -ING, -ES** to stretch out or put forth

REACHER *n* pl. **-S** one that reaches

REACT *v* **-ED, -ING, -S** to respond to a stimulus

REACTANT *n* pl. **-S** one that reacts

REACTION *n* pl. **-S** the act of reacting

REACTIVE *adj* tending to react

REACTOR *n* pl. **-S** one that reacts

READ *v* **READ, READING, READS** to look at so as to take in the meaning of, as something written or printed **READABLE** *adj* **READABLY** *adv*

READER *n* pl. **-S** one that reads

READERLY *adj* typical of a reader

READIED past tense of ready

READIER comparative of ready

READIES present 3d person sing. of ready

READIEST superlative of ready

READILY *adv* in a ready manner

READING *n* pl. **-S** material that is read

READOUT *n* pl. **-S** a presentation of computer data

READY *adj* **READIER, READIEST** prepared

READY *v* **READIED, READYING, READIES** to make ready

REAGENT *n* pl. **-S** a substance used in a chemical reaction to ascertain the nature or composition of another

REAGIN *n* pl. **-S** a type of antibody **REAGINIC** *adj*

REAL *adj* **REALER, REALEST** having actual existence

REAL *n* pl. **-S** or **-ES** a former monetary unit of Spain

REAL *n* pl. **REIS** a former monetary unit of Portugal and Brazil

REALGAR *n* pl. **-S** a mineral

REALIA *n/pl* objects used by a teacher to illustrate everyday living

REALISE *v* **-ISED, -ISING, -ISES** to realize

REALISER *n* pl. **-S** one that realises

REALISM *n* pl. **-S** concern with fact or reality

REALIST *n* pl. **-S** one who is concerned with fact or reality

REALITY *n* pl. **-TIES** something that is real

REALIZE *v* **-IZED, -IZING, -IZES** to understand completely

REALIZER *n* pl. **-S** one that realizes

REALLY *adv* actually

REALM *n* pl. **-S** a kingdom

REALNESS *n* pl. **-ES** the state of being real

REALTY *n* pl. **-TIES** property in buildings and land

REAM *v* **-ED, -ING, -S** to enlarge with a reamer

REAMER *n* pl. **-S** a tool used to enlarge holes

REAP *v* **-ED, -ING, -S** to cut for harvest **REAPABLE** *adj*

REAPER *n* pl. **-S** one that reaps

REAPHOOK *n* pl. **-S** an implement used in reaping

REAR *v* **-ED, -ING, -S** to lift upright

List of self-explanatory verbs containing the prefix RE- (continued):

REATTACH	*v* **-ED, -ING, -ES**	**REBIND**	*v* **-BOUND,**	**REBOTTLE**	*v* **-TLED, -TLING,**
REATTACK	*v* **-ED, -ING, -S**		**-BINDING,**		**-TLES**
REATTAIN	*v* **-ED, -ING, -S**		**-BINDS**	**REBOUGHT**	past tense of
REAVAIL	*v* **-ED, -ING, -S**	**REBLEND**	*v* **-BLENDED** or		rebuy
REAVOW	*v* **-ED, -ING, -S**		**-BLENT,**	**REBOUND**	past tense of
REAWAKE	*v* **-AWAKED** or		**-BLENDING,**		rebind
	-AWOKE,		**-BLENDS**	**REBREED**	*v* **-BRED,**
	-AWOKEN,	**REBLOOM**	*v* **-ED, -ING, -S**		**-BREEDING,**
	-AWAKING,	**REBOARD**	*v* **-ED, -ING, -S**		**-BREEDS**
	-AWAKES	**REBODY**	*v* **-BODIED,**	**REBUILD**	*v* **-BUILT** or
REAWAKEN	*v* **-ED, -ING, -S**		**-BODYING,**		**-BUILDED,**
REBAIT	*v* **-ED, -ING, -S**		**-BODIES**		**-BUILDING,**
REBEGIN	*v* **-GAN, -GUN,**	**REBOIL**	*v* **-ED, -ING, -S**		**-BUILDS**
	-GINNING,	**REBOOK**	*v* **-ED, -ING, -S**	**REBURY**	*v* **-BURIED,**
	-GINS	**REBOOT**	*v* **-ED, -ING, -S**		**-BURYING,**
REBID	*v* **-BID, -BIDDEN,**	**REBORE**	*v* **-BORED,**		**-BURIES**
	-BIDDING, -BIDS		**-BORING,**	**REBUTTON**	*v* **-ED, -ING,**
REBILL	*v* **-ED, -ING, -S**		**-BORES**		**-S**

REARER	*n* pl. **-S** one that rears	**REBOP**	*n* pl. **-S** a type of music
REARMICE	*n/pl* reremice	**REBORN**	*adj* born again
REARMOST	*adj* coming or situated last	**REBOUND**	*v* **-ED, -ING, -S** to spring back
REARWARD	*n* pl. **-S** the rearmost division of an army	**REBOZO**	*n* pl. **-ZOS** a long scarf
REASCENT	*n* pl. **-S** a new or second ascent	**REBRANCH**	*v* **-ED, -ING, -ES** to form secondary branches
REASON	*v* **-ED, -ING, -S** to derive inferences or conclusions from known or presumed facts	**REBUFF**	*v* **-ED, -ING, -S** to reject or refuse curtly
REASONER	*n* pl. **-S** one that reasons	**REBUKE**	*v* **-BUKED, -BUKING, -BUKES** to criticize sharply
REATA	*n* pl. **-S** riata	**REBUKER**	*n* pl. **-S** one that rebukes
REAVE	*v* **REAVED** or **REFT, REAVING, REAVES** to plunder	**REBURIAL**	*n* pl. **-S** a second burial
REAVER	*n* pl. **-S** one that reaves	**REBUS**	*n* pl. **-ES** a type of puzzle
REB	*n* pl. **-S** a Confederate soldier	**REBUT**	*v* **-BUTTED, -BUTTING, -BUTS** to refute
REBAR	*n* pl. **-S** a steel rod for use in reinforced concrete	**REBUTTAL**	*n* pl. **-S** argument or proof that rebuts
REBATE	*v* **-BATED, -BATING, -BATES** to deduct or return from a payment or bill	**REBUTTER**	*n* pl. **-S** one that rebuts
		REBUTTING	present participle of rebut
REBATER	*n* pl. **-S** one that rebates	**REC**	*n* pl. **-S** recreation
REBATO	*n* pl. **-TOS** rabato	**RECALL**	*v* **-ED, -ING, -S** to call back
REBBE	*n* pl. **-S** a rabbi	**RECALLER**	*n* pl. **-S** one that recalls
REBEC	*n* pl. **-S** an ancient stringed instrument	**RECAMIER**	*n* pl. **-S** a backless couch
REBECK	*n* pl. **-S** rebec	**RECANT**	*v* **-ED, -ING, -S** to make a formal retraction or disavowal of
REBEL	*v* **-BELLED, -BELLING, -BELS** to oppose the established government of one's land	**RECANTER**	*n* pl. **-S** one that recants
REBELDOM	*n* pl. **-S** an area controlled by rebels	**RECAP**	*v* **-CAPPED, -CAPPING, -CAPS** to review by a brief summary
REBIRTH	*n* pl. **-S** a new or second birth	**RECCE**	*n* pl. **-S** a preliminary survey
REBOANT	*adj* resounding loudly	**RECEDE**	*v* **-CEDED, -CEDING, -CEDES** to move back or away

---

List of self-explanatory verbs containing the prefix RE- (continued):

REBUY	*v* **-BOUGHT, -BUYING, -BUYS**	**RECHARGE**	*v* **-CHARGED, -CHARGING, -CHARGES**	**RECLOTHE**	*v* **-CLOTHED** or **-CLAD, -CLOTHING, -CLOTHES**
RECANE	*v* **-CANED, -CANING, -CANES**	**RECHART**	*v* **-ED, -ING, -S**	**RECOAL**	*v* **-ED, -ING, -S**
		RECHECK	*v* **-ED, -ING, -S**	**RECOAT**	*v* **-ED, -ING, -S**
		RECHEW	*v* **-ED, -ING, -S**	**RECOCK**	*v* **-ED, -ING, -S**
RECARPET	*v* **-ED, -ING, -S**	**RECHOOSE**	*v* **-CHOSE, -CHOSEN, -CHOOSING, -CHOOSES**	**RECODE**	*v* **-CODED, -CODING, -CODES**
RECARRY	*v* **-RIED, -RYING, -RIES**				
RECAST	*v* **-CAST, -CASTING, -CASTS**	**RECIRCLE**	*v* **-CLED, -CLING, -CLES**	**RECODIFY**	*v* **-FIED, -FYING, -FIES**
RECEMENT	*v* **-ED, -ING, -S**	**RECLAD**	*v* **-CLADDED, -CLADDING, -CLADS**	**RECOIN**	*v* **-ED, -ING, -S**
RECENSOR	*v* **-ED, -ING, -S**			**RECOLOR**	*v* **-ED, -ING, -S**
				RECOMB	*v* **-ED, -ING, -S**
RECHANGE	*v* **-CHANGED, -CHANGING, -CHANGES**	**RECLASP**	*v* **-ED, -ING, -S**	**RECOMMIT**	*v* **-MITTED, -MITTING, -MITS**
		RECLEAN	*v* **-ED, -ING, -S**		

RECEIPT	*v* **-ED, -ING, -S** to mark as having been paid	**RECLAME**	*n* pl. **-S** publicity
RECEIVE	*v* **-CEIVED, -CEIVING, -CEIVES** to come into possession of	**RECLINE**	*v* **-CLINED, -CLINING, -CLINES** to lean or lie back
RECEIVER	*n* pl. **-S** one that receives	**RECLINER**	*n* pl. **-S** one that reclines
RECENCY	*n* pl. **-CIES** the state of being recent	**RECLUSE**	*n* pl. **-S** one who lives in solitude and seclusion
RECENT	*adj* **-CENTER, -CENTEST** of or pertaining to a time not long past **RECENTLY** *adv*	**RECOIL**	*v* **-ED, -ING, -S** to draw back in fear or disgust
		RECOILER	*n* pl. **-S** one that recoils
RECEPT	*n* pl. **-S** a type of mental image	**RECON**	*v* **-CONNED, -CONNING, -CONS** to reconnoiter
RECEPTOR	*n* pl. **-S** a nerve ending specialized to receive stimuli	**RECONVEY**	*v* **-ED, -ING, -S** to convey back to a previous position
RECESS	*v* **-ED, -ING, -ES** to place in a receding space or hollow	**RECORD**	*v* **-ED, -ING, -S** to set down for preservation
RECHEAT	*n* pl. **-S** a hunting call	**RECORDER**	*n* pl. **-S** one that records
RECIPE	*n* pl. **-S** a set of instructions for making something	**RECOUNT**	*v* **-ED, -ING, -S** to relate in detail
RECISION	*n* pl. **-S** a cancellation	**RECOUP**	*v* **-ED, -ING, -S** to get back the equivalent of
RECIT	*n* pl. **-S** the part of a story in which the events are related without enhancement	**RECOUPE**	*adj* divided twice
		RECOURSE	*n* pl. **-S** a turning or applying to someone or something for aid
RECITAL	*n* pl. **-S** a detailed account	**RECOVER**	*v* **-ED, -ING, -S** to obtain again after losing
RECITE	*v* **-CITED, -CITING, -CITES** to declaim or say from memory		
RECITER	*n* pl. **-S** one that recites	**RECOVERY**	*n* pl. **-ERIES** an economic upturn
RECK	*v* **-ED, -ING, -S** to be concerned about	**RECREANT**	*n* pl. **-S** a coward
		RECREATE	*v* **-ATED, -ATING, -ATES** to refresh mentally or physically
RECKLESS	*adj* foolishly heedless of danger	**RECRUIT**	*v* **-ED, -ING, -S** to engage for military service
RECKON	*v* **-ED, -ING, -S** to count or compute		
RECKONER	*n* pl. **-S** one that reckons	**RECTA**	*a* pl. of rectum
RECLAIM	*v* **-ED, -ING, -S** to make suitable for cultivation or habitation	**RECTAL**	*adj* pertaining to the rectum **RECTALLY** *adv*

List of self-explanatory verbs containing the prefix RE- (continued):

RECONFER	*v* **-FERRED, -FERRING, -FERS**	**REDATE**	*v* **-DATED, -DATING, -DATES**	**REDIAL**	*v* **-DIALED, -DIALING, -DIALS** or **-DIALLED, -DIALLING, -DIALS**
RECOOK	*v* **-ED, -ING, -S**				
RECOPY	*v* **-COPIED, -COPYING, -COPIES**	**REDECIDE**	*v* **-CIDED, -CIDING, -CIDES**		
				REDID	past tense of redo
RECORK	*v* **-ED, -ING, -S**	**REDEFEAT**	*v* **-ED, -ING, -S**	**REDIGEST**	*v* **-ED, -ING, -S**
RECOUPLE	*v* **-PLED, -PLING, -PLES**	**REDEFECT**	*v* **-ED, -ING, -S**	**REDIP**	*v* **-DIPPED** or **-DIPT, -DIPPING, -DIPS**
		REDEFINE	*v* **-FINED, -FINING, -FINES**		
RECRATE	*v* **-CRATED, -CRATING, -CRATES**			**REDIVIDE**	*v* **-VIDED, -VIDING, -VIDES**
		REDEFY	*v* **-FIED, -FYING, -FIES**		
RECROSS	*v* **-ED, -ING, -ES**			**REDO**	*v* **-DID, -DONE, -DOING, -DOES**
RECROWN	*v* **-ED, -ING, -S**	**REDEMAND**	*v* **-ED, -ING, -S**		
RECUT	*v* **-CUT, -CUTTING, -CUTS**	**REDENY**	*v* **-NIED, -NYING, -NIES**	**REDOCK**	*v* **-ED, -ING, -S**
		REDEPLOY	*v* **-ED, -ING, -S**	**REDON**	*v* **-DONNED, -DONNING, -DONS**
REDAMAGE	*v* **-AGED, -AGING, -AGES**	**REDESIGN**	*v* **-ED, -ING, -S**		

RECTI	pl. of rectus
RECTIFY	*v* **-FIED, -FYING, -FIES** to correct
RECTO	*n* pl. **-TOS** a right-hand page of a book
RECTOR	*n* pl. **-S** a clergyman in charge of a parish
RECTORY	*n* pl. **-RIES** a rector's dwelling
RECTRIX	*n* pl. **-TRICES** a feather of a bird's tail
RECTUM	*n* pl. **-TUMS** or **-TA** the terminal portion of the large intestine
RECTUS	*n* pl. **-TI** a straight muscle
RECUR	*v* **-CURRED, -CURRING, -CURS** to happen again
RECURVE	*v* **-CURVED, -CURVING, -CURVES** to curve backward or downward
RECUSAL	*n* pl. **-S** the act of recusing
RECUSANT	*n* pl. **-S** one who refuses to accept established authority
RECUSE	*v* **-CUSED, -CUSING, -CUSES** to disqualify or challenge as judge in a particular case
RECYCLE	*v* **-CLED, -CLING, -CLES** to process in order to extract useful materials
RECYCLER	*n* pl. **-S** one that recycles
RED	*adj* **REDDER, REDDEST** of the color of blood
RED	*v* **REDDED, REDDING, REDS** to redd
REDACT	*v* **-ED, -ING, -S** to prepare for publication
REDACTOR	*n* pl. **-S** one that redacts
REDAN	*n* pl. **-S** a type of fortification
REDARGUE	*v* **-GUED, -GUING, -GUES** to disprove
REDBAIT	*v* **-ED, -ING, -S** to denounce as Communist
REDBAY	*n* pl. **-BAYS** a small tree
REDBIRD	*n* pl. **-S** a bird with red plumage
REDBONE	*n* pl. **-S** a hunting dog
REDBRICK	*n* pl. **-S** a modern British university
REDBUD	*n* pl. **-S** a small tree
REDBUG	*n* pl. **-S** a chigger
REDCAP	*n* pl. **-S** a porter
REDCOAT	*n* pl. **-S** a British soldier during the American Revolution
REDD	*v* **-ED, -ING, -S** to put in order
REDDED	past tense of red and redd
REDDEN	*v* **-ED, -ING, -S** to make or become red
REDDER	*n* pl. **-S** one that redds
REDDEST	superlative of red
REDDING	present participle of red and redd
REDDISH	*adj* somewhat red
REDDLE	*v* **-DLED, -DLING, -DLES** to ruddle
REDE	*v* **REDED, REDING, REDES** to advise
REDEAR	*n* pl. **-S** a common sunfish
REDEEM	*v* **-ED, -ING, -S** to buy back
REDEEMER	*n* pl. **-S** one that redeems
REDEYE	*n* pl. **-S** a railroad danger signal
REDFIN	*n* pl. **-S** a freshwater fish
REDFISH	*n* pl. **-ES** an edible rockfish
REDHEAD	*n* pl. **-S** a person with red hair

List of self-explanatory verbs containing the prefix RE- (continued):

REDRAW	*v* **-DREW, -DRAWN, -DRAWING, -DRAWS**	**REDYE**	*v* **-DYED, -DYEING, -DYES**	**REENACT**	*v* **-ED, -ING, -S**
		REEARN	*v* **-ED, -ING, -S**	**REENDOW**	*v* **-ED, -ING, -S**
		REECHO	*v* **-ED, -ING, -ES**	**REENGAGE**	*v* **-GAGED, -GAGING, -GAGES**
REDREAM	*v* **-DREAMED** or **-DREAMT, -DREAMING, -DREAMS**	**REEDIT**	*v* **-ED, -ING, -S**		
		REEJECT	*v* **-ED, -ING, -S**	**REENJOY**	*v* **-ED, -ING, -S**
		REELECT	*v* **-ED, -ING, -S**	**REENLIST**	*v* **-ED, -ING, -S**
		REEMBARK	*v* **-ED, -ING, -S**	**REENROLL**	*v* **-ED, -ING, -S**
REDRILL	*v* **-ED, -ING, -S**	**REEMBODY**	*v* **-BODIED, -BODYING, -BODIES**	**REENTER**	*v* **-ED, -ING, -S**
REDRIVE	*v* **-DROVE, -DRIVEN, -DRIVING, -DRIVES**			**REEQUIP**	*v* **-EQUIPPED, -EQUIPPING, -EQUIPS**
		REEMERGE	*v* **-EMERGED, -EMERGING, -EMERGES**		
REDRY	*v* **-DRIED, -DRYING, -DRIES**			**REERECT**	*v* **-ED, -ING, -S**
		REEMIT	*v* **-EMITTED, -EMITTING, -EMITS**	**REEVOKE**	*v* **-EVOKED, -EVOKING, -EVOKES**
REDUB	*v* **-DUBBED, -DUBBING, -DUBS**				
		REEMPLOY	*v* **-ED, -ING, -S**	**REEXPEL**	*v* **-PELLED, -PELLING, -PELS**

REDHORSE	*n* pl. **-S** a freshwater fish	**REDSHIFT**	*n* pl. **-S** a displacement of the spectrum of a celestial body toward the longer wavelengths
REDIA	*n* pl. **-DIAS** or **-DIAE** the larva of certain flatworms **REDIAL** *adj*	**REDSHIRT**	*v* **-ED, -ING, -S** to keep a college athlete out of varsity play in order to extend his eligibility
REDING	present participle of rede		
REDIRECT	*v* **-ED, -ING, -S** to change the course or direction of		
REDLEG	*n* pl. **-S** a bird with red legs	**REDSTART**	*n* pl. **-S** a small songbird
REDLINE	*v* **-LINED, -LINING, -LINES** to withhold loans or insurance from certain neighborhoods	**REDTAIL**	*n* pl. **-S** a type of hawk
		REDTOP	*n* pl. **-S** a type of grass
		REDUCE	*v* **-DUCED, -DUCING, -DUCES** to diminish
REDLINER	*n* pl. **-S** one that redlines	**REDUCER**	*n* pl. **-S** one that reduces
REDLY	*adv* with red color	**REDUCTOR**	*n* pl. **-S** an apparatus for the reduction of metallic ions in solution
REDNESS	*n* pl. **-ES** the state of being red		
REDO	*n* pl. **-DOS** something that is done again		
		REDUVIID	*n* pl. **-S** a bloodsucking insect
REDOLENT	*adj* fragrant	**REDUX**	*adj* brought back
REDOUBLE	*v* **-BLED, -BLING, -BLES** to double	**REDWARE**	*n* pl. **-S** an edible seaweed
		REDWING	*n* pl. **-S** a European thrush
REDOUBT	*n* pl. **-S** an enclosed fortification	**REDWOOD**	*n* pl. **-S** a very tall evergreen tree
REDOUND	*v* **-ED, -ING, -S** to have an effect	**REE**	*n* pl. **-S** the female Eurasian sandpiper
REDOUT	*n* pl. **-S** a condition in which blood is driven to the head		
		REECHY	*adj* **REECHIER, REECHIEST** foul, rancid
REDOWA	*n* pl. **-S** a lively dance		
REDOX	*n* pl. **-ES** a type of chemical reaction	**REED**	*v* **-ED, -ING, -S** to fasten with reeds (the stalks of tall grasses)
REDPOLL	*n* pl. **-S** a small finch	**REEDBIRD**	*n* pl. **-S** the bobolink
REDRAFT	*v* **-ED, -ING, -S** to make a revised copy of	**REEDBUCK**	*n* pl. **-S** an African antelope
		REEDIER	comparative of reedy
REDRAWER	*n* pl. **-S** one that redraws	**REEDIEST**	superlative of reedy
REDRESS	*v* **-ED, -ING, -ES** to set right	**REEDIFY**	*v* **-FIED, -FYING, -FIES** to rebuild
REDROOT	*n* pl. **-S** a perennial herb	**REEDILY**	*adv* with a thin, piping sound
REDSHANK	*n* pl. **-S** a shore bird	**REEDING**	*n* pl. **-S** a convex molding

List of self-explanatory verbs containing the prefix RE- (continued):

REEXPORT	*v* **-ED, -ING, -S**	**REFIGHT**	*v* **-FOUGHT, -FIGHTING, -FIGHTS**	**REFLOAT**	*v* **-ED, -ING, -S**
REEXPOSE	*v* **-POSED, -POSING, -POSES**			**REFLOOD**	*v* **-ED, -ING, -S**
				REFLOW	*v* **-ED, -ING, -S**
REFALL	*v* **-FELL, -FALLEN, -FALLING, -FALLS**	**REFIGURE**	*v* **-URED, -URING, -URES**	**REFLOWER**	*v* **-ED, -ING, -S**
		REFILE	*v* **-FILED, -FILING, -FILES**	**REFLY**	*v* **-FLEW, -FLOWN, -FLYING, -FLIES**
REFASTEN	*v* **-ED, -ING, -S**	**REFILL**	*v* **-ED, -ING, -S**		
REFEED	*v* **-FED, -FEEDING, -FEEDS**	**REFILM**	*v* **-ED, -ING, -S**	**REFOCUS**	*v* **-CUSED, -CUSING, -CUSES** or **-CUSSED, -CUSSING, -CUSSES**
		REFILTER	*v* **-ED, -ING, -S**		
		REFIND	*v* **-FOUND, -FINDING, -FINDS**		
REFEEL	*v* **-FELT, -FEELING, -FEELS**	**REFIRE**	*v* **-FIRED, -FIRING, -FIRES**	**REFOLD**	*v* **-ED, -ING, -S**
				REFORGE	*v* **-FORGED, -FORGING, -FORGES**
REFELL	past tense of refall	**REFIX**	*v* **-ED, -ING, -ES**		
REFENCE	*v* **-FENCED, -FENCING, -FENCES**	**REFLEW**	past tense of refly	**REFORMAT**	*v* **-MATTED, -MATTING, -MATS**
		REFLIES	present 3d person sing. of refly		

REEDLIKE	*adj* resembling a reed
REEDLING	*n* pl. **-S** a marsh bird
REEDMAN	*n* pl. **-MEN** one who plays a reed instrument
REEDY	*adj* **REEDIER, REEDIEST** abounding in reeds
REEF	*v* **-ED, -ING, -S** to reduce the area of a sail **REEFABLE** *adj*
REEFER	*n* pl. **-S** one that reefs
REEFY	*adj* **REEFIER, REEFIEST** abounding in ridges of rock
REEK	*v* **-ED, -ING, -S** to give off a strong, unpleasant odor
REEKER	*n* pl. **-S** one that reeks
REEKY	*adj* **REEKIER, REEKIEST** reeking
REEL	*v* **-ED, -ING, -S** to wind on a type of rotary device **REELABLE** *adj*
REELER	*n* pl. **-S** one that reels
REELING	*n* pl. **-S** sustained noise
REENTRY	*n* pl. **-TRIES** a new or second entry
REEST	*v* **-ED, -ING, -S** to balk
REEVE	*v* **REEVED** or **ROVE, ROVEN, REEVING, REEVES** to fasten by passing through or around something
REF	*v* **REFFED, REFFING, REFS** to referee
REFACE	*v* **-FACED, -FACING, -FACES** to repair the outer surface of
REFECT	*v* **-ED, -ING, -S** to refresh with food and drink
REFEL	*v* **-FELLED, -FELLING, -FELS** to reject

REFER	*v* **-FERRED, -FERRING, -FERS** to direct to a source for help or information
REFEREE	*v* **-EED, -EEING, -EES** to supervise the play in certain sports
REFERENT	*n* pl. **-S** something referred to
REFERRAL	*n* pl. **-S** one that is referred
REFERRED	past tense of refer
REFERRER	*n* pl. **-S** one that refers
REFERRING	present participle of refer
REFFED	past tense of ref
REFFING	present participle of ref
REFINE	*v* **-FINED, -FINING, -FINES** to free from impurities
REFINER	*n* pl. **-S** one that refines
REFINERY	*n* pl. **-ERIES** a place where crude material is refined
REFINISH	*v* **-ED, -ING, -ES** to give a new surface to
REFIT	*v* **-FITTED, -FITTING, -FITS** to prepare and equip for additional use
REFLAG	*v* **-FLAGGED, -FLAGGING, -FLAGS** to give a new registered nationality to (a ship)
REFLATE	*v* **-FLATED, -FLATING, -FLATES** to inflate again
REFLECT	*v* **-ED, -ING, -S** to turn or throw back from a surface
REFLET	*n* pl. **-S** special brilliance of surface
REFLEX	*v* **-ED, -ING, -ES** to bend back
REFLEXLY	*adv* in a reflexed manner
REFLUENT	*adj* flowing back

List of self-explanatory verbs containing the prefix RE- (continued):

REFOUGHT	past tense of refight	**REGATHER**	*v* -ED, -ING, -S	**REGRADE**	*v* -GRADED, -GRADING, -GRADES
REFOUND	*v* -ED, -ING, -S	**REGAUGE**	*v* -GAUGED, -GAUGING, -GAUGES		
REFRAME	*v* -FRAMED, -FRAMING, -FRAMES			**REGRAFT**	*v* -ED, -ING, -S
		REGEAR	*v* -ED, -ING, -S	**REGRANT**	*v* -ED, -ING, -S
		REGILD	*v* -GILDED or -GILT, -GILDING, -GILDS	**REGREEN**	*v* -ED, -ING, -S
REFREEZE	*v* -FROZE, -FROZEN, -FREEZING, -FREEZES			**REGREW**	past tense of regrow
		REGIVE	*v* -GAVE, -GIVEN, -GIVING, -GIVES	**REGRIND**	*v* -GROUND, -GRINDING, -GRINDS
REFRONT	*v* -ED, -ING, -S	**REGLAZE**	*v* -GLAZED, -GLAZING, -GLAZES		
REFRY	*v* -FRIED, -FRYING, -FRIES			**REGROOM**	*v* -ED, -ING, -S
		REGLOSS	*v* -ED, -ING, -ES	**REGROOVE**	*v* -GROOVED, -GROOVING, -GROOVES
		REGLOW	*v* -ED, -ING, -S		
REFUEL	*v* -ELED, -ELING, -ELS or -ELLED, -ELLING, -ELS	**REGLUE**	*v* -GLUED, -GLUING, -GLUES	**REGROUND**	past tense of regrind
REGAIN	*v* -ED, -ING, -S			**REGROUP**	*v* -ED, -ING, -S

REFLUX	*v* **-ED, -ING, -ES** to cause to flow back	**REGAINER**	*n* pl. **-S** one that regains	
REFOREST	*v* **-ED, -ING, -S** to replant with trees	**REGAL**	*adj* of or befitting a king	
REFORM	*v* **-ED, -ING, -S** to change to a better state	**REGALE**	*v* **-GALED, -GALING, -GALES** to delight	
REFORMER	*n* pl. **-S** one that reforms	**REGALER**	*n* pl. **-S** one that regales	
REFRACT	*v* **-ED, -ING, -S** to deflect in a particular manner, as a ray of light	**REGALIA**	*n/pl* the rights and privileges of a king	

REFLUX   *v* **-ED, -ING, -ES** to cause to flow back

REFOREST   *v* **-ED, -ING, -S** to replant with trees

REFORM   *v* **-ED, -ING, -S** to change to a better state

REFORMER   *n* pl. **-S** one that reforms

REFRACT   *v* **-ED, -ING, -S** to deflect in a particular manner, as a ray of light

REFRAIN   *v* **-ED, -ING, -S** to keep oneself back

REFRESH   *v* **-ED, -ING, -ES** to restore the well-being and vigor of

REFT   a past tense of reave

REFUGE   *v* **-UGED, -UGING, -UGES** to give or take shelter

REFUGEE   *n* pl. **-S** one who flees for safety

REFUGIUM   *n* pl. **-GIA** a stable area during a period of continental climactic change

REFUND   *v* **-ED, -ING, -S** to give back

REFUNDER   *n* pl. **-S** one that refunds

REFUSAL   *n* pl. **-S** the act of refusing

REFUSE   *v* **-FUSED, -FUSING, -FUSES** to express oneself as unwilling to accept, do, or comply with

REFUSER   *n* pl. **-S** one that refuses

REFUSNIK   *n* pl. **-S** a Soviet citizen who is refused permission to emigrate

REFUTAL   *n* pl. **-S** the act of refuting

REFUTE   *v* **-FUTED, -FUTING, -FUTES** to prove to be false or erroneous

REFUTER   *n* pl. **-S** one that refutes

REG   *n* pl. **-S** a regulation

REGAINER   *n* pl. **-S** one that regains

REGAL   *adj* of or befitting a king

REGALE   *v* **-GALED, -GALING, -GALES** to delight

REGALER   *n* pl. **-S** one that regales

REGALIA   *n/pl* the rights and privileges of a king

REGALITY   *n* pl. **-TIES** regal authority

REGALLY   *adv* in a regal manner

REGARD   *v* **-ED, -ING, -S** to look upon with a particular feeling

REGATTA   *n* pl. **-S** a boat race

REGELATE   *v* **-LATED, -LATING, -LATES** to refreeze ice by reducing the pressure

REGENCY   *n* pl. **-CIES** the office of a regent

REGENT   *n* pl. **-S** one who rules in the place of a sovereign **REGENTAL** *adj*

REGES   pl. of rex

REGGAE   *n* pl. **-S** a form of popular Jamaican music

REGICIDE   *n* pl. **-S** the killing of a king

REGIME   *n* pl. **-S** a system of government

REGIMEN   *n* pl. **-S** a systematic plan

REGIMENT   *v* **-ED, -ING, -S** to form into military units

REGINA   *n* pl. **-NAS** or **-NAE** queen **REGINAL** *adj*

REGION   *n* pl. **-S** an administrative area or division

REGIONAL   *n* pl. **-S** something that serves as a region

REGISTER   *v* **-ED, -ING, -S** to record officially

List of self-explanatory verbs containing the prefix RE- (continued):

REGROW	*v* **-GREW, -GROWN, -GROWING, -GROWS**	**REHEM**	*v* **-HEMMED, -HEMMING, -HEMS**	**REINCITE**	*v* **-CITED, -CITING, -CITES**
		REHINGE	*v* **-HINGED, -HINGING, -HINGES**	**REINCUR**	*v* **-CURRED, -CURRING, -CURS**
REHAMMER	*v* **-ED, -ING, -S**				
REHANDLE	*v* **-DLED, -DLING, -DLES**	**REHIRE**	*v* **-HIRED, -HIRING, -HIRES**	**REINDEX**	*v* **-ED, -ING, -ES**
REHANG	*v* **-HUNG** or **-HANGED, -HANGING, -HANGS**	**REHUNG**	a past tense of rehang	**REINDICT**	*v* **-ED, -ING, -S**
				REINDUCE	*v* **-DUCED, -DUCING, -DUCES**
REHARDEN	*v* **-ED, -ING, -S**	**REIGNITE**	*v* **-NITED, -NITING, -NITES**	**REINDUCT**	*v* **-ED, -ING, -S**
REHASH	*v* **-ED, -ING, -ES**	**REIMAGE**	*v* **-AGED, -AGING, -AGES**	**REINFECT**	*v* **-ED, -ING, -S**
REHEAR	*v* **-HEARD, -HEARING, -HEARS**			**REINFORM**	*v* **-ED, -ING, -S**
		REIMPORT	*v* **-ED, -ING, -S**	**REINFUSE**	*v* **-FUSED, -FUSING, -FUSES**
		REIMPOSE	*v* **-POSED, -POSING, -POSES**	**REINJECT**	*v* **-ED, -ING, -S**
REHEAT	*v* **-ED, -ING, -S**			**REINJURE**	*v* **-JURED, -JURING, -JURES**
REHEEL	*v* **-ED, -ING, -S**				

REGISTRY	*n* pl. **-TRIES** the act of registering
REGIUS	*adj* holding a professorship founded by the sovereign
REGLET	*n* pl. **-S** a flat, narrow molding
REGMA	*n* pl. **-MATA** a type of fruit
REGNA	pl. of regnum
REGNAL	*adj* pertaining to a king or his reign
REGNANCY	*n* pl. **-CIES** the state of being regnant
REGNANT	*adj* reigning
REGNUM	*n* pl. **-NA** dominion
REGOLITH	*n* pl. **-S** a layer of loose rock
REGORGE	*v* **-GORGED, -GORGING, -GORGES** to vomit
REGOSOL	*n* pl. **-S** a type of soil
REGRATE	*v* **-GRATED, -GRATING, -GRATES** to buy up in order to sell for a higher price in the same area
REGREET	*v* **-ED, -ING, -S** to greet in return
REGRESS	*v* **-ED, -ING, -ES** to go back
REGRET	*v* **-GRETTED, -GRETTING, -GRETS** to look back upon with sorrow or remorse
REGROWTH	*n* pl. **-S** a new or second growth
REGULAR	*n* pl. **-S** a habitual customer
REGULATE	*v* **-LATED, -LATING, -LATES** to control according to rule
REGULUS	*n* pl. **-LUSES** or **-LI** a mass that forms beneath the slag in a furnace **REGULINE** *adj*
REHAB	*v* **-HABBED, -HABBING, -HABS** to restore to a good condition
REHABBER	*n* pl. **-S** one that rehabs
REHEARSE	*v* **-HEARSED, -HEARSING, -HEARSES** to practice in preparation for a public appearance
REHEATER	*n* pl. **-S** one that reheats
REHOBOAM	*n* pl. **-S** a wine bottle
REHOUSE	*v* **-HOUSED, -HOUSING, -HOUSES** to establish in a new housing unit
REI	*n* pl. **-S** an erroneous English form for a former Portuguese coin
REIF	*n* pl. **-S** robbery
REIFIER	*n* pl. **-S** one that reifies
REIFY	*v* **-IFIED, -IFYING, -IFIES** to regard as real or concrete
REIGN	*v* **-ED, -ING, -S** to exercise sovereign power
REIN	*v* **-ED, -ING, -S** to restrain
REINDEER	*n* pl. **-S** a large deer
REINJURY	*n* pl. **-RIES** a second injury
REINLESS	*adj* unrestrained
REINSMAN	*n* pl. **-MEN** a skilled rider of horses
REIS	pl. of real
REISSUER	*n* pl. **-S** one that reissues
REITBOK	*n* pl. **-S** the reedbuck
REIVE	*v* **REIVED, REIVING, REIVES** to plunder
REIVER	*n* pl. **-S** one that reives
REJECT	*v* **-ED, -ING, -S** to refuse to accept, consider, or make use of
REJECTEE	*n* pl. **-S** one that is rejected
REJECTER	*n* pl. **-S** one that rejects
REJECTOR	*n* pl. **-S** rejecter

List of self-explanatory verbs containing the prefix RE- (continued):

REINK	*v* **-ED, -ING, -S**	**REJUDGE**	*v* **-JUDGED, -JUDGING, -JUDGES**	**RELACE**	*v* **-LACED, -LACING, -LACES**
REINSERT	*v* **-ED, -ING, -S**				
REINSURE	*v* **-SURED, -SURING, -SURES**	**REJUGGLE**	*v* **-GLED, -GLING, -GLES**	**RELAND**	*v* **-ED, -ING, -S**
REINTER	*v* **-TERRED, -TERRING, -TERS**	**REKEY**	*v* **-ED, -ING, -S**	**RELAUNCH**	*v* **-ED, -ING, -ES**
REINVADE	*v* **-VADED, -VADING, -VADES**	**REKINDLE**	*v* **-DLED, -DLING, -DLES**	**RELAY**	*v* **-LAID, -LAYING, -LAYS**
REINVENT	*v* **-ED, -ING, -S**	**REKNIT**	*v* **-KNITTED, -KNITTING, -KNITS**	**RELEARN**	*v* **-LEARNED** or **-LEARNT, -LEARNING, -LEARNS**
REINVEST	*v* **-ED, -ING, -S**				
REINVITE	*v* **-VITED, -VITING, -VITES**	**REKNOT**	*v* **-KNOTTED, -KNOTTING, -KNOTS**	**RELEND**	*v* **-LENT, -LENDING, -LENDS**
REINVOKE	*v* **-VOKED, -VOKING, -VOKES**	**RELABEL**	*v* **-BELED, -BELING, -BELS** or **-BELLED, -BELLING, -BELS**	**RELET**	*v* **-LET, -LETTING, -LETS**
REISSUE	*v* **-SUED, -SUING, -SUES**				
REJACKET	*v* **-ED, -ING, -S**				
REJOIN	*v* **-ED, -ING, -S**			**RELETTER**	*v* **-ED, -ING, -S**

REJIG   *v* **-JIGGED, -JIGGING, -JIGS** to rejigger

REJIGGER   *v* **-ED, -ING, -S** to alter

REJOICE   *v* **-JOICED, -JOICING, -JOICES** to feel joyful

REJOICER   *n* pl. **-S** one that rejoices

RELAPSE   *v* **-LAPSED, -LAPSING, -LAPSES** to fall or slip back into a former state

RELAPSER   *n* pl. **-S** one that relapses

RELATE   *v* **-LATED, -LATING, -LATES** to give an account of

RELATER   *n* pl. **-S** one that relates

RELATION   *n* pl. **-S** a significant association between two or more things

RELATIVE   *n* pl. **-S** one who is connected with another by blood or marriage

RELATOR   *n* pl. **-S** relater

RELAX   *v* **-ED, -ING, -ES** to make less tense or rigid

RELAXANT   *n* pl. **-S** a drug that relieves muscular tension

RELAXER   *n* pl. **-S** one that relaxes

RELAXIN   *n* pl. **-S** a female hormone

RELAY   *v* **-ED, -ING, -S** to send along by using fresh sets to replace tired ones

RELEASE   *v* **-LEASED, -LEASING, -LEASES** to set free

RELEASER   *n* pl. **-S** one that releases

RELEGATE   *v* **-GATED, -GATING, -GATES** to assign

RELENT   *v* **-ED, -ING, -S** to become less severe

RELEVANT   *adj* pertaining to the matter at hand

RELEVE   *n* pl. **-S** a raising onto the toe in ballet

RELIABLE   *n* pl. **-S** one that can be relied on

RELIABLY   *adv* in a manner that can be relied on

RELIANCE   *n* pl. **-S** confident or trustful dependence

RELIANT   *adj* showing reliance

RELIC   *n* pl. **-S** a surviving memorial of something past

RELICT   *n* pl. **-S** an organism surviving in a changed environment

RELIED   past tense of rely

RELIEF   *n* pl. **-S** aid in the form of money or necessities

RELIER   *n* pl. **-S** one that relies

RELIES   present 3d person sing. of rely

RELIEVE   *v* **-LIEVED, -LIEVING, -LIEVES** to lessen or free from pain or discomfort

RELIEVER   *n* pl. **-S** one that relieves

RELIEVO   *n* pl. **-VOS** the projection of figures or forms from a flat background

RELIGION   *n* pl. **-S** the worship of a god or the supernatural

RELIQUE   *n* pl. **-S** relic

RELISH   *v* **-ED, -ING, -ES** to enjoy

RELIVE   *v* **-LIVED, -LIVING, -LIVES** to experience again

RELLENO   *n* pl. **-S** a Mexican dish of a stuffed and fried green chile

RELOADER   *n* pl. **-S** one that reloads

List of self-explanatory verbs containing the prefix RE- (continued):

RELIGHT	*v* **-LIGHTED** or **-LIT, -LIGHTING, -LIGHTS**	**REMAP**	*v* **-MAPPED, -MAPPING, -MAPS**	**REMET**	past tense of remeet
RELINE	*v* **-LINED, -LINING, -LINES**	**REMARKET**	*v* **-ED, -ING, -S**	**REMIX**	*v* **-MIXED** or **-MIXT, -MIXING, -MIXES**
RELINK	*v* **-ED, -ING, -S**	**REMARRY**	*v* **-RIED, -RYING, -RIES**	**REMODIFY**	*v* **-FIED, -FYING, -FIES**
RELIST	*v* **-ED, -ING, -S**	**REMASTER**	*v* **-ED, -ING, -S**	**REMOLD**	*v* **-ED, -ING, -S**
RELIT	a past tense of relight	**REMATCH**	*v* **-ED, -ING, -ES**	**REMOUNT**	*v* **-ED, -ING, -S**
		REMATE	*v* **-MATED, -MATING, -MATES**	**RENAIL**	*v* **-ED, -ING, -S**
RELOAD	*v* **-ED, -ING, -S**	**REMEET**	*v* **-MET, -MEETING, -MEETS**	**RENAME**	*v* **-NAMED, -NAMING, -NAMES**
RELOAN	*v* **-ED, -ING, -S**				
RELOCK	*v* **-ED, -ING, -S**				
RELOOK	*v* **-ED, -ING, -S**	**REMELT**	*v* **-ED, -ING, -S**	**RENEST**	*v* **-ED, -ING, -S**
REMAIL	*v* **-ED, -ING, -S**	**REMEND**	*v* **-ED, -ING, -S**	**RENOTIFY**	*v* **-FIED, -FYING, -FIES**
REMAKE	*v* **-MADE, -MAKING, -MAKES**	**REMERGE**	*v* **-MERGED, -MERGING, -MERGES**	**RENUMBER**	*v* **-ED, -ING, -S**
				REOBJECT	*v* **-ED, -ING, -S**

RELOCATE	*v* **-CATED, -CATING, -CATES** to establish in a new place	**REMIND**	*v* **-ED, -ING, -S** to cause to remember
RELUCENT	*adj* reflecting light	**REMINDER**	*n* pl. **-S** one that reminds
RELUCT	*v* **-ED, -ING, -S** to show opposition	**REMINT**	*v* **-ED, -ING, -S** to melt down and make into new coin
RELUME	*v* **-LUMED, -LUMING, -LUMES** to light again	**REMISE**	*v* **-MISED, -MISING, -MISES** to give up a claim to
RELUMINE	*v* **-MINED, -MINING, -MINES** to relume	**REMISS**	*adj* careless **REMISSLY** *adv*
RELY	*v* **-LIED, -LYING, -LIES** to place trust or confidence	**REMIT**	*v* **-MITTED, -MITTING, -MITS** to send money in payment
REM	*n* pl. **-S** a quantity of ionizing radiation	**REMITTAL**	*n* pl. **-S** the act of remitting
REMAIN	*v* **-ED, -ING, -S** to continue in the same state	**REMITTER**	*n* pl. **-S** one that remits
		REMITTOR	*n* pl. **-S** remitter
REMAKER	*n* pl. **-S** one that remakes	**REMNANT**	*n* pl. **-S** something remaining
REMAN	*v* **-MANNED, -MANNING, -MANS** to furnish with a fresh supply of men	**REMODEL**	*v* **-ELED, -ELING, -ELS** or **-ELLED, -ELLING, -ELS** to make over
REMAND	*v* **-ED, -ING, -S** to send back	**REMOLADE**	*n* pl. **-S** a piquant sauce
REMANENT	*adj* remaining	**REMORA**	*n* pl. **-S** a type of marine fish **REMORID** *adj*
REMANNED	past tense of reman		
REMANNING	present participle of reman	**REMORSE**	*n* pl. **-S** deep anguish caused by a sense of guilt
REMARK	*v* **-ED, -ING, -S** to say or write briefly or casually	**REMOTE**	*adj* **-MOTER, -MOTEST** situated far away **REMOTELY** *adv*
REMARKER	*n* pl. **-S** one that remarks	**REMOTE**	*n* pl. **-S** a broadcast originating outside a studio
REMARQUE	*n* pl. **-S** a mark made in the margin of an engraved plate		
		REMOTION	*n* pl. **-S** the act of removing
REMEDIAL	*adj* intended to correct something	**REMOVAL**	*n* pl. **-S** the act of removing
REMEDY	*v* **-DIED, -DYING, -DIES** to relieve or cure	**REMOVE**	*v* **-MOVED, -MOVING, -MOVES** to take or move away
REMEMBER	*v* **-ED, -ING, -S** to bring to mind again	**REMOVER**	*n* pl. **-S** one that removes
		REMUDA	*n* pl. **-S** a herd of horses
REMEX	*n* pl. **REMIGES** a flight feather of a bird's wing **REMIGIAL** *adj*	**RENAL**	*adj* pertaining to the kidneys

List of self-explanatory verbs containing the prefix RE- (continued):

REOBTAIN	*v* **-ED, -ING, -S**	**REPACK**	*v* **-ED, -ING, -S**	**REPHRASE**	*v* **-PHRASED,**
REOCCUPY	*v* **-PIED, -PYING,**	**REPAINT**	*v* **-ED, -ING, -S**		**-PHRASING,**
	-PIES	**REPANEL**	*v* **-ELED, -ELING,**		**-PHRASES**
REOCCUR	*v* **-CURRED,**		**-ELS** or **-ELLED,**	**REPIN**	*v* **-PINNED,**
	-CURRING,		**-ELLING, -ELS**		**-PINNING,**
	-CURS	**REPAPER**	*v* **-ED, -ING, -S**		**-PINS**
REOIL	*v* **-ED, -ING, -S**	**REPARK**	*v* **-ED, -ING, -S**	**REPLAN**	*v* **-PLANNED,**
REOPEN	*v* **-ED, -ING, -S**	**REPASS**	*v* **-ED, -ING, -ES**		**-PLANNING,**
REOPPOSE	*v* **-POSED,**	**REPATCH**	*v* **-ED, -ING, -ES**		**-PLANS**
	-POSING,	**REPAVE**	*v* **-PAVED,**	**REPLANT**	*v* **-ED, -ING, -S**
	-POSES		**-PAVING,**	**REPLATE**	*v* **-PLATED,**
REORDAIN	*v* **-ED, -ING, -S**		**-PAVES**		**-PLATING,**
REORDER	*v* **-ED, -ING, -S**	**REPEG**	*v* **-PEGGED,**		**-PLATES**
REORIENT	*v* **-ED, -ING, -S**		**-PEGGING,**	**REPLAY**	*v* **-ED, -ING, -S**
REOUTFIT	*v* **-FITTED,**		**-PEGS**	**REPLEAD**	*v* **-PLEADED** or
	-FITTING, -FITS	**REPEOPLE**	*v* **-PLED, -PLING,**		**-PLED,**
REPACIFY	*v* **-FIED, -FYING,**		**-PLES**		**-PLEADING,**
	-FIES	**REPERK**	*v* **-ED, -ING, -S**		**-PLEADS**

RENATURE	*v* **-TURED, -TURING, -TURES** to restore natural qualities	**RENOUNCE**	*v* **-NOUNCED, -NOUNCING, -NOUNCES** to disown
REND	*v* **RENT** or **RENDED, RENDING, RENDS** to tear apart forcibly	**RENOVATE**	*v* **-VATED, -VATING, -VATES** to make like new
RENDER	*v* **-ED, -ING, -S** to cause to be or become	**RENOWN**	*v* **-ED, -ING, -S** to make famous
		RENT	*v* **-ED, -ING, -S** to obtain temporary use of in return for compensation **RENTABLE** *adj*
RENDERER	*n* pl. **-S** one that renders		
RENDIBLE	*adj* capable of being rent		
RENDZINA	*n* pl. **-S** a type of soil	**RENTAL**	*n* pl. **-S** an amount paid or collected as rent
RENEGADE	*v* **-GADED, -GADING, -GADES** to become a traitor	**RENTE**	*n* pl. **-S** annual income under French law
RENEGADO	*n* pl. **-DOS** or **-DOES** a traitor	**RENTER**	*n* pl. **-S** one that rents
RENEGE	*v* **-NEGED, -NEGING, -NEGES** to fail to carry out a promise or commitment	**RENTIER**	*n* pl. **-S** one that receives a fixed income
RENEGER	*n* pl. **-S** one that reneges	**RENVOI**	*n* pl. **-S** the expulsion by a government of an alien
RENEW	*v* **-ED, -ING, -S** to make new or as if new again	**REOFFER**	*v* **-ED, -ING, -S** to offer for public sale
RENEWAL	*n* pl. **-S** the act of renewing	**REOVIRUS**	*n* pl. **-ES** a type of virus
RENEWER	*n* pl. **-S** one that renews	**REP**	*v* **REPPED, REPPING, REPS** to represent
RENIFORM	*adj* kidney-shaped		
RENIG	*v* **-NIGGED, -NIGGING, -NIGS** to renege	**REPAID**	past tense of repay
		REPAIR	*v* **-ED, -ING, -S** to restore to good condition
RENIN	*n* pl. **-S** an enzyme		
RENITENT	*adj* resisting physical pressure	**REPAIRER**	*n* pl. **-S** one that repairs
RENMINBI	*n* pl. **RENMINBI** currency in the People's Republic of China	**REPAND**	*adj* having a wavy margin **REPANDLY** *adv*
RENNASE	*n* pl. **-S** rennin	**REPARTEE**	*n* pl. **-S** a quick, witty reply
RENNET	*n* pl. **-S** a lining membrane in the stomach of certain young animals	**REPAST**	*v* **-ED, -ING, -S** to eat or feast
		REPAY	*v* **-PAID, -PAYING, -PAYS** to pay back
RENNIN	*n* pl. **-S** an enzyme		
RENOGRAM	*n* pl. **-S** a photographic depiction of the course of renal excretion	**REPEAL**	*v* **-ED, -ING, -S** to revoke
		REPEALER	*n* pl. **-S** one that repeals

List of self-explanatory verbs containing the prefix RE- (continued):

REPLEDGE	*v* **-PLEDGED, -PLEDGING, -PLEDGES**	**REPOWER**	*v* **-ED, -ING, -S**	**REREAD**	*v* **-READ, -READING, -READS**
REPLOT	*v* **-PLOTTED, -PLOTTING, -PLOTS**	**REPRICE**	*v* **-PRICED, -PRICING, -PRICES**	**RERECORD**	*v* **-ED, -ING, -S**
				REREMIND	*v* **-ED, -ING, -S**
REPLOW	*v* **-ED, -ING, -S**	**REPRINT**	*v* **-ED, -ING, -S**		
REPLUMB	*v* **-ED, -ING, -S**	**REPROBE**	*v* **-PROBED, -PROBING, -PROBES**	**RERENT**	*v* **-ED, -ING, -S**
REPLUNGE	*v* **-PLUNGED, -PLUNGING, -PLUNGES**			**REREPEAT**	*v* **-ED, -ING, -S**
		REPUMP	*v* **-ED, -ING, -S**		
REPOLISH	*v* **-ED, -ING, -ES**	**REPURIFY**	*v* **-FIED, -FYING, -FIES**	**REREVIEW**	*v* **-ED, -ING, -S**
REPOLL	*v* **-ED, -ING, -S**	**REPURSUE**	*v* **-SUED, -SUING, -SUES**	**RERIG**	*v* **-RIGGED, -RIGGING, -RIGS**
REPOT	*v* **-POTTED, -POTTING, -POTS**	**RERACK**	*v* **-ED, -ING, -S**		
		RERAISE	*v* **-RAISED, -RAISING, -RAISES**	**RERISE**	*v* **-ROSE, -RISEN, -RISING, -RISES**
REPOUR	*v* **-ED, -ING, -S**				

REPEAT	v **-ED, -ING, -S** to say or do again	**REPOSAL**	n pl. **-S** the act of reposing
REPEATER	n pl. **-S** one that repeats	**REPOSE**	v **-POSED, -POSING, -POSES** to lie at rest
REPEL	v **-PELLED, -PELLING, -PELS** to drive back	**REPOSER**	n pl. **-S** one that reposes
REPELLER	n pl. **-S** one that repels	**REPOSIT**	v **-ED, -ING, -S** to put away
REPENT	v **-ED, -ING, -S** to feel remorse or self-reproach for a past action	**REPOUSSE**	n pl. **-S** a raised design hammered in metal
REPENTER	n pl. **-S** one that repents	**REPP**	n pl. **-S** a cross-ribbed fabric
REPETEND	n pl. **-S** a phrase or sound that is repeated	**REPPED**	adj resembling repp
REPINE	v **-PINED, -PINING, -PINES** to express discontent	**REPRESS**	v **-ED, -ING, -ES** to keep under control
REPINER	n pl. **-S** one that repines	**REPRIEVE**	v **-PRIEVED, -PRIEVING, -PRIEVES** to postpone the punishment of
REPLACE	v **-PLACED, -PLACING, -PLACES** to take the place of	**REPRISAL**	n pl. **-S** an act of retaliation
REPLACER	n pl. **-S** one that replaces	**REPRISE**	v **-PRISED, -PRISING, -PRISES** to take back by force
REPLETE	n pl. **-S** a worker ant that serves as a living storehouse for liquid food	**REPRO**	n pl. **-PROS** a trial sheet of printed material suitable for photographic reproduction
REPLEVIN	v **-ED, -ING, -S** to replevy		
REPLEVY	v **-PLEVIED, -PLEVYING, -PLEVIES** to regain possession of by legal action	**REPROACH**	v **-ED, -ING, -ES** to find fault with
		REPROOF	n pl. **-S** criticism for a fault
REPLICA	n pl. **-S** a close copy or reproduction	**REPROVAL**	n pl. **-S** reproof
REPLICON	n pl. **-S** a section of nucleic acid that replicates as a unit	**REPROVE**	v **-PROVED, -PROVING, -PROVES** to rebuke
REPLIER	n pl. **-S** one that replies	**REPROVER**	n pl. **-S** one that reproves
REPLY	v **-PLIED, -PLYING, -PLIES** to answer	**REPTANT**	adj creeping or crawling
REPO	n pl. **-POS** something repossessed	**REPTILE**	n pl. **-S** any of a class of cold-blooded, air-breathing vertebrates
REPORT	v **-ED, -ING, -S** to give an account of	**REPTILIA**	n/pl buildings for housing reptiles
		REPUBLIC	n pl. **-S** a constitutional form of government
REPORTER	n pl. **-S** one that reports	**REPUGN**	v **-ED, -ING, -S** to oppose

List of self-explanatory verbs containing the prefix RE- (continued):

REROLL	v **-ED, -ING, -S**	**RESAMPLE**	v **-PLED, -PLING, -PLES**	**RESEASON**	v **-ED, -ING, -S**
REROOF	v **-ED, -ING, -S**	**RESAW**	v **-SAWED, -SAWN, -SAWING, -SAWS**	**RESEAT**	v **-ED, -ING, -S**
REROSE	past tense of rerise			**RESECURE**	v **-CURED, -CURING, -CURES**
REROUTE	v **-ROUTED, -ROUTING, -ROUTES**	**RESAY**	v **-SAID, -SAYING, -SAYS**	**RESEE**	v **-SAW, -SEEN, -SEEING, -SEES**
		RESCHOOL	v **-ED, -ING, -S**		
RESADDLE	v **-DLED, -DLING, -DLES**	**RESCORE**	v **-SCORED, -SCORING, -SCORES**	**RESEED**	v **-ED, -ING, -S**
RESAID	past tense of resay	**RESCREEN**	v **-ED, -ING, -S**	**RESEEK**	v **-SOUGHT, -SEEKING, -SEEKS**
RESAIL	v **-ED, -ING, -S**	**RESCULPT**	v **-ED, -ING, -S**		
RESALUTE	v **-LUTED, -LUTING, -LUTES**	**RESEAL**	v **-ED, -ING, -S**	**RESEEN**	past participle of resee

REPULSE	*v* -PULSED, -PULSING, -PULSES to drive back
REPULSER	*n* pl. **-S** one that repulses
REPUTE	*v* -PUTED, -PUTING, -PUTES to consider to be as specified
REQUEST	*v* -ED, -ING, -S to express a desire for
REQUIEM	*n* pl. **-S** a musical composition for the dead
REQUIN	*n* pl. **-S** a voracious shark
REQUIRE	*v* -QUIRED, -QUIRING, -QUIRES to have need of
REQUIRER	*n* pl. **-S** one that requires
REQUITAL	*n* pl. **-S** something given in return, compensation, or retaliation
REQUITE	*v* -QUITED, -QUITING, -QUITES to make equivalent return for
REQUITER	*n* pl. **-S** one that requites
RERAN	past tense of rerun
REREDOS	*n* pl. **-ES** an ornamental screen behind an altar
REREMICE	*n/pl* bats (flying mammals)
REREWARD	*n* pl. **-S** rearward
REROLLER	*n* pl. **-S** one that rerolls
RERUN	*v* -RAN, -RUNNING, -RUNS to present a repetition of a recorded performance
RES	*n* pl. **RES** a particular thing or matter
RESALE	*n* pl. **-S** the act of selling again
RESCALE	*v* -SCALED, -SCALING, -SCALES to plan on a new scale
RESCIND	*v* -ED, -ING, -S to annul
RESCRIPT	*n* pl. **-S** something rewritten
RESCUE	*v* -CUED, -CUING, -CUES to free from danger
RESCUER	*n* pl. **-S** one that rescues
RESEARCH	*v* -ED, -ING, -ES to investigate thoroughly
RESEAU	*n* pl. **-SEAUS** or **-SEAUX** a filter screen for making color films
RESECT	*v* -ED, -ING, -S to excise part of an organ or structure surgically
RESEDA	*n* pl. **-S** a flowering plant
RESELLER	*n* pl. **-S** one that resells
RESEMBLE	*v* -BLED, -BLING, -BLES to be similar to
RESENT	*v* -ED, -ING, -S to feel or express annoyance or ill will at
RESERVE	*v* -SERVED, -SERVING, -SERVES to keep back for future use
RESERVER	*n* pl. **-S** one that reserves
RESETTER	*n* pl. **-S** one that resets
RESH	*n* pl. **-ES** a Hebrew letter
RESHAPER	*n* pl. **-S** one that reshapes something
RESID	*n* pl. **-S** a type of fuel oil
RESIDE	*v* -SIDED, -SIDING, -SIDES to dwell permanently or continuously
RESIDENT	*n* pl. **-S** one who resides
RESIDER	*n* pl. **-S** a resident
RESIDUAL	*n* pl. **-S** something left over
RESIDUE	*n* pl. **-S** something remaining after the removal of a part
RESIDUUM	*n* pl. **-SIDUUMS** or **-SIDUA** residue

List of self-explanatory verbs containing the prefix RE- (continued):

RESEIZE	*v* -SEIZED, -SEIZING, -SEIZES	**RESHAPE**	*v* -SHAPED, -SHAPING, -SHAPES	**RESHONE**	a past tense of reshine
RESELECT	*v* -ED, -ING, -S	**RESHAVE**	*v* -SHAVED, -SHAVEN, -SHAVING, -SHAVES	**RESHOOT**	*v* -SHOT, -SHOOTING, -SHOOTS
RESELL	*v* -SOLD, -SELLING, -SELLS	**RESHINE**	*v* -SHINED or -SHONE, -SHINING, -SHINES	**RESHOW**	*v* -SHOWED, -SHOWN, -SHOWING, -SHOWS
RESEND	*v* -SENT, -SENDING, -SENDS			**RESHOWER**	*v* -ED, -ING, -S
				RESIFT	*v* -ED, -ING, -S
RESET	*v* -SET, -SETTING, -SETS	**RESHIP**	*v* -SHIPPED, -SHIPPING, -SHIPS	**RESIGHT**	*v* -ED, -ING, -S
				RESILVER	*v* -ED, -ING, -S
RESETTLE	*v* -TLED, -TLING, -TLES	**RESHOE**	*v* -SHOD or -SHOED, -SHOEING, -SHOES	**RESIT**	*v* -SAT, -SITTING, -SITS
RESEW	*v* -SEWED, -SEWN, -SEWING, -SEWS			**RESITE**	*v* -SITED, -SITING, -SITES

RESIGN	v -**ED, -ING, -S** to give up one's office or position	**RESORT**	v -**ED, -ING, -S** to go frequently or habitually
RESIGNER	n pl. -**S** one that resigns	**RESORTER**	n pl. -**S** one that resorts
RESILE	v -**SILED, -SILING, -SILES** to spring back	**RESOUND**	v -**ED, -ING, -S** to make a loud, long, or echoing sound
RESILIN	n pl. -**S** an elastic substance in the cuticles of many insects	**RESOURCE**	n pl. -**S** an available supply
RESIN	v -**ED, -ING, -S** to treat with resin (a viscous substance obtained from certain plants)	**RESPECT**	v -**ED, -ING, -S** to have a high regard for
		RESPIRE	v -**SPIRED, -SPIRING, -SPIRES** to breathe
RESINATE	v -**ATED, -ATING, -ATES** to resin	**RESPITE**	v -**SPITED, -SPITING, -SPITES** to relieve temporarily
RESINIFY	v -**FIED, -FYING, -FIES** to convert into resin		
RESINOID	n pl. -**S** a resinous substance	**RESPOND**	v -**ED, -ING, -S** to say or act in return
RESINOUS	adj resembling resin	**RESPONSA**	n/pl written rabbinic decisions
RESINY	adj resinous	**RESPONSE**	n pl. -**S** a reply or reaction
RESIST	v -**ED, -ING, -S** to strive against	**REST**	v -**ED, -ING, -S** to refresh oneself by ceasing work or activity
RESISTER	n pl. -**S** one that resists	**RESTER**	n pl. -**S** one that rests
RESISTOR	n pl. -**S** a device in an electric circuit	**RESTFUL**	adj -**FULLER, -FULLEST** tranquil
RESOJET	n pl. -**S** a pulsejet	**RESTIVE**	adj difficult to control
RESOLUTE	adj -**LUTER, -LUTEST** characterized by firmness or determination	**RESTLESS**	adj unable or disinclined to remain at rest
		RESTORAL	n pl. -**S** the act of restoring
RESOLUTE	n pl. -**S** one who is resolute	**RESTORE**	v -**STORED, -STORING, -STORES** to bring back to a former or original condition
RESOLVE	v -**SOLVED, -SOLVING, -SOLVES** to make a firm decision about		
RESOLVER	n pl. -**S** one that resolves	**RESTORER**	n pl. -**S** one that restores
RESONANT	n pl. -**S** a resounding sound	**RESTRAIN**	v -**ED, -ING, -S** to hold back from action
RESONATE	v -**NATED, -NATING, -NATES** to resound	**RESTRICT**	v -**ED, -ING, -S** to keep within certain boundaries
RESORB	v -**ED, -ING, -S** to absorb again	**RESTROOM**	n pl. -**S** a room furnished with toilets and sinks
RESORCIN	n pl. -**S** a chemical compound		

List of self-explanatory verbs containing the prefix RE- (continued):

RESIZE	v -**SIZED, -SIZING, -SIZES**	**RESOLE**	v -**SOLED, -SOLING, -SOLES**	**RESPELL**	v -**SPELLED** or -**SPELT, -SPELLING, -SPELLS**
RESKETCH	v -**ED, -ING, -ES**	**RESOUGHT**	past tense of reseek		
RESLATE	v -**SLATED, -SLATING, -SLATES**	**RESOW**	v -**SOWED, -SOWN, -SOWING, -SOWS**	**RESPLICE**	v -**SPLICED, -SPLICING, -SPLICES**
RESMELT	v -**ED, -ING, -S**			**RESPLIT**	v -**SPLIT, -SPLITTING, -SPLITS**
RESMOOTH	v -**ED, -ING, -S**	**RESPACE**	v -**SPACED, -SPACING, -SPACES**		
RESOAK	v -**ED, -ING, -S**			**RESPOKE**	past tense of respeak
RESOD	v -**SODDED, -SODDING, -SODS**	**RESPADE**	v -**SPADED, -SPADING, -SPADES**	**RESPOKEN**	past participle of respeak
RESOFTEN	v -**ED, -ING, -S**				
RESOLD	past tense of resell	**RESPEAK**	v -**SPOKE, -SPOKEN, -SPEAKING, -SPEAKS**	**RESPOOL**	v -**ED, -ING, -S**
RESOLDER	v -**ED, -ING, -S**			**RESPOT**	v -**SPOTTED, -SPOTTING, -SPOTS**

RESULT	*v* **-ED, -ING, -S** to occur as a consequence
RESUME	*v* **-SUMED, -SUMING, -SUMES** to take up again after interruption
RESUMER	*n* pl. **-S** one that resumes
RESUPINE	*adj* lying on the back
RESURGE	*v* **-SURGED, -SURGING, -SURGES** to rise again
RET	*v* **RETTED, RETTING, RETS** to soak in order to loosen the fiber from the woody tissue
RETABLE	*n* pl. **-S** a raised shelf above an altar
RETAIL	*v* **-ED, -ING, -S** to sell in small quantities
RETAILER	*n* pl. **-S** one that retails
RETAIN	*v* **-ED, -ING, -S** to keep possession of
RETAINER	*n* pl. **-S** one that retains
RETAKE	*v* **-TOOK, -TAKEN, -TAKING, -TAKES** to take back
RETAKER	*n* pl. **-S** one that retakes
RETARD	*v* **-ED, -ING, -S** to slow the progress of
RETARDER	*n* pl. **-S** one that retards
RETCH	*v* **-ED, -ING, -ES** to make an effort to vomit
RETE	*n* pl. **-TIA** an anatomical mesh or network
RETEM	*n* pl. **-S** a desert shrub
RETENE	*n* pl. **-S** a chemical compound
RETIAL	*adj* pertaining to a rete
RETIARII	*n/pl* ancient Roman gladiators
RETIARY	*adj* resembling a net
RETICENT	*adj* tending to be silent
RETICLE	*n* pl. **-S** a network of lines in the eyepiece of an optical instrument
RETICULA	*n/pl* netlike structures
RETICULE	*n* pl. **-S** a woman's handbag
RETIFORM	*adj* arranged like a net
RETINA	*n* pl. **-NAS** or **-NAE** a membrane of the eye
RETINAL	*n* pl. **-S** retinene
RETINE	*n* pl. **-S** a substance in cells that retards growth and cell division
RETINENE	*n* pl. **-S** a pigment in the retina
RETINITE	*n* pl. **-S** a fossil resin
RETINOID	*n* pl. **-S** a compound analogous to vitamin A
RETINOL	*n* pl. **-S** a liquid hydrocarbon
RETINUE	*n* pl. **-S** a group of attendants **RETINUED** *adj*
RETINULA	*n* pl. **-LAS** or **-LAE** a neural receptor of an arthropod's eye
RETIRANT	*n* pl. **-S** a retiree
RETIRE	*v* **-TIRED, -TIRING, -TIRES** to go away or withdraw
RETIREE	*n* pl. **-S** one who has retired from his vocation
RETIRER	*n* pl. **-S** one that retires
RETIRING	*adj* shy
RETOOK	past tense of retake
RETOOL	*v* **-ED, -ING, -S** to reequip with tools
RETORT	*v* **-ED, -ING, -S** to answer back sharply

List of self-explanatory verbs containing the prefix RE- (continued):

RESPRANG	a past tense of respring	**RESTAMP**	*v* **-ED, -ING, -S**	**RESTRIVE**	*v* **-STROVE, -STRIVEN, -STRIVING, -STRIVES**
RESPRAY	*v* **-ED, -ING, -S**	**RESTART**	*v* **-ED, -ING, -S**		
RESPREAD	*v* **-SPREAD, -SPREADING, -SPREADS**	**RESTATE**	*v* **-STATED, -STATING, -STATES**	**RESTRUCK**	past tense of restrike
		RESTITCH	*v* **-ED, -ING, -ES**	**RESTRUNG**	past tense of restring
RESPRING	*v* **-SPRANG** or **-SPRUNG, -SPRINGING, -SPRINGS**	**RESTOCK**	*v* **-ED, -ING, -S**	**RESTUDY**	*v* **-STUDIED, -STUDYING, -STUDIES**
		RESTOKE	*v* **-STOKED, -STOKING, -STOKES**		
RESPROUT	*v* **-ED, -ING, -S**	**RESTRESS**	*v* **-ED, -ING, -ES**	**RESTUFF**	*v* **-ED, -ING, -S**
RESTABLE	*v* **-BLED, -BLING, -BLES**	**RESTRIKE**	*v* **-STRUCK, -STRICKEN, -STRIKING, -STRIKES**	**RESTYLE**	*v* **-STYLED, -STYLING, -STYLES**
RESTACK	*v* **-ED, -ING, -S**				
RESTAFF	*v* **-ED, -ING, -S**	**RESTRING**	*v* **-STRUNG, -STRINGING, -STRINGS**	**RESUBMIT**	*v* **-MITTED, -MITTING, -MITS**
RESTAGE	*v* **-STAGED, -STAGING, -STAGES**			**RESUMMON**	*v* **-ED, -ING, -S**

RETORTER	*n* pl. **-S** one that retorts	**RETURNER**	*n* pl. **-S** one that returns
RETOUCH	*v* **-ED, -ING, -ES** to add new details or touches to	**RETUSE**	*adj* having a rounded apex with a shallow notch — used of leaves
RETRACE	*v* **-TRACED, -TRACING, -TRACES** to go back over	**REUNION**	*n* pl. **-S** a reuniting of persons after separation
RETRACER	*n* pl. **-S** one that retraces	**REUNITER**	*n* pl. **-S** one that reunites
RETRACT	*v* **-ED, -ING, -S** to take back	**REUPTAKE**	*n* pl. **-S** the reabsorption of a chemical into the cell that released it
RETRAL	*adj* situated toward the back **RETRALLY** *adv*		
RETREAD	*v* **-ED, -ING, -S** to furnish with a new tread	**REUSABLE**	*n* pl. **-S** something that can be reused
RETREAT	*v* **-ED, -ING, -S** to go back or backward	**REV**	*v* **REVVED, REVVING, REVS** to increase the speed of
RETRENCH	*v* **-ED, -ING, -ES** to curtail	**REVAMP**	*v* **-ED, -ING, -S** to make over
RETRIAL	*n* pl. **-S** a second trial	**REVAMPER**	*n* pl. **-S** one that revamps
RETRIEVE	*v* **-TRIEVED, -TRIEVING, -TRIEVES** to get back	**REVANCHE**	*n* pl. **-S** a political policy designed to regain lost territory
RETRO	*n* pl. **-ROS** a rocket on a spacecraft that produces thrust in a direction opposite to the line of flight	**REVEAL**	*v* **-ED, -ING, -S** to make known
		REVEALER	*n* pl. **-S** one that reveals
RETROACT	*v* **-ED, -ING, -S** to act in return	**REVEHENT**	*adj* carrying back
RETROFIT	*v* **-FITTED, -FITTING, -FITS** to furnish with new parts not originally available	**REVEILLE**	*n* pl. **-S** a morning bugle call
		REVEL	*v* **-ELED, -ELING, -ELS** or **-ELLED, -ELLING, -ELS** to engage in revelry
RETRONYM	*n* pl. **-S** a term coined to distinguish the original referent from a later development	**REVELER**	*n* pl. **-S** one that revels
		REVELLER	*n* pl. **-S** reveler
RETRORSE	*adj* bent backward	**REVELRY**	*n* pl. **-RIES** noisy merrymaking
RETSINA	*n* pl. **-S** a resin-flavored Greek wine	**REVENANT**	*n* pl. **-S** one that returns
RETTED	past tense of ret	**REVENGE**	*v* **-VENGED, -VENGING, -VENGES** to inflict injury in return for
RETTING	present participle of ret		
RETURN	*v* **-ED, -ING, -S** to come or go back		
RETURNEE	*n* pl. **-S** one that has returned	**REVENGER**	*n* pl. **-S** one that revenges

List of self-explanatory verbs containing the prefix RE- (continued):

RESUPPLY	*v* **-PLIED, -PLYING, -PLIES**	**RETEACH**	*v* **-TAUGHT, -TEACHING, -TEACHES**	**RETILE**	*v* **-TILED, -TILING, -TILES**
RESURVEY	*v* **-ED, -ING, -S**			**RETIME**	*v* **-TIMED, -TIMING, -TIMES**
RETACK	*v* **-ED, -ING, -S**	**RETEAM**	*v* **-ED, -ING, -S**		
RETACKLE	*v* **-LED, -LING, -LES**	**RETEAR**	*v* **-TORE, -TORN, -TEARING, -TEARS**	**RETINT**	*v* **-ED, -ING, -S**
RETAG	*v* **-TAGGED, -TAGGING, -TAGS**	**RETELL**	*v* **-TOLD, -TELLING, -TELLS**	**RETITLE**	*v* **-TLED, -TLING, -TLES**
RETAILOR	*v* **-ED, -ING, -S**			**RETOLD**	past tense of retell
RETALLY	*v* **-LIED, -LYING, -LIES**	**RETEMPER**	*v* **-ED, -ING, -S**	**RETORE**	past tense of retear
RETAPE	*v* **-TAPED, -TAPING, -TAPES**	**RETEST**	*v* **-ED, -ING, -S**	**RETORN**	past participle of retear
		RETHINK	*v* **-THOUGHT, -THINKING, -THINKS**		
RETARGET	*v* **-ED, -ING, -S**			**RETOTAL**	*v* **-TALED, -TALING, -TALS** or **-TALLED, -TALLING, -TALS**
RETASTE	*v* **-TASTED, -TASTING, -TASTES**	**RETHREAD**	*v* **-ED, -ING, -S**		
RETAX	*v* **-ED, -ING, -ES**	**RETIE**	*v* **-TIED, -TYING,** or **-TIEING, -TIES**		

REVENUE	*n* pl. **-S** the income of a government **REVENUAL, REVENUED** *adj*	**REVISAL**	*n* pl. **-S** a revision
		REVISE	*v* **-VISED, -VISING, -VISES** to make a new or improved version of
REVENUER	*n* pl. **-S** a revenue officer	**REVISER**	*n* pl. **-S** one that revises
REVERB	*v* **-ED, -ING, -S** to continue in a series of echoes	**REVISION**	*n* pl. **-S** a revised version
REVERE	*v* **-VERED, -VERING, -VERES** to regard with great respect	**REVISOR**	*n* pl. **-S** reviser
		REVISORY	*adj* pertaining to revision
REVEREND	*n* pl. **-S** a clergyman	**REVIVAL**	*n* pl. **-S** renewed attention to or interest in something
REVERENT	*adj* deeply respectful		
REVERER	*n* pl. **-S** one that reveres	**REVIVE**	*v* **-VIVED, -VIVING, -VIVES** to bring back to life or consciousness
REVERIE	*n* pl. **-S** a daydream		
REVERIES	pl. of revery	**REVIVER**	*n* pl. **-S** one that revives
REVERING	present participle of revere	**REVIVIFY**	*v* **-FIED, -FYING, -FIES** to give new life to
REVERS	*n* pl. **REVERS** a part of a garment turned back to show the inside	**REVOKE**	*v* **-VOKED, -VOKING, -VOKES** to annul by taking back
REVERSAL	*n* pl. **-S** the act of reversing	**REVOKER**	*n* pl. **-S** one that revokes
REVERSE	*v* **-VERSED, -VERSING, -VERSES** to turn or move in the opposite direction	**REVOLT**	*v* **-ED, -ING, -S** to rise up against authority
		REVOLTER	*n* pl. **-S** one that revolts
REVERSER	*n* pl. **-S** one that reverses	**REVOLUTE**	*adj* rolled backward or downward
REVERSO	*n* pl. **-VERSOS** verso	**REVOLVE**	*v* **-VOLVED, -VOLVING, -VOLVES** to turn about an axis
REVERT	*v* **-ED, -ING, -S** to return to a former state		
		REVOLVER	*n* pl. **-S** a type of handgun
REVERTER	*n* pl. **-S** one that reverts	**REVUE**	*n* pl. **-S** a type of musical show
REVERY	*n* pl. **-ERIES** reverie	**REVUIST**	*n* pl. **-S** a writer of revues
REVET	*v* **-VETTED, -VETTING, -VETS** to face with masonry	**REVULSED**	*adj* affected with revulsion
		REVVED	past tense of rev
REVIEWAL	*n* pl. **-S** the act of reviewing	**REVVING**	present participle of rev
REVIEWER	*n* pl. **-S** one that reviews	**REWARD**	*v* **-ED, -ING, -S** to give recompense to for worthy behavior
REVILE	*v* **-VILED, -VILING, -VILES** to denounce with abusive language		
REVILER	*n* pl. **-S** one that reviles	**REWARDER**	*n* pl. **-S** one that rewards

---

List of self-explanatory verbs containing the prefix RE- (continued):

RETRACK	*v* **-ED, -ING, -S**	**REUNITE**	*v* **-UNITED, -UNITING, -UNITES**	**REWAKE**	*v* **-WAKED** or **-WOKE, -WOKEN, -WAKING, -WAKES**
RETRAIN	*v* **-ED, -ING, -S**				
RETRIM	*v* **-TRIMMED, -TRIMMING, -TRIMS**				
		REUSE	*v* **-USED, -USING, -USES**	**REWAKEN**	*v* **-ED, -ING, -S**
RETRY	*v* **-TRIED, -TRYING, -TRIES**	**REUTTER**	*v* **-ED, -ING, -S**	**REWAN**	a past tense of rewin
		REVALUE	*v* **-UED, -UING, -UES**		
RETUNE	*v* **-TUNED, -TUNING, -TUNES**			**REWARM**	*v* **-ED, -ING, -S**
		REVERIFY	*v* **-FIED, -FYING, -FIES**	**REWASH**	*v* **-ED, -ING, -ES**
				REWAX	*v* **-ED, -ING, -ES**
RETWIST	*v* **-ED, -ING, -S**	**REVEST**	*v* **-ED, -ING, -S**	**REWEAR**	*v* **-WORE, -WORN, -WEARING, -WEARS**
RETYING	present participle of retie	**REVIEW**	*v* **-ED, -ING, -S**		
		REVISIT	*v* **-ED, -ING, -S**		
RETYPE	*v* **-TYPED, -TYPING, -TYPES**	**REVOICE**	*v* **-VOICED, -VOICING, -VOICES**	**REWEAVE**	*v* **-WOVE** or **-WEAVED, -WOVEN, -WEAVING, -WEAVES**
REUNIFY	*v* **-FIED, -FYING, -FIES**	**REVOTE**	*v* **-VOTED, -VOTING, -VOTES**		

REWINDER	*n* pl. **-S** one that rewinds	**RHEOPHIL**	*adj* living in flowing water
REWORD	*v* **-ED, -ING, -S** to state again in other words	**RHEOSTAT**	*n* pl. **-S** a resistor used to control electric current
REWRITER	*n* pl. **-S** one that rewrites	**RHESUS**	*n* pl. **-ES** an Asian monkey
REX	*n* pl. **-ES** an animal with a single wavy layer of hair	**RHETOR**	*n* pl. **-S** a teacher of rhetoric
REX	*n* pl. **REGES** king	**RHETORIC**	*n* pl. **-S** the study of effective speech and writing
REYNARD	*n* pl. **-S** a fox	**RHEUM**	*n* pl. **-S** a watery discharge from the eyes or nose **RHEUMIC** *adj*
REZERO	*v* **-ED, -ING, -ES** or **-S** to reset (a gauge) back to zero	**RHEUMY**	*adj* **RHEUMIER, RHEUMIEST** marked by rheum
RHABDOM	*n* pl. **-S** a rodlike structure in the retinula	**RHINAL**	*adj* pertaining to the nose
RHABDOME	*n* pl. **-S** rhabdom	**RHINITIS**	*n* pl. **RHINITIDES** inflammation of the mucous membranes of the nose
RHACHIS	*n* pl. **-CHISES** or **-CHIDES** rachis		
RHAMNOSE	*n* pl. **-S** a sugar found in plants	**RHINO**	*n* pl. **-NOS** a rhinoceros
RHAMNUS	*n* pl. **-ES** a thorny tree or shrub	**RHIZOBIA**	*n/pl* rod-shaped bacteria
RHAPHE	*n* pl. **-PHES** or **-PHAE** raphe	**RHIZOID**	*n* pl. **-S** a rootlike structure
RHAPSODE	*n* pl. **-S** a reciter of epic poetry in ancient Greece	**RHIZOMA**	*n* pl. **-MATA** rhizome
RHAPSODY	*n* pl. **-DIES** an exalted expression of feeling	**RHIZOME**	*n* pl. **-S** a rootlike, underground stem **RHIZOMIC** *adj*
RHATANY	*n* pl. **-NIES** a South American shrub	**RHIZOPOD**	*n* pl. **-S** any of a class of protozoans
RHEA	*n* pl. **-S** a flightless bird	**RHIZOPUS**	*n* pl. **-PUSES** or **-PI** any of a genus of mold fungi
RHEBOK	*n* pl. **-S** a large antelope		
RHEMATIC	*adj* pertaining to a verb	**RHO**	*n* pl. **RHOS** a Greek letter
RHEME	*n* pl. **-S** a statement of fact or opinion	**RHODAMIN**	*n* pl. **-S** a red dye
RHENIUM	*n* pl. **-S** a metallic element	**RHODIUM**	*n* pl. **-S** a metallic element **RHODIC** *adj*
RHEOBASE	*n* pl. **-S** the smallest amount of electricity required to stimulate a nerve	**RHODORA**	*n* pl. **-S** a flowering shrub
		RHOMB	*n* pl. **-S** a rhombus
RHEOLOGY	*n* pl. **-GIES** the study of matter in the fluid state	**RHOMBIC**	*adj* having the shape of a rhombus
		RHOMBOID	*n* pl. **-S** a type of geometric figure

List of self-explanatory verbs containing the prefix RE- (continued):

REWED	*v* **-WEDDED, -WEDDING, -WEDS**	**REWIRE**	*v* **-WIRED, -WIRING, -WIRES**	**REWOVEN**	past participle of reweave
REWEIGH	*v* **-ED, -ING, -S**	**REWOKE**	a past tense of rewake	**REWRAP**	*v* **-WRAPPED** or **-WRAPT, -WRAPPING, -WRAPS**
REWELD	*v* **-ED, -ING, -S**	**REWOKEN**	past participle of rewake		
REWET	*v* **-WETTED, -WETTING, -WETS**	**REWON**	a past tense of rewin	**REWRITE**	*v* **-WROTE, -WRITTEN, -WRITING, -WRITES**
REWIDEN	*v* **-ED, -ING, -S**	**REWORK**	*v* **-WORKED** or **-WROUGHT, -WORKING, -WORKS**		
REWIN	*v* **-WON** or **-WAN, -WINNING, -WINS**			**REWROUGHT**	a past tense of rework
REWIND	*v* **-WOUND** or **-WINDED, -WINDING, -WINDS**	**REWOUND**	a past tense of rewind	**REZONE**	*v* **-ZONED, -ZONING, -ZONES**
		REWOVE	a past tense of reweave		

RHOMBUS	*n* pl. **-BUSES** or **-BI** a type of geometric figure	**RIBES**	*n* pl. **RIBES** a flowering shrub
RHONCHUS	*n* pl. **-CHI** a rattling respiratory sound **RHONCHAL** *adj*	**RIBGRASS**	*n* pl. **-ES** a weedy plant
		RIBIER	*n* pl. **-S** a large, black grape
		RIBLESS	*adj* having no ribs
RHOTIC	*adj* pertaining to a dialect of English in which the letter r at the end of a syllable is pronounced	**RIBLET**	*n* pl. **-S** the rib end in a breast of lamb or veal
RHUBARB	*n* pl. **-S** a perennial herb	**RIBLIKE**	*adj* resembling a rib
RHUMB	*n* pl. **-S** a point of the mariner's compass	**RIBOSE**	*n* pl. **-S** a pentose sugar
RHUMBA	*v* **-ED, -ING, -S** to rumba	**RIBOSOME**	*n* pl. **-S** a particle composed of protein and ribonucleic acid
RHUS	*n* pl. **-ES** any of a genus of shrubs and trees	**RIBOZYME**	*n* pl. **-S** a molecule of RNA that functions as an enzyme
RHYME	*v* **RHYMED, RHYMING, RHYMES** to compose verse with corresponding terminal sounds	**RIBWORT**	*n* pl. **-S** ribgrass
		RICE	*v* **RICED, RICING, RICES** to press through a ricer
RHYMER	*n* pl. **-S** one that rhymes	**RICEBIRD**	*n* pl. **-S** the bobolink
RHYOLITE	*n* pl. **-S** a volcanic rock	**RICER**	*n* pl. **-S** a kitchen utensil consisting of a container perforated with small holes
RHYTHM	*n* pl. **-S** movement or procedure with uniform recurrence of strong and weak elements		
RHYTHMIC	*n* pl. **-S** the science of rhythm	**RICERCAR**	*n* pl. **-S** an instrumental composition
RHYTON	*n* pl. **-TONS** or **-TA** an ancient Greek drinking horn	**RICH**	*adj* **RICHER, RICHEST** having wealth
RIA	*n* pl. **-S** a long, narrow inlet	**RICHEN**	*v* **-ED, -ING, -S** to make rich
RIAL	*n* pl. **-S** a monetary unit of Iran	**RICHES**	*n/pl* wealth
RIALTO	*n* pl. **-TOS** a marketplace	**RICHLY**	*adv* in a rich manner
RIANT	*adj* cheerful **RIANTLY** *adv*	**RICHNESS**	*n* pl. **-ES** the state of being rich
RIATA	*n* pl. **-S** a lasso	**RICHWEED**	*n* pl. **-S** a flowering plant
RIB	*v* **RIBBED, RIBBING, RIBS** to poke fun at	**RICIN**	*n* pl. **-S** a poisonous protein
		RICING	present participle of rice
RIBALD	*n* pl. **-S** one who uses crude language	**RICINUS**	*n* pl. **-ES** a large-leaved plant
RIBALDLY	*adv* crudely	**RICK**	*v* **-ED, -ING, -S** to pile hay in stacks
RIBALDRY	*n* pl. **-RIES** crude language	**RICKETS**	*n/pl* a disease resulting from vitamin D deficiency
RIBAND	*n* pl. **-S** a ribbon		
RIBBAND	*n* pl. **-S** a long, narrow strip used in shipbuilding	**RICKETY**	*adj* **-ETIER, -ETIEST** likely to fall or collapse
RIBBED	past tense of rib	**RICKEY**	*n* pl. **-EYS** an alcoholic beverage containing lime juice, sugar, and soda water
RIBBER	*n* pl. **-S** one that ribs		
RIBBIER	comparative of ribby		
RIBBIEST	superlative of ribby	**RICKRACK**	*n* pl. **-S** a flat braid used as a trimming
RIBBING	*n* pl. **-S** the act of one that ribs	**RICKSHA**	*n* pl. **-S** rickshaw
RIBBON	*v* **-ED, -ING, -S** to decorate with ribbons (narrow strips of fine fabric)	**RICKSHAW**	*n* pl. **-S** a small, two-wheeled passenger vehicle
		RICOCHET	*v* **-CHETED, -CHETING, -CHETS** or **-CHETTED, -CHETTING, -CHETS** to rebound from a surface
RIBBONY	*adj* resembling ribbon		
RIBBY	*adj* **-BIER, -BIEST** marked by prominent ribs (curved bony rods in the body)	**RICOTTA**	*n* pl. **-S** an Italian cheese
		RICRAC	*n* pl. **-S** rickrack

RICTUS | *n* pl. **-ES** the expanse of the open mouth **RICTAL** *adj*

RID | *v* **RID** or **RIDDED, RIDDING, RIDS** to free from something objectionable

RIDABLE | *adj* capable of being ridden

RIDDANCE | *n* pl. **-S** deliverance

RIDDEN | past participle of ride

RIDDER | *n* pl. **-S** one that rids

RIDDING | present participle of rid

RIDDLE | *v* **-DLED, -DLING, -DLES** to pierce with many holes

RIDDLER | *n* pl. **-S** one that riddles

RIDE | *v* **RODE, RIDDEN, RIDING, RIDES** to sit on, control, and be conveyed by an animal or machine

RIDEABLE | *adj* ridable

RIDENT | *adj* laughing

RIDER | *n* pl. **-S** one that rides

RIDGE | *v* **RIDGED, RIDGING, RIDGES** to form into ridges (long, narrow elevations)

RIDGEL | *n* pl. **-S** a ridgling

RIDGETOP | *n* pl. **-S** the crest of a ridge

RIDGIER | comparative of ridgy

RIDGIEST | superlative of ridgy

RIDGIL | *n* pl. **-S** a ridgling

RIDGING | present participle of ridge

RIDGLING | *n* pl. **-S** a male animal with undescended testicles

RIDGY | *adj* **RIDGIER, RIDGIEST** having ridges

RIDICULE | *v* **-CULED, -CULING, -CULES** to make fun of

RIDING | *n* pl. **-S** the act of one that rides

RIDLEY | *n* pl. **-LEYS** a sea turtle

RIDOTTO | *n* pl. **-TOS** a public musical entertainment in 18th century England

RIEL | *n* pl. **-S** a monetary unit of Cambodia

RIESLING | *n* pl. **-S** a white Rhine wine

RIEVER | *n* pl. **-S** reaver

RIF | *v* **RIFFED, RIFFING, RIFS** to dismiss from employment

RIFAMPIN | *n* pl. **-S** an antibiotic

RIFE | *adj* **RIFER, RIFEST** abundant **RIFELY** *adv*

RIFENESS | *n* pl. **-ES** the state of being rife

RIFF | *v* **-ED, -ING, -S** to riffle

RIFFED | past tense of rif

RIFFING | present participle of rif

RIFFLE | *v* **-FLED, -FLING, -FLES** to flip through hastily

RIFFLER | *n* pl. **-S** a filing and scraping tool

RIFFRAFF | *n* pl. **-S** the disreputable element of society

RIFLE | *v* **-FLED, -FLING, -FLES** to search through and rob

RIFLEMAN | *n* pl. **-MEN** a soldier armed with a rifle (a type of firearm)

RIFLER | *n* pl. **-S** one that rifles

RIFLERY | *n* pl. **-RIES** the practice of shooting at targets with a rifle

RIFLING | *n* pl. **-S** the system of grooves in a gun barrel

RIFLIP | *n* pl. **-S** a fragment of DNA

RIFT | *v* **-ED, -ING, -S** to form rifts (clefts)

RIFTLESS | *adj* having no rift

RIG | *v* **RIGGED, RIGGING, RIGS** to put in proper condition for use

RIGADOON | *n* pl. **-S** a lively dance

RIGATONI | *n* pl. **-S** a tubular pasta

RIGAUDON | *n* pl. **-S** rigadoon

RIGGED | past tense of rig

RIGGER | *n* pl. **-S** one that rigs

RIGGING | *n* pl. **-S** the system of lines, chains, and tackle used aboard a ship

RIGHT | *adj* **RIGHTER, RIGHTEST** being in accordance with what is good, proper, or just

RIGHT | *v* **-ED, -ING, -S** to put in proper order or condition

RIGHTER | *n* pl. **-S** one that rights

RIGHTFUL | *adj* just or proper

RIGHTIES | pl. of righty

RIGHTISM | *n* pl. **-S** a conservative political philosophy

RIGHTIST | *n* pl. **-S** an advocate of rightism

RIGHTLY | *adv* in a right manner

RIGHTO | *interj* — used to express cheerful consent

RIGHTY | *n* pl. **RIGHTIES** a right-handed person

RIGID | *adj* not flexible

RIGIDIFY | *v* **-FIED, -FYING, -FIES** to make rigid

RIGIDITY | *n* pl. **-TIES** the state of being rigid

RIGIDLY	*adv* in a rigid manner
RIGOR	*n* pl. **-S** strictness or severity
RIGORISM	*n* pl. **-S** strictness or severity in conduct or attitude
RIGORIST	*n* pl. **-S** one that professes rigorism
RIGOROUS	*adj* characterized by rigor
RIGOUR	*n* pl. **-S** rigor
RIKISHA	*n* pl. **-S** rickshaw
RIKSHAW	*n* pl. **-S** rickshaw
RILE	*v* **RILED, RILING, RILES** to anger
RILEY	*adj* angry
RILIEVO	*n* pl. **-VI** relievo
RILL	*v* **-ED, -ING, -S** to flow like a rill (a small brook)
RILLE	*n* pl. **-S** a valley on the moon's surface
RILLET	*n* pl. **-S** a small rill
RIM	*v* **RIMMED, RIMMING, RIMS** to provide with a rim (an outer edge)
RIME	*v* **RIMED, RIMING, RIMES** to rhyme
RIMER	*n* pl. **-S** one that rimes
RIMESTER	*n* pl. **-S** a rimer
RIMFIRE	*n* pl. **-S** a cartridge having the primer set in the rim of the shell
RIMIER	comparative of rimy
RIMIEST	superlative of rimy
RIMINESS	*n* pl. **-ES** the condition of being rimy
RIMING	present participle of rime
RIMLAND	*n* pl. **-S** an outlying area
RIMLESS	*adj* having no rim
RIMMED	past tense of rim
RIMMER	*n* pl. **-S** a reamer
RIMMING	present participle of rim
RIMOSE	*adj* marked by cracks **RIMOSELY** *adv*
RIMOSITY	*n* pl. **-TIES** the state of being rimose
RIMOUS	*adj* rimose
RIMPLE	*v* **-PLED, -PLING, -PLES** to wrinkle
RIMROCK	*n* pl. **-S** a type of rock formation
RIMSHOT	*n* pl. **-S** a sound made by a drumstick striking the rim and head of a drum
RIMY	*adj* **RIMIER, RIMIEST** frosty
RIN	*v* **RAN, RINNING, RINS** to run or melt
RIND	*n* pl. **-S** a thick and firm outer covering **RINDED, RINDY** *adj*
RINDLESS	*adj* lacking a rind
RING	*v* **-ED, -ING, -S** to form a ring (a circular band) around
RING	*v* **RANG, RUNG, RINGING, RINGS** to give forth a clear, resonant sound
RINGBARK	*v* **-ED, -ING, -S** to make an encircling cut through the bark of
RINGBOLT	*n* pl. **-S** a type of eyebolt
RINGBONE	*n* pl. **-S** a bony growth on a horse's foot
RINGDOVE	*n* pl. **-S** a European pigeon
RINGENT	*adj* having open liplike parts
RINGER	*n* pl. **-S** one that rings
RINGGIT	*n* pl. **-S** a monetary unit of Malaysia
RINGHALS	*n* pl. **-ES** a venomous snake
RINGLET	*n* pl. **-S** a small ring
RINGLIKE	*adj* resembling a ring
RINGNECK	*n* pl. **-S** a bird having a ring of color around the neck
RINGSIDE	*n* pl. **-S** the area just outside a boxing or wrestling ring (a square enclosure)
RINGTAIL	*n* pl. **-S** an animal having a tail with ringlike markings
RINGTAW	*n* pl. **-S** a game of marbles
RINGTOSS	*n* pl. **-ES** a game in which the object is to toss a ring onto an upright stick
RINGWORM	*n* pl. **-S** a skin disease
RINK	*n* pl. **-S** a surface of ice for skating
RINNING	present participle of rin
RINSE	*v* **RINSED, RINSING, RINSES** to cleanse with clear water **RINSABLE, RINSIBLE** *adj*
RINSER	*n* pl. **-S** one that rinses
RINSING	*n* pl. **-S** the act of one that rinses
RIOJA	*n* pl. **-S** a dry red Spanish wine
RIOT	*v* **-ED, -ING, -S** to take part in a violent public disturbance
RIOTER	*n* pl. **-S** one that riots
RIOTOUS	*adj* characterized by rioting
RIP	*v* **RIPPED, RIPPING, RIPS** to tear or cut apart roughly
RIPARIAN	*adj* pertaining to the bank of a river
RIPCORD	*n* pl. **-S** a cord pulled to release a parachute

RIPE	*adj* **RIPER, RIPEST** fully developed **RIPELY** *adv*	**RISKY**	*adj* **RISKIER, RISKIEST** dangerous **RISKILY** *adv*
RIPE	*v* **RIPED, RIPING, RIPES** to cleanse	**RISOTTO**	*n* pl. **-TOS** a rice dish
RIPEN	*v* **-ED, -ING, -S** to become ripe	**RISQUE**	*adj* bordering on impropriety or indecency
RIPENER	*n* pl. **-S** one that ripens	**RISSOLE**	*n* pl. **-S** a small roll filled with meat or fish
RIPENESS	*n* pl. **-ES** the state of being ripe	**RISTRA**	*n* pl. **-S** a string on which foodstuffs are tied for storage
RIPER	comparative of ripe		
RIPEST	superlative of ripe	**RISUS**	*n* pl. **-ES** a grin or laugh
RIPIENO	*n* pl. **-NOS** or **-NI** tutti	**RITARD**	*n* pl. **-S** a musical passage with a gradual slackening in tempo
RIPING	present participle of ripe		
RIPOFF	*n* pl. **-S** an instance of stealing	**RITE**	*n* pl. **-S** a ceremonial act or procedure
RIPOST	*v* **-ED, -ING, -S** to riposte		
RIPOSTE	*v* **-POSTED, -POSTING, -POSTES** to make a return thrust in fencing	**RITTER**	*n* pl. **-S** a knight
		RITUAL	*n* pl. **-S** a system of rites
RIPPABLE	*adj* capable of being ripped	**RITUALLY**	*adv* ceremonially
RIPPED	past tense of rip	**RITZ**	*n* pl. **-ES** pretentious display
RIPPER	*n* pl. **-S** one that rips	**RITZY**	*adj* **RITZIER, RITZIEST** elegant **RITZILY** *adv*
RIPPING	*adj* excellent		
RIPPLE	*v* **-PLED, -PLING, -PLES** to form ripples (small waves)	**RIVAGE**	*n* pl. **-S** a coast, shore, or bank
		RIVAL	*v* **-VALED, -VALING, -VALS** or **-VALLED, -VALLING, -VALS** to strive to equal or surpass
RIPPLER	*n* pl. **-S** a toothed tool for cleaning flax fiber		
RIPPLET	*n* pl. **-S** a small ripple	**RIVALRY**	*n* pl. **-RIES** competition
RIPPLING	present participle of ripple	**RIVE**	*v* **RIVED, RIVEN, RIVING, RIVES** to tear apart
RIPPLY	*adj* **-PLIER, -PLIEST** marked by ripples		
		RIVER	*n* pl. **-S** a large, natural stream of water
RIPRAP	*v* **-RAPPED, -RAPPING, -RAPS** to strengthen with a foundation of broken stones		
		RIVERBED	*n* pl. **-S** the area covered or once covered by a river
RIPSAW	*v* **-SAWED, -SAWN, -SAWING, -SAWS** to saw wood by cutting with the grain	**RIVERINE**	*adj* pertaining to a river
		RIVET	*v* **-ETED, -ETING, -ETS** or **-ETTED, -ETTING, -ETS** to fasten with a type of metal bolt
RIPSTOP	*n* pl. **-S** a fabric woven so that small tears do not spread		
RIPTIDE	*n* pl. **-S** a tide that opposes other tides	**RIVETER**	*n* pl. **-S** one that rivets
		RIVIERA	*n* pl. **-S** a coastal resort area
RISE	*v* **ROSE, RISEN, RISING, RISES** to move upward	**RIVIERE**	*n* pl. **-S** a necklace of precious stones
RISER	*n* pl. **-S** one that rises	**RIVING**	present participle of rive
RISHI	*n* pl. **-S** a Hindu sage	**RIVULET**	*n* pl. **-S** a small stream
RISIBLE	*adj* inclined to laugh **RISIBLY** *adv*	**RIVULOSE**	*adj* having narrow, winding lines
RISIBLES	*n/pl* a sense of the ridiculous	**RIYAL**	*n* pl. **-S** a monetary unit of Saudi Arabia
RISING	*n* pl. **-S** the act of one that rises		
RISK	*v* **-ED, -ING, -S** to expose to a risk (a chance of injury or loss)	**ROACH**	*v* **-ED, -ING, -ES** to cause to arch
		ROAD	*n* pl. **-S** an open way for public passage
RISKER	*n* pl. **-S** one that risks		
RISKLESS	*adj* free of risk	**ROADBED**	*n* pl. **-S** the foundation for a railroad track

ROADEO *n pl.* **-EOS** a competition for truck drivers

ROADIE *n pl.* **-S** a person who works for traveling entertainers

ROADKILL *n pl.* **-S** an animal that has been killed on a road

ROADLESS *adj* having no roads

ROADSHOW *n pl.* **-S** a theatrical show on tour

ROADSIDE *n pl.* **-S** the area along the side of a road

ROADSTER *n pl.* **-S** a light, open automobile

ROADWAY *n pl.* **-WAYS** a road

ROADWORK *n pl.* **-S** outdoor running as a form of physical conditioning

ROAM *v* **-ED, -ING, -S** to move about without purpose or plan

ROAMER *n pl.* **-S** one that roams

ROAN *n pl.* **-S** an animal having a coat sprinkled with white or gray

ROAR *v* **-ED, -ING, -S** to utter a loud, deep sound

ROARER *n pl.* **-S** one that roars

ROARING *n pl.* **-S** a loud, deep sound

ROAST *v* **-ED, -ING, -S** to cook with dry heat

ROASTER *n pl.* **-S** one that roasts

ROB *v* **ROBBED, ROBBING, ROBS** to take property from illegally

ROBALO *n pl.* **-LOS** a marine food fish

ROBAND *n pl.* **-S** a piece of yarn used to fasten a sail

ROBBER *n pl.* **-S** one that robs

ROBBERY *n pl.* **-BERIES** the act of one who robs

ROBBIN *n pl.* **-S** a roband

ROBBING present participle of rob

ROBE *v* **ROBED, ROBING, ROBES** to cover with a robe (a long, loose outer garment)

ROBIN *n pl.* **-S** a songbird

ROBLE *n pl.* **-S** an oak tree

ROBORANT *n pl.* **-S** an invigorating drug

ROBOT *n pl.* **-S** a humanlike machine that performs various functions **ROBOTIC** *adj*

ROBOTICS *n/pl* a field of interest concerned with robots

ROBOTISM *n pl.* **-S** the state of being a robot

ROBOTIZE *v* **-IZED, -IZING, -IZES** to make automatic

ROBOTRY *n pl.* **-RIES** the science of robots

ROBUST *adj* **-BUSTER, -BUSTEST** strong and healthy **ROBUSTLY** *adv*

ROBUSTA *n pl.* **-S** a coffee grown in Africa

ROC *n pl.* **-S** a legendary bird of prey

ROCAILLE *n pl.* **-S** rococo

ROCHET *n pl.* **-S** a linen vestment

ROCK *v* **-ED, -ING, -S** to move back and forth **ROCKABLE** *adj*

ROCKABY *n pl.* **-BIES** a song used to lull a child to sleep

ROCKABYE *n pl.* **-S** rockaby

ROCKAWAY *n pl.* **-WAYS** a light carriage

ROCKER *n pl.* **-S** a rocking chair

ROCKERY *n pl.* **-ERIES** a rock garden

ROCKET *v* **-ED, -ING, -S** to convey by means of a rocket (a device propelled by the reaction of escaping gases)

ROCKETER *n pl.* **-S** one that designs or launches rockets

ROCKETRY *n pl.* **-RIES** the science of rockets

ROCKFALL *n pl.* **-S** a mass of fallen rocks

ROCKFISH *n pl.* **-ES** a fish living around rocks

ROCKIER comparative of rocky

ROCKIEST superlative of rocky

ROCKLESS *adj* having no rocks

ROCKLIKE *adj* resembling a rock (a large mass of stone)

ROCKLING *n pl.* **-S** a marine fish

ROCKOON *n pl.* **-S** a small rocket

ROCKROSE *n pl.* **-S** a flowering plant

ROCKWEED *n pl.* **-S** a brown seaweed

ROCKWORK *n pl.* **-S** a natural mass of rocks

ROCKY *adj* **ROCKIER, ROCKIEST** unsteady

ROCOCO *n pl.* **-COS** a style of architecture and decoration

ROD *v* **RODDED, RODDING, RODS** to provide with a rod (a straight, slender piece of material)

RODE *n pl.* **-S** a cable attached to the anchor of a small boat

RODENT *n pl.* **-S** a gnawing mammal

RODEO *v* **-ED, -ING, -S** to perform cowboy skills in a contest

RODLESS *adj* having no rod

RODLIKE *adj* resembling a rod

RODMAN *n pl.* **-MEN** a surveyor's assistant

RODSMAN _n_ pl. **-MEN** rodman

ROE _n_ pl. **-S** the mass of eggs within a female fish

ROEBUCK _n_ pl. **-S** the male of a small Eurasian deer

ROENTGEN _n_ pl. **-S** a unit of radiation dosage

ROGATION _n_ pl. **-S** the proposal of a law in ancient Rome

ROGATORY _adj_ requesting information

ROGER _v_ **-ED, -ING, -S** to indicate that a message has been received

ROGUE _v_ **ROGUED, ROGUEING** or **ROGUING, ROGUES** to defraud

ROGUERY _n_ pl. **-ERIES** roguish conduct

ROGUISH _adj_ dishonest

ROIL _v_ **-ED, -ING, -S** to make muddy

ROILY _adj_ **ROILIER, ROILIEST** muddy

ROISTER _v_ **-ED, -ING, -S** to revel

ROLAMITE _n_ pl. **-S** a nearly frictionless mechanical device

ROLE _n_ pl. **-S** a part played by an actor

ROLF _v_ **-ED, -ING, -S** to practice a type of massage

ROLFER _n_ pl. **-S** one that rolfs

ROLL _v_ **-ED, -ING, -S** to move along by repeatedly turning over

ROLLAWAY _n_ pl. **-WAYS** a piece of furniture that can be rolled away when not in use

ROLLBACK _n_ pl. **-S** a return to a lower level of prices or wages

ROLLER _n_ pl. **-S** a rotating cylinder

ROLLICK _v_ **-ED, -ING, -S** to frolic

ROLLICKY _adj_ given to rollicking

ROLLING _n_ pl. **-S** the act of one that rolls

ROLLMOP _n_ pl. **-S** a fillet of herring

ROLLOUT _n_ pl. **-S** a type of play in football

ROLLOVER _n_ pl. **-S** a motor vehicle accident in which the vehicle overturns

ROLLTOP _adj_ having a flexible, sliding cover

ROLLWAY _n_ pl. **-WAYS** an incline for rolling logs

ROM _n_ pl. **-S** a Gypsy man or boy

ROMAINE _n_ pl. **-S** a variety of lettuce

ROMAJI _n_ pl. **-S** a system of transliterating Japanese into the Latin alphabet

ROMAN _n_ pl. **-S** a metrical narrative of medieval France

ROMANCE _v_ **-MANCED, -MANCING, -MANCES** to woo

ROMANCER _n_ pl. **-S** one that romances

ROMANISE _v_ **-ISED, -ISING, -ISES** to romanize

ROMANIZE _v_ **-IZED, -IZING, -IZES** to write in the Roman alphabet

ROMANO _n_ pl. **-NOS** an Italian cheese

ROMANTIC _n_ pl. **-S** a fanciful person

ROMAUNT _n_ pl. **-S** a long, medieval tale

ROMEO _n_ pl. **-MEOS** a male lover

ROMP _v_ **-ED, -ING, -S** to play boisterously

ROMPER _n_ pl. **-S** one that romps

ROMPISH _adj_ inclined to romp

RONDEAU _n_ pl. **-DEAUX** a short poem of fixed form

RONDEL _n_ pl. **-S** a rondeau of 14 lines

RONDELET _n_ pl. **-S** a rondeau of 5 or 7 lines

RONDELLE _n_ pl. **-S** rondel

RONDO _n_ pl. **-DOS** a type of musical composition

RONDURE _n_ pl. **-S** a circle or sphere

RONION _n_ pl. **-S** a mangy animal or person

RONNEL _n_ pl. **-S** an insecticide

RONTGEN _n_ pl. **-S** roentgen

RONYON _n_ pl. **-S** ronion

ROOD _n_ pl. **-S** a crucifix

ROOF _v_ **-ED, -ING, -S** to provide with a roof (the external upper covering of a building)

ROOFER _n_ pl. **-S** one that builds or repairs roofs

ROOFIE _n_ pl. **-S** a tablet of a powerful sedative

ROOFING _n_ pl. **-S** material for a roof

ROOFLESS _adj_ having no roof

ROOFLIKE _adj_ resembling a roof

ROOFLINE _n_ pl. **-S** the profile of a roof

ROOFTOP _n_ pl. **-S** a roof

ROOFTREE _n_ pl. **-S** a horizontal timber in a roof

ROOK _v_ **-ED, -ING, -S** to swindle

ROOKERY _n_ pl. **-ERIES** a colony of rooks (European crows)

ROOKIE _n_ pl. **-S** a novice

ROOKY _adj_ **ROOKIER, ROOKIEST** abounding in rooks

ROOM _v_ **-ED, -ING, -S** to occupy a room (a walled space within a building)

ROOMER _n_ pl. **-S** a lodger

ROOMETTE *n* pl. **-S** a small room

ROOMFUL *n* pl. **-S** as much as a room can hold

ROOMIE *n* pl. **-S** a roommate

ROOMMATE *n* pl. **-S** one with whom a room is shared

ROOMY *adj* **ROOMIER, ROOMIEST** spacious **ROOMILY** *adv*

ROORBACH *n* pl. **-S** roorback

ROORBACK *n* pl. **-S** a false story used for political advantage

ROOSE *v* **ROOSED, ROOSING, ROOSES** to praise

ROOSER *n* pl. **-S** one that rooses

ROOST *v* **-ED, -ING, -S** to settle down for rest or sleep

ROOSTER *n* pl. **-S** a male chicken

ROOT *v* **-ED, -ING, -S** to put forth a root (an underground portion of a plant)

ROOTAGE *n* pl. **-S** a system of roots

ROOTCAP *n* pl. **-S** the loose mass of cells that covers the tip of some roots

ROOTER *n* pl. **-S** one that gives encouragement or support

ROOTHOLD *n* pl. **-S** the embedding of a plant to soil through the growing of roots

ROOTIER comparative of rooty

ROOTIEST superlative of rooty

ROOTLE *v* **-TLED, -TLING, -TLES** to dig in the ground as with the snout

ROOTLESS *adj* having no roots

ROOTLET *n* pl. **-S** a small root

ROOTLIKE *adj* resembling a root

ROOTWORM *n* pl. **-S** a beetle whose larvae feed on the roots of crop plants

ROOTY *adj* **ROOTIER, ROOTIEST** full of roots

ROPE *v* **ROPED, ROPING, ROPES** to bind with a rope (a thick line of twisted fibers) **ROPABLE** *adj*

ROPELIKE *adj* resembling a rope

ROPER *n* pl. **-S** one that ropes

ROPERY *n* pl. **-ERIES** a place where ropes are made

ROPEWALK *n* pl. **-S** a long path where ropes are made

ROPEWAY *n* pl. **-WAYS** an aerial cable used to transport freight

ROPEY *adj* **ROPIER, ROPIEST** ropy

ROPIER comparative of ropy

ROPIEST superlative of ropy

ROPILY *adv* in a ropy manner

ROPINESS *n* pl. **-ES** the quality of being ropy

ROPING present participle of rope

ROPY *adj* **ROPIER, ROPIEST** resembling a rope or ropes

ROQUE *n* pl. **-S** a form of croquet

ROQUET *v* **-ED, -ING, -S** to cause one's own ball to hit another in croquet

ROQUETTE *n* pl. **-S** an arugula

RORQUAL *n* pl. **-S** a large whale

ROSACEA *n* pl. **-S** a chronic inflammation of parts of the face

ROSARIAN *n* pl. **-S** a cultivator of roses

ROSARIUM *n* pl. **-IUMS** or **-IA** a rose garden

ROSARY *n* pl. **-RIES** a series of prayers in the Roman Catholic Church

ROSCOE *n* pl. **-S** a pistol

ROSE *v* **ROSED, ROSING, ROSES** to make the color of a rose (a reddish flower)

ROSEATE *adj* rose-colored

ROSEBAY *n* pl. **-BAYS** an evergreen shrub

ROSEBUD *n* pl. **-S** the bud of a rose

ROSEBUSH *n* pl. **-ES** a shrub that bears roses

ROSED past tense of rose

ROSEFISH *n* pl. **-ES** a marine food fish

ROSEHIP *n* pl. **-S** the aggregate fruit of the rose plant

ROSELIKE *adj* resembling a rose

ROSELLE *n* pl. **-S** a tropical plant

ROSEMARY *n* pl. **-MARIES** an evergreen shrub

ROSEOLA *n* pl. **-S** a rose-colored skin rash **ROSEOLAR** *adj*

ROSEROOT *n* pl. **-S** a perennial herb

ROSERY *n* pl. **-ERIES** a place where roses are grown

ROSESLUG *n* pl. **-S** a larval sawfly that eats rose leaves

ROSET *n* pl. **-S** resin

ROSETTE *n* pl. **-S** an ornament resembling a rose

ROSEWOOD *n* pl. **-S** a tropical tree

ROSHI *n* pl. **-S** the spiritual leader of a group of Zen Buddhists

ROSIER comparative of rosy

ROSIEST superlative of rosy

ROSILY *adv* in a rosy manner

ROSIN *v* **-ED, -ING, -S** to treat with rosin (a brittle resin)

ROSINESS *n* pl. **-ES** the state of being rosy

ROSING present participle of rose

ROSINOL *n* pl. **-S** rosin oil

ROSINOUS *adj* resembling rosin

ROSINY *adj* rosinous

ROSOLIO *n* pl. **-LIOS** a liqueur made from raisins and brandy

ROSTELLA *n/pl* small, beaklike structures

ROSTER *n* pl. **-S** a list of names

ROSTRA a pl. of rostrum

ROSTRAL *adj* pertaining to a rostrum

ROSTRATE *adj* having a rostrum

ROSTRUM *n* pl. **-TRUMS** or **-TRA** a beaklike process or part

ROSULATE *adj* arranged in the form of a rosette

ROSY *adj* **ROSIER, ROSIEST** rose-colored

ROT *v* **ROTTED, ROTTING, ROTS** to decompose

ROTA *n* pl. **-S** a roster

ROTARY *n* pl. **-RIES** a rotating part or device

ROTATE *v* **-TATED, -TATING, -TATES** to turn about an axis

ROTATION *n* pl. **-S** the act or an instance of rotating **ROTATIVE** *adj*

ROTATOR *n* pl. **-ES** or **-S** one that rotates

ROTATORY *adj* pertaining to rotation

ROTCH *n* pl. **-ES** rotche

ROTCHE *n* pl. **-S** a seabird

ROTE *n* pl. **-S** mechanical routine

ROTENONE *n* pl. **-S** an insecticide

ROTGUT *n* pl. **-S** inferior liquor

ROTI *n* pl. **-S** an unleavened bread

ROTIFER *n* pl. **-S** a microscopic aquatic organism

ROTIFORM *adj* shaped like a wheel

ROTL *n* pl. **ROTLS** or **ARTAL** a unit of weight in Muslim countries

ROTO *n* pl. **-TOS** a type of printing process

ROTOR *n* pl. **-S** a rotating part of a machine

ROTOTILL *v* **-ED, -ING, -S** to till soil with a type of farming implement

ROTTE *n* pl. **-S** a medieval stringed instrument

ROTTED past tense of rot

ROTTEN *adj* **-TENER, -TENEST** being in a state of decay **ROTTENLY** *adv*

ROTTER *n* pl. **-S** a scoundrel

ROTTING present participle of rot

ROTUND *adj* marked by roundness **ROTUNDLY** *adv*

ROTUNDA *n* pl. **-S** a round building

ROTURIER *n* pl. **-S** a commoner

ROUBLE *n* pl. **-S** ruble

ROUCHE *n* pl. **-S** ruche

ROUE *n* pl. **-S** a lecherous man

ROUEN *n* pl. **-S** any of a breed of domestic ducks

ROUGE *v* **ROUGED, ROUGING, ROUGES** to color with a red cosmetic

ROUGH *adj* **ROUGHER, ROUGHEST** having an uneven surface

ROUGH *v* **-ED, -ING, -S** to make rough

ROUGHAGE *n* pl. **-S** coarse, bulky food

ROUGHDRY *v* **-DRIED, -DRYING, -DRIES** to dry without ironing, as washed clothes

ROUGHEN *v* **-ED, -ING, -S** to make rough

ROUGHER *n* pl. **-S** one that roughs

ROUGHHEW *v* **-HEWED, -HEWN, -HEWING, -HEWS** to shape roughly

ROUGHISH *adj* somewhat rough

ROUGHLEG *n* pl. **-S** a large hawk

ROUGHLY *adv* in a rough manner

ROUGHY *n* pl. **ROUGHIES** a small fish having rough scales

ROUGING present participle of rouge

ROUILLE *n* pl. **-S** a peppery garlic sauce

ROULADE *n* pl. **-S** a musical embellishment

ROULEAU *n* pl. **-LEAUS** or **-LEAUX** a roll of coins wrapped in paper

ROULETTE *v* **-LETTED, -LETTING, -LETTES** to make tiny slits in

ROUND *adj* **ROUNDER, ROUNDEST** shaped like a sphere

ROUND *v* **-ED, -ING, -S** to make round

ROUNDEL *n* pl. **-S** a round figure or object

ROUNDER *n* pl. **-S** a tool for rounding

ROUNDISH *adj* somewhat round

ROUNDLET *n* pl. **-S** a small circle

ROUNDLY *adv* in a round manner

ROUNDUP *n* pl. **-S** the driving together of cattle scattered over a range

ROUP *v* **-ED, -ING, -S** to auction

ROUPET *adj* roupy

ROUPY *adj* **ROUPIER, ROUPIEST** hoarse **ROUPILY** *adv*

ROUSE *v* **ROUSED, ROUSING, ROUSES** to bring out of a state of sleep or inactivity

ROUSER *n* pl. **-S** one that rouses

ROUSSEAU *n* pl. **-S** fried pemmican

ROUST *v* **-ED, -ING, -S** to arouse and drive out

ROUSTER *n* pl. **-S** a wharf laborer and deckhand

ROUT *v* **-ED, -ING, -S** to defeat overwhelmingly

ROUTE *v* **ROUTED, ROUTING, ROUTES** to send on a particular course

ROUTEMAN *n* pl. **-MEN** one who conducts business on a customary course

ROUTER *n* pl. **-S** a scooping tool

ROUTEWAY *n* pl. **-WAYS** an established course of travel

ROUTH *n* pl. **-S** an abundance

ROUTINE *n* pl. **-S** a regular course of procedure

ROUTING present participle of route

ROUX *n* pl. **ROUX** a mixture of butter and flour

ROVE *v* **ROVED, ROVING, ROVES** to roam

ROVEN a past participle of reeve

ROVER *n* pl. **-S** one that roves

ROVING *n* pl. **-S** a roll of textile fibers

ROVINGLY *adv* in a roving manner

ROW *v* **-ED, -ING, -S** to propel by means of oars **ROWABLE** *adj*

ROWAN *n* pl. **-S** a Eurasian tree

ROWBOAT *n* pl. **-S** a small boat designed to be rowed

ROWDY *adj* **-DIER, -DIEST** disorderly in behavior **ROWDILY** *adv*

ROWDY *n* pl. **-DIES** a rowdy person

ROWDYISH *adj* tending to be rowdy

ROWDYISM *n* pl. **-S** disorderly behavior

ROWEL *v* **-ELED, -ELING, -ELS** or **-ELLED, -ELLING, -ELS** to prick with a spiked wheel in order to urge forward

ROWEN *n* pl. **-S** a second growth of grass

ROWER *n* pl. **-S** one that rows

ROWING *n* pl. **-S** the sport of racing in light, long, and narrow rowboats

ROWLOCK *n* pl. **-S** an oarlock

ROWTH *n* pl. **-S** routh

ROYAL *n* pl. **-S** a size of printing paper

ROYALISM *n* pl. **-S** support of a monarch or monarchy

ROYALIST *n* pl. **-S** a supporter of a monarch or monarchy

ROYALLY *adv* in a kingly manner

ROYALTY *n* pl. **-TIES** the status or power of a monarch

ROYSTER *v* **-ED, -ING, -S** to roister

ROZZER *n* pl. **-S** a policeman

RUANA *n* pl. **-S** a woolen poncho

RUB *v* **RUBBED, RUBBING, RUBS** to move along the surface of a body with pressure

RUBABOO *n* pl. **-BOOS** a type of soup

RUBACE *n* pl. **-S** rubasse

RUBAIYAT *n* pl. **RUBAIYAT** four-lined stanzas in Persian poetry

RUBASSE *n* pl. **-S** a variety of quartz

RUBATO *n* pl. **-TOS** or **-TI** a fluctuation of speed within a musical phrase

RUBBABOO *n* pl. **-BOOS** rubaboo

RUBBED past tense of rub

RUBBER *v* **-ED, -ING, -S** to stretch one's neck in looking at something

RUBBERY *adj* **-BERIER, -BERIEST** resembling rubber (an elastic substance)

RUBBIES pl. of rubby

RUBBING *n* pl. **-S** an image produced by rubbing

RUBBISH *n* pl. **-ES** worthless, unwanted matter **RUBBISHY** *adj*

RUBBLE *v* **-BLED, -BLING, -BLES** to reduce to rubble (broken pieces)

RUBBLY *adj* **-BLIER, -BLIEST** abounding in rubble

RUBBOARD *n* pl. **-S** a corrugated rectangular board used as a percussion instrument

RUBBY *n* pl. **-BIES** an alcoholic given to drinking rubbing alcohol

RUBDOWN *n* pl. **-S** a brisk rubbing of the body

RUBE *n* pl. **-S** a rustic

RUBEL *n* pl. **-S** a monetary unit of Belarus

RUBELLA *n* pl. **-S** a virus disease

RUBEOLA *n* pl. **-S** a virus disease **RUBEOLAR** *adj*

RUBICUND *adj* ruddy

RUBIDIUM *n* pl. **-S** a metallic element **RUBIDIC** *adj*

RUBIED past tense of ruby

RUBIER comparative of ruby

RUBIES present 3d person sing. of ruby

RUBIEST superlative of ruby

RUBIGO *n* pl. **-GOS** red iron oxide

RUBIOUS *adj* ruby-colored

RUBLE *n* pl. **-S** a monetary unit of Russia

RUBOFF *n* pl. **-S** a deep impression made by close contact

RUBOUT *n* pl. **-S** an instance of obliterating something

RUBRIC *n* pl. **-S** a part of a manuscript or book that appears in red **RUBRICAL** *adj*

RUBUS *n* pl. **RUBUS** a plant of the rose family

RUBY *adj* **-BIER, -BIEST** of a deep-red color

RUBY *v* **-BIED, -BYING, -BIES** to tint with the color of a ruby (a deep-red precious stone)

RUBYLIKE *adj* resembling a ruby

RUCHE *n* pl. **-S** a pleated strip of fine fabric

RUCHED *adj* trimmed with a ruche

RUCHING *n* pl. **-S** a ruche

RUCK *v* **-ED, -ING, -S** to wrinkle or crease

RUCKLE *v* **-LED, -LING, -LES** to ruck

RUCKSACK *n* pl. **-S** a knapsack

RUCKUS *n* pl. **-ES** a noisy disturbance

RUCTION *n* pl. **-S** a ruckus

RUCTIOUS *adj* quarrelsome

RUDD *n* pl. **-S** a freshwater fish

RUDDER *n* pl. **-S** a vertical blade used to direct the course of a vessel

RUDDIER comparative of ruddy

RUDDIEST superlative of ruddy

RUDDILY *adv* in a ruddy manner

RUDDLE *v* **-DLED, -DLING, -DLES** to color with a red dye

RUDDOCK *n* pl. **-S** a European bird

RUDDY *adj* **-DIER, -DIEST** having a healthy, reddish color

RUDE *adj* **RUDER, RUDEST** discourteous or impolite **RUDELY** *adv*

RUDENESS *n* pl. **-ES** the quality of being rude

RUDERAL *n* pl. **-S** a plant growing in poor land

RUDERY *n* pl. **-ERIES** a rude act

RUDESBY *n* pl. **-BIES** a rude person

RUDEST superlative of rude

RUDIMENT *n* pl. **-S** a basic principle or element

RUE *v* **RUED, RUING, RUES** to feel sorrow or remorse for

RUEFUL *adj* feeling sorrow or remorse **RUEFULLY** *adv*

RUER *n* pl. **-S** one that rues

RUFF *v* **-ED, -ING, -S** to trump

RUFFE *n* pl. **-S** a freshwater fish

RUFFIAN *n* pl. **-S** a tough, lawless person

RUFFLE *v* **-FLED, -FLING, -FLES** to destroy the smoothness of

RUFFLER *n* pl. **-S** one that ruffles

RUFFLIKE *adj* resembling a ruff (a pleated collar)

RUFFLING present participle of ruffle

RUFFLY *adj* **-FLIER, -FLIEST** not smooth

RUFIYAA *n* pl. **RUFIYAA** a monetary unit of the Maldives

RUFOUS *adj* reddish

RUG *v* **RUGGED, RUGGING, RUGS** to tear roughly

RUGA *n* pl. **-GAE** an anatomical fold or wrinkle **RUGAL, RUGATE** *adj*

RUGALACH *n* pl. **RUGALACH** rugelach

RUGBY *n* pl. **-BIES** a form of football

RUGELACH *n* pl. **RUGELACH** a cookie of cream-cheese dough spread with a filling and rolled up

RUGGED *adj* **-GEDER, -GEDEST** having an uneven surface **RUGGEDLY** *adv*

RUGGER *n* pl. **-S** rugby

RUGGING present participle of rug

RUGLIKE *adj* resembling a rug (a thick fabric used as a floor covering)

RUGOLA *n* pl. **-S** arugula

RUGOSA *n* pl. **-S** a flowering plant

RUGOSE *adj* full of wrinkles **RUGOSELY** *adv*

RUGOSITY   *n pl.* **-TIES** the state of being rugose

RUGOUS   *adj* rugose

RUGULOSE   *adj* having small wrinkles

RUIN   *v* **-ED, -ING, -S** to destroy **RUINABLE** *adj*

RUINATE   *v* **-ATED, -ATING, -ATES** to ruin

RUINER   *n pl.* **-S** one that ruins

RUING   present participle of rue

RUINOUS   *adj* destructive

RULE   *v* **RULED, RULING, RULES** to exercise control over **RULABLE** *adj*

RULELESS   *adj* not restrained or regulated by law

RULER   *n pl.* **-S** one that rules

RULING   *n pl.* **-S** an authoritative decision

RULY   *adj* **RULIER, RULIEST** orderly

RUM   *adj* **RUMMER, RUMMEST** odd

RUM   *n pl.* **-S** an alcoholic liquor

RUMAKI   *n pl.* **-S** chicken liver wrapped together with water chestnuts in a bacon slice

RUMBA   *v* **-ED, -ING, -S** to perform a ballroom dance

RUMBLE   *v* **-BLED, -BLING, -BLES** to make a deep, thunderous sound

RUMBLER   *n pl.* **-S** one that rumbles

RUMBLING   *n pl.* **-S** a thunderous sound

RUMBLY   *adj* tending to rumble

RUMEN   *n pl.* **-MENS** or **-MINA** a part of the stomach of a ruminant **RUMINAL** *adj*

RUMINANT   *n pl.* **-S** a hoofed, even-toed mammal

RUMINATE   *v* **-NATED, -NATING, -NATES** to chew again

RUMMAGE   *v* **-MAGED, -MAGING, -MAGES** to search thoroughly through

RUMMAGER   *n pl.* **-S** one that rummages

RUMMER   *n pl.* **-S** a large drinking glass

RUMMEST   superlative of rum

RUMMY   *adj* **-MIER, -MIEST** odd

RUMMY   *n pl.* **-MIES** a card game

RUMOR   *v* **-ED, -ING, -S** to spread by hearsay

RUMOUR   *v* **-ED, -ING, -S** to rumor

RUMP   *n pl.* **-S** the lower and back part of the trunk **RUMPLESS** *adj*

RUMPLE   *v* **-PLED, -PLING, -PLES** to wrinkle

RUMPLY   *adj* **-PLIER, -PLIEST** rumpled

RUMPUS   *n pl.* **-ES** a noisy disturbance

RUN   *v* **RAN, RUNNING, RUNS** to move by rapid steps

RUNABOUT   *n pl.* **-S** a small, open auto

RUNAGATE   *n pl.* **-S** a deserter

RUNAWAY   *n pl.* **-AWAYS** one that runs away

RUNBACK   *n pl.* **-S** a type of run in football

RUNDLE   *n pl.* **-S** a rung

RUNDLET   *n pl.* **-S** a small barrel

RUNDOWN   *n pl.* **-S** a summary

RUNE   *n pl.* **-S** a letter of an ancient alphabet **RUNELIKE** *adj*

RUNG   *n pl.* **-S** a crosspiece forming a step of a ladder **RUNGLESS** *adj*

RUNIC   *adj* pertaining to a rune

RUNKLE   *v* **-KLED, -KLING, -KLES** to wrinkle

RUNLESS   *adj* scoring no runs in baseball

RUNLET   *n pl.* **-S** a small stream

RUNNEL   *n pl.* **-S** a small stream

RUNNER   *n pl.* **-S** one that runs

RUNNING   *n pl.* **-S** a race

RUNNY   *adj* **-NIER, -NIEST** tending to drip

RUNOFF   *n pl.* **-S** rainfall that is not absorbed by the soil

RUNOUT   *n pl.* **-S** the end of a film strip

RUNOVER   *n pl.* **-S** matter for publication that exceeds the allotted space

RUNROUND   *n pl.* **-S** evasive action

RUNT   *n pl.* **-S** a small person or animal **RUNTISH** *adj*

RUNTY   *adj* **RUNTIER, RUNTIEST** small

RUNWAY   *n pl.* **-WAYS** a landing and takeoff strip for aircraft

RUPEE   *n pl.* **-S** a monetary unit of India

RUPIAH   *n pl.* **-S** a monetary unit of Indonesia

RUPTURE   *v* **-TURED, -TURING, -TURES** to burst

RURAL   *adj* pertaining to the country

RURALISE   *v* **-ISED, -ISING, -ISES** to ruralize

RURALISM   *n pl.* **-S** the state of being rural

RURALIST   *n pl.* **-S** one who lives in the country

RURALITE   *n pl.* **-S** a ruralist

RURALITY   *n pl.* **-TIES** the state of being rural

RURALIZE *v* **-IZED, -IZING, -IZES** to make rural

RURALLY *adv* in a rural manner

RURBAN *adj* partially rural and urban

RUSE *n* pl. **-S** a deception

RUSH *v* **-ED, -ING, -ES** to move swiftly

RUSHEE *n* pl. **-S** a college student seeking admission to a fraternity or sorority

RUSHER *n* pl. **-S** one that rushes

RUSHIER comparative of rushy

RUSHIEST superlative of rushy

RUSHING *n* pl. **-S** yardage gained in football by running plays

RUSHLIKE *adj* resembling a rush (a grasslike marsh plant)

RUSHY *adj* **RUSHIER, RUSHIEST** abounding in rushes

RUSINE *adj* pertaining to a genus of deer

RUSK *n* pl. **-S** a sweetened biscuit

RUSSET *n* pl. **-S** a reddish or yellowish brown color **RUSSETY** *adj*

RUSSIFY *v* **-FIED, -FYING, -FIES** to make Russian

RUST *v* **-ED, -ING, -S** to form rust (a reddish coating that forms on iron) **RUSTABLE** *adj*

RUSTIC *n* pl. **-S** one who lives in the country

RUSTICAL *n* pl. **-S** a rustic

RUSTICLY *adv* in a rural manner

RUSTIER comparative of rusty

RUSTIEST superlative of rusty

RUSTILY *adv* in a rusty manner

RUSTLE *v* **-TLED, -TLING, -TLES** to make a succession of slight, soft sounds

RUSTLER *n* pl. **-S** one that rustles

RUSTLESS *adj* free from rust

RUSTY *adj* **RUSTIER, RUSTIEST** covered with rust

RUT *v* **RUTTED, RUTTING, RUTS** to make ruts (grooves) in

RUTABAGA *n* pl. **-S** a plant having a thick, edible root

RUTH *n* pl. **-S** compassion

RUTHENIC *adj* pertaining to a rare, metallic element

RUTHFUL *adj* full of compassion

RUTHLESS *adj* having no compassion

RUTILANT *adj* having a reddish glow

RUTILE *n* pl. **-S** a mineral

RUTIN *n* pl. **-S** a chemical compound

RUTTED past tense of rut

RUTTIER comparative of rutty

RUTTIEST superlative of rutty

RUTTILY *adv* in a rutty manner

RUTTING present participle of rut

RUTTISH *adj* lustful

RUTTY *adj* **-TIER, -TIEST** marked by ruts

RYA *n* pl. **-S** a Scandinavian handwoven rug

RYE *n* pl. **-S** a cereal grass

RYEGRASS *n* pl. **-ES** a European grass

RYKE *v* **RYKED, RYKING, RYKES** to reach

RYND *n* pl. **-S** an iron support

RYOKAN *n* pl. **-S** a Japanese inn

RYOT *n* pl. **-S** a tenant farmer in India

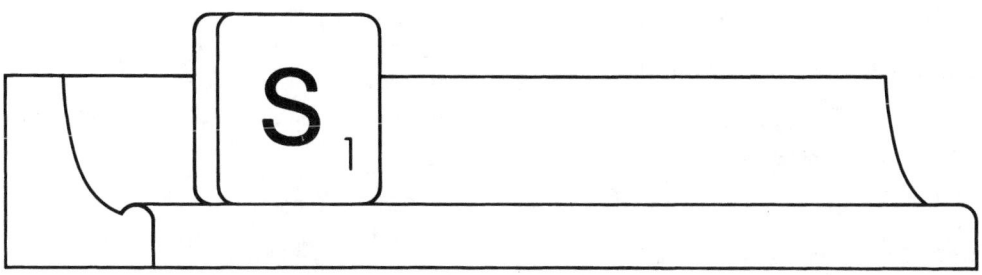

SAB	v **SABBED, SABBING, SABS** to sob
SABAL	n pl. **-S** a palmetto
SABATON	n pl. **-S** a piece of armor for the foot
SABAYON	n pl. **-S** a sauce of whipped egg yolks, sugar, and wine
SABBAT	n pl. **-S** an assembly of demons and witches
SABBATH	n pl. **-S** sabbat
SABBATIC	n pl. **-S** a year of release from normal teaching duties
SABBED	past tense of sab
SABBING	present participle of sab
SABE	v **SABED, SABEING, SABES** to savvy
SABER	v **-ED, -ING, -S** to strike with a saber (a type of sword)
SABIN	n pl. **-S** a unit of sound absorption
SABINE	n pl. **-S** savin
SABIR	n pl. **-S** a French-based pidgin language
SABLE	n pl. **-S** a carnivorous mammal
SABOT	n pl. **-S** a wooden shoe
SABOTAGE	v **-TAGED, -TAGING, -TAGES** to destroy maliciously
SABOTEUR	n pl. **-S** one who sabotages
SABRA	n pl. **-S** a native Israeli
SABRE	v **-BRED, -BRING, -BRES** to saber
SABULOSE	adj sabulous
SABULOUS	adj sandy
SAC	n pl. **-S** a pouchlike structure in an animal or plant
SACATON	n pl. **-S** a perennial grass
SACBUT	n pl. **-S** sackbut
SACCADE	n pl. **-S** a rapid, jerky movement of the eye **SACCADIC** adj
SACCATE	adj having a sac

SACCULAR	adj resembling a sac
SACCULE	n pl. **-S** a small sac
SACCULUS	n pl. **-LI** saccule
SACHEM	n pl. **-S** a North American Indian chief **SACHEMIC** adj
SACHET	n pl. **-S** a small bag containing perfumed powder **SACHETED** adj
SACK	v **-ED, -ING, -S** to put into a sack (a large bag)
SACKBUT	n pl. **-S** a medieval trombone
SACKER	n pl. **-S** one that sacks
SACKFUL	n pl. **SACKFULS** or **SACKSFUL** as much as a sack can hold
SACKING	n pl. **-S** material for making sacks
SACKLIKE	adj resembling a sack
SACLIKE	adj resembling a sac
SACQUE	n pl. **-S** a loose-fitting dress
SACRA	pl. of sacrum
SACRAL	n pl. **-S** a vertebra or nerve situated near the sacrum
SACRARIA	n/pl ancient Roman shrines
SACRED	adj dedicated to or set apart for the worship of a deity **SACREDLY** adv
SACRING	n pl. **-S** the consecration of bread and wine of the Eucharist
SACRIST	n pl. **-S** a person in charge of a sacristy
SACRISTY	n pl. **-TIES** a room in which sacred vessels and vestments are kept
SACRUM	n pl. **-CRUMS** or **-CRA** a bone of the pelvis
SAD	adj **SADDER, SADDEST** unhappy
SADDEN	v **-ED, -ING, -S** to make sad
SADDHU	n pl. **-S** sadhu
SADDLE	v **-DLED, -DLING, -DLES** to put a saddle (a leather seat for a rider) on

SADDLER *n* pl. **-S** one that makes, repairs, or sells saddles

SADDLERY *n* pl. **-DLERIES** the shop of a saddler

SADE *n* pl. **-S** a Hebrew letter

SADHE *n* pl. **-S** sade

SADHU *n* pl. **-S** a Hindu holy man

SADI *n* pl. **-S** sade

SADIRON *n* pl. **-S** a heavy flatiron

SADISM *n* pl. **-S** a tendency to take delight in inflicting pain

SADIST *n* pl. **-S** one marked by sadism **SADISTIC** *adj*

SADLY *adv* in a sad manner

SADNESS *n* pl. **-ES** the state of being sad

SAE *adv* so

SAFARI *v* **-ED, -ING, -S** to go on a hunting expedition

SAFE *adj* **SAFER, SAFEST** free from danger **SAFELY** *adv*

SAFE *n* pl. **-S** a metal receptacle for storing valuables

SAFENESS *n* pl. **-ES** the quality of being safe

SAFETY *v* **-TIED, -TYING, -TIES** to protect against failure, breakage, or accident

SAFFRON *n* pl. **-S** a flowering plant

SAFRANIN *n* pl. **-S** a red dye

SAFROL *n* pl. **-S** safrole

SAFROLE *n* pl. **-S** a poisonous liquid

SAG *v* **SAGGED, SAGGING, SAGS** to bend or sink downward from weight or pressure

SAGA *n* pl. **-S** a medieval Scandinavian narrative

SAGACITY *n* pl. **-TIES** wisdom

SAGAMAN *n* pl. **-MEN** a writer of sagas

SAGAMORE *n* pl. **-S** an Algonquian Indian chief

SAGANASH *n* pl. **-ES** a white man — an Algonquian Indian term

SAGBUT *n* pl. **-S** sackbut

SAGE *adj* **SAGER, SAGEST** wise **SAGELY** *adv*

SAGE *n* pl. **-S** an aromatic herb used as seasoning

SAGENESS *n* pl. **-ES** wisdom

SAGGAR *v* **-ED, -ING, -S** to bake in a saggar (a protective clay casing)

SAGGARD *n* pl. **-S** a saggar

SAGGED past tense of sag

SAGGER *v* **-ED, -ING, -S** to saggar

SAGGING present participle of sag

SAGGY *adj* **-GIER, -GIEST** characterized by sagging

SAGIER comparative of sagy

SAGIEST superlative of sagy

SAGITTAL *adj* resembling an arrow or arrowhead

SAGO *n* pl. **-GOS** a tropical tree

SAGUARO *n* pl. **-ROS** a tall cactus

SAGUM *n* pl. **-GA** a cloak worn by ancient Roman soldiers

SAGY *adj* **SAGIER, SAGIEST** flavored with sage

SAHIB *n* pl. **-S** sir; master — used as a term of respect in colonial India

SAHIWAL *n* pl. **-S** any of a breed of humped dairy cattle

SAHUARO *n* pl. **-ROS** saguaro

SAICE *n* pl. **-S** syce

SAID *n* pl. **-S** sayyid

SAIGA *n* pl. **-S** a small antelope

SAIL *v* **-ED, -ING, -S** to move across the surface of water by the action of wind **SAILABLE** *adj*

SAILBOAT *n* pl. **-S** a boat that sails

SAILER *n* pl. **-S** a vessel that sails

SAILFISH *n* pl. **-ES** a large marine fish

SAILING *n* pl. **-S** the act of one that sails

SAILLESS *adj* lacking a sail

SAILOR *n* pl. **-S** a member of a ship's crew **SAILORLY** *adj*

SAIMIN *n* pl. **-S** a Hawaiian noodle soup

SAIN *v* **-ED, -ING, -S** to make the sign of the cross on

SAINFOIN *n* pl. **-S** a perennial herb

SAINT *v* **-ED, -ING, -S** to declare to be a saint (a person of exceptional holiness)

SAINTDOM *n* pl. **-S** the condition of being a saint

SAINTLY *adj* **-LIER, -LIEST** of or befitting a saint

SAITH a present 3d person sing. of say

SAITHE *n* pl. **SAITHE** a marine food fish

SAIYID *n* pl. **-S** sayyid

SAJOU *n* pl. **-S** a capuchin

SAKE *n pl.* **-S** benefit, interest, or advantage

SAKER *n pl.* **-S** a Eurasian falcon

SAKI *n pl.* **-S** a Japanese liquor

SAL *n pl.* **-S** salt

SALAAM *v* **-ED, -ING, -S** to greet with a low bow

SALABLE *adj* capable of being or fit to be sold **SALABLY** *adv*

SALACITY *n pl.* **-TIES** lewdness

SALAD *n pl.* **-S** a dish of green, raw vegetables

SALADANG *n pl.* **-S** a wild ox

SALAL *n pl.* **-S** a small shrub

SALAMI *n pl.* **-S** a seasoned sausage

SALARIAT *n pl.* **-S** the class of salaried persons

SALARY *v* **-RIED, -RYING, -RIES** to pay a periodic, fixed compensation to

SALCHOW *n pl.* **-S** a figure-skating jump

SALE *n pl.* **-S** the act or an instance of selling

SALEABLE *adj* salable **SALEABLY** *adv*

SALEP *n pl.* **-S** a starchy meal ground from the roots of certain orchids

SALEROOM *n pl.* **-S** a room in which goods are displayed for sale

SALESMAN *n pl.* **-MEN** a man who sells merchandise

SALIC *adj* pertaining to a group of igneous rocks

SALICIN *n pl.* **-S** a chemical compound

SALICINE *n pl.* **-S** salicin

SALIENCE *n pl.* **-S** a projecting feature or detail

SALIENCY *n pl.* **-CIES** salience

SALIENT *n pl.* **-S** the part of a fortification projecting closest to the enemy

SALIFY *v* **-FIED, -FYING, -FIES** to combine with a salt

SALINA *n pl.* **-S** a pond, marsh, or lake containing salt water

SALINE *n pl.* **-S** a salt solution

SALINITY *n pl.* **-TIES** a concentration of salt

SALINIZE *v* **-NIZED, -NIZING, -NIZES** to treat with salt

SALIVA *n pl.* **-S** a fluid secreted by the glands of the mouth **SALIVARY** *adj*

SALIVATE *v* **-VATED, -VATING, -VATES** to secrete saliva

SALL *v* shall — SALL is the only form of this verb; it cannot be conjugated

SALLET *n pl.* **-S** a light medieval helmet

SALLIED past tense of sally

SALLIER *n pl.* **-S** one that sallies

SALLIES present 3d person sing. of sally

SALLOW *adj* **-LOWER, -LOWEST** of a sickly yellowish color **SALLOWLY** *adv*

SALLOW *v* **-ED, -ING, -S** to make sallow

SALLOWY *adj* abounding in willow trees

SALLY *v* **-LIED, -LYING, -LIES** to rush out suddenly

SALMI *n pl.* **-S** a dish of roasted game birds

SALMON *n pl.* **-S** a food fish

SALMONID *n pl.* **-S** a fish of the salmon family

SALOL *n pl.* **-S** a chemical compound

SALON *n pl.* **-S** a large room in which guests are received

SALOON *n pl.* **-S** a tavern

SALOOP *n pl.* **-S** a hot drink made from an infusion of aromatic herbs

SALP *n pl.* **-S** salpa

SALPA *n pl.* **-PAS** or **-PAE** a free-swimming tunicate

SALPIAN *n pl.* **-S** salpa

SALPID *n pl.* **-S** salpa

SALPINX *n pl.* **-PINGES** an anatomical tube

SALSA *n pl.* **-S** a spicy sauce of tomatoes, onions, and peppers

SALSIFY *n pl.* **-FIES** a European herb

SALSILLA *n pl.* **-S** a tropical plant

SALT *adj* **SALTER, SALTEST** salty

SALT *v* **-ED, -ING, -S** to treat with salt (a crystalline compound used as a seasoning and preservative)

SALTANT *adj* jumping or dancing

SALTBOX *n pl.* **-ES** a type of house

SALTBUSH *n pl.* **-ES** a salt-tolerant plant

SALTER *n pl.* **-S** one that salts

SALTERN *n pl.* **-S** a place where salt is produced

SALTIE *n pl.* **-S** a deep-sea vessel sailing the Great Lakes

SALTIER *n pl.* **-S** saltire

SALTIEST superlative of salty

SALTILY	*adv* in a salty manner
SALTINE	*n* pl. **-S** a salted cracker
SALTING	*n* pl. **-S** land regularly flooded by tides
SALTIRE	*n* pl. **-S** a heraldic design
SALTISH	*adj* somewhat salty
SALTLESS	*adj* having no salt
SALTLIKE	*adj* resembling salt
SALTNESS	*n* pl. **-ES** the state of being salty
SALTPAN	*n* pl. **-S** a large pan for making salt by evaporation
SALTWORK	*n* pl. **-S** a saltern
SALTWORT	*n* pl. **-S** a seaside herb
SALTY	*adj* **SALTIER, SALTIEST** tasting of or containing salt
SALUKI	*n* pl. **-S** a tall, slender dog
SALUTARY	*adj* producing a beneficial effect
SALUTE	*v* **-LUTED, -LUTING, -LUTES** to greet with a sign of welcome or respect
SALUTER	*n* pl. **-S** one that salutes
SALVABLE	*adj* capable of being saved **SALVABLY** *adv*
SALVAGE	*v* **-VAGED, -VAGING, -VAGES** to save from loss or destruction
SALVAGEE	*n* pl. **-S** one in whose favor salvage has been effected
SALVAGER	*n* pl. **-S** one that salvages
SALVE	*v* **SALVED, SALVING, SALVES** to soothe
SALVER	*n* pl. **-S** a tray or serving platter
SALVIA	*n* pl. **-S** a flowering plant
SALVIFIC	*adj* having the power to save
SALVING	present participle of salve
SALVO	*v* **-ED, -ING, -S** or **-ES** to discharge firearms simultaneously
SALVOR	*n* pl. **-S** a salvager
SAMADHI	*n* pl. **-S** a state of concentration in yoga
SAMARA	*n* pl. **-S** a dry, one-seeded fruit
SAMARIUM	*n* pl. **-S** a metallic element
SAMBA	*v* **-ED, -ING, -S** to perform a Brazilian dance
SAMBAL	*n* pl. **-S** a spicy condiment
SAMBAR	*n* pl. **-S** a large Asian deer
SAMBHAR	*n* pl. **-S** sambar
SAMBHUR	*n* pl. **-S** sambar
SAMBO	*n* pl. **-BOS** a Latin American of mixed black and Indian ancestry
SAMBUCA	*n* pl. **-S** an ancient stringed instrument
SAMBUKE	*n* pl. **-S** sambuca
SAMBUR	*n* pl. **-S** sambar
SAME	*adj* resembling in every relevant respect
SAMECH	*n* pl. **-S** samek
SAMEK	*n* pl. **-S** a Hebrew letter
SAMEKH	*n* pl. **-S** samek
SAMENESS	*n* pl. **-ES** lack of change or variety
SAMIEL	*n* pl. **-S** the simoom
SAMISEN	*n* pl. **-S** a Japanese stringed instrument
SAMITE	*n* pl. **-S** a silk fabric
SAMIZDAT	*n* pl. **-S** a system in the Soviet Union for printing and distributing unauthorized literature
SAMLET	*n* pl. **-S** a young salmon
SAMOSA	*n* pl. **-S** a filled pastry turnover
SAMOVAR	*n* pl. **-S** a metal urn for heating water
SAMP	*n* pl. **-S** coarsely ground corn
SAMPAN	*n* pl. **-S** a flat-bottomed Chinese skiff
SAMPHIRE	*n* pl. **-S** a European herb
SAMPLE	*v* **-PLED, -PLING, -PLES** to test a representative portion of a whole
SAMPLER	*n* pl. **-S** one that samples
SAMPLING	*n* pl. **-S** a small part selected for analysis
SAMSARA	*n* pl. **-S** the cycle of birth, death, and rebirth in Buddhism
SAMSHU	*n* pl. **-S** a Chinese liquor
SAMURAI	*n* pl. **-S** a Japanese warrior
SANATIVE	*adj* having the power to cure or heal
SANCTA	a pl. of sanctum
SANCTIFY	*v* **-FIED, -FYING, -FIES** to make holy
SANCTION	*v* **-ED, -ING, -S** to authorize
SANCTITY	*n* pl. **-TIES** holiness
SANCTUM	*n* pl. **-TUMS** or **-TA** a sacred place
SAND	*v* **-ED, -ING, -S** to smooth by rubbing with an abrasive **SANDABLE** *adj*

SANDAL v **-DALED, -DALING, -DALS** or **-DALLED, -DALLING, -DALS** to provide with sandals (light, open shoes)

SANDARAC n pl. **-S** an aromatic resin

SANDBAG v **-BAGGED, -BAGGING, -BAGS** to surround with bags of sand (loose granular rock material)

SANDBANK n pl. **-S** a large mass of sand

SANDBAR n pl. **-S** a ridge of sand formed in a river or sea

SANDBOX n pl. **-ES** a box containing sand for children to play in

SANDBUR n pl. **-S** an annual herb

SANDBURR n pl. **-S** sandbur

SANDDAB n pl. **-S** a small flatfish

SANDER n pl. **-S** one that sands

SANDFISH n pl. **-ES** a marine fish

SANDFLY n pl. **-FLIES** a biting fly

SANDHI n pl. **-S** a process of phonetic modification

SANDHOG n pl. **-S** a worker who digs or works in sand

SANDIER comparative of sandy

SANDIEST superlative of sandy

SANDLESS adj lacking sand

SANDLIKE adj resembling sand

SANDLING n pl. **-S** a marine fish

SANDLOT n pl. **-S** a vacant lot

SANDMAN n pl. **-MEN** a mythical person who makes children sleepy by sprinkling sand in their eyes

SANDPEEP n pl. **-S** a wading bird

SANDPILE n pl. **-S** a pile of sand

SANDPIT n pl. **-S** a pit dug in sandy soil

SANDSHOE n pl. **-S** a lightweight sneaker

SANDSOAP n pl. **-S** a type of soap

SANDSPUR n pl. **-S** a sandbur

SANDWICH v **-ED, -ING, -ES** to place between two layers or objects

SANDWORM n pl. **-S** a sand-dwelling worm

SANDWORT n pl. **-S** a flowering plant

SANDY adj **SANDIER, SANDIEST** containing or covered with sand

SANE adj **SANER, SANEST** mentally sound **SANELY** adv

SANE v **SANED, SANING, SANES** to sain

SANENESS n pl. **-ES** sanity

SANG past tense of sing

SANGA n pl. **-S** sangar

SANGAR n pl. **-S** a temporary fortification for two or three men

SANGAREE n pl. **-S** an alcoholic beverage

SANGER n pl. **-S** sangar

SANGH n pl. **-S** an association promoting unity between the different groups in Hinduism

SANGRIA n pl. **-S** an alcoholic beverage

SANGUINE n pl. **-S** a red color

SANICLE n pl. **-S** a medicinal herb

SANIDINE n pl. **-S** a glassy variety of feldspar

SANIES n pl. **SANIES** a fluid discharged from wounds **SANIOUS** adj

SANING present participle of sane

SANITARY n pl. **-TARIES** a public urinal

SANITATE v **-TATED, -TATING, -TATES** to sanitize

SANITISE v **-TISED, -TISING, -TISES** to sanitize

SANITIZE v **-TIZED, -TIZING, -TIZES** to guard against infection or disease by cleaning or sterilizing

SANITY n pl. **-TIES** the state of being sane

SANJAK n pl. **-S** an administrative district of Turkey

SANK past tense of sink

SANNOP n pl. **-S** sannup

SANNUP n pl. **-S** a married male American Indian

SANNYASI n pl. **-S** a Hindu monk

SANS prep without

SANSAR n pl. **-S** sarsar

SANSEI n pl. **-S** a grandchild of Japanese immigrants to the United States

SANSERIF n pl. **-S** a typeface without serifs

SANTALIC adj pertaining to sandalwood

SANTALOL n pl. **-S** sandalwood oil

SANTERA n pl. **-S** a priestess of santeria

SANTERIA n pl. **-S** a religion of the Caribbean region

SANTERO n pl. **-ROS** a priest of santeria

SANTIMS n pl. **-TIMI** or **-TIMU** a formerly used coin of Latvia

SANTIR n pl. **-S** a Persian dulcimer

SANTO n pl. **-TOS** a wooden image of a saint

SANTOL n pl. **-S** a tropical tree

SANTONIN	n pl. **-S** a chemical compound
SANTOOR	n pl. **-S** santir
SANTOUR	n pl. **-S** santir
SANTUR	n pl. **-S** santir
SAP	v **SAPPED, SAPPING, SAPS** to deplete or weaken gradually
SAPAJOU	n pl. **-S** a capuchin
SAPHEAD	n pl. **-S** a foolish, stupid, or gullible person
SAPHENA	n pl. **-NAS** or **-NAE** a vein of the leg
SAPID	adj pleasant to the taste
SAPIDITY	n pl. **-TIES** the state of being sapid
SAPIENCE	n pl. **-S** wisdom
SAPIENCY	n pl. **-CIES** sapience
SAPIENS	adj pertaining to recent man
SAPIENT	n pl. **-S** a wise person
SAPLESS	adj lacking vitality
SAPLING	n pl. **-S** a young tree
SAPONIFY	v **-FIED, -FYING, -FIES** to convert into soap
SAPONIN	n pl. **-S** a soapy substance obtained from plants
SAPONINE	n pl. **-S** saponin
SAPONITE	n pl. **-S** a mineral found in veins and cavities of rocks
SAPOR	n pl. **-S** flavor **SAPOROUS** adj
SAPOTA	n pl. **-S** an evergreen tree
SAPOTE	n pl. **-S** a tropical American tree
SAPOUR	n pl. **-S** sapor
SAPPED	past tense of sap
SAPPER	n pl. **-S** a military engineer
SAPPHIC	n pl. **-S** a type of verse form
SAPPHIRE	n pl. **-S** a blue gem
SAPPHISM	n pl. **-S** lesbianism
SAPPHIST	n pl. **-S** a lesbian
SAPPING	present participle of sap
SAPPY	adj **-PIER, -PIEST** silly **SAPPILY** adv
SAPREMIA	n pl. **-S** a form of blood poisoning **SAPREMIC** adj
SAPROBE	n pl. **-S** an organism that derives its nourishment from decaying organic matter **SAPROBIC** adj
SAPROPEL	n pl. **-S** mud consisting chiefly of decaying organic matter
SAPSAGO	n pl. **-GOS** a hard green cheese
SAPWOOD	n pl. **-S** the newly formed outer wood of a tree
SARABAND	n pl. **-S** a stately Spanish dance
SARAN	n pl. **-S** a thermoplastic resin
SARAPE	n pl. **-S** serape
SARCASM	n pl. **-S** a sharply mocking or contemptuous remark
SARCENET	n pl. **-S** a silk fabric
SARCINA	n pl. **-NAS** or **-NAE** a spherical bacterium
SARCOID	n pl. **-S** a disease of horses
SARCOMA	n pl. **-MAS** or **-MATA** a type of tumor
SARCOUS	adj composed of flesh or muscle
SARD	n pl. **-S** a variety of quartz
SARDANA	n pl. **-S** a Spanish folk dance
SARDAR	n pl. **-S** sirdar
SARDINE	v **-DINED, -DINING, -DINES** to pack tightly
SARDIUS	n pl. **-ES** sard
SARDONIC	adj mocking
SARDONYX	n pl. **-ES** a variety of quartz
SAREE	n pl. **-S** sari
SARGASSO	n pl. **-GASSOS** a brownish seaweed
SARGE	n pl. **-S** sergeant
SARGO	n pl. **-GOS** a silvery marine fish
SARI	n pl. **-S** an outer garment worn by Hindu women
SARIN	n pl. **-S** a toxic gas
SARK	n pl. **-S** a shirt
SARKY	adj **SARKIER, SARKIEST** sarcastic
SARMENT	n pl. **-S** a type of plant stem
SARMENTA	n/pl sarments
SAROD	n pl. **-S** a lute of northern India
SARODE	n pl. **-S** sarod
SARODIST	n pl. **-S** one who plays the sarod
SARONG	n pl. **-S** an outer garment worn in the Pacific islands
SAROS	n pl. **-ES** the eclipse cycle of the sun and moon
SARSAR	n pl. **-S** a cold, whistling wind
SARSEN	n pl. **-S** a large sandstone block
SARSENET	n pl. **-S** sarcenet
SARSNET	n pl. **-S** sarcenet
SARTOR	n pl. **-S** a tailor

SARTORII	*n/pl* flat, narrow thigh muscles	**SATINPOD**	*n* pl. **-S** a flowering plant
SASH	*v* **-ED, -ING, -ES** to furnish with a frame in which glass is set	**SATINY**	*adj* resembling satin
		SATIRE	*n* pl. **-S** the use of derisive wit to attack folly or wickedness **SATIRIC** *adj*
SASHAY	*v* **-ED, -ING, -S** to flounce		
SASHIMI	*n* pl. **-S** a Japanese dish of sliced raw fish	**SATIRISE**	*v* **-RISED, -RISING, -RISES** to satirize
SASHLESS	*adj* lacking a sash (a long band worn around the waist)	**SATIRIST**	*n* pl. **-S** one who satirizes
SASIN	*n* pl. **-S** an antelope of India	**SATIRIZE**	*v* **-RIZED, -RIZING, -RIZES** to subject to satire
SASS	*v* **-ED, -ING, -ES** to talk impudently to	**SATISFY**	*v* **-FIED, -FYING, -FIES** to provide fully with what is desired, expected, or needed
SASSABY	*n* pl. **-BIES** an African antelope		
SASSIER	comparative of sassy	**SATORI**	*n* pl. **-S** the illumination of spirit sought by Zen Buddhists
SASSIES	pl. of sassy		
SASSIEST	superlative of sassy	**SATRAP**	*n* pl. **-S** a governor of a province in ancient Persia
SASSILY	*adv* in a sassy manner		
SASSWOOD	*n* pl. **-S** an African tree	**SATRAPY**	*n* pl. **-PIES** the territory of a satrap
SASSY	*adj* **SASSIER, SASSIEST** impudent	**SATSUMA**	*n* pl. **-S** a variety of orange
		SATURANT	*n* pl. **-S** a substance used to saturate
SASSY	*n* pl. **-SIES** sasswood		
SASTRUGA	*n* pl. **-GI** a ridge of snow formed by the wind in polar regions	**SATURATE**	*v* **-RATED, -RATING, -RATES** to fill completely with something that permeates
SAT	past tense of sit	**SATYR**	*n* pl. **-S** a woodland deity of Greek mythology **SATYRIC** *adj*
SATANG	*n* pl. **-S** a monetary unit of Thailand		
SATANIC	*adj* extremely evil	**SATYRID**	*n* pl. **-S** a brownish butterfly
SATANISM	*n* pl. **-S** worship of the powers of evil	**SAU**	*n* pl. **SAU** xu
		SAUCE	*v* **SAUCED, SAUCING, SAUCES** to season with sauce (a flavorful liquid dressing)
SATANIST	*n* pl. **-S** one who practices satanism		
SATARA	*n* pl. **-S** a woolen fabric	**SAUCEBOX**	*n* pl. **-ES** a saucy person
SATAY	*n* pl. **-TAYS** marinated meat that is skewered and broiled and dipped in peanut sauce	**SAUCEPAN**	*n* pl. **-S** a deep cooking pan with a handle
		SAUCEPOT	*n* pl. **-S** a deep cooking pot with two handles
SATCHEL	*n* pl. **-S** a small carrying bag		
SATE	*v* **SATED, SATING, SATES** to satiate	**SAUCER**	*n* pl. **-S** a small, shallow dish
		SAUCH	*n* pl. **-S** saugh
SATEEN	*n* pl. **-S** a cotton fabric	**SAUCIER**	*n* pl. **-S** a chef who specializes in sauces
SATEM	*adj* pertaining to a group of Indo-European languages		
		SAUCING	present participle of sauce
SATI	*n* pl. **-S** suttee	**SAUCY**	*adj* **SAUCIER, SAUCIEST** impudent **SAUCILY** *adv*
SATIABLE	*adj* capable of being satiated **SATIABLY** *adv*		
		SAUGER	*n* pl. **-S** a freshwater fish
SATIATE	*v* **-ATED, -ATING, -ATES** to satisfy to or beyond capacity	**SAUGH**	*n* pl. **-S** a willow tree **SAUGHY** *adj*
		SAUL	*n* pl. **-S** soul
SATIETY	*n* pl. **-ETIES** the state of being satiated	**SAULT**	*n* pl. **-S** a waterfall
		SAUNA	*v* **-ED, -ING, -S** to take a dry heat bath
SATIN	*n* pl. **-S** a smooth fabric		
SATINET	*n* pl. **-S** a thin satin	**SAUNTER**	*v* **-ED, -ING, -S** to walk in a leisurely manner
SATING	present participle of sate		

SAUREL *n* pl. **-S** a marine fish

SAURIAN *n* pl. **-S** any of a suborder of reptiles

SAUROPOD *n* pl. **-S** any of a suborder of large dinosaurs

SAURY *n* pl. **-RIES** a marine fish

SAUSAGE *n* pl. **-S** finely chopped and seasoned meat stuffed into a casing

SAUTE *v* **-TEED** or **-TED**, **-TEING**, **-TES** to fry in a small amount of fat

SAUTERNE *n* pl. **-S** a sweet white wine

SAUTOIR *n* pl. **-S** a saltire

SAUTOIRE *n* pl. **-S** sautoir

SAVABLE *adj* capable of being saved

SAVAGE *adj* **-AGER**, **-AGEST** fierce **SAVAGELY** *adv*

SAVAGE *v* **-AGED**, **-AGING**, **-AGES** to attack or treat brutally

SAVAGERY *n* pl. **-RIES** the quality of being savage

SAVAGISM *n* pl. **-S** savagery

SAVANNA *n* pl. **-S** a flat, treeless grassland

SAVANNAH *n* pl. **-S** savanna

SAVANT *n* pl. **-S** a man of profound learning

SAVARIN *n* pl. **-S** a yeast cake baked in a ring mold

SAVATE *n* pl. **-S** a pugilistic sport

SAVE *v* **SAVED**, **SAVING**, **SAVES** to rescue from danger, injury, or loss **SAVEABLE** *adj*

SAVELOY *n* pl. **-LOYS** a highly seasoned sausage

SAVER *n* pl. **-S** one that saves

SAVIN *n* pl. **-S** an evergreen shrub

SAVINE *n* pl. **-S** savin

SAVING *n* pl. **-S** the act or an instance of saving

SAVINGLY *adv* in a thrifty manner

SAVIOR *n* pl. **-S** one that saves

SAVIOUR *n* pl. **-S** savior

SAVOR *v* **-ED**, **-ING**, **-S** to taste or smell with pleasure

SAVORER *n* pl. **-S** one that savors

SAVOROUS *adj* savory

SAVORY *adj* **-VORIER**, **-VORIEST** pleasant to the taste or smell **SAVORILY** *adv*

SAVORY *n* pl. **-VORIES** a savory dish served before or after a meal

SAVOUR *v* **-ED**, **-ING**, **-S** to savor

SAVOURER *n* pl. **-S** savorer

SAVOURY *adj* **-VOURIER**, **-VOURIEST** savory

SAVOURY *n* pl. **-VOURIES** a savory

SAVOY *n* pl. **-VOYS** a variety of cabbage

SAVVY *adj* **-VIER**, **-VIEST** shrewd

SAVVY *v* **-VIED**, **-VYING**, **-VIES** to understand **SAVVILY** *adv*

SAW *v* **SAWED**, **SAWN**, **SAWING**, **SAWS** to cut or divide with a saw (a type of cutting tool)

SAWBILL *n* pl. **-S** a tropical bird

SAWBONES *n* pl. **-BONESES** a surgeon

SAWBUCK *n* pl. **-S** a sawhorse

SAWDUST *n* pl. **-S** small particles of wood produced in sawing **SAWDUSTY** *adj*

SAWER *n* pl. **-S** one that saws

SAWFISH *n* pl. **-ES** a marine fish

SAWFLY *n* pl. **-FLIES** a winged insect

SAWHORSE *n* pl. **-S** a rack used to support a piece of wood being sawed

SAWLIKE *adj* resembling a saw

SAWLOG *n* pl. **-S** a log large enough to saw into boards

SAWMILL *n* pl. **-S** a place where logs are sawed

SAWN a past participle of saw

SAWNEY *n* pl. **-NEYS** a foolish person

SAWTOOTH *n* pl. **-TEETH** a cutting edge on a saw

SAWYER *n* pl. **-S** one that saws wood for a living

SAX *n* pl. **-ES** a saxophone

SAXATILE *adj* living or growing among rocks

SAXHORN *n* pl. **-S** a brass wind instrument

SAXONY *n* pl. **-NIES** a woolen fabric

SAXTUBA *n* pl. **-S** a bass saxhorn

SAY *v* **SAID**, **SAYING** present sing. 2d person **SAY**, **SAYEST** or **SAYST** 3d person **SAYS** or **SAITH** to utter **SAYABLE** *adj*

SAYED *n* pl. **-S** sayyid

SAYER *n* pl. **-S** one that says

SAYID *n* pl. **-S** sayyid

SAYING *n* pl. **-S** a maxim

SAYONARA *n* pl. **-S** goodby

SAYST a present 2d person sing. of say

SAYYID	*n* pl. **-S** lord; sir — used as a title of respect for a Muslim dignitary	**SCALING**	present participle of scale
SCAB	*v* **SCABBED, SCABBING, SCABS** to become covered with a scab (a crust that forms over a healing wound)	**SCALL**	*n* pl. **-S** a scaly eruption of the skin
		SCALLION	*n* pl. **-S** an onion-like plant
		SCALLOP	*v* **-ED, -ING, -S** to bake in a sauce topped with bread crumbs
SCABBARD	*v* **-ED, -ING, -S** to put into a sheath, as a sword	**SCALP**	*v* **-ED, -ING, -S** to remove an upper part from
SCABBLE	*v* **-BLED, -BLING, -BLES** to shape roughly	**SCALPEL**	*n* pl. **-S** a small surgical knife
SCABBY	*adj* **-BIER, -BIEST** covered with scabs **SCABBILY** *adv*	**SCALPER**	*n* pl. **-S** one that scalps
		SCALY	*adj* **SCALIER, SCALIEST** peeling off in flakes
SCABIES	*n* pl. **SCABIES** a skin disease	**SCAM**	*v* **SCAMMED, SCAMMING, SCAMS** to cheat or swindle
SCABIOSA	*n* pl. **-S** scabious		
SCABIOUS	*n* pl. **-ES** a flowering plant	**SCAMMER**	*n* pl. **-S** one that scams
SCABLAND	*n* pl. **-S** rocky land with little soil cover	**SCAMMONY**	*n* pl. **-NIES** a climbing plant
		SCAMP	*v* **-ED, -ING, -S** to perform in a hasty or careless manner
SCABLIKE	*adj* resembling a scab		
SCABROUS	*adj* roughened with small projections	**SCAMPER**	*v* **-ED, -ING, -S** to run playfully about
SCAD	*n* pl. **-S** a marine fish	**SCAMPI**	*n* pl. **SCAMPI** or **SCAMPIES** large shrimp used in Italian cooking
SCAFFOLD	*v* **-ED, -ING, -S** to provide with a scaffold (a temporary platform for workmen)		
		SCAMPISH	*adj* rascally
		SCAMSTER	*n* pl. **-S** one that scams
SCAG	*n* pl. **-S** heroin	**SCAN**	*v* **SCANNED, SCANNING, SCANS** to examine closely
SCALABLE	*adj* capable of being scaled **SCALABLY** *adv*		
		SCANDAL	*v* **-DALED, -DALING, -DALS** or **-DALLED, -DALLING, -DALS** to defame
SCALADE	*n* pl. **-S** an act of scaling the walls of a fortification		
SCALADO	*n* pl. **-DOS** scalade	**SCANDENT**	*adj* climbing, as a plant
SCALAGE	*n* pl. **-S** a percentage deduction to compensate for shrinkage	**SCANDIA**	*n* pl. **-S** an oxide of scandium
		SCANDIUM	*n* pl. **-S** a metallic element **SCANDIC** *adj*
SCALAR	*n* pl. **-S** a mathematical quantity possessing only magnitude		
		SCANNED	past tense of scan
SCALARE	*n* pl. **-S** a tropical fish	**SCANNER**	*n* pl. **-S** one that scans
SCALAWAG	*n* pl. **-S** a rascal	**SCANNING**	*n* pl. **-S** close examination
SCALD	*v* **-ED, -ING, -S** to burn with hot liquid or steam	**SCANSION**	*n* pl. **-S** the analysis of verse into metrical feet and rhythm patterns
SCALDIC	*adj* skaldic		
SCALE	*v* **SCALED, SCALING, SCALES** to climb up or over	**SCANT**	*adj* **SCANTER, SCANTEST** meager
SCALENE	*adj* designating a triangle having no two sides equal	**SCANT**	*v* **-ED, -ING, -S** to provide with a meager portion
		SCANTIES	*n/pl* brief panties for women
SCALENUS	*n* pl. **-NI** a muscle of the neck	**SCANTLY**	*adv* in a scant manner
SCALEPAN	*n* pl. **-S** a pan on a weighing scale	**SCANTY**	*adj* **SCANTIER, SCANTIEST** meager **SCANTILY** *adv*
SCALER	*n* pl. **-S** one that scales		
SCALEUP	*n* pl. **-S** an increase based on a fixed ratio	**SCAPE**	*v* **SCAPED, SCAPING, SCAPES** to escape
SCALIER	comparative of scaly	**SCAPHOID**	*n* pl. **-S** a bone of the wrist
SCALIEST	superlative of scaly	**SCAPOSE**	*adj* bearing a leafless stalk

SCAPULA _n_ pl. **-LAS** or **-LAE** a bone of the shoulder

SCAPULAR _n_ pl. **-S** a sleeveless outer garment worn by monks

SCAR _v_ **SCARRED, SCARRING, SCARS** to form a scar (a mark left by the healing of injured tissue)

SCARAB _n_ pl. **-S** a large, black beetle

SCARCE _adj_ **SCARCER, SCARCEST** infrequently seen or found

SCARCELY _adv_ by a narrow margin

SCARCITY _n_ pl. **-TIES** the quality of being scarce

SCARE _v_ **SCARED, SCARING, SCARES** to frighten

SCARED _adj_ **SCAREDER, SCAREDEST** afraid

SCARER _n_ pl. **-S** one that scares

SCAREY _adj_ **SCARIER, SCARIEST** scary

SCARF _n_ pl. **SCARFS** or **SCARVES** a piece of cloth worn for warmth or protection

SCARF _v_ **-ED, -ING, -S** to cover with a scarf

SCARFER _n_ pl. **-S** one that eats or drinks voraciously

SCARFPIN _n_ pl. **-S** a tiepin

SCARIER comparative of scarey and scary

SCARIEST superlative of scarey and scary

SCARIFY _v_ **-FIED, -FYING, -FIES** to make superficial cuts in

SCARILY _adv_ in a scary manner

SCARING present participle of scare

SCARIOSE _adj_ scarious

SCARIOUS _adj_ thin, dry, and membranous

SCARLESS _adj_ having no scars

SCARLET _n_ pl. **-S** a red color

SCARP _v_ **-ED, -ING, -S** to cut or make into a steep slope

SCARPER _v_ **-ED, -ING, -S** to flee

SCARPH _v_ **-ED, -ING, -S** to unite by means of a type of joint

SCARRED past tense of scar

SCARRING present participle of scar

SCARRY _adj_ **-RIER, -RIEST** marked with scars

SCART _v_ **-ED, -ING, -S** to scratch

SCARVES a pl. of scarf

SCARY _adj_ **SCARIER, SCARIEST** frightening

SCAT _v_ **SCATTED, SCATTING, SCATS** to leave hastily

SCATBACK _n_ pl. **-S** a type of player in football

SCATHE _v_ **SCATHED, SCATHING, SCATHES** to criticize severely

SCATT _n_ pl. **-S** a tax

SCATTED past tense of scat

SCATTER _v_ **-ED, -ING, -S** to go or send in various directions

SCATTING present participle of scat

SCATTY _adj_ **-TIER, -TIEST** crazy

SCAUP _n_ pl. **-S** a sea duck

SCAUPER _n_ pl. **-S** an engraving tool

SCAUR _n_ pl. **-S** a protruding, isolated rock

SCAVENGE _v_ **-ENGED, -ENGING, -ENGES** to search through rubbish for usable items

SCENA _n_ pl. **-S** an elaborate composition for a single voice

SCENARIO _n_ pl. **-IOS** a summary of the plot of a dramatic work

SCEND _v_ **-ED, -ING, -S** to rise upward, as a ship on a wave

SCENE _n_ pl. **-S** the place where some action or event occurs

SCENERY _n_ pl. **-ERIES** a picturesque landscape or view

SCENIC _n_ pl. **-S** a depiction of natural scenery

SCENICAL _adj_ pertaining to scenery

SCENT _v_ **-ED, -ING, -S** to fill with an odor

SCEPTER _v_ **-ED, -ING, -S** to invest with royal authority

SCEPTIC _n_ pl. **-S** skeptic

SCEPTRAL _adj_ pertaining to royal authority

SCEPTRE _v_ **-TRED, -TRING, -TRES** to scepter

SCHAPPE _n_ pl. **-S** a silk fabric

SCHAV _n_ pl. **-S** a chilled soup

SCHEDULE _v_ **-ULED, -ULING, -ULES** to assign to a certain date or time

SCHEMA _n_ pl. **-MAS** or **-MATA** a generalized diagram or plan

SCHEME _v_ **SCHEMED, SCHEMING, SCHEMES** to plan or plot

SCHEMER _n_ pl. **-S** one that schemes

SCHERZO _n_ pl. **-ZOS** or **-ZI** a lively musical movement

SCHILLER _n_ pl. **-S** a brownish luster occurring on certain minerals

SCHISM *n* pl. **-S** a division into opposing parties

SCHIST *n* pl. **-S** a rock that readily splits into parallel layers

SCHIZIER comparative of schizy

SCHIZIEST superlative of schizy

SCHIZO *n* pl. **SCHIZOS** a schizoid

SCHIZOID *n* pl. **-S** a person affected with a type of psychotic disorder

SCHIZONT *n* pl. **-S** an organism that reproduces by a form of asexual reproduction

SCHIZY *adj* **SCHIZIER, SCHIZIEST** affected with schizophrenia

SCHIZZY *adj* **SCHIZZIER, SCHIZZIEST** schizy

SCHLEP *v* **SCHLEPPED, SCHLEPPING, SCHLEPS** to lug or drag

SCHLEPP *v* **-ED, -ING, -S** to schlep

SCHLIERE *n* pl. **-REN** a small streak in an igneous rock

SCHLOCK *n* pl. **-S** inferior merchandise

SCHLOCKY *adj* **SCHLOCKIER, SCHLOCKIEST** of inferior quality

SCHLUB *n* pl. **-S** a stupid or unattractive person

SCHLUMP *v* **-ED, -ING, -S** to go about lazily or sloppily dressed

SCHLUMPY *adj* **SCHLUMPIER, SCHLUMPIEST** unattractive, slovenly

SCHMALTZ *n* pl. **-ES** excessive sentimentality

SCHMALZ *n* pl. **-ES** schmaltz

SCHMALZY *adj* **SCHMALZIER, SCHMALZIEST** characterized by schmaltz

SCHMATTE *n* pl. **-S** a ragged garment

SCHMEAR *v* **-ED, -ING, -S** to schmeer

SCHMEER *v* **-ED, -ING, -S** to bribe

SCHMELZE *n* pl. **-S** a type of decorative glass

SCHMO *n* pl. **SCHMOES** or **SCHMOS** a stupid person

SCHMOE *n* pl. **-S** schmo

SCHMOOS *v* **-ED, -ING, -ES** to schmooze

SCHMOOSE *v* **SCHMOOSED, SCHMOOSING, SCHMOOSES** to schmooze

SCHMOOZE *v* **SCHMOOZED, SCHMOOZING, SCHMOOZES** to gossip

SCHMOOZY *adj* **SCHMOOZIER, SCHMOOZIEST** given to schmoozing

SCHMUCK *n* pl. **-S** a foolish or clumsy person

SCHNAPPS *n* pl. **SCHNAPPS** a strong liquor

SCHNAPS *n* pl. **SCHNAPS** schnapps

SCHNECKE *n* pl. **-KEN** a sweet roll

SCHNOOK *n* pl. **-S** an easily deceived person

SCHNOZ *n* pl. **-ES** the nose

SCHNOZZ *n* pl. **-ES** schnoz

SCHOLAR *n* pl. **-S** a learned person

SCHOLIUM *n* pl. **-LIUMS** or **-LIA** an explanatory marginal note

SCHOOL *v* **-ED, -ING, -S** to educate in an institution of learning

SCHOONER *n* pl. **-S** a sailing vessel

SCHORL *n* pl. **-S** a mineral

SCHRIK *n* pl. **-S** sudden fright

SCHROD *n* pl. **-S** scrod

SCHTICK *n* pl. **-S** shtick

SCHTIK *n* pl. **-S** shtick

SCHUIT *n* pl. **-S** a Dutch sailing vessel

SCHUL *n* pl. **SCHULS** or **SCHULN** shul

SCHUSS *v* **-ED, -ING, -ES** to make a fast, straight run in skiing

SCHUSSER *n* pl. **-S** one that schusses

SCHWA *n* pl. **-S** a type of vowel sound

SCIAENID *n* pl. **-S** a carnivorous fish

SCIATIC *n* pl. **-S** a nerve, vein, or artery situated near the hip

SCIATICA *n* pl. **-S** a painful disorder of the hip and adjoining areas

SCIENCE *n* pl. **-S** a department of systematized knowledge

SCILICET *adv* namely

SCILLA *n* pl. **-S** a flowering plant

SCIMETAR *n* pl. **-S** scimitar

SCIMITAR *n* pl. **-S** a curved sword used by Arabs and Turks

SCIMITER *n* pl. **-S** scimitar

SCINCOID *n* pl. **-S** one of a family of smooth, short-limbed lizards

SCIOLISM *n* pl. **-S** superficial knowledge

SCIOLIST *n* pl. **-S** one whose knowledge is superficial

SCION *n* pl. **-S** a child or descendant

SCIROCCO *n* pl. **-COS** sirocco

SCIRRHUS *n* pl. **-RHUSES** or **-RHI** a hard tumor

SCISSILE *adj* capable of being cut or split easily

SCISSION *n* pl. **-S** the act of cutting or splitting

SCISSOR *v* **-ED, -ING, -S** to cut with a two-bladed cutting implement

SCISSURE *n* pl. **-S** a lengthwise cut

SCIURID *n* pl. **-S** a sciurine

SCIURINE *n* pl. **-S** a rodent of the squirrel family

SCIUROID *adj* resembling a squirrel

SCLAFF *v* **-ED, -ING, -S** to strike the ground with the club before hitting the ball in golf

SCLAFFER *n* pl. **-S** one that sclaffs

SCLERA *n* pl. **-RAS** or **-RAE** the white, fibrous outer coat of the eyeball **SCLERAL** *adj*

SCLEREID *n* pl. **-S** a type of plant cell

SCLERITE *n* pl. **-S** one of the hard plates forming the outer covering of an arthropod

SCLEROID *adj* sclerous

SCLEROMA *n* pl. **-MAS** or **-MATA** a hardened patch of cellular tissue

SCLEROSE *v* **-ROSED, -ROSING, -ROSES** to become hard, as tissue

SCLEROUS *adj* hardened

SCOFF *v* **-ED, -ING, -S** to express rude doubt or derision

SCOFFER *n* pl. **-S** one that scoffs

SCOFFLAW *n* pl. **-S** a habitual law violator

SCOLD *v* **-ED, -ING, -S** to rebuke harshly

SCOLDER *n* pl. **-S** one that scolds

SCOLDING *n* pl. **-S** a harsh reproof

SCOLEX *n* pl. **-LECES** or **-LICES** the knoblike head of a tapeworm

SCOLIOMA *n* pl. **-S** abnormal curvature of the spine

SCOLLOP *v* **-ED, -ING, -S** to scallop

SCOMBRID *n* pl. **-S** a fish of the mackerel family

SCONCE *v* **SCONCED, SCONCING, SCONCES** to fine

SCONE *n* pl. **-S** a flat, round cake

SCOOCH *v* **-ED, -ING, -ES** to slide with short movements

SCOOP *v* **-ED, -ING, -S** to take up with a scoop (a spoonlike utensil)

SCOOPER *n* pl. **-S** one that scoops

SCOOPFUL *n* pl. **SCOOPFULS** or **SCOOPSFUL** as much as a scoop will hold

SCOOT *v* **-ED, -ING, -S** to go quickly

SCOOTCH *v* **-ED, -ING, -ES** to scooch

SCOOTER *n* pl. **-S** a two-wheeled vehicle

SCOP *n* pl. **-S** an Old English poet

SCOPE *v* **SCOPED, SCOPING, SCOPES** to look at in order to evaluate

SCOPULA *n* pl. **-LAS** or **-LAE** a dense tuft of hairs

SCORCH *v* **-ED, -ING, -ES** to burn slightly so as to alter the color or taste

SCORCHER *n* pl. **-S** one that scorches

SCORE *v* **SCORED, SCORING, SCORES** to make a point in a game or contest

SCOREPAD *n* pl. **-S** a pad on which scored points are recorded

SCORER *n* pl. **-S** one that scores

SCORIA *n* pl. **-RIAE** the refuse of a smelted metal or ore

SCORIFY *v* **-FIED, -FYING, -FIES** to reduce to scoria

SCORING present participle of score

SCORN *v* **-ED, -ING, -S** to treat or regard with contempt

SCORNER *n* pl. **-S** one that scorns

SCORNFUL *adj* feeling or expressing contempt

SCORPION *n* pl. **-S** a stinging arachnid

SCOT *n* pl. **-S** a tax

SCOTCH *v* **-ED, -ING, -ES** to put a definite end to

SCOTER *n* pl. **-S** a sea duck

SCOTIA *n* pl. **-S** a concave molding

SCOTOMA *n* pl. **-MAS** or **-MATA** a blind spot in the field of vision

SCOTOPIA *n* pl. **-S** vision in dim light **SCOTOPIC** *adj*

SCOTTIE *n* pl. **-S** a short-legged terrier

SCOUR *v* **-ED, -ING, -S** to cleanse or polish by hard rubbing

SCOURER *n* pl. **-S** one that scours

SCOURGE *v* **SCOURGED, SCOURGING, SCOURGES** to punish severely

SCOURGER *n* pl. **-S** one that scourges

SCOURING *n* pl. **-S** material removed by scouring

SCOUSE *n* pl. **-S** a type of meat stew

SCOUT *v* **-ED, -ING, -S** to observe for the purpose of obtaining information

SCOUTER *n* pl. **-S** one that scouts

SCOUTH *n* pl. **-S** plenty

SCOUTHER *v* **-ED, -ING, -S** to scorch

SCOUTING *n* pl. **-S** the act of one that scouts

SCOW *v* **-ED, -ING, -S** to transport by scow (a flat-bottomed boat)

SCOWDER *v* **-ED, -ING, -S** to scouther

SCOWL *v* **-ED, -ING, -S** to frown angrily

SCOWLER *n* pl. **-S** one that scowls

SCRABBLE *v* **-BLED, -BLING, -BLES** to claw or grope about frantically

SCRABBLY *adj* **-BLIER, -BLIEST** raspy

SCRAG *v* **SCRAGGED, SCRAGGING, SCRAGS** to wring the neck of

SCRAGGLY *adj* **-GLIER, -GLIEST** uneven

SCRAGGY *adj* **-GIER, -GIEST** scrawny

SCRAICH *v* **-ED, -ING, -S** to utter a shrill cry

SCRAIGH *v* **-ED, -ING, -S** to scraich

SCRAM *v* **SCRAMMED, SCRAMMING, SCRAMS** to leave quickly

SCRAMBLE *v* **-BLED, -BLING, -BLES** to move or climb hurriedly

SCRAMJET *n* pl. **-S** a type of aircraft engine

SCRANNEL *n* pl. **-S** a thin person

SCRAP *v* **SCRAPPED, SCRAPPING, SCRAPS** to discard

SCRAPE *v* **SCRAPED, SCRAPING, SCRAPES** to rub so as to remove an outer layer

SCRAPER *n* pl. **-S** one that scrapes

SCRAPIE *n* pl. **-S** a disease of sheep

SCRAPING *n* pl. **-S** something scraped off

SCRAPPED past tense of scrap

SCRAPPER *n* pl. **-S** a fighter

SCRAPPING present participle of scrap

SCRAPPLE *n* pl. **-S** a seasoned mixture of ground meat and cornmeal

SCRAPPY *adj* **-PIER, -PIEST** marked by fighting spirit

SCRATCH *v* **-ED, -ING, -ES** to make a thin, shallow cut or mark on

SCRATCHY *adj* **SCRATCHIER, SCRATCHIEST** made by scratching

SCRAWL *v* **-ED, -ING, -S** to write hastily or illegibly

SCRAWLER *n* pl. **-S** one that scrawls

SCRAWLY *adj* **SCRAWLIER, SCRAWLIEST** written hastily or illegibly

SCRAWNY *adj* **-NIER, -NIEST** extremely thin

SCREAK *v* **-ED, -ING, -S** to screech

SCREAKY *adj* screechy

SCREAM *v* **-ED, -ING, -S** to utter a prolonged, piercing cry

SCREAMER *n* pl. **-S** one that screams

SCREE *n* pl. **-S** a mass of rocks at the foot of a slope

SCREECH *v* **-ED, -ING, -ES** to utter a harsh, shrill cry

SCREECHY *adj* **SCREECHIER, SCREECHIEST** screeching

SCREED *v* **-ED, -ING, -S** to shred

SCREEN *v* **-ED, -ING, -S** to provide with a screen (a device designed to divide, conceal, or protect)

SCREENER *n* pl. **-S** one that screens

SCREW *v* **-ED, -ING, -S** to attach with a screw (a type of metal fastener)

SCREWER *n* pl. **-S** one that screws

SCREWUP *n* pl. **-S** an instance of bungling

SCREWY *adj* **SCREWIER, SCREWIEST** crazy

SCRIBAL *adj* pertaining to a public clerk or secretary

SCRIBBLE *v* **-BLED, -BLING, -BLES** to write hastily or carelessly

SCRIBBLY *adj* consisting of scribbles (careless writings)

SCRIBE *v* **SCRIBED, SCRIBING, SCRIBES** to mark with a scriber

SCRIBER *n* pl. **-S** a pointed instrument used for marking off material to be cut

SCRIED past tense of scry

SCRIES present 3d person sing. of scry

SCRIEVE *v* **SCRIEVED, SCRIEVING, SCRIEVES** to move along swiftly and smoothly

SCRIM *n* pl. **-S** a cotton fabric

SCRIMP *v* **-ED, -ING, -S** to be very or overly thrifty

SCRIMPER *n* pl. **-S** one that scrimps

SCRIMPIT *adj* meager

SCRIMPY *adj* **SCRIMPIER, SCRIMPIEST** meager

SCRIP *n* pl. **-S** a small piece of paper

SCRIPT *v* **-ED, -ING, -S** to prepare a written text for, as a play or motion picture

SCRIPTER *n* pl. **-S** one that scripts

SCRIVE *v* **SCRIVED, SCRIVING, SCRIVES** to engrave

SCROD *n* pl. **-S** a young cod

SCROFULA *n* pl. **-S** a disease of the lymph glands

SCROGGY *adj* **-GIER, -GIEST** of stunted growth

SCROLL *v* **-ED, -ING, -S** to move text across a display screen

SCROOCH *v* **-ED, -ING, -ES** to crouch

SCROOGE *n* pl. **-S** a miserly person

SCROOP *v* **-ED, -ING, -S** to make a harsh, grating sound

SCROOTCH *v* **-ED, -ING, -ES** to scrooch

SCROTUM *n* pl. **-TUMS** or **-TA** the pouch of skin that contains the testes **SCROTAL** *adj*

SCROUGE *v* **SCROUGED, SCROUGING, SCROUGES** to crowd

SCROUNGE *v* **SCROUNGED, SCROUNGING, SCROUNGES** to gather by foraging

SCROUNGY *adj* **SCROUNGIER, SCROUNGIEST** dirty

SCRUB *v* **SCRUBBED, SCRUBBING, SCRUBS** to rub hard in order to clean

SCRUBBER *n* pl. **-S** one that scrubs

SCRUBBY *adj* **-BIER, -BIEST** inferior in size or quality

SCRUFF *n* pl. **-S** the back of the neck

SCRUFFY *adj* **-FIER, -FIEST** shabby

SCRUM *v* **SCRUMMED, SCRUMMING, SCRUMS** to engage in a scrummage (a formation around the ball in rugby)

SCRUNCH *v* **-ED, -ING, -ES** to crush

SCRUNCHY *n* pl. **SCRUNCHIES** an elastic band for fastening the hair

SCRUPLE *v* **-PLED, -PLING, -PLES** to hesitate because of ethical considerations

SCRUTINY *n* pl. **-NIES** a close examination

SCRY *v* **SCRIED, SCRYING, SCRIES** to engage in crystal gazing

SCUBA *v* **-ED, -ING, -S** to swim underwater using a breathing device with compressed air

SCUD *v* **SCUDDED, SCUDDING, SCUDS** to run or move swiftly

SCUDO *n* pl. **-DI** a former Italian coin

SCUFF *v* **-ED, -ING, -S** to walk without lifting the feet

SCUFFER *n* pl. **-S** one that scuffs

SCUFFLE *v* **-FLED, -FLING, -FLES** to struggle in a rough, confused manner

SCUFFLER *n* pl. **-S** one that scuffles

SCULCH *n* pl. **-ES** clean trash

SCULK *v* **-ED, -ING, -S** to skulk

SCULKER *n* pl. **-S** skulker

SCULL *v* **-ED, -ING, -S** to propel with a type of oar

SCULLER *n* pl. **-S** one that sculls

SCULLERY *n* pl. **-LERIES** a room in which kitchen utensils are cleaned and stored

SCULLION *n* pl. **-S** a kitchen servant who does menial work

SCULP *v* **-ED, -ING, -S** to sculpt

SCULPIN *n* pl. **-S** a freshwater fish

SCULPT *v* **-ED, -ING, -S** to form an image or representation of from solid material

SCULPTOR *n* pl. **-S** one that sculpts

SCULTCH *n* pl. **-ES** sculch

SCUM *v* **SCUMMED, SCUMMING, SCUMS** to remove the scum (impure or extraneous matter) from

SCUMBAG *n* pl. **-S** a dirtbag

SCUMBLE *v* **-BLED, -BLING, -BLES** to soften the outlines or colors of by rubbing lightly

SCUMLESS *adj* having no scum

SCUMLIKE *adj* resembling scum

SCUMMED past tense of scum

SCUMMER *n* pl. **-S** one that scums

SCUMMING present participle of scum

SCUMMY *adj* **-MIER, -MIEST** covered with scum **SCUMMILY** *adv*

SCUNNER *v* **-ED, -ING, -S** to feel loathing or disgust

SCUP *n* pl. **-S** a marine food fish

SCUPPAUG *n* pl. **-S** scup

SCUPPER *v* **-ED, -ING, -S** to ambush

SCURF *n* pl. **-S** scaly or shredded dry skin

SCURFY *adj* **SCURFIER, SCURFIEST** covered with scurf

SCURRIL *adj* scurrile

SCURRILE *adj* expressed in coarse and abusive language

SCURRY *v* **-RIED, -RYING, -RIES** to move hurriedly

SCURVY	adj **-VIER, -VIEST** base or contemptible **SCURVILY** adv		**SEAFRONT**	n pl. **-S** an area along the edge of the sea
SCURVY	n pl. **-VIES** a disease resulting from vitamin C deficiency		**SEAGIRT**	adj surrounded by the sea
SCUT	n pl. **-S** a short tail, as of a rabbit		**SEAGOING**	adj designed for use on the sea
SCUTA	pl. of scutum		**SEAGULL**	n pl. **-S** a gull frequenting the sea
SCUTAGE	n pl. **-S** a tax exacted by a feudal lord in lieu of military service		**SEAHORSE**	n pl. **-S** a fish of the pipefish family
SCUTATE	adj shaped like a shield		**SEAL**	v **-ED, -ING, -S** to close or make secure against access, leakage, or passage **SEALABLE** adj
SCUTCH	v **-ED, -ING, -ES** to separate the woody fiber from by beating		**SEALANT**	n pl. **-S** a sealing agent
SCUTCHER	n pl. **-S** one that scutches		**SEALER**	n pl. **-S** one that seals
SCUTE	n pl. **-S** a horny plate or scale		**SEALERY**	n pl. **-ERIES** the occupation of hunting seals
SCUTELLA	n/pl small, scutate organs or parts		**SEALIFT**	v **-ED, -ING, -S** to transport (military personnel and equipment) by ship
SCUTTER	v **-ED, -ING, -S** to scurry			
SCUTTLE	v **-TLED, -TLING, -TLES** to scurry		**SEALLIKE**	adj resembling a seal (an aquatic mammal)
SCUTUM	n pl. **-TA** scute		**SEALSKIN**	n pl. **-S** the skin of a seal
SCUTWORK	n pl. **-S** tedious or menial work		**SEAM**	v **-ED, -ING, -S** to join with a seam (a line formed by sewing two pieces of fabric together)
SCUZZ	n pl. **-ES** a dirty or contemptible person			
SCUZZY	adj **-ZIER, -ZIEST** dirty or shabby		**SEAMAN**	n pl. **-MEN** a sailor **SEAMANLY** adj
SCYPHATE	adj shaped like a cup		**SEAMARK**	n pl. **-S** a landmark serving as a navigational guide to mariners
SCYPHUS	n pl. **-PHI** a Greek cup with two handles		**SEAMER**	n pl. **-S** one that seams
SCYTHE	v **SCYTHED, SCYTHING, SCYTHES** to cut with a scythe (a single-bladed cutting implement)		**SEAMIER**	comparative of seamy
			SEAMIEST	superlative of seamy
			SEAMLESS	adj having no seam
SEA	n pl. **-S** the ocean		**SEAMLIKE**	adj resembling a seam
SEABAG	n pl. **-S** a bag used by a sailor		**SEAMOUNT**	n pl. **-S** an undersea mountain
SEABEACH	n pl. **-ES** a beach lying along the sea		**SEAMSTER**	n pl. **-S** a person whose occupation is sewing
SEABED	n pl. **-S** a seafloor		**SEAMY**	adj **SEAMIER, SEAMIEST** unpleasant
SEABIRD	n pl. **-S** a bird frequenting the ocean or seacoast			
SEABOARD	n pl. **-S** the seacoast		**SEANCE**	n pl. **-S** a meeting of persons seeking spiritualistic messages
SEABOOT	n pl. **-S** a waterproof boot		**SEAPIECE**	n pl. **-S** a seascape
SEABORNE	adj carried on or over the sea		**SEAPLANE**	n pl. **-S** an airplane designed to take off from or land on the water
SEACOAST	n pl. **-S** land bordering on the sea			
SEACOCK	n pl. **-S** a valve in a ship's hull		**SEAPORT**	n pl. **-S** a harbor or town accessible to seagoing ships
SEACRAFT	n pl. **-S** skill in sea navigation			
SEADOG	n pl. **-S** a fogbow		**SEAQUAKE**	n pl. **-S** an undersea earthquake
SEADROME	n pl. **-S** an airport in the sea		**SEAR**	adj **SEARER, SEAREST** sere
SEAFARER	n pl. **-S** a sailor		**SEAR**	v **-ED, -ING, -S** to burn the surface of
SEAFLOOR	n pl. **-S** the bottom of a sea			
SEAFOOD	n pl. **-S** edible fish or shellfish from the sea		**SEARCH**	v **-ED, -ING, -ES** to look through or over carefully in order to find something
SEAFOWL	n pl. **-S** a seabird		**SEARCHER**	n pl. **-S** one that searches

SEAROBIN *n* pl. **-S** a marine fish

SEASCAPE *n* pl. **-S** a picture of the sea

SEASCOUT *n* pl. **-S** a boy scout trained in water activities

SEASHELL *n* pl. **-S** the shell of a marine mollusk

SEASHORE *n* pl. **-S** land bordering on the sea

SEASICK *adj* affected with nausea caused by the motion of a vessel at sea

SEASIDE *n* pl. **-S** the seashore

SEASON *v* **-ED, -ING, -S** to heighten or improve the flavor of by adding savory ingredients

SEASONAL *n* pl. **-S** an employee or product associated with a time of the year

SEASONER *n* pl. **-S** one that seasons

SEAT *v* **-ED, -ING, -S** to place on a seat (something on which one sits)

SEATBACK *n* pl. **-S** the back of a seat

SEATBELT *n* pl. **-S** an arrangement of straps to keep a person steady in a seat

SEATER *n* pl. **-S** one that seats

SEATING *n* pl. **-S** material for covering seats

SEATLESS *adj* having no seat

SEATMATE *n* pl. **-S** one with whom one shares a seat

SEATRAIN *n* pl. **-S** a ship equipped to carry railroad cars

SEATROUT *n* pl. **-S** a marine fish

SEATWORK *n* pl. **-S** work done at one's seat

SEAWALL *n* pl. **-S** a wall to protect a shoreline from erosion

SEAWAN *n* pl. **-S** wampum

SEAWANT *n* pl. **-S** seawan

SEAWARD *n* pl. **-S** the direction toward the open sea

SEAWARE *n* pl. **-S** seaweed used as fertilizer

SEAWATER *n* pl. **-S** water from the sea

SEAWAY *n* pl. **-WAYS** the headway made by a ship

SEAWEED *n* pl. **-S** a plant growing in the sea

SEBACIC *adj* derived from a certain acid

SEBASIC *adj* sebacic

SEBUM *n* pl. **-S** a fatty matter secreted by certain glands of the skin

SEC *n* pl. **-S** secant

SECALOSE *n* pl. **-S** a complex carbohydrate

SECANT *n* pl. **-S** a trigonometric function of an angle

SECANTLY *adv* in an intersecting manner

SECATEUR *n* pl. **-S** a pruning tool

SECCO *n* pl. **-COS** the art of painting on dry plaster

SECEDE *v* **-CEDED, -CEDING, -CEDES** to withdraw formally from an alliance or association

SECEDER *n* pl. **-S** one that secedes

SECERN *v* **-ED, -ING, -S** to discern as separate

SECLUDE *v* **-CLUDED, -CLUDING, -CLUDES** to remove or set apart from others

SECOND *v* **-ED, -ING, -S** to give support or encouragement to

SECONDE *n* pl. **-S** a position in fencing

SECONDER *n* pl. **-S** one that seconds

SECONDLY *adv* in the next place after the first

SECONDO *n* pl. **-DI** the lower part in a piano duet

SECPAR *n* pl. **-S** a parsec

SECRECY *n* pl. **-CIES** the condition of being secret

SECRET *adj* **-CRETER, -CRETEST** kept from knowledge or view

SECRET *n* pl. **-S** something kept from the knowledge of others

SECRETE *v* **-CRETED, -CRETING, -CRETES** to generate and separate out from cells or bodily fluids

SECRETIN *n* pl. **-S** a hormone

SECRETLY *adv* in a secret manner

SECRETOR *n* pl. **-S** one that secretes

SECT *n* pl. **-S** a group of people united by common beliefs or interests

SECTARY *n* pl. **-RIES** a member of a sect

SECTILE *adj* capable of being cut smoothly

SECTION *v* **-ED, -ING, -S** to divide into sections (distinct parts)

SECTOR *v* **-ED, -ING, -S** to divide into sectors (sections)

SECTORAL *adj* of or pertaining to a sector

SECULAR *n* pl. **-S** a layman

SECUND *adj* having the parts or organs arranged on one side only **SECUNDLY** *adv*

SECUNDUM *adv* according to

SECURE *adj* **-CURER, -CUREST** free from danger **SECURELY** *adv*

SECURE   *v* **-CURED, -CURING, -CURES** to make firm or tight

SECURING   present participle of secure

SECURITY   *n* pl. **-TIES** the state of being secure

SEDAN   *n* pl. **-S** a type of automobile

SEDARIM   a pl. of seder

SEDATE   *adj* **-DATER, -DATEST** calm **SEDATELY** *adv*

SEDATE   *v* **-DATED, -DATING, -DATES** to administer a sedative to

SEDATION   *n* pl. **-S** the reduction of stress or excitement by the use of sedatives

SEDATIVE   *n* pl. **-S** a drug that induces a calm state

SEDER   *n* pl. **-DERS** or **-DARIM** a Jewish ceremonial dinner

SEDERUNT   *n* pl. **-S** a prolonged sitting

SEDGE   *n* pl. **-S** a marsh plant

SEDGY   *adj* **SEDGIER, SEDGIEST** abounding in sedge

SEDILE   *n* pl. **-LIA** one of the seats in a church for the use of the officiating clergy

SEDILIUM   *n* pl. **-LIA** sedile

SEDIMENT   *v* **-ED, -ING, -S** to settle to the bottom of a liquid

SEDITION   *n* pl. **-S** incitement of rebellion against a government

SEDUCE   *v* **-DUCED, -DUCING, -DUCES** to lead astray **SEDUCIVE** *adj*

SEDUCER   *n* pl. **-S** one that seduces

SEDULITY   *n* pl. **-TIES** the state of being sedulous

SEDULOUS   *adj* diligent

SEDUM   *n* pl. **-S** a flowering plant

SEE   *v* **SAW, SEEN, SEEING, SEES** to perceive with the eyes **SEEABLE** *adj*

SEECATCH   *n* pl. **-CATCHIE** an adult male fur seal

SEED   *v* **-ED, -ING, -S** to plant seeds (propagative plant structures) in

SEEDBED   *n* pl. **-S** land prepared for seeding

SEEDCAKE   *n* pl. **-S** a sweet cake containing aromatic seeds

SEEDCASE   *n* pl. **-S** a pericarp

SEEDER   *n* pl. **-S** one that seeds

SEEDIER   comparative of seedy

SEEDIEST   superlative of seedy

SEEDILY   *adv* in a seedy manner

SEEDLESS   *adj* having no seeds

SEEDLIKE   *adj* resembling a seed

SEEDLING   *n* pl. **-S** a young plant

SEEDMAN   *n* pl. **-MEN** seedsman

SEEDPOD   *n* pl. **-S** a type of seed vessel

SEEDSMAN   *n* pl. **-MEN** a dealer in seeds

SEEDTIME   *n* pl. **-S** the season for sowing seeds

SEEDY   *adj* **SEEDIER, SEEDIEST** containing seeds; inferior in condition or quality

SEEING   *n* pl. **-S** the act of one that sees

SEEK   *v* **SOUGHT, SEEKING, SEEKS** to go in search of

SEEKER   *n* pl. **-S** one that seeks

SEEL   *v* **-ED, -ING, -S** to stitch closed the eyes of, as a falcon during training

SEELY   *adj* frail

SEEM   *v* **-ED, -ING, -S** to give the impression of being

SEEMER   *n* pl. **-S** one that seems

SEEMING   *n* pl. **-S** outward appearance

SEEMLY   *adj* **-LIER, -LIEST** of pleasing appearance

SEEN   past participle of see

SEEP   *v* **-ED, -ING, -S** to pass slowly through small openings

SEEPAGE   *n* pl. **-S** the quantity of fluid that has seeped

SEEPY   *adj* **SEEPIER, SEEPIEST** soaked or oozing with water

SEER   *n* pl. **-S** a prophet

SEERESS   *n* pl. **-ES** a female seer

SEESAW   *v* **-ED, -ING, -S** to move up and down or back and forth

SEETHE   *v* **SEETHED, SEETHING, SEETHES** to surge or foam as if boiling

SEG   *n* pl. **-S** one who advocates racial segregation

SEGETAL   *adj* growing in fields of grain

SEGGAR   *n* pl. **-S** a saggar

SEGMENT   *v* **-ED, -ING, -S** to divide into sections

SEGNO   *n* pl. **-GNOS** or **-GNI** a musical sign

SEGO   *n* pl. **-GOS** a perennial herb

SEGUE *v* **-GUED, -GUEING, -GUES** to proceed without pause from one musical theme to another

SEI *n* pl. **-S** a rorqual

SEICENTO *n* pl. **-TOS** the seventeenth century

SEICHE *n* pl. **-S** an oscillation of the surface of a lake or landlocked sea

SEIDEL *n* pl. **-S** a large beer glass

SEIF *n* pl. **-S** a long, narrow sand dune

SEIGNEUR *n* pl. **-S** seignior

SEIGNIOR *n* pl. **-S** a feudal lord

SEIGNORY *n* pl. **-GNORIES** the power of a seignior

SEINE *v* **SEINED, SEINING, SEINES** to catch fish with a large, vertically hanging net

SEINER *n* pl. **-S** one that seines

SEISE *v* **SEISED, SEISING, SEISES** to seize **SEISABLE** *adj*

SEISER *n* pl. **-S** seizer

SEISIN *n* pl. **-S** seizin

SEISING *n* pl. **-S** seizing

SEISM *n* pl. **-S** an earthquake **SEISMAL, SEISMIC** *adj*

SEISMISM *n* pl. **-S** the natural activity involved in earthquakes

SEISOR *n* pl. **-S** seizor

SEISURE *n* pl. **-S** seizure

SEITAN *n* pl. **-S** a food made from wheat gluten

SEIZE *v* **SEIZED, SEIZING, SEIZES** to take hold of suddenly and forcibly **SEIZABLE** *adj*

SEIZER *n* pl. **-S** one that seizes

SEIZIN *n* pl. **-S** legal possession of land

SEIZING *n* pl. **-S** the act of one that seizes

SEIZOR *n* pl. **-S** one that takes seizin

SEIZURE *n* pl. **-S** the act of seizing

SEJANT *adj* represented in a sitting position — used of a heraldic animal

SEJEANT *adj* sejant

SEL *n* pl. **-S** self

SELADANG *n* pl. **-S** saladang

SELAH *n* pl. **-S** a word of unknown meaning often marking the end of a verse in the Psalms

SELAMLIK *n* pl. **-S** the portion of a Turkish house reserved for men

SELCOUTH *adj* unusual

SELDOM *adj* infrequent **SELDOMLY** *adv*

SELECT *v* **-ED, -ING, -S** to choose

SELECTEE *n* pl. **-S** one that is selected

SELECTLY *adv* by selection

SELECTOR *n* pl. **-S** one that selects

SELENATE *n* pl. **-S** a chemical salt

SELENIC *adj* pertaining to selenium

SELENIDE *n* pl. **-S** a compound of selenium

SELENITE *n* pl. **-S** a variety of gypsum

SELENIUM *n* pl. **-S** a nonmetallic element **SELENOUS** *adj*

SELF *n* pl. **SELVES** the total, essential, or particular being of one person

SELF *v* **-ED, -ING, -S** to inbreed

SELFDOM *n* pl. **-S** selfhood

SELFHEAL *n* pl. **-S** a perennial herb

SELFHOOD *n* pl. **-S** the state of being an individual person

SELFISH *adj* concerned chiefly or only with oneself

SELFLESS *adj* unselfish

SELFNESS *n* pl. **-ES** selfhood

SELFSAME *adj* identical

SELFWARD *adv* toward oneself

SELKIE *n* pl. **-S** a creature in Scottish and Irish folklore

SELL *v* **SOLD, SELLING, SELLS** to give up to another for money or other valuable consideration **SELLABLE** *adj*

SELLE *n* pl. **-S** a saddle

SELLER *n* pl. **-S** one that sells

SELLOFF *n* pl. **-S** the sale of a large number of stocks, bonds, or commodities

SELLOUT *n* pl. **-S** a performance for which all seats have been sold

SELSYN *n* pl. **-S** a type of remote-control device

SELTZER *n* pl. **-S** carbonated mineral water

SELVA *n* pl. **-S** a tropical rain forest

SELVAGE *n* pl. **-S** the edge of a woven fabric finished to prevent raveling **SELVAGED** *adj*

SELVEDGE *n* pl. **-S** selvage

SELVES pl. of self

SEMANTIC *adj* pertaining to meaning

SEMATIC *adj* serving as a warning

SEME *n* pl. **-S** a type of ornamental pattern

SEMEME *n* pl. **-S** the meaning of a morpheme **SEMEMIC** *adj*

SEMEN *n* pl. **-MENS** or **-MINA** a fluid produced in the male reproductive organs

SEMESTER *n* pl. **-S** a period constituting half of an academic year

SEMI *n* pl. **-S** a freight trailer

SEMIARID *adj* characterized by light rainfall

SEMIBALD *adj* partly bald

SEMICOMA *n* pl. **-S** a coma from which a person can be aroused

SEMIDEAF *adj* partly deaf

SEMIDOME *n* pl. **-S** a half dome

SEMIDRY *adj* moderately dry

SEMIFIT *adj* conforming somewhat to the lines of the body

SEMIGALA *adj* somewhat gala

SEMIHARD *adj* moderately hard

SEMIHIGH *adj* moderately high

SEMIHOBO *n* pl. **-BOS** or **-BOES** a person having some of the characteristics of a hobo

SEMILLON *n* pl. **-S** a white grape grown in France

SEMILOG *adj* having one scale logarithmic and the other arithmetic

SEMIMAT *adj* having a slight luster

SEMIMATT *adj* semimat

SEMIMILD *adj* moderately mild

SEMIMUTE *adj* having partially lost the faculty of speech

SEMINA *a* pl. of semen

SEMINAL *adj* pertaining to semen

SEMINAR *n* pl. **-S** an advanced study group at a college or university

SEMINARY *n* pl. **-NARIES** a school for the training of priests, ministers, or rabbis

SEMINOMA *n* pl. **-MAS** or **-MATA** a malignant tumor of the testis

SEMINUDE *adj* partly nude

SEMIOPEN *adj* partly open

SEMIOSIS *n* pl. **-OSES** a process in which something functions as a sign to an organism

SEMIOTIC *n* pl. **-S** a general theory of signs and symbolism

SEMIOVAL *adj* somewhat oval

SEMIPRO *n* pl. **-PROS** one who is engaged in some field or sport for pay on a part-time basis

SEMIRAW *adj* somewhat raw

SEMIS *n* pl. **-MISES** a coin of ancient Rome

SEMISOFT *adj* moderately soft

SEMITIST *n* pl. **-S** one who favors Jewish interests

SEMITONE *n* pl. **-S** a type of musical tone

SEMIWILD *adj* somewhat wild

SEMOLINA *n* pl. **-S** a granular product of wheat used for pasta

SEMPLE *adj* of humble birth

SEMPLICE *adj* simple — used as a musical direction

SEMPRE *adv* in the same manner throughout — used as a musical direction

SEN *n* pl. **SEN** a monetary unit of Japan

SENARIUS *n* pl. **-NARII** a Greek or Latin verse consisting of six metrical feet

SENARY *adj* pertaining to the number six

SENATE *n* pl. **-S** an assembly having high deliberative and legislative functions

SENATOR *n* pl. **-S** a member of a senate

SEND *v* **-ED, -ING, -S** to scend

SEND *v* **SENT, SENDING, SENDS** to cause to go **SENDABLE** *adj*

SENDAL *n* pl. **-S** a silk fabric

SENDER *n* pl. **-S** one that sends

SENDOFF *n* pl. **-S** a farewell celebration

SENDUP *n* pl. **-S** a parody

SENE *n* pl. **SENE** a monetary unit of Samoa

SENECA *n* pl. **-S** senega

SENECIO *n* pl. **-CIOS** a flowering plant

SENEGA *n* pl. **-S** a medicinal plant root

SENGI *n* pl. **SENGI** a monetary unit of Zaire

SENHOR *n* pl. **-S** or **-ES** a Portuguese or Brazilian gentleman

SENHORA *n* pl. **-S** a married Portuguese or Brazilian woman

SENILE *n* pl. **-S** one who exhibits senility

SENILELY *adv* in a senile manner

SENILITY *n* pl. **-TIES** mental and physical infirmity due to old age

SENIOR   *n* pl. **-S** a person who is older than another

SENITI   *n* pl. **SENITI** a monetary unit of Tonga

SENNA   *n* pl. **-S** a medicinal plant

SENNET   *n* pl. **-S** a call sounded on a trumpet signaling the entrance or exit of actors

SENNIGHT   *n* pl. **-S** a week

SENNIT   *n* pl. **-S** braided straw used in making hats

SENOPIA   *n* pl. **-S** an improvement of near vision

SENOR   *n* pl. **-S** or **-ES** a Spanish gentleman

SENORA   *n* pl. **-S** a married Spanish woman

SENORITA   *n* pl. **-S** an unmarried Spanish girl or woman

SENRYU   *n* pl. **SENRYU** a Japanese poem

SENSA   pl. of sensum

SENSATE   *v* **-SATED, -SATING, -SATES** to sense

SENSE   *v* **SENSED, SENSING, SENSES** to perceive by the senses (any of certain agencies through which an individual receives impressions of the external world)

SENSEFUL   *adj* sensible

SENSEI   *n* pl. **-S** a teacher of Japanese martial arts

SENSIBLE   *adj* **-BLER, -BLEST** having or showing good judgment **SENSIBLY** *adv*

SENSIBLE   *n* pl. **-S** something that can be sensed

SENSILLA   *n* pl. **-LAE** a simple sense organ

SENSING   present participle of sense

SENSOR   *n* pl. **-S** a device that receives and responds to a stimulus

SENSORIA   *n/pl* the parts of the brain concerned with the reception and interpretation of sensory stimuli

SENSORY   *adj* pertaining to the senses or sensation

SENSUAL   *adj* pertaining to the physical senses

SENSUM   *n* pl. **-SA** an object of perception or sensation

SENSUOUS   *adj* pertaining to or derived from the senses

SENT   past tense of send (to cause to go)

SENTE   *n* pl. **LICENTE** or **LISENTE** a monetary unit of Lesotho

SENTENCE   *v* **-TENCED, -TENCING, -TENCES** to declare judicially the extent of punishment to be imposed

SENTI   *n* pl. **SENTI** a former monetary unit of Tanzania

SENTIENT   *n* pl. **-S** a person or thing capable of sensation

SENTIMO   *n* pl. **-MOS** a monetary unit of the Philippines

SENTINEL   *v* **-NELED, -NELING, -NELS** or **-NELLED, -NELLING, -NELS** to stand guard

SENTRY   *n* pl. **-TRIES** one who stands guard

SEPAL   *n* pl. **-S** one of the individual leaves of a calyx **SEPALED, SEPALINE, SEPALLED, SEPALOID, SEPALOUS** *adj*

SEPARATE   *v* **-RATED, -RATING, -RATES** to set or keep apart

SEPIA   *n* pl. **-S** a brown pigment **SEPIC** *adj*

SEPOY   *n* pl. **-POYS** a native of India serving in the British army

SEPPUKU   *n* pl. **-S** a Japanese form of suicide

SEPSIS   *n* pl. **SEPSES** bacterial invasion of the body

SEPT   *n* pl. **-S** a clan

SEPTA   pl. of septum

SEPTAGE   *n* pl. **-S** the waste in a septic tank

SEPTAL   *adj* pertaining to a septum

SEPTARIA   *n/pl* limestone nodules

SEPTATE   *adj* having a septum

SEPTET   *n* pl. **-S** a group of seven

SEPTETTE   *n* pl. **-S** septet

SEPTIC   *n* pl. **-S** an agent producing sepsis **SEPTICAL** *adj*

SEPTIME   *n* pl. **-S** a position in fencing

SEPTUM   *n* pl. **-TUMS** or **-TA** a dividing membrane or partition

SEPTUPLE   *v* **-PLED, -PLING, -PLES** to make seven times as great

SEQUEL   *n* pl. **-S** something that follows and serves as a continuation

SEQUELA   *n* pl. **-QUELAE** an abnormal condition resulting from a preceding disease

SEQUENCE   *v* **-QUENCED, -QUENCING, -QUENCES** to arrange in consecutive order

SEQUENCY	*n* pl. **-CIES** the following of one thing after another
SEQUENT	*n* pl. **-S** something that follows
SEQUIN	*v* **-ED, -ING, -S** to affix sequins (shiny ornamental discs) to
SEQUITUR	*n* pl. **-S** the conclusion of an inference
SEQUOIA	*n* pl. **-S** a large evergreen tree
SER	*n* pl. **-S** a unit of weight of India
SERA	a pl. of serum
SERAC	*n* pl. **-S** a large mass of ice broken off of a glacier
SERAGLIO	*n* pl. **-GLIOS** a harem
SERAI	*n* pl. **-S** a Turkish palace
SERAIL	*n* pl. **-S** a seraglio
SERAL	*adj* pertaining to a series of ecological changes
SERAPE	*n* pl. **-S** a colorful woolen shawl
SERAPH	*n* pl. **-APHS** or **-APHIM** or **-APHIN** a winged celestial being **SERAPHIC** *adj*
SERAPHIM	*n* pl. **-S** seraph
SERDAB	*n* pl. **-S** a chamber within an ancient Egyptian tomb
SERE	*adj* **SERER, SEREST** withered; dry
SERE	*v* **SERED, SERING, SERES** to sear
SEREIN	*n* pl. **-S** a fine rain falling from an apparently clear sky
SERENADE	*v* **-NADED, -NADING, -NADES** to perform an honorific evening song for
SERENATA	*n* pl. **-TAS** or **-TE** a dramatic cantata
SERENE	*adj* **SERENER, SERENEST** calm; tranquil **SERENELY** *adv*
SERENE	*n* pl. **-S** a serene condition or expanse
SERENITY	*n* pl. **-TIES** the state of being serene
SERER	comparative of sere
SEREST	superlative of sere
SERF	*n* pl. **-S** a feudal slave
SERFAGE	*n* pl. **-S** serfdom
SERFDOM	*n* pl. **-S** the state of being a serf
SERFHOOD	*n* pl. **-S** serfdom
SERFISH	*adj* characteristic of a serf
SERFLIKE	*adj* serfish
SERGE	*v* **SERGED, SERGING, SERGES** to finish (a cut edge of a seam) with overcast stitches
SERGEANT	*n* pl. **-S** a noncommissioned military officer
SERGER	*n* pl. **-S** a machine for serging
SERGING	*n* pl. **-S** a process of finishing the raw edges of a fabric
SERIAL	*n* pl. **-S** a literary or dramatic work presented in successive installments
SERIALLY	*adv* in the manner or form of a serial
SERIATE	*v* **-ATED, -ATING, -ATES** to put into a series
SERIATIM	*adv* serially
SERICIN	*n* pl. **-S** a kind of protein
SERIEMA	*n* pl. **-S** a Brazilian bird
SERIES	*n* pl. **SERIES** an arrangement of one after another
SERIF	*n* pl. **-S** a fine line used to finish off the main stroke of a letter **SERIFED, SERIFFED** *adj*
SERIN	*n* pl. **-S** a European finch
SERINE	*n* pl. **-S** an amino acid
SERING	present participle of sere
SERINGA	*n* pl. **-S** a Brazilian tree
SERIOUS	*adj* thoughtful or subdued in appearance or manner
SERJEANT	*n* pl. **-S** sergeant
SERMON	*n* pl. **-S** a religious discourse **SERMONIC** *adj*
SEROLOGY	*n* pl. **-GIES** the science of serums
SEROSA	*n* pl. **-SAS** or **-SAE** a thin membrane lining certain bodily cavities **SEROSAL** *adj*
SEROSITY	*n* pl. **-TIES** the quality or state of being serous
SEROTINE	*n* pl. **-S** a European bat
SEROTINY	*n* pl. **-NIES** the condition of having late or gradual seed dispersal
SEROTYPE	*v* **-TYPED, -TYPING, -TYPES** to classify (microorganisms) according to a characteristic set of antigens
SEROUS	*adj* of or resembling serum
SEROVAR	*n* pl. **-S** a group of microorganisms having a characteristic set of antigens
SEROW	*n* pl. **-S** an Asian antelope
SERPENT	*n* pl. **-S** a snake

SERPIGO *n* pl. **-GOS** or **-GOES** or **-GINES** a spreading skin eruption

SERRANID *n* pl. **-S** a marine fish

SERRANO *n* pl. **-NOS** a small hot pepper

SERRATE *v* **-RATED, -RATING, -RATES** to furnish with toothlike projections

SERRY *v* **-RIED, -RYING, -RIES** to crowd together

SERUM *n* pl. **-RUMS** or **-RA** the watery portion of whole blood **SERUMAL** *adj*

SERVABLE *adj* capable of serving or being served

SERVAL *n* pl. **-S** an African wildcat

SERVANT *n* pl. **-S** one that serves others

SERVE *v* **SERVED, SERVING, SERVES** to work for

SERVER *n* pl. **-S** one that serves another

SERVICE *v* **-VICED, -VICING, -VICES** to repair

SERVICER *n* pl. **-S** one that services

SERVILE *adj* slavishly submissive

SERVING *n* pl. **-S** a portion of food

SERVITOR *n* pl. **-S** a male servant

SERVO *n* pl. **-VOS** an automatic device used to control another mechanism

SESAME *n* pl. **-S** an East Indian plant

SESAMOID *n* pl. **-S** a nodular mass of bone or cartilage

SESSILE *adj* permanently attached

SESSION *n* pl. **-S** a meeting of a legislative or judicial body for the transaction of business

SESSPOOL *n* pl. **-S** cesspool

SESTERCE *n* pl. **-S** a coin of ancient Rome

SESTET *n* pl. **-S** a stanza of six lines

SESTINA *n* pl. **-S** a type of verse form

SESTINE *n* pl. **-S** sestina

SET *v* **SET, SETTING, SETS** to put in a particular position

SETA *n* pl. **-TAE** a coarse, stiff hair **SETAL** *adj*

SETBACK *n* pl. **-S** a defeat

SETENANT *n* pl. **-S** a postage stamp that differs in design from others in the same sheet

SETIFORM *adj* having the form of a seta

SETLINE *n* pl. **-S** a strong fishing line

SETOFF *n* pl. **-S** something that offsets something else

SETON *n* pl. **-S** a type of surgical thread

SETOSE *adj* covered with setae

SETOUS *adj* setose

SETOUT *n* pl. **-S** a display

SETSCREW *n* pl. **-S** a type of screw

SETT *n* pl. **-S** the burrow of a badger

SETTEE *n* pl. **-S** a long seat with a high back

SETTER *n* pl. **-S** one that sets

SETTING *n* pl. **-S** the scenery used in a dramatic production

SETTLE *v* **-TLED, -TLING, -TLES** to place in a desired state or order

SETTLER *n* pl. **-S** one that settles

SETTLING *n* pl. **-S** sediment

SETTLOR *n* pl. **-S** one that makes a legal settlement

SETULOSE *adj* covered with seta

SETULOUS *adj* setulose

SETUP *n* pl. **-S** the way something is arranged

SEVEN *n* pl. **-S** a number

SEVENTH *n* pl. **-S** one of seven equal parts

SEVENTY *n* pl. **-TIES** a number

SEVER *v* **-ED, -ING, -S** to divide or cut into parts

SEVERAL *n* pl. **-S** a few persons or things

SEVERE *adj* **-VERER, -VEREST** unsparing in the treatment of others **SEVERELY** *adv*

SEVERITY *n* pl. **-TIES** the quality or state of being severe

SEVICHE *n* pl. **-S** a dish of raw fish

SEVRUGA *n* pl. **-S** caviar from the Caspian Sea

SEW *v* **SEWED, SEWN, SEWING, SEWS** to mend or fasten with a needle and thread **SEWABLE** *adj*

SEWAGE *n* pl. **-S** the waste matter carried off by sewers

SEWAN *n* pl. **-S** seawan

SEWAR *n* pl. **-S** a medieval servant

SEWER *v* **-ED, -ING, -S** to clean or maintain sewers (underground conduits for waste)

SEWERAGE *n* pl. **-S** sewage

SEWING *n* pl. **-S** material that has been or is to be sewed

SEWN	a past participle of sew
SEX	v **-ED, -ING, -ES** to determine the sex (the property by which organisms are classified according to reproductive functions) of
SEXIER	comparative of sexy
SEXIEST	superlative of sexy
SEXILY	adv in a sexy manner
SEXINESS	n pl. **-ES** the quality or state of being sexy
SEXISM	n pl. **-S** prejudice or discrimination against women
SEXIST	n pl. **-S** one that practices sexism
SEXLESS	adj lacking sexual characteristics
SEXOLOGY	n pl. **-GIES** the study of human sexual behavior
SEXPOT	n pl. **-S** a sexually attractive woman
SEXT	n pl. **-S** one of seven canonical daily periods for prayer and devotion
SEXTAIN	n pl. **-S** a stanza of six lines
SEXTAN	n pl. **-S** a recurrent malarial fever
SEXTANT	n pl. **-S** an instrument for measuring angular distances
SEXTARII	n/pl ancient Roman units of liquid measure
SEXTET	n pl. **-S** a group of six
SEXTETTE	n pl. **-S** sextet
SEXTILE	n pl. **-S** the position of two celestial bodies when they are sixty degrees apart
SEXTO	n pl. **-TOS** sixmo
SEXTON	n pl. **-S** a maintenance worker of a church
SEXTUPLE	v **-PLED, -PLING, -PLES** to make six times as great
SEXTUPLY	adv to six times as much or as many
SEXUAL	adj pertaining to sex **SEXUALLY** adv
SEXY	adj **SEXIER, SEXIEST** arousing sexual desire
SFERICS	n/pl an electronic detector of storms
SFORZATO	n pl. **-TOS** the playing of a tone or chord with sudden force
SFUMATO	n pl. **-TOS** a technique used in painting
SH	interj — used to urge silence
SHA	interj — used to urge silence
SHABBY	adj **-BIER, -BIEST** ragged **SHABBILY** adv
SHACK	v **-ED, -ING, -S** to live or dwell
SHACKLE	v **-LED, -LING, -LES** to confine with metal fastenings placed around the wrists or ankles
SHACKLER	n pl. **-S** one that shackles
SHACKO	n pl. **-KOS** or **-KOES** shako
SHAD	n pl. **-S** a food fish
SHADBLOW	n pl. **-S** a shadbush
SHADBUSH	n pl. **-ES** a flowering tree or shrub
SHADCHAN	n pl. **-CHANS** or **-CHANIM** a Jewish marriage broker
SHADDOCK	n pl. **-S** a citrus fruit
SHADE	v **SHADED, SHADING, SHADES** to screen from light or heat
SHADER	n pl. **-S** one that shades
SHADFLY	n pl. **-FLIES** a winged insect
SHADIER	comparative of shady
SHADIEST	superlative of shady
SHADILY	adv in a shady manner
SHADING	n pl. **-S** protection against light or heat
SHADKHAN	n pl. **-KHANS** or **-KHANIM** shadchan
SHADOOF	n pl. **-S** a device used in Egypt for raising water for irrigation
SHADOW	v **-ED, -ING, -S** to make dark or gloomy
SHADOWER	n pl. **-S** one that shadows
SHADOWY	adj **-OWIER, -OWIEST** dark
SHADRACH	n pl. **-S** a mass of unfused material in the hearth of a blast furnace
SHADUF	n pl. **-S** shadoof
SHADY	adj **SHADIER, SHADIEST** shaded
SHAFT	v **-ED, -ING, -S** to push or propel with a pole
SHAFTING	n pl. **-S** a system of rods for transmitting motion or power
SHAG	v **SHAGGED, SHAGGING, SHAGS** to make shaggy
SHAGBARK	n pl. **-S** a hardwood tree
SHAGGY	adj **-GIER, -GIEST** covered with long, coarse hair **SHAGGILY** adv
SHAGREEN	n pl. **-S** the rough skin of certain sharks
SHAH	n pl. **-S** an Iranian ruler
SHAHDOM	n pl. **-S** the territory ruled by a shah

SHAIRD	*n* pl. **-S** shard
SHAIRN	*n* pl. **-S** sharn
SHAITAN	*n* pl. **-S** an evil spirit
SHAKE	*v* **SHOOK, SHAKEN, SHAKING, SHAKES** to move to and fro with short, rapid movements **SHAKABLE** *adj*
SHAKEOUT	*n* pl. **-S** a minor economic recession
SHAKER	*n* pl. **-S** one that shakes
SHAKEUP	*n* pl. **-S** a total reorganization
SHAKIER	comparative of shaky
SHAKIEST	superlative of shaky
SHAKILY	*adv* in a shaky manner
SHAKING	present participle of shake
SHAKO	*n* pl. **-KOS** or **-KOES** a type of military hat
SHAKY	*adj* **SHAKIER, SHAKIEST** shaking
SHALE	*n* pl. **-S** a fissile rock
SHALED	*adj* having a shell or husk
SHALEY	*adj* **SHALIER, SHALIEST** shaly
SHALIER	comparative of shaly
SHALIEST	superlative of shaly
SHALL	*v* present sing. 2d person **SHALL** or **SHALT,** past sing. 2d person **SHOULD** or **SHOULDST** or **SHOULDEST** — used as an auxiliary to express futurity, inevitability, or command
SHALLOON	*n* pl. **-S** a woolen fabric
SHALLOP	*n* pl. **-S** a small, open boat
SHALLOT	*n* pl. **-S** a plant resembling an onion
SHALLOW	*adj* **-LOWER, -LOWEST** having little depth
SHALLOW	*v* **-ED, -ING, -S** to make shallow
SHALOM	*n* pl. **-S** a word used as a Jewish greeting or farewell
SHALT	a present 2d person sing. of shall
SHALY	*adj* **SHALIER, SHALIEST** resembling shale
SHAM	*v* **SHAMMED, SHAMMING, SHAMS** to feign
SHAMABLE	*adj* capable of being shamed **SHAMABLY** *adv*
SHAMAN	*n* pl. **-S** a medicine man among certain North American Indians **SHAMANIC** *adj*
SHAMAS	*n* pl. **-MOSIM** shammes

SHAMBLE	*v* **-BLED, -BLING, -BLES** to walk awkwardly
SHAME	*v* **SHAMED, SHAMING, SHAMES** to cause to feel a painful sense of guilt or degradation
SHAMEFUL	*adj* disgraceful
SHAMES	*n* pl. **-MOSIM** shammes
SHAMISEN	*n* pl. **-S** samisen
SHAMMAS	*n* pl. **-MASIM** shammes
SHAMMASH	*n* pl. **-MASHIM** shammes
SHAMMED	past tense of sham
SHAMMER	*n* pl. **-S** one that shams
SHAMMES	*n* pl. **-MOSIM** a minor official of a synagogue
SHAMMIED	past tense of shammy
SHAMMIES	present 3d person sing. of shammy
SHAMMING	present participle of sham
SHAMMOS	*n* pl. **-MOSIM** shammes
SHAMMOSIM	pl. of shammes
SHAMMY	*v* **-MIED, -MYING, -MIES** to chamois
SHAMOIS	*n* pl. **SHAMOIS** chamois
SHAMOS	*n* pl. **-MOSIM** shammes
SHAMOSIM	pl. of shamos
SHAMOY	*v* **-ED, -ING, -S** to chamois
SHAMPOO	*v* **-ED, -ING, -S** to cleanse with a special preparation
SHAMROCK	*n* pl. **-S** a three-leaved plant
SHAMUS	*n* pl. **-ES** a private detective
SHANDY	*n* pl. **-DIES** an alcoholic drink
SHANGHAI	*v* **-ED, -ING, -S** to kidnap for service aboard a ship
SHANK	*v* **-ED, -ING, -S** to hit sharply to the right, as a golf ball
SHANNY	*n* pl. **-NIES** a marine fish
SHANTEY	*n* pl. **-TEYS** chantey
SHANTI	*n* pl. **-S** peace
SHANTIES	pl. of shanty
SHANTIH	*n* pl. **-S** shanti
SHANTUNG	*n* pl. **-S** a silk fabric
SHANTY	*n* pl. **-TIES** a small, crudely built dwelling
SHAPE	*v* **SHAPED, SHAPEN, SHAPING, SHAPES** to give shape (outward form) to **SHAPABLE** *adj*
SHAPELY	*adj* **-LIER, -LIEST** having a pleasing shape

SHAPER *n* pl. **-S** one that shapes

SHAPEUP *n* pl. **-S** a system of hiring a work crew

SHAPING present participle of shape

SHARD *n* pl. **-S** a fragment of broken pottery

SHARE *v* **SHARED, SHARING, SHARES** to have, get, or use in common with another or others **SHARABLE** *adj*

SHARER *n* pl. **-S** one that shares

SHARIA *n* pl. **-S** Islamic law based on the Koran

SHARIAH *n* pl. **-S** sharia

SHARIF *n* pl. **-S** sherif

SHARING present participle of share

SHARK *v* **-ED, -ING, -S** to live by trickery

SHARKER *n* pl. **-S** one that sharks

SHARN *n* pl. **-S** cow dung **SHARNY** *adj*

SHARP *adj* **SHARPER, SHARPEST** suitable for or capable of cutting or piercing

SHARP *v* **-ED, -ING, -S** to raise in pitch, as a musical tone

SHARPEN *v* **-ED, -ING, -S** to make sharp

SHARPER *n* pl. **-S** a swindler

SHARPIE *n* pl. **-S** a very alert person

SHARPLY *adv* in a sharp manner

SHARPY *n* pl. **SHARPIES** sharpie

SHASHLIK *n* pl. **-S** kabob

SHASLIK *n* pl. **-S** shashlik

SHATTER *v* **-ED, -ING, -S** to break into pieces

SHAUGH *n* pl. **-S** a thicket

SHAUL *v* **-ED, -ING, -S** to shoal

SHAVE *v* **SHAVED, SHAVEN, SHAVING, SHAVES** to sever the hair close to the roots **SHAVABLE** *adj*

SHAVER *n* pl. **-S** one that shaves

SHAVIE *n* pl. **-S** a trick or prank

SHAVING *n* pl. **-S** something shaved off

SHAW *v* **SHAWED, SHAWN, SHAWING, SHAWS** to show

SHAWL *v* **-ED, -ING, -S** to wrap in a shawl (a piece of cloth worn as a covering)

SHAWM *n* pl. **-S** an early woodwind instrument

SHAY *n* pl. **SHAYS** a chaise

SHAZAM *interj* — used to signify a magical occurrence

SHE *n* pl. **-S** a female person

SHEA *n* pl. **-S** an African tree

SHEAF *v* **-ED, -ING, -S** to sheave

SHEAL *n* pl. **-S** shealing

SHEALING *n* pl. **-S** a shepherd's hut

SHEAR *v* **SHEARED** or **SHORE, SHORN, SHEARING, SHEARS** to cut the hair or wool from

SHEARER *n* pl. **-S** one that shears

SHEARING *n* pl. **-S** an instance of cutting hair or wool

SHEATH *v* **-ED, -ING, -S** to sheathe

SHEATHE *v* **SHEATHED, SHEATHING, SHEATHES** to put into a protective case

SHEATHER *n* pl. **-S** one that sheathes

SHEAVE *v* **SHEAVED, SHEAVING, SHEAVES** to gather into a bundle

SHEBANG *n* pl. **-S** a situation, organization, or matter

SHEBEAN *n* pl. **-S** shebeen

SHEBEEN *n* pl. **-S** a place where liquor is sold illegally

SHED *v* **SHEDDED, SHEDDING, SHEDS** to house in a shed (a small, low structure)

SHEDABLE *adj* capable of being cast off

SHEDDER *n* pl. **-S** one that casts off something

SHEDLIKE *adj* resembling a shed

SHEEN *v* **-ED, -ING, -S** to shine

SHEENFUL *adj* shining

SHEENY *adj* **SHEENIER, SHEENIEST** shining

SHEEP *n* pl. **SHEEP** a ruminant mammal

SHEEPCOT *n* pl. **-S** an enclosure for sheep

SHEEPDOG *n* pl. **-S** a dog trained to guard and herd sheep

SHEEPISH *adj* embarrassed

SHEEPMAN *n* pl. **-MEN** a person who raises sheep

SHEER *adj* **SHEERER, SHEEREST** of very thin texture **SHEERLY** *adv*

SHEER *v* **-ED, -ING, -S** to swerve

SHEESH *interj* — used to express mild annoyance

SHEET	*v* **-ED, -ING, -S** to cover with a sheet (a thin, rectangular piece of material)
SHEETER	*n* pl. **-S** one that sheets
SHEETFED	*adj* pertaining to a type of printing press
SHEETING	*n* pl. **-S** material in the form of sheets
SHEEVE	*n* pl. **-S** a grooved pulley wheel
SHEIK	*n* pl. **-S** an Arab chief
SHEIKDOM	*n* pl. **-S** the area ruled by a sheik
SHEIKH	*n* pl. **-S** sheik
SHEILA	*n* pl. **-S** a young woman
SHEITAN	*n* pl. **-S** shaitan
SHEKEL	*n* pl. **SHEKELS** or **SHEKELIM** or **SHEKALIM** an ancient unit of weight and money
SHELDUCK	*n* pl. **-S** a European duck
SHELF	*n* pl. **SHELVES** a flat rigid structure used to support articles
SHELFFUL	*n* pl. **-S** as much as a shelf can hold
SHELL	*v* **-ED, -ING, -S** to divest of a shell (a hard outer covering)
SHELLAC	*v* **-LACKED, -LACKING, -LACS** to cover with a thin varnish
SHELLACK	*v* **-ED, -ING, -S** to shellac
SHELLER	*n* pl. **-S** one that shells
SHELLY	*adj* **SHELLIER, SHELLIEST** abounding in seashells
SHELTA	*n* pl. **-S** an esoteric jargon of Gaelic
SHELTER	*v* **-ED, -ING, -S** to provide cover or protection for
SHELTIE	*n* pl. **-S** a small, shaggy pony
SHELTY	*n* pl. **-TIES** sheltie
SHELVE	*v* **SHELVED, SHELVING, SHELVES** to place on a shelf
SHELVER	*n* pl. **-S** one that shelves
SHELVES	pl. of shelf
SHELVING	*n* pl. **-S** material for shelves
SHELVY	*adj* **SHELVIER, SHELVIEST** inclining gradually
SHEND	*v* **SHENT, SHENDING, SHENDS** to disgrace
SHEOL	*n* pl. **-S** hell
SHEPHERD	*v* **-ED, -ING, -S** to watch over carefully
SHEQEL	*n* pl. **SHEQELS** or **SHEQALIM** shekel
SHERBERT	*n* pl. **-S** sherbet
SHERBET	*n* pl. **-S** a frozen fruit-flavored mixture
SHERD	*n* pl. **-S** shard
SHEREEF	*n* pl. **-S** sherif
SHERIF	*n* pl. **-S** an Arab ruler
SHERIFF	*n* pl. **-S** a law-enforcement officer of a county
SHERLOCK	*n* pl. **-S** a detective
SHEROOT	*n* pl. **-S** cheroot
SHERPA	*n* pl. **-S** a soft fabric for linings
SHERRIS	*n* pl. **-RISES** sherry
SHERRY	*n* pl. **-RIES** a type of wine
SHETLAND	*n* pl. **-S** a wool yarn
SHEUCH	*n* pl. **-S** sheugh
SHEUGH	*n* pl. **-S** a ditch
SHEW	*v* **SHEWED, SHEWN, SHEWING, SHEWS** to show
SHEWER	*n* pl. **-S** one that shews
SHH	*interj* sh
SHIATSU	*n* pl. **-S** a massage using finger pressure
SHIATZU	*n* pl. **-S** shiatsu
SHIBAH	*n* pl. **-S** shiva
SHICKER	*n* pl. **-S** a drunkard
SHIED	past tense of shy
SHIEL	*n* pl. **-S** shieling
SHIELD	*v* **-ED, -ING, -S** to provide with a protective cover or shelter
SHIELDER	*n* pl. **-S** one that shields
SHIELING	*n* pl. **-S** shealing
SHIER	*n* pl. **-S** a horse having a tendency to shy
SHIES	present 3d person sing. of shy
SHIEST	a superlative of shy
SHIFT	*v* **-ED, -ING, -S** to move from one position to another
SHIFTER	*n* pl. **-S** one that shifts
SHIFTY	*adj* **SHIFTIER, SHIFTIEST** tricky **SHIFTILY** *adv*
SHIGELLA	*n* pl. **-LAS** or **-LAE** any of a genus of aerobic bacteria
SHIITAKE	*n* pl. **-S** a dark Oriental mushroom
SHIKAR	*v* **-KARRED, -KARRING, -KARS** to hunt
SHIKAREE	*n* pl. **-S** a big game hunter
SHIKARI	*n* pl. **-S** shikaree

SHIKKER	*n* pl. **-S** shicker
SHILINGI	*n* pl. **SHILINGI** a monetary unit of Tanzania
SHILL	*v* **-ED, -ING, -S** to act as a decoy
SHILLALA	*n* pl. **-S** a short, thick club
SHILLING	*n* pl. **-S** a former monetary unit of Great Britain
SHILPIT	*adj* sickly
SHILY	*adv* in a shy manner
SHIM	*v* **SHIMMED, SHIMMING, SHIMS** to fill out or level by inserting a thin wedge
SHIMMER	*v* **-ED, -ING, -S** to glimmer
SHIMMERY	*adj* shimmering
SHIMMY	*v* **-MIED, -MYING, -MIES** to vibrate or wobble
SHIN	*v* **SHINNED, SHINNING, SHINS** to climb by gripping and pulling alternately with the hands and legs
SHINBONE	*n* pl. **-S** the tibia
SHINDIG	*n* pl. **-S** an elaborate dance or party
SHINDY	*n* pl. **-DYS** or **-DIES** a shindig
SHINE	*v* **SHONE** or **SHINED, SHINING, SHINES** to emit light
SHINER	*n* pl. **-S** one that shines
SHINGLE	*v* **-GLED, -GLING, -GLES** to cover with shingles (thin, oblong pieces of building material)
SHINGLER	*n* pl. **-S** one that shingles
SHINGLY	*adj* covered with small, loose stones
SHINIER	comparative of shiny
SHINIEST	superlative of shiny
SHINILY	*adv* in a shiny manner
SHINING	*adj* emitting or reflecting light
SHINLEAF	*n* pl. **-LEAFS** or **-LEAVES** a perennial herb
SHINNED	past of shin
SHINNERY	*n* pl. **-NERIES** a dense growth of small trees
SHINNEY	*v* **-ED, -ING, -S** to play a form of hockey
SHINNING	present participle of shin
SHINNY	*v* **-NIED, -NYING, -NIES** to shin
SHINY	*adj* **SHINIER, SHINIEST** filled with light
SHIP	*v* **SHIPPED, SHIPPING, SHIPS** to transport by ship (a vessel suitable for navigation in deep water)
SHIPLAP	*n* pl. **-S** an overlapping joint used in carpentry
SHIPLESS	*adj* lacking a ship
SHIPLOAD	*n* pl. **-S** as much as a ship can carry
SHIPMAN	*n* pl. **-MEN** a sailor
SHIPMATE	*n* pl. **-S** a fellow sailor
SHIPMENT	*n* pl. **-S** something that is shipped
SHIPPED	past tense of ship
SHIPPEN	*n* pl. **-S** a cowshed
SHIPPER	*n* pl. **-S** one that ships
SHIPPING	*n* pl. **-S** the business of one that ships
SHIPPON	*n* pl. **-S** shippen
SHIPSIDE	*n* pl. **-S** the area alongside a ship
SHIPWAY	*n* pl. **-WAYS** a canal deep enough to serve ships
SHIPWORM	*n* pl. **-S** a wormlike mollusk
SHIPYARD	*n* pl. **-S** a place where ships are built or repaired
SHIRE	*n* pl. **-S** a territorial division of Great Britain
SHIRK	*v* **-ED, -ING, -S** to avoid work or duty
SHIRKER	*n* pl. **-S** one that shirks
SHIRR	*v* **-ED, -ING, -S** to draw into three or more parallel rows, as cloth
SHIRRING	*n* pl. **-S** a shirred arrangement of cloth
SHIRT	*n* pl. **-S** a garment for the upper part of the body
SHIRTING	*n* pl. **-S** fabric used for making shirts
SHIRTY	*adj* **SHIRTIER, SHIRTIEST** angry
SHIST	*n* pl. **-S** schist
SHITAKE	*n* pl. **-S** shiitake
SHITTAH	*n* pl. **-S** a hardwood tree
SHITTIM	*n* pl. **-S** the wood of the shittah
SHIV	*n* pl. **-S** a knife
SHIVA	*n* pl. **-S** a period of mourning
SHIVAH	*n* pl. **-S** shiva
SHIVAREE	*v* **-REED, -REEING, -REES** to chivaree
SHIVE	*n* pl. **-S** a thin fragment
SHIVER	*v* **-ED, -ING, -S** to tremble with fear or cold
SHIVERER	*n* pl. **-S** one that shivers
SHIVERY	*adj* shivering

SHIVITI *n* pl. **-S** a plaque with a Hebrew verse

SHLEMIEL *n* pl. **-S** an unlucky bungler

SHLEP *v* **SHLEPPED, SHLEPPING, SHLEPS** to schlep

SHLEPP *v* **-ED, -ING, -S** to schlep

SHLOCK *n* pl. **-S** schlock

SHLOCKY *adj* **SHLOCKIER, SHLOCKIEST** schlocky

SHLUB *n* pl. **-S** schlub

SHLUMP *v* **-ED, -ING, -S** to schlump

SHLUMPY *adj* slovenly

SHMALTZ *n* pl. **-ES** schmaltz

SHMALTZY *adj* **SHMALTZIER, SHMALTZIEST** schmalzy

SHMEAR *n* pl. **-S** schmear

SHMO *n* pl. **SHMOES** schmo

SHMOOZE *v* **SHMOOZED, SHMOOZING, SHMOOZES** to schmooze

SHMUCK *n* pl. **-S** schmuck

SHNAPPS *n* pl. **SHNAPPS** schnapps

SHNAPS *n* pl. **SHNAPS** schnapps

SHNOOK *n* pl. **-S** schnook

SHNORRER *n* pl. **-S** one who takes advantage of the generosity of others

SHOAL *adj* **SHOALER, SHOALEST** shallow

SHOAL *v* **-ED, -ING, -S** to become shallow

SHOALY *adj* **SHOALIER, SHOALIEST** full of shallow areas

SHOAT *n* pl. **-S** a young hog

SHOCK *v* **-ED, -ING, -S** to strike with great surprise, horror, or disgust

SHOCKER *n* pl. **-S** one that shocks

SHOD a past tense of shoe

SHODDEN a past participle of shoe

SHODDY *adj* **-DIER, -DIEST** of inferior quality **SHODDILY** *adv*

SHODDY *n* pl. **-DIES** a low-quality wool

SHOE *n* pl. **SHOES** or **SHOON** a covering for the foot

SHOE *v* **SHOD** or **SHOED, SHODDEN, SHOEING, SHOES** to provide with shoes

SHOEBILL *n* pl. **-S** a wading bird

SHOEBOX *n* pl. **-ES** an oblong box for holding a pair of shoes

SHOEHORN *v* **-ED, -ING, -S** to force into a small space

SHOELACE *n* pl. **-S** a lace for fastening a shoe

SHOELESS *adj* having no shoe

SHOEPAC *n* pl. **-S** a waterproof boot

SHOEPACK *n* pl. **-S** shoepac

SHOER *n* pl. **-S** one that shoes horses

SHOETREE *n* pl. **-S** a device shaped like a foot that is inserted into a shoe to preserve its shape

SHOFAR *n* pl. **SHOFARS** or **SHOFROTH** a ram's-horn trumpet blown in certain Jewish rituals

SHOG *v* **SHOGGED, SHOGGING, SHOGS** to move along

SHOGI *n* pl. **-S** a Japanese game like chess

SHOGUN *n* pl. **-S** a former military leader of Japan **SHOGUNAL** *adj*

SHOJI *n* pl. **-S** a paper screen used as a partition or door in a Japanese house

SHOLOM *n* pl. **-S** shalom

SHONE a past tense of shine

SHOO *v* **-ED, -ING, -S** to drive away

SHOOFLY *n* pl. **-FLIES** a child's rocker

SHOOK *n* pl. **-S** a set of parts for assembling a barrel or packing

SHOOL *v* **-ED, -ING, -S** to shovel

SHOON a pl. of shoe

SHOOT *v* **SHOT, SHOOTING, SHOOTS** to hit, wound, or kill with a missile discharged from a weapon

SHOOTER *n* pl. **-S** one that shoots

SHOOTING *n* pl. **-S** the act of one that shoots

SHOOTOUT *n* pl. **-S** a battle fought with handguns or rifles

SHOP *v* **SHOPPED, SHOPPING, SHOPS** to examine goods with intent to buy

SHOPBOY *n* pl. **-BOYS** a salesclerk

SHOPGIRL *n* pl. **-S** a salesgirl

SHOPHAR *n* pl. **-PHARS** or **-PHROTH** shofar

SHOPLIFT *v* **-ED, -ING, -S** to steal goods from a store

SHOPMAN *n* pl. **-MEN** one who owns or operates a small store

SHOPPE *n* pl. **-S** a small store

SHOPPED past tense of shop

SHOPPER *n* pl. **-S** one that shops

SHOPPING *n* pl. **-S** the act of one that shops

SHOPTALK	*n* pl. **-S** conversation concerning one's business or occupation
SHOPWORN	*adj* worn out from being on display in a store
SHORAN	*n* pl. **-S** a type of navigational system
SHORE	*v* **SHORED, SHORING, SHORES** to prop with a supporting timber
SHORING	*n* pl. **-S** a system of supporting timbers
SHORL	*n* pl. **-S** schorl
SHORN	a past participle of shear
SHORT	*adj* **SHORTER, SHORTEST** having little length
SHORT	*v* **-ED, -ING, -S** to cause a type of electrical malfunction in
SHORTAGE	*n* pl. **-S** an insufficient supply or amount
SHORTCUT	*v* **-CUT, -CUTTING, -CUTS** to take a shorter or quicker way
SHORTEN	*v* **-ED, -ING, -S** to make or become shorter
SHORTIA	*n* pl. **-S** a perennial herb
SHORTIE	*n* pl. **-S** shorty
SHORTIES	pl. of shorty
SHORTISH	*adj* somewhat short
SHORTLY	*adv* in a short time
SHORTY	*n* pl. **SHORTIES** one that is short
SHOT	*v* **SHOTTED, SHOTTING, SHOTS** to load with shot (small lead or steel pellets)
SHOTE	*n* pl. **-S** shoat
SHOTGUN	*v* **-GUNNED, -GUNNING, -GUNS** to shoot with a type of gun
SHOTHOLE	*n* pl. **-S** a hole drilled in rock to hold explosives
SHOTT	*n* pl. **-S** chott
SHOTTED	past tense of shot
SHOTTEN	*adj* having spawned — used of a fish
SHOTTING	present participle of shot
SHOULD	past tense of shall
SHOULDER	*v* **-ED, -ING, -S** to assume the burden or responsibility of
SHOULDEST	a 2d person sing. past tense of shall
SHOULDST	a 2d person sing. past tense of shall
SHOUT	*v* **-ED, -ING, -S** to utter loudly
SHOUTER	*n* pl. **-S** one that shouts
SHOVE	*v* **SHOVED, SHOVING, SHOVES** to push roughly
SHOVEL	*v* **-ELED, -ELING, -ELS** or **-ELLED, -ELLING, -ELS** to take up with a shovel (a digging implement)
SHOVELER	*n* pl. **-S** one that shovels
SHOVER	*n* pl. **-S** one that shoves
SHOVING	present participle of shove
SHOW	*v* **SHOWED, SHOWN, SHOWING, SHOWS** to cause or permit to be seen **SHOWABLE** *adj*
SHOWBIZ	*n* pl. **-BIZZES** show business
SHOWBOAT	*v* **-ED, -ING, -S** to show off
SHOWCASE	*v* **-CASED, -CASING, -CASES** to exhibit
SHOWDOWN	*n* pl. **-S** an event that forces the conclusion of an issue
SHOWER	*v* **-ED, -ING, -S** to bathe in a spray of water
SHOWERER	*n* pl. **-S** one that showers
SHOWERY	*adj* abounding with brief periods of rain
SHOWGIRL	*n* pl. **-S** a chorus girl
SHOWIER	comparative of showy
SHOWIEST	superlative of showy
SHOWILY	*adv* in a showy manner
SHOWING	*n* pl. **-S** an exhibition or display
SHOWMAN	*n* pl. **-MEN** a theatrical producer
SHOWN	past participle of show
SHOWOFF	*n* pl. **-S** one given to pretentious display
SHOWRING	*n* pl. **-S** a ring where animals are displayed
SHOWROOM	*n* pl. **-S** a room used for the display of merchandise
SHOWTIME	*n* pl. **-S** the time at which an entertainment is to start
SHOWY	*adj* **SHOWIER, SHOWIEST** making a great or brilliant display
SHOYU	*n* pl. **-S** soy sauce
SHRANK	past tense of shrink
SHRAPNEL	*n* pl. **SHRAPNEL** fragments from an exploding bomb, mine, or shell
SHRED	*v* **SHREDDED, SHREDDING, SHREDS** to tear into small strips
SHREDDER	*n* pl. **-S** one that shreds
SHREW	*v* **-ED, -ING, -S** to curse
SHREWD	*adj* **SHREWDER, SHREWDEST** having keen insight **SHREWDLY** *adv*

SHREWDIE *n* pl. **-S** a shrewd person

SHREWISH *adj* ill-tempered

SHRI *n* pl. **-S** sri

SHRIEK *v* **-ED, -ING, -S** to utter a shrill cry

SHRIEKER *n* pl. **-S** one that shrieks

SHRIEKY *adj* **SHRIEKIER, SHRIEKIEST** shrill

SHRIEVAL *adj* pertaining to a sheriff

SHRIEVE *v* **SHRIEVED, SHRIEVING, SHRIEVES** to shrive

SHRIFT *n* pl. **-S** the act of shriving

SHRIKE *n* pl. **-S** a predatory bird

SHRILL *adj* **SHRILLER, SHRILLEST** having a high-pitched and piercing quality **SHRILLY** *adv*

SHRILL *v* **-ED, -ING, -S** to utter a shrill sound

SHRIMP *v* **-ED, -ING, -S** to catch shrimps (small marine decapods)

SHRIMPER *n* pl. **-S** a shrimp fisher

SHRIMPY *adj* **SHRIMPIER, SHRIMPIEST** abounding in shrimp

SHRINE *v* **SHRINED, SHRINING, SHRINES** to place in a shrine (a receptacle for sacred relics)

SHRINK *v* **SHRANK, SHRUNK** or **SHRUNKEN, SHRINKING, SHRINKS** to contract or draw back

SHRINKER *n* pl. **-S** one that shrinks

SHRIVE *v* **SHROVE** or **SHRIVED, SHRIVEN, SHRIVING, SHRIVES** to hear the confession of and grant absolution to

SHRIVEL *v* **-ELED, -ELING, -ELS** or **-ELLED, -ELLING, -ELS** to contract into wrinkles

SHRIVER *n* pl. **-S** one that shrives

SHROFF *v* **-ED, -ING, -S** to test the genuineness of, as a coin

SHROUD *v* **-ED, -ING, -S** to wrap in burial clothing

SHROVE a past tense of shrive

SHRUB *n* pl. **-S** a low, woody plant

SHRUBBY *adj* **-BIER, -BIEST** covered with shrubs

SHRUG *v* **SHRUGGED, SHRUGGING, SHRUGS** to raise and contract the shoulders

SHRUNK a past tense of shrink

SHRUNKEN a past participle of shrink

SHTETEL *n* pl. **SHTETELS** or **SHTETLACH** a Jewish village

SHTETL *n* pl. **SHTETLS** or **SHTETLACH** shtetel

SHTICK *n* pl. **-S** an entertainment routine

SHTICKY *adj* **SHTICKIER, SHTICKIEST** resembling a shtick

SHTIK *n* pl. **-S** shtick

SHUCK *v* **-ED, -ING, -S** to remove the husk or shell from

SHUCKER *n* pl. **-S** one that shucks

SHUCKING *n* pl. **-S** the act of one that shucks

SHUDDER *v* **-ED, -ING, -S** to tremble

SHUDDERY *adj* shuddering

SHUFFLE *v* **-FLED, -FLING, -FLES** to walk without lifting the feet

SHUFFLER *n* pl. **-S** one that shuffles

SHUL *n* pl. **SHULS** or **SHULN** a synagogue

SHUN *v* **SHUNNED, SHUNNING, SHUNS** to avoid

SHUNNER *n* pl. **-S** one that shuns

SHUNPIKE *v* **-PIKED, -PIKING, -PIKES** to travel on side roads to avoid expressways

SHUNT *v* **-ED, -ING, -S** to turn aside

SHUNTER *n* pl. **-S** one that shunts

SHUSH *v* **-ED, -ING, -ES** to silence

SHUSHER *n* pl. **-S** one that shushes

SHUT *v* **SHUT, SHUTTING, SHUTS** to close

SHUTDOWN *n* pl. **-S** a temporary closing of an industrial plant

SHUTE *v* **SHUTED, SHUTING, SHUTES** to chute

SHUTEYE *n* pl. **-S** sleep

SHUTOFF *n* pl. **-S** a device that shuts something off

SHUTOUT *n* pl. **-S** a game in which one team fails to score

SHUTTER *v* **-ED, -ING, -S** to provide with shutters (hinged window covers)

SHUTTING present participle of shut

SHUTTLE *v* **-TLED, -TLING, -TLES** to move or travel back and forth

SHUTTLER *n* pl. **-S** one that shuttles

SHWA *n* pl. **-S** schwa

SHWANPAN *n* pl. **-S** swanpan

SHY *adj* **SHIER, SHIEST** or **SHYER, SHYEST** timid

SHY   v **SHIED, SHYING, SHIES** to move suddenly back or aside, as in fear

SHYER   n pl. **-S** shier

SHYLOCK   v **-ED, -ING, -S** to lend money at high interest rates

SHYLY   adv in a shy manner

SHYNESS   n pl. **-ES** the state of being shy

SHYSTER   n pl. **-S** an unscrupulous lawyer or politician

SI   n pl. **-S** ti

SIAL   n pl. **-S** a type of rock formation **SIALIC** adj

SIALID   n pl. **-S** an alderfly

SIALIDAN   n pl. **-S** sialid

SIALOID   adj resembling saliva

SIAMANG   n pl. **-S** a large, black gibbon

SIAMESE   n pl. **-S** a water pipe with a connection for two hoses

SIB   n pl. **-S** a sibling

SIBB   n pl. **-S** sib

SIBILANT   n pl. **-S** a speech sound produced by the fricative passage of breath through a narrow orifice

SIBILATE   v **-LATED, -LATING, -LATES** to hiss

SIBLING   n pl. **-S** one having the same parents as another

SIBYL   n pl. **-S** a female prophet **SIBYLIC, SIBYLLIC** adj

SIC   v **SICCED, SICCING, SICS** to urge to attack

SICCAN   adj such

SICE   n pl. **-S** syce

SICK   adj **SICKER, SICKEST** affected with disease or ill health

SICK   v **-ED, -ING, -S** to sic

SICKBAY   n pl. **-BAYS** a ship's hospital

SICKBED   n pl. **-S** a sick person's bed

SICKEE   n pl. **-S** sickie

SICKEN   v **-ED, -ING, -S** to make sick

SICKENER   n pl. **-S** one that sickens

SICKERLY   adv securely

SICKIE   n pl. **-S** an emotionally sick person

SICKISH   adj somewhat sick

SICKLE   v **-LED, -LING, -LES** to cut with an agricultural implement having a single blade

SICKLY   adj **-LIER, -LIEST** appearing as if sick **SICKLILY** adv

SICKLY   v **-LIED, -LYING, -LIES** to make sickly

SICKNESS   n pl. **-ES** the state of being sick

SICKO   n pl. **SICKOS** sickie

SICKOUT   n pl. **-S** an organized absence of workers claiming to be sick

SICKROOM   n pl. **-S** a room occupied by a sick person

SIDDUR   n pl. **-DURS** or **-DURIM** a Jewish prayer book

SIDE   v **SIDED, SIDING, SIDES** to agree with or support

SIDEARM   n pl. **-S** a weapon worn at the side

SIDEBAND   n pl. **-S** a band of radio frequencies

SIDEBAR   n pl. **-S** a short news story accompanying a major story

SIDECAR   n pl. **-S** a passenger car attached to a motorcycle

SIDED   past tense of side

SIDEHILL   n pl. **-S** a hillside

SIDEKICK   n pl. **-S** a close friend

SIDELINE   v **-LINED, -LINING, -LINES** to put out of action

SIDELING   adj sloping

SIDELONG   adj directed to one side

SIDEMAN   n pl. **-MEN** a member of a jazz band

SIDEREAL   adj pertaining to the stars

SIDERITE   n pl. **-S** a mineral

SIDESHOW   n pl. **-S** a small show offered in addition to a main attraction

SIDESLIP   v **-SLIPPED, -SLIPPING, -SLIPS** to slip to one side

SIDESPIN   n pl. **-S** a type of spin imparted to a ball

SIDESTEP   v **-STEPPED, -STEPPING, -STEPS** to step to one side

SIDEWALK   n pl. **-S** a paved walk for pedestrians

SIDEWALL   n pl. **-S** a side surface of a tire

SIDEWARD   adv toward one side

SIDEWAY   adv sideways

SIDEWAYS   adv toward or from one side

SIDEWISE   adv sideways

SIDH   n pl. **SIDHE** a hill inhabited by supernatural beings in Irish folklore

SIDING   n pl. **-S** material used for surfacing a frame building

SIDLE *v* **-DLED, -DLING, -DLES** to move sideways

SIDLER *n* pl. **-S** one that sidles

SIEGE *v* **SIEGED, SIEGING, SIEGES** to attempt to capture or gain

SIEMENS *n* pl. **SIEMENS** a unit of electrical conductance

SIENITE *n* pl. **-S** syenite

SIENNA *n* pl. **-S** a brown pigment

SIEROZEM *n* pl. **-S** a type of soil

SIERRA *n* pl. **-S** a mountain range **SIERRAN** *adj*

SIESTA *n* pl. **-S** an afternoon nap or rest

SIEUR *n* pl. **-S** an old French title of respect for a man

SIEVE *v* **SIEVED, SIEVING, SIEVES** to pass through a sieve (a utensil for separating the coarse parts from the fine parts of loose matter)

SIEVERT *n* pl. **-S** a unit of ionizing radiation

SIFAKA *n* pl. **-S** a lemur of Madagascar

SIFFLEUR *n* pl. **-S** an animal that makes a whistling noise

SIFT *v* **-ED, -ING, -S** to sieve

SIFTER *n* pl. **-S** one that sifts

SIFTING *n* pl. **-S** the work of a sifter

SIGANID *n* pl. **-S** any of a family of fishes

SIGH *v* **-ED, -ING, -S** to let out a sigh (a deep, audible breath)

SIGHER *n* pl. **-S** one that sighs

SIGHLESS *adj* uttering no sigh

SIGHLIKE *adj* resembling a sigh

SIGHT *v* **-ED, -ING, -S** to observe or notice

SIGHTER *n* pl. **-S** one that sights

SIGHTING *n* pl. **-S** an observation

SIGHTLY *adj* **-LIER, -LIEST** pleasing to look at

SIGHTSEE *v* **-SAW, -SEEN, -SEEING, -SEES** to visit and view places of interest

SIGIL *n* pl. **-S** an official seal

SIGLOS *n* pl. **-LOI** an ancient Persian coin

SIGLUM *n* pl. **SIGLA** an abbreviation to indicate the source of an edited text

SIGMA *n* pl. **-S** a Greek letter **SIGMATE** *adj*

SIGMOID *n* pl. **-S** an S-shaped curve in a bodily part

SIGN *v* **-ED, -ING, -S** to write one's name on

SIGNA *v* write on the label — no other form of this imperative verb is used

SIGNAGE *n* pl. **-S** a system of signs in a community

SIGNAL *v* **-NALED, -NALING, -NALS** or **-NALLED, -NALLING, -NALS** to notify by a means of communication

SIGNALER *n* pl. **-S** one that signals

SIGNALLY *adv* notably

SIGNEE *n* pl. **-S** a signer of a document

SIGNER *n* pl. **-S** one that signs

SIGNET *v* **-ED, -ING, -S** to mark with an official seal

SIGNIFY *v* **-FIED, -FYING, -FIES** to make known

SIGNIOR *n* pl. **-GNIORS** or **-GNIORI** signor

SIGNIORY *n* pl. **-GNIORIES** signory

SIGNOR *n* pl. **-GNORS** or **-GNORI** an Italian title of courtesy for a man

SIGNORA *n* pl. **-GNORAS** or **-GNORE** an Italian title of courtesy for a married woman

SIGNORE *n* pl. **-GNORI** signor

SIGNORY *n* pl. **-GNORIES** seignory

SIGNPOST *v* **-ED, -ING, -S** to provide with signposts (posts bearing signs)

SIKA *n* pl. **-S** a small deer native to Asia

SIKE *n* pl. **-S** syke

SIKER *adj* secure

SILAGE *n* pl. **-S** fodder that has been preserved in a silo

SILANE *n* pl. **-S** a chemical compound

SILD *n* pl. **-S** a young herring

SILENCE *v* **-LENCED, -LENCING, -LENCES** to make silent

SILENCER *n* pl. **-S** one that silences

SILENI pl. of silenus

SILENT *adj* **-LENTER, -LENTEST** making no sound or noise **SILENTLY** *adv*

SILENTS *n/pl* silent movies

SILENUS *n* pl. **-NI** a woodland deity of Greek mythology

SILESIA *n* pl. **-S** a cotton fabric

SILEX *n* pl. **-ES** silica

SILICA *n* pl. **-S** a form of silicon

SILICATE *n* pl. **-S** a chemical salt

SILICIC *adj* pertaining to silicon

SILICIDE *n* pl. **-S** a silicon compound

SILICIFY *v* **-FIED, -FYING, -FIES** to convert into silica

SILICIUM *n* pl. **-S** silicon

SILICLE *n* pl. **-S** a short, flat silique

SILICON *n* pl. **-S** a nonmetallic element

SILICONE *n* pl. **-S** a silicon compound

SILICULA *n* pl. **-LAE** a silicle

SILIQUA *n* pl. **-QUAE** silique

SILIQUE *n* pl. **-LIQUES** a type of seed capsule

SILK *v* **-ED, -ING, -S** to cover with silk (a soft, lustrous fabric)

SILKEN *adj* made of silk

SILKIE *n* pl. **-S** selkie

SILKIER comparative of silky

SILKIES pl. of silky

SILKIEST superlative of silky

SILKILY *adv* in a silky manner

SILKLIKE *adj* resembling silk

SILKWEED *n* pl. **-S** milkweed

SILKWORM *n* pl. **-S** a caterpillar that spins a cocoon of silk fibers

SILKY *adj* **SILKIER, SILKIEST** resembling silk

SILKY *n* pl. **SILKIES** a glossy-coated terrier

SILL *n* pl. **-S** the horizontal piece at the base of a window

SILLABUB *n* pl. **-S** an alcoholic dessert

SILLER *n* pl. **-S** silver

SILLIBUB *n* pl. **-S** sillabub

SILLY *adj* **-LIER, -LIEST** showing a lack of good sense **SILLILY** *adv*

SILLY *n* pl. **-LIES** a silly person

SILO *v* **-ED, -ING, -S** to store in a silo (a tall, cylindrical structure)

SILOXANE *n* pl. **-S** a chemical compound

SILT *v* **-ED, -ING, -S** to fill with silt (a sedimentary material)

SILTY *adj* **SILTIER, SILTIEST** full of silt

SILURID *n* pl. **-S** any of a family of catfishes

SILUROID *n* pl. **-S** a silurid

SILVA *n* pl. **-VAS** or **-VAE** sylva

SILVAN *n* pl. **-S** sylvan

SILVER *v* **-ED, -ING, -S** to cover with silver (a metallic element)

SILVERER *n* pl. **-S** one that silvers

SILVERLY *adv* with a silvery appearance

SILVERN *adj* silvery

SILVERY *adj* resembling silver

SILVEX *n* pl. **-ES** an herbicide

SILVICAL *adj* pertaining to silvics

SILVICS *n/pl* the study of forest trees

SIM *n* pl. **-S** simulation

SIMA *n* pl. **-S** an igneous rock

SIMAR *n* pl. **-S** a woman's light jacket or robe

SIMARUBA *n* pl. **-S** a tropical tree

SIMAZINE *n* pl. **-S** an herbicide

SIMIAN *n* pl. **-S** an ape or monkey

SIMILAR *adj* being like but not completely identical to

SIMILE *n* pl. **-S** a figure of speech

SIMIOID *adj* simious

SIMIOUS *adj* pertaining to simians

SIMITAR *n* pl. **-S** scimitar

SIMLIN *n* pl. **-S** cymling

SIMMER *v* **-ED, -ING, -S** to cook below or just at the boiling point

SIMNEL *n* pl. **-S** a crisp bread

SIMOLEON *n* pl. **-S** a dollar

SIMONIAC *n* pl. **-S** one who practices simony

SIMONIES pl. of simony

SIMONIST *n* pl. **-S** a simoniac

SIMONIZE *v* **-NIZED, -NIZING, -NIZES** to polish with wax

SIMONY *n* pl. **-NIES** the buying or selling of a church office

SIMOOM *n* pl. **-S** a hot, dry desert wind

SIMOON *n* pl. **-S** simoom

SIMP *n* pl. **-S** a foolish person

SIMPER *v* **-ED, -ING, -S** to smile in a silly manner

SIMPERER *n* pl. **-S** one that simpers

SIMPLE *adj* **SIMPLER, SIMPLEST** not complex or complicated

SIMPLE *n* pl. **-S** something that is simple

SIMPLEX *n* pl. **-PLEXES** or **-PLICES** or **-PLICIA** a simple word

SIMPLIFY *v* **-FIED, -FYING, -FIES** to make simple

SIMPLISM *n* pl. **-S** the tendency to oversimplify an issue or problem

SIMPLIST	*n* pl. **-S** a person given to simplism
SIMPLY	*adv* in a simple manner
SIMULANT	*n* pl. **-S** one that simulates
SIMULAR	*n* pl. **-S** a simulant
SIMULATE	*v* **-LATED, -LATING, -LATES** to take on the appearance of
SIN	*v* **SINNED, SINNING, SINS** to commit a sin (an offense against religious or moral law)
SINAPISM	*n* pl. **-S** a pasty mixture applied to an irritated part of the body
SINCE	*adv* from then until now
SINCERE	*adj* **-CERER, -CEREST** free from hypocrisy or falseness
SINCIPUT	*n* pl. **-CIPUTS** or **-CIPITA** the forehead
SINE	*n* pl. **-S** a trigonometric function of an angle
SINECURE	*n* pl. **-S** an office or position requiring little or no work
SINEW	*v* **-ED, -ING, -S** to strengthen
SINEWY	*adj* lean and muscular
SINFONIA	*n* pl. **-NIAS** or **-NIE** a symphony
SINFUL	*adj* marked by sin **SINFULLY** *adv*
SING	*v* **SANG, SUNG, SINGING, SINGS** to utter with musical inflections of the voice **SINGABLE** *adj*
SINGE	*v* **SINGED, SINGEING, SINGES** to burn slightly
SINGER	*n* pl. **-S** one that sings
SINGLE	*v* **-GLED, -GLING, -GLES** to select from a group
SINGLET	*n* pl. **-S** a man's undershirt or jersey
SINGLY	*adv* without the company of others
SINGSONG	*n* pl. **-S** monotonous cadence in speaking or reading
SINGULAR	*n* pl. **-S** a word form that denotes one person or thing
SINH	*n* pl. **-S** a hyperbolic function of an angle
SINICIZE	*v* **-CIZED, -CIZING, -CIZES** to modify by Chinese influence
SINISTER	*adj* threatening or portending evil
SINK	*v* **SANK, SUNK** or **SUNKEN, SINKING, SINKS** to move to a lower level **SINKABLE** *adj*
SINKAGE	*n* pl. **-S** the act, process, or degree of sinking
SINKER	*n* pl. **-S** one that sinks
SINKHOLE	*n* pl. **-S** a natural depression in a land surface
SINLESS	*adj* free from sin
SINNED	past tense of sin
SINNER	*n* pl. **-S** one that sins
SINNING	present participle of sin
SINOLOGY	*n* pl. **-GIES** the study of the Chinese
SINOPIA	*n* pl. **-PIAS** or **-PIE** a red pigment
SINSYNE	*adv* since
SINTER	*v* **-ED, -ING, -S** to make cohesive by the combined action of heat and pressure
SINUATE	*v* **-ATED, -ATING, -ATES** to curve in and out
SINUOUS	*adj* characterized by curves, bends, or turns
SINUS	*n* pl. **-ES** a cranial cavity
SINUSOID	*n* pl. **-S** a mathematical curve
SIP	*v* **SIPPED, SIPPING, SIPS** to drink in small quantities
SIPE	*v* **SIPED, SIPING, SIPES** to seep
SIPHON	*v* **-ED, -ING, -S** to draw off through a siphon (a type of tube)
SIPHONAL	*adj* of or pertaining to a siphon
SIPHONIC	*adj* siphonal
SIPING	present participle of sipe
SIPPED	past tense of sip
SIPPER	*n* pl. **-S** one that sips
SIPPET	*n* pl. **-S** a small piece of bread soaked in gravy
SIPPING	present participle of sip
SIR	*n* pl. **-S** a respectful form of address used to a man
SIRDAR	*n* pl. **-S** a person of rank in India
SIRE	*v* **SIRED, SIRING, SIRES** to beget
SIREE	*n* pl. **-S** sirree
SIREN	*n* pl. **-S** a device that produces a penetrating warning sound
SIRENIAN	*n* pl. **-S** any of an order of aquatic mammals
SIRING	present participle of sire
SIRLOIN	*n* pl. **-S** a cut of beef
SIROCCO	*n* pl. **-COS** a hot, dry wind
SIRRA	*n* pl. **-S** sirrah
SIRRAH	*n* pl. **-S** a form of address used to inferiors
SIRREE	*n* pl. **-S** sir

SIRUP	*v* **-ED, -ING, -S** to syrup
SIRUPY	*adj* **-UPIER, -UPIEST** syrupy
SIRVENTE	*n* pl. **-S** a satirical medieval song or poem
SIS	*n* pl. **SISES** or **SISSES** sister
SISAL	*n* pl. **-S** a strong fiber used for rope
SISKIN	*n* pl. **-S** a Eurasian finch
SISSY	*adj* **SISSIER, SISSIEST** sissyish
SISSY	*n* pl. **-SIES** an effeminate man or boy
SISSYISH	*adj* resembling a sissy
SISTER	*v* **-ED, -ING, -S** to treat like a sister (a female sibling)
SISTERLY	*adj* of or resembling a sister
SISTROID	*adj* included between the convex sides of two intersecting curves
SISTRUM	*n* pl. **-TRUMS** or **-TRA** an ancient Egyptian percussion instrument
SIT	*v* **SAT, SAT** or **SITTEN, SITTING, SITS** to rest on the buttocks
SITAR	*n* pl. **-S** a lute of India
SITARIST	*n* pl. **-S** one who plays the sitar
SITCOM	*n* pl. **-S** a television comedy series with continuing characters
SITE	*v* **SITED, SITING, SITES** to place in position for operation
SITH	*adv* since
SITHENCE	*adv* since
SITHENS	*adv* since
SITING	present participle of site
SITOLOGY	*n* pl. **-GIES** the science of nutrition and diet
SITTEN	a past participle of sit
SITTER	*n* pl. **-S** one that sits
SITTING	*n* pl. **-S** a meeting or session
SITUATE	*v* **-ATED, -ATING, -ATES** to place in a certain position
SITUP	*n* pl. **-S** an exercise in which one moves from a lying to a sitting position
SITUS	*n* pl. **-TUSES** a position or location
SITZMARK	*n* pl. **-S** a mark left in the snow by a skier who has fallen backward
SIVER	*n* pl. **-S** a sewer
SIX	*n* pl. **-ES** a number
SIXFOLD	*adj* being six times as great as
SIXMO	*n* pl. **-MOS** a paper size
SIXPENCE	*n* pl. **-S** a formerly used British coin worth six pennies
SIXPENNY	*adj* worth sixpence
SIXTE	*n* pl. **-S** a fencing parry
SIXTEEN	*n* pl. **-S** a number
SIXTH	*n* pl. **-S** one of six equal parts
SIXTHLY	*adv* in the sixth place
SIXTIETH	*n* pl. **-S** one of sixty equal parts
SIXTY	*n* pl. **-TIES** a number
SIXTYISH	*adj* being about sixty years old
SIZABLE	*adj* of considerable size **SIZABLY** *adv*
SIZAR	*n* pl. **-S** a British student who receives financial assistance from his college
SIZE	*v* **SIZED, SIZING, SIZES** to arrange according to size (physical proportions)
SIZEABLE	*adj* sizable **SIZEABLY** *adv*
SIZER	*n* pl. **-S** sizar
SIZINESS	*n* pl. **-ES** the quality or state of being sizy
SIZING	*n* pl. **-S** a substance used as a glaze or filler for porous materials
SIZY	*adj* **SIZIER, SIZIEST** viscid
SIZZLE	*v* **-ZLED, -ZLING, -ZLES** to burn or fry with a hissing sound
SIZZLER	*n* pl. **-S** a very hot day
SJAMBOK	*v* **-ED, -ING, -S** to strike with a whip used in South Africa
SKA	*n* pl. **-S** a popular music of Jamaica
SKAG	*n* pl. **-S** heroin
SKALD	*n* pl. **-S** an ancient Scandinavian poet **SKALDIC** *adj*
SKANK	*v* **-ED, -ING, -S** to dance in a loose-limbed manner
SKANKER	*n* pl. **-S** one that skanks
SKANKY	*adj* **SKANKIER, SKANKIEST** filthy or sleazy
SKAT	*n* pl. **-S** a card game
SKATE	*v* **SKATED, SKATING, SKATES** to glide over ice or the ground on skates (shoes fitted with runners or wheels)
SKATER	*n* pl. **-S** one that skates
SKATING	*n* pl. **-S** the sport of gliding on skates
SKATOL	*n* pl. **-S** skatole
SKATOLE	*n* pl. **-S** a chemical compound
SKEAN	*n* pl. **-S** a type of dagger

SKEANE *n* pl. **-S** a length of yarn wound in a loose coil

SKEE *v* **SKEED, SKEEING, SKEES** to ski

SKEEN *n* pl. **-S** skean

SKEET *n* pl. **-S** the sport of shooting at clay pigeons hurled in the air by spring traps

SKEETER *n* pl. **-S** a skeet shooter

SKEG *n* pl. **-S** a timber that connects the keel and sternpost of a ship

SKEIGH *adj* proud

SKEIN *v* **-ED, -ING, -S** to wind into long, loose coils

SKELETON *n* pl. **-S** the supporting or protective framework of a human or animal body **SKELETAL** *adj*

SKELL *n* pl. **-S** a homeless person

SKELLUM *n* pl. **-S** a rascal

SKELM *n* pl. **-S** skellum

SKELP *v* **SKELPED** or **SKELPIT, SKELPING, SKELPS** to slap

SKELTER *v* **-ED, -ING, -S** to scurry

SKENE *n* pl. **-S** skean

SKEP *n* pl. **-S** a beehive

SKEPSIS *n* pl. **-SISES** the attitude or outlook of a skeptic

SKEPTIC *n* pl. **-S** a person who doubts generally accepted ideas

SKERRY *n* pl. **-RIES** a small, rocky island

SKETCH *v* **-ED, -ING, -ES** to make a rough, hasty drawing of

SKETCHER *n* pl. **-S** one that sketches

SKETCHY *adj* **SKETCHIER, SKETCHIEST** lacking in completeness or clearness

SKEW *v* **-ED, -ING, -S** to turn aside

SKEWBACK *n* pl. **-S** a sloping surface against which the end of an arch rests

SKEWBALD *n* pl. **-S** a horse having patches of brown and white

SKEWER *v* **-ED, -ING, -S** to pierce with a long pin, as meat

SKEWNESS *n* pl. **-ES** lack of symmetry

SKI *v* **-ED, -ING, -S** to travel on skis (long, narrow strips of wood or metal)

SKIABLE *adj* capable of being skied over

SKIAGRAM *n* pl. **-S** a picture made up of shadows or outlines

SKIBOB *n* pl. **-S** a vehicle used for traveling over snow

SKID *v* **SKIDDED, SKIDDING, SKIDS** to slide sideways as a result of a loss of traction

SKIDDER *n* pl. **-S** one that skids

SKIDDOO *v* **-ED, -ING, -S** to go away

SKIDDY *adj* **-DIER, -DIEST** likely to cause skidding

SKIDOO *v* **-ED, -ING, -S** to skiddoo

SKIDWAY *n* pl. **-WAYS** a platform on which logs are piled for loading or sawing

SKIED past tense of ski and sky

SKIER *n* pl. **-S** one that skis

SKIES present 3d person sing. of sky

SKIEY *adj* skyey

SKIFF *n* pl. **-S** a small, open boat

SKIFFLE *v* **-FLED, -FLING, -FLES** to play a particular style of music

SKIING *n* pl. **-S** the sport of traveling on skis

SKIJORER *n* pl. **-S** a skier who is drawn over snow by dogs, a horse, or vehicle

SKILFUL *adj* skillful

SKILL *n* pl. **-S** the ability to do something well **SKILLED** *adj*

SKILLESS *adj* having no skill

SKILLET *n* pl. **-S** a frying pan

SKILLFUL *adj* having skill

SKILLING *n* pl. **-S** a former coin of Scandinavian countries

SKIM *v* **SKIMMED, SKIMMING, SKIMS** to remove floating matter from the surface of

SKIMMER *n* pl. **-S** one that skims

SKIMMING *n* pl. **-S** something that is skimmed from a liquid

SKIMP *v* **-ED, -ING, -S** to scrimp

SKIMPY *adj* **SKIMPIER, SKIMPIEST** scanty **SKIMPILY** *adv*

SKIN *v* **SKINNED, SKINNING, SKINS** to strip or deprive of skin (the membranous tissue covering the body of an animal)

SKINFUL *n* pl. **-S** as much as a skin container can hold

SKINHEAD *n* pl. **-S** one whose hair is cut very short

SKINK *v* **-ED, -ING, -S** to pour out or serve, as liquor

SKINKER *n* pl. **-S** one that skinks

SKINLESS *adj* having no skin

SKINLIKE *adj* resembling skin

SKINNED past tense of skin

SKINNER *n* pl. **-S** one that skins

SKINNING present participle of skin

SKINNY *adj* **-NIER, -NIEST** very thin

SKINT *adj* having no money

SKIORING *n* pl. **-S** a form of skiing

SKIP *v* **SKIPPED, SKIPPING, SKIPS** to move with light springing steps

SKIPJACK *n* pl. **-S** a marine fish

SKIPLANE *n* pl. **-S** an airplane designed to take off from or land on snow

SKIPPED past tense of skip

SKIPPER *v* **-ED, -ING, -S** to act as master or captain of

SKIPPET *n* pl. **-S** a small box for protecting an official seal

SKIPPING present participle of skip

SKIRL *v* **-ED, -ING, -S** to produce a shrill sound

SKIRMISH *v* **-ED, -ING, -ES** to engage in a minor battle

SKIRR *v* **-ED, -ING, -S** to move rapidly

SKIRRET *n* pl. **-S** an Asian herb

SKIRT *v* **-ED, -ING, -S** to go or pass around

SKIRTER *n* pl. **-S** one that skirts

SKIRTING *n* pl. **-S** a board at the base of a wall

SKIT *n* pl. **-S** a short dramatic scene

SKITE *v* **SKITED, SKITING, SKITES** to move away quickly

SKITTER *v* **-ED, -ING, -S** to move lightly or rapidly along a surface

SKITTERY *adj* **-TERIER, -TERIEST** skittish

SKITTISH *adj* easily frightened

SKITTLE *n* pl. **-S** a wooden pin used in a bowling game

SKIVE *v* **SKIVED, SKIVING, SKIVES** to pare

SKIVER *n* pl. **-S** one that skives

SKIVVY *v* **-VIED, -VYING, -VIES** to work as a female servant

SKIWEAR *n* pl. **SKIWEAR** clothing suitable for wear while skiing

SKLENT *v* **-ED, -ING, -S** to slant

SKOAL *v* **-ED, -ING, -S** to drink to the health of

SKOOKUM *adj* excellent

SKORT *n* pl. **-S** a pair of shorts that resembles a skirt

SKOSH *n* pl. **-ES** a small amount

SKREEGH *v* **-ED, -ING, -S** to screech

SKREIGH *v* **-ED, -ING, -S** to screech

SKUA *n* pl. **-S** a predatory seabird

SKULK *v* **-ED, -ING, -S** to move about stealthily

SKULKER *n* pl. **-S** one that skulks

SKULL *v* **-ED, -ING, -S** to hit on the head

SKULLCAP *n* pl. **-S** a close-fitting cap

SKUNK *v* **-ED, -ING, -S** to defeat overwhelmingly

SKUNKY *adj* **SKUNKIER, SKUNKIEST** having a smell suggestive of a skunk (a mammal that can spray a foul-smelling liquid)

SKY *v* **SKIED** or **SKYED, SKYING, SKIES** to hit or throw toward the sky (the upper atmosphere)

SKYBOARD *n* pl. **-S** a board with foot bindings that is used for skysurfing

SKYBORNE *adj* airborne

SKYBOX *n* pl. **-ES** an enclosure of seats situated high in a stadium

SKYCAP *n* pl. **-S** a porter at an airport

SKYDIVE *v* **-DIVED** or **-DOVE, -DIVING, -DIVES** to parachute from an airplane for sport

SKYDIVER *n* pl. **-S** one that skydives

SKYEY *adj* resembling the sky

SKYHOOK *n* pl. **-S** a hook conceived as being suspended from the sky

SKYJACK *v* **-ED, -ING, -S** to hijack an airplane

SKYLARK *v* **-ED, -ING, -S** to frolic

SKYLIGHT *n* pl. **-S** a window in a roof or ceiling

SKYLIKE *adj* resembling the sky

SKYLINE *n* pl. **-S** the horizon

SKYLIT *adj* having a skylight

SKYMAN *n* pl. **-MEN** an aviator

SKYPHOS *n* pl. **-PHOI** a drinking vessel used in ancient Greece

SKYSAIL *n* pl. **-S** a type of sail

SKYSURF *v* **-ED, -ING, -S** to perform maneuvers during free fall while riding on a skyboard

SKYWALK *n* pl. **-S** an elevated walkway between two buildings

SKYWARD *adv* toward the sky

SKYWARDS *adv* skyward

SKYWAY *n* pl. **-WAYS** an elevated highway

SKYWRITE *v* **-WROTE, -WRITTEN, -WRITING, -WRITES** to write in the sky by releasing a visible vapor from an airplane

SLAB *v* **SLABBED, SLABBING, SLABS** to cover with slabs (broad, flat pieces of solid material)

SLABBER *v* **-ED, -ING, -S** to slobber

SLABBERY *adj* slobbery

SLABLIKE *adj* resembling a slab

SLACK *adj* **SLACKER, SLACKEST** not tight or taut

SLACK *v* **-ED, -ING, -S** to slacken

SLACKEN *v* **-ED, -ING, -S** to make less tight or taut

SLACKER *n* pl. **-S** a shirker

SLACKLY *adv* in a slack manner

SLAG *v* **SLAGGED, SLAGGING, SLAGS** to convert into slag (the fused residue of a smelted ore)

SLAGGY *adj* **-GIER, -GIEST** resembling slag

SLAIN past participle of slay

SLAINTE *interj* — used to toast one's health

SLAKE *v* **SLAKED, SLAKING, SLAKES** to quench **SLAKABLE** *adj*

SLAKER *n* pl. **-S** one that slakes

SLALOM *v* **-ED, -ING, -S** to ski in a zigzag course

SLALOMER *n* pl. **-S** one that slaloms

SLAM *v* **SLAMMED, SLAMMING, SLAMS** to shut forcibly and noisily

SLAMMER *n* pl. **-S** a jail

SLAMMING *n* pl. **-S** the practice of switching a person's telephone service from one company to another without permission

SLANDER *v* **-ED, -ING, -S** to defame

SLANG *v* **-ED, -ING, -S** to use slang (extremely informal or vulgar language)

SLANGY *adj* **SLANGIER, SLANGIEST** being or containing slang **SLANGILY** *adv*

SLANK a past tense of slink

SLANT *v* **-ED, -ING, -S** to deviate from the horizontal or vertical

SLANTY *adj* deviating from the horizontal or vertical **SLANTLY** *adv*

SLAP *v* **SLAPPED, SLAPPING, SLAPS** to strike with the open hand

SLAPDASH *n* pl. **-ES** careless work

SLAPJACK *n* pl. **-S** a pancake

SLAPPER *n* pl. **-S** one that slaps

SLAPPING present participle of slap

SLASH *v* **-ED, -ING, -ES** to cut with violent sweeping strokes

SLASHER *n* pl. **-S** one that slashes

SLASHING *n* pl. **-S** the act of one that slashes

SLAT *v* **SLATTED, SLATTING, SLATS** to provide with slats (narrow strips of wood or metal)

SLATCH *n* pl. **-ES** a calm between breaking waves

SLATE *v* **SLATED, SLATING, SLATES** to cover with slate (a roofing material)

SLATER *n* pl. **-S** one that slates

SLATEY *adj* **SLATIER, SLATIEST** slaty

SLATHER *v* **-ED, -ING, -S** to spread thickly

SLATIER comparative of slaty

SLATIEST superlative of slaty

SLATING *n* pl. **-S** the act of one that slates

SLATTED past tense of slat

SLATTERN *n* pl. **-S** a slovenly woman

SLATTING *n* pl. **-S** material for making slats

SLATY *adj* **SLATIER, SLATIEST** resembling slate

SLAVE *v* **SLAVED, SLAVING, SLAVES** to work like a slave (one who is owned by another)

SLAVER *v* **-ED, -ING, -S** to drool

SLAVERER *n* pl. **-S** one that slavers

SLAVERY *n* pl. **-ERIES** ownership of one person by another

SLAVEY *n* pl. **-EYS** a female servant

SLAVING present participle of slave

SLAVISH *adj* pertaining to or characteristic of a slave

SLAW *n* pl. **-S** coleslaw

SLAY *v* **SLEW** or **SLAYED, SLAIN, SLAYING, SLAYS** to kill violently **SLAYABLE** *adj*

SLAYER *n* pl. **-S** one that slays

SLEAVE *v* **SLEAVED, SLEAVING, SLEAVES** to separate into filaments

SLEAZE *n* pl. **-S** a sleazy quality

SLEAZO *adj* sleazy

SLEAZOID   *n* pl. **-S** a person of low morals or character

SLEAZY   *adj* **SLEAZIER, SLEAZIEST** shoddy **SLEAZILY** *adv*

SLED   *v* **SLEDDED, SLEDDING, SLEDS** to convey on a sled (a vehicle for carrying people or loads over snow or ice)

SLEDDER   *n* pl. **-S** one that sleds

SLEDDING   *n* pl. **-S** the act of one that sleds

SLEDGE   *v* **SLEDGED, SLEDGING, SLEDGES** to convey on a type of sled

SLEEK   *adj* **SLEEKER, SLEEKEST** smooth and glossy

SLEEK   *v* **-ED, -ING, -S** to make sleek

SLEEKEN   *v* **-ED, -ING, -S** to sleek

SLEEKER   *n* pl. **-S** one that sleeks

SLEEKIT   *adj* sleek

SLEEKLY   *adv* in a sleek manner

SLEEKY   *adj* **SLEEKIER, SLEEKIEST** sleek

SLEEP   *v* **SLEPT, SLEEPING, SLEEPS** to be in a natural, periodic state of rest

SLEEPER   *n* pl. **-S** one that sleeps

SLEEPING   *n* pl. **-S** the act of one that sleeps

SLEEPY   *adj* **SLEEPIER, SLEEPIEST** ready or inclined to sleep **SLEEPILY** *adv*

SLEET   *v* **-ED, -ING, -S** to shower sleet (frozen rain)

SLEETY   *adj* **SLEETIER, SLEETIEST** resembling sleet

SLEEVE   *v* **SLEEVED, SLEEVING, SLEEVES** to furnish with a sleeve (the part of a garment covering the arm)

SLEIGH   *v* **-ED, -ING, -S** to ride in a sled

SLEIGHER   *n* pl. **-S** one that sleighs

SLEIGHT   *n* pl. **-S** deftness

SLENDER   *adj* **-DERER, -DEREST** thin

SLEPT   past tense of sleep

SLEUTH   *v* **-ED, -ING, -S** to act as a detective

SLEW   *v* **-ED, -ING, -S** to slue

SLICE   *v* **SLICED, SLICING, SLICES** to cut into thin, flat pieces

SLICER   *n* pl. **-S** one that slices

SLICK   *adj* **SLICKER, SLICKEST** smooth and slippery

SLICK   *v* **-ED, -ING, -S** to make slick

SLICKEN   *v* **-ED, -ING, -S** to make slick

SLICKER   *n* pl. **-S** an oilskin raincoat

SLICKLY   *adv* in a slick manner

SLIDE   *v* **SLID, SLIDDEN, SLIDING, SLIDES** to move smoothly along a surface **SLIDABLE** *adj*

SLIDER   *n* pl. **-S** one that slides

SLIDEWAY   *n* pl. **-WAYS** a route along which something slides

SLIER   a comparative of sly

SLIEST   a superlative of sly

SLIEVE   *n* pl. **-S** a mountain

SLIGHT   *adj* **SLIGHTER, SLIGHTEST** small in size or amount **SLIGHTLY** *adv*

SLIGHT   *v* **-ED, -ING, -S** to treat with disregard

SLIGHTER   *n* pl. **-S** one that slights

SLILY   *adv* in a sly manner

SLIM   *adj* **SLIMMER, SLIMMEST** slender

SLIM   *v* **SLIMMED, SLIMMING, SLIMS** to make slim

SLIME   *v* **SLIMED, SLIMING, SLIMES** to cover with slime (viscous mud)

SLIMIER   comparative of slimy

SLIMIEST   superlative of slimy

SLIMILY   *adv* in a slimy manner

SLIMING   present participle of slime

SLIMLY   *adv* in a slim manner

SLIMMED   past tense of slim

SLIMMER   *n* pl. **-S** a dieter

SLIMMEST   superlative of slim

SLIMMING   present participle of slim

SLIMNESS   *n* pl. **-ES** the state of being slim

SLIMPSY   *adj* **-SIER, -SIEST** slimsy

SLIMSY   *adj* **-SIER, -SIEST** flimsy

SLIMY   *adj* **SLIMIER, SLIMIEST** resembling slime

SLING   *v* **SLUNG, SLINGING, SLINGS** to throw with a sudden motion

SLINGER   *n* pl. **-S** one that slings

SLINK   *v* **SLUNK** or **SLANK** or **SLINKED, SLINKING, SLINKS** to move stealthily

SLINKY   *adj* **SLINKIER, SLINKIEST** stealthy **SLINKILY** *adv*

SLIP   *v* **SLIPPED** or **SLIPT, SLIPPING, SLIPS** to slide suddenly and accidentally

SLIPCASE   *n* pl. **-S** a protective box for a book

SLIPE   *v* **SLIPED, SLIPING, SLIPES** to peel

SLIPFORM   *v* **-ED, -ING, -S** to construct with the use of a mold in which concrete is placed to set

SLIPKNOT   *n* pl. **-S** a type of knot

SLIPLESS   *adj* free from errors

SLIPOUT   *n* pl. **-S** an insert in a newspaper

SLIPOVER   *n* pl. **-S** a pullover

SLIPPAGE   *n* pl. **-S** a falling off from a standard or level

SLIPPED   a past tense of slip

SLIPPER   *n* pl. **-S** a light, low shoe

SLIPPERY   *adj* **-PERIER, -PERIEST** causing or tending to cause slipping

SLIPPING   present participle of slip

SLIPPY   *adj* **-PIER, -PIEST** slippery **SLIPPILY** *adv*

SLIPSHOD   *adj* carelessly done or made

SLIPSLOP   *n* pl. **-S** watery food

SLIPSOLE   *n* pl. **-S** a thin insole

SLIPT   a past tense of slip

SLIPUP   *n* pl. **-S** a mistake

SLIPWARE   *n* pl. **-S** a type of pottery

SLIPWAY   *n* pl. **-WAYS** an area sloping toward the water in a shipyard

SLIT   *v* **SLITTED, SLITTING, SLITS** to make a slit (a long, narrow cut) in

SLITHER   *v* **-ED, -ING, -S** to slide from side to side

SLITHERY   *adj* slippery

SLITLESS   *adj* having no slits

SLITLIKE   *adj* resembling a slit

SLITTED   past tense of slit

SLITTER   *n* pl. **-S** one that slits

SLITTING   present participle of slit

SLITTY   *adj* **-TIER, -TIEST** being long and narrow

SLIVER   *v* **-ED, -ING, -S** to cut into long, thin pieces

SLIVERER   *n* pl. **-S** one that slivers

SLIVOVIC   *n* pl. **-ES** a plum brandy

SLOB   *n* pl. **-S** a slovenly or boorish person

SLOBBER   *v* **-ED, -ING, -S** to drool

SLOBBERY   *adj* slobbering

SLOBBISH   *adj* resembling a slob

SLOBBY   *adj* **SLOBBIER, SLOBBIEST** characteristic of a slob

SLOE   *n* pl. **-S** a plumlike fruit

SLOG   *v* **SLOGGED, SLOGGING, SLOGS** to plod

SLOGAN   *n* pl. **-S** a motto adopted by a group

SLOGGER   *n* pl. **-S** one that slogs

SLOID   *n* pl. **-S** sloyd

SLOJD   *n* pl. **-S** sloyd

SLOOP   *n* pl. **-S** a type of sailing vessel

SLOP   *v* **SLOPPED, SLOPPING, SLOPS** to spill or splash

SLOPE   *v* **SLOPED, SLOPING, SLOPES** to slant

SLOPER   *n* pl. **-S** one that slopes

SLOPPY   *adj* **-PIER, -PIEST** messy **SLOPPILY** *adv*

SLOPWORK   *n* pl. **-S** the manufacture of cheap clothing

SLOSH   *v* **-ED, -ING, -ES** to move with a splashing motion

SLOSHY   *adj* **SLOSHIER, SLOSHIEST** slushy

SLOT   *v* **SLOTTED, SLOTTING, SLOTS** to cut a long, narrow opening in

SLOTBACK   *n* pl. **-S** a type of football player

SLOTH   *n* pl. **-S** a slow-moving arboreal mammal

SLOTHFUL   *adj* sluggish

SLOTTED   past tense of slot

SLOTTER   *n* pl. **-S** a machine for slotting

SLOTTING   present participle of slot

SLOUCH   *v* **-ED, -ING, -ES** to sit, stand, or move with a drooping posture

SLOUCHER   *n* pl. **-S** one that slouches

SLOUCHY   *adj* **SLOUCHIER, SLOUCHIEST** slouching

SLOUGH   *v* **-ED, -ING, -S** to cast off

SLOUGHY   *adj* **SLOUGHIER, SLOUGHIEST** miry

SLOVEN   *n* pl. **-S** a slovenly person

SLOVENLY   *adj* **-LIER, -LIEST** habitually untidy or unclean

SLOW   *adj* **SLOWER, SLOWEST** moving with little speed

SLOW   *v* **-ED, -ING, -S** to lessen the speed of

SLOWDOWN   *n* pl. **-S** a lessening of pace

SLOWISH   *adj* somewhat slow

SLOWLY *adv* in a slow manner

SLOWNESS *n* pl. **-ES** the state of being slow

SLOWPOKE *n* pl. **-S** a slow individual

SLOWWORM *n* pl. **-S** a European lizard having no legs

SLOYD *n* pl. **-S** a Swedish system of manual training

SLUB *v* **SLUBBED, SLUBBING, SLUBS** to draw out and twist slightly

SLUBBER *v* **-ED, -ING, -S** to stain or dirty

SLUBBING *n* pl. **-S** a slightly twisted roll of textile fibers

SLUDGE *v* **SLUDGED, SLUDGING, SLUDGES** to form sludge (a muddy mass or sediment)

SLUDGY *adj* **SLUDGIER, SLUDGIEST** covered with sludge

SLUE *v* **SLUED, SLUING, SLUES** to cause to move sideways

SLUFF *v* **-ED, -ING, -S** to discard a card or cards

SLUG *v* **SLUGGED, SLUGGING, SLUGS** to strike heavily

SLUGABED *n* pl. **-S** one inclined to stay in bed out of laziness

SLUGFEST *n* pl. **-S** a vigorous fight

SLUGGARD *n* pl. **-S** a habitually lazy person

SLUGGED past tense of slug

SLUGGER *n* pl. **-S** one that slugs

SLUGGING present participle of slug

SLUGGISH *adj* displaying little movement or activity

SLUICE *v* **SLUICED, SLUICING, SLUICES** to wash with a sudden flow of water

SLUICY *adj* falling in streams

SLUING present participle of slue

SLUM *v* **SLUMMED, SLUMMING, SLUMS** to visit slums (squalid urban areas)

SLUMBER *v* **-ED, -ING, -S** to sleep

SLUMBERY *adj* sleepy

SLUMGUM *n* pl. **-S** the residue remaining after honey is extracted from a honeycomb

SLUMISM *n* pl. **-S** the prevalence of slums

SLUMLORD *n* pl. **-S** a landlord of slum property

SLUMMED past tense of slum

SLUMMER *n* pl. **-S** one that slums

SLUMMING present participle of slum

SLUMMY *adj* **-MIER, -MIEST** resembling a slum

SLUMP *v* **-ED, -ING, -S** to fall or sink suddenly

SLUNG past tense of sling

SLUNK a past tense of slink

SLUR *v* **SLURRED, SLURRING, SLURS** to pass over lightly or carelessly

SLURB *n* pl. **-S** a poorly planned suburban area **SLURBAN** *adj*

SLURP *v* **-ED, -ING, -S** to eat or drink noisily

SLURRY *v* **-RIED, -RYING, -RIES** to convert into a type of watery mixture

SLUSH *v* **-ED, -ING, -ES** to splash with slush (partly melted snow)

SLUSHY *adj* **SLUSHIER, SLUSHIEST** resembling slush **SLUSHILY** *adv*

SLUT *n* pl. **-S** a slovenly woman **SLUTTISH** *adj*

SLUTTY *adj* **SLUTTIER, SLUTTIEST** characteristic of a slut

SLY *adj* **SLIER, SLIEST** or **SLYER, SLYEST** crafty **SLYLY** *adv*

SLYBOOTS *n* pl. **SLYBOOTS** a sly person

SLYNESS *n* pl. **-ES** the quality or state of being sly

SLYPE *n* pl. **-S** a narrow passage in an English cathedral

SMACK *v* **-ED, -ING, -S** to strike sharply

SMACKER *n* pl. **-S** one that smacks

SMALL *adj* **SMALLER, SMALLEST** of limited size or quantity

SMALL *n* pl. **-S** a small part

SMALLAGE *n* pl. **-S** a wild celery

SMALLISH *adj* somewhat small

SMALLPOX *n* pl. **-ES** a virus disease

SMALT *n* pl. **-S** a blue pigment

SMALTI a pl. of smalto

SMALTINE *n* pl. **-S** smaltite

SMALTITE *n* pl. **-S** a mineral

SMALTO *n* pl. **-TOS** or **-TI** colored glass used in mosaics

SMARAGD *n* pl. **-S** an emerald

SMARAGDE *n* pl. **-S** smaragd

SMARM *n* pl. **-S** trite sentimentality

SMARMY *adj* **SMARMIER, SMARMIEST** marked by excessive flattery **SMARMILY** *adv*

SMART	*adj* **SMARTER, SMARTEST** characterized by mental acuity
SMART	*v* **-ED, -ING, -S** to cause a sharp, stinging pain
SMARTASS	*n* pl. **-ES** a smarty
SMARTEN	*v* **-ED, -ING, -S** to improve in appearance
SMARTIE	*n* pl. **-S** smarty
SMARTLY	*adv* in a smart manner
SMARTY	*n* pl. **SMARTIES** an obnoxiously conceited person
SMASH	*v* **-ED, -ING, -ES** to shatter violently
SMASHER	*n* pl. **-S** one that smashes
SMASHUP	*n* pl. **-S** a collision of motor vehicles
SMATTER	*v* **-ED, -ING, -S** to speak with little knowledge
SMAZE	*n* pl. **-S** an atmospheric mixture of smoke and haze
SMEAR	*v* **-ED, -ING, -S** to spread with a sticky, greasy, or dirty substance
SMEARER	*n* pl. **-S** one that smears
SMEARY	*adj* **SMEARIER, SMEARIEST** smeared
SMECTIC	*adj* pertaining to a phase of a liquid crystal
SMECTITE	*n* pl. **-S** a clayey mineral
SMEDDUM	*n* pl. **-S** ground malt powder
SMEEK	*v* **-ED, -ING, -S** to smoke
SMEGMA	*n* pl. **-S** sebum
SMELL	*v* **SMELLED** or **SMELT, SMELLING, SMELLS** to perceive by means of the olfactory nerves
SMELLER	*n* pl. **-S** one that smells
SMELLY	*adj* **SMELLIER, SMELLIEST** having an unpleasant odor
SMELT	*v* **-ED, -ING, -S** to melt or fuse, as ores
SMELTER	*n* pl. **-S** one that smelts
SMELTERY	*n* pl. **-ERIES** a place for smelting
SMERK	*v* **-ED, -ING, -S** to smirk
SMEW	*n* pl. **-S** a Eurasian duck
SMIDGE	*n* pl. **-S** a smidgen
SMIDGEN	*n* pl. **-S** a very small amount
SMIDGEON	*n* pl. **-S** smidgen
SMIDGIN	*n* pl. **-S** smidgen
SMILAX	*n* pl. **-ES** a twining plant
SMILE	*v* **SMILED, SMILING, SMILES** to upturn the corners of the mouth in pleasure
SMILER	*n* pl. **-S** one that smiles
SMILEY	*n* pl. **-EYS** a representation of a smiling face
SMIRCH	*v* **-ED, -ING, -ES** to soil
SMIRK	*v* **-ED, -ING, -S** to smile in an affected or smug manner
SMIRKER	*n* pl. **-S** one that smirks
SMIRKY	*adj* **SMIRKIER, SMIRKIEST** smirking **SMIRKILY** *adv*
SMITE	*v* **SMOTE, SMIT** or **SMITTEN, SMITING, SMITES** to strike heavily
SMITER	*n* pl. **-S** one that smites
SMITH	*n* pl. **-S** a worker in metals
SMITHERS	*n/pl* small fragments
SMITHERY	*n* pl. **-ERIES** the trade of a smith
SMITHY	*n* pl. **SMITHIES** the workshop of a smith
SMITING	present participle of smite
SMITTEN	a past participle of smite
SMOCK	*v* **-ED, -ING, -S** to furnish with a smock (a loose outer garment)
SMOCKING	*n* pl. **-S** a type of embroidery
SMOG	*n* pl. **-S** an atmospheric mixture of smoke and fog **SMOGLESS** *adj*
SMOGGY	*adj* **-GIER, -GIEST** filled with smog
SMOKE	*v* **SMOKED, SMOKING, SMOKES** to emit smoke (the gaseous product of burning materials) **SMOKABLE** *adj*
SMOKEPOT	*n* pl. **-S** a container for giving off smoke
SMOKER	*n* pl. **-S** one that smokes
SMOKEY	*adj* **SMOKIER, SMOKIEST** smoky
SMOKING	present participle of smoke
SMOKY	*adj* **SMOKIER, SMOKIEST** filled with smoke **SMOKILY** *adv*
SMOLDER	*v* **-ED, -ING, -S** to burn with no flame
SMOLT	*n* pl. **-S** a young salmon
SMOOCH	*v* **-ED, -ING, -ES** to kiss
SMOOCHER	*n* pl. **-S** one that smooches
SMOOCHY	*adj* smudgy
SMOOSH	*v* **-ED, -ING, -ES** to squash
SMOOTH	*adj* **SMOOTHER, SMOOTHEST** having a surface that is free from irregularities

SMOOTH *v* **-ED, -ING, -S** or **-ES** to make smooth

SMOOTHEN *v* **-ED, -ING, -S** to smooth

SMOOTHER *n* pl. **-S** one that smooths

SMOOTHIE *n* pl. **-S** a person with polished manners

SMOOTHLY *adv* in a smooth manner

SMOOTHY *n* pl. **SMOOTHIES** smoothie

SMOTE past tense of smite

SMOTHER *v* **-ED, -ING, -S** to prevent from breathing

SMOTHERY *adj* tending to smother

SMOULDER *v* **-ED, -ING, -S** to smolder

SMUDGE *v* **SMUDGED, SMUDGING, SMUDGES** to smear or dirty

SMUDGY *adj* **SMUDGIER, SMUDGIEST** smudged **SMUDGILY** *adv*

SMUG *adj* **SMUGGER, SMUGGEST** highly self-satisfied

SMUGGLE *v* **-GLED, -GLING, -GLES** to import or export illicitly

SMUGGLER *n* pl. **-S** one that smuggles

SMUGLY *adv* in a smug manner

SMUGNESS *n* pl. **-ES** the quality or state of being smug

SMUSH *v* **-ED, -ING, -ES** to smoosh

SMUT *v* **SMUTTED, SMUTTING, SMUTS** to soil

SMUTCH *v* **-ED, -ING, -ES** to smudge

SMUTCHY *adj* **SMUTCHIER, SMUTCHIEST** smudgy

SMUTTY *adj* **-TIER, -TIEST** obscene **SMUTTILY** *adv*

SNACK *v* **-ED, -ING, -S** to eat a light meal

SNACKER *n* pl. **-S** one that snacks

SNAFFLE *v* **-FLED, -FLING, -FLES** to obtain by devious means

SNAFU *v* **-ED, -ING, -S** to bring into a state of confusion

SNAG *v* **SNAGGED, SNAGGING, SNAGS** to catch on a snag (a jagged protuberance)

SNAGGY *adj* **-GIER, -GIEST** full of snags

SNAGLIKE *adj* resembling a snag

SNAIL *v* **-ED, -ING, -S** to move slowly

SNAKE *v* **SNAKED, SNAKING, SNAKES** to move like a snake (a limbless reptile)

SNAKEBIT *adj* unlucky

SNAKEPIT *n* pl. **-S** a psychiatric hospital

SNAKEY *adj* **SNAKIER, SNAKIEST** snaky

SNAKY *adj* **SNAKIER, SNAKIEST** resembling a snake **SNAKILY** *adv*

SNAP *v* **SNAPPED, SNAPPING, SNAPS** to make a sharp cracking sound

SNAPBACK *n* pl. **-S** a sudden rebound or recovery

SNAPLESS *adj* lacking a snap (a type of fastening device)

SNAPPER *n* pl. **-S** one that snaps

SNAPPIER comparative of snappy

SNAPPIEST superlative of snappy

SNAPPILY *adv* in a snappy manner

SNAPPING present participle of snap

SNAPPISH *adj* tending to speak in an impatient or irritable manner

SNAPPY *adj* **-PIER, -PIEST** snappish

SNAPSHOT *v* **-SHOTTED, -SHOTTING, -SHOTS** to photograph informally and quickly

SNAPWEED *n* pl. **-S** a flowering plant

SNARE *v* **SNARED, SNARING, SNARES** to trap

SNARER *n* pl. **-S** one that snares

SNARF *v* **-ED, -ING, -S** to eat or drink greedily

SNARK *n* pl. **-S** an imaginary animal

SNARKY *adj* **SNARKIER, SNARKIEST** snappish **SNARKILY** *adv*

SNARL *v* **-ED, -ING, -S** to growl viciously

SNARLER *n* pl. **-S** one that snarls

SNARLY *adj* **SNARLIER, SNARLIEST** tangled

SNASH *n* pl. **-ES** abusive language

SNATCH *v* **-ED, -ING, -ES** to seize suddenly

SNATCHER *n* pl. **-S** one that snatches

SNATCHY *adj* **SNATCHIER, SNATCHIEST** occurring irregularly

SNATH *n* pl. **-S** the handle of a scythe

SNATHE *n* pl. **-S** snath

SNAW *v* **-ED, -ING, -S** to snow

SNAZZY *adj* **-ZIER, -ZIEST** very stylish

SNEAK *v* **SNEAKED** or **SNUCK, SNEAKING, SNEAKS** to move stealthily

SNEAKER *n* pl. **-S** one that sneaks

SNEAKY *adj* **SNEAKIER, SNEAKIEST** deceitful **SNEAKILY** *adv*

SNEAP *v* **-ED, -ING, -S** to chide

SNECK	*n* pl. **-S** a latch
SNED	*v* **SNEDDED, SNEDDING, SNEDS** to prune
SNEER	*v* **-ED, -ING, -S** to curl the lip in contempt
SNEERER	*n* pl. **-S** one that sneers
SNEERFUL	*adj* given to sneering
SNEERY	*adj* **SNEERIER, SNEERIEST** marked by sneering
SNEESH	*n* pl. **-ES** snuff
SNEEZE	*v* **SNEEZED, SNEEZING, SNEEZES** to make a sudden, involuntary expiration of breath
SNEEZER	*n* pl. **-S** one that sneezes
SNEEZY	*adj* **SNEEZIER, SNEEZIEST** tending to sneeze
SNELL	*adj* **SNELLER, SNELLEST** keen
SNELL	*v* **-ED, -ING, -S** to attach a short line to a fishhook
SNIB	*v* **SNIBBED, SNIBBING, SNIBS** to latch
SNICK	*v* **-ED, -ING, -S** to nick
SNICKER	*v* **-ED, -ING, -S** to utter a partly stifled laugh
SNICKERY	*adj* tending to snicker
SNIDE	*adj* **SNIDER, SNIDEST** maliciously derogatory **SNIDELY** *adv*
SNIFF	*v* **-ED, -ING, -S** to inhale audibly through the nose
SNIFFER	*n* pl. **-S** one that sniffs
SNIFFIER	comparative of sniffy
SNIFFIEST	superlative of sniffy
SNIFFILY	*adv* in a sniffy manner
SNIFFISH	*adj* haughty
SNIFFLE	*v* **-FLED, -FLING, -FLES** to sniff repeatedly
SNIFFLER	*n* pl. **-S** one that sniffles
SNIFFLY	*adj* that sniffles
SNIFFY	*adj* **-FIER, -FIEST** sniffish
SNIFTER	*n* pl. **-S** a pear-shaped liquor glass
SNIGGER	*v* **-ED, -ING, -S** to snicker
SNIGGLE	*v* **-GLED, -GLING, -GLES** to fish for eels
SNIGGLER	*n* pl. **-S** one that sniggles
SNIGLET	*n* pl. **-S** a word coined for something not having a name
SNIP	*v* **SNIPPED, SNIPPING, SNIPS** to cut with a short, quick stroke
SNIPE	*v* **SNIPED, SNIPING, SNIPES** to shoot at individuals from a concealed place
SNIPER	*n* pl. **-S** one that snipes
SNIPPER	*n* pl. **-S** one that snips
SNIPPET	*n* pl. **-S** a small piece snipped off
SNIPPETY	*adj* **-PETIER, -PETIEST** snippy
SNIPPING	present participle of snip
SNIPPY	*adj* **-PIER, -PIEST** snappish **SNIPPILY** *adv*
SNIT	*n* pl. **-S** a state of agitation
SNITCH	*v* **-ED, -ING, -ES** to tattle
SNITCHER	*n* pl. **-S** one that snitches
SNIVEL	*v* **-ELED, -ELING, -ELS** or **-ELLED, -ELLING, -ELS** to cry or whine with sniffling
SNIVELER	*n* pl. **-S** one that snivels
SNOB	*n* pl. **-S** one who tends to avoid or rebuff those regarded as inferior
SNOBBERY	*n* pl. **-BERIES** snobbish behavior
SNOBBIER	comparative of snobby
SNOBBIEST	superlative of snobby
SNOBBILY	*adv* in a snobby manner
SNOBBISH	*adj* characteristic of a snob
SNOBBISM	*n* pl. **-S** snobbery
SNOBBY	*adj* **-BIER, -BIEST** snobbish
SNOG	*v* **SNOGGED, SNOGGING, SNOGS** to kiss
SNOOD	*v* **-ED, -ING, -S** to secure with a snood (a net or fabric cap for the hair)
SNOOK	*v* **-ED, -ING, -S** to sniff
SNOOKER	*v* **-ED, -ING, -S** to trick
SNOOL	*v* **-ED, -ING, -S** to yield meekly
SNOOP	*v* **-ED, -ING, -S** to pry about
SNOOPER	*n* pl. **-S** one that snoops
SNOOPY	*adj* **SNOOPIER, SNOOPIEST** given to snooping **SNOOPILY** *adv*
SNOOT	*v* **-ED, -ING, -S** to treat with disdain
SNOOTY	*adj* **SNOOTIER, SNOOTIEST** snobbish **SNOOTILY** *adv*
SNOOZE	*v* **SNOOZED, SNOOZING, SNOOZES** to sleep lightly
SNOOZER	*n* pl. **-S** one that snoozes
SNOOZLE	*v* **-ZLED, -ZLING, -ZLES** to nuzzle
SNOOZY	*adj* **SNOOZIER, SNOOZIEST** drowsy
SNORE	*v* **SNORED, SNORING, SNORES** to breathe loudly while sleeping

SNORER	*n* pl. **-S** one that snores
SNORKEL	*v* **-ED, -ING, -S** to swim underwater with a type of breathing device
SNORT	*v* **-ED, -ING, -S** to exhale noisily through the nostrils
SNORTER	*n* pl. **-S** one that snorts
SNOT	*n* pl. **-S** nasal mucus
SNOTTY	*adj* **-TIER, -TIEST** arrogant **SNOTTILY** *adv*
SNOUT	*v* **-ED, -ING, -S** to provide with a nozzle
SNOUTISH	*adj* snouty
SNOUTY	*adj* **SNOUTIER, SNOUTIEST** resembling a long, projecting nose
SNOW	*v* **-ED, -ING, -S** to fall as snow (precipitation in the form of ice crystals)
SNOWBALL	*v* **-ED, -ING, -S** to increase at a rapidly accelerating rate
SNOWBANK	*n* pl. **-S** a mound of snow
SNOWBELL	*n* pl. **-S** a flowering shrub
SNOWBELT	*n* pl. **-S** a region that receives an appreciable amount of snow each year
SNOWBIRD	*n* pl. **-S** a small bird
SNOWBUSH	*n* pl. **-ES** a flowering shrub
SNOWCAP	*n* pl. **-S** a covering of snow
SNOWCAT	*n* pl. **-S** a tracklaying vehicle for travel on snow
SNOWDROP	*n* pl. **-S** a European herb
SNOWFALL	*n* pl. **-S** a fall of snow
SNOWIER	comparative of snowy
SNOWIEST	superlative of snowy
SNOWILY	*adv* in a snowy manner
SNOWLAND	*n* pl. **-S** an area marked by a great amount of snow
SNOWLESS	*adj* having no snow
SNOWLIKE	*adj* resembling snow
SNOWMAN	*n* pl. **-MEN** a figure of a person that is made of snow
SNOWMELT	*n* pl. **-S** water produced by the melting of snow
SNOWMOLD	*n* pl. **-S** a fungus disease of grasses near the edge of melting snow
SNOWPACK	*n* pl. **-S** an accumulation of packed snow
SNOWPLOW	*v* **-ED, -ING, -S** to execute a type of skiing maneuver
SNOWSHED	*n* pl. **-S** a structure built to provide protection against snow
SNOWSHOE	*v* **-SHOED, -SHOEING, -SHOES** to walk on snowshoes (oval frames that allow a person to walk on deep snow)
SNOWSUIT	*n* pl. **-S** a child's garment for winter wear
SNOWY	*adj* **SNOWIER, SNOWIEST** abounding in snow
SNUB	*v* **SNUBBED, SNUBBING, SNUBS** to treat with contempt or neglect
SNUBBER	*n* pl. **-S** one that snubs
SNUBBY	*adj* **-BIER, -BIEST** blunt
SNUBNESS	*n* pl. **-ES** bluntness
SNUCK	a past tense of sneak
SNUFF	*v* **-ED, -ING, -S** to use or inhale snuff (powdered tobacco)
SNUFFBOX	*n* pl. **-ES** a box for holding snuff
SNUFFER	*n* pl. **-S** one that snuffs
SNUFFIER	comparative of snuffy
SNUFFIEST	superlative of snuffy
SNUFFILY	*adv* in a snuffy manner
SNUFFLE	*v* **-FLED, -FLING, -FLES** to sniffle
SNUFFLER	*n* pl. **-S** one that snuffles
SNUFFLY	*adj* **-FLIER, -FLIEST** tending to snuffle
SNUFFY	*adj* **SNUFFIER, SNUFFIEST** dingy
SNUG	*adj* **SNUGGER, SNUGGEST** warmly comfortable
SNUG	*v* **SNUGGED, SNUGGING, SNUGS** to make snug
SNUGGERY	*n* pl. **-GERIES** a snug place
SNUGGEST	superlative of snug
SNUGGIES	*n/pl* women's long underwear
SNUGGING	present participle of snug
SNUGGLE	*v* **-GLED, -GLING, -GLES** to lie or press closely
SNUGLY	*adv* in a snug manner
SNUGNESS	*n* pl. **-ES** the quality or state of being snug
SNYE	*n* pl. **-S** a side channel in a river or creek
SO	*n* pl. **SOS** sol
SOAK	*v* **-ED, -ING, -S** to saturate thoroughly in liquid
SOAKAGE	*n* pl. **-S** the act of soaking
SOAKER	*n* pl. **-S** one that soaks

SOAP	v **-ED, -ING, -S** to treat with soap (a cleansing agent)	**SOCIETY**	n pl. **-ETIES** an organized group of persons **SOCIETAL** adj
SOAPBARK	n pl. **-S** a tropical tree	**SOCK**	n pl. **SOCKS** or **SOX** a knitted or woven covering for the foot
SOAPBOX	v **-ED, -ING, -ES** to deliver an informal impassioned speech on the street	**SOCK**	v **-ED, -ING, -S** to strike forcefully
SOAPER	n pl. **-S** a serial melodrama on radio or television	**SOCKET**	v **-ED, -ING, -S** to furnish with a socket (an opening for receiving something)
SOAPIER	comparative of soapy	**SOCKEYE**	n pl. **-S** a food fish
SOAPIEST	superlative of soapy	**SOCKLESS**	adj having no socks
SOAPILY	adv in a soapy manner	**SOCKMAN**	n pl. **-MEN** socman
SOAPLESS	adj having no soap	**SOCKO**	adj strikingly impressive
SOAPLIKE	adj resembling soap	**SOCLE**	n pl. **-S** a block used as a base for a column or pedestal
SOAPSUDS	n/pl suds (soapy water)		
SOAPWORT	n pl. **-S** a perennial herb	**SOCMAN**	n pl. **-MEN** a socager
SOAPY	adj **SOAPIER, SOAPIEST** containing or resembling soap	**SOD**	v **SODDED, SODDING, SODS** to cover with sod (turf)
SOAR	v **-ED, -ING, -S** to fly at a great height	**SODA**	n pl. **-S** a type of chemical compound **SODALESS** adj
SOARER	n pl. **-S** one that soars	**SODALIST**	n pl. **-S** a member of a sodality
SOARING	n pl. **-S** the sport of flying in a heavier-than-air craft without power	**SODALITE**	n pl. **-S** a mineral
		SODALITY	n pl. **-TIES** a society
SOAVE	n pl. **-S** an Italian wine	**SODAMIDE**	n pl. **-S** a chemical compound
SOB	v **SOBBED, SOBBING, SOBS** to cry with a convulsive catching of the breath	**SODDED**	past tense of sod
		SODDEN	v **-ED, -ING, -S** to make soggy
SOBA	n pl. **-S** a Japanese noodle made from buckwheat flour	**SODDENLY**	adv in a soggy manner
		SODDING	present participle of sod
SOBBER	n pl. **-S** one that sobs	**SODDY**	n pl. **-DIES** a house built of sod
SOBEIT	conj provided that	**SODIUM**	n pl. **-S** a metallic element **SODIC** adj
SOBER	adj **SOBERER, SOBEREST** having control of one's faculties		
SOBER	v **-ED, -ING, -S** to make sober	**SODOM**	n pl. **-S** a place notorious for vice and corruption
SOBERIZE	v **-IZED, -IZING, -IZES** to sober	**SODOMIST**	n pl. **-S** a sodomite
SOBERLY	adv in a sober manner	**SODOMITE**	n pl. **-S** one who practices sodomy
SOBFUL	adj given to sobbing	**SODOMIZE**	v **-IZED, -IZING, -IZES** to engage in sodomy with
SOBRIETY	n pl. **-ETIES** the quality or state of being sober		
		SODOMY	n pl. **-OMIES** unnatural copulation
SOCA	n pl. **-S** a blend of soul and calypso music	**SOEVER**	adv at all
SOCAGE	n pl. **-S** a form of feudal land tenure	**SOFA**	n pl. **-S** a long, upholstered seat
		SOFABED	n pl. **-S** a sofa that can be made into a bed
SOCAGER	n pl. **-S** a tenant by socage	**SOFAR**	n pl. **-S** a system for locating underwater explosions
SOCCAGE	n pl. **-S** socage		
SOCCER	n pl. **-S** a type of ball game	**SOFFIT**	n pl. **-S** the underside of an architectural structure
SOCIABLE	n pl. **-S** a social		
SOCIABLY	adv in a friendly manner	**SOFT**	adj **SOFTER, SOFTEST** yielding readily to pressure
SOCIAL	n pl. **-S** a friendly gathering		
SOCIALLY	adv with respect to society	**SOFT**	n pl. **-S** a soft object or part

SOFTA *n* pl. **-S** a Muslim theological student

SOFTBACK *n* pl. **-S** a book bound in a flexible paper cover

SOFTBALL *n* pl. **-S** a type of ball

SOFTCORE *adj* less than explicit in depicting sex acts

SOFTEN *v* **-ED, -ING, -S** to make soft

SOFTENER *n* pl. **-S** one that softens

SOFTHEAD *n* pl. **-S** a foolish person

SOFTIE *n* pl. **-S** softy

SOFTIES pl. of softy

SOFTISH *adj* somewhat soft

SOFTLY *adv* in a soft manner

SOFTNESS *n* pl. **-ES** the quality or state of being soft

SOFTWARE *n* pl. **-S** written or printed data used in computer operations

SOFTWOOD *n* pl. **-S** the soft wood of various trees

SOFTY *n* pl. **SOFTIES** a sentimental person

SOGGED *adj* soggy

SOGGY *adj* **-GIER, -GIEST** heavy with moisture **SOGGILY** *adv*

SOIGNE *adj* carefully done

SOIGNEE *adj* soigne

SOIL *v* **-ED, -ING, -S** to make dirty

SOILAGE *n* pl. **-S** green crops for feeding animals

SOILLESS *adj* carried on without soil (finely divided rock mixed with organic matter)

SOILURE *n* pl. **-S** a stain or smudge

SOIREE *n* pl. **-S** an evening party

SOJA *n* pl. **-S** the soybean

SOJOURN *v* **-ED, -ING, -S** to stay temporarily

SOKE *n* pl. **-S** a feudal right to administer justice within a certain territory

SOKEMAN *n* pl. **-MEN** socman

SOKOL *n* pl. **-S** an international group promoting physical fitness

SOL *n* pl. **-S** the fifth tone of the diatonic musical scale

SOLA a pl. of solum

SOLACE *v* **-LACED, -LACING, -LACES** to console

SOLACER *n* pl. **-S** one that solaces

SOLAN *n* pl. **-S** a gannet

SOLAND *n* pl. **-S** solan

SOLANDER *n* pl. **-S** a protective box for library materials

SOLANIN *n* pl. **-S** solanine

SOLANINE *n* pl. **-S** a poisonous alkaloid

SOLANO *n* pl. **-NOS** a strong, hot wind

SOLANUM *n* pl. **-S** any of a genus of herbs and shrubs

SOLAR *adj* pertaining to the sun

SOLARIA a pl. of solarium

SOLARISE *v* **-ISED, -ISING, -ISES** to solarize

SOLARISM *n* pl. **-S** an interpretation of folk tales as concepts of the nature of the sun

SOLARIUM *n* pl. **-IUMS** or **-IA** a room exposed to the sun

SOLARIZE *v* **-IZED, -IZING, -IZES** to expose to sunlight

SOLATE *v* **-ATED, -ATING, -ATES** to change to a fluid colloidal system

SOLATION *n* pl. **-S** the act of solating

SOLATIUM *n* pl. **-TIA** a compensation given for damage to the feelings

SOLD past tense of sell

SOLDAN *n* pl. **-S** a Muslim ruler

SOLDER *v* **-ED, -ING, -S** to join closely together

SOLDERER *n* pl. **-S** one that solders

SOLDIER *v* **-ED, -ING, -S** to perform military service

SOLDIERY *n* pl. **-DIERIES** the military profession

SOLDO *n* pl. **-DI** a former coin of Italy

SOLE *v* **SOLED, SOLING, SOLES** to furnish with a sole (the bottom surface of a shoe or boot)

SOLECISE *v* **-CISED, -CISING, -CISES** to solecize

SOLECISM *n* pl. **-S** an ungrammatical combination of words in a sentence

SOLECIST *n* pl. **-S** one who solecizes

SOLECIZE *v* **-CIZED, -CIZING, -CIZES** to use solecisms

SOLED past tense of sole

SOLEI a pl. of soleus

SOLELESS *adj* having no sole

SOLELY *adv* singly

SOLEMN *adj* **-EMNER, -EMNEST** serious **SOLEMNLY** *adv*

SOLENESS *n* pl. **-ES** the state of being the only one

SOLENOID *n* pl. **-S** a type of electric coil

SOLERET *n* pl. **-S** solleret

SOLEUS *n* pl. **-LEUSES** or **-LEI** a muscle in the calf of the leg

SOLFEGE *n* pl. **-S** a type of singing exercise

SOLFEGGI *n/pl* solfeges

SOLGEL *adj* involving some changes in the state of a colloidal system

SOLI a pl. of solo

SOLICIT *v* **-ED, -ING, -S** to ask for earnestly

SOLID *adj* **-IDER, -IDEST** having definite shape and volume

SOLID *n* pl. **-S** a solid substance

SOLIDAGO *n* pl. **-GOS** a flowering plant

SOLIDARY *adj* united

SOLIDI pl. of solidus

SOLIDIFY *v* **-FIED, -FYING, -FIES** to make solid

SOLIDITY *n* pl. **-TIES** the quality or state of being solid

SOLIDLY *adv* in a solid manner

SOLIDUS *n* pl. **-DI** a coin of ancient Rome

SOLING present participle of sole

SOLION *n* pl. **-S** an electronic detecting and amplifying device

SOLIQUID *n* pl. **-S** a fluid colloidal system

SOLITARY *n* pl. **-TARIES** one who lives alone

SOLITON *n* pl. **-S** a solitary wave in physics

SOLITUDE *n* pl. **-S** the state of being alone

SOLLERET *n* pl. **-S** a sabaton

SOLO *n* pl. **-LOS** or **-LI** a musical composition for a single voice or instrument

SOLO *v* **-ED, -ING, -S** to perform alone

SOLOIST *n* pl. **-S** one that performs a solo

SOLON *n* pl. **-S** a wise lawgiver

SOLONETS *n* pl. **-ES** solonetz

SOLONETZ *n* pl. **-ES** a type of soil

SOLSTICE *n* pl. **-S** the time of the year when the sun is at its greatest distance from the celestial equator

SOLUBLE *n* pl. **-S** something that is soluble (capable of being dissolved)

SOLUBLY *adv* in a soluble manner

SOLUM *n* pl. **-LUMS** or **-LA** a soil layer

SOLUNAR *adj* listing the rising and setting times of the sun and moon

SOLUS *adj* alone

SOLUTE *n* pl. **-S** a dissolved substance

SOLUTION *n* pl. **-S** a homogeneous liquid mixture

SOLVABLE *adj* capable of being solved

SOLVATE *v* **-VATED, -VATING, -VATES** to convert into a type of ion

SOLVE *v* **SOLVED, SOLVING, SOLVES** to find the answer or explanation for

SOLVENCY *n* pl. **-CIES** the ability to pay all debts

SOLVENT *n* pl. **-S** a substance capable of dissolving others

SOLVER *n* pl. **-S** one that solves

SOLVING present participle of solve

SOM *n* pl. **SOMS** a monetary unit of Kyrgyzstan

SOMA *n* pl. **-MAS** or **-MATA** the body of an organism **SOMATIC** *adj*

SOMAN *n* pl. **-S** a toxic chemical warfare agent

SOMBER *adj* gloomy **SOMBERLY** *adv*

SOMBRE *adj* somber **SOMBRELY** *adv*

SOMBRERO *n* pl. **-ROS** a broad-brimmed hat

SOMBROUS *adj* somber

SOME *adj* being an unspecified number or part

SOMEBODY *n* pl. **-BODIES** an important person

SOMEDAY *adv* at some future time

SOMEDEAL *adv* to some degree

SOMEHOW *adv* by some means

SOMEONE *n* pl. **-S** a somebody

SOMERSET *v* **-SETED, -SETING, -SETS** or **-SETTED, -SETTING, -SETS** to roll the body in a complete circle, head over heels

SOMETIME *adv* at some future time

SOMEWAY *adv* somehow

SOMEWAYS *adv* someway

SOMEWHAT *n* pl. **-S** an unspecified number or part

SOMEWHEN *adv* sometime

SOMEWISE *adv* somehow

SOMITE *n* pl. **-S** a longitudinal segment of the body of some animals **SOMITAL, SOMITIC** *adj*

SOMONI *n* pl. **SOMONI** a monetary unit of Tajikistan

SON *n* pl. **-S** a male child

SONANCE *n* pl. **-S** sound

SONANT *n* pl. **-S** a sound uttered with vibration of the vocal cords **SONANTAL, SONANTIC** *adj*

SONAR *n* pl. **-S** an underwater locating device

SONARMAN *n* pl. **-MEN** a person who operates sonar equipment

SONATA *n* pl. **-S** a type of musical composition

SONATINA *n* pl. **-TINAS** or **-TINE** a short sonata

SONDE *n* pl. **-S** a device for observing atmospheric phenomena

SONDER *n* pl. **-S** a class of small yachts

SONE *n* pl. **-S** a unit of loudness

SONG *n* pl. **-S** a musical composition written or adapted for singing

SONGBIRD *n* pl. **-S** a bird that utters a musical call

SONGBOOK *n* pl. **-S** a book of songs

SONGFEST *n* pl. **-S** an informal gathering for group singing

SONGFUL *adj* melodious

SONGLESS *adj* incapable of singing

SONGLIKE *adj* resembling a song

SONGSTER *n* pl. **-S** a singer

SONHOOD *n* pl. **-S** the state of being a son

SONIC *adj* pertaining to sound

SONICATE *v* **-CATED, -CATING, -CATES** to disrupt with sound waves

SONICS *n/pl* the science dealing with the practical applications of sound

SONLESS *adj* having no son

SONLIKE *adj* resembling a son

SONLY *adj* pertaining to a son

SONNET *v* **-NETED, -NETING, -NETS** or **-NETTED, -NETTING, -NETS** to compose a sonnet (a type of poem)

SONNY *n* pl. **-NIES** a small boy

SONOBUOY *n* pl. **-BUOYS** a buoy that detects and transmits underwater sounds

SONOGRAM *n* pl. **-S** an image produced by ultrasound

SONORANT *n* pl. **-S** a type of voiced sound

SONORITY *n* pl. **-TIES** the quality or state of being sonorous

SONOROUS *adj* characterized by a full and loud sound

SONOVOX *n* pl. **-ES** a sound effects device

SONSHIP *n* pl. **-S** the state of being a son

SONSIE *adj* **-SIER, -SIEST** sonsy

SONSY *adj* **-SIER, -SIEST** comely

SOOCHONG *n* pl. **-S** souchong

SOOEY *interj* — used in calling pigs

SOOK *n* pl. **-S** souk

SOON *adv* **SOONER, SOONEST** in the near future

SOONER *n* pl. **-S** one who settles on government land before it is officially opened for settlement

SOOT *v* **-ED, -ING, -S** to cover with soot (a black substance produced by combustion)

SOOTH *adj* **SOOTHER, SOOTHEST** true

SOOTH *n* pl. **-S** truth

SOOTHE *v* **SOOTHED, SOOTHING, SOOTHES** to restore to a quiet or normal state

SOOTHER *n* pl. **-S** one that soothes

SOOTHLY *adv* in truth

SOOTHSAY *v* **-SAID, -SAYING, -SAYS** to predict

SOOTY *adj* **SOOTIER, SOOTIEST** covered with soot **SOOTILY** *adv*

SOP *v* **SOPPED, SOPPING, SOPS** to dip or soak in a liquid

SOPH *n* pl. **-S** a sophomore

SOPHIES pl. of sophy

SOPHISM *n* pl. **-S** a plausible but fallacious argument

SOPHIST *n* pl. **-S** one that uses sophisms

SOPHY *n* pl. **-PHIES** a ruler of Persia

SOPITE *v* **-PITED, -PITING, -PITES** to put to sleep

SOPOR *n* pl. **-S** an abnormally deep sleep

SOPPED past tense of sop

SOPPING *adj* very wet

SOPPY *adj* **-PIER, -PIEST** very wet

SOPRANO *n* pl. **-NOS** or **-NI** the highest singing voice

SORA *n* pl. **-S** a marsh bird

SORB *v* **-ED, -ING, -S** to take up and hold by absorption or adsorption **SORBABLE** *adj*

SORBATE *n* pl. **-S** a sorbed substance

SORBENT   *n* pl. **-S** a substance that sorbs

SORBET   *n* pl. **-S** sherbet

SORBIC   *adj* pertaining to a type of fruit

SORBITOL   *n* pl. **-S** a chemical compound

SORBOSE   *n* pl. **-S** a type of sugar

SORCERER   *n* pl. **-S** one who practices sorcery

SORCERY   *n* pl. **-CERIES** alleged use of supernatural powers

SORD   *n* pl. **-S** a flight of mallards

SORDID   *adj* filthy **SORDIDLY** *adv*

SORDINE   *n* pl. **-S** a device used to muffle the tone of a musical instrument

SORDINO   *n* pl. **-NI** sordine

SORDOR   *n* pl. **-S** a sordid state

SORE   *v* **SORED, SORING, SORES** to mutilate the feet of (a horse) so as to force a particular gait

SORE   *adj* **SORER, SOREST** painfully sensitive to the touch

SOREHEAD   *n* pl. **-S** a person who is easily angered or offended

SOREL   *n* pl. **-S** sorrel

SORELY   *adv* in a sore manner

SORENESS   *n* pl. **-ES** the quality or state of being sore

SORER   comparative of sore

SOREST   superlative of sore

SORGHO   *n* pl. **-GHOS** sorgo

SORGHUM   *n* pl. **-S** a cereal grass

SORGO   *n* pl. **-GOS** a variety of sorghum

SORI   pl. of sorus

SORICINE   *adj* belonging to the shrew family of mammals

SORING   *n* pl. **-S** the practice of making a horse's front feet sore to force high stepping

SORITES   *n* pl. **SORITES** a type of argument used in logic **SORITIC** *adj*

SORN   *v* **-ED, -ING, -S** to force oneself on others for food and lodging

SORNER   *n* pl. **-S** one that sorns

SOROCHE   *n* pl. **-S** mountain sickness

SORORAL   *adj* sisterly

SORORATE   *n* pl. **-S** the marriage of a man usually with his deceased wife's sister

SORORITY   *n* pl. **-TIES** a social club for women

SOROSIS   *n* pl. **-ROSISES** or **-ROSES** a women's club or society

SORPTION   *n* pl. **-S** the act or process of sorbing **SORPTIVE** *adj*

SORREL   *n* pl. **-S** a reddish brown color

SORRIER   comparative of sorry

SORRIEST   superlative of sorry

SORRILY   *adv* in a sorry manner

SORROW   *v* **-ED, -ING, -S** to grieve

SORROWER   *n* pl. **-S** one that sorrows

SORRY   *adj* **-RIER, -RIEST** feeling grief or penitence

SORT   *v* **-ED, -ING, -S** to arrange according to kind, class, or size **SORTABLE** *adj* **SORTABLY** *adv*

SORTER   *n* pl. **-S** one that sorts

SORTIE   *v* **-TIED, -TIEING, -TIES** to attack suddenly from a defensive position

SORUS   *n* pl. **-RI** a cluster of plant reproductive bodies

SOT   *n* pl. **-S** a habitual drunkard

SOTH   *n* pl. **-S** sooth

SOTOL   *n* pl. **-S** a flowering plant

SOTTED   *adj* besotted **SOTTEDLY** *adv*

SOTTISH   *adj* resembling a sot

SOU   *n* pl. **-S** a formerly used French coin

SOUARI   *n* pl. **-S** a tropical tree

SOUBISE   *n* pl. **-S** a sauce of onions and butter

SOUCAR   *n* pl. **-S** a Hindu banker

SOUCHONG   *n* pl. **-S** a Chinese tea

SOUDAN   *n* pl. **-S** soldan

SOUFFLE   *n* pl. **-S** a light, baked dish

SOUFFLED   *adj* made puffy by beating and baking

SOUGH   *v* **-ED, -ING, -S** to make a moaning or sighing sound

SOUGHT   past tense of seek

SOUK   *n* pl. **-S** a marketplace in northern Africa and the Middle East

SOUKOUS   *n* pl. **-ES** a dance music in the Democratic Republic of the Congo

SOUL   *n* pl. **-S** the spiritual aspect of human beings **SOULED, SOULLESS, SOULLIKE** *adj*

SOULFUL   *adj* full of emotion

SOULMATE   *n* pl. **-S** a person with whom one is perfectly suited

SOUND   *adj* **SOUNDER, SOUNDEST** being in good health or condition

SOUND	*v* **-ED, -ING, -S** to make a sound (something that stimulates the auditory receptors)
SOUNDBOX	*n* pl. **-ES** a resonant cavity in a musical instrument
SOUNDER	*n* pl. **-S** one that sounds
SOUNDING	*n* pl. **-S** a sampling of opinions
SOUNDLY	*adv* in a sound manner
SOUNDMAN	*n* pl. **-MEN** a person who controls the quality of sound being recorded
SOUP	*v* **-ED, -ING, -S** to increase the power or efficiency of
SOUPCON	*n* pl. **-S** a minute amount
SOUPLESS	*adj* having no soup (a liquid food often having solid ingredients)
SOUPLIKE	*adj* resembling soup
SOUPY	*adj* **SOUPIER, SOUPIEST** foggy
SOUR	*adj* **SOURER, SOUREST** sharp or biting to the taste
SOUR	*v* **-ED, -ING, -S** to make or become sour
SOURBALL	*n* pl. **-S** a sour candy
SOURCE	*v* **SOURCED, SOURCING, SOURCES** to obtain from a point of origin
SOURDINE	*n* pl. **-S** sordine
SOURISH	*adj* somewhat sour
SOURLY	*adv* in a sour manner
SOURNESS	*n* pl. **-ES** the quality or state of being sour
SOURPUSS	*n* pl. **-ES** a grouchy person
SOURSOP	*n* pl. **-S** a tropical tree
SOURWOOD	*n* pl. **-S** a flowering tree
SOUSE	*v* **SOUSED, SOUSING, SOUSES** to immerse
SOUSLIK	*n* pl. **-S** suslik
SOUTACHE	*n* pl. **-S** a flat, narrow braid
SOUTANE	*n* pl. **-S** a cassock
SOUTER	*n* pl. **-S** a shoemaker
SOUTH	*v* **-ED, -ING, -S** to move toward the south (a cardinal point of the compass)
SOUTHER	*n* pl. **-S** a wind or storm from the south
SOUTHERN	*n* pl. **-S** a person living in the south
SOUTHING	*n* pl. **-S** movement toward the south
SOUTHPAW	*n* pl. **-S** a left-handed person
SOUTHRON	*n* pl. **-S** a southern
SOUVENIR	*n* pl. **-S** a memento
SOUVLAKI	*n* pl. **-S** a Greek shish kebab
SOVIET	*n* pl. **-S** a legislative body in a Communist country
SOVKHOZ	*n* pl. **-KHOZES** or **-KHOZY** a state-owned farm in the former Soviet Union
SOVRAN	*n* pl. **-S** a monarch
SOVRANLY	*adv* supremely
SOVRANTY	*n* pl. **-TIES** a monarchy
SOW	*v* **SOWED, SOWN, SOWING, SOWS** to scatter over land for growth, as seed **SOWABLE** *adj*
SOWANS	*n* pl. **SOWANS** sowens
SOWAR	*n* pl. **-S** a mounted native soldier in India
SOWBELLY	*n* pl. **-LIES** pork cured in salt
SOWBREAD	*n* pl. **-S** a flowering plant
SOWCAR	*n* pl. **-S** soucar
SOWENS	*n* pl. **SOWENS** porridge made from oat husks
SOWER	*n* pl. **-S** one that sows
SOWN	past participle of sow
SOX	a pl. of sock
SOY	*n* pl. **SOYS** the soybean
SOYA	*n* pl. **-S** soy
SOYBEAN	*n* pl. **-S** the seed of a cultivated Asian herb
SOYMILK	*n* pl. **-S** a milk substitute made from soybeans
SOYUZ	*n* pl. **-ES** a manned spacecraft of the former Soviet Union
SOZIN	*n* pl. **-S** a type of protein
SOZINE	*n* pl. **-S** sozin
SOZZLED	*adj* drunk
SPA	*n* pl. **-S** a mineral spring
SPACE	*v* **SPACED, SPACING, SPACES** to set some distance apart
SPACEMAN	*n* pl. **-MEN** an astronaut
SPACER	*n* pl. **-S** one that spaces
SPACEY	*adj* **SPACIER, SPACIEST** weird in behavior
SPACIAL	*adj* spatial
SPACING	*n* pl. **-S** the distance between any two objects
SPACIOUS	*adj* vast or ample in extent
SPACKLE	*v* **-LED, -LING, -LES** to fill cracks or holes in a surface with paste
SPACY	*adj* **SPACIER, SPACIEST** spacey

SPADE | *v* **SPADED, SPADING, SPADES** to take up with a spade (a digging implement)

SPADEFUL | *n* pl. **-S** as much as a spade can hold

SPADER | *n* pl. **-S** one that spades

SPADICES | pl. of spadix

SPADILLE | *n* pl. **-S** the highest trump in certain card games

SPADING | present participle of spade

SPADIX | *n* pl. **-DIXES** or **-DICES** a flower cluster

SPADO | *n* pl. **-DONES** a castrated man or animal

SPAE | *v* **SPAED, SPAEING, SPAES** to foretell

SPAEING | *n* pl. **-S** the act of foretelling

SPAETZLE | *n* pl. **-S** a tiny dumpling

SPAGYRIC | *n* pl. **-S** a person skilled in alchemy

SPAHEE | *n* pl. **-S** spahi

SPAHI | *n* pl. **-S** a Turkish cavalryman

SPAIL | *n* pl. **-S** spale

SPAIT | *n* pl. **-S** spate

SPAKE | a past tense of speak

SPALDEEN | *n* pl. **-S** a small hollow rubber ball

SPALE | *n* pl. **-S** a splinter or chip

SPALL | *v* **-ED, -ING, -S** to break up into fragments

SPALLER | *n* pl. **-S** one that spalls

SPALPEEN | *n* pl. **-S** a rascal

SPAM | *v* **SPAMMED, SPAMMING, SPAMS** to send unsolicited e-mail to a large number of addresses

SPAMBOT | *n* pl. **-S** a computer program that sends out unsolicited e-mail

SPAMMER | *n* pl. **-S** one that spams

SPAN | *v* **SPANNED, SPANNING, SPANS** to extend over or across

SPANCEL | *v* **-CELED, -CELING, -CELS** or **-CELLED, -CELLING, -CELS** to bind or fetter with a rope

SPANDEX | *n* pl. **-ES** a synthetic elastic fiber

SPANDREL | *n* pl. **-S** a space between two adjoining arches

SPANDRIL | *n* pl. **-S** spandrel

SPANG | *adv* directly

SPANGLE | *v* **-GLED, -GLING, -GLES** to adorn with spangles (bits of sparkling metal)

SPANGLY | *adj* **-GLIER, -GLIEST** covered with spangles

SPANIEL | *n* pl. **-S** a dog with silky hair

SPANK | *v* **-ED, -ING, -S** to slap on the buttocks

SPANKER | *n* pl. **-S** one that spanks

SPANKING | *n* pl. **-S** the act of one that spanks

SPANLESS | *adj* having no extent

SPANNED | past tense of span

SPANNER | *n* pl. **-S** one that spans

SPANNING | present participle of span

SPANWORM | *n* pl. **-S** an inchworm

SPAR | *v* **SPARRED, SPARRING, SPARS** to provide with spars (stout poles used to support rigging)

SPARABLE | *n* pl. **-S** a type of nail

SPARE | *adj* **SPARER, SPAREST** meager **SPARELY** *adv*

SPARE | *v* **SPARED, SPARING, SPARES** to refrain from punishing, harming, or destroying

SPARER | *n* pl. **-S** one that spares

SPARERIB | *n* pl. **-S** a cut of pork

SPARGE | *v* **SPARGED, SPARGING, SPARGES** to sprinkle

SPARGER | *n* pl. **-S** one that sparges

SPARID | *n* pl. **-S** any of a family of marine fishes

SPARING | present participle of spare

SPARK | *v* **-ED, -ING, -S** to give off sparks (small fiery particles)

SPARKER | *n* pl. **-S** something that sparks

SPARKIER | comparative of sparky

SPARKIEST | superlative of sparky

SPARKILY | *adv* in a lively manner

SPARKISH | *adj* jaunty

SPARKLE | *v* **-KLED, -KLING, -KLES** to give off or reflect flashes of light

SPARKLER | *n* pl. **-S** something that sparkles

SPARKLET | *n* pl. **-S** a small spark

SPARKLY | *adj* **-KLIER, -KLIEST** tending to sparkle

SPARKY | *adj* **SPARKIER, SPARKIEST** lively

SPARLIKE | *adj* resembling a spar

SPARLING | *n* pl. **-S** a young herring

SPAROID | *n* pl. **-S** a sparid

SPARRED | past tense of spar

SPARRING | present participle of spar

SPARROW *n* pl. **-S** a small bird

SPARRY *adj* **-RIER, -RIEST** resembling spar (a lustrous mineral)

SPARSE *adj* **SPARSER, SPARSEST** thinly distributed **SPARSELY** *adv*

SPARSITY *n* pl. **-TIES** the quality or state of being sparse

SPARTAN *adj* avoiding luxury and comfort

SPARTINA *n* pl. **-S** a salt-marsh grass of coastal regions

SPASM *v* **-ED, -ING, -S** to undergo an involuntary muscular contraction

SPASTIC *n* pl. **-S** one suffering from a paralysis with muscle spasms

SPAT *v* **SPATTED, SPATTING, SPATS** to strike lightly

SPATE *n* pl. **-S** a freshet

SPATHE *n* pl. **-S** a leaflike organ of certain plants **SPATHAL, SPATHED, SPATHOSE** *adj*

SPATHIC *adj* sparry

SPATIAL *adj* of or pertaining to space

SPATTED past tense of spat

SPATTER *v* **-ED, -ING, -S** to scatter in drops

SPATTING present participle of spat

SPATULA *n* pl. **-S** a mixing implement **SPATULAR** *adj*

SPATZLE *n* pl. **-S** spaetzle

SPAVIE *n* pl. **-S** spavin **SPAVIET** *adj*

SPAVIN *n* pl. **-S** a disease of horses **SPAVINED** *adj*

SPAWN *v* **-ED, -ING, -S** to deposit eggs

SPAWNER *n* pl. **-S** one that spawns

SPAY *v* **-ED, -ING, -S** to remove the ovaries of

SPEAK *v* **SPOKE** or **SPAKE, SPOKEN, SPEAKING, SPEAKS** to utter words

SPEAKER *n* pl. **-S** one that speaks

SPEAKING *n* pl. **-S** a speech or discourse

SPEAN *v* **-ED, -ING, -S** to wean

SPEAR *v* **-ED, -ING, -S** to pierce with a spear (a long, pointed weapon)

SPEARER *n* pl. **-S** one that spears

SPEARGUN *n* pl. **-S** a gun that shoots a spear

SPEARMAN *n* pl. **-MEN** a person armed with a spear

SPEC *v* **SPECCED, SPECCING, SPECS** to write specifications for

SPECIAL *adj* **-CIALER, -CIALEST** of a distinct kind or character

SPECIAL *n* pl. **-S** a special person or thing

SPECIATE *v* **-ATED, -ATING, -ATES** to undergo a type of evolutionary process

SPECIE *n* pl. **-S** coined money

SPECIFIC *n* pl. **-S** a remedy intended for a particular disease

SPECIFY *v* **-FIED, -FYING, -FIES** to state in detail

SPECIMEN *n* pl. **-S** a part or individual representative of a group or whole

SPECIOUS *adj* having a false look of truth or authenticity

SPECK *v* **-ED, -ING, -S** to mark with small spots

SPECKLE *v* **-LED, -LING, -LES** to speck

SPECS *n/pl* eyeglasses

SPECTATE *v* **-TATED, -TATING, -TATES** to attend and view

SPECTER *n* pl. **-S** a visible disembodied spirit

SPECTRA a pl. of spectrum

SPECTRAL *adj* resembling a specter

SPECTRE *n* pl. **-S** specter

SPECTRUM *n* pl. **-TRUMS** or **-TRA** an array of the components of a light wave

SPECULUM *n* pl. **-LUMS** or **-LA** a medical instrument **SPECULAR** *adj*

SPEECH *n* pl. **-ES** the faculty or act of speaking

SPEED *v* **SPED** or **SPEEDED, SPEEDING, SPEEDS** to move swiftly

SPEEDER *n* pl. **-S** one that speeds

SPEEDIER comparative of speedy

SPEEDIEST superlative of speedy

SPEEDILY *adv* in a speedy manner

SPEEDING *n* pl. **-S** the act of driving faster than the law allows

SPEEDO *n* pl. **SPEEDOS** a speedometer

SPEEDUP *n* pl. **-S** an acceleration of production without an increase in pay

SPEEDWAY *n* pl. **-WAYS** a road designed for rapid travel

SPEEDY *adj* **SPEEDIER, SPEEDIEST** swift

SPEEL *v* **-ED, -ING, -S** to climb

SPEER *v* **-ED, -ING, -S** to inquire

SPEERING *n* pl. **-S** inquiry

SPEIL	*v* **-ED, -ING, -S** to speel	**SPHERIEST**	superlative of sphery
SPEIR	*v* **-ED, -ING, -S** to speer	**SPHERING**	present participle of sphere
SPEISE	*n* pl. **-S** speiss	**SPHEROID**	*n* pl. **-S** a type of geometric solid
SPEISS	*n* pl. **-ES** a metallic mixture obtained in smelting certain ores	**SPHERULE**	*n* pl. **-S** a small sphere
SPELAEAN	*adj* spelean	**SPHERY**	*adj* **SPHERIER, SPHERIEST** resembling a sphere
SPELEAN	*adj* living in caves	**SPHINGES**	a pl. of sphinx
SPELL	*v* **SPELLED** or **SPELT, SPELLING, SPELLS** to name or write the letters of in order	**SPHINGID**	*n* pl. **-S** the hawkmoth
		SPHINX	*n* pl. **SPHINXES** or **SPHINGES** a monster in Egyptian mythology
SPELLER	*n* pl. **-S** one that spells words	**SPHYGMUS**	*n* pl. **-ES** the pulse **SPHYGMIC** *adj*
SPELLING	*n* pl. **-S** a sequence of letters composing a word	**SPHYNX**	*n* pl. **-ES** a cat of a breed of hairless cats
SPELT	*n* pl. **-S** a variety of wheat	**SPICA**	*n* pl. **-CAS** or **-CAE** an ear of grain **SPICATE, SPICATED** *adj*
SPELTER	*n* pl. **-S** zinc in the form of ingots		
SPELTZ	*n* pl. **-ES** spelt	**SPICCATO**	*n* pl. **-TOS** a method of playing a stringed instrument
SPELUNK	*v* **-ED, -ING, -S** to explore caves		
SPENCE	*n* pl. **-S** a pantry	**SPICE**	*v* **SPICED, SPICING, SPICES** to season with a spice (an aromatic vegetable substance)
SPENCER	*n* pl. **-S** a trysail		
SPEND	*v* **SPENT, SPENDING, SPENDS** to pay out	**SPICER**	*n* pl. **-S** one that spices
		SPICERY	*n* pl. **-ERIES** a spicy quality
SPENDER	*n* pl. **-S** one that spends	**SPICEY**	*adj* **SPICIER, SPICIEST** spicy
SPENDY	*adj* **SPENDIER, SPENDIEST** expensive	**SPICIER**	comparative of spicy
		SPICIEST	superlative of spicy
SPENSE	*n* pl. **-S** spence	**SPICILY**	*adv* in a spicy manner
SPENT	past tense of spend	**SPICING**	present participle of spice
SPERM	*n* pl. **-S** a male gamete **SPERMIC** *adj*	**SPICULA**	*n* pl. **-LAE** spicule **SPICULAR** *adj*
SPERMARY	*n* pl. **-RIES** an organ in which sperms are formed	**SPICULE**	*n* pl. **-S** a needlelike structure
		SPICULUM	*n* pl. **-LA** spicule
SPERMINE	*n* pl. **-S** a chemical compound	**SPICY**	*adj* **SPICIER, SPICIEST** containing spices
SPERMOUS	*adj* resembling or made up of sperms		
		SPIDER	*n* pl. **-S** a type of arachnid
SPEW	*v* **-ED, -ING, -S** to vomit	**SPIDERY**	*adj* **-DERIER, -DERIEST** resembling a spider
SPEWER	*n* pl. **-S** one that spews		
SPHAGNUM	*n* pl. **-S** a grayish moss	**SPIED**	past tense of spy
SPHENE	*n* pl. **-S** a mineral	**SPIEGEL**	*n* pl. **-S** a type of cast iron
SPHENIC	*adj* shaped like a wedge	**SPIEL**	*v* **-ED, -ING, -S** to talk at length
SPHENOID	*n* pl. **-S** a bone of the skull	**SPIELER**	*n* pl. **-S** one that spiels
SPHERAL	*adj* of, pertaining to, or having the form of a sphere	**SPIER**	*v* **-ED, -ING, -S** to speer
		SPIES	present 3d person sing. of spy
SPHERE	*v* **SPHERED, SPHERING, SPHERES** to form into a sphere (a type of geometric solid)	**SPIFF**	*v* **-ED, -ING, -S** to make spiffy
		SPIFFING	*adj* spiffy
		SPIFFY	*v* **-FIED, -FYING, -FIES** to make stylish
SPHERIC	*adj* spheral		
SPHERICS	*n/pl* the geometry of figures on the surface of a sphere	**SPIFFY**	*adj* **-FIER, -FIEST** stylish **SPIFFILY** *adv*
SPHERIER	comparative of sphery	**SPIGOT**	*n* pl. **-S** a faucet

SPIKE   *v* **SPIKED, SPIKING, SPIKES** to fasten with a spike (a long, thick nail)

SPIKELET   *n* pl. **-S** a type of flower cluster

SPIKER   *n* pl. **-S** one that spikes

SPIKEY   *adj* **SPIKIER, SPIKIEST** spiky

SPIKING   present participle of spike

SPIKY   *adj* **SPIKIER, SPIKIEST** resembling a spike **SPIKILY** *adv*

SPILE   *v* **SPILED, SPILING, SPILES** to stop up with a wooden plug

SPILIKIN   *n* pl. **-S** a strip of wood used in a game

SPILING   *n* pl. **-S** a piling

SPILL   *v* **SPILLED** or **SPILT, SPILLING, SPILLS** to cause to run out of a container

SPILLAGE   *n* pl. **-S** something that is spilled

SPILLER   *n* pl. **-S** one that spills

SPILLWAY   *n* pl. **-WAYS** a channel for surplus water in a reservoir

SPILT   a past tense of spill

SPILTH   *n* pl. **-S** spillage

SPIN   *v* **SPUN, SPINNING, SPINS** to draw out and twist into threads

SPINACH   *n* pl. **-ES** a cultivated herb **SPINACHY** *adj*

SPINAGE   *n* pl. **-S** spinach

SPINAL   *n* pl. **-S** an injection of an anesthetic into the spinal cord

SPINALLY   *adv* with respect to the spine

SPINATE   *adj* bearing thorns

SPINDLE   *v* **-DLED, -DLING, -DLES** to impale on a slender rod

SPINDLER   *n* pl. **-S** one that spindles

SPINDLY   *adj* **-DLIER, -DLIEST** long and slender

SPINE   *n* pl. **-S** the vertebral column **SPINED** *adj*

SPINEL   *n* pl. **-S** a mineral

SPINELLE   *n* pl. **-S** spinel

SPINET   *n* pl. **-S** a small piano

SPINIER   comparative of spiny

SPINIEST   superlative of spiny

SPINIFEX   *n* pl. **-ES** an Australian grass

SPINLESS   *adj* having no rotation

SPINNER   *n* pl. **-S** one that spins

SPINNERY   *n* pl. **-NERIES** a spinning mill

SPINNEY   *n* pl. **-NEYS** a thicket

SPINNING   *n* pl. **-S** the act of one that spins

SPINNY   *n* pl. **-NIES** spinney

SPINOFF   *n* pl. **-S** a new application or incidental result

SPINOR   *n* pl. **-S** a type of mathematical vector

SPINOSE   *adj* spiny

SPINOUS   *adj* spiny

SPINOUT   *n* pl. **-S** a rotational skid by an automobile

SPINSTER   *n* pl. **-S** an unmarried woman who is past the usual age for marrying

SPINTO   *n* pl. **-TOS** a singing voice that is lyric and dramatic

SPINULA   *n* pl. **-LAE** spinule

SPINULE   *n* pl. **-S** a small thorn

SPINY   *adj* **SPINIER, SPINIEST** bearing or covered with thorns

SPIRACLE   *n* pl. **-S** an orifice through which breathing occurs

SPIRAEA   *n* pl. **-S** spirea

SPIRAL   *v* **-RALED, -RALING, -RALS** or **-RALLED, -RALLING, -RALS** to move like a spiral (a type of plane curve)

SPIRALLY   *adv* in a spiral manner

SPIRANT   *n* pl. **-S** a speech sound produced by the forcing of breath through a narrow passage

SPIRE   *v* **SPIRED, SPIRING, SPIRES** to rise in a tapering manner

SPIREA   *n* pl. **-S** a flowering shrub

SPIREM   *n* pl. **-S** spireme

SPIREME   *n* pl. **-S** a filament forming part of a cell nucleus during mitosis

SPIRIER   comparative of spiry

SPIRIEST   superlative of spiry

SPIRILLA   *n/pl* spirally twisted, aerobic bacteria

SPIRING   present participle of spire

SPIRIT   *v* **-ED, -ING, -S** to carry off secretly

SPIROID   *adj* resembling a spiral

SPIRT   *v* **-ED, -ING, -S** to spurt

SPIRULA   *n* pl. **-LAS** or **-LAE** a spiral-shelled mollusk

SPIRY   *adj* **SPIRIER, SPIRIEST** tall, slender, and tapering

SPIT   *v* **SPITTED, SPITTING, SPITS** to impale on a spit (a pointed rod on which meat is turned)

SPITAL   *n* pl. **-S** a hospital

SPITBALL   *n* pl. **-S** a type of pitch in baseball

SPITE   *v* **SPITED, SPITING, SPITES** to treat with malice

SPITEFUL   *adj* **-FULLER, -FULLEST** malicious

SPITFIRE   *n* pl. **-S** a quick-tempered person

SPITTED   past tense of spit

SPITTER   *n* pl. **-S** a spitball

SPITTING   present participle of spit

SPITTLE   *n* pl. **-S** saliva

SPITTOON   *n* pl. **-S** a receptacle for saliva

SPITZ   *n* pl. **-ES** a dog having a heavy coat

SPIV   *n* pl. **-S** a petty criminal **SPIVVY** *adj*

SPLAKE   *n* pl. **-S** a freshwater fish

SPLASH   *v* **-ED, -ING, -ES** to scatter a liquid about

SPLASHER   *n* pl. **-S** one that splashes

SPLASHY   *adj* **SPLASHIER, SPLASHIEST** showy

SPLAT   *v* **SPLATTED, SPLATTING, SPLATS** to flatten on impact

SPLATTER   *v* **-ED, -ING, -S** to spatter

SPLAY   *v* **-ED, -ING, -S** to spread out

SPLEEN   *n* pl. **-S** a ductless organ of the body

SPLEENY   *adj* **SPLEENIER, SPLEENIEST** peevish

SPLENDID   *adj* **-DIDER, -DIDEST** magnificent

SPLENDOR   *n* pl. **-S** magnificence

SPLENIAL   *adj* pertaining to the splenius

SPLENIC   *adj* pertaining to the spleen

SPLENIUM   *n* pl. **-NIA** a surgical bandage

SPLENIUS   *n* pl. **-NII** a muscle of the neck

SPLENT   *n* pl. **-S** a splint

SPLICE   *v* **SPLICED, SPLICING, SPLICES** to join at the ends

SPLICER   *n* pl. **-S** one that splices

SPLIFF   *n* pl. **-S** a marijuana cigarette

SPLINE   *v* **SPLINED, SPLINING, SPLINES** to provide with a spline (a key that connects two rotating mechanical parts)

SPLINT   *v* **-ED, -ING, -S** to brace with a splint (a thin piece of wood)

SPLINTER   *v* **-ED, -ING, -S** to split into sharp, slender pieces

SPLIT   *v* **SPLIT, SPLITTING, SPLITS** to separate lengthwise

SPLITTER   *n* pl. **-S** one that splits

SPLODGE   *v* **SPLODGED, SPLODGING, SPLODGES** to splotch

SPLORE   *n* pl. **-S** a carousal

SPLOSH   *v* **-ED, -ING, -ES** to splash

SPLOTCH   *v* **-ED, -ING, -ES** to mark with large, irregular spots

SPLOTCHY   *adj* **SPLOTCHIER, SPLOTCHIEST** splotched

SPLURGE   *v* **SPLURGED, SPLURGING, SPLURGES** to spend money lavishly

SPLURGER   *n* pl. **-S** one that splurges

SPLURGY   *adj* **SPLURGIER, SPLURGIEST** tending to splurge

SPLUTTER   *v* **-ED, -ING, -S** to speak rapidly and confusedly

SPODE   *n* pl. **-S** a fine china

SPODOSOL   *n* pl. **-S** an acidic forest soil

SPOIL   *v* **SPOILED** or **SPOILT, SPOILING, SPOILS** to impair the value or quality of

SPOILAGE   *n* pl. **-S** something that is spoiled or wasted

SPOILER   *n* pl. **-S** one that spoils

SPOKE   *v* **SPOKED, SPOKING, SPOKES** to provide with spokes (rods that support the rim of a wheel)

SPOKEN   past participle of speak

SPOLIATE   *v* **-ATED, -ATING, -ATES** to plunder

SPONDAIC   *n* pl. **-S** a spondee

SPONDEE   *n* pl. **-S** a type of metrical foot

SPONGE   *v* **SPONGED, SPONGING, SPONGES** to wipe with a sponge (a mass of absorbent material)

SPONGER   *n* pl. **-S** one that sponges

SPONGIER   comparative of spongy

SPONGIEST   superlative of spongy

SPONGILY   *adv* in a spongy manner

SPONGIN   *n* pl. **-S** a fibrous material

SPONGING   present participle of sponge

SPONGY   *adj* **SPONGIER, SPONGIEST** resembling a sponge

SPONSAL   *adj* pertaining to marriage

SPONSION   *n* pl. **-S** the act of sponsoring

SPONSON   *n* pl. **-S** a projection from the side of a ship

SPONSOR *v* **-ED, -ING, -S** to make oneself responsible for

SPONTOON *n* pl. **-S** a spear-like weapon

SPOOF *v* **-ED, -ING, -S** to ridicule in fun

SPOOFER *n* pl. **-S** one that spoofs

SPOOFERY *n* pl. **-ERIES** good-natured ridicule

SPOOFY *adj* humorously satiric

SPOOK *v* **-ED, -ING, -S** to scare

SPOOKERY *n* pl. **-ERIES** something spooky

SPOOKISH *adj* spooky

SPOOKY *adj* **SPOOKIER, SPOOKIEST** scary **SPOOKILY** *adv*

SPOOL *v* **-ED, -ING, -S** to wind on a small cylinder

SPOOLER *n* pl. **-S** one that spools

SPOOLING *n* pl. **-S** the temporary storage of data for later output

SPOON *v* **-ED, -ING, -S** to take up with a spoon (a type of eating utensil)

SPOONEY *adj* **SPOONIER, SPOONIEST** spoony

SPOONEY *n* pl. **-EYS** a spoony

SPOONFUL *n* pl. **SPOONFULS** or **SPOONSFUL** as much as a spoon can hold

SPOONSFUL a pl. of spoonful

SPOONY *adj* **SPOONIER, SPOONIEST** overly sentimental **SPOONILY** *adv*

SPOONY *n* pl. **SPOONIES** a spoony person

SPOOR *v* **-ED, -ING, -S** to track

SPORADIC *adj* occurring at irregular intervals

SPORAL *adj* of, pertaining to, or resembling a spore

SPORE *v* **SPORED, SPORING, SPORES** to produce spores (asexual, usually single-celled reproductive bodies)

SPOROID *adj* resembling a spore

SPOROZOA *n/pl* parasitic one-celled animals

SPORRAN *n* pl. **-S** a large purse worn by Scottish Highlanders

SPORT *v* **-ED, -ING, -S** to frolic

SPORTER *n* pl. **-S** one that sports

SPORTFUL *adj* sportive

SPORTIF *adj* sporty

SPORTIVE *adj* playful

SPORTY *adj* **SPORTIER, SPORTIEST** showy **SPORTILY** *adv*

SPORULE *n* pl. **-S** a small spore **SPORULAR** *adj*

SPOT *v* **SPOTTED, SPOTTING, SPOTS** to mark with spots (small, roundish discolorations)

SPOTLESS *adj* perfectly clean

SPOTLIT a past tense of spotlight

SPOTTER *n* pl. **-S** one that spots

SPOTTING present participle of spot

SPOTTY *adj* **-TIER, -TIEST** marked with spots **SPOTTILY** *adv*

SPOUSAL *n* pl. **-S** marriage

SPOUSE *v* **SPOUSED, SPOUSING, SPOUSES** to marry

SPOUT *v* **-ED, -ING, -S** to eject in a rapid stream

SPOUTER *n* pl. **-S** one that spouts

SPOUTING *n* pl. **-S** a channel for draining off water from a roof

SPRADDLE *v* **-DLED, -DLING, -DLES** to straddle

SPRAG *n* pl. **-S** a device used to prevent a vehicle from rolling backward

SPRAIN *v* **-ED, -ING, -S** to weaken by a sudden and violent twisting or wrenching

SPRANG *n* pl. **-S** a weaving technique to form an openwork mesh

SPRAT *n* pl. **-S** a small herring

SPRATTLE *v* **-TLED, -TLING, -TLES** to struggle

SPRAWL *v* **-ED, -ING, -S** to stretch out ungracefully

SPRAWLER *n* pl. **-S** one that sprawls

SPRAWLY *adj* **SPRAWLIER, SPRAWLIEST** tending to sprawl

SPRAY *v* **-ED, -ING, -S** to disperse in fine particles

SPRAYER *n* pl. **-S** one that sprays

SPREAD *v* **SPREAD, SPREADING, SPREADS** to open or expand over a larger area

SPREADER *n* pl. **-S** one that spreads

SPREE *n* pl. **-S** an unrestrained indulgence in an activity

SPRENT *adj* sprinkled over

SPRIER a comparative of spry

SPRIEST a superlative of spry

SPRIG *v* **SPRIGGED, SPRIGGING, SPRIGS** to fasten with small, thin nails

SPRIGGER *n* pl. **-S** one that sprigs

SPRIGGY *adj* **-GIER, -GIEST** having small branches

SPRIGHT *n* pl. **-S** sprite

SPRING *v* **SPRANG** or **SPRUNG, SPRINGING, SPRINGS** to move upward suddenly and swiftly

SPRINGAL *n* pl. **-S** a young man

SPRINGE *v* **SPRINGED, SPRINGEING, SPRINGES** to catch with a type of snare

SPRINGER *n* pl. **-S** one that springs

SPRINGY *adj* **SPRINGIER, SPRINGIEST** resilient

SPRINKLE *v* **-KLED, -KLING, -KLES** to scatter drops or particles on

SPRINT *v* **-ED, -ING, -S** to run at top speed

SPRINTER *n* pl. **-S** one that sprints

SPRIT *n* pl. **-S** a ship's spar

SPRITE *n* pl. **-S** an elf or fairy

SPRITZ *v* **-ED, -ING, -ES** to spray

SPRITZER *n* pl. **-S** a beverage of white wine and soda water

SPROCKET *n* pl. **-S** a toothlike projection that engages with the links of a chain

SPROUT *v* **-ED, -ING, -S** to begin to grow

SPRUCE *adj* **SPRUCER, SPRUCEST** neat and trim in appearance **SPRUCELY** *adv*

SPRUCE *v* **SPRUCED, SPRUCING, SPRUCES** to make spruce

SPRUCY *adj* **SPRUCIER, SPRUCIEST** spruce

SPRUE *n* pl. **-S** a tropical disease

SPRUG *n* pl. **-S** a sparrow

SPRUNG a past tense of spring

SPRY *adj* **SPRYER, SPRYEST** or **SPRIER, SPRIEST** nimble **SPRYLY** *adv*

SPRYNESS *n* pl. **-ES** the quality or state of being spry

SPUD *v* **SPUDDED, SPUDDING, SPUDS** to remove with a spade-like tool

SPUDDER *n* pl. **-S** a tool for removing bark from trees

SPUE *v* **SPUED, SPUING, SPUES** to spew

SPUME *v* **SPUMED, SPUMING, SPUMES** to foam

SPUMIER comparative of spumy

SPUMIEST superlative of spumy

SPUMING present participle of spume

SPUMONE *n* pl. **-S** an Italian ice cream

SPUMONI *n* pl. **-S** spumone

SPUMOUS *adj* spumy

SPUMY *adj* **SPUMIER, SPUMIEST** foamy

SPUN past tense of spin

SPUNK *v* **-ED, -ING, -S** to begin to burn

SPUNKIE *n* pl. **-S** a light caused by the combustion of marsh gas

SPUNKY *adj* **SPUNKIER, SPUNKIEST** plucky **SPUNKILY** *adv*

SPUR *v* **SPURRED, SPURRING, SPURS** to urge on with a spur (a horseman's goad)

SPURGALL *v* **-ED, -ING, -S** to injure with a spur

SPURGE *n* pl. **-S** a tropical plant

SPURIOUS *adj* not genuine

SPURN *v* **-ED, -ING, -S** to reject with contempt

SPURNER *n* pl. **-S** one that spurns

SPURRED past tense of spur

SPURRER *n* pl. **-S** one that spurs

SPURREY *n* pl. **-REYS** spurry

SPURRIER *n* pl. **-S** one that makes spurs

SPURRING present participle of spur

SPURRY *n* pl. **-RIES** a European weed

SPURT *v* **-ED, -ING, -S** to gush forth

SPURTER *n* pl. **-S** one that spurts

SPURTLE *n* pl. **-S** a stick for stirring porridge

SPUTNIK *n* pl. **-S** a Soviet artificial earth satellite

SPUTTER *v* **-ED, -ING, -S** to eject particles in short bursts

SPUTTERY *adj* ejecting in short bursts

SPUTUM *n* pl. **-TA** saliva

SPY *v* **SPIED, SPYING, SPIES** to watch secretly

SPYGLASS *n* pl. **-ES** a small telescope

SQUAB *n* pl. **-S** a young pigeon

SQUABBLE *v* **-BLED, -BLING, -BLES** to quarrel

SQUABBY *adj* **-BIER, -BIEST** short and fat

SQUAD *v* **SQUADDED, SQUADDING, SQUADS** to form into squads (small organized groups)

SQUADRON *v* **-ED, -ING, -S** to arrange in squadrons (units of military organization)

SQUALENE *n* pl. **-S** a chemical compound

SQUALID *adj* **-IDER, -IDEST** marked by filthiness caused by neglect or poverty

SQUALL *v* **-ED, -ING, -S** to cry or scream loudly

SQUALLER *n pl.* **-S** one that squalls

SQUALLY *adj* **SQUALLIER, SQUALLIEST** gusty

SQUALOR *n pl.* **-S** the quality or state of being squalid

SQUAMA *n pl.* **-MAE** a scale **SQUAMOSE, SQUAMOUS** *adj*

SQUAMATE *n pl.* **-S** any of an order of reptiles

SQUANDER *v* **-ED, -ING, -S** to spend wastefully

SQUARE *adj* **SQUARER, SQUAREST** having four equal sides and four right angles; rigidly conventional

SQUARE *v* **SQUARED, SQUARING, SQUARES** to make square

SQUARELY *adv* in a straightforward and honest manner

SQUARER *n pl.* **-S** one that squares

SQUAREST superlative of square

SQUARING present participle of square

SQUARISH *adj* somewhat square

SQUARK *n pl.* **-S** the hypothetical boson analogue of a quark

SQUASH *v* **-ED, -ING, -ES** to press into a pulp or flat mass

SQUASHER *n pl.* **-S** one that squashes

SQUASHY *adj* **SQUASHIER, SQUASHIEST** soft and moist

SQUAT *adj* **SQUATTER, SQUATTEST** short and thick **SQUATLY** *adv*

SQUAT *v* **SQUATTED, SQUATTING, SQUATS** to bend one's knees and sit on one's heels

SQUATTER *v* **-ED, -ING, -S** to move through water

SQUATTY *adj* **-TIER, -TIEST** squat

SQUAWK *v* **-ED, -ING, -S** to utter a loud, harsh cry

SQUAWKER *n pl.* **-S** one that squawks

SQUEAK *v* **-ED, -ING, -S** to make a sharp, high-pitched sound

SQUEAKER *n pl.* **-S** one that squeaks

SQUEAKY *adj* **SQUEAKIER, SQUEAKIEST** tending to squeak

SQUEAL *v* **-ED, -ING, -S** to utter a sharp, shrill cry

SQUEALER *n pl.* **-S** one that squeals

SQUEEGEE *v* **-GEED, -GEEING, -GEES** to wipe with a squeegee (an implement for removing water from a surface)

SQUEEZE *v* **SQUEEZED, SQUEEZING, SQUEEZES** to press hard upon

SQUEEZER *n pl.* **-S** one that squeezes

SQUEG *v* **SQUEGGED, SQUEGGING, SQUEGS** to oscillate in an irregular manner

SQUELCH *v* **-ED, -ING, -ES** to squash

SQUELCHY *adj* **SQUELCHIER, SQUELCHIEST** squashy

SQUIB *v* **SQUIBBED, SQUIBBING, SQUIBS** to lampoon

SQUID *v* **SQUIDDED, SQUIDDING, SQUIDS** to fish for squid (ten-armed marine mollusks)

SQUIFFED *adj* drunk

SQUIFFY *adj* **-FIER, -FIEST** squiffed

SQUIGGLE *v* **-GLED, -GLING, -GLES** to wriggle

SQUIGGLY *adj* **-GLIER, -GLIEST** wriggly

SQUILGEE *v* **-GEED, -GEEING, -GEES** to squeegee

SQUILL *n pl.* **-S** a Eurasian herb

SQUILLA *n pl.* **-LAS** or **-LAE** a burrowing crustacean

SQUINCH *v* **-ED, -ING, -ES** to squint

SQUINNY *adj* **-NIER, -NIEST** squinty

SQUINNY *v* **-NIED, -NYING, -NIES** to squint

SQUINT *adj* **SQUINTER, SQUINTEST** cross-eyed

SQUINT *v* **-ED, -ING, -S** to look with the eyes partly closed

SQUINTER *n pl.* **-S** one that squints

SQUINTY *adj* **SQUINTIER, SQUINTIEST** marked by squinting

SQUIRE *v* **SQUIRED, SQUIRING, SQUIRES** to serve as a squire (an escort)

SQUIREEN *n pl.* **-S** an owner of a small estate

SQUIRISH *adj* of, resembling, or befitting a squire

SQUIRM *v* **-ED, -ING, -S** to wriggle

SQUIRMER *n pl.* **-S** one that squirms

SQUIRMY *adj* **SQUIRMIER, SQUIRMIEST** wriggly

SQUIRREL *v* **-RELED, -RELING, -RELS** or **-RELLED, -RELLING, -RELS** to store up for future use

SQUIRT	*v* **-ED, -ING, -S** to eject in a thin, swift stream
SQUIRTER	*n* pl. **-S** one that squirts
SQUISH	*v* **-ED, -ING, -ES** to squash
SQUISHY	*adj* **SQUISHIER, SQUISHIEST** squashy
SQUOOSH	*v* **-ED, -ING, -ES** to squash
SQUOOSHY	*adj* **SQUOOSHIER, SQUOOSHIEST** squashy
SQUUSH	*v* **-ED, -ING, -ES** to squash
SRADDHA	*n* pl. **-S** sradha
SRADHA	*n* pl. **-S** a Hindu ceremonial offering
SRI	*n* pl. **-S** mister; sir — used as a Hindu title of respect
STAB	*v* **STABBED, STABBING, STABS** to pierce with a pointed weapon
STABBER	*n* pl. **-S** one that stabs
STABILE	*n* pl. **-S** a stationary abstract sculpture
STABLE	*adj* **-BLER, -BLEST** resistant to sudden change or position or condition
STABLE	*v* **-BLED, -BLING, -BLES** to put in a stable (a shelter for domestic animals)
STABLER	*n* pl. **-S** one that keeps a stable
STABLING	*n* pl. **-S** accommodation for animals in a stable
STABLISH	*v* **-ED, -ING, -ES** to establish
STABLY	*adv* in a stable manner
STACCATO	*n* pl. **-TOS** or **-TI** a musical passage marked by the short, clear-cut playing of tones
STACK	*v* **-ED, -ING, -S** to pile
STACKER	*n* pl. **-S** one that stacks
STACKUP	*n* pl. **-S** an arrangement of circling airplanes over an airport waiting to land
STACTE	*n* pl. **-S** a spice used by the ancient Jews in making incense
STADDLE	*n* pl. **-S** a platform on which hay is stacked
STADE	*n* pl. **-S** an ancient Greek unit of length
STADIA	*n* pl. **-S** a method of surveying distances
STADIUM	*n* pl. **-S** a structure in which athletic events are held
STAFF	*v* **-ED, -ING, -S** to provide with a staff (a body of assistants)
STAFFER	*n* pl. **-S** a member of a staff
STAG	*v* **STAGGED, STAGGING, STAGS** to attend a social function without a female companion
STAGE	*v* **STAGED, STAGING, STAGES** to produce for public view
STAGEFUL	*n* pl. **-S** as much or as many as a stage can hold
STAGER	*n* pl. **-S** an experienced person
STAGEY	*adj* **STAGIER, STAGIEST** stagy
STAGGARD	*n* pl. **-S** a full-grown male red deer
STAGGART	*n* pl. **-S** staggard
STAGGED	past tense of stag
STAGGER	*v* **-ED, -ING, -S** to walk or stand unsteadily
STAGGERY	*adj* unsteady
STAGGIE	*n* pl. **-S** a colt
STAGGING	present participle of stag
STAGGY	*adj* **-GIER, -GIEST** having the appearance of a mature male
STAGIER	comparative of stagey and stagy
STAGIEST	superlative of stagey and stagy
STAGILY	*adv* in a stagy manner
STAGING	*n* pl. **-S** a temporary platform
STAGNANT	*adj* not moving or flowing
STAGNATE	*v* **-NATED, -NATING, -NATES** to become stagnant
STAGY	*adj* **STAGIER, STAGIEST** having a theatrical quality
STAID	*adj* **STAIDER, STAIDEST** sober and sedate **STAIDLY** *adv*
STAIG	*n* pl. **-S** a colt
STAIN	*v* **-ED, -ING, -S** to discolor or dirty
STAINER	*n* pl. **-S** one that stains
STAIR	*n* pl. **-S** a rest for the foot used in going from one level to another
STAIRWAY	*n* pl. **-WAYS** a flight of stairs
STAITHE	*n* pl. **-S** a wharf equipped for transferring coal from railroad cars into ships
STAKE	*v* **STAKED, STAKING, STAKES** to fasten with a stake (a pointed piece of wood or metal)
STAKEOUT	*n* pl. **-S** a surveillance of an area especially by the police
STALAG	*n* pl. **-S** a German prisoner-of-war camp
STALE	*adj* **STALER, STALEST** not fresh **STALELY** *adv*

STALE   *v* **STALED, STALING, STALES** to become stale

STALK   *v* **-ED, -ING, -S** to pursue stealthily

STALKER   *n* pl. **-S** one that stalks

STALKING   *n* pl. **-S** the act of one that stalks

STALKY   *adj* **STALKIER, STALKIEST** long and slender **STALKILY** *adv*

STALL   *v* **-ED, -ING, -S** to stop the progress of

STALLION   *n* pl. **-S** an uncastrated male horse

STALWART   *n* pl. **-S** an unwavering partisan

STAMEN   *n* pl. **-S** the pollen-bearing organ of flowering plants **STAMENED** *adj*

STAMINA   *n* pl. **-S** endurance **STAMINAL** *adj*

STAMMEL   *n* pl. **-S** a red color

STAMMER   *v* **-ED, -ING, -S** to speak with involuntary breaks and pauses

STAMP   *v* **-ED, -ING, -S** to bring the foot down heavily

STAMPEDE   *v* **-PEDED, -PEDING, -PEDES** to cause to run away in headlong panic

STAMPER   *n* pl. **-S** one that stamps

STANCE   *n* pl. **-S** a manner of standing

STANCH   *adj* **STANCHER, STANCHEST** staunch

STANCH   *v* **-ED, -ING, -ES** to stop the flow of blood from

STANCHER   *n* pl. **-S** one that stanches

STANCHLY   *adv* in a stanch manner

STAND   *v* **STOOD, STANDING, STANDS** to assume or maintain an upright position

STANDARD   *n* pl. **-S** an established measure of comparison

STANDBY   *n* pl. **-BYS** one that can be relied on

STANDEE   *n* pl. **-S** one who stands because of the lack of seats

STANDER   *n* pl. **-S** one that stands

STANDING   *n* pl. **-S** a position or condition in society

STANDISH   *n* pl. **-ES** a receptacle for pens and ink

STANDOFF   *n* pl. **-S** a tie or draw, as in a game

STANDOUT   *n* pl. **-S** one that shows marked superiority

STANDPAT   *adj* resisting or opposing change

STANDUP   *n* pl. **-S** a comic monologue by a performer alone on a stage

STANE   *v* **STANED, STANING, STANES** to stone

STANG   *v* **-ED, -ING, -S** to sting

STANHOPE   *n* pl. **-S** a light, open carriage

STANINE   *n* pl. **-S** one of the nine classes into which a set of scores are divided

STANING   present participle of stane

STANK   *n* pl. **-S** a pond

STANNARY   *n* pl. **-RIES** a tin-mining region

STANNIC   *adj* pertaining to tin

STANNITE   *n* pl. **-S** an ore of tin

STANNOUS   *adj* pertaining to tin

STANNUM   *n* pl. **-S** tin

STANOL   *n* pl. **-S** a fully saturated phytosterol

STANZA   *n* pl. **-S** a division of a poem **STANZAED, STANZAIC** *adj*

STAPEDES   pl. of stapes

STAPELIA   *n* pl. **-S** an African plant

STAPES   *n* pl. **-PEDES** a bone of the middle ear

STAPH   *n* pl. **-S** any of various spherical bacteria

STAPLE   *v* **-PLED, -PLING, -PLES** to fasten by means of a U-shaped metal loop

STAPLER   *n* pl. **-S** a stapling device

STAR   *v* **STARRED, STARRING, STARS** to shine as a star (a natural luminous body visible in the sky)

STARCH   *v* **-ED, -ING, -ES** to treat with starch (a solid carbohydrate)

STARCHY   *adj* **STARCHIER, STARCHIEST** containing starch

STARDOM   *n* pl. **-S** the status of a preeminent performer

STARDUST   *n* pl. **-S** a romantic quality

STARE   *v* **STARED, STARING, STARES** to gaze fixedly

STARER   *n* pl. **-S** one that stares

STARETS   *n* pl. **STARTSY** a spiritual adviser in the Eastern Orthodox Church

STARFISH   *n* pl. **-ES** a star-shaped marine animal

STARGAZE   *v* **-GAZED, -GAZING, -GAZES** to gaze at the stars

STARING   present participle of stare

STARK   *adj* **STARKER, STARKEST** harsh in appearance **STARKLY** *adv*

STARKERS   *adj* naked

STARLESS *adj* having no stars

STARLET *n* pl. **-S** a small star

STARLIKE *adj* resembling a star

STARLING *n* pl. **-S** a European bird

STARLIT *adj* lighted by the stars

STARNOSE *n* pl. **-S** a burrowing mammal

STARRED past tense of star

STARRING present participle of star

STARRY *adj* **-RIER, -RIEST** abounding with stars

STARSHIP *n* pl. **-S** a spaceship for interstellar travel

START *v* **-ED, -ING, -S** to set out

STARTER *n* pl. **-S** one that starts

STARTLE *v* **-TLED, -TLING, -TLES** to frighten or surprise suddenly

STARTLER *n* pl. **-S** one that startles

STARTSY pl. of starets

STARTUP *n* pl. **-S** the act of starting something

STARVE *v* **STARVED, STARVING, STARVES** to die from lack of food

STARVER *n* pl. **-S** one that starves

STARWORT *n* pl. **-S** a flowering plant

STASES pl. of stasis

STASH *v* **-ED, -ING, -ES** to store in a secret place

STASIMON *n* pl. **-MA** a choral ode in ancient Greek drama

STASIS *n* pl. **STASES** a stoppage of the normal flow of bodily fluids

STAT *n* pl. **-S** a statistic

STATABLE *adj* capable of being stated

STATAL *adj* pertaining to a national government

STATANT *adj* standing with all feet on the ground — used of a heraldic animal

STATE *v* **STATED, STATING, STATES** to set forth in words

STATEDLY *adv* regularly

STATELY *adj* **-LIER, -LIEST** dignified

STATER *n* pl. **-S** one that states

STATIC *n* pl. **-S** random noise produced in a radio or television receiver **STATICAL** *adj*

STATICE *n* pl. **-S** a flowering plant

STATICKY *adj* marked by static

STATIN *n* pl. **-S** any of a class of drugs that reduce serum cholesterol levels

STATING present participle of state

STATION *v* **-ED, -ING, -S** to assign to a position

STATISM *n* pl. **-S** a theory of government

STATIST *n* pl. **-S** an adherent of statism

STATIVE *n* pl. **-S** a verb that expresses a condition

STATOR *n* pl. **-S** the part of a machine about which the rotor revolves

STATUARY *n* pl. **-ARIES** a group of statues

STATUE *n* pl. **-S** a three-dimensional work of art **STATUED** *adj*

STATURE *n* pl. **-S** the natural height of a human or animal body

STATUS *n* pl. **-ES** relative position

STATUSY *adj* conferring prestige

STATUTE *n* pl. **-S** a law enacted by the legislative branch of a government

STAUMREL *n* pl. **-S** a dolt

STAUNCH *adj* **STAUNCHER, STAUNCHEST** firm and dependable

STAUNCH *v* **-ED, -ING, -ES** to stanch

STAVE *v* **STAVED** or **STOVE, STAVING, STAVES** to drive or thrust away

STAW a past tense of steal

STAY *v* **STAYED** or **STAID, STAYING, STAYS** to continue in a place or condition

STAYER *n* pl. **-S** one that stays

STAYSAIL *n* pl. **-S** a type of sail

STEAD *v* **-ED, -ING, -S** to be of advantage to

STEADIED past tense of steady

STEADIER *n* pl. **-S** one that steadies

STEADING *n* pl. **-S** a small farm

STEADY *adj* **STEADIER, STEADIEST** firm in position **STEADILY** *adv*

STEADY *v* **STEADIED, STEADYING, STEADIES** to make steady

STEAK *n* pl. **-S** a slice of meat

STEAL *v* **STOLE** or **STAW, STOLEN, STEALING, STEALS** to take without right or permission

STEALAGE *n* pl. **-S** theft

STEALER *n* pl. **-S** one that steals

STEALING *n* pl. **-S** the act of one that steals

STEALTH *n* pl. **-S** stealthy procedure

STEALTHY	*adj* **STEALTHIER, STEALTHIEST** intended to escape observation	**STELE**	*n* pl. **-S** the central portion of vascular tissue in a plant stem **STELIC** *adj*
STEAM	*v* **-ED, -ING, -S** to expose to steam (water in the form of vapor)	**STELLA**	*n* pl. **-S** a formerly used coin of the United States
STEAMER	*v* **-ED, -ING, -S** to travel by steamship	**STELLAR**	*adj* pertaining to the stars
STEAMY	*adj* **STEAMIER, STEAMIEST** marked by steam **STEAMILY** *adv*	**STELLATE**	*adj* shaped like a star
STEAPSIN	*n* pl. **-S** an enzyme	**STELLIFY**	*v* **-FIED, -FYING, -FIES** to convert into a star
STEARATE	*n* pl. **-S** a chemical salt	**STEM**	*v* **STEMMED, STEMMING, STEMS** to remove stems (ascending axes of a plant) from
STEARIN	*n* pl. **-S** the solid portion of a fat **STEARIC** *adj*		
STEARINE	*n* pl. **-S** stearin	**STEMLESS**	*adj* having no stem
STEATITE	*n* pl. **-S** a variety of talc	**STEMLIKE**	*adj* resembling a stem
STEDFAST	*adj* staunch	**STEMMA**	*n* pl. **-MAS** or **-MATA** a scroll recording the genealogy of a family in ancient Rome
STEED	*n* pl. **-S** a horse		
STEEK	*v* **-ED, -ING, -S** to shut	**STEMMED**	past tense of stem
STEEL	*v* **-ED, -ING, -S** to cover with steel (a tough iron alloy)	**STEMMER**	*n* pl. **-S** one that removes stems
STEELIE	*n* pl. **-S** a steel playing marble	**STEMMERY**	*n* pl. **-MERIES** a place where tobacco leaves are stripped
STEELY	*adj* **STEELIER, STEELIEST** resembling steel	**STEMMING**	present participle of stem
STEENBOK	*n* pl. **-S** an African antelope	**STEMMY**	*adj* **-MIER, -MIEST** abounding in stems
STEEP	*adj* **STEEPER, STEEPEST** inclined sharply	**STEMSON**	*n* pl. **-S** a supporting timber of a ship
STEEP	*v* **-ED, -ING, -S** to soak in a liquid	**STEMWARE**	*n* pl. **-S** a type of glassware
STEEPEN	*v* **-ED, -ING, -S** to make steep	**STENCH**	*n* pl. **-ES** a foul odor
STEEPER	*n* pl. **-S** one that steeps	**STENCHY**	*adj* **STENCHIER, STENCHIEST** having a stench
STEEPISH	*adj* somewhat steep	**STENCIL**	*v* **-CILED, -CILING, -CILS** or **-CILLED, -CILLING, -CILS** to mark by means of a perforated sheet of material
STEEPLE	*n* pl. **-S** a tapering structure on a church tower **STEEPLED** *adj*		
STEEPLY	*adv* in a steep manner		
STEER	*v* **-ED, -ING, -S** to direct the course of	**STENGAH**	*n* pl. **-S** a mixed drink
STEERAGE	*n* pl. **-S** the act of steering	**STENO**	*n* pl. **STENOS** a stenographer
STEERER	*n* pl. **-S** one that steers	**STENOKY**	*n* pl. **-KIES** the ability of an organism to live only under a narrow range of conditions
STEEVE	*v* **STEEVED, STEEVING, STEEVES** to stow in the hold of a ship		
		STENOSED	*adj* affected with stenosis
STEEVING	*n* pl. **-S** the angular elevation of a bowsprit from a ship's keel	**STENOSIS**	*n* pl. **-NOSES** a narrowing of a bodily passage **STENOTIC** *adj*
STEGODON	*n* pl. **-S** an extinct elephant-like mammal	**STENT**	*n* pl. **-S** a tubular device inserted into a blood vessel
STEIN	*n* pl. **-S** a beer mug	**STENTOR**	*n* pl. **-S** a person having a very loud voice
STEINBOK	*n* pl. **-S** steenbok	**STEP**	*v* **STEPPED, STEPPING, STEPS** to move by lifting the foot and setting it down in another place
STELA	*n* pl. **-LAE** or **-LAI** an inscribed slab used as a monument **STELAR, STELENE** *adj*		
		STEPDAME	*n* pl. **-S** a stepmother
		STEPLIKE	*adj* resembling a stair

STEPPE	*n* pl. **-S** a vast treeless plain	**STHENIA**	*n* pl. **-S** excessive energy **STHENIC** *adj*
STEPPED	past tense of step		
STEPPER	*n* pl. **-S** one that steps	**STIBIAL**	*adj* pertaining to stibium
STEPPING	present participle of step	**STIBINE**	*n* pl. **-S** a poisonous gas
STEPSON	*n* pl. **-S** a son of one's spouse by a former marriage	**STIBIUM**	*n* pl. **-S** antimony
		STIBNITE	*n* pl. **-S** an ore of antimony
STEPWISE	*adj* marked by a gradual progression	**STICH**	*n* pl. **-S** a line of poetry **STICHIC** *adj*
STERE	*n* pl. **-S** a unit of volume	**STICK**	*v* **-ED, -ING, -S** to support with slender pieces of wood
STEREO	*v* **-ED, -ING, -S** to make a type of printing plate	**STICK**	*v* **STUCK, STICKING, STICKS** to pierce with a pointed object
STERIC	*adj* pertaining to the spatial relationships of atoms in a molecule	**STICKER**	*n* pl. **-S** an adhesive label
		STICKFUL	*n* pl. **-S** an amount of set type
STERICAL	*adj* steric	**STICKIER**	comparative of sticky
STERIGMA	*n* pl. **-MAS** or **-MATA** a spore-bearing stalk of certain fungi	**STICKIES**	pl. of sticky
		STICKIEST	superlative of sticky
STERILE	*adj* incapable of producing offspring	**STICKILY**	*adv* in a sticky manner
STERLET	*n* pl. **-S** a small sturgeon	**STICKIT**	*adj* unsuccessful
STERLING	*n* pl. **-S** British money	**STICKLE**	*v* **-LED, -LING, -LES** to argue stubbornly
STERN	*adj* **STERNER, STERNEST** unyielding	**STICKLER**	*n* pl. **-S** one that stickles
STERN	*n* pl. **-S** the rear part of a ship	**STICKMAN**	*n* pl. **-MEN** one who supervises the play at a dice table
STERNA	a pl. of sternum		
STERNAL	*adj* pertaining to the sternum	**STICKOUT**	*n* pl. **-S** one that is conspicuous
STERNITE	*n* pl. **-S** a somitic sclerite	**STICKPIN**	*n* pl. **-S** a decorative tiepin
STERNLY	*adv* in a stern manner	**STICKUM**	*n* pl. **-S** a substance that causes adhesion
STERNSON	*n* pl. **-S** a reinforcing post of a ship	**STICKUP**	*n* pl. **-S** a robbery at gunpoint
STERNUM	*n* pl. **-NUMS** or **-NA** a long, flat supporting bone of most vertebrates	**STICKY**	*n* pl. **STICKIES** a slip of notepaper having an adhesive strip on the back
STERNWAY	*n* pl. **-WAYS** the backward movement of a vessel	**STICKY**	*adj* **STICKIER, STICKIEST** tending to adhere
STEROID	*n* pl. **-S** a type of chemical compound	**STICTION**	*n* pl. **-S** the force required to begin to move a body that is in contact with another body
STEROL	*n* pl. **-S** a type of solid alcohol		
STERTOR	*n* pl. **-S** a deep snoring sound	**STIED**	a past tense of sty
STET	*v* **STETTED, STETTING, STETS** to cancel a previously made printing correction	**STIES**	present 3d person sing. of sty
		STIFF	*adj* **STIFFER, STIFFEST** difficult to bend or stretch
STEW	*v* **-ED, -ING, -S** to cook by boiling slowly **STEWABLE** *adj*	**STIFF**	*v* **-ED, -ING, -S** to cheat someone by not paying
STEWARD	*v* **-ED, -ING, -S** to manage	**STIFFEN**	*v* **-ED, -ING, -S** to make stiff
STEWBUM	*n* pl. **-S** a drunken bum (a vagrant)	**STIFFISH**	*adj* somewhat stiff
STEWPAN	*n* pl. **-S** a pan used for stewing	**STIFFLY**	*adv* in a stiff manner
STEWY	*adj* having the characteristics of a stew (food cooked by stewing)	**STIFLE**	*v* **-FLED, -FLING, -FLES** to smother
STEY	*adj* steep	**STIFLER**	*n* pl. **-S** one that stifles

STIGMA *n* pl. **-MAS** or **-MATA** a mark of disgrace **STIGMAL** *adj*

STILBENE *n* pl. **-S** a chemical compound

STILBITE *n* pl. **-S** a mineral

STILE *n* pl. **-S** a series of steps for passing over a fence or wall

STILETTO *v* **-ED, -ING, -S** or **-ES** to stab with a stiletto (a short dagger)

STILL *adj* **STILLER, STILLEST** free from sound or motion

STILL *v* **-ED, -ING, -S** to make still

STILLMAN *n* pl. **-MEN** one who operates a distillery

STILLY *adj* **STILLIER, STILLIEST** still

STILT *v* **-ED, -ING, -S** to raise on stilts (long, slender poles)

STIME *n* pl. **-S** a glimpse

STIMULUS *n* pl. **-LI** something that causes a response

STIMY *v* **-MIED, -MYING, -MIES** to stymie

STING *v* **STUNG, STINGING, STINGS** to prick painfully

STINGER *n* pl. **-S** one that stings

STINGIER comparative of stingy

STINGIEST superlative of stingy

STINGILY *adv* in a stingy manner

STINGO *n* pl. **-GOS** a strong ale or beer

STINGRAY *n* pl. **-RAYS** a flat-bodied marine fish

STINGY *adj* **-GIER, -GIEST** unwilling to spend or give

STINK *v* **STANK** or **STUNK, STINKING, STINKS** to emit a foul odor

STINKARD *n* pl. **-S** a despicable person

STINKBUG *n* pl. **-S** an insect that emits a foul odor

STINKER *n* pl. **-S** one that stinks

STINKO *adj* drunk

STINKPOT *n* pl. **-S** a jar containing foul-smelling combustibles formerly used in warfare

STINKY *adj* **STINKIER, STINKIEST** emitting a foul odor

STINT *v* **-ED, -ING, -S** to limit

STINTER *n* pl. **-S** one that stints

STIPE *n* pl. **-S** a slender supporting part of a plant **STIPED** *adj*

STIPEL *n* pl. **-S** a small stipule

STIPEND *n* pl. **-S** a fixed sum of money paid periodically

STIPES *n* pl. **STIPITES** a stipe

STIPPLE *v* **-PLED, -PLING, -PLES** to draw, paint, or engrave by means of dots or short touches

STIPPLER *n* pl. **-S** one that stipples

STIPULE *n* pl. **-S** an appendage at the base of a leaf in certain plants **STIPULAR, STIPULED** *adj*

STIR *v* **STIRRED, STIRRING, STIRS** to pass an implement through in circular motions

STIRK *n* pl. **-S** a young cow

STIRP *n* pl. **-S** lineage

STIRPS *n* pl. **STIRPES** a family or branch of a family

STIRRED past tense of stir

STIRRER *n* pl. **-S** one that stirs

STIRRING *n* pl. **-S** a beginning of motion

STIRRUP *n* pl. **-S** a support for the foot of a horseman

STITCH *v* **-ED, -ING, -ES** to join by making in-and-out movements with a threaded needle

STITCHER *n* pl. **-S** one that stitches

STITHY *v* **STITHIED, STITHYING, STITHIES** to forge on an anvil

STIVER *n* pl. **-S** a formerly used Dutch coin

STOA *n* pl. **STOAE** or **STOAI** or **STOAS** an ancient Greek covered walkway

STOAT *n* pl. **-S** a weasel with a black-tipped tail

STOB *v* **STOBBED, STOBBING, STOBS** to stab

STOCCADO *n* pl. **-DOS** a thrust with a rapier

STOCCATA *n* pl. **-S** stoccado

STOCK *v* **-ED, -ING, -S** to keep for future sale or use

STOCKADE *v* **-ADED, -ADING, -ADES** to build a type of protective fence around

STOCKAGE *n* pl. **-S** the amount of supplies on hand

STOCKCAR *n* pl. **-S** a boxcar for carrying livestock

STOCKER *n* pl. **-S** a young animal suitable for being fattened for market

STOCKIER comparative of stocky

STOCKIEST superlative of stocky

STOCKILY *adv* in a stocky manner

STOCKING *n* pl. **-S** a knitted or woven covering for the foot and leg

STOCKISH *adj* stupid

STOCKIST *n pl.* **-S** one who stocks goods

STOCKMAN *n pl.* **-MEN** one who owns or raises livestock

STOCKPOT *n pl.* **-S** a pot in which broth is prepared

STOCKY *adj* **STOCKIER, STOCKIEST** having a short, thick body

STODGE *v* **STODGED, STODGING, STODGES** to stuff full with food

STODGY *adj* **STODGIER, STODGIEST** boring **STODGILY** *adv*

STOGEY *n pl.* **-GEYS** stogy

STOGIE *n pl.* **-S** stogy

STOGY *n pl.* **-GIES** a long, slender cigar

STOIC *n pl.* **-S** one who is indifferent to pleasure or pain **STOICAL** *adj*

STOICISM *n pl.* **-S** indifference to pleasure or pain

STOKE *v* **STOKED, STOKING, STOKES** to supply a furnace with fuel

STOKER *n pl.* **-S** one that stokes

STOKESIA *n pl.* **-S** a perennial herb

STOLE *n pl.* **-S** a long wide scarf **STOLED** *adj*

STOLEN past participle of steal

STOLID *adj* **-IDER, -IDEST** showing little or no emotion **STOLIDLY** *adv*

STOLLEN *n pl.* **-S** a sweet bread

STOLON *n pl.* **-S** a type of plant stem **STOLONIC** *adj*

STOLPORT *n pl.* **-S** an airport for aircraft needing comparatively short runways

STOMA *n pl.* **-MAS** or **-MATA** a minute opening in the epidermis of a plant organ

STOMACH *v* **-ED, -ING, -S** to tolerate

STOMACHY *adj* paunchy

STOMAL *adj* stomatal

STOMATA a *pl.* of stoma

STOMATAL *adj* pertaining to a stoma

STOMATE *n pl.* **-S** a stoma

STOMATIC *adj* pertaining to the mouth

STOMODEA *n/pl* embryonic oral cavities

STOMP *v* **-ED, -ING, -S** to tread heavily

STOMPER *n pl.* **-S** one that stomps

STONE *v* **STONED, STONING, STONES** to pelt with stones (pieces of concreted earthy or mineral matter) **STONABLE** *adj*

STONEFLY *n pl.* **-FLIES** a winged insect

STONER *n pl.* **-S** one that stones

STONEY *adj* **STONIER, STONIEST** stony

STONIER comparative of stony

STONIEST superlative of stony

STONILY *adv* in a stony manner

STONING present participle of stone

STONISH *v* **-ED, -ING, -ES** to astonish

STONY *adj* **STONIER, STONIEST** abounding in stones

STOOD past tense of stand

STOOGE *v* **STOOGED, STOOGING, STOOGES** to act as a comedian's straight man

STOOK *v* **-ED, -ING, -S** to stack upright in a field for drying, as bundles of grain

STOOKER *n pl.* **-S** one that stooks

STOOL *v* **-ED, -ING, -S** to defecate

STOOLIE *n pl.* **-S** an informer

STOOP *v* **-ED, -ING, -S** to bend the body forward and down

STOOPER *n pl.* **-S** one that stoops

STOP *v* **STOPPED** or **STOPT, STOPPING, STOPS** to discontinue the progress or motion of

STOPBANK *n pl.* **-S** an embankment along a river

STOPCOCK *n pl.* **-S** a type of faucet

STOPE *v* **STOPED, STOPING, STOPES** to excavate in layers, as ore

STOPER *n pl.* **-S** one that stopes

STOPGAP *n pl.* **-S** a temporary substitute

STOPOFF *n pl.* **-S** a stopover

STOPOVER *n pl.* **-S** a brief stop in the course of a journey

STOPPAGE *n pl.* **-S** the act of stopping

STOPPED a past tense of stop

STOPPER *v* **-ED, -ING, -S** to plug

STOPPING present participle of stop

STOPPLE *v* **-PLED, -PLING, -PLES** to stopper

STOPT a past tense of stop

STOPWORD *n pl.* **-S** a frequently used word that is not searchable by search engines

STORABLE *n pl.* **-S** something that can be stored

STORAGE *n pl.* **-S** a place for storing

STORAX *n pl.* **-ES** a fragrant resin

STORE	*v* **STORED, STORING, STORES** to put away for future use
STORER	*n* pl. **-S** one that stores
STOREY	*n* pl. **-REYS** a horizontal division of a building **STOREYED** *adj*
STORIED	past tense of story
STORIES	present 3d person sing. of story
STORING	present participle of store
STORK	*n* pl. **-S** a wading bird
STORM	*v* **-ED, -ING, -S** to blow violently
STORMY	*adj* **STORMIER, STORMIEST** storming **STORMILY** *adv*
STORY	*v* **-RIED, -RYING, -RIES** to relate as a story (an account of an event or series of events)
STOSS	*adj* facing the direction from which a glacier moves
STOT	*v* **STOTTED, STOTTING, STOTS** to bound with a stiff-legged gait
STOTIN	*n* pl. **-TINS** or **-TINOV** a monetary unit of Slovenia
STOTINKA	*n* pl. **-KI** a monetary unit of Bulgaria
STOTT	*v* **-ED, -ING, -S** to stot
STOUND	*v* **-ED, -ING, -S** to ache
STOUP	*n* pl. **-S** a basin for holy water
STOUR	*n* pl. **-S** dust
STOURE	*n* pl. **-S** stour
STOURIE	*adj* stoury
STOURY	*adj* dusty
STOUT	*adj* **STOUTER, STOUTEST** fat
STOUT	*n* pl. **-S** a strong, dark ale
STOUTEN	*v* **-ED, -ING, -S** to make stout
STOUTISH	*adj* somewhat stout
STOUTLY	*adv* in a stout manner
STOVE	*n* pl. **-S** a heating apparatus
STOVER	*n* pl. **-S** coarse food for cattle
STOW	*v* **-ED, -ING, -S** to pack **STOWABLE** *adj*
STOWAGE	*n* pl. **-S** goods in storage
STOWAWAY	*n* pl. **-AWAYS** one who hides aboard a conveyance to obtain free passage
STOWP	*n* pl. **-S** stoup
STRADDLE	*v* **-DLED, -DLING, -DLES** to sit, stand, or walk with the legs wide apart
STRAFE	*v* **STRAFED, STRAFING, STRAFES** to attack with machine-gun fire from an airplane
STRAFER	*n* pl. **-S** one that strafes
STRAGGLE	*v* **-GLED, -GLING, -GLES** to stray
STRAGGLY	*adj* **-GLIER, -GLIEST** irregularly spread out
STRAIGHT	*adj* **STRAIGHTER, STRAIGHTEST** extending uniformly in one direction without bends or irregularities
STRAIGHT	*v* **-ED, -ING, -S** to make straight
STRAIN	*v* **-ED, -ING, -S** to exert to the utmost
STRAINER	*n* pl. **-S** a utensil used to separate liquids from solids
STRAIT	*adj* **STRAITER, STRAITEST** narrow **STRAITLY** *adv*
STRAIT	*n* pl. **-S** a narrow waterway connecting two larger bodies of water
STRAITEN	*v* **-ED, -ING, -S** to make strait
STRAKE	*n* pl. **-S** a line of planking extending along a ship's hull **STRAKED** *adj*
STRAMASH	*n* pl. **-ES** an uproar
STRAMONY	*n* pl. **-NIES** a poisonous weed
STRAND	*v* **-ED, -ING, -S** to leave in an unfavorable situation
STRANDER	*n* pl. **-S** a machine that twists fibers into rope
STRANG	*adj* strong
STRANGE	*n* pl. **-S** a fundamental quark
STRANGE	*adj* **STRANGER, STRANGEST** unusual or unfamiliar
STRANGER	*v* **-ED, -ING, -S** to estrange
STRANGLE	*v* **-GLED, -GLING, -GLES** to choke to death
STRAP	*v* **STRAPPED, STRAPPING, STRAPS** to fasten with a strap (a narrow strip of flexible material)
STRAPPER	*n* pl. **-S** one that straps
STRAPPY	*adj* **STRAPPIER, STRAPPIEST** having straps
STRASS	*n* pl. **-ES** a brilliant glass used in making imitation gems
STRATA	*n* pl. **-S** a stratum
STRATAL	*adj* pertaining to a stratum
STRATEGY	*n* pl. **-GIES** a plan for obtaining a specific goal
STRATH	*n* pl. **-S** a wide river valley

STRATI pl. of stratus

STRATIFY v **-FIED, -FYING, -FIES** to form or arrange in layers

STRATOUS adj stratal

STRATUM n pl. **-TUMS** or **-TA** a layer of material

STRATUS n pl. **-TI** a type of cloud

STRAVAGE v **-VAGED, -VAGING, -VAGES** to stroll

STRAVAIG v **-ED, -ING, -S** to stravage

STRAW v **-ED, -ING, -S** to cover with straw (stalks of threshed grain)

STRAWHAT adj pertaining to a summer theater situated in a resort area

STRAWY adj **STRAWIER, STRAWIEST** resembling straw

STRAY v **-ED, -ING, -S** to wander from the proper area or course

STRAYER n pl. **-S** one that strays

STREAK v **-ED, -ING, -S** to cover with streaks (long, narrow marks)

STREAKER n pl. **-S** one that streaks

STREAKY adj **STREAKIER, STREAKIEST** covered with streaks

STREAM v **-ED, -ING, -S** to flow in a steady current

STREAMER n pl. **-S** a long, narrow flag

STREAMY adj **STREAMIER, STREAMIEST** streaming

STREEK v **-ED, -ING, -S** to stretch

STREEKER n pl. **-S** one that streeks

STREEL v **-ED, -ING, -S** to saunter

STREET n pl. **-S** a public thoroughfare

STRENGTH n pl. **-S** capacity for exertion or endurance

STREP n pl. **-S** any of various spherical or oval bacteria

STRESS v **-ED, -ING, -ES** to place emphasis on

STRESSOR n pl. **-S** a type of stimulus

STRETCH v **-ED, -ING, -ES** to draw out or open to full length

STRETCHY adj **STRETCHIER, STRETCHIEST** having a tendency to stretch

STRETTA n pl. **-TAS** or **-TE** stretto

STRETTO n pl. **-TOS** or **-TI** a concluding musical passage played at a faster tempo

STREUSEL n pl. **-S** a topping for coffee cakes

STREW v **STREWED, STREWN, STREWING, STREWS** to scatter about

STREWER n pl. **-S** one that strews

STRIA n pl. **STRIAE** a thin groove, stripe, or streak

STRIATE v **-ATED, -ATING, -ATES** to mark with striae

STRIATUM n pl. **-TA** a mass of nervous tissue within the brain

STRICK n pl. **-S** a bunch of flax fibers

STRICKEN adj strongly affected or afflicted

STRICKLE v **-LED, -LING, -LES** to shape or smooth with a strickle (an instrument for leveling off grain)

STRICT adj **STRICTER, STRICTEST** kept within narrow and specific limits **STRICTLY** adv

STRIDE v **STRODE, STRIDDEN, STRIDING, STRIDES** to walk with long steps

STRIDENT adj shrill

STRIDER n pl. **-S** one that strides

STRIDING present participle of stride

STRIDOR n pl. **-S** a strident sound

STRIFE n pl. **-S** bitter conflict or dissension

STRIGIL n pl. **-S** a scraping instrument

STRIGOSE adj covered with short, stiff hairs

STRIKE v **STRUCK** or **STROOK, STRICKEN** or **STRUCKEN, STRIKING, STRIKES** to come or cause to come into contact with

STRIKER n pl. **-S** one that strikes

STRING v **STRUNG** or **STRINGED, STRINGING, STRINGS** to provide with strings (slender cords)

STRINGER n pl. **-S** one that strings

STRINGY adj **STRINGIER, STRINGIEST** resembling a string or strings

STRIP v **STRIPPED** or **STRIPT, STRIPPING, STRIPS** to remove the outer covering from

STRIPE v **STRIPED, STRIPING, STRIPES** to mark with stripes (long, distinct bands)

STRIPER n pl. **-S** a food and game fish

STRIPIER comparative of stripy

STRIPIEST superlative of stripy

STRIPING n pl. **-S** the stripes marked or painted on something

STRIPPED a past tense of strip

STRIPPER	*n* pl. **-S** one that strips	**STRUDEL**	*n* pl. **-S** a type of pastry
STRIPPING	present participle of strip	**STRUGGLE**	*v* **-GLED, -GLING, -GLES** to make strenuous efforts against opposition
STRIPT	a past tense of strip		
STRIPY	*adj* **STRIPIER, STRIPIEST** marked with stripes	**STRUM**	*v* **STRUMMED, STRUMMING, STRUMS** to play a stringed instrument by running the fingers lightly across the strings
STRIVE	*v* **STROVE** or **STRIVED, STRIVEN, STRIVING, STRIVES** to exert much effort or energy		
		STRUMA	*n* pl. **-MAS** or **-MAE** scrofula
STRIVER	*n* pl. **-S** one that strives	**STRUMMER**	*n* pl. **-S** one that strums
STROBE	*n* pl. **-S** a device that produces brief, high-intensity flashes of light	**STRUMMING**	present participle of strum
		STRUMOSE	*adj* having a struma
STROBIC	*adj* spinning	**STRUMOUS**	*adj* having or pertaining to a struma
STROBIL	*n* pl. **-S** strobile		
STROBILA	*n* pl. **-LAE** the entire body of a tapeworm	**STRUMPET**	*n* pl. **-S** a prostitute
		STRUNG	a past tense of string
STROBILE	*n* pl. **-S** the conical, multiple fruit of certain trees	**STRUNT**	*v* **-ED, -ING, -S** to strut
STROBILI	*n/pl* strobiles	**STRUT**	*v* **STRUTTED, STRUTTING, STRUTS** to walk with a pompous air
STRODE	a past tense of stride		
STROKE	*v* **STROKED, STROKING, STROKES** to rub gently	**STRUTTER**	*n* pl. **-S** one that struts
		STUB	*v* **STUBBED, STUBBING, STUBS** to strike accidentally against a projecting object
STROKER	*n* pl. **-S** one that strokes		
STROLL	*v* **-ED, -ING, -S** to walk in a leisurely manner	**STUBBIER**	comparative of stubby
		STUBBIEST	superlative of stubby
STROLLER	*n* pl. **-S** one that strolls	**STUBBILY**	*adv* in a stubby manner
STROMA	*n* pl. **-MATA** the substance that forms the framework of an organ or cell **STROMAL** *adj*	**STUBBING**	present participle of stub
		STUBBLE	*n* pl. **-S** a short, rough growth of beard **STUBBLED** *adj*
STRONG	*adj* **STRONGER, STRONGEST** having great strength **STRONGLY** *adv*	**STUBBLY**	*adj* **-BLIER, -BLIEST** covered with stubble
		STUBBORN	*adj* **-BORNER, -BORNEST** unyielding
STRONGYL	*n* pl. **-S** a parasitic worm		
STRONTIA	*n* pl. **-S** a chemical compound **STRONTIC** *adj*	**STUBBY**	*adj* **-BIER, -BIEST** short and thick
		STUCCO	*v* **-ED, -ING, -ES** or **-S** to coat with a type of plaster
STROOK	a past tense of strike		
STROP	*v* **STROPPED, STROPPING, STROPS** to sharpen on a strip of leather	**STUCCOER**	*n* pl. **-S** one that stuccoes
		STUCK	past tense of stick
		STUD	*v* **STUDDED, STUDDING, STUDS** to set thickly with small projections
STROPHE	*n* pl. **-S** a part of an ancient Greek choral ode **STROPHIC** *adj*		
		STUDBOOK	*n* pl. **-S** a record of the pedigree of purebred animals
STROPPER	*n* pl. **-S** one that strops		
STROPPY	*adj* **-PIER, -PIEST** unruly	**STUDDIE**	*n* pl. **-S** an anvil
STROUD	*n* pl. **-S** a coarse woolen blanket	**STUDDING**	*n* pl. **-S** the framework of a wall
STROVE	a past tense of strive	**STUDENT**	*n* pl. **-S** a person formally engaged in learning
STROW	*v* **STROWED, STROWN, STROWING, STROWS** to strew		
		STUDFISH	*n* pl. **-ES** a freshwater fish
STROY	*v* **-ED, -ING, -S** to destroy	**STUDIED**	past tense of study
STROYER	*n* pl. **-S** one that stroys	**STUDIER**	*n* pl. **-S** one that studies
STRUCK	a past tense of strike		
STRUCKEN	a past participle of strike		

STUDIES	present 3d person sing. of study
STUDIO	n pl. **-DIOS** an artist's workroom
STUDIOUS	adj given to study
STUDLY	adj **-LIER, -LIEST** muscular and attractive
STUDWORK	n pl. **-S** studding
STUDY	v **STUDIED, STUDYING, STUDIES** to apply the mind to the acquisition of knowledge
STUFF	v **-ED, -ING, -S** to fill or pack tightly
STUFFER	n pl. **-S** one that stuffs
STUFFING	n pl. **-S** material with which something is stuffed
STUFFY	adj **STUFFIER, STUFFIEST** poorly ventilated **STUFFILY** adv
STUIVER	n pl. **-S** stiver
STULL	n pl. **-S** a supporting timber in a mine
STULTIFY	v **-FIED, -FYING, -FIES** to cause to appear absurd
STUM	v **STUMMED, STUMMING, STUMS** to increase the fermentation of by adding grape juice
STUMBLE	v **-BLED, -BLING, -BLES** to miss one's step in walking or running
STUMBLER	n pl. **-S** one that stumbles
STUMP	v **-ED, -ING, -S** to baffle
STUMPAGE	n pl. **-S** uncut marketable timber
STUMPER	n pl. **-S** a baffling question
STUMPY	adj **STUMPIER, STUMPIEST** short and thick
STUN	v **STUNNED, STUNNING, STUNS** to render senseless or incapable of action
STUNG	past tense of sting
STUNK	a past tense of stink
STUNNER	n pl. **-S** one that stuns
STUNNING	adj strikingly beautiful or attractive
STUNSAIL	n pl. **-S** a type of sail
STUNT	v **-ED, -ING, -S** to hinder the normal growth of
STUNTMAN	n pl. **-MEN** a person who substitutes for an actor in scenes involving dangerous activities
STUPA	n pl. **-S** a Buddhist shrine
STUPE	n pl. **-S** a medicated cloth to be applied to a wound
STUPEFY	v **-FIED, -FYING, -FIES** to dull the senses of

STUPID	adj **-PIDER, -PIDEST** mentally slow **STUPIDLY** adv
STUPID	n pl. **-S** a stupid person
STUPOR	n pl. **-S** a state of reduced sensibility
STURDY	adj **-DIER, -DIEST** strong and durable **STURDILY** adv
STURDY	n pl. **-DIES** a disease of sheep **STURDIED** adj
STURGEON	n pl. **-S** an edible fish
STURT	n pl. **-S** contention
STUTTER	v **-ED, -ING, -S** to speak with spasmodic repetition
STY	v **STIED** or **STYED, STYING, STIES** to keep in a pigpen
STYE	n pl. **-S** an inflamed swelling of the eyelid
STYGIAN	adj gloomy
STYLAR	adj pertaining to a stylus
STYLATE	adj bearing a stylet
STYLE	v **STYLED, STYLING, STYLES** to name
STYLER	n pl. **-S** one that styles
STYLET	n pl. **-S** a small, stiff organ or appendage of certain animals
STYLI	a pl. of stylus
STYLING	n pl. **-S** the way in which something is styled
STYLISE	v **-ISED, -ISING, -ISES** to stylize
STYLISER	n pl. **-S** one that stylises
STYLISH	adj fashionable
STYLIST	n pl. **-S** one who is a master of a literary or rhetorical style
STYLITE	n pl. **-S** an early Christian ascetic **STYLITIC** adj
STYLIZE	v **-IZED, -IZING, -IZES** to make conventional
STYLIZER	n pl. **-S** one that stylizes
STYLOID	adj slender and pointed
STYLUS	n pl. **-LUSES** or **-LI** a pointed instrument for writing, marking, or engraving
STYMIE	v **-MIED, -MIEING, -MIES** to thwart
STYMY	v **-MIED, -MYING, -MIES** to stymie
STYPSIS	n pl. **-SISES** the use of a styptic
STYPTIC	n pl. **-S** a substance used to check bleeding
STYRAX	n pl. **-ES** storax
STYRENE	n pl. **-S** a liquid hydrocarbon

SUABLE *adj* capable of being sued **SUABLY** *adv*

SUASION *n* pl. **-S** persuasion **SUASIVE, SUASORY** *adj*

SUAVE *adj* **SUAVER, SUAVEST** smoothly affable and polite **SUAVELY** *adv*

SUAVITY *n* pl. **-TIES** the state of being suave

SUB *v* **SUBBED, SUBBING, SUBS** to act as a substitute

SUBA *n* pl. **-S** subah

SUBABBOT *n* pl. **-S** a subordinate abbot

SUBACID *adj* slightly sour

SUBACRID *adj* somewhat acrid

SUBACUTE *adj* somewhat acute

SUBADAR *n* pl. **-S** subahdar

SUBADULT *n* pl. **-S** an individual approaching adulthood

SUBAGENT *n* pl. **-S** a subordinate agent

SUBAH *n* pl. **-S** a province of India

SUBAHDAR *n* pl. **-S** a governor of a subah

SUBALAR *adj* situated under the wings

SUBAREA *n* pl. **-S** a subdivision of an area

SUBARID *adj* somewhat arid

SUBATOM *n* pl. **-S** a component of an atom

SUBAURAL *adj* scarcely hearable

SUBAXIAL *adj* somewhat axial

SUBBASE *n* pl. **-S** the lowest part of a base

SUBBASIN *n* pl. **-S** a section of an area drained by a river

SUBBASS *n* pl. **-ES** a pedal stop producing the lowest tones of an organ

SUBBED past tense of sub

SUBBING *n* pl. **-S** a thin coating on the support of a photographic film

SUBBLOCK *n* pl. **-S** a subdivision of a block

SUBBREED *n* pl. **-S** a distinguishable strain within a breed

SUBCASTE *n* pl. **-S** a subdivision of a caste

SUBCAUSE *n* pl. **-S** a subordinate cause

SUBCELL *n* pl. **-S** a subdivision of a cell

SUBCHIEF *n* pl. **-S** a subordinate chief

SUBCLAIM *n* pl. **-S** a subordinate claim

SUBCLAN *n* pl. **-S** a subdivision of a clan

SUBCLASS *v* **-ED, -ING, -ES** to place in a subdivision of a class

SUBCLERK *n* pl. **-S** a subordinate clerk

SUBCODE *n* pl. **-S** a subdivision of a code

SUBCOOL *v* **-ED, -ING, -S** to cool below the freezing point without solidification

SUBCULT *n* pl. **-S** a subdivision of a cult

SUBCUTIS *n* pl. **-CUTISES** or **-CUTES** the deeper part of the dermis

SUBDEAN *n* pl. **-S** a subordinate dean

SUBDEB *n* pl. **-S** a girl the year before she becomes a debutante

SUBDEPOT *n* pl. **-S** a military depot that operates under the jurisdiction of another depot

SUBDUAL *n* pl. **-S** the act of subduing

SUBDUCE *v* **-DUCED, -DUCING, -DUCES** to take away

SUBDUCT *v* **-ED, -ING, -S** to subduce

SUBDUE *v* **-DUED, -DUING, -DUES** to bring under control

SUBDUER *n* pl. **-S** one that subdues

SUBDURAL *adj* situated under the dura mater

SUBDWARF *n* pl. **-S** a small star of relatively low luminosity

SUBECHO *n* pl. **-ECHOES** an inferior echo

SUBEDIT *v* **-ED, -ING, -S** to act as the assistant editor of

SUBENTRY *n* pl. **-TRIES** an entry made under a more general entry

SUBEPOCH *n* pl. **-S** a subdivision of an epoch

SUBER *n* pl. **-S** phellem

SUBERECT *adj* nearly erect

SUBERIC *adj* pertaining to cork

SUBERIN *n* pl. **-S** a substance found in cork cells

SUBERISE *v* **-ISED, -ISING, -ISES** to suberize

SUBERIZE *v* **-IZED, -IZING, -IZES** to convert into cork tissue

SUBEROSE *adj* corky

SUBEROUS *adj* suberose

SUBFIELD *n* pl. **-S** a subset of a mathematical field that is itself a field

SUBFILE *n* pl. **-S** a subdivision of a file

SUBFIX *n* pl. **-ES** a distinguishing symbol or letter written below another character

SUBFLOOR *n* pl. **-S** a rough floor laid as a base for a finished floor

SUBFLUID *adj* somewhat fluid

SUBFRAME *n* pl. **-S** a frame for the attachment of a finish frame

SUBFUSC *n* pl. **-S** dark dull clothing

SUBGENRE *n* pl. **-S** a subdivision of a genre

SUBGENUS *n* pl. **-GENUSES** or **-GENERA** a subdivision of a genus

SUBGOAL *n* pl. **-S** a subordinate goal

SUBGRADE *n* pl. **-S** a surface on which a pavement is placed

SUBGRAPH *n* pl. **-S** a graph contained within a larger graph

SUBGROUP *v* **-ED, -ING, -S** to divide into smaller groups

SUBGUM *n* pl. **-S** a Chinese dish of mixed vegetables

SUBHEAD *n* pl. **-S** the heading of a subdivision

SUBHUMAN *n* pl. **-S** one that is less than human

SUBHUMID *adj* somewhat humid

SUBIDEA *n* pl. **-S** an inferior idea

SUBINDEX *n* pl. **-DEXES** or **-DICES** a subfix

SUBITEM *n* pl. **-S** an item that forms a subdivision of a larger topic

SUBITO *adv* quickly — used as a musical direction

SUBJECT *v* **-ED, -ING, -S** to cause to experience

SUBJOIN *v* **-ED, -ING, -S** to add at the end

SUBLATE *v* **-LATED, -LATING, -LATES** to cancel

SUBLEASE *v* **-LEASED, -LEASING, -LEASES** to sublet

SUBLET *v* **-LET, -LETTING, -LETS** to rent leased property to another

SUBLEVEL *n* pl. **-S** a lower level

SUBLIME *adj* **-LIMER, -LIMEST** of elevated or noble quality

SUBLIME *v* **-LIMED, -LIMING, -LIMES** to make sublime

SUBLIMER *n* pl. **-S** one that sublimes

SUBLIMEST superlative of sublime

SUBLIMIT *n* pl. **-S** a limit within a limit

SUBLINE *n* pl. **-S** an inbred line within a strain

SUBLOT *n* pl. **-S** a subdivision of a lot

SUBLUNAR *adj* pertaining to the earth

SUBMENU *n* pl. **-S** a secondary list of options for a computer

SUBMERGE *v* **-MERGED, -MERGING, -MERGES** to place below the surface of a liquid

SUBMERSE *v* **-MERSED, -MERSING, -MERSES** to submerge

SUBMISS *adj* inclined to submit

SUBMIT *v* **-MITTED, -MITTING, -MITS** to yield to the power of another

SUBNASAL *adj* situated under the nose

SUBNET *n* pl. **-S** a system of interconnections within a communications system

SUBNICHE *n* pl. **-S** a subdivision of a habitat

SUBNODAL *adj* situated under a node

SUBOCEAN *adj* existing below the floor of the ocean

SUBOPTIC *adj* situated under the eyes

SUBORAL *adj* situated under the mouth

SUBORDER *n* pl. **-S** a category of related families within an order

SUBORN *v* **-ED, -ING, -S** to induce to commit perjury

SUBORNER *n* pl. **-S** one that suborns

SUBOVAL *adj* nearly oval

SUBOVATE *adj* nearly ovate

SUBOXIDE *n* pl. **-S** an oxide containing relatively little oxygen

SUBPANEL *n* pl. **-S** a subdivision of a panel

SUBPAR *adj* below par

SUBPART *n* pl. **-S** a subdivision of a part

SUBPENA *v* **-ED, -ING, -S** to subpoena

SUBPHASE *n* pl. **-S** a subdivision of a phase

SUBPHYLA *n/pl* divisions within a phylum

SUBPLOT *n* pl. **-S** a secondary literary plot

SUBPOENA *v* **-ED, -ING, -S** to summon with a type of judicial writ

SUBPOLAR *adj* situated just outside the polar circles

SUBPUBIC *adj* situated under the pubis

SUBRACE *n* pl. **-S** a subdivision of a race

SUBRENT *n* pl. **-S** rent from a subtenant

SUBRING *n* pl. **-S** a subset of a mathematical ring that is itself a ring

SUBRULE *n* pl. **-S** a subordinate rule

SUBSALE *n* pl. **-S** a resale of purchased goods

SUBSCALE *n* pl. **-S** a subdivision of a scale

SUBSEA *adj* situated below the surface of the sea

SUBSECT *n* pl. **-S** a sect directly derived from another

SUBSENSE *n* pl. **-S** a subdivision of a sense

SUBSERE *n* pl. **-S** a type of ecological succession

SUBSERVE *v* **-SERVED, -SERVING, -SERVES** to serve to promote

SUBSET *n* pl. **-S** a mathematical set contained within a larger set

SUBSHAFT *n* pl. **-S** a shaft that is beneath another shaft

SUBSHELL *n* pl. **-S** one of the orbitals making up an electron shell of an atom

SUBSHRUB *n* pl. **-S** a low shrub

SUBSIDE *v* **-SIDED, -SIDING, -SIDES** to sink to a lower or normal level

SUBSIDER *n* pl. **-S** one that subsides

SUBSIDY *n* pl. **-DIES** a grant or contribution of money

SUBSIST *v* **-ED, -ING, -S** to continue to exist

SUBSITE *n* pl. **-S** a subdivision of a site

SUBSKILL *n* pl. **-S** a subordinate skill

SUBSOIL *v* **-ED, -ING, -S** to plow so as to turn up the subsoil (the layer of earth beneath the surface soil)

SUBSOLAR *adj* situated directly beneath the sun

SUBSONIC *adj* moving at a speed less than that of sound

SUBSPACE *n* pl. **-S** a subset of a mathematical space

SUBSTAGE *n* pl. **-S** a part of a microscope for supporting accessories

SUBSTATE *n* pl. **-S** a subdivision of a state

SUBSUME *v* **-SUMED, -SUMING, -SUMES** to include within a larger group

SUBTASK *n* pl. **-S** a subordinate task

SUBTAXON *n* pl. **-TAXONS** or **-TAXA** a subdivision of a taxon

SUBTEEN *n* pl. **-S** a person approaching the teenage years

SUBTEND *v* **-ED, -ING, -S** to extend under or opposite to

SUBTEST *n* pl. **-S** a subdivision of a test

SUBTEXT *n* pl. **-S** written or printed matter under a more general text

SUBTHEME *n* pl. **-S** a subordinate theme

SUBTILE *adj* **-TILER, -TILEST** subtle

SUBTILIN *n* pl. **-S** an antibiotic

SUBTILTY *n* pl. **-TIES** subtlety

SUBTITLE *v* **-TLED, -TLING, -TLES** to give a secondary title to

SUBTLE *adj* **-TLER, -TLEST** so slight as to be difficult to detect **SUBTLY** *adv*

SUBTLETY *n* pl. **-TIES** the state of being subtle

SUBTONE *n* pl. **-S** a low or subdued tone

SUBTONIC *n* pl. **-S** a type of musical tone

SUBTOPIA *n* pl. **-S** the suburbs of a city

SUBTOPIC *n* pl. **-S** a secondary topic

SUBTOTAL *v* **-TALED, -TALING, -TALS** or **-TALLED, -TALLING, -TALS** to total a portion of

SUBTRACT *v* **-ED, -ING, -S** to take away

SUBTREND *n* pl. **-S** a subordinate trend

SUBTRIBE *n* pl. **-S** a subdivision of a tribe

SUBTUNIC *n* pl. **-S** a tunic worn under another tunic

SUBTYPE *n* pl. **-S** a type that is subordinate to or included in another type

SUBULATE *adj* slender and tapering to a point

SUBUNIT *n* pl. **-S** a unit that is a part of a larger unit

SUBURB *n* pl. **-S** a residential area adjacent to a city **SUBURBED** *adj*

SUBURBAN *n* pl. **-S** one who lives in a suburb

SUBURBIA *n* pl. **-S** the suburbs of a city

SUBVENE *v* **-VENED, -VENING, -VENES** to arrive or occur as a support or relief

SUBVERT *v* **-ED, -ING, -S** to destroy completely

SUBVICAR *n* pl. **-S** a subordinate vicar

SUBVIRAL *adj* pertaining to a part of a virus

SUBVIRUS *n* pl. **-ES** a viral protein smaller than a virus

SUBVOCAL *adj* mentally formulated as words

SUBWAY *v* **-ED, -ING, -S** to travel by an underground railroad

SUBWORLD *n* pl. **-S** a subdivision of a sphere of interest or activity

SUBZERO *adj* registering less than zero

SUBZONE *n* pl. **-S** a subdivision of a zone

SUCCAH *n* pl. **-CAHS** or **-COTH** sukkah

SUCCEED *v* **-ED, -ING, -S** to accomplish something desired or intended

SUCCESS *n* pl. **-ES** the attainment of something desired or intended

SUCCINCT *adj* **-CINCTER, -CINCTEST** clearly expressed in few words

SUCCINIC *adj* pertaining to amber

SUCCINYL *n* pl. **-S** a univalent radical

SUCCOR *v* **-ED, -ING, -S** to go to the aid of

SUCCORER *n* pl. **-S** one that succors

SUCCORY *n* pl. **-RIES** chicory

SUCCOTH	a pl. of succah
SUCCOUR	v **-ED, -ING, -S** to succor
SUCCUBA	n pl. **-BAS** or **-BAE** a succubus
SUCCUBUS	n pl. **-BUSES** or **-BI** a female demon
SUCCUMB	v **-ED, -ING, -S** to yield to superior force
SUCCUSS	v **-ED, -ING, -ES** to shake violently
SUCH	adj of that kind
SUCHLIKE	adj of a similar kind
SUCHNESS	n pl. **-ES** essential or characteristic quality
SUCK	v **-ED, -ING, -S** to draw in by establishing a partial vacuum
SUCKER	v **-ED, -ING, -S** to strip of lower shoots or branches
SUCKFISH	n pl. **-ES** a remora
SUCKLE	v **-LED, -LING, -LES** to give milk to from the breast
SUCKLER	n pl. **-S** one that suckles
SUCKLESS	adj having no juice
SUCKLING	n pl. **-S** an unweaned mammal
SUCKY	adj **SUCKIER, SUCKIEST** extremely objectionable
SUCRASE	n pl. **-S** an enzyme
SUCRE	n pl. **-S** a monetary unit of Ecuador
SUCROSE	n pl. **-S** a type of sugar
SUCTION	v **-ED, -ING, -S** to remove by the process of sucking
SUDARIUM	n pl. **-IA** a cloth for wiping the face
SUDARY	n pl. **-RIES** sudarium
SUDATION	n pl. **-S** excessive sweating
SUDATORY	n pl. **-RIES** a hot-air bath for inducing sweating
SUDD	n pl. **-S** a floating mass of vegetation
SUDDEN	adj happening quickly and without warning **SUDDENLY** adv
SUDDEN	n pl. **-S** a sudden occurrence
SUDOR	n pl. **-S** sweat **SUDORAL** adj
SUDS	v **-ED, -ING, -ES** to wash in soapy water
SUDSER	n pl. **-S** one that sudses
SUDSLESS	adj having no suds
SUDSY	adj **SUDSIER, SUDSIEST** foamy
SUE	v **SUED, SUING, SUES** to institute legal proceedings against
SUEDE	v **SUEDED, SUEDING, SUEDES** to finish leather with a soft, napped surface
SUER	n pl. **-S** one that sues
SUET	n pl. **-S** the hard, fatty tissue around the kidneys of cattle and sheep **SUETY** adj
SUFFARI	n pl. **-S** a safari
SUFFER	v **-ED, -ING, -S** to feel pain or distress
SUFFERER	n pl. **-S** one that suffers
SUFFICE	v **-FICED, -FICING, -FICES** to be adequate
SUFFICER	n pl. **-S** one that suffices
SUFFIX	v **-ED, -ING, -ES** to add as a suffix (a form affixed to the end of a root word)
SUFFIXAL	adj pertaining to or being a suffix
SUFFLATE	v **-FLATED, -FLATING, -FLATES** to inflate
SUFFRAGE	n pl. **-S** the right to vote
SUFFUSE	v **-FUSED, -FUSING, -FUSES** to spread through or over
SUGAR	v **-ED, -ING, -S** to cover with sugar (a sweet carbohydrate)
SUGARER	n pl. **-S** one that makes sugar
SUGARY	adj **-ARIER, -ARIEST** containing or resembling sugar
SUGGEST	v **-ED, -ING, -S** to bring or put forward for consideration
SUGH	v **-ED, -ING, -S** to sough
SUICIDAL	adj self-destructive
SUICIDE	v **-CIDED, -CIDING, -CIDES** to kill oneself intentionally
SUING	present participle of sue
SUINT	n pl. **-S** a natural grease found in the wool of sheep
SUIT	v **-ED, -ING, -S** to be appropriate to
SUITABLE	adj appropriate **SUITABLY** adv
SUITCASE	n pl. **-S** a flat, rectangular piece of luggage
SUITE	n pl. **-S** a series of things forming a unit
SUITER	n pl. **-S** a suitcase holding a specified number of suits (sets of garments)
SUITING	n pl. **-S** fabric for making suits
SUITLIKE	adj resembling a suit (a set of garments)

SUITOR   *n* pl. **-S** one that is courting a woman

SUK   *n* pl. **-S** souk

SUKIYAKI   *n* pl. **-S** a Japanese dish

SUKKAH   *n* pl. **-KAHS** or **-KOTH** or **-KOT** a temporary shelter in which meals are eaten during a Jewish festival

SULCATE   *adj* having long, narrow furrows

SULCATED   *adj* sulcate

SULCUS   *n* pl. **-CI** a narrow furrow **SULCAL** *adj*

SULDAN   *n* pl. **-S** soldan

SULFA   *n* pl. **-S** a bacteria-inhibiting drug

SULFATE   *v* **-FATED, -FATING, -FATES** to treat with sulfuric acid

SULFID   *n* pl. **-S** sulfide

SULFIDE   *n* pl. **-S** a sulfur compound

SULFINYL   *n* pl. **-S** a bivalent radical

SULFITE   *n* pl. **-S** a chemical salt **SULFITIC** *adj*

SULFO   *adj* sulfonic

SULFONE   *n* pl. **-S** a sulfur compound

SULFONIC   *adj* containing a certain univalent radical

SULFONYL   *n* pl. **-S** a bivalent radical

SULFUR   *v* **-ED, -ING, -S** to treat with sulfur (a nonmetallic element)

SULFURET   *v* **-RETED, -RETING, -RETS** or **-RETTED, -RETTING, -RETS** to treat with sulfur

SULFURIC   *adj* pertaining to sulfur

SULFURY   *adj* resembling sulfur

SULFURYL   *n* pl. **-S** sulfonyl

SULK   *v* **-ED, -ING, -S** to be sulky

SULKER   *n* pl. **-S** one that sulks

SULKY   *adj* **SULKIER, SULKIEST** sullenly aloof or withdrawn **SULKILY** *adv*

SULKY   *n* pl. **SULKIES** a light horse-drawn vehicle

SULLAGE   *n* pl. **-S** sewage

SULLEN   *adj* **-LENER, -LENEST** showing a brooding ill humor or resentment **SULLENLY** *adv*

SULLY   *v* **-LIED, -LYING, -LIES** to soil

SULPHA   *n* pl. **-S** sulfa

SULPHATE   *v* **-PHATED, -PHATING, -PHATES** to sulfate

SULPHID   *n* pl. **-S** sulfide

SULPHIDE   *n* pl. **-S** sulfide

SULPHITE   *n* pl. **-S** sulfite

SULPHONE   *n* pl. **-S** sulfone

SULPHUR   *v* **-ED, -ING, -S** to sulfur

SULPHURY   *adj* sulfury

SULTAN   *n* pl. **-S** the ruler of a Muslim country **SULTANIC** *adj*

SULTANA   *n* pl. **-S** a sultan's wife

SULTRY   *adj* **-TRIER, -TRIEST** very hot and humid **SULTRILY** *adv*

SULU   *n* pl. **-S** a Melanesian skirt

SUM   *v* **SUMMED, SUMMING, SUMS** to add into one total

SUMAC   *n* pl. **-S** a flowering tree or shrub

SUMACH   *n* pl. **-S** sumac

SUMLESS   *adj* too large for calculation

SUMMA   *n* pl. **-MAS** or **-MAE** a comprehensive work on a topic

SUMMABLE   *adj* capable of being summed

SUMMAND   *n* pl. **-S** an addend

SUMMARY   *n* pl. **-RIES** a short restatement

SUMMATE   *v* **-MATED, -MATING, -MATES** to sum

SUMMED   past tense of sum

SUMMER   *v* **-ED, -ING, -S** to pass the summer (the warmest season of the year)

SUMMERLY   *adj* summery

SUMMERY   *adj* **-MERIER, -MERIEST** characteristic of summer

SUMMING   present participle of sum

SUMMIT   *v* **-ED, -ING, -S** to participate in a highest-level conference

SUMMITAL   *adj* pertaining to the highest point

SUMMITRY   *n* pl. **-RIES** the use of conferences between chiefs of state for international negotiation

SUMMON   *v* **-ED, -ING, -S** to order to appear

SUMMONER   *n* pl. **-S** one that summons

SUMMONS   *v* **-ED, -ING, -ES** to summon with a court order

SUMO   *n* pl. **-MOS** a Japanese form of wrestling

SUMOIST   *n* pl. **-S** a sumo wrestler

SUMP   *n* pl. **-S** a low area serving as a drain or receptacle for liquids

SUMPTER   *n* pl. **-S** a pack animal

SUMPWEED   *n* pl. **-S** a marsh plant

SUN   *v* **SUNNED, SUNNING, SUNS** to expose to the sun (the star around which the earth revolves)

SUNBACK *adj* cut low to expose the back to sunlight

SUNBAKED *adj* baked by the sun

SUNBATH *n* pl. **-S** an exposure to sunlight

SUNBATHE *v* **-BATHED, -BATHING, -BATHES** to take a sunbath

SUNBEAM *n* pl. **-S** a beam of sunlight **SUNBEAMY** *adj*

SUNBELT *n* pl. **-S** the southern and southwestern states of the U.S.

SUNBIRD *n* pl. **-S** a tropical bird

SUNBLOCK *n* pl. **-S** a preparation to protect the skin from the sun's rays

SUNBOW *n* pl. **-S** an arc of spectral colors formed by the sun shining through a mist

SUNBURN *v* **-BURNED** or **-BURNT, -BURNING, -BURNS** to burn or discolor from exposure to the sun

SUNBURST *n* pl. **-S** a burst of sunlight

SUNCHOKE *n* pl. **-S** a type of sunflower

SUNDAE *n* pl. **-S** a dish of ice cream served with a topping

SUNDECK *n* pl. **-S** a deck that is exposed to the sun

SUNDER *v* **-ED, -ING, -S** to break apart

SUNDERER *n* pl. **-S** one that sunders

SUNDEW *n* pl. **-S** a marsh plant

SUNDIAL *n* pl. **-S** a type of time-telling device

SUNDOG *n* pl. **-S** a small rainbow

SUNDOWN *v* **-ED, -ING, -S** to experience nighttime confusion

SUNDRESS *n* pl. **-ES** a dress with an abbreviated bodice

SUNDRIES *n/pl* miscellaneous items

SUNDROPS *n* pl. **SUNDROPS** a flowering plant

SUNDRY *adj* miscellaneous **SUNDRILY** *adv*

SUNFAST *adj* resistant to fading by the sun

SUNFISH *n* pl. **-ES** a marine fish

SUNG past participle of sing

SUNGLASS *n* pl. **-ES** a lens for concentrating the sun's rays in order to produce heat

SUNGLOW *n* pl. **-S** a glow in the sky caused by the sun

SUNK a past participle of sink

SUNKEN a past participle of sink

SUNKET *n* pl. **-S** a tidbit

SUNLAMP *n* pl. **-S** a lamp that radiates ultraviolet rays

SUNLAND *n* pl. **-S** an area marked by a great amount of sunshine

SUNLESS *adj* having no sunlight

SUNLIGHT *n* pl. **-S** the light of the sun

SUNLIKE *adj* resembling the sun

SUNLIT *adj* lighted by the sun

SUNN *n* pl. **-S** an East Indian shrub

SUNNA *n* pl. **-S** the body of traditional Muslim law

SUNNAH *n* pl. **-S** sunna

SUNNED past tense of sun

SUNNING present participle of sun

SUNNY *adj* **-NIER, -NIEST** filled with sunlight **SUNNILY** *adv*

SUNPORCH *n* pl. **-ES** a porch that admits much sunlight

SUNPROOF *adj* resistant to damage by sunlight

SUNRAY *n* pl. **-RAYS** a ray of sunlight

SUNRISE *n* pl. **-S** the ascent of the sun above the horizon in the morning

SUNROOF *n* pl. **-S** an automobile roof having an openable panel

SUNROOM *n* pl. **-S** a room built to admit a great amount of sunlight

SUNSCALD *n* pl. **-S** an injury of woody plants caused by the sun

SUNSET *n* pl. **-S** the descent of the sun below the horizon in the evening

SUNSHADE *n* pl. **-S** something used as a protection from the sun

SUNSHINE *n* pl. **-S** the light of the sun **SUNSHINY** *adj*

SUNSPOT *n* pl. **-S** a dark spot on the surface of the sun

SUNSTONE *n* pl. **-S** a variety of quartz

SUNSUIT *n* pl. **-S** a type of playsuit

SUNTAN *v* **-TANNED, -TANNING, -TANS** to become tan

SUNUP *n* pl. **-S** sunrise

SUNWARD *adv* toward the sun

SUNWARDS *adv* sunward

SUNWISE *adv* from left to right

SUP *v* **SUPPED, SUPPING, SUPS** to eat supper

SUPE *n* pl. **-S** an actor without a speaking part

SUPER *v* **-ED, -ING, -S** to reinforce with a thin cotton mesh, as a book

SUPERADD	*v* **-ED, -ING, -S** to add further
SUPERB	*adj* **-PERBER, -PERBEST** of excellent quality **SUPERBLY** *adv*
SUPERBAD	*adj* exceedingly bad
SUPERBUG	*n* pl. **-S** a strain of bacteria that is resistant to all antibiotics
SUPERCAR	*n* pl. **-S** a superior car
SUPERCOP	*n* pl. **-S** a superior police officer
SUPEREGO	*n* pl. **-EGOS** a part of the psyche
SUPERFAN	*n* pl. **-S** an exceedingly devoted enthusiast
SUPERFIX	*n* pl. **-ES** a recurrent pattern of stress in speech
SUPERHIT	*n* pl. **-S** something exceedingly successful
SUPERHOT	*adj* exceedingly hot
SUPERIOR	*n* pl. **-S** one of higher rank, quality, or authority than another
SUPERJET	*n* pl. **-S** a type of jet airplane
SUPERLIE	*v* **-LAY, -LAIN, -LYING, -LIES** to lie above
SUPERMAN	*n* pl. **-MEN** a hypothetical superior man
SUPERMOM	*n* pl. **-S** a superior mom
SUPERNAL	*adj* pertaining to the sky
SUPERPRO	*n* pl. **-PROS** a superior professional
SUPERSEX	*n* pl. **-ES** a type of sterile organism
SUPERSPY	*n* pl. **-SPIES** a superior spy
SUPERTAX	*n* pl. **-ES** an additional tax
SUPINATE	*v* **-NATED, -NATING, -NATES** to turn so that the palm is facing upward
SUPINE	*n* pl. **-S** a Latin verbal noun
SUPINELY	*adv* in an inactive manner
SUPPED	past tense of sup
SUPPER	*n* pl. **-S** an evening meal
SUPPING	present participle of sup
SUPPLANT	*v* **-ED, -ING, -S** to take the place of
SUPPLE	*adj* **-PLER, -PLEST** pliant **SUPPLELY** *adv*
SUPPLE	*v* **-PLED, -PLING, -PLES** to make supple
SUPPLIER	*n* pl. **-S** one that supplies
SUPPLY	*v* **-PLIED, -PLYING, -PLIES** to furnish with what is needed
SUPPORT	*v* **-ED, -ING, -S** to hold up or add strength to
SUPPOSAL	*n* pl. **-S** something supposed
SUPPOSE	*v* **-POSED, -POSING, -POSES** to assume to be true
SUPPOSER	*n* pl. **-S** one that supposes
SUPPRESS	*v* **-ED, -ING, -ES** to put an end to forcibly
SUPRA	*adv* above
SUPREME	*n* pl. **-S** a smooth white sauce made with chicken stock
SUPREME	*adj* **-PREMER, -PREMEST** highest in power or authority
SUPREMO	*n* pl. **-MOS** one who is highest in authority
SUQ	*n* pl. **-S** souk
SURA	*n* pl. **-S** a chapter of the Koran
SURAH	*n* pl. **-S** a silk fabric
SURAL	*adj* pertaining to the calf of the leg
SURBASE	*n* pl. **-S** a molding or border above the base of a structure **SURBASED** *adj*
SURCEASE	*v* **-CEASED, -CEASING, -CEASES** to cease
SURCOAT	*n* pl. **-S** an outer coat or cloak
SURD	*n* pl. **-S** a voiceless speech sound
SURE	*adj* **SURER, SUREST** free from doubt
SUREFIRE	*adj* sure to meet expectations
SURELY	*adv* certainly
SURENESS	*n* pl. **-ES** the state of being sure
SURER	comparative of sure
SUREST	superlative of sure
SURETY	*n* pl. **-TIES** sureness
SURF	*v* **-ED, -ING, -S** to ride breaking waves on a long, narrow board **SURFABLE** *adj*
SURFACE	*v* **-FACED, -FACING, -FACES** to apply an outer layer to
SURFACER	*n* pl. **-S** one that surfaces
SURFBIRD	*n* pl. **-S** a shore bird
SURFBOAT	*n* pl. **-S** a strong rowboat
SURFEIT	*v* **-ED, -ING, -S** to supply to excess
SURFER	*n* pl. **-S** one that surfs
SURFFISH	*n* pl. **-ES** a marine fish
SURFIER	comparative of surfy
SURFIEST	superlative of surfy
SURFING	*n* pl. **-S** the act or sport of riding the surf (breaking waves)
SURFLIKE	*adj* resembling breaking waves
SURFMAN	*n* pl. **-MEN** one who is skilled in handling a boat in surf

SURFSIDE	*adj* situated near the seashore
SURFY	*adj* **SURFIER, SURFIEST** abounding in breaking waves
SURGE	*v* **SURGED, SURGING, SURGES** to move in a swelling manner
SURGEON	*n* pl. **-S** one who practices surgery
SURGER	*n* pl. **-S** one that surges
SURGERY	*n* pl. **-GERIES** the treatment of medical problems by operation
SURGICAL	*adj* pertaining to surgery
SURGING	present participle of surge
SURGY	*adj* surging
SURICATE	*n* pl. **-S** a burrowing mammal
SURIMI	*n* pl. **-S** an inexpensive fish product
SURLY	*adj* **-LIER, -LIEST** sullenly rude **SURLILY** *adv*
SURMISE	*v* **-MISED, -MISING, -MISES** to infer with little evidence
SURMISER	*n* pl. **-S** one that surmises
SURMOUNT	*v* **-ED, -ING, -S** to get over or across
SURNAME	*v* **-NAMED, -NAMING, -NAMES** to give a family name to
SURNAMER	*n* pl. **-S** one that surnames
SURPASS	*v* **-ED, -ING, -ES** to go beyond
SURPLICE	*n* pl. **-S** a loose-fitting vestment
SURPLUS	*v* **-PLUSED, -PLUSING, -PLUSES** or **-PLUSSED, -PLUSSING, -PLUSSES** to treat as being in excess of what is needed
SURPRINT	*v* **-ED, -ING, -S** to print over something already printed
SURPRISE	*v* **-PRISED, -PRISING, -PRISES** to come upon unexpectedly
SURPRIZE	*v* **-PRIZED, -PRIZING, -PRIZES** to surprise
SURRA	*n* pl. **-S** a disease of domestic animals
SURREAL	*adj* having dreamlike qualities
SURREY	*n* pl. **-REYS** a light carriage
SURROUND	*v* **-ED, -ING, -S** to extend completely around
SURROYAL	*n* pl. **-S** the topmost prong of a stag's antler
SURTAX	*v* **-ED, -ING, -ES** to assess with an extra tax
SURTITLE	*n* pl. **-S** a translation of a foreign-language dialogue displayed above a screen or stage
SURTOUT	*n* pl. **-S** a close-fitting overcoat
SURVEIL	*v* **-VEILLED, -VEILLING, -VEILS** to watch closely
SURVEY	*v* **-ED, -ING, -S** to determine the boundaries, area, or elevations of by measuring angles and distances
SURVEYOR	*n* pl. **-S** one that surveys land
SURVIVAL	*n* pl. **-S** a living or continuing longer than another person or thing
SURVIVE	*v* **-VIVED, -VIVING, -VIVES** to remain in existence
SURVIVER	*n* pl. **-S** survivor
SURVIVOR	*n* pl. **-S** one that survives
SUSHI	*n* pl. **-S** a dish of cold rice cakes topped with strips of raw fish
SUSLIK	*n* pl. **-S** a Eurasian rodent
SUSPECT	*v* **-ED, -ING, -S** to think guilty on slight evidence
SUSPEND	*v* **-ED, -ING, -S** to cause to stop for a period
SUSPENSE	*n* pl. **-S** a state of mental uncertainty or excitement
SUSPIRE	*v* **-PIRED, -PIRING, -PIRES** to sigh
SUSS	*v* **-ED, -ING, -ES** to figure out
SUSTAIN	*v* **-ED, -ING, -S** to maintain by providing with food and drink
SUSURRUS	*n* pl. **-ES** a soft rustling sound
SUTLER	*n* pl. **-S** one that peddles goods to soldiers
SUTRA	*n* pl. **-S** a Hindu aphorism
SUTTA	*n* pl. **-S** sutra
SUTTEE	*n* pl. **-S** a Hindu widow cremated on her husband's funeral pile to show her devotion to him
SUTURAL	*adj* pertaining to the line of junction between two bones
SUTURE	*v* **-TURED, -TURING, -TURES** to unite by sewing
SUZERAIN	*n* pl. **-S** a feudal lord
SVARAJ	*n* pl. **-ES** swaraj
SVEDBERG	*n* pl. **-S** a unit of time
SVELTE	*adj* **SVELTER, SVELTEST** gracefully slender **SVELTELY** *adv*
SWAB	*v* **SWABBED, SWABBING, SWABS** to clean with a large mop
SWABBER	*n* pl. **-S** one that swabs
SWABBIE	*n* pl. **-S** a sailor
SWABBING	present participle of swab

SWABBY   *n* pl. **-BIES** swabbie

SWACKED   *adj* drunk

SWADDLE   *v* **-DLED, -DLING, -DLES** to wrap in bandages

SWAG   *v* **SWAGGED, SWAGGING, SWAGS** to sway

SWAGE   *v* **SWAGED, SWAGING, SWAGES** to shape with a hammering tool

SWAGER   *n* pl. **-S** one that swages

SWAGGER   *v* **-ED, -ING, -S** to walk with a pompous air

SWAGGIE   *n* pl. **-S** a swagman

SWAGGING   present participle of swag

SWAGING   present participle of swage

SWAGMAN   *n* pl. **-MEN** a hobo

SWAIL   *n* pl. **-S** swale

SWAIN   *n* pl. **-S** a country boy **SWAINISH** *adj*

SWALE   *n* pl. **-S** a tract of low, marshy ground

SWALLOW   *v* **-ED, -ING, -S** to take through the mouth and esophagus into the stomach

SWAM   past tense of swim

SWAMI   *n* pl. **-S** a Hindu religious teacher

SWAMIES   pl. of swamy

SWAMP   *v* **-ED, -ING, -S** to inundate

SWAMPER   *n* pl. **-S** one that lives in a swampy area

SWAMPISH   *adj* swampy

SWAMPY   *adj* **SWAMPIER, SWAMPIEST** marshy

SWAMY   *n* pl. **-MIES** swami

SWAN   *v* **SWANNED, SWANNING, SWANS** to swear

SWANG   a past tense of swing

SWANHERD   *n* pl. **-S** one who tends swans (large aquatic birds)

SWANK   *adj* **SWANKER, SWANKEST** imposingly elegant

SWANK   *v* **-ED, -ING, -S** to swagger

SWANKY   *adj* **SWANKIER, SWANKIEST** swank **SWANKILY** *adv*

SWANLIKE   *adj* resembling a swan

SWANNED   past tense of swan

SWANNERY   *n* pl. **-NERIES** a place where swans are raised

SWANNING   present participle of swan

SWANNY   *v* to declare — used only in the 1st person sing.

SWANPAN   *n* pl. **-S** a Chinese abacus

SWANSKIN   *n* pl. **-S** the skin of a swan

SWAP   *v* **SWAPPED, SWAPPING, SWAPS** to trade

SWAPPER   *n* pl. **-S** one that swaps

SWARAJ   *n* pl. **-ES** self-government in British India

SWARD   *v* **-ED, -ING, -S** to cover with turf

SWARE   a past tense of swear

SWARF   *n* pl. **-S** material removed by a cutting tool

SWARM   *v* **-ED, -ING, -S** to move in a large group

SWARMER   *n* pl. **-S** one that swarms

SWART   *adj* swarthy

SWARTH   *n* pl. **-S** turf

SWARTHY   *adj* **-THIER, -THIEST** having a dark complexion

SWARTY   *adj* swarthy

SWASH   *v* **-ED, -ING, -ES** to swagger

SWASHER   *n* pl. **-S** one that swashes

SWASTICA   *n* pl. **-S** swastika

SWASTIKA   *n* pl. **-S** a geometrical figure used as a symbol or ornament

SWAT   *v* **SWATTED, SWATTING, SWATS** to hit sharply

SWATCH   *n* pl. **-ES** a sample piece of cloth

SWATH   *n* pl. **-S** a row of cut grass or grain

SWATHE   *v* **SWATHED, SWATHING, SWATHES** to wrap in bandages

SWATHER   *n* pl. **-S** one that swathes

SWATTED   past tense of swat

SWATTER   *n* pl. **-S** one that swats

SWATTING   present participle of swat

SWAY   *v* **-ED, -ING, -S** to move slowly back and forth **SWAYABLE** *adj*

SWAYBACK   *n* pl. **-S** an abnormal sagging of the back

SWAYER   *n* pl. **-S** one that sways

SWAYFUL   *adj* capable of influencing

SWEAR   *v* **SWORE** or **SWARE, SWORN, SWEARING, SWEARS** to utter a solemn oath

SWEARER   *n* pl. **-S** one that swears

SWEAT   *v* **-ED, -ING, -S** to perspire

SWEATBOX   *n* pl. **-ES** a small enclosure in which one is made to sweat

SWEATER *n* pl. **-S** a knitted outer garment

SWEATY *adj* **SWEATIER, SWEATIEST** covered with perspiration **SWEATILY** *adv*

SWEDE *n* pl. **-S** a rutabaga

SWEENEY *n* pl. **-NEYS** sweeny

SWEENY *n* pl. **-NIES** atrophy of the shoulder muscles in horses

SWEEP *v* **SWEPT, SWEEPING, SWEEPS** to clear or clean with a brush or broom

SWEEPER *n* pl. **-S** one that sweeps

SWEEPING *n* pl. **-S** the act of one that sweeps

SWEEPY *adj* **SWEEPIER, SWEEPIEST** of wide range or scope

SWEER *adj* lazy

SWEET *adj* **SWEETER, SWEETEST** pleasing to the taste

SWEET *n* pl. **-S** something that is sweet

SWEETEN *v* **-ED, -ING, -S** to make sweet

SWEETIE *n* pl. **-S** darling

SWEETING *n* pl. **-S** a sweet apple

SWEETISH *adj* somewhat sweet

SWEETLY *adv* in a sweet manner

SWEETSOP *n* pl. **-S** a tropical tree

SWELL *adj* **SWELLER, SWELLEST** stylish

SWELL *v* **SWELLED, SWOLLEN, SWELLING, SWELLS** to increase in size or volume

SWELLING *n* pl. **-S** something that is swollen

SWELTER *v* **-ED, -ING, -S** to suffer from oppressive heat

SWELTRY *adj* **-TRIER, -TRIEST** oppressively hot

SWEPT past tense of sweep

SWERVE *v* **SWERVED, SWERVING, SWERVES** to turn aside suddenly from a straight course

SWERVER *n* pl. **-S** one that swerves

SWEVEN *n* pl. **-S** a dream or vision

SWIDDEN *n* pl. **-S** an agricultural plot produced by burning off the vegetative cover

SWIFT *adj* **SWIFTER, SWIFTEST** moving with a great rate of motion

SWIFT *n* pl. **-S** a fast-flying bird

SWIFTER *n* pl. **-S** a rope on a ship

SWIFTLET *n* pl. **-S** a cave-dwelling swift

SWIFTLY *adv* in a swift manner

SWIG *v* **SWIGGED, SWIGGING, SWIGS** to drink deeply or rapidly

SWIGGER *n* pl. **-S** one that swigs

SWILL *v* **-ED, -ING, -S** to swig

SWILLER *n* pl. **-S** one that swills

SWIM *v* **SWAM, SWUM, SWIMMING, SWIMS** to propel oneself in water by natural means

SWIMMER *n* pl. **-S** one that swims

SWIMMING *n* pl. **-S** the act of one that swims

SWIMMY *adj* **-MIER, -MIEST** dizzy **SWIMMILY** *adv*

SWIMSUIT *n* pl. **-S** a bathing suit

SWIMWEAR *n* pl. **SWIMWEAR** clothing suitable for swimming

SWINDLE *v* **-DLED, -DLING, -DLES** to take money or property from by fraudulent means

SWINDLER *n* pl. **-S** one that swindles

SWINE *n* pl. **SWINE** a domestic pig

SWINEPOX *n* pl. **-ES** a disease of swine

SWING *v* **SWUNG** or **SWANG, SWINGING, SWINGS** to move freely back and forth

SWINGBY *n* pl. **-BYS** a mission in which a spacecraft uses a planet's gravitational pull for making course changes

SWINGE *v* **SWINGED, SWINGEING, SWINGES** to flog

SWINGER *n* pl. **-S** one that swings

SWINGIER comparative of swingy

SWINGIEST superlative of swingy

SWINGING *adj* **SWINGINGEST** lively and hip

SWINGING *n* pl. **-S** the practice of swapping sex partners

SWINGLE *v* **-GLED, -GLING, -GLES** to scutch

SWINGMAN *n* pl. **-MEN** a basketball player who can play guard or forward

SWINGY *adj* **SWINGIER, SWINGIEST** marked by swinging

SWINISH *adj* resembling or befitting swine

SWINK *v* **-ED, -ING, -S** to toil

SWINNEY *n* pl. **-NEYS** sweeny

SWIPE *v* **SWIPED, SWIPING, SWIPES** to strike with a sweeping blow

SWIPES *n/pl* spoiled beer

SWIPLE *n* pl. **-S** a part of a threshing device

SWIPPLE	*n* pl. **-S** swiple
SWIRL	*v* **-ED, -ING, -S** to move with a whirling motion
SWIRLY	*adj* **SWIRLIER, SWIRLIEST** swirling
SWISH	*v* **-ED, -ING, -ES** to move with a prolonged hissing sound
SWISHER	*n* pl. **-S** one that swishes
SWISHY	*adj* **SWISHIER, SWISHIEST** swishing
SWISS	*n* pl. **-ES** a cotton fabric
SWITCH	*v* **-ED, -ING, -ES** to beat with a flexible rod
SWITCHER	*n* pl. **-S** one that switches
SWITH	*adv* quickly
SWITHE	*adv* swith
SWITHER	*v* **-ED, -ING, -S** to doubt
SWITHLY	*adv* swith
SWIVE	*v* **SWIVED, SWIVING, SWIVES** to copulate with
SWIVEL	*v* **-ELED, -ELING, -ELS** or **-ELLED, -ELLING, -ELS** to turn on a pivoted support
SWIVET	*n* pl. **-S** a state of nervous excitement
SWIZZLE	*v* **-ZLED, -ZLING, -ZLES** to drink excessively
SWIZZLER	*n* pl. **-S** one that swizzles
SWOB	*v* **SWOBBED, SWOBBING, SWOBS** to swab
SWOBBER	*n* pl. **-S** swabber
SWOLLEN	past participle of swell
SWOON	*v* **-ED, -ING, -S** to faint
SWOONER	*n* pl. **-S** one that swoons
SWOONY	*adj* **SWOONIER, SWOONIEST** languid, dazed
SWOOP	*v* **-ED, -ING, -S** to make a sudden descent
SWOOPER	*n* pl. **-S** one that swoops
SWOOPY	*adj* **SWOOPIER, SWOOPIEST** having sweeping lines or features
SWOOSH	*v* **-ED, -ING, -ES** to move with a rustling sound
SWOP	*v* **SWOPPED, SWOPPING, SWOPS** to swap
SWORD	*n* pl. **-S** a weapon having a long blade for cutting or thrusting
SWORDMAN	*n* pl. **-MEN** one skilled in the use of a sword
SWORE	a past tense of swear
SWORN	past participle of swear
SWOT	*v* **SWOTTED, SWOTTING, SWOTS** to swat
SWOTTER	*n* pl. **-S** one that swots
SWOUN	*v* **-ED, -ING, -S** to swoon
SWOUND	*v* **-ED, -ING, -S** to swoon
SWUM	past participle of swim
SWUNG	a past tense of swing
SYBARITE	*n* pl. **-S** a person devoted to pleasure and luxury
SYBO	*n* pl. **-BOES** the cibol
SYCAMINE	*n* pl. **-S** the mulberry tree
SYCAMORE	*n* pl. **-S** a North American tree
SYCE	*n* pl. **-S** a male servant in India
SYCEE	*n* pl. **-S** fine uncoined silver formerly used in China as money
SYCOMORE	*n* pl. **-S** sycamore
SYCONIUM	*n* pl. **-NIA** a fleshy multiple fruit
SYCOSIS	*n* pl. **-COSES** an inflammatory disease of the hair follicles
SYENITE	*n* pl. **-S** an igneous rock **SYENITIC** *adj*
SYKE	*n* pl. **-S** a small stream
SYLI	*n* pl. **-S** a former monetary unit of Guinea
SYLLABI	a pl. of syllabus
SYLLABIC	*n* pl. **-S** a speech sound of high sonority
SYLLABLE	*v* **-BLED, -BLING, -BLES** to pronounce syllables (units of spoken language)
SYLLABUB	*n* pl. **-S** sillabub
SYLLABUS	*n* pl. **-BUSES** or **-BI** an outline of a course of study
SYLPH	*n* pl. **-S** a slender, graceful girl or woman **SYLPHIC, SYLPHISH, SYLPHY** *adj*
SYLPHID	*n* pl. **-S** a young sylph
SYLVA	*n* pl. **-VAS** or **-VAE** the forest trees of an area
SYLVAN	*n* pl. **-S** one that lives in a forest
SYLVATIC	*adj* pertaining to a forest
SYLVIN	*n* pl. **-S** sylvite
SYLVINE	*n* pl. **-S** sylvite
SYLVITE	*n* pl. **-S** an ore of potassium
SYMBION	*n* pl. **-S** symbiont
SYMBIONT	*n* pl. **-S** an organism living in close association with another
SYMBIOT	*n* pl. **-S** symbiont

SYMBIOTE *n pl.* **-S** symbiont

SYMBOL *v* **-BOLED, -BOLING, -BOLS** or **-BOLLED, -BOLLING, -BOLS** to serve as a symbol (a representation) of

SYMBOLIC *adj* pertaining to a symbol

SYMMETRY *n pl.* **-TRIES** an exact correspondence between the opposite halves of a figure

SYMPATHY *n pl.* **-THIES** a feeling of compassion for another's suffering

SYMPATRY *n pl.* **-RIES** the state of occupying the same area without loss of identity from interbreeding

SYMPHONY *n pl.* **-NIES** an orchestral composition

SYMPODIA *n/pl* plant stems made up of a series of superposed branches

SYMPOSIA *n/pl* conferences for the purpose of discussion

SYMPTOM *n pl.* **-S** an indication of something

SYN *adv* syne

SYNAGOG *n pl.* **-S** a building for Jewish worship

SYNANON *n pl.* **-S** a method of group therapy for drug addicts

SYNAPSE *v* **-APSED, -APSING, -APSES** to come together in synapsis

SYNAPSID *n pl.* **-S** one of a group of extinct reptiles

SYNAPSIS *n pl.* **-APSES** the point at which a nervous impulse passes from one neuron to another **SYNAPTIC** *adj*

SYNC *v* **-ED, -ING, -S** to cause to operate in unison

SYNCARP *n pl.* **-S** a fleshy multiple fruit

SYNCARPY *n pl.* **-PIES** the state of being a syncarp

SYNCH *v* **-ED, -ING, -S** to sync

SYNCHRO *n pl.* **-CHROS** a selsyn

SYNCLINE *n pl.* **-S** a type of rock formation

SYNCOM *n pl.* **-S** a type of communications satellite

SYNCOPE *n pl.* **-S** the contraction of a word by omitting one or more sounds from the middle **SYNCOPAL, SYNCOPIC** *adj*

SYNCYTIA *n/pl* masses of protoplasm resulting from cell fusion

SYNDESIS *n pl.* **-DESISES** or **-DESES** synapsis

SYNDET *n pl.* **-S** a synthetic detergent

SYNDETIC *adj* serving to connect

SYNDIC *n pl.* **-S** a business agent **SYNDICAL** *adj*

SYNDROME *n pl.* **-S** a group of symptoms that characterize a particular disorder

SYNE *adv* since

SYNECTIC *adj* pertaining to a system of problem solving

SYNERGIA *n pl.* **-S** synergy

SYNERGID *n pl.* **-S** a cell found in the embryo sac of a seed plant

SYNERGY *n pl.* **-GIES** combined action **SYNERGIC** *adj*

SYNESIS *n pl.* **-SISES** a type of grammatical construction

SYNFUEL *n pl.* **-S** a fuel derived from fossil fuels

SYNGAMY *n pl.* **-MIES** the union of two gametes **SYNGAMIC** *adj*

SYNGAS *n pl.* **-GASES** or **-GASSES** a mixture of carbon monoxide and hydrogen used in chemical synthesis

SYNGENIC *adj* relating to or being genetically identical individuals with respect to reaction to antigens

SYNKARYA *n/pl* cell nuclei formed by the fusion of two preexisting nuclei

SYNOD *n pl.* **-S** a church council **SYNODAL, SYNODIC** *adj*

SYNONYM *n pl.* **-S** a word having the same meaning as another

SYNONYME *n pl.* **-S** synonym

SYNONYMY *n pl.* **-MIES** equivalence of meaning

SYNOPSIS *n pl.* **-OPSES** a summary **SYNOPTIC** *adj*

SYNOVIA *n pl.* **-S** a lubricating fluid secreted by certain membranes **SYNOVIAL** *adj*

SYNTAGM *n pl.* **-S** syntagma

SYNTAGMA *n pl.* **-MAS** or **-MATA** a syntactic element

SYNTAX *n pl.* **-ES** the way in which words are put together to form phrases and sentences

SYNTH *n pl.* **-S** a synthesizer

SYNTHPOP *n pl.* **-S** popular music played with synthesizers

SYNTONY *n pl.* **-NIES** the tuning of transmitters and receivers with each other **SYNTONIC** *adj*

SYNURA *n* pl. **-RAE** any of a genus of protozoa

SYPH *n* pl. **-S** syphilis

SYPHER *v* **-ED, -ING, -S** to overlap so as to make an even surface, as beveled plank edges

SYPHILIS *n* pl. **-LISES** a venereal disease

SYPHON *v* **-ED, -ING, -S** to siphon

SYREN *n* pl. **-S** siren

SYRETTE *n* pl. **-S** a small tube fitted with a hypodermic needle containing a single dose of medication

SYRINGA *n* pl. **-S** an ornamental shrub

SYRINGE *v* **-RINGED, -RINGING, -RINGES** to cleanse or treat with injected fluid

SYRINX *n* pl. **-INXES** or **-INGES** the vocal organ of a bird

SYRPHIAN *n* pl. **-S** syrphid

SYRPHID *n* pl. **-S** a winged insect

SYRUP *v* **-ED, -ING, -S** to sweeten with a thick sweet liquid

SYRUPY *adj* **-UPIER, -UPIEST** resembling a thick, sticky, sweet liquid

SYSADMIN *n* pl. **-S** a system administrator

SYSOP *n* pl. **-S** the administrator of a computer bulletin board

SYSTEM *n* pl. **-S** a group of interacting elements forming a unified whole

SYSTEMIC *n* pl. **-S** a type of pesticide

SYSTOLE *n* pl. **-S** the normal rhythmic contraction of the heart **SYSTOLIC** *adj*

SYZYGY *n* pl. **-GIES** the configuration of the earth, moon, and sun lying in a straight line **SYZYGAL, SYZYGIAL** *adj*

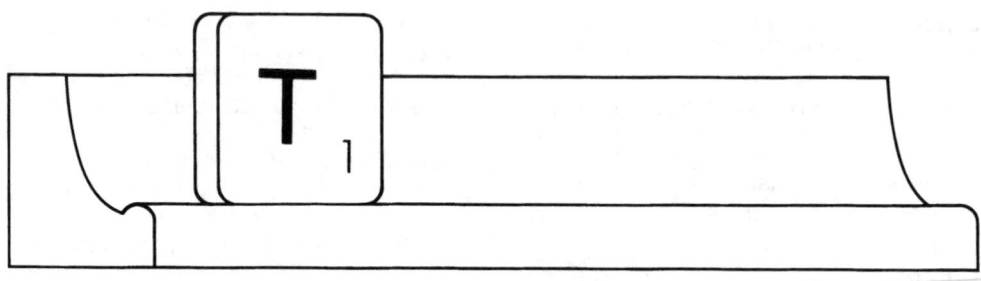

TA	*n* pl. **-S** an expression of gratitude
TAB	*v* **TABBED, TABBING, TABS** to name or designate
TABANID	*n* pl. **-S** a bloodsucking insect
TABARD	*n* pl. **-S** a sleeveless outer garment **TABARDED** *adj*
TABARET	*n* pl. **-S** a silk fabric
TABBED	past tense of tab
TABBING	present participle of tab
TABBIS	*n* pl. **-BISES** a silk fabric
TABBY	*v* **-BIED, -BYING, -BIES** to give a wavy appearance to
TABER	*v* **-ED, -ING, -S** to tabor
TABES	*n* pl. **TABES** a syphilitic disease
TABETIC	*n* pl. **-S** one affected with tabes
TABID	*adj* affected with tabes
TABLA	*n* pl. **-S** a small drum
TABLE	*v* **-BLED, -BLING, -BLES** to place on a table (a piece of furniture having a flat upper surface)
TABLEAU	*n* pl. **-LEAUS** or **-LEAUX** a picture
TABLEFUL	*n* pl. **TABLEFULS** or **TABLESFUL** as much as a table can hold
TABLET	*v* **-LETED, -LETING, -LETS** or **-LETTED, -LETTING, -LETS** to inscribe on a small, flat surface
TABLETOP	*n* pl. **-S** the top of a table
TABLING	present participle of table
TABLOID	*n* pl. **-S** a small newspaper
TABOO	*v* **-ED, -ING, -S** to exclude from use, approach, or mention
TABOOLEY	*n* pl. **-LEYS** tabouli
TABOR	*v* **-ED, -ING, -S** to beat on a small drum
TABORER	*n* pl. **-S** one that tabors
TABORET	*n* pl. **-S** a small drum
TABORIN	*n* pl. **-S** taborine
TABORINE	*n* pl. **-S** a taboret

TABOULEH	*n* pl. **-S** tabouli
TABOULI	*n* pl. **-S** a Lebanese salad containing bulgur wheat, tomatoes, parsley, onions, and mint
TABOUR	*v* **-ED, -ING, -S** to tabor
TABOURER	*n* pl. **-S** taborer
TABOURET	*n* pl. **-S** taboret
TABU	*v* **-ED, -ING, -S** to taboo
TABULAR	*adj* of or pertaining to a list
TABULATE	*v* **-LATED, -LATING, -LATES** to arrange in a list
TABULI	*n* pl. **-S** tabouli
TABUN	*n* pl. **-S** a chemical compound
TACE	*n* pl. **-S** tasse
TACET	*interj* be silent — used as a musical direction
TACH	*n* pl. **-S** a device for indicating speed of rotation
TACHE	*n* pl. **-S** a clasp or buckle
TACHINID	*n* pl. **-S** a grayish fly
TACHISM	*n* pl. **-S** action painting
TACHISME	*n* pl. **-S** tachism
TACHIST	*n* pl. **-S** an action painter
TACHISTE	*n* pl. **-S** tachist
TACHYON	*n* pl. **-S** a theoretical subatomic particle
TACIT	*adj* unspoken **TACITLY** *adv*
TACITURN	*adj* habitually silent
TACK	*v* **-ED, -ING, -S** to fasten with tacks (short, sharp-pointed nails)
TACKER	*n* pl. **-S** one that tacks
TACKET	*n* pl. **-S** a hobnail
TACKEY	*adj* **TACKIER, TACKIEST** tacky
TACKIER	comparative of tacky
TACKIEST	superlative of tacky
TACKIFY	*v* **-FIED, -FYING, -FIES** to make tacky

TACKILY	*adv* in a tacky manner
TACKLE	*v* **-LED, -LING, -LES** to seize and throw to the ground
TACKLER	*n* pl. **-S** one that tackles
TACKLESS	*adj* having no tacks
TACKLING	*n* pl. **-S** equipment
TACKY	*adj* **TACKIER, TACKIEST** adhesive
TACNODE	*n* pl. **-S** a point of contact between two curves
TACO	*n* pl. **-COS** a tortilla folded around a filling
TACONITE	*n* pl. **-S** a low-grade iron ore
TACRINE	*n* pl. **-S** a drug for treating Alzheimer's disease
TACT	*n* pl. **-S** skill in dealing with delicate situations
TACTFUL	*adj* having tact
TACTIC	*n* pl. **-S** a maneuver for gaining an objective **TACTICAL** *adj*
TACTILE	*adj* pertaining to the sense of touch
TACTION	*n* pl. **-S** the act of touching
TACTLESS	*adj* lacking tact
TACTUAL	*adj* tactile
TAD	*n* pl. **-S** a small boy
TADPOLE	*n* pl. **-S** the aquatic larva of an amphibian
TAE	*prep* to
TAEL	*n* pl. **-S** a Chinese unit of weight
TAENIA	*n* pl. **-NIAS** or **-NIAE** a headband worn in ancient Greece
TAFFAREL	*n* pl. **-S** taffrail
TAFFEREL	*n* pl. **-S** taffrail
TAFFETA	*n* pl. **-S** a lustrous fabric
TAFFIA	*n* pl. **-S** tafia
TAFFRAIL	*n* pl. **-S** a rail around the stern of a ship
TAFFY	*n* pl. **-FIES** a chewy candy
TAFIA	*n* pl. **-S** an inferior rum
TAG	*v* **TAGGED, TAGGING, TAGS** to provide with a tag (an identifying marker)
TAGALONG	*n* pl. **-S** one that follows another
TAGBOARD	*n* pl. **-S** a material for making shipping tags
TAGGANT	*n* pl. **-S** a substance added to a product to indicate its source of manufacture
TAGGED	past tense of tag
TAGGER	*n* pl. **-S** one that tags
TAGGING	present participle of tag
TAGLIKE	*adj* resembling a tag
TAGLINE	*n* pl. **-S** the final line of a play or joke that makes the point
TAGMEME	*n* pl. **-S** the smallest unit of meaningful grammatical relation
TAGMEMIC	*adj* pertaining to a grammar in which a tagmeme is the basic unit
TAGRAG	*n* pl. **-S** riffraff
TAHINI	*n* pl. **-S** a paste of sesame seeds
TAHR	*n* pl. **-S** a goatlike mammal
TAHSIL	*n* pl. **-S** a district in India
TAIGA	*n* pl. **-S** a subarctic evergreen forest
TAIGLACH	*n* pl. **TAIGLACH** teiglach
TAIL	*v* **-ED, -ING, -S** to provide with a tail (a hindmost part)
TAILBACK	*n* pl. **-S** a member of the backfield in some football formations
TAILBONE	*n* pl. **-S** the coccyx
TAILCOAT	*n* pl. **-S** a man's coat
TAILER	*n* pl. **-S** one that secretly follows another
TAILFAN	*n* pl. **-S** a fanlike swimming organ at the rear of some crustaceans
TAILFIN	*n* pl. **-S** a fin at the posterior end of a fish
TAILGATE	*v* **-GATED, -GATING, -GATES** to drive dangerously close behind another vehicle
TAILING	*n* pl. **-S** the part of a projecting stone or brick that is inserted into a wall
TAILLAMP	*n* pl. **-S** a light at the rear of a vehicle
TAILLE	*n* pl. **-S** a former French tax
TAILLESS	*adj* having no tail
TAILLEUR	*n* pl. **-S** a woman's tailored suit
TAILLIKE	*adj* resembling a tail
TAILOR	*v* **-ED, -ING, -S** to fit with clothes
TAILPIPE	*n* pl. **-S** an exhaust pipe
TAILRACE	*n* pl. **-S** a part of a millrace
TAILSKID	*n* pl. **-S** a support on which the tail of an airplane rests
TAILSPIN	*v* **-SPINNED, -SPINNING, -SPINS** to spin headlong down toward earth
TAILWIND	*n* pl. **-S** a wind coming from behind a moving vehicle

TAIN *n* pl. **-S** a thin plate

TAINT *v* **-ED, -ING, -S** to touch or affect slightly with something bad

TAIPAN *n* pl. **-S** a venomous snake

TAJ *n* pl. **-ES** a tall, conical cap worn in Muslim countries

TAKA *n* pl. **-S** a monetary unit of Bangladesh

TAKAHE *n* pl. **-S** a flightless bird

TAKE *v* **TOOK, TAKEN, TAKING, TAKES** to get possession of **TAKABLE, TAKEABLE** *adj*

TAKEAWAY *n* pl. **-AWAYS** prepared food to be taken away from its place of sale

TAKEDOWN *n* pl. **-S** an article that can be taken apart easily

TAKEOFF *n* pl. **-S** the act of rising in flight

TAKEOUT *n* pl. **-S** the act of removing

TAKEOVER *n* pl. **-S** the act of assuming control

TAKER *n* pl. **-S** one that takes

TAKEUP *n* pl. **-S** the act of taking something up

TAKIN *n* pl. **-S** a goatlike mammal

TAKING *n* pl. **-S** a seizure

TAKINGLY *adv* in an attractive manner

TALA *n* pl. **-S** a traditional rhythmic pattern of music in India

TALAPOIN *n* pl. **-S** a small African monkey

TALAR *n* pl. **-S** a long cloak

TALARIA *n/pl* winged sandals worn by various figures of classical mythology

TALC *v* **TALCKED, TALCKING, TALCS** or **TALCED, TALCING, TALCS** to treat with talc (a soft mineral with a soapy texture) **TALCKY, TALCOSE, TALCOUS** *adj*

TALCUM *n* pl. **-S** a powder made from talc

TALE *n* pl. **-S** a story

TALEGGIO *n* pl. **-GIOS** a soft creamy cheese

TALENT *n* pl. **-S** a special natural ability **TALENTED** *adj*

TALER *n* pl. **-S** a formerly used German coin

TALESMAN *n* pl. **-MEN** a person summoned to fill a vacancy on a jury

TALI pl. of talus

TALION *n* pl. **-S** a retaliation for a crime

TALIPED *n* pl. **-S** a person afflicted with clubfoot

TALIPES *n* pl. **TALIPES** clubfoot

TALIPOT *n* pl. **-S** a tall palm tree

TALISMAN *n* pl. **-S** an object believed to possess magical powers

TALK *v* **-ED, -ING, -S** to communicate by speaking

TALKABLE *adj* able to be talked about

TALKBACK *n* pl. **-S** a one-way communications link between a control booth and a recording studio

TALKER *n* pl. **-S** one that talks

TALKIE *n* pl. **-S** a moving picture with synchronized sound

TALKING *n* pl. **-S** conversation

TALKY *adj* **TALKIER, TALKIEST** tending to talk a great deal

TALL *n* pl. **-S** a garment size for tall persons

TALL *adj* **TALLER, TALLEST** having great height

TALLAGE *v* **-LAGED, -LAGING, -LAGES** to tax

TALLBOY *n* pl. **-BOYS** a highboy

TALLIED past tense of tally

TALLIER *n* pl. **-S** one that tallies

TALLIES present 3d person sing. of tally

TALLIS *n* pl. **-LISES** or **-LISIM** tallith

TALLISH *adj* somewhat tall

TALLIT *n* pl. **-LITS** or **-LITIM** tallith

TALLITH *n* pl. **-LITHS** or **-LITHIM** a Jewish prayer shawl

TALLNESS *n* pl. **-ES** the state of being tall

TALLOL *n* pl. **-S** a resinous liquid

TALLOW *v* **-ED, -ING, -S** to smear with tallow (a mixture of animal fats)

TALLOWY *adj* resembling tallow

TALLY *v* **-LIED, -LYING, -LIES** to count

TALLYHO *v* **-ED, -ING, -S** to make an encouraging shout to hunting hounds

TALLYMAN *n* pl. **-MEN** a person who tallies

TALMUDIC *adj* pertaining to the body of Jewish civil and religious law

TALON *n* pl. **-S** a claw of a bird of prey **TALONED** *adj*

TALOOKA *n* pl. **-S** taluk

TALUK *n* pl. **-S** an estate in India

TALUKA *n* pl. **-S** taluk

TALUS	*n* pl. **-ES** a slope formed by an accumulation of rock debris	**TAMPALA**	*n* pl. **-S** an annual herb
TALUS	*n* pl. **-LI** a bone of the foot	**TAMPAN**	*n* pl. **-S** a biting insect
TAM	*n* pl. **-S** a tight-fitting Scottish cap	**TAMPER**	*v* **-ED, -ING, -S** to interfere in a harmful manner
TAMABLE	*adj* capable of being tamed	**TAMPERER**	*n* pl. **-S** one that tampers
TAMAL	*n* pl. **-S** tamale	**TAMPION**	*n* pl. **-S** a plug for the muzzle of a cannon
TAMALE	*n* pl. **-S** a Mexican dish		
TAMANDU	*n* pl. **-S** tamandua	**TAMPON**	*v* **-ED, -ING, -S** to plug with a cotton pad
TAMANDUA	*n* pl. **-S** an arboreal anteater		
TAMARACK	*n* pl. **-S** a timber tree	**TAN**	*adj* **TANNER, TANNEST** brown from the sun's rays
TAMARAO	*n* pl. **-RAOS** tamarau		
TAMARAU	*n* pl. **-S** a small buffalo of the Philippines	**TAN**	*v* **TANNED, TANNING, TANS** to convert hide into leather by soaking in chemicals
TAMARI	*n* pl. **-S** a Japanese soy sauce	**TANAGER**	*n* pl. **-S** a brightly colored bird
TAMARIN	*n* pl. **-S** a South American monkey	**TANBARK**	*n* pl. **-S** a tree bark used as a source of tannin
TAMARIND	*n* pl. **-S** a tropical tree		
TAMARISK	*n* pl. **-S** an evergreen shrub	**TANDEM**	*n* pl. **-S** a bicycle built for two
TAMASHA	*n* pl. **-S** a public entertainment in India	**TANDOOR**	*n* pl. **-DOORS** or **-DOORI** a clay oven
TAMBAC	*n* pl. **-S** tombac	**TANDOORI**	*n* pl. **-S** food cooked in a tandoor
TAMBAK	*n* pl. **-S** tombac	**TANG**	*v* **-ED, -ING, -S** to provide with a pungent flavor
TAMBALA	*n* pl. **-S** or **MATAMBALA** a monetary unit of Malawi		
		TANGA	*n* pl. **TANGA** a former monetary unit of Tajikistan
TAMBOUR	*v* **-ED, -ING, -S** to embroider on a round wooden frame		
		TANGELO	*n* pl. **-LOS** a citrus fruit
TAMBOURA	*n* pl. **-S** tambura	**TANGENCE**	*n* pl. **-S** tangency
TAMBUR	*n* pl. **-S** tambura	**TANGENCY**	*n* pl. **-CIES** the state of being in immediate physical contact
TAMBURA	*n* pl. **-S** a stringed instrument		
TAME	*adj* **TAMER, TAMEST** gentle or docile	**TANGENT**	*n* pl. **-S** a straight line in contact with a curve at one point
TAME	*v* **TAMED, TAMING, TAMES** to make tame	**TANGIBLE**	*n* pl. **-S** something palpable
		TANGIBLY	*adv* palpably
TAMEABLE	*adj* tamable	**TANGIER**	comparative of tangy
TAMEIN	*n* pl. **-S** a garment worn by Burmese women	**TANGIEST**	superlative of tangy
		TANGLE	*v* **-GLED, -GLING, -GLES** to bring together in intricate confusion
TAMELESS	*adj* not capable of being tamed		
TAMELY	*adv* in a tame manner	**TANGLER**	*n* pl. **-S** one that tangles
TAMENESS	*n* pl. **-ES** the state of being tame	**TANGLY**	*adj* **-GLIER, -GLIEST** tangled
TAMER	*n* pl. **-S** one that tames	**TANGO**	*v* **-ED, -ING, -S** to perform a Latin-American dance
TAMEST	superlative of tame		
TAMING	present participle of tame	**TANGRAM**	*n* pl. **-S** a Chinese puzzle
TAMIS	*n* pl. **-ISES** a strainer made of cloth mesh	**TANGY**	*adj* **TANGIER, TANGIEST** pungent
		TANIST	*n* pl. **-S** the heir apparent to a Celtic chief
TAMMIE	*n* pl. **-S** tammy		
TAMMY	*n* pl. **-MIES** a fabric of mixed fibers	**TANISTRY**	*n* pl. **-RIES** the system of electing a tanist
TAMP	*v* **-ED, -ING, -S** to pack down by tapping	**TANK**	*v* **-ED, -ING, -S** to store in a tank (a container usually for liquids)
		TANKA	*n* pl. **-S** a Japanese verse form

TANKAGE *n pl.* **-S** the capacity of a tank

TANKARD *n pl.* **-S** a tall drinking vessel

TANKER *n pl.* **-S** a ship designed to transport liquids

TANKFUL *n pl.* **-S** the amount a tank can hold

TANKINI *n pl.* **-S** a woman's swimsuit consisting of bikini briefs and a tank top

TANKLESS *adj* having no tank

TANKLIKE *adj* resembling a tank

TANKSHIP *n pl.* **-S** a tanker

TANNABLE *adj* capable of being tanned

TANNAGE *n pl.* **-S** the process of tanning

TANNATE *n pl.* **-S** a chemical salt

TANNED past tense of tan

TANNER *n pl.* **-S** one that tans

TANNERY *n pl.* **-NERIES** a place where hides are tanned

TANNEST superlative of tan

TANNIC *adj* pertaining to tannin

TANNIN *n pl.* **-S** a chemical compound used in tanning

TANNING *n pl.* **-S** the process of converting hides into leather

TANNISH *adj* somewhat tan

TANREC *n pl.* **-S** tenrec

TANSY *n pl.* **-SIES** a perennial herb

TANTALUM *n pl.* **-S** a metallic element **TANTALIC** *adj*

TANTALUS *n pl.* **-ES** a case for wine bottles

TANTARA *n pl.* **-S** the sound of a trumpet or horn

TANTIVY *n pl.* **-TIVIES** a hunting cry

TANTO *adv* so much — used as a musical direction

TANTRA *n pl.* **-S** one of a class of Hindu religious writings **TANTRIC** *adj*

TANTRISM *n pl.* **-S** a school of Buddhism incorporating Hindu and pagan elements

TANTRUM *n pl.* **-S** a fit of rage

TANUKI *n pl.* **-S** a raccoon dog

TANYARD *n pl.* **-S** the section of a tannery containing the vats

TAO *n pl.* **-S** the path of virtuous conduct according to a Chinese philosophy

TAP *v* **TAPPED, TAPPING, TAPS** to strike gently

TAPA *n pl.* **-S** a cloth made from tree bark

TAPADERA *n pl.* **-S** a part of a saddle

TAPADERO *n pl.* **-ROS** tapadera

TAPALO *n pl.* **-LOS** a scarf worn in Latin-American countries

TAPE *v* **TAPED, TAPING, TAPES** to fasten with tape (a long, narrow strip or band) **TAPEABLE** *adj*

TAPELESS *adj* being without tape

TAPELIKE *adj* resembling tape

TAPELINE *n pl.* **-S** a tape for measuring distances

TAPENADE *n pl.* **-S** a spread made with black olives, capers, and anchovies

TAPER *v* **-ED, -ING, -S** to become gradually narrower toward one end

TAPERER *n pl.* **-S** one that carries a candle in a religious procession

TAPESTRY *v* **-TRIED, -TRYING, -TRIES** to decorate with woven wall hangings

TAPETUM *n pl.* **-TA** a layer of cells in some plants **TAPETAL** *adj*

TAPEWORM *n pl.* **-S** a parasitic worm

TAPHOLE *n pl.* **-S** a hole in a blast furnace

TAPHOUSE *n pl.* **-S** a tavern

TAPING present participle of tape

TAPIOCA *n pl.* **-S** a starchy food

TAPIR *n pl.* **-S** a hoofed mammal

TAPIS *n pl.* **-PISES** material used for wall hangings and floor coverings

TAPPABLE *adj* capable of being tapped

TAPPED past tense of tap

TAPPER *n pl.* **-S** one that taps

TAPPET *n pl.* **-S** a sliding rod that causes another part of a mechanism to move

TAPPING *n pl.* **-S** the process or means by which something is tapped

TAPROOM *n pl.* **-S** a barroom

TAPROOT *n pl.* **-S** the main root of a plant

TAPSTER *n pl.* **-S** one that dispenses liquor in a barroom

TAQUERIA *n pl.* **-S** a restaurant specializing in tacos and burritos

TAR *v* **TARRED, TARRING, TARS** to cover with tar (a black viscous liquid)

TARAMA *n pl.* **-S** a Greek paste of fish roe, garlic, lemon juice, and olive oil

TARANTAS *n* pl. **-ES** a Russian carriage

TARBOOSH *n* pl. **-ES** a cap worn by Muslim men

TARBUSH *n* pl. **-ES** tarboosh

TARDIER comparative of tardy

TARDIES pl. of tardy

TARDIVE *adj* having symptoms that develop slowly

TARDO *adj* slow — used as a musical direction

TARDY *adj* **TARDIER, TARDIEST** late **TARDILY** *adv*

TARDY *n* pl. **-DIES** an instance of being late

TARDYON *n* pl. **-S** a subatomic particle that travels slower than the speed of light

TARE *v* **TARED, TARING, TARES** to determine the weight of a container holding goods

TARGE *n* pl. **-S** a small, round shield

TARGET *v* **-ED, -ING, -S** to make a goal of

TARIFF *v* **-ED, -ING, -S** to tax imported or exported goods

TARING present participle of tare

TARLATAN *n* pl. **-S** a cotton fabric

TARLETAN *n* pl. **-S** tarlatan

TARMAC *v* **-MACKED, -MACKING, -MACS** to cause (an aircraft) to sit on a taxiway

TARN *n* pl. **-S** a small mountain lake

TARNAL *adj* damned **TARNALLY** *adv*

TARNISH *v* **-ED, -ING, -ES** to dull the luster of

TARO *n* pl. **-ROS** a tropical plant

TAROC *n* pl. **-S** tarok

TAROK *n* pl. **-S** a card game

TAROT *n* pl. **-S** any of a set of playing cards used for fortune-telling

TARP *n* pl. **-S** a protective canvas covering

TARPAN *n* pl. **-S** an Asian wild horse

TARPAPER *n* pl. **-S** a heavy paper coated with tar

TARPON *n* pl. **-S** a marine game fish

TARRAGON *n* pl. **-S** a perennial herb

TARRE *v* **TARRED, TARRING, TARRES** to urge to action

TARRED past tense of tar

TARRIER *n* pl. **-S** one that tarries

TARRING present participle of tar and tarre

TARRY *adj* **-RIER, -RIEST** resembling tar

TARRY *v* **-RIED, -RYING, -RIES** to delay or be slow in acting or doing

TARSAL *n* pl. **-S** a bone of the foot

TARSI pl. of tarsus

TARSIA *n* pl. **-S** intarsia

TARSIER *n* pl. **-S** a nocturnal primate

TARSUS *n* pl. **TARSI** a part of the foot

TART *adj* **TARTER, TARTEST** having a sharp, sour taste

TART *v* **-ED, -ING, -S** to dress up

TARTAN *n* pl. **-S** a patterned woolen fabric

TARTANA *n* pl. **-S** a Mediterranean sailing vessel

TARTAR *n* pl. **-S** a crust on the teeth **TARTARIC** *adj*

TARTARE *adj* served raw

TARTIER comparative of tarty

TARTIEST superlative of tarty

TARTISH *adj* somewhat tart

TARTLET *n* pl. **-S** a small pie

TARTLY *adv* in a tart manner

TARTNESS *n* pl. **-ES** the state of being tart

TARTRATE *n* pl. **-S** a chemical salt

TARTUFE *n* pl. **-S** tartuffe

TARTUFFE *n* pl. **-S** a hypocrite

TARTY *adj* **TARTIER, TARTIEST** suggestive of a prostitute **TARTILY** *adv*

TARWEED *n* pl. **-S** a flowering plant

TARZAN *n* pl. **-S** a person of superior strength and agility

TASK *v* **-ED, -ING, -S** to assign a job to

TASKBAR *n* pl. **-S** a row of graphical controls on a computer screen

TASKWORK *n* pl. **-S** hard work

TASS *n* pl. **-ES** a drinking cup

TASSE *n* pl. **-S** tasset

TASSEL *v* **-SELED, -SELING, -SELS** or **-SELLED, -SELLING, -SELS** to adorn with dangling ornaments

TASSET *n* pl. **-S** a piece of plate armor for the upper thigh

TASSIE *n* pl. **-S** tass

TASTE *v* **TASTED, TASTING, TASTES** to perceive the flavor of by taking into the mouth **TASTABLE** *adj*

TASTEFUL   *adj* tasty

TASTER   *n* pl. **-S** one that tastes

TASTY   *adj* **TASTIER, TASTIEST** pleasant to the taste **TASTILY** *adv*

TAT   *v* **TATTED, TATTING, TATS** to make tatting

TATAMI   *n* pl. **-S** straw matting used as a floor covering

TATAR   *n* pl. **-S** a ferocious person

TATE   *n* pl. **-S** a tuft of hair

TATER   *n* pl. **-S** a potato

TATOUAY   *n* pl. **-AYS** a South American armadillo

TATSOI   *n* pl. **-S** an Asian mustard

TATTED   past tense of tat

TATTER   *v* **-ED, -ING, -S** to become torn and worn

TATTIE   *n* pl. **-S** a potato

TATTIER   comparative of tatty

TATTIEST   superlative of tatty

TATTILY   *adv* in a tatty manner

TATTING   *n* pl. **-S** delicate handmade lace

TATTLE   *v* **-TLED, -TLING, -TLES** to reveal the activities of another

TATTLER   *n* pl. **-S** one that tattles

TATTOO   *v* **-ED, -ING, -S** to mark the skin with indelible pigments

TATTOOER   *n* pl. **-S** one that tattoos

TATTY   *adj* **-TIER, -TIEST** shabby

TAU   *n* pl. **-S** a Greek letter

TAUGHT   past tense of teach

TAUNT   *v* **-ED, -ING, -S** to challenge or reproach sarcastically

TAUNTER   *n* pl. **-S** one that taunts

TAUON   *n* pl. **-S** an unstable lepton

TAUPE   *n* pl. **-S** a dark gray color

TAURINE   *n* pl. **-S** a chemical compound

TAUT   *adj* **TAUTER, TAUTEST** fully stretched, so as not to be slack

TAUT   *v* **-ED, -ING, -S** to tangle

TAUTAUG   *n* pl. **-S** tautog

TAUTEN   *v* **-ED, -ING, -S** to make taut

TAUTLY   *adv* in a taut manner

TAUTNESS   *n* pl. **-ES** the state of being taut

TAUTOG   *n* pl. **-S** a marine fish

TAUTOMER   *n* pl. **-S** a type of chemical compound

TAUTONYM   *n* pl. **-S** a type of taxonomic designation

TAV   *n* pl. **-S** a Hebrew letter

TAVERN   *n* pl. **-S** a place where liquor is sold to be drunk on the premises

TAVERNA   *n* pl. **-S** a cafe in Greece

TAVERNER   *n* pl. **-S** one that runs a tavern

TAW   *v* **-ED, -ING, -S** to convert into white leather by the application of minerals

TAWDRY   *adj* **-DRIER, -DRIEST** gaudy **TAWDRILY** *adv*

TAWDRY   *n* pl. **-DRIES** gaudy finery

TAWER   *n* pl. **-S** one that taws

TAWIE   *adj* docile

TAWNEY   *n* pl. **-NEYS** tawny

TAWNY   *adj* **-NIER, -NIEST** light brown **TAWNILY** *adv*

TAWNY   *n* pl. **-NIES** a light brown color

TAWPIE   *n* pl. **-S** a foolish young person

TAWSE   *v* **TAWSED, TAWSING, TAWSES** to flog

TAX   *v* **-ED, -ING, -ES** to place a tax (a charge imposed by authority for public purposes) on

TAXA   a pl. of taxon

TAXABLE   *adj* subject to tax **TAXABLY** *adv*

TAXABLE   *n* pl. **-S** a taxable item

TAXATION   *n* pl. **-S** the process of taxing

TAXEME   *n* pl. **-S** a minimum grammatical feature of selection **TAXEMIC** *adj*

TAXER   *n* pl. **-S** one that taxes

TAXI   *v* **TAXIED, TAXIING** or **TAXYING, TAXIS** or **TAXIES** to travel in a taxicab

TAXICAB   *n* pl. **-S** an automobile for hire

TAXIMAN   *n* pl. **-MEN** the operator of a taxicab

TAXINGLY   *adv* in an onerous manner

TAXITE   *n* pl. **-S** a volcanic rock **TAXITIC** *adj*

TAXIWAY   *n* pl. **-WAYS** a paved strip at an airport

TAXLESS   *adj* free from taxation

TAXMAN   *n* pl. **-MEN** one who collects taxes

TAXOL   *n* pl. **-S** a medicinal substance from a yew tree

TAXON   *n* pl. **TAXONS** or **TAXA** a unit of scientific classification

TAXONOMY *n* pl. **-MIES** the study of scientific classification

TAXPAID *adj* paid for by taxes

TAXPAYER *n* pl. **-S** one that pays taxes

TAXUS *n* pl. **TAXUS** an evergreen tree or shrub

TAXWISE *adj* pertaining to taxes

TAXYING a present participle of taxi

TAZZA *n* pl. **-ZAS** or **-ZE** an ornamental bowl

TEA *n* pl. **-S** a beverage made by infusing dried leaves in boiling water

TEABERRY *n* pl. **-RIES** a North American shrub

TEABOARD *n* pl. **-S** a tray for serving tea

TEABOWL *n* pl. **-S** a teacup having no handle

TEABOX *n* pl. **-ES** a box for tea leaves

TEACAKE *n* pl. **-S** a small cake served with tea

TEACART *n* pl. **-S** a wheeled table used in serving tea

TEACH *v* **TAUGHT, TEACHING, TEACHES** to impart knowledge or skill to

TEACHER *n* pl. **-S** one that teaches

TEACHING *n* pl. **-S** a doctrine

TEACUP *n* pl. **-S** a cup in which tea is served

TEAHOUSE *n* pl. **-S** a public establishment serving tea

TEAK *n* pl. **-S** an East Indian tree

TEAKWOOD *n* pl. **-S** the wood of the teak

TEAL *n* pl. **-S** a river duck

TEALIKE *adj* resembling tea

TEAM *v* **-ED, -ING, -S** to form a team (a group of persons associated in a joint action)

TEAMAKER *n* pl. **-S** one that makes tea

TEAMMATE *n* pl. **-S** a member of the same team

TEAMSTER *n* pl. **-S** a truck driver

TEAMWORK *n* pl. **-S** cooperative effort to achieve a common goal

TEAPOT *n* pl. **-S** a vessel used in making and serving tea

TEAPOY *n* pl. **-POYS** a small table used in serving tea

TEAR *v* **-ED, -ING, -S** to emit tears (drops of saline liquid secreted by a gland of the eye)

TEAR *v* **TORE, TORN, TEARING, TEARS** to pull apart or into pieces **TEARABLE** *adj*

TEARAWAY *n* pl. **-AWAYS** a rebellious person

TEARDOWN *n* pl. **-S** the process of disassembling

TEARDROP *n* pl. **-S** a tear

TEARER *n* pl. **-S** one that tears or rips

TEARFUL *adj* full of tears

TEARGAS *v* **-GASSED, -GASSING, -GASES** or **-GASSES** to subject to a gas that irritates the eyes

TEARIER comparative of teary

TEARIEST superlative of teary

TEARILY *adv* in a teary manner

TEARLESS *adj* being without tears

TEAROOM *n* pl. **-S** a restaurant serving tea

TEARY *adj* **TEARIER, TEARIEST** tearful

TEASE *v* **TEASED, TEASING, TEASES** to make fun of **TEASABLE** *adj*

TEASEL *v* **-SELED, -SELING, -SELS** or **-SELLED, -SELLING, -SELS** to raise a soft surface on fabric with a bristly flower head

TEASELER *n* pl. **-S** one that teasels

TEASER *n* pl. **-S** one that teases

TEASHOP *n* pl. **-S** a tearoom

TEASING present participle of tease

TEASPOON *n* pl. **-S** a small spoon

TEAT *n* pl. **-S** a mammary gland **TEATED** *adj*

TEATIME *n* pl. **-S** the customary time for tea

TEAWARE *n* pl. **-S** a tea service

TEAZEL *v* **-ZELED, -ZELING, -ZELS** or **-ZELLED, -ZELLING, -ZELS** to teasel

TEAZLE *v* **-ZLED, -ZLING, -ZLES** to teasel

TECH *n* pl. **-S** a technician

TECHED *adj* crazy

TECHIE *n* pl. **-S** a technician

TECHNIC *n* pl. **-S** technique

TECHNO *n* pl. **-NOS** a style of disco music

TECHY *adj* **TECHIER, TECHIEST** tetchy **TECHILY** *adv*

TECTA a pl. of tectum

TECTAL *adj* pertaining to a tectum

TECTITE *n* pl. **-S** tektite

TECTONIC *adj* pertaining to construction

TECTRIX *n* pl. **-TRICES** a small feather of a bird's wing

TECTUM *n* pl. **-TUMS** or **-TA** a rooflike structure

TED *v* **TEDDED, TEDDING, TEDS** to spread for drying

TEDDER *v* **-ED, -ING, -S** to ted (hay) with a machine

TEDDY *n* pl. **-DIES** a woman's undergarment

TEDIOUS *adj* causing weariness

TEDIUM *n* pl. **-S** the state of being tedious

TEE *v* **TEED, TEEING, TEES** to place a golf ball on a small peg

TEEL *n* pl. **-S** sesame

TEEM *v* **-ED, -ING, -S** to be full to overflowing

TEEMER *n* pl. **-S** one that teems

TEEN *n* pl. **-S** a teenager

TEENAGE *adj* pertaining to teenagers

TEENAGED *adj* teenage

TEENAGER *n* pl. **-S** a person between the ages of thirteen and nineteen

TEENER *n* pl. **-S** a teenager

TEENFUL *adj* filled with grief

TEENSY *adj* **-SIER, -SIEST** tiny

TEENTSY *adj* **-SIER, -SIEST** tiny

TEENY *adj* **-NIER, -NIEST** tiny

TEENYBOP *adj* pertaining to a young teenager

TEEPEE *n* pl. **-S** tepee

TEETER *v* **-ED, -ING, -S** to move unsteadily

TEETH pl. of tooth

TEETHE *v* **TEETHED, TEETHING, TEETHES** to cut teeth

TEETHER *n* pl. **-S** an object for a baby to bite on during teething

TEETHING *n* pl. **-S** the first growth of teeth

TEETOTAL *v* **-TALED, -TALING, -TALS** or **-TALLED, -TALLING, -TALS** to abstain completely from alcoholic beverages

TEETOTUM *n* pl. **-S** a spinning toy

TEFF *n* pl. **-S** a cereal grass

TEFILLIN *n/pl* the phylacteries worn by Jews

TEG *n* pl. **-S** a yearling sheep

TEGG *n* pl. **-S** a sheep in its second year

TEGMEN *n* pl. **-MINA** a covering

TEGMENTA *n/pl* anatomical coverings

TEGMINAL *adj* pertaining to a tegmen

TEGUA *n* pl. **-S** a type of moccasin

TEGULAR *adj* resembling a tile

TEGUMEN *n* pl. **-MINA** tegmen

TEGUMENT *n* pl. **-S** a covering

TEIGLACH *n* pl. **TEIGLACH** a confection consisting of balls of dough boiled in honey

TEIID *n* pl. **-S** a tropical American lizard

TEIND *n* pl. **-S** a tithe

TEKKIE *n* pl. **-S** techie

TEKTITE *n* pl. **-S** a glassy body believed to be of meteoritic origin **TEKTITIC** *adj*

TEL *n* pl. **-S** an ancient mound in the Middle East

TELA *n* pl. **-LAE** an anatomical tissue

TELAMON *n* pl. **-ES** a male figure used as a supporting column

TELCO *n* pl. **-COS** a telecommunications company

TELE *n* pl. **-S** a television set

TELECAST *v* **-ED, -ING, -S** to broadcast by television

TELECOM *n* pl. **-S** telecommunication

TELEDU *n* pl. **-S** a carnivorous mammal

TELEFAX *n* pl. **-ES** a system for transmitting graphic material over telephone lines

TELEFILM *n* pl. **-S** a motion picture made for television

TELEGA *n* pl. **-S** a Russian wagon

TELEGONY *n* pl. **-NIES** the supposed influence of a previous sire on the offspring of later matings of the mother with other males

TELEGRAM *v* **-GRAMMED, -GRAMMING, -GRAMS** to send a message by telegraph

TELEMAN *n* pl. **-MEN** a naval officer

TELEMARK *n* pl. **-S** a type of turn in skiing

TELEOST *n* pl. **-S** a bony fish

TELEPATH *n* pl. **-S** one who can communicate with another by some means other than the senses

TELEPLAY *n* pl. **-PLAYS** a play written for television

TELEPORT *v* **-ED, -ING, -S** to transport by a process that involves no physical means

TELERAN *n* pl. **-S** a system of air navigation

TELESHOP *v* **-SHOPPED, -SHOPPING, -SHOPS** to shop by interactive telecommunications systems

TELESIS *n* pl. **TELESES** planned progress

TELESTIC *n* pl. **-S** a type of acrostic

TELETEXT *n* pl. **-S** a communications system in which printed matter is telecast to subscribers

TELETHON *n* pl. **-S** a fund-raising television program

TELETYPE *v* **-TYPED, -TYPING, -TYPES** to send by teletypewriter

TELEVIEW *v* **-ED, -ING, -S** to observe by means of television

TELEVISE *v* **-VISED, -VISING, -VISES** to broadcast by television (an electronic system of transmitting images and sound)

TELEX *v* **-ED, -ING, -ES** to send a message by a type of telegraphic system

TELFER *v* **-ED, -ING, -S** to telpher

TELFORD *n* pl. **-S** a road made of stones

TELIAL *adj* pertaining to a telium

TELIC *adj* directed toward a goal

TELIUM *n* pl. **-LIA** a sorus on the host plant of a rust fungus

TELL *v* **TOLD, TELLING, TELLS** to give a detailed account of **TELLABLE** *adj*

TELLER *n* pl. **-S** one that tells

TELLIES a pl. of telly

TELLTALE *n* pl. **-S** a tattler

TELLURIC *adj* pertaining to the earth

TELLY *n* pl. **-LYS** or **-LIES** a television set

TELNET *v* **-NETTED, -NETTING, -NETS** or **-NETED, -NETING, -NETS** to access an acount over the Internet using an appropriate procedure

TELOME *n* pl. **-S** a structural unit of a vascular plant **TELOMIC** *adj*

TELOMERE *n* pl. **-S** the natural end of a chromosome

TELOS *n* pl. **TELOI** an ultimate end

TELPHER *v* **-ED, -ING, -S** to transport by a system of aerial cable cars

TELSON *n* pl. **-S** the terminal segment of an arthropod **TELSONIC** *adj*

TEMBLOR *n* pl. **-S** or **-ES** an earthquake

TEMERITY *n* pl. **-TIES** foolish boldness

TEMP *v* **-ED, -ING, -S** to work as a temporary employee

TEMPEH *n* pl. **-S** an Asian food

TEMPER *v* **-ED, -ING, -S** to moderate by adding a counterbalancing agent

TEMPERA *n* pl. **-S** a technique of painting

TEMPERER *n* pl. **-S** one that tempers

TEMPEST *v* **-ED, -ING, -S** to agitate violently

TEMPI a pl. of tempo

TEMPLAR *n* pl. **-S** a lawyer or student of law in London

TEMPLATE *n* pl. **-S** a pattern used as a guide in making something

TEMPLE *n* pl. **-S** a house of worship **TEMPLED** *adj*

TEMPLET *n* pl. **-S** template

TEMPO *n* pl. **-POS** or **-PI** the rate of speed of a musical piece

TEMPORAL *n* pl. **-S** a bone of the skull

TEMPT *v* **-ED, -ING, -S** to entice to commit an unwise or immoral act

TEMPTER *n* pl. **-S** one that tempts

TEMPURA *n* pl. **-S** a Japanese dish

TEN *n* pl. **-S** a number

TENABLE *adj* capable of being held **TENABLY** *adv*

TENACE *n* pl. **-S** a combination of two high cards in some card games

TENACITY *n* pl. **-TIES** perseverance or persistence

TENACULA *n/pl* hooked surgical instruments

TENAIL *n* pl. **-S** tenaille

TENAILLE *n* pl. **-S** an outer defense

TENANCY *n* pl. **-CIES** the temporary occupancy of something that belongs to another

TENANT *v* **-ED, -ING, -S** to inhabit

TENANTRY *n* pl. **-RIES** tenancy

TENCH *n* pl. **-ES** a freshwater fish

TEND *v* **-ED, -ING, -S** to be disposed or inclined

TENDANCE *n* pl. **-S** watchful care

TENDENCE *n* pl. **-S** tendance

TENDENCY *n* pl. **-CIES** an inclination to act or think in a particular way

TENDER *adj* **-DERER, -DEREST** soft or delicate

TENDER *v* **-ED, -ING, -S** to present for acceptance

TENDERER *n* pl. **-S** one that tenders

TENDERLY *adv* in a tender manner

TENDON	*n* pl. **-S** a band of tough, fibrous tissue	**TENSOR**	*n* pl. **-S** a muscle that stretches a body part
TENDRIL	*n* pl. **-S** a leafless organ of climbing plants	**TENT**	*v* **-ED, -ING, -S** to live in a tent (a type of portable shelter)
TENDU	*n* pl. **-S** an Asian ebony tree	**TENTACLE**	*n* pl. **-S** an elongated, flexible appendage of some animals
TENEBRAE	*n/pl* a religious service		
TENEMENT	*n* pl. **-S** an apartment house	**TENTAGE**	*n* pl. **-S** a supply of tents
TENESMUS	*n* pl. **-ES** an urgent but ineffectual effort to defecate or urinate **TENESMIC** *adj*	**TENTER**	*v* **-ED, -ING, -S** to stretch on a type of frame
		TENTH	*n* pl. **-S** one of ten equal parts
TENET	*n* pl. **-S** a principle, belief, or doctrine held to be true	**TENTHLY**	*adv* in the tenth place
		TENTIE	*adj* **TENTIER, TENTIEST** tenty
TENFOLD	*n* pl. **-S** an amount ten times as great as a given unit	**TENTIER**	comparative of tenty
		TENTIEST	superlative of tenty
TENGE	*n* pl. **TENGE** a monetary unit of Kazakhstan	**TENTLESS**	*adj* having no tent
		TENTLIKE	*adj* resembling a tent
TENIA	*n* pl. **-NIAS** or **-NIAE** a tapeworm	**TENTORIA**	*n/pl* the internal skeletons of the heads of insects
TENIASIS	*n* pl. **TENIASES** infestation with tapeworms		
		TENTY	*adj* **TENTIER, TENTIEST** watchful
TENNER	*n* pl. **-S** a ten-dollar bill	**TENUIS**	*n* pl. **-UES** a voiceless phonetic stop
TENNIES	*n/pl* low-cut sneakers		
TENNIS	*n* pl. **-NISES** an outdoor ball game	**TENUITY**	*n* pl. **-ITIES** lack of substance or strength
TENNIST	*n* pl. **-S** a tennis player		
TENON	*v* **-ED, -ING, -S** to unite by means of a tenon (a projection on the end of a piece of wood)	**TENUOUS**	*adj* having little substance or strength
		TENURE	*v* **-URED, -URING, -URES** to grant tenure (the status of holding one's position on a permanent basis) to
TENONER	*n* pl. **-S** one that tenons		
TENOR	*n* pl. **-S** a high male singing voice		
TENORIST	*n* pl. **-S** one who sings tenor or plays a tenor instrument	**TENURIAL**	*adj* of or pertaining to tenure (the status of holding one's position on a permanent basis)
TENORITE	*n* pl. **-S** a mineral		
TENOTOMY	*n* pl. **-MIES** the surgical division of a tendon	**TENUTO**	*n* pl. **-TOS** or **-TI** a musical note or chord held longer than its normal duration
TENOUR	*n* pl. **-S** tenor		
TENPENCE	*n* pl. **-S** the sum of ten pennies	**TEOCALLI**	*n* pl. **-S** an Aztec temple
TENPENNY	*adj* worth tenpence	**TEOPAN**	*n* pl. **-S** a teocalli
TENPIN	*n* pl. **-S** a bowling pin	**TEOSINTE**	*n* pl. **-S** an annual grass
TENREC	*n* pl. **-S** a mammal that feeds on insects	**TEPA**	*n* pl. **-S** a chemical compound
		TEPAL	*n* pl. **-S** a division of a perianth
TENSE	*adj* **TENSER, TENSEST** taut **TENSELY** *adv*	**TEPEE**	*n* pl. **-S** a conical tent of some North American Indians
TENSE	*v* **TENSED, TENSING, TENSES** to make tense	**TEPEFY**	*v* **-FIED, -FYING, -FIES** to make tepid
TENSIBLE	*adj* capable of being stretched **TENSIBLY** *adv*	**TEPHRA**	*n* pl. **-S** solid material ejected from a volcano
TENSILE	*adj* tensible	**TEPHRITE**	*n* pl. **-S** a volcanic rock
TENSION	*v* **-ED, -ING, -S** to make tense	**TEPID**	*adj* moderately warm **TEPIDLY** *adv*
TENSITY	*n* pl. **-TIES** the state of being tense	**TEPIDITY**	*n* pl. **-TIES** the state of being tepid
		TEPOY	*n* pl. **-POYS** teapoy
TENSIVE	*adj* causing tensity	**TEQUILA**	*n* pl. **-S** a Mexican liquor

TERABYTE *n* pl. **-S** one trillion bytes

TERAFLOP *n* pl. **-S** a measure of computing speed

TERAI *n* pl. **-S** a sun hat with a wide brim

TERAOHM *n* pl. **-S** one trillion ohms

TERAPH *n* pl. **-APHIM** an image of a Semitic household god

TERATISM *n* pl. **-S** a malformed fetus **TERATOID** *adj*

TERATOMA *n* pl. **-MAS** or **-MATA** a type of tumor

TERAWATT *n* pl. **-S** one trillion watts

TERBIA *n* pl. **-S** an oxide of terbium

TERBIUM *n* pl. **-S** a metallic element **TERBIC** *adj*

TERCE *n* pl. **-S** tierce

TERCEL *n* pl. **-S** a male falcon

TERCELET *n* pl. **-S** tercel

TERCET *n* pl. **-S** a group of three lines of verse

TEREBENE *n* pl. **-S** a mixture of terpenes

TEREBIC *adj* pertaining to an acid derived from oil of turpentine

TEREDO *n* pl. **-DOS** or **-DINES** a bivalve mollusk

TEREFAH *adj* tref

TERETE *adj* cylindrical and slightly tapering

TERGAL *adj* pertaining to a tergum

TERGITE *n* pl. **-S** a tergum

TERGUM *n* pl. **-GA** a back part of a segment of an arthropod

TERIYAKI *n* pl. **-S** a Japanese food

TERM *v* **-ED, -ING, -S** to give a name to

TERMER *n* pl. **-S** a prisoner serving a specified sentence

TERMINAL *n* pl. **-S** an end or extremity

TERMINUS *n* pl. **-NUSES** or **-NI** a terminal

TERMITE *n* pl. **-S** an insect resembling an ant **TERMITIC** *adj*

TERMLESS *adj* having no limits

TERMLY *adv* periodically

TERMOR *n* pl. **-S** one that holds land for a certain number of years

TERMTIME *n* pl. **-S** the time when a school or court is in session

TERN *n* pl. **-S** a seabird

TERNARY *n* pl. **-RIES** a group of three

TERNATE *adj* arranged in groups of three

TERNE *n* pl. **-S** an alloy of lead and tin

TERNION *n* pl. **-S** a group of three

TERPENE *n* pl. **-S** a chemical compound **TERPENIC** *adj*

TERPINOL *n* pl. **-S** a fragrant liquid

TERRA *n* pl. **-RAE** earth; land

TERRACE *v* **-RACED, -RACING, -RACES** to provide with a terrace (a raised embankment)

TERRAIN *n* pl. **-S** a tract of land

TERRANE *n* pl. **-S** a rock formation

TERRAPIN *n* pl. **-S** a North American tortoise

TERRARIA *n/pl* glass enclosures for plants or small animals

TERRAS *n* pl. **-ES** trass

TERRAZZO *n* pl. **-ZOS** a mosaic flooring

TERREEN *n* pl. **-S** terrine

TERRELLA *n* pl. **-S** a spherical magnet

TERRENE *n* pl. **-S** a land area

TERRET *n* pl. **-S** a metal ring on a harness

TERRIBLE *adj* very bad **TERRIBLY** *adv*

TERRIER *n* pl. **-S** a small, active dog

TERRIES pl. of terry

TERRIFIC *adj* very good; fine

TERRIFY *v* **-FIED, -FYING, -FIES** to fill with terror

TERRINE *n* pl. **-S** an earthenware jar

TERRIT *n* pl. **-S** terret

TERROR *n* pl. **-S** intense fear

TERRY *n* pl. **-RIES** an absorbent fabric

TERSE *adj* **TERSER, TERSEST** succinct **TERSELY** *adv*

TERTIAL *n* pl. **-S** a flight feather of a bird's wing

TERTIAN *n* pl. **-S** a recurrent fever

TERTIARY *n* pl. **-ARIES** a tertial

TESLA *n* pl. **-S** a unit of magnetic induction

TESSERA *n* pl. **-SERAE** a small square used in mosaic work

TEST *v* **-ED, -ING, -S** to subject to an examination **TESTABLE** *adj*

TESTA *n* pl. **-TAE** the hard outer coating of a seed

TESTACY *n* pl. **-CIES** the state of being testate

TESTATE *n* pl. **-S** a testator

TESTATOR *n* pl. **-S** one that makes a will

TESTEE	*n* pl. **-S** one that is tested
TESTER	*n* pl. **-S** one that tests
TESTES	pl. of testis
TESTICLE	*n* pl. **-S** a testis
TESTIER	comparative of testy
TESTIEST	superlative of testy
TESTIFY	*v* **-FIED, -FYING, -FIES** to make a declaration of truth under oath
TESTILY	*adv* in a testy manner
TESTIS	*n* pl. **TESTES** a male reproductive gland
TESTON	*n* pl. **-S** a former French coin
TESTOON	*n* pl. **-S** teston
TESTUDO	*n* pl. **-DOS** or **-DINES** a portable screen used as a shield by the ancient Romans
TESTY	*adj* **TESTIER, TESTIEST** irritable
TET	*n* pl. **-S** teth
TETANAL	*adj* pertaining to tetanus
TETANIC	*n* pl. **-S** a drug capable of causing convulsions
TETANIES	pl. of tetany
TETANISE	*v* **-NISED, -NISING, -NISES** to tetanize
TETANIZE	*v* **-NIZED, -NIZING, -NIZES** to affect with convulsions
TETANUS	*n* pl. **-ES** an infectious disease **TETANOID** *adj*
TETANY	*n* pl. **-NIES** a condition marked by painful muscular spasms
TETCHED	*adj* crazy
TETCHY	*adj* **TETCHIER, TETCHIEST** irritable **TETCHILY** *adv*
TETH	*n* pl. **-S** a Hebrew letter
TETHER	*v* **-ED, -ING, -S** to fasten to a fixed object with a rope
TETOTUM	*n* pl. **-S** teetotum
TETRA	*n* pl. **-S** a tropical fish
TETRACID	*n* pl. **-S** a type of acid
TETRAD	*n* pl. **-S** a group of four **TETRADIC** *adj*
TETRAGON	*n* pl. **-S** a four-sided polygon
TETRAMER	*n* pl. **-S** a type of polymer
TETRAPOD	*n* pl. **-S** a four-footed animal
TETRARCH	*n* pl. **-S** one of four joint rulers
TETRI	*n* pl. **-S** a monetary unit of the Republic of Georgia
TETRODE	*n* pl. **-S** a type of electron tube
TETROXID	*n* pl. **-S** a type of oxide
TETRYL	*n* pl. **-S** a chemical compound
TETTER	*n* pl. **-S** a skin disease
TEUCH	*adj* teugh
TEUGH	*adj* tough **TEUGHLY** *adv*
TEVATRON	*n* pl. **-S** a particle accelerator
TEW	*v* **-ED, -ING, -S** to work hard
TEXAS	*n* pl. **-ES** the uppermost structure on a steamboat
TEXT	*n* pl. **-S** the main body of a written or printed work
TEXTBOOK	*n* pl. **-S** a book used in the study of a subject
TEXTILE	*n* pl. **-S** a woven fabric
TEXTLESS	*adj* having no text
TEXTUAL	*adj* pertaining to a text
TEXTUARY	*n* pl. **-ARIES** a specialist in the study of the Scriptures
TEXTURAL	*adj* pertaining to the surface characteristics of something
TEXTURE	*v* **-TURED, -TURING, -TURES** to make by weaving
THACK	*v* **-ED, -ING, -S** to thatch
THAE	*adj* these; those
THAIRM	*n* pl. **-S** tharm
THALAMUS	*n* pl. **-MI** a part of the brain **THALAMIC** *adj*
THALER	*n* pl. **-S** taler
THALLIUM	*n* pl. **-S** a metallic element **THALLIC, THALLOUS** *adj*
THALLUS	*n* pl. **-LUSES** or **-LI** a plant body without true root, stem, or leaf **THALLOID** *adj*
THALWEG	*n* pl. **-S** the line defining the lowest points along the length of a riverbed
THAN	*conj* — used to introduce the second element of a comparison
THANAGE	*n* pl. **-S** the land held by a thane
THANATOS	*n* pl. **-ES** an instinctual desire for death
THANE	*n* pl. **-S** a man holding land by military service in Anglo-Saxon England
THANK	*v* **-ED, -ING, -S** to express gratitude to
THANKER	*n* pl. **-S** one that thanks
THANKFUL	*adj* **-FULLER, -FULLEST** feeling gratitude
THARM	*n* pl. **-S** the belly

THAT *pron* pl. **THOSE** the one indicated

THATAWAY *adv* in that direction

THATCH *v* **-ED, -ING, -ES** to cover with thatch (plant stalks or foliage)

THATCHER *n* pl. **-S** one that thatches

THATCHY *adj* **THATCHIER, THATCHIEST** resembling thatch

THAW *v* **-ED, -ING, -S** to melt

THAWER *n* pl. **-S** one that thaws

THAWLESS *adj* never thawing

THE *definite article* — used to specify or make particular

THEARCHY *n* pl. **-CHIES** rule by a god

THEATER *n* pl. **-S** a building for dramatic presentations **THEATRIC** *adj*

THEATRE *n* pl. **-S** theater

THEBAINE *n* pl. **-S** a poisonous alkaloid

THEBE *n* pl. **-S** a monetary unit of Botswana

THECA *n* pl. **-CAE** a protective anatomical covering **THECAL, THECATE** *adj*

THEE *pron* the objective case of the pronoun thou

THEELIN *n* pl. **-S** estrone

THEELOL *n* pl. **-S** estriol

THEFT *n* pl. **-S** the act of stealing

THEGN *n* pl. **-S** thane **THEGNLY** *adj*

THEIN *n* pl. **-S** theine

THEINE *n* pl. **-S** caffeine

THEIR *pron* a possessive form of the pronoun they

THEIRS *pron* a possessive form of the pronoun they

THEISM *n* pl. **-S** belief in the existence of a god

THEIST *n* pl. **-S** one who believes in the existence of a god **THEISTIC** *adj*

THELITIS *n* pl. **-TISES** inflammation of the nipple

THEM *pron* the objective case of the pronoun they

THEMATIC *n* pl. **-S** a stamp collected according to its subject

THEME *v* **THEMED, THEMING, THEMES** to plan something according to a central subject

THEN *n* pl. **-S** that time

THENAGE *n* pl. **-S** thanage

THENAL *adj* pertaining to the palm of the hand

THENAR *n* pl. **-S** the palm of the hand

THENCE *adv* from that place

THEOCRAT *n* pl. **-S** a person who rules as a representative of a god

THEODICY *n* pl. **-CIES** a defense of God's goodness in respect to the existence of evil

THEOGONY *n* pl. **-NIES** an account of the origin of the gods

THEOLOG *n* pl. **-S** a student of theology

THEOLOGY *n* pl. **-GIES** the study of religion

THEONOMY *n* pl. **-MIES** rule by a god

THEORBO *n* pl. **-BOS** a stringed musical instrument

THEOREM *n* pl. **-S** a proposition that is demonstrably true or is assumed to be so

THEORIES pl. of theory

THEORISE *v* **-RISED, -RISING, -RISES** to theorize

THEORIST *n* pl. **-S** one that theorizes

THEORIZE *v* **-RIZED, -RIZING, -RIZES** to form theories

THEORY *n* pl. **-RIES** a group of propositions used to explain a class of phenomena

THERAPY *n* pl. **-PIES** the treatment of illness or disability

THERE *n* pl. **-S** that place

THEREAT *adv* at that place or time

THEREBY *adv* by that means

THEREFOR *adv* for that

THEREIN *adv* in that place

THEREMIN *n* pl. **-S** a musical instrument

THEREOF *adv* of that

THEREON *adv* on that

THERETO *adv* to that

THERIAC *n* pl. **-S** molasses

THERIACA *n* pl. **-S** theriac

THERIAN *n* pl. **-S** any of a subclass of mammals

THERM *n* pl. **-S** a unit of quantity of heat

THERMAE *n/pl* hot springs

THERMAL *n* pl. **-S** a rising mass of warm air

THERME *n* pl. **-S** therm

THERMEL *n* pl. **-S** a device for temperature measurement

THERMIC *adj* pertaining to heat

THERMION *n* pl. **-S** an ion emitted by a heated body

THERMITE *n* pl. **-S** a metallic mixture that produces intense heat when ignited

THERMOS *n* pl. **-ES** a container used to keep liquids either hot or cold

THEROID *adj* resembling a beast

THEROPOD *n* pl. **-S** a carnivorous dinosaur

THESAURI *n/pl* dictionaries of synonyms and antonyms

THESE pl. of this

THESIS *n* pl. **THESES** a proposition put forward for discussion

THESP *n* pl. **-S** an actor

THESPIAN *n* pl. **-S** an actor or actress

THETA *n* pl. **-S** a Greek letter

THETIC *adj* arbitrary

THETICAL *adj* thetic

THEURGY *n* pl. **-GIES** divine intervention in human affairs **THEURGIC** *adj*

THEW *n* pl. **-S** a well-developed muscle

THEWLESS *adj* weak

THEWY *adj* **THEWIER, THEWIEST** brawny

THEY *pron* the 3d person pl. pronoun in the nominative case

THIAMIN *n* pl. **-S** thiamine

THIAMINE *n* pl. **-S** a B vitamin

THIAZIDE *n* pl. **-S** a drug used to treat high blood pressure

THIAZIN *n* pl. **-S** thiazine

THIAZINE *n* pl. **-S** a chemical compound

THIAZOL *n* pl. **-S** thiazole

THIAZOLE *n* pl. **-S** a chemical compound

THICK *adj* **THICKER, THICKEST** having relatively great extent from one surface to its opposite

THICK *n* pl. **-S** the thickest part

THICKEN *v* **-ED, -ING, -S** to make thick

THICKET *n* pl. **-S** a dense growth of shrubs or small trees **THICKETY** *adj*

THICKISH *adj* somewhat thick

THICKLY *adv* in a thick manner

THICKSET *n* pl. **-S** a thicket

THIEF *n* pl. **THIEVES** one that steals

THIEVE *v* **THIEVED, THIEVING, THIEVES** to steal

THIEVERY *n* pl. **-ERIES** the act or practice of stealing

THIEVISH *adj* given to stealing

THIGH *n* pl. **-S** a part of the leg **THIGHED** *adj*

THILL *n* pl. **-S** a shaft of a vehicle

THIMBLE *n* pl. **-S** a cap used to protect the fingertip during sewing

THIN *adj* **THINNER, THINNEST** having relatively little density or thickness

THIN *v* **THINNED, THINNING, THINS** to make thin

THINCLAD *n* pl. **-S** a runner on a track team

THINDOWN *n* pl. **-S** a lessening in the number of atomic particles and cosmic rays passing through the earth's atmosphere

THINE *pron* a possessive form of the pronoun thou

THING *n* pl. **-S** an inanimate object

THINK *v* **THOUGHT, THINKING, THINKS** to formulate in the mind

THINKER *n* pl. **-S** one that thinks

THINKING *n* pl. **-S** an opinion or judgment

THINLY *adv* in a thin manner

THINNED past tense of thin

THINNER *n* pl. **-S** one that thins

THINNESS *n* pl. **-ES** the quality or state of being thin

THINNEST superlative of thin

THINNING present participle of thin

THINNISH *adj* somewhat thin

THIO *adj* containing sulfur

THIOL *n* pl. **-S** a sulfur compound **THIOLIC** *adj*

THIONATE *n* pl. **-S** a chemical salt

THIONIC *adj* pertaining to sulfur

THIONIN *n* pl. **-S** a violet dye

THIONINE *n* pl. **-S** thionin

THIONYL *n* pl. **-S** sulfinyl

THIOPHEN *n* pl. **-S** a chemical compound

THIOTEPA *n* pl. **-S** a chemical compound

THIOUREA *n* pl. **-S** a chemical compound

THIR *pron* these

THIRAM *n* pl. **-S** a chemical compound

THIRD *n* pl. **-S** one of three equal parts

THIRDLY *adv* in the third place

THIRL *v* **-ED, -ING, -S** to thrill

THIRLAGE *n* pl. **-S** an obligation requiring feudal tenants to grind grain at a certain mill

THIRST *v* **-ED, -ING, -S** to feel a desire or need to drink

THIRSTER *n* pl. **-S** one that thirsts

THIRSTY *adj* **THIRSTIER, THIRSTIEST** feeling a desire or need to drink

THIRTEEN *n* pl. **-S** a number

THIRTY *n* pl. **-TIES** a number

THIS *pron* pl. **THESE** the person or thing just mentioned

THISAWAY *adv* this way

THISTLE *n* pl. **-S** a prickly plant

THISTLY *adj* **-TLIER, -TLIEST** prickly

THITHER *adv* in that direction

THO *conj* though

THOLE *v* **THOLED, THOLING, THOLES** to endure

THOLEPIN *n* pl. **-S** a pin that serves as an oarlock

THOLOS *n* pl. **-LOI** a circular, underground tomb

THONG *n* pl. **-S** a narrow strip of leather used for binding **THONGED** *adj*

THORAX *n* pl. **-RAXES** or **-RACES** the part of the body between the neck and the abdomen **THORACAL, THORACIC** *adj*

THORIA *n* pl. **-S** an oxide of thorium

THORIC *adj* pertaining to thorium

THORITE *n* pl. **-S** a thorium ore

THORIUM *n* pl. **-S** a metallic element

THORN *v* **-ED, -ING, -S** to prick with a thorn (a sharp, rigid projection on a plant)

THORNY *adj* **THORNIER, THORNIEST** full of thorns **THORNILY** *adv*

THORO *adj* thorough

THORON *n* pl. **-S** a radioactive isotope of radon

THOROUGH *adj* **THOROUGHER, THOROUGHEST** complete in all respects

THORP *n* pl. **-S** a small village

THORPE *n* pl. **-S** thorp

THOSE pl. of that

THOU *v* **-ED, -ING, -S** to address as "thou" (the 2d person sing. pronoun in the nominative case)

THOUGH *conj* despite the fact that

THOUGHT *n* pl. **-S** a product of thinking

THOUSAND *n* pl. **-S** a number

THOWLESS *adj* listless

THRALDOM *n* pl. **-S** servitude

THRALL *v* **-ED, -ING, -S** to enslave

THRASH *v* **-ED, -ING, -ES** to beat

THRASHER *n* pl. **-S** one that thrashes

THRAVE *n* pl. **-S** a unit of measure for grain

THRAW *v* **-ED, -ING, -S** to twist

THRAWART *adj* stubborn

THRAWN *adj* twisted **THRAWNLY** *adv*

THREAD *v* **-ED, -ING, -S** to pass a thread (a very slender cord) through

THREADER *n* pl. **-S** one that threads

THREADY *adj* **THREADIER, THREADIEST** resembling a thread

THREAP *v* **-ED, -ING, -S** to dispute

THREAPER *n* pl. **-S** one that threaps

THREAT *v* **-ED, -ING, -S** to threaten

THREATEN *v* **-ED, -ING, -S** to be a source of danger to

THREE *n* pl. **-S** a number

THREEP *v* **-ED, -ING, -S** to threap

THRENODE *n* pl. **-S** a threnody

THRENODY *n* pl. **-DIES** a song of lamentation

THRESH *v* **-ED, -ING, -ES** to separate the grain or seeds from a plant mechanically

THRESHER *n* pl. **-S** one that threshes

THREW past tense of throw

THRICE *adv* three times

THRIFT *n* pl. **-S** care and wisdom in the management of one's resources

THRIFTY *adj* **THRIFTIER, THRIFTIEST** displaying thrift

THRILL *v* **-ED, -ING, -S** to excite greatly

THRILLER *n* pl. **-S** one that thrills

THRIP *n* pl. **-S** a British coin

THRIVE *v* **THROVE** or **THRIVED, THRIVEN, THRIVING, THRIVES** to grow vigorously

THRIVER *n* pl. **-S** one that thrives

THRO *prep* through

THROAT *v* **-ED, -ING, -S** to utter in a hoarse voice

THROATY *adj* **THROATIER, THROATIEST** hoarse

THROB	*v* **THROBBED, THROBBING, THROBS** to pulsate
THROBBER	*n* pl. **-S** one that throbs
THROE	*n* pl. **-S** a violent spasm of pain
THROMBIN	*n* pl. **-S** an enzyme
THROMBUS	*n* pl. **-BI** a clot occluding a blood vessel
THRONE	*v* **THRONED, THRONING, THRONES** to place on a throne (a royal chair)
THRONG	*v* **-ED, -ING, -S** to crowd into
THROSTLE	*n* pl. **-S** a songbird
THROTTLE	*v* **-TLED, -TLING, -TLES** to strangle
THROUGH	*prep* by way of
THROVE	a past tense of thrive
THROW	*v* **THREW, THROWN, THROWING, THROWS** to propel through the air with a movement of the arm
THROWER	*n* pl. **-S** one that throws
THRU	*prep* through
THRUM	*v* **THRUMMED, THRUMMING, THRUMS** to play a stringed instrument idly or monotonously
THRUMMER	*n* pl. **-S** one that thrums
THRUMMY	*adj* **-MIER, -MIEST** shaggy
THRUPUT	*n* pl. **-S** the amount of raw material processed within a given time
THRUSH	*n* pl. **-ES** a songbird
THRUST	*v* **-ED, -ING, -S** to push forcibly
THRUSTER	*n* pl. **-S** one that thrusts
THRUSTOR	*n* pl. **-S** thruster
THRUWAY	*n* pl. **-WAYS** an express highway
THUD	*v* **THUDDED, THUDDING, THUDS** to make a dull, heavy sound
THUG	*n* pl. **-S** a brutal ruffian or assassin
THUGGEE	*n* pl. **-S** thuggery in India
THUGGERY	*n* pl. **-GERIES** thuggish behavior
THUGGISH	*adj* characteristic of a thug
THUJA	*n* pl. **-S** an evergreen tree or shrub
THULIA	*n* pl. **-S** an oxide of thulium
THULIUM	*n* pl. **-S** a metallic element
THUMB	*v* **-ED, -ING, -S** to leaf through with the thumb (the short, thick digit of the human hand)
THUMBKIN	*n* pl. **-S** a screw that is turned by the thumb and fingers
THUMBNUT	*n* pl. **-S** a nut that is turned by the thumb and fingers
THUMP	*v* **-ED, -ING, -S** to strike so as to make a dull, heavy sound
THUMPER	*n* pl. **-S** one that thumps
THUNDER	*v* **-ED, -ING, -S** to produce a loud, resounding sound
THUNDERY	*adj* accompanied with thunder
THUNK	*v* **-ED, -ING, -S** to make a sudden, muffled sound
THURIBLE	*n* pl. **-S** a censer
THURIFER	*n* pl. **-S** one who carries a thurible in a religious ceremony
THURL	*n* pl. **-S** the hip joint in cattle
THUS	*adv* in this manner
THUSLY	*adv* thus
THUYA	*n* pl. **-S** thuja
THWACK	*v* **-ED, -ING, -S** to strike with something flat
THWACKER	*n* pl. **-S** one that thwacks
THWART	*v* **-ED, -ING, -S** to prevent the accomplishment of
THWARTER	*n* pl. **-S** one that thwarts
THWARTLY	*adv* athwart
THY	*pron* a possessive form of the pronoun thou
THYME	*n* pl. **-S** an aromatic herb
THYMEY	*adj* **THYMIER, THYMIEST** thymy
THYMI	a pl. of thymus
THYMIC	*adj* pertaining to thyme
THYMIER	comparative of thymey and thymy
THYMIEST	superlative of thymey and thymy
THYMINE	*n* pl. **-S** a chemical compound
THYMOL	*n* pl. **-S** a chemical compound
THYMOSIN	*n* pl. **-S** a hormone secreted by the thymus
THYMUS	*n* pl. **-MUSES** or **-MI** a glandular structure in the body
THYMY	*adj* **THYMIER, THYMIEST** abounding in thyme
THYREOID	*adj* pertaining to the thyroid
THYROID	*n* pl. **-S** an endocrine gland
THYROXIN	*n* pl. **-S** an amino acid
THYRSE	*n* pl. **-S** thyrsus
THYRSUS	*n* pl. **-SI** a type of flower cluster **THYRSOID** *adj*
THYSELF	*pron* yourself
TI	*n* pl. **-S** the seventh tone of the diatonic musical scale

TIARA   *n* pl. **-S** a jeweled headpiece worn by women **TIARAED** *adj*

TIBIA   *n* pl. **-IAS** or **-IAE** a bone of the leg **TIBIAL** *adj*

TIC   *v* **TICCED, TICCING, TICS** to have an involuntary muscular contraction

TICAL   *n* pl. **-S** a former Thai unit of weight

TICK   *v* **-ED, -ING, -S** to make a recurrent clicking sound

TICKER   *n* pl. **-S** one that ticks

TICKET   *v* **-ED, -ING, -S** to attach a tag to

TICKING   *n* pl. **-S** a strong cotton fabric

TICKLE   *v* **-LED, -LING, -LES** to touch lightly so as to produce a tingling sensation

TICKLER   *n* pl. **-S** one that tickles

TICKLISH   *adj* sensitive to tickling

TICKSEED   *n* pl. **-S** a flowering plant

TICKTACK   *v* **-ED, -ING, -S** to ticktock

TICKTOCK   *v* **-ED, -ING, -S** to make the ticking sound of a clock

TICTAC   *v* **-TACKED, -TACKING, -TACS** to ticktack

TICTOC   *v* **-TOCKED, -TOCKING, -TOCS** to ticktock

TIDAL   *adj* pertaining to the tides **TIDALLY** *adv*

TIDBIT   *n* pl. **-S** a choice bit of food

TIDDLER   *n* pl. **-S** a small fish

TIDDLY   *adj* slightly drunk

TIDE   *v* **TIDED, TIDING, TIDES** to flow like the tide (the rise and fall of the ocean's waters)

TIDELAND   *n* pl. **-S** land alternately covered and uncovered by the tide

TIDELESS   *adj* lacking a tide

TIDELIKE   *adj* resembling a tide

TIDEMARK   *n* pl. **-S** a mark showing the highest or lowest point of a tide

TIDERIP   *n* pl. **-S** a riptide

TIDEWAY   *n* pl. **-WAYS** a tidal channel

TIDIED   past tense of tidy

TIDIER   *n* pl. **-S** one that tidies

TIDIES   present 3d person sing. of tidy

TIDIEST   superlative of tidy

TIDILY   *adv* in a tidy manner

TIDINESS   *n* pl. **-ES** the state of being tidy

TIDING   *n* pl. **-S** a piece of news

TIDY   *adj* **-DIER, -DIEST** neat and orderly

TIDY   *v* **-DIED, -DYING, -DIES** to make tidy

TIDYTIPS   *n* pl. **TIDYTIPS** an annual herb

TIE   *v* **TIED, TYING** or **TIEING, TIES** to fasten with a cord or rope

TIEBACK   *n* pl. **-S** a loop for holding a curtain back to one side

TIEBREAK   *n* pl. **-S** a contest to select a winner from among contestants with a tied score

TIECLASP   *n* pl. **-S** a clasp for securing a necktie

TIED   past tense of tie

TIELESS   *adj* having no necktie

TIEPIN   *n* pl. **-S** a pin for securing a necktie

TIER   *v* **-ED, -ING, -S** to arrange in tiers (rows placed one above another)

TIERCE   *n* pl. **-S** one of seven canonical daily periods for prayer and devotion

TIERCED   *adj* divided into three equal parts

TIERCEL   *n* pl. **-S** tercel

TIFF   *v* **-ED, -ING, -S** to have a petty quarrel

TIFFANY   *n* pl. **-NIES** a thin, mesh fabric

TIFFIN   *v* **-ED, -ING, -S** to lunch

TIGER   *n* pl. **-S** a large feline mammal

TIGEREYE   *n* pl. **-S** a gemstone

TIGERISH   *adj* resembling a tiger

TIGHT   *adj* **TIGHTER, TIGHTEST** firmly or closely fixed in place **TIGHTLY** *adv*

TIGHTEN   *v* **-ED, -ING, -S** to make tight

TIGHTS   *n/pl* a close-fitting garment

TIGHTWAD   *n* pl. **-S** a miser

TIGLON   *n* pl. **-S** the offspring of a male tiger and a female lion

TIGON   *n* pl. **-S** tiglon

TIGRESS   *n* pl. **-ES** a female tiger

TIGRISH   *adj* tigerish

TIKE   *n* pl. **-S** tyke

TIKI   *n* pl. **-S** a wood or stone image of a Polynesian god

TIKKA   *n* pl. **-S** an Indian dish of meat cooked on a skewer

TIL   *n* pl. **-S** the sesame plant

TILAK   *n* pl. **-S** a mark worn on the forehead by Hindus

TILAPIA   *n* pl. **-S** an African fish

TILBURY   *n* pl. **-BURIES** a carriage having two wheels

TILDE   *n* pl. **-S** a mark placed over a letter to indicate its sound

TILE   *v* **TILED, TILING, TILES** to cover with tiles (thin slabs of baked clay)

TILEFISH   *n* pl. **-ES** a marine food fish

TILELIKE   *adj* resembling a tile

TILER   *n* pl. **-S** one that tiles

TILING   *n* pl. **-S** a surface of tiles

TILL   *v* **-ED, -ING, -S** to prepare land for crops by plowing **TILLABLE** *adj*

TILLAGE   *n* pl. **-S** cultivated land

TILLER   *v* **-ED, -ING, -S** to put forth stems from a root

TILLITE   *n* pl. **-S** rock made up of consolidated clay, sand, gravel, and boulders

TILT   *v* **-ED, -ING, -S** to cause to slant **TILTABLE** *adj*

TILTER   *n* pl. **-S** one that tilts

TILTH   *n* pl. **-S** tillage

TILTYARD   *n* pl. **-S** an area for jousting contests

TIMARAU   *n* pl. **-S** tamarau

TIMBAL   *n* pl. **-S** a large drum

TIMBALE   *n* pl. **-S** a pastry shell shaped like a drum

TIMBER   *v* **-ED, -ING, -S** to furnish with timber (wood used as a building material) **TIMBERY** *adj*

TIMBRE   *n* pl. **-S** the quality given to a sound by its overtones **TIMBRAL** *adj*

TIMBREL   *n* pl. **-S** a percussion instrument

TIME   *v* **TIMED, TIMING, TIMES** to determine the speed or duration of

TIMECARD   *n* pl. **-S** a card for recording an employee's times of arrival and departure

TIMELESS   *adj* having no beginning or end

TIMELINE   *n* pl. **-S** a schedule of events

TIMELY   *adj* **-LIER, -LIEST** occurring at the right moment

TIMEOUS   *adj* timely

TIMEOUT   *n* pl. **-S** a brief suspension of activity

TIMER   *n* pl. **-S** one that times

TIMEWORK   *n* pl. **-S** work paid for by the hour or by the day

TIMEWORN   *adj* showing the effects of long use or wear

TIMID   *adj* **-IDER, -IDEST** lacking courage or self-confidence **TIMIDLY** *adv*

TIMIDITY   *n* pl. **-TIES** the quality of being timid

TIMING   *n* pl. **-S** the selection of the proper moment for doing something

TIMOLOL   *n* pl. **-S** a drug used to treat glaucoma

TIMOROUS   *adj* fearful

TIMOTHY   *n* pl. **-THIES** a European grass

TIMPANO   *n* pl. **-NI** a kettledrum

TIMPANUM   *n* pl. **-NUMS** or **-NA** tympanum

TIN   *v* **TINNED, TINNING, TINS** to coat with tin (a metallic element)

TINAMOU   *n* pl. **-S** a South American game bird

TINCAL   *n* pl. **-S** crude borax

TINCT   *v* **-ED, -ING, -S** to tinge

TINCTURE   *v* **-TURED, -TURING, -TURES** to tinge

TINDER   *n* pl. **-S** readily combustible material **TINDERY** *adj*

TINE   *v* **TINED, TINING, TINES** to lose

TINEA   *n* pl. **-S** a fungous skin disease **TINEAL** *adj*

TINEID   *n* pl. **-S** one of a family of moths

TINFOIL   *n* pl. **-S** a thin metal sheeting

TINFUL   *n* pl. **-S** as much as a tin container can hold

TING   *v* **-ED, -ING, -S** to emit a high-pitched metallic sound

TINGE   *v* **TINGED, TINGEING** or **TINGING, TINGES** to apply a trace of color to

TINGLE   *v* **-GLED, -GLING, -GLES** to cause a prickly, stinging sensation

TINGLER   *n* pl. **-S** one that tingles

TINGLY   *adj* **-GLIER, -GLIEST** tingling

TINHORN   *n* pl. **-S** a showily pretentious person

TINIER   comparative of tiny

TINIEST   superlative of tiny

TINILY   *adv* in a tiny manner

TININESS   *n* pl. **-ES** the quality of being tiny

TINING   present participle of tine

TINKER   *v* **-ED, -ING, -S** to repair in an unskilled or experimental manner

TINKERER   *n* pl. **-S** one that tinkers

TINKLE	*v* **-KLED, -KLING, -KLES** to make slight, sharp, metallic sounds		**TIPPED**	past tense of tip
TINKLER	*n* pl. **-S** one that tinkles		**TIPPER**	*n* pl. **-S** one that tips
TINKLING	*n* pl. **-S** the sound made by something that tinkles		**TIPPET**	*n* pl. **-S** a covering for the shoulders
TINKLY	*adj* **-KLIER, -KLIEST** producing a tinkling sound		**TIPPIER**	comparative of tippy
TINLIKE	*adj* resembling tin		**TIPPIEST**	superlative of tippy
TINMAN	*n* pl. **-MEN** a tinsmith		**TIPPING**	present participle of tip
TINNED	past tense of tin		**TIPPLE**	*v* **-PLED, -PLING, -PLES** to drink alcoholic beverages
TINNER	*n* pl. **-S** a tin miner		**TIPPLER**	*n* pl. **-S** one that tipples
TINNIER	comparative of tinny		**TIPPY**	*adj* **-PIER, -PIEST** unsteady
TINNIEST	superlative of tinny		**TIPPYTOE**	*v* **-TOED, -TOEING, -TOES** to tiptoe
TINNILY	*adv* in a tinny manner			
TINNING	present participle of tin		**TIPSHEET**	*n* pl. **-S** a publication with tips for betting on races or investing in stocks
TINNITUS	*n* pl. **-ES** a ringing sound in the ears			
TINNY	*adj* **-NIER, -NIEST** of or resembling tin		**TIPSIER**	comparative of tipsy
			TIPSIEST	superlative of tipsy
TINPLATE	*n* pl. **-S** thin sheet iron coated with tin		**TIPSILY**	*adv* in a tipsy manner
TINPOT	*adj* of little importance		**TIPSTAFF**	*n* pl. **-STAFFS** or **-STAVES** an attendant in a court of law
TINSEL	*v* **-SELED, -SELING, -SELS** or **-SELLED, -SELLING, -SELS** to give a showy or gaudy appearance to		**TIPSTER**	*n* pl. **-S** one that sells information to gamblers
			TIPSTOCK	*n* pl. **-S** a part of a gun
TINSELLY	*adj* cheaply gaudy		**TIPSY**	*adj* **-SIER, -SIEST** slightly drunk
TINSMITH	*n* pl. **-S** one who works with tin		**TIPTOE**	*v* **-TOED, -TOEING, -TOES** to walk on the tips of one's toes
TINSNIPS	*n/pl* a tool for cutting sheet metal			
TINSTONE	*n* pl. **-S** a tin ore		**TIPTOP**	*n* pl. **-S** the highest point
TINT	*v* **-ED, -ING, -S** to color slightly or delicately		**TIRADE**	*n* pl. **-S** a long, vehement speech
			TIRAMISU	*n* pl. **-S** a dessert made with ladyfingers, mascarpone, chocolate, and espresso
TINTER	*n* pl. **-S** one that tints			
TINTING	*n* pl. **-S** the process of one that tints		**TIRE**	*v* **TIRED, TIRING, TIRES** to grow tired
TINTLESS	*adj* lacking color		**TIRED**	*adj* **TIREDER, TIREDEST** sapped of strength **TIREDLY** *adv*
TINTYPE	*n* pl. **-S** a kind of photograph			
TINWARE	*n* pl. **-S** articles made of tinplate		**TIRELESS**	*adj* seemingly incapable of tiring
TINWORK	*n* pl. **-S** something made of tin		**TIRESOME**	*adj* tedious
TINY	*adj* **TINIER, TINIEST** very small		**TIRING**	present participle of tire
TIP	*v* **TIPPED, TIPPING, TIPS** to tilt		**TIRL**	*v* **-ED, -ING, -S** to make a vibrating sound
TIPCART	*n* pl. **-S** a type of cart			
TIPCAT	*n* pl. **-S** a game resembling baseball		**TIRO**	*n* pl. **-ROS** tyro
			TIRRIVEE	*n* pl. **-S** a tantrum
TIPI	*n* pl. **-S** tepee		**TISANE**	*n* pl. **-S** a ptisan
TIPLESS	*adj* having no point or extremity		**TISSUAL**	*adj* pertaining to tissue
TIPOFF	*n* pl. **-S** a hint or warning		**TISSUE**	*v* **-SUED, -SUING, -SUES** to weave into tissue (a fine sheer fabric)
TIPPABLE	*adj* capable of being tipped		**TISSUEY**	*adj* resembling tissue

TISSULAR *adj* affecting an organism's tissue (structural material)

TIT *n* pl. **-S** a small bird

TITAN *n* pl. **-S** a person of great size

TITANATE *n* pl. **-S** a chemical salt

TITANESS *n* pl. **-ES** a female titan

TITANIA *n* pl. **-S** a mineral

TITANIC *adj* of great size

TITANISM *n* pl. **-S** revolt against social conventions

TITANITE *n* pl. **-S** a mineral

TITANIUM *n* pl. **-S** a metallic element

TITANOUS *adj* pertaining to titanium

TITBIT *n* pl. **-S** tidbit

TITER *n* pl. **-S** the strength of a chemical solution

TITFER *n* pl. **-S** a hat

TITHABLE *adj* subject to the payment of tithes

TITHE *v* **TITHED, TITHING, TITHES** to pay a tithe (a small tax)

TITHER *n* pl. **-S** one that tithes

TITHING *n* pl. **-S** the act of levying tithes

TITHONIA *n* pl. **-S** a tall herb

TITI *n* pl. **-S** an evergreen shrub or tree

TITIAN *n* pl. **-S** a reddish brown color

TITIVATE *v* **-VATED, -VATING, -VATES** to dress smartly

TITLARK *n* pl. **-S** a songbird

TITLE *v* **-TLED, -TLING, -TLES** to furnish with a title (a distinctive appellation)

TITLIST *n* pl. **-S** a sports champion

TITMAN *n* pl. **-MEN** the smallest of a litter of pigs

TITMOUSE *n* pl. **-MICE** a small bird

TITRABLE *adj* capable of being titrated

TITRANT *n* pl. **-S** the reagent used in titration

TITRATE *v* **-TRATED, -TRATING, -TRATES** to determine the strength of a solution by adding a reagent until a desired reaction occurs

TITRATOR *n* pl. **-S** one that titrates

TITRE *n* pl. **-S** titer

TITTER *v* **-ED, -ING, -S** to utter a restrained, nervous laugh

TITTERER *n* pl. **-S** one that titters

TITTIE *n* pl. **-S** a sister

TITTIES pl. of titty

TITTLE *n* pl. **-S** a very small mark in writing or printing

TITTUP *v* **-TUPED, -TUPING, -TUPS** or **-TUPPED, -TUPPING, -TUPS** to move in a lively manner

TITTUPPY *adj* shaky; unsteady

TITTY *n* pl. **-TIES** a teat

TITUBANT *adj* marked by wavering

TITULAR *n* pl. **-S** one who holds a title

TITULARY *n* pl. **-LARIES** a titular

TIVY *adv* with great speed

TIZZY *n* pl. **-ZIES** a state of nervous confusion

TMESIS *n* pl. **TMESES** the separation of the parts of a compound word by an intervening word or words

TO *prep* in the direction of

TOAD *n* pl. **-S** a tailless, jumping amphibian

TOADFISH *n* pl. **-ES** a marine fish

TOADFLAX *n* pl. **-ES** a perennial herb

TOADIED past tense of toady

TOADIES present 3d person sing. of toady

TOADISH *adj* resembling a toad

TOADLESS *adj* having no toads

TOADLIKE *adj* resembling a toad

TOADY *v* **TOADIED, TOADYING, TOADIES** to engage in servile flattering

TOADYISH *adj* characteristic of one that toadies

TOADYISM *n* pl. **-S** toadyish behavior

TOAST *v* **-ED, -ING, -S** to brown by exposure to heat

TOASTER *n* pl. **-S** a device for toasting

TOASTY *adj* **TOASTIER, TOASTIEST** comfortably warm

TOBACCO *n* pl. **-COS** or **-COES** an annual herb cultivated for its leaves

TOBOGGAN *v* **-ED, -ING, -S** to ride on a long, narrow sled

TOBY *n* pl. **-BIES** a type of drinking mug

TOCCATA *n* pl. **-TAS** or **-TE** a musical composition usually for an organ

TOCHER *v* **-ED, -ING, -S** to give a dowry to

TOCOLOGY *n* pl. **-GIES** the branch of medicine dealing with childbirth

TOCSIN *n* pl. **-S** an alarm sounded on a bell

TOD *n* pl. **-S** a British unit of weight

TODAY *n* pl. **-DAYS** the present day

TODDLE v **-DLED, -DLING, -DLES** to walk unsteadily

TODDLER n pl. **-S** one that toddles

TODDY n pl. **-DIES** an alcoholic beverage

TODY n pl. **-DIES** a West Indian bird

TOE v **TOED, TOEING, TOES** to touch with the toe (one of the terminal members of the foot)

TOEA n pl. **-S** a monetary unit of Papua New Guinea

TOECAP n pl. **-S** a covering for the tip of a shoe or boot

TOEHOLD n pl. **-S** a space that supports the toes in climbing

TOELESS adj having no toes

TOELIKE adj resembling a toe

TOENAIL v **-ED, -ING, -S** to fasten with obliquely driven nails

TOEPIECE n pl. **-S** a piece of a shoe designed to cover the toes

TOEPLATE n pl. **-S** a metal tab attached to the tip of a shoe

TOESHOE n pl. **-S** a dance slipper without a heel

TOFF n pl. **-S** a dandy

TOFFEE n pl. **-S** a chewy candy

TOFFY n pl. **-FIES** toffee

TOFT n pl. **-S** a hillock

TOFU n pl. **-S** a soft food product made from soybean milk

TOG v **TOGGED, TOGGING, TOGS** to clothe

TOGA n pl. **-GAS** or **-GAE** an outer garment worn in ancient Rome **TOGAED** adj

TOGATE adj pertaining to ancient Rome

TOGATED adj wearing a toga

TOGETHER adv into a union or relationship

TOGGED past tense of tog

TOGGERY n pl. **-GERIES** clothing

TOGGING present participle of tog

TOGGLE v **-GLED, -GLING, -GLES** to fasten with a type of pin or short rod

TOGGLER n pl. **-S** one that toggles

TOGUE n pl. **-S** a freshwater fish

TOIL v **-ED, -ING, -S** to work strenuously

TOILE n pl. **-S** a sheer linen fabric

TOILER n pl. **-S** one that toils

TOILET v **-ED, -ING, -S** to dress and groom oneself

TOILETRY n pl. **-TRIES** an article used in dressing and grooming oneself

TOILETTE n pl. **-S** the act of dressing and grooming oneself

TOILFUL adj toilsome

TOILSOME adj demanding much exertion

TOILWORN adj worn by toil

TOIT v **-ED, -ING, -S** to saunter

TOKAMAK n pl. **-S** a doughnut-shaped nuclear reactor

TOKAY n pl. **-KAYS** a Malaysian gecko

TOKE v **TOKED, TOKING, TOKES** to take a puff on a marijuana cigarette

TOKEN v **-ED, -ING, -S** to serve as a sign of

TOKENISM n pl. **-S** the policy of making only a superficial effort

TOKER n pl. **-S** one that tokes

TOKING present participle of toke

TOKOLOGY n pl. **-GIES** tocology

TOKOMAK n pl. **-S** tokamak

TOKONOMA n pl. **-S** a small alcove in a Japanese house

TOLA n pl. **-S** a unit of weight used in India

TOLAN n pl. **-S** a chemical compound

TOLANE n pl. **-S** tolan

TOLAR n pl. **-LARS** or **-LARJEV** a monetary unit of Slovenia

TOLBOOTH n pl. **-S** a prison

TOLD past tense of tell

TOLE v **TOLED, TOLING, TOLES** to allure

TOLEDO n pl. **-DOS** a finely tempered sword

TOLERANT adj inclined to tolerate

TOLERATE v **-ATED, -ATING, -ATES** to allow without active opposition

TOLIDIN n pl. **-S** tolidine

TOLIDINE n pl. **-S** a chemical compound

TOLING present participle of tole

TOLL v **-ED, -ING, -S** to collect or impose a toll (a fixed charge for a service or privilege)

TOLLAGE n pl. **-S** a toll

TOLLBAR n pl. **-S** a tollgate

TOLLER n pl. **-S** a collector of tolls

TOLLGATE n pl. **-S** a gate where a toll is collected

TOLLMAN n pl. **-MEN** a toller

TOLLWAY n pl. **-WAYS** a road on which tolls are collected

TOLU n pl. **-S** a fragrant resin

TOLUATE n pl. **-S** a chemical salt

TOLUENE n pl. **-S** a flammable liquid

TOLUIC adj pertaining to any of four isomeric acids derived from toluene

TOLUID n pl. **-S** toluide

TOLUIDE n pl. **-S** an amide

TOLUIDIN n pl. **-S** an amine

TOLUOL n pl. **-S** toluene

TOLUOLE n pl. **-S** toluol

TOLUYL n pl. **-S** a univalent chemical radical

TOLYL n pl. **-S** a univalent chemical radical

TOM n pl. **-S** the male of various animals

TOMAHAWK v **-ED, -ING, -S** to strike with a light ax

TOMALLEY n pl. **-LEYS** the liver of a lobster

TOMAN n pl. **-S** a formerly used coin of Iran

TOMATO n pl. **-TOES** the fleshy, edible fruit of a perennial plant **TOMATOEY** adj

TOMB v **-ED, -ING, -S** to place in a tomb (a burial vault or chamber)

TOMBAC n pl. **-S** an alloy of copper and zinc

TOMBACK n pl. **-S** tombac

TOMBAK n pl. **-S** tombac

TOMBAL adj pertaining to a tomb

TOMBLESS adj having no tomb

TOMBLIKE adj resembling a tomb

TOMBOLA n pl. **-S** a gambling game that is a type of lottery

TOMBOLO n pl. **-LOS** a sandbar connecting an island to the mainland

TOMBOY n pl. **-BOYS** a girl who prefers boyish activities

TOMCAT v **-CATTED, -CATTING, -CATS** to engage in sexually promiscuous behavior — used of a male

TOMCOD n pl. **-S** a marine fish

TOME n pl. **-S** a large book

TOMENTUM n pl. **-TA** a network of small blood vessels

TOMFOOL n pl. **-S** a foolish person

TOMMY n pl. **-MIES** a loaf of bread

TOMMYROT n pl. **-S** nonsense

TOMOGRAM n pl. **-S** a photograph made with X-rays

TOMORROW n pl. **-S** the day following today

TOMPION n pl. **-S** tampion

TOMTIT n pl. **-S** any of various small active birds

TON n pl. **-S** a unit of weight

TONAL adj pertaining to tone **TONALLY** adv

TONALITY n pl. **-TIES** a system of tones

TONDO n pl. **-DOS** or **-DI** a circular painting

TONE v **TONED, TONING, TONES** to give a particular tone (a sound of definite pitch and vibration) to

TONEARM n pl. **-S** the pivoted part of a record player that holds the needle

TONELESS adj lacking in tone

TONEME n pl. **-S** a tonal unit of speech **TONEMIC** adj

TONER n pl. **-S** one that tones

TONETICS n/pl the phonetic study of tone in language **TONETIC** adj

TONETTE n pl. **-S** a simple flute

TONEY adj **TONIER, TONIEST** tony

TONG v **-ED, -ING, -S** to lift with a type of grasping device

TONGA n pl. **-S** a light cart used in India

TONGER n pl. **-S** one that tongs

TONGMAN n pl. **-MEN** a member of a Chinese secret society

TONGUE v **TONGUED, TONGUING, TONGUES** to touch with the tongue (an organ of the mouth)

TONGUING n pl. **-S** the use of the tongue in articulating notes on a wind instrument

TONIC n pl. **-S** something that invigorates or refreshes

TONICITY n pl. **-TIES** normal, healthy bodily condition

TONIER comparative of toney and tony

TONIEST superlative of toney and tony

TONIGHT n pl. **-S** the present night

TONING present participle of tone

TONISH adj stylish **TONISHLY** adv

TONLET n pl. **-S** a skirt of plate armor

TONNAGE	*n* pl. **-S** total weight in tons
TONNE	*n* pl. **-S** a unit of weight
TONNEAU	*n* pl. **-NEAUS** or **-NEAUX** the rear seating compartment of an automobile
TONNER	*n* pl. **-S** an object having a specified tonnage
TONNISH	*adj* tonish
TONSIL	*n* pl. **-S** a lymphoid organ **TONSILAR** *adj*
TONSURE	*v* **-SURED, -SURING, -SURES** to shave the head of
TONTINE	*n* pl. **-S** a form of collective life insurance
TONUS	*n* pl. **-ES** a normal state of tension in muscle tissue
TONY	*adj* **TONIER, TONIEST** stylish
TOO	*adv* in addition
TOOK	past tense of take
TOOL	*v* **-ED, -ING, -S** to form or finish with a tool (an implement used in manual work)
TOOLBAR	*n* pl. **-S** a row of icons on a computer screen that activate functions
TOOLBOX	*n* pl. **-ES** a box for tools
TOOLER	*n* pl. **-S** one that tools
TOOLHEAD	*n* pl. **-S** a part of a machine
TOOLING	*n* pl. **-S** ornamentation done with tools
TOOLLESS	*adj* having no tools
TOOLROOM	*n* pl. **-S** a room where tools are stored
TOOLSHED	*n* pl. **-S** a building where tools are stored
TOOM	*adj* empty
TOON	*n* pl. **-S** an East Indian tree
TOONIE	*n* pl. **-S** a Canadian two-dollar coin
TOOT	*v* **-ED, -ING, -S** to sound a horn or whistle in short blasts
TOOTER	*n* pl. **-S** one that toots
TOOTH	*n* pl. **TEETH** one of the hard structures attached in a row to each jaw
TOOTH	*v* **-ED, -ING, -S** to furnish with toothlike projections
TOOTHY	*adj* **TOOTHIER, TOOTHIEST** having or showing prominent teeth **TOOTHILY** *adv*
TOOTLE	*v* **-TLED, -TLING, -TLES** to toot softly or repeatedly

TOOTLER	*n* pl. **-S** one that tootles
TOOTS	*n* pl. **-ES** a woman or girl — usually used as a form of address
TOOTSIE	*n* pl. **-S** tootsy
TOOTSY	*n* pl. **-SIES** a foot
TOP	*v* **TOPPED, TOPPING, TOPS** to cut off the top (the highest part, point, or surface) of
TOPAZ	*n* pl. **-ES** a mineral **TOPAZINE** *adj*
TOPCOAT	*n* pl. **-S** a lightweight overcoat
TOPCROSS	*n* pl. **-ES** a cross between a purebred male and inferior female stock
TOPE	*v* **TOPED, TOPING, TOPES** to drink liquor to excess
TOPEE	*n* pl. **-S** topi
TOPER	*n* pl. **-S** one that topes
TOPFUL	*adj* topfull
TOPFULL	*adj* full to the top
TOPH	*n* pl. **-S** tufa
TOPHE	*n* pl. **-S** tufa
TOPHUS	*n* pl. **-PHI** a deposit of urates in the tissue around a joint
TOPI	*n* pl. **-S** a sun helmet
TOPIARY	*n* pl. **-ARIES** the art of trimming shrubs into shapes
TOPIC	*n* pl. **-S** a subject of discourse **TOPICAL** *adj*
TOPING	present participle of tope
TOPKICK	*n* pl. **-S** a first sergeant
TOPKNOT	*n* pl. **-S** an ornament for the hair
TOPLESS	*adj* having no top
TOPLINE	*n* pl. **-S** the outline of the top of an animal's body
TOPLOFTY	*adj* **-LOFTIER, -LOFTIEST** haughty
TOPMAST	*n* pl. **-S** a mast of a ship
TOPMOST	*adj* highest
TOPNOTCH	*adj* excellent
TOPO	*adj* topographic
TOPOI	pl. of topos
TOPOLOGY	*n* pl. **-GIES** a branch of mathematics
TOPONYM	*n* pl. **-S** the name of a place
TOPONYMY	*n* pl. **-MIES** the study of toponyms
TOPOS	*n* pl. **-POI** a stock rhetorical theme
TOPOTYPE	*n* pl. **-S** a specimen selected from a locality typical of a species

TOPPED past tense of top

TOPPER *n* pl. **-S** one that tops

TOPPING *n* pl. **-S** something that forms a top

TOPPLE *v* **-PLED, -PLING, -PLES** to fall forward

TOPSAIL *n* pl. **-S** a sail of a ship

TOPSIDE *n* pl. **-S** the upper portion of a ship

TOPSIDER *n* pl. **-S** one who is at the highest level of authority

TOPSOIL *v* **-ED, -ING, -S** to remove the surface layer of soil from

TOPSPIN *n* pl. **-S** a forward spin imparted to a ball

TOPSTONE *n* pl. **-S** the stone at the top of a structure

TOPWORK *v* **-ED, -ING, -S** to graft scions of another variety of plant on the main branches of

TOQUE *n* pl. **-S** a close-fitting woman's hat

TOQUET *n* pl. **-S** toque

TOR *n* pl. **-S** a high, craggy hill

TORA *n* pl. **-S** torah

TORAH *n* pl. **-RAHS** or **-ROTH** or **-ROT** a law or precept

TORC *n* pl. **-S** a metal collar or necklace

TORCH *v* **-ED, -ING, -ES** to set on fire

TORCHERE *n* pl. **-S** a type of electric lamp

TORCHIER *n* pl. **-S** torchere

TORCHON *n* pl. **-S** a coarse lace

TORCHY *adj* **TORCHIER, TORCHIEST** characteristic of a torch song

TORE *n* pl. **-S** a torus

TOREADOR *n* pl. **-S** a bullfighter

TORERO *n* pl. **-ROS** a bullfighter

TOREUTIC *adj* pertaining to a type of metalwork

TORI pl. of torus

TORIC *n* pl. **-S** a lens designed to correct astigmatism

TORIES pl. of tory

TORII *n* pl. **TORII** the gateway of a Japanese temple

TORMENT *v* **-ED, -ING, -S** to inflict with great bodily or mental suffering

TORN past participle of tear

TORNADO *n* pl. **-DOS** or **-DOES** a violent windstorm **TORNADIC** *adj*

TORNILLO *n* pl. **-LOS** a flowering shrub

TORO *n* pl. **-ROS** a bull

TOROID *n* pl. **-S** a type of geometric surface **TOROIDAL** *adj*

TOROSE *adj* cylindrical and swollen at intervals

TOROSITY *n* pl. **-TIES** the quality or state of being torose

TOROT a pl. of torah

TOROTH a pl. of torah

TOROUS *adj* torose

TORPEDO *v* **-ED, -ING, -ES** or **-S** to damage or sink with an underwater missile

TORPID *n* pl. **-S** a racing boat

TORPIDLY *adv* in a sluggish manner

TORPOR *n* pl. **-S** mental or physical inactivity

TORQUATE *adj* having a torques

TORQUE *v* **TORQUED, TORQUING, TORQUES** to cause to twist

TORQUER *n* pl. **-S** one that torques

TORQUES *n* pl. **-QUESES** a band of feathers, hair, or coloration around the neck

TORR *n* pl. **-S** a unit of pressure

TORREFY *v* **-FIED, -FYING, -FIES** to subject to intense heat

TORRENT *n* pl. **-S** a rapid stream of water

TORRID *adj* **-RIDER, -RIDEST** extremely hot **TORRIDLY** *adv*

TORRIFY *v* **-FIED, -FYING, -FIES** to torrefy

TORSADE *n* pl. **-S** a twisted cord

TORSE *n* pl. **-S** a wreath of twisted silks

TORSI a pl. of torso

TORSION *n* pl. **-S** the act of twisting

TORSK *n* pl. **-S** a marine food fish

TORSO *n* pl. **-SOS** or **-SI** the trunk of the human body

TORT *n* pl. **-S** a civil wrong

TORTA *n* pl. **-S** an elaborate dessert

TORTE *n* pl. **TORTES** or **TORTEN** a rich cake

TORTILE *adj* twisted; coiled

TORTILLA *n* pl. **-S** a round, flat cake of unleavened cornmeal

TORTIOUS *adj* of the nature of a tort

TORTOISE *n* pl. **-S** any of an order of reptiles having the body enclosed in a bony shell

TORTONI *n* pl. **-S** a type of ice cream

TORTRIX *n* pl. **-ES** a small moth

TORTUOUS *adj* marked by repeated turns or bends

TORTURE	*v* **-TURED, -TURING, -TURES** to subject to severe physical pain	**TOTTERY**	*adj* shaky
TORTURER	*n* pl. **-S** one that tortures	**TOTTING**	present participle of tot
TORULA	*n* pl. **-LAS** or **-LAE** a type of fungus	**TOUCAN**	*n* pl. **-S** a tropical bird
		TOUCH	*v* **-ED, -ING, -ES** to be in or come into contact with
TORUS	*n* pl. **-RI** a large convex molding	**TOUCHE**	*interj* — used to acknowledge a hit in fencing
TORY	*n* pl. **-RIES** a political conservative		
TOSH	*n* pl. **-ES** nonsense	**TOUCHER**	*n* pl. **-S** one that touches
TOSS	*v* **TOSSED** or **TOST, TOSSING, TOSSES** to throw lightly	**TOUCHPAD**	*n* pl. **-S** a keypad sensitized to finger movement or pressure
TOSSER	*n* pl. **-S** one that tosses	**TOUCHUP**	*n* pl. **-S** an act of finishing by adding minor improvements
TOSSPOT	*n* pl. **-S** a drunkard		
TOSSUP	*n* pl. **-S** an even choice or chance	**TOUCHY**	*adj* **TOUCHIER, TOUCHIEST** overly sensitive **TOUCHILY** *adv*
TOST	a past tense of toss	**TOUGH**	*adj* **TOUGHER, TOUGHEST** strong and resilient
TOSTADA	*n* pl. **-S** a tortilla fried in deep fat		
TOSTADO	*n* pl. **-DOS** tostada	**TOUGH**	*v* **-ED, -ING, -S** to endure hardship
TOT	*v* **TOTTED, TOTTING, TOTS** to total	**TOUGHEN**	*v* **-ED, -ING, -S** to make tough
TOTABLE	*adj* capable of being toted	**TOUGHIE**	*n* pl. **-S** a tough person
TOTAL	*v* **-TALED, -TALING, -TALS** or **-TALLED, -TALLING, -TALS** to ascertain the entire amount of	**TOUGHISH**	*adj* somewhat tough
		TOUGHLY	*adv* in a tough manner
		TOUGHY	*n* pl. **TOUGHIES** toughie
TOTALISE	*v* **-ISED, -ISING, -ISES** to totalize	**TOUPEE**	*n* pl. **-S** a wig worn to cover a bald spot
TOTALISM	*n* pl. **-S** centralized control by an autocratic authority		
		TOUR	*v* **-ED, -ING, -S** to travel from place to place
TOTALIST	*n* pl. **-S** one who tends to regard things as a unified whole		
		TOURACO	*n* pl. **-COS** an African bird
TOTALITY	*n* pl. **-TIES** the quality or state of being complete	**TOURER**	*n* pl. **-S** a large, open automobile
		TOURING	*n* pl. **-S** cross-country skiing for pleasure
TOTALIZE	*v* **-IZED, -IZING, -IZES** to make complete		
		TOURISM	*n* pl. **-S** the practice of touring for pleasure
TOTALLED	a past tense of total		
TOTALLING	a present participle of total	**TOURIST**	*n* pl. **-S** one who tours for pleasure **TOURISTY** *adj*
TOTALLY	*adv* completely		
TOTE	*v* **TOTED, TOTING, TOTES** to carry by hand **TOTEABLE** *adj*	**TOURISTA**	*n* pl. **-S** turista
		TOURNEY	*v* **-ED, -ING, -S** to compete in a tournament
TOTEM	*n* pl. **-S** a natural object serving as the emblem of a family or clan **TOTEMIC** *adj*		
		TOUSE	*v* **TOUSED, TOUSING, TOUSES** to tousle
		TOUSLE	*v* **-SLED, -SLING, -SLES** to dishevel
TOTEMISM	*n* pl. **-S** a system of tribal division according to totems		
TOTEMIST	*n* pl. **-S** a specialist in totemism	**TOUT**	*v* **-ED, -ING, -S** to solicit brazenly
TOTEMITE	*n* pl. **-S** a totemist	**TOUTER**	*n* pl. **-S** one that touts
TOTER	*n* pl. **-S** one that totes	**TOUZLE**	*v* **-ZLED, -ZLING, -ZLES** to tousle
TOTHER	*pron* the other	**TOVARICH**	*n* pl. **-ES** comrade
TOTING	present participle of tote	**TOVARISH**	*n* pl. **-ES** tovarich
TOTTED	past tense of tot	**TOW**	*v* **-ED, -ING, -S** to pull by means of a rope or chain **TOWABLE** *adj*
TOTTER	*v* **-ED, -ING, -S** to walk unsteadily		
TOTTERER	*n* pl. **-S** one that totters	**TOWAGE**	*n* pl. **-S** the price paid for towing

TOWARD	*prep* in the direction of
TOWARDLY	*adj* favorable
TOWARDS	*prep* toward
TOWAWAY	*n* pl. **-AWAYS** the act of towing away a vehicle
TOWBOAT	*n* pl. **-S** a tugboat
TOWEL	*v* **-ELED, -ELING, -ELS** or **-ELLED, -ELLING, -ELS** to wipe with a towel (an absorbent cloth)
TOWELING	*n* pl. **-S** material used for towels
TOWER	*v* **-ED, -ING, -S** to rise to a great height
TOWERY	*adj* **-ERIER, -ERIEST** very tall
TOWHEAD	*n* pl. **-S** a head of light blond hair
TOWHEE	*n* pl. **-S** a common finch
TOWIE	*n* pl. **-S** a form of contract bridge for three players
TOWLINE	*n* pl. **-S** a line used in towing
TOWMOND	*n* pl. **-S** a year
TOWMONT	*n* pl. **-S** towmond
TOWN	*n* pl. **-S** a center of population smaller than a city
TOWNEE	*n* pl. **-S** a townsman
TOWNFOLK	*n/pl* the inhabitants of a town
TOWNHOME	*n* pl. **-S** one of a series of contiguous houses of two or three stories
TOWNIE	*n* pl. **-S** a nonstudent who lives in a college town
TOWNIES	pl. of towny
TOWNISH	*adj* characteristic of a town
TOWNLESS	*adj* having no towns
TOWNLET	*n* pl. **-S** a small town
TOWNSHIP	*n* pl. **-S** an administrative division of a county
TOWNSMAN	*n* pl. **-MEN** a resident of a town
TOWNWEAR	*n* pl. **TOWNWEAR** apparel that is suitable for wear in the city
TOWNY	*n* pl. **TOWNIES** townie
TOWPATH	*n* pl. **-S** a path along a river that is used by animals towing boats
TOWPLANE	*n* pl. **-S** an airplane that tows gliders
TOWROPE	*n* pl. **-S** a rope used in towing
TOWSACK	*n* pl. **-S** a sack made of a coarse fabric
TOWY	*adj* resembling coarse hemp or flax fiber
TOXAEMIA	*n* pl. **-S** toxemia **TOXAEMIC** *adj*
TOXEMIA	*n* pl. **-S** the condition of having toxins in the blood **TOXEMIC** *adj*
TOXIC	*n* pl. **-S** a poisonous substance
TOXICAL	*adj* toxic
TOXICANT	*n* pl. **-S** a poisonous substance
TOXICITY	*n* pl. **-TIES** the quality of being poisonous
TOXIN	*n* pl. **-S** a poisonous substance
TOXINE	*n* pl. **-S** toxin
TOXOID	*n* pl. **-S** a type of toxin
TOY	*v* **-ED, -ING, -S** to amuse oneself as if with a toy (a child's plaything)
TOYER	*n* pl. **-S** one that toys
TOYISH	*adj* frivolous
TOYLESS	*adj* having no toy
TOYLIKE	*adj* resembling a toy
TOYO	*n* pl. **-YOS** a smooth straw used in making hats
TOYON	*n* pl. **-S** an ornamental evergreen shrub
TOYSHOP	*n* pl. **-S** a shop where toys are sold
TRABEATE	*adj* constructed with horizontal beams
TRACE	*v* **TRACED, TRACING, TRACES** to follow the course of
TRACER	*n* pl. **-S** one that traces
TRACERY	*n* pl. **-ERIES** ornamental work of interlaced lines
TRACHEA	*n* pl. **-CHEAS** or **-CHEAE** the passage for conveying air to the lungs **TRACHEAL** *adj*
TRACHEID	*n* pl. **-S** a long, tubular plant cell
TRACHLE	*v* **-LED, -LING, -LES** to draggle
TRACHOMA	*n* pl. **-S** a disease of the eye
TRACHYTE	*n* pl. **-S** a light-colored igneous rock
TRACING	*n* pl. **-S** something that is traced
TRACK	*v* **-ED, -ING, -S** to follow the marks left by an animal, a person, or a vehicle
TRACKAGE	*n* pl. **-S** the track system of a railroad
TRACKER	*n* pl. **-S** one that tracks
TRACKING	*n* pl. **-S** the placement of students within a curriculum
TRACKMAN	*n* pl. **-MEN** a railroad worker
TRACKPAD	*n* pl. **-S** a touchpad
TRACKWAY	*n* pl. **-WAYS** a trodden path
TRACT	*n* pl. **-S** an expanse of land

TRACTATE *n* pl. **-S** a treatise

TRACTILE *adj* capable of being drawn out in length

TRACTION *n* pl. **-S** the act of pulling or drawing over a surface **TRACTIVE** *adj*

TRACTOR *n* pl. **-S** a motor vehicle used in farming

TRAD *adj* traditional

TRADE *v* **TRADED, TRADING, TRADES** to give in exchange for another commodity **TRADABLE** *adj*

TRADEOFF *n* pl. **-S** a giving up of one thing in return for another

TRADER *n* pl. **-S** one that trades

TRADITOR *n* pl. **-ES** a traitor among the early Christians

TRADUCE *v* **-DUCED, -DUCING, -DUCES** to defame

TRADUCER *n* pl. **-S** one that traduces

TRAFFIC *v* **-FICKED, -FICKING, -FICS** to engage in buying and selling

TRAGEDY *n* pl. **-DIES** a disastrous event

TRAGI pl. of tragus

TRAGIC *n* pl. **-S** the element of a drama that produces tragedy

TRAGICAL *adj* of the nature of a tragedy

TRAGOPAN *n* pl. **-S** an Asian pheasant

TRAGUS *n* pl. **-GI** a part of the external opening of the ear

TRAIK *v* **-ED, -ING, -S** to trudge

TRAIL *v* **-ED, -ING, -S** to drag along a surface

TRAILER *v* **-ED, -ING, -S** to transport by means of a trailer (a vehicle drawn by another)

TRAIN *v* **-ED, -ING, -S** to instruct systematically

TRAINEE *n* pl. **-S** a person receiving training

TRAINER *n* pl. **-S** one that trains

TRAINFUL *n* pl. **-S** as much as a railroad train can hold

TRAINING *n* pl. **-S** systematic instruction

TRAINMAN *n* pl. **-MEN** a railroad employee

TRAINWAY *n* pl. **-WAYS** a railway

TRAIPSE *v* **TRAIPSED, TRAIPSING, TRAIPSES** to walk about in an idle or aimless manner

TRAIT *n* pl. **-S** a distinguishing characteristic

TRAITOR *n* pl. **-S** one who betrays another

TRAJECT *v* **-ED, -ING, -S** to transmit

TRAM *v* **TRAMMED, TRAMMING, TRAMS** to convey in a tramcar

TRAMCAR *n* pl. **-S** a streetcar

TRAMEL *v* **-ELED, -ELING, -ELS** or **-ELLED, -ELLING, -ELS** to trammel

TRAMELL *v* **-ED, -ING, -S** to trammel

TRAMLESS *adj* having no tramcar

TRAMLINE *n* pl. **-S** a streetcar line

TRAMMED past tense of tram

TRAMMEL *v* **-MELED, -MELING, -MELS** or **-MELLED, -MELLING, -MELS** to hinder

TRAMMING present participle of tram

TRAMP *v* **-ED, -ING, -S** to walk with a firm, heavy step

TRAMPER *n* pl. **-S** one that tramps

TRAMPISH *adj* resembling a vagabond

TRAMPLE *v* **-PLED, -PLING, -PLES** to tread on heavily

TRAMPLER *n* pl. **-S** one that tramples

TRAMPY *adj* **TRAMPIER, TRAMPIEST** having the characteristics of a vagrant

TRAMROAD *n* pl. **-S** a railway in a mine

TRAMWAY *n* pl. **-WAYS** a tramline

TRANCE *v* **TRANCED, TRANCING, TRANCES** to put into a trance (a semiconscious state)

TRANCHE *n* pl. **-S** a portion

TRANGAM *n* pl. **-S** a gewgaw

TRANK *n* pl. **-S** a drug that tranquilizes

TRANNY *n* pl. **-NIES** a transmission

TRANQ *n* pl. **-S** trank

TRANQUIL *adj* **-QUILER, -QUILEST** or **-QUILLER, -QUILLEST** free from disturbance

TRANS *adj* characterized by the arrangement of different atoms on opposite sides of the molecule

TRANSACT *v* **-ED, -ING, -S** to carry out

TRANSECT *v* **-ED, -ING, -S** to cut across

TRANSEPT *n* pl. **-S** a major transverse part of the body of a church

TRANSFER *v* **-FERRED, -FERRING, -FERS** to convey from one source to another

TRANSFIX *v* **-FIXED** or **-FIXT, -FIXING, -FIXES** to impale

TRANSHIP *v* **-SHIPPED, -SHIPPING, -SHIPS** to transfer from one conveyance to another

TRANSIT *v* **-ED, -ING, -S** to pass across or through

TRANSMIT *v* **-MITTED, -MITTING, -MITS** to send from one place or person to another

TRANSOM *n pl.* **-S** a small window above a door or another window

TRANSUDE *v* **-SUDED, -SUDING, -SUDES** to pass through a membrane

TRAP *v* **TRAPPED** or **TRAPT, TRAPPING, TRAPS** to catch in a trap (a device for capturing and holding animals)

TRAPAN *v* **-PANNED, -PANNING, -PANS** to trepan

TRAPBALL *n pl.* **-S** a type of ball game

TRAPDOOR *n pl.* **-S** a lifting or sliding door covering an opening

TRAPES *v* **-ED, -ING, -ES** to traipse

TRAPEZE *n pl.* **-S** a gymnastic apparatus

TRAPEZIA *n/pl* four-sided polygons having no parallel sides

TRAPEZII *n/pl* triangular muscles of the back

TRAPLIKE *adj* resembling a trap

TRAPLINE *n pl.* **-S** a series of traps

TRAPNEST *v* **-ED, -ING, -S** to determine the productivity of hens with a type of nest

TRAPPEAN *adj* pertaining to traprock

TRAPPED a past tense of trap

TRAPPER *n pl.* **-S** one that traps

TRAPPING *n pl.* **-S** a covering for a horse

TRAPPOSE *adj* trappean

TRAPPOUS *adj* trappean

TRAPROCK *n pl.* **-S** an igneous rock

TRAPT a past tense of trap

TRAPUNTO *n pl.* **-TOS** a decorative quilted design

TRASH *v* **-ED, -ING, -ES** to free from trash (worthless or waste matter)

TRASHER *n pl.* **-S** one that destroys or damages

TRASHMAN *n pl.* **-MEN** a person who removes trash

TRASHY *adj* **TRASHIER, TRASHIEST** resembling trash **TRASHILY** *adv*

TRASS *n pl.* **-ES** a volcanic rock

TRAUCHLE *v* **-LED, -LING, -LES** to trachle

TRAUMA *n pl.* **-MAS** or **-MATA** a severe emotional shock

TRAVAIL *v* **-ED, -ING, -S** to toil

TRAVE *n pl.* **-S** a frame for confining a horse

TRAVEL *v* **-ELED, -ELING, -ELS** or **-ELLED, -ELLING, -ELS** to go from one place to another

TRAVELER *n pl.* **-S** one that travels

TRAVELOG *n pl.* **-S** a lecture or film on traveling

TRAVERSE *v* **-VERSED, -VERSING, -VERSES** to pass across or through

TRAVESTY *v* **-TIED, -TYING, -TIES** to parody

TRAVOIS *n pl.* **-ES** a type of sled

TRAVOISE *n pl.* **-S** travois

TRAWL *v* **-ED, -ING, -S** to fish by dragging a net along the sea bottom

TRAWLER *n pl.* **-S** a boat used for trawling

TRAWLEY *n pl.* **-LEYS** a small truck or car for conveying material

TRAWLNET *n pl.* **-S** the large net used in trawling

TRAY *n pl.* **TRAYS** a flat, shallow receptacle

TRAYFUL *n pl.* **-S** as much as a tray will hold

TREACLE *n pl.* **-S** molasses

TREACLY *adj* **-CLIER, -CLIEST** cloyingly sweet and sentimental

TREAD *v* **TROD** or **TRODE** or **TREADED, TRODDEN, TREADING, TREADS** to walk on, over, or along

TREADER *n pl.* **-S** one that treads

TREADLE *v* **-LED, -LING, -LES** to work a foot lever

TREADLER *n pl.* **-S** one that treadles

TREASON *n pl.* **-S** violation of allegiance toward one's country

TREASURE *v* **-URED, -URING, -URES** to value highly

TREASURY *n pl.* **-URIES** a place where funds are received, kept, and disbursed

TREAT *v* **-ED, -ING, -S** to behave in a particular way toward

TREATER *n pl.* **-S** one that treats

TREATISE *n pl.* **-S** a formal and systematic written account of a subject

TREATY *n pl.* **-TIES** a formal agreement between two or more nations

TREBLE *v* **-BLED, -BLING, -BLES** to triple

TREBLY *adv* triply

TRECENTO *n* pl. **-TOS** the fourteenth century

TREDDLE *v* **-DLED, -DLING, -DLES** to treadle

TREE *v* **TREED, TREEING, TREES** to drive up a tree (a tall, woody plant)

TREELAWN *n* pl. **-S** the strip of lawn between the street and the sidewalk

TREELESS *adj* having no tree

TREELIKE *adj* resembling a tree

TREEN *n* pl. **-S** an article made from wood

TREENAIL *n* pl. **-S** a wooden peg used for fastening timbers

TREETOP *n* pl. **-S** the top of a tree

TREF *adj* unfit for use according to Jewish law

TREFAH *adj* tref

TREFOIL *n* pl. **-S** a plant having ternate leaves

TREHALA *n* pl. **-S** a sweet, edible substance forming the pupal case of certain weevils

TREK *v* **TREKKED, TREKKING, TREKS** to make a slow or arduous journey

TREKKER *n* pl. **-S** one that treks

TRELLIS *v* **-ED, -ING, -ES** to provide with a trellis (a frame used as a support for climbing plants)

TREMBLE *v* **-BLED, -BLING, -BLES** to shake involuntarily

TREMBLER *n* pl. **-S** one that trembles

TREMBLY *adj* **-BLIER, -BLIEST** marked by trembling

TREMOLO *n* pl. **-LOS** a vibrating musical effect

TREMOR *n* pl. **-S** a shaking movement

TRENAIL *n* pl. **-S** treenail

TRENCH *v* **-ED, -ING, -ES** to dig a long, narrow excavation in the ground

TRENCHER *n* pl. **-S** a wooden platter for serving food

TREND *v* **-ED, -ING, -S** to take a particular course

TRENDOID *n* pl. **-S** a trendy person

TRENDY *adj* **TRENDIER, TRENDIEST** very fashionable **TRENDILY** *adv*

TRENDY *n* pl. **TRENDIES** a trendy person

TREPAN *v* **-PANNED, -PANNING, -PANS** to trephine

TREPANG *n* pl. **-S** a marine animal

TREPHINE *v* **-PHINED, -PHINING, -PHINES** to operate on with a surgical saw

TREPID *adj* timorous

TRESPASS *v* **-ED, -ING, -ES** to enter upon the land of another unlawfully

TRESS *n* pl. **-ES** a long lock of hair **TRESSED** *adj*

TRESSEL *n* pl. **-S** trestle

TRESSOUR *n* pl. **-S** tressure

TRESSURE *n* pl. **-S** a type of heraldic design

TRESSY *adj* **TRESSIER, TRESSIEST** abounding in tresses

TRESTLE *n* pl. **-S** a framework for supporting a bridge

TRET *n* pl. **-S** an allowance formerly paid to purchasers for waste incurred in transit

TREVALLY *n* pl. **-LIES** or **-LYS** an Australian food fish

TREVET *n* pl. **-S** trivet

TREWS *n/pl* close-fitting tartan trousers

TREY *n* pl. **TREYS** a three in cards, dice, or dominoes

TRIABLE *adj* subject to judicial examination

TRIAC *n* pl. **-S** an electronic device used to control power

TRIACID *n* pl. **-S** a type of acid

TRIAD *n* pl. **-S** a group of three

TRIADIC *n* pl. **-S** a member of a triad

TRIADISM *n* pl. **-S** the quality or state of being a triad

TRIAGE *v* **-AGED, -AGING, -AGES** to practice a system of treating disaster victims

TRIAL *n* pl. **-S** a judicial examination

TRIANGLE *n* pl. **-S** a polygon having three sides

TRIARCHY *n* pl. **-CHIES** government by three persons

TRIAXIAL *adj* having three axes

TRIAZIN *n* pl. **-S** triazine

TRIAZINE *n* pl. **-S** a chemical compound

TRIAZOLE *n* pl. **-S** a chemical compound

TRIBADE *n* pl. **-S** a lesbian **TRIBADIC** *adj*

TRIBAL *n* pl. **-S** a member of an aboriginal people of India

TRIBALLY *adv* in a manner characteristic of a tribe

TRIBASIC *adj* having three replaceable hydrogen atoms

TRIBE *n* pl. **-S** a group of people sharing a common ancestry and culture

TRIBRACH *n* pl. **-S** a type of metrical foot

TRIBUNAL   *n* pl. **-S** a court of justice

TRIBUNE   *n* pl. **-S** a defender of the rights of the people

TRIBUTE   *n* pl. **-S** something given to show respect, gratitude, or admiration

TRICE   *v* **TRICED, TRICING, TRICES** to haul up with a rope

TRICEP   *n* pl. **-S** a triceps

TRICEPS   *n* pl. **-ES** an arm muscle

TRICHINA   *n* pl. **-NAS** or **-NAE** a parasitic worm

TRICHITE   *n* pl. **-S** a minute mineral body found in volcanic rocks

TRICHOID   *adj* hairlike

TRICHOME   *n* pl. **-S** a hairlike outgrowth

TRICING   present participle of trice

TRICK   *v* **-ED, -ING, -S** to deceive

TRICKER   *n* pl. **-S** one that tricks

TRICKERY   *n* pl. **-ERIES** deception

TRICKIE   *adj* **TRICKIER, TRICKIEST** tricky

TRICKIER   comparative of tricky

TRICKIEST   superlative of tricky

TRICKILY   *adv* in a tricky manner

TRICKISH   *adj* tricky

TRICKLE   *v* **-LED, -LING, -LES** to flow or fall in drops

TRICKLY   *adj* **-LIER, -LIEST** marked by trickling

TRICKSY   *adj* **-SIER, -SIEST** mischievous

TRICKY   *adj* **TRICKIER, TRICKIEST** characterized by deception

TRICLAD   *n* pl. **-S** an aquatic flatworm

TRICOLOR   *n* pl. **-S** a flag having three colors

TRICORN   *n* pl. **-S** a hat with the brim turned up on three sides

TRICORNE   *n* pl. **-S** tricorn

TRICOT   *n* pl. **-S** a knitted fabric

TRICTRAC   *n* pl. **-S** a form of backgammon

TRICYCLE   *n* pl. **-S** a vehicle having three wheels

TRIDENT   *n* pl. **-S** a spear having three prongs

TRIDUUM   *n* pl. **-S** a period of three days of prayer

TRIED   past tense of try

TRIENE   *n* pl. **-S** a type of chemical compound

TRIENNIA   *n/pl* periods of three years

TRIENS   *n* pl. **-ENTES** a coin of ancient Rome

TRIER   *n* pl. **-S** one that tries

TRIES   present 3d person sing. of try

TRIETHYL   *adj* containing three ethyl groups

TRIFECTA   *n* pl. **-S** a system of betting

TRIFID   *adj* divided into three parts

TRIFLE   *v* **-FLED, -FLING, -FLES** to waste time

TRIFLER   *n* pl. **-S** one that trifles

TRIFLING   *n* pl. **-S** a waste of time

TRIFOCAL   *n* pl. **-S** a type of lens

TRIFOLD   *adj* having three parts

TRIFORIA   *n/pl* galleries in a church

TRIFORM   *adj* having three forms

TRIG   *adj* **TRIGGER, TRIGGEST** neat

TRIG   *v* **TRIGGED, TRIGGING, TRIGS** to make trig

TRIGGER   *v* **-ED, -ING, -S** to actuate

TRIGLY   *adv* in a trig manner

TRIGLYPH   *n* pl. **-S** an architectural ornament

TRIGNESS   *n* pl. **-ES** the quality or state of being trig

TRIGO   *n* pl. **-GOS** wheat

TRIGON   *n* pl. **-S** an ancient stringed instrument

TRIGONAL   *adj* shaped like a triangle

TRIGRAM   *n* pl. **-S** a cluster of three successive letters

TRIGRAPH   *n* pl. **-S** a group of three letters representing one sound

TRIHEDRA   *n/pl* figures having three plane surfaces meeting at a point

TRIJET   *n* pl. **-S** an airplane powered by three jet engines

TRIKE   *n* pl. **-S** a tricycle

TRILBY   *n* pl. **-BIES** a soft felt hat

TRILITH   *n* pl. **-S** a prehistoric structure of three large stones

TRILL   *v* **-ED, -ING, -S** to sing or play with a vibrating effect

TRILLER   *n* pl. **-S** one that trills

TRILLION   *n* pl. **-S** a number

TRILLIUM   *n* pl. **-S** a flowering plant

TRILOBAL   *adj* trilobed

TRILOBED   *adj* having three lobes

TRILOGY   *n* pl. **-GIES** a group of three related literary works

TRIM	*adj* **TRIMMER, TRIMMEST** neat and orderly
TRIM	*v* **TRIMMED, TRIMMING, TRIMS** to make trim by cutting
TRIMARAN	*n* pl. **-S** a sailing vessel
TRIMER	*n* pl. **-S** a type of chemical compound **TRIMERIC** *adj*
TRIMETER	*n* pl. **-S** a verse of three metrical feet
TRIMLY	*adv* in a trim manner
TRIMMED	past tense of trim
TRIMMER	*n* pl. **-S** one that trims
TRIMMEST	superlative of trim
TRIMMING	*n* pl. **-S** something added as a decoration
TRIMNESS	*n* pl. **-ES** the state of being trim
TRIMORPH	*n* pl. **-S** a substance existing in three forms
TRIMOTOR	*n* pl. **-S** an airplane powered by three engines
TRINAL	*adj* having three parts
TRINARY	*adj* consisting of three parts
TRINDLE	*v* **-DLED, -DLING, -DLES** to trundle
TRINE	*v* **TRINED, TRINING, TRINES** to place in a particular astrological position
TRINITY	*n* pl. **-TIES** a group of three
TRINKET	*v* **-ED, -ING, -S** to deal secretly
TRINKUMS	*n/pl* small ornaments
TRINODAL	*adj* having three nodes
TRIO	*n* pl. **TRIOS** a group of three
TRIODE	*n* pl. **-S** a type of electron tube
TRIOL	*n* pl. **-S** a type of chemical compound
TRIOLET	*n* pl. **-S** a short poem of fixed form
TRIOSE	*n* pl. **-S** a simple sugar
TRIOXID	*n* pl. **-S** trioxide
TRIOXIDE	*n* pl. **-S** a type of oxide
TRIP	*v* **TRIPPED, TRIPPING, TRIPS** to stumble
TRIPACK	*n* pl. **-S** a type of film pack
TRIPART	*adj* divided into three parts
TRIPE	*n* pl. **-S** a part of the stomach of a ruminant that is used as food
TRIPEDAL	*adj* having three feet
TRIPHASE	*adj* having three phases
TRIPLANE	*n* pl. **-S** a type of airplane
TRIPLE	*v* **-PLED, -PLING, -PLES** to make three times as great
TRIPLET	*n* pl. **-S** a group of three of one kind
TRIPLEX	*n* pl. **-ES** an apartment having three floors
TRIPLITE	*n* pl. **-S** a mineral
TRIPLOID	*n* pl. **-S** a cell having a chromosome number that is three times the basic number
TRIPLY	*adv* in a triple degree, manner, or number
TRIPOD	*n* pl. **-S** a stand having three legs **TRIPODAL, TRIPODIC** *adj*
TRIPODY	*n* pl. **-DIES** a verse of three metrical feet
TRIPOLI	*n* pl. **-S** a soft, friable rock
TRIPOS	*n* pl. **-ES** a tripod
TRIPPED	past tense of trip
TRIPPER	*n* pl. **-S** one that trips
TRIPPET	*n* pl. **-S** a part of a mechanism designed to strike another part
TRIPPING	*n* pl. **-S** the act of one that trips
TRIPPY	*adj* **-PIER, -PIEST** suggesting a trip on psychedelic drugs
TRIPTAN	*n* pl. **-S** a drug for treating migraine attacks
TRIPTANE	*n* pl. **-S** a chemical compound
TRIPTYCA	*n* pl. **-S** a triptych
TRIPTYCH	*n* pl. **-S** an ancient writing tablet
TRIPWIRE	*n* pl. **-S** a low-placed hidden wire that sets off an alarm or a trap
TRIREME	*n* pl. **-S** an ancient Greek or Roman warship
TRISCELE	*n* pl. **-S** triskele
TRISECT	*v* **-ED, -ING, -S** to divide into three equal parts
TRISEME	*n* pl. **-S** a type of metrical foot **TRISEMIC** *adj*
TRISHAW	*n* pl. **-S** a pedicab
TRISKELE	*n* pl. **-S** a figure consisting of three branches radiating from a center
TRISMUS	*n* pl. **-ES** lockjaw **TRISMIC** *adj*
TRISOME	*n* pl. **-S** an organism having one chromosome in addition to the usual diploid number
TRISOMIC	*n* pl. **-S** a trisome
TRISOMY	*n* pl. **-MIES** the condition of being a trisome
TRISTATE	*adj* pertaining to an area made up of three adjoining states

TRISTE	*adj* sad
TRISTEZA	*n* pl. **-S** a disease of citrus trees
TRISTFUL	*adj* sad
TRISTICH	*n* pl. **-S** a stanza of three lines
TRITE	*adj* **TRITER, TRITEST** used so often as to be made commonplace **TRITELY** *adv*
TRITHING	*n* pl. **-S** an administrative division in England
TRITICUM	*n* pl. **-S** a cereal grass
TRITIUM	*n* pl. **-S** an isotope of hydrogen
TRITOMA	*n* pl. **-S** an African herb
TRITON	*n* pl. **-S** a marine mollusk
TRITONE	*n* pl. **-S** a musical interval of three whole tones
TRIUMPH	*v* **-ED, -ING, -S** to be victorious
TRIUMVIR	*n* pl. **-VIRS** or **-VIRI** one of a ruling body of three in ancient Rome
TRIUNE	*n* pl. **-S** a trinity
TRIUNITY	*n* pl. **-TIES** a trinity
TRIVALVE	*n* pl. **-S** a type of shell
TRIVET	*n* pl. **-S** a small stand having three legs
TRIVIA	*n/pl* insignificant matters
TRIVIAL	*adj* insignificant
TRIVIUM	*n* pl. **-IA** a group of studies in medieval schools
TROAK	*v* **-ED, -ING, -S** to troke
TROCAR	*n* pl. **-S** a surgical instrument
TROCHAIC	*n* pl. **-S** a trochee
TROCHAL	*adj* shaped like a wheel
TROCHAR	*n* pl. **-S** trocar
TROCHE	*n* pl. **-S** a medicated lozenge
TROCHEE	*n* pl. **-S** a type of metrical foot
TROCHIL	*n* pl. **-S** an African bird
TROCHILI	*n/pl* trochils
TROCHLEA	*n* pl. **-LEAS** or **-LEAE** an anatomical structure resembling a pulley
TROCHOID	*n* pl. **-S** a type of geometric curve
TROCK	*v* **-ED, -ING, -S** to troke
TROD	a past tense of tread
TRODDEN	past participle of tread
TRODE	a past tense of tread
TROFFER	*n* pl. **-S** a fixture for fluorescent lighting
TROG	*n* pl. **-S** a hooligan
TROGON	*n* pl. **-S** a tropical bird
TROIKA	*n* pl. **-S** a Russian carriage
TROILISM	*n* pl. **-S** sexual relations involving three persons
TROILITE	*n* pl. **-S** a mineral
TROILUS	*n* pl. **-ES** a large butterfly
TROIS	*n* pl. **TROIS** the number three
TROKE	*v* **TROKED, TROKING, TROKES** to exchange
TROLAND	*n* pl. **-S** a unit of measurement of retinal response to light
TROLL	*v* **-ED, -ING, -S** to fish with a slowly trailing line
TROLLER	*n* pl. **-S** one that trolls
TROLLEY	*v* **-ED, -ING, -S** to convey by streetcar
TROLLING	*n* pl. **-S** the act of one that trolls
TROLLOP	*n* pl. **-S** a prostitute **TROLLOPY** *adj*
TROLLY	*v* **-LIED, -LYING, -LIES** to trolley
TROMBONE	*n* pl. **-S** a brass wind instrument
TROMMEL	*n* pl. **-S** a screen used for sifting rock, ore, or coal
TROMP	*v* **-ED, -ING, -S** to tramp
TROMPE	*n* pl. **-S** a device used for supplying air to a furnace
TRONA	*n* pl. **-S** a mineral
TRONE	*n* pl. **-S** a weighing device
TROOP	*v* **-ED, -ING, -S** to move or gather in crowds
TROOPER	*n* pl. **-S** a cavalryman
TROOPIAL	*n* pl. **-S** troupial
TROOZ	*n/pl* trews
TROP	*adv* too much
TROPE	*n* pl. **-S** the figurative use of a word
TROPHIC	*adj* pertaining to nutrition
TROPHY	*v* **-PHIED, -PHYING, -PHIES** to honor with a trophy (a symbol of victory)
TROPIC	*n* pl. **-S** either of two circles of the celestial sphere on each side of the equator
TROPICAL	*n* pl. **-S** a plant of the region lying between the tropics
TROPIN	*n* pl. **-S** tropine
TROPINE	*n* pl. **-S** a poisonous alkaloid
TROPISM	*n* pl. **-S** the involuntary response of an organism to an external stimulus
TROPONIN	*n* pl. **-S** a protein of muscle

TROT	v **TROTTED, TROTTING, TROTS** to go at a gait between a walk and a run	**TRUCK**	v **-ED, -ING, -S** to transport by truck (an automotive vehicle designed to carry loads)
TROTH	v **-ED, -ING, -S** to betroth	**TRUCKAGE**	n pl. **-S** transportation of goods by trucks
TROTLINE	n pl. **-S** a strong fishing line	**TRUCKER**	n pl. **-S** a truck driver
TROTTER	n pl. **-S** a horse that trots	**TRUCKFUL**	n pl. **-S** as much as a truck can hold
TROTTING	present participle of trot		
TROTYL	n pl. **-S** an explosive	**TRUCKING**	n pl. **-S** truckage
TROUBLE	v **-BLED, -BLING, -BLES** to distress	**TRUCKLE**	v **-LED, -LING, -LES** to yield weakly
TROUBLER	n pl. **-S** one that troubles	**TRUCKLER**	n pl. **-S** one that truckles
TROUGH	n pl. **-S** a long, narrow receptacle	**TRUCKMAN**	n pl. **-MEN** a trucker
TROUNCE	v **TROUNCED, TROUNCING, TROUNCES** to beat severely	**TRUDGE**	v **TRUDGED, TRUDGING, TRUDGES** to walk tiredly
TROUNCER	n pl. **-S** one that trounces	**TRUDGEN**	n pl. **-S** a swimming stroke
TROUPE	v **TROUPED, TROUPING, TROUPES** to tour with a theatrical company	**TRUDGEON**	n pl. **-S** trudgen
		TRUDGER	n pl. **-S** one that trudges
		TRUDGING	present participle of trudge
TROUPER	n pl. **-S** a member of a theatrical company	**TRUE**	adj **TRUER, TRUEST** consistent with fact or reality
TROUPIAL	n pl. **-S** a tropical bird	**TRUE**	v **TRUED, TRUING** or **TRUEING, TRUES** to bring to conformity with a standard or requirement
TROUSER	adj pertaining to trousers	
TROUSERS	n/pl a garment for the lower part of the body	**TRUEBLUE**	n pl. **-S** a person of unwavering loyalty
TROUT	n pl. **-S** a freshwater fish	**TRUEBORN**	adj genuinely such by birth
TROUTY	adj **TROUTIER, TROUTIEST** abounding in trout	**TRUEBRED**	adj designating an animal of unmixed stock
TROUVERE	n pl. **-S** a medieval poet	**TRUED**	past tense of true
TROUVEUR	n pl. **-S** trouvere	**TRUELOVE**	n pl. **-S** a sweetheart
TROVE	n pl. **-S** a valuable discovery	**TRUENESS**	n pl. **-ES** the quality or state of being true
TROVER	n pl. **-S** a type of legal action	
TROW	v **-ED, -ING, -S** to suppose	**TRUER**	comparative of true
TROWEL	v **-ELED, -ELING, -ELS** or **-ELLED, -ELLING, -ELS** to smooth with a trowel (a hand tool having a flat blade)	**TRUEST**	superlative of true
		TRUFFE	n pl. **-S** truffle
		TRUFFLE	n pl. **-S** an edible fungus **TRUFFLED** adj
TROWELER	n pl. **-S** one that trowels	
TROWSERS	n/pl trousers	**TRUG**	n pl. **-S** a gardener's basket
TROWTH	n pl. **-S** truth	**TRUING**	a present participle of true
TROY	n pl. **TROYS** a system of weights	**TRUISM**	n pl. **-S** an obvious truth **TRUISTIC** adj
TRUANCY	n pl. **-CIES** an act of truanting	
TRUANT	v **-ED, -ING, -S** to stay out of school without permission	**TRULL**	n pl. **-S** a prostitute
		TRULY	adv in conformity with fact or reality
TRUANTLY	adv in a manner of one who shirks duty	**TRUMEAU**	n pl. **-MEAUX** a column supporting part of a doorway
TRUANTRY	n pl. **-RIES** truancy	
TRUCE	v **TRUCED, TRUCING, TRUCES** to suspend hostilities by mutual agreement	**TRUMP**	v **-ED, -ING, -S** to outdo
		TRUMPERY	n pl. **-ERIES** worthless finery

TRUMPET	v **-ED, -ING, -S** to sound on a trumpet (a brass wind instrument)
TRUNCATE	v **-CATED, -CATING, -CATES** to shorten by cutting off a part
TRUNDLE	v **-DLED, -DLING, -DLES** to propel by causing to rotate
TRUNDLER	n pl. **-S** one that trundles
TRUNK	n pl. **-S** the main stem of a tree **TRUNKED** adj
TRUNKFUL	n pl. **-S** as much as a trunk (a storage box) can hold
TRUNNEL	n pl. **-S** treenail
TRUNNION	n pl. **-S** a pin or pivot on which something can be rotated
TRUSS	v **-ED, -ING, -ES** to secure tightly
TRUSSER	n pl. **-S** one that trusses
TRUSSING	n pl. **-S** the framework of a structure
TRUST	v **-ED, -ING, -S** to place confidence in
TRUSTEE	v **-TEED, -TEEING, -TEES** to commit to the care of an administrator
TRUSTER	n pl. **-S** one that trusts
TRUSTFUL	adj inclined to trust
TRUSTOR	n pl. **-S** one that trustees his property
TRUSTY	adj **TRUSTIER, TRUSTIEST** worthy of trust **TRUSTILY** adv
TRUSTY	n pl. **TRUSTIES** one worthy of trust
TRUTH	n pl. **-S** conformity to fact or reality
TRUTHFUL	adj telling the truth
TRY	v **TRIED, TRYING, TRIES** to attempt
TRYINGLY	adv in a distressing manner
TRYMA	n pl. **-MATA** a type of nut
TRYOUT	n pl. **-S** a test of ability
TRYPSIN	n pl. **-S** an enzyme **TRYPTIC** adj
TRYSAIL	n pl. **-S** a type of sail
TRYST	v **-ED, -ING, -S** to agree to meet
TRYSTE	n pl. **-S** a market
TRYSTER	n pl. **-S** one that trysts
TRYWORKS	n/pl a type of furnace
TSADDIK	n pl. **-DIKIM** zaddik
TSADE	n pl. **-S** sade
TSADI	n pl. **-S** sade
TSAR	n pl. **-S** czar
TSARDOM	n pl. **-S** czardom

TSAREVNA	n pl. **-S** czarevna
TSARINA	n pl. **-S** czarina
TSARISM	n pl. **-S** czarism
TSARIST	n pl. **-S** czarist
TSARITZA	n pl. **-S** czaritza
TSATSKE	n pl. **-S** chachka
TSETSE	n pl. **-S** an African fly
TSIMMES	n pl. **TSIMMES** tzimmes
TSK	v **-ED, -ING, -S** to utter an exclamation of annoyance
TSKTSK	v **-ED, -ING, -S** to tsk
TSOORIS	n pl. **TSOORIS** tsuris
TSORES	n pl. **TSORES** tsuris
TSORIS	n pl. **TSORIS** tsuris
TSORRISS	n pl. **TSORRISS** tsuris
TSOURIS	n pl. **TSOURIS** tsuris
TSUBA	n pl. **TSUBA** a part of a Japanese sword
TSUNAMI	n pl. **-S** a very large ocean wave **TSUNAMIC** adj
TSURIS	n pl. **TSURIS** a series of misfortunes
TUATARA	n pl. **-S** a large reptile
TUATERA	n pl. **-S** tuatara
TUB	v **TUBBED, TUBBING, TUBS** to wash in a tub (a round, open vessel)
TUBA	n pl. **-BAS** or **-BAE** a brass wind instrument
TUBAIST	n pl. **-S** a tuba player
TUBAL	adj pertaining to a tube
TUBATE	adj tubular
TUBBABLE	adj suitable for washing in a tub
TUBBED	past tense of tub
TUBBER	n pl. **-S** one that tubs
TUBBING	present participle of tub
TUBBY	adj **-BIER, -BIEST** short and fat
TUBE	v **TUBED, TUBING, TUBES** to provide with a tube (a long, hollow cylinder)
TUBELESS	adj having no tube
TUBELIKE	adj resembling a tube
TUBENOSE	n pl. **-S** a bird having tubular nostrils
TUBER	n pl. **-S** a thick underground stem
TUBERCLE	n pl. **-S** a small, rounded swelling
TUBEROID	adj pertaining to a tuber

TUBEROSE *n* pl. **-S** a Mexican herb

TUBEROUS *adj* pertaining to a tuber

TUBEWORK *n* pl. **-S** tubing

TUBEWORM *n* pl. **-S** a marine worm that builds and lives in a tube

TUBFUL *n* pl. **-S** as much as a tub will hold

TUBIFEX *n* pl. **-ES** an aquatic worm

TUBIFORM *adj* tubular

TUBING *n* pl. **-S** material in the form of a tube

TUBIST *n* pl. **-S** a tubaist

TUBLIKE *adj* resembling a tub

TUBULAR *adj* shaped like a tube

TUBULATE *v* **-LATED, -LATING, -LATES** to form into a tube

TUBULE *n* pl. **-S** a small tube

TUBULIN *n* pl. **-S** a protein that polymerizes to form tiny tubules

TUBULOSE *adj* tubular

TUBULOUS *adj* tubular

TUBULURE *n* pl. **-S** a short tubular opening

TUCHUN *n* pl. **-S** a Chinese military governor

TUCK *v* **-ED, -ING, -S** to fold under

TUCKAHOE *n* pl. **-S** the edible root of certain arums

TUCKER *v* **-ED, -ING, -S** to weary

TUCKET *n* pl. **-S** a trumpet fanfare

TUCKSHOP *n* pl. **-S** a confectioner's shop

TUFA *n* pl. **-S** a porous limestone

TUFF *n* pl. **-S** a volcanic rock

TUFFET *n* pl. **-S** a clump of grass

TUFOLI *n* pl. **TUFOLI** a large macaroni shell

TUFT *v* **-ED, -ING, -S** to form into tufts (clusters of flexible outgrowths attached at the base)

TUFTER *n* pl. **-S** one that tufts

TUFTING *n* pl. **-S** a cluster of tufts used for decoration

TUFTY *adj* **TUFTIER, TUFTIEST** abounding in tufts **TUFTILY** *adv*

TUG *v* **TUGGED, TUGGING, TUGS** to pull with force

TUGBOAT *n* pl. **-S** a boat built for towing

TUGGER *n* pl. **-S** one that tugs

TUGGING present participle of tug

TUGHRIK *n* pl. **-S** tugrik

TUGLESS *adj* being without a rope or chain with which to pull

TUGRIK *n* pl. **-S** a monetary unit of Mongolia

TUI *n* pl. **-S** a bird of New Zealand

TUILLE *n* pl. **-S** a tasset

TUITION *n* pl. **-S** a fee for instruction

TULADI *n* pl. **-S** a freshwater fish

TULE *n* pl. **-S** a tall marsh plant

TULIP *n* pl. **-S** a flowering plant

TULLE *n* pl. **-S** a silk material

TULLIBEE *n* pl. **-S** a freshwater fish

TUMBLE *v* **-BLED, -BLING, -BLES** to fall or roll end over end

TUMBLER *n* pl. **-S** one that tumbles

TUMBLING *n* pl. **-S** the sport of gymnastics

TUMBREL *n* pl. **-S** a type of cart

TUMBRIL *n* pl. **-S** tumbrel

TUMEFY *v* **-FIED, -FYING, -FIES** to swell

TUMESCE *v* **-MESCED, -MESCING, -MESCES** to become swollen

TUMID *adj* swollen **TUMIDLY** *adv*

TUMIDITY *n* pl. **-TIES** the quality or state of being tumid

TUMMLER *n* pl. **-S** an entertainer who encourages audience participation

TUMMY *n* pl. **-MIES** the stomach

TUMOR *n* pl. **-S** an abnormal swelling **TUMORAL, TUMOROUS** *adj*

TUMOUR *n* pl. **-S** tumor

TUMP *v* **-ED, -ING, -S** to tip over

TUMPLINE *n* pl. **-S** a strap for supporting a load on the back

TUMULAR *adj* having the form of a mound

TUMULI a pl. of tumulus

TUMULOSE *adj* full of mounds

TUMULOUS *adj* tumulose

TUMULT *n* pl. **-S** a great din and commotion

TUMULUS *n* pl. **-LUSES** or **-LI** a mound over a grave

TUN *v* **TUNNED, TUNNING, TUNS** to store in a large cask

TUNA *n* pl. **-S** a marine food fish

TUNABLE *adj* capable of being tuned **TUNABLY** *adv*

TUNDISH *n* pl. **-ES** a receptacle for molten metal

TUNDRA   *n* pl. **-S** a level, treeless expanse of arctic land

TUNE   *v* **TUNED, TUNING, TUNES** to put into the proper pitch

TUNEABLE   *adj* tunable **TUNEABLY** *adv*

TUNEFUL   *adj* melodious

TUNELESS   *adj* not tuneful

TUNER   *n* pl. **-S** one that tunes

TUNEUP   *n* pl. **-S** an adjustment to insure efficient operation

TUNG   *n* pl. **-S** a Chinese tree

TUNGSTEN   *n* pl. **-S** a metallic element **TUNGSTIC** *adj*

TUNIC   *n* pl. **-S** a loose-fitting garment

TUNICA   *n* pl. **-CAE** an enveloping membrane or layer of body tissue

TUNICATE   *n* pl. **-S** a small marine animal

TUNICLE   *n* pl. **-S** a type of vestment

TUNING   present participle of tune

TUNNAGE   *n* pl. **-S** tonnage

TUNNED   past tense of tun

TUNNEL   *v* **-NELED, -NELING, -NELS** or **-NELLED, -NELLING, -NELS** to dig a tunnel (an underground passageway)

TUNNELER   *n* pl. **-S** one that tunnels

TUNNING   present participle of tun

TUNNY   *n* pl. **-NIES** a tuna

TUP   *v* **TUPPED, TUPPING, TUPS** to copulate with a ewe

TUPELO   *n* pl. **-LOS** a softwood tree

TUPIK   *n* pl. **-S** an Eskimo tent

TUPPENCE   *n* pl. **-S** twopence

TUPPENNY   *adj* twopenny

TUPPING   present participle of tup

TUQUE   *n* pl. **-S** a knitted woolen cap

TURACO   *n* pl. **-COS** touraco

TURACOU   *n* pl. **-S** touraco

TURBAN   *n* pl. **-S** a head covering worn by Muslims **TURBANED** *adj*

TURBARY   *n* pl. **-RIES** a place where peat can be dug

TURBETH   *n* pl. **-S** turpeth

TURBID   *adj* thick or opaque with roiled sediment **TURBIDLY** *adv*

TURBINAL   *n* pl. **-S** a bone of the nasal passage

TURBINE   *n* pl. **-S** a type of engine

TURBIT   *n* pl. **-S** a domestic pigeon

TURBITH   *n* pl. **-S** turpeth

TURBO   *n* pl. **-BOS** a turbine

TURBOCAR   *n* pl. **-S** an auto powered by a gas turbine

TURBOFAN   *n* pl. **-S** a type of jet engine

TURBOJET   *n* pl. **-S** a type of jet engine

TURBOT   *n* pl. **-S** a European flatfish

TURDINE   *adj* belonging to a large family of singing birds

TUREEN   *n* pl. **-S** a large, deep bowl

TURF   *n* pl. **TURFS** or **TURVES** a surface layer of earth containing a dense growth of grass

TURF   *v* **-ED, -ING, -S** to cover with turf

TURFIER   comparative of turfy

TURFIEST   superlative of turfy

TURFLESS   *adj* having no turf

TURFLIKE   *adj* resembling turf

TURFMAN   *n* pl. **-MEN** a person who is devoted to horse racing

TURFSKI   *n* pl. **-S** a type of ski

TURFY   *adj* **TURFIER, TURFIEST** covered with turf

TURGENCY   *n* pl. **-CIES** turgor

TURGENT   *adj* turgid

TURGID   *adj* swollen **TURGIDLY** *adv*

TURGITE   *n* pl. **-S** an iron ore

TURGOR   *n* pl. **-S** the quality or state of being turgid

TURION   *n* pl. **-S** a thick new growth on a plant

TURISTA   *n* pl. **-S** intestinal sickness affecting a tourist in a foreign country

TURK   *n* pl. **-S** one who eagerly advocates change

TURKEY   *n* pl. **-KEYS** a large American bird

TURKOIS   *n* pl. **-ES** turquois

TURMERIC   *n* pl. **-S** an East Indian herb

TURMOIL   *v* **-ED, -ING, -S** to throw into an uproar

TURN   *v* **-ED, -ING, -S** to move around a central point **TURNABLE** *adj*

TURNCOAT   *n* pl. **-S** a traitor

TURNDOWN   *n* pl. **-S** a rejection

TURNER   *n* pl. **-S** one that turns

TURNERY   *n* pl. **-ERIES** the process of shaping articles on a lathe

TURNHALL *n* pl. **-S** a building where gymnasts practice

TURNING *n* pl. **-S** a rotation about an axis

TURNIP *n* pl. **-S** an edible plant root

TURNKEY *n* pl. **-KEYS** a person who has charge of a prison's keys

TURNOFF *n* pl. **-S** a road that branches off from a larger one

TURNON *n* pl. **-S** something that arouses interest

TURNOUT *n* pl. **-S** an assemblage of people

TURNOVER *n* pl. **-S** an upset or overthrow

TURNPIKE *n* pl. **-S** a toll road

TURNSOLE *n* pl. **-S** a plant that turns with the sun

TURNSPIT *n* pl. **-S** one that turns a roasting spit

TURNUP *n* pl. **-S** a part of a garment that is turned up

TURPETH *n* pl. **-S** a medicinal plant root

TURPS *n* pl. **TURPS** turpentine

TURQUOIS *n* pl. **-ES** a greenish blue gem

TURRET *n* pl. **-S** a small tower **TURRETED** *adj*

TURRICAL *adj* resembling a turret

TURTLE *v* **-TLED, -TLING, -TLES** to catch turtles (tortoises)

TURTLER *n* pl. **-S** one that turtles

TURTLING *n* pl. **-S** the act of one that turtles

TURVES a pl. of turf

TUSCHE *n* pl. **-S** a liquid used in lithography

TUSH *v* **-ED, -ING, -ES** to tusk

TUSHERY *n* pl. **-ERIES** pretentious writing

TUSHIE *n* pl. **-S** the buttocks

TUSHY *n* pl. **TUSHIES** tushie

TUSK *v* **-ED, -ING, -S** to gore with a tusk (a long, pointed tooth extending outside of the mouth)

TUSKER *n* pl. **-S** an animal with tusks

TUSKLESS *adj* having no tusk

TUSKLIKE *adj* resembling a tusk

TUSSAH *n* pl. **-S** an Asian silkworm

TUSSAL *adj* pertaining to a cough

TUSSAR *n* pl. **-S** tussah

TUSSEH *n* pl. **-S** tussah

TUSSER *n* pl. **-S** tussah

TUSSIS *n* pl. **TUSSISES** or **TUSSES** a cough **TUSSIVE** *adj*

TUSSLE *v* **-SLED, -SLING, -SLES** to struggle

TUSSOCK *n* pl. **-S** a clump of grass **TUSSOCKY** *adj*

TUSSOR *n* pl. **-S** tussah

TUSSORE *n* pl. **-S** tussah

TUSSUCK *n* pl. **-S** tussock

TUSSUR *n* pl. **-S** tussah

TUT *v* **TUTTED, TUTTING, TUTS** to utter an exclamation of impatience

TUTEE *n* pl. **-S** one who is being tutored

TUTELAGE *n* pl. **-S** the act of tutoring

TUTELAR *n* pl. **-S** a tutelary

TUTELARY *n* pl. **-LARIES** one who has the power to protect

TUTOR *v* **-ED, -ING, -S** to instruct privately

TUTORAGE *n* pl. **-S** tutelage

TUTORESS *n* pl. **-ES** a female who tutors

TUTORIAL *n* pl. **-S** a session of tutoring

TUTOYER *v* **-TOYERED** or **-TOYED, -TOYERING, -TOYERS** to address familiarly

TUTTED past tense of tut

TUTTI *n* pl. **-S** a musical passage performed by all the performers

TUTTING present participle of tut

TUTTY *n* pl. **-TIES** an impure zinc oxide

TUTU *n* pl. **-S** a short ballet skirt **TUTUED** *adj*

TUX *n* pl. **-ES** a tuxedo

TUXEDO *n* pl. **-DOS** or **-DOES** a man's semiformal dinner coat **TUXEDOED** *adj*

TUYER *n* pl. **-S** tuyere

TUYERE *n* pl. **-S** a pipe through which air is forced into a blast furnace

TWA *n* pl. **-S** two

TWADDLE *v* **-DLED, -DLING, -DLES** to talk foolishly

TWADDLER *n* pl. **-S** one that twaddles

TWAE *n* pl. **-S** two

TWAIN *n* pl. **-S** a set of two

TWANG *v* **-ED, -ING, -S** to make a sharp, vibrating sound

TWANGER *n* pl. **-S** one that twangs

TWANGLE *v* **-GLED, -GLING, -GLES** to twang

TWANGLER *n* pl. **-S** one that twangles

TWANGY *adj* **TWANGIER, TWANGIEST** twanging

TWANKY   *n* pl. **-KIES** a variety of green tea

TWASOME   *n* pl. **-S** twosome

TWATTLE   *v* **-TLED, -TLING, -TLES** to twaddle

TWEAK   *v* **-ED, -ING, -S** to pinch and twist sharply

TWEAKY   *adj* **TWEAKIER, TWEAKIEST** twitchy

TWEE   *adj* affectedly cute or dainty

TWEED   *n* pl. **-S** a coarse woolen fabric

TWEEDLE   *v* **-DLED, -DLING, -DLES** to perform casually on a musical instrument

TWEEDY   *adj* **TWEEDIER, TWEEDIEST** resembling tweed

TWEEN   *n* pl. **-S** a child typically of an age eight through twelve

TWEENER   *n* pl. **-S** a player having some but not all of the qualifications for two or more positions

TWEENESS   *n* pl. **-ES** the state of being twee

TWEENY   *n* pl. **TWEENIES** a housemaid

TWEET   *v* **-ED, -ING, -S** to chirp

TWEETER   *n* pl. **-S** a loudspeaker designed to reproduce high-pitched sounds

TWEEZE   *v* **TWEEZED, TWEEZING, TWEEZES** to pluck with a tweezer

TWEEZER   *n* pl. **-S** a pincerlike tool

TWELFTH   *n* pl. **-S** the number twelve in a series

TWELVE   *n* pl. **-S** a number

TWELVEMO   *n* pl. **-MOS** a page size

TWENTY   *n* pl. **-TIES** a number

TWERP   *n* pl. **-S** a small, impudent person

TWIBIL   *n* pl. **-S** a battle-ax with two cutting edges

TWIBILL   *n* pl. **-S** twibil

TWICE   *adv* two times

TWIDDLE   *v* **-DLED, -DLING, -DLES** to play idly with something

TWIDDLER   *n* pl. **-S** one that twiddles

TWIDDLY   *adj* **-DLIER, -DLIEST** having many turns

TWIER   *n* pl. **-S** tuyere

TWIG   *v* **TWIGGED, TWIGGING, TWIGS** to observe

TWIGGEN   *adj* made of twigs (small branches)

TWIGGY   *adj* **-GIER, -GIEST** twiglike

TWIGLESS   *adj* having no twigs

TWIGLIKE   *adj* resembling a twig

TWILIGHT   *n* pl. **-S** the early evening light

TWILIT   *adj* lighted by twilight

TWILL   *v* **-ED, -ING, -S** to weave so as to produce a diagonal pattern

TWILLING   *n* pl. **-S** a twilled fabric

TWIN   *v* **TWINNED, TWINNING, TWINS** to bring together in close association

TWINBORN   *adj* born at the same birth

TWINE   *v* **TWINED, TWINING, TWINES** to twist together

TWINER   *n* pl. **-S** one that twines

TWINGE   *v* **TWINGED, TWINGING** or **TWINGEING, TWINGES** to affect with a sharp pain

TWINIER   comparative of twiny

TWINIEST   superlative of twiny

TWINIGHT   *adj* pertaining to a baseball doubleheader that begins in the late afternoon

TWINING   present participle of twine

TWINJET   *n* pl. **-S** an aircraft with two jet engines

TWINKIE   *n* pl. **-S** a young, attractive person of little experience

TWINKLE   *v* **-KLED, -KLING, -KLES** to shine with a flickering or sparkling light

TWINKLER   *n* pl. **-S** one that twinkles

TWINKLY   *adj* twinkling

TWINNED   past tense of twin

TWINNING   *n* pl. **-S** the bearing of two children at the same birth

TWINSET   *n* pl. **-S** a matching pair of sweaters to be worn together

TWINSHIP   *n* pl. **-S** close similarity or association

TWINY   *adj* **TWINIER, TWINIEST** resembling twine (a strong string)

TWIRL   *v* **-ED, -ING, -S** to rotate rapidly

TWIRLER   *n* pl. **-S** one that twirls

TWIRLY   *adj* **TWIRLIER, TWIRLIEST** curved

TWIRP   *n* pl. **-S** twerp

TWIST   *v* **-ED, -ING, -S** to combine by winding together

TWISTER   *n* pl. **-S** one that twists

TWISTING   *n* pl. **-S** a form of trickery used in selling life insurance

TWISTY   *adj* **TWISTIER, TWISTIEST** full of curves

TWIT *v* **TWITTED, TWITTING, TWITS** to ridicule

TWITCH *v* **-ED, -ING, -ES** to move or pull with a sudden motion

TWITCHER *n* pl. **-S** one that twitches

TWITCHY *adj* **TWITCHIER, TWITCHIEST** fidgety

TWITTED past tense of twit

TWITTER *v* **-ED, -ING, -S** to utter a succession of chirping sounds

TWITTERY *adj* nervously agitated

TWITTING present participle of twit

TWIXT *prep* between

TWO *n* pl. **TWOS** a number

TWOFER *n* pl. **-S** something sold at the rate of two for the price of one

TWOFOLD *n* pl. **-S** an amount twice as great as a given unit

TWOONIE *n* pl. **-S** toonie

TWOPENCE *n* pl. **-S** a British coin worth two pennies

TWOPENNY *adj* worth twopence

TWOSOME *n* pl. **-S** a group of two

TWYER *n* pl. **-S** tuyere

TYCOON *n* pl. **-S** a wealthy and powerful business person

TYE *n* pl. **-S** a chain on a ship

TYEE *n* pl. **-S** a food fish

TYER *n* pl. **-S** one that ties

TYIN *n* pl. **TYIN** a monetary unit of Kazakhstan

TYING a present participle of tie

TYIYN *n* pl. **TYIYN** a monetary unit of Kyrgyzstan

TYKE *n* pl. **-S** a small child

TYLOSIN *n* pl. **-S** an antibiotic

TYMBAL *n* pl. **-S** timbal

TYMPAN *n* pl. **-S** a drum

TYMPANA a pl. of tympanum

TYMPANAL *adj* tympanic

TYMPANIC *adj* pertaining to the tympanum

TYMPANO *n* pl. **-NI** timpano

TYMPANUM *n* pl. **-NUMS** or **-NA** the middle ear

TYMPANY *n* pl. **-NIES** a swelling of the abdomen

TYNE *v* **TYNED, TYNING, TYNES** to tine

TYPAL *adj* typical

TYPE *v* **TYPED, TYPING, TYPES** to write with a typewriter **TYPABLE, TYPEABLE** *adj*

TYPEBAR *n* pl. **-S** a part of a typewriter

TYPECASE *n* pl. **-S** a tray for holding printing type

TYPECAST *v* **-CAST, -CASTING, -CASTS** to cast in an acting role befitting one's own nature

TYPED past tense of type

TYPEFACE *n* pl. **-S** the face of printing type

TYPESET *v* **-SET, -SETTING, -SETS** to set in type

TYPEY *adj* **TYPIER, TYPIEST** typy

TYPHOID *n* pl. **-S** an infectious disease

TYPHON *n* pl. **-S** a type of signal horn

TYPHOON *n* pl. **-S** a tropical hurricane **TYPHONIC** *adj*

TYPHOSE *adj* pertaining to typhoid

TYPHUS *n* pl. **-ES** an infectious disease **TYPHOUS** *adj*

TYPIC *adj* typical

TYPICAL *adj* having the nature of a representative specimen

TYPIER comparative of typey and typy

TYPIEST superlative of typey and typy

TYPIFIER *n* pl. **-S** one that typifies

TYPIFY *v* **-FIED, -FYING, -FIES** to serve as a typical example of

TYPING present participle of type

TYPIST *n* pl. **-S** one who types

TYPO *n* pl. **-POS** a typographical error

TYPOLOGY *n* pl. **-GIES** the study of classification according to common characteristics

TYPP *n* pl. **-S** a unit of yarn size

TYPY *adj* **TYPIER, TYPIEST** characterized by strict conformance to the characteristics of a group

TYRAMINE *n* pl. **-S** a chemical compound

TYRANNIC *adj* characteristic of a tyrant

TYRANNY *n* pl. **-NIES** the rule of a tyrant

TYRANT *n* pl. **-S** an absolute ruler

TYRE *v* **TYRED, TYRING, TYRES** to furnish with a covering for a wheel

TYRO *n* pl. **-ROS** a beginner **TYRONIC** *adj*

TYROSINE *n* pl. **-S** an amino acid

TYTHE	*v* **TYTHED, TYTHING, TYTHES** to tithe	**TZARITZA**	*n* pl. **-S** czaritza
		TZETZE	*n* pl. **-S** tsetse
TZADDIK	*n* pl. **-DIKIM** zaddik	**TZIGANE**	*n* pl. **-S** a gypsy
TZAR	*n* pl. **-S** czar	**TZIMMES**	*n* pl. **TZIMMES** a vegetable stew
TZARDOM	*n* pl. **-S** czardom	**TZITZIS**	*n/pl* zizith
TZAREVNA	*n* pl. **-S** czarevna	**TZITZIT**	*n/pl* zizith
TZARINA	*n* pl. **-S** czarina	**TZITZITH**	*n/pl* zizith
TZARISM	*n* pl. **-S** czarism	**TZURIS**	*n* pl. **TZURIS** tsuris
TZARIST	*n* pl. **-S** czarist		

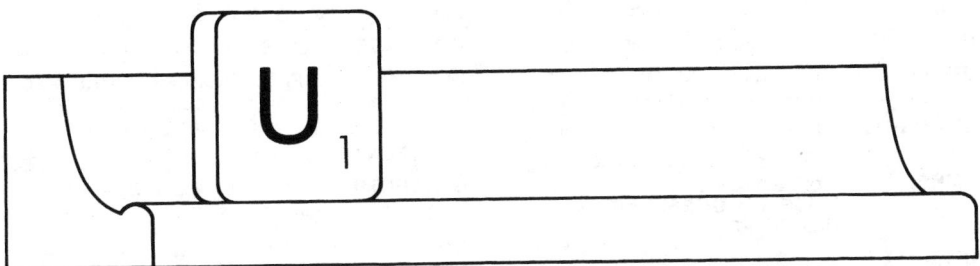

UAKARI   *n* pl. **-S** a South American monkey

UBIETY   *n* pl. **-ETIES** the state of having a definite location

UBIQUE   *adv* everywhere

UBIQUITY   *n* pl. **-TIES** the state of being everywhere at the same time

UDDER   *n* pl. **-S** a mammary gland

UDO   *n* pl. **UDOS** a Japanese herb

UDOMETER   *n* pl. **-S** a rain gauge

UDOMETRY   *n* pl. **-TRIES** the measurement of rain

UDON   *n* pl. **-S** a Japanese noodle made with wheat flour

UFOLOGY   *n* pl. **-GIES** the study of unidentified flying objects

UGH   *n* pl. **-S** the sound of a cough or grunt

UGLIER   comparative of ugly

UGLIES   pl. of ugly

UGLIEST   superlative of ugly

UGLIFIER   *n* pl. **-S** one that uglifies

UGLIFY   *v* **-FIED, -FYING, -FIES** to make ugly

UGLINESS   *n* pl. **-ES** the state of being ugly

UGLY   *adj* **-LIER, -LIEST** displeasing to the sight **UGLILY** *adv*

UGLY   *n* pl. **-LIES** one that is ugly

UGSOME   *adj* disgusting

UH   *interj* — used to express hesitation

UHLAN   *n* pl. **-S** one of a body of Prussian cavalry

UINTAITE   *n* pl. **-S** a variety of asphalt

UKASE   *n* pl. **-S** an edict

UKE   *n* pl. **-S** ukelele

UKELELE   *n* pl. **-S** ukulele

UKULELE   *n* pl. **-S** a small guitar-like instrument

ULAMA   *n* pl. **-S** ulema

ULAN   *n* pl. **-S** uhlan

ULCER   *v* **-ED, -ING, -S** to affect with an ulcer (a type of lesion)

ULCERATE   *v* **-ATED, -ATING, -ATES** to ulcer

ULCEROUS   *adj* being or affected with an ulcer

ULEMA   *n* pl. **-S** a Muslim scholar

ULEXITE   *n* pl. **-S** a mineral

ULLAGE   *n* pl. **-S** the amount that a container lacks of being full **ULLAGED** *adj*

ULNA   *n* pl. **-NAS** or **-NAE** a bone of the forearm **ULNAR** *adj*

ULNAD   *adv* toward the ulna

ULPAN   *n* pl. **-PANIM** a school in Israel for teaching Hebrew

ULSTER   *n* pl. **-S** a long, loose overcoat

ULTERIOR   *adj* more remote

ULTIMA   *n* pl. **-S** the last syllable of a word

ULTIMACY   *n* pl. **-CIES** an ultimate

ULTIMATA   *n/pl* final proposals

ULTIMATE   *v* **-MATED, -MATING, -MATES** to come to an end

ULTIMO   *adj* of or occurring in the preceding month

ULTRA   *n* pl. **-S** an ultraist

ULTRADRY   *adj* extremely dry

ULTRAHIP   *adj* extremely hip

ULTRAHOT   *adj* extremely hot

ULTRAISM   *n* pl. **-S** advocacy of extreme measures

ULTRAIST   *n* pl. **-S** an advocate of extreme measures

ULTRALOW   *adj* extremely low

ULTRARED   *n* pl. **-S** infrared

ULU   *n* pl. **-S** an Eskimo knife

ULULANT   *adj* howling

ULULATE   *v* **-LATED, -LATING, -LATES** to howl

ULVA *n pl.* **-S** an edible seaweed

UM *interj* — used to indicate hesitation

UMAMI *n pl.* **-S** a taste characteristic of monosodium glutamate

UMANGITE *n pl.* **-S** a mineral consisting of copper selenide

UMBEL *n pl.* **-S** a type of flower cluster **UMBELED, UMBELLAR, UMBELLED** *adj*

UMBELLET *n pl.* **-S** a small umbel

UMBELULE *n pl.* **-S** a secondary umbel

UMBER *v* **-ED, -ING, -S** to color with a brown pigment

UMBILICI *n/pl* navels

UMBLES *n/pl* the entrails of a deer

UMBO *n pl.* **-BOS** or **-BONES** the rounded elevation at the center of a shield **UMBONAL, UMBONATE, UMBONIC** *adj*

UMBRA *n pl.* **-BRAS** or **-BRAE** a dark area **UMBRAL** *adj*

UMBRAGE *n pl.* **-S** resentment

UMBRELLA *v* **-ED, -ING, -S** to provide with an umbrella (a portable cover for protection from rain or sun)

UMBRETTE *n pl.* **-S** a wading bird

UMIAC *n pl.* **-S** umiak

UMIACK *n pl.* **-S** umiak

UMIAK *n pl.* **-S** an open Eskimo boat

UMIAQ *n pl.* **-S** umiak

UMLAUT *v* **-ED, -ING, -S** to modify a vowel sound by partial assimilation to a succeeding sound

UMM *interj* um

UMP *v* **-ED, -ING, -S** to umpire

UMPIRAGE *n pl.* **-S** the function of an umpire

UMPIRE *v* **-PIRED, -PIRING, -PIRES** to act as umpire (a person appointed to rule on the plays in a game)

UMPTEEN *adj* indefinitely numerous

UMTEENTH *adj* being the last in an indefinitely numerous series

UN *pron pl.* **-S** one

UNAI *n pl.* **-S** unau

UNAKITE *n pl.* **-S** an igneous rock

UNANCHOR *v* **-ED, -ING, -S** to loosen from an anchor

UNARM *v* **-ED, -ING, -S** to disarm

UNARY *adj* consisting of a single element

UNAU *n pl.* **-S** a two-toed sloth

UNAWARES *adv* without warning

UNBALE *v* **-BALED, -BALING, -BALES** to loosen from a compressed bundle

UNBAN *v* **-BANNED, -BANNING, -BANS** to remove a prohibition against

UNBAR *v* **-BARRED, -BARRING, -BARS** to remove a bar from

UNBATED *adj* unabated

UNBE *v* **UNBEING** to cease to have being

UNBEAR *v* **-BEARED, -BEARING, -BEARS** to free from the pressure of a rein

UNBELIEF *n pl.* **-S** lack of belief

UNBELT *v* **-ED, -ING, -S** to remove the belt of

UNBEND *v* **-BENT** or **-BENDED, -BENDING, -BENDS** to make or allow to become straight

---

Following is a list of self-explanatory adjectives and adverbs containing the prefix UN- (not):

UNABATED	*adj*	**UNAIDED**	*adj*	**UNASKED**	*adj*
UNABLE	*adj*	**UNAIMED**	*adj*	**UNATONED**	*adj*
UNABUSED	*adj*	**UNAIRED**	*adj*	**UNAVOWED**	*adj*
UNACIDIC	*adj*	**UNAKIN**	*adj*	**UNAWAKE**	*adj*
UNACTED	*adj*	**UNALIKE**	*adj*	**UNAWAKED**	*adj*
UNADDED	*adj*	**UNALLIED**	*adj*	**UNAWARE**	*adj*
UNADEPT	*adj*	**UNAMAZED**	*adj*	**UNAWED**	*adj*
UNADULT	*adj*	**UNAMUSED**	*adj*	**UNAXED**	*adj*
UNAFRAID	*adj*	**UNANELED**	*adj*	**UNBACKED**	*adj*
UNAGED	*adj*	**UNAPT**	*adj*	**UNBAKED**	*adj*
UNAGEING	*adj*	**UNAPTLY**	*adv*	**UNBANDED**	*adj*
UNAGILE	*adj*	**UNARCHED**	*adj*	**UNBANNED**	*adj*
UNAGING	*adj*	**UNARGUED**	*adj*	**UNBARBED**	*adj*
UNAGREED	*adj*	**UNARTFUL**	*adj*	**UNBASED**	*adj*

UNBID	*adj* unbidden
UNBIDDEN	*adj* not invited
UNBIND	*v* **-BOUND, -BINDING, -BINDS** to free from bindings
UNBLOCK	*v* **-ED, -ING, -S** to free from being blocked
UNBODIED	*adj* having no body
UNBOLT	*v* **-ED, -ING, -S** to open by withdrawing a bolt (a metal bar)
UNBONNET	*v* **-ED, -ING, -S** to uncover the head
UNBOSOM	*v* **-ED, -ING, -S** to reveal
UNBOTTLE	*v* **-TLED, -TLING, -TLES** to release from or as if from a bottle
UNBOUND	past tense of unbind
UNBOX	*v* **-ED, -ING, -ES** to remove from a box
UNBRACE	*v* **-BRACED, -BRACING, -BRACES** to free from braces
UNBRAID	*v* **-ED, -ING, -S** to separate the strands of
UNBRAKE	*v* **-BRAKED, -BRAKING, -BRAKES** to release a brake
UNBREECH	*v* **-ED, -ING, -ES** to remove the breeches of
UNBRIDLE	*v* **-DLED, -DLING, -DLES** to set loose
UNBUCKLE	*v* **-LED, -LING, -LES** to loosen a buckle
UNBUILD	*v* **-BUILT, -BUILDING, -BUILDS** to demolish
UNBUNDLE	*v* **-DLED, -DLING, -DLES** to price separately
UNBURDEN	*v* **-ED, -ING, -S** to free from a burden

UNBUTTON	*v* **-ED, -ING, -S** to unfasten the buttons of
UNCAGE	*v* **-CAGED, -CAGING, -CAGES** to release from a cage
UNCAKE	*v* **-CAKED, -CAKING, -CAKES** to break up a cake (a block of compacted matter)
UNCANNY	*adj* **-NIER, -NIEST** strange and inexplicable
UNCAP	*v* **-CAPPED, -CAPPING, -CAPS** to remove the cap from
UNCASE	*v* **-CASED, -CASING, -CASES** to remove from a case
UNCHAIN	*v* **-ED, -ING, -S** to free by removing a chain
UNCHAIR	*v* **-ED, -ING, -S** to remove from a chairmanship
UNCHANCY	*adj* unlucky
UNCHARGE	*v* **-CHARGED, -CHARGING, -CHARGES** to acquit
UNCHOKE	*v* **-CHOKED, -CHOKING, -CHOKES** to free from obstruction
UNCHURCH	*v* **-ED, -ING, -ES** to expel from a church
UNCI	pl. of uncus
UNCIA	*n* pl. **-CIAE** a coin of ancient Rome
UNCIAL	*n* pl. **-S** a style of writing
UNCIALLY	*adv* in the uncial style
UNCIFORM	*n* pl. **-S** a bone of the wrist
UNCINAL	*adj* uncinate
UNCINATE	*adj* bent at the end like a hook
UNCINUS	*n* pl. **-NI** an uncinate structure
UNCLAD	a past tense of unclothe

List of self-explanatory adjectives and adverbs containing the prefix UN- (continued):

UNBASTED	*adj*	**UNBORN**	*adj*	**UNCANNED**	*adj*
UNBATHED	*adj*	**UNBOUGHT**	*adj*	**UNCARDED**	*adj*
UNBEATEN	*adj*	**UNBOUNCY**	*adj*	**UNCARING**	*adj*
UNBENIGN	*adj*	**UNBOWED**	*adj*	**UNCARTED**	*adj*
UNBIASED	*adj*	**UNBOWING**	*adj*	**UNCARVED**	*adj*
UNBILLED	*adj*	**UNBRED**	*adj*	**UNCASHED**	*adj*
UNBITTED	*adj*	**UNBRIGHT**	*adj*	**UNCASKED**	*adj*
UNBITTEN	*adj*	**UNBROKE**	*adj*	**UNCAST**	*adj*
UNBITTER	*adj*	**UNBROKEN**	*adj*	**UNCATCHY**	*adj*
UNBLAMED	*adj*	**UNBULKY**	*adj*	**UNCAUGHT**	*adj*
UNBLEST	*adj*	**UNBURIED**	*adj*	**UNCAUSED**	*adj*
UNBLOODY	*adj*	**UNBURNED**	*adj*	**UNCEDED**	*adj*
UNBOBBED	*adj*	**UNBURNT**	*adj*	**UNCHARY**	*adj*
UNBOILED	*adj*	**UNBUSTED**	*adj*	**UNCHASTE**	*adj* **-CHASTER, -CHASTEST**
UNBONDED	*adj*	**UNBUSY**	*adj*		
UNBONED	*adj*	**UNCALLED**	*adj*	**UNCHEWED**	*adj*
UNBOOTED	*adj*	**UNCANDID**	*adj*	**UNCHIC**	*adj*

UNCLAMP	*v* **-ED, -ING, -S** to free from a clamp	**UNCREATE**	*v* **-ATED, -ATING, -ATES** to deprive of existence
UNCLASP	*v* **-ED, -ING, -S** to free from a clasp	**UNCROSS**	*v* **-ED, -ING, -ES** to change from a crossed position
UNCLE	*n* pl. **-S** the brother of one's father or mother	**UNCROWN**	*v* **-ED, -ING, -S** to deprive of a crown
UNCLENCH	*v* **-ED, -ING, -ES** to open from a clenched position	**UNCTION**	*n* pl. **-S** the act of anointing
UNCLINCH	*v* **-ED, -ING, -ES** to unclench	**UNCTUOUS**	*adj* greasy
UNCLIP	*v* **-CLIPPED, -CLIPPING, -CLIPS** to remove a clip (a fastening device) from	**UNCUFF**	*v* **-ED, -ING, -S** to remove handcuffs from
UNCLOAK	*v* **-ED, -ING, -S** to remove a cloak from	**UNCURB**	*v* **-ED, -ING, -S** to remove restraints from
UNCLOG	*v* **-CLOGGED, -CLOGGING, -CLOGS** to free from a difficulty or obstruction	**UNCURL**	*v* **-ED, -ING, -S** to straighten the curls of
UNCLOSE	*v* **-CLOSED, -CLOSING, -CLOSES** to open	**UNCUS**	*n* pl. **-CI** a hook-shaped anatomical part
UNCLOTHE	*v* **-CLOTHED** or **-CLAD, -CLOTHING, -CLOTHES** to divest of clothing	**UNDE**	*adj* wavy
		UNDEAD	*n* pl. **UNDEAD** a vampire
UNCLOUD	*v* **-ED, -ING, -S** to free from clouds	**UNDEE**	*adj* unde
UNCO	*n* pl. **-COS** a stranger	**UNDER**	*prep* in a lower position than
UNCOCK	*v* **-ED, -ING, -S** to remove from a cocked position	**UNDERACT**	*v* **-ED, -ING, -S** to act subtly and with restraint
UNCOFFIN	*v* **-ED, -ING, -S** to remove from a coffin	**UNDERAGE**	*n* pl. **-S** a shortage
		UNDERARM	*n* pl. **-S** the armpit
UNCOIL	*v* **-ED, -ING, -S** to release from a coiled position	**UNDERATE**	past tense of undereat
UNCORK	*v* **-ED, -ING, -S** to draw the cork	**UNDERBID**	*v* **-BID, -BIDDING, -BIDS** to bid lower than
UNCOUPLE	*v* **-PLED, -PLING, -PLES** to disconnect	**UNDERBUD**	*v* **-BUDDED, -BUDDING, -BUDS** to bud from beneath
UNCOVER	*v* **-ED, -ING, -S** to remove the covering from	**UNDERBUY**	*v* **-BOUGHT, -BUYING, -BUYS** to buy at a lower price than
UNCRATE	*v* **-CRATED, -CRATING, -CRATES** to remove from a crate	**UNDERCUT**	*v* **-CUT, -CUTTING, -CUTS** to cut under

---

List of self-explanatory adjectives and adverbs containing the prefix UN- (continued):

UNCHICLY	*adv*	**UNCOMIC**	*adj*	**UNDATED**	*adj*
UNCHOSEN	*adj*	**UNCOMMON**	*adj* **-MONER,**	**UNDECKED**	*adj*
UNCIVIL	*adj*		**-MONEST**	**UNDENIED**	*adj*
UNCLASSY	*adj*	**UNCOOKED**	*adj*	**UNDENTED**	*adj*
UNCLAWED	*adj*	**UNCOOL**	*adj*	**UNDEVOUT**	*adj*
UNCLEAN	*adj* **-CLEANER,**	**UNCOOLED**	*adj*	**UNDIMMED**	*adj*
	-CLEANEST	**UNCOUTH**	*adj*	**UNDOABLE**	*adj*
UNCLEAR	*adj* **-CLEARER,**	**UNCOY**	*adj*	**UNDOCILE**	*adj*
	-CLEAREST	**UNCRAZY**	*adj*	**UNDOTTED**	*adj*
UNCLEFT	*adj*	**UNCREWED**	*adj*	**UNDREAMT**	*adj*
UNCLOUDY	*adj*	**UNCUFFED**	*adj*	**UNDRIED**	*adj*
UNCLOYED	*adj*	**UNCURED**	*adj*	**UNDUBBED**	*adj*
UNCOATED	*adj*	**UNCURSED**	*adj*	**UNDULLED**	*adj*
UNCODED	*adj*	**UNCUT**	*adj*	**UNDYED**	*adj*
UNCOINED	*adj*	**UNCUTE**	*adj*	**UNEAGER**	*adj*
UNCOMBED	*adj*	**UNDAMPED**	*adj*	**UNEARNED**	*adj*
UNCOMELY	*adj*	**UNDARING**	*adj*	**UNEATEN**	*adj*

UNDERDO	*v* **-DID, -DONE, -DOING, -DOES** to do insufficiently		**UNDERTOW**	*n* pl. **-S** the seaward pull of receding waves breaking on a shore
UNDERDOG	*n* pl. **-S** one who is expected to lose		**UNDERUSE**	*v* **-USED, -USING, -USES** to use less than fully
UNDEREAT	*v* **-ATE, -EATEN, -EATING, -EATS** to eat an insufficient amount		**UNDERWAY**	*adv* in progress
UNDERFED	*adj* fed an insufficient amount		**UNDERWENT**	past tense of undergo
UNDERFUR	*n* pl. **-S** the thick, soft fur beneath the outer coat of certain mammals		**UNDID**	past tense of undo
			UNDIES	*n/pl* underwear
UNDERGO	*v* **-WENT, -GONE, -GOING, -GOES** to be subjected to		**UNDINE**	*n* pl. **-S** a female water spirit
UNDERGOD	*n* pl. **-S** a lesser god		**UNDO**	*v* **-DID, -DONE, -DOING, -DOES** to bring to ruin
UNDERJAW	*n* pl. **-S** the lower jaw		**UNDOCK**	*v* **-ED, -ING, -S** to move away from a dock
UNDERLAIN	past participle of underlie			
UNDERLAP	*v* **-LAPPED, -LAPPING, -LAPS** to extend partly under		**UNDOER**	*n* pl. **-S** one that undoes
			UNDOING	*n* pl. **-S** a cause of ruin
UNDERLAY	*v* **-LAID, -LAYING, -LAYS** to place under		**UNDONE**	past participle of undo
UNDERLET	*v* **-LET, -LETTING, -LETS** to lease at less than the usual value		**UNDOUBLE**	*v* **-BLED, -BLING, -BLES** to unfold
			UNDRAPE	*v* **-DRAPED, -DRAPING, -DRAPES** to strip of drapery
UNDERLIE	*v* **-LAY, -LAIN, -LYING, -LIES** to lie under		**UNDRAW**	*v* **-DREW, -DRAWN, -DRAWING, -DRAWS** to draw open
UNDERLIP	*n* pl. **-S** the lower lip			
UNDERLIT	*adj* lacking adequate light		**UNDRESS**	*v* **-DRESSED** or **-DREST, -DRESSING, -DRESSES** to remove one's clothing
UNDERPAY	*v* **-PAID, -PAYING, -PAYS** to pay less than is deserved			
			UNDRUNK	*adj* not swallowed
UNDERPIN	*v* **-PINNED, -PINNING, -PINS** to support from below		**UNDUE**	*adj* exceeding what is appropriate or normal
UNDERRUN	*v* **-RAN, -RUNNING, -RUNS** to pass or extend under		**UNDULANT**	*adj* undulating
			UNDULAR	*adj* undulating
UNDERSEA	*adv* beneath the surface of the sea		**UNDULATE**	*v* **-LATED, -LATING, -LATES** to move with a wavelike motion
UNDERSET	*n* pl. **-S** a current below the surface of the ocean			
			UNDULY	*adv* in an undue manner
UNDERTAX	*v* **-ED, -ING, -ES** to tax less than the usual amount		**UNDY**	*adj* unde

---

List of self-explanatory adjectives and adverbs containing the prefix UN- (continued):

UNEDIBLE	*adj*	**UNFAIR**	*adj* **-FAIRER, -FAIREST**	**UNFLASHY**	*adj*	
UNEDITED	*adj*			**UNFLAWED**	*adj*	
UNENDED	*adj*	**UNFAIRLY**	*adv*	**UNFLEXED**	*adj*	
UNENDING	*adj*	**UNFAKED**	*adj*	**UNFLUTED**	*adj*	
UNENVIED	*adj*	**UNFALLEN**	*adj*	**UNFOILED**	*adj*	
UNERASED	*adj*	**UNFAMOUS**	*adj*	**UNFOND**	*adj*	
UNEROTIC	*adj*	**UNFANCY**	*adj*	**UNFORCED**	*adj*	
UNERRING	*adj*	**UNFAZED**	*adj*	**UNFORGED**	*adj*	
UNEVADED	*adj*	**UNFEARED**	*adj*	**UNFORKED**	*adj*	
UNEVEN	*adj* **-EVENER, -EVENEST**	**UNFED**	*adj*	**UNFORMED**	*adj*	
		UNFELT	*adj*	**UNFOUGHT**	*adj*	
UNEVENLY	*adv*	**UNFELTED**	*adj*	**UNFOUND**	*adj*	
UNEXOTIC	*adj*	**UNFILIAL**	*adj*	**UNFRAMED**	*adj*	
UNEXPERT	*adj*	**UNFILLED**	*adj*	**UNFUNDED**	*adj*	
UNFADED	*adj*	**UNFILMED**	*adj*	**UNFUNNY**	*adj*	
UNFADING	*adj*	**UNFIRED**	*adj*	**UNFUSED**	*adj*	
		UNFISHED	*adj*	**UNFUSSY**	*adj*	

UNDYING	*adj* not subject to death
UNEARTH	*v* **-ED, -ING, -S** to dig up
UNEASE	*n* pl. **-S** mental or physical discomfort
UNEASY	*adj* **-EASIER, -EASIEST** marked by mental or physical discomfort **UNEASILY** *adv*
UNEQUAL	*n* pl. **-S** one that is not equal to another
UNFAITH	*n* pl. **-S** lack of faith
UNFASTEN	*v* **-ED, -ING, -S** to release from fastenings
UNFENCE	*v* **-FENCED, -FENCING, -FENCES** to remove a fence from
UNFETTER	*v* **-ED, -ING, -S** to free from fetters
UNFIT	*v* **-FITTED, -FITTING, -FITS** to make unsuitable
UNFITLY	*adv* in an unsuitable manner
UNFIX	*v* **-FIXED** or **-FIXT, -FIXING, -FIXES** to unfasten
UNFOLD	*v* **-ED, -ING, -S** to open something that is folded
UNFOLDER	*n* pl. **-S** one that unfolds
UNFORGOT	*adj* not forgotten
UNFREE	*v* **-FREED, -FREEING, -FREES** to deprive of freedom
UNFREEZE	*v* **-FROZE, -FROZEN, -FREEZING, -FREEZES** to cause to thaw
UNFROCK	*v* **-ED, -ING, -S** to divest of ecclesiastical authority
UNFURL	*v* **-ED, -ING, -S** to unroll
UNGAINLY	*adj* **-LIER, -LIEST** awkward
UNGIRD	*v* **-GIRDED** or **-GIRT, -GIRDING, -GIRDS** to remove a belt from
UNGLOVE	*v* **-GLOVED, -GLOVING, -GLOVES** to uncover by removing a glove
UNGLUE	*v* **-GLUED, -GLUING, -GLUES** to disjoin
UNGODLY	*adj* **-LIER, -LIEST** impious
UNGOT	*adj* ungotten
UNGOTTEN	*adj* not obtained
UNGUAL	*adj* pertaining to an unguis
UNGUARD	*v* **-ED, -ING, -S** to leave unprotected
UNGUENT	*n* pl. **-S** an ointment
UNGUENTA	*n/pl* ointments
UNGUIS	*n* pl. **-GUES** a nail, claw, or hoof
UNGULA	*n* pl. **-LAE** an unguis **UNGULAR** *adj*
UNGULATE	*n* pl. **-S** a hoofed mammal
UNHAIR	*v* **-ED, -ING, -S** to remove the hair from
UNHAIRER	*n* pl. **-S** one that unhairs
UNHALLOW	*v* **-ED, -ING, -S** to profane
UNHAND	*v* **-ED, -ING, -S** to remove the hand from
UNHANDY	*adj* **-HANDIER, -HANDIEST** difficult to handle
UNHANG	*v* **-HUNG** or **-HANGED, -HANGING, -HANGS** to detach from a hanging support
UNHAT	*v* **-HATTED, -HATTING, -HATS** to remove one's hat
UNHELM	*v* **-ED, -ING, -S** to remove the helmet of
UNHINGE	*v* **-HINGED, -HINGING, -HINGES** to remove from hinges

---

List of self-explanatory adjectives and adverbs containing the prefix UN- (continued):

UNGALLED	*adj*	**UNHAILED**	*adj*	**UNHOLY**	*adj* **-LIER, -LIEST**
UNGARBED	*adj*	**UNHALVED**	*adj*	**UNHUMAN**	*adj*
UNGATED	*adj*	**UNHAPPY**	*adj* **-PIER, -PIEST**	**UNHUNG**	*adj*
UNGAZING	*adj*			**UNHURT**	*adj*
UNGELDED	*adj*	**UNHARMED**	*adj*	**UNIDEAL**	*adj*
UNGENIAL	*adj*	**UNHASTY**	*adj*	**UNIMBUED**	*adj*
UNGENTLE	*adj*	**UNHEALED**	*adj*	**UNIRONED**	*adj*
UNGENTLY	*adv*	**UNHEARD**	*adj*	**UNIRONIC**	*adj*
UNGIFTED	*adj*	**UNHEATED**	*adj*	**UNISSUED**	*adj*
UNGIVING	*adj*	**UNHEDGED**	*adj*	**UNJADED**	*adj*
UNGLAZED	*adj*	**UNHEEDED**	*adj*	**UNJOINED**	*adj*
UNGOWNED	*adj*	**UNHELPED**	*adj*	**UNJOYFUL**	*adj*
UNGRACED	*adj*	**UNHEROIC**	*adj*	**UNJUDGED**	*adj*
UNGRADED	*adj*	**UNHEWN**	*adj*	**UNJUST**	*adj*
UNGREEDY	*adj*	**UNHIP**	*adj*	**UNJUSTLY**	*adv*
UNGROUND	*adj*	**UNHIRED**	*adj*	**UNKEELED**	*adj*
UNGUIDED	*adj*	**UNHOLILY**	*adv*	**UNKEPT**	*adj*

UNHITCH	*v* **-ED, -ING, -ES** to free from being hitched	**UNIFORM**	*adj* **-FORMER, -FORMEST** unchanging
UNHOOD	*v* **-ED, -ING, -S** to remove a hood from	**UNIFORM**	*v* **-ED, -ING, -S** to make uniform
UNHOOK	*v* **-ED, -ING, -S** to remove from a hook	**UNIFY**	*v* **-FIED, -FYING, -FIES** to make into a coherent whole
UNHOPED	*adj* not hoped for or expected	**UNILOBED**	*adj* having one lobe
UNHORSE	*v* **-HORSED, -HORSING, -HORSES** to cause to fall from a horse	**UNION**	*n* pl. **-S** a number of persons, parties, or political entities united for a common purpose
UNHOUSE	*v* **-HOUSED, -HOUSING, -HOUSES** to deprive of a protective shelter	**UNIONISE**	*v* **-ISED, -ISING, -ISES** to unionize
UNHUSK	*v* **-ED, -ING, -S** to remove the husk from	**UNIONISM**	*n* pl. **-S** the principle of forming a union
UNIALGAL	*adj* pertaining to a single algal cell	**UNIONIST**	*n* pl. **-S** an advocate of unionism
UNIAXIAL	*adj* having one axis	**UNIONIZE**	*v* **-IZED, -IZING, -IZES** to form into a union
UNIBODY	*adj* being a type of construction in which parts are welded together to form one unit	**UNIPOD**	*n* pl. **-S** a one-legged support
		UNIPOLAR	*adj* showing only one kind of polarity
UNICOLOR	*adj* of one color	**UNIQUE**	*adj* **UNIQUER, UNIQUEST** existing as the only one of its kind; very unusual **UNIQUELY** *adv*
UNICORN	*n* pl. **-S** a mythical horselike creature		
UNICYCLE	*v* **-CLED, -CLING, -CLES** to ride a one-wheeled vehicle	**UNIQUE**	*n* pl. **-S** something that is unique
		UNISEX	*n* pl. **-ES** the condition of not being distinguishable as to sex
UNIDEAED	*adj* lacking ideas		
UNIFACE	*n* pl. **-S** a coin having a design on only one side	**UNISIZE**	*adj* made to fit all sizes
		UNISON	*n* pl. **-S** complete agreement **UNISONAL** *adj*
UNIFIC	*adj* unifying		
UNIFIED	past tense of unify	**UNIT**	*n* pl. **-S** a specific quantity used as a standard of measurement
UNIFIER	*n* pl. **-S** one that unifies		
UNIFIES	present 3d person sing. of unify	**UNITAGE**	*n* pl. **-S** amount in units
UNIFILAR	*adj* having only one thread, wire, or fiber	**UNITARD**	*n* pl. **-S** a leotard that also covers the legs
		UNITARY	*adj* pertaining to a unit

List of self-explanatory adjectives and adverbs containing the prefix UN- (continued):

UNKIND	*adj* **-KINDER, -KINDEST**	**UNLISTED**	*adj*	**UNMATTED**	*adj*
		UNLIT	*adj*	**UNMEANT**	*adj*
UNKINDLY	*adv* **-LIER, -LIEST**	**UNLIVELY**	*adj*	**UNMELLOW**	*adj*
UNKINGLY	*adj*	**UNLOBED**	*adj*	**UNMELTED**	*adj*
UNKISSED	*adj*	**UNLOVED**	*adj*	**UNMENDED**	*adj*
UNKOSHER	*adj*	**UNLOVELY**	*adj* **-LIER, -LIEST**	**UNMERRY**	*adj*
UNLAWFUL	*adj*	**UNLOVING**	*adj*	**UNMET**	*adj*
UNLEASED	*adj*	**UNLUCKY**	*adj* **-LUCKIER, -LUCKIEST**	**UNMILLED**	*adj*
UNLED	*adj*			**UNMINED**	*adj*
UNLETHAL	*adj*	**UNMACHO**	*adj*	**UNMIXED**	*adj*
UNLETTED	*adj*	**UNMAILED**	*adj*	**UNMIXT**	*adj*
UNLEVIED	*adj*	**UNMANFUL**	*adj*	**UNMODISH**	*adj*
UNLICKED	*adj*	**UNMANLY**	*adj* **-LIER, -LIEST**	**UNMOLTEN**	*adj*
UNLIKE	*adj*	**UNMAPPED**	*adj*	**UNMOVED**	*adj*
UNLIKED	*adj*	**UNMARKED**	*adj*	**UNMOVING**	*adj*
UNLIKELY	*adj* **-LIER, -LIEST**	**UNMARRED**	*adj*	**UNMOWN**	*adj*
UNLINED	*adj*	**UNMATED**	*adj*	**UNNAMED**	*adj*

UNITE	*v* **UNITED, UNITING, UNITES** to bring together so as to form a whole **UNITEDLY** *adv*	**UNKNOT**	*v* **-KNOTTED, -KNOTTING, -KNOTS** to undo a knot in
UNITER	*n* pl. **-S** one that unites	**UNKNOWN**	*n* pl. **-S** one that is not known
UNITIES	pl. of unity	**UNLACE**	*v* **-LACED, -LACING, -LACES** to unfasten the laces of
UNITIVE	*adj* serving to unite	**UNLADE**	*v* **-LADED, -LADEN, -LADING, -LADES** to unload
UNITIZE	*v* **-IZED, -IZING, -IZES** to divide into units	**UNLASH**	*v* **-ED, -ING, -ES** to untie the lashing (a type of binding) of
UNITIZER	*n* pl. **-S** one that unitizes		
UNITRUST	*n* pl. **-S** a type of annuity trust	**UNLATCH**	*v* **-ED, -ING, -ES** to open by lifting the latch (a fastening device)
UNITY	*n* pl. **-TIES** the state of being one single entity	**UNLAY**	*v* **-LAID, -LAYING, -LAYS** to untwist
UNIVALVE	*n* pl. **-S** a mollusk having a single shell	**UNLEAD**	*v* **-ED, -ING, -S** to remove the lead from
UNIVERSE	*n* pl. **-S** the totality of all existing things	**UNLEADED**	*n* pl. **-S** a product containing no lead
UNIVOCAL	*n* pl. **-S** a word having only one meaning	**UNLEARN**	*v* **-LEARNED** or **-LEARNT, -LEARNING, -LEARNS** to put out of one's knowledge or memory
UNJAM	*v* **-JAMMED, -JAMMING, -JAMS** to undo things tightly crammed together	**UNLEASH**	*v* **-ED, -ING, -ES** to free from a leash
UNJOINT	*v* **-ED, -ING, -S** to separate at a juncture	**UNLESS**	*conj* except on the condition that
UNKEMPT	*adj* untidy	**UNLET**	*adj* not rented
UNKEND	*adj* unkenned	**UNLEVEL**	*v* **-ELED, -ELING, -ELS** or **-ELLED, -ELLING, -ELS** to make uneven
UNKENNED	*adj* not known or recognized	**UNLIMBER**	*v* **-ED, -ING, -S** to prepare for action
UNKENNEL	*v* **-NELED, -NELING, -NELS** or **-NELLED, -NELLING, -NELS** to release from a kennel	**UNLINK**	*v* **-ED, -ING, -S** to unfasten the links (connecting devices) of
UNKENT	*adj* unkenned	**UNLIVE**	*v* **-LIVED, -LIVING, -LIVES** to live so as to make amends for
UNKINK	*v* **-ED, -ING, -S** to remove curls from	**UNLOAD**	*v* **-ED, -ING, -S** to remove the load or cargo from
UNKNIT	*v* **-KNITTED, -KNITTING, -KNITS** to unravel	**UNLOADER**	*n* pl. **-S** one that unloads

---

List of self-explanatory adjectives and adverbs containing the prefix UN- (continued):

UNNEEDED	*adj*	**UNPLACED**	*adj*	**UNPROVEN**	*adj*
UNNOISY	*adj*	**UNPLAYED**	*adj*	**UNPRUNED**	*adj*
UNNOTED	*adj*	**UNPLIANT**	*adj*	**UNPURE**	*adj*
UNOILED	*adj*	**UNPLOWED**	*adj*	**UNPURELY**	*adv*
UNOPEN	*adj*	**UNPOETIC**	*adj*	**UNPURGED**	*adj*
UNOPENED	*adj*	**UNPOISED**	*adj*	**UNQUIET**	*adj* **-ETER, -ETEST**
UNORNATE	*adj*	**UNPOLITE**	*adj*		
UNOWNED	*adj*	**UNPOLLED**	*adj*	**UNRAISED**	*adj*
UNPADDED	*adj*	**UNPOSED**	*adj*	**UNRAKED**	*adj*
UNPAID	*adj*	**UNPOSTED**	*adj*	**UNRANKED**	*adj*
UNPAIRED	*adj*	**UNPOTTED**	*adj*	**UNRATED**	*adj*
UNPARTED	*adj*	**UNPRETTY**	*adj*	**UNRAZED**	*adj*
UNPAVED	*adj*	**UNPRICED**	*adj*	**UNREAD**	*adj*
UNPAYING	*adj*	**UNPRIMED**	*adj*	**UNREADY**	*adj* **-READIER, -READIEST**
UNPEELED	*adj*	**UNPRIZED**	*adj*		
UNPITIED	*adj*	**UNPROBED**	*adj*	**UNREAL**	*adj*
UNPITTED	*adj*	**UNPROVED**	*adj*	**UNREALLY**	*adv*

UNLOCK	*v* **-ED, -ING, -S** to unfasten the lock of	**UNNERVE**	*v* **-NERVED, -NERVING, -NERVES** to deprive of courage
UNLOOSE	*v* **-LOOSED, -LOOSING, -LOOSES** to set free	**UNPACK**	*v* **-ED, -ING, -S** to remove the contents of
UNLOOSEN	*v* **-ED, -ING, -S** to unloose	**UNPACKER**	*n* pl. **-S** one that unpacks
UNMAKE	*v* **-MADE, -MAKING, -MAKES** to destroy	**UNPAGED**	*adj* having no page numbers
UNMAKER	*n* pl. **-S** one that unmakes	**UNPEG**	*v* **-PEGGED, -PEGGING, -PEGS** to remove the pegs from
UNMAN	*v* **-MANNED, -MANNING, -MANS** to deprive of courage	**UNPEN**	*v* **-PENNED** or **-PENT, -PENNING, -PENS** to release from confinement
UNMASK	*v* **-ED, -ING, -S** to remove a mask from	**UNPEOPLE**	*v* **-PLED, -PLING, -PLES** to remove people from
UNMASKER	*n* pl. **-S** one that unmasks	**UNPERSON**	*n* pl. **-S** one who is removed completely from recognition
UNMEET	*adj* improper **UNMEETLY** *adv*		
UNMESH	*v* **-ED, -ING, -ES** to disentangle	**UNPICK**	*v* **-ED, -ING, -S** to remove the stitches from
UNMEW	*v* **-ED, -ING, -S** to set free	**UNPILE**	*v* **-PILED, -PILING, -PILES** to take or disentangle from a pile
UNMINGLE	*v* **-GLED, -GLING, -GLES** to separate things that are mixed		
UNMITER	*v* **-ED, -ING, -S** to depose from the rank of bishop	**UNPIN**	*v* **-PINNED, -PINNING, -PINS** to remove the pins from
UNMITRE	*v* **-TRED, -TRING, -TRES** to unmiter	**UNPLAIT**	*v* **-ED, -ING, -S** to undo the plaits of
		UNPLUG	*v* **-PLUGGED, -PLUGGING, -PLUGS** to take a plug out of
UNMIX	*v* **-MIXED** or **-MIXT, -MIXING, -MIXES** to separate from a mixture	**UNPUCKER**	*v* **-ED, -ING, -S** to remove the wrinkles from
UNMOLD	*v* **-ED, -ING, -S** to remove from a mold	**UNPUZZLE**	*v* **-ZLED, -ZLING, -ZLES** to work out the obscured meaning of
UNMOOR	*v* **-ED, -ING, -S** to release from moorings	**UNQUIET**	*n* pl. **-S** a state of unrest
UNMORAL	*adj* amoral	**UNQUOTE**	*v* **-QUOTED, -QUOTING, -QUOTES** to close a quotation
UNMUFFLE	*v* **-FLED, -FLING, -FLES** to free from something that muffles	**UNRAVEL**	*v* **-ELED, -ELING, -ELS** or **-ELLED, -ELLING, -ELS** to separate the threads of
UNMUZZLE	*v* **-ZLED, -ZLING, -ZLES** to remove a muzzle from		
UNNAIL	*v* **-ED, -ING, -S** to remove the nails from	**UNREASON**	*v* **-ED, -ING, -S** to disrupt the sanity of

---

List of self-explanatory adjectives and adverbs containing the prefix UN- (continued):

UNRENTED	*adj*	**UNSATED**	*adj*	**UNSHADED**	*adj*
UNREPAID	*adj*	**UNSAVED**	*adj*	**UNSHAKEN**	*adj*
UNRESTED	*adj*	**UNSAVORY**	*adj*	**UNSHAMED**	*adj*
UNRHYMED	*adj*	**UNSAWED**	*adj*	**UNSHAPED**	*adj*
UNRIBBED	*adj*	**UNSAWN**	*adj*	**UNSHAPEN**	*adj*
UNRIFLED	*adj*	**UNSCALED**	*adj*	**UNSHARED**	*adj*
UNRIMED	*adj*	**UNSEARED**	*adj*	**UNSHARP**	*adj*
UNRINSED	*adj*	**UNSEEDED**	*adj*	**UNSHAVED**	*adj*
UNRISEN	*adj*	**UNSEEING**	*adj*	**UNSHAVEN**	*adj*
UNROPED	*adj*	**UNSEEMLY**	*adj* **-LIER,**	**UNSHED**	*adj*
UNROUGH	*adj*		**-LIEST**	**UNSHOD**	*adj*
UNRULED	*adj*	**UNSEEN**	*adj*	**UNSHORN**	*adj*
UNRUSHED	*adj*	**UNSEIZED**	*adj*	**UNSHOWY**	*adj*
UNRUSTED	*adj*	**UNSENT**	*adj*	**UNSHRUNK**	*adj*
UNSAFE	*adj*	**UNSERVED**	*adj*	**UNSHUT**	*adj*
UNSAFELY	*adv*	**UNSEXUAL**	*adj*	**UNSIFTED**	*adj*
UNSALTED	*adj*	**UNSEXY**	*adj*	**UNSIGNED**	*adj*

UNREEL *v* **-ED, -ING, -S** to unwind from a reel

UNREELER *n* pl. **-S** one that unreels

UNREEVE *v* **-REEVED** or **-ROVE, -ROVEN, -REEVING, -REEVES** to withdraw a rope from an opening

UNRENT *adj* not torn

UNREPAIR *n* pl. **-S** lack of repair

UNREST *n* pl. **-S** a disturbed or uneasy state

UNRETIRE *v* **-TIRED, -TIRING, -TIRES** to return to work after having taken retirement

UNRIDDLE *v* **-DLED, -DLING, -DLES** to solve

UNRIG *v* **-RIGGED, -RIGGING, -RIGS** to divest of rigging

UNRIP *v* **-RIPPED, -RIPPING, -RIPS** to rip open

UNRIPE *adj* **-RIPER, -RIPEST** not ripe **UNRIPELY** *adv*

UNROBE *v* **-ROBED, -ROBING, -ROBES** to undress

UNROLL *v* **-ED, -ING, -S** to open something that is rolled up

UNROOF *v* **-ED, -ING, -S** to strip off the roof of

UNROOT *v* **-ED, -ING, -S** to uproot

UNROUND *v* **-ED, -ING, -S** to articulate without rounding the lips

UNROVE a past tense of unreeve

UNROVEN a past participle of unreeve

UNRULY *adj* **-LIER, -LIEST** difficult to control

UNSADDLE *v* **-DLED, -DLING, -DLES** to remove the saddle from

UNSAFETY *n* pl. **-TIES** lack of safety

UNSAY *v* **-SAID, -SAYING, -SAYS** to retract something said

UNSCREW *v* **-ED, -ING, -S** to remove the screws from

UNSEAL *v* **-ED, -ING, -S** to remove the seal of

UNSEAM *v* **-ED, -ING, -S** to open the seams of

UNSEAT *v* **-ED, -ING, -S** to remove from a seat

UNSELL *v* **-SOLD, -SELLING, -SELLS** to persuade to change an opinion or belief

UNSET *v* **-SET, -SETTING, -SETS** to unsettle

UNSETTLE *v* **-TLED, -TLING, -TLES** to make unstable

UNSEW *v* **-SEWED, -SEWN, -SEWING, -SEWS** to undo the sewing of

UNSEX *v* **-ED, -ING, -ES** to deprive of sexual power

UNSHELL *v* **-ED, -ING, -S** to remove the shell from

UNSHIFT *v* **-ED, -ING, -S** to release the shift key on a typewriter

UNSHIP *v* **-SHIPPED, -SHIPPING, -SHIPS** to unload from a ship

UNSICKER *adj* unreliable

UNSIGHT *v* **-ED, -ING, -S** to prevent from seeing

UNSLING *v* **-SLUNG, -SLINGING, -SLINGS** to remove from a slung position

UNSNAG *v* **-SNAGGED, -SNAGGING, -SNAGS** to free of snags

UNSNAP *v* **-SNAPPED, -SNAPPING, -SNAPS** to undo the snaps of

---

List of self-explanatory adjectives and adverbs containing the prefix UN- (continued):

UNSILENT	*adj*	UNSOUND	*adj* **-SOUNDER, -SOUNDEST**	UNSTUFFY	*adj*
UNSINFUL	*adj*			UNSTUNG	*adj*
UNSIZED	*adj*	UNSOURED	*adj*	UNSUBTLE	*adj*
UNSLAKED	*adj*	UNSOWED	*adj*	UNSUBTLY	*adv*
UNSLICED	*adj*	UNSOWN	*adj*	UNSUITED	*adj*
UNSLICK	*adj*	UNSPENT	*adj*	UNSUNG	*adj*
UNSMART	*adj*	UNSPILT	*adj*	UNSUNK	*adj*
UNSMOKED	*adj*	UNSPLIT	*adj*	UNSURE	*adj*
UNSOAKED	*adj*	UNSPOILT	*adj*	UNSURELY	*adv*
UNSOBER	*adj*	UNSPRUNG	*adj*	UNSWAYED	*adj*
UNSOCIAL	*adj*	UNSPUN	*adj*	UNSWEPT	*adj*
UNSOILED	*adj*	UNSTABLE	*adj* **-BLER, -BLEST**	UNTAGGED	*adj*
UNSOLD	*adj*			UNTAKEN	*adj*
UNSOLID	*adj*	UNSTABLY	*adv*	UNTAME	*adj*
UNSOLVED	*adj*	UNSTEADY	*adj* **-STEADIER, -STEADIEST**	UNTAMED	*adj*
UNSORTED	*adj*			UNTANNED	*adj*
UNSOUGHT	*adj*	UNSTONED	*adj*	UNTAPPED	*adj*

UNSNARL	*v* **-ED, -ING, -S** to untangle	**UNSWATHE**	*v* **-SWATHED, -SWATHING, -SWATHES** to unbind
UNSOLDER	*v* **-ED, -ING, -S** to separate	**UNSWEAR**	*v* **-SWORE, -SWORN, -SWEARING, -SWEARS** to retract something sworn
UNSONCY	*adj* unsonsie		
UNSONSIE	*adj* unlucky	**UNTACK**	*v* **-ED, -ING, -S** to remove a tack from
UNSONSY	*adj* unsonsie		
UNSPEAK	*v* **-SPOKE, -SPOKEN, -SPEAKING, -SPEAKS** to unsay	**UNTANGLE**	*v* **-GLED, -GLING, -GLES** to free from tangles
UNSPHERE	*v* **-SPHERED, -SPHERING, -SPHERES** to remove from a sphere	**UNTEACH**	*v* **-TAUGHT, -TEACHING, -TEACHES** to cause to unlearn something
UNSPOOL	*v* **-ED, -ING, -S** to unwind from a small cylinder	**UNTENTED**	*adj* not probed or attended to
		UNTETHER	*v* **-ED, -ING, -S** to free from a tether
UNSTACK	*v* **-ED, -ING, -S** to remove from a stack	**UNTHINK**	*v* **-THOUGHT, -THINKING, -THINKS** to dismiss from the mind
UNSTATE	*v* **-STATED, -STATING, -STATES** to deprive of status	**UNTHREAD**	*v* **-ED, -ING, -S** to remove the thread from
UNSTAYED	*adj* not secured with ropes or wires	**UNTHRONE**	*v* **-THRONED, -THRONING, -THRONES** to remove from a throne
UNSTEADY	*v* **-STEADIED, -STEADYING, -STEADIES** to make unsteady		
UNSTEEL	*v* **-ED, -ING, -S** to make soft	**UNTIDY**	*v* **-DIED, -DYING, -DIES** to make untidy
UNSTEP	*v* **-STEPPED, -STEPPING, -STEPS** to remove from a socket	**UNTIE**	*v* **-TIED, -TYING** or **-TIEING, -TIES** to free from something that ties
UNSTICK	*v* **-STUCK, -STICKING, -STICKS** to disjoin	**UNTIL**	*prep* up to the time of
UNSTITCH	*v* **-ED, -ING, -ES** to remove the stitches from	**UNTO**	*prep* to
		UNTOWARD	*adj* unruly
UNSTOP	*v* **-STOPPED, -STOPPING, -STOPS** to remove a stopper from	**UNTRACK**	*v* **-ED, -ING, -S** to cause to escape from a slump
UNSTRAP	*v* **-STRAPPED, -STRAPPING, -STRAPS** to remove a strap from	**UNTREAD**	*v* **-TROD** or **-TREADED, -TRODDEN, -TREADING, -TREADS** to tread back
UNSTRESS	*n* pl. **-ES** a syllable having relatively weak stress		
UNSTRING	*v* **-STRUNG, -STRINGING, -STRINGS** to remove from a string	**UNTRIM**	*v* **-TRIMMED, -TRIMMING, -TRIMS** to strip of trimming
UNSTUCK	past tense of unstick		

List of self-explanatory adjectives and adverbs containing the prefix UN- (continued):

UNTASTED	*adj*	**UNTORN**	*adj*	**UNVEINED**	*adj*
UNTAXED	*adj*	**UNTRACED**	*adj*	**UNVERSED**	*adj*
UNTENDED	*adj*	**UNTRENDY**	*adj*	**UNVESTED**	*adj*
UNTESTED	*adj*	**UNTRIED**	*adj*	**UNVEXED**	*adj*
UNTHAWED	*adj*	**UNTRUE**	*adj* **-TRUER, -TRUEST**	**UNVEXT**	*adj*
UNTIDILY	*adv*			**UNVIABLE**	*adj*
UNTIDY	*adj* **-DIER, -DIEST**	**UNTRULY**	*adv*	**UNVOCAL**	*adj*
UNTILLED	*adj*	**UNTRUSTY**	*adj*	**UNWALLED**	*adj*
UNTILTED	*adj*	**UNTUFTED**	*adj*	**UNWANING**	*adj*
UNTIMED	*adj*	**UNTURNED**	*adj*	**UNWANTED**	*adj*
UNTIMELY	*adj* **-LIER, -LIEST**	**UNUNITED**	*adj*	**UNWARIER**	comparative of unwary
UNTINGED	*adj*	**UNURGED**	*adj*		
UNTIPPED	*adj*	**UNUSABLE**	*adj*	**UNWARIEST**	superlative of unwary
UNTIRED	*adj*	**UNUSED**	*adj*		
UNTIRING	*adj*	**UNUSUAL**	*adj*	**UNWARILY**	*adv*
UNTITLED	*adj*	**UNVALUED**	*adj*	**UNWARMED**	*adj*
UNTOLD	*adj*	**UNVARIED**	*adj*	**UNWARNED**	*adj*

UNTRUSS	*v* **-ED, -ING, -ES** to free from a truss
UNTRUTH	*n* pl. **-S** something that is untrue
UNTUCK	*v* **-ED, -ING, -S** to release from being tucked up
UNTUNE	*v* **-TUNED, -TUNING, -TUNES** to put out of tune
UNTWINE	*v* **-TWINED, -TWINING, -TWINES** to separate the twisted or tangled parts of
UNTWIST	*v* **-ED, -ING, -S** to untwine
UNTYING	present participle of untie
UNUNBIUM	*n* pl. **-S** a synthetic element
UNVEIL	*v* **-ED, -ING, -S** to remove a covering from
UNVOICE	*v* **-VOICED, -VOICING, -VOICES** to deprive of voice or vocal quality
UNWASHED	*n* pl. **-S** an ignorant or underprivileged group
UNWEAVE	*v* **-WOVE, -WOVEN, -WEAVING, -WEAVES** to undo something woven
UNWEIGHT	*v* **-ED, -ING, -S** to reduce the weight of
UNWIND	*v* **-WOUND, -WINDING, -WINDS** to reverse the winding of
UNWINDER	*n* pl. **-S** one that unwinds
UNWISDOM	*n* pl. **-S** lack of wisdom
UNWISH	*v* **-ED, -ING, -ES** to cease to wish for
UNWIT	*v* **-WITTED, -WITTING, -WITS** to make insane
UNWONTED	*adj* unusual
UNWORTHY	*n* pl. **-THIES** an unworthy person
UNWOUND	past tense of unwind
UNWOVE	past tense of unweave
UNWOVEN	past participle of unweave
UNWRAP	*v* **-WRAPPED, -WRAPPING, -WRAPS** to remove the wrapping from
UNYEANED	*adj* unborn
UNYOKE	*v* **-YOKED, -YOKING, -YOKES** to free from a yoke
UNZIP	*v* **-ZIPPED, -ZIPPING, -ZIPS** to open the zipper of
UP	*v* **UPPED, UPPING, UPS** to raise
UPAS	*n* pl. **-ES** an Asian tree
UPBEAR	*v* **-BORE, -BORNE, -BEARING, -BEARS** to raise aloft
UPBEARER	*n* pl. **-S** one that upbears
UPBEAT	*n* pl. **-S** an unaccented beat in a musical measure
UPBIND	*v* **-BOUND, -BINDING, -BINDS** to bind completely
UPBOIL	*v* **-ED, -ING, -S** to boil up
UPBORE	past tense of upbear
UPBORNE	past participle of upbear
UPBOUND	past tense of upbind
UPBOW	*n* pl. **-S** a type of stroke in playing a bowed instrument
UPBRAID	*v* **-ED, -ING, -S** to reproach severely
UPBUILD	*v* **-BUILT, -BUILDING, -BUILDS** to build up
UPBY	*adv* upbye
UPBYE	*adv* a little farther on
UPCAST	*v* **-CAST, -CASTING, -CASTS** to cast up
UPCHUCK	*v* **-ED, -ING, -S** to vomit
UPCLIMB	*v* **-ED, -ING, -S** to climb up
UPCOAST	*adv* up the coast
UPCOIL	*v* **-ED, -ING, -S** to coil up
UPCOMING	*adj* about to happen or appear
UPCOURT	*adv* in the opposite half of a basketball court

List of self-explanatory adjectives and adverbs containing the prefix UN- (continued):

UNWARPED	*adj*	**UNWELL**	*adj*	**UNWISELY**	*adv*
UNWARY	*adj* **-WARIER, -WARIEST**	**UNWEPT**	*adj*	**UNWON**	*adj*
		UNWET	*adj*	**UNWOODED**	*adj*
UNWASTED	*adj*	**UNWETTED**	*adj*	**UNWOOED**	*adj*
UNWAXED	*adj*	**UNWHITE**	*adj*	**UNWORKED**	*adj*
UNWEANED	*adj*	**UNWIELDY**	*adj* **-WIELDIER, -WIELDIEST**	**UNWORN**	*adj*
UNWEARY	*adj*			**UNWORTHY**	*adj* **-THIER, -THIEST**
UNWED	*adj*	**UNWIFELY**	*adj*		
UNWEDDED	*adj*	**UNWILLED**	*adj*	**UNWRUNG**	*adj*
UNWEEDED	*adj*	**UNWISE**	*adj* **-WISER, -WISEST**	**UNYOUNG**	*adj*
UNWELDED	*adj*			**UNZONED**	*adj*

UPCURL   *v* **-ED, -ING, -S** to curl up

UPCURVE   *v* **-CURVED, -CURVING, -CURVES** to curve upward

UPDART   *v* **-ED, -ING, -S** to dart up

UPDATE   *v* **-DATED, -DATING, -DATES** to bring up to date

UPDATER   *n* pl. **-S** one that updates

UPDIVE   *v* **-DIVED** or **-DOVE, -DIVING, -DIVES** to spring upward

UPDO   *n* pl. **-DOS** an upswept hairdo

UPDRAFT   *n* pl. **-S** an upward movement of air

UPDRY   *v* **-DRIED, -DRYING, -DRIES** to dry completely

UPEND   *v* **-ED, -ING, -S** to set or stand on end

UPFIELD   *adv* into the part of the field toward which the offensive team is going

UPFLING   *v* **-FLUNG, -FLINGING, -FLINGS** to fling up

UPFLOW   *v* **-ED, -ING, -S** to flow up

UPFOLD   *v* **-ED, -ING, -S** to fold up

UPFRONT   *adj* honest; candid

UPGATHER   *v* **-ED, -ING, -S** to gather up

UPGAZE   *v* **-GAZED, -GAZING, -GAZES** to gaze up

UPGIRD   *v* **-GIRDED** or **-GIRT, -GIRDING, -GIRDS** to gird completely

UPGOING   *adj* going up

UPGRADE   *v* **-GRADED, -GRADING, -GRADES** to raise to a higher grade or standard

UPGROW   *v* **-GREW, -GROWN, -GROWING, -GROWS** to grow up

UPGROWTH   *n* pl. **-S** the process of growing up

UPHEAP   *v* **-ED, -ING, -S** to heap up

UPHEAVAL   *n* pl. **-S** the act of upheaving

UPHEAVE   *v* **-HEAVED** or **-HOVE, -HEAVING, -HEAVES** to heave up

UPHEAVER   *n* pl. **-S** one that upheaves

UPHILL   *n* pl. **-S** an upward slope

UPHOARD   *v* **-ED, -ING, -S** to hoard up

UPHOLD   *v* **-HELD, -HOLDING, -HOLDS** to hold aloft

UPHOLDER   *n* pl. **-S** one that upholds

UPHOVE   a past tense of upheave

UPHROE   *n* pl. **-S** euphroe

UPKEEP   *n* pl. **-S** the cost of maintaining something in good condition

UPLAND   *n* pl. **-S** the higher land of a region

UPLANDER   *n* pl. **-S** an inhabitant of an upland

UPLEAP   *v* **-LEAPED** or **-LEAPT, -LEAPING, -LEAPS** to leap up

UPLIFT   *v* **-ED, -ING, -S** to lift up

UPLIFTER   *n* pl. **-S** one that uplifts

UPLIGHT   *v* **-LIGHTED** or **-LIT, -LIGHTING, -LIGHTS** to light to a higher degree

UPLINK   *v* **-ED, -ING, -S** to transmit (data) to a spacecraft or satellite

UPLOAD   *v* **-ED, -ING, -S** to transfer information from a small computer to a larger computer

UPMARKET   *adj* upscale

UPMOST   *adj* highest

UPO   *prep* upon

UPON   *prep* on

UPPED   past tense of up

UPPER   *n* pl. **-S** the part of a boot or shoe above the sole

UPPERCUT   *v* **-CUT, -CUTTING, -CUTS** to strike an upward blow

UPPILE   *v* **-PILED, -PILING, -PILES** to pile up

UPPING   *n* pl. **-S** the process of marking young swans for identification purposes

UPPISH   *adj* uppity **UPPISHLY** *adv*

UPPITY   *adj* tending to be snobbish and arrogant

UPPROP   *v* **-PROPPED, -PROPPING, -PROPS** to prop up

UPRAISE   *v* **-RAISED, -RAISING, -RAISES** to raise up

UPRAISER   *n* pl. **-S** one that upraises

UPRATE   *v* **-RATED, -RATING, -RATES** to improve the power output of an engine

UPREACH   *v* **-ED, -ING, -ES** to reach up

UPREAR   *v* **-ED, -ING, -S** to upraise

UPRIGHT   *v* **-ED, -ING, -S** to make vertical

UPRISE   *v* **-ROSE, -RISEN, -RISING, -RISES** to rise up

UPRISER   *n* pl. **-S** one that uprises

UPRISING   *n* pl. **-S** a revolt

UPRIVER   *n* pl. **-S** an area lying toward the source of a river

UPROAR   *n* pl. **-S** a state of noisy excitement and confusion

UPROOT   *v* **-ED, -ING, -S** to pull up by the roots

UPROOTAL *n* pl. **-S** the act of uprooting

UPROOTER *n* pl. **-S** one that uproots

UPROSE past tense of uprise

UPROUSE *v* **-ROUSED, -ROUSING, -ROUSES** to rouse up

UPRUSH *v* **-ED, -ING, -ES** to rush up

UPSCALE *v* **-SCALED, -SCALING, -SCALES** to make appealing to affluent consumers

UPSEND *v* **-SENT, -SENDING, -SENDS** to send upward

UPSET *v* **-SET, -SETTING, -SETS** to overturn

UPSETTER *n* pl. **-S** one that upsets

UPSHIFT *v* **-ED, -ING, -S** to shift into a higher gear

UPSHOOT *v* **-SHOT, -SHOOTING, -SHOOTS** to shoot upward

UPSHOT *n* pl. **-S** the final result

UPSIDE *n* pl. **-S** a positive aspect

UPSILON *n* pl. **-S** a Greek letter

UPSIZE *v* **-SIZED, -SIZING, -SIZES** to increase in size

UPSLOPE *adv* toward the top of a slope

UPSOAR *v* **-ED, -ING, -S** to soar upward

UPSPRING *v* **-SPRANG** or **-SPRUNG, -SPRINGING, -SPRINGS** to spring up

UPSTAGE *v* **-STAGED, -STAGING, -STAGES** to outdo theatrically

UPSTAGER *n* pl. **-S** one that upstages

UPSTAIR *adj* pertaining to an upper floor

UPSTAIRS *adv* up the stairs

UPSTAND *v* **-STOOD, -STANDING, -STANDS** to stand up on one's feet

UPSTARE *v* **-STARED, -STARING, -STARES** to stare upward

UPSTART *v* **-ED, -ING, -S** to spring up suddenly

UPSTATE *n* pl. **-S** the northern region of a state

UPSTATER *n* pl. **-S** an inhabitant of an upstate region

UPSTEP *v* **-STEPPED, -STEPPING, -STEPS** to step up

UPSTIR *v* **-STIRRED, -STIRRING, -STIRS** to stir up

UPSTOOD past tense of upstand

UPSTREAM *adv* toward the source of a stream

UPSTROKE *n* pl. **-S** an upward stroke

UPSURGE *v* **-SURGED, -SURGING, -SURGES** to surge up

UPSWEEP *v* **-SWEPT, -SWEEPING, -SWEEPS** to sweep upward

UPSWELL *v* **-SWELLED, -SWOLLEN, -SWELLING, -SWELLS** to swell up

UPSWING *v* **-SWUNG, -SWINGING, -SWINGS** to swing upward

UPTAKE *n* pl. **-S** an upward ventilating shaft

UPTALK *n* pl. **-S** a manner of ending a declarative sentence with a rising intonation

UPTEAR *v* **-TORE, -TORN, -TEARING, -TEARS** to tear out by the roots

UPTEMPO *n* pl. **-POS** a fast or lively tempo

UPTHROW *v* **-THREW, -THROWN, -THROWING, -THROWS** to throw upward

UPTHRUST *v* **-ED, -ING, -S** to thrust up

UPTICK *n* pl. **-S** an increase or rise

UPTIGHT *adj* nervous

UPTILT *v* **-ED, -ING, -S** to tilt upward

UPTIME *n* pl. **-S** the time during which machinery is functioning

UPTORE past tense of uptear

UPTORN past participle of uptear

UPTOSS *v* **-ED, -ING, -ES** to toss upward

UPTOWN *n* pl. **-S** the upper part of a city

UPTOWNER *n* pl. **-S** one that lives uptown

UPTREND *n* pl. **-S** a tendency upward or toward growth

UPTURN *v* **-ED, -ING, -S** to turn up or over

UPWAFT *v* **-ED, -ING, -S** to waft upward

UPWARD *adv* toward a higher place or position **UPWARDLY** *adv*

UPWARDS *adv* upward

UPWELL *v* **-ED, -ING, -S** to well up

UPWIND *n* pl. **-S** a wind that blows against one's course

URACIL *n* pl. **-S** a chemical compound

URAEMIA *n* pl. **-S** uremia **URAEMIC** *adj*

URAEUS *n* pl. **URAEUSES** or **URAEI** the figure of the sacred serpent on the headdress of ancient Egyptian rulers

URALITE *n* pl. **-S** a mineral **URALITIC** *adj*

URANIA *n* pl. **-S** uranium dioxide

URANIC *adj* pertaining to uranium

URANIDE *n* pl. **-S** uranium

URANISM	*n* pl. **-S** homosexuality	**URETIC**	*adj* pertaining to urine
URANITE	*n* pl. **-S** a mineral **URANITIC** *adj*	**URGE**	*v* **URGED, URGING, URGES** to force forward
URANIUM	*n* pl. **-S** a radioactive element	**URGENCY**	*n* pl. **-CIES** the quality of being urgent
URANOUS	*adj* pertaining to uranium		
URANYL	*n* pl. **-S** a bivalent radical **URANYLIC** *adj*	**URGENT**	*adj* requiring immediate attention **URGENTLY** *adv*
URARE	*n* pl. **-S** curare	**URGER**	*n* pl. **-S** one that urges
URARI	*n* pl. **-S** curare	**URGING**	present participle of urge
URASE	*n* pl. **-S** urease	**URGINGLY**	*adv* in an urging manner
URATE	*n* pl. **-S** a chemical salt **URATIC** *adj*	**URIAL**	*n* pl. **-S** a wild Asian sheep
URB	*n* pl. **-S** an urban area	**URIC**	*adj* pertaining to urine
URBAN	*adj* pertaining to a city	**URIDINE**	*n* pl. **-S** a chemical compound
URBANE	*adj* **-BANER, -BANEST** refined and elegant **URBANELY** *adv*	**URINAL**	*n* pl. **-S** a fixture used for urinating
URBANISE	*v* **-ISED, -ISING, -ISES** to urbanize	**URINARY**	*n* pl. **-NARIES** a urinal
URBANISM	*n* pl. **-S** the lifestyle of city dwellers	**URINATE**	*v* **-NATED, -NATING, -NATES** to discharge urine
URBANIST	*n* pl. **-S** a specialist in city planning	**URINATOR**	*n* pl. **-S** one that urinates
URBANITE	*n* pl. **-S** one who lives in a city	**URINE**	*n* pl. **-S** a liquid containing body wastes
URBANITY	*n* pl. **-TIES** the quality of being urbane	**URINEMIA**	*n* pl. **-S** uremia **URINEMIC** *adj*
URBANIZE	*v* **-IZED, -IZING, -IZES** to cause to take on urban characteristics	**URINOSE**	*adj* pertaining to urine
		URINOUS	*adj* pertaining to urine
URBIA	*n* pl. **-S** cities collectively	**URN**	*n* pl. **-S** a type of vase **URNLIKE** *adj*
URCHIN	*n* pl. **-S** a mischievous boy		
URD	*n* pl. **-S** an annual bean grown in India	**UROCHORD**	*n* pl. **-S** a rodlike structure in certain lower vertebrates
UREA	*n* pl. **-S** a chemical compound **UREAL** *adj*	**URODELE**	*n* pl. **-S** a type of amphibian
		UROLITH	*n* pl. **-S** a concretion in the urinary tract
UREASE	*n* pl. **-S** an enzyme	**UROLOGY**	*n* pl. **-GIES** the branch of medicine dealing with the urinary tract **UROLOGIC** *adj*
UREDIA	pl. of uredium		
UREDIAL	*adj* pertaining to a uredium		
UREDINIA	*n/pl* uredia	**UROPOD**	*n* pl. **-S** an abdominal limb of an arthropod **UROPODAL** *adj*
UREDIUM	*n* pl. **-DIA** a spore-producing organ of certain fungi	**UROPYGIA**	*n/pl* the humps from which birds' tail feathers grow
UREDO	*n* pl. **-DOS** a skin irritation	**UROSCOPY**	*n* pl. **-PIES** analysis of the urine as a means of diagnosis
UREIC	*adj* pertaining to urea		
UREIDE	*n* pl. **-S** a chemical compound	**UROSTYLE**	*n* pl. **-S** a part of the vertebral column of frogs and toads
UREMIA	*n* pl. **-S** an abnormal condition of the blood **UREMIC** *adj*	**URP**	*v* **-ED, -ING, -S** to vomit
URETER	*n* pl. **-S** the duct that conveys urine from the kidney to the bladder **URETERAL, URETERIC** *adj*	**URSA**	*n* pl. **-SAE** a female bear
		URSID	*n* pl. **-S** a mammal of the family Ursidae
URETHAN	*n* pl. **-S** urethane	**URSIFORM**	*adj* having the form of a bear
URETHANE	*n* pl. **-S** a chemical compound	**URSINE**	*adj* pertaining to a bear
URETHRA	*n* pl. **-THRAS** or **-THRAE** the duct through which urine is discharged from the bladder **URETHRAL** *adj*	**URTEXT**	*n* pl. **-S** the original text
		URTICANT	*n* pl. **-S** an urticating substance

URTICATE	*v* **-CATED, -CATING, -CATES** to cause itching or stinging
URUS	*n* pl. **-ES** an extinct European ox
URUSHIOL	*n* pl. **-S** a toxic liquid
US	*pron* the objective case of the pronoun we
USABLE	*adj* capable of being used **USABLY** *adv*
USAGE	*n* pl. **-S** a firmly established and generally accepted practice or procedure
USANCE	*n* pl. **-S** usage
USAUNCE	*n* pl. **-S** usance
USE	*v* **USED, USING, USES** to put into service
USEABLE	*adj* usable **USEABLY** *adv*
USEFUL	*adj* serving a purpose **USEFULLY** *adv*
USELESS	*adj* serving no purpose
USER	*n* pl. **-S** one that uses
USERNAME	*n* pl. **-S** an identifying sequence of characters used for logging on to a computer system
USHER	*v* **-ED, -ING, -S** to conduct to a place
USING	present participle of use
USNEA	*n* pl. **-S** any of a genus of lichens
USQUABAE	*n* pl. **-S** usquebae
USQUE	*n* pl. **-S** usquebae
USQUEBAE	*n* pl. **-S** whiskey
USTULATE	*adj* scorched
USUAL	*n* pl. **-S** something that is usual (ordinary)
USUALLY	*adv* ordinarily
USUFRUCT	*n* pl. **-S** the legal right to use another's property so long as it is not damaged or altered
USURER	*n* pl. **-S** one that practices usury
USURIES	pl. of usury
USURIOUS	*adj* practicing usury
USURP	*v* **-ED, -ING, -S** to seize and hold without legal authority
USURPER	*n* pl. **-S** one that usurps
USURY	*n* pl. **-RIES** the lending of money at an exorbitant interest rate
UT	*n* pl. **-S** the musical tone C in the French solmization system now replaced by do

UTA	*n* pl. **-S** any of a genus of large lizards
UTE	*n* pl. **-S** a utility vehicle
UTENSIL	*n* pl. **-S** a useful implement
UTERUS	*n* pl. **UTERUSES** or **UTERI** an organ of female mammals **UTERINE** *adj*
UTILE	*adj* useful
UTILIDOR	*n* pl. **-S** an insulated system of pipes for use in arctic regions
UTILISE	*v* **-LISED, -LISING, -LISES** to utilize
UTILISER	*n* pl. **-S** utilizer
UTILITY	*n* pl. **-TIES** the quality of being useful
UTILIZE	*v* **-LIZED, -LIZING, -LIZES** to make use of
UTILIZER	*n* pl. **-S** one that utilizes
UTMOST	*n* pl. **-S** the greatest degree or amount
UTOPIA	*n* pl. **-S** a place of ideal perfection
UTOPIAN	*n* pl. **-S** one who believes in the perfectibility of human society
UTOPISM	*n* pl. **-S** the body of ideals or principles of a utopian
UTOPIST	*n* pl. **-S** a utopian
UTRICLE	*n* pl. **-S** a saclike cavity in the inner ear
UTRICULI	*n/pl* utricles
UTTER	*v* **-ED, -ING, -S** to give audible expression to
UTTERER	*n* pl. **-S** one that utters
UTTERLY	*adv* totally
UVEA	*n* pl. **-S** a layer of the eye **UVEAL** *adj*
UVEITIS	*n* pl. **-ITISES** inflammation of the uvea **UVEITIC** *adj*
UVEOUS	*adj* pertaining to the uvea
UVULA	*n* pl. **-LAS** or **-LAE** the pendent, fleshy portion of the soft palate
UVULAR	*n* pl. **-S** a uvularly produced sound
UVULARLY	*adv* with the use of the uvula
UVULITIS	*n* pl. **-TISES** inflammation of the uvula
UXORIAL	*adj* pertaining to a wife
UXORIOUS	*adj* excessively submissive or devoted to one's wife

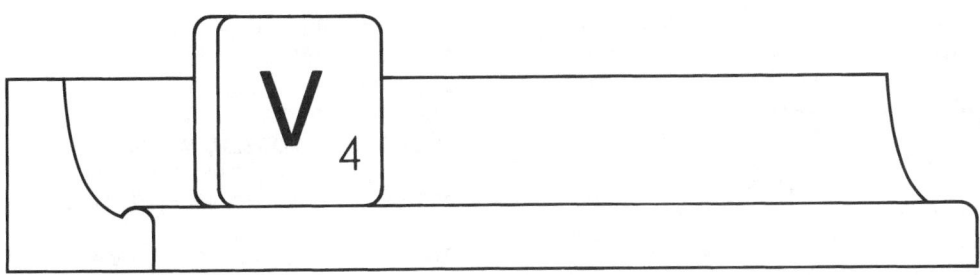

VAC *n* pl. **-S** a vacuum cleaner

VACANCY *n* pl. **-CIES** the quality or state of being vacant

VACANT *adj* empty **VACANTLY** *adv*

VACATE *v* **-CATED, -CATING, -CATES** to make vacant

VACATION *v* **-ED, -ING, -S** to take a vacation (a period of time devoted to rest and relaxation)

VACCINA *n* pl. **-S** vaccinia

VACCINE *n* pl. **-S** a preparation given to produce immunity to a specific disease **VACCINAL** *adj*

VACCINEE *n* pl. **-S** one that is vaccinated

VACCINIA *n* pl. **-S** cowpox

VACUA a pl. of vacuum

VACUITY *n* pl. **-ITIES** an empty space

VACUOLE *n* pl. **-S** a small cavity in organic tissue **VACUOLAR** *adj*

VACUOUS *adj* empty

VACUUM *n* pl. **VACUUMS** or **VACUA** a space entirely devoid of matter

VACUUM *v* **-ED, -ING, -S** to use a device that cleans by suction

VADOSE *adj* located above the permanent groundwater level

VAGABOND *v* **-ED, -ING, -S** to live like a vagabond (a vagrant)

VAGAL *adj* pertaining to the vagus nerve **VAGALLY** *adv*

VAGARY *n* pl. **-RIES** a whim

VAGI pl. of vagus

VAGILE *adj* free to move about

VAGILITY *n* pl. **-TIES** freedom of movement

VAGINA *n* pl. **-NAS** or **-NAE** the passage leading from the uterus to the vulva **VAGINAL** *adj*

VAGINATE *adj* enclosed in a sheath

VAGOTOMY *n* pl. **-MIES** surgical division of the vagus nerve

VAGRANCY *n* pl. **-CIES** the state of being a vagrant

VAGRANT *n* pl. **-S** a wanderer with no apparent means of support

VAGROM *adj* wandering

VAGUE *adj* **VAGUER, VAGUEST** not clearly expressed or understood **VAGUELY** *adv*

VAGUS *n* pl. **-GI** a cranial nerve

VAHINE *n* pl. **-S** wahine

VAIL *v* **-ED, -ING, -S** to lower

VAIN *adj* **VAINER, VAINEST** filled with undue admiration for oneself **VAINLY** *adv*

VAINNESS *n* pl. **-ES** the quality or state of being vain

VAIR *n* pl. **-S** a fur used for lining and trimming medieval garments

VAKEEL *n* pl. **-S** a native lawyer in India

VAKIL *n* pl. **-S** vakeel

VALANCE *v* **-LANCED, -LANCING, -LANCES** to furnish with a short drapery

VALE *n* pl. **-S** a valley

VALENCE *n* pl. **-S** the degree of combining power of an element or radical

VALENCIA *n* pl. **-S** a woven fabric

VALENCY *n* pl. **-CIES** valence

VALERATE *n* pl. **-S** a chemical salt

VALERIAN *n* pl. **-S** a perennial herb **VALERIC** *adj*

VALET *v* **-ED, -ING, -S** to act as a personal servant to

VALGUS *n* pl. **-ES** the position of a joint that is abnormally turned outward **VALGOID** *adj*

VALIANCE *n* pl. **-S** valor

VALIANCY *n* pl. **-CIES** valor

VALIANT *n* pl. **-S** a courageous person

VALID *adj* based on evidence that can be supported

VALIDATE *v* **-DATED, -DATING, -DATES** to give legal force to

VALIDITY *n* pl. **-TIES** the quality or state of being valid

VALIDLY *adv* in a valid manner

VALINE *n* pl. **-S** an amino acid

VALISE *n* pl. **-S** a small piece of hand luggage

VALKYR *n* pl. **-S** valkyrie

VALKYRIE *n* pl. **-S** a maiden in Norse mythology

VALLATE *adj* bordered by a raised edge

VALLEY *n* pl. **-LEYS** a depression of the earth's surface **VALLEYED** *adj*

VALONIA *n* pl. **-S** a substance obtained from dried acorn cups and used in tanning and dyeing

VALOR *n* pl. **-S** courage

VALORISE *v* **-ISED, -ISING, -ISES** to valorize

VALORIZE *v* **-IZED, -IZING, -IZES** to establish and maintain the price of by governmental action

VALOROUS *adj* courageous

VALOUR *n* pl. **-S** valor

VALSE *n* pl. **-S** a concert waltz

VALUABLE *n* pl. **-S** a possession of value

VALUABLY *adv* with value

VALUATE *v* **-ATED, -ATING, -ATES** to appraise

VALUATOR *n* pl. **-S** one that valuates

VALUE *v* **-UED, -UING, -UES** to estimate the value (the quality that renders a thing useful or desirable) of

VALUER *n* pl. **-S** one that values

VALUTA *n* pl. **-S** the agreed or exchange value of a currency

VALVAL *adj* resembling or pertaining to a valve

VALVAR *adj* valval

VALVATE *adj* having valves or parts resembling valves

VALVE *v* **VALVED, VALVING, VALVES** to provide with a valve (a device for controlling the flow of a liquid or gas)

VALVELET *n* pl. **-S** a small valve

VALVULA *n* pl. **-LAE** valvule

VALVULAR *adj* pertaining to a valve

VALVULE *n* pl. **-S** a small valve

VAMBRACE *n* pl. **-S** a piece of armor for the forearm

VAMOOSE *v* **-MOOSED, -MOOSING, -MOOSES** to leave quickly

VAMOSE *v* **-MOSED, -MOSING, -MOSES** to vamoose

VAMP *v* **-ED, -ING, -S** to repair or patch

VAMPER *n* pl. **-S** one that vamps

VAMPIRE *n* pl. **-S** a reanimated corpse believed to feed on sleeping persons' blood **VAMPIRIC** *adj*

VAMPISH *adj* seductive

VAMPY *adj* **VAMPIER, VAMPIEST** seductive

VAN *v* **VANNED, VANNING, VANS** to transport in a van (a type of motor vehicle)

VANADATE *n* pl. **-S** a chemical salt

VANADIUM *n* pl. **-S** a metallic element **VANADIC, VANADOUS** *adj*

VANDA *n* pl. **-S** a tropical orchid

VANDAL *n* pl. **-S** one who willfully destroys or defaces property **VANDALIC** *adj*

VANDYKE *n* pl. **-S** a short, pointed beard **VANDYKED** *adj*

VANE *n* pl. **-S** a device for showing the direction of the wind **VANED** *adj*

VANG *n* pl. **-S** a rope on a ship

VANGUARD *n* pl. **-S** the forefront of a movement

VANILLA *n* pl. **-S** a flavoring extract **VANILLIC** *adj*

VANILLIN *n* pl. **-S** a chemical compound used in flavoring

VANISH *v* **-ED, -ING, -ES** to disappear

VANISHER *n* pl. **-S** one that vanishes

VANITORY *n* pl. **-RIES** a combined dressing table and basin

VANITY *n* pl. **-TIES** inflated pride in oneself **VANITIED** *adj*

VANLOAD *n* pl. **-S** the quantity that a van can carry

VANMAN *n* pl. **-MEN** a person who drives a van

VANNED past tense of van

VANNER *n* pl. **-S** a person who owns a van

VANNING present participle of van

VANPOOL	*n* pl. **-S** an arrangement whereby several commuters travel in one van
VANQUISH	*v* **-ED, -ING, -ES** to defeat in battle
VANTAGE	*n* pl. **-S** superiority over a competitor
VANWARD	*adv* toward the front
VAPID	*adj* insipid **VAPIDLY** *adv*
VAPIDITY	*n* pl. **-TIES** the quality or state of being vapid
VAPOR	*v* **-ED, -ING, -S** to emit vapor (visible floating moisture)
VAPORER	*n* pl. **-S** one that vapors
VAPORING	*n* pl. **-S** boastful talk
VAPORISE	*v* **-ISED, -ISING, -ISES** to vaporize
VAPORISH	*adj* resembling vapor
VAPORIZE	*v* **-IZED, -IZING, -IZES** to convert into vapor
VAPOROUS	*adj* vaporish
VAPORY	*adj* vaporish
VAPOUR	*v* **-ED, -ING, -S** to vapor
VAPOURER	*n* pl. **-S** vaporer
VAPOURY	*adj* vapory
VAQUERO	*n* pl. **-ROS** a cowboy
VAR	*n* pl. **-S** a unit of reactive power
VARA	*n* pl. **-S** a Spanish unit of length
VARACTOR	*n* pl. **-S** a capacitor with variable capacitance
VARIA	*n* pl. **-S** a miscellany of literary works
VARIABLE	*n* pl. **-S** something that varies
VARIABLY	*adv* in a varying manner
VARIANCE	*n* pl. **-S** a license to perform an act contrary to the usual rule
VARIANT	*n* pl. **-S** a variable
VARIATE	*v* **-ATED, -ATING, -ATES** to vary
VARICES	pl. of varix
VARICOSE	*adj* abnormally swollen or dilated
VARIED	past tense of vary
VARIEDLY	*adv* in a varied manner
VARIER	*n* pl. **-S** one that varies
VARIES	present 3d person sing. of vary
VARIETAL	*n* pl. **-S** a wine designated by the variety of grape
VARIETY	*n* pl. **-ETIES** something differing from others of the same general kind
VARIFORM	*adj* having various forms

VARIOLA	*n* pl. **-S** smallpox **VARIOLAR** *adj*
VARIOLE	*n* pl. **-S** a foveola
VARIORUM	*n* pl. **-S** an edition containing various versions of a text
VARIOUS	*adj* of diverse kinds
VARISTOR	*n* pl. **-S** a type of electrical resistor
VARIX	*n* pl. **VARICES** a varicose vein
VARLET	*n* pl. **-S** a knave
VARLETRY	*n* pl. **-RIES** a group of common people
VARMENT	*n* pl. **-S** varmint
VARMINT	*n* pl. **-S** an animal considered to be a pest
VARNA	*n* pl. **-S** any of the four main Hindu social classes
VARNISH	*v* **-ED, -ING, -ES** to give a glossy appearance to
VARNISHY	*adj* glossy
VAROOM	*v* **-ED, -ING, -S** to vroom
VARSITY	*n* pl. **-TIES** the principal team representing a university, college, or school in any activity
VARUS	*n* pl. **-ES** a malformation of a bone or joint
VARVE	*n* pl. **-S** a deposit of sedimentary material **VARVED** *adj*
VARY	*v* **VARIED, VARYING, VARIES** to become or make different
VAS	*n* pl. **VASA** an anatomical duct **VASAL** *adj*
VASCULAR	*adj* pertaining to ducts that convey body fluids
VASCULUM	*n* pl. **-LUMS** or **-LA** a box used to hold plant specimens
VASE	*n* pl. **-S** a rounded, decorative container **VASELIKE** *adj*
VASIFORM	*adj* having the form of a vase
VASOTOMY	*n* pl. **-MIES** a surgical cutting of the vas deferens
VASSAL	*n* pl. **-S** a person granted the use of land by a feudal lord in return for homage and allegiance
VAST	*adj* **VASTER, VASTEST** of great extent or size
VAST	*n* pl. **-S** a vast space
VASTIER	comparative of vasty
VASTIEST	superlative of vasty
VASTITY	*n* pl. **-TIES** vastness
VASTLY	*adv* to a vast extent or degree

VASTNESS *n pl.* **-ES** the quality or state of being vast

VASTY *adj* **VASTIER, VASTIEST** vast

VAT *v* **VATTED, VATTING, VATS** to put into a vat (a large container for holding liquids)

VATFUL *n pl.* **-S** as much as a vat can hold

VATIC *adj* pertaining to a prophet

VATICAL *adj* vatic

VATICIDE *n pl.* **-S** the killing of a prophet

VATTED past tense of vat

VATTING present participle of vat

VATU *n pl.* **-S** a monetary unit of Vanuatu

VAU *n pl.* **-S** vav

VAULT *v* **-ED, -ING, -S** to provide with a vault (an arched ceiling)

VAULTER *n pl.* **-S** one that leaps

VAULTING *n pl.* **-S** the structure forming a vault

VAULTY *adj* **VAULTIER, VAULTIEST** resembling a vault

VAUNT *v* **-ED, -ING, -S** to brag

VAUNTER *n pl.* **-S** one that vaunts

VAUNTFUL *adj* boastful

VAUNTIE *adj* boastful

VAUNTY *adj* vauntie

VAV *n pl.* **-S** a Hebrew letter

VAVASOR *n pl.* **-S** a high-ranking vassal

VAVASOUR *n pl.* **-S** vavasor

VAVASSOR *n pl.* **-S** vavasor

VAW *n pl.* **-S** vav

VAWARD *n pl.* **-S** the foremost part

VAWNTIE *adj* vaunty

VEAL *v* **-ED, -ING, -S** to kill and prepare a calf for food

VEALER *n pl.* **-S** a calf raised for food

VEALY *adj* **VEALIER, VEALIEST** immature

VECTOR *v* **-ED, -ING, -S** to guide in flight by means of radioed directions

VEDALIA *n pl.* **-S** an Australian ladybug

VEDETTE *n pl.* **-S** a small boat used for scouting

VEE *n pl.* **-S** the letter V

VEEJAY *n pl.* **-JAYS** an announcer on a program of music videos

VEENA *n pl.* **-S** vina

VEEP *n pl.* **-S** a vice president

VEEPEE *n pl.* **-S** veep

VEER *v* **-ED, -ING, -S** to change direction

VEERY *n pl.* **-RIES** a songbird

VEG *v* **VEGGED, VEGGING, VEGES** to spend time idly

VEGAN *n pl.* **-S** one that eats only plant products

VEGANISM *n pl.* **-S** the practice of eating only plant products

VEGETAL *adj* pertaining to plants

VEGETANT *adj* characteristic of plant life

VEGETATE *v* **-TATED, -TATING, -TATES** to grow in the manner of a plant

VEGETE *adj* healthy

VEGETIST *n pl.* **-S** one that eats only plant products

VEGETIVE *adj* growing or capable of growing

VEGGIE *n pl.* **-S** a vegetable

VEGIE *n pl.* **-S** veggie

VEHEMENT *adj* ardent

VEHICLE *n pl.* **-S** a device used as a means of conveyance

VEIL *v* **-ED, -ING, -S** to provide with a veil (a piece of sheer fabric worn over the face)

VEILEDLY *adv* in a disguised manner

VEILER *n pl.* **-S** one that veils

VEILING *n pl.* **-S** a veil

VEILLIKE *adj* resembling a veil

VEIN *v* **-ED, -ING, -S** to fill with veins (tubular blood vessels)

VEINAL *adj* of or pertaining to the veins

VEINER *n pl.* **-S** a tool used in wood carving

VEINIER comparative of veiny

VEINIEST superlative of veiny

VEINING *n pl.* **-S** a network of veins

VEINLESS *adj* having no veins

VEINLET *n pl.* **-S** a small vein

VEINLIKE *adj* resembling a vein

VEINULE *n pl.* **-S** venule

VEINULET *n pl.* **-S** venule

VEINY *adj* **VEINIER, VEINIEST** full of veins

VELA pl. of velum

VELAMEN *n pl.* **-MINA** a velum

VELAR *n pl.* **-S** a kind of speech sound

VELARIUM *n* pl. **-IA** an awning over an ancient Roman theater

VELARIZE *v* **-IZED, -IZING, -IZES** to pronounce with the back of the tongue touching the soft palate

VELATE *adj* having a velum

VELD *n* pl. **-S** veldt

VELDT *n* pl. **-S** a grassland of southern Africa

VELIGER *n* pl. **-S** a larval stage of certain mollusks

VELITES *n/pl* foot soldiers of ancient Rome

VELLEITY *n* pl. **-ITIES** a very low degree of desire

VELLUM *n* pl. **-S** a fine parchment

VELOCE *adv* rapidly — used as a musical direction

VELOCITY *n* pl. **-TIES** rapidity of motion

VELOUR *n* pl. **-S** a fabric resembling velvet

VELOUTE *n* pl. **-S** a type of sauce

VELUM *n* pl. **-LA** a thin membranous covering or partition

VELURE *v* **-LURED, -LURING, -LURES** to smooth with a velvet or silk pad, as a hat

VELVERET *n* pl. **-S** a fabric resembling velvet

VELVET *n* pl. **-S** a soft, smooth fabric **VELVETED** *adj*

VELVETY *adj* **-VETIER, -VETIEST** resembling velvet in texture

VENA *n* pl. **-NAE** a vein

VENAL *adj* open to bribery **VENALLY** *adv*

VENALITY *n* pl. **-TIES** the quality or state of being venal

VENATIC *adj* pertaining to hunting

VENATION *n* pl. **-S** an arrangement of veins

VEND *v* **-ED, -ING, -S** to sell

VENDABLE *n* pl. **-S** vendible

VENDACE *n* pl. **-S** a European fish

VENDEE *n* pl. **-S** a buyer

VENDER *n* pl. **-S** vendor

VENDETTA *n* pl. **-S** a feud between two families

VENDEUSE *n* pl. **-S** a saleswoman

VENDIBLE *n* pl. **-S** a salable article

VENDIBLY *adv* salably

VENDOR *n* pl. **-S** a seller

VENDUE *n* pl. **-S** a public sale

VENEER *v* **-ED, -ING, -S** to overlay with thin layers of material

VENEERER *n* pl. **-S** one that veneers

VENENATE *v* **-NATED, -NATING, -NATES** to poison

VENENE *n* pl. **-S** venin

VENENOSE *adj* poisonous

VENERATE *v* **-ATED, -ATING, -ATES** to revere

VENEREAL *adj* involving the genital organs

VENERY *n* pl. **-ERIES** sexual intercourse

VENETIAN *n* pl. **-S** a flexible window screen

VENGE *v* **VENGED, VENGING, VENGES** to avenge

VENGEFUL *adj* seeking to avenge

VENIAL *adj* easily excused or forgiven **VENIALLY** *adv*

VENIN *n* pl. **-S** a toxin found in snake venom

VENINE *n* pl. **-S** venin

VENIRE *n* pl. **-S** a type of judicial writ

VENISON *n* pl. **-S** the edible flesh of a deer

VENOGRAM *n* pl. **-S** a roentgenogram of a vein

VENOLOGY *n* pl. **-GIES** the study of veins

VENOM *v* **-ED, -ING, -S** to inject with venom (a poisonous secretion of certain animals)

VENOMER *n* pl. **-S** one that venoms

VENOMOUS *adj* poisonous

VENOSE *adj* venous

VENOSITY *n* pl. **-TIES** the quality or state of being venous

VENOUS *adj* full of veins **VENOUSLY** *adv*

VENT *v* **-ED, -ING, -S** to provide with a vent (an opening for the escape of gas or liquid)

VENTAGE *n* pl. **-S** a small opening

VENTAIL *n* pl. **-S** the adjustable front of a medieval helmet

VENTER *n* pl. **-S** the abdomen

VENTLESS *adj* having no vent

VENTRAL *n* pl. **-S** a fin located on the underside of a fish

VENTURE *v* **-TURED, -TURING, -TURES** to risk

VENTURER *n* pl. **-S** one that ventures

VENTURI *n* pl. **-S** a device for measuring the flow of a fluid

VENUE *n* pl. **-S** the locale of an event

VENULE	*n* pl. **-S** a small vein **VENULAR, VENULOSE, VENULOUS** *adj*
VERA	*adj* very
VERACITY	*n* pl. **-TIES** conformity to truth
VERANDA	*n* pl. **-S** a type of porch
VERANDAH	*n* pl. **-S** veranda
VERATRIA	*n* pl. **-S** veratrin
VERATRIN	*n* pl. **-S** a poisonous mixture of alkaloids
VERATRUM	*n* pl. **-S** a poisonous herb
VERB	*n* pl. **-S** a word used to express an act, occurrence, or mode of being
VERBAL	*n* pl. **-S** a word derived from a verb
VERBALLY	*adv* in a spoken manner
VERBATIM	*adv* word for word
VERBENA	*n* pl. **-S** a flowering plant
VERBIAGE	*n* pl. **-S** an excess of words
VERBID	*n* pl. **-S** a verbal
VERBIFY	*v* **-FIED, -FYING, -FIES** to use as a verb
VERBILE	*n* pl. **-S** one whose mental imagery consists of words
VERBLESS	*adj* lacking a verb
VERBOSE	*adj* wordy
VERBOTEN	*adj* forbidden
VERDANCY	*n* pl. **-CIES** the quality or state of being verdant
VERDANT	*adj* green with vegetation
VERDERER	*n* pl. **-S** an officer in charge of the royal forests of England
VERDEROR	*n* pl. **-S** verderer
VERDICT	*n* pl. **-S** the decision of a jury at the end of a legal proceeding
VERDIN	*n* pl. **-S** a small bird
VERDITER	*n* pl. **-S** a blue or green pigment
VERDURE	*n* pl. **-S** green vegetation **VERDURED** *adj*
VERECUND	*adj* shy
VERGE	*v* **VERGED, VERGING, VERGES** to come near
VERGENCE	*n* pl. **-S** a movement of one eye in relation to the other
VERGER	*n* pl. **-S** a church official
VERGLAS	*n* pl. **-ES** a thin coating of ice on rock
VERIDIC	*adj* truthful
VERIER	comparative of very
VERIEST	superlative of very
VERIFIER	*n* pl. **-S** one that verifies
VERIFY	*v* **-FIED, -FYING, -FIES** to prove to be true
VERILY	*adv* in truth
VERISM	*n* pl. **-S** realism in art or literature **VERISTIC** *adj*
VERISMO	*n* pl. **-MOS** verism
VERIST	*n* pl. **-S** one who practices verism
VERITAS	*n* pl. **-TATES** truth
VERITE	*n* pl. **-S** the technique of filming so as to convey candid realism
VERITY	*n* pl. **-TIES** truth
VERJUICE	*n* pl. **-S** the juice of sour or unripe fruit
VERMEIL	*n* pl. **-S** a red color
VERMES	pl. of vermis
VERMIAN	*adj* pertaining to worms
VERMIN	*n* pl. **VERMIN** small, common, harmful, or objectionable animals
VERMIS	*n* pl. **-MES** a part of the brain
VERMOULU	*adj* eaten by worms
VERMOUTH	*n* pl. **-S** a liqueur
VERMUTH	*n* pl. **-S** vermouth
VERNACLE	*n* pl. **-S** vernicle
VERNAL	*adj* pertaining to spring **VERNALLY** *adv*
VERNICLE	*n* pl. **-S** veronica
VERNIER	*n* pl. **-S** an auxiliary scale used with a main scale to obtain fine measurements
VERNIX	*n* pl. **-ES** a fatty substance covering the skin of a fetus
VERONICA	*n* pl. **-S** a handkerchief bearing the image of Christ's face
VERRUCA	*n* pl. **-CAS** or **-CAE** a wart
VERSAL	*adj* entire
VERSANT	*n* pl. **-S** the slope of a mountain or mountain chain
VERSE	*v* **VERSED, VERSING, VERSES** to versify
VERSEMAN	*n* pl. **-MEN** one who versifies
VERSER	*n* pl. **-S** a verseman
VERSET	*n* pl. **-S** a versicle
VERSICLE	*n* pl. **-S** a short line of metrical writing
VERSIFY	*v* **-FIED, -FYING, -FIES** to change from prose into metrical form
VERSINE	*n* pl. **-S** a trigonometric function of an angle

VERSING	present participle of verse
VERSION	*n* pl. **-S** an account or description from a particular point of view
VERSO	*n* pl. **-SOS** a left-hand page of a book
VERST	*n* pl. **-S** a Russian measure of distance
VERSTE	*n* pl. **-S** verst
VERSUS	*prep* against
VERT	*n* pl. **-S** the heraldic color green
VERTEBRA	*n* pl. **-BRAS** or **-BRAE** any of the bones or segments forming the spinal column
VERTEX	*n* pl. **-TEXES** or **-TICES** the highest point of something
VERTICAL	*n* pl. **-S** something that is vertical (extending up and down)
VERTICIL	*n* pl. **-S** a circular arrangement, as of flowers or leaves, about a point on an axis
VERTIGO	*n* pl. **-GOES** or **-GOS** or **-GINES** a disordered state in which the individual or his surroundings seem to whirl dizzily
VERTU	*n* pl. **-S** virtu
VERVAIN	*n* pl. **-S** a flowering plant
VERVE	*n* pl. **-S** vivacity
VERVET	*n* pl. **-S** an African monkey
VERY	*adj* **VERIER, VERIEST** absolute
VESICA	*n* pl. **-CAE** a bladder **VESICAL** *adj*
VESICANT	*n* pl. **-S** a chemical warfare agent that induces blistering
VESICATE	*v* **-CATED, -CATING, -CATES** to blister
VESICLE	*n* pl. **-S** a small bladder
VESICULA	*n* pl. **-LAE** a vesicle
VESPER	*n* pl. **-S** an evening service, prayer, or song
VESPERAL	*n* pl. **-S** a covering for an altar cloth
VESPIARY	*n* pl. **-ARIES** a nest of wasps
VESPID	*n* pl. **-S** a wasp
VESPINE	*adj* pertaining to wasps
VESSEL	*n* pl. **-S** a craft for traveling on water **VESSELED** *adj*
VEST	*v* **-ED, -ING, -S** to place in the control of
VESTA	*n* pl. **-S** a short friction match
VESTAL	*n* pl. **-S** a chaste woman
VESTALLY	*adv* chastely
VESTEE	*n* pl. **-S** a garment worn under a woman's jacket or blouse
VESTIARY	*n* pl. **-ARIES** a dressing room
VESTIGE	*n* pl. **-S** a visible sign of something that is no longer in existence
VESTIGIA	*n/pl* vestiges
VESTING	*n* pl. **-S** the right of an employee to share in and withdraw from a pension fund without penalty
VESTLESS	*adj* being without a vest
VESTLIKE	*adj* resembling a vest (a short, sleeveless garment)
VESTMENT	*n* pl. **-S** one of the ceremonial garments of the clergy
VESTRY	*n* pl. **-TRIES** a room in which vestments are kept **VESTRAL** *adj*
VESTURAL	*adj* pertaining to clothing
VESTURE	*v* **-TURED, -TURING, -TURES** to clothe
VESUVIAN	*n* pl. **-S** a mineral
VET	*v* **VETTED, VETTING, VETS** to treat animals medically
VETCH	*n* pl. **-ES** a climbing plant
VETERAN	*n* pl. **-S** a former member of the armed forces
VETIVER	*n* pl. **-S** an Asian grass
VETIVERT	*n* pl. **-S** the essential oil of the vetiver
VETO	*v* **-ED, -ING, -ES** to forbid or prevent authoritatively
VETOER	*n* pl. **-S** one that vetoes
VETTED	past tense of vet
VETTER	*n* pl. **-S** one that evaluates something for approval
VETTING	present participle of vet
VEX	*v* **VEXED** or **VEXT, VEXING, VEXES** to annoy
VEXATION	*n* pl. **-S** a cause of trouble
VEXEDLY	*adv* in a vexed manner
VEXER	*n* pl. **-S** one that vexes
VEXIL	*n* pl. **-S** vexillum
VEXILLUM	*n* pl. **-LA** the web or vane of a feather **VEXILLAR** *adj*
VEXINGLY	*adv* in a vexing manner
VEXT	a past tense of vex
VIA	*prep* by way of
VIABLE	*adj* capable of living **VIABLY** *adv*
VIADUCT	*n* pl. **-S** a type of bridge

VIAL	*v* **VIALED, VIALING, VIALS** or **VIALLED, VIALLING, VIALS** to put in a vial (a small container for liquids)
VIAND	*n* pl. **-S** an article of food
VIATIC	*adj* pertaining to traveling
VIATICAL	*n* pl. **-S** a type of life insurance arrangement
VIATICUM	*n* pl. **-CUMS** or **-CA** an allowance for traveling expenses
VIATOR	*n* pl. **-ES** or **-S** a traveler
VIBE	*n* pl. **-S** a vibration
VIBIST	*n* pl. **-S** one who plays the vibraphone
VIBRANCE	*n* pl. **-S** vibrancy
VIBRANCY	*n* pl. **-CIES** the quality or state of being vibrant
VIBRANT	*n* pl. **-S** a sonant
VIBRATE	*v* **-BRATED, -BRATING, -BRATES** to move back and forth rapidly
VIBRATO	*n* pl. **-TOS** a tremulous or pulsating musical effect
VIBRATOR	*n* pl. **-S** something that vibrates
VIBRIO	*n* pl. **-RIOS** any of a genus of bacteria shaped like a comma **VIBRIOID** *adj*
VIBRION	*n* pl. **-S** vibrio
VIBRISSA	*n* pl. **-SAE** one of the stiff hairs growing about the mouth of certain mammals
VIBRONIC	*adj* pertaining to changes in molecular energy states resulting from vibrational energy
VIBURNUM	*n* pl. **-S** a flowering shrub
VICAR	*n* pl. **-S** a church official
VICARAGE	*n* pl. **-S** the office of a vicar
VICARATE	*n* pl. **-S** vicarage
VICARIAL	*adj* pertaining to a vicar
VICARLY	*adj* vicarial
VICE	*v* **VICED, VICING, VICES** to vise
VICELESS	*adj* having no immoral habits
VICENARY	*adj* pertaining to the number twenty
VICEROY	*n* pl. **-ROYS** one who rules as the representative of a sovereign
VICHY	*n* pl. **-CHIES** a type of mineral water
VICINAGE	*n* pl. **-S** vicinity
VICINAL	*adj* nearby
VICING	present participle of vice
VICINITY	*n* pl. **-TIES** the region near or about a place
VICIOUS	*adj* dangerously aggressive
VICOMTE	*n* pl. **-S** a French nobleman
VICTIM	*n* pl. **-S** one who suffers from a destructive or injurious action
VICTOR	*n* pl. **-S** one who defeats an adversary
VICTORIA	*n* pl. **-S** a light carriage
VICTORY	*n* pl. **-RIES** a successful outcome in a contest or struggle
VICTRESS	*n* pl. **-ES** a female victor
VICTUAL	*v* **-UALED, -UALING, -UALS** or **-UALLED, -UALLING, -UALS** to provide with food
VICUGNA	*n* pl. **-S** vicuna
VICUNA	*n* pl. **-S** a ruminant mammal
VID	*n* pl. **-S** a video
VIDE	*v* see — used to direct a reader to another item; VIDE is the only form of this verb; it cannot be conjugated
VIDEO	*n* pl. **-EOS** a recording for playing on a television set
VIDEOTEX	*n* pl. **-ES** an electronic system for transmitting data to a subscriber's video screen
VIDETTE	*n* pl. **-S** vedette
VIDICON	*n* pl. **-S** a type of television camera tube
VIDUITY	*n* pl. **-ITIES** the quality or state of being a widow
VIE	*v* **VIED, VYING, VIES** to strive for superiority
VIER	*n* pl. **-S** one that vies
VIEW	*v* **-ED, -ING, -S** to look at **VIEWABLE** *adj*
VIEWDATA	*n* pl. **VIEWDATA** a videotex
VIEWER	*n* pl. **-S** one that views
VIEWIER	comparative of viewy
VIEWIEST	superlative of viewy
VIEWING	*n* pl. **-S** an act of seeing, watching, or looking
VIEWLESS	*adj* having no opinions
VIEWY	*adj* **VIEWIER, VIEWIEST** showy
VIG	*n* pl. **-S** a vigorish
VIGA	*n* pl. **-S** a ceiling beam in Spanish architecture
VIGIA	*n* pl. **-S** a warning on a navigational chart

VIGIL   *n* pl. **-S** a period of watchfulness maintained during normal sleeping hours

VIGILANT   *adj* watchful

VIGNERON   *n* pl. **-S** a winegrower

VIGNETTE   *v* **-GNETTED, -GNETTING, -GNETTES** to describe briefly

VIGOR   *n* pl. **-S** active strength or force

VIGORISH   *n* pl. **-ES** a charge paid to a bookie on a bet

VIGOROSO   *adv* with emphasis and spirit — used as a musical direction

VIGOROUS   *adj* full of vigor

VIGOUR   *n* pl. **-S** vigor

VIKING   *n* pl. **-S** a Scandinavian pirate

VILAYET   *n* pl. **-S** an administrative division of Turkey

VILE   *adj* **VILER, VILEST** morally despicable or physically repulsive **VILELY** *adv*

VILENESS   *n* pl. **-ES** the state of being vile

VILIFIER   *n* pl. **-S** one that vilifies

VILIFY   *v* **-FIED, -FYING, -FIES** to defame

VILIPEND   *v* **-ED, -ING, -S** to vilify

VILL   *n* pl. **-S** a village

VILLA   *n* pl. **-LAS** or **-LAE** an agricultural estate of ancient Rome

VILLADOM   *n* pl. **-S** the world constituted by suburban residences and their occupants

VILLAGE   *n* pl. **-S** a small community in a rural area

VILLAGER   *n* pl. **-S** one who lives in a village

VILLAIN   *n* pl. **-S** a cruelly malicious person

VILLAINY   *n* pl. **-LAINIES** conduct characteristic of a villain

VILLATIC   *adj* rural

VILLEIN   *n* pl. **-S** a type of serf

VILLUS   *n* pl. **-LI** one of the hairlike projections found on certain membranes **VILLOSE, VILLOUS** *adj*

VIM   *n* pl. **-S** energy

VIMEN   *n* pl. **-MINA** a long, flexible branch of a plant **VIMINAL** *adj*

VINA   *n* pl. **-S** a stringed instrument of India

VINAL   *n* pl. **-S** a synthetic textile fiber

VINASSE   *n* pl. **-S** a residue left after the distillation of liquor

VINCA   *n* pl. **-S** a flowering plant

VINCIBLE   *adj* capable of being conquered **VINCIBLY** *adv*

VINCULUM   *n* pl. **-LUMS** or **-LA** a unifying bond

VINDALOO   *n* pl. **-LOOS** a curried dish made with meat, garlic, and wine

VINE   *v* **VINED, VINING, VINES** to grow like a vine (a climbing plant)

VINEAL   *adj* vinous

VINEGAR   *n* pl. **-S** a sour liquid used as a condiment or preservative **VINEGARY** *adj*

VINERY   *n* pl. **-ERIES** a place in which grapevines are grown

VINEYARD   *n* pl. **-S** an area planted with grapevines

VINIC   *adj* derived from wine

VINIER   comparative of viny

VINIEST   superlative of viny

VINIFERA   *n* pl. **-S** a European grape

VINIFY   *v* **-FIED, -FYING, -FIES** to convert into wine by fermentation

VINING   present participle of vine

VINO   *n* pl. **-NOS** wine

VINOSITY   *n* pl. **-TIES** the character of a wine

VINOUS   *adj* pertaining to wine **VINOUSLY** *adv*

VINTAGE   *n* pl. **-S** a season's yield of wine from a vineyard

VINTAGER   *n* pl. **-S** one that harvests wine grapes

VINTNER   *n* pl. **-S** a wine merchant

VINY   *adj* **VINIER, VINIEST** covered with vines

VINYL   *n* pl. **-S** a type of plastic **VINYLIC** *adj*

VIOL   *n* pl. **-S** a stringed instrument

VIOLA   *n* pl. **-S** a stringed instrument

VIOLABLE   *adj* capable of being violated **VIOLABLY** *adv*

VIOLATE   *v* **-LATED, -LATING, -LATES** to break or disregard the terms or requirements of

VIOLATER   *n* pl. **-S** violator

VIOLATOR   *n* pl. **-S** one that violates

VIOLENCE   *n* pl. **-S** violent action

VIOLENT   *adj* marked by intense physical force or roughness

VIOLET   *n* pl. **-S** a flowering plant

VIOLIN   *n* pl. **-S** a stringed instrument

VIOLIST   *n* pl. **-S** one who plays the viol or viola

VIOLONE   *n* pl. **-S** a stringed instrument

VIOMYCIN   *n* pl. **-S** an antibiotic

VIPER   *n* pl. **-S** a venomous snake **VIPERINE, VIPERISH, VIPEROUS** *adj*

VIRAGO   *n* pl. **-GOS** or **-GOES** a noisy, domineering woman

VIRAL   *adj* pertaining to or caused by a virus **VIRALLY** *adv*

VIRELAI   *n* pl. **-S** virelay

VIRELAY   *n* pl. **-LAYS** a medieval French verse form

VIREMIA   *n* pl. **-S** the presence of a virus in the blood **VIREMIC** *adj*

VIREO   *n* pl. **-EOS** a small bird

VIRES   pl. of vis

VIRGA   *n* pl. **-S** wisps of precipitation evaporating before reaching ground

VIRGATE   *n* pl. **-S** an early English measure of land area

VIRGIN   *n* pl. **-S** a person who has never had sexual intercourse

VIRGINAL   *n* pl. **-S** a musical instrument

VIRGULE   *n* pl. **-S** a diagonal printing mark used to separate alternatives

VIRICIDE   *n* pl. **-S** a substance that destroys viruses

VIRID   *adj* verdant

VIRIDIAN   *n* pl. **-S** a bluish-green pigment

VIRIDITY   *n* pl. **-TIES** verdancy

VIRILE   *adj* having masculine vigor **VIRILELY** *adv*

VIRILISM   *n* pl. **-S** the development of male secondary sex characteristics in a female

VIRILITY   *n* pl. **-TIES** the quality or state of being virile

VIRILIZE   *v* **-IZED, -IZING, -IZES** to induce male characteristics in (a female)

VIRION   *n* pl. **-S** a virus particle

VIRL   *n* pl. **-S** a metal ring or cap put around a shaft to prevent splitting

VIROID   *n* pl. **-S** a viruslike plant pathogen

VIROLOGY   *n* pl. **-GIES** the study of viruses

VIROSIS   *n* pl. **-ROSES** infection with a virus

VIRTU   *n* pl. **-S** a love or taste for the fine arts

VIRTUAL   *adj* having the effect but not the actual form of what is specified

VIRTUE   *n* pl. **-S** moral excellence

VIRTUOSA   *n* pl. **-SAS** or **-SE** a female virtuoso

VIRTUOSO   *n* pl. **-SOS** or **-SI** a highly skilled artistic performer

VIRTUOUS   *adj* characterized by virtue

VIRUCIDE   *n* pl. **-S** viricide

VIRULENT   *adj* extremely poisonous

VIRUS   *n* pl. **-ES** any of a class of submicroscopic pathogens

VIRUSOID   *n* pl. **-S** a particle of RNA associated with some plant viruses

VIS   *n* pl. **VIRES** force or power

VISA   *v* **-ED, -ING, -S** to put an official endorsement on, as a passport

VISAGE   *n* pl. **-S** the face or facial expression of a person **VISAGED** *adj*

VISARD   *n* pl. **-S** vizard

VISCACHA   *n* pl. **-S** a burrowing rodent

VISCERA   pl. of viscus

VISCERAL   *adj* pertaining to the internal organs

VISCID   *adj* thick and adhesive **VISCIDLY** *adv*

VISCOID   *adj* somewhat viscid

VISCOSE   *n* pl. **-S** a viscous solution

VISCOUNT   *n* pl. **-S** a British nobleman

VISCOUS   *adj* having relatively high resistance to flow

VISCUS   *n* pl. **-CERA** an internal organ

VISE   *v* **VISED, VISING, VISES** to hold in a vise (a clamping device)

VISE   *v* **VISEED, VISEING, VISES** to visa

VISELIKE   *adj* resembling a vise

VISIBLE   *adj* capable of being seen **VISIBLY** *adv*

VISION   *v* **-ED, -ING, -S** to imagine

VISIONAL   *adj* imaginary

VISIT   *v* **-ED, -ING, -S** to go or come to see someone or something

VISITANT   *n* pl. **-S** a visitor

VISITER   *n* pl. **-S** visitor

VISITOR   *n* pl. **-S** one that visits

VISIVE   *adj* visible

VISOR   *v* **-ED, -ING, -S** to provide with a visor (a projecting brim)

VISTA   *n* pl. **-S** a distant view **VISTAED** *adj*

VISUAL   *n* pl. **-S** something that illustrates by pictures or diagrams

VISUALLY   *adv* with regard to sight

VITA   *n* pl. **-TAE** a brief, autobiographical sketch

VITAL   *adj* necessary to life

VITALISE   *v* **-ISED, -ISING, -ISES** to vitalize

VITALISM   *n* pl. **-S** a philosophical doctrine

VITALIST   *n* pl. **-S** an advocate of vitalism

VITALITY   *n* pl. **-TIES** exuberant physical strength or mental vigor

VITALIZE   *v* **-IZED, -IZING, -IZES** to give life to

VITALLY   *adv* in a vital manner

VITALS   *n/pl* vital organs

VITAMER   *n* pl. **-S** a type of chemical compound

VITAMIN   *n* pl. **-S** any of various organic substances essential to proper nutrition

VITAMINE   *n* pl. **-S** vitamin

VITELLIN   *n* pl. **-S** a protein found in egg yolk

VITELLUS   *n* pl. **-ES** the yolk of an egg

VITESSE   *n* pl. **-S** speed

VITIATE   *v* **-ATED, -ATING, -ATES** to impair the value or quality of **VITIABLE** *adj*

VITIATOR   *n* pl. **-S** one that vitiates

VITILIGO   *n* pl. **-GOS** a skin disease

VITRAIN   *n* pl. **-S** the material in the vitreous layers of banded bituminous coal

VITREOUS   *n* pl. **-ES** the jelly that fills the eyeball

VITRIC   *adj* pertaining to glass

VITRICS   *n/pl* the art of making or decorating glass articles

VITRIFY   *v* **-FIED, -FYING, -FIES** to convert into glass

VITRINE   *n* pl. **-S** a glass showcase for art objects

VITRIOL   *v* **-OLED, -OLING, -OLS** or **-OLLED, -OLLING, -OLS** to treat with sulfuric acid

VITTA   *n* pl. **-TAE** a streak or band of color **VITTATE** *adj*

VITTLE   *v* **-TLED, -TLING, -TLES** to victual

VITULINE   *adj* pertaining to a calf

VIVA   *n* pl. **-S** a shout or cry used to express approval

VIVACE   *n* pl. **-S** a musical passage played in a brisk spirited manner

VIVACITY   *n* pl. **-TIES** the quality or state of being lively

VIVARIUM   *n* pl. **-IUMS** or **-IA** a place for raising and keeping live animals

VIVARY   *n* pl. **-RIES** vivarium

VIVE   *interj* — used as an exclamation of approval

VIVERRID   *n* pl. **-S** any of a family of small carnivorous mammals

VIVERS   *n/pl* food

VIVID   *adj* **-IDER, -IDEST** strikingly bright or intense **VIVIDLY** *adv*

VIVIFIC   *adj* vivifying

VIVIFIER   *n* pl. **-S** one that vivifies

VIVIFY   *v* **-FIED, -FYING, -FIES** to give life to

VIVIPARA   *n/pl* animals that bring forth living young

VIVISECT   *v* **-ED, -ING, -S** to dissect the living body of

VIXEN   *n* pl. **-S** a shrewish woman **VIXENISH, VIXENLY** *adj*

VIZARD   *n* pl. **-S** a mask **VIZARDED** *adj*

VIZCACHA   *n* pl. **-S** viscacha

VIZIER   *n* pl. **-S** a high official in some Muslim countries

VIZIR   *n* pl. **-S** vizier **VIZIRIAL** *adj*

VIZIRATE   *n* pl. **-S** the office of a vizir

VIZOR   *v* **-ED, -ING, -S** to visor

VIZSLA   *n* pl. **-S** a Hungarian breed of dog

VOCAB   *n* pl. **-S** a vocabulary

VOCABLE   *n* pl. **-S** a word

VOCABLY   *adv* in a manner that may be voiced aloud

VOCAL   *n* pl. **-S** a sound produced with the voice

VOCALESE   *n* pl. **-S** a form of jazz singing

VOCALIC   *n* pl. **-S** a vowel sound

VOCALISE   *v* **-ISED, -ISING, -ISES** to vocalize

VOCALISM   *n* pl. **-S** the act of vocalizing

VOCALIST   *n* pl. **-S** a singer

VOCALITY   *n* pl. **-TIES** possession or exercise of vocal powers

VOCALIZE   *v* **-IZED, -IZING, -IZES** to produce with the voice

VOCALLY *adv* with the voice

VOCATION *n* pl. **-S** the work in which a person is regularly employed

VOCATIVE *n* pl. **-S** a grammatical case used in some languages

VOCES pl. of vox

VOCODER *n* pl. **-S** an electronic device used in transmitting speech signals

VODKA *n* pl. **-S** a liquor

VODOU *n* pl. **-S** vodun

VODOUN *n* pl. **-S** vodun

VODUN *n* pl. **-S** a primitive religion of the West Indies

VOE *n* pl. **-S** a small bay, creek, or inlet

VOGIE *adj* vain

VOGUE *v* **VOGUED, VOGUING** or **VOGUEING, VOGUES** to imitate poses of fashion models

VOGUEING *n* pl. **-S** voguing

VOGUER *n* pl. **-S** one that vogues

VOGUING *n* pl. **-S** a dance consisting of a series of styled poses

VOGUISH *adj* fashionable

VOICE *v* **VOICED, VOICING, VOICES** to express or utter

VOICEFUL *adj* sonorous

VOICER *n* pl. **-S** one that voices

VOICING *n* pl. **-S** the tonal quality of an instrument in an ensemble

VOID *v* **-ED, -ING, -S** to make void (of no legal force or effect) **VOIDABLE** *adj*

VOIDANCE *n* pl. **-S** the act or process of voiding

VOIDER *n* pl. **-S** one that voids

VOIDNESS *n* pl. **-ES** the quality or state of being void

VOILA *interj* — used to call attention to something

VOILE *n* pl. **-S** a sheer fabric

VOLANT *adj* flying or capable of flying

VOLANTE *adj* moving with light rapidity — used as a musical direction

VOLAR *adj* pertaining to flight

VOLATILE *n* pl. **-S** a winged creature

VOLCANIC *n* pl. **-S** a rock produced by a volcano

VOLCANO *n* pl. **-NOS** or **-NOES** an opening in the earth's crust through which molten rock and gases are ejected

VOLE *v* **VOLED, VOLING, VOLES** to win all the tricks in a card game

VOLERY *n* pl. **-ERIES** a large birdcage

VOLITANT *adj* volant

VOLITION *n* pl. **-S** the power of choosing or determining

VOLITIVE *adj* pertaining to volition

VOLLEY *v* **-ED, -ING, -S** to return a tennis ball before it touches the ground

VOLLEYER *n* pl. **-S** one that volleys

VOLOST *n* pl. **-S** an administrative district in Russia

VOLPLANE *v* **-PLANED, -PLANING, -PLANES** to glide in an airplane

VOLT *n* pl. **-S** a unit of electromotive force

VOLTA *n* pl. **-TE** a turning

VOLTAGE *n* pl. **-S** electromotive force expressed in volts

VOLTAISM *n* pl. **-S** electricity produced by chemical action **VOLTAIC** *adj*

VOLTE *n* pl. **-S** a fencing movement

VOLTI *interj* — used to direct musicians to turn the page

VOLUBLE *adj* talkative **VOLUBLY** *adv*

VOLUME *v* **-UMED, -UMING, -UMES** to send or give out in large quantities

VOLUTE *n* pl. **-S** a spiral architectural ornament **VOLUTED** *adj*

VOLUTIN *n* pl. **-S** a granular substance that is common in microorganisms

VOLUTION *n* pl. **-S** a spiral

VOLVA *n* pl. **-S** a membranous sac that encloses certain immature mushrooms **VOLVATE** *adj*

VOLVOX *n* pl. **-ES** any of a genus of freshwater protozoa

VOLVULUS *n* pl. **-LUSES** or **-LI** a twisting of the intestine that causes obstruction

VOMER *n* pl. **-S** a bone of the skull **VOMERINE** *adj*

VOMICA *n* pl. **-CAE** a cavity in the body containing pus

VOMIT *v* **-ED, -ING, -S** to eject the contents of the stomach through the mouth

VOMITER *n* pl. **-S** one that vomits

VOMITIVE *n* pl. **-S** an emetic

VOMITO *n* pl. **-TOS** the black vomit of yellow fever

VOMITORY   *n* pl. **-RIES** an emetic

VOMITOUS   *adj* pertaining to vomiting

VOMITUS   *n* pl. **-ES** vomited matter

VOODOO   *v* **-ED, -ING, -S** to hex

VORACITY   *n* pl. **-TIES** the quality or state of being ravenous

VORLAGE   *n* pl. **-S** a position in skiing

VORTEX   *n* pl. **-TEXES** or **-TICES** a whirling mass of fluid **VORTICAL** *adj*

VOTABLE   *adj* capable of being voted on

VOTARESS   *n* pl. **-ES** a female votary

VOTARIST   *n* pl. **-S** a votary

VOTARY   *n* pl. **-RIES** a person who is bound by religious vows

VOTE   *v* **VOTED, VOTING, VOTES** to cast a vote (a formal expression of will or opinion)

VOTEABLE   *adj* votable

VOTELESS   *adj* having no vote

VOTER   *n* pl. **-S** one that votes

VOTING   present participle of vote

VOTIVE   *n* pl. **-S** a small squat candle

VOTIVELY   *adv* in a manner expressing devotion or gratitude

VOTRESS   *n* pl. **-ES** votaress

VOUCH   *v* **-ED, -ING, -ES** to give one's personal assurance or guarantee

VOUCHEE   *n* pl. **-S** one for whom another vouches

VOUCHER   *v* **-ED, -ING, -S** to establish the authenticity of

VOUDON   *n* pl. **-S** vodun

VOUDOUN   *n* pl. **-S** vodun

VOUSSOIR   *n* pl. **-S** a wedge-shaped building stone

VOUVRAY   *n* pl. **-VRAYS** a French white wine

VOW   *v* **-ED, -ING, -S** to make a vow (a solemn promise)

VOWEL   *n* pl. **-S** a type of speech sound

VOWELIZE   *v* **-IZED, -IZING, -IZES** to provide with symbols used to indicate vowels

VOWER   *n* pl. **-S** one that vows

VOWLESS   *adj* having made no vow

VOX   *n* pl. **VOCES** voice

VOYAGE   *v* **-AGED, -AGING, -AGES** to travel

VOYAGER   *n* pl. **-S** one that voyages

VOYAGEUR   *n* pl. **-S** a person employed by a fur company to transport goods between distant stations

VOYEUR   *n* pl. **-S** one who is sexually gratified by looking at sexual objects or acts

VROOM   *v* **-ED, -ING, -S** to run an engine at high speed

VROUW   *n* pl. **-S** a Dutch woman

VROW   *n* pl. **-S** vrouw

VUG   *n* pl. **-S** a small cavity in a rock or lode

VUGG   *n* pl. **-S** vug

VUGGY   *adj* **-GIER, -GIEST** abounding in vugs

VUGH   *n* pl. **-S** vug

VULCANIC   *adj* pertaining to a volcano

VULGAR   *adj* **-GARER, -GAREST** crude **VULGARLY** *adv*

VULGAR   *n* pl. **-S** a common person

VULGATE   *n* pl. **-S** the common speech of a people

VULGO   *adv* commonly

VULGUS   *n* pl. **-ES** an exercise in Latin formerly required of pupils in some English public schools

VULPINE   *adj* pertaining to a fox

VULTURE   *n* pl. **-S** a bird of prey

VULVA   *n* pl. **-VAS** or **-VAE** the external genital organs of a female **VULVAL, VULVAR, VULVATE** *adj*

VULVITIS   *n* pl. **-TISES** inflammation of the vulva

VUM   *interj* — used to express surprise

VYING   present participle of vie

VYINGLY   *adv* in a vying manner

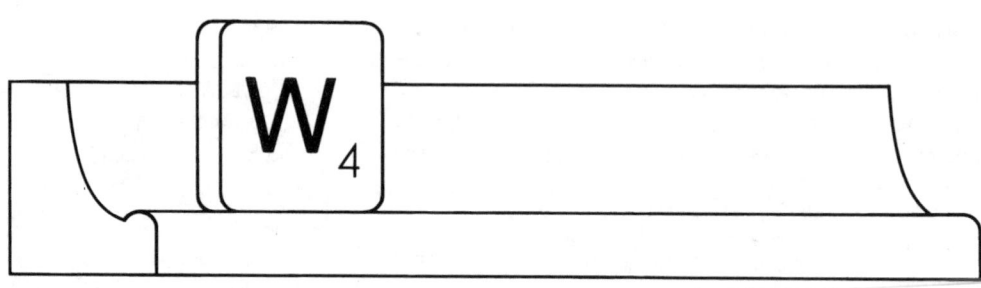

WAB	*n* pl. **-S** a web	**WADMEL**	*n* pl. **-S** wadmal
WABBLE	*v* **-BLED, -BLING, -BLES** to wobble	**WADMOL**	*n* pl. **-S** wadmal
		WADMOLL	*n* pl. **-S** wadmal
WABBLER	*n* pl. **-S** one that wabbles	**WADSET**	*v* **-SETTED, -SETTING, -SETS** to mortgage
WABBLY	*adj* **-BLIER, -BLIEST** wobbly		
WACK	*adj* **WACKER, WACKEST** very bad	**WADY**	*n* pl. **-DIES** wadi
WACK	*n* pl. **-S** a wacky person	**WAE**	*n* pl. **-S** woe
WACKE	*n* pl. **-S** a type of basaltic rock	**WAEFUL**	*adj* woeful
WACKO	*n* pl. **WACKOS** a wacky person	**WAENESS**	*n* pl. **-ES** woeness
WACKY	*adj* **WACKIER, WACKIEST** very irrational **WACKILY** *adv*	**WAESUCK**	*interj* waesucks
		WAESUCKS	*interj* — used to express pity
WAD	*v* **WADDED, WADDING, WADS** to form into a wad (a small mass of soft material)	**WAFER**	*v* **-ED, -ING, -S** to seal with an adhesive disk
		WAFERY	*adj* resembling a wafer (a thin, crisp biscuit)
WADABLE	*adj* wadeable		
WADDER	*n* pl. **-S** one that wads	**WAFF**	*v* **-ED, -ING, -S** to wave
WADDIE	*n* pl. **-S** a cowboy	**WAFFIE**	*n* pl. **-S** a vagabond
WADDIED	past tense of waddy	**WAFFLE**	*v* **-FLED, -FLING, -FLES** to talk vaguely or indecisively
WADDIES	present 3d person sing. of waddy		
WADDING	*n* pl. **-S** a wad	**WAFFLER**	*n* pl. **-S** one that waffles
WADDLE	*v* **-DLED, -DLING, -DLES** to walk with short, swaying steps	**WAFFLING**	*n* pl. **-S** an indecisive statement or position
WADDLER	*n* pl. **-S** one that waddles	**WAFFLY**	*adj* **-FLIER, -FLIEST** indecisive
WADDLY	*adj* having or being a waddling gait	**WAFT**	*v* **-ED, -ING, -S** to carry lightly over air or water
WADDY	*v* **-DIED, -DYING, -DIES** to strike with a thick club	**WAFTAGE**	*n* pl. **-S** the act of wafting
		WAFTER	*n* pl. **-S** one that wafts
WADE	*v* **WADED, WADING, WADES** to walk through water	**WAFTURE**	*n* pl. **-S** waftage
WADEABLE	*adj* capable of being passed through by wading	**WAG**	*v* **WAGGED, WAGGING, WAGS** to move briskly up and down or to and fro
WADER	*n* pl. **-S** one that wades		
WADI	*n* pl. **-S** the bed of a usually dry watercourse	**WAGE**	*v* **WAGED, WAGING, WAGES** to engage in or carry on
		WAGELESS	*adj* unpaid
WADIES	pl. of wady	**WAGER**	*v* **-ED, -ING, -S** to risk on an uncertain outcome
WADING	present participle of wade		
WADMAAL	*n* pl. **-S** wadmal	**WAGERER**	*n* pl. **-S** one that wagers
WADMAL	*n* pl. **-S** a thick woolen fabric	**WAGGED**	past tense of wag

WAGGER *n* pl. **-S** one that wags

WAGGERY *n* pl. **-GERIES** waggish behavior

WAGGING present participle of wag

WAGGISH *adj* playfully humorous

WAGGLE *v* **-GLED, -GLING, -GLES** to wag

WAGGLY *adj* **-GLIER, -GLIEST** unsteady

WAGGON *v* **-ED, -ING, -S** to wagon

WAGGONER *n* pl. **-S** wagoner

WAGING present participle of wage

WAGON *v* **-ED, -ING, -S** to convey by wagon (a four-wheeled, horse-drawn vehicle)

WAGONAGE *n* pl. **-S** conveyance by wagon

WAGONER *n* pl. **-S** one who drives a wagon

WAGSOME *adj* waggish

WAGTAIL *n* pl. **-S** a songbird

WAHCONDA *n* pl. **-S** wakanda

WAHINE *n* pl. **-S** a Hawaiian woman

WAHOO *n* pl. **-HOOS** a flowering shrub

WAIF *v* **-ED, -ING, -S** to throw away

WAIFISH *adj* waiflike

WAIFLIKE *adj* resembling a waif (a homeless child)

WAIL *v* **-ED, -ING, -S** to utter a long, mournful cry

WAILER *n* pl. **-S** one that wails

WAILFUL *adj* mournful

WAILSOME *adj* wailful

WAIN *n* pl. **-S** a large, open wagon

WAINSCOT *v* **-SCOTED, -SCOTING, -SCOTS** or **-SCOTTED, -SCOTTING, -SCOTS** to line the walls of with wooden paneling

WAIR *v* **-ED, -ING, -S** to spend

WAIST *n* pl. **-S** the part of the body between the ribs and the hips **WAISTED** *adj*

WAISTER *n* pl. **-S** a seaman stationed in the middle section of a ship

WAISTING *n* pl. **-S** a type of dressmaking material

WAIT *v* **-ED, -ING, -S** to stay in expectation of

WAITER *v* **-ED, -ING, -S** to work as a male server in a restaurant

WAITING *n* pl. **-S** the act of one who waits

WAITLIST *v* **-ED, -ING, -S** to put on a list of persons waiting

WAITRESS *v* **-ED, -ING, -ES** to work as a female server in a restaurant

WAITRON *n* pl. **-S** a server in a restaurant

WAIVE *v* **WAIVED, WAIVING, WAIVES** to give up intentionally

WAIVER *n* pl. **-S** the act of waiving something

WAKAME *n* pl. **-S** a brown seaweed native to Asia

WAKANDA *n* pl. **-S** a supernatural force in Sioux beliefs

WAKE *v* **WAKED** or **WOKE, WOKEN, WAKING, WAKES** to rouse from sleep

WAKEFUL *adj* not sleeping or able to sleep

WAKELESS *adj* unbroken — used of sleep

WAKEN *v* **-ED, -ING, -S** to wake

WAKENER *n* pl. **-S** one that wakens

WAKENING *n* pl. **-S** the act of one that wakens

WAKER *n* pl. **-S** one that wakes

WAKERIFE *adj* wakeful

WAKIKI *n* pl. **-S** shell money of the South Sea Islands

WAKING present participle of wake

WALE *v* **WALED, WALING, WALES** to mark with welts

WALER *n* pl. **-S** an Australian-bred saddle horse

WALIES pl. of waly

WALK *v* **-ED, -ING, -S** to advance on foot **WALKABLE** *adj*

WALKAWAY *n* pl. **-AWAYS** an easy victory

WALKER *n* pl. **-S** one that walks

WALKING *n* pl. **-S** the act of one that walks

WALKOUT *n* pl. **-S** a strike by workers

WALKOVER *n* pl. **-S** a walkaway

WALKUP *n* pl. **-S** an apartment house having no elevator

WALKWAY *n* pl. **-WAYS** a passage for walking

WALKYRIE *n* pl. **-S** valkyrie

WALL *v* **-ED, -ING, -S** to provide with a wall (an upright structure built to enclose an area)

WALLA *n* pl. **-S** wallah

WALLABY *n* pl. **-BIES** a small kangaroo

WALLAH *n* pl. **-S** a person engaged in a particular occupation or activity

WALLAROO *n* pl. **-ROOS** a large kangaroo

WALLET *n* pl. **-S** a flat folding case

WALLEYE *n* pl. **-S** an eye having a white cornea **WALLEYED** *adj*

WALLIE *n* pl. **-S** a valet

WALLIES pl. of wally

WALLOP *v* **-ED, -ING, -S** to beat soundly

WALLOPER *n* pl. **-S** one that wallops

WALLOW *v* **-ED, -ING, -S** to roll about

WALLOWER *n* pl. **-S** one that wallows

WALLY *n* pl. **-LIES** waly

WALNUT *n* pl. **-S** an edible nut

WALRUS *n* pl. **-ES** a marine mammal

WALTZ *v* **-ED, -ING, -ES** to perform a ballroom dance

WALTZER *n* pl. **-S** one that waltzes

WALY *n* pl. **WALIES** something visually pleasing

WAMBLE *v* **-BLED, -BLING, -BLES** to move unsteadily

WAMBLY *adj* **-BLIER, -BLIEST** unsteady

WAME *n* pl. **-S** the belly

WAMEFOU *n* pl. **-S** a bellyful

WAMEFUL *n* pl. **-S** wamefou

WAMMUS *n* pl. **-ES** wamus

WAMPISH *v* **-ED, -ING, -ES** to throw about

WAMPUM *n* pl. **-S** a form of currency formerly used by North American Indians

WAMPUS *n* pl. **-ES** wamus

WAMUS *n* pl. **-ES** a heavy outer jacket

WAN *adj* **WANNER, WANNEST** unnaturally pale

WAN *v* **WANNED, WANNING, WANS** to become wan

WAND *n* pl. **-S** a slender rod

WANDER *v* **-ED, -ING, -S** to move about with no destination or purpose

WANDERER *n* pl. **-S** one that wanders

WANDEROO *n* pl. **-ROOS** an Asian monkey

WANDLE *adj* supple

WANE *v* **WANED, WANING, WANES** to decrease in size or extent

WANEY *adj* **WANIER, WANIEST** wany

WANGAN *n* pl. **-S** wanigan

WANGLE *v* **-GLED, -GLING, -GLES** to obtain or accomplish by contrivance

WANGLER *n* pl. **-S** one that wangles

WANGUN *n* pl. **-S** wanigan

WANIER comparative of waney and wany

WANIEST superlative of waney and wany

WANIGAN *n* pl. **-S** a supply chest used in a logging camp

WANING present participle of wane

WANION *n* pl. **-S** vengeance

WANLY *adv* in a wan manner

WANNABE *n* pl. **-S** one who aspires to be like someone else

WANNABEE *n* **-S** wannabe

WANNED past tense of wan

WANNER comparative of wan

WANNESS *n* pl. **-ES** the quality of being wan

WANNEST superlative of wan

WANNIGAN *n* pl. **-S** wanigan

WANNING present participle of wan

WANT *v* **-ED, -ING, -S** to have a desire for

WANTAGE *n* pl. **-S** something that is lacking

WANTER *n* pl. **-S** one that wants

WANTON *v* **-ED, -ING, -S** to behave immorally

WANTONER *n* pl. **-S** one that wantons

WANTONLY *adv* immorally

WANY *adj* **WANIER, WANIEST** waning in some parts

WAP *v* **WAPPED, WAPPING, WAPS** to wrap

WAPITI *n* pl. **-S** a large deer

WAR *v* **WARRED, WARRING, WARS** to engage in war (a state of open, armed conflict)

WARBLE *v* **-BLED, -BLING, -BLES** to sing with melodic embellishments

WARBLER *n* pl. **-S** one that warbles

WARCRAFT *n* pl. **-S** the art of war

WARD *v* **-ED, -ING, -S** to turn aside

WARDEN *n* pl. **-S** the chief officer of a prison

WARDENRY *n* pl. **-RIES** the office of a warden

WARDER *n* pl. **-S** a person who guards something

WARDLESS *adj* having no ward (part of a lock casing)

WARDRESS *n* pl. **-ES** a female warden

WARDROBE *n* pl. **-S** a collection of garments

WARDROBE *v* **-ROBED, -ROBING, -ROBES** to provide with a collection of garments

WARDROOM *n* pl. **-S** a dining area for officers on a warship

WARDSHIP	*n* pl. **-S** the state of being under a guardian
WARE	*v* **WARED, WARING, WARES** to beware of
WAREROOM	*n* pl. **-S** a room in which goods are displayed for sale
WARFARE	*n* pl. **-S** the act of engaging in war
WARFARIN	*n* pl. **-S** a chemical compound
WARHEAD	*n* pl. **-S** the front part of a missile containing the explosive
WARHORSE	*n* pl. **-S** a musical or dramatic work that has been performed to excess
WARIER	comparative of wary
WARIEST	superlative of wary
WARILY	*adv* in a wary manner
WARINESS	*n* pl. **-ES** the state of being wary
WARING	present participle of ware
WARISON	*n* pl. **-S** a call to attack
WARK	*v* **-ED, -ING, -S** to endure pain
WARLESS	*adj* free from war
WARLIKE	*adj* disposed to engage in war
WARLOCK	*n* pl. **-S** a sorcerer
WARLORD	*n* pl. **-S** a military leader of a warlike nation
WARM	*adj* **WARMER, WARMEST** moderately hot
WARM	*v* **-ED, -ING, -S** to make warm
WARMAKER	*n* pl. **-S** one that wars
WARMER	*n* pl. **-S** one that warms
WARMISH	*adj* somewhat warm
WARMLY	*adv* in a warm manner
WARMNESS	*n* pl. **-ES** the state of being warm
WARMOUTH	*n* pl. **-S** a freshwater fish
WARMTH	*n* pl. **-S** warmness
WARMUP	*n* pl. **-S** a preparatory exercise or procedure
WARN	*v* **-ED, -ING, -S** to make aware of impending or possible danger
WARNER	*n* pl. **-S** one that warns
WARNING	*n* pl. **-S** something that warns
WARP	*v* **-ED, -ING, -S** to turn or twist out of shape
WARPAGE	*n* pl. **-S** the act of warping
WARPATH	*n* pl. **-S** the route taken by attacking American Indians
WARPER	*n* pl. **-S** one that warps
WARPLANE	*n* pl. **-S** an airplane armed for combat

WARPOWER	*n* pl. **-S** the power to make war
WARPWISE	*adv* in a vertical direction
WARRAGAL	*n* pl. **-S** warrigal
WARRANT	*v* **-ED, -ING, -S** to give authority to
WARRANTY	*v* **-TIED, -TYING, -TIES** to provide a written guarantee for
WARRED	past tense of war
WARREN	*n* pl. **-S** a place where rabbits live and breed
WARRENER	*n* pl. **-S** the keeper of a warren
WARRIGAL	*n* pl. **-S** a dingo
WARRING	present participle of war
WARRIOR	*n* pl. **-S** one engaged or experienced in warfare
WARSAW	*n* pl. **-S** a marine fish
WARSHIP	*n* pl. **-S** a ship armed for combat
WARSLE	*v* **-SLED, -SLING, -SLES** to wrestle
WARSLER	*n* pl. **-S** a wrestler
WARSTLE	*v* **-TLED, -TLING, -TLES** to wrestle
WARSTLER	*n* pl. **-S** a wrestler
WART	*n* pl. **-S** a protuberance on the skin **WARTED** *adj*
WARTHOG	*n* pl. **-S** an African wild hog
WARTIER	comparative of warty
WARTIEST	superlative of warty
WARTIME	*n* pl. **-S** a time of war
WARTLESS	*adj* having no warts
WARTLIKE	*adj* resembling a wart
WARTY	*adj* **WARTIER, WARTIEST** covered with warts
WARWORK	*n* pl. **-S** work done during a war
WARWORN	*adj* showing the effects of war
WARY	*adj* **WARIER, WARIEST** watchful
WAS	1st and 3d person sing. past indicative of be
WASABI	*n* pl. **-S** a pungent herb
WASH	*v* **-ED, -ING, -ES** to cleanse by immersing in or applying a liquid
WASHABLE	*n* pl. **-S** something that can be washed without damage
WASHBOWL	*n* pl. **-S** a bowl used for washing oneself
WASHDAY	*n* pl. **-DAYS** a day set aside for washing clothes
WASHER	*n* pl. **-S** one that washes
WASHIER	comparative of washy

WASHIEST	superlative of washy
WASHING	*n* pl. **-S** articles washed or to be washed
WASHOUT	*n* pl. **-S** an erosion of earth by the action of water
WASHRAG	*n* pl. **-S** a small cloth used for washing oneself
WASHROOM	*n* pl. **-S** a lavatory
WASHTUB	*n* pl. **-S** a tub used for washing clothes
WASHUP	*n* pl. **-S** the act of washing clean
WASHY	*adj* **WASHIER, WASHIEST** overly diluted
WASP	*n* pl. **-S** a stinging insect **WASPISH, WASPLIKE** *adj*
WASPY	*adj* **WASPIER, WASPIEST** resembling a wasp **WASPILY** *adv*
WASSAIL	*v* **-ED, -ING, -S** to drink to the health of
WAST	*n* pl. **-S** west
WASTABLE	*adj* capable of being wasted
WASTAGE	*n* pl. **-S** something that is wasted
WASTE	*v* **WASTED, WASTING, WASTES** to use thoughtlessly
WASTEFUL	*adj* tending to waste
WASTELOT	*n* pl. **-S** a vacant lot
WASTER	*n* pl. **-S** one that wastes
WASTERIE	*n* pl. **-S** wastry
WASTERY	*n* pl. **-RIES** wastry
WASTEWAY	*n* pl. **-WAYS** a channel for excess water
WASTING	present participle of waste
WASTREL	*n* pl. **-S** one that wastes
WASTRIE	*n* pl. **-S** wastry
WASTRY	*n* pl. **-RIES** reckless extravagance
WAT	*adj* **WATTER, WATTEST** wet
WAT	*n* pl. **-S** a hare
WATAP	*n* pl. **-S** a thread made from the roots of various trees
WATAPE	*n* pl. **-S** watap
WATCH	*v* **-ED, -ING, -ES** to observe carefully
WATCHCRY	*n* pl. **-CRIES** a password
WATCHDOG	*v* **-DOGGED, -DOGGING, -DOGS** to act as a guardian for
WATCHER	*n* pl. **-S** one that watches
WATCHEYE	*n* pl. **-S** a walleye
WATCHFUL	*adj* closely observant or alert
WATCHMAN	*n* pl. **-MEN** a man employed to stand guard
WATCHOUT	*n* pl. **-S** the act of looking out for something
WATER	*v* **-ED, -ING, -S** to sprinkle with water (a transparent, odorless, tasteless liquid)
WATERAGE	*n* pl. **-S** the conveyance of goods by water
WATERBED	*n* pl. **-S** a bed whose mattress is a plastic bag filled with water
WATERBUS	*n* pl. **-BUSES** or **-BUSSES** a large motorboat for carrying passengers
WATERDOG	*n* pl. **-S** a large salamander
WATERER	*n* pl. **-S** one that waters
WATERHEN	*n* pl. **-S** the American coot
WATERIER	comparative of watery
WATERIEST	superlative of watery
WATERILY	*adv* in a watery manner
WATERING	*n* pl. **-S** the act of one that waters
WATERISH	*adj* watery
WATERJET	*n* pl. **-S** a stream of water forced through a small opening
WATERLOG	*v* **-LOGGED, -LOGGING, -LOGS** to soak with water
WATERLOO	*n* pl. **-LOOS** a decisive defeat
WATERMAN	*n* pl. **-MEN** a boatman
WATERSKI	*n* pl. **-S** a ski for skiing on water
WATERWAY	*n* pl. **-WAYS** a navigable body of water
WATERY	*adj* **-TERIER, -TERIEST** containing water
WATT	*n* pl. **-S** a unit of power
WATTAGE	*n* pl. **-S** an amount of power in terms of watts
WATTAPE	*n* pl. **-S** watap
WATTER	comparative of wat
WATTEST	superlative of wat
WATTHOUR	*n* pl. **-S** a unit of energy
WATTLE	*v* **-TLED, -TLING, -TLES** to weave into a network
WATTLESS	*adj* denoting a type of electric current
WAUCHT	*v* **-ED, -ING, -S** to waught
WAUGH	*adj* damp
WAUGHT	*v* **-ED, -ING, -S** to drink deeply
WAUK	*v* **-ED, -ING, -S** to wake
WAUL	*v* **-ED, -ING, -S** to cry like a cat
WAUR	*adj* worse

WAVE   *v* **WAVED, WAVING, WAVES** to move freely back and forth or up and down

WAVEBAND   *n* pl. **-S** a range of radio frequencies

WAVEFORM   *n* pl. **-S** a type of mathematical graph

WAVELESS   *adj* having no waves (moving ridges on the surface of a liquid)

WAVELET   *n* pl. **-S** a small wave

WAVELIKE   *adj* resembling a wave

WAVEOFF   *n* pl. **-S** the act of denying landing permission to an approaching aircraft

WAVER   *v* **-ED, -ING, -S** to move back and forth

WAVERER   *n* pl. **-S** one that wavers

WAVERY   *adj* wavering

WAVEY   *n* pl. **-VEYS** the snow goose

WAVICLE   *n* pl. **-S** a subatomic particle that can act like both a wave and a particle

WAVIER   comparative of wavy

WAVIES   pl. of wavy

WAVIEST   superlative of wavy

WAVILY   *adv* in a wavy manner

WAVINESS   *n* pl. **-ES** the state of being wavy

WAVING   present participle of wave

WAVY   *adj* **WAVIER, WAVIEST** having waves

WAVY   *n* pl. **-VIES** wavey

WAW   *n* pl. **-S** vav

WAWL   *v* **-ED, -ING, -S** to waul

WAX   *v* **-ED, -ING, -ES** to coat with wax (a natural, heat-sensitive substance) **WAXABLE** *adj*

WAXBERRY   *n* pl. **-RIES** a berry with a waxy coating

WAXBILL   *n* pl. **-S** a tropical bird

WAXEN   *adj* covered with wax

WAXER   *n* pl. **-S** one that waxes

WAXIER   comparative of waxy

WAXIEST   superlative of waxy

WAXILY   *adv* in a waxy manner

WAXINESS   *n* pl. **-ES** the quality of being waxy

WAXING   *n* pl. **-S** the act of one that waxes

WAXLIKE   *adj* resembling wax

WAXPLANT   *n* pl. **-S** a tropical plant

WAXWEED   *n* pl. **-S** an annual herb

WAXWING   *n* pl. **-S** a type of passerine bird

WAXWORK   *n* pl. **-S** an effigy made of wax

WAXWORM   *n* pl. **-S** a moth that infests beehives

WAXY   *adj* **WAXIER, WAXIEST** resembling wax

WAY   *n* pl. **WAYS** a method of doing something

WAYBILL   *n* pl. **-S** a list of goods relative to a shipment

WAYFARER   *n* pl. **-S** a traveler

WAYGOING   *n* pl. **-S** the act of leaving

WAYLAY   *v* **-LAID, -LAYING, -LAYS** to ambush

WAYLAYER   *n* pl. **-S** one that waylays

WAYLESS   *adj* having no road or path

WAYPOINT   *n* pl. **-S** a point between major points along a route

WAYSIDE   *n* pl. **-S** the side of a road

WAYWARD   *adj* willful

WAYWORN   *adj* fatigued by travel

WE   *pron* 1st person pl. pronoun in the nominative case

WEAK   *adj* **WEAKER, WEAKEST** lacking strength

WEAKEN   *v* **-ED, -ING, -S** to make weak

WEAKENER   *n* pl. **-S** one that weakens

WEAKFISH   *n* pl. **-ES** a marine fish

WEAKISH   *adj* somewhat weak

WEAKLING   *n* pl. **-S** a weak person

WEAKLY   *adj* **-LIER, -LIEST** weak and sickly

WEAKNESS   *n* pl. **-ES** the state of being weak

WEAKON   *n* pl. **-S** a subatomic particle

WEAKSIDE   *n* pl. **-S** the side of a basketball court with fewer players

WEAL   *n* pl. **-S** a welt

WEALD   *n* pl. **-S** a woodland

WEALTH   *n* pl. **-S** a great quantity of valuable material

WEALTHY   *adj* **WEALTHIER, WEALTHIEST** having wealth

WEAN   *v* **-ED, -ING, -S** to withhold mother's milk from and substitute other nourishment

WEANER   *n* pl. **-S** one that weans

WEANLING   *n* pl. **-S** a recently weaned child or animal

WEAPON *v* **-ED, -ING, -S** to supply with a weapon (an instrument used in combat)

WEAPONRY *n pl.* **-RIES** an aggregate of weapons

WEAR *v* **WORE, WORN, WEARING, WEARS** to have on one's person

WEARABLE *n pl.* **-S** a garment

WEARER *n pl.* **-S** one that wears something

WEARIED past tense of weary

WEARIER comparative of weary

WEARIES present 3d person sing. of weary

WEARIFUL *adj* tiresome

WEARISH *adj* tasteless

WEARY *adj* **-RIER, -RIEST** tired **WEARILY** *adv*

WEARY *v* **-RIED, -RYING, -RIES** to make or become weary

WEASAND *n pl.* **-S** the throat

WEASEL *v* **-SELED, -SELING, -SELS** or **-SELLED, -SELLING, -SELS** to act evasively

WEASELLY *adj* resembling a weasel (a small carnivorous mammal)

WEASELY *adj* weaselly

WEASON *n pl.* **-S** weasand

WEATHER *v* **-ED, -ING, -S** to expose to atmospheric conditions

WEAVE *v* **WOVE** or **WEAVED, WOVEN, WEAVING, WEAVES** to form by interlacing threads

WEAVER *n pl.* **-S** one that weaves

WEAZAND *n pl.* **-S** weasand

WEB *v* **WEBBED, WEBBING, WEBS** to provide with a web (an interlaced fabric or structure)

WEBBING *n pl.* **-S** a woven strip of fiber

WEBBY *adj* **-BIER, -BIEST** weblike

WEBCAM *n pl.* **-S** a camera used for transmitting live images over the World Wide Web

WEBCAST *v* **-ED, -ING, -S** to transmit sound and images via the World Wide Web

WEBER *n pl.* **-S** a unit of magnetic flux

WEBFED *adj* designed to print a continuous roll of paper

WEBFOOT *n pl.* **-FEET** a foot having the toes joined by a membrane

WEBLESS *adj* having no webs

WEBLIKE *adj* resembling a web

WEBLOG *n pl.* **-S** a website that contains an online personal journal

WEBPAGE *n pl.* **-S** a single document on the World Wide Web

WEBSITE *n pl.* **-S** a set of interconnected webpages maintained by an individual or organization

WEBSTER *n pl.* **-S** a weaver

WEBWORK *n pl.* **-S** a weblike pattern or structure

WEBWORM *n pl.* **-S** a web-spinning caterpillar

WECHT *n pl.* **-S** weight

WED *v* **WEDDED, WEDDING, WEDS** to marry

WEDDER *n pl.* **-S** one that weds

WEDDING *n pl.* **-S** a marriage ceremony

WEDEL *v* **-ED, -ING, -S** to perform a wedeln

WEDELN *n pl.* **-S** a skiing technique

WEDGE *v* **WEDGED, WEDGING, WEDGES** to force apart with a wedge (a tapering piece of wood or metal)

WEDGIE *n pl.* **-S** a type of woman's shoe

WEDGY *adj* **WEDGIER, WEDGIEST** resembling a wedge

WEDLOCK *n pl.* **-S** the state of being married

WEE *adj* **WEER, WEEST** very small

WEE *n pl.* **-S** a short time

WEED *v* **-ED, -ING, -S** to remove weeds (undesirable plants)

WEEDER *n pl.* **-S** one that weeds

WEEDIER comparative of weedy

WEEDIEST superlative of weedy

WEEDILY *adv* in a weedy manner

WEEDLESS *adj* having no weeds

WEEDLIKE *adj* resembling a weed

WEEDY *adj* **WEEDIER, WEEDIEST** resembling a weed

WEEK *n pl.* **-S** a period of seven days

WEEKDAY *n pl.* **-DAYS** any day of the week except Saturday and Sunday

WEEKEND *v* **-ED, -ING, -S** to spend the weekend (the end of the week)

WEEKLONG *adj* continuing for a week

WEEKLY *n pl.* **-LIES** a publication issued once a week

WEEL *adj* well

WEEN *v* **-ED, -ING, -S** to suppose

WEENIE *n pl.* **-S** a wiener

WEENSY *adj* **-SIER, -SIEST** tiny

WEENY *adj* **-NIER, -NIEST** tiny

WEEP *v* **WEPT, WEEPING, WEEPS** to express sorrow by shedding tears

WEEPER *n* pl. **-S** one that weeps

WEEPIE *n* pl. **-S** a very maudlin movie

WEEPING *n* pl. **-S** the act of one that weeps

WEEPY *adj* **WEEPIER, WEEPIEST** tending to weep

WEER comparative of wee

WEEST superlative of wee

WEET *v* **-ED, -ING, -S** to know

WEEVER *n* pl. **-S** a marine fish

WEEVIL *n* pl. **-S** a small beetle **WEEVILED, WEEVILLY, WEEVILY** *adj*

WEEWEE *v* **-WEED, -WEEING, -WEES** to urinate

WEFT *n* pl. **-S** a woven fabric or garment

WEFTWISE *adv* in a horizontal direction

WEIGELA *n* pl. **-S** a flowering shrub

WEIGELIA *n* pl. **-S** weigela

WEIGH *v* **-ED, -ING, -S** to determine the weight of

WEIGHER *n* pl. **-S** one that weighs

WEIGHMAN *n* pl. **-MEN** one whose occupation is weighing goods

WEIGHT *v* **-ED, -ING, -S** to add weight (heaviness) to

WEIGHTER *n* pl. **-S** one that weights

WEIGHTY *adj* **WEIGHTIER, WEIGHTIEST** having great weight

WEINER *n* pl. **-S** wiener

WEIR *n* pl. **-S** a fence placed in a stream to catch fish

WEIRD *v* **-ED, -ING, -S** to cause to experience a strange sensation

WEIRD *adj* **WEIRDER, WEIRDEST** mysteriously strange

WEIRD *n* pl. **-S** destiny

WEIRDIE *n* pl. **-S** a very strange person

WEIRDIES pl. of weirdy

WEIRDLY *adv* in a weird manner

WEIRDO *n* pl. **WEIRDOES** or **WEIRDOS** a weirdie

WEIRDY *n* pl. **WEIRDIES** weirdie

WEKA *n* pl. **-S** a flightless bird

WELCH *v* **-ED, -ING, -ES** to welsh

WELCHER *n* pl. **-S** one that welshes

WELCOME *v* **-COMED, -COMING, -COMES** to greet cordially

WELCOMER *n* pl. **-S** one that welcomes

WELD *v* **-ED, -ING, -S** to join by applying heat **WELDABLE** *adj*

WELDER *n* pl. **-S** one that welds

WELDLESS *adj* having no welded joints

WELDMENT *n* pl. **-S** a unit composed of welded pieces

WELDOR *n* pl. **-S** welder

WELFARE *n* pl. **-S** general well-being

WELKIN *n* pl. **-S** the sky

WELL *v* **-ED, -ING, -S** to rise to the surface and flow forth

WELLADAY *n* pl. **-DAYS** wellaway

WELLAWAY *n* pl. **-WAYS** an expression of sorrow

WELLBORN *adj* of good birth or ancestry

WELLCURB *n* pl. **-S** the stone ring around a well (a hole dug in the ground to obtain water)

WELLDOER *n* pl. **-S** a doer of good deeds

WELLHEAD *n* pl. **-S** the source of a spring or stream

WELLHOLE *n* pl. **-S** the shaft of a well

WELLIE *n* pl. **-S** a Wellington boot

WELLIES pl. of welly

WELLNESS *n* pl. **-ES** the state of being healthy

WELLSITE *n* pl. **-S** a mineral

WELLY *n* pl. **-LIES** wellie

WELSH *v* **-ED, -ING, -ES** to fail to pay a debt

WELSHER *n* pl. **-S** one that welshes

WELT *v* **-ED, -ING, -S** to mark with welts (ridges or lumps raised on the skin)

WELTER *v* **-ED, -ING, -S** to roll about

WELTING *n* pl. **-S** a cord or strip used to reinforce a seam

WEN *n* pl. **-S** a benign tumor of the skin

WENCH *v* **-ED, -ING, -ES** to consort with prostitutes

WENCHER *n* pl. **-S** one that wenches

WEND *v* **-ED, -ING, -S** to proceed along

WENDIGO *n* pl. **-GOS** windigo

WENNISH *adj* wenny

WENNY *adj* **-NIER, -NIEST** resembling a wen

WENT past tense of go

WEPT	past tense of weep
WERE	a pl. and 2d person sing. past indicative, and past subjunctive of be
WEREGILD	n pl. **-S** wergeld
WEREWOLF	n pl. **-WOLVES** a person capable of assuming the form of a wolf
WERGELD	n pl. **-S** a price paid for the taking of a man's life in Anglo-Saxon law
WERGELT	n pl. **-S** wergeld
WERGILD	n pl. **-S** wergeld
WERT	a 2d person sing. past tense of be
WERWOLF	n pl. **-WOLVES** werewolf
WESKIT	n pl. **-S** a vest
WESSAND	n pl. **-S** weasand
WEST	n pl. **-S** a cardinal point of the compass
WESTER	v **-ED, -ING, -S** to move toward the west
WESTERLY	n pl. **-LIES** a wind from the west
WESTERN	n pl. **-S** one who lives in the west
WESTING	n pl. **-S** a shifting west
WESTMOST	adj farthest west
WESTWARD	n pl. **-S** a direction toward the west
WET	adj **WETTER, WETTEST** covered or saturated with a liquid
WET	v **WETTED, WETTING, WETS** to make wet
WETHER	n pl. **-S** a gelded male sheep
WETLAND	n pl. **-S** land containing much soil moisture
WETLY	adv in a wet manner
WETNESS	n pl. **-ES** the state of being wet
WETPROOF	adj waterproof
WETSUIT	n pl. **-S** a close-fitting rubberlike suit worn in cold water by skin divers
WETTABLE	adj capable of being wetted
WETTED	past tense of wet
WETTER	n pl. **-S** one that wets
WETTEST	superlative of wet
WETTING	n pl. **-S** a liquid used in moistening something
WETTISH	adj somewhat wet
WETWARE	n pl. **-S** the human brain when considered as functionally equivalent to a computer
WHA	pron who
WHACK	v **-ED, -ING, -S** to strike sharply

WHACKER	n pl. **-S** one that whacks
WHACKO	n pl. **WHACKOS** wacko
WHACKY	adj **WHACKIER, WHACKIEST** wacky
WHALE	v **WHALED, WHALING, WHALES** to engage in the hunting of whales (large marine mammals)
WHALEMAN	n pl. **-MEN** a whaler
WHALER	n pl. **-S** a person engaged in whaling
WHALING	n pl. **-S** the industry of hunting and processing whales
WHAM	v **WHAMMED, WHAMMING, WHAMS** to hit with a loud impact
WHAMMO	interj — used to indicate a startling event
WHAMMY	n pl. **-MIES** a supernatural spell bringing bad luck
WHAMO	interj whammo
WHANG	v **-ED, -ING, -S** to beat with a whip
WHANGEE	n pl. **-S** an Asian grass
WHAP	v **WHAPPED, WHAPPING, WHAPS** to whop
WHAPPER	n pl. **-S** whopper
WHARF	v **-ED, -ING, -S** to moor to a wharf (a docking place for vessels)
WHARFAGE	n pl. **-S** the use of a wharf
WHARVE	n pl. **-S** a round piece of wood used in spinning thread
WHAT	n pl. **-S** the true nature of something
WHATEVER	adj being what or who it may be
WHATNESS	n pl. **-ES** the true nature of something
WHATNOT	n pl. **-S** an ornamental set of shelves
WHATSIS	n pl. **-SISES** whatsit
WHATSIT	n pl. **-S** something whose name is unknown or forgotten
WHAUP	n pl. **-S** a European bird
WHEAL	n pl. **-S** a welt
WHEAT	n pl. **-S** a cereal grass
WHEATEAR	n pl. **-S** a small bird of northern regions
WHEATEN	n pl. **-S** a pale yellowish color
WHEE	interj — used to express delight
WHEEDLE	v **-DLED, -DLING, -DLES** to attempt to persuade by flattery
WHEEDLER	n pl. **-S** one that wheedles

WHEEL *v* **-ED, -ING, -S** to convey on wheels (circular frames designed to turn on an axis)

WHEELER *n* pl. **-S** one that wheels

WHEELIE *n* pl. **-S** a maneuver made on a wheeled vehicle

WHEELING *n* pl. **-S** the condition of a road for vehicles

WHEELMAN *n* pl. **-MEN** a helmsman

WHEEN *n* pl. **-S** a fairly large amount

WHEEP *v* **-ED, -ING, -S** to wheeple

WHEEPLE *v* **-PLED, -PLING, -PLES** to give forth a prolonged whistle

WHEEZE *v* **WHEEZED, WHEEZING, WHEEZES** to breathe with a whistling sound

WHEEZER *n* pl. **-S** one that wheezes

WHEEZY *adj* **WHEEZIER, WHEEZIEST** characterized by wheezing **WHEEZILY** *adv*

WHELK *n* pl. **-S** a pustule

WHELKY *adj* **WHELKIER, WHELKIEST** marked with whelks

WHELM *v* **-ED, -ING, -S** to cover with water

WHELP *v* **-ED, -ING, -S** to give birth to

WHEN *n* pl. **-S** the time in which something is done or occurs

WHENAS *conj* at which time

WHENCE *conj* from what place

WHENEVER *conj* at whatever time

WHERE *n* pl. **-S** the place at or in which something is located or occurs

WHEREAS *n* pl. **-ES** an introductory statement of a formal document

WHEREAT *conj* at which

WHEREBY *conj* by which

WHEREIN *conj* in which

WHEREOF *conj* of which

WHEREON *conj* on which

WHERETO *conj* to which

WHEREVER *conj* in or to whatever place

WHERRY *v* **-RIED, -RYING, -RIES** to transport in a light rowboat

WHERVE *n* pl. **-S** wharve

WHET *v* **WHETTED, WHETTING, WHETS** to sharpen by friction

WHETHER *conj* if it be the case that

WHETTER *n* pl. **-S** one that whets

WHEW *n* pl. **-S** a whistling sound

WHEY *n* pl. **WHEYS** the watery part of milk **WHEYEY, WHEYISH** *adj*

WHEYFACE *n* pl. **-S** a pale, sallow face

WHEYLIKE *adj* resembling whey

WHICH *pron* what particular one or ones

WHICKER *v* **-ED, -ING, -S** to whinny

WHID *v* **WHIDDED, WHIDDING, WHIDS** to move rapidly and quietly

WHIDAH *n* pl. **-S** whydah

WHIFF *v* **-ED, -ING, -S** to blow or convey with slight gusts of air

WHIFFER *n* pl. **-S** one that whiffs

WHIFFET *n* pl. **-S** an insignificant person

WHIFFLE *v* **-FLED, -FLING, -FLES** to move or think erratically

WHIFFLER *n* pl. **-S** one that whiffles

WHIG *n* pl. **-S** one who interprets history as a continuing victory of progress over reactionary forces

WHILE *v* **WHILED, WHILING, WHILES** to cause to pass pleasantly

WHILOM *adv* formerly

WHILST *conj* during the time that

WHIM *n* pl. **-S** an impulsive idea

WHIMBREL *n* pl. **-S** a shore bird

WHIMPER *v* **-ED, -ING, -S** to cry with plaintive, broken sounds

WHIMSEY *n* pl. **-SEYS** whimsy

WHIMSY *n* pl. **-SIES** a whim **WHIMSIED** *adj*

WHIN *n* pl. **-S** furze

WHINCHAT *n* pl. **-S** a songbird

WHINE *v* **WHINED, WHINING, WHINES** to utter a plaintive, high-pitched sound

WHINER *n* pl. **-S** one that whines

WHINEY *adj* **WHINIER, WHINIEST** whiny

WHINGE *v* **WHINGED, WHINGEING** or **WHINGING, WHINGES** to whine

WHINGER *n* pl. **-S** one that whinges

WHINIER comparative of whiny

WHINIEST superlative of whiny

WHINING present participle of whine

WHINNY *adj* **-NIER, -NIEST** abounding in whin

WHINNY *v* **-NIED, -NYING, -NIES** to neigh in a low or gentle manner

WHINY *adj* **WHINIER, WHINIEST** tending to whine

WHIP	*v* **WHIPPED** or **WHIPT, WHIPPING, WHIPS** to strike with a whip (an instrument for administering corporal punishment)
WHIPCORD	*n* pl. **-S** a strong, twisted cord
WHIPLASH	*n* pl. **-ES** the lash of a whip
WHIPLIKE	*adj* resembling a whip
WHIPPED	a past tense of whip
WHIPPER	*n* pl. **-S** one that whips
WHIPPET	*n* pl. **-S** a small, swift dog
WHIPPING	*n* pl. **-S** material used to whip
WHIPPY	*adj* **-PIER, -PIEST** pertaining to or resembling a whip
WHIPRAY	*n* pl. **-RAYS** a stingray
WHIPSAW	*v* **-SAWED, -SAWN, -SAWING, -SAWS** to cut with a narrow, tapering saw
WHIPT	a past tense of whip
WHIPTAIL	*n* pl. **-S** a lizard having a long, slender tail
WHIPWORM	*n* pl. **-S** a parasitic worm
WHIR	*v* **WHIRRED, WHIRRING, WHIRS** to move with a buzzing sound
WHIRL	*v* **-ED, -ING, -S** to revolve rapidly
WHIRLER	*n* pl. **-S** one that whirls
WHIRLY	*adj* **WHIRLIER, WHIRLIEST** marked by a whirling motion
WHIRLY	*n* pl. **WHIRLIES** a small tornado
WHIRR	*v* **-ED, -ING, -S** to whir
WHIRRED	past tense of whir
WHIRRING	present participle of whir
WHIRRY	*v* **-RIED, -RYING, -RIES** to hurry
WHISH	*v* **-ED, -ING, -ES** to move with a hissing sound
WHISHT	*v* **-ED, -ING, -S** to hush
WHISK	*v* **-ED, -ING, -S** to move briskly
WHISKER	*n* pl. **-S** a hair on a man's face **WHISKERY** *adj*
WHISKEY	*n* pl. **-KEYS** a liquor
WHISKY	*n* pl. **-KIES** whiskey
WHISPER	*v* **-ED, -ING, -S** to speak softly
WHISPERY	*adj* resembling a whisper
WHIST	*v* **-ED, -ING, -S** to hush
WHISTLE	*v* **-TLED, -TLING, -TLES** to make a shrill, clear musical sound
WHISTLER	*n* pl. **-S** one that whistles
WHIT	*n* pl. **-S** a particle
WHITE	*adj* **WHITER, WHITEST** of the color of pure snow
WHITE	*v* **WHITED, WHITING, WHITES** to whiten
WHITECAP	*n* pl. **-S** a wave with a crest of foam
WHITEFLY	*n* pl. **-FLIES** a small whitish insect
WHITELY	*adv* in a white manner
WHITEN	*v* **-ED, -ING, -S** to make white
WHITENER	*n* pl. **-S** one that whitens
WHITEOUT	*n* pl. **-S** an arctic weather condition
WHITER	comparative of white
WHITEST	superlative of white
WHITEY	*adj* whity
WHITHER	*adv* to what place
WHITIER	comparative of whity
WHITIEST	superlative of whity
WHITING	*n* pl. **-S** a marine food fish
WHITISH	*adj* somewhat white
WHITLOW	*n* pl. **-S** an inflammation of the finger or toe
WHITRACK	*n* pl. **-S** a weasel
WHITTER	*n* pl. **-S** a large draft of liquor
WHITTLE	*v* **-TLED, -TLING, -TLES** to cut or shave bits from
WHITTLER	*n* pl. **-S** one that whittles
WHITTRET	*n* pl. **-S** a weasel
WHITY	*adj* **WHITIER, WHITIEST** whitish
WHIZ	*v* **WHIZZED, WHIZZING, WHIZZES** to move with a buzzing or hissing sound
WHIZBANG	*n* pl. **-S** a type of explosive shell
WHIZZ	*v* **-ED, -ING, -ES** to whiz
WHIZZER	*n* pl. **-S** one that whizzes
WHIZZES	present 3d person sing. of whiz
WHIZZING	present participle of whiz
WHIZZY	*adj* **-ZIER, -ZIEST** marvelous in construction or operation
WHO	*pron* what or which person or persons
WHOA	*interj* — used to command an animal to stop
WHODUNIT	*n* pl. **-S** a mystery story
WHOEVER	*pron* whatever person
WHOLE	*n* pl. **-S** all the parts or elements entering into and making up a thing
WHOLISM	*n* pl. **-S** holism
WHOLLY	*adv* totally

WHOM *pron* the objective case of who

WHOMEVER *pron* the objective case of whoever

WHOMP *v* **-ED, -ING, -S** to defeat decisively

WHOMSO *pron* the objective case of whoso

WHOOF *v* **-ED, -ING, -S** to make a deep snorting sound

WHOOP *v* **-ED, -ING, -S** to utter loud cries

WHOOPEE *n pl.* **-S** boisterous fun

WHOOPER *n pl.* **-S** one that whoops

WHOOPIE *n pl.* **-S** whoopee

WHOOPLA *n pl.* **-S** a noisy commotion

WHOOSH *v* **-ED, -ING, -ES** to move with a hissing sound

WHOOSIS *n pl.* **-SISES** an object or person whose name is not known

WHOP *v* **WHOPPED, WHOPPING, WHOPS** to strike forcibly

WHOPPER *n pl.* **-S** something unusually large

WHORE *v* **WHORED, WHORING, WHORES** to consort with prostitutes

WHOREDOM *n pl.* **-S** prostitution

WHORESON *n pl.* **-S** a bastard

WHORISH *adj* lewd

WHORL *n pl.* **-S** a circular arrangement of similar parts **WHORLED** *adj*

WHORT *n pl.* **-S** an edible berry

WHORTLE *n pl.* **-S** whort

WHOSE *pron* the possessive case of who

WHOSEVER *pron* the possessive case of whoever

WHOSIS *n pl.* **-SISES** whoosis

WHOSO *pron* whoever

WHUMP *v* **-ED, -ING, -S** to thump

WHUP *v* **WHUPPED, WHUPPING, WHUPS** to defeat decisively

WHY *n pl.* **WHYS** the reason or cause of something

WHYDAH *n pl.* **-S** an African bird

WICCA *n pl.* **-S** a form of nature-oriented witchcraft

WICCAN *n pl.* **-S** one who practices wicca

WICH *n pl.* **-ES** wych

WICK *n pl.* **-S** a bundle of loosely twisted fibers in a candle or oil lamp

WICKAPE *n pl.* **-S** wicopy

WICKED *adj* **-EDER, -EDEST** evil **WICKEDLY** *adv*

WICKER *n pl.* **-S** a slender, pliant twig or branch

WICKET *n pl.* **-S** a small door or gate

WICKING *n pl.* **-S** material for wicks

WICKIUP *n pl.* **-S** an American Indian hut

WICKLESS *adj* having no wick

WICKYUP *n pl.* **-S** wickiup

WICOPY *n pl.* **-PIES** a flowering shrub

WIDDER *n pl.* **-S** a widow

WIDDIE *n pl.* **-S** widdy

WIDDLE *v* **-DLED, -DLING, -DLES** to wriggle

WIDDY *n pl.* **-DIES** a hangman's noose

WIDE *adj* **WIDER, WIDEST** having great extent from side to side **WIDELY** *adv*

WIDE *n pl.* **-S** a type of bowled ball in cricket

WIDEBAND *adj* operating over a wide band of frequencies

WIDEBODY *n pl.* **-BODIES** a jet aircraft having a wide fuselage

WIDEN *v* **-ED, -ING, -S** to make wide or wider

WIDENER *n pl.* **-S** one that widens

WIDENESS *n pl.* **-ES** the state of being wide

WIDEOUT *n pl.* **-S** a receiver in football

WIDER comparative of wide

WIDEST superlative of wide

WIDGEON *n pl.* **-S** a river duck

WIDGET *n pl.* **-S** a gadget

WIDISH *adj* somewhat wide

WIDOW *v* **-ED, -ING, -S** to deprive of a husband

WIDOWER *n pl.* **-S** a man whose wife has died and who has not remarried

WIDTH *n pl.* **-S** extent from side to side

WIDTHWAY *adv* from side to side

WIELD *v* **-ED, -ING, -S** to handle or use effectively

WIELDER *n pl.* **-S** one that wields

WIELDY *adj* **WIELDIER, WIELDIEST** easily wielded

WIENER *n pl.* **-S** a frankfurter

WIENIE *n pl.* **-S** a wiener

WIFE *n pl.* **WIVES** a woman married to a man

WIFE *v* **WIFED, WIFING, WIFES** to wive

WIFEDOM *n* pl. **-S** the status or function of a wife

WIFEHOOD *n* pl. **-S** the state of being a wife

WIFELESS *adj* having no wife

WIFELIKE *adj* wifely

WIFELY *adj* **-LIER, -LIEST** of or befitting a wife

WIFEY *n* pl. **WIFEYS** a wife

WIFING present participle of wife

WIFTY *adj* **-TIER, -TIEST** ditsy

WIG *v* **WIGGED, WIGGING, WIGS** to provide with a wig (an artificial covering of hair for the head)

WIGAN *n* pl. **-S** a stiff fabric

WIGEON *n* pl. **-S** widgeon

WIGGED past tense of wig

WIGGERY *n* pl. **-GERIES** a wig

WIGGIER comparative of wiggy

WIGGIEST superlative of wiggy

WIGGING *n* pl. **-S** a scolding

WIGGLE *v* **-GLED, -GLING, -GLES** to move with short, quick movements from side to side

WIGGLER *n* pl. **-S** one that wiggles

WIGGLY *adj* **-GLIER, -GLIEST** tending to wiggle

WIGGY *adj* **-GIER, -GIEST** crazy

WIGHT *n* pl. **-S** a living being

WIGLESS *adj* having no wig

WIGLET *n* pl. **-S** a small wig

WIGLIKE *adj* resembling a wig

WIGMAKER *n* pl. **-S** one that makes wigs

WIGWAG *v* **-WAGGED, -WAGGING, -WAGS** to move back and forth

WIGWAM *n* pl. **-S** an American Indian dwelling

WIKIUP *n* pl. **-S** wickiup

WILCO *interj* — used to indicate that a message received will be complied with

WILD *v* **-ED, -ING, -S** to go about in a group attacking others

WILD *adj* **WILDER, WILDEST** living in a natural state

WILDCARD *n* pl. **-S** a symbol used in a database search to represent unspecified characters

WILDCAT *v* **-CATTED, -CATTING, -CATS** to search for oil in an area of doubtful productivity

WILDER *v* **-ED, -ING, -S** to bewilder

WILDFIRE *n* pl. **-S** a raging, destructive fire

WILDFOWL *n* pl. **-S** a wild game bird

WILDING *n* pl. **-S** a wild plant or animal

WILDISH *adj* somewhat wild

WILDLAND *n* pl. **-S** uncultivated land

WILDLIFE *n* pl. **WILDLIFE** wild animals and vegetation

WILDLING *n* pl. **-S** a wilding

WILDLY *adv* in a wild manner

WILDNESS *n* pl. **-ES** the state of being wild

WILDWOOD *n* pl. **-S** natural forest land

WILE *v* **WILED, WILING, WILES** to entice

WILFUL *adj* willful **WILFULLY** *adv*

WILIER comparative of wily

WILIEST superlative of wily

WILILY *adv* in a wily manner

WILINESS *n* pl. **-ES** the quality of being wily

WILING present participle of wile

WILL *v* **-ED, -ING, -S** to decide upon **WILLABLE** *adj*

WILL *v* past sing. 2d person **WOULD** or **WOULDEST** or **WOULDST** — used as an auxiliary followed by a simple infinitive to express futurity, inclination, likelihood, or requirement

WILLER *n* pl. **-S** one that wills

WILLET *n* pl. **-S** a shore bird

WILLFUL *adj* bent on having one's own way

WILLIED past tense of willy

WILLIES present 3d person sing. of willy

WILLING *adj* **-INGER, -INGEST** inclined or favorably disposed in mind

WILLIWAU *n* pl. **-S** williwaw

WILLIWAW *n* pl. **-S** a violent gust of cold wind

WILLOW *v* **-ED, -ING, -S** to clean textile fibers with a certain machine

WILLOWER *n* pl. **-S** one that willows

WILLOWY *adj* **-LOWIER, -LOWIEST** pliant

WILLY *v* **-LIED, -LYING, -LIES** to willow

WILLYARD *adj* willful

WILLYART *adj* willyard

WILLYWAW *n* pl. **-S** williwaw

WILT *v* **-ED, -ING, -S** to become limp

WILY *adj* **WILIER, WILIEST** crafty

WIMBLE	*v* **-BLED, -BLING, -BLES** to bore with a hand tool
WIMP	*v* **-ED, -ING, -S** to act in a timid manner
WIMPISH	*adj* wimpy
WIMPLE	*v* **-PLED, -PLING, -PLES** to pleat
WIMPY	*adj* **WIMPIER, WIMPIEST** weak, ineffectual
WIN	*v* **WINNED, WINNING, WINS** to winnow
WIN	*v* **WON** or **WAN, WINNING, WINS** to be victorious
WINCE	*v* **WINCED, WINCING, WINCES** to flinch
WINCER	*n* pl. **-S** one that winces
WINCEY	*n* pl. **-CEYS** a type of fabric
WINCH	*v* **-ED, -ING, -ES** to raise with a winch (a hoisting machine)
WINCHER	*n* pl. **-S** one that winches
WINCING	present participle of wince
WIND	*v* **WOUND** or **WINDED, WINDING, WINDS** to pass around an object or fixed center **WINDABLE** *adj*
WINDAGE	*n* pl. **-S** the effect of the wind (air in natural motion) on a projectile
WINDBAG	*n* pl. **-S** a talkative person
WINDBELL	*n* pl. **-S** a light bell that can be sounded by the wind
WINDBURN	*v* **-BURNED** or **-BURNT, -BURNING, -BURNS** to be affected with skin irritation caused by exposure to the wind
WINDER	*n* pl. **-S** one that winds
WINDFALL	*n* pl. **-S** a sudden and unexpected gain
WINDFLAW	*n* pl. **-S** a gust of wind
WINDGALL	*n* pl. **-S** a swelling on a horse's leg
WINDIER	comparative of windy
WINDIEST	superlative of windy
WINDIGO	*n* pl. **-GOS** an evil demon in Algonquian mythology
WINDILY	*adv* in a windy manner
WINDING	*n* pl. **-S** material wound about an object
WINDLASS	*v* **-ED, -ING, -ES** to raise with a windlass (a hoisting machine)
WINDLE	*v* **-DLED, -DLING, -DLES** to wind
WINDLESS	*adj* being without wind
WINDLING	*n* pl. **-S** a bundle of straw
WINDMILL	*v* **-ED, -ING, -S** to rotate solely under the force of a passing airstream
WINDOW	*v* **-ED, -ING, -S** to provide with a window (an opening in a wall to admit light and air)
WINDOWY	*adj* having many windows
WINDPIPE	*n* pl. **-S** the trachea
WINDROW	*v* **-ED, -ING, -S** to arrange in long rows, as hay or grain
WINDSOCK	*n* pl. **-S** a device used to indicate wind direction
WINDSURF	*v* **-ED, -ING, -S** to sail on a sailboard
WINDUP	*n* pl. **-S** a conclusion
WINDWARD	*n* pl. **-S** the direction from which the wind blows
WINDWAY	*n* pl. **-WAYS** a passage for air
WINDY	*adj* **WINDIER, WINDIEST** marked by strong wind
WINE	*v* **WINED, WINING, WINES** to provide with wine (the fermented juice of the grape)
WINELESS	*adj* having no wine
WINERY	*n* pl. **-ERIES** an establishment for making wine
WINESAP	*n* pl. **-S** a red apple with somewhat tart flesh
WINESHOP	*n* pl. **-S** a shop where wine is sold
WINESKIN	*n* pl. **-S** a goatskin bag for holding wine
WINESOP	*n* pl. **-S** a food sopped in wine
WINEY	*adj* **WINIER, WINIEST** winy
WING	*v* **-ED, -ING, -S** to travel by means of wings (organs of flight)
WINGBACK	*n* pl. **-S** a certain player in football
WINGBOW	*n* pl. **-S** a mark on the wing of a domestic fowl
WINGDING	*n* pl. **-S** a lively party
WINGEDLY	*adv* swiftly
WINGER	*n* pl. **-S** a certain player in soccer
WINGIER	comparative of wingy
WINGIEST	superlative of wingy
WINGLESS	*adj* having no wings
WINGLET	*n* pl. **-S** a small wing
WINGLIKE	*adj* resembling a wing
WINGMAN	*n* pl. **-MEN** a pilot behind the leader of a flying formation
WINGOVER	*n* pl. **-S** a flight maneuver

WINGSPAN *n* pl. **-S** the distance from the tip of one of a pair of wings to that of the other

WINGTIP *n* pl. **-S** a type of man's shoe

WINGY *adj* **WINGIER, WINGIEST** swift

WINIER comparative of winey and winy

WINIEST superlative of winey and winy

WINING present participle of wine

WINISH *adj* winy

WINK *v* **-ED, -ING, -S** to close and open one eye quickly

WINKER *n* pl. **-S** one that winks

WINKLE *v* **-KLED, -KLING, -KLES** to displace, extract, or evict from a position

WINLESS *adj* having no wins

WINNABLE *adj* able to be won

WINNED past tense of win (to winnow)

WINNER *n* pl. **-S** one that wins

WINNING *n* pl. **-S** money won in a game or competition

WINNOCK *n* pl. **-S** a window

WINNOW *v* **-ED, -ING, -S** to free grain from impurities

WINNOWER *n* pl. **-S** one that winnows

WINO *n* pl. **WINOS** or **WINOES** one who is habitually drunk on wine

WINSOME *adj* **-SOMER, -SOMEST** charming

WINTER *v* **-ED, -ING, -S** to pass the winter (the coldest season of the year)

WINTERER *n* pl. **-S** one that winters

WINTERLY *adj* wintry

WINTERY *adj* **-TERIER, -TERIEST** wintry

WINTLE *v* **-TLED, -TLING, -TLES** to stagger

WINTRY *adj* **-TRIER, -TRIEST** characteristic of winter **WINTRILY** *adv*

WINY *adj* **WINIER, WINIEST** having the taste or qualities of wine

WINZE *n* pl. **-S** a steeply inclined mine shaft

WIPE *v* **WIPED, WIPING, WIPES** to rub lightly in order to clean or dry

WIPEOUT *n* pl. **-S** a fall from a surfboard

WIPER *n* pl. **-S** one that wipes

WIRE *v* **WIRED, WIRING, WIRES** to fasten with wire (a slender rod, strand, or thread of ductile metal) **WIRABLE** *adj*

WIREDRAW *v* **-DREW, -DRAWN, -DRAWING, -DRAWS** to draw into wire

WIREHAIR *n* pl. **-S** a dog having a wiry coat

WIRELESS *v* **-ED, -ING, -ES** to radio

WIRELIKE *adj* resembling wire

WIREMAN *n* pl. **-MEN** one who makes or works with wire

WIRER *n* pl. **-S** one that wires

WIRETAP *v* **-TAPPED, -TAPPING, -TAPS** to intercept messages by means of a concealed monitoring device

WIREWAY *n* pl. **-WAYS** a tube for protecting electric wires

WIREWORK *n* pl. **-S** an article made of wire

WIREWORM *n* pl. **-S** a wirelike worm

WIRIER comparative of wiry

WIRIEST superlative of wiry

WIRILY *adv* in a wiry manner

WIRINESS *n* pl. **-ES** the quality of being wiry

WIRING *n* pl. **-S** a system of electric wires

WIRRA *interj* — used to express sorrow

WIRY *adj* **WIRIER, WIRIEST** resembling wire

WIS *v* past tense **WIST** to know — WIS and WIST are the only accepted forms of this verb; it cannot be conjugated further

WISDOM *n* pl. **-S** the power of true and right discernment

WISE *adj* **WISER, WISEST** having wisdom

WISE *v* **WISED, WISING, WISES** to become aware or informed

WISEACRE *n* pl. **-S** a pretentiously wise person

WISEASS *n* pl. **-ES** a wiseacre

WISED past tense of wise

WISEGUY *n* pl. **-GUYS** a mobster

WISELY *adv* **-LIER, -LIEST** in a wise manner

WISENESS *n* pl. **-ES** wisdom

WISENT *n* pl. **-S** a European bison

WISER comparative of wise

WISEST superlative of wise

WISH *v* **-ED, -ING, -ES** to feel an impulse toward attainment or possession of something

WISHA *interj* — used to express surprise

WISHBONE *n* pl. **-S** a forked bone in front of a bird's breastbone

WISHER *n* pl. **-S** one that wishes

WISHFUL *adj* desirous

WISHLESS *adj* not wishful

WISING present participle of wise

WISP *v* **-ED, -ING, -S** to twist into a wisp (a small bunch or bundle)

WISPIER comparative of wispy

WISPIEST superlative of wispy

WISPILY *adv* in a wispy manner

WISPISH *adj* wispy

WISPLIKE *adj* wispy

WISPY *adj* **WISPIER, WISPIEST** resembling a wisp

WISS *v* **-ED, -ING, -ES** to wish

WIST *v* **-ED, -ING, -S** to know

WISTARIA *n* pl. **-S** wisteria

WISTERIA *n* pl. **-S** a flowering shrub

WISTFUL *adj* yearning

WIT *n* pl. **-S** intelligence

WIT *v* **WIST, WITING** or **WITTING,** present sing. 1st person **WOT,** 2d **WOST,** 3d **WOT,** present pl. **WITE** to know

WITAN *n* pl. **-S** an Anglo-Saxon council to the king

WITCH *v* **-ED, -ING, -ES** to bewitch

WITCHERY *n* pl. **-ERIES** sorcery

WITCHING *n* pl. **-S** sorcery

WITCHY *adj* **WITCHIER, WITCHIEST** malicious

WITE *v* **WITED, WITING, WITES** to blame

WITH *prep* in the company of

WITHAL *adv* in addition

WITHDRAW *v* **-DREW, -DRAWN, -DRAWING, -DRAWS** to move back or away

WITHE *v* **WITHED, WITHING, WITHES** to bind with flexible twigs

WITHER *v* **-ED, -ING, -S** to dry up and wilt

WITHERER *n* pl. **-S** one that withers

WITHEROD *n* pl. **-S** a North American shrub

WITHHOLD *v* **-HELD, -HOLDING, -HOLDS** to hold back

WITHIER comparative of withy

WITHIES pl. of withy

WITHIEST superlative of withy

WITHIN *n* pl. **-S** an interior place or area

WITHING present participle of withe

WITHOUT *n* pl. **-S** an exterior place or area

WITHY *adj* **WITHIER, WITHIEST** flexible and tough

WITHY *n* pl. **WITHIES** a flexible twig

WITING present participle of wit and wite

WITLESS *adj* lacking intelligence

WITLING *n* pl. **-S** one who considers himself witty

WITLOOF *n* pl. **-S** chicory

WITNESS *v* **-ED, -ING, -ES** to see or know by personal experience

WITNEY *n* pl. **-NEYS** a heavy woolen fabric

WITTED *adj* having intelligence

WITTIER comparative of witty

WITTIEST superlative of witty

WITTILY *adv* in a witty manner

WITTING *n* pl. **-S** knowledge

WITTOL *n* pl. **-S** a man who tolerates his wife's infidelity

WITTY *adj* **-TIER, -TIEST** humorously clever

WIVE *v* **WIVED, WIVING, WIVES** to marry a woman

WIVER *n* pl. **-S** wivern

WIVERN *n* pl. **-S** a two-legged dragon

WIVES pl. of wife

WIVING present participle of wive

WIZ *n* pl. **WIZZES** or **WIZES** a very clever or skillful person

WIZARD *n* pl. **-S** a sorcerer **WIZARDLY** *adj*

WIZARDRY *n* pl. **-RIES** sorcery

WIZEN *v* **-ED, -ING, -S** to shrivel

WIZZEN *n* pl. **-S** weasand

WO *n* pl. **WOS** woe

WOAD *n* pl. **-S** a blue dye **WOADED** *adj*

WOADWAX *n* pl. **-ES** an ornamental shrub

WOALD *n* pl. **-S** a yellow pigment

WOBBLE *v* **-BLED, -BLING, -BLES** to move unsteadily

WOBBLER *n* pl. **-S** one that wobbles

WOBBLY *adj* **-BLIER, -BLIEST** unsteady

WOBBLY *n* pl. **-BLIES** a member of the Industrial Workers of the World

WOBEGONE *adj* affected with woe

WODGE *n* pl. **-S** a chunk of something

WOE *n* pl. **-S** tremendous grief

WOEFUL	*adj* **-FULLER, -FULLEST** full of woe **WOEFULLY** *adv*
WOENESS	*n* pl. **-ES** sadness
WOESOME	*adj* woeful
WOFUL	*adj* **-FULLER, -FULLEST** woeful **WOFULLY** *adv*
WOK	*n* pl. **-S** a cooking utensil
WOKE	a past tense of wake
WOKEN	a past participle of wake
WOLD	*n* pl. **-S** an elevated tract of open land
WOLF	*n* pl. **WOLVES** a carnivorous mammal
WOLF	*v* **-ED, -ING, -S** to devour voraciously
WOLFER	*n* pl. **-S** one who hunts wolves
WOLFFISH	*n* pl. **-ES** a marine fish
WOLFISH	*adj* wolflike
WOLFLIKE	*adj* resembling a wolf
WOLFRAM	*n* pl. **-S** tungsten
WOLVER	*n* pl. **-S** wolfer
WOLVES	pl. of wolf
WOMAN	*n* pl. **WOMEN** an adult human female
WOMAN	*v* **-ED, -ING, -S** to play the part of a woman
WOMANISE	*v* **-ISED, -ISING, -ISES** to womanize
WOMANISH	*adj* characteristic of a woman
WOMANISM	*n* pl. **-S** a belief in or respect for women
WOMANIST	*n* pl. **-S** a supporter of womanism
WOMANIZE	*v* **-IZED, -IZING, -IZES** to make effeminate
WOMANLY	*adj* **-LIER, -LIEST** having the qualities of a woman
WOMB	*n* pl. **-S** the uterus **WOMBED** *adj*
WOMBAT	*n* pl. **-S** a nocturnal mammal
WOMBY	*adj* **WOMBIER, WOMBIEST** hollow
WOMEN	pl. of woman
WOMERA	*n* pl. **-S** a device used to propel spears
WOMMERA	*n* pl. **-S** womera
WOMYN	*n/pl* women
WON	*v* **WONNED, WONNING, WONS** to dwell
WONDER	*v* **-ED, -ING, -S** to have a feeling of curiosity or doubt
WONDERER	*n* pl. **-S** one that wonders
WONDROUS	*adj* marvelous
WONK	*n* pl. **-S** an overly studious student
WONKY	*adj* **-KIER, -KIEST** unsteady
WONNED	past tense of won
WONNER	*n* pl. **-S** a prodigy
WONNING	present participle of won
WONT	*v* **-ED, -ING, -S** to make accustomed to
WONTEDLY	*adv* in a usual manner
WONTON	*n* pl. **-S** a pork-filled dumpling used in Chinese cooking
WOO	*v* **-ED, -ING, -S** to seek the affection of
WOOD	*v* **-ED, -ING, -S** to furnish with wood (the hard, fibrous substance beneath the bark of a tree or shrub)
WOODBIN	*n* pl. **-S** a bin for holding firewood
WOODBIND	*n* pl. **-S** woodbine
WOODBINE	*n* pl. **-S** a European shrub
WOODBOX	*n* pl. **-ES** a woodbin
WOODCHAT	*n* pl. **-S** a European shrike
WOODCOCK	*n* pl. **-S** a game bird
WOODCUT	*n* pl. **-S** an engraved block of wood
WOODEN	*adj* **-ENER, -ENEST** resembling wood in stiffness **WOODENLY** *adv*
WOODHEN	*n* pl. **-S** the weka
WOODIE	*n* pl. **-S** woody
WOODIER	comparative of woody
WOODIES	pl. of woody
WOODIEST	superlative of woody
WOODLAND	*n* pl. **-S** land covered with trees
WOODLARK	*n* pl. **-S** a songbird
WOODLESS	*adj* having no wood
WOODLORE	*n* pl. **-S** knowledge of the forest
WOODLOT	*n* pl. **-S** an area restricted to the growing of forest trees
WOODMAN	*n* pl. **-MEN** woodsman
WOODNOTE	*n* pl. **-S** a song or call of a forest bird
WOODPILE	*n* pl. **-S** a pile of wood
WOODRUFF	*n* pl. **-S** an aromatic herb
WOODSHED	*v* **-SHEDDED, -SHEDDING, -SHEDS** to practice on a musical instrument
WOODSIA	*n* pl. **-S** a small fern
WOODSMAN	*n* pl. **-MEN** one who works or lives in the forest

WOODSY *adj* **WOODSIER, WOODSIEST** suggestive of a forest

WOODTONE *n pl.* **-S** a finish that imitates wood

WOODWAX *n pl.* **-ES** woadwax

WOODWIND *n pl.* **-S** a musical wind instrument

WOODWORK *n pl.* **-S** work made of wood

WOODWORM *n pl.* **-S** a wood-boring worm

WOODY *adj* **WOODIER, WOODIEST** containing or resembling wood

WOODY *n pl.* **WOODIES** a wood-paneled station wagon

WOOER *n pl.* **-S** one that woos

WOOF *v* **-ED, -ING, -S** to utter a gruff barking sound

WOOFER *n pl.* **-S** a loudspeaker designed to reproduce low-pitched sounds

WOOINGLY *adv* attractively

WOOL *n pl.* **-S** the dense, soft hair forming the coat of certain mammals

WOOLED *adj* having wool of a specified kind

WOOLEN *n pl.* **-S** a fabric made of wool

WOOLER *n pl.* **-S** a domestic animal raised for its wool

WOOLFELL *n pl.* **-S** woolskin

WOOLHAT *n pl.* **-S** one who works a small farm

WOOLIE *n pl.* **-S** a woolly

WOOLIER comparative of wooly

WOOLIES pl. of wooly

WOOLIEST superlative of wooly

WOOLLED *adj* wooled

WOOLLEN *n pl.* **-S** woolen

WOOLLIES pl. of woolly

WOOLLIKE *adj* resembling wool

WOOLLY *adj* **-LIER, -LIEST** consisting of or resembling wool **WOOLLILY** *adv*

WOOLLY *n pl.* **-LIES** a garment made of wool

WOOLMAN *n pl.* **-MEN** a dealer in wool

WOOLPACK *n pl.* **-S** a bag for packing a bale of wool

WOOLSACK *n pl.* **-S** a sack of wool

WOOLSHED *n pl.* **-S** a building in which sheep are sheared

WOOLSKIN *n pl.* **-S** a sheepskin with the wool still on it

WOOLWORK *n pl.* **-S** needlework

WOOLY *adj* **WOOLIER, WOOLIEST** woolly

WOOLY *n pl.* **WOOLIES** a woolly

WOOMERA *n pl.* **-S** womera

WOOPS *v* **-ED, -ING, -ES** to vomit

WOORALI *n pl.* **-S** curare

WOORARI *n pl.* **-S** curare

WOOSH *v* **-ED, -ING, -ES** to whoosh

WOOZY *adj* **-ZIER, -ZIEST** dazed **WOOZILY** *adv*

WORD *v* **-ED, -ING, -S** to express in words (speech sounds that communicate meaning)

WORDAGE *n pl.* **-S** the number of words used

WORDBOOK *n pl.* **-S** a dictionary

WORDIER comparative of wordy

WORDIEST superlative of wordy

WORDILY *adv* in a wordy manner

WORDING *n pl.* **-S** the act or style of expressing in words

WORDLESS *adj* being without words

WORDPLAY *n pl.* **-PLAYS** a witty exchange of words

WORDY *adj* **WORDIER, WORDIEST** using many or too many words

WORE past tense of wear

WORK *v* **WORKED** or **WROUGHT, WORKING, WORKS** to exert one's powers of body or mind for some purpose

WORKABLE *adj* capable of being done **WORKABLY** *adv*

WORKADAY *adj* everyday

WORKBAG *n pl.* **-S** a bag for holding work instruments and materials

WORKBOAT *n pl.* **-S** a boat used for commercial purposes

WORKBOOK *n pl.* **-S** an exercise book for a student

WORKBOX *n pl.* **-ES** a box for holding work instruments and materials

WORKDAY *n pl.* **-DAYS** a day on which work is done

WORKER *n pl.* **-S** one that works

WORKFARE *n pl.* **-S** a welfare program that requires recipients to perform public-service work

WORKFLOW *n pl.* **-S** the amount of work to and from an office or employee

WORKFOLK *n/pl* manual laborers

WORKHOUR *n pl.* **-S** any of the hours of the day during which work is done

WORKING *n pl.* **-S** a mining excavation

WORKLESS *adj* unemployed

WORKLOAD *n* pl. **-S** the amount of work assigned to an employee

WORKMAN *n* pl. **-MEN** a male worker

WORKMATE *n* pl. **-S** a fellow worker

WORKOUT *n* pl. **-S** a period of physical exercise

WORKROOM *n* pl. **-S** a room in which work is done

WORKSHOP *n* pl. **-S** a workroom

WORKUP *n* pl. **-S** an intensive diagnostic study

WORKWEEK *n* pl. **-S** the number of hours worked in a week

WORLD *n* pl. **-S** the earth and all its inhabitants

WORLDLY *adj* **-LIER, -LIEST** pertaining to the world

WORM *v* **-ED, -ING, -S** to rid of worms (small, limbless invertebrates)

WORMER *n* pl. **-S** one that worms

WORMGEAR *n* pl. **-S** a gear wheel driven by a worm (a rotating shaft with threads)

WORMHOLE *n* pl. **-S** a hole made by a burrowing worm

WORMIER comparative of wormy

WORMIEST superlative of wormy

WORMIL *n* pl. **-S** a lump in the skin of an animal's back

WORMISH *adj* wormlike

WORMLIKE *adj* resembling a worm

WORMROOT *n* pl. **-S** pinkroot

WORMSEED *n* pl. **-S** a tropical plant

WORMWOOD *n* pl. **-S** a European herb

WORMY *adj* **WORMIER, WORMIEST** infested with worms

WORN *adj* affected by wear or use

WORNNESS *n* pl. **-ES** the state of being worn

WORRIER *n* pl. **-S** one that worries

WORRIT *v* **-ED, -ING, -S** to worry

WORRY *v* **-RIED, -RYING, -RIES** to feel anxious and uneasy about something

WORSE *n* pl. **-S** something that is worse (bad in a greater degree)

WORSEN *v* **-ED, -ING, -S** to make or become worse

WORSER *adj* worse

WORSET *n* pl. **-S** worsted

WORSHIP *v* **-SHIPED, -SHIPING, -SHIPS** or **-SHIPPED, -SHIPPING, -SHIPS** to honor and love as a divine being

WORST *v* **-ED, -ING, -S** to defeat

WORSTED *n* pl. **-S** a woolen yarn

WORT *n* pl. **-S** a plant, herb, or vegetable

WORTH *v* **-ED, -ING, -S** to befall

WORTHFUL *adj* worthy

WORTHY *adj* **-THIER, -THIEST** having value or merit **WORTHILY** *adv*

WORTHY *n* pl. **-THIES** a worthy person

WOST a present 2d person sing. of wit

WOT *v* **WOTTED, WOTTING, WOTS** to know

WOULD past tense of will

WOULDEST a 2d person sing. past tense of will

WOULDST a 2d person sing. past tense of will

WOUND *v* **-ED, -ING, -S** to inflict an injury upon

WOVE a past tense of weave

WOVEN *n* pl. **-S** a woven fabric

WOW *v* **-ED, -ING, -S** to excite to enthusiastic approval

WOWSER *n* pl. **-S** a puritanical person

WRACK *v* **-ED, -ING, -S** to wreck

WRACKFUL *adj* destructive

WRAITH *n* pl. **-S** a ghost

WRANG *n* pl. **-S** a wrong

WRANGLE *v* **-GLED, -GLING, -GLES** to argue noisily

WRANGLER *n* pl. **-S** one that wrangles

WRAP *v* **WRAPPED** or **WRAPT, WRAPPING, WRAPS** to enclose in something wound or folded about

WRAPPER *n* pl. **-S** one that wraps

WRAPPING *n* pl. **-S** the material in which something is wrapped

WRASSE *n* pl. **-S** a marine fish

WRASSLE *v* **-SLED, -SLING, -SLES** to wrastle

WRASTLE *v* **-TLED, -TLING, -TLES** to wrestle

WRATH *v* **-ED, -ING, -S** to make wrathful

WRATHFUL *adj* extremely angry

WRATHY *adj* **WRATHIER, WRATHIEST** wrathful **WRATHILY** *adv*

WREAK *v* **-ED, -ING, -S** to inflict

WREAKER *n* pl. **-S** one that wreaks

WREATH *n* pl. **-S** a band of flowers **WREATHY** *adj*

WREATHE   *v* **WREATHED, WREATHEN, WREATHING, WREATHES** to shape into a wreath

WREATHER   *n* pl. **-S** one that wreathes

WRECK   *v* **-ED, -ING, -S** to cause the ruin of

WRECKAGE   *n* pl. **-S** the act of wrecking

WRECKER   *n* pl. **-S** one that wrecks

WRECKFUL   *adj* destructive

WRECKING   *n* pl. **-S** the occupation of salvaging wrecked objects

WREN   *n* pl. **-S** a small songbird

WRENCH   *v* **-ED, -ING, -ES** to twist suddenly and forcibly

WRENCHER   *n* pl. **-S** one that wrenches

WREST   *v* **-ED, -ING, -S** to take away by force

WRESTER   *n* pl. **-S** one that wrests

WRESTLE   *v* **-TLED, -TLING, -TLES** to engage in a type of hand-to-hand contest

WRESTLER   *n* pl. **-S** one that wrestles

WRETCH   *n* pl. **-ES** a wretched person

WRETCHED   *adj* **-EDER, -EDEST** extremely unhappy

WRICK   *v* **-ED, -ING, -S** to wrench

WRIED   past tense of wry

WRIER   a comparative of wry

WRIES   present 3d person sing. of wry

WRIEST   a superlative of wry

WRIGGLE   *v* **-GLED, -GLING, -GLES** to turn or twist in a sinuous manner

WRIGGLER   *n* pl. **-S** one that wriggles

WRIGGLY   *adj* **-GLIER, -GLIEST** wriggling

WRIGHT   *n* pl. **-S** one who constructs or creates

WRING   *v* **WRUNG** or **WRINGED, WRINGING, WRINGS** to twist so as to compress

WRINGER   *n* pl. **-S** one that wrings

WRINKLE   *v* **-KLED, -KLING, -KLES** to make wrinkles (small ridges or furrows) in

WRINKLY   *adj* **-KLIER, -KLIEST** having wrinkles

WRIST   *n* pl. **-S** the junction between the hand and forearm

WRISTLET   *n* pl. **-S** a band worn around the wrist

WRISTY   *adj* **WRISTIER, WRISTIEST** using much wrist action

WRIT   *n* pl. **-S** a written legal order

WRITE   *v* **WROTE, WRITTEN, WRITING, WRITES** to form characters or symbols on a surface with an instrument **WRITABLE** *adj*

WRITER   *n* pl. **-S** one that writes

WRITERLY   *adj* characteristic of a writer

WRITHE   *v* **WRITHED, WRITHING, WRITHES** to squirm or twist in pain

WRITHEN   *adj* twisted

WRITHER   *n* pl. **-S** one that writhes

WRITING   *n* pl. **-S** a written composition

WRITTEN   past participle of write

WRONG   *adj* **WRONGER, WRONGEST** not according to what is right, proper, or correct

WRONG   *v* **-ED, -ING, -S** to treat injuriously or unjustly

WRONGER   *n* pl. **-S** one that wrongs

WRONGFUL   *adj* wrong

WRONGLY   *adv* in a wrong manner

WROTE   past tense of write

WROTH   *adj* very angry

WROTHFUL   *adj* wroth

WROUGHT   a past tense of work

WRUNG   a past tense of wring

WRY   *adj* **WRIER, WRIEST** or **WRYER, WRYEST** contorted **WRYLY** *adv*

WRY   *v* **WRIED, WRYING, WRIES** to contort

WRYNECK   *n* pl. **-S** a European bird

WRYNESS   *n* pl. **-ES** the state of being wry

WUD   *adj* insane

WURST   *n* pl. **-S** sausage

WURTZITE   *n* pl. **-S** a mineral

WURZEL   *n* pl. **-S** a variety of beet

WUSHU   *n* pl. **WUSHU** Chinese martial arts

WUSS   *n* pl. **-ES** a wimp (a weak, ineffectual person)

WUSSY   *adj* **WUSSIER, WUSSIEST** wimpy

WUSSY   *n* pl. **-SIES** a wuss

WUTHER   *v* **-ED, -ING, -S** to blow with a dull roaring sound

WYCH   *n* pl. **-ES** a European elm

WYE   *n* pl. **-S** the letter Y

WYLE   *v* **WYLED, WYLING, WYLES** to beguile

WYN   *n* pl. **-S** wynn

WYND   *n* pl. **-S** a narrow street

WYNN   *n* pl. **-S** the rune for W

WYTE   *v* **WYTED, WYTING, WYTES** to wite

WYVERN   *n* pl. **-S** wivern

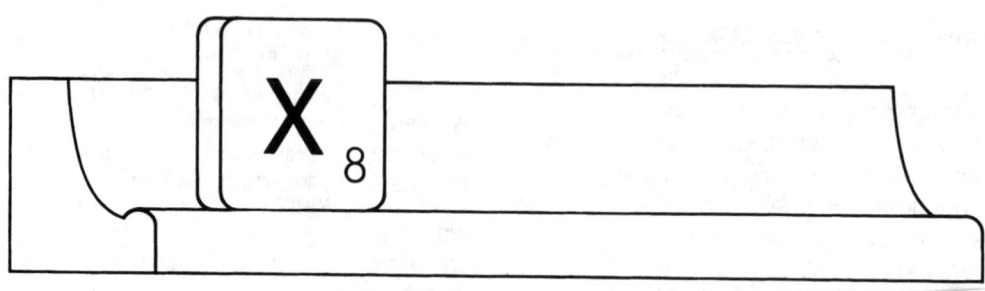

XANTHAN *n* pl. **-S** a gum produced by bacterial fermentation

XANTHATE *n* pl. **-S** a chemical salt

XANTHEIN *n* pl. **-S** the water-soluble part of the coloring matter in yellow flowers

XANTHENE *n* pl. **-S** a chemical compound

XANTHIC *adj* tending to have a yellow color

XANTHIN *n* pl. **-S** a yellow pigment

XANTHINE *n* pl. **-S** a chemical compound

XANTHOMA *n* pl. **-MAS** or **-MATA** a skin disease

XANTHONE *n* pl. **-S** a chemical compound

XANTHOUS *adj* yellow

XEBEC *n* pl. **-S** a Mediterranean sailing vessel

XENIA *n* pl. **-S** the effect of pollen on certain plant structures **XENIAL** *adj*

XENIC *adj* pertaining to a type of culture medium

XENOGAMY *n* pl. **-MIES** the transfer of pollen from one plant to another

XENOGENY *n* pl. **-NIES** the supposed production of offspring totally different from the parent

XENOLITH *n* pl. **-S** a rock fragment included in another rock

XENON *n* pl. **-S** a gaseous element

XENOPUS *n* pl. **-PUSES** a frog native to southern Africa

XERARCH *adj* developing in a dry area

XERIC *adj* requiring only a small amount of moisture

XEROSERE *n* pl. **-S** a dry-land sere

XEROSIS *n* pl. **-ROSES** abnormal dryness of a body part or tissue **XEROTIC** *adj*

XEROX *v* **-ED, -ING, -ES** to copy on a xerographic copier

XERUS *n* pl. **-ES** an African ground squirrel

XI *n* pl. **-S** a Greek letter

XIPHOID *n* pl. **-S** a part of the sternum

XU *n* pl. **XU** a monetary unit of Vietnam

XYLAN *n* pl. **-S** a substance found in cell walls of plants

XYLEM *n* pl. **-S** a complex plant tissue

XYLENE *n* pl. **-S** a flammable hydrocarbon

XYLIDIN *n* pl. **-S** xylidine

XYLIDINE *n* pl. **-S** a chemical compound

XYLITOL *n* pl. **-S** an alcohol

XYLOCARP *n* pl. **-S** a hard, woody fruit

XYLOID *adj* resembling wood

XYLOL *n* pl. **-S** xylene

XYLOSE *n* pl. **-S** a type of sugar

XYLOTOMY *n* pl. **-MIES** the preparation of sections of wood for microscopic examination

XYLYL *n* pl. **-S** a univalent radical

XYST *n* pl. **-S** xystus

XYSTER *n* pl. **-S** a surgical instrument for scraping bones

XYSTOS *n* pl. **-TOI** xystus

XYSTUS *n* pl. **-TI** a roofed area where athletes trained in ancient Greece

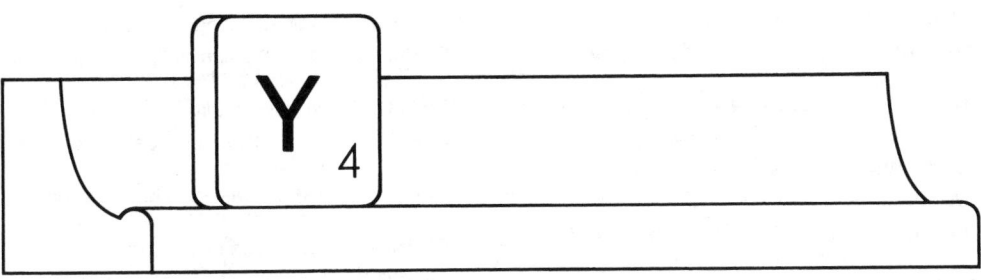

YA *pron* you

YABBER *v* **-ED, -ING, -S** to jabber

YABBIE *n* pl. **-S** yabby

YABBY *n* pl. **-BIES** an Australian crayfish

YACHT *v* **-ED, -ING, -S** to sail in a yacht (a vessel used for pleasure cruising or racing)

YACHTER *n* pl. **-S** one who sails a yacht

YACHTING *n* pl. **-S** the sport of sailing in yachts

YACHTMAN *n* pl. **-MEN** a yachter

YACK *v* **-ED, -ING, -S** to yak

YAFF *v* **-ED, -ING, -S** to bark

YAG *n* pl. **-S** a synthetic garnet

YAGER *n* pl. **-S** jaeger

YAGI *n* pl. **-S** a type of shortwave antenna

YAH *interj* — used as an exclamation of disgust

YAHOO *n* pl. **-HOOS** a coarse, uncouth person

YAHOOISM *n* pl. **-S** coarse, uncouth behavior

YAHRZEIT *n* pl. **-S** an anniversary of the death of a family member observed by Jews

YAIRD *n* pl. **-S** a garden

YAK *v* **YAKKED, YAKKING, YAKS** to chatter

YAKITORI *n* pl. **-S** marinated chicken pieces on skewers

YAKKER *n* pl. **-S** one that yaks

YAKUZA *n* pl. **YAKUZA** an alliance of Japanese criminal organizations

YALD *adj* yauld

YAM *n* pl. **-S** a plant having an edible root

YAMALKA *n* pl. **-S** yarmulke

YAMEN *n* pl. **-S** the residence of a Chinese public official

YAMMER *v* **-ED, -ING, -S** to whine or complain peevishly

YAMMERER *n* pl. **-S** one that yammers

YAMULKA *n* pl. **-S** yarmulke

YAMUN *n* pl. **-S** yamen

YANG *n* pl. **-S** the masculine active principle in Chinese cosmology

YANK *v* **-ED, -ING, -S** to pull suddenly

YANQUI *n* pl. **-S** a United States citizen

YANTRA *n* pl. **-S** a geometrical diagram used in meditation

YAP *v* **YAPPED, YAPPING, YAPS** to bark shrilly

YAPOCK *n* pl. **-S** an aquatic mammal

YAPOK *n* pl. **-S** yapock

YAPON *n* pl. **-S** yaupon

YAPPED past tense of yap

YAPPER *n* pl. **-S** one that yaps

YAPPING present participle of yap

YAR *adj* yare

YARD *v* **-ED, -ING, -S** to put in a yard (a tract of ground adjacent to a building)

YARDAGE *n* pl. **-S** the use of an enclosure for livestock at a railroad station

YARDARM *n* pl. **-S** either end of a ship's spar

YARDBIRD *n* pl. **-S** an army recruit

YARDER *n* pl. **-S** one having a specified number of yards in length

YARDLAND *n* pl. **-S** an old English unit of land measure

YARDMAN *n* pl. **-MEN** a man employed to do outdoor work

YARDWAND *n* pl. **-S** a measuring stick

YARDWORK *n* pl. **-S** the work of caring for a lawn

YARE *adj* **YARER, YAREST** nimble **YARELY** *adv*

YARMELKE *n* pl. **-S** yarmulke

YARMULKE *n* pl. **-S** a skullcap worn by Jewish males

YARN *v* **-ED, -ING, -S** to tell a long story

YARNER *n* pl. **-S** one that yarns

YARROW *n* pl. **-S** a perennial herb

YASHMAC *n* pl. **-S** yashmak

YASHMAK *n* pl. **-S** a veil worn by Muslim women

YASMAK *n* pl. **-S** yashmak

YATAGAN *n* pl. **-S** yataghan

YATAGHAN *n* pl. **-S** a Turkish sword

YATTER *v* **-ED, -ING, -S** to talk idly

YAUD *n* pl. **-S** an old mare

YAULD *adj* vigorous

YAUP *v* **-ED, -ING, -S** to yawp

YAUPER *n* pl. **-S** one that yaups

YAUPON *n* pl. **-S** an evergreen shrub

YAUTIA *n* pl. **-S** a tropical plant

YAW *v* **-ED, -ING, -S** to deviate from an intended course

YAWEY *adj* pertaining to yaws (an infectious disease)

YAWL *v* **-ED, -ING, -S** to yowl

YAWMETER *n* pl. **-S** an instrument in an aircraft

YAWN *v* **-ED, -ING, -S** to open the mouth wide with a deep inhalation of air

YAWNER *n* pl. **-S** one that yawns

YAWP *v* **-ED, -ING, -S** to utter a loud, harsh cry

YAWPER *n* pl. **-S** one that yawps

YAWPING *n* pl. **-S** a loud, harsh cry

YAY *n* pl. **YAYS** yea

YCLAD *adj* clothed

YCLEPED *adj* yclept

YCLEPT *adj* called; named

YE *pron* you

YEA *n* pl. **-S** an affirmative vote

YEAH *n* pl. **-S** an affirmative reply

YEALING *n* pl. **-S** a person of the same age

YEAN *v* **-ED, -ING, -S** to bear young

YEANLING *n* pl. **-S** the young of a sheep or goat

YEAR *n* pl. **-S** a period of time consisting of 365 or 366 days

YEARBOOK *n* pl. **-S** a book published each year by a graduating class

YEAREND *n* pl. **-S** the end of a year

YEARLING *n* pl. **-S** an animal past its first year and not yet two years old

YEARLONG *adj* lasting through a year

YEARLY *n* pl. **-LIES** a publication appearing once a year

YEARN *v* **-ED, -ING, -S** to have a strong or deep desire

YEARNER *n* pl. **-S** one that yearns

YEARNING *n* pl. **-S** a strong or deep desire

YEASAYER *n* pl. **-S** one that affirms something

YEAST *v* **-ED, -ING, -S** to foam

YEASTY *adj* **YEASTIER, YEASTIEST** foamy **YEASTILY** *adv*

YECCH *n* pl. **-S** something disgusting

YECH *n* pl. **-S** yecch

YECHY *adj* disgusting

YEELIN *n* pl. **-S** yealing

YEGG *n* pl. **-S** a burglar

YEGGMAN *n* pl. **-MEN** a yegg

YEH *adv* yeah

YELD *adj* not giving milk

YELK *n* pl. **-S** yolk

YELL *v* **-ED, -ING, -S** to cry out loudly

YELLER *n* pl. **-S** one that yells

YELLOW *adj* **-LOWER, -LOWEST** of a bright color like that of ripe lemons **YELLOWLY** *adv*

YELLOW *v* **-ED, -ING, -S** to make or become yellow

YELLOWY *adj* somewhat yellow

YELP *v* **-ED, -ING, -S** to utter a sharp, shrill cry

YELPER *n* pl. **-S** one that yelps

YEN *v* **YENNED, YENNING, YENS** to yearn

YENTA *n* pl. **-S** a gossipy woman

YENTE *n* pl. **-S** yenta

YEOMAN *n* pl. **-MEN** an independent farmer **YEOMANLY** *adj*

YEOMANRY *n* pl. **-RIES** the collective body of yeomen

YEP *n* pl. **-S** an affirmative reply

YERBA *n* pl. **-S** a South American beverage resembling tea

YERK *v* **-ED, -ING, -S** to beat vigorously

YES *v* **YESSED, YESSING, YESSES** or **YESES** to give an affirmative reply to

YESHIVA	*n* pl. **-VAS** or **-VOT** or **-VOTH** an orthodox Jewish school	**YOGA**	*n* pl. **-S** a Hindu philosophy involving physical and mental disciplines
YESHIVAH	*n* pl. **-S** yeshiva		
YESTER	*adj* pertaining to yesterday	**YOGEE**	*n* pl. **-S** yogi
YESTERN	*adj* yester	**YOGH**	*n* pl. **-S** a Middle English letter
YESTREEN	*n* pl. **-S** the previous evening	**YOGHOURT**	*n* pl. **-S** yogurt
		YOGHURT	*n* pl. **-S** yogurt
YET	*adv* up to now	**YOGI**	*n* pl. **-S** a person who practices yoga
YETI	*n* pl. **-S** the abominable snowman		
YETT	*n* pl. **-S** a gate	**YOGIC**	*adj* pertaining to yoga
YEUK	*v* **-ED, -ING, -S** to itch	**YOGIN**	*n* pl. **-S** yogi
YEUKY	*adj* itchy	**YOGINI**	*n* pl. **-S** a female yogi
YEW	*n* pl. **-S** an evergreen tree or shrub	**YOGURT**	*n* pl. **-S** a food made from milk
YIELD	*v* **-ED, -ING, -S** to give up	**YOHIMBE**	*n* pl. **-S** a topical African tree
YIELDER	*n* pl. **-S** one that yields	**YOICKS**	*interj* — used to encourage hunting hounds
YIKES	*interj* — used to express fear or pain		
		YOK	*n* pl. **-S** a boisterous laugh
YILL	*n* pl. **-S** ale	**YOKE**	*v* **YOKED, YOKING, YOKES** to fit with a yoke (a wooden frame for joining together draft animals)
YIN	*n* pl. **-S** the feminine passive principle in Chinese cosmology		
YINCE	*adv* once	**YOKEL**	*n* pl. **-S** a naive or gullible rustic
YIP	*v* **YIPPED, YIPPING, YIPS** to yelp	**YOKELESS**	*adj* having no yoke
YIPE	*interj* — used to express fear or surprise	**YOKELISH**	*adj* resembling a yokel
		YOKEMATE	*n* pl. **-S** a companion in work
YIPES	*interj* yipe	**YOKING**	present participle of yoke
YIPPEE	*interj* — used to express joy	**YOKOZUNA**	*n* pl. **-S** a champion sumo wrestler
YIPPIE	*n* pl. **-S** a politically radical hippie	**YOLK**	*n* pl. **-S** the yellow portion of an egg **YOLKED** *adj*
YIPPING	present participle of yip		
YIRD	*n* pl. **-S** earth	**YOLKY**	*adj* **YOLKIER, YOLKIEST** resembling a yolk
YIRR	*v* **-ED, -ING, -S** to snarl		
YIRTH	*n* pl. **-S** yird	**YOM**	*n* pl. **YOMIM** day
YLEM	*n* pl. **-S** hypothetical matter from which the elements are derived	**YON**	*adv* yonder
		YOND	*adv* yonder
YO	*interj* — used to call attention or to express affirmation	**YONDER**	*adv* over there
		YONI	*n* pl. **-S** a symbol for the vulva in Hindu religion **YONIC** *adj*
YOB	*n* pl. **-S** a hooligan		
YOBBO	*n* pl. **-BOS** or **-BOES** a yob	**YONKER**	*n* pl. **-S** younker
YOCK	*v* **-ED, -ING, -S** to laugh boisterously	**YORE**	*n* pl. **-S** time past
		YOU	*n* pl. **-S** something identified with the person addressed
YOD	*n* pl. **-S** a Hebrew letter		
YODEL	*v* **-DELED, -DELING, -DELS** or **-DELLED, -DELLING, -DELS** to sing with a fluctuating voice	**YOUNG**	*adj* **YOUNGER, YOUNGEST** being in the early period of life or growth
		YOUNG	*n* pl. **-S** offspring
YODELER	*n* pl. **-S** one that yodels	**YOUNGER**	*n* pl. **-S** an inferior in age
YODELLER	*n* pl. **-S** yodeler	**YOUNGISH**	*adj* somewhat young
YODH	*n* pl. **-S** yod	**YOUNKER**	*n* pl. **-S** a young gentleman
YODLE	*v* **-DLED, -DLING, -DLES** to yodel	**YOUPON**	*n* pl. **-S** yaupon
YODLER	*n* pl. **-S** yodeler		

YOUR	*adj* a possessive form of the pronoun you
YOURN	*pron* yours
YOURS	*pron* a possessive form of the pronoun you
YOURSELF	*pron* pl. **-SELVES** a form of the 2d person pronoun
YOUSE	*pron* you
YOUTH	*n* pl. **-S** a young person
YOUTHEN	*v* **-ED, -ING, -S** to make youthful
YOUTHFUL	*adj* young
YOW	*v* **-ED, -ING, -S** to yowl
YOWE	*n* pl. **-S** a ewe
YOWIE	*n* pl. **-S** a small ewe
YOWL	*v* **-ED, -ING, -S** to utter a loud, long, mournful cry
YOWLER	*n* pl. **-S** one that yowls
YPERITE	*n* pl. **-S** a poisonous gas
YTTERBIA	*n* pl. **-S** a chemical compound **YTTERBIC** *adj*
YTTRIA	*n* pl. **-S** a chemical compound
YTTRIUM	*n* pl. **-S** a metallic element **YTTRIC** *adj*
YUAN	*n* pl. **-S** a monetary unit of China
YUCA	*n* pl. **-S** yucca
YUCCA	*n* pl. **-S** a tropical plant
YUCCH	*interj* — used to express disgust
YUCH	*interj* yucch
YUCK	*v* **-ED, -ING, -S** to yuk
YUCKY	*adj* **YUCKIER, YUCKIEST** disgusting
YUGA	*n* pl. **-S** an age of time in Hinduism
YUK	*v* **YUKKED, YUKKING, YUKS** to laugh loudly
YUKKY	*adj* **YUKKIER, YUKKIEST** yucky
YULAN	*n* pl. **-S** a Chinese tree
YULE	*n* pl. **-S** Christmas time
YULETIDE	*n* pl. **-S** yule
YUM	*interj* — used to express pleasurable satisfaction
YUMMY	*adj* **-MIER, -MIEST** delicious
YUMMY	*n* pl. **-MIES** something delicious
YUP	*n* pl. **-S** a yuppie
YUPON	*n* pl. **-S** yaupon
YUPPIE	*n* pl. **-S** a young professional person working in a city
YUPPIFY	*v* **-FIED, -FYING, -FIES** to make appealing to yuppies
YUPPY	*n* pl. **-PIES** yuppie
YURT	*n* pl. **YURTS** or **YURTA** a portable tent
YUTZ	*n* pl. **-ES** a stupid, foolish, or ineffectual person
YWIS	*adv* iwis

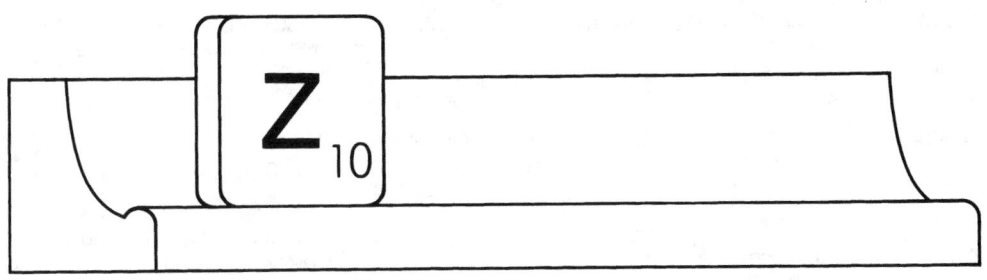

ZA   *n* pl. **-S** a pizza

ZABAIONE   *n* pl. **-S** a dessert resembling custard

ZABAJONE   *n* pl. **-S** zabaione

ZACATON   *n* pl. **-S** a Mexican grass

ZADDICK   *n* pl. **-DIKIM** zaddik

ZADDIK   *n* pl. **-DIKIM** a virtuous person by Jewish religious standards

ZAFFAR   *n* pl. **-S** zaffer

ZAFFER   *n* pl. **-S** a blue ceramic coloring

ZAFFIR   *n* pl. **-S** zaffer

ZAFFRE   *n* pl. **-S** zaffer

ZAFTIG   *adj* full-bosomed

ZAG   *v* **ZAGGED, ZAGGING, ZAGS** to turn sharply

ZAIBATSU   *n* pl. **ZAIBATSU** a powerful family combine in Japan

ZAIKAI   *n* pl. **-S** the business community of Japan

ZAIRE   *n* pl. **-S** a monetary unit of Zaire

ZAMARRA   *n* pl. **-S** a sheepskin coat

ZAMARRO   *n* pl. **-ROS** zamarra

ZAMIA   *n* pl. **-S** a tropical plant

ZAMINDAR   *n* pl. **-S** a tax collector in precolonial India

ZANANA   *n* pl. **-S** zenana

ZANDER   *n* pl. **-S** a freshwater fish

ZANINESS   *n* pl. **-ES** the quality or state of being zany

ZANY   *adj* **ZANIER, ZANIEST** ludicrously comical **ZANILY** *adv*

ZANY   *n* pl. **-NIES** a zany person

ZANYISH   *adj* somewhat zany

ZANZA   *n* pl. **-S** an African musical instrument

ZAP   *v* **ZAPPED, ZAPPING, ZAPS** to kill or destroy instantaneously

ZAPATEO   *n* pl. **-TEOS** a Spanish dance

ZAPPER   *n* pl. **-S** a device that zaps

ZAPPY   *adj* **-PIER, -PIEST** zippy

ZAPTIAH   *n* pl. **-S** a Turkish policeman

ZAPTIEH   *n* pl. **-S** zaptiah

ZARATITE   *n* pl. **-S** a chemical compound

ZAREBA   *n* pl. **-S** an improvised stockade

ZAREEBA   *n* pl. **-S** zareba

ZARF   *n* pl. **-S** a metal holder for a coffee cup

ZARIBA   *n* pl. **-S** zareba

ZARZUELA   *n* pl. **-S** a Spanish operetta

ZASTRUGA   *n* pl. **-GI** sastruga

ZAX   *n* pl. **-ES** a tool for cutting roof slates

ZAYIN   *n* pl. **-S** a Hebrew letter

ZAZEN   *n* pl. **-S** meditation in Zen Buddhism

ZEAL   *n* pl. **-S** enthusiastic devotion

ZEALOT   *n* pl. **-S** one who is zealous

ZEALOTRY   *n* pl. **-RIES** excessive zeal

ZEALOUS   *adj* filled with zeal

ZEATIN   *n* pl. **-S** a chemical compound found in maize

ZEBEC   *n* pl. **-S** xebec

ZEBECK   *n* pl. **-S** xebec

ZEBRA   *n* pl. **-S** an African mammal that is related to the horse **ZEBRAIC** *adj*

ZEBRANO   *n* pl. **-BRANOS** a tree having striped wood

ZEBRASS   *n* pl. **-ES** the offspring of a zebra and an ass

ZEBRINE   *n* pl. **-S** the offspring of a male horse and a female zebra

ZEBROID   *adj* resembling a zebra

ZEBU   *n* pl. **-S** an Asian ox

ZECCHIN   *n* pl. **-S** zecchino

ZECCHINO   *n* pl. **-NOS** or **-NI** a former gold coin of Italy

ZECHIN   *n* pl. **-S** zecchino

ZED   *n* pl. **-S** the letter Z

ZEDOARY   *n* pl. **-ARIES** the medicinal root of a tropical plant

ZEE   *n* pl. **-S** the letter Z

ZEIN   *n* pl. **-S** a simple protein

ZEK   *n* pl. **-S** an inmate in a Soviet labor camp

ZELKOVA   *n* pl. **-S** a Japanese tree

ZEMINDAR   *n* pl. **-S** zamindar

ZEMSTVO   *n* pl. **-VOS** or **-VA** an elective council in czarist Russia

ZENAIDA   *n* pl. **-S** a wild dove

ZENANA   *n* pl. **-S** the section of a house in India reserved for women

ZENITH   *n* pl. **-S** the highest point **ZENITHAL** *adj*

ZEOLITE   *n* pl. **-S** a mineral **ZEOLITIC** *adj*

ZEP   *n* pl. **-S** a long sandwich

ZEPHYR   *n* pl. **-S** a gentle breeze

ZEPPELIN   *n* pl. **-S** a long, rigid airship

ZEPPOLE   *n* pl. **-POLES** or **-POLI** a deep-fried pastry

ZERK   *n* pl. **-S** a grease fitting

ZERO   *v* **-ED, -ING, -ES** or **-S** to aim at the exact center of a target

ZEROTH   *adj* being numbered zero in a series

ZEST   *v* **-ED, -ING, -ES** to fill with zest (invigorating excitement)

ZESTER   *n* pl. **-S** a utensil for peeling citrus rind

ZESTFUL   *adj* full of zest

ZESTLESS   *adj* lacking zest

ZESTY   *adj* **ZESTIER, ZESTIEST** marked by zest **ZESTILY** *adv*

ZETA   *n* pl. **-S** a Greek letter

ZEUGMA   *n* pl. **-S** the use of a word to modify or govern two or more words, while applying to each in a different sense

ZIBELINE   *n* pl. **-S** a soft fabric

ZIBET   *n* pl. **-S** an Asian civet

ZIBETH   *n* pl. **-S** zibet

ZIG   *v* **ZIGGED, ZIGGING, ZIGS** to turn sharply

ZIGGURAT   *n* pl. **-S** an ancient Babylonian temple tower

ZIGZAG   *v* **-ZAGGED, -ZAGGING, -ZAGS** to proceed on a course marked by sharp turns

ZIGZAGGY   *adj* marked by sharp turns

ZIKKURAT   *n* pl. **-S** ziggurat

ZIKURAT   *n* pl. **-S** ziggurat

ZILCH   *n* pl. **-ES** nothing

ZILL   *n* pl. **-S** one of a pair of finger cymbals

ZILLAH   *n* pl. **-S** an administrative district in India

ZILLION   *n* pl. **-S** an indeterminately large number

ZIN   *n* pl. **-S** a dry red wine

ZINC   *v* **ZINCED, ZINCING, ZINCS** or **ZINCKED, ZINCKING, ZINCS** to coat with zinc (a metallic element)

ZINCATE   *n* pl. **-S** a chemical salt

ZINCIC   *adj* pertaining to zinc

ZINCIFY   *v* **-FIED, -FYING, -FIES** to coat with zinc

ZINCITE   *n* pl. **-S** an ore of zinc

ZINCKED   a past tense of zinc

ZINCKING   a present participle of zinc

ZINCKY   *adj* resembling zinc

ZINCOID   *adj* zincic

ZINCOUS   *adj* zincic

ZINCY   *adj* zincky

ZINE   *n* pl. **-S** a magazine

ZINEB   *n* pl. **-S** an insecticide

ZING   *v* **-ED, -ING, -S** to move with a high-pitched humming sound

ZINGANO   *n* pl. **-NI** zingaro

ZINGARA   *n* pl. **-RE** a female gypsy

ZINGARO   *n* pl. **-RI** a gypsy

ZINGER   *n* pl. **-S** a pointed witty retort or remark

ZINGY   *adj* **ZINGIER, ZINGIEST** enjoyably exciting

ZINKIFY   *v* **-FIED, -FYING, -FIES** to zincify

ZINKY   *adj* zincky

ZINNIA   *n* pl. **-S** a tropical plant

ZIP   *v* **ZIPPED, ZIPPING, ZIPS** to move with speed and vigor

ZIPLESS   *adj* lacking vigor or energy

ZIPLOCK   *adj* having a groove and ridge that form a tight seal when joined

ZIPPER   *v* **-ED, -ING, -S** to fasten with a zipper (a fastener consisting of two rows of interlocking teeth)

ZIPPY   *adj* **-PIER, -PIEST** full of energy

ZIRAM   *n* pl. **-S** a chemical salt

ZIRCALOY   *n* pl. **-S** a zirconium alloy

ZIRCON   *n* pl. **-S** a mineral

ZIRCONIA   *n* pl. **-S** a chemical compound

ZIRCONIC   *adj* pertaining to the metallic element zirconium

ZIT   *n* pl. **-S** a pimple

ZITHER   *n* pl. **-S** a stringed instrument

ZITHERN   *n* pl. **-S** zither

ZITI   *n* pl. **-S** a tubular pasta

ZIZIT   *n/pl* zizith

ZIZITH   *n/pl* the tassels on the four corners of a Jewish prayer shawl

ZIZZLE   *v* **-ZLED, -ZLING, -ZLES** to sizzle

ZLOTY   *n* pl. **ZLOTYS** a monetary unit of Poland

ZOA   a pl. of zoon

ZOARIUM   *n* pl. **-IA** a colony of bryozoans **ZOARIAL** *adj*

ZOCALO   *n* pl. **-LOS** the public square in a Mexican city or town

ZODIAC   *n* pl. **-S** an imaginary belt encircling the celestial sphere **ZODIACAL** *adj*

ZOEA   *n* pl. **ZOEAS** or **ZOEAE** a larval form of certain crustaceans **ZOEAL** *adj*

ZOECIUM   *n* pl. **-CIA** zooecium

ZOFTIG   *adj* zaftig

ZOIC   *adj* pertaining to animals or animal life

ZOISITE   *n* pl. **-S** a mineral

ZOMBI   *n* pl. **-S** zombie

ZOMBIE   *n* pl. **-S** a will-less human capable only of automatic movement

ZOMBIFY   *v* **-FIED, -FYING, -FIES** to turn into a zombie

ZOMBIISM   *n* pl. **-S** the system of beliefs connected with a West African snake god

ZONA   *n* pl. **-NAE** a transparent substance surrounding the ovum of mammals

ZONAL   *adj* pertaining to a zone **ZONALLY** *adv*

ZONARY   *adj* zonal

ZONATE   *adj* arranged in zones

ZONATED   *adj* zonate

ZONATION   *n* pl. **-S** arrangement in zones

ZONE   *v* **ZONED, ZONING, ZONES** to arrange in zones (areas distinguished from other adjacent areas)

ZONELESS   *adj* having no zone or belt

ZONER   *n* pl. **-S** one that zones

ZONETIME   *n* pl. **-S** standard time used at sea

ZONING   present participle of zone

ZONK   *v* **-ED, -ING, -S** to stupefy

ZONULA   *n* pl. **-LAS** or **-LAE** zonule

ZONULE   *n* pl. **-S** a small zone **ZONULAR** *adj*

ZOO   *n* pl. **ZOOS** a place where animals are kept for public exhibition

ZOOCHORE   *n* pl. **-S** a plant dispersed by animals

ZOOECIUM   *n* pl. **-CIA** a sac secreted and lived in by an aquatic organism

ZOOEY   *adj* **ZOOIER, ZOOIEST** resembling a zoo

ZOOGENIC   *adj* caused by animals or their activities

ZOOGENY   *n* pl. **-NIES** the development or evolution of animals

ZOOGLEA   *n* pl. **-GLEAS** or **-GLEAE** a jellylike mass of bacteria **ZOOGLEAL** *adj*

ZOOGLOEA   *n* pl. **-GLOEAS** or **-GLOEAE** zooglea

ZOOID   *n* pl. **-S** an organic cell or body capable of independent movement **ZOOIDAL** *adj*

ZOOKS   *interj* — used as a mild oath

ZOOLATER   *n* pl. **-S** one that worships animals

ZOOLATRY   *n* pl. **-TRIES** the worship of animals

ZOOLOGY   *n* pl. **-GIES** the science that deals with animals **ZOOLOGIC** *adj*

ZOOM   *v* **-ED, -ING, -S** to move with a loud humming sound

ZOOMANIA   *n* pl. **-S** an excessive interest in animals

ZOOMETRY   *n* pl. **-TRIES** the measurement of animals or animal parts

ZOOMORPH   *n* pl. **-S** something in the form of an animal

ZOON   *n* pl. **ZOONS** or **ZOA** the whole product of one fertilized egg **ZOONAL** *adj*

ZOON *v* **-ED, -ING, -S** to zoom

ZOONOSIS *n* pl. **-NOSES** a disease that can be transmitted from animals to humans **ZOONOTIC** *adj*

ZOOPHILE *n* pl. **-S** a lover of animals

ZOOPHILY *n* pl. **-LIES** a love of animals

ZOOPHOBE *n* pl. **-S** one who fears or hates animals

ZOOPHYTE *n* pl. **-S** an invertebrate animal

ZOOSPERM *n* pl. **-S** the male fertilizing element of an animal

ZOOSPORE *n* pl. **-S** a type of spore

ZOOTOMY *n* pl. **-MIES** the dissection of animals **ZOOTOMIC** *adj*

ZOOTY *adj* **ZOOTIER, ZOOTIEST** flashy in manner or style

ZORI *n* pl. **-S** a type of sandal

ZORIL *n* pl. **-S** a small African mammal

ZORILLA *n* pl. **-S** zoril

ZORILLE *n* pl. **-S** zoril

ZORILLO *n* pl. **-LOS** zoril

ZOSTER *n* pl. **-S** a virus disease

ZOUAVE *n* pl. **-S** a French infantryman

ZOUK *n* pl. **-S** a dance music of the French West Indies

ZOUNDS *interj* — used as a mild oath

ZOWIE *interj* — used to express surprise or pleasure

ZOYSIA *n* pl. **-S** a perennial grass

ZUCCHINI *n* pl. **-S** a vegetable

ZUGZWANG *n* pl. **-S** a situation in chess that forces a disadvantageous move

ZUZ *n* pl. **ZUZIM** an ancient Hebrew silver coin

ZWIEBACK *n* pl. **-S** a sweetened bread

ZYDECO *n* pl. **-COS** popular music of southern Louisiana

ZYGOID *adj* pertaining to a zygote

ZYGOMA *n* pl. **-MAS** or **-MATA** the cheekbone

ZYGOSIS *n* pl. **-GOSES** the union of two gametes **ZYGOSE** *adj*

ZYGOSITY *n* pl. **-TIES** the makeup of a particular zygote

ZYGOTE *n* pl. **-S** a cell formed by the union of two gametes **ZYGOTIC** *adj*

ZYGOTENE *n* pl. **-S** a stage in meiosis

ZYMASE *n* pl. **-S** an enzyme

ZYME *n* pl. **-S** an enzyme

ZYMOGEN *n* pl. **-S** a substance that develops into an enzyme when suitably activated

ZYMOGENE *n* pl. **-S** zymogen

ZYMOGRAM *n* pl. **-S** a record of separated proteins after electrophoresis

ZYMOLOGY *n* pl. **-GIES** the science of fermentation

ZYMOSAN *n* pl. **-S** an insoluble fraction of yeast cell walls

ZYMOSIS *n* pl. **-MOSES** fermentation **ZYMOTIC** *adj*

ZYMURGY *n* pl. **-GIES** a branch of chemistry dealing with fermentation

ZYZZYVA *n* pl. **-S** a tropical weevil

ZZZ *interj* — used to suggest the sound of snoring

A SELECTION OF USEFUL WORDS FOR PLAYERS

Q words not followed by U

BUQSHA	MBAQANGAS	QAID	QIS	QIVIUTS	SHEQALIM
BUQSHAS	QABALA	QAIDS	QINDAR	QOPH	SUQ
BURQA	QABALAS	QANAT	QINDARS	QOPHS	SUQS
BURQAS	QABALAH	QANATS	QINDARKA	QWERTY	TRANQ
FAQIR	QABALAHS	QAT	QINTAR	QWERTYS	TRANQS
FAQIRS	QADI	QATS	QINTARS	SHEQEL	UMIAQ
MBAQANGA	QADIS	QI	QIVIUT	SHEQELS	UMIAQS

2- to 5-letter words with no AEIOU vowels

BY	NTH	WYN	RYND	CYSTS	SLYLY
HM	PHT	ZZZ	SCRY	DRYLY	STYMY
MM	PLY		SPRY	FLYBY	SYLPH
MY	PRY	BRRR	SYNC	GHYLL	SYNCS
SH	PST	BYRL	SYPH	GLYPH	SYNCH
	PYX	CWMS	TSKS	GYPSY	SYNTH
BRR	SHH	CYST	TYPP	HYMNS	SYPHS
BYS	SHY	DRYS	TYPY	LYMPH	THYMY
CRY	SKY	GYMS	WHYS	LYNCH	TRYST
CWM	SLY	GYPS	WYCH	MYRRH	TYPPS
DRY	SPY	HYMN	WYNS	MYTHS	WRYLY
FLY	STY	HYPS	WYND	MYTHY	WYNDS
FRY	SYN	LYCH	WYNN	NYMPH	WYNNS
GYM	THY	LYNX	XYST	PHPHT	XYLYL
GYP	TRY	MYCS		PSYCH	XYSTS
HMM	TSK	MYTH	BYRLS	PYGMY	
HYP	WHY	PFFT	CRWTH	RYNDS	
MYC	WRY	PSST	CRYPT	SHYLY	

2- to 5-letter words with high vowel count

AA	AIM	AVE	DUI	FEE
AE	AIN	AVO	DUO	FEU
AI	AIR	AWA	EAR	FIE
OE	AIS	AWE	EAT	FOE
OI	AIT	AXE	EAU	FOU
	ALA	AYE	ECU	GAE
AAH	ALE	AZO	EEK	GEE
AAL	AMA	BAA	EEL	GIE
AAS	AMI	BEE	EGO	GOA
ABA	AMU	BIO	EKE	GOO
ACE	ANA	BOA	EME	HAE
ADO	ANE	BOO	EMU	HAO
AGA	ANI	CEE	EON	HIE
AGE	APE	COO	ERA	HOE
AGO	APO	CUE	ERE	HUE
AHA	ARE	DEE	ETA	ICE
AHI	ATE	DIE	EVE	ION
AID	AUK	DOE	EWE	IRE
AIL	AVA	DUE	EYE	JEE

JEU OOH TIE AMIA OLEA
JOE OOT TOE AMIE OLEO
KAE OPE TOO ANOA OLIO
KEA ORA TUI AQUA OOZE
KOA ORE UDO AREA OUZO
KOI OSE UKE ARIA QUAI
KUE OUD ULU ASEA RAIA
LEA OUR UPO AURA ROUE
LEE OUT USE AUTO TOEA
LEI OVA UTA AWEE UNAI
LEU OWE UTE BEAU UNAU
LIE OXO VAU CIAO UREA
LOO PEA VEE EASE UVEA
MAE PEE VIA EAUX ZOEA
MOA PIA VIE EAVE
MOO PIE VOE EIDE AALII
NAE PIU WAE EMEU ADIEU
NEE POI WEE EPEE AECIA
NOO QUA WOE ETUI AERIE
OAF RAI WOO EURO AIOLI
OAK REE YEA IDEA AQUAE
OAR REI YOU ILEA AREAE
OAT RIA ZEE ILIA AUDIO
OBA ROE ZOA INIA AURAE
OBE RUE ZOO IOTA AUREI
OBI SAE IXIA COOEE
OCA SAU AEON JIAO EERIE
ODA SEA AERO LIEU LOOIE
ODE SEE AGEE LUAU LOUIE
OES SEI AGIO MEOU MIAOU
OHO SOU AGUE MOUE OIDIA
OIL SUE AIDE NAOI OORIE
OKA TAE AJEE OBIA OURIE
OKE TAO AKEE OBOE QUEUE
OLE TAU ALAE ODEA URAEI
ONE TEA ALEE OGEE ZOEAE
ONO TEE ALOE OHIA

2- to 5-letter words containing J, Q, X or Z

AX GOX JUN REX ZIG
EX HAJ JUS SAX ZIN
JO HEX JUT SEX ZIP
OX JAB KEX SIX ZIT
QI JAG LAX SOX ZOA
XI JAM LEX SUQ ZOO
XU JAR LOX TAJ ZUZ
ZA JAW LUX TAX ZZZ
JAY MAX TUX
ADZ JEE MIX VEX ADZE
AXE JET NIX VOX AJAR
AZO JEU OXO WAX AJEE
BIZ JIB OXY WIZ APEX
BOX JIG PAX XIS AQUA
COX JIN PIX ZAG AXAL
COZ JOB POX ZAP AXED
DEX JOE PYX ZAS AXEL
FAX JOG QAT ZAX AXES
FEZ JOT QIS ZED AXIL
FIX JOW QUA ZEE AXIS
FIZ JOY RAJ ZEK AXLE
FOX JUG RAX ZEP AXON

AZAN	JAMS	JUGA	RAJA	AMAZE	CODEX
AZON	JANE	JUGS	RAZE	ANNEX	COLZA
BIZE	JAPE	JUJU	RAZZ	AQUAE	COMIX
BOXY	JARL	JUKE	RITZ	AQUAS	COXAE
BOZO	JARS	JUKU	ROUX	ATAXY	COXAL
BRUX	JATO	JUMP	SEXT	AUXIN	COXED
BUZZ	JAUK	JUNK	SEXY	AXELS	COXES
CALX	JAUP	JUPE	SIZE	AXIAL	COZEN
CHEZ	JAVA	JURA	SIZY	AXILE	COZES
COAX	JAWS	JURY	SOJA	AXILS	COZEY
COXA	JAYS	JUST	SUQS	AXING	COZIE
COZY	JAZZ	JUTE	TAXA	AXIOM	CRAZE
CRUX	JEAN	JUTS	TAXI	AXION	CRAZY
CZAR	JEED	KOJI	TEXT	AXITE	CROZE
DAZE	JEEP	LAZE	TZAR	AXLED	CULEX
DEXY	JEER	LAZY	VEXT	AXLES	CYLIX
DITZ	JEES	LUTZ	WAXY	AXMAN	CZARS
DJIN	JEEZ	LUXE	WHIZ	AXMEN	DAZED
DOJO	JEFE	LYNX	XYST	AXONE	DAZES
DOUX	JEHU	MAXI	YUTZ	AXONS	DEOXY
DOXY	JELL	MAZE	ZAGS	AZANS	DESEX
DOZE	JEON	MAZY	ZANY	AZIDE	DETOX
DOZY	JERK	MEZE	ZAPS	AZIDO	DEWAX
EAUX	JESS	MINX	ZARF	AZINE	DEXES
EXAM	JEST	MIXT	ZEAL	AZLON	DEXIE
EXEC	JETE	MOJO	ZEBU	AZOIC	DIAZO
EXED	JETS	MOXA	ZEDS	AZOLE	DITZY
EXES	JEUX	MOZO	ZEES	AZONS	DIXIT
EXIT	JIAO	NAZI	ZEIN	AZOTE	DIZEN
EXON	JIBB	NEXT	ZEKS	AZOTH	DIZZY
EXPO	JIBE	NIXE	ZEPS	AZUKI	DJINN
FALX	JIBS	NIXY	ZERK	AZURE	DJINS
FAUX	JIFF	ONYX	ZERO	BAIZA	DOJOS
FAZE	JIGS	OOZE	ZEST	BAIZE	DOOZY
FIXT	JILL	OOZY	ZETA	BANJO	DOXIE
FIZZ	JILT	ORYX	ZIGS	BAZAR	DOZED
FLAX	JIMP	ORZO	ZILL	BAZOO	DOZEN
FLEX	JINK	OUZO	ZINC	BEAUX	DOZER
FLUX	JINN	OXEN	ZINE	BEMIX	DOZES
FOXY	JINS	OXES	ZING	BEZEL	EJECT
FOZY	JINX	OXID	ZINS	BEZIL	ENJOY
FRIZ	JIVE	OXIM	ZIPS	BIJOU	ENZYM
FUJI	JIVY	OYEZ	ZITI	BIZES	EPOXY
FUTZ	JOBS	PHIZ	ZITS	BLAZE	EQUAL
FUZE	JOCK	PIXY	ZOEA	BLITZ	EQUID
FUZZ	JOES	PLEX	ZOIC	BONZE	EQUIP
GAZE	JOEY	POXY	ZONA	BOOZE	EXACT
GEEZ	JOGS	PREX	ZONE	BOOZY	EXALT
HADJ	JOHN	PREZ	ZONK	BORAX	EXAMS
HAJI	JOIN	PUJA	ZOOM	BORTZ	EXCEL
HAJJ	JOKE	PUTZ	ZOON	BOXED	EXECS
HAZE	JOKY	QADI	ZOOS	BOXER	EXERT
HAZY	JOLE	QAID	ZORI	BOXES	EXILE
HOAX	JOLT	QATS	ZOUK	BOZOS	EXINE
IBEX	JOSH	QOPH	ZYME	BRAXY	EXING
ILEX	JOSS	QUAD		BRAZA	EXIST
IXIA	JOTA	QUAG	ABUZZ	BRAZE	EXITS
IZAR	JOTS	QUAI	ADDAX	BURQA	EXONS
JABS	JOUK	QUAY	ADMIX	BUXOM	EXPAT
JACK	JOWL	QUEY	ADOZE	CAJON	EXPEL
JADE	JOWS	QUID	ADZED	CALIX	EXPOS
JAGG	JOYS	QUIN	ADZES	CALYX	EXTOL
JAGS	JUBA	QUIP	AFFIX	CAPIZ	EXTRA
JAIL	JUBE	QUIT	AGAZE	CAREX	EXUDE
JAKE	JUCO	QUIZ	AJIVA	CIMEX	EXULT
JAMB	JUDO	QUOD	AJUGA	CLOZE	EXURB

FAQIR	HEXAD	JETON	JUKES	MUJIK
FAXED	HEXED	JETTY	JUKUS	MUREX
FAXES	HEXER	JEWEL	JULEP	MUZZY
FAZED	HEXES	JIBBS	JUMBO	NAZIS
FAZES	HEXYL	JIBED	JUMPS	NERTZ
FEAZE	HIJAB	JIBER	JUMPY	NEXUS
FEDEX	HIJRA	JIBES	JUNCO	NINJA
FEEZE	HUZZA	JIFFS	JUNKS	NIXED
FEZES	HYRAX	JIFFY	JUNKY	NIXES
FEZZY	IMMIX	JIGGY	JUNTA	NIXIE
FIQUE	INDEX	JIHAD	JUNTO	NIZAM
FIXED	INFIX	JILLS	JUPES	NUDZH
FIXER	IXIAS	JILTS	JUPON	OBJET
FIXES	IXORA	JIMMY	JURAL	OOZED
FIXIT	IXTLE	JIMPY	JURAT	OOZES
FIZZY	IZARS	JINGO	JUREL	ORZOS
FJELD	JABOT	JINKS	JUROR	OUZEL
FJORD	JACAL	JINNI	JUSTS	OUZOS
FLAXY	JACKS	JINNS	JUTES	OXBOW
FOXED	JACKY	JIVED	JUTTY	OXEYE
FOXES	JADED	JIVER	KANJI	OXIDE
FRITZ	JADES	JIVES	KANZU	OXIDS
FRIZZ	JAGER	JIVEY	KAZOO	OXIME
FROZE	JAGGS	JNANA	KEXES	OXIMS
FUJIS	JAGGY	JOCKO	KLUTZ	OXLIP
FURZE	JAGRA	JOCKS	KOJIS	OXTER
FURZY	JAILS	JOEYS	KOPJE	OZONE
FUZED	JAKES	JOHNS	KUDZU	PAXES
FUZEE	JALAP	JOINS	KYLIX	PHLOX
FUZES	JALOP	JOINT	LATEX	PIQUE
FUZIL	JAMBE	JOIST	LAXER	PIXEL
FUZZY	JAMBS	JOKED	LAXES	PIXES
GALAX	JAMMY	JOKER	LAXLY	PIXIE
GANJA	JANES	JOKES	LAZAR	PIZZA
GAUZE	JANTY	JOKEY	LAZED	PLAZA
GAUZY	JAPAN	JOLES	LAZES	PLOTZ
GAZAR	JAPED	JOLLY	LEXES	POXED
GAZED	JAPER	JOLTS	LEXIS	POXES
GAZER	JAPES	JOLTY	LOXED	PREXY
GAZES	JARLS	JOMON	LOXES	PRIZE
GHAZI	JATOS	JONES	LUXES	PROXY
GIZMO	JAUKS	JORAM	MAIZE	PUJAH
GLAZE	JAUNT	JORUM	MAJOR	PUJAS
GLAZY	JAUPS	JOTAS	MAQUI	PUNJI
GLITZ	JAVAS	JOTTY	MATZA	PYXES
GLOZE	JAWAN	JOUAL	MATZO	PYXIE
GONZO	JAWED	JOUKS	MAXED	PYXIS
GOXES	JAZZY	JOULE	MAXES	QADIS
GRAZE	JEANS	JOUST	MAXIM	QAIDS
GROSZ	JEBEL	JOWAR	MAXIS	QANAT
GYOZA	JEEPS	JOWED	MAZED	QOPHS
HADJI	JEERS	JOWLS	MAZER	QUACK
HAFIZ	JEFES	JOWLY	MAZES	QUADS
HAJES	JEHAD	JOYED	MEZES	QUAFF
HAJIS	JEHUS	JUBAS	MEZZO	QUAGS
HAJJI	JELLS	JUBES	MIREX	QUAIL
HAMZA	JELLY	JUCOS	MIRZA	QUAIS
HAPAX	JEMMY	JUDAS	MIXED	QUAKE
HAZAN	JENNY	JUDGE	MIXER	QUAKY
HAZED	JERID	JUDOS	MIXES	QUALE
HAZEL	JERKS	JUGAL	MIXUP	QUALM
HAZER	JERKY	JUGUM	MIZEN	QUANT
HAZES	JERRY	JUICE	MOJOS	QUARE
HEEZE	JESSE	JUICY	MOXAS	QUARK
HELIX	JESTS	JUJUS	MOXIE	QUART
HERTZ	JETES	JUKED	MOZOS	QUASH

QUASI	QUOTH	SILEX	THUJA	WIZEN	ZILCH
QUASS	QURSH	SIXES	TIZZY	WIZES	ZILLS
QUATE	RADIX	SIXMO	TOPAZ	WOOZY	ZINCS
QUAYS	RAJAH	SIXTE	TOQUE	XEBEC	ZINCY
QUBIT	RAJAS	SIXTH	TOXIC	XENIA	ZINEB
QUEAN	RAJES	SIXTY	TOXIN	XENIC	ZINES
QUEEN	RAXED	SIZAR	TRANQ	XENON	ZINGS
QUEER	RAXES	SIZED	TROOZ	XERIC	ZINGY
QUELL	RAZED	SIZER	TUQUE	XEROX	ZINKY
QUERN	RAZEE	SIZES	TUXES	XERUS	ZIPPY
QUERY	RAZER	SLOJD	TWIXT	XYLAN	ZIRAM
QUEST	RAZES	SMAZE	TZARS	XYLEM	ZITIS
QUEUE	RAZOR	SOJAS	UMIAQ	XYLOL	ZIZIT
QUEYS	REDOX	SOYUZ	UNBOX	XYLYL	ZLOTY
QUICK	REDUX	SOZIN	UNFIX	XYSTI	ZOEAE
QUIDS	REFIX	SPITZ	UNJAM	XYSTS	ZOEAL
QUIET	REJIG	SQUAB	UNMIX	ZAIRE	ZOEAS
QUIFF	RELAX	SQUAD	UNSEX	ZAMIA	ZOMBI
QUILL	REMEX	SQUAT	UNZIP	ZANZA	ZONAE
QUILT	REMIX	SQUEG	USQUE	ZAPPY	ZONAL
QUINS	RETAX	SQUIB	VARIX	ZARFS	ZONED
QUINT	REWAX	SQUID	VEXED	ZAXES	ZONER
QUIPS	REXES	TAJES	VEXER	ZAYIN	ZONES
QUIPU	RIOJA	TAXED	VEXES	ZAZEN	ZONKS
QUIRE	RITZY	TAXER	VEXIL	ZEALS	ZOOEY
QUIRK	ROQUE	TAXES	VIXEN	ZEBEC	ZOOID
QUIRT	SAJOU	TAXIS	VIZIR	ZEBRA	ZOOKS
QUITE	SAXES	TAXOL	VIZOR	ZEBUS	ZOOMS
QUITS	SCUZZ	TAXON	WALTZ	ZEINS	ZOONS
QUODS	SEIZE	TAXUS	WAXED	ZERKS	ZOOTY
QUOIN	SEXED	TAZZA	WAXEN	ZEROS	ZORIL
QUOIT	SEXES	TAZZE	WAXER	ZESTS	ZORIS
QUOLL	SEXTO	TELEX	WAXES	ZESTY	ZOUKS
QUOTA	SEXTS	TEXAS	WHIZZ	ZETAS	ZOWIE
QUOTE	SHOJI	TEXTS	WINZE	ZIBET	ZYMES